C000039400

John Locke, Toleration and Early Enlightenment Culture

This book is a major new intellectual and cultural history of intolerance and toleration in early modern and 'early Enlightenment' Europe. John Marshall offers an extensive study of late seventeenth-century practices of religious intolerance and toleration in England, Ireland, France, Piedmont, and the Netherlands, and of the arguments which John Locke and his associates made in defence of 'universal religious toleration' against contemporary justifications of intolerance. He analyses early modern and especially 'early Enlightenment' discussions of toleration; debates over toleration for Jews and Muslims as well as for Christians; the limits of toleration for the intolerant, Catholics, atheists, 'libertines', and 'sodomites', and the complex relationships between intolerance and resistance theories, including Locke's own *Treatises*. This study is a significant contribution to the history of the 'republic of letters' of the 1680s and the development of 'early Enlightenment' culture and will be essential reading for scholars of early modern European history, religion, political science, and philosophy.

JOHN MARSHALL is Professor of History at the Johns Hopkins University. He is also the author of *John Locke: Resistance, Religion, and Responsibility* (1994).

Cambridge Studies in Early Modern British History

Series editors

ANTHONY FLETCHER
Emeritus Professor of English Social History, University of London

JOHN GUY
Visiting Fellow, Clare College, Cambridge

JOHN MORRILL
*Professor of British and Irish History, University of Cambridge,
and Vice-Master of Selwyn College*

This is a series of monographs and studies covering many aspects of the history of the British Isles between the late fifteenth century and the early eighteenth century. It includes the work of established scholars and pioneering work by a new generation of scholars. It includes both reviews and revisions of major topics and books, which open up new historical terrain or which reveal startling new perspectives on familiar subjects. All the volumes set detailed research into our broader perspectives, and the books are intended for the use of students as well as of their teachers.

For a list of titles in the series, see end of book.

JOHN LOCKE, TOLERATION AND EARLY ENLIGHTENMENT CULTURE

Religious Intolerance and Arguments for Religious Toleration in Early Modern and 'Early Enlightenment' Europe

JOHN MARSHALL
Johns Hopkins University

CAMBRIDGE
UNIVERSITY PRESS

CAMBRIDGE UNIVERSITY PRESS
Cambridge, New York, Melbourne, Madrid, Cape Town, Singapore,
São Paulo, Delhi, Dubai, Tokyo

Cambridge University Press
The Edinburgh Building, Cambridge CB2 8RU, UK

Published in the United States of America by Cambridge University Press, New York

www.cambridge.org
Information on this title: www.cambridge.org/9780521129572

First published 2006
Reprinted 2008
This digitally printed version 2009

A catalogue record for this publication is available from the British Library

ISBN 978-0-521-65114-1 Hardback
ISBN 978-0-521-12957-2 Paperback

CONTENTS

v

FIGURES

ACKNOWLEDGMENTS

Many of the chapters of this book have been improved by their presentation at many conferences and seminars and due to the comments of numerous colleagues over many years. While at the University of Denver, I presented an early version of Chapter 16 on the 'republic of letters', and earlier versions of parts of Chapters 1 and 3 on Locke and the law. This book was completed at The Johns Hopkins University, with portions of the research undertaken as a By-Fellow at Churchill College, Cambridge University. To colleagues at all of these institutions I owe my gratitude for many conversations and comments. Various versions of many of these chapters were presented to a large number of conferences and seminars between 1995 and 2001, including: The American Society of Legal Historians; The University of Denver; The Cambridge University Seminar in Early Modern British History; The Institute of Historical Research Seminar on Seventeenth-Century Britain; The Conference on Conspiracies and Conspiracy Theory in Early Modern Europe organised by Michael Hunter; the British Society for the History of Philosophy Conferences on 'The Furly Circle' and on 'Libertinism and Liberty' organised by Sarah Hutton and Justin Champion; the UCLA/Clark Library Conference 'Materialist Philosophy, Religious Heresy and Political Radicalism' organised by Margaret Jacob and Lynn Hunt; the Seventeenth-Century Studies Conference 'Orthodoxies and Heterodoxy' at Durham, England, and the National Humanities Centre, North Carolina, seminar on the Enlightenment. I am grateful to all of the members of all of these many audiences for their comments, and to colleagues for invitations to speak in these locations. I have enjoyed conversations with Luisa Simonutti and am grateful to her for supplying me with copies of some of her pieces. Many colleagues have also offered words of encouragement over the years, together with comments which have sharpened the arguments of this book. I am particularly grateful to David Bell, Justin Champion, Jonathan Israel, Mark Goldie, Mary Fissell, Gabrielle Spiegel, and my former PhD supervisor, J. G. A. Pocock. Many of my colleagues, some of these individuals, and some anonymous referees suffered through a very much longer version of this book in 2001 or 2002, and I am grateful to them all for their patience. Most of all I owe my thanks to my family, including my mother, Eileen, my wife, Nina, and my daughter, Sarah.

Introduction

This book centres on a study of the practices, representations, and justifications of religious intolerance in France, Piedmont, England, Ireland, and the Netherlands in the late seventeenth century, and the arguments for 'universal religious toleration' which were articulated by a small but crucial 'early Enlightenment' group of writers in the 1680s and 1690s in order to combat these practices and justifications of intolerance. It simultaneously studies late seventeenth-century defences of religious intolerance as reiterating many long-standing patristic, late medieval, and early modern justifications of intolerance, and analyses the arguments for religious toleration of the 1680s and 1690s as restatements and expansions of preceding arguments for religious toleration. This book will show that many advocates of 'universal religious toleration' in the 1680s and 1690s, including John Locke, Jean Le Clerc, and Pierre Bayle, were crucial contributors to the development of the 'republic of letters' in the late seventeenth century, and will stress the importance of this 'republic of letters'. It will demonstrate that these thinkers not merely articulated many elements of 'High Enlightenment' thought, such as support for 'civility', 'humanity', and 'tolerance' against 'superstition', 'barbarism', and 'ignorance', but also described their period as one of 'reason' and 'light' against traditional authority and against 'implicit faith'. Religious toleration was the central value of this 'early Enlightenment', and the 'republic of letters' was the central cultural form of the 'early Enlightenment'. Their intellectual and cultural symbiosis will be analysed.

Since Paul Hazard's *La Crise de la Conscience Européenne* identified the late seventeenth century as the crucial revolutionary period in the construction of 'the Enlightenment' nearly seventy years ago, relatively little work has been done on the final two decades of the seventeenth century. Scholarship on 'the Enlightenment' has continued to be dominated by work on the 'High Enlightenment' of the late eighteenth century. Such scholarship has, moreover, tended to focus on the atheistic and materialistic strands of 'the Enlightenment' rather than on arguments of 'the Enlightenment' developed

1

within Christianity.[1] While scholars of the history of political thought associated with the 'Cambridge school' have over recent years paid considerable attention to discourses of resistance and popular sovereignty, natural rights, liberty, and 'reason of state' as foundations of modern political thought, they have paid relatively little attention to religious toleration as another key issue of modern political thought. While Locke has often been discussed as an apologist of religious toleration, Locke's arguments for toleration have not been placed sufficiently in their multiple and international practical and intellectual contexts. Locke has too often been studied in isolation from most or all of his predecessors and contemporaries who advocated religious toleration.[2] The recent outpouring of scholarship on the 'republic of letters' in the eighteenth century has identified this 'republic' as crucial to eighteenth-century sociability and criticism, egalitarianism and participation, and, as such, central to the development of both the 'public sphere' and 'the Enlightenment', but there has been relatively little scholarly attention paid to the 'republic of letters' in the late seventeenth century, to the emergence of its ethos as a 'republic' of virtuous citizens serving the 'public good', and to the central commitment of many in the 'republic of letters' during these years in their advocacy of universal religious toleration at a moment of very considerable religious intolerance.[3]

Travelling widely through European space and time, the chronological focus of this book is on the decade of the 1680s, and the geographical focus of this book is on France, England, and the Netherlands. During the 1680s religious intolerance reached extremely high levels in France preceding and

---

[1] Two particularly important recent works which have studied respectively the radical or 'Spinozist' strains of the 'early Enlightenment' and some of their Christian components as important to the later Enlightenment of Gibbon, are J. Israel, *Radical Enlightenment* (Oxford 2001) and J. G. A. Pocock, *Barbarism and Religion* (Cambridge 1999–).

[2] For the methodology and works of the 'Cambridge school' with which this author is associated, see especially the works of J. G. A. Pocock, Quentin Skinner, John Dunn, Richard Tuck, James Tully, Mark Goldie, Justin Champion, Peter Miller, and David Armitage. Aspects of tolerationist and anti-tolerationist arguments have often been briefly but brilliantly discussed by some of these authors. Other useful recent studies of toleration with greater or lesser historical density and acumen have included: J. C. Laursen (ed.), *Beyond the Persecuting Society* (Pennsylvania 1998); O. Grell and R. Porter, *Toleration in Enlightenment Europe* (Cambridge 1999); O. Grell and R. Scribner, *Tolerance and Intolerance in the European Reformation* (Cambridge 1996); J. Coffey, *Persecution and Toleration in Protestant England 1558–1689* (Harlow 2000); C. Berkvens-Stevelinck (ed.), *The Emergence of Tolerance in the Dutch Republic* (Leiden 1997).

[3] P. Hazard, *The European Mind 1680–1715* (1935; tr. 1953–64); D. Goodman, *The Republic of Letters* (Ithaca 1994); D. Gordon, *Citizens Without Sovereignty* (Princeton 1994); R. Chartier, *The Cultural Origins of the French Revolution* (Durham 1991); M. Jacob, *Living the Enlightenment* (Oxford 1991); J. Habermas, *The Structural Transformation of the Public Sphere* (Cambridge 1996); A. Goldgar, *Impolite Learning* (Yale 1995). On the late seventeenth century 'republic of letters', also see the valuable works cited in Chapter 16 of this book.

following the Revocation of the Edict of Nantes in 1685; 200,000 Huguenots fled from France in these years, and 700,000 Huguenots were prevented from leaving France and coerced to attend Catholic worship. Huguenots who resisted were incarcerated, tortured, forced into slavery on galleys, or executed. Catholic intolerance towards Protestants was also significant in Piedmont, where in 1686 Protestant Waldensians who refused to convert to Catholicism were either killed or imprisoned and then forced into exile by a joint French and Piedmontese army. In England from the 1660s to the mid-1680s an extremely high level of Protestant intolerance involved fines, imprisonments, and the deaths of many Protestant dissenters and some Catholic recusants. Such Protestant religious intolerance in England continued at the beginning of the reign of the Catholic James II in 1685–6, and when in 1687–8 James II attempted to provide a large degree of religious toleration this was undermined by reports and representations of Catholic intolerance in France and Piedmont. Protestant intolerance was also significant in Ireland before the reign of James II, and a brief period of religious toleration under James II was followed first by war between an Irish and French Catholic force in support of James II and an international Protestant army led by William III, and then by the reimposition of Protestant intolerance in the 1690s.

As we will see, the Netherlands provided shelter during the 1680s for many religious and political refugees and was the most religiously tolerant society in Western Europe in the seventeenth century. This book will describe in detail the practical toleration in the seventeenth-century Netherlands for Catholics, many unorthodox Protestants, and Jews, alongside the orthodox Calvinist 'public church'. But we will see that in the seventeenth century religious toleration in the Netherlands had significant limits, was practised by failure to enforce intolerant legislation rather than by legislative enactment of toleration, and faced considerable opposition. In the later 1680s, toleration was under increasing challenge as representations of Catholic violence against Huguenots and Waldensians led to the growth of anti-Catholicism in the Netherlands, and as a chorus of 'orthodox' Huguenot refugees added their voices to long-standing Dutch Reformed hostility to toleration of 'unorthodox' or 'heretical' Protestants such as Socinians. The few refugees to the Netherlands who supported a universal religious toleration in the 1680s recognised that such 'universal' toleration was not established in the Netherlands, and realistically feared that intolerance was gaining support. Bayle spoke in the early 1690s of his fear of a developing Protestant Inquisition in the Netherlands which would become worse than the Catholic Inquisition, while Locke and Limborch also compared contemporary Protestant persecution to the Inquisition.

This book will not merely trace the impact of practices of religious violence but also discuss the impact of representations of religious intolerance in the

1680s in France, Piedmont, England, Ireland, the Netherlands, and among the Huguenot community in exile. It will emphasise the significance in England, Ireland, and the Netherlands of exaggerated representations of Catholic violence in anti-Catholic propaganda during the 'Exclusion Crisis' of 1678–81 in England, in propaganda undermining the tolerationist regime of James II, and in propaganda generating Dutch and English support for William's military and political campaigns in England and Ireland in 1688–91. It will be shown that such representations of Catholic violence against Huguenots and Waldensians drew significance from the communities against whom they were directed: the massacre of Huguenots on St Bartholomew's Day in 1572 had long provided a staple of English and Dutch anti-Catholic propaganda, and Huguenots remained a crucial sister church in many English Protestant eyes, while the Waldensians were viewed as the only visible church which had managed to preserve the 'true religion' in medieval Europe, and previous persecutions of the Waldensians had been central to British and Dutch anti-Catholic propaganda long before the 1680s, most notably in 1655.

This book will briefly describe the provision of religious toleration and its limits in England and Ireland in and after 1689–91, after they came to be ruled by the Dutch stadtholder, William of Orange, and his Protestant English wife Mary. It will stress the importance of statutory provision of toleration to orthodox Protestant dissenters in 1689 as ending the incarcerations, financial ruin, and deaths of orthodox Protestant dissenters, and the significance of the statutory denial after 1689 of toleration to Catholics, to unorthodox Protestants such as anti-Trinitarians or Socinians, and to 'atheists' and 'libertines'. It will indicate that the degree of religious toleration and intolerance actually practised depended not merely on statutory provision but also on royal intervention, and that by these means a limited toleration of Jews was allowed in England before and after 1689, and practised for Catholics in England after 1689. A careful examination of the practices of toleration is also provided for the Netherlands, where toleration was often practised while legally proscribed, and where private religious practice was usually free but public worship and public expression of one's religious commitments were disallowed or subject to significant restrictions. In Part 3 of this book the arguments for toleration composed in the Netherlands in the 1680s will be shown to have been influenced by these restrictions.

At many points the story of intolerance told in this book will intersect with arguments for and against resistance to political tyranny, including most notably the arguments for resistance of John Locke. As these many intersections are encountered they will be studied. We will analyse the ways in which practices and representations of Catholic intolerance towards Protestants in France and Piedmont provided Locke with significant reasons to fear the growth of absolutism in England, and thus provided a part of the background to his justification of resistance in the Second Treatise. And we will study the ways in which the practices of High Anglican intolerance towards Protestant dissenters also provided a part of the background to Locke's justification of resistance in the Second Treatise as the Crown tried to remove Protestant dissenters from the Church of England from sitting on grand juries, where they had been crucial to providing security of life for political opponents of the drive towards absolutism of Charles II. Nonetheless, this book will stress that Locke's argument for resistance in the Second Treatise does not make a case for resistance on religious grounds, and probes some of the reasons for that absence. That Locke was arguing for rights of resistance *in extremis* will be emphasised. Examination of the defence of individual rights of resistance to tyranny by others who supported religious toleration, including Locke's close friend Jean Le Clerc, will indicate that Le Clerc similarly constructed arguments for resistance *in extremis* and repudiated the actions of the regicides who had executed Charles I as a tyrant in 1649. Other defences of toleration and resistance will be examined, including Gilbert Burnet's arguments, which received wide circulation both in the Netherlands and in England.

But while in these instances defence of rights of resistance was generally aligned with support for rights of religious toleration, we will see in the course of this book that this was a highly contingent alignment. We will see that the leading Huguenot theologian Pierre Jurieu's early works supported a limited religious toleration and opposed rights of resistance to tyranny, and that when he became an avid defender of rights of resistance to tyranny, Jurieu simultaneously wrote works against universal religious toleration. Pierre Bayle was one of the most important advocates of universal religious toleration in the Netherlands in the 1680s and 1690s, but he was an opponent of rights of resistance to political tyranny. As we will see, Bayle defended toleration and non-resistance against Jurieu. I indicated in my book *John Locke: Resistance, Religion, and Responsibility* the contingent relationships between Locke's commitments to rights of religious toleration and rights of individual resistance to political tyranny, as in 1660 he opposed both, in 1667 he supported the former but opposed the latter (like the early Jurieu and the consistent Bayle), and by about 1682–3 he came to support both toleration and resistance. In examining the thought of Locke, Le Clerc, Jurieu, Bayle, Burnet, and others, this book will again indicate some of the complexity of associations between commitments to toleration and resistance in the 1680s. In its examination of the ways in which some Protestant defences of rights of resistance and condemnations of Catholic intolerance were combined with defences of denial of toleration to Catholics, most notably in Ireland, this book will delineate further complexities in the associations between commitments to resistance and to toleration in the 1680s and 1690s.

The advocates of religious toleration in the 1680s and 1690s were writing to combat not merely contemporary practices of religious intolerance but also to oppose contemporary justifications of religious intolerance. This book will study the justifications of religious intolerance by Anglicans, Huguenots, the Dutch Reformed Church, and Catholics in the late seventeenth century, as Catholics defended the use of force against Protestants, and many Protestants justified the use of force not merely against Catholics but also against unorthodox or dissenting Protestants as 'heretics' and 'schismatics'. It will show that the voices raised in justification of universal religious toleration in this context were few, and that the voices in defence of religious intolerance were legion. In order to understand these multiple Catholic and Protestant justifications of intolerance in the late seventeenth century, which explicitly rehearsed and expanded upon many long-standing themes of anti-tolerationist literature, and in order to understand the character of the response to these arguments by the advocates of toleration, this book will place the arguments against religious toleration of the 1680s and 1690s into the context of arguments against religious toleration developed over the preceding history of Christianity. It will emphasise the sources for later arguments against religious toleration in the fourth century of 'late patristic' Christianity, most notably in the thought of Augustine, and the repetition of many of these arguments in late medieval Christianity, in the time of development of the inquisition against the Waldensians – significantly, the ancestors of the Waldensians against whom Catholics used armed force in 1686. But it will concentrate most heavily on documenting support for religious intolerance in sixteenth-century and early seventeenth-century Europe as 'magisterial Reformation' Protestants (that is, mainstream Reformation Protestants such as Luther, Calvin, Zwingli, Bullinger, and their followers, who supported the role of the magistrate in enforcing religion) joined hands with Catholics in defending religious intolerance.

The intolerance of Calvinism will be stressed as influential in sixteenth-century justifications of intolerance against Catholics, anti-Trinitarians and Anabaptists, influential again in early and mid-seventeenth-century defences of intolerance against Catholics, Arminians, Baptists, Quakers, and anti-Trinitarians, and central to 'orthodox' Dutch Reformed ministers and to 'orthodox' Huguenot ministers of the 1680s. The Huguenot Church, Dutch Reformed Church, and Waldensians had adopted the same confession of faith in the sixteenth century as parts of the movement of international Calvinism, which also gained considerable support in England, and defined 'orthodoxy' in terms of the strict Calvinism supported against Arminianism at the Synod of Dort in 1618. Defences of religious intolerance in the 1680s by Huguenot and Dutch Reformed ministers were thus late moments of intolerant international Calvinism.

As this book will show, many early modern assaults on religious toleration were structured around very similar sets of accusations against 'heretics' and 'schismatics'. 'Heretics' and 'schismatics' were associated repeatedly with treason and sedition, communism and anarchy, poison and pestilence, 'libertinism' and 'sodomy'. It will be shown that an understanding of 'heresies' and 'schisms' as repeated through the centuries was central to early modern European anti-heretical and anti-schismatic literature which identified 'new heresies' and 'schisms' as 'old heresies and schisms revived'. Many 'new heresies', such as Protestantism to Catholics, or Anabaptism or anti-Trinitarianism to 'magisterial Reformation' Protestants, were therefore understood in terms that had formerly been deployed against the medieval Waldensians and Albigensians (or Cathars), and before that against fourth-century and medieval anti-Trinitarians. In the Western Europe whose Christianity had fissured after the Reformation into the division between Catholic and Protestant and into a host of Protestant denominations and sects, preceding accusations against 'heretics' and 'schismatics' intensified as the number of such 'heretics' and 'schismatics' was understood to have multiplied. This book will show the ways in which these increased accusations were combined in early modern Europe with accusations that 'heretics' and 'schismatics' were 'witches' or 'monsters' in a period increasingly understood as that of the 'Last Days' before the millennium, a period when biblical prophecies were interpreted as having forecast that 'heresies' and 'schisms' would multiply alongside witches and monsters, comets and eclipses. Most thinkers, both Catholic and Protestant, treated monsters, comets, and eclipses as signs and portents from God, and concluded that magistrates needed to act ever more forcefully against 'heretics' and 'schismatics' in order to ward off God's punishments of their communities by famines, plagues, and wars. To most sixteenth- and seventeenth-century thinkers in England, France, and the Netherlands, both 'magisterial Reformation' Protestants and Catholics, religious toleration was itself a 'poisonous' and a 'diabolical' doctrine. This book will indicate further reasons why the accusations against 'heretics' and 'schismatics' seemed to anti-heretical and anti-schismatic writers to be evidenced by the actual events of early modern Europe, as some individuals pilloried as 'heretical' and 'schismatic' did indeed support communism, seemed to cause civil war, and challenged 'orthodox sexual and familial morality'. But this book will show that anti-heretical and anti-schismatic writers very often mischaracterised the commitments of 'heretics' and 'schismatics', and will stress that the challenges that were posed only by the minority of such 'heretics' and 'schismatics' to political, familial, or social hierarchy were ascribed by anti-heretical and anti-schismatic writers to all 'heretics' and 'schismatics'.

In the course of thus examining in detail the anti-heretical and anti-schismatic literature of sixteenth- and early seventeenth-century Europe, this book will describe the arguments for religious toleration advanced in this period. It will note the infrequency of such arguments, and trace some limitations or tensions within such accounts, such as support by largely tolerationist Polish Socinians for the imprisonment of the Socinian Francis David for challenging the invocation of Christ, and the defence of intolerance towards Catholics of the largely tolerationist Arian Arminian John Milton. And it will indicate that most of the arguments for religious toleration were generated by those accused by most of their contemporaries of being 'heretics' and 'schismatics', and thus by those who were accused of being seditious communists, murderers, 'libertines' and 'sodomites'. This book will consider very briefly also *politique* advocacy of toleration on grounds of 'reason of state'. While such *politique* arguments were important in supporting the practice of religious toleration for orthodox Huguenots and Catholics in late sixteenth-century France, the double-edged nature of much *politique* argument for toleration will be indicated: religious minorities who lost the capacity to defend themselves by force of arms became in such *politique* accounts legitimately subject to intolerance, since it was their very capacity to disrupt the state which underpinned the case for their toleration. In the sixteenth century, Lipsius' *politique* argument favoured the toleration of Huguenots; by the late seventeenth, it favoured intolerance, and it was as an argument against toleration that Bayle anathematised Lipsius' thought.

In analysing the development of arguments for religious toleration in the sixteenth and early seventeenth centuries, this book will also trace the importance of arguments from patristic and late medieval writers that Jews, Muslims, and pagans should be tolerated, whereas 'heretics' and 'schismatics' should be punished. Anti-heretical and anti-schismatic writers argued that toleration should be extended to those who had never known Christianity and needed to be persuaded to adopt it, but not to those who had 'fallen' from the 'truth'. It will be shown that much argument for religious toleration in early modern Europe generally, and in the 1680s and 1690s specifically, revolved around suggesting that the accepted toleration for Jews and Muslims should be extended to 'heretics' and 'schismatics'. It will, moreover, be indicated that many supporters of religious toleration in the seventeenth century pointed to Islamic societies as providing a degree of religious toleration which ought to be imitated by contemporary Christian societies. This example of Islamic tolerance was combined in tolerationist argument with the example of the Netherlands as a society tolerating both Jews and Christians in the seventeenth century.

Many limitations on support for toleration for Jews and Muslims even in the Netherlands will nonetheless be stressed, with discussion, for instance, of the limitations which Grotius sought to place on Jews, and of his unwillingness to repudiate allegations of ritual murder by Jews. Debates over toleration of Jewish worship and readmission to England in the mid-seventeenth century similarly saw accusations of child murder and cannibalism by Jews rehearsed as reasons to maintain the medieval exclusion of Jews from England. Only a very limited number of Jews were allowed to resettle in England at the end of this debate, and then by prerogative action by Oliver Cromwell, not by statutory permission; it was this prerogative action that was to be repeated by Charles II, James II, and then expanded by William III in the wake of the Revolutions of 1688–91. It will be indicated that in Christian arguments, Jews and Muslims were represented on many occasions as being 'evildoers', 'sodomites', and 'obstinate' opponents of Christianity. While these representations of Jews and Muslims had often been combined since patristic and medieval writing with support for their toleration on the ground that Jews and Muslims needed to be persuaded to adopt Christianity, at other times in late medieval Europe these accusations had been involved in justifications of punishments, pogroms, and banishments. Early modern Europeans inherited and redeployed these accusations, and anti-heretical and anti-schismatic writers often responded to the example of the toleration of Jews in the Netherlands by arguing that it gave further grounds to indict religious toleration.

Having thus described in Part 1 of this book the practices and representations of religious intolerance in France, Piedmont, England, Ireland, the Netherlands, and among the Huguenot community in exile, and having described in Part 2 of this book the weight of anti-tolerationist argument in early modern Europe and in the 1680s while sketching important arguments for religious toleration in sixteenth- and early seventeenth-century Europe, the final third of this book will be devoted to an extensive and intensive account of the arguments for religious toleration issued by a small group of writers in the 1680s and 1690s in order to combat the contemporary practices and justifications of religious intolerance. Most of the writers defending universal religious toleration in the 1680s were based in the Netherlands in the 1680s. Some were Dutch, but most were refugees. All were composing their defences of religious toleration with an international perspective, intending to combat Protestant and Catholic arguments for intolerance, and writing with a strong awareness that contemporary arguments for intolerance reiterated arguments expressed throughout the past millennium of Christian intolerance.

The third part of this book will also situate these defenders of universal religious toleration by showing that these authors, including Locke, were attempting to develop and to define in the 1680s and 1690s an 'early Enlightenment culture' which centred on advocacy of religious toleration and on development of the culture of the 'republic of letters'. This 'early

Enlightenment culture' and the emergent 'republic of letters' of the 1680s and 1690s will be discussed at length. It will be shown that these advocates of universal religious toleration offered to each other many important forms of mutual support, including assistance in improving, publishing, and publicising their tolerationist arguments themselves. It will be shown that they viewed such services to each other as contributions to the 'republic of letters', and that they celebrated an ethos of 'virtuous' service to that 'republic' which was itself 'republican': based on the duties of citizens to serve the common or public good, realising their own liberty through performance of that service, and defending liberty against 'slavery' in the international intellectual society that was the 'republic of letters' by those actions. In 1685, Bayle depicted the 'republic of letters' as the antithesis of 'the Inquisition', the institutional epitome of religious persecution and restriction of intellectual enquiry. Locke drew a similar contrast in the 1680s between the conversational circles of the 'republic of letters' and 'the Inquisition', which he viewed as a central part of the 'Empire of Darkness'. Many linkages between the cultural practices and ethos of the 'republic of letters' and the defence of religious toleration will be analysed.

These thinkers advanced a series of political, economic, epistemological, religious, historical, and scientific arguments for universal religious toleration. Each of these arguments will be examined in turn. These advocates of religious toleration particularly stressed that (almost all forms of) religious worship and all 'speculative opinions' were intrinsically 'harmless'. This argument was applied against notions of the magisterial duty to establish the 'true religion' drawn from the Mosaic theocracy and from the Constantinian Christianisation of the Roman Empire. Magisterial attempts to institute a religion for all of their subjects and to back that with punishments were defined as 'tyrannical'. These advocates of religious toleration replied explicitly to the accusations that 'heretics' and 'schismatics' were evil and intolerable, treasonous and communist, 'poisonous' and 'pestilential', 'libertine' and 'sodomitical'. They argued for toleration of the worship of Jews and Muslims, and while they did so in the attempt to extend the general acceptance of toleration of Jews and Muslims and 'pagans' to the toleration of 'heretics' and 'schismatics' by arguing that it was incongruous for Christians to tolerate Jews and Muslims but not their fellow Christians, their arguments were also practical arguments for the religious toleration of Jews and 'pagans' and perhaps of Muslims. Locke argued for citizenship as well as toleration for Jews and Muslims, in full recognition of the toleration of Jews in the Netherlands and in argument for its desirability in England, and argued for the toleration of 'pagans' as a colonial administrator.

These advocates of religious toleration in the 1680s and 1690s argued that religious toleration had been practised and supported in the 'primitive

Christianity' of the first three centuries, and that 'enlightened' Christianity should now revive such toleration in practice and principle. They repudiated the fourth century for its development of credalism and coercion, criticised the Constantinian Christianisation of the church, and assaulted the authority of Augustine. And they anathematised the 'Middle Ages' – a term which came into currency in the 1690s – as the period when already considerable late patristic intolerance had been further developed by the institutionalisation of 'the Inquisition', a set of institutions and practices in whose reductive image as one institution, 'the Inquisition', they represented all religious persecution. They celebrated their time as a time of 'enlightenment', of 'civility', 'politeness', and 'humanity', in direct opposition to the 'superstition' and 'barbarity' of the 'Middle Ages', to the Constantinian corruption of Christianity, and to the retention of 'Popery' at the Reformation. And they looked back to the 'tolerant' Roman republic and Roman Empire before its Christianisation (and to Athens) as a time of 'civility' and 'humanity' and 'politeness', as well as religious toleration which should now be revived. Their notion of their time as one of 'enlightenment' challenged the notion of the repetition and intensification of diabolic 'heresies' and schisms in the 'Last Days' central to early modern anti-heretical and anti-schismatic literature, and undermined explanations of monsters and comets as supernatural signs from God which had been used to support much early modern persecution. Such beliefs in supernatural portents were declared 'superstitions', and naturalistic or 'scientific' explanations for many of these events were instead advanced. Here, the development of 'natural philosophy' by the late seventeenth century joined hands with the cause of religious toleration, and itself helped to reinforce the notion that this was a time of 'progress' and of 'enlightenment'. The 'republic of letters' drew from notions of a religiously impartial scientific community, and from models of scientific enquiry which stressed 'civility' and 'probability' and impartially attested 'fact'; both were strongly associated in the 1680s and 1690s with the cause of religious toleration and the culture of the 'republic of letters'. This period was thus crucial in handing on to the 'High Enlightenment' many of its leitmotifs – of religious toleration, of 'humanity' and 'civility', and of the notion of progress against the alleged 'barbarism', 'superstition', and 'inhumanity' of preceding ages.

Thus far in this introduction the emphasis has been on the extensiveness of support for universal religious toleration by its advocates. But it is important to stress that this was a commitment to religious toleration, and not to toleration or to liberty more generally. There were important limits in the support for religious toleration in the 1680s and 1690s which will be discussed in this book. Several of these advocates of toleration were explicitly supporters of intolerance towards the intolerant. Many advocates of religious toleration in the 1680s and 1690s questioned whether toleration could be extended to Catholics on the political grounds of the threat posed by those who were committed to intolerance, who believed that 'faith did not need to be kept with heretics', or who obeyed 'a foreign prince' such as the Pope. We will situate these discussions of toleration for Catholics in simultaneous contexts of the actual Catholic religious violence of 1685–6, of religious propaganda about Catholic violence and Catholic political principles, and of contemporary Dutch and English practices of toleration for Catholics. We will see that in many works of the 1680s depicting Catholic violence in France and Piedmont, intolerance was said to be required by Catholicism and all or many Catholics were alleged to believe that faith did not need to be kept with heretics. We will stress that several of the advocates of universal religious toleration, including Bayle and Burnet, argued that a number of their principles rendered contemporary Catholics dangerous subjects in Protestant countries and required intolerance towards many of their priests, and simultaneously argued that the private worship of many or all lay Catholics should be tolerated, as it was in practice in the Netherlands. Support for toleration of lay Catholics was also voiced in England under James II by William Popple, the English translator of Locke's *Letter Concerning Toleration*. I will discuss Locke's own treatment of the question of Catholic toleration, stressing simultaneously his fear of what he perceived as the encircling menace of intolerant and politically subversive Roman Catholicism, his explicit exclusion from toleration of the intolerant and of those who held that faith did not have to be kept with heretics, and his statements that Catholic worship deserved toleration in suggesting that in the mid- and later 1680s Locke was struggling to find a way to extend toleration to at least some lay Catholics, while holding many Catholics intolerable.

Several of these advocates of religious toleration explicitly and straight-forwardly denied toleration to 'atheists'. They argued that 'atheists' were untrustworthy: there was no security of their keeping their promises without divine sanctions for oaths. They suggested that 'atheists' were such because they were desirous that there be no God in order to avoid punishment for their sins. And they suggested that 'atheists' could make no claim to religious toleration since they were not religious. One could not claim a duty to worship a God in whom one did not believe. Unlike heretics, 'atheists' could not claim the duty and therefore the right to evangelise on behalf of a gospel to which they did not subscribe. Facing the accusation that 'heretics' and 'schismatics' were close to 'atheists' and as such evil and intolerable, advocates of universal religious toleration replied that 'heretics' and 'schis-matics' were good and tolerable but that 'atheists' were indeed evil and intolerable. I will note that the exclusion of 'atheists' from 'toleration' was apparently supported even by Bayle in the *Philosophical Commentary*, and suggest – with Mori and others – that Bayle's position even in this text was complex if read carefully, and that there were good reasons to think that Bayle was indirectly supporting toleration for 'atheists' in other works. I will examine Bayle's various arguments on the issue of 'atheists' at some length. And I will note that there is a hint in Locke's *Essay Concerning Human Understanding* that Locke was at least considering the issue of 'atheists'' political viability in the 1690s in the light of his reading of travel literature, even though Locke adamantly denied toleration to 'atheists' in many of his works, including the *Essay*.

Finally, I will examine the exclusion from toleration of 'libertinism' and 'sodomy' by these advocates of universal religious toleration. Although at points the advocates of universal religious toleration indicated that some kinds of 'libertine' activities were not subject to magisterial action as they did not threaten the security of the society nor harm others, they usually indicated this in order to point out the incongruity of contemporary punishment of 'morally' upstanding religious dissenters while 'libertines' went unpunished and not in order to defend 'libertinism' itself. Facing anti-heretical and anti-schismatic arguments that 'heretics' and 'schismatics' were 'libertines' and 'sodomites', and writing in a context in which a very small number of writers defended 'libertinism' and 'sodomy' together with religious toleration, most notably the avowed 'libertine' Earl of Rochester, these advocates of religious toleration argued that 'libertines' and 'sodomites' were evil and intolerable. They attacked the toleration of 'libertinism', and supported the toleration of 'liberty'. These advocates of religious toleration may even be said to have contributed thereby to the atmosphere which supported prosecution of homosexuals in the Netherlands, where many homosexuals were to be executed in the 1730s, and in England, where an accused 'sodomite' was punished in the 1690s and where homosexuals were severely punished in ways that occasionally led to their deaths in the eighteenth century. As we will see, at the end of the eighteenth century Joseph Priestley and Thomas Jefferson criticised the advocates of religious toleration of the 1680s and 1690s for denying toleration to Catholics and 'atheists', and expanded their arguments to support toleration for Catholics and 'atheists' by declaring Catholics and 'atheists' harmless, and Jeremy Bentham constructed arguments for the toleration of homosexual acts and declared them harmless (although he did not print these arguments because of his fear that they would be used to condemn his utilitarianism). This book will thus not merely show that the arguments for religious toleration constructed in the 1680s and 1690s provided very important replies to prevailing anti-tolerationist arguments and violence; it will also indicate the limitations of these arguments in the 1680s and 1690s.

In order to study the arguments for religious toleration of the 1680s and early 1690s in their practical and intellectual contexts, this book navigates across a number of national and chronological boundaries. Centred on

Locke, like Locke's interests this book crosses boundaries between English, French, Dutch, Irish, Piedmontese, and Genevan history. It navigates a course between intellectual history, cultural history, religious history, political history, the history of science, and the histories of sexuality and gender. It travels between the immediate period of the 1680s and 1690s and the broader history of toleration and persecution. Bringing all of these different stories and sub-fields of history into relation to each other, it intends to appeal above all others to an audience interested in early modern British history, while wishing to speak also to those interested in other areas of early modern history, to those interested in Locke, or to those interested in the history of toleration. Drawing materials from scholars in many different sub-specialties and from scholars of several nations in order to tell its story, I am conscious of particularly significant debts to the works of Elisabeth Labrousse on intolerance and toleration in France, of Jonathan Israel on intolerance and toleration in the Netherlands, and of Mark Goldie, Tim Harris, John Coffey, and Michael Watts on toleration and intolerance in seventeenth-century England. I am conscious also of particular debts to: Stuart Clark, R. I. Moore, and J. C. Davis on demonology and anti-heretical thought and polemic; to Lorraine Daston, Katherine Park, Robert Scribner, Barbara Shapiro, and Margaret Jacob on the topics of monsters and comets and on the history of science and Latitudinarianism; also to Justin Champion, David Katz, and Nabil Matar on polemic representations of Islam and Judaism and issues of toleration of Jews and Muslims in seventeenth-century British thought.

A full account of the 'early Enlightenment' stands beyond the time and space available. This book concentrates on analysing 'early Enlightenment culture' and its arguments for religious toleration on the thought of Locke and his associates. Locke looms far larger in the 'early Enlightenment' described in this book than he would in an account of the entire 'early Enlightenment'; other figures, most notably Spinoza, loom far less large than they would in an account of the entire 'early Enlightenment'. I enthusiastically recommend on Spinozist and other aspects of radical Enlightenment thought Jonathan Israel's *Radical Enlightenment* and the important works of such scholars as Justin Champion, Margaret Jacob, Anthony McKenna, and Miguel Benitez. A considerably lengthier draft of this book was completed in 2001–2. Since then it has been cut massively; I have only very sparingly addressed books published since 2002.[4]

---

[4] Two particularly valuable books on toleration published after composition of this book are R. Po-Chia Hsia and A. van Nierop (eds.), *Calvinism and Religious Toleration in the Dutch Golden Age* (Cambridge 2002) and P. Zagorin, *How the Idea of Religious Toleration Came to the West* (Princeton 2003).

PART 1

Catholic and Protestant intolerance in the later seventeenth century

1

Catholic intolerance, its representations in England, c. 1678–86, and Locke's Second Treatise

The 1680s constituted one of the most religiously repressive decades in European history. The most significant of many persecutions of religious minorities in the 1680s involved the 1685 Revocation of the Edict of Nantes in France. Before 1680, there were approximately 850,000–900,000 Protestants in France – or about 5 per cent of the French population.[1] Under considerable duress, the decade of the 1680s saw the apparent conversion to Roman Catholicism of perhaps 700,000 of these Huguenots, while approximately 200,000 went into exile.[2] England and the Netherlands each welcomed about 50,000–70,000 refugees, most of whom settled in London, Canterbury, Rotterdam, and Amsterdam. In 1700, more than 23,000 inhabitants of London and its immediate environs were Huguenots, while in 1687 a Huguenot refugee declared that Rotterdam had become 'nearly French by the arrival there of a great number of the inhabitants of Rouen and Dieppe', and in Amsterdam several thousand new refugees arrived in 1685–8 to add to already considerable immigration from 1681.[3]

---

[1] D. Parker, 'The Huguenots in Seventeenth-century France' in A. C. Hepburn (ed.), *Minorities in History* (New York 1979), 11–30, at 11; J. McManners, *Church and Society in Eighteenth-Century France* (Oxford 1998), 565. Significant parts of this chapter were presented to the Cambridge University seminar in early modern British history; the University of London seminar in seventeenth-century history; the Centre for British Christian Thought at the United Theological College, Aberystwyth; the North American conference on British Studies; the Seventeenth-Century Studies conference on 'Orthodoxies and Heterodoxy'; and the Huguenot Society conference. I wish to thank all of these audiences for their comments and their convenors for the invitations to speak, including John Morrill, Mark Goldie, John Miller, Justin Champion, and Alan Sell. The final section of this chapter (and part of Chapter 3) was given as a paper, 'Locke, liberty and the law', at the American Society for Legal Historians conference in Houston, Texas, in 1995. I am grateful to Tim Harris, Michael Mendle and Joyce Lee Malcolm for their comments at that conference, and to Joyce Malcolm for the invitation.

[2] J. Garrisson, *L'Édit de Nantes et sa révocation* (Paris 1985); P. Joutard, *Les Camisards* (Paris 1994).

[3] Quotation on Rotterdam in C. Gibbs, 'Some Intellectual and Political Influences of the Huguenot Emigres in the United Provinces c. 1680–1730', *Bijdragen en mededelingen de geschiedenis des Nederlanden* 90 (1975), 255–87, at 257n.8; figures for London in Gwynn,

It was this exile of Huguenots to England and to the Netherlands that gave first circulation to the term 'refugees', now central to our language in designating those fleeing religious or political persecution. It was first used in the minutes of the Threadneedle Street consistory in London in 1681, and in the Netherlands in 1690.[4] The process of forced conversion and exile of Huguenots was, moreover, one of the two largest forced conversions and forced migrations of peoples within Europe in the entire early modern period,[5] the other being the forced conversion of Muslims, and the forced conversion or expulsion of Jews from Spain (and other countries) commencing in 1492.[6] The Huguenots themselves often compared these two processes of forced conversion or exile. In the 1706 *History of the Jews* by a tolerationist Huguenot refugee to the Netherlands, Jacques Basnage, the description of 1492 was designed to apply equally to the 1680s, with the change of the words 'Jews' and 'Spain' to 'Huguenots' and 'France':

Will it not be acknowledged, that in civil Society, Exile is one of the severest and most mortifying Punishments?...Are not the loss of Estates, confiscated by the Sovereign, pecuniary Taxes, the depriving of the means of livelihood, the ruin and starving of a Family caused by Edicts, so many cruel Punishments in all Nations of the world?...Shall we say, that those Thousands of Jews that were banished from Spain, and perished with Famine and Misery did not suffer?'[7]

Huguenot Heritage (London 1985), 36; for Amsterdam in C. Gibbs, 'The European Origins of the Glorious Revolution' in W. A. Maguire (ed.), *Kings in Conflict* (Belfast 1990), 9–28, at 14. The Huguenot migration of 1681–1705, concentrated in the 1680s, has been very variously estimated; but most scholars (e.g. Garrisson, *L'Édit de Nantes*, 250) now estimate about 200,000, with about 50,000–70,000 going to each of England and the Netherlands (although one scholar has argued for a much lower figure of c. 100,000–130,000: H. P. H. Nusteling, 'The Netherlands and the Huguenot Emigres' in *La Révocation de L'Édit de Nantes et les provinces-unies 1685* (Amsterdam 1986), 17–34). Gibbs 'Some Intellectual and Political Influences', 255–7, expresses scepticism about ever knowing the figures accurately.

[4] R. Gwynn, 'England's First Refugees', *History Today* (May 1985); M. Waller, *1700: Scenes from London Life* (London 2000), 265; J. Stouten, 'Quelques textes littéraires sur la Révocation de L'Édit de Nantes' in *La Révocation de L'Édit de Nantes*, 77–84, at 77. I am grateful to Dr Gwynn for conversations about the Huguenot emigration to England and its relationship to English political life.

[5] The largest forced migration of peoples caused by early modern Europeans was, of course, the enslavement and transportation of millions of people from Africa to the Americas; 1685 was not merely the year of the Revocation of the Edict of Nantes, but was also the year of promulgation of the Code Noir.

[6] Estimates of Jews expelled from Spain in 1492 vary, but are often thought to be in the range 50,000–100,000, with about the same number 'converting'. Jonathan Israel has appropriately emphasised that these Spanish actions need to be understood as part of a wave of expulsion from Western Europe: *European Jewry in the Age of Mercantilism* (Oxford 1985): ch. 1. See also E. W. Monter, 'The Death of Co-existence: Jews and Moslems in Christian Spain 1480–1502' in *The Expulsion of the Jews: 1492 and After* (ed.) R. B. Waddington and A. Williamson (New York 1994); J. Hale, *The Civilization of Europe in the Renaissance*, (New York 1994), 167, 475–7.

[7] J. Basnage, *History of the Jews* (London 1708), VII, xi, 638–40. Part of this passage is discussed in J. Elukin, 'Jacques Basnage and the History of the Jews: Anti-Catholic Polemic and

The paralleling of measures taken against the Huguenots in the 1680s and against Jews in the 1490s was strongly stated in the 1680s themselves. The leading Huguenot minister Pierre Jurieu's 1682 *Last Efforts of Afflicted Innocence* compared removal of children from Huguenot homes to be educated as Catholics to the forced baptism of Jews by King Manuel I in Portugal in 1497 under the influence of the 'infernal...Spanish and Portuguese Inquisitions'. The 1681 *Humble Address of the Distressed Protestants in France* declared that parents had the right to educate their children by the 'Law of Nature' and argued that the kings of Spain and Portugal had been condemned for undue 'zeal' for similar actions against Jewish children. And the persecutions of 1492 and 1685 were compared by the single most influential of the tolerationist authors in the Netherlands, Pierre Bayle, in his 1685 *New Letters*.[8]

The Revocation of the Edict of Nantes in October 1685 is the most notorious moment of the persecution of the Huguenots, but it was actually the culmination of an escalation of measures against Huguenots since 1661, which had included offering financial incentives for conversion and ordering Protestant temples to be destroyed.[9] Of about 700 Protestant temples in 1660, only about 100 remained standing in France by 1680. In those areas where bishops were to be avid advocates of the Revocation, almost no Protestant temples remained by October 1685. In order to prevent Protestant worship, soldiers had torn down these temples, carting away or destroying the pulpits, pews, furniture, and the fabric of the buildings. On many occasions, the objects of worship were ritually destroyed by soldiers. In order to continue to worship, many Protestants were forced to worship in the fields and woods in the early 1680s.[10] From 1680 to 1685 the number and

Historical Allegory in the Republic of Letters', *Journal of the History of Ideas* (1992), 603–30, at 607. Cf. also E. Peters, *The Inquisition* (Berkeley 1989), 162. The year 1686 saw the lifting of expulsion orders against Jews in France: Israel, *European Jewry*, 133–4.

[8] Jurieu, *Last Efforts* (1682), 58, 62–9; Jurieu, *Policy*, 226–9; *Humble Address*, 4 (also printed in J. Quick, *Synodicon in Gallia Reformata or the Acts, Decisions and Canons of Those Famous National Councils of the Reformed Church in France* (London 1692), cxxv–vii); Bayle, *Nouvelles* in OD, II, 211 A (and discussed in M. Yardeni, 'Bayle and Basnage on Post-Commonwealth Jewish History', *European Studies Review* (1977), 245–58, at 246); T. Lennon, *Reading Bayle* (Toronto 1999), 90–1; W. Rex, *Essays on Pierre Bayle and Religious Controversy* (The Hague 1965), 183. Bayle was to accuse Jurieu of being a 'Turncoat' for contradicting the arguments of the *Policy* in Note H of Augustine in the *Historical and Critical Dictionary*, but Jurieu's reversal was less substantial on this issue than Bayle alleged: see below, ch. 14. For earlier uses of these arguments, see below, ch. 12; for uses in the 'republic of letters' in the 1680s, see pp. 593–4.

[9] Labrousse, *Bayle* (Oxford 1983). Robert Ferguson's 1682 *Third Part of No Protestant Plot* was to identify the persecution of Huguenots in France as starting in 1660, and thus to parallel it directly with the Restoration of the English monarchy and its persecution of Protestant dissent.

[10] E. Benoist, *Histoire de L'Édit de Nantes* (Delft 1693–5), 5 vols. in 3, III, *passim* (where, for instance, Benoist notes that by as early as 1671 the sixty-one churches of Poitou had been

impact of measures against Protestants increased significantly. Protestants were forbidden to hold many offices, including those of judges and attorneys. These measures created informers against Protestant worship of some who abjured in order to keep their positions, such as the 'pettifoggin[g]' attorney Agoust, whom the Huguenot minister Jacques Fontaine recorded as abjuring in order 'to retain his employment' and giving 'information by which he might ingratiate himself with those in power' by listing sixty Huguenot worshippers who had met for worship in the woods in 1684 when their church at Vaux had been 'levelled with the ground', together with 'most of the Protestant places of worship in our province'.[11] Summer 1681 saw the closure of the Protestant Academy at Sedan, quickly followed by the first dragonnades in Poitou, a practice in which large numbers of soldiers were billeted in the homes of Protestants until their hosts converted. It was also extended to Languedoc in 1681, before being extended to the nation as a whole in 1685. Perhaps the harshest new measure of the early 1680s, however, was the edict of June 1681 providing that Huguenot children could 'choose' Catholicism at age seven and were then to be taken from their parents in order to be educated as Catholics. A manuscript list of Huguenot children drawn up in 1680 in the town of Alençon has the chilling instructions written in the margins: 'Take Jean and Anne Marie;' 'Take Louise and Marie;' and, next to the 'weakly' Anne, 'Take Anne if she is in [sufficient] condition'.[12] Jurieu's 1682 *Last Efforts* declared this a 'terrible law' and 'repugnant to the Laws of Nature', while the English ambassador Henry Savile called it a 'terrible new edict' of which the Huguenots were 'more sensible' than of 'any previous measure'.[13] It was immediately after this edict that large-scale Huguenot emigration to the Netherlands and England started; probably more than 3,000 families left in 1681 alone.[14] As Savile recorded, the 'poor people are in such fear that they hurry their

---

reduced to thirteen); P. Bolle, 'Deux évêques devant la Révocation: Le Camus et Cosnac' in *La Révocation de L'Édit de Nantes et le protestantisme français en 1685*, ed. R. Zuber and L. Theis (*BSHPF*: Paris 1986), 59–74; S. Deyon, 'La destruction des temples' in *ibid.*, 239–59, esp. at 255–6; R. M. Golden (ed.), *The Huguenot Connection: The Edict of Nantes, its Revocation, and Early French Migration to South Carolina* (Dordrecht 1988), 18; E. Labrousse, *Une foi, une loi, un roi?: Essai sur la Révocation de L'Édit de Nantes* (Paris 1985), 167ff.; *idem, Bayle*, 4–5, 8.

[11] James Fontaine, *Memoirs of a Huguenot Family* (Suffolk 1986; originally published 1722), 46–9, 70, 80; also published as Jacques Fontaine, *Mémoires d'une Famille Huguenote*, ed. B. Cottret (Languedoc 1992).

[12] E. Benoist, *Histoire de L'Édit*, III, ii, 437–8, 445–58; H. M. Baird, *The Huguenots and the Revocation of the Edict of Nantes* (New York 1895), I, 497–8.

[13] Jurieu, *Last Efforts* (1682), 58, 62–9; *Savile Correspondence*, ed. W. D. Cooper (London 1858), 201, 206; cf. also 97–8; Benoist, *Histoire de L'Édit*, III, ii, 446–7; C. Johnston, 'Elie Benoist, Historian of the Edict of Nantes', *Church History* (1988), 468–88.

[14] W. J. Stankiewicz, *Politics and Religion in Seventeenth Century France* (Berkeley 1960), 196.

children out of France in shoals'.[15] An English newsletter in 1681 described boats arriving in England from France 'with few men in them, they sending their wives and children away first, and most of these having run great hazards at sea'.[16] Such emigration was illegal and dangerous even before setting out to sea. Halifax noted that some 300 Huguenots had been forcibly prevented from leaving France at Dieppe in 1681, and Robert Ferguson's February 1682 *Third Part of No Protestant Plot* declared that 'many thousands have forsaken their native Country...and the rest are ready to do the like, were they not debarred all ways of...escape'.[17] In order to escape dragoons in Poitiers, methods were devised such as those used by Jean François de Portal in sending his sons to England: they were first concealed in a bread oven to leave town, and were then sent on a boat to Southampton hidden in an empty wine cask.[18]

In the early 1680s, several years before the Revocation of the Edict of Nantes, many pastors and professors were also being forced into exile. Two such individuals deserve particular note, as they will be met repeatedly throughout this book. Jurieu was among those leaving in the early 1680s for the Netherlands, where he was to become pastor and professor of theology in the École Illustre and the dominant and domineering theologian of the refugees throughout the Huguenot diaspora. Jurieu was closely related to the du Moulin family and to André Rivet, and thus in France to the leading theologians of Huguenot orthodoxy of the early seventeenth century; in England to two significant mid-century Calvinist controversialists; and in the Netherlands to the governor of William II and to an intimate of William III who had been involved in Dutch anti-French anti-Catholic propaganda in the 1670s. Jurieu unsurprisingly possessed a strongly internationalist perspective on the interrelated fate of Protestantism in the Netherlands, England, and France. Until closure of the Protestant Academy at Sedan, Jurieu had been its professor of theology. He had long been an advocate of Huguenot orthodoxy within France and simultaneously a defender of civil 'toleration' for orthodox Huguenots under the Edict of Nantes. We will meet Jurieu many times later in this book as the leading Huguenot opponent of the toleration of Protestant *un*orthodoxy of the 1680s and 1690s. Jurieu chose exile in order to maintain a faith which he firmly believed to be required in order to obtain salvation, and he was to be a fierce opponent of that faith being undermined in exile from within the Huguenot

---

[15] Baird, *Huguenots*, 494, 512; *Savile Correspondence*, 201, 206, and cf. also 97–8.
[16] R. Gwynn, 'England's First Refugees'.
[17] [R. Ferguson], *Third Part of No Protestant Plot* (1682), 8.
[18] T. Murdoch, 'The Quiet Conquest: The Huguenots 1685–1985', *History Today* (1985); R. Gwynn, 'The Arrival of Huguenot Refugees in England 1680–1705', *Proceedings of the Huguenot Society* 21 (1969), 366–73.

community.[19] In October 1681, Jurieu was joined in the Netherlands by the most influential Huguenot tolerationist of the 1680s, Pierre Bayle, whom we will also meet many times in this book. Like Jurieu, Bayle had been a professor at Sedan, and with Jurieu's help he obtained in exile a position at the École Illustre as Professor of Philosophy and History. By 1681, Bayle had already written the first version of his famous *Pensées diverses sur la Comète (Miscellaneous Reflections on the Comet)*, but had been refused permission to publish it in France by the Lieutenant-General of Police of Paris; he fled into exile with the manuscript and had it published (as the *Lettre sur la Comète*) in Rotterdam in March 1682. As Professor of Philosophy at Sedan from 1675, Bayle had been not merely Jurieu's colleague, but to a significant extent Jurieu's friend and client. Their later fierce opposition as Bayle wrote tolerationist works against Jurieu, and Jurieu secured Bayle's dismissal in October 1693 from his post at the École Illustre as an alleged 'libertine' and 'atheist', surely owed something to each thinking that the other had betrayed them.[20]

Huguenot ministers and professors like Jurieu and Bayle who managed to flee in 1681 were fortunate. Bayle's brother Jacob, minister of Carla in Foix, was imprisoned in June 1685 in retaliation against publication of Pierre Bayle's *General Criticism of the History of Calvinism*, and he died in prison just after the Revocation. Protestant accounts, such as John Quick's *Synodicon*, emphasised that Jacob Bayle had been denied even 'a cup of cold water to quench his burning thirst', and that his guards had treated him 'with all manner of Barbarities, that by those Torments he might be enforced to apostasise from the Truth'. The fierceness of Pierre Bayle's attack on intolerant Christianity for the rest of his life probably owed much to his personal loss.[21] And as Jacob Bayle's death was painful to his brother, so to all Huguenots were the widely publicised deaths of hundreds of Protestant worshippers and at least one minister in the stronghold of Protestantism in France in the Cévennes, Vivarais, and Dauphiné who were killed in battle or by execution when they attempted to continue their worship in 1683 after their temples had been demolished. In the most notorious incident, several

---

[19] On Jurieu, see below, Chapter 14; R. Howells, *Pierre Jurieu: Antinomian Radical* (Durham 1983), 11; E. Labrousse, 'The Political Ideas of the Huguenot Diaspora (Bayle and Jurieu)' in R. M. Golden (ed.), *Church, State and Society under the Bourbon Kings of France* (Lawrence, Kansas 1982), 222–83, at 245–6, 273–4n. For a very important article on the fierce commitment to maintenance of the faith of the exilic communities, see R. Whelan, 'Persecution and Toleration: The Changing Identities of Ireland's Huguenot Refugees', *Proceedings of the Huguenot Society* (1998), 20–35.

[20] Dodge, *The Political Thought of the Huguenots of the Dispersion* (New York 1947), 12; Rex, *Essays*, 141–5; Labrousse, 'les frères enemis: Bayle et Jurieu' in *idem, Conscience et Conviction* (Paris and Oxford 1996); Bayle, *Pensées*, ed. A. Prat (Paris 1939) xiv–xvi.

[21] Quick, *Synodicon*, cxxxiii–cxxxvi.

thousand lightly armed worshippers and their pastors attempted unsuccessfully to defend themselves against dragoons. Bishop Daniel de Cosnac, in whose diocese this occurred, recorded that the soldiers had burned to death perhaps 200 Huguenots who had taken refuge in a barn, and that 'a large number were taken prisoner and all were condemned to die by the hand of the executioner. All of the prisons in my diocese were filled'. Many executions followed, even though those who abjured Protestantism were pardoned. The lawyer Daniel Chamier, grandson of a famous Huguenot pastor, was broken upon the wheel; Protestants alleged that he had received some thirty blows from an iron bar and had then taken three painful days to die. The aged pastor Isaac Homel was similarly broken on the wheel and allegedly took two excruciating days to die, after receiving some forty blows which had broken his arms and legs.[22]

The increasing pace of measures taken by the court against Huguenots in the early 1680s was paralleled by an increasing number of Catholic works attacking Huguenots and declaring the desirability of the union of the nation in one faith. Among these 'preparatory Machin[es] used by the Persecutors' to dispose people to the 'utter extirpation' of Protestants, as the English minister Quick was to put it in the 1690s, were: the 1680 reissue of Paul Hay du Châtelet's 1666 *Treatise on the Policy of France*; Pierre Nicole's 1684 *Protestants Convicted of Schism*; Bossuet's *Exposition of the Catholic Faith*, which deployed the authority of Tertullian against schism and Augustine's justification of compulsion against the Donatists and condemned Protestants for their variations in the faith, and thereby advanced the twinned themes of Bossuet's later defences of the Revocation; and Antoine Arnauld's 1681–2 *Apology for the Catholics*, 'venting his Choler against the Calvinists', as Quick put it. Most influential of all was the former Jesuit Louis Maimbourg's 1682 indictment of Huguenot rebelliousness and plea for uniformity, the *History of Calvinism*, a work which sparked a huge controversy in the early 1680s and brought replies which included most notably Pierre Bayle's *General Criticism* and Jurieu's *History of Calvinism*.[23] The Assembly of the Clergy had long been campaigning for the king to act against heresy and schism, professing in 1675 that liberty of conscience was opposed by all Catholics and that it opened the door to 'libertinism'. The Assembly added in 1 July 1682, in its *Pastoral Exhortation*, a still darker note in threatening unconverted Huguenots with 'misfortunes far more fearsome

---

[22] Quick, *Synodicon*, cxxxiii–cxxxvi; Benoist, *Histoire de L'Édit* (1695), III, iii, 638–69, esp. 651, 669; Labrousse, *Bayle*, 20–2, 26–33; *idem*, *Avertissement aux Protestants des provinces* (1684; Paris 1986), introduction and *passim*.

[23] On these works, see below, ch. 13; on Locke's reading of Jurieu, see below, p. 550; on Maimbourg, see Labrousse, *Bayle*.

and fatal than those which you have already incurred by your rebellion and schism'.[24]

In this 1682 Assembly of the Clergy which called for increased measures to be taken against Huguenots in France the coadjutor archbishop of Arles decried the 'Fury of Babylon' then raging against Catholicism in England.[25] It is important to emphasise that Catholic clerical promotion of measures against Huguenots in the early 1680s was fostered in part by news of the execution of many Catholic priests in 1679.[26] These executions were due both specifically to the 'Popish Plot' allegations that Catholics had plotted to assassinate King Charles II in order to place on the throne his Catholic brother James, Duke of York, and had then assassinated the Protestant magistrate, Sir Edmund Berry Godfrey, before whom these allegations had been sworn, and due more generally to the fiercely anti-Catholic bigotry and zeal of English Protestants. As Mark Goldie has noted, 1679 saw more Catholic martyrs created in England than any other year except that of the Spanish Armada. In England, Jesuit priests who declared their innocence immediately before their execution were identified in pamphlet literature as giving the false statements of those whose theology allowed them to lie and equivocate as well as assassinate; in France, however, their dying speeches were immediately given wide publicity and their deaths were widely represented as bigoted Protestant executions of entirely innocent Catholics.[27]

---

[24] Quick, *Synodicon*, cxxiv–v, discussed all of these works other than Bossuet's as among the preparations for the 'extirpation' of Protestantism; Jean Claude's *Account*, 17–18, also identified the works of Maimbourg, Arnauld, and Nicole as the crucial texts supporting persecution; Benoist's *Histoire de L'Édit*, III, ii, 556–7, stressed not merely Maimbourg and Nicole but also Bossuet's arguments and use of Augustine and Tertullian, while he also pointed out that the Assemblies of the Clergy had long pressed the king to extirpate heresy. Generally, see also: I. Perry, *From Theology to History* (the Hague 1973), 166–7 and notes; Garrisson, *L'Édit de Nantes*, 146–50, 190–2; J. Orcibal, *Louis XIV et les Protestants* (Paris 1951), 23; P. Blet, *Les Assemblées du Clergé et Louis XIV* (Paris 1972), 423–44, 467–76.

[25] McManners, *Church*, 580.

[26] R. Briggs, *Communities of Belief* (Oxford 1994), 218–9, argues for a limited influence of clerics on the Revocation; J. Armogathe, *Croire en liberté* (Paris 1985), 84–6, suggests reservations on the part of Harlay about the Revocation and its implementation; and E. Labrousse argued in *Une foi* that it was absolutist 'reason of state' which primarily motivated the Revocation. I do not wish to dispute these interpretations of the primary motivations of the Revocation, nor to intimate that these clerics intended to support all of the violence used against Huguenots, but wish to emphasise that contemporary Huguenots perceived their arguments as being crucial as preparations for and justifications of the Revocation, and that Catholic clerics issued strongly anti-Huguenot works before the Revocation and rushed to its justification: on the latter, see below, ch. 13. I concur with the judgment of McManners, *Church*, 578, that the clerics were perhaps not 'inspirers' but were 'accomplices'.

[27] M. A. Goldie, 'Sir Peter Pett, Sceptical Toryism and the Science of Toleration in the 1680s' in W. Sheils (ed.), *Persecution and Toleration* (Oxford 1984), 247–74, at 247; as Thomas Whitehead put it, 'I go out of the world as innocent…as I came into the world'. Anthony Turner concurred: 'I am as free from the Treason I am accused of, as the child that is unborn'. Many English Protestant prints and works nonetheless depicted the executions as causes for

In 1679, Henry Savile declared in Paris that their dying speeches had been read by 'everybody', had a 'terrible effect heer', and that:

The Archbishop of Paris, and the Père de la Chaise, [the king's confessor] do all they can to prevail with this King to make him revenge the quarrel of the English Catholics upon the French Protestants, who tremble for fear of some violent persecution.[28]

The Revocation of the Edict of Nantes in October 1685 was, then, a final link in a long chain of actions which had intensified considerably during the early 1680s in an increasingly hostile atmosphere of clerical polemic against Huguenots that was due in part to reports of contemporary English Protestant executions of Catholics. In many areas of France, the October 1685 Revocation itself was preceded in summer 1685 by a further escalation of measures including fines, bribes, destruction of temples, imprisonment of those caught worshipping in the fields and woods where those temples had been destroyed, substantial use of dragonnades, confiscation of Huguenot property followed by its undervalued sale to Catholic neighbours, imprisonment of male Huguenots in prisons and galleys and of Huguenot women in monasteries, taking of family members as hostages to induce 'conversion', incessant drumming by soldiers to prevent Huguenots from sleeping, verbal abuse, and, in some cases – although rape was officially outlawed – probably both the torture and rape of Huguenots to force 'conversion'. Hoping that without its ministers Protestant worship would wither on the vine, at the moment of the Revocation pastors were required to convert or to leave France within two weeks to avoid being 'sent to the Galleys'; from 1 July 1686 punishments up to execution were instituted for ministering to Protestants or for attending Protestant worship.[29] Exile for lay Huguenots

celebration, and depicted the protestations of innocence by the priests but declared them false. *A True Narrative of the Horrid, Hellish Popish Plot, the Second Part* came complete with a series of twelve engravings telling the story of the 'Popish Plot'. The final one showed the priests being hung and cut into pieces and protesting their innocence, and explained these protestations by the caption: 'And to be cut into Quarters/Cause they' d be canoniz' d for Martirs': *The True Speeches of Thomas Whitebread, William Harcourt, John Fenwick, John Gavan, and Anthony Turner before their execution at Tyburn June 20th 1679* (1679), *passim*.

28 *Savile Correspondence*, 93–4, 97, 112, 113, 209–10; I. Dunlop, *Louis XIV* (London 1999), 268. This was not the first occasion in the seventeenth century of substantial French reaction to English anti-Catholic executions for alleged popish conspiracy. In 1642, there were processions in Paris carrying pictures of priests executed for conspiracy and it was declared that they had been murdered by Protestants. The Dutch Protestant visitor Peter de la Court wrote in his diary: 'In Paris and elsewhere I saw the printed pictures of priests whom I had seen hanged in London some two months before. Their deaths were solemnly celebrated with many lies as though they had been true martyrs', in F. P. van Stam, *The Controversy over the Theology of Saumur* (Amsterdam 1988), 10.

29 Benoist, *Histoire de L'Édit*; C. Johnston, 'Elie Benoist'. For criticisms of Elie Benoist's tone and emphases more than of his accuracy, see Labrousse, *Une foi* and the comments of Johnston; F. Deijk, 'Elie Benoist: Historiographer and Politician after the Revocation of the Edict of Nantes', *Nederlands Archief voor Kerkgeschiedenis* 69 (1989), 54–92, also supports Benoist's accuracy.

was illegal. Men who were caught attempting to emigrate were sent to the galleys 'in perpetuity', while similarly captured women were sent to prison. At Grenoble alone in 1686–7, magistrates sentenced 57 men to the galleys, 8 to execution, and 182 to prison.[30] After 1687, if caught, guides employed by escapees were sent to the gallows. Fugitives were paraded shackled to discourage others from fleeing. In many areas the 'Coasts, Bridges, Passages unto Rivers, and the Highways' were 'strictly guarded night and day'. Informers were offered rewards, strict surveillance was instituted at borders, and in some ports authorities inspecting ships about to sail burned sulphur in order to asphyxiate stowaways. As the exiled pastor Isaac Jacquelot was to put it, in 1686 for Huguenots France itself had been turned into a 'vast prison'.[31]

There are no 'independent' accounts of the processes of 'conversion' for those Protestants who did not leave France, and it is highly likely that Protestants significantly exaggerated the scale of the violence and that Catholics minimised it. In many cases, the first appearance of troops in villages in 1685 was sufficient to cause ostensible abjuration by Protestants as soldiers' brutal reputations preceded them. But it is clear even from Catholic accounts that significant degrees of force were used to promote 'conversion' in many places. While Catholics such as Bishop Bossuet described the Huguenots' 'conversion' in works such as his *Pastoral Letter* to the 'new converts' of his diocese in March 1686 as having been peaceful and easy, and the 1685 Assembly of the Clergy spoke of Louis as having 'opened before' the Huguenots a 'road strewn with flowers' to conquer 'the obstinacy of their spirit', they thereafter shifted when confronted by Protestant reports of the violence to defending the use of force as legitimate because used against 'heretics and schismatics' who were 'evil-doers' against whom princes were armed.[32] The Intendant of Poitou, Foucault, recorded in his *Memoirs* that many Huguenots were 'converted' when troops first appeared, but also recorded fines and incarceration and by 1686 was sentencing nobles and a lawyer to the galleys 'in perpetuity'. In 1687, he recorded that he had been commanded by Louvois, the Minister of War, to

---

[30] McManners, *Church*, II, 586.
[31] Quick, *Synodicon*, cxliii; [I. Jacquelot], *Reponce à la lettre pastorale* (Amsterdam 1686) cited in E. Labrousse, 'Les Réponses du Refuge a la *Pastorale* aux N. C. De Meaux' in T. Goyet and J.-P. Collinet (eds.), *Journées Bossuet* (Paris 1980), 343–60, at 349; P. Joutard, 'The Revocation of the Edict of Nantes: End or Renewal of French Calvinism?' in M. Prestwich (ed.), *International Calvinism 1541–1715* (Oxford 1985), 339–68, at 350; Benoist, *Histoire de L'Édit*, III, iii, 964; S. Smiles, *The Huguenots* (New York 1868; reprint Baltimore 1972), 154, 159; McManners, *Church*, ch. 44.
[32] Joutard, 'Revocation', 339–68; C. Johnston, 'Elie Benoist', 468–88, at 481. Some Catholics were opponents of violence and helped Huguenots to escape: See J. McManners, *Church*, ch. 44 and, with caution – note McManners, 583 – Bolle, 'Deux évêques'.

'promptly inflict so severe a punishment' on Protestant worshippers that it would serve as 'an example' to others, and that when he condemned only one to death, and others to the galleys, he was reprimanded by Louvois for being 'too indulgent'. Louvois ordered that the dragoons were to 'live very licentiously'; their officers were ordered to allow them 'such disorder as needed to force these folk'. This encouragement of disorder was, of course, represented as having promoted extreme brutality in Protestant accounts, such as that of the Huguenot minister Jacques Fontaine, who settled in Ireland in exile, and declared in his *Memoirs* that a dragoon who 'had ingenuity enough to invent any new species of torture was sure of applause, and even reward for his discovery'. According to Fontaine, the dragoons had 'ravaged and pillaged without mercy, resembling in the process a lawless and victorious army taking possession of an enemy's country'. While this was probably somewhat exaggerated, Louvois had informed the Marquis de Vérac in November 1685 that 'those who would have the stupid glory of wanting to be the last [to abjure] should be pushed to the last extremities'.[33] Louvois' pressure maintained violence in some areas where the intendants were reluctant to continue the use of force. By 1686, Intendant Basville of Languedoc was asking for a relaxation of what he called the 'extreme rigour' being employed in his territory; he was refused.[34]

Protestant accounts are chilling in their depictions of the violence used in conversion. Jean Migault, Huguenot schoolmaster at Moulle in Poitou, kept a journal for the children he had earlier sent away to safety, in which he recorded that the first use of dragonnades, in 1681, had involved the billeting of fifteen dragoons on his household, and that they had forced his wife, who had just given birth, to come downstairs and having suggested 'that in her condition, it was necessary to keep her as warm as possible', they had then created a fire of the Migaults' furniture and threatened 'to burn her at once if she did not at once abjure her Protestantism'. Migault recorded that the local curé had intervened to prevent her execution, but that all other Protestants in the village had abjured in the face of the violence, while 'Our beds, our linen, our clothes, everything we possessed was either sold or destroyed'.[35] Others signed abjurations under duress and later recanted them in exile. Isaac Dumont de Bostaquet, who took with him into exile in Ireland deep hostility to Catholic priests as 'devils', recorded that he abjured Protestantism 'in the

---

33 N.-J. Foucault, *Mémoires* (Paris 1862), in W. Church, *The Impact of Absolutism in France* (New York 1969), 87–94; J. McManners, *Church*, 573; I. Dunlop, *Louis XIV*, 270; J. Fontaine, *Memoirs of a Huguenot Family* (Suffolk 1986; originally published 1722), 92.

34 J.-R. Armogathe and P. Joutard, 'Basville et la guerre des Camisards', *Rev. hist. mod. contemp* (1972), 66, in McManners, *Church*, 585.

35 J. Migault, *Journal de Jean Migault* (Paris 1995), ed. Y. Krumenacker, *passim*; Dunlop, *Louis XIV*, 271–2.

face of the order given to billet twenty-five soldiers' at his house, as 'the fear of seeing so many women and girls exposed to the insolence of the soldiers, who were permitted to take every liberty, forced me to sign'.[36]

As many historians have stressed, the increasing restrictions placed on Huguenots in the early 1680s and their culmination in and after 1685 were widely reported in England.[37] The focus of seventeenth-century British Protestants on the fate of international Protestantism has been the subject of much British historiography, perhaps most notably in the work of Patrick Collinson, Peter Lake, John Morrill, Robin Clifton, William Hunt, and Thomas Cogswell on the early seventeenth century, and in that of John Miller, Jonathan Scott, Tim Harris, Richard Ashcraft, Mark Goldie, Steven Pincus, and myself on the Restoration. Many of these historians have further underlined the extent to which fear of 'popery' was intimately linked to fear of absolutism. And Scott has valuably stressed that increased fear of Catholicism by the late seventeenth century was due in part to the increase of Catholic power and territory in Europe as that of Protestantism dwindled. The recent emphasis on 'British and Irish history' has similarly indicated the importance of concern in England about predominantly Catholic Ireland and fear of Catholic conquest of England, fed by massively exaggerated accounts of the anti-Protestant massacre in Ireland in 1641. In 1681–3, Locke was to declare that in England popery 'so nearly surrounds and threatens us'; this mind-set was shared by many Protestant Englishmen.[38]

---

[36] Isaac Dumont de Bostaquet, *Mémoires sur les temps qui ont précédé et suivi la Révocation de L'Édit de Nantes*, ed. M. Richard (Paris 1968), 102–5 in Whelan, 'Persecution', 23.

[37] See, *inter alia*, M. Goldie, 'The Huguenot Experience and the Problem of Toleration in England' in C. E. F. Caldicott et al. (eds.), *The Huguenots and Ireland* (Dublin 1987), 175–203, at 175; J. Miller, 'The Immediate Impact of the Revocation in England' in *ibid.*, 161–74; *idem, James II* (Hove 1978); T. Harris, 'The Parties and the People: The Press, the Crowd and Politics "Out-of-doors" in Restoration England' in L. K. Glassey (ed.), *The Reigns of Charles II and James VII and II* (London), 125–51, at 130; Gwynn, 'Arrival', 366–73; *idem, Huguenot Heritage*; B. Cottret, *The Huguenots in England* (Cambridge 1991); C. Gibbs, 'Some Intellectual and Political Influences', 255–87; *idem*, 'European Origins', 14–15; *La Révocation de L'Édit de Nantes et les provinces-unies 1685* (Amsterdam 1986); M. Magdelaine and R. von Thadden (eds.), *Le Refuge Huguenot* (Paris 1985); J. Israel, *The Dutch Republic*, (Oxford 1995), 646.

[38] J. Morrill, 'The Religious Context of the English Civil War', *TRHS* (1984), 155–78; *idem, The Nature of the English Revolution* (London 1993), Part 1; P. Lake, 'The Significance of the Elizabethan Identification of the Pope as Antichrist', *Journal of Ecclesiastical History* (1980), 161–78; *idem*, 'Antipopery: The Structure of a Prejudice' in R. Cust and A. Hugues (eds.), *Conflict in Early Stuart England: Studies in Religion and Politics 1603–42* (London 1989); R. Clifton, 'The Fear of Popery' in C. Russell (ed.), *The Origins of the English Civil*

Restoration politics had been dominated by anti-Catholicism even before the years of the 'Popish Plot' and 'Exclusion Crisis' from 1678 to 1681. The 1666 Great Fire of London led to the execution of a Catholic, Robert Hubbert, alleged to have started it, and fear of another such fire was rampant throughout the Restoration, even if it was to reach new heights in the later 1670s and early 1680s.[39] After 1670, there were increasing worries that Charles II was a crypto-Catholic and that his true allegiances were to 'popery' and absolutism. He was alleged to have signed – and had indeed signed – a secret treaty with Louis XIV in 1670, and was alleged to intend to establish absolutism and Catholicism in England. His court was depicted as including a 'popish faction' around the Catholic James, Duke of York, which was conspiring to introduce Catholicism and absolutism in the person of James, if not Charles. After the public expression by James of his Catholicism, the fear of Catholics holding civic and military office led to a 1673 Test Act prohibiting all Catholics other than the monarch from holding any civic or military office, and this act was reinforced in 1678 by excluding Catholics from Parliament.[40] Fear of absolutism and popery, influentially expressed in the later 1670s by Marvell's 1677 *Account of the Growth of Popery And Arbitrary Power*, was central to nascent Whig politics. Marvell's *Account* alleged that 'there has now for

War (Oxford 1973); A. Milton, *Catholic and Reformed* (Cambridge 1995); W. Hunt, 'Spectral Origins of the English Revolution' in G. Eley and W. Hunt (eds.), *Reviving the English Revolution* (1988), 305–32; T. Cogswell, *The Blessed Revolution* (Cambridge 1989); C. Hibbard, *Charles I and the Popish Plot*; J. Scott, *England's Troubles* (Cambridge 2000); J. Kenyon, *The Popish Plot* (London 1972), 1–2; R. Ashcraft, *Revolutionary Politics and Locke's Two Treatises of Government* (Princeton 1990); J. Miller, *Popery and Politics* (Cambridge 1973); S. Pincus, *Protestantism and Patriotism* (Cambridge 1996); T. Harris, *London Crowds* (Cambridge 1987); idem, *Politics Under the Later Stuarts* (London 1993); my *Locke*; J. G. A. Pocock, 'British History: A Plea for a New Subject', *New Zealand Historical Journal* (1974), 3–21; idem, 'The Limits and Divisions of British History: In Search of the Unknown Subject', *American Historical Review* 87 (1982); C. Russell, *The Fall of the British Monarchies* (Oxford 1991); B. Bradshaw and J. Morrill (eds.), *The British Problem* (Basingstoke 1996); S. Ellis and S. Barber, *Conquest and Union* (London 1995); R. Asch (ed.), *Three Nations* (Bochum 1992); S. Connolly (ed.), *United Kingdoms?* (Dublin 1998); G. Burgess, *The New British History* (London 1999); T. Claydon and I. McBride (eds.), *Protestantism and National Identity* (Cambridge 1998); J. Ohlmeyer (ed.), *Ireland from Independence to Occupation* (Cambridge 1995); D. Armitage, *The Ideological Origins of the British Empire* (Cambridge 2000), 6–9, 66, 152–3; Scott, *England's Troubles*. We await an important study from Tim Harris of the revolutions of 1688–91 in all three kingdoms. I am grateful to John Miller for his comments in personal conversations and at his University of London seminar, and to Jonathan Scott for many conversations.

[39] The monument on the site recorded that the fire was due to the 'treachery and malice of the Popish Faction...in order to the carrying on their horrid plot for extirpating the Protestant religion'; in 1681, a stone was inscribed with the words 'Here by the permission of Heaven, Hell broke loose upon this Protestant city from the malicious hearts of barbarous Papists': Speck, *Reluctant Revolutionaries* (Oxford 1988), 168.

[40] Miller, *Popery*, passim; Harris, *Politics*; idem, *London*; Scott, *Algernon Sidney and the Restoration Crisis* (Cambridge 1991); idem, *Troubles*; Knights, *Politics and Public Opinion* (Cambridge 1995); Marshall, *Locke*; Ashcraft, *Revolutionary Politics*.

divers years a design been carried on to change the lawful government of England into an absolute tyranny; and to convert the established protestant religion into downright popery', introducing 'French slavery and Roman idolatry'. Marvell declared Louis XIV the 'Champion of Popery' and 'slavery'. For Marvell, Catholic monarchy in England would mean that every 'considerable estate in England' would 'have a piece torn out of it upon the title of piety, and the rest subject to be wholly forfeited upon the account of Heresy'.[41]

The 'Popish Plot' and 'Exclusion Crisis' of 1678–81, the latter name being given because the political opposition argued that, as a Catholic, James, Duke of York, should be excluded from the succession to the throne, were thus expressions of a long-standing but increasing Restoration fear of European Catholicism and of a 'popish' conspiracy at court. Majorities of the members of the House of Commons elected in three fiercely fought elections from 1679 to 1681 maintained the reality of the 'Popish Plot', execrated English Catholics as 'enemies' within the realm, and demanded either James' exclusion from the throne or that substantial limitations be placed upon any future ruler to prevent him from being able to Catholicise England by force. James' unconditional succession was secured firstly because Charles II resolutely refused to comply, successively proroguing and dissolving the 'Exclusionist' Parliaments and then not calling another before his 1685 death and James' succession, and secondly because in the wake of the turmoil and regicide of the English Civil Wars and Revolution of 1642–60, the majority of the political nation feared the prospect of another civil war and revolution even more than they feared either Charles' own absolutism or the prospects of a Catholic successor. The allegations of the 'Popish Plot' and the anti-Catholic propaganda which poured out of the English presses after 1678 therefore did not secure the Exclusion of James, but they did cause the execution of many Catholics in 1678–80 in a fervidly anti-Catholic atmosphere. The alleged 'evidence' of a 'Popish Plot' provided by a host of 'witnesses' led between November 1678 and July 1681 to the trials and executions of lay Catholics, including Viscount Stafford, the gentlemen Coleman and Grove, and three labourers, Green, Berry, and Hill. Twenty-four Jesuit priests died by execution, in prison, or as a result of their sufferings, and twenty secular priests were tried, of whom six were executed, and three more died in prison. Archbishop Plunkett of Armagh, brought to England for trial, was executed in July 1681. All but one of the Catholic laity among those executed suffered the punishment for treason in this period, being 'hanged by the neck' then 'cut down alive' in order to have

---

[41] Marvell, *Account, passim*, esp. 258–61 and its discussions in Knights, *Politics*, 17–18; Scott, *Restoration*, 8, 15–6, 31, 36, 53, 80, 185; Marshall, *Locke*; A. Patterson, *Marvell: The Writer in Public Life* (New York 2000), ch. 6.

their 'privy members' cut off and to have 'bowels taken out, and...burnt in [their] view' before their 'heads' were 'severed'.[42]

It is important to stress that throughout the years of the 'Popish Plot' and 'Exclusion Crisis', anti-Catholic agitation repeatedly linked the fate of Protestantism in England with that in continental Europe and in Ireland and asserted that there was a French-led conspiracy to overthrow English Protestantism. A manuscript among the Shaftesbury papers entitled 'The Present State of the Kingdom at the Opening of the Parliament', presumably of 1678, declared that 'all the wise Protestants' talked of a 'secret Catholic league carried on by the clergy for the utter extirpation of the Protestant religion out of the world. And this they all say cannot be carried on without the full concurrence of the English court'. Such a vision drew on an estimate of the intentions of Louis XIV, on the widely rumoured 1670 secret Treaty of Dover, and on the perception that James and others around the king were ardent Catholics aligned ever more closely with France following James' recent marriage to Mary of Modena. But sustenance came also from the correspondence discovered between Louis XIV's confessor La Chaise and Edmund Coleman, a Jesuit-educated secretary first of the Duke of York and then of the Duchess of York. In this correspondence, Coleman had not merely documented attempts to arrange a subsidy from Louis XIV for Charles' 1675 dissolution of Parliament, evidencing Catholic French absolutist support for English absolutism, but had expressed his hopes for the 'mighty work upon our hands' of the 'conversion of three kingdoms' and the 'subduing of a pestilent heresy'. This passage was central in Coleman's trial and execution as a conspirator.[43]

In March 1679, Shaftesbury gave a speech in Parliament in which he very famously declared that 'Popery and slavery, like two little sisters, go hand in hand'. This line alone is often quoted, but the rest of his quickly printed speech is equally noteworthy. Shaftesbury used the text of the Song of Songs to introduce his theme:

We have a little sister, and she hath no breasts; what shall we do for our sister in the day when she shall be spoken for? if she be a wall, we will build on her a palace of silver; if she be a door, we will enclose her with bonds of cedar.

He then identified the 'little sisters without breasts' as the French Protestant churches, a 'defence' to England, and the kingdoms of Scotland and Ireland

---

[42] T. Harris, *Politics*, ch. 4; J. Scott, *Restoration*; J. Miller, *Popery*; J. Kenyon, *Popish*; M. Knights, *Politics*; R. Ashcraft, *Revolutionary Politics*; K. H. D. Haley, *Shaftesbury*, (Oxford 1968), ch. 21; my *Locke*.

[43] Haley, *Shaftesbury*, 455–6, 470, 502; Kenyon, *Popish*, 88, 123; S. Pincus, 'From Butterboxes to Wooden Shoes: The Shift in English Popular Sentiment from Anti-Dutch to Anti-French in the 1670s', *Historical Journal* (1995), 333–61, esp. 351–61.

as the doors 'either to let in good or mischief on us', arguing that in Ireland many 'Papists' were armed and that the kingdom would not be held in 'English hands' without great force. Shaftesbury's was thus an international perspective which allied the fate of England with that of the Huguenots and of the Protestants in Ireland. The 1679 *Popery and Tyranny or the Present State of France* similarly aligned the fate of English and French Protestantism by attacking the 'Absolute Monarchy' of France 'imposed upon the people by a standing, illegal, and oppressive Army' which was establishing the 'double Tyranny of Popery and Arbitrary Power' in corrupting the 'best tempered' government by laying aside the States in France, and in weakening the Protestants. It itemised the measures that Louis had at that point already taken against Protestants, including the demolition of 'Multitudes' of temples.[44]

Similar themes were sounded in translations of two 'particularly influential' works by Jurieu documenting the increase of violence against the Huguenots in 1681–2, the 1681 *Policy of the Clergy of France to Destroy the Protestants of that Kingdom* and its 1682 continuation, *The Last Efforts of Afflicted Innocence*.[45] Jurieu's 1681 *Policy*, written in autumn 1680, first published in the Netherlands at the beginning of 1681, and translated into English before March 1681, described the efforts in France over the past twenty years to 'root out the Protestant religion', focusing on the 'Design of ruining' Protestants since 1660 by deprivations of liberty of preaching, the razing of 'Temples', the persecuting, fining, imprisoning, and banishing of ministers, the removal of employment for the laity, and the taking of children to 'be instructed in the Catholick Religion' (at this date, at age fourteen for boys and twelve for girls). While Jurieu – in a fictional dialogue between a Parisian and a Provincial Catholic – denied that the King would use 'Sword, Fire and Banishment' against the Huguenots in what was in effect a plea to the monarchy not to do just that, one character was already made to forecast that the end-point of the current diminution of liberties 'little by little' would be the 'sudden' revocation of 'all their Edicts'. Indeed, the *Policy* declared as early as 1681 that when people were banished, had their 'goods confiscated for Religion's sake', and there was no true 'liberty of conscience', the only thing missing in order to establish in France 'that terrible Tribunal of the Inquisition' was 'Fire'. For Jurieu, all Catholics were committed to the teaching that 'faith did not need to be kept with heretics'.

We saw earlier that the reporting in France of executions of Catholics in England in 1679–81 helped to fuel measures against the Huguenots in

---

[44] Haley, *Shaftesbury*, 510; *Popery and Tyranny or the Present State of France* (London 1679), 1, 5–6.
[45] Goldie, 'Huguenot Experience', 174 and 196n.4 describes Jurieu's works as 'particularly influential publications' in spreading 'the news of the first dragonnades in the early 1680s'.

France. With Jurieu's *Policy* we meet the reverse: reports of the increased restrictions placed upon Huguenots in France further fuelling English anti-Catholicism. Jurieu's *Policy* was published in English translation to influence the final Exclusion Parliament at Oxford in March 1681. The translation supported the Exclusion or the 'bridling' of James in England by declaring:

When there is a Prince to be established, the States of the Kingdom, who are obliged to be careful of the Preservation of the Religion, are authorised to take all their Sureties, that no change may be made therein: Thus they must either remove from the Throne, if they have the right to do so, he who would mount into it to ruin the Religion; or at least, they ought to bridle his Authority for the hindring him from making any changes.

At this date, before leaving France for the Netherlands, Jurieu supported Exclusion in England and declared that Catholics there desired to extirpate Protestants while he simultaneously attempted to persuade the king in France that Protestants were loyal subjects who would not resist their ruler, stressed the irrevocability of the Edict of Nantes as a perpetual law lying at the foundation of peace in the state, and emphasised that any legal revocation would require the consent of the Estates and not merely a royal edict. He condemned the Catholic clergy for recently organising measures undermining the Edict of Nantes. Even though he had not explicitly criticised the king, Jurieu had sailed too close to the wind in emphasis on the irrevocability of the Edict and its multiple recent violations. Publication of the *Policy* made it imperative for him to leave France for the Netherlands in 1681.[46]

In response to the calls by the French Catholic clergy for increased measures against the Huguenots due to the execution of Catholics in England, and in response to the Catholic clergy's accusation that the 'Popish Plot' was a farrago of lies, Jurieu's *Policy* discussed the reality of the 'Popish Plot' for over twenty pages. A Huguenot character in the text denied French Catholic reports that the 'Popish Plot' was a fabrication, supporting the reality of the 'late Conspiracy' of England 'by which half the Kingdom was to have had their Throats cut'. Jurieu underlined the point by having two Catholic characters in the text record that they were persuaded that the 'Popish Plot' was real, concluding that the accusations that the plot was fabricated 'spread on this side of the sea' were themselves 'Fables'. Jurieu also supported the allegations that French Jesuits had been actively promoting 'the design of re-establishing the Roman Catholick religion in England, by fire and by the effusion of Blood' and desired to 'make a St Bartholemew beyond the seas'. Jurieu then used the 'Popish Plot' and its support by French Jesuits to interpret prospects in France for his Huguenot audience, asking: 'What

---

[46] Jurieu, *Policy, passim*, esp. 132–43; Howells, *Jurieu*, 30, 33, 78n.17.

may not the Protestants of France fear' given 'the design of cutting the Throats of so many millions of Protestants'. Thus, Jurieu's early 1681 *Policy*, issued both in the Netherlands and in a rapid English translation, read events in England and France as mutually supportive evidence of an international clerical Catholic commitment to violence against Protestants.[47]

Jurieu's 1682 *Last Efforts* returned to the same themes. Like the *Policy*, the *Last Efforts* spent more than twenty pages justifying the reality of the 'Popish Plot' to its international audience, with assertion that it was 'ordinary with the misguided Zealots' of Catholicism 'to make Parties and enter into Conspiracies for exterminating by Poison, Fire and Sword, those they call Hereticks'. It attacked the 'Miseries of Protestants under Princes infected with the Doctrine of Rome' which declared 'Protestants hereticks, and reputes Hereticks, Outlaws and Enemies of Mankind, with whom no Faith is to be kept'. By this time, however, Jurieu was in exile in the Netherlands, and since the issue of the 1681 *Policy* measures against Huguenots had been increased by the dragonnades in Poitou, the Edict allowing removal of Protestant children at age seven, and closure of the Protestant Academy at Sedan. For Jurieu, this escalation confirmed that in France, as a Catholic character put it to a Huguenot character, 'there is a settled design for extirpating your religion'. Jurieu's text was issued as a final plea to end this escalation of measures against Huguenots by continuing to declare them loyal subjects, but that this plea was 'final' prophesied that it would be ignored in its very title, and the text was simultaneously a documentation of the escalation of measures against Protestants issued for audiences in the Netherlands and England if its plea should indeed fall on deaf ears. More than fifty pages of the *Last Efforts* were devoted to describing to its Protestant audiences in the Netherlands and England the dragonnades in Poitou, which it declared 'a Terror' to all Protestants. Jurieu depicted in gruesome detail troops 'with orders to commit the worst of outrages, till they had forced their hosts to go to mass'. According to Jurieu, Marillac had 'dispersd all the congregations, interdicted the ministers, rob'd their houses, plundering and carrying away all their goods, [and] burnt, beat, imprison'd or put to flight all those who would not change their religion'. Jurieu said that to force conversion troops had taken measures such as taking the 'master' of a house and 'burn[ing] the soles of his feet with a gentle fire'; torturing others 'with vices and other instruments to screw in their thumbs'; and hanging 'some women up at the rafters'. He depicted the 'tying of three women' to benches and troops who 'pour'd in water at their mouths'.[48]

---

[47] Jurieu, *Policy*, 110–30.   [48] Jurieu, *Last Efforts*, 85–101, 218; Howells, *Jurieu*, 33–4.

Jurieu's *Last Efforts* was a particularly influential work in its international circulation, but it was one among many accounts of events in Poitou being published in England in 1681–2 which added further fuel to the fierce fires of English anti-Catholicism. Events in Poitou were quickly reported in England in other works such as *The Horrible Persecution of the French Protestants in the Province of Poitou* (London 1681), and E[dmund] E[verard]'s *The Great Pressures and Grievances of the Protestants in France* (London 1681). Many works interpreted the absolute power of Louis XIV twinned with his Catholic persecution of Protestants as very dangerous precedents for the English monarchy.[49] The linkage was clear in the declaration of the 1681 *Letter From a Person of Quality Concerning His Majesty's Late Declaration* that 'never were our Liberties and Properties more in danger, nor the Protestant religion more expos'd to an utter extirpation *both at home and abroad*'.[50]

JOHN LOCKE 1676–83: HUGUENOTS, THE 'POPISH PLOT', THE 'POPISH CONSPIRACY' AGAINST SHAFTESBURY, AND THE DEFENCE OF RESISTANCE IN THE SECOND TREATISE

The contemporary treatment of Huguenots was central to the international Protestant perspective of John Locke in the 1670s and 1680s. Locke spent the period from 1676 to 1679 in France, visiting many Huguenots and living in the Huguenot community at Montpellier for over a year in 1676–7. As early as 1676, Locke recorded that at Nîmes the Protestants had 'but one Temple' (the other by the king's order having been pulled down about four years since), and that the Protestants of Uzès were losing their church 'the only one they had left there, though 3/4 of the town be Protestants' on the grounds that their singing of psalms 'disturbed the service' in the nearby Catholic church. In 1676, he was informed that '160 churches' had been destroyed in the last decade, and he noted that nine of the thirteen churches at Aix had been demolished and that 'those who are garantie of the Edict of Nantes interpose nothing in their behalf'. By 1679, he was recording that 'The Protestants within these twenty years have had above three hundred churches demolished, and within these two months fifteen more condemned'. Locke recorded on many occasions other new restrictions placed on Protestants, such as his note in 1676 that Protestant ministers were 'forbid to teach above two scholars at once'. In a later note, he recorded simply that Huguenots 'daily loose some privilege or other'.[51] Among the books which he left in Paris to be sent back to England was one referred to as 'Edict of Nantes';

---

[49] Jurieu, *Last Efforts*, 31, 218; Harris, 'The Parties and the People', 130 and 269n.10, n.11.
[50] *Letter From a Person of Quality*; my italics.
[51] J. Lough, *Locke's Travels in France* (Cambridge 1953), *passim*.

in his library catalogue is an unidentified entry, *Révocations de L'Édit de Nantes*.[52] It is possible that in these years Locke came to know Jean Claude, and he took many notes from Claude's 1673 *Defence of the Reformation* in 1678–9.[53] This was one of two works attacking the Catholic Pierre Nicole's *Well-grounded Prejudices against the Calvinists* which Locke possessed; he also possessed Claude Pajon's 1673 *Examination of the Prejudices*. Locke translated Nicole's *Moral Essays* in 1676, and where Nicole's original had stressed the need for individuals to submit their judgment to the Catholic Church, Locke's translation attacked the 'monstrous presumption' of commanding interpretations of Scripture desired because of the 'sweet of dominion over men's consciences'. Such dominion Locke indicted as 'slavery'.[54] In January 1676, Locke was recording that the oft-alleged Catholic principle that 'faith does not have to be kept with heretics' was playing an important role in France in the move to increasing intolerance towards Huguenots, noting specifically: 'Teaching biding to cheat the Huguenots: Nulla fides servanda cum Hereticis, nisi satis validi sunt ad se defendos'.[55] In 1676, Locke had discussed with a French Carthusian monk the return of England to Catholicism; Locke had said that there would need to be a restoration of church lands, and the monk had declared him a 'good divine'.[56] Having thus spent time in the Huguenot communities in France, and worshipping with Huguenots at Montpellier, Charenton, and Bègles, after his 1679 return to England Locke carefully followed the further measures taken against Huguenots, purchasing works itemising the developing persecution for himself or for Shaftesbury, whose political adviser he was. Locke supplied further copies of these works about persecution of the Huguenots to Whig friends in 1679–82; in May 1681, Locke lent the English translation of Jurieu's *Policy* to his Whig tolerationist friend James Tyrrell. Locke owned the 1682 final edition of the French *Politique*, Jurieu's *Last Efforts*, and the 1682 Paris *Actes de l' Assemblée (Générale) du Clergé de France*, the assembly which threatened the Huguenots with 'fearsome' and 'fatal' misfortunes.[57]

It was, then, after extensive recent personal acquaintance with increasing restrictions upon Huguenots in the 1670s, and in part in the context of reading about further measures against Huguenots in the early 1680s, that

---

[52] MS Locke b2, 21; Lough, 'Locke's Reading During His Stay in France', *The Library* (1953), 256; Locke, *The Library Catalogue of John Locke*, ed. P. Laslett and J. Harrison (Oxford 1965), 1018.

[53] Lough, *Locke's Travels*, 256n.; MS Locke f3, 380–1; MS Locke d1, 9, 37, 49, 77, 85; Lough, 'Locke's Reading', 250–1.

[54] Marshall, *Locke*, 89–90; Locke, *Library*, 2168.   [55] Lough, *Locke's Travels*, 20.

[56] *Ibid.*, 86; Ashcraft, *Revolutionary Politics*; Marshall, *Locke*.

[57] Lough, *Locke's Travels*, lx–lxi; Ashcraft, *Revolutionary Politics*; Marshall, *Locke*, 357; MS Locke f5, 54; Locke, *Library*, 779, 779a, 780, 2397; Dodge, *Political Thought*, 12ff. (Locke recorded Jurieu's *Last Efforts* by its other French title, *Suite de la politique du clergé*.)

Locke wrote his lengthy 167-page unpublished 1681–3 manuscript which is now known as the 'Critical Notes on Edward Stillingfleet'.[58] This is Locke's longest still unpublished manuscript defence of religious toleration, probably largely composed by dictation to Locke's Swiss Protestant amanuensis Sylvanus Brownover, and to his Anglican tolerationist Whig friend James Tyrrell, to whom he lent Jurieu's *Policy*, and in whose house he spent much of 1681.[59] While in one place in this manuscript Locke spoke of a 'regulated toleration' for Catholics, and while he clearly declared that for their worship alone Catholics deserved toleration – very important points within Locke's tolerationist thought to which we will return in Chapter 22 – Locke also declared in this manuscript straightforwardly that 'all Protestants ought now by all ways to be stirred up against them [Catholics] as People that have declared themselves ready by blood, violence, and destruction to ruine our Religion and Government'. It was in this manuscript in 1681–3 that Locke registered that 'popery so nearly surrounds and threatens us'. For Locke, Catholics were to be looked on as 'either Enemyes in our bowells or spies among us, whilst their General Commanders whom they blindly obey declare Warr, and an unalterable design to destroy us'. He called for the uniting of Protestants against this 'common Enemy'.[60]

The 'Critical Notes' was composed by Locke in a period when Whigs were still attempting to maintain the fervent anti-Catholicism in England of the height of the 'Popish Plot' and 'Exclusion Crisis' in 1678–81, and the description of England as surrounded and threatened by Catholics was most probably composed during 1681, and thus during the central period of allegations of the 'Irish plot' component of the 'Popish Plot' by Shaftesbury from spring 1680 to July 1681. Shaftesbury was throughout the years of the 'Popish Plot' and 'Exclusion Crisis' the leader of the campaign to exclude James from the succession, famously declaring of the 'Popish Plot' allegations that 'I will not say who started the Game, but I am sure I had the full hunting of it'.[61] Shaftesbury's campaign drew heavily on images of the suffering of Protestants at the hands of Catholic rulers, and repeatedly referred to prospects of Irish Catholic violence against English Protestants. Issued from the Shaftesbury circle, the 1680 *Letter From a Gentleman in the City to One in the Country* declared it 'an indispensable duty' of a Catholic ruler to destroy subjects disagreeing with him 'in faith and worship'. A manuscript draft among the Shaftesbury papers of a work

---

[58] MS Locke c34; Marshall, *Locke*. I am in the process of editing this manuscript for publication in the Clarendon edition of the *Works of John Locke*, Oxford University Press.

[59] Marshall, *Locke*; P. Milton, 'John Locke and the Rye House Plot', *Historical Journal* (2000), 647–68.

[60] *My Locke*, 110.   [61] J. R. Jones, *First Whigs* (London 1961), 23.

intended for publication in support of Exclusion, *A Word in Season to All True Protestants*, forecast the future fate of English Protestants on the basis of the history of Catholic intolerance through the centuries. *An Appeal from the Country to the City* was perhaps by Shaftesbury's chaplain Ferguson, but is usually ascribed to Charles Blount, brother-in-law of James Tyrrell and probably a visitor at Tyrrell's house during 1681, when Locke spent time with Tyrrell. It called on the reader to imagine London in flames with 'troops of papists ravishing your wives and your daughters, dashing your litttle children's brains out against the walls, plundering your houses, and cutting your own throats, by the name of heretic dogs'. The troops invoked here were Irish 'bog-trotters'.[62]

Allegations of plans for an Irish Catholic rising against Protestants with French Catholic support were central to the 'Popish Plot' and particularly to its 'Irish Plot' phase of 1680–1. *The Several Informations of John McNamara, Maurice Fitzgerald and James Nash relating to the Horrid Popish Plot in Ireland* were among many informations claiming that Irish Catholics had been commissioned as officers in French forces, with 'hardly a county in Ireland, but persons were appointed by the French king' to help to 'banish the English very soon' from Ireland, and as part of a joint French and papal plan to invade England and Ireland and 'wash the hands of Hereticks out of the Estates of our Ancestors'. Such plans allegedly called for many of the English in Ireland to be massacred by being 'murdered in their beds'. Led by Shaftesbury, both the House of Commons and House of Lords unanimously declared themselves satisfied that a plot existed by those 'of the Popish Religion in Ireland, for massacring the English, and subverting the Protestant Religion'.[63] Shaftesbury's assistant in exploiting the 'Popish Plot' and accenting its Irish dimensions in 1680–1 was the Earl of Essex, who as Viceroy in Ireland from 1672 to 1677 had issued a proclamation that unlicensed arms could not be kept by Catholics because of 'the insolency of Irish papists'. Essex was to be a professed believer in the reality of the Irish component of the conspiracies in the 'Popish Plot' until April 1681 when, as Shaftesbury put it, he 'did of a sudden fall from it'.[64] Many other members of the Irish Protestant elite remained supporters of the reality of the 'Popish Plot' and of its Irish dimensions throughout 1681. Roger, Earl of Orrery, and Lady Ranelagh, both siblings of Robert Boyle, stressed that there was a

---

[62] The printer of the *Appeal*, Benjamin Harris, spent much of 1680 in prison. On the *Appeal*, see: G. Kitchin, *Sir Roger L' Estrange* (London 1913), 271–2; R. L. Greaves, *Secrets of the Kingdom* (Stanford 1992), 17–18; Haley, *Shaftesbury*, 552–5; *A Narrative of Popish Plots*; Jones, *First Whigs*, 22; on Locke's movements, P. Milton, 'Rye House'.

[63] *The Several Informations of John McNamara, Maurice Fitzgerald and James Nash relating to the Horrid Popish Plot in Ireland* (London 1680), 3–9, 11.

[64] R. Bagwell, *Ireland under the Stuarts* (London 1909–16), III, ch. 46; Haley, *Shaftesbury*, 487, 572.

substantial Irish conspiracy to repeat the 1641 massacres of Protestants; their father, Richard, Earl of Cork, had fought in 1641–2 against what he had then called 'the Conspiracy to roote out all the Protestants in this Kingdome' so 'generall' that 'every Irish and English Papist...had vowed...to roote us all out of Ireland, both roote and branche'.[65]

Locke was close to several members of the Protestant elite in Ireland, and by 1681 had long supported the maintenance of the power and property of that elite. He was friends with Robert Boyle and was to be his literary executor. Locke's friend John Parry became Dean of Christ Church, Dublin, in 1666, and offered Locke help in gaining the post of chaplain to the Lord Lieutenant. Locke considered marrying Parry's sister Elinor. When she became a refugee from Ireland in 1689, Locke helped her with a loan, and assisted her son Benjamin Hawkshaw. And Locke seems to have been associated with the defence of the huge transfer of land to Protestants in the mid-seventeenth century on the grounds that it had been forfeited by Catholics by their rebellion in 1641. Many of the Shaftesbury papers in the PRO discuss the land settlement in Ireland and itemise the land distributed to Protestants as 'forfeit' by Catholics in the 'rebellion' of 1641. These papers include a manuscript itemising revenues in Ireland in 1680, and a manuscript of answers to objections to the forfeiture of lands by the rebellion endorsed 'Ireland' in a hand that appears to be Locke's own. The transfers of land in Ireland, confirmed by the Act of Settlement of 1662, had been justified in significant part by rehearsal of the alleged massacre of Protestants in the rebellion of 1641 and by declaration that because of their rebellion 'the Irish Popish rebels and enemies...lives, liberties and estates were at his majesty's disposition'. In the later seventeenth century, further 'justification' was offered with the allegation that Protestant settlers 'improved the land' and made it much more productive than its former native Irish owners. Like many others among the Protestant elite, the fortune of Locke's close friend of the 1690s, William Molyneux, was based on the 1641 forfeiture.[66] Scholars have recently identified England and America as Locke's foci in constructing

---

[65] Lismore 2nd sr 5:19 in J. Jacob, *Robert Boyle and the English Revolution* (New York 1977), 11, 13, 50, 122–4.

[66] S. J. Connolly, *Religion, Law and Power: The Making of Protestant Ireland* (Oxford 1992), 13–14; J. Froude, *The English in Ireland in the Eighteenth Century* (London 1901), I, 165; J. Simms, *William Molyneux* (Dublin 1982); Jacob, *Boyle, passim*; T. C. Barnard, 'The Cult and Culture of Improvement in Ireland' in M. Greengrass (ed.), *Samuel Hartlib and Universal Reformation* (Cambridge 1994), 281–97; W. King, *The State of the Protestants of Ireland under James* (London 1691), 342, 389, 396; J. Bardon, *A History of Ulster* (Belfast 1992), 148–9; PRO 30/24/50/7; PRO 30/24/50/29–40; PRO 30/24/50/45ff. incl. 125, 170ff., 250ff. Justice Keating alleged that Ireland was the 'most improved and improving Spot of Ground in Europe' because of Protestant settlers' activities; King printed his arguments as an appendix to his *The State of the Protestants*, on which, see pp. 91–2 below.

the arguments on property in the *Treatises*, which rendered those who allegedly used 'unjust force' – allegedly American Indians – subject to loss
of estates, and which spoke extensively of 'improvement' of the land as
justifying ownership of land – thereby further 'justifying' English settlers
in America and also 'justifying' the practices of enclosure in England employed
by Shaftesbury. Given that the manuscripts on Irish land associated with
Locke and Shaftesbury date from around 1680, it is quite possible that
Locke also had in mind in constructing his series of arguments in the
Treatises the acquisitions of property by the Protestant elite in Ireland with
their 'justifications' by allegations of 'unjust force' and of 'improvement'.[67]

Locke was not merely Shaftesbury's adviser and close to many members of
the Protestant elite in Ireland; in 1678–81, he helped to 'raise that spirit in the
nation which was necessary against the prevailing "popish party"', as the
third Earl of Shaftesbury declared. Locke was involved in Shaftesbury's
campaign at many levels, from preparing instructions for newly elected
members of Parliament to obtaining accommodation for Whig members
of Parliament and preparing readings for Shaftesbury. Shaftesbury had
probably speeded up the hanging, drawing, and quartering of the Jesuits
in 1679 just one week after their trial in an attempt to make one or more
accuse the Duke of York of involvement in the alleged plot. He personally
visited two of them on the day before their execution. Shaftesbury's reaction
to the executions of the Jesuits was allegedly that 'hanging so many on
one occasion had been a mistake, because now that the popular mind
was pacified, it would be impossible to stir it up again without a great
expenditure of careful effort over a long period of time'. Shaftesbury's
household then co-ordinated the depositions of Irish witnesses alleging
newly discovered Irish dimensions to the 'Popish Plot' in 1680–1, at
a point when most historians declare that these allegations stretched credulity farthest, when the witnesses were most corrupt, and when they were
certainly paid, and probably suborned into 'improved' testimony, by
Shaftesbury and others. That the accusations being made in this period
might not all be true was even recognised in Whig polemic in 1680: E. C.'s
A Full and Final Proof of the Plot was willing to declare explicitly that
'in cases of this moment and weight relating to the Body-politick, 'tis better
that now and then an Innocent suffer, than that all the Malefactors escape'.[68]
Locke's friend and Shaftesbury's steward Thomas Stringer took many of the

---

[67] J. Tully, *Strange Multiplicity* (Cambridge 1995); N. Wood, *Locke and Agrarian Capitalism*
(Berkeley 1984); D. Armitage, *Ideological Origins*.

[68] A. Curtayne, *The Trial of Oliver Plunkett* (London 1953); Haley, *Shaftesbury*, 541, 572;
Marshall, *Locke*, 111–12; Ashcraft, *Revolutionary Politics*, 192, 203; Jones, *Whigs*, 166; *Full
and Final Proof* (1680), 7, in Tumbleson, *Catholicism in the English Protestant Imagination*
(Cambridge 1998), 75.

depositions from witnesses who had been recruited by Shaftesbury's agent Hetherington, and while they left Ireland very poor, they were said to have returned after their testimony as rich as gentlemen. The witnesses included an accused horse-thief, and others described as 'drunken vagabonds' and 'such creatures' that they would not have been trusted 'with the design of robbing an orchard'. As Patrick Kelly has shown, Locke himself spent time with some of the Irish witnesses testifying to the Irish plot in 1680–1: Locke's manuscripts include some veterinary recipes that he recorded receiving from them. Horse-thieves were thought by Locke to have more than one skill, it seems.[69]

From 1678–81, Shaftesbury, assisted by Locke, thus rode the crest of a wave of anti-Catholicism and fostered executions for treason based in part on testimony from highly disreputable witnesses, together with inferences from the actual desires for re-Catholicisation of England of Coleman, from James' Catholicism, from Charles II's suspected Catholicism, and from Charles' alliance with France. After Charles' dismissal of the Oxford Parliament in 1681, however, 'the weapon which Shaftesbury had sharpened was...turned against him', as Charles II accused Shaftesbury of treason by using some of the disreputable witnesses that had formerly been used by Shaftesbury against Catholics. Buckingham commented that it was the first case that he had known where a man had been betrayed by his own witnesses. Burnet, willing to accept these witnesses when they were testifying against Catholics, now allegedly told Charles II that these witnesses were unreliable; knowing that they had been used by Shaftesbury to gain the execution of innocent Catholics, Charles II allegedly replied that 'at dooms-day we shall see whose arse is blackest'. As the political pendulum swung toward the Tories, the first significant Whig swung at the gallows. The Whig propagandist Stephen College, whose first attempted indictment for treason at London was prevented by a Whig grand jury, was convicted and executed in September 1681 when he was indicted and tried at Royalist Oxford where Tories controlled the juries as well as the judge.[70]

In November 1681, Shaftesbury was not indicted for treason because at that point he still had the backing of a Whig grand jury appointed by Whig

---

[69] *The Further Information of Stephen Dugdale* (London 1680); *The Information of Robert Jennison* (London 1680); *The Information of Edward Turberville* (London 1680); P. Kelly, 'Locke and Molyneux: The Anatomy of a Friendship', *Hermathena* (1979), 38–54, at 40–1, discussing MS Locke c42, MS Locke d9, 87, MS Locke c1, 46–7; Haley, *Shaftesbury*, 570–1, and Locke, *The Correspondence of John Locke*, ed. E. S. de Beer (Oxford 1978–), III, 640, 689. Kelly indicates that PRO 30/24/98/16 is a list of witnesses in Locke's hand, but I have not been able to find such a list. Kelly suggests that PRO 30/24/24/63 has a deposition from Brian Haynes in Locke's hand; on this, see below, p. 49 and n. 86.

[70] R. Bagwell, *Ireland*, III, 139; Jones, *Whigs*, 189; Hutton, *Charles II* (Oxford 1989), 408; Marshall, *Locke*.

sheriffs. This jury had among its leading members the rich second-generation immigrant Huguenot Whig merchant Papillon, a schoolboy friend of Shaftesbury, since then involved in financial investments with Shaftesbury, and in 1682 a Whig candidate for sheriff. And it had four Members of Parliament who had supported Exclusion. In November, this Whig grand jury not merely refused to indict Shaftesbury, but it also questioned the witnesses and pointed out that some had even signed a Whig petition to the Common Council protesting against efforts to suborn them. In the Shaftesbury papers are instructions giving grounds for protesting the charge itself and detailed suggestions for questioning and 'incriminating' the witnesses if that proved possible. These instructions, copied into two small notebooks for easy handling in court, appear to have been closely followed at the trial by the leading jury members Papillon and Barnardiston.[71]

Immediately after his initial arrest in July 1681, and before this November refusal of the grand jury to indict him, the Shaftesbury circle issued *A Brief Account of the Designs which the Papists have had Against the Earl of Shaftesbury, Occasioned by his Commitment, July 2 1681*. This argued that the sole source of accusations against him were his 'faithful and unwearied cares and endeavours to obviate the formidable growth of France, and to prevent the re-establishment of Popery in these nations, and thereby the enslaving them again to Rome'. His efforts against 'a French and Popish Party and Faction', the 'abettors of Arbitrariness and Popery at home', were declared to have fostered 'Popish rage' against him. The *Brief Account* declared that Shaftesbury had therefore 'expected every night to have his throat cut' and had been forced to keep a 'constant watch' in his house to 'prevent his being murdered and assassinated'. His prosecution of the 'Popish Plot' was said to have caused 'many Designs' against him and the contracting of 'the killing of him'. It was only when such plans of 'violence and force' failed, the *Brief Account* declared, that they had turned to ruining him 'under the countenance of the Law'.[72] The rhetoric in this text, then, was that the accusation of treason against Shaftesbury under 'countenance of the Law' was a continuation by legal means of the attempts to use force against Shaftesbury in plots against his life which had taken more direct forms up

---

[71] PRO 30/24/43/63 fos. 375ff., 413ff.; *The Proceedings against the Right Honorable Earl of Shaftesbury 24 November 1681* (1681), *passim*, esp. 12ff.; *State Trials*, VIII, 809, 816; Jones, *Whigs*, 191–205. The next sections of this chapter on the legal contexts of Locke's *Two Treatises* are based on a paper 'Locke, the Law and Liberty' which was given to the American Society of Legal Historians in Houston, Texas, in 1995. I wish to thank my co-panellists Tim Harris and Joyce Lee Malcolm, the Chair Michael Mendle, and the audience for their comments.

[72] *A Brief Account of the Designs which the Papists have had Against the Earl of Shaftesbury, Occasioned by his Commitment, July 2 1681*, 1–4. Bedloe had claimed that the 'Popish Plot' included plans to assassinate Shaftesbury: Kenyon, *Popish*, 95–6.

to this point. It was a rhetoric that placed desires for 'popery' and arbitrary power together as preludes to Catholicisation of England. Locke was in this period helping to co-ordinate Shaftsbury's legal defence.[73] He owned a copy of the *Brief Account*.[74] It is possible that he shared the perspective of the *Brief Account* on the legal attempts to try Shaftesbury for treason as parts of a 'popish' plan to execute Shaftesbury in order to establish absolutism and Catholicism in England. If so, it is equally important that there was no hint in the *Brief Account* that armed resistance was yet thought to be legitimate to repulse such an attempt against Shaftesbury's life. Locke and Shaftesbury at this point in 1681 seem to have been focused on using legal means to repulse the king. In 1681, the London (Middlesex) grand juries were still in Whig hands, and as long as they could protect the constitution of those juries by Whig sheriffs, Shaftesbury was secure.

The *Brief Account* was one 1681 work associated with the Shaftesbury circle which described a Catholic or popish 'conspiracy' as behind the attempts to try Shaftesbury. A second work making the same allegation was issued from the Shaftesbury circle, probably by Shaftesbury's chaplain Robert Ferguson, the October 1681 *No Protestant Plot, or The Present Pretended Conspiracy of Protestants Against the King, and Government, Discovered to be a Conspiracy of the Papists Against the King and his Protestant Subjects*. Its anonymous author depicted his text as supporting the 'Loyalty of persons barely accused', and attacked the accusations against Shaftesbury of plotting against the king as the suborned testimony of entirely untrustworthy witnesses. It asserted that the 'base and villanous arts the Papists will use to destroy my Lord Shaftesbury' were 'evident by their many endeavours to have him stab'd' and their counterfeiting of letters to accuse him falsely of treason. The plot 'under the guilt whereof they would involve the Earl of Shaftesbury' was 'nothing but a forgery of the Papists' and an attempt to 'destroy such as have any zeal for Protestancy, or the Laws and Liberties of the Land'. Ferguson argued that the executing of an innocent person was 'the ready way to cause such as are loyal to waver in their fidelity, and instigate them if they apprehend themselves in danger, to fly to unlawful means for defence and shelter'. Like the *Brief Account*, Ferguson thus did not suggest that there was a right of resistance, but rather suggested that such was 'unlawful'.[75]

John Somers' 1681 [*The Security of Englishmen's Lives or*] *The Trust, Power, and Duty of the Grand Juries*, issued at the end of 1681 and in

---

[73] J. R. Milton and P. Milton, 'Selecting the Grand Jury: A Tract by John Locke', *HJ* (1997), 185–94.

[74] Locke, *Library*, 2641.

[75] [R. Ferguson], *No Protestant Plot* (1681), *passim*, esp. 1–3, 16–18, 22, 24, 35.

circulation mainly in 1682, made much the same case of a Catholic conspiracy against Protestants' lives, and stressed the importance of grand juries
to prevent this. Somers had been a supporter of Exclusion, and a friend of
Lords Essex and Russell – the first of whom was arguably to be murdered in
prison by agents of the Crown in 1683, and the second of whom was to be
executed for complicity in the 'Rye House Plot' in 1683. Somers was a lawyer
for the Whig outgoing and incoming sheriffs charged with inciting a riot
around the disputed election of sheriffs; among the activities of these Whig
sheriffs had been impanelling the Whig grand jury which refused to indict
Shaftesbury. Somers was a friend of Shaftesbury, and of Locke's friends and
MPs Edward Clarke and John Freke. By the 1690s, Locke was close to
Somers, in the years after Somers chaired the committee which composed
the 1689 Declaration of Rights; Somers was to help Locke gain his position
with the Board of Trade. Such patronage suggests a longer standing relation-
ship. It is likely that Locke knew Somers by the early 1680s in the context of
Whig legal manoeuvring to protect Shaftesbury. He then possessed a copy of
Grand Juries.[76] Somers declared in his *Grand Juries* that the work was
'Published for the Prevention of Popish Designs against the Lives of Many
Protestant Lords and Commoners, who stand firm to the Religion and
ancient Government of England'. The first lines of the book declared that
'The Principal Ends of all Civil Government, and of Humane Society, were
the Security of Men's Lives, Liberties and Properties'. Somers argued that the
'fundamental of government' was the jury system and identified the 'trust' of
Grand Juries as next to Parliament, attacked judges as creatures of passion
and interest dependent on those who appointed and dismissed them, and
asserted the need for independent juries to counteract their pernicious influences. According to Somers, 'our lawmakers foresaw' that corrupt ministers
of state might accuse and 'commit the most odious of murders in the form
and course of justice; either by corrupting of judges, as dependant upon
them...or by bribing...to swear falsely'. For Somers, it was vital that
grand juries 'neither be cheated nor frighted from their Duty'.[77]

That Shaftesbury had been innocent of treason when the Crown had
attempted to indict him in 1681, and that the Crown had attempted to indict
him due to a 'popish' and Catholic 'conspiracy' because Shaftesbury had
attacked Catholics who were attempting to erect absolutism and persecution
in England, was strongly asserted again in either late 1681 or early 1682 in a
further work probably by Robert Ferguson, the *Second Part of No Protestant
Plot*. The *Second Part* again asserted that the attempt to try him had been

---

[76] L. Schwoerer, *The Declaration of Rights 1689* (Baltimore 1981), 34, 47–50; W. Sachse, *John,
Lord Somers*, (Manchester 1975), 16–20; MS Locke f28, 68.
[77] [Somers], *Grand Juries, passim.*

generated by a papist conspiracy utilising suborned witnesses with the ultimate aim of re-establishing 'Papal superstition and Idolatry in these Kingdoms'. And it declared the danger of a situation in which men were assured of the protection of the laws and yet they were applied 'to the ruine of the innocent' and left 'no man safe', and was much worse than 'either the poysoning or assassinating men' because of the dangers posed by 'studying to destroy them in a pretended legal way, upon the Testimony and Oaths of suborned and perjured rascals'. Yet it asserted in this context that juries were vital to protect the 'Lives of innocent men' and that it was therefore the 'inestimable privilege of our constitution' that 'twelve impartial, honest, and substantial Men' among the neighbours of any accused were needed for pronouncing men guilty. It defended the juries returned in London 'by the last sheriffs and those now in office' as the best men returned in the last twenty years 'for Quality and Estate, and for unblameableness and integrity of life', and it defended the role of sheriffs in nominating juries. It too, in other words, suggests a moment when the protection provided by juries for Whigs like Shaftesbury was under attack in England, but in which it still had not yet been lost. John and Philip Milton have pointed to Ferguson's *Second Part of No Protestant Plot* as including arguments which may have been suggested to Ferguson by Locke himself.[78]

The first eighteen pages of Ferguson's February 1682 *Third Part of No Protestant Plot, with Observations on the Bill of Indictment against the Earl of Shafesbury* then placed its repetition of the accusation of the plots, conspiracies, and designs of the Papists in England against Protestants' religion, lives and liberties into a context of international Catholic violence against Protestants, including in England under Queen Mary, in the Netherlands under Spanish rule, in the Irish rebellion of 1641, in the persecution of the Waldensians in Piedmont, and in the persecution of the Huguenots in France. The text opened with the declaration:

How much the Papists are not only justified in destroying those who differ from them in Faith and Worship, but obliged by the Principles of their Religion, to extirpate all Christians, who have withdrawn from the Communion of their Church; we may be easily informed, if we would but give our selves the trouble of consulting the canons of their Councils, the Decrees of their Popes, and the publick writings of their most approved Authors...For besides, millions of men and Women professing and obeying the Gospel, that have been destroyed in other nations, for no other offence, but because they have dissented from the Church of Rome, there have been several hundred thousands been murther'd, kill'd and massacr'd in these three Kingdoms.

---

[78] [Ferguson], *The Second Part of No Protestant Plot* (London 1682), *passim*, esp. 2–3, 7, 10, 20, 23, 32; Haley, *Shaftesbury*, 691; J. and P. Milton, 'Selecting'.

Ferguson declared that 'we may yet more fully satisfy ourselves, what we are to expect from Papists, and what their Religion guides them unto, and justifeth them in, if we will but consider what the sufferings of the Protestants in France at present are, and what methods are pursued for the extirpating of them'. It would 'take a volume rather than a Paragraph' he declared, 'to recount the many late Edicts which have been published against them, and the several steps and methods which have been taken to ruin them'. Those he did itemise included the demolition of 'an infinite number of churches', punishment of ministers, loss of offices, and taking of children. He continued 'the sufferings and calamities of the Protestants in France, are grown to such a height, that many thousands have forsaken their native country' and these were 'but a Copy of what we in these Nations are to look for, in case we should come under a Popish Prince'. According to Ferguson, popish conspirators held an 'intimate and dayly correspondence with' the court in France, which had committed itself to provide 'Supplies of Power and Succcour' whenever the moment appeared ripe to 'set upon destroying our religion, and altering the Government'. The accusation against Shaftesbury was declared part of a 'popish conspiracy' which would, if successful against Shaftesbury, have seen sworn testimony against 'all... whom out of malice, or for the facilitating the Introduction of Popery, and arbitrary power, they had a mind to get destroyed'. Like its preceding two parts, it attacked the credibility of the witnesses against Shaftesbury, and argued that Shaftsbury had taken part in no plans to assassinate or resist the king. It again offered no defence of resistance against the king; it again suggested that only by trial by jury could security of lives, liberties, estates, and religion be preserved.[79]

The Whig English translation of Jurieu's 1682 *Last Efforts* by W. Vaughan[80] similarly strongly stated Shaftesbury's innocence when the Crown attempted to indict him in 1681, and that it was due to a popish and Catholic conspiracy that the court had attempted to have him indicted. This accusation served in its French original as a warning to Huguenots in France and the Netherlands of the kinds of actions that would be taken in countries dominated by Catholic conspiracies against Protestantism. In its English translation, it served to support Shaftesbury's actions to defend England from Catholic absolutism and persecution, and to condemn the court's actions against Shaftesbury by

---

[79] [Ferguson], *The Third Part of No Protestant Plot* (London 1682), *passim*.

[80] Vaughan is obscure: he has no DNB entry, and the only other work with which I suspect him to be associated – for obvious reasons – is the 1689 *A Caveat to Protestants* in a dialogue between a Huguenot and a papist about the extirpation of Protestantism in France. The only surviving copy of this work I have so far traced is at UCLA; I have not yet been able to consult it. He would appear from the reasons given below to be a client of the Earl of Bedford and a firm Whig.

paralleling them with evidence of the French Catholic absolute ruler's persecution of Huguenots in France. Jurieu declared that the charge against Shaftesbury was 'a Counter-battery raised by your Catholiques'. The Catholic witnesses against Shaftesbury were described as 'suborning' themselves in order, they believed, to serve God in attacking Shaftesbury because he was 'the great Enemy of the Roman Church'.[81]

Thus, whereas Jurieu's 1681 *Policy* had focused on the Estates being able to defend the edicts of toleration in France and the Parliament being able to secure a Protestant succession in England, the text of the 1682 *Last Efforts* focused instead on the legal moves against Shaftesbury in England and on the legal moves against Huguenots in France, establishing a more worrying parallel between England and France. It was the Epistle Dedicatory to the English translation of Jurieu's 1682 *Last Efforts* which drew out the implications of this different emphasis. This epistle was dedicated to the Whig Exclusionist Earl of Bedford, a close associate of Shaftesbury in opposition to royal absolutism from 1675 and father of Lord Russell, who was to be a co-conspirator with Shaftesbury in plans for armed resistance to the king, and who was to be executed in 1683, although Bedford himself was to refrain from armed resistance.[82] Against the background in England in 1682 of moves against the charters of corporations which secured the sheriffs who held the power to appoint juries, the Epistle Dedicatory offered its interpretation of events in France as a warning to English Protestants that Catholic persecution in France was occurring via Catholics' corruption of legal protections offered by edicts and privileges now revoked in the denial of 'impartial law' by use of 'subtilty' and 'artifice' 'to make Law an instrument of Oppression, and Justice itself a Minister of Injury' in a government where a 'prevalent Faction doth by colour of Law and pretence of Religion, destroy the Religion and Rights of their adversaries, who are therefore the more miserable, because they suffer unjustly under a form of justice'. Jurieu's interpretation of events in France, and its issue with English translation and dedication in 1682 at a point when the king was moving in England to try Shaftesbury by 'colour of law' but with suborned witnesses and rigged juries, was thus being used to provide collateral evidence for the Whig interpretation of events in England in 1682: that popishly inclined or Catholic-dominated absolute monarchies used the 'colour of law' to remove 'impartial justice', the legal protection of Protestants' rights of religious worship, and Protestants' liberties.[83] The *Last Efforts* describes the most pressing threat from Catholic absolutism as being channelled through ostensibly legal means against which Parliament and the Estates were increasingly

---

[81] Jurieu, *Last Efforts*, Epistle Dedicatory and *passim.*   [82] Haley, *Shaftesbury*, 561.
[83] Jurieu, *Last Efforts*, Epistle Dedicatory.

powerless. Yet it stresses that resistance is invalid: it explicitly advocates toleration towards Huguenots as necessary in France because they are loyal subjects, and it explicitly condemns resistance as a 'black crime'. Jurieu's original *Last Efforts* was published a year before armed resistance would be justified by Jurieu in 1683 in response to a situation made even more desperate for Huguenots in France, and its English translation as *Last Efforts* was published some months before resistance would be justified in England in a situation which had been made even more desperate for political opponents of absolute monarchy in England. In 1681 to mid-1682, both in England and in France, the situation had not yet reached the level of desperation which it was later to reach.

Having failed to obtain an indictment of Shaftesbury for treason in 1681, the Crown turned from late 1681 to 1683 to various legal manoeuvres, including challenges to the London electorate and the corporation charter, in efforts to obtain compliant sheriffs and thereby compliant juries. It maintained propaganda suggesting that Shaftesbury's head would look good displayed 'on a pike'. In July 1682, as the result of a contested election, the Crown succeeded in gaining a Tory shrievalty, and thus gained the capacity to indict Shaftesbury for treason in front of a compliant jury after the swearing in of new sheriffs on 30 September 1682. Shaftesbury was very probably involved in plotting armed resistance to the king in about September to November 1682, and went into hiding and then fled into exile in the Netherlands in mid-November when this resistance did not materialise. On the day on which the new sheriffs were sworn in, Shaftesbury allegedly cried out 'Popery, Slavery, Murder, Irish witnesses'. According to the accounts provided by Ferguson and West among others, the gaining of control of the sheriffs and thereby of the juries was the crucial moment in turning Shaftesbury and others to immediate planning of resistance, and shortly before the planned date set for a rising – 19 November 1682 – Ferguson and Shaftesbury turned from focusing on the prospect of a future Catholic king to attacking the 'present majesty' for 'attempts. . .to introduce Popery and arbitrary government', and both 'concluded that the government was dissolved and the people at liberty to settle another'. According to West, Ferguson had argued in late 1682 that it was 'the duty of a people invaded in their rights, and under oppression, to defend themselves by the ordinary means of taking arms'. West called such resistance the plan of a 'desperate' Shaftesbury.[84]

---

[84] BM Add MSS 38847 'Robert West's Full confession to the King', 2–4, 7, 10; R. Ferguson, 'Concerning the Rye House Business' in J. Ferguson, *Robert Ferguson the Plotter* (Edinburgh 1887), 410, 412–14; Scott, *Restoration*; Marshall, *Locke*. I am grateful to Michael Mendle for his comments as Chair/Commentator on my paper, in which he stressed the importance of the 'desperation' of Shaftesbury and Locke at this moment.

As John and Philip Milton very importantly have shown, in late 1681 Locke had composed a manuscript challenging the Crown's attempts to change the composition of the Whig grand jury; we will examine this manuscript and these attempts in Chapter 3 as they concerned the Crown's attempt to exclude Protestant dissenters from the jury.[85] Locke was also the author of a manuscript in the Shaftesbury papers which attempted to demonstrate that Brian Haynes, one of the Irish witnesses who was now about to testify against Shaftesbury, was offering false testimony, by using the deposition that Haynes had himself provided to the Recorder of London in March 1681 – when he was still testifying for the Whigs – that he was being promised money to testify falsely against the Whigs that there was a Presbyterian plot against the monarch led by Shaftesbury. Locke was thus deeply involved in the extended legal campaign to defend Shaftesbury in late 1681 and with arguing that the evidence against Shaftesbury was false. Haynes had also been one of the witnesses against College in 1681, and John and Philip Milton have given reason to believe that Locke was involved in the failed legal defence of College in September 1681.[86] The many depositions that now form the bulk of PRO 30/24/43/63 show that a large number of testimonies had been collected in order to defend Shaftesbury in 1681 by alleging the suborned and false testimony of Irish witnesses who had formerly testified for the Whigs against Catholics and who now testified for the court against the Whigs. The legal campaign to defend Shaftesbury by incriminating witnesses was the central preoccupation of the Whigs in late 1681, and Locke was deeply involved in this legal campaign, in the claim that the witnesses against Shaftesbury were offering false testimony, and in the general case that juries were vital to protect lives where judges were controlled and witnesses offered false testimony.[87] Locke was to follow Shaftesbury into exile in the Netherlands, fleeing from England soon after the 'Rye House Plot' was discovered by the king in 1683. As a visitor to Essex's house at Cassiobury both in September 1682 and in April 1683 – the

---

[85] Milton and Milton, 'Selecting'; below, pp. 120–4. This manuscript is now most readily available in Goldie (ed.), *Locke: Political Essays*.

[86] PRO 30/24/43/63 fo. 171r; Milton and Milton, 'Selecting'. Kelly, 'Locke and Molyneux', misattributes this manuscript itself to March 1681. It is headed 'Dated 6 March 1681' because that was the date of Haynes' earlier deposition that there had been an attempt to suborn him. It is dated on the back 6 November 1681, probably the date of its composition or of its amalgamation into the documents to be used at indictment, and it is surely part of the legal plans for challenges to witnesses to be used against Shaftesbury. Milton and Milton note the existence of this manuscript and call it 'an annotated copy of the deposition made by Brian Haynes'. It would be more accurate to call it 'some reflexions on a deposition made by Brian Haynes'. Cf. PRO 30/24/43/63 265ff.; 375ff., esp. 382–3, 452ff.; *The Proceedings against the Right Honorable Earl of Shaftesbury 24 November 1681*, 14ff.

[87] PRO 30/24/43/63, *passim*.

latter during a period when Ashcraft and Scott have identified justifications
for resistance were being composed at Essex's house and the former at about
the date that Ferguson and West indicate that serious discussions of resistance were under way and that Shaftesbury was coming to declare the
government 'dissolved' – Locke was probably, although not definitely,
aware of and involved in plans of resistance not merely from about late
September to November 1682, in alliance with his patron Shaftesbury, but
even after Shaftesbury had fled to the Netherlands and died.[88] I have argued
in my *Locke: Resistance, Religion and Responsibility* that it is probable that
Locke composed the greatest part of the Second Treatise in the dual context
of 1682–3, firstly of legal moves against leading Whigs which posed a direct
threat to their lives as they replaced the security of Whig-controlled grand
juries with Tory juries which would indict and convict for treason on the
slimmest of accusations, and secondly of actual planning of armed resistance
from 1682 due to those actions by the Crown.[89]

[88] Ashcraft, *Revolutionary Politics*; my *Locke*; Haley, *Shaftesbury*; Scott, *Restoration*; Hutton,
Charles II, 419–20. For an article identifying Locke as physically distancing himself from
locations of the planning of resistance and assassination, see Milton, 'Rye House'. Milton
does indicate that Locke did visit Essex's house in 1683, and that his visit in September 1682
occurred after the arrest of Monmouth and not before it, but he makes much less of either
point than I do. Locke's correspondence for late October 1682, as Milton notes, includes a
letter from Edward Clarke to Locke at Christ Church, Oxford, when Shaftesbury was in
hiding in London, which suggested that Locke's 'Freinds in the citty are verie desirous of your
Company' and that they now needed the 'best Advise and Assistance of theire wisest and
Truest friends', of whose number Locke deserved 'first place'. The letter could be read as
confirming Milton's stress on Locke physically distancing himself from plans for resistance,
but it could also be read as suggesting that Clarke thought that Locke might have something
of intellectual importance and assistance to offer to his friends at that moment when
resistance was being planned by Locke's patron-in-hiding Shaftesbury: *Correspondence*, ii,
739. Milton gives many reasons to doubt pieces of evidence that Ashcraft adduced for Locke's
involvement in the conspiracies planning resistance, but even he argues: 'It is, of course, unlikely
that he was wholly unaware of Shaftesbury's insurrectionary plans, and it is evident from the
final chapters of the Second Treatise that he regarded resistance as a legitimate response to
governmental abuse of power'. It still seems to me that the most persuasive combination of
these two points is to suggest that composition was related to awareness of the planning.
[89] For varied datings and purposes urged over recent years, see in addition to my *Locke*, Ashcraft,
Revolutionary Politics; Scott, *Restoration*; *idem*, *England's Troubles*; A. Patterson, *Early
Modern Liberalism* (Cambridge 1997); M. Knights, *Politics*; D. Wootton (ed.), *Locke:
Political Writings* (London 1993); J. R. Milton, 'Dating Locke's Second Treatise', *History of
Political Thought* (1995), 356–90; Tuck, *The Rights of War and Peace* (Oxford 1999), 168–9;
cf. also Milton, 'Rye House'. Richard Tuck has suggested on completely different grounds than
those adduced here that a very significant portion of Locke's arguments were a response to
Pufendorf from June 1681 or later, writing of 'the critique of Pufendorf in chapter V' that it
belongs 'most naturally to 1681 or later': *Rights*, 168. The Miltons initially seemed to favour
composition of the later sections of the Second Treatise in autumn 1682 but gave reasons for
arguing against mid- to late 1681; I still find their arguments for arguing against mid- to late
1681 persuasive and their arguments for composition of the later sections of the Second
Treatise in 1682 persuasive and in agreement with my own arguments, and Richard Tuck's
argument for composition in mid-1681 or later persuasive – and all as reinforcing my initial

Here I wish briefly to restate this argument, and simultaneously both to associate and also in one sense to dissociate this suggested context for composition of the Second Treatise with the accusations of 'popish conspiracy' by 'perversion of the law' and suborned testimony in trials of opponents given in the *Brief Account*, Somers' *Grand Juries*, Ferguson's three parts of *No Protestant Plot*, and the English dedication to Jurieu's *Last Efforts*. Shaftesbury had long been arguing that there was a 'popish conspiracy' at court, and these works by Shaftesbury's close associates, and the work by Jurieu translated by a Whig who dedicated the translation to Shaftesbury's Whig associate Bedford, argued that the legal moves against Shaftesbury were continuations of this 'popish conspiracy'. Yet they had concentrated on arguing that this was a 'popish conspiracy' around the king and against the king and his subjects, and they had not included the king himself within their attack. Moreover, they had condemned resistance in arguing that the attack on Shaftesbury was an unjustified attack on a loyal subject. They were written and published when the Whigs still controlled the juries. Locke's attack, which I will examine in a moment, did not mention the word 'conspiracy' and did not refer to it, except perhaps briefly in arguing that when a religion most conducive to absolutism was 'underhand favoured though publicly proclaimed against' this gave further evidence that there were moves to establish absolutism. It was a direct attack on the prince himself as a 'noxious beast' deserving to be slain by armed resistance as himself intent on establishing absolutism, and not an allegation of 'popish conspiracy' around the king. The arguments defending individual rights of armed resistance against the moves towards absolutism in Locke's text were written, I suggest again here, when the move had been made to justification of resistance, when the Whigs had lost control of sheriffs and thereby of juries. There is a relatively thin line between the works of Somers, Ferguson, and the English translator of Jurieu, who argued that juries provided the only security of lives, liberty, property, and religion, and justification of resistance by arguing that subjects have now lost the security of life itself, but it is an important one both chronologically and in terms of the division between Whig strategies of resistance by law to the drive towards absolutism and the final, desperate plans of resistance by arms. We await an important book on

contention that the text is most likely to date from 1682, when the evidence discussed in my *Locke* indicates that actual planning of resistance was begun in the Shaftesbury circle. By focusing here on the legal context and that of plans of armed resistance in terms of immediate motivations for composition of major parts of the Second Treatise I do not wish to exclude the intellectual significance of Locke having responded to Pufendorf in '1681 or later', nor of his having been thinking about composition of such a response from the point of purchase of Pufendorf in mid-1681. Cf now also D. Armitage, 'Locke, Carolina and the *Two Treatises*', *Political Theory* (2004), 602–27, which appeared while this book was already going through the press.

this division among Whigs in London between resistance 'by arms' and 'by law' by Gary de Krey.[90] Bedford, supporter of Exclusion and dedicatee of the English translation of Jurieu's *Last Efforts*, did not support resistance by arms, although his son Russell did and was to be executed as a conspirator. I am suggesting that Locke's arguments are a logical extension of the arguments that juries provided the only security of life against a 'popish conspiracy' raised by Ferguson, Somers, and Vaughan's translation of Jurieu, and that they involve simultaneously what was a significant step beyond those arguments. Many Whigs were willing to try to withstand Charles II by all possible legal means, but few were willing to take up arms against the king. Simultaneously, I want here also to note that part of this context is formed by the parallels being drawn between France's most recent moves against Huguenots and English moves towards legal absolutism that were traced most explicitly by Ferguson's *Third Part of No Protestant Plot* and in the Epistle Dedicatory and text of Jurieu's *Last Efforts*. In the forced removal of Huguenot children for Catholic education at age seven and the dragonnades in Poitou, Catholic absolutism in France had by 1682 given evidence for what Locke and Shaftesbury had long been alleging, that absolutist Catholic kings would persecute Protestantism and violate Protestants' rights to property even when they had promised on many occasions to be respectful of both religion and property, and even when they had taken many oaths that they would continue edicts of toleration protecting property and religion.

The opposition of absolute monarchy to the security provided by 'impartial law' was structurally central to Locke's Second Treatise, which attacked the threat to life, liberty, and property posed by a loss of 'impartial justice', and which included specifically the charge that the political opponents of absolutism were now being tried for their opposition to absolutism under 'colour of law'. It is important to emphasise that the argument for resistance in the Second Treatise focused even more upon the legal actions of the Crown and their threat to life itself than it did upon the issue of Parliament meeting when the 'public good' demanded this; while that issue was significant, and has long been the focus of scholars' analyses of the text, the first justification of resistance in political society in the Second Treatise that is met by a reader – as early as the twentieth paragraph, and thus immediately after the conceptual groundwork for the right of resistance has been laid in the opening sections on men outside political society having a right to kill aggressors – is that men join political society to achieve a common authority to punish with a 'fair determination of law' and that

---

[90] G. De Krey, *London and the Restoration*, (Cambridge, 2005) appeared only after this book was already going through the press.

where an appeal to the Law and constituted judges lies open, but the remedy is denyd by a manifest perverting of justice, and a barefaced wresting of the laws...there it is hard to imagine anything but a state of war. For wherever violence is used, and injury done, though by the hands appointed to administer justice, it is still violence and injury, however colourd with the Name, Pretences, or Forms of Law, the end whereof is to protect and redress the innocent...War is made upon the Sufferers, who having no appeal on Earth to right them, they are left to the only remedy in such Cases, an appeal to Heaven.

Such an appeal to heaven was, of course, resistance with a sword.[91]

Listing the reasons for which men should conclude that absolutism was about to be imposed, and that therefore they legitimately could and should resist, Locke surely had in mind the legal actions against Shaftesbury and others when he described a situation 'under pretence of lawful authority' of the prince gaining power 'to terrify or suppress opposers as factious, seditious, and enemies to the government'. The *Treatises* further declared that it should 'be put past doubt' what a prince was doing, and justify resistance, when 'all the arts of perverted law' were 'made use of, to take off and destroy all that stand in the way of such a design, and will not comply and consent to betray the Liberties of their country'. According to Locke, people would not, and by implication should not, fail to be persuaded that 'their Estates, Liberties and Lives are in danger'

if either...illegal acts have extended to the Majority of the People, or if the Mischief and Oppression has light only on some few, but in such Cases, as the Precedent, and Consequences seem to threaten all.

More generally, the primary argument for resistance and against absolutism of the Second Treatise was that 'wherever law ends tyranny begins if the law is transgressed to anothers harm'. 'Where there is no longer the administration of Justice, for the securing mens Rights' Locke declared that no government existed any longer; where an executive power made its own will law instead of executing the law, obligation to it from oaths ceased; it became instead of a superior, a noxious beast to be slain. The association of rule by indifferent law with liberty, and resistance as justified when this was violated, was thus structurally central to Locke's entire argument in the Second Treatise as we have it. For Locke, in political terms, liberty in the Second Treatise was fundamentally defined in terms of security from threat

---

[91] Locke, Second Treatise, *passim*, esp. paragraph 20. It should be stressed, for those who wish still to date composition of the bulk of the Second Treatise before 1681 (Laslett, Knights), that an argument that the executive has removed indifferent law makes less sense before mid-1681 than it does from mid-1681 or most especially from mid-1682 onwards: up until mid-1681, it was Shaftesbury and Locke, and not the king, who could much more accurately have been accused of perverting the law and not providing impartial justice in executing the innocent by wresting the laws.

to life. As he put it, 'liberty is to be free from...violence from others'. Locke's fundamental argument about liberty in the *Treatises* was that men exchanged their natural liberty to dispose of themselves, their actions, and possessions, within the bounds of the law of nature, for liberty in political society in being under laws made by the legislature because they thereby gained security that violence would be prevented. It was because of the absence of a standing, settled law and a known indifferent judge that men gave up their natural liberty to join political society; it was that very purpose which excluded the possibility of a legitimate absolute government. In what I remain persuaded is the most probable immediate context of composition of the Second Treatise, it was the threat to life itself actually being posed by trials in 1682–3 that provided both the conceptual centre of Locke's argument as we have it and his primary immediate motivation for its composition.[92]

---

[92] Locke, *Second Treatise, passim.* While I stress here the motivational importance of the issue of the threats to life and juries and the structural importance of the threat to life itself that they posed to composition of justifications of resistance and plans for resistance, I do not mean thereby to reduce the arguments of the *Treatises* to the issue of the preservation of life and juries: they also, of course, make important arguments about the importance of Parliament sitting when needed, and arguments about elections and electors that are also about representative government and not merely the appointment of juries, and they responded extensively to issues of property in the Americas, for instance, among other issues.

2

Catholic intolerance and the significance of its representations in England, Ireland, and the Netherlands, c. 1687–92

THE 1685–6 PERSECUTION OF THE WALDENSIANS
AND ITS REPRESENTATIONS IN ENGLAND

The persecution of Huguenots culminating in the Revocation of the Edict of Nantes is familiar to historians who have long recognised its impact in England and the Netherlands. But it was not the only significant Catholic persecution of Protestants which commenced in 1685, and the now less familiar persecution of the Waldensians was also extremely significant and often cited in the 1680s alongside the treatment of Huguenots as clear evidence of the international commitment of contemporary Catholicism to persecution. In December 1685, less than two months after Louis XIV revoked the Edict of Nantes, the Catholic Duke of Savoy, Victor Amadeus II, ended toleration for 14,000 Waldensians, members of a community which had lived for centuries in mountain valleys in his territories in Piedmont. These valleys bordered south-eastern France (where the Waldensians had also formerly lived), and the Waldensians both maintained considerable contact with Huguenots and had adopted as their own confession of faith in 1655 a shortened version of the Huguenot confession of faith. Victor Amadeus II was encouraged to revoke his protection by Louis XIV, partly in order to prevent Waldensians from sheltering Huguenot refugees. In April 1686, a joint Catholic French and Piedmontese army was sent to crush the resistance of Waldensians who would not convert or accept forced exile, leading first to the massacre of more than 1,000 Waldensians, and then to the disease-ridden imprisonment of some 8,500 survivors in makeshift prison camps, followed by exile of survivors to the Swiss cantons and the Netherlands. Perhaps 3,000 of the 14,000 pre-1685 Waldensians ostensibly converted to Catholicism, but most fought and died or were forcibly exiled. Louis XIV's reaction to the diseases which killed many of the prisoners was that they delivered Victor Amadeus from needing to guard them and that he should 'easily console himself for the loss of such subjects'.[1]

---

[1] P. Stephens, *The Waldensian Story* (Lewes 1998), 199ff., esp. 208.

In exile in the Netherlands from 1685 to 1688, Gilbert Burnet published in 1687 in both Amsterdam and London a *History of the Persecution in the Valleys of Piedmont*, which celebrated the Waldensians as 'the most ancient of all, that from the top of the alpes, had illuminated a great part of the universe'. For Burnet, God had preserved them through many persecutions, but the most recent was the most 'cruel and...unjust' and 'should draw tears from eyes of all good Christians'. Burnet declared it 'requisite' in order to know the 'spirit of persecutors' to take a prospect of 'the Outrages and Cruelties they have committed'. He then described 'barbarous enormities' in page after page dripping with blood, describing 'many little children cut in pieces', prisoners skinned alive, the pregnant, blind and old being slaughtered, parents being killed trying to defend their children or witnessing their children being killed, and the killing of women after which the soldiers 'satiated their infamous lusts on the very Bodies of those whom they had deprived of life'.[2] In Burnet's *Some Letters* and its *Supplement*, a 1686 account of his travels which quickly received several editions in England and the Netherlands, Burnet similarly declared 'shameful' the persecution of the Waldensians and compared it to that in France, recording that the persecution in France went beyond even the 'common measures of Barbarity or Cruelty' and sarcastically declaring that he did 'not so much blame the King' since his religion 'doth certainly oblige him to devest himself of Humanity'. 'What I saw and knew there at first hand', he said, 'confirmed eveything learned from books of cruelty of religion'.[3]

Jurieu made the persecution of the Waldensians significant in two of his most famous works, the first of which was the *Accomplishment of the Scripture Prophecies*, published in French in the Netherlands in 1686, and in English in London in 1687. The *Accomplishment* sold 3,000 copies in its first 6 months, and almost 10,000 in French, German, Dutch, and English by late 1687.[4] In the *Accomplishment* Jurieu argued that Revelation forecast a 'last persecution' by the Antichrist before his 'total ruin', and stressed that the French Catholic Church was currently making herself the 'executioner of arrests' in Piedmont 'the most singular example of the spirit of persecution...ever seen' since all other persecutors had stopped at persecuting only

[2] G. Burnet, *History of the Persecution in the Valleys of Piedmont* (Amsterdam and London 1687), 31–45.

[3] Burnet, *Some Letters* (Amsterdam 1686), 58, 254–7; J. Jacob, *Boyle*, 124–6; M. Jacob, *The Newtonians and the English Revolution* (Hassocks 1976), 120–1. Locke thought Burnet's *Some Letters* unusually significant, possessing three separate editions, and later giving one to Anthony Collins.

[4] Howells, *Jurieu*, 50. On the importance of prophecy to Dutch Calvinist thought, see E. van der Wall, '"Antichrist Stormed": The Glorious Revolution and the Dutch Prophetic Tradition' in D. Hoak and M. Feingold (eds.), *The World of William and Mary*, 152–64.

their own subjects. For Jurieu, the biblical prophecy of three and a half years of the death of the witnesses before their rising again in the book of Revelations might 'be reckoned from the destruction of these Waldenses' – a date which led Jurieu to forecast in 1686 their rising again in 1689 as a major stage in the inauguration of the millennium.[5]

Perhaps no one painted the picture of Waldensian persecution in more emotionally provoking detail in the 1680s, however, than the anonymous author of the 1688 *A Short Account of the Persecution of the Waldensians*, which quickly came to be recommended as the source to consult to understand recent events in Piedmont by other authors of works on Piedmont, such as the leading Huguenot exile minister Pierre Allix. The *Short Account* personalised its many stories of violence, telling, for instance, of 'Daniel Moudon, one of the Elders of the Church' who 'having bin the Spectator of the death of John, and James Moudon his two children, (whose heads the Soldiers cut off) after he had seen the body of the wife of John ript up from the Navil, and her daughter's brains beat out, who was not above 6 weeks old, and the two children of James cut in Pieces, (one of which was 4 years old, and the other 14 months) was constrained by these Monsters, to carry cross his shoulders the heads of his two sons, and to march barefoot 2 hours journy, near Lucerna, where he was hang'd in the midst of these two heads, which were fastnd to a Gibbet'.[6]

Such emotive and personalised accounts of violence gave the persecution of the Waldensians signifance beyond their numbers to Protestants across Europe; in describing the Waldensians as anciently 'illuminating' the universe and in attributing to them a central apocalyptic role in the overthrow of the Antichrist, Burnet and Jurieu voiced two further reasons why the fate of the Waldensians held a significance for Protestants in the 1680s that far outweighed their numbers. Accounts of violence against the Waldensians were also enormously significant to English and Dutch Protestants in the 1680s because in the seventeenth century the Waldensians held a central place in Protestant accounts of their ancestry as the sole 'visible' church preserving the apostolic faith against its Roman Catholic 'perversion' in the Middle Ages, being the only 'heresy' of the twelfth century to survive 'in unbroken continuity into the sixteenth century to...link hands with the Protestant Reformation'.[7] The most important seventeenth-century Protestant apologists, from the Anglo-Irish bishop James Ussher to John Milton, responded to the Catholic challenge that Protestantism lacked apostolic succession by focusing on the Waldensians' maintenance of 'apostolic purity'. When Ussher's 1613 *Gravissimae Quaestionis de Christianum*

---

[5] Jurieu, *Accomplishment, passim.*   [6] *Short Account, passim.*
[7] Lambert, *Medieval Heresy* (Cambridge 1992), 147.

Ecclesiarum in Occidentis was reissued in 1687 in the wake of renewed persecution of the Waldensians in 1685–6, attention was drawn to the importance of the Waldensians as securing Protestant continuity by Jean Le Clerc in the *Bibliothèque universelle et historique*.[8] And even before Jurieu accorded the Waldensians millennial significance, seventeenth-century accounts of the fight against the papal Antichrist, including Joseph Mede's influential 1627 *A Key to the Revelation*, had discussed the decline and fall of the Pope as the Antichrist in a millenarian chronology which commenced with the Waldensians' medieval break with Rome. Mede's work was of particular interest to Locke in the 1680s and 1690s when he studied and discussed it with his friend Isaac Newton.[9]

Thus central to Protestant continuity and millenarianism, the 1685–6 persecution of the Waldensians also assumed great importance to Protestants because it was depicted as a reiteration of Catholic violence against Protestants in the burning of Protestants in England by Queen Mary, in the St Bartholomew's Day Massacre of 1572 in France, in the rule of the Duke of Alva in the Netherlands, in the devastations of the Thirty Years War in Germany, in the violence against English Protestant settlers in Ireland in 1641, and in the widely publicised massacre of Waldensians in 1655. And these incidents were understood as reiterations of Catholic violence against medieval 'heretics', including the Waldensians.[10] When Burnet remarked that witnessing recent persecutions had evidenced for him at first hand what he

---

[8] J. Ussher, *Gravissimae Quaestionis de Christianum Ecclesiarum in Occidentis* (1687); Le Clerc, *Bibliothèque universelle et historique* (April 1688), 1–48, at 2, 30, 44. Ussher's thought had long interested Locke, an avid reader of the *Bibliothèque universelle* in these years; Ussher was grandfather of Locke's friend Tyrrell: Marshall, *Locke*, 3–4, 9; Bayle, *Dictionary* (1734), Usher. An emphatic asserter of Protestant continuity through the Waldensians, Ussher was also designer of the Irish articles of the Church of Ireland of 1615 which identified the Pope as the Antichrist. On Ussher, see the chapter in H. Trevor-Roper, *Catholics, Anglicans, and Puritans* (London 1989); A. Ford, 'The Protestant Reformation in Ireland' in C. Brady and R. Gillespie (eds.), *Natives and Newcomers* (Dublin 1986), 65.

[9] J. Milton, *Considerations Touching the Likeliest Means to Remove Hirelings Out of the Church* (London 1659), 64, 80–1, 87; J. Mede, *A Key to the Revelation* (London 1627), *passim*.

[10] Modern historians usually estimate Protestants 'massacred' in Ireland in 1641 at between 2,000 and 12,000; contemporary Protestant estimates often spoke of 150,000 and 300,000: R. Foster, *Modern Ireland* (London 1988), 85; J. Bardon, *A History of Ulster*, 185. In the most careful recent account of N. Canny, there is a sophisticated attempt to isolate the trustworthy evidence, reducing the number 'massacred' very considerably. Canny does indicate that there is some evidence of pronouncements such as 'it was no more pity to kill English than to kill dogs, calling the English heretics and saying they were Gods enemies': N. Canny, 'What Really Happened in 1641' in Ohlmeyer, *Ireland*, 24–42. Cromwell declared that his much larger massacre of Catholic men, women and children in Drogheda was 'a righteous judgment of God upon these barbarous wretches who have imbrued their hands in so much innocent blood': R. Kee, *Ireland* (London 1995), 46. Mr John Ball of Johns Hopkins is currently completing a PhD thesis on the violence in Ireland in 1641.

already knew from books of cruelty in religion, he was indicating the importance of preceding images of Catholic violence in shaping his own perception of contemporary events in the 1680s. Burnet had been concerned with violence against the Waldensians long before their 1685 persecution. His 1673 *Mystery of Iniquity* gave as its first 'proof' that the Catholic Church was anti-Christian the 'enraged cruelty [which] appeared against the poor Waldenses, for the separating from their Corruption; how many of all Sexes and ages were cruelly butchered'.[11] And Burnet had often trained his eye on centuries of Catholic violence against the Albigensians and Waldensians in combination with that against the Huguenots. Burnet's 1678 account of the St Bartholomew's Day Massacre, *A Relation of the Barbarous and Bloody Massacre of About an Hundred Thousand Protestants*, which dwelt on allegations such as the opening of 'the bellies of the fattest, to sell their greese to apothecaries', had declared that the 'likest things in History to it for Barbarity' were during 'the precedent which the Church of Rome had formerly given in the Massacre of the Albigenses'. For Burnet, the argument that 'faith was not to be kept with heretics' was the central justification of Catholic atrocities throughout the centuries, and the nature of Catholicism was unchangingly barbaric: such massacres were not merely allowed, but required, by Catholicism. For Burnet, the Pope's celebration of the massacre was a sign of the character of the Antichrist, being – as Burnet followed Revelation in putting it – 'drunk with the blood of the saints'.[12]

The 1655 massacre of the Waldensians had caused a national campaign in England and Ireland for their relief, with churches painted red to symbolise the bloodshed, newsletters such as the *Weekly Post* reporting on the massacre committed by those 'drunk with the blood of saints', and many texts rehearsing a repertoire of Catholic violence later reiterated in descriptions of the persecutions of the 1680s. Thus Stouppe's *A Collection of the Several Papers Sent to his Highness the Lord Protector* etched a gruesome picture of Waldensians burned alive, tossed from the edge of precipices, torn in pieces, slashed with salt and pepper put in their wounds, nailed to the ground by stakes through the belly, or, in the case of many men, castrated then executed, and of many women, raped then executed. The cutting off of the heads of 150 women and children was described 'whereof they did boyl many, and eat their brains out, but left off, saying, they were too unsavoury'.[13] The

[11] G. Burnet, *Mystery of Iniquity* (London 1673); H. Foxcroft, *Life of Burnet* (Cambridge 1907), 153ff.
[12] G. Burnet, *A Relation of the Barbarous and Bloody Massacre of About an Hundred Thousand Protestants* (London 1678), 27, 34.
[13] J. Stouppe, *A Collection of the Several Papers Sent to his Highness the Lord Protector* (London 1655), *passim*; Stephens, *Waldensian*; R. Vigne, 'Avenge O Lord Thy Slaughtered Saints: Cromwell's intervention on behalf of the Vaudois', *Proceedings of the Huguenot Society* (1983), 10–25.

English Ambassador to Piedmont, Samuel Morland, issued a 1658 *The History of the Evangelical Churches of the Valleys of Piedmont* complete with twenty-five pages of images of atrocities, commencing with the image of a severed head being placed into a boiling pot to cook it before consumption. Morland's text dwelled on the slaughter of babies 'torn in pieces limb-meal' or with their brains 'dashed out against the Rocks', and on the 'ravishing' and executing of women, and stressed that Catholic attempts to 'convert' Protestants were made by tearing out people's nails with 'red hot pincers'.[14]

This denunciation of Catholic violence against the Waldensians, uttered without any questioning of its complete veracity and unaccompanied by any condemnation of English Protestant violence against Catholics in Ireland, had served instead as a further justification of Protestant violence against Catholics in Ireland, as it was combined with reference to the massacre of Protestants in Ireland in 1641, whose scale was itself inflated in accounts such as Sir John Temple's 1646 *The Irish Rebellion*, which depicted Irish Catholics disembowelling, boiling, hanging, and drowning English Protestants in Ireland, cutting children 'into quarters and gobbets', hanging infants on 'tenterhooks', and making 'candles' from the 'grease' of some victims.[15] Further tying events in Piedmont and Ireland together, Stouppe's *Collection* identified the Catholic troops who had attacked Protestants in Piedmont as including 'severall Irish regiments'. Transplantation of Catholic Irish landed families to the wastes of Connaught was ordered when reports from Piedmont were received. Charles Fleetwood, Cromwell's son-in-law, urged against 'an unsafe pity of those whose principles in all ages carry them forth to such brutish and inhuman practices' and declared 'Let such be not untransplanted here whose continuance amongst us do palpably hazard the very being of the Protestant interest in these nations'.[16] Cromwell planned to send a force to relieve the Waldensians, used that threat to gain restoration of their toleration, and was described as saying that their fate lay 'nearer his heart than if it had concerned his nearest and dearest Relations'. Indeed, Cromwell's dying words were about the need to protect the Waldensians.[17]

It would, then, be difficult to overstate the importance of the Waldensians in mid-century English and Irish Protestant religious thought, dominated by

---

[14] S. Morland, *The History of the Evangelical Churches of the Valleys of Piedmont* (London 1658), *passim*, esp. 336–61.

[15] On the untrustworthiness of Temple and his influence, see T. Bartlett, *The Fall and Rise of the Irish Nation: The Catholic Question 1690–1830* (Savage, Md. 1992), ch. 1; Sir John Temple, *The Irish Rebellion* (London 1646), 9–10, 123 in Tumbleson, *Catholicism*, 88.

[16] Stouppe, *Collection*, title-page; Vigne, 'Avenge', 14–15; Stephens, *Waldensian*.

[17] Vigne, 'Avenge'; A. Sell, 'Through Suffering to Liberty: 1689 in the English and Vaudois Experience', in *idem, Commemorations* (Cardiff 1993), v. 119–46; I owe the final point to John Morrill.

the perceived threats of 'Popery' and 'Catholicism' and by alleged Catholic atrocities. The Waldensians then continued to occupy a central place in sermons on 'popery' in the Restoration as evidence of what should be expected in England if Catholic kings came to rule there.[18] Milton had penned one of his most famous sonnets on the 1655 massacre, and it received Restoration circulation in the 1673 edition of his poems:

Avenge O Lord thy slaughter'd Saints, whose bones/Lie scatter'd on the Alpine mountains cold/Ev'n them who kept thy truth so pure of old/When all our Fathers worship't Stocks and Stones/Forget not: in thy book record their groanes/Who were thy Sheep and in their antient Fold/Slayn by the bloody Piemontese that roll'd/ Mother with Infant down the Rocks. Their moans/The vales redoubl'd to the Hills, and they/To Heav'n. Their martyr'd blood and ashes sow/O're all th'Italian fields where still doth sway/The triple Tyrant: that from these may grow/A hundred-fold, who having learnt thy way/Early may fly the Babylonian wo.[19]

In the 1677 republication of Samuel Clarke's *General Martyrology*, which surveyed all persecutions since the Creation, the medieval Waldensians and Albigensians received eighty-five pages in an account which emphasised their persecutors' alleged sexual transgressions, torture, and murders. The recent massacres in Piedmont in 1655 received thirty-seven pages, which followed immediately after twelve pages on the alleged 'Popish' massacres in Ireland in 1641, while the St Bartholomew's Day Massacre of Huguenots in 1572 also featured prominently in Clarke's text.[20] In his 1679 *Word in Season*, the Whig polemicist Henry Care similarly paralleled the 'barbarous and cruel murders and massacres' of Protestants in the Netherlands, France, Ireland, Piedmont, and the Albigenses – thus including 1572 in France, 1641 in Ireland, and 1655 in Piedmont, together with medieval actions against the Albigensians as parallel examples of Catholic violence. And Care ran the example of Piedmont directly into the example of England, and the Fire of London into the alleged assassination of Sir Edmund Berry Godfrey during the 'Popish Plot': 'So in Piedmont how many quiet peaceable souls were murdered there? Shall I not bring in their Design of firing London Sept 2 1666 as a witness in this matter? Let me not forget Sir Edmund Berry Godfrey'.[21]

---

[18] T. Harris, 'The Parties and the People', 125–151, at 129–30.

[19] J. Milton, 'On the Late Massacre in Piedmont' in *Poems* (London 1673).

[20] S. Clarke, *A General Martyrology* (London 1677), 76–125, 269–81, 282–5, 290–325. For Clarke, Waldensians and Albigensians differed only in name 'from habitation': 105. On Clarke's importance, see Miller, *Popery*, 75.

[21] H. Care, *A Word in Season* (London 1679), preface, 36; Haley, *Shaftesbury*, 552–5.

REPRESENTATIONS OF THE PERSECUTION OF WALDENSIANS AND
HUGUENOTS IN THE NETHERLANDS AND THEIR SIGNIFICANCE IN
GENERATING SUPPORT FOR WILLIAM'S INVASION OF ENGLAND

For many reasons, Protestants in the Netherlands were nearly as steeped in
the history of Catholic atrocity and attention to the fate of Waldensians and
Huguenots as were Protestants in England. While the Netherlands experienced no 'Popish Plot' and 'Exclusion Crisis' in the 1670s and 1680s, the
identity of the Netherlands was defined in significant part by its sixteenth-
century expulsion of the Inquisition, and images of Catholic persecution of
Protestants remained central in the Netherlands in the seventeenth century,
preparing the ground for reception of reports of Catholic persecution in
France and Piedmont in the 1680s in much the same way that reading
books of 'cruelty in religion' had prepared Burnet to 'witness' the persecutions of the 1680s. The particularly close associations of the Dutch and
French Reformed Churches fostered considerable Dutch attention to
the fate of the Huguenots even before the 1685 Revocation. In 1682,
French forces occupied the Principality of Orange and commenced forced
conversion of Protestants there. By then, significant Huguenot immigration
to the Netherlands had already begun. Dutch attention to the fate of the
Waldensians in 1655 had been considerable, and to many in the Netherlands
the actions of Victor Amadeus at Louis' instigation in 1685–6 were a repeat
of Charles Emmanuel's actions in 1655 at Mazarin's behest.

Under Spanish rule, the Netherlands had seen more Protestants burned as
heretics than in any other country in Europe, causing deep hostility to the
severe repression of the reign of Charles V, symbolised by his 'blood placard'
of 1550, and to the executions of over 1,000 Protestants under the Duke of
Alva.[22] In the 1560s 'the Inquisition' was attacked as creating 'perpetual
slaves of the Inquisitors' and as 'against all human and divine laws, surpass-
ing the worst barbarism ever practised by tyrants'. These sentiments were
then further reinforced by Alva's brutal rule. The resistance of the
Netherlands was repeatedly justified as self-defence against the power of
a foreign Inquisition.[23] Much Dutch propaganda of the late sixteenth and
early seventeenth century focused on the brutality of the Spanish Inquisition

---

[22] A. Pettegree, *Emden and the Dutch Revolt* (Oxford 1992); A. Duke, *Reformation and Revolt
in the Low Countries* (London 1990); M. van Gelderen, *The Political Thought of the Dutch
Revolt*, (Cambridge 1992), 36, 40; A. Duke, 'Salvation by Coercion: The Controversy
Surrounding the "Inquisition" in the Low Countries on the Eve of the Revolt' in
P. N. Brooks (ed.), *Reformation Principle and Practice: Essays in Honour of A. G. Dickens*
(London 1986); reprinted in *idem, Reformation*, 152–74, esp. 173–4; Israel, *Dutch Republic*.
[23] Israel, *Dutch Republic*, 146; Peters, *The Inquisition*, 150–2; van Gelderen, *Political Thought*,
151–3; *Apologie*, ed. Lacroix, 106–7 in Le Cler, *Toleration*, II, 248.

together with the St Bartholomew's Day Massacre in France. Jan Evertszoon's 1620 account of the war in the Netherlands, 'Le Miroire de la Tyrannie Espagnole', was published with an account of St Bartholomew's Day. Many works provided gruesome depictions of violence enacted against Protestants, often focusing on particular individuals or families being butchered and raped, murders of the aged and bedridden, mutilation of babies, throwing of pregnant or nursing mothers into icy rivers, and slaughters at weddings, and came complete with graphic illustrations of the methods used by Catholics against 'heretics', such as the 1621 image of the 'Council of Blood' in *Warachtige Beschrijvinghe. . .vande meer dan onmenschelijke ende Barbarische Tyrannije*, which depicted the gallows, burning at the stake, breaking on the wheel, stretching on the rack, and water torture being used against Protestants.[24]

Images of sixteenth-century Catholic violence against Dutch Protestants continued to be reprinted in the late 1680s, including in the 1687 'latest edition' of the *Spiegel der Jeught Oft Spaense Tyrannye* (*The Mirror of Youth, or Spanish Tyranny*), a pamphlet which showed both churches and Protestants burning, Protestants being hung and dragged behind horses, and Protestant babies being skewered by soldiers. The 1685 reprint of the martyrology of Anabaptist victims of sixteenth-century Catholic persecution, Thieleman Janz van Braght's *Martyr's Mirror*, was full of etchings of burnings and torture.[25] The ground was thereby prepared in the Netherlands for works documenting the violence against Waldensians and Huguenots, many of which – such as the works of Burnet and Jurieu – we have already discussed as a result of their circulation in England as well as the Netherlands. Burnet and Jurieu's depictions were paralleled in dozens of works issued by the Huguenot community in the Netherlands and having received quick translation into English, including the leading Huguenot controversialist Jean Claude's *Les plaintes des protestans cruellement opprimez du royaume de France* (Cologne 1686), published in an abridged version as *An Account of the Persecutions and Oppressions of the Protestants in France* (1686). Claude described the force used against the Huguenots as extremely violent in a series of images which were seared into Protestant imaginations across north-western Europe:

They strung up their victims, men or women, by their hair or by their feet, to the rafters in the roof, or the hooks in the chimney, and then set fire to bundles of mouldy hay heaped up beneath them. They plucked out their beards, and tore at their heads till not a hair was left. They flung them into huge fires which they lit for the purpose,

---

[24] Several such images are reproduced in S. Schama, *The Embarrassment of Riches* (New York 1987), 83–93.
[25] J. Horsch, *Mennonites in Europe* (Scottsdale, Penn. 1950), 312–13.

and left them there till they were half-roasted. They fastened ropes underneath their arms, and lowered them into wells, pulling them up and down till they promised to change their religion.

Claude indicated that they had also been cut with knives, tortured with red-hot pincers, beaten, had fingernails ripped out, and were blown up by bellows until they were about to burst.[26]

Many Dutch works and images of the 1680s and 1690s similarly recorded Catholic violence. Numerological and typological interpretations of the Bible carried weight in this period, in which many clerics remained committed to prophetic understandings of the Bible; *Aanmerkingh, Op dese onderstaande Syffer Letteren* (1687) was one offering such an account in giving 'Proof that Louis XIV is the Beast of the Apocalypse' and identifying Louis XIV as the Antichrist by itemising the letters in LUDOVICUS as summing to 666, and those in Ludovicus Magnus XIV to 1019, which, when added to 666, made 1685.[27] Publicity was given in this most mercantile of nations to the French preventing Dutch merchants who had become naturalised French citizens from leaving France, and to the torture of the Dutch consul at Nantes to force his conversion. And the fumigation of ships leaving Bordeaux which were feared to be carrying Huguenots hit home very hard indeed in the Netherlands: the results included a poisoned cargo of prunes, whose consumption in the Netherlands led to several deaths.[28]

The 1685 dragonnades in Orange, until very recently Dutch territory, were widely reported and depicted in engravings, such as those by the Mennonite Jan Luyken, whose prints were used to illustrate the refugee minister Elie Benoist's *Historie der Gereformeerde Kerken van Vankryk* (see Figure 2.1). The image showed soldiers killing people, preparation for whipping of Protestants, and soldiers drumming in order to keep someone permanently awake – a very common form of pressure to convert in Orange as it was in France in 1685.[29]

---

[26] [J. Claude], *An Account of the Persecutions and Oppressions of the Protestants in France* (London 1686), 19–21; also in Hazard, *The European Mind*, 84; C. R. Gillett, *Burned Books* (New York 1932), II, 525ff.

[27] P. Rietbergen, 'William III of Orange (1650–1702) Between European Politics and European Protestantism: The Case of the Huguenots' in *La Révocation de L'Édit de Nantes et les Provinces-Unies 1685* (Amsterdam 1986), 35–50; C. Johnston, 'Elie Benoist', 468–88, at 475; *Aanmerkingh* in H. Bots et al. (eds.), *Vlucht naar de Vrijheid de Huguenoten in Nederland* (Amsterdam 1985), 71; H. Bots, 'L'Écho de la Révocation dans les Provinces-Unies' in R. Zuber and L. Theiss (eds.), *La Révocation de L'Édit de Nantes et le protestantisme français en 1685* (Paris 1986), 281–98.

[28] S. Baxter, *William III and the Defense of European Liberty* (Connecticut 1976, reprint of 1966), 210–11.

[29] Image from Benoist, *Historie der Gereformeerde kerken van Vankryk* (Amsterdam 1696); cf. H. Bots et al. (eds.), *Vlucht*, 25.

Figure 2.1 *The Dragonnades in Orange 1685*, by Jan Luyken. From E. Benoist, *Historie der Gereformeerde Kerken van Vankryk* (Amsterdam 1696). By permission of Duke University Library Special Collections.

Romeyn de Hooghe's 1685 bilingual French and Dutch *Tableau of the Persecution of the Protestants in France (Tafereel dervolginge tegen de Gereformeerde in Vrankrück)* contained twelve small images surrounding one large image in the centre (see Figure 2.2). The twelve small images commenced in the upper left corner with an image of the St Bartholomew's Day Massacre, and included a depiction of the executions in Vivarais in 1683–4, which it declared based on 'false reports of sedition'. The majority of the small images, however, were of Intendants ordering people to surrender their goods or their religion, dragoons committing theft, the sale of goods to Jesuits and other Catholics, the forced exile of pastors and their families and destruction of temples, the incarceration in nunneries of Protestant women, the means used to force Protestants to mass, and several images of torture by fire, pincers, and sexual abuse in order to 'persuade' people to 'convert'. Its central image showed Protestant executions, the destruction of Protestant temples, and the gathering of money and goods by monks. Its text recorded that Jesuit counsels and 'damnable doctrine' had created this

Figure 2.2 *Tableau of the Persecution of the Protestants in France*, by Romeyn de Hooghe. By permission of the Albertina Museum, Vienna.

N DE GEREFORMEERDE IN VRANKRIICK.

TION CONTRE
ES ENFRANCE

persecution. At its centre was an image of France trampling on the Edict of Nantes, persuaded to this act both by a bishop and by a Jesuit with a demon perched on his shoulder breathing into his ear. At the feet of the Jesuit was placed the declaration that 'faith does not need to be kept with heretics'.

After 1685, as Jonathan Israel has written, 'The resurgence of anti-Catholic sentiment, in reaction to persecution of the Huguenots in France, pervaded the entire religious and political climate of the Republic'.[30] Fear of the encircling menace of Catholic force and of the inability of the Netherlands to withstand this alone grew as 1685 brought both a new Catholic ruler to England and a new Catholic Elector Palatine who was described by Gilbert Burnet as the member of 'a most bigotted Popish family'. Due to the simultaneity of these events, Burnet called this year that of the 'fifth great crisis of the Protestant religion' and the year 'the most fatal to the Protestant religion'.[31] The Protestant stadtholder of the Netherlands, William of Orange, devoted considerable effort to building support for opposition to Catholic France by supporting propaganda about the violence of Catholic armies enforcing the faith on their own and other populations, including the persecution of Protestants in his own principality of Orange which had been occupied by French troops in 1682, of the Huguenots in France in 1685, and of the Waldensians in Piedmont in 1686, even as he pursued an alliance with the rulers of Catholic countries by emphasising the need to combat French aggression rather than Catholicism. William subsidised Claude, author of the *Account of the Cruel Oppressions*. Elie Benoist's multi-volume *History of the Edict of Nantes* was begun as 'an extension' of Claude's work in 1687 when the States of Holland and West Friesland voted Benoist a pension of 315 guilders 'to write a history of the religious persecution in France'. Louis XIV himself recognised that reports of the campaign against the Huguenots in France were having a major impact on Protestant opinion in the Netherlands, as William made 'use of the good success that God is giving to my efforts to convert my subjects to turn the States General against my interests'.[32]

By 1687–8, the combination of French commercial and military aggression with reports of the increased persecution of Huguenots and Waldensians and fear of Catholicisation and absolutism in England under James II convinced even those in the States-General who had long maintained relations with the French court that the Dutch would now have to

---

[30] Israel, *The Dutch Republic*, 646; Barnouw, *Philippus van Limborch* (The Hague 1963), 42–3.

[31] G. Burnet, *History of His Own Time* (London 1724–30), II, 344–5 in D. Katz, 'The Jews of England and 1688' in O. Grell et al. (eds.), *From Persecution to Toleration* (Oxford 1991), 217–49, at 224; Dunlop, *Louis XIV*, 283.

[32] Louis XIV to D'Avaux, in Miller, *James II*, 143.

fight against France in order to maintain their own independence, and that they should support William's invasion of England.[33] In October 1688 the Dutch States-General expressed their increased fear of absolutism and Catholicism in France and England in declaring their support for William's forces because:

> The French king having often, yea upon all occasions, showed the ill-will he bore to this Republick, it is to be feared that if the King of Great Britain reach his mark, to wit, an absolute power over his people, then will both these kings, partly out of maxime of state, and partly out of hatred and zeale against the Protestant religion, endevour to ruine, and if possible extirpate this Republick.[34]

THE SIGNIFICANCE OF REPRESENTATIONS OF CATHOLIC INTOLERANCE AGAINST HUGUENOTS AND WALDENSIANS IN UNDERMINING THE TOLERATIONIST REGIME OF JAMES II AND THE EFFORTS OF HIS SUPPORTERS TO DEFEND TOLERATION

The huge outpouring of Protestant propaganda about the violence used against Huguenots and Waldensians was thus important in the Netherlands in the late 1680s in generating increased fear of France and mobilising Dutch support for the 1688 invasion of England. And such propaganda was as important in helping this invasion to succeed by undermining support in England, and among Protestants in Ireland, for the reign of James II (1685–8), a Catholic ruler who attempted to provide toleration for Protestant dissenters and Catholics in the final two years of his four-year reign. The example of the actions taken by Louis and Victor Amadeus against Huguenots and Waldensians was proof for many English Protestants of the untrustworthiness of all Catholic rulers with Protestant subjects. Those who sought to defend James' toleration in 1687–8 were therefore battling wind and wave. And many Huguenots and other Protestants from across Europe fought for William in Ireland against James' largely Irish and French Catholic army in part as a result of personal experience of, or reading the propaganda about, the actions of Louis XIV and Victor Amadeus against their Protestant populations.

[33] J. Israel, 'The Dutch Contribution to the Glorious Revolution' in *idem, The Anglo-Dutch Moment; idem, The Dutch Republic*, 841–53; *idem, Dutch Primacy in World Trade* (Oxford 1989), 341–2; Gibbs, 'European Origins'.

[34] Gibbs, 'European Origins', 17; Bardon, *History of Ulster*, 151; Rietbergen, 'William III of Orange', 35–50; H. Bots and R. Bastiaanse, 'Le Refuge huguenot et les Provinces-Unies, une esquisse sommaire' in *Le Refuge huguenot* (ed.) M. Magdelaine and R. von Thadden (Paris 1985), 63–82, at 77; B. Cottret, 'Glorieuse révolution, révocation honteuse? Protestants Français et Protestants d'Angleterre' in *ibid.*, 83–96, at 89.

It remains the subject of dispute among historians, as it was the subject of dispute among his contemporaries, why James II wished to provide religious toleration in the final two years of his reign in 1687–8. To some, James personally was genuinely and permanently tolerationist, committed to every individual having 'liberty of conscience'. To others, James believed that provision of such liberty would secure the rapid conversion of the English population to Catholicism by persuasion, as he had been persuaded to convert to Catholicism. But many were convinced that toleration was in his eyes only a temporary expedient to allow Catholics to gain power in the army, offices of state, and universities, franchise, and justiceships, prior to imposition of Catholicism by force. There is some evidence that James had long been committed to a genuine liberty of conscience, but was worried about how it was compatible with security given the association of Protestant dissent with resistance, and there is evidence that once James came to understand the levels of force used by Louis' soldiers he disapproved of the persecution of the Huguenots as both impolitic and unchristian, even as he was reluctant to express public criticism of his fellow Catholic ruler. Certainly, James' April 1687 Declaration of Indulgence, providing toleration by suspending the penal statutes for all who did not attend worship in the Church of England, recorded that its monarch was a supporter of 'an intire liberty of conscience, it having always been his Majesty's opinion, as most suitable to the principles of Christianity, that no man should be persecuted for conscience's sake, which his Majesty thinks is not to be forced'.[35]

Yet James was probably also convinced to become a Catholic in part because of the strength of his opposition to sectarianism: he allegedly told Burnet that part of his reason for conversion to Catholicism was the 'necessity of having but one church, otherwise he saw what swarms of sects did rise up on our revolt from Rome'. James grew up in the Catholic French Court, his father having been executed by the predecessors of those Protestant sects. The French ambassador Barrillon claimed that James believed that 'the Anglican church is so little removed from the Catholic that it should not be difficult to bring the majority of them to declare themselves openly…they are Roman Catholics without knowing it'. While James was at the least to become more reticent as it became clearer to him how much force had been used against Protestants to gain their conversion, during the initial period when Catholic works were depicting such violence as insignificant Barillon also reported to Louis XIV that when shown the decree revoking the Edict of Nantes, James had shown such 'delight' at the measure to 'complete the extirpation of heresy from your kingdom' that it would have been 'impossible to be more delighted'.[36] In the

---

[35] On the dispensing power and suspending power, see Miller, *James II*, 165.
[36] M. Ashley, *James II* (Minneapolis 1977), 186.

first years of his reign, as we will see in the next chapter, James maintained a great deal of the persecution of most Protestant dissenters instituted by his brother.[37]

Believing James' support for toleration genuine, and desirous of an end to their fierce persecution in the Restoration, James was supported strongly in works written to defend his provision of toleration by the leading Quaker William Penn, and by some other Quaker apologists; he was also supported by some Baptists, and by a few other Protestant dissenters, such as the tolerationist Presbyterian Vincent Alsop and the Whig polemicist Henry Care. He was defended by William Popple, author of *A Letter to Mr Penn* (1688) and in this period close to Penn.[38] He unsurprisingly gained the support of many Catholics, and of some Anglicans, including some long-standing supporters of toleration, such as the Dorset rector Samuel Bold. The most significant of these propagandists for toleration was the leading Quaker William Penn, and his central arguments were also those rehearsed by most defenders of James' toleration. Penn repeated the same basic case for toleration in many works, sometimes explicitly as a list of 'reasons' or 'considerations'. Penn's 1685 *Considerations Moving to a Toleration and Liberty of Conscience*, for instance, gave ten clearly demarcated reasons for toleration, many of which were repeated in his other works of 1685–6 before James' Declarations of Indulgence and then in 1687–8 in his defences of James' toleration. This work may therefore stand as a summary of the central arguments for toleration issued in England in these years; it was very similar to many of the central arguments for toleration that were issued in the 1680s in the Netherlands which we will discuss in Part 3 of this book. According to Penn's *Considerations*, God had not appointed 'forcible ways', and Christ's successors were to imitate his preaching by attempting to 'inform the judgment, convince the conscience, and so to perswade'. In the first centuries, Christians had not merely not practised intolerance but had argued against it.

---

[37] The many complex and conflicting motivations of and forces operating on James II are summarised excellently in Miller, 'The Immediate Impact of the Revocation'; *idem, James II*, 125ff., esp. 144, on the disapproval of Louis' actions as impolitic and unchristian; *idem*, 'James II and Toleration' in E. Cruickshanks (ed.), *By Force or Default?* (Edinburgh 1989), 13–14, on the need for one Catholic authority against the swarms of sects and on the closeness of Anglicanism to Roman Catholicism. For a work stressing James' intolerance more strongly, see Gwynn, *Huguenot Heritage*; for works stressing James' tolerationism more strongly, see M. Goldie, 'James II and the Whig Collaborators', *Historical Journal* (1992), and J. Champion, 'Willing to Suffer' in McLaren and H. Coward (eds.), *Religious Conscience, State and Law* (Albany 1999), 13–28.

[38] Lawton's memoir of William Penn, in *Memoirs of the Historical Society of Pennsylvania* (Philadelphia 1836), III, pt 2, 215–31, at 218, records dining in 1687 near Windsor with Penn and Popple, 'who Mr Penn was then bringing out of trouble', and states that Penn was 'going to the French Embassadours to solicit Mr Popple's business'; C. Robbins, *Absolute Liberty* (Hamden, Connecticut 1982), 12–13.

Force created only 'hypocrisy' and so was actively harmful. Penn argued that 'All sorts of persons' were 'for Liberty of conscience for themselves' but many for 'Imposing on others', and that this clearly violated the precept that 'whatsoever things ye would that Men should do unto you, do ye so unto them'. Intolerance was said to violate moreover the duties of 'humanity' and of 'civility'. Those who urged punishment now were urged to reflect on Queen Mary's time and their punishment by others on the same grounds they now advanced. This provided the platform for Penn to discuss France not in order to argue that this showed the danger of tolerating Catholics but rather to show that those who were condemning 'the French King' for persecuting his 'peaceable subjects' were to be attacked for doing 'the same things in our Kingdome which we condemn in another'. Union in affection was held possible with 'disagreement of Opinion'. Liberty of conscience was declared good for trade and for population growth, and thus central to the economy.[39] In various works, Penn urged specifically that toleration should be extended to Catholics as well as dissenters, and in his 1687 *Great and Popular Objection* he supported the abolition of restrictions on Catholic officeholding as well as worship, as Catholics were peaceable subjects.[40] Penn trumpeted his support for James' measure as support for an irrevocable order for toleration, as a 'perpetual edict' or great 'charter', and encouraged its statutory adoption by Parliament.[41]

Recognising that in the wake of the widely publicised Revocation of the allegedly irrevocable Edict of Nantes he was in difficult waters, Henry Care argued explicitly in the *Answer to the Letter to a Dissenter* (1687) that James would never imitate the violence, suffering, and economic dislocation involved in the Revocation of the Edict of Nantes, because he understood that the costs to his own nation would be too great. He supported opening office to Catholics and providing toleration for Catholics[42] William Popple was in these years close to Penn and a supporter of the toleration of Catholic worship and of the opening of office to Catholics. Popple's *Three Letters* argued that 'No man ought to be Persecuted for Matters of Meer Religion...there is nothing requisite but Honesty and Sense...the Interest

---

[39] W. Penn, *Considerations Moving to a Toleration* (London 1685), *passim.*

[40] W. Penn, *The Great and Popular Objection Against the Repeal of the Penal Laws and Tests Briefly Stated and Considered* (1687, 1688), *passim.*

[41] W. Penn, *Good Advice to the Church of England, Roman Catholick, and Protestant Dissenter* (London 1687), 45; *Great and Popular Objection*, 6, 22; James Stewart, *James Stewart's Answer*, 4; H. Care, *The Legality of the Court* (London 1688), 38; *idem*, *A Discourse for Taking off the Tests and Penal Laws* (London 1687), sig. A3r, 98, all in Goldie, 'Huguenot Experience', 177.

[42] H. Care, *Answer*, 9–10 discussed in J. R. Jones, *The Revolutions of 1688 in England* (New York 1978), 112.

of this Nation, as wel as the Laws of Christianity, requires an Absolute, Universal, Equal, and Inviolable Liberty of Conscience'.[43]

To these Protestant dissenting voices raised in defence of James' toleration were added those of a tiny number of Anglican clerics, including the former staunch opponent of dissent, now Bishop of Oxford, Samuel Parker, whose motives surely involved more of ambition than of allegiance to toleration. A few other Anglicans were attracted by James' tolerance and advocated support for his provision of toleration. Samuel Bold, later to be a friend of Locke, who had in 1682 been prosecuted by his fellow Anglicans for his tolerance towards dissenters, was willing to have toleration extended to Catholics as well as Protestant dissenters. And James gained the support of some Whiggish gentlemen who had wished to see him excluded, but who had defended toleration in 1678–83 and saw an end to the proscription of Whigs as James reversed course. But James' support from Anglicans paled in comparison to the numbers of Anglican gentry and clergy alienated by James' actions. Few Anglican clerics and polemicists advocated James' provision both of liberty of worship and opening of office to dissenters and Catholics. As Gordon Schochet has emphasised, Parker's reversal from attacking the dissenters as 'unreasoning beasts' needing to be 'scourged' into better manners in his 1670 *Discourse of Ecclesiastical Polity* to support of James' toleration probably fostered Anglican and dissenting scepticism more than it helped James' cause.[44] And as Mark Goldie has emphasised, Bold's 1688 *A Brief Account of the First Rise of the Name Protestant*, defending a general toleration for Catholics as well as Protestants, gained him no more Anglican friends in the late 1680s than he had had in the early 1680s, when his support for toleration had led to prosecution by his Anglican superiors.[45]

There was thus a small number of strong advocates of James' toleration for and opening of office to Catholics, and they included many viewed as problematic by many Anglicans. In England, Catholics probably numbered only about 60,000, or just over 1 per cent of an English population of more than 5 million.[46] Quakers and Baptists were far smaller denominations than

---

[43] [W. Popple], *Three Letters Tending to Demonstrate How the Security of This Nation Against All Future Persecution for Religion Lys in the Abolishment of the Present Penal Laws...and the Establishment of a New Law for Universal Liberty of Conscience* (London 1688), 4–5; cf. C. Robbins on attribution of this work to Popple.

[44] G. Schochet, 'Between Lambeth and Leviathan' in Philippson (ed.), *Political Discourse in Early Modern Britain* (Cambridge 1993); M. A. Goldie, 'Sir Peter Pett, Sceptical Toryism and the Science of Toleration in the 1680s' in W. Sheils (ed.), *Persecution and Toleration* (Oxford 1984), 247–74; Speck, *Reluctant*, 65–6.

[45] M. A. Goldie, 'John Locke's Circle and James II', *Historical Journal* (1992), 557–86, discusses the support of Locke's English friends for James' tolerationism in 1687–8.

[46] J. Bossy, *The English Catholic Community 1570–1850* (Oxford 1976), 189; J. Miller, *Popery*, 11.

were Presbyterians and Independents, numbering together less than 100,000. Quakers and Baptists had suffered more than other denominations in previous years, giving them greater incentive to support James II, and had always been more tolerationist than these other groups, giving them greater principled reasons for support of toleration, but both were deeply unpopular among their fellow Protestant dissenters. To many Protestants, Baptists were direct descendants of the vilified Dutch Anabaptists. Quakers were, if anything, even worse; many of their fellow dissenters did not view them as Protestant at all. There was, moreover, a huge literature holding Quakers and Baptists to be Catholics in disguise.[47] Their tolerationism was said to be intended to break apart Protestants and thereby to provide the ground for a return of England to Rome. Given that this was a long-standing accusation by the late 1680s, Quaker support for James' tolerationism served to reinforce rather than dispel suspicion about James' intentions. This was itself recognised in William Popple's *Letter to Mr Penn*, a work which went through three editions in 1688.[48] Popple pleaded in this work for Penn to respond to the charges that he was a 'Jesuit in disguise' both in order to defend his reputation, and because for Popple the accusation fostered people's 'jealousy' that James intended 'to settle Popery in this Nation, not only in a fair and secure liberty, but even in a predominating Superiority over all other Professions' because 'the Aspersion of Popery and Jesuitism, that has been cast upon you, has reflected upon His Majesty; for having made use, in that Affair, of so disguised a personage as you are supposed to have been'.[49]

A general atmosphere of deep suspicion thus marked many of the tolerationist arguments connected with James II. When he did advance the toleration of Protestant dissenters and Catholics in 1687–8, James' attempts to establish toleration for such generally unpopular groups required him to use the powers of the monarchy in their most expansive definition, wielding the dispensing power to add legal stays to prosecutions of Quakers and Baptists in late 1686 and thwarting the penal statutes of Parliament.[50] He used monarchical power to suspend the operation of Parliamentary statutes against nonconformity and Catholic recusancy, suspending the Test Acts

---

[47] For this charge against Baptists, see L. McBeth, *English Baptist Literature on Religious Liberty to 1689* (New York 1980), 243; on Quakers, see 463–4 below.

[48] Robbins, *Absolute*, 13. The Duke of Buckingham was also a defender of toleration, including under James II, for which he was defended by Penn in *A Defence of the Duke of Buckingham's Book of Religion* (London 1685). Cf. N.H. Keeble, 'Why transpose the Rehearsal?' in W. Chernaik and M. Dzelzanis (eds.), *Marvell and Liberty* (Basingstoke 1999), 249–68, at 253–4.

[49] [Popple], *Letter to Mr Penn*, 5–7; Penn appended an *Answer* to Popple's *Letter*, in which he denied that he was a Catholic, supported an entire liberty of conscience, and declared this 'the natural right of all men': 14–16.

[50] D. Lacey, *Dissent and Parliamentary Politics* (New Brunswick 1969), 178.

barring Catholics (and dissenters) from office, and then appointing many Catholics to positions in the armed forces, colleges of Oxford and Cambridge, and justiceships of the peace, often against fierce opposition. The Parliament elected in 1685 under a franchise remodelled by Charles II in order to provide a Tory-high Anglican majority supportive of monarchy was unwilling to support measures to tolerate Catholics or to admit them to office. In order to secure support in Parliament for a more permanent enactment of toleration, James then undertook an even more extensive campaign of remodelling the electorate into a dissenting 'Whig Anglican tolerationist' Catholic alliance, like Charles changing corporation charters, but this time doing so in order to create a Parliament willing to enact toleration, and thus undertaking the removal of staunch high church Anglicans from the electorate and from office. And James pressured judges into finding that all of these actions and the most capacious definition of his powers to dispense with or suspend statutes were legal exercises of monarchical power, removing several who opposed this extensive a definition of monarchical power from the bench. It is worth stressing that while James unquestionably held an exalted notion of monarchy, the central desire reflected in his many actions was not for an undifferentiated absolutism in itself, but for the power necessary for his religious agenda of gaining toleration for Catholics. As John Miller has remarked, 'In accusing him of trying to establish absolutism, his contemporaries and later historians confused means with ends...James's abuses of power...were highly selective; all were geared to allowing Catholics to worship freely and hold office'.[51]

In his Protestant subjects' interpretation of James' actions it was crucial that they had been nursed on allegations of Catholic atrocities and nourished by a steady diet of Restoration anti-Catholic propaganda. James' actions served in the minds of most of these Protestant subjects to reinforce rather than to dispel the associations between his intentions and those of Louis XIV and Victor Amadeus II. James' Declaration of Indulgence itself registered: 'We cannot but heartily wish, as it will easily be believed, that all the people of our dominions were members of the Catholic Church'.[52] James suppressed much of the information about the persecution of Protestant subjects in France and Piedmont, had Jean Claude's *Account* burned by the public hangman, and ordered burned *An Edict of the French King, Prohibiting all Exercise of the Pretended Reformed Religion in his Kingdom*.[53] The official London *Gazette* carried no news of the violence in France, leading John

---

[51] Miller, *James II*, 128; Speck, *Reluctant*, has argued that James showed absolutist tendencies outside England, but does not effectively challenge the central point that Miller has made.

[52] J. Kenyon, *The Stuart Constitution* (Cambridge 1986), 410.

[53] Gwynn, *Huguenot Heritage*, 135.

Evelyn to record that it 'appeared very extraordinary in a Protestant country, that we should know nothing of what Protestants suffered' by official means. Evelyn lamented the burning of Claude's work, declaring that it related 'only matters of fact concerning the horrid massacres and barbarous proceedings of the French King against his Protestant subjects'. And Evelyn recorded that 'About this time also the Duke of Savoy, instigated by the French king to extirpate the Protestants of Piedmont, slew many thousands of these innocent people, so that there seemed to be a universal design to destroy all that would not go to mass, throughout Europe. Quod avertat D.O.M.! No faith in princes!'[54] James allowed English ships to be searched in French ports to allow French authorities to find any refugees trying to flee to England.[55] And James not merely received a papal nuncio, Ferdinand D'Adda, but had his elevation into an Archbishop *in partibus infidelium* – in heretical countries – celebrated in the Chapel Royal.[56] When the bishop of Valence, Cosnac, spoke in 1685 of James' rule as giving Louis XIV 'one of the most glorious opportunities he could wish for...to restore true religion everywhere', and of 'the pious sovereign of England' as looking to 'the Most Christian King, the eldest son of the Church, for support against a heretical nation', his speech was read in the House of Lords and its implications discussed.[57]

Interpreting the actions by James II in the wake of the recent actions of Louis XIV and of Victor Amadeus II, it was difficult for many Protestants in England to believe that there was such a thing as Penn and Care identified, a Catholic ruler's 'perpetual' edict of toleration for Protestant subjects. Penn lamented the way that 'We look on France till we frighten our selves from the best means of our worldly Happiness'.[58] The justifications given in France by Catholics for the Revocation seemed to make clear to Protestants throughout Europe that there was no such thing as a Catholic ruler's 'perpetual' edict of toleration. Most Catholics in France had justified the Edict of Nantes during the eighty-seven years of its existence from 1598 to 1685 almost entirely on the *politique* grounds that Catholic co-existence with Protestants was temporarily necessary in order to prevent the continuation of the bloody civil wars of the sixteenth century, rather than because Catholics had stopped viewing their Protestant neighbours as 'heretics' and 'schismatics'.[59] In the years leading up to the Revocation, Catholic writers had then increasingly stressed that the Edict had only ever been a temporary measure, and not irrevocable, even though they explicitly recognised that later rulers,

---

[54] *Gazette*, number 2136, 10 May 1686 quoted in Gillett, *Burned Books*, II, 528; J. Evelyn, *Diary*, 5 May 1686, in C. Whiting, *Studies in English Puritanism* (London 1931), 357.
[55] Miller, *James II*, 148.   [56] Ashley, *James II*, 202.
[57] J. Orcibal, *Louis XIV*, 105n.65; Smiles, *Huguenots*, 185; Miller, 'The Immediate Impact of the Revocation', 161–74, at 163; Burnet, *History of My Own Time*, III, 69.
[58] Penn, *Great and Popular Objection*, 9.   [59] See pp. 275ff.; ch. 13 below.

including Louis XIV, had promised to maintain it on many occasions. Paul Hay du Châtelet's 1666 *Treatise*, reissued in 1680, declared that the Huguenots were 'ill advised to make so much noise...about the Edict of Nantes...an interim settlement, until such time as they should have seen the light of truth – for which they have had sufficient time'. Granted for the 'well-being' of the state, for Châtelet it could now be revoked on the same grounds.[60] Maimbourg's 1682 *History of Calvinism* trumpeted the change to come in 1685 in arguing that the Edict of Nantes had only been made because of its time in order to secure peace, and that times had now changed. It was for Maimbourg a duty of magistrates to act against heresy whenever they could do so without imperilling the society.[61] The initial rhetoric of Bossuet's 1686 *Pastoral Letter*, disclaiming that violence had in fact been used against Protestants, followed by his move to justify violence against Protestants as heretics and schismatics, provided further reason for English scepticism: Catholic bishops could not be trusted to be straightforward in their depiction of the methods of conversion they supported. James' licensing of Bossuet's text further corroded trust in James' truthfulness. When pressed about the reality of violence, Bossuet turned to refurbishment of sixteenth-century Catholic arguments that magistrates were armed against 'evil-doers', among whom were to be numbered all Protestants as 'heretics' and 'schismatics'. This latter 1686 declaration by Bossuet that violence was legitimate against 'evil-doers' was republished by Jean Rou and Pierre Bayle among others in the Netherlands, and subjected to withering scorn in England in 1687 in *A Second Defense of the Exposition of the Church of England* by the future Archbishop William Wake, who had just returned from a visit to the Netherlands.[62]

Unsurprisingly, then, to many Protestants Louis' and Victor Amadeus' actions showed that Catholic rulers' promises were untrustworthy. This became the central theme rung out in many works issued in the mid-1680s in the Netherlands and in England.[63] Halifax argued in his *Letter to a Dissenter* in 1687 that 'The Church of Rome doth not only dislike the allowing liberty, but by its principles it cannot do it. Wine is more expressly forbid to the Mahometans, than giving heretics liberty to the Papists'. Even if

---

[60] P. Hay du Châtelet, *Traité de la Politique de France* (1666), ch. 5, tr. A. Soman in O. Ranum, *The Century of Louis XIV*, 354.

[61] L. Maimbourg, *Histoire du calvinism* (1682), VI, 499; Perry, *Theology*, 166.

[62] W. Wake, *A Second Defense of the Exposition of the Doctrine of the Church of England* (London 1687), 25–9.

[63] [C. Ancillon] *L'irrévocabilité de L'Édit de Nantes, prouvée par les principes de droit & de la politique* (Amsterdam 1688); *Popish Treachery, or a Short Account of the Horrid Cruelties Exercised on the Protestans in France. Being a True Prospect of What is to be Expected From the Most Solemn Promises of Roman Catholic Princes* (London 1689); Claude, *Account*.

they wished to tolerate you, he asserted, 'The continuance of their kindness would be a habit of sin, of which they are to repent...You are therefore to be hugged now, onely that you may be the better squeezed at another time'. Halifax's *Letter* was spread 'industriously', reprinted, and circulated in every 'Corner in the Land'.[64] Burnet's 1686 *Reflections* similarly assaulted the 'ambition and superstition' of Princes which had produced the violation of 'edicts' formerly sworn by those rulers.[65] Burnet's 1687 *Apology*, quickly issued in French in the Netherlands and in English in London, noted that the king of France 'even after he had resolved to break the Edict of Nantes, yet repeated in above an hundred Edicts, a clause confirmatory of the Edict of Nantes, declaring that "he would never violate it"'.[66] Burnet's 1687 *Six Papers* repeatedly compared James to Louis XIV, noting that in France edicts, coronation oaths, laws and promises were all 'feeble things', and stressed that the councils of church decreed 'extirpation' of heretics and placed 'severe sanctions' on princes who failed in their duty of 'being hangmen of the Inquisitors'. He interpreted James' claims of absolute power in Scotland in February 1687 as leading to the power to 'declare us all heretics' and make us 'obey without reserve' or 'be burnt without reserve'. Analysing the Declaration of Indulgence of April 1687 in England, he argued that the king's religion committed him to extirpating heretics, and that promises of toleration were aimed at 'nothing but' to 'divide us or to lay us asleep till time to destroy us'.[67] And Burnet's 1687 *History of the Persecution* emphasised that Victor Amadeus II had rescinded edicts that were not 'simple tolerations, but perpetual concessions' and suggested that the Revocation was undertaken at Louis XIV's instigation.[68]

Throughout these many works, Burnet was an avid defender of the Test Acts of 1673 and 1678 that had prohibited Catholics from holding office and from sitting in Parliament. He argued that Catholics should themselves be tolerated in their worship, but was adamant that they should not be allowed to hold any office. He excoriated the arguments of his fellow Anglican Samuel Parker that if one was to tolerate, then one must also allow service in the state, firmly distinguishing public service from public worship, and suggesting that the only security of the state when the monarch was a

---

[64] Miller, *James II*, 114–15; George Savile, Marquis of Halifax, *A Letter to a Dissenter* (1687) in M. Brown (ed.), *The Works of George Savile, Marquis of Halifax* (Oxford 1989), 3. See also G. Schochet, 'The Act of Toleration and the Failure of Comprehension: Persecution, Nonconformity, and Religious Indifference' in D. Hoak and M. Feingold (eds.), *The World of William and Mary* (Stanford 1996), 179; Henry Care, *Animadversions* (Amsterdam 1687), 7.

[65] G. Burnet, *Reflections on Mr Varrillas' History of the Great Revolutions which have Happened in Europe in Matters of Religion* (Amsterdam 1686), 4.

[66] G. Burnet, *An Apology for the Church of England with Relation to the Spirit of Persecution for which she is Accused* (London 1688); Gwynn, *Huguenot Heritage*, 142.

[67] G. Burnet, *Six Papers* (London 1687), 9–13.   [68] Burnet, *History of the Persecution*, 7.

Catholic and the majority of his subjects were Protestants came from legal prohibition of office to Catholic subjects. This line was also taken in William's and Mary's responses to James' actions, some of which were translated into English by Burnet: it was declared that they supported an entire liberty of conscience for Catholics as well as Protestants, but that they were adamantly opposed to allowing Catholics to hold office. It was reported to James in April 1688 that Fagel's *Letter*, translated by Burnet, and other pamphlets 'are industriously spread through all parts with discourses and endeavours to prejudice the minds' of those faithful to him.[69]

In 1688, John Westbrown of Harwich questioned 'whether the usage of the Protestants in France and Savoy for these three years past be not a sufficient warning not to trust to the declarations, promises, or oaths in religion of any papist whatsoever'.[70] In 1688, the arrival of William's and Mary's forces in Torbay was greeted by a *Memorial from the English Protestants to their Highnesses the Prince and Princess of Orange*, which declared that:

Suppression of the Protestants of England hath always been esteemed the principal part of the Popish Design to extirpate the Protestant Religion...and our king proceeds in the same methods against us, wherein the French king hath been successful to destroy the Protestants of his kingdom...He seeks to make his proclamations and declarations to have as much power over our Laws, as the French king's Edicts. And after his Example he establishes a mercenary army to master and subdue the People to his will.

He could then as easily destroy the liberty of conscience 'however seemingly settled by him' because he could as 'easily destroy it as the French king has abolished the irrevocable Edicts, Treatises or Laws of his kingdom, confirmed by his oath, which were as good security to those Protestants as any Magna Charta which our king may make for us'.[71]

In the atmosphere created by account after account of the dragoons' violence in France, and of the massacre in Piedmont, James' actions in preferring Catholic officers in the army, increasing its size from the Caroline level of 8,575 men to 19,778 men, and unusually maintaining it in time of peace, were understood by many English Protestants to provide the clear evidence that James intended English persecution directly modelled on Louis' actions.[72] The poem 'Hounslow-Heath 1686' described James'

---

[69] Bodleian Rawlinson MSS A 139b fo. 178 in Speck, *Reluctant*, 134.

[70] BM Add MS 41805 fo. 50 in Gwynn, *Huguenot Heritage*, 142. Even before the Revocation, Claude Brusson had attempted to prove edicts in religion irrevocable in *État des réformez en france* (1684); he was later executed for ministering to the Reformed of the Midi: Perry, *Theology*, 17.

[71] *Memorial* in State Tracts (1705), I, 1–37, at 9–10 quoted in Cottret, *Huguenots*, 190.

[72] Speck, *Reluctant*, 55–7.

standing army with its newly admitted Catholic officers and men in terms
which stressed the 'Tridentine' method of conversion:

> Now pause, and view the Army Royal,
> Compos'd of valiant souls and loyal,
> Not rais'd (as ill men say) to hurt ye,
> But to defend, or to convert ye,
> For that's the method now in use,
> The faith Tridentine to diffuse,
> Time was, the Word was powerful;
> But now 'tis thought remiss and dull,
> Has not that energy and force,
> Which is in well-arm'd foot and horse.[73]

It was thus not merely, nor even primarily, suspicion of James' 'arbitrary'
actions – his use of monarchical powers – that explains the hostility of many
Protestant dissenters to his Declarations of Indulgence. There was, in fact,
good reason at this moment in European history to see them as untrustworthy, as made by a Catholic ruler. While Baptists and Quakers were the
first to issue addresses to James thanking him for his toleration, the Baptist
leaders William Kiffin and Joseph Stennett refused to issue addresses to the
king in support of his 1687 Declaration of Indulgence. Although some
Independents and even some Presbyterians had come to voice increasing
support for toleration outside of a national or established church as the
Restoration wore on, many Independents and Presbyterians still desired
comprehension in a national church as the best form of 'toleration'; most
were reluctant to accept toleration by royal indulgence rather than through
parliamentary statute; some questioned toleration of worship for Catholics,
and many were strongly opposed to the opening of offices to Catholics. The
Presbyterian leaders Richard Baxter, John Howe, and Dr Bates all refused to
issue addresses of thanks to the king in 1687. So did the leading Independent
Richard Stretton.[74] These dissenting leaders thereby joined hands in 1688
with a number of Latitudinarian Anglicans in the Church of England who
had long been supportive of Protestant toleration, especially through comprehension of the majority of Protestants within the Church of England by
accommodating objections to its liturgy, and who might be willing to tolerate English Catholics' worship, but only if Catholics were kept out of office.
These Latitudinarians attacked Catholicism fiercely in the early years of
James' reign. Several had been supporters of James' Exclusion in 1678–81.
And James was opposed as strongly by the majority of Anglicans, who
desired neither comprehension nor toleration, whose commitment to the
Church of England was greater than their commitment to their monarch,

---

[73] Gwynn, *Huguenot Heritage*, 141.   [74] Lacey, *Dissent*, 180.

and who feared both the forced Catholicisation of England and the indirect Catholicisation they forecast as the result of toleration dividing English Protestants. These Anglican ministers continued to argue against Catholics and against toleration, even while they preached passive (dis)obedience. When James ordered his second Declaration of Indulgence read from churches in April 1688, the vast majority of Anglican minsters throughout the land refused to comply with his order. Seven bishops who petitioned against the Declarations were tried for 'seditious libel' by James; when they were incarcerated in the Tower, a print was issued of the Protestant bishops who had been burned under Mary. When the bishops were found not guilty, the result was greeted by bonfires throughout London, and the bishop William Lloyd was greeted by a crowd which thought it a 'blessing to kiss any of these bishops' hands or garments'.[75]

James II was thus faced with lukewarm support or opposition from the majority of Protestant dissenters, and with deep hostility from many Anglicans. It was in this unpropitious situation that James finally fathered a son and heir who could perpetuate Catholic rule, a child whose legitimacy as James' own child was quickly held by many Protestants to be spurious.[76] It was fear of Catholicism triumphant in England, perpetuated in the rule of a Catholic son, at least as much as opposition to James 'arbitrary' government – and probably far more – that then led many leading figures in England in 1688 to issue an invitation to William of Orange, husband of James' daughter Mary. This invitation helped to give the excuse for William to invade England with an army in 1688. William wished to ensure that the joint force of England and the Netherlands would combat the advance of French Catholicism.[77] In the wake of Louis' and Victor Amadeus' actions, the leading Englishmen who flocked to William's support, and the majority of the political nation who remained quiescent rather than repulsing this 'invading force', wished to prevent the Catholicisation of England by James and by his newly born successor. Faced with this loss of English support, James fled, and the Revolution of 1688–9 was born. This revolution, tellingly, was first to be called 'the glorious Revolution' by the Anglo-Irish Protestant community, to whose domination over the Catholic majority of the Irish population William quickly devoted his troops in bloody battles that give the lie direct to the notion of 1688–9 as a 'bloodless revolution'. William's army included literally thousands of Huguenot exiles in its ranks, officers, and preachers,

---

[75] M. A. Goldie, 'The Political Thought of the Anglican Revolution' in R. A. Beddard, *The Revolutions of 1688* (Oxford 1991), 102–36, esp. 125, 123; see also the important work of Miller, *James II*, 187, and Speck, *Reluctant*; T. Harris, 'London Crowds and the Revolution of 1688' in Cruickshanks (ed.), *By Force or by Default* (Edinburgh 1989), 50, 52.

[76] See R. Weil, *Political Passions* (Manchester 2000), ch. 3.

[77] Israel, 'The Dutch Contribution'.

and they understood themselves to be fighting for the international fate of Protestantism. Over 500 Huguenot officers alone were to obtain pensions on the Irish establishment when the Huguenot regiments were disbanded after the Treaty of Ryswick, and large Huguenot communities were to be founded in the 1690s in Portarlington, Dublin, Cork, Lisburn, and Waterford.[78]

Symbolic of the fight to defend Protestantism against Catholicism on an international terrain, some of these troops were led by the Marquis de Ruvigny. Ruvigny was soon to be Lord Galway, Lord Justice of Ireland, and the leading Huguenot nobleman in England and Ireland in the 1690s, but a few years earlier in life it had been Ruvigny who had taken to the king the 1681 protest of the Huguenot consistory at Charenton against the edict allowing removal of Protestant children from parental homes at seven, and it was to be Ruvigny who commanded British forces in Piedmont in 1693–4, including four Huguenot regiments, and who convened a Huguenot synod in Piedmont. Symbolic of the international affiliations of Whig anti-Catholicism, Ruvigny's first cousin was Rachel Russell, wife of the Rye House plotter and 1683 Whig martyr Lord Russell.[79] Moreover, the aged Marshal Shomberg was recorded by an Huguenot exile officer in that army, Rapin de Thoyras, as having rallied the Huguenot regiments at the battle of the Boyne itself by shouting 'voila vos persecuteurs', because, equally symbolically, the Protestant troops in Ireland, drawn from England, the Netherlands, and the Huguenot community, fought in Ireland against an army composed jointly of Irish and French Catholics. The French commander of the Irish army was Charles Chalmont, Marquis de Saint-Ruth, who had led troops destroying Huguenot temples in the south of France in 1683–4, including the armed force which had put down the Huguenot attempts to maintain worship in 1683, during which Cosnac recorded that his troops had burned perhaps 200 Huguenots sheltering in a barn. And he had been involved in the attack on the Waldensians in Piedmont. Saint-Ruth died in battle, and in his 1692 *Synodicon* the English minister Quick pointed to these burnings and celebrated that their commander had 'paid his reckoning' in the Siege of Limerick in 1691 by being cut off by 'God's sword of Justice'.[80]

William's invasion of England and the conquest of Ireland were, then, understood by many in William's forces as battles for the fate of

---

[78] J. G. Simms, 'Protestant Ascendancy 1691–1714', 26, in M. Vaughn (ed.), *A New History of Ireland* (Oxford 1986), IV.

[79] R. Vigne, 'The Good Lord Galway. The Irish and English Careers of a Huguenot leader: biographical notes', *Proceedings of the Huguenot Society*, xxiv (1988), 532–50; Benoist, *Histoire de L'Édit*, III, ii, 458. P. Kelly, 'Lord Galway and the Penal Laws' in *The Huguenots and Ireland*, 239–55.

[80] Quick, *Synodicon*, cxxxv; Smiles, *Huguenots*, 215; R. F. Foster, *Modern Ireland*, 149–50.

Protestantism internationally as well as domestically. While William's own motivations were multiple and complex, and included the desire to gain and maintain support of Catholic rulers in an alliance against France, William clearly stated what he understood to be the priorities of the English population in his *Declaration* issued from the Hague and widely circulated across Europe, which declared that public peace could not be preserved when laws, liberties and customs were transgressed, 'more especially where the alteration of Religion is endeavoured, and that a religion, which is contrary to law, is endeavoured to be introduced', obliging the people to the attempt to preserve these laws, liberties and customs 'and, *above all*, the Religion and Worship of God, that is established among them'.[81]

THE CENTRAL ROLES OF DISCUSSIONS OF CATHOLIC VIOLENCE AGAINST HUGUENOTS AND WALDENSIANS IN DEFENCES OF THE REVOLUTIONS OF 1688–1691 IN ENGLAND AND IRELAND

James' reign was thus brought abruptly to an end in England by the invasion of William of Orange and by James' flight, and in Ireland by bloody battles in which thousands of Huguenot refugees fought in William's army. But Huguenots and Waldensians were not merely martyrs in Protestant propaganda and soldiers in William's armies in 1688–91; their treatment at the hands of their Catholic rulers also provided central topics in the late 1680s in the Netherlands and in England for discussions about the legitimacy of resistance to the use of force by a ruler that were then made applicable to resistance to James in England, and to legitimation of the Revolutions of 1688–91. Such arguments were applied not merely in England, but also in Ireland in defence of the reimposition of Protestant rule over the majority Catholic population, and in the Netherlands in the early 1690s as part of European debate about the events of 1688–91. Remarkably, due in part to the Duke of Savoy changing sides and in part to the support of William, in 1689 a few hundred Waldensians recovered their valleys in Piedmont by force of arms in guerilla warfare against French forces, an event which confirmed to many Protestants in England, Ireland, and the Netherlands that God was miraculously protecting Protestantism. This in turn helped to confirm to many that William was the providential deliverer of both England and Ireland from the Catholic James and should therefore be obeyed as God's providentially chosen ruler, leading to even greater discussion of the Waldensians in 1689–92 than in the immediate wake of their 1685–6 persecution. Bayle declared in 1691 that more had been spoken about the

---

[81] Speck, *Reluctant*, 74 (my italics); Israel, *Anglo-Dutch Moment; idem, Dutch Republic*; Scott, *England's Troubles.*

Waldensians recently than ever before, and cited this reconquest of their valleys as one of the two major reasons.[82]

To many who accorded prophetic significance to the Waldensians, their fate in the 1680s was central to acceptance of the Revolution in England and Ireland as 'providential'. We have already seen that Jurieu had forecast the rising again of Protestantism in his 1686 *Accomplishment*. Jurieu's thought was providentially and prophetically structured, holding that God gave many signs and portents of his will and intervened directly in the world to protect the true faith. The success of the Waldensians in 1689 was to Jurieu the 'miraculous' fulfilment of his prophetic forecast of God's providential intervention on behalf of the true faith. In 1686, Jurieu's *Accomplishment* had identified 1689 as the year in which he expected the restoration of true religion in France, when 'France will renounce Papistry and the kingdom shall be converted'. Whereas the Catholics justifying the Revocation of the Edict of Nantes thought of the conversion of less than 5 per cent of the French population, Jurieu thus expected the conversion of the other 95 per cent! For Jurieu, this was the beginning of the end of the reign of the Antichrist, which would be completed between 1710 and 1715 with great bloodshed and reduction 'to ashes' of the 'empire's capital' of Rome [Babylon].[83] Such providentialist millenarianism formed one of two strands of justification of 1688–9 which intertwined in Jurieu's thought. Jurieu's famous series of *Pastoral Letters*, written from exile in the late 1680s, were ostensibly directed only to those Protestants still in France to confirm them in their faith, but they also circulated widely in the Netherlands and in England. In one of these letters at the beginning of 1689, issued by itself in London, Jurieu attacked Bishop Bossuet's attempted distinction that it was not valid for the church itself to use force in matters of religion, but that it was valid for rulers to use it on behalf of the church. For Jurieu, this made Catholic practices over the centuries invalid: he questioned rhetorically why, then, had

they imployed the Armies of the Cross, to massacre an hundred thousand Waldenses, and Albigenses? Why does the Tribunal of the Inquisition find Imployment for Hangmen, Fires, Tortures, Executions...?

It was on exactly the same ground, he declared, that they had recently employed 'dragoons, and soldiers to violate consciences'. Jurieu then made what he considered a firm distinction between legitimate defence of a religion by force

[82] Goldie, 'Huguenot Experience'; Goldie, 'The Revolution of 1689 and the Structure of Political Argument', *Bulletin of the Institute for Research in the Humanities* (1980); J. Kenyon, *Revolution Principles* (Cambridge 1977); L. Schwoerer, *Declaration, passim*; Bayle, *OD*, IV, 652.

[83] Jurieu, *Accomplishment*, 18–36, 141, 151–2, 182; J. Delumeau, *Sin and Fear* (New York 1990), 529–30.

of arms and illegitimate establishment of a religion by force of arms. It was on the grounds of 'self-defence' that he held that the Waldensians could defend themselves by force of arms, proclaiming in this context a 'natural right' to 'self-defence'. For Jurieu, the English similarly had the 'natural right' to take up arms in self-defence against James' transparent attempts to impose Catholicism.[84]

Jurieu's *Accomplishment* and *Pastoral Letters* in combination thus served to legitimate the Revolution of 1688–9 in England by God's 'providential protection' of Protestantism and by the 'natural right' to resist unjust force – the latter concerned far more with the natural right to defend one's religion by force of arms when it was attacked by the Inquisition than with any broader series of secular rights. And Jurieu's works made this case by linking the legitimacy of resistance of the Waldensians, the Dutch, and the English. In this, Jurieu was not alone. Burnet's 1687 *History of the Persecution*, issued both in the Netherlands and in England after the most recent massacre of 1686, but before the Waldensians' campaign to regain their valleys, was similarly clear that the Waldensians had been loyal to their ruler, that they had fought for their ruler in wars, and that they had only used arms to defend themselves from massacre when they were attacked. This was for Burnet 'a natural and warrantable defence against the unjust and violent oppression' of the council of the propagation of the faith whose task was 'to extirpate heresy'. Burnet's 1687 work on the Waldensians was thus in part an extremely powerful martyrological exhibition of his ceaselessly repeated refrain that Catholic kings were untrustworthy, in part a defence of the miraculous preservation of religion by God, and in part a justification of the use of arms in natural and warrantable defence against unjust oppression. It was thus cognate to the arguments he was to use to justify – in advance – the events of 1688–9 in England in works such as his 1688 *Enquiry*, which justified resistance to arbitrary authority on the basis of natural rights and the 'dissolution of the Government' which Burnet said James had created by his abuse of prerogative powers in suspending Test Acts and providing toleration. Burnet argued in the *Enquiry* that in general one was not to defend religion by force of arms, but rather to flee or submit, but he also argued that men were born free, had joined civil society to protect their property, and that if the laws had made religion a 'property' then it became a right of the subject which could be defended. For Burnet, men were to judge of that 'invasion' of their property like all other 'invasions' and were justified in repulsing such 'invasion'.[85] Burnet's other works of these years repeatedly returned to this theme. They were all enormously influential both in the Netherlands, where they were translated into French and where they received

---

[84] P. Jurieu, *Pastoral Letters*, 1 Jan 1689.
[85] Burnet, *History of the Persecution*, 25; *idem, An Enquiry into the Measures of Submission* (London 1688), *passim*, esp. 4.

many reviews in the new journals of the 'republic of letters' – including seven in the *Nouvelles de la république des lettres* and fourteen in the *Histoire des Ouvrages des Savans* – and in England, where all were published in English in London in the period 1685–9. Burnet's *History of the Reformation* (1679–80) had made him in these years the most significant living British writer on the church for continental audiences, and his political tracts as a propagandist for William and Mary made him hold the same status in these years on issues of the state. When in his 1689 *Critique of Jurieu's Pastoral Letters* the Catholic Pierre Paulian declared Burnet the 'Jurieu d'Angleterre', and Jurieu 'le Burnet Français', he was recognising their elevated status internationally as the two most important Protestant voices of 1688–9.[86]

Burnet's defences of the Revolution issued after his return from exile in 1688 and his rapid elevation to Bishop of Salisbury continued to stress the avoidance in England of intolerant Catholic rule which he imaged to his audience through the Waldensians and Huguenots, even as they turned in a more providentialist than juristic direction. Burnet's Thanksgiving sermon before the Commons on January 31 1689, which decried 'the fierceness of Inquisitors' in the recent persecution in France, stressed not merely the need for fences to liberty and property and an end to 'precarious Judges and suborned Juries' in an 'exact conduct of Public Justice', but demanded 'the avoiding of every Invasion upon the Freedom of Conscience, which is the first, and most sacred of all a Man's Rights'. Burnet's sermon on 5 November 1689 before the Lords emphasised that the Revolution was crucial in preventing Catholic force, and placed it into a context of God's protection for Protestantism against the 'many rebellions' of the Irish. He declared that 'our late conspirators were not so cautious as to hide the Fuel that was preparing for our Destruction, since we saw them persecute in so many other places of Europe at the same time that they talked of toleration here'. He declared 'when I have named France, I have said all that is necessary to give you a complete idea of the Blackest Tyranny over Men's Consciences, Persons and Estates, that can possibly be imagined'.[87]

William Lloyd was, with Burnet, the central episcopal propagandist of the new regime in 1688–9. He had formerly been a central propagandist for the 'Popish Plot' and the preacher of Sir Edmund Berry Godfrey's funeral sermon, mounting the pulpit on that occasion flanked by two other clerics as bodyguards because he feared assassination.[88] Lloyd was, quite simply,

---

[86] Quoted in Dodge, *Political Thought*, 11n.

[87] Burnet, *Sermon 5 November 1689*, 1, 5; cf. Burnet, *Sermon...December 1688; idem, Sermon...31 Jan 1689*.

[88] W. Lloyd, *A Sermon Preached at the Funeral of Sir Edmund Berry Godfrey* (London 1678); A. Tindal Hart, *William Lloyd, 1627–1717: Bishop, Politician and Prophet* (London 1952), *passim*.

eschatologically obsessed with the Waldensians. In 1689 itself, two weeks after the Coronation, Lloyd met with the then Archbishop of Canterbury, William Sancroft, and John Evelyn. Evelyn recorded Lloyd and Sancroft holding a discussion 'concerning the final destruction of Antichrist, both of them concluding that the third trumpet and vial were now pouring out. My lord St Asaph considered the killing of the two witnesses, to be the utter destruction of the Cevennes Protestants by the French and Duke of Savoy, and the other the Waldenses and Pyrennean Christians, (who by all appearance from good history had kept the primitive faith from the very Apostles'-time)'. They had 'both agreed it would be good to employ some intelligent French minister to travel as far as the Pyrenees to understand the present state of the Church there'. Lloyd, who later described his entire understanding of prophecy as dependent on the fate of the Waldensians, seems to have carried through on the suggestion. In 1690, Evelyn recorded that Lloyd's 'conversation' was again 'on the Vaudois in Savoy, who had been thought so near destruction and final extirpation by the French, being totally given up to slaughter, so that there were no hopes for them' but that they had been restored to their country and to the exercise of their religion. These were, recorded Evelyn,

the remainder of those persecuted Christians which the bishop of St Asaph had so long affirmed to be the two witnesses spokn of in Revelation, who should be killed and brought to life again, it was looked on as an extraordinary thing that this prophesying bishop should persuade two fugitive ministers of the Vaudois to return to their country, and furnished them with 20 towards their journey, at that very time when nothing but universal destruction was to be expected, assuring them and showing them from the Apocalypse that their countrymen should be returned safely to their country before they arrived. This happening contrary to all expectation and experience, did exceedingly credit the Bishop's confidence how that prophecy of the witnesses should come to pass, just at that time, and the very month he had spoken of some years before.

According to Calamy, Lloyd had not merely foretold the return of the Waldensians, 'those venerable remains of the primitive church' soon after 'the Revolution compassed by King William', but had told two young Waldensians that if they lived until 1716 they 'might hope to be in a manner able, standing on the top of their mountains, and lifting up their hands, to warm themselves with the flames of the City of Rome, which would then be consumed to ashes'.[89]

---

[89] E. S. de Beer (ed.), *The Diary of John Evelyn* (1955), IV, 636 in Jacob, *Newtonians*, 120–1; Hart, *Lloyd, passim*. The book of Revelation spoke of two witnesses of God killed in the street of the great city, whose bodies lie unburied for three-and-a-half days, and are then returned to life and ascend to heaven.

It is unsurprising, then, that in his defences of the new regime after 1689, Lloyd often combined the examples of violence against Huguenots and Waldensians to establish the danger to Protestant England removed by William and Mary. Preaching the sermon before William and Mary on 5 November 1689, Lloyd declared that in France there had been 'a Government by Laws, and there were two Millions of Protestants under the Protection of those Laws. But where are they now? There are no Laws but the King's Will: and it is his Will that there must be no Protestants'. So Protestants were hunted by dogs 'like wild Beasts'. Louis had then 'lent. . .his Dogs' to the Duke of Savoy who had 'hunted the Vaudois, till they had Kill'd above half that poor People. . .the few that remain'd were forced to abjure their Religion. . .God knows how soon the like might have been done in England'. He that 'gave the example, and lent hands to the Duke of Savoy, would have seen that hands should not have been wanting in England'. It was, however, then that God had raised up a 'deliverer' for England in the person of William, 'Blessed be God'. It was as such a 'deliverer' that for Lloyd William was providential ruler of England.[90] Since this wonderful preservation there had, for Lloyd, been added further 'marks of God's hand' in reducing Ireland.[91]

Lloyd was not alone in celebrating William as 'deliverer' of the English in works focusing on the violence against the Waldensians and the Huguenots. The leading Huguenot defender of the Revolution in England was Pierre Allix, described by Evelyn as early as 1686 as the 'famous preacher and writer', and in 1689 a fierce defender of the Revolution. Allix was to be the most published of all the defenders of the new Whig regime in the 1705 collected *State Tracts*, with no less than three separate defences of the Revolution of 1688–9. He was also author of two works in these years on the Waldensians and the Albigensians. For Allix, the Waldensians had advanced 'only pure doctrine from the gospel' and 'Never did the Church of Rome give a more incontestable evidence of her own Antichristianism, than by her insatiable Thirst after the Blood of those Christians'. Allix's *Some Remarks* was printed on paper imported from Holland without duty for the purpose by special order of the House of Commons, and was dedicated to William, who had given these 'dispersed christians' a 'happy retreat' in his dominions.[92] And Archbishop John Tillotson's 1692 sermon before the king and queen at Whitehall compared Louis XIV to the biblical King of Babylon, who had sworn destruction on Zion just as the French king had

[90] W. Lloyd, *A Sermon Preached before their Majesties. . .5 November 1689*, 28–9.
[91] W. Lloyd, *A Sermon Preached. . .29 May 1692, passim*; Hart, *Lloyd*.
[92] P. Allix, *Some Remarks Upon the Ecclesiastical History of the Ancient Churches of Piedmont* (London 1690), *passim*.

planned to 'destroy the Reformation [and] extirpate the northern heresy'. Giving thanks for the fleet victory at Honfleur, Tillotson had wondered, he said, 'why at the destruction of Modern and Mystical Babylon the Scripture should make mention of great wailing and lamentation for the loss of Her Ships and Seamen [Revelation 18:7]; he knew now that 'The Scripture saith nothing in vain'.[93]

Waldensians and Huguenots in justifications of the Revolution in Ireland

The Waldensians and Huguenots often were concentrated upon jointly in accounts which did not merely justify the Revolutions of 1688–9 in England, but also offered justifications of the Revolution of 1688–91 in Ireland which reinforced the rule of the minority Protestant elite and their 'protective laws' against the majority Catholic population. Pierre Boyer published an *Abstract of the History of the Waldensians* at the Hague in 1691, extensively celebrating their fulfilment of Revelation. Its English translation in 1692, *The History of the Vaudois*, was dedicated to William, who had seen in Ireland and England 'the God of Armies march before you, as anciently he marched before the Camp of Israel' and as he had marched before the Waldensians. Boyer declared the Waldensians the only church in the West that had been preserved pure, numbered the time from corruption of the faith by Popery to the dissipation of the Waldensians in 1686 as 1260 years – the prophetical '1260 days' that the church was to be 'nourished in the desert', and then interpreted the re-establishment of the true church as occurring three-and-a-half years later – the prophetical 'three-and-a-half days' spoken of in Revelation as occurring after the killing of the 'two witnesses' (the Protestants of France and Piedmont) where 'truth had been driven out', or 'killed'.[94] Boyer thus voiced a common apocalyptic interpretation of events, expressed also by Jurieu and Lloyd among others, in defence of Protestant hegemony in Ireland. The English divine and scientist Thomas Burnet similarly declared in 1691 that 'the Resurrection of the Witnesses goes on very well in Savoy and Dauphiné' as an argument to hope that 'all will end well' in the fighting in Ireland.[95]

The 1694 *Défense de la nation Britannique*, published in the Hague, won the favour of William III for its author, Jacques Abbadie, in the early 1690s a preacher with William's armies in Ireland and a minister in the French church

[93] S. Barton, *A Sermon Preached...16th July...1690* (1690), 23–4; T. Shadwell, *The Scowrers* (1691), 7; J. Tillotson, *A Sermon Preached...27th October...1692*, 30–1, in C. Rose, *England in the 1690s* (Oxford 1999), 105–10. Tillotson was a close friend of Locke. It was in the year of this sermon, 1692, that Locke was visiting Tillotson frequently and requesting permission for his friend Philip van Limborch to dedicate to Tillotson his 1692 *History of the Inquisition*, a work composed at Locke's instigation.
[94] P. Boyer, *The History of the Vaudois* (London 1692), *passim.*   [95] Jacob, *Newtonians*, 124.

at the Savoy, and then promoted to Dean of Killaloe. Abbadie combined defence of the Revolutions of 1688–9 in England and Ireland with defence of the 'valiant' Piedmontese against 'the inhumane orders of a foreign inquisition'. For Abbadie, no prince committed to Catholicism could be trusted to keep promises made to 'heretics'. The Catholic religion required the extermination of heretics. James' actions in England had for Abbadie provided the evidence that he intended to fulfil his duty to exterminate heretics and to render England 'the victim of the Roman Inquisition'. Abbadie's *Défense* included a litany of massacres, placing the persecution of the Waldensians alongside the alleged massacre of Protestants in Ireland in 1641. For Abbadie, the Waldensians had exercised a 'just and natural defense which is allowed by right of god and of nature'; man was possessed of natural rights; political authority was based on a voluntary act of association; members of a commonwealth could never cede their right to preservation; rulers could be deposed by the people; and the Convention in England had acted for the safety of the country in placing the crown in the hands of William and Mary. While on these grounds Abbadie justified the resistance of the Waldensians and of the English to Catholic tyranny, he simultaneously justifed penal laws in Ireland against Catholics and condemned Irish resistance as rebellion. For Abbadie, the 'Irish have been treated as rebels because they rose up against the English government to which they owe allegiance, but we do not persecute them on religious grounds...These laws are so many precautions taken to guarantee the safety and preservation of the state...a just precaution which we are obliged to take in order to ensure that we do not become the victims of the perpetrators of superstition who have pronounced a thousand death sentences against us'.[96]

Samuel D'Assigny performed the same tripartite defence of the Revolutions of 1688–9 in England, Waldensian resistance, and the rule of Protestants in Ireland, in his 1699 Dublin *A Short Relation of the Brave Exploits of the Vaudois*, dedicated to the Huguenot Lord Galway, one of the Lords Justices of Ireland and formerly commander of Huguenot regiments in Piedmont. D'Assigny recalled the 'Popish massacres' in Ireland – but no Protestant massacres of Catholics – declared God's miraculous providence in the preservation of the Waldensians, and urged his new countrymen to imitate their courage if need be. For D'Assigny, it was a 'real betraying the

[96] J. Abbadie, *Défense de la nation Britannique* (1694), 113–7, 229, 309–23, 327–31, 336, 353, 366–75, 424–7, 464, 470; final quotations from Whelan, 'Persecution', 26–7. Whelan's article is an extremely important one on the theme of justification of Protestant domination in the eyes of Huguenots in Ireland, and we await an important book by Tim Harris on the Revolution of 1688–91 in Scotland, Ireland, and England. See also R. P. Hylton, 'The Less-favoured Refuge: Ireland's Nonconformist Huguenots at the Turn of the Eighteenth Century' in K. Herlihy (ed.), *The Religion of Irish Dissent 1650–1800* (Dublin 1996), 83–99.

true Cause of God and Religion, to suffer ourselves to be exterminated and expell'd out of a Countrey and Nation by Papists, when we are in a power to defend ourselves'. These words were voiced about the Waldensians, but D'Assigny then ran consideration of the Waldensians straight into the 'late revolution' in 'these kingdoms' required by 'necessity, self-preservation and the vindication of the laws and religion of a country in visible danger to be overturned' which had driven men, 'a whole nation, and those who are intrusted with the Government as well as the prince, to seek a Remedy in arms'. D'Assigny thus depicted it as exactly the same cause to 'vindicate' the Waldensians and 'our present Government'.[97]

It was not merely Huguenot immigrants to Ireland who defended the Protestant regime in Ireland by citing the examples of Huguenot and Waldensian persecution. Having been one of many Protestant ministers in Ireland imprisoned by the Jacobite regime in 1689, after William's victory, William King became successively dean, bishop, and archbishop in the Church of Ireland. In his Thanksgiving sermon on 16 November 1690 on the occasion of William's departure following the Battle of the Boyne, *Europe's Deliverance from France and Slavery*, King detailed a Europe-wide Catholic design for 'The Extirpation of the Pestilent Northern Heresie', and identified James as 'chiefly' desiring absolute power over his subjects 'that he might compel them to come into the Bosom of his church'. Specifically interpreting James as imitating Louis' actions against the Huguenots, King asked 'What business had he with a standing army, or numerous troops of dragoons, but to employ them as Missionaries to convert his heretical Subjects? The example of France had taught him their use; and that dragooning was a much more effectual way to Reconcile men than Sermons, or Arguments'. Tying together the fate of the Huguenots, the Waldensians, and Irish Protestants, King continued 'by this conspiracy, the Protestants of France are already destroyed: those of Savoy turned out of their country...And as for us in Ireland, I need not tell you how we have been used'. In his popular 1691 *State of the Protestants*, King again asserted that James intended 'prosecuting the same, if not worse methods towards the Protestants in Ireland, that the King of France did with Huguenots in his dominions' and that 'both kings' had the 'same design, to root out not only the Protestants of these kingdoms, but likewise of Europe'. For King, a king could be resisted if he designed to 'destroy and utterly ruin the Protestant religion, the liberty and property of the Subjects' and to alter the 'very frame and constitution of government'. Since 'the immediate end of government is to preserve property', for King government 'dissolves itself' if it attacks property. For King, both Protestants' lives and their estates, largely

---

[97] S. D'Assigny, *Short Relation, passim*, esp. 10–13.

gained in 1641, were under threat from James, and 'Every Roman Catholic King if he thoroughly understands his religion and do in earnest believe the principles of it, is obliged if he be able to destroy his Protestant subjects'.[98]

Locke on the Revolutions of 1688–91

Locke was among those for whom recent Catholic violence against Huguenots and Waldensians provided evidence about the prospects for Protestants in England and Ireland under James II. As we saw in Chapter 1, Locke was deeply concerned about the fate of the Huguenots in the late 1670s and early 1680s, and this only intensified as he sheltered in the Netherlands among huge influxes of Huguenot refugees in the later 1680s and wrote his *Letter Concerning Toleration* in significant part in immediate reaction to the Revocation of the Edict of Nantes. And as early as 1677, Locke had been interested in the late medieval persecution of those considered 'heretical' predecessors of Protestantism in France, the Waldensians and Albigensians, taking notes from a document on the history of the Inquisition against the Waldensians and Albigensians and endorsing a sheet 'waldenses 1677. Out of a manuscript record now at Nismes concerning the condemnation of several Albigenses'. In exile in the Netherlands in the later 1680s and then back in England after 1689, Locke continued to be interested in this manuscript when he studied it at the household of Benjamin Furly and persuaded Limborch to publish it as part of his *History of the Inquisition*. Further indicating his concern with the persecution of the Waldensians, Locke wrote in his 1692 *Third Letter for Toleration* about the preservation of the 'truth' in Piedmont and France through 'many ages' of persecution.[99]

It is unsurprising, then, that Locke's interpretation of events in England and Ireland in 1689–91 was structured within a perspective of an international fight between Protestantism and Catholicism. Locke was among many Protestant Englishmen who saw the war in Ireland in 1689–91 as determining the 'security of Christendom' itself, and the fate of England as poised between a ruler, William, who would protect the 'Protestant Interest' internationally and domestically and prevent 'popery and slavery' in England, and a ruler, James II, who would bring in 'a foreign force' of dragoons to coerce English Protestants as they had formerly coerced other Protestants elsewhere. This was precisely the stark choice that Locke posed in 1690 in writing a manuscript paper on allegiance to the new regime. This referred to the arrival of the Prince of

---

[98] King, *Europe's Deliverance*, 1–10; *idem, State of the Protestants*, 1–5, 12–13, 15, 109, 129–31, 186–91, 217ff., 235, 246.
[99] Lough, 'Locke's Reading', 236n.; Locke, *A Third Letter for Toleration* in *idem, Works* (1823), VI, 444; Chapter 20 below.

Orange as the beginning of 'our delivery from popery and slavery' and saw its completion in 'William's settlement in the throne'. This was for Locke 'the fence set up against popery and France, for King James' name, however made use of, can be but a stale [decoy/pretext] to these two. If ever he return, under what pretences soever, Jesuits must govern and France be our master. He is too much wedded to the one and relies too much on the other ever to part with either. He that has ventured and lost three crowns for his blind obedience to those guides of his conscience and for his following the counsels and pattern of the French king cannot be hoped, after the provocations he has had to heighten his natural aversion, should ever return with calm thoughts and good intentions to Englishmen, their liberties, and religion'. Support for William was depicted by Locke as the only alternative to being a 'contemned popish convert' and being exposed to 'popish rage and revenge'. For Locke, 'we have a war upon our hands of no small weight. We have a potent and vigilant enemy at our doors' and any breach among English Protestants would let 'in him and his dragoons inevitably upon us'. This 'foreign force, enemy to our religion and nation' would make England 'the scene of blood, slaughter, and devastation' with every Protestant Englishman's estate and family ruined, with his 'children stripped and his wife ravished' by the 'insolence and rapine of foreigners with swords in their hands' used against 'those of a contrary religion'. That choice was of a 'French or Irish master' – James II at the moment of composition controlled Catholic Ireland, and was fighting the English with a mixture of Irish and French troops – 'that turns him out of all and forces even his conscience to a compliance'. The 'religion, liberty, safety of himself and his country' were at stake. It was for these reasons, Locke argued in 1690, that there was a need for all to renounce publicly the doctrine which would make them 'an avowed enemy to King William and the present government', the doctrine of *jure divino* monarchy. Such a renunciation would show support for 'that throne on which our peace and religion depends'. Since William's 'rise and right' to coming and to the throne depended on 'the miscarriages of the former reigns', it was required moreover to join in a 'public condemnation and abhorrence of them'. It was required to support the 'justice' of William's armed force to 'recover our oppressed and sinking laws, liberties, and religion', and to reject any distinction between a king *de jure* and *de facto*. It was to such a purpose of making secure William's title that Locke's *Treatises* gave, moreover, their published support in 1689–90.[100]

---

[100] J. Locke, 'Allegiance and the Revolution' in *Locke: Political Essays*, ed. M. Goldie (Cambridge 1997); cf. also Farr and Roberts 'John Locke on the Glorious Revolution: A Rediscovered Document', *Historical Journal* (1985), 385–98; Goldie, 'The Revolution of 1689', 473–564.

3

Protestant religious intolerance in England, c. 1660–c. 1700

As Mark Goldie has declared, 'Restoration England was a persecuting society'.[1] The twenty-five-year reign of Charles II (1660–85) saw several lengthy periods of repression of Protestant nonconformists. After 1662, the four largest Protestant nonconformist denominations of Presbyterians, Independents, Baptists, and Quakers together numbered nearly 200,000 people, or about 4 per cent of the English population, and thus almost exactly the same percentage of the population as were Huguenots in pre-Revocation France.[2] The fiercest persecution of Protestant dissenters in England occurred from 1681 to 1685, and thus in the period of escalating intolerance in France, contributing to parallels being drawn in those years between English and French moves towards absolutism and intolerance. But for most of the period from 1660 to 1681, it was the persecution of Protestant dissenters in England, and not the restrictions placed on Huguenots in France, which involved the more severe punishments for religious dissent, and in these years France was cited by advocates of toleration in England as a country whose relative tolerance should be imitated.[3]

In the early 1660s, the 'high Anglican and Cavalier' Parliament elected at the end of the English Revolution (1642–60) confirmed pre-existing penal statutes against nonconformity and added new statutes that became known as 'the Clarendon Code'. The vast majority of the population were members of the restored national episcopal Church of England, and considerable hostility was directed against dissenters, who were blamed

---

[1] M. A. Goldie, 'The Theory of Religious Intolerance in Restoration England' in Sheils, *Persecution and Toleration*, 331. Cf also Coffey, *Persecution*, ch. 7.

[2] R. Greaves, *John Bunyan and English Nonconformity* (Hambledon 1992), 2; N. Keeble, *The Literary Culture of Nonconformity* (Leicester 1987), 137–8.

[3] For a superb article which powerfully documents this case, see Goldie, 'Huguenot Experience', *passim*.

for having caused the civil wars and Revolution with their bloodshed, heavy taxation, unpopular regicide, unpopular proscription of Anglicanism, and unpopular descent into sectarianism. Hostility towards Protestant dissenters was especially strong against Baptists, repeatedly excoriated as Anabaptists, and against Quakers, who were seen as having 'turned the world upside down' in the Revolution by their challenges to hierarchies in family, church, and state by refusal of 'hat honour' to social superiors, refusal of oaths, address to others as 'thee' and 'thou', allowance of preaching and prophesying by women and the poor, and preaching against luxury and corruption.[4] Hostility to dissenters undergirded Restoration Protestant – Anglican – persecution of their fellow Protestants. Due to Restoration laws against nonconformity, thousands of dissenters were fined, imprisoned, and financially ruined, and hundreds, and perhaps thousands, died.[5] This persecution was interrupted by periods of lax enforcement of the laws, and softened locally by some sympathetic officials and clerics, but official removal of statutory penalties against nonconformity was only provided twice between 1660 and 1685, under royal Declarations of Indulgence of 1662 and 1672, and each Declaration had to be quickly withdrawn due to 'high Anglican and Cavalier' opposition in Parliament. For most of the Restoration, especially after 1681, persecution was severe. Surveying the Restoration in 1687, the Quaker William Penn noted that the English had protested against Catholic persecution in France but 'will not look at home upon greater cruelties'.[6]

As early as January 1661, following a Fifth Monarchist Venner's rising in London supported by only about fifty people but perceived as evidence that religious dissidents still intended to establish a republic, a royal proclamation forbade all meetings of Quakers, Baptists and Fifth Monarchists. Thousands of Quakers and Baptists were quickly imprisoned. Baptists were dragged from bed by armed soldiers in the middle of the

---

[4] See especially J. Morrill (ed.), *The Impact of the English Civil War* (London 1991); *idem*, *Revolution and Restoration* (London 1992); *idem*, *The Nature of the English Revolution*; D. Underdown, *Revel, Riot and Rebellion* (Oxford 1985); T. Harris, 'Lives, Liberties and Estates: Rhetorics of Liberty in the Reign of Charles II' in *idem* (ed.), *The Politics of Religion in Restoration England* (Oxford 1990), 217–42; J. Marshall, 'Some Intellectual Consequences of the English Revolution', *The European Legacy* (2000), 515–30; B. Reay, *Quakers in the English Revolution* (New York 1985); C. Hill, *World Turned Upside Down* (New York 1972); P. Mack, *Visionary Women* (Berkeley 1992).

[5] William Penn estimated that more than 5,000 dissenters died in prison in the Restoration: *Good Advice*, conclusion; Jeremy White, Cromwell's chaplain, estimated the figure for Charles' and James' reigns at 5,000: A. W. Braithwaite, *The Second Period of Quakerism* (Cambridge 1961), 114. These figures are surely too high, but since 450 Quakers alone died, and many other dissenters were imprisoned, it is likely that the death toll in prison alone was above 1,000.

[6] Penn, *Great and Popular Objection*, 9 in Goldie, 'Huguenot Experience', 180.

night, and the Baptist pastor John James was arrested while preaching and sentenced to be hanged, drawn and quartered for treason.[7] Thus began Restoration religious repression. The Quaker Act of 1662 provided penalties including fines, imprisonment, and transportation for attending Quaker meetings. These meetings were raided, and hundreds imprisoned in 1662. The Conventicle Act of 1664 extended the provisions of that Quaker Act to all Protestant dissenters, so that the first offence of worship in a nonconformist meeting could bring a fine of 5 pounds or three months' imprisonment, the second offence a fine of 10 pounds or six months' imprisonment, and the third offence a fine of 100 pounds or transportation. Dissenters unable to pay fines languished in jail; many refused to pay on grounds of conscience and were imprisoned. Due to reconfirmation of an Elizabethan statute of 1593 against conventicles, anyone convicted of separation had to conform to the Church of England within three months or abjure the country, forfeiting land and goods, with death the penalty for failure to comply. While none were actually executed on this basis in the Restoration, twelve Baptists were sentenced to death in 1664 and reprieved only because of royal intervention, and a Quaker merchant was sentenced to death in the 1680s and then reprieved. The imprisoned Baptist John Bunyan spent much of the Restoration expecting execution, imagining himself 'on the Ladder, with the Rope about my neck', and giving himself solace that a large crowd would attend and that his dying words might be useful to convert some sinner.[8] Indefinite imprisonment awaited adults who refused to take the Oaths of Supremacy and Allegiance, especially Quakers and some Baptists who refused oaths on the ground that God forbade them.[9]

The Second Conventicle Act of 1670 significantly increased fines for ministers in the belief that dissent would wither on the vine when left untended. It maintained the significant financial rewards for informing on those who did not come to Anglican worship first instituted under Elizabeth I, rather as informers were later to be used in France in the early 1680s to record names of Huguenots attending proscribed worship. Informers officially gained one third of the goods confiscated in fines, but often helped bailiffs to collect amounts far in excess of the fines. Dissenters' goods were often sold significantly below market value, rather as Huguenots were to have their goods distrained and undersold by dragoons in France from

---

[7] M. Watts, *The Dissenters* (Oxford 1978), I, 223; Whiting, *Studies*, 84, 108; R. Greaves, *Deliver us from Evil* (Oxford 1986), ch. 2 and *passim*.

[8] Harris, 'Lives', 225–6; Keeble, *Literary Culture*, 45; Greaves, *Bunyan*, 101.

[9] C. Horle, *The Quakers and the English Legal System 1660–89* (Pennsylvania 1988); Keeble, *Literary Culture*, 45–6; A. W. Braithwaite, 'Imprisonment upon a Praemunire', *JFHS* (1962), 38–40.

1681.[10] Informers' evidence was almost always accepted, even though it was shown in trials that it was often false. The accused did not even have the chance to testify until appeal, and often had not been told that informers had testified against them and that a warrant had been sworn out in a closed hearing, creating what the Quaker George Whitehead accurately called a 'clandestine conviction'.[11] *To the King and Both Houses...the Suffering Condition of the...Quakers* (?1685) complained: 'These informers being accepted for credible witnesses, yet parties, swearing for their own profit and gain in the absence of the persons prosecuted...we think is...not consistent with common law or justice. As also convicting and fining us upon their depositions, unsummon'd and unheard in our own defence'.[12] The Presbyterian John Howe declared that informers had committed 'multitudes of Perjuries' leading to 'Convictions made without a Jury, and without any Hearing of the Persons accused; Penalties inflicted; Goods rifled; Estates seized and imbezl'd; Houses broken up...without any Cause, or Shadow of a Cause, if only a Malicious Villain could pretend to suspect a Meeting there'.[13] Given the level of hostility to informers, it is unsurprising that crowds sometimes attacked informers. In 1664, it was noted in London that an informer 'dare hardly owne his employment' for fear of being stoned, and when an informer came out of the Exchange in 1670, Richard Boylstone called apprentices to 'pelt him with stones'. At Wrentham in Norfolk, two informers were 'dragged through a foul hog sty, and from thence through a pond'; one of them died.[14] Rhetorical revenge was also common. The 1675, *An Elegy Upon Marsh* invited 'Stay reader! And piss here, for it is said/Under this dirt there's an informer laid'. An informer depicted in a tree observing worship in a field in John Bunyan's 1680 *The Life and Death of Mr Badman* had the threatening words: 'Informer, art thou in the Tree?/Take heed, lest thou there hanged be'.[15]

As Craig Horle has shown, Quakers organised legal efforts to defend their worship against informers. The high church Anglican Sir John

---

[10] See, for instance, *To the King, Lords and Commons in Parliament Assembled, the Case of the People Called Quakers Stated* (1680), 2–3, 39 and *passim*; [G. Whitehead], *A Brief Account of Some of the Late and Present Sufferings of the People called Quakers* (London 1680), *passim*.

[11] Whitehead, *A Brief Account*; 'To the King', *passim*; Horle, *Quakers*, 122–5, 202–3; Whitehead in M. A. Goldie, 'James II and the Dissenters' Revenge', *Bulletin of the Institute for Historical Research* (1993), 53–88 at 58; *idem*, 'The Hilton Gang', *History Today* (1998), x, 26–32; *The Informer's Lecture to his Sons* (1682), 5, in *ibid*.

[12] *To the King...the Suffering Condition of the...Quakers* (1685?), 3, in Horle, *Quakers*, 157n.98.

[13] J. Howe, *The Case of the Protestant Dissenters* (1689), 2, in Keeble, *Literary Culture*, 47.

[14] Harris, *London Crowds*, 72, 182–3; Watts, *Dissenters*, 246.

[15] *An Elegy upon Marsh* (1675); J. Bunyan, *Life and Death of Mr Badman* (1680) both in J. Spurr, *England in the 1670s* (Oxford 2000), 232.

Knightley recorded sorrowfully in 1671: 'Such is the insolence of that party and so resolved they are to fright all persons from being informers of their seditious meetings, that...they arrested the informer with five severall actions, the expense of which must necessarily undo a poor man'.[16] More common were attempts to avoid arrest by concealing worship or ministers. Dissenting churches, such as the Baptist Broadmead Church in Bristol in 1674, appointed members of the congregation to guard the doors 'to watch when...informers or officers were coming' or to crowd the stairs 'soe ye informers might not too Suddainely come in upon us'. Fearful of informers, they made those they did not know who came to their worship sit behind a curtain to prevent identification of the ministers, and built a trapdoor to convey the preacher away before he could be arrested. Their meetings were infiltrated and the trapdoor was needed.[17] Nathaniel Vincent's Presbyterian meeting-house in Southwark was similarly constructed so that worshippers could flee quickly: 'Almost every seat that adjoins to the sides of the Conventicle has a door like the Sally Port of a Fireship to make their escape by. And in each door, a smal Peep-hole...to Ken the Person before they let them in'.[18] Stepney Congregationalists built a concealed room above the ceiling of their meeting-house.[19] Trying to avoid the proscription in the Conventicle Act of meetings of more than five people outside a household, many congregations took to meeting in small 'parcels'; preachers would preach to each in succession. Some congregations knocked holes in walls or had preachers preach from windows in order to allow hearers in adjoining buildings to participate without exceeding the allowed numbers in any one house.[20] Baptists attended the Broadmead meetings in plain clothing so that they did not advertise to onlookers that they were attending worship. Other dissenters pretended to be going to or from work in order to conceal from informers that they were going to worship. The Presbyterian Richard Chantrye recorded going to meetings 'in the twilight to escape the informers, with a Bible in his pocket and a fork on his shoulder'.[21] Many dissenting congregations started worship at 4 am or very late at night in the hopes that they would not be observed. Some meetings were even held from 2 am to sunrise to thwart informers. But even when the Broadmead Church met at 6 am in the house of the Baptist elder Edward Terrill, it was still not safe: a sheriff and his assistants used crowbars on the doors and smashed shutters on the windows in their attempts to gain entry. In the process of persecuting

---

[16] *CSPD* 1671 20–1 in A. Fletcher, 'The Enforcement of the Conventicle Acts' in W. Sheils (ed.), *Persecution and Toleration* (Oxford 1984), 235–46, at 242; Goldie, 'The Hilton Gang', *History Today* (1998), x, 26–32.

[17] Harris, *Politics*, 41; L. McBeth, *The Baptist Heritage* (Nashville 1989), 117–19.

[18] Quotation from Greaves, *Secrets*, 92. [19] Watts, *Dissenters*, 230.

[20] Watts, *Dissenters*, 228–30. [21] Keeble, *Literary Culture*, 49.

nonconformist meetings as though they were conspiratorial meetings, Anglicans thus forced the nonconformists to meet secretly, thereby exacerbating their fears.

Dissenters often tried to avoid informers by meeting in private houses and for worship in woods and meadows. They were, moreover, forced to scatter and meet in woods and meadows when informers and bailiffs arrived at their meeting-place with warrants, or when their meeting-houses had been forcibly closed. Worship was so frequently held in these locations that the Second Conventicle Act expanded the definition of a conventicle from a meeting of four or five adults 'above the members of the household' to include meetings held in 'any place...house, field or place where there is no family inhabiting'. The Independent preacher Joseph Oddy preached in the woods at night and on horseback in order to avoid arrest. The Congregationalist John Flavell held services on a rock in Kingsbridge estuary (near Dartmouth) at low tide.[22] Welsh Quakers were recorded meeting in 'a Barne' and 'by stealth...in a Cave'; Derbyshire Quakers were recorded going into 'a Moore' where they kept their Conventicle'. Others recorded meeting among 'the rocks'.[23] Just as in the early 1680s across the Channel Huguenots were being forced to meet in the woods and meadows after the demolition of their temples, by January 1682 all dissenting congregations in Bristol other than the Quakers were meeting in the fields and woods because their meeting-houses had been destroyed.[24] And meeting in the woods also did not guarantee safety. When the Broadmead Church tried to meet in the woods near Bristol, they were pursued and had to flee; the long chase of some of the worshippers led two to try to swim across the river Avon to safety, leading to the immediate drowning of one, and the later death of the other.[25] And many nonconformists, especially Baptists and Quakers, held that they should meet in public and suffer persecution if that was required. Bessell's Green General Baptist Church in Kent excluded from its membership any who endeavoured to 'make our knees feeble...by creeping into corners, and meeting by fours'. The minister of the Broadmead Baptist Church, George Fownes, wrote from prison – where he died – to encourage his fellow Baptists not to meet in private but to meet publicly until 'made to cease by force'. Quakers preached openly in the streets, offering themselves for arrest. George Fox recorded that the Governor of Dover Castle had told the king that if 'he did imprison them and break them up, they would meet again; and, if he should beat them and knock them down or kill some of them, all was one, they would meet, and not resist again'.[26] The

---

[22] Watts, *Dissenters*, 230–1.   [23] Keeble, *Literary Culture*, 49.   [24] Watts, *Dissenters*, 254.
[25] G. Cragg, *Puritanism in the Age of the Great Persecution* (Cambridge 1957), 40, 42, 161; Watts, *Dissenters*, 255.
[26] *Epistles*, 5, in Braithwaite, *Second Period*, 75; Watts, *Dissenters*, 228.

Presbyterian Richard Baxter recorded in his *Reliquiae Baxterianae* that Quakers 'gloried in their constancy and sufferings' and so met openly 'and were dragged away daily to the common gaol...Abundance of them died in prison, and yet they continued their assemblies still'.[27]

Having been arrested, many dissenters were sentenced to makeshift, unsanitary, and overcrowded prisons. Isaac Pennington, John Whitehead, and sixty or seventy other Quakers were incarcerated in 1660 in a jail which was an old malt-house, 'so decayed that it was scarce fit for a dog house'.[28] Joseph Fuce was incarcerated at Dover Castle in 1660 in 'a dungeon-like hole under the bell-tower, a place very filthy...overrun with maggots and other insects, having no windows for light'.[29] In 1663, the Quaker leader George Fox was imprisoned in Lancaster Castle awaiting trial in a room so smoky he could not see the candle 'and so starved with cold and rain that my body was almost numbed, and my body swelled with the cold'.[30] Many prisons were damp and never cleaned; the prisoners at Leominster recorded that their dungeon became 'so loathsome that those who came to speak to them through the hole of the door could hardly endure the stench for a few minutes'.[31] Major periods of persecution created severe overcrowding. Edward Burrough, who died in Newgate prison in London, wrote in 1662 'here is now near 250 of us prisoners in Newgate, Bridewell, Southwark, and New Prison. In Newgate we are extremely thronged...there is near a hundred in one room'. Thomas Ellwood described the conditions in that room, where hammocks were fastened in 'storeys', below which were beds 'in which the sick and such weak persons as could not get into the hammocks lay'.[32] In 1682 in Bristol, there were so many inmates that prisoners could not lie down to sleep at the same time.[33] Unsurprisingly, diseases spread quickly. In an eight-month period in 1662, twenty-eight Quakers died in Newgate; in 1664–5, during an outbreak of the plague, another seventy-six died there.[34] Richard Flavel and his wife were jailed in London during the plague in 1666 and both quickly succumbed to the disease of their fellow prisoners.[35] Burrough died of a fever aged twenty-eight in 1663, lying on a damp straw mattress next to an open drain.[36] During the plague of 1665, fifty-two Quakers died of the plague in Newgate prison, and another twenty-seven died on a ship awaiting transportation.[37] Leading

---

[27] Watts, *Dissenters*, 228, 255; Horle, *Quakers*.   [28] Braithwaite, *Second Period*, 10.

[29] *Ibid.*, 12.   [30] G. Fox, *Cambridge Journal*, II, 83, in *ibid.*, 36; Cragg, *Puritanism*, 109.

[31] Cragg, *Puritanism*, 92, 96.

[32] Letter of Burrough, 9 November 1662; Ellwood, *Life* (1714), 137–200 in Braithwaite, *Second Period*, 26–8.

[33] Greaves, *Bunyan*, 13.   [34] Horle, *Quakers*, 148.   [35] Cragg, *Puritanism*, 108.

[36] Watts, *Dissenters*, 235.

[37] *GBS* 3, 30, 38–9 in Horle, *Quakers*, 148; S. Porter, *The Great Plague* (Sutton 1999), 67.

Baptist defenders of liberty of conscience such as Thomas Delaune, author of the 1683 *Plea for Non-conformists*, died in prison, as did his wife and two children, who had joined him out of solidarity.[38]

While release after a number of months was common for nonconformist ministers if they gave recognisance for good behaviour, those unwilling to do so stayed in prison for much longer periods, often viewing themselves as 'witnessing' by their suffering. John Bunyan spent no less than twelve years of the Restoration in prison in Bedford, from 1660 to 1672, and was imprisoned again in 1676. He was joined there at various times by many Quakers, Congregationalists, and Baptists. The Quaker William Dewsbury spent nineteen years in jail between 1663 and 1686, while the Quaker Thomas Stordy died in prison in 1684, having spent twenty-four years in prison since his refusal to take the Oath of Allegiance. The Quaker George Fox spent about six years in jail, having been arrested eight times; as he wrote in his *Concerning Persecution in all Ages to this Day* (1682), prisons 'have been made my Home a great part of my time'. The Baptist Abraham Cheare spent most of the period from 1660 to 1668, when he died, in prison. The Presbyterian John Cole spent eight years in prison. The Congregationalist Francis Colcroft spent nine years in prison. The Baptist Francis Bampfield died in 1684, after ten years in prison.[39]

Other dissenters died or were seriously injured as the result of attacks by soldiers and crowds. Quaker collections of their 'Sufferings' record many instances of violence against Quakers, such as some forced to march after their meeting was broken up by the militia in Portsmouth in 1660–1 'which was done with much cruelty, beating and kicking them on their backs' until they reached the town gate and the guards 'joined in',[40] and others being dragged out of a meeting-house in London in 1662 by soldiers who knocked down and trampled on John Trowell, who later died, 'his body being black with bruises'. In 1663, the king's regiment attacked Friends in Horslydown, London, with staves and pikes. Seven years later, in the same location, soldiers threw dirt and mire at the Quakers, and then assaulted them, 'striking and knocking them down without regard to age or sex...until they shed blood from many'. Soldiers and the militia were often commanded to destroy meeting-houses, and such occasions often sparked violence, as in this incident.

---

[38] McBeth, *Baptist Heritage*, 116–7, 119.

[39] Cragg, *Puritanism*, 90, 112–13; A. W. Braithwaite, 'Early Tithe Prosecutions', *JFHS* (1960), 148–56; Horle, *Quakers*; Whiting, *Studies*, 147–50; R. Greaves and R. Zaller, *Biographical Dictionary of British Radicals in the Seventeenth Century* (Brighton 1982), I, 139; Sell, 'Through Suffering', V, 135–6; Watts, *Dissenters*, 229, 238, 254; Fox, *Concerning Persecution*, 341.

[40] Horle, *Quakers*, 52, 127.

Following passage of the second Conventicle Act, Charles II ordered all seats and pulpits in dissenting meeting-houses destroyed. The order went to Sir Christopher Wren as surveyor-general, who therefore spent part of the Restoration building beautiful Anglican churches and St Paul's Cathedral, and part of it commanding the destruction of dissenting churches. In August and September 1670, soldiers pulled down the Ratcliffe meeting-house in Schoolhouse Lane, taking away 'twelve cart loads of doors, windows and floors'. In Bristol, meeting-houses for several nonconformist denominations were destroyed in 1681 and crowds were allowed to haul away whatever they could salvage.[41] More common still was forcing Quakers to meet in the street by padlocking the doors, as at Plymouth in 1676, where soldiers and 'the scum of the people', as the Quakers put it, were recorded as having then pelted them with hot coals, and marched them up and down, 'bedaubing them with filthy excrements'.[42] In 1670, the meeting-house in Colchester was twice 'planked and bricked up', forcing Friends to 'Meet in the Street in the Winter in Rain and Snow'. Quakers who tried to break open the doors so that they could return to worship inside were imprisoned.[43] In the early 1680s, Whig crowds would sometimes rescue conventiclers,[44] but other crowds joined in destroying dissenting meeting-houses and some initiated attacks on dissenting houses. William Kiffin's Baptist meeting-house on St Dunstan's Hill, in the heart of the City of London, was attacked by a 'rude multitude' of the 'looser sort of people' in 1660 with 'all the doors, seats, windows, galleries, and floors etc to the value of about 200 pounds carried away'.[45]

Such direct action against meeting-houses and churches, together with such physical attacks on dissenters, were part of a more widespread atmosphere of threat and of ritualised violence. Oliver Heywood noted that a Yorkshire farmer had declared of the Presbyterian meeting-house that 'if the house was his he would burn us out'. A mob at Wiscanton burned the nonconformist minister in effigy. In Suffolk, an old hog trough was called the 'phanaticks pulpit' and burned. The pelting of Quaker crowds with hot coals involved symbolic as well as real violence. As Bernard Capp has recently argued, threats of 'burning' were directed against those 'seen as likely to divide or contaminate the community' in a culture in which burning was a central action against 'pollution'.[46]

Natalie Zemon Davis has pointed out that in sixteenth-century France alternative forms of worship and belief (of Catholics and Protestants)

---

[41] Cragg, *Puritanism*, 38–9; Watts, *Dissenters*, 254; Horle, *Quakers*, 127–8, 139–40.
[42] In Horle, *Quakers*, 140.   [43] Keeble, *Literary Culture*, 73.
[44] Harris, *London Crowds*, 182; Greaves, *Bunyan*, 219.   [45] Harris, *London Crowds*, 52.
[46] B. Capp, 'Arson, Threats of Arson, and Incivility' in Harrison and Slack (eds.), *Civil Histories* (Oxford 2000), 206.

often produced incidents of violence as they enacted expressions of the sacred community against the 'polluters' of worship, involving ritual desacralisations in order to demonstrate the lack of power in the other religion. Among the acts were the leaving by Protestants of excrement on holy-water basins and the pelting of Protestants with dung.[47] Religious festivals in Restoration England similarly provided the source of much violence, and the repeated use of 'dung' or 'mire' surely involved not merely an object to hand on the streets but also ritual desacralisation and invocation of the 'pollution' felt to come from dissenters. In 1661, the Huntingdon Quaker shopkeeper Robert Raby and his friends had 'Dirt and Mire cast upon them' because he had kept his shop open on Christmas Day; Quakers believed Christmas Day a pagan festival and Anglicans a central day of worship and festivity. Just before the Restoration a 'rabble' was recorded attacking the worship of the Quakers in Sawbridgeworth, Hertfordshire, throwing 'Showers of Stones, Dirt, rotten Eggs, human Dung and Urine' into the meeting-house. Quakers refused to take off their hats to alleged social superiors, identifying such deference as due to God alone. The crowds took the Quakers' hats, filled them with Dirt, and put them back on their heads.[48] Quaker meetings in the streets were responded to by violence that included the pelting of worshippers with dung; Whitehead's account of an attack on Plymouth Quakers stressed that they had been pelted with 'nasty filthy excrements'.[49]

Davis has drawn our attention to funerals and burials as occasions of violence in France as they symbolised and enacted the division of the sacred community, while Philip Benedict has told the story of a Protestant whose funeral in Rouen in 1568 was interrupted by a Catholic mob which dragged away the cadaver in order to prevent the defiling of the holy ground that such a burial would have involved; for Benedict, few events of the period 'demonstrate more strikingly that the Catholics came to view the Huguenots as agents of pollution'.[50] Similarly, contestations over funerals and burials were frequent in Restoration England. At Amersham in 1665, a Quaker funeral was disrupted by a crowd of constables 'and rude fellows' who assaulted the bearers and threw the coffin to the ground.[51] At Croft in Lincolnshire, a General Baptist's body was removed

---

[47] N. Z. Davis, 'The Rites of Violence' in *idem, Culture and Society in Early Modern France* (Stanford 1975), 152–87, esp. 180.

[48] Huntingdon Monthly Meeting Sufferings Book 1656–1793, Cambs RO R59/25/3/1; Besse, *Sufferings*, I, 241 both quoted in W. Stevenson, 'Social Integration' in M. Spufford (ed.), *The World of Rural Dissenters 1520–1725* (Cambridge 1995), 360–87, at 366.

[49] Whitehead, *A Brief Account*, 24.

[50] P. Benedict, *Rouen during the Wars of Religion* (Cambridge 1981), 64.

[51] Watts, *Dissenters*, 233–4.

from the parish burial ground, dragged on a sledge, and left outside his home. In Breconshire, a young Baptist woman was dug up out of the churchyard and 'buried at the cross-roads like a common suicide' – a location which declared her outside the boundaries of the sacred community. Similar in its symbolism, the Muggletonian widow Mary Cundy of Orwell, Cambridgeshire, was excommunicated in 1682, then given the 'burial of an Asse' in 1686.[52]

It is impossible to put an exact figure on Protestant dissenters who were financially 'ruined', but Tim Harris has shown that many thousands were fined and that since many of these were tradesman or labourers, often not only 'sheep, cows, horses, hogs, wool' but also 'pewter, pans and pots' and in some cases even sheets, pillowcases, and clothes were taken to pay the fines.[53] The heel-maker Thomas Cooper of Beford 'a poor man, and living only upon making heels and lasts' had 'three cart loads of wood' distrained. A blacksmith lost his shovels and anvil.[54] William Bingley, a prominent London Quaker, recorded that he had initially had goods taken in October 1685 'so much as my coals and candles and mine and my wife's wearing clothes', but the distraint was then made more threatening by the taking of the keys of his house and for four days inviting others to sit in it, 'smoking and drinking', before they left in a final volley of threats to both family and servants and the taking of dishes, chairs, stools, and the kitchen table. The parallel with distraint of Huguenots' goods by dragoons was not lost on dissenters in England: one work recorded that many dissenters had 'had their Houses broken open by the Informers, Constables, and other Officers, who, like so many Dragoons, have for a long time kept the Possession, plundering and stealing, as well as distreining their Goods'.[55]

The taking of dissenters' tools left individuals complaining about their loss of trades and of the 'looms, leads, and tenters' which were the 'upholders of their families'.[56] Tithe-impropriators could sue Quakers for treble damages, and take property to pay the costs. John Moon of Cabus was thus fined treble costs in 1683. To pay the fine, two acres of wheat, oats and barley were seized, his barn was broken into and hay and turf taken, and pewter, brass and bedding was taken 'leaving him very naked, not a bed to lie on'.[57] Ministers faced the most serious fines under the terms of the Second Conventicle Act and some were ruined. John Miller, pastor of the General

[52] Stevenson, 'Social Integration', 386–7; Watts, *Dissenters*, 233–4. For an interpretation of the symbolism of burial (of a bull) at a crossroads, see D. Sabean, *Power in the Blood* (Cambridge 1984).

[53] Harris, 'Lives'; also Horle, *Quakers*, 132–6.   [54] Watts, *Dissenters*, 232.

[55] Keeble, *Literary Culture*, 76; Horle, *Quakers*, 132–3.   [56] Harris, 'Lives'.

[57] *Transcripts*, III, 15–16, in A. B. Anderson, 'Sociology of Persecution', *Journal of Religious History* (1977), 259.

Baptist Church at Minterne in Dorset had 'four hundred sheep, twenty cows, seven horses, six or seven hogs', 'all the hay, corn, and wool of the last year's produce', and even his family's own malt and hops taken in 1684. Robert Collins of Devon was fined repeatedly until he fled to the Netherlands 'to maintain his person and family in their distracted, shattered condition'.[58]

At least 11,000 Quakers were imprisoned during the Restoration, and since the incarceration of employers left many employees without work, further thousands suffered. Imprisonment was particularly devastating if it occurred at crucial moments of the agricultural calendar. As early as 1660, Bridget Fell was worrying that 'if they keep men in custody that should till the ground, the time of seeding being now, it cannot be expected that we should be able to maintain them in prison,[and] hire our tillage at home'.[59] The threat to sustenance posed by imprisonment of the head of the household may have lessened the punishments some magistrates meted out, but a Justice of the Peace was recorded as telling the wife of the imprisoned Wisbech Quaker William Williams in 1664 that 'If she wanted Food, she might take her children, fry them for stakes, and eat them'.[60]

The Second Conventicle Act took away security of property from dissenters by the processes of statutory law, based on the activities of informers whose evidence was often perjured but accepted by biased magistrates, in the administration of a 'justice' by judges who came increasingly to be referred to by dissenters derisively as 'called a justice'. It is, then, unsurprising that the Second Conventicle Act was called the 'horrid law...most principally grievous to us' by which 'our Magna Carta was torn in Pieces' by the Presbyterian John Howe. In a private letter to his nephew William Popple – who was in 1689 to be the translator of Locke's *Letter Concerning Toleration* into English – Andrew Marvell called the Second Conventicle Act a 'terrible bill' and 'the quintessence of arbitrary malice'.[61] Many dissenters wrote of the denial of their rights as a denial of English liberties, of the ancient constitution, and of the Magna Carta. George Whitehead's 1680 *A Brief Account* declared that Quakers faced the 'arbitrary determination of one Justice of the Peace' who was 'both Judge and Jury' and that if an appeal was lodged it was to be laid 'before the Parties themselves' who often overawed juries or were 'forced to bring in such a verdict' as pleased judges being 'expressly against the constitution of our English government, and the ancient fundamental laws

---

[58] Watts, *Dissenters*, 232.
[59] Braithwaite, *Second Period*, 10; W. Stevenson,'The Social and Economic Status of Post-Restoration Dissenters 1660–1725' in M. Spufford (ed.), *The World of Rural Dissenters 1520–1725* (Cambridge 1995), 332–59, e.g. 338–9, 357–8.
[60] Quoted in Stevenson, 'Social Integration', 367.
[61] J. Howe, *The Case of the Protestant Dissenters* (1689), 2, in Keeble, *Literary Culture*, 47; Fletcher, 'Conventicle'; Keeble, *Literary Culture*, 80.

of the Kingdom, which did expressly forbid the seizure of men's Liberties and Estates, without a lawful judgment of their peers'.[62]

Some justices encouraged informers and even accompanied constables and bailiffs. The Suffolk magistrate Edmund Bohun recorded his 'great contentment' at convictions in 1673, writing that he had 'first raised up the informers and then assisted them with much labour and expense'.[63] In 1679, it was reported that 'the Justices and their men, the informers and witnesses. . .ate and drank in one afternoon to the value of 50/-' after raiding the Quaker shoemaker James Harrison.[64] George Whitehead's 1680 *A Brief Account* itemised among its 'most remarkable Instances of Injustice and cruelty' that in one incident 'A Justice beat several [Quakers] pulling them by the hair of the Head, and drew his knife in a great passion' before being restrained. And Whitehead alleged that another Justice had become so frustrated by his inability to prevent Quaker meetings that he went 'and beat several of them', knocking one to the ground with a blow to the head whose effects persisted until his death several months later.[65] Some magistrates ensured immunity for such violence by constables and bailiffs. Thomas Masters accompanied his officers in Cirencester in 1670 in an attack on the Quakers that saw some thrown down the stairs, one of whom, Elizabeth Hewlings, then died. Masters packed the coroner's jury with his own tenants, who declared she had died from 'God's visitation', while his clerk informed Quaker witnesses who attempted to testify otherwise that they 'did not deserve the benefit of the law'. In another case, a Quaker was recorded as 'pistoled' to death, but the coroner and town clerk picked a jury of 'tenants and vassals' of the mayor and aldermen, and a not guilty verdict followed. It became impossible for dissenters to believe that an impartial execution of justice was being offered in England.[66]

Tim Harris has importantly stressed the resonance to dissenters of a rhetoric of liberty and property being protected by an impartial law.[67] Such rhetoric contrasted English liberty based on fundamental laws and juries with tyranny imaged through the Spanish Inquisition and based on the excessive power of judges, never more importantly than when in 1670 William Penn challenged his prosecution for riot for holding a Quaker religious meeting in the streets. Penn declaimed to the jury that 'if these ancient fundamental laws which relate to liberty and property, and are not limited to particular persuasions in matters of religion, must not be

---

[62] Whitehead, *A Brief Account*, preface.
[63] F. Bate, *Declaration of Indulgence* (London 1908), 134; Fletcher, 'Conventicle', 243.
[64] *Transcripts of the Lancashire Sufferings Records*, II, 77, in Anderson, 'Sociology', 247–62, at 257.
[65] Whitehead, *A Brief Account*, 31–2, 91.
[66] Whitehead, *A Brief Account*, 83, 91; Horle, *Quakers*, 130.   [67] Harris, 'Lives'.

indispensably maintained and observed, who can say he hath right to the coat upon his back? Certainly our liberties are openly to be invaded, our wives to be ravished, our children slaved, our families ruined and our estates led away in triumph, by every sturdy beggar and malicious informer, as their trophies but our pretended forfeits for conscience' sake'. The jury refused to convict Penn, leading to a remarkable declaration from the Recorder, Sir John Howell, that until then he had never understood the 'reason of the policy and prudence of the Spaniards, in suffering the Inquisition among them. And certainly it will never be well with us, till something like the Spanish Inquisition be in England'. When the jury steadfastly refused to convict, he imprisoned the jury, and kept Penn and his associate Meade in prison for failure to pay a fine for keeping their hats on in court. It took a year before other judges reviewing the case reversed the punishments inflicted *on the jury*, indicating clearly to many dissenters and moderate Anglican opponents of intolerance how precarious were the rights and liberties not merely of dissenters but also of juries under the law administered by justices willing to declare the Spanish Inquisition a desirable model of authority, and simultaneously how essential juries were to restrain such judges – a message that was to resurface even more urgently in and after 1681 as juries became the only security against royal absolutism being established by royally appointed judges.[68]

The peak of Restoration intolerance: the 1680s

Restoration persecution of Protestant dissenters reached its height in the early 1680s. In 1682, the Broadmead Baptist Church in Bristol calculated that of the nine separate periods of persecution since the Restoration, the current one was the most severe.[69] Reflecting on this period in the late 1680s, the radical Whig nonconformist pamphleteer Henry Care argued that Anglican clerics were the 'Authors of the late Violences towards Dissenters' who 'by Concert throughout the Nation both in Pulpits, Prints, and Practices, instigate and warrantise those Outrages'. Care was correct that many Anglican clerics helped to lead the call for persecution in the early 1680s. The Bishop of Exeter was one among many who described the corporations and boroughs in 1681 as 'nurseries of faction, sedition, and disloyalty' and demanded that the laws 'restraining Nonconformists from entering in corporations' were 'put in execution'. His prebendary, Francis Fulwood, preached to the congregation of the cathedral against 'schism or separation, yea sedition and faction' and then promptly signed warrants for

---

[68] Braithwaite, *Second Period*, 68–74; Keeble, *Literary Culture*, 86–7.
[69] *Broadmead Records*, 229, 253, in Watts, *Dissenters*, 228; Goldie, 'The Hilton Gang'.

the distraint of dissenters' goods as the 'severest of the laws' was put into force against 'the sectaries and fanatics'.[70] And these Exeter voices were raised as part of a chorus of clerical demands for prosecution of dissent. Many Anglican preachers asked magistrates to 'give the law the swinge of its power' in these years, as John Rainsthorp put it in the sermon *Loyalty Recommended* in 1684. John Allen's assize sermon at Chester in 1682 concurred, arguing bluntly that 'those that pretend to complain of arbitrary power, they, methinks, ought to have law enough, their belly full, that they may complain for something'. Miles Barne called in an assize sermon at Hertford in 1684 for a 'constant, vigorous and resolute execution of all the laws' against dissent.[71]

Thus, in England, as in France in the early 1680s, clerical promotion of the use of force against religious dissenters was important. In these years, however, an even greater impetus towards persecution came from the court. Charles II increasingly spoke of all Protestant dissenters as 'fanatics', and in September 1681 declared that he would 'have all the laws put in execution and none of the dissenters spared'.[72] Parliamentary campaigns for Exclusion in 1679–81 had drawn significant and disproportionate support from among the dissenting population. Dissenters were prominent in support for the Whigs in elections in 1679–81 and in petitions for the sitting of the multiply prorogued Exclusion Parliaments. Quakers sent out 'general letters' to Friends in 1681 to support 'moderate men such as...are against persecution and popery and that deport themselves tenderly towards our friends'. Leading Whigs reached out to nonconformist voters. In response, Charles desired to punish dissenters for their support for the campaign to exclude or limit the power of his brother James. His desire to punish dissenters increased still further as plans for armed resistance in 1682–3 were discovered which drew significant and disproportionate support from Protestant dissenters, with Baptists and some Congregationalists prominent amongst the small number who supported resistance in 1682–3, although only one Presbyterian (the 'freethinking' John Hampden) and no Quakers seem to have been involved in supporting resistance, and most supporters of the plans for resistance seem to have been Whig Anglicans rather than dissenters.[73]

---

[70] Tanner MSS 36, fo. 91 in Lacey, *Dissent*, 152; Goldie, 'James II and the Dissenters' Revenge', 74.
[71] All in Harris, 'Lives', 234–5.   [72] Speck, *Reluctant*, 40; Harris, 'Lives'.
[73] Lacey, *Dissent*, 93–4, 106, 108–9, 113, 117, 158–9; Scott, *Restoration*, 128–38, 155–61; Knights, *Politics*; Greaves, *Secrets*; Ashcraft, *Revolutionary Politics*; see pp. 121–4 below. In making the important point that Whig support for Exclusion in 1678–81 came disproportionately and significantly from dissenters and that radical Whig support for resistance in 1682–3 also came significantly from Baptists and Congregationalists, it is important to register that most support for opposition to the king in 1678–81 and most apparent support for the plans for resistance in 1682–3 came from Whig Anglicans who were sympathetic to the plight of dissent and desirous of toleration for dissenters. This is what one should expect when only

From 1681, the Privy Council called for vigorous enforcement of the penal laws, and magistrates who failed to prosecute were publicly rebuked. In December 1681 the Privy Council rebuked Surrey justices for failing to enforce the laws and ordered Middlesex judges to put them into effect against Papists, Quakers, Presbyterians, Baptists, 'and such like other vermin, which swarm in the land'.[74] As Ronald Hutton has written, from 1681 to 1685 'Any man ambitious for royal favour now knew that he might obtain it by turning savagely upon the local presbyterians, sectaries, or Quakers. The persecution which followed was, for all these groups, the most sustained of the reign and indeed, in history'.[75] Henry Care noted ironically in his *Courant* that England was sheltering French Protestant Calvinist refugees, and yet prosecuting English Protestant dissenters of similar views in Bristol: 'I could not but snicker the other day to see a parcel of wooden-shoed French heretics that had fled for shelter, how sillily they looked when they saw a parcel of English calvinists dragged out of their meetings and hurried to the gaol'.[76]

Importantly resisting this royal pressure for persecution, many individual magistrates, some corporation officials, and the Whig grand juries of London up to mid-1682 sought to mitigate or forestall punishments of dissenters. The Whig sheriffs of London warned nonconformists in early 1682 when they were about to be arrested, and the Whig grand jury returned an ignoramus verdict in early 1682 when the Presbyterian Nathaniel Vincent was prosecuted for holding a seditious conventicle. As late as January 1682, the Lord Mayor Sir John Moore was even persuaded to hand to the king a petition in defence of conventicles that had been subscribed by several thousand citizens.[77] But those who thus resisted prosecution of dissenters were then themselves attacked by the court. In 1681, the Whig-dominated Parliament had voted that dissenters should not be prosecuted, and the Whig-dominated grand jury had agreed, but by the time that the Whig pamphleteer Langley Curtis republished the Parliamentary vote that 'they ought not to prosecute the Dissenters' in his *Impartial Protestant Mercury* of 7 February 1682, the

some 4 per cent of the population were Protestant dissenters but when the political nation was electing a majority of 'Whig' members of Parliament in the contested elections of 1678–81. G. de Krey, 'London Radicals and Revolutionary Politics' in *The Politics of Religion in Restoration England*, ed. T. Harris, P. Seaward and M. Goldie (Blackwell 1990), 133–62. The terms Whig and Tory did not come into prevalent use until 1681 but the positions taken were in process of formation earlier and so I do not attempt here to use an awkward circumlocution to designate those who in 1681 were to be called Whigs. Ashcraft's *Revolutionary Politics* tends to overstate the significance of dissenters and to understate the important of Whig Anglican tolerationist sympathy for dissent.

74 Quoted in C. F. Mullett, 'Toleration and Persecution in England 1660–89', *Church History* (1949), 18–43, at 35.

75 Hutton, *Charles II*, 424.   76 *Courant*, 5, 136, in Kitchin, *L'Estrange*, 351.

77 Harris, *London Crowds*, 184.

pendulum of power had swung towards the Tories. Both he and the grand jury were brought before the Bar of King's Bench at the order of the Attorney General. In order to save themselves, the grand jury presented Curtis and he was prosecuted.[78] Leading 'Whigs' in the period of Exclusion had included Latitudinarian Anglican clerics such as John Tillotson and Edward Fowler, both close to Shaftesbury and Locke, and they preached against persecution in the early 1680s and faced hostility from their high church Anglican superiors. As Burnet later recorded, 'such of the clergy as would not engage in that fury were cried out on as the betrayers of the church, and as secret favourers of the dissenters'.[79] Such Latitudinarians were significant to Locke as his closest friends among clergy both then and later, and many of his attitudes were very close to theirs.[80] Fowler's A Sermon Preached before the Judges (1681) and A Discourse of Offences (1683) were pleas against Anglican persecution; he was prosecuted by his fellow Anglicans and suspended.[81] The Dorset vicar Samuel Bold, later defender of James' toleration and then of Locke's Reasonableness of Christianity, wrote a 1682 Plea for Moderation towards Dissenters; he was prosecuted in the church courts.[82] Daniel Whitby, later a correspondent of Locke, wrote against the 'stiff imposers of unnecessary things' in The Protestant Reconciler (1682); his work was condemned to the flames in 1683 by the 'Decree and Judgment of Oxford University'.[83]

As the period from 1681–5 wore on, those who resisted the drive towards prosecution of dissenters were increasingly removed from power in royal revocations of corporation charters: indeed, their very support for nonconformity when Charles had turned decisively to repression of dissenters was a major part of the motivation for Charles' campaign of removal of corporation charters in 1682–5 and for his restriction of electors to Tory Anglicans. By late 1682, the new Tory sheriffs in London were enforcing laws against conventicles, and controlled appointments to the grand juries to facilitate prosecution in London. Already in 1681, dissenting religious meetings had been vigorously suppressed in Salisbury, Leicestershire, Essex, Norfolk, Middlesex, Southwark, Stepney, Bristol, and Canterbury. In some cases, dissenters were assaulted. By 1682, suppression had extended to Cornwall,

[78] Kitchin, L'Estrange, 296–7.

[79] Burnet, History of His Own Time, II, 290 in Spurr, The Restoration Church (Yale 1991), 83.

[80] Marshall, Locke.

[81] E. Fowler, The Great Wickedness, and Mischievous Effects of Slandering (London 1685); Harris, London Crowds, 223; Spurr, Restoration, 84; M. A. Goldie and J. Spurr, 'Politics and the Restoration Paris: Edward Fowler and the Struggle for St Giles Cripplegate', English Historical Review (1994), 572–96.

[82] Spurr, Restoration, 83; Goldie, 'Huguenot Experience', 186–8; J. O'Higgins, Anthony Collins (The Hague 1970), 10.

[83] Gillett, Burned Books, II, 505–6; D. Wootton, Divine Right and Democracy (London 1986).

Devon, Gloucestershire, Hertfordshire, Dorset, the Isle of Ely, Nottingham, and Newcastle. By late 1682, London had finally been forced to join the bandwagon of fierce persecution.[84]

By late 1682, then, the Crown was aggressively excluding dissenting votes in local elections for crucial offices such as the shrievalty and the Lord Mayor of London, and aggressively calling for the prosecution of dissenting worship. Assize judges often encouraged the actions against nonconformity. The assize judge in York in April 1682 told the mayor and aldermen on the bench that 'if a Quo Warranto were brought against them' their charter would be forfeit for 'misgovernment and for suffering conventicles to be held'.[85] Justices in Gloucestershire in 1682 accused dissenters at the quarter sessions of living

in open disobedience and contempt of his Majesties Lawes by withdrawing his Majesties Subjects from their natural obedience...and corrupting them in their principles and religion as also by holding seditious Conventicles...in such great numbers as may be of dangerous consequence to the peace and tranquility of his Majesties Government.[86]

In Taunton in April 1684, Chief Justice George Jeffries called for a severe execution of the laws and told local justices 'that if they would not do it, he would put in them that should'.[87] In many areas, local authorities joined in the demand for punishment of dissenters. The Wiltshire grand jury accused dissenters of terrorising loyal subjects in 1681. The loyal address of Kent in March 1683 condemned not merely 'fanaticism' but 'all such as pretend to moderation in execution of the laws, where the government is apparently assaulted'. The jurymen of Devon added their voice in 1683: nonconformist preachers were responsible for the 'Rye House Plot' and all should be punished.[88] Halifax was later to note that it became a maxim in these years that to be a 'dissenter' was to be a 'rebel'. By October 1684, it was reported to the Earl of Sunderland that 'in general all the Dissenters lie...under the lash of the penal statutes'.[89] By December 1684, it was reported that Charles II had even begun to order the use of dragoons: 'The King being given to understand that a dangerous conventicle continues to be kept at Oldbury...and that several hundreds resort thither, many whereof are armed, has ordered two troops of dragoons to be quartered in the neighbourhood to be assistant in suppressing the said dangerous meeting and apprehending the offenders, whom he would have proceeded against with all severity according to law'.[90]

---

[84] Greaves, *Secrets*, 91ff.
[85] Leeds RO Mexborough MSS 20/14, 8 Apr 1682 in Speck, *Reluctant*, 40.
[86] PRO SP 29/418/26.1 in Greaves, *Bunyan*, 219.   [87] *GBS* 6, 125, in Horle, *Quakers*, 258.
[88] Greaves, *Bunyan*, 219; D. Ogg, *England in the Reign of Charles II* (Oxford 1934), II, 653.
[89] *CSPD* 1684–5,187–8, in Lacey, *Dissent*, 163. Keeble, *Literary Culture*, 29.
[90] *CSPD* 1684–5, 237, quoted in J. Miller, *The Glorious Revolution* (London 1983), 98; Ogg, *England*, II, 653–4.

By 1685, over 1,500 Quakers alone were in prison in England. In the Winter of 1683–4 – the harshest winter ever recorded in Britain – over 100 dissenters died in prison.[91] Many Quaker meeting-houses were pulled down or nailed shut, forcing them to meet in the streets through the 'great, severe, and long frost and snow in the year 1683...when the river Thames was so frozen up that horses, coaches, and carts could pass to and fro on it'. Such meetings often ended after two or three sentences of the ministers by trained bands who arrested the preachers and worshippers and sent them to prison.[92] When children attempted to keep meetings going in the absence of their incarcerated parents, some of the children were put in the stocks, beaten, whipped, or imprisoned.[93] The 'Morning Meeting' of the Quakers in 1684 issued a declaration noting that they had suffered 'the most of any people in the nation. We have been counted as sheep for the slaughter, persecuted and despised, beaten, stoned, wounded, stocked, whipped, imprisoned...cast into dungeons and noisome vaults, where many have died'.[94] Although some Baptists and Congregationalists had probably been part of plans for resistance against the king in 1682–3, there is no evidence of Quaker involvement. On 8 August 1683 the Quakers presented to the king an address which asserted that they were 'clear in the sight of God, angels, and men from all hellish plots and traiterous conspiracies, and from all murderous designs against the King, his brother, or any person on earth whatsoever'. It was signed by over 1,000 people. The 1684 Declaration of the Morning Meeting, penned by George Fox and Richard Hubberthorne, stressed that the Quakers eschewed violence and armed resistance, and that Quakers had been 'found in no plots nor guilty of any sedition'. Quaker pacifism and commitment to witnessing for the truth by suffering martyrdom if necessary had taken hold. Neither their petition nor their declaration helped to abate their persecution in the early 1680s, but they may have helped to persuade James II, who had already intervened to help the Quaker William Penn escape persecution in the 1670s, that Quakers were indeed tolerable.[95]

In 1681–5, as throughout the Restoration, Quakers suffered disproportionately, but in these years all dissenters were targeted. By March 1682, the prisons in Bristol were overflowing with incarcerated dissenters – including not just eighty-five Quakers, but also fifty-two Presbyterians.[96] The

---

[91] G. Manley, '1684: The Coldest Winter in the English Historical Record', *Weather* (1975), 382–8 in Porter, *Great Plague*, 173. Braithwaite, *Second Period*, 109.

[92] G. Whitehead, *Christian Progress*, 543–4, in Braithwaite, *Second Period*, 110.

[93] Braithwaite, *Second Period*, 102–3.   [94] Braithwaite, *Second Period*, 12–13.

[95] Braithwaite, *Second Period*, 12–13; Whiting, *Studies*, 179; Greaves, *Secrets*; idem, 'Shattered Expectations? George Fox, the Quakers, and the Restoration State 1660–85', *Albion* (1992) 237–59.

[96] Greaves, *Secrets*, 92–3.

Congregationalist minister Oliver Heywood declared that God had 'set up the right hand of the enemy' because 'Never were meetings so universally broken in London, in all cities, towns, countreys' with 'Ministers driven into corners'.[97] Continuing the policy of prosecuting ministers particularly fiercely, in November 1681 eleven dissenting ministers prosecuted under the Recusancy Act were fined the staggering sum of 4,840 pounds (at a time when a gentleman's annual income might be only a few hundred pounds). Mainly Presbyterians and Independents, those fined included Shaftsbury's chaplain Robert Ferguson; the leading Independent to whom Ferguson had been an assistant, John Owen; and several Presbyterian leaders, such as Edmund Calamy, who was later to write a defence of moderate nonconformity which Locke would praise highly in the early eighteenth century.[98] And it was not merely ministers who were targeted in these years but all dissenting congregations. In 1683, in Bristol fines totalling 16,440 pounds were levied on 191 Quakers, and in Suffolk in 1685 exchequer processes against Quakers totalled 33,300 pounds. In the early 1680s, 500 serge-makers lost work as a result of the imprisonment of their dissenting employers in Devon, and 200 people lost work due to the imprisonment of 1 Quaker woollen manufacturer in Suffolk. As a Quaker petition to the Taunton assizes of 1685 complained, they were being 'exposed to great sufferings, in our persons, liberties and estates'.[99]

1685-7

While James II was to attempt in the second half of his reign to establish toleration for both Catholics and Protestant dissenters, and while his first significant moves towards that policy were made in 1686 as he began to release individual Protestant dissenters from prison soon after being crowned, nonetheless many Quakers languished in jail until Spring 1686 – over a year into James' reign – and it was not until August 1686 that James intervened to provide legal stays in cases against Baptists. Even after their release in March 1686, Quakers received only partial protection; the later 1680s saw the greatest numbers of Quakers fined in Lancashire for non-payment of the tithe of the entire Restoration.[100] As John Miller has noted, 'more conventiclers were convicted in Middlesex in six months in 1686 than there were papists convicted of recusancy in 1679, the worst year of the [Popish] Plot'.[101] In the first months of James' reign, leading Presbyterians were included in the prosecution of dissent. In 1685–6, Richard Baxter served seventeen months in prison, having been prosecuted for seditious libel for

[97] *The Rev. Oliver Heywood 1630–1702: His Autobiography, Diaries, Anecdotes, and Event Books*, ed. J. Horsfall Turner (4 vols. 1882), II, 223, in Speck, *Reluctant*, 40.
[98] Greaves, *Secrets*, 93 and note 14.   [99] Harris, 'Lives', 224–7.
[100] Ashley, *James II*, 185; Anderson, 'Sociology', 251.   [101] Miller, *Popery*, 205.

having written a criticism of the bishops of the Church of England – a charge made out by excising the references of various of his comments to the bishops of the Church of Rome so that they would appear to have been aimed at the Anglican episcopate.[102] In May 1686, the Dutch ambassador noted that soldiers had 'disturbed a presbyterian conventicle' in London.[103] In the summer of 1686, there was severe prosecution of conventicles and meetings 'made up of such as go ordinarily to Church', as the Presbyterian Morrice reported, and in late 1686 Morrice described the Church of England as desiring to 'fall upon and utterly break in pieces all such Dissenters'.[104]

There was much reason from James' record and contemporary actions to believe in 1685–6 that he would not support toleration for Protestant nonconformists. Required to be out of England during the Exclusion Crisis, in Scotland in 1680 James had violently suppressed field conventicles, using torture as well as executions, allowed under Scottish law. The high church Archbishop Sancroft thought he shared his father Charles I's concern for the church.[105] Back in England from 1682, James was involved in ecclesiastical promotions that aided the Tory reaction against dissent.[106] The Monmouth rebels of 1685 demanded that 'all the Penal laws against Protestant dissenters be repealed' and received significant nonconformist support; James' reaction was to order the arrest of 'disaffected and suspicious persons, particularly all nonconformist ministers'.[107] James initially confirmed the Tory–Anglican representation in Parliament secured by Charles' remodelling of corporation charters in the 1680s to remove dissenters. The confirmation of the Charter of Berwick in September 1686, for instance, invoked the king's duty 'to defend the Church of England in the beauty of holiness against factious sectaries and separatists'.[108] James told Archbishop Sancroft and Bishop Turner at his accession that 'he would never give any sort of countenance to Dissenters, knowing it must needs be faction and not religion if men could not be content to meet five besides their own family, which the law dispenses with'.[109] While James began widespread release of

---

[102] L. Levy, *Blasphemy* (Chapel Hill 1993), 213.　　　[103] Lacey, *Dissent*, 176.

[104] Lacey, *Dissent*, 177.

[105] R. Beddard, 'The Restoration Church' in J. R. Jones (ed.), *The Restored Monarchy 1660–88* (London 1979), 174 ; Smiles, *Huguenots*, 183 (on Scotland).

[106] R. A. Beddard, 'The Commission for Ecclesiastical Promotions 1681–4: An Instrument of Tory Reaction', *Historical Journal* (1967), 11–40.

[107] Keeble, *Literary Culture*, 61.

[108] P. Halliday, *Dismembering the Body Politic* (Cambridge 1998), 238. Not until July 1687 did James dismiss the Tory–Anglican parliament of 1685. Miller argues (*James II*, 155) that James slowly and painfully rethought his attitudes towards dissent in 1686 and was genuinely tolerationist only in 1687–8.

[109] Miller, *James II*, 120.

dissenters in Spring 1686, not until April 1687 did he institute in England his full toleration of Protestant dissenters and Catholics by Declaration of Indulgence. Until that date, persecution in England was causing those in the religious minority to suffer at least imprisonment for their religious convictions; in 1681–5, as in France and Piedmont in 1685–6, many in England had died for these convictions.

Locke's responses to the persecution of Protestant dissent in England

In the early 1690s, in his *Third Letter for Toleration*, Locke was to describe in appropriately purple prose the penalties against Protestant dissenters in the Restoration, attacking the Anglican Jonas Proast's regret that 'moderate' penalties against Protestant dissenters had been removed in 1689:

And I beseech you what penalties were they? Such whereby many have been ruined in their fortunes; such whereby many have lost their liberties, and some their lives in prisons; such as have sent some into banishment, stripped of all they had.

Locke anatomised the growth of penal laws under Elizabeth, which had started with a fine of 1 shilling for missing common prayer but had 'gradually' increased over the course of her reign to include larger fines, forfeiture of goods and land, imprisonment, exile, and then death as a felon for those who returned from exile. And he noted that these penalties which had 'reached men's estates, liberties, and lives' had been the laws until their penalties were 'in respect of Protestant dissenters, lately taken off'. While Proast denied supporting penalties which involved loss of estate, maiming and 'starving and tormenting in noisome prisons', Locke emphasised in reply that these were indeed laws 'by which men have lost their estates, liberties, and lives too, in noisome prisons'.[110]

Locke owned a series of the protests written by Quakers against the severity of their punishment, including George Whitehead's *A Brief Account*; the 1680 *Of the Great Sufferings and Oppressions of the Quackers*; *Their Suffering Condition Presented to K[ing] and Parliament* (?1685), and William Penn's [anonymous] (1675) *The Continued Cry of the*

---

[110] Locke, *Third Letter*, 286–9. For strong and appropriate emphases on the need for Locke's thought on toleration to be placed into the context of persecution of dissenters see J. Tully (ed.), Locke, *A Letter Concerning Toleration*, introduction; and J. Dunn 'The Claim to Freedom of Conscience' in *idem*, *The History of Political Theory* (Cambridge 1996); for a similar suggestion about the *Treatises*, see Harris, 'Lives'. For a somewhat divergent account of Locke's relation to such a context of persecution from that presented here, see Ashcraft, *Revolutionary Politics*; for criticisms of Ashcraft, see my *Locke*; G. de Krey, 'Rethinking the Restoration: Dissenting Cases for Conscience 1667–72', *HJ* (1995), and Schochet's review of Ashcraft's book in the *JHI*.

Oppressed for Justice: Being a Farther Account of the Late Unjust and Cruel Proceedings Against the Quakers. Some forty-two pages of Whitehead's *A Brief Account* were taken up by 'An account of such as dyed in prison and prisoners for the testimony of truth and a good conscience from the year 1660 to the year 1680'. Whitehead's work moreover itemised among its 'most remarkable Instances of Injustice and cruelty' justices beating Quakers. As we saw earlier, *To the King and Both Houses...the Suffering Condition of the...Quakers* (?1685) had indicted the system as unjust as based on informers 'swearing for their own profit' and convictions of those 'unheard in our own defence'. That Locke read these and other Quaker works in the late 1670s and 1680s is extremely likely. Douglas Lacey noted that in the late 1670s Quaker leaders frequently 'approached the Anglican wing of opposition' to the king, including Shaftesbury, in order to provide them with such accounts of their sufferings. Whitehead's work was one of a series of 1680s works, which also included *To the King, Lords and Commons in Parliament Assembled. The Case of the People called Quakers stated*, which specifically pleaded with king and Parliament to stop prosecuting Quakers. In the Exclusionist Parliaments, the Whigs attempted to provide toleration for Protestant dissenters and explicitly included Quakers within that toleration. Shaftesbury vehemently protested when in 1680 the bishops and courtiers carried a motion in the Lords that Quakers were to be banished from London alongside Catholics, as both were dissenters from the established church. While Quakers were by far the most organised of the dissenters in presenting evidence of their 'sufferings', in March 1678 the Baptist merchant who had occasional financial dealings with Shaftesbury and Locke, William Kiffin, also presented a 'book' on behalf of the 'Anabaptists' to the Committee 'for the discrimination of Quakers *etc* from Papists'.[111]

Originally from what appears to have been an Anglican–Presbyterian and broadly Calvinist background, Locke had spent the 1650s questioning the anarchic tendencies of such Quakers as James Nayler, disparaging the religious chaos of 'Bedlam' England, and celebrating Cromwell for maintaining the 'peace'. At the Restoration, Locke was an apologist for Anglican intolerance, limiting liberty of conscience to that of 'belief' and not of public worship, and criticising what seemed to him then the excessive and hypocritical claims of 'conscience' of most revolutionary dissenters. Supportive of an inclusive national church, in the early 1660s he had become friends with leading English 'lay Latitudinarians' such as Robert Boyle and Peter Pett who supported limited indulgence for dissenters outside of the

---

[111] Lacey, *Dissent*, 107–8; Locke, *Library*, 2412, 2415, 2416, 2417; Whitehead, *A Brief Account*, 85–127; Haley, *Shaftesbury*, 514–15 (there was an important Quaker meeting-house, the Bull and Mouth, near Shaftesbury's London residence at Thanet House: *ibid.*, 411).

church but whose primary desire for toleration was of a variety of opinions within an inclusive accommodating national church. Locke had suggested that Quakers might need to be suppressed in the first three of his four drafts of his 1667 'Essay on Toleration' even when he had first become an apologist for religious toleration, very probably when he had just become a political adviser to Shaftesbury, who was in 1667 a member of the Cabal administration which advised the king to provide toleration. But after Locke had removed this passage on suppression of the Quakers in the final draft of the 'Essay' in 1667 and emphasised that toleration would prevent sedition, he was to be a supporter of toleration for all Protestant dissenters who maintained the peace, while still wishing to see most tolerantly accommodated within a more inclusive church allowing a wide latitude in belief. He criticised the necessity of 'one church' for maintenance of the peace voiced by Samuel Parker in 1670, and probably helped to compose the assault on the intolerant regime of 'high episcopal man and old cavalier' of the 1675 *Letter From a Person of Quality*. He again supported both toleration outside of the church and within the church in 1681–3 in his lengthy unpublished manuscript, 'Critical Notes on Edward Stillingfleet's *Unreasonableness of Separation*'. On both practical and intellectual grounds, in the 1680s Locke was deeply opposed to the persecution of Protestant dissenters described in this chapter, a decade before his *Second* and *Third Letter for Toleration* publicly assaulted the persecutionary regime of Restoration Anglicanism. Locke surely understood in the 1680s as well as the 1690s that this persecutionary regime had left dissenters with no secure rights to property, to liberty, or even to life itself.[112]

Locke was also, as John and Philip Milton have recently shown in an extremely important article, deeply concerned during the Tory or court reaction beginning in 1681 with the legal actions taken against Protestant dissenters in London and Middlesex.[113] In late 1681, as we saw in Chapter 1, Locke's patron Shaftesbury faced indictment for treason for having led the political opposition to the king and allegedly (and probably at this date inaccurately) for planning to use armed force against the king. During this period in late 1681, Shaftesbury attempted to negotiate with Charles, offering that he would leave the country, but Charles proved implacable: he wanted Shaftesbury executed. Charles and his agents attempted to get dissenters excluded from the jury, and argued that justices in oyer and

---

[112] For a lengthier analysis, see Marshall, *Locke*.

[113] Milton and Milton, 'Selecting'. This section of this chapter is indebted above all to the research of Milton and Milton, and was explored in my paper 'Locke, Liberty, and the Law' at the American Society of Legal Historians conference in 1995. As noted in Chapter 1, I am grateful to Tim Harris, Michael Mendle, and Joyce Lee Malcolm for comments.

terminer could overturn the nominations of sheriffs. In late 1681, Locke was very concerned that justices, who were appointed and dismissed at the king's pleasure, and who had in August been summoned to Whitehall to aid in the preparation of the indictment of Shaftesbury, should not be allowed the power to exclude Protestant dissenters from the grand juries which issued indictments. Whig sheriffs had up until this point controlled appointment to these juries, and had appointed dissenters to such juries in London (Middlesex) as well as Whig Anglicans; it was these juries which had provided the crucial protection for the political opponents of the king and refused to return indictments.

As John and Philip Milton have shown, in late 1681 Locke feared that the judges would attempt to remove dissenters on the grounds that they had not taken the sacrament in the Church of England. He researched the issue, and produced a document which argued that under the operative Statute of 3H8, only issues such as being such men of 'ill fame' as 'probably make noe conscience of an oath' allowed the judges to reform a jury panel, overturning shrieval nomination. Locke continued, 'But every breach of law, or repeated breaches of law espetially of some penall laws the observation of which is not rigorously exacted will not render a man suspected of being guilty of wilfull perjury which the Statute takes notice of. For at this rate every one that eats flesh on Fridays or that doth not exactly keep Lent or observe all the holy days will be made incapeable'. Moreover, Locke added,

as to the Dissenters from the Rites and Ceremonys of the church of England (which hath been objected) they cannot be brought within the meaning of that Act. Because the dissent is in such things wherein wise and good men have heretofore differed and doe and will always herein more or lesse differ. And the dissent being soe much against the profit and secular interest of the Dissenters it can not be presumed to proceed from any thing but impulse of conscience: wherein although they may erre and therefor be or be thought weake: yet there can be noe reason to conclude them wicked, but rather that they feare & therefor will keepe their Oaths lawfully administred and taken. Besides that, Dissenters cease not thereby to be free men of England but are equally with others capeable of the same priviledges & lyable to the same burthens & services & the law makes noe such destinction nor is there any reason for it.

The Crown's plan to reform the jury by excluding dissenters did not succeed, and it was therefore before a Whig-controlled jury which included several dissenters that the court attempted to obtain an indictment of Shaftesbury; in November, this jury rendered an ignoramus verdict, refusing to indict Shaftesbury. Such refusal was among the reasons which prompted actions that the court then took in 1682–5 against the Whig shrievalty itself and which prompted the court moves to exclude dissenters from the electorate for Lord Mayor. The attack on the corporation of London by *quo warranto* proceedings came simultaneously with court-sponsored propaganda which indicated that Shaftesbury's head should be displayed upon 'a pike'. In 1683, the king obtained the forfeiture of the corporation in the Court of King's Bench on the dubious legal grounds that the common council had illegally imposed its own tolls on goods and had illegally petitioned the king for a Parliament in 1679. To save its existence, the common council narrowly voted the king power of approval and in effect power of appointment of mayors and sheriffs. By late 1682, following dubious electoral processes in the election of a new Lord Mayor and of new sheriffs, in which many Whigs were disenfranchised as dissenters, had their votes disregarded, or refused to participate, Charles had obtained Tory sheriffs, who would then appoint the members of grand juries, and a Tory Lord Mayor. The election of Sir William Pritchard as Lord Mayor of London in 1682 followed the striking out of a significant number of Whig votes as being the 'disqualified' votes of Quakers and other dissenters; only those taking the sacrament in the Church of England were held to be qualified electors.

Other dissenters were thereafter removed from office and from the franchises in the rest of England as parts of the processes of royal recalls of charters of other towns, as the royal prerogative was extended in and after 1681 in order to obtain compliant towns and corporations around England who would elect Tory Members of Parliament should Charles ever call another Parliament, who would put into force the laws against dissenters, and who would appoint as juries individuals who would not refuse to indict opponents of the regime.[114] To many Whigs, the sheriffs and the rights of common council were central to the 'liberties' of London; the attempt of the Lord Mayor to impose his own sheriff as early as 1675 had caused major opposition to the Crown as an attack on the 'liberties' of the city, and many of those involved in Whig opposition to the king in the city and in Parliament in 1678–81 had been involved in support of the right to appoint sheriffs as early as 1675.[115] To many Whigs, the rights of the corporation of London and its control of its franchise and of sheriffs were a microcosm of the rights of the kingdom; as the legal manoeuvrings against the corporation and the imposition of new regulations were being conducted under 'colour of law', so it was felt that the king could attack many other liberties and franchises established by the law. This was prescient: after Charles gained forfeiture of London, many town charters were surrendered. As Charles' propagandist North was to put it (in 1684), Judge Jeffries on the northern circuit had 'made all the charters, like the walls of Jericho fall down before him, and returned laden with surrenders, the spoils of towns'. Once it had gained such powers the Crown tried and executed a number of leading opponents of the

---

[114] Harris, *London Crowds*, 185 ff.; Marshall, *Locke*; Scott, *Restoration*.
[115] G. de Krey, 'London Radicals'.

regime, alleging that they had plotted to resist the monarchy in the 'Rye House Plot' and associated plans for assassination and armed resistance. Those executed in 1683 included Algernon Sidney and Lord Russell; the Earl of Essex either committed suicide or was murdered while incarcerated. By 1683, all three were probably in fact guilty of treason as plotters or at the least very serious discussants of armed resistance against the king, but it was believed by some Whigs even in this period that the evidence against them was concocted and that they had been judicially murdered. Tried as a co-conspirator in plots to resist the king in 1682–3, Russell at his 1683 execution was effectively to admit that he had discussed resistance but not actively plotted it, and to declare defiantly that his conscience would not have allowed him to 'run Men down by Strains and Fetches, impose on easie and willing juries to the Ruine of Innocent Men: For to kill by Forms and Subtilities of Law, is the worst sort of Murder'.[116]

In Chapter 1 we examined the Crown's attempts to try and to execute the opponents of 'popery' and 'arbitrary' government as being responded to in 1681–2 by the Shaftesbury circle and other Whig accounts with accusations of an alleged 'popish conspiracy' at court.[117] Here I wish to emphasise that the tracts which made the accusation of a 'popish conspiracy' against the security of fair trial by grand jury were simultaneously voicing arguments which would have been understood by their authors and audiences in 1682–3 as concerned with the status of Protestant dissenters, identifying the security provided by the law for opponents of monarchical absolutism as removed when dissenters were disabled from sitting on grand juries and from being part of the electorate. According to Somers' *Grand Juries*, such juries provided security of lives themselves. Since 'our law makers foresaw', Somers argued, that corrupt ministers of state might accuse and 'commit the most odious of murders in the form and course of justice; either by corrupting of judges, as dependant upon them...or by bribing...to swear falsely', they had understood that it was vital that grand juries 'neither be cheated nor frighted from their Duty'. It was impossible that 'satisfaction or reparation should be made for innocent Bloodshed in the forms of Justice'. These and similar words in late 1681 and 1682 were surely intended to be read as being above all else a defence of the famous ignoramus grand jury of Shaftesbury which had rejected the suborned witnesses against Shaftesbury and which

---

[116] H. Nenner, *By Colour of Law* (Chicago 1977), 29; M. Zook, *Radical Whigs and Conspiratorial Politics in Late Stuart England* (Pennsylvania 1999).

[117] John and Philip Milton have shown in 'Selecting' that Locke was almost certainly involved in College's legal defence. His 1681 trial and execution had shown the 'artifices and arts' that the Crown was willing to use to execute its opponents: in the trial, College's own notes for his defence were confiscated by the judges and used by the prosecution, and witnesses were suborned against him by the Crown.

had insisted on examining these witnesses in order to discredit them. More broadly, they would have been understood as a defence of composition of that grand jury which included several dissenters, including its leading member, Papillon.[118]

We saw also in Chapter 1 that the same notion of the centrality of legal protections for life by juries was expressed in the *Third Part of No Protestant Plot*, embedded within a defence of Protestant nonconformists from accusations of a plot against the monarchy. This work declared that the law existed centrally to protect men 'in reputation and lives if innocent'. Discussing the illegality of proceedings against Shaftesbury, it declared that 'no kind of procedure is further for the kings honour and interest, than as it is according to law, which is the standard of the kings prerogative, glory and safety'. This text thus identified the defence of life with the defence of the law in a text whose overarching theme was denial that there had been a 'Protestant' – that was, a dissenters' – plot against the monarchy, again tying together defence of dissenters' rights and liberties with those of everyone. The rights of dissenters will have been central to such rights in the minds of its author, Robert Ferguson, a Congregationalist and close associate of John Owen, as well as Shaftesbury's chaplain.[119]

An extremely important intersection between Locke's defence of resistance and issues of the legal status of dissenters was provided by the moves by the Crown in 1681–3 to remove dissenters from juries and from the franchise. These Crown actions rendered the arguments in the Second Treatise for impartial law, and against executive corruptions of electorate and legal process, significantly about the rights of dissenters in the English polity, as crucial to the protection of the lives of opponents of monarchical absolutism. This perspective underlies Locke's manuscript defence of those rights in late 1681, when Shaftesbury was facing indictment and execution, and it underlies the response of Shaftesbury to the Tories being sworn into the London shrievalty in 1682: he immediately went into hiding. As I argued in Chapter 1, listing the reasons for which men should conclude that absolutism was about to be imposed and that therefore they must and legitimately could resist, Locke surely had in mind the legal actions against Shaftesbury and others when he described a situation 'under pretence of lawful authority' of the prince gaining power 'to terrify or suppress opposers as factious, seditious, and enemies to the government'. The broad rhetoric here was, I wish now to suggest, intended to include within those being suppressed dissenters and London Whigs who had been attempting to resist by law the king's actions in 1681–2, but who by mid-1682 were finally losing

---

[118] Somers, *Grand Juries, passim*; Schwoerer, *Declaration*, 49.
[119] [R. Ferguson], *Third Part of No Protestant Plot, passim*.

that battle. According to Locke, people would not, and by implication should not, fail to be persuaded that 'their Estates, Liberties and Lives are in danger' 'if either...illegal acts have extended to the Majority of the People, or if the Mischief and Oppression has light only on some few, but in such Cases, as the Precedent, and Consequences seem to threaten all'. They would not avoid this conclusion, he argued, surely with the Corporation of London and actions against its magistrates by removal of dissenters from the franchise in mind, if they 'shall observe...arts used to elude the law, and...the ministers and subordinate magistrates chosen suitable to such ends and favoured or laid by proportionately as they promote or oppose them'. It was surely the attack on the corporation and the shrievalty elections of mid- to late 1682, which was simultaneously an abrogation of legal customs in London, the gaining of royal control over juries, and the removal of the political voice of Protestant dissenters, that prompted Locke to define governments as dissolved from within 'when by the arbitrary power of the Prince, the Electors or the ways of Election are altered, without the consent and contrary to the common Interest of the People'.[120]

Locke's set of arguments in the *Treatises* were surely designed to appeal to Whig gentlemen, both tolerantly lay Anglican and nonconformist, and to leading Anglican and dissenting property owners. Whiggish Anglicans had long argued that the right to trial by jury was the cynosure of English law, and they saw this as being overturned by the Crown's actions against dissenters, against the London magistracy and electorate, and against Shaftesbury. The language of Locke's *Treatises* in speaking of liberty and property as needing to be protected by impartial law probably also needs to be understood, as Tim Harris has suggested, as in part directed both at dissenters and at Latitudinarian Anglicans who were sympathetic to the dissenters' plight. Dissenters' liberty and property had repeatedly been removed during the Restoration by markedly partial laws, and many dissenters had lost their lives in prison. Dissenters had reason to see the vicious Tory reaction against dissent after 1681 as taking to new levels the long partial administration of law in the actions against Shaftesbury, long among the most important advocates for their toleration, and in the actions against many of the corporation officers who had attempted to shelter dissenters from the effects of statutory intolerance. Their repeated attack on the Restoration regime as abrogating fundamental laws in taking away their liberty and property and in threatening their lives has been described earlier in this chapter. Locke was surely aware of these resonances of language speaking of rights to liberty, property and estate as a tolerationist Whig

---

[120] Locke, *Treatises*; cf. also Scott, *Troubles*; *idem*, *Restoration*; Marshall, *Locke*, and now also G. De Krey, *London*, which appeared while this book was going through the press.

Anglican deeply sympathetic to the sufferings of dissent.[121] But it is clear that Locke's argument was highly secular and abstract, and if its language was surely resonant for dissenters who had suffered deprivations of property, liberty and life in the Restoration and were suffering the peak of such deprivations in the early 1680s, Locke included no specific arguments about the status of religious dissenters. He surely wrote knowing that resistance for religious reasons – because of religious persecution – would not be supported by many dissenters nor by Anglicans.

Dissenters had been suffering persecution throughout the Restoration, and almost none had resisted, and almost all had repeatedly denied the legitimacy of resistance for religious reasons. Anglicans were generally even more hostile to resistance on the grounds of religious persecution. Since resistance was not raised in 1682–3, but only discussed and planned, it is not possible to specify who might have been involved in planning and intending to support it. In his 'full confession' of the 'Rye House Plot', however, Robert West recorded that in spring 1683 the people were 'encouraged' to take up arms 'as necessary for their preservation from that ruine to which the vigorous execution of the penall laws against dissenters, made them lyable'. He noted that a Baptist preacher Hicks had said that Baptists would have supported resistance in 1683, and that the Congregationalist Stephen Lobb was attempting to gain support in his congregation for resistance. Some other Baptists and Congregationalists seem to have been supporters of plans for resistance, and among the grounds for their support seems to have been their opposition to the penal laws. Yet West simultaneously provided evidence of the limited support of nonconformists, and the active opposition of many nonconformists, regarding plans for armed resistance.

West recorded that he had himself 'told' the Congregationalist Ferguson that 'the Nonconformists, as well as the churchmen, had put shackles upon the people by preaching up the doctrine of passive obedience, though under another phrase, viz waiting upon the Lord's time'. Ferguson had allegedly replied not by denying that this was so, but by saying that such nonconformists misunderstood God's providence, which actually required men to help themselves. West recorded moreover that Ferguson had told him that 'some Nonconformist ministers suspected that he was carrying on this design to kill the King and Duke and begged him to desist, because it would bring a reproach on all dissenters whatsoever the result might otherwise be, and that he was forced to deny it lest they should have betrayed it'. Ferguson had then allegedly said 'alas...they are weak and silly men, and not fit for these things, who cannot distinguish betwixt destroying a king meerly for his opinion in Religion, though otherwise an excellent person, and destroying

---

[121] Harris, 'Lives'. I hereby register my continued disagreement on this issue with Ashcraft's somewhat reductive account in *Revolutionary Politics* of Locke as an 'ideologist of dissent'.

tyrants who design to overthrow our laws, Religion and civil rights, and have the nation'. West asked him if 'more of them [dissenting ministers] knew and approved of it, because they might otherwise ruine the effects of it by their power with the Dissenters'. Ferguson replied that 'some of them were sensible men and looked upon it as both lawfull and necessary and that they and himself had prepared sermons ready, suitable to the occasion'. The clear implication of West's account is first that only a few dissenting ministers knew of the plans for resistance and supported them, and that the majority of nonconformist ministers would not have supported resistance but rather supported the duty of nonresistance that they had been preaching throughout the Restoration. Indeed, such nonconformist ministers were said to have opposed planning resistance if they suspected it, causing Ferguson to deny its existence to them because he was convinced that otherwise they would have revealed the plans to the government.[122]

PROTESTANT INTOLERANCE C. 1660–C. 1700 TOWARDS HERETICS, ATHEISTS, LIBERTINES, AND CATHOLICS

Restoration punishment of 'heresy' and proposed legislation against 'heresy'

The vast majority of the thousands of Protestant dissenters who suffered for their religious commitments in Restoration England were punished for a separation from the Church of England that was understood as 'schism' and not 'heresy'. Nonconformists such as Presbyterians, Independents, and most Baptists were understood by most Anglicans to have separated in worship despite agreeing with Anglicans in doctrine, and the allegation that most nonconformists had thus 'unreasonably' separated from Anglican worship was endlessly repeated in Anglican arguments and gave the title to such works as Edward Stillingfleet's 1681 *Unreasonableness of Separation*. In the Restoration, more allegations of heretical beliefs, and more allegations of unacceptable toleration of others' heretical beliefs in too doctrinally 'latitudinarian' a church, were made against Anglicans by nonconformists challenging Anglicans' alleged 'Arminian' or 'Socinian' tendencies than were made by Anglicans against nonconformists. Many leading members of the Restoration Church of England became Arminian and stressed the expansiveness of the articles of the Church of England. Several of the most doctrinally ecumenical 'latitudinarian' Anglicans, including Locke's close friends Edward Fowler and John Tillotson, redescribed heresy as a failure of the will and not of the understanding, stressed particularly heavily the

---

[122] BM Add MSS 38847: 'West's confession', *passim.*

wide latitude in 'speculative' opinions allowed in the Church of England, were friends with anti-Trinitarian Anglicans such as Thomas Firmin, and were themselves repeatedly attacked as 'Socinians' by nonconformists. Some nonconformists even gave as their reason for refusing communion that Anglicanism was too tolerant of 'heresy'.[123]

Some Restoration punishments of nonconformists, were, however, for heresy and blasphemy, and these centred on allegations of anti-Trinitarianism. Among those punished were William Penn and Lodowick Muggleton. Penn was imprisoned in the Tower in 1668 for publishing his *Sandy Foundation Shaken*, which departed from the orthodox doctrine of the Trinity in that it opposed 'those so generally believed and applauded doctrines of one God, subsisting in three distinct and separate persons, the impossibility of God's pardoning sinners without a plenary satisfaction, the justification of impure persons by a putative righteousness'. For Penn, 'since the Father is God, and the Son is God, and the Spirit is God, then unless the Father, Son, and Spirit are three distinct nothings, they must be three distinct substances, and consequently three distinct Gods'. He continued 'If each person be God, and that God subsists in three persons, then in each person are three persons or Gods, and from them three, they will increase to nine and so ad infinitum'.[124] For these sentiments, Penn's book was quickly called a 'horrid and abominable piece against the Holy Trinity' and the Presbyterian Thomas Vincent attacked it as full of 'hideous blasphemies, Socinian and damnably-heretical opinions'. Its printer was arrested, and its author was committed to the Tower. There, Penn was visited by Stillingfleet in an effort to persuade him to recant his 'blasphemous and heretical opinions'. He was told that the Bishop of London was resolved that he should either recant, or die a prisoner.[125] In a letter to Lord Arlington, Penn affirmed his faith in the 'eternal deity of jesus christ and the substantial unity of father word and spirit', and in *Innocency With her Open Face Presented* he argued that he supported the 'eternal Deity' of Christ while denying the Trinity of persons in the Godhead except as 'operations' of the one God – a largely Sabellian understanding of the Trinity and still for most orthodox thinkers

[123] Spurr, *Restoration*; Marshall, *Locke*; Goldie, 'Theory of Religious Intolerance'; Philanglus, *Englands Alarm*, 3–12 in Harris, *Politics*, 94; Corbet in Greaves, *Bunyan*, 10; R. Colie, *Light and Enlightenment* (Cambridge 1957), 40, 43; N. Tyacke, 'Arminianism and the Theology of the Restoration Church' in S. Groenveld and M. Wintle (eds.), *The Exchange of Ideas* (Zutphen 1991), 68–83. Locke was far closer to Tillotson and Fowler than to any dissenting minister. Unitarians were to point out in the 1690s – accurately – that the Church of England was more tolerant of their views than nonconformists.

[124] Levy, *Blasphemy*, 216–17; Braithwaite, *Second Period*, 61.

[125] Braithwaite, *Second Period*, 61, 64.

anti-Trinitarian heresy. Penn was only released after eight months due to the intercession of James, Duke of York.[126]

A thoroughgoing opponent of the Quakers, Lodowick Muggleton, also denied the orthodox doctrine of the Trinity in various works, including *The Neck of the Quaker Broken* (1663) and the *Answer to William Penn* (1673). He went into hiding for six years to escape arrest after one of his works was ordered burned in 1668, and a warrant for his arrest was issued in 1670. Having been traced, he was tried in 1677 for his 1663 work *Neck of the Quaker*. When he was convicted, Rainsford summed up that Muggleton deserved punishment as a 'murderer of souls'. Muggleton was sentenced to stand in the pillory in three separate places wearing a placard proclaiming him 'blasphemer' and to imprisonment until he could pay a large fine. In each place, crowds gathered and pelted him with clay, rotten eggs, and 'dirt'; at the last, he was pelted with stones as 'thick as hail' and his head was broken open. Muggleton then spent six months in Newgate prison.[127]

And while such prosecution for anti-Trinitarian heresy was rare in Restoration England, this was not because such views were seen as tolerable, but rather because anti-Trinitarianism had limited support and because most anti-Trinitarians were prevented from publishing their views by licensing laws and fear of punishment. Anti-Trinitarians like Milton usually either kept their views private, or circulated them via manuscript to a select group of like-minded or inquisitive individuals. And fear of punishment was generated not merely by trials, such as those of Penn and Muggleton, but also by repeated proposals of further legislation against anti-Trinitarianism. In the wake of the Plague and Great Fire of London in 1665–6, which many saw as God's punishments for a nation insufficiently intolerant towards sins and blasphemies, the Anglican Cavalier-dominated House of Commons established a Committee to consider a bill 'touching such books as tend to atheism, blasphemy, and profaneness, or against the essence powers or attributes of God the Father, Son or Holy Ghost, given to them in Scripture', or 'in denial of the immortality of souls, resurrection of the body' and 'eternal rewards' in heaven or 'eternal torments' in hell. Here, then, was a bill directed simultaneously against atheism and against heresy in which almost all of the specified religious tenets were those associated with Socinianism. The Commons' Committee discussed reviving the writ *de haeretico comburendo* under which heretics had been burned in the centuries after 1401. The bill failed. But it reappeared for enactment in February 1674,

---

[126] Braithwaite, *Second Period*, 61–4. It was, notably, under James II that there was the relaxation of the press that allowed Socinian works to be published and so caused the 'Unitarian Controversy' of c. 1687–95.

[127] Levy, *Blasphemy*, 222–3.

in November 1675, and December 1680. And while Hobbes argued that *de haeretico* had been abolished long before and should not now be revived, it was not clear to contemporaries that *de haeretico comburendo* was not simply still in force. In the early 1670s, Andrew Marvell wrote that 'some of our ruling clergy, who yet would be content to be accounted good protestants, are so loath to part with any hank they have got, at what time soever over the poor laity, or what other reason, that the writ *de haeretico comburendo*, though desired to be abolished, is still kept in force to this day'. The writ *de haeretico comburendo* was only officially repealed in 1677. Even thereafter, however, by reproposal of the 1666 legislation, as Richard Tuck has written, 'the goal of an intolerant, orthodoxly Christian regime was kept constantly before the public gaze from 1666 to 1681'.[128]

The 'Toleration Act' of 1689 in England marked a major advance in English legislative practices of tolerationism by providing Parliamentary indulgence of nonconformist worship, thereby ending after 1689 the persecution and imprisonment of Protestant dissenters which had led to the deaths of over 450 Quakers in the reign of Charles II alone, and which had caused the deaths, imprisonment, and financial ruin of many other dissenters. But such toleration of worship and belief was provided in 1689 only to Trinitarians. The Act excluded from its benefits 'any person that shall deny in his preaching or writing the doctrine of the Blessed Trinity, as it is declared in the aforesaid articles of religion'. Archbishop Wake was thus able to celebrate in the 1710s that toleration was *not* provided in England to Arians and Socinians. When the Licensing Act expired in 1696, it was quickly followed by the Blasphemy Act of 1698, which imposed fines and prison sentences for repeated public denials of the Trinity. One was guilty of blasphemy if, as a Christian, one denied 'any one of the Persons of the Holy Trinity to be God', 'the Christian religion to be true', or the 'divine authority of the Bible'. A first offence disabled from office; a second resulted in three years' imprisonment 'without bail'. The House of Commons called on the king to suppress pernicious books containing 'impious doctrine against the Holy Trinity', or against 'other fundamental articles of our faith'. Locke's close friend and collaborator in biblical interpretation, Isaac Newton, kept his anti-Trinitarianism secret; scholars are still excavating his views from unpublished manuscripts today. Arthur Bury was excommunicated and fined, and his 1690 *Naked Gospel* was burned. William Freke's 1694 *Brief*

---

[128] Marvell, *Mr Smirke*, 23 in Spurr, *Restoration*, 225. Tuck, 'Hobbes and Locke on Toleration' in M.G. Dietz, *Thomas Hobbes and Political Theory* (Kansas 1990) 153–71, at 157–8. J. Edwards, *Some Thoughts Concerning...Atheism* (London 1695), most famous for attacking Locke's Socinianism, makes a stronger case for Hobbes' closeness to these parts of Socinian thought. For a broad account of some significant similarities between Socinian thought and Spinoza, see L. Strauss, *Spinoza's Critique of Religion* (New York 1965).

but Clear Confutation of the Doctrine of the Trinity was burned by the public hangman, and Freke was fined. Both books were read by Locke.[129] In the early eighteenth century, anti-Trinitarian Anglicans such as William Whiston and Samuel Clarke were to lose posts or preferment for their anti-Trinitarianism. The Unitarianism of individuals such as Joseph Priestley and Richard Price was still to cause attacks upon them near the end of the eighteenth century, and when John Wilkes expressed scurrilous anti-Trinitarianism in a privately printed *Essay on Women* he was prosecuted under the Blasphemy Statute and convicted in the House of Lords of having composed a 'most wicked and blasphemous attempt to ridicule and vilify the person of our most blessed Saviour'. Wilkes' sentence for anti-Trinitarianism was longer than that for mocking a royal speech in *North Briton*. As late as a full century after the 'Toleration Act' of 1689, ridicule of divine majesty remained a more serious crime in England than ridicule of human majesty.[130]

Intolerance towards 'libertines' and 'atheists' c. 1660–c. 1700

As we saw earlier, in the Restoration new legislation was often proposed simultaneously against the 'heresy' of anti-Trinitarianism and against 'atheism', the latter being defined to include not merely those who denied the very existence of God but also those who denied the providence of God or ridiculed Christianity. There were only a tiny number of prosecutions for public denial of Christianity or ridicule of Christianity, both alternately referred to in the period as 'atheism' or 'libertinism'. Two notable cases of prosecution of 'atheists' and 'libertines' stand out in Restoration England. A dramatist and a rake closely associated with many 'libertines' in the Restoration, Sir Charles Sedley, went onto a balcony of an inn near Covent Garden roaring drunk in 1663, pulled down 'his breeches' and 'excrementised in the Street'. He then preached a 'mountebank sermon' full of 'Blasphemy' to a crowd that Pepys estimated at 1,000 people, 'acting all the postures of lust and buggery that could be imagined'. He abused 'the Scripture', suggested that he could sell a powder to 'make all the cunts in town to run after him', and ended by washing 'his prick' in a glass of wine which he then drank and followed by a toast to the king. For this remarkable performance, Sedley was tried in 1663 in the Court of King's Bench on the charge that his 'profane' actions against Christianity tended to 'the disturbance of the peace'. He was fined heavily, imprisoned for a week, and bound over for three years. When spoken in a public setting in front of

---

[129] J. Champion, *The Pillars of Priestcraft Shaken* (Cambridge 1992), 107.
[130] Levy, *Blasphemy*, 323–4.

a London crowd in a way that could disturb the peace, even the 'libertinism' of the Restoration rake and courtier drew punishment.

In 1675, the otherwise obscure yeoman John Taylor of Guildford was prosecuted for having said that 'Christ is a whore-master, and religion is a cheat, and profession [of Christianity] is a cloak, and they are both cheats'. He had allegedly further declared that all the earth was his, that he was the 'younger brother' to Christ and 'an angel of God', that Christ was 'a bastard', and ended by damning all gods. The initial response of the House of Lords was, perhaps unsurprisingly, to declare that Taylor had to be mad, and to send him to Bedlam. But when Bedlam interestingly denied that he was mad, and he publicly maintained his views, he was prosecuted in the Court of King's Bench for a 'high Misdemeanor' for words that 'tend immediately to the destruction of all Religion and Government'. Chief Justice Hale sentenced him to stand in the pillory wearing a sign saying 'for blasphemous words, tending to the subversion of all government' together with a large fine and sureties for good behaviour. In accounts of Hale's decision, it was said that he argued that Taylor's words by 'taking away religion', left no basis for oaths, and so tended to the 'dissolution of all government'. Hale further held that injuries to God and Christianity were punishable by criminal courts 'because the Christian religion is part of the law'. To say 'religion is a cheat, is to dissolve all those obligations whereby the civil societies are preserved', and Christianity 'is parcel of the laws of England; and therefore to reproach the Christian religion is to speak in subversion of the law'.[131]

But while these two prosecutions were notable, they were exceptional. Whereas thousands of orthodox Protestant nonconformists were prosecuted and incarcerated in the Restoration, in contrast it appeared to many that 'libertinism' and 'atheism' was undesirably tolerated. It was widely understood that the court was itself 'libertine', dominated by a 'libertine' king who kept many mistresses and fathered at least fourteen illegitimate children, by a Duke of York who might risk his crown for his religion but was unwilling to give up his mistress for his religion, and by other similarly inclined courtiers. Charles II remains in English memory 'the merry monarch' beloved of Nell Gwynn, and his court remains the epitome of courtly dissolution – of wits, rakes, and libertines – in the entirety of British history. The king even sponsored propaganda which attempted to make the sexual prowess exemplified in his mistresses and bastard children central to royal authority, including Dryden's *Absalom and Achitophel*, which celebrated them in terms of his elevation above other mortals and even as a proof of his 'piety' aligned with 'pious times ere priestcraft did begin' when monogamy had not

---

[131] Levy, *Blasphemy*, 214–22; A. Cromartie, *Sir Matthew Hale 1609–76* (Cambridge 1995), 174–5.

been required. Unsurprisingly, 'Country' and 'Whig' attacks on the court frequently condemned the king's sexual appetites as representative of his tyrannical desires. Depicted as desiring to sleep with every woman in the kingdom, Charles' desires were directly related to his alleged desires for his subjects' property as women were held to be men's property, either as wives to husbands, or daughters to fathers. Charles II was depicted in this literature as attempting by his example to 'withdraw both men and women from the laws of nature and morality, and to pollute and infect the people with all manner of debauchery and wickedness'.[132] The king and court provided patronage for Hobbes, widely execrated as an 'atheist' and 'libertine', and sheltered the Earl of Rochester, the most notorious sexual 'libertine' in the country apart from the king himself. While at moments Rochester was banished from the court for expressing poetic criticism of the king's libertinism and laziness, there was no attempt to prosecute Rochester for his 'libertinism' or 'sodomy', as these were apparently evidenced in acts as well as in his poetic imagination, and Rochester's poetry reached a significant circulation via pirated printing and manuscript circulation. Rochester, indeed, is responsible for having coined the phrase 'merry monarch' for Charles II in a poem which famously anatomised Charles' sole motivation as the pursuit of pleasure, encapsulated in the suggestion that 'his pintle and his sceptre are of a length'.[133]

Restoration nonconformists convinced that 'libertinism' and 'atheism' should not be tolerated looked at the court and read Hobbes' works, and Rochester's or Behn's 'libertine' literature, and were convinced that apart from extremely rare cases of prosecution such as that of Sedley, 'atheism' and 'sexual libertinism' were tolerated and celebrated at the highest levels in Restoration England. To many nonconformists, for most of the Restoration the effective toleration of 'libertinism' – even while it was legally proscribed by laws against adultery, fornication, and 'sodomy' at the same time that pious Protestant nonconformists were violently persecuted – was an abhorrent inversion of the legitimate organisation of a polity in which 'libertinism' would have been prosecuted and religious nonconformity tolerated. Such antagonism to toleration of 'libertinism' surfaced in nonconformist texts, which repeatedly complained about the failure of the Restoration regime to prosecute 'debauchery' and attacked the incongruity of enforcing worship on the 'godly' while leaving unpunished the 'manifest sins' of sexual nonconformity.[134] As Tim Harris has shown, nonconformist

---

[132] Weil, *Political Passions*; S. Kent, *Gender and Power in Britain 1640–1990* (London 1999), ch. 2.
[133] Kent, *Gender*, 31; R. Weil, 'Sometimes a Scepter is only a Scepter: Pornography and Politics in Restoration England' in L. Hunt, *The Invention of Pornography* (New York 1993), 125–53.
[134] *CSPD* 23: 562 quoted in Zook, *Radical Whigs*, 87.

hostility to the failure to enforce sexual morality by neglecting the laws against prostitution at the exact moment of enforcing religious intolerance by imprisoning nonconformists surfaced in riots against 'bawdy-houses' in London in 1668 after the court failed to deliver an attempted toleration and comprehension of Protestant dissenters in 1667. Rioters not merely destroyed London bawdy-houses but drew up 'mock petitions' from the 'poor whores' which stressed the support for whores by Catholics and by Anglicans leading the campaign against nonconformist worship. And a satire made the point explicit in discussion of a bill to be passed in Parliament for a 'full Toleration of all Bawdy-houses' but for the suppression of 'all Preaching, Printing, Private Meetings, Conventicles, etc'. As Harris puts it, 'In their minds it must have seemed that the Court was adopting a double standard; openly violating the laws against brothels and bawds, and yet demanding a rigid enforcement of the laws against dissenters'.[135] At the height of Restoration persecution in the early 1680s, the 1682 *A Word of Advice to the Two New Sherriffs of London* similarly argued that 'Meetings have been disturb'd too often by those, That to a Bawdy-House were never foes'.[136]

Such hostility to the allowance of sexual licence while punishing religious nonconformity was not merely expressed by many nonconformists but also by leading Latitudinarians such as Stillingfleet and Burnet, who chastised the king and court and attacked the toleration of libertinism, indicting 'libertinism' as contrary to the 'laws of nature' as well as to those of religion. The Latitudinarians stressed moral performance as the essence of Christianity and voiced considerable hostility to 'sexual immorality' or 'license'. It is perhaps unsurprising, then, that the Revolution of 1688–91 which brought Burnet and Stillingfleet to episcopal power did not provide toleration for 'libertinism' or 'atheism'. The public expression of atheism remained subject to many forms of censorship, and the Blasphemy Act of 1698, which replaced the lapsed Licensing Act, provided prison terms not merely for those who attacked the doctrine of the Trinity but also for any who attacked the divine revelation of the Gospels or the providence of God. Although William III himself was probably bisexual and was attacked in the 1690s for 'sodomitical' relationships with his 'favourite' Portland, in the 1690s the court officially repudiated 'libertine' and 'sodomitical' behaviour and supported an extensive campaign of 'moral reformation' that targeted sexual 'libertinism' and 'sodomy'. The Revolution of 1688–9 was quickly called a 'moral revolution' by Gilbert Burnet. Burnet's 23 December 1688

---

[135] Bodleian MS Don b8 fos. 190–3; Marvell, *Last Instructions to a Painter* in *Poems on Affairs of States* (New Haven 1963–75), I, 133; Pepys, *Diary*, VIII, 585, 596; *The Gracious Answer*; all in T. Harris, 'The Bawdy House Riots of 1668', *Historical Journal* 29, 3 (1986), 537–56.
[136] Harris, *London Crowds*, 81, 85, 128; Cragg, *Puritanism*, 118.

sermon excoriated the 'criminal excess' of 'debauchery' in the Restoration, and his Coronation sermon itself declared that the 'chief design' of William's and Mary's rule was that 'impiety and Vice are punished'. The 1690s were marked by a series of laws and proclamations against 'debauchery' and 'vice', and by calls for parishioners to inform Justices of the Peace of sexual offenders to be punished. Under such pressure, the 1690s included a series of trials of prostitutes, their clients, and an accused 'sodomite', Captain Rigby.[137] The passage of 'religious toleration' for orthodox Protestant dissenters in 1689 with nonconformist and Latitudinarian Anglican support thus involved the fulfilment of the long-standing desire of both groups to see 'libertinism' and 'debauchery' punished and orthodox nonconformist religious worship tolerated.

It is important, then, to approach the issue of the toleration of 'libertinism' and 'atheism' in Restoration England from two different angles. Firstly, while legislation against 'atheism' and anti-Trinitarianism was proposed repeatedly in Parliament, such legislation did not pass and the number of 'atheists' prosecuted was tiny. From this perspective, the practical toleration of 'libertinism' and 'atheism' was greater than that for nonconformity until 1688–9. Many nonconformists were hostile to such toleration of what they considered 'immorality' and 'atheism', a hostility reinforced by suffering for their beliefs and worship while 'libertinism' seemed unpunished. And to the extent that atheists were punished (Sedley and Taylor) and others repeatedly threatened with new legislation against atheism, it could be said that in contrast to religious nonconformists who believed themselves to have a duty to express their beliefs in worship and evangelisation, 'atheists' and 'libertines' had no 'duty' of testifying to their belief. However, from another angle of vision, the prosecutions of Taylor and Sedley, involving declaration that Christianity was the 'law of the land' in England, together with extensive practices of pre-publication censorship, threats of substantial punishment for authors and printers convicted of involvement in a 'libertine' work, and repeated threats that further legislation against 'atheism' might be passed, combined to make committed 'atheists' and 'libertines' perceive themselves as facing significant persecution in the Restoration. They kept most of their ideas to themselves, placed them in limited manuscript circulation, or issued them in print with a veil of theological piety. The intellectual freedom to question religion publicly in the Restoration was severely circumscribed, however much the 'wits' might dominate at court. Rather than experiencing himself as being tolerated in his convictions, a figure such as the Earl of

---

[137] C. Herrup, *A House in Gross Disorder* (Oxford 1999); Burnet, *Sermon*; T. Claydon, *William III and the Godly Revolution* (Cambridge 1996).

Rochester, or his friends Charles Blount and Thomas Hobbes, had reason to perceive themselves as facing censorship, in significant danger of punishment for their views, and needing to create plausible deniability in expressing their views in a veiled manner if they wished to print them.

Toleration and intolerance towards Catholics in England and Ireland c. 1660–c. 1710

Between the Restoration of monarchy and Church of England in 1660–2 and the Revolution of 1688–9, English Catholics remained under threat of prosecution under Elizabethan and Jacobean recusancy statutes, except for the brief periods when Charles II and James II provided dispensation through prerogative indulgence. Prosecution varied widely. Most Catholics in England were gentlemen and aristocrats and members of their households who could worship in private chapels on their estates, and had social equals as magistrates who usually sheltered them from prosecution. Charles II was a secret Catholic, understood that English Catholics were his loyal subjects, and for most of his reign did not seek their prosecution. After 1673, and especially after 1678, however, prosecution of English Catholics reached significant levels both for recusancy and for treason during the 'Popish Plot', and there was also considerable crowd violence against Catholics and Catholic chapels. After 1673, as John Miller has written, magistrates 'began to convict Catholics of recusancy in large numbers and, to a lesser extent, to levy fines on them and confiscate their lands'.[138] Such action was due initially to 'Whig' Parliamentary pressure, and after 1678 Catholic houses and even a nunnery were broken into by Whigs in searches for evidence of plotting, and Whig crowds attacked Catholic chapels and Catholics going to worship during the years of the 'Popish Plot' and 'Exclusion Crisis'. The Whig-instigated executions of Catholics for treason in these years were described in Chapter 1. During the Tory Anglican reaction after 1681 such executions ceased, but the Privy Council demanded enforcement of the recusancy laws against 'Papists' because the court was denying the reality of a 'popish conspiracy' at court and was therefore anxious to show that it was a vigorous enforcer of laws against Catholics. Many Catholics were fined heavily in 1681–5. And Whig crowd actions against Catholics continued. In 1682, the Countess of Soissons was 'most dreadfully abused. . .in one of the Duke of Yorks Coaches by a number of Boyes that fell upon there Coach as she was going to Somerset House to publick masse'; they broke all the windows and forced the coach to turn

---

[138] Miller, *Popery*, 59.

back.[139] Thus in the period 1660–85, with the brief exceptions of 1662 and 1672, English Catholics lacked freedom of worship and security of property, and in the Whig-dominated period after 1678 they lacked security of life itself.

Under the officially tolerant regime of James II, governmental prosecution of English Catholics ceased and offices were opened to Catholics. But crowd violence was still directed against Catholic worship and worshippers. In 1686, youths disturbed the first mass held in the newly opened chapel in Lime Street, dragging one Catholic worshipper through the gutter. On the following Sunday, they stole a cross and mocked it 'paying a very disorderly adoration to it with hollowing, and then going back and taking a crucifix, and saying they would have no wooden gods worshipped there'. Thereafter, worshippers had to be protected by soldiers on their way to worship. By May 1686, the Bishop of Durham recorded to James II that such chapels were 'daily made the occasion of so much Disturbance and Mischief here' that their very continuance would 'unavoidably endanger the peace and Safety of Your great City'.[140] On 30 September 1688, the Jesuit Charles Petre was dragged from the pulpit at the Catholic chapel in Lime Street, London, by a crowd. On the following Sunday, they pulled down the pulpit and broke the altar, and he fled. Other crowds attacked Catholic chapels throughout England on many occasions in late 1688. In Norwich, a 'mob' of over a thousand 'ill-used' the priest and had to be dispersed by soldiers; a mass-house in Newcastle was 'sacked' and a chapel in York was destroyed. In Oxford, there was an anti-Catholic riot, while in Bristol there were attacks on the houses of Catholics. On Lord Mayor's Day 1688, a crowd burned the altar furnishings of a chapel in Bucklesbury. On 11 November 1688, crowds attacked mass-houses throughout London. In early December, a spurious declaration was issued, claiming that 'great numbers of Armed Papists' were preparing 'some desperate Attempts' on Londoners 'by a Fire, or a Sudden Massacre, or both'; further attacks on Catholic chapels followed.[141] In December 1688, chapels were reported demolished in York, Bristol, Gloucester, Worcester, Shrewsbury, Stafford, Wolverhampton, Birmingham, Cambridge, Bury St Edmunds, Hull, Newcastle, and Northamptonshire. Even Catholic worship conducted in the private chapels of the gentry and aristocracy was not secure from crowd violence by 1688, as the estates of several Catholic Lords

---

[139] Harris, *London Crowds*, 183.
[140] PRO SP 31/3 fo. 64 in W. L. Sachse, 'The Mob and the Revolution of 1688', *Journal of British Studies* (1964), 23–40; Harris, *London Crowds*, 47.
[141] Sachse, 'The Mob', 27–8; Harris, 'London Crowds', *passim*; cf. also Goldie, 'Political Thought', 102–36, esp. 123, 125; Miller, *James II*, 187 and Speck, *Reluctant*.

were attacked, including those of Lord Dover, Lord Ashton, and Henry Mordaunt, Earl of Peterborough (uncle of a friend of Locke, and a Catholic convert whose steward was allegedly threatened with being burned alive). Their chapels were destroyed and furniture burned.[142]

While the Revolution of 1688–9 brought statutory relief in England for orthodox Protestant dissenters, it denied this to Catholics, who remained subject to the Elizabethan recusancy laws. And many other restrictions were placed on English Catholics in the 1690s and early eighteenth century, limiting Catholic education and inheritance. Liberty was understood in 1689 in England as preserved by Test Acts disabling Catholics from office. William and Mary supported such Test Acts. In Fagel's *Letter to Stewart*, translated by Burnet – 50,000 copies of which circulated in England in 1688 – William had declared that he supported repeal of the penal laws provided the Test Acts 'still remained in their full vigour, by which Roman Catholics are shut out of both Houses of Parliament, and out of all public employments, Ecclesiastical, civil and military'. This remained his policy in the 1690s. William did, however, press for toleration of worship to be provided for Catholics by statute, and when this was refused he attempted to mitigate the effects of penal laws.[143] By 1710, as Anne continued William's policy of mitigating the effects of the penal laws, it was possible to report that English Catholics were 'totally free' in exercise of their religion. Not until 1778, however, were English Catholics brought under the terms of the Toleration Act, and not until the nineteenth century was Catholic emancipation provided in England.[144]

Whereas in England Catholics formed about 1 per cent of the population, in Ireland they formed the majority, with 800,000 Catholics to 300,000 Protestants. In the early years of Charles' reign, lay Irish Catholics were largely tacitly tolerated in their worship, with few fines and penalties imposed for worship. But priests could not hold worship freely, and many were banished for refusal to testify their allegiance to the Crown by signing a remonstrance to that effect and by taking an oath of allegiance which required the explicit denial of papal deposing power. These oaths were condemned by the Pope. As anti-Catholicism escalated in the 1670s, in 1673 Essex (Shaftesbury's assistant in campaigning for Exclusion and the

---

[142] Sachse, 'The mob', 30–1.
[143] G. Fagel, *A Letter Writ by...Fagel...to James Stewart* (1688), *passim*; *The Prince of Orange's Engagement for Maintaining and Securing the Protestant Religion, and Liberties of the People of England* (London 1689), 1–4.
[144] A. Seaton, *The Theory of Toleration under the Later Stuarts* (Cambridge 1911), 280–1. The 1778 measures to remove Catholic disabilites provoked the Gordon Riots, and anti-Catholicism was central to English and British identity in the eighteenth century: on this topic generally, see L. Colley, *Britons* (Yale 1992).

reality of the 'Irish Plot' in early 1681) ordered all regular clergy banished, and all convents, seminaries, and 'public popish schools' suspended. In the early 1680s, as 'Popish Plot' and 'Exclusion Crisis' agitation fuelled even greater anti-Catholicism and Archbishop Plunkett was brought to England and executed, many of the remaining Catholic clergy fled from Ireland to France. In 1683, chapels in Kilkenny were closed and mass forbidden, the Jesuit superior arrested, and the rest of the regular clergy forced to flee. And all such restrictions of Catholic worship and priests occurred against the backdrop of the Restoration confirmation of Protestants' titles to the majority of the vast Cromwellian confiscations of lands from Catholics as alleged rebels.[145]

The restored toleration of priests and Catholic worship in Ireland in James' reign was extremely important, and was combined with questioning of Protestants' titles to confiscated lands. But this restored toleration under James II was also short-lived, and was succeeded by reinstitution and expansion of measures against Irish Catholics after the victories of William's army in 1690–1. The exclusively Protestant Irish Parliament refused to repeal the Elizabethan laws against Catholic worship and confirmed Protestants' titles to formerly Catholic lands. In Ireland, as in England, William seems to have wanted to allow greater freedom for Catholics than did Parliament. He helped to reduce the lands ceded from Catholics to Protestants and he initially prevented the banishment of members of religious orders from Ireland in 1695. But a 'violently anti-Irish' Capel ministry, led by a former leading Whig Exclusionist, came to power in 1695 and demanded banishment of priests. In an atmosphere created in part by the Protestant propaganda about Catholic violence in continental Europe and by further rehearsals of the massacre of 1641 in Ireland, the Irish Parliament thereafter established in the later 1690s and early 1700s a regime in which the Catholic majority of the population were declared threatening to the Protestant minority's religion and property, and restricted in education, inheritance, land-holding, and possession of arms and horses. In 1697, Catholic bishops and priests were again banished from Ireland, with 424 regular priests transported and a further 300 fleeing in 1698 alone. The measure banished not merely all regular priests but also secular bishops. In 1704, important Catholic forms of worship such as pilgrimages were declared illegal 'riots'. Although a number of these measures were to prove unenforceable in the eighteenth century, with many 'registered' priests allowed after 1704, and

---

[145] Connolly, *Religion*, ch. 1; Bagwell, *Ireland*, III, ch. 46; Chapter 1 above, pp. 24–5 (citing McManners, *Church*).

many Catholic pilgrimages continuing even if legally proscribed, it was not until the late eighteenth century that full relief from such measures was provided in Ireland.[146]

---

[146] Connolly, *Religion*; W. A. Maguire, 'The Land Settlement' in *idem* (ed.), *Kings in Conflict*, 139–56; S. J. Connolly, 'The Penal Laws' in *ibid.*, 157–72; Bartlett, *The Fall and Rise of the Irish Nation*, ch. 1; J. G. Simms, 'The Establishment of Protestant Ascendancy 1691–1714' in T. Moody and M. Vaughn (eds.), *A New History of Ireland* (Oxford 1986), 16–17. While Patrick Kelly has indicated that Galway was not the fanatic supporter of the 1697 penal laws against Catholic priests in revenge for persecution of Huguenots that Catholic propaganda alleged, he does indicate that Galway supported banishment of regular priests in 1697: Kelly, 'Galway'.

4

Religious toleration and intolerance in the Netherlands and in the Huguenot community in exile

The significant degree of religious toleration in the Netherlands

In the years of increasing and severe religious persecution in the early and mid-1680s in England, France, and Piedmont, the Netherlands provided in practice a great degree of religious toleration and a home for many thousands fleeing persecution. In the late sixteenth and early seventeenth centuries it had been common to speak of Poland, Transylvania, and the Netherlands as the three most tolerant countries in Europe. But the image of Polish toleration was lost first as severe persecution of Jews was instituted in 1648, and it was reported in 1655 that Jews had been 'soundly pillaged, and many massacred', and then when Socinians were restricted in the 1640s and 1650s and banished in 1658–60. By 1660, the recognised 'tolerant' countries in Christian Europe had dwindled to just Transylvania and the Netherlands.[1]

By the 1680s, extensive religious freedom was almost exactly a century old in the Netherlands. 'Freedom of religion' or 'freedom of conscience' were declared to be at the centre of Dutch identity from the period of the Dutch Revolt against Spanish rule. The 1579 Union of Utrecht officially provided for 'freedom of conscience'. Such freedom – and competition over its definition – was thus placed at the legal and constitutional centre of the 'republic' created by the Dutch Revolt against Spanish rule. The Revolt ended the major period of executions of Protestants as 'heretics' under Charles V in the mid-sixteenth century and then under the Duke of Alva as part of his 'Council of Troubles' in the late 1560s and early 1570s. Saravia's 1568 pamphlet, *The Heartfelt Desire of the Noble, Forbearing Highborn Prince of Orange*, justified

---

[1] On Poland, see Bayle, *Dictionary* Socinus F and K; Le Cler, *Toleration*; J. Tazbir, *A State Without Stakes. Polish Religious Toleration in the Sixteenth and Seventeenth Centuries* (New York 1973), esp. 94–5, 133–4, on French, Dutch, and English citations of Polish toleration in the sixteenth century; M. Greengrass, *The Longman Companion to the European Reformation c. 1500–1618* (London 1998), 166–70; on the reporting of Polish massacres, see D. Katz, 'English Charity and Jewish Qualms' in A. Rapoport-Albert and S. Zipperstein (eds.), *Jewish History* (London 1988), 245–66. The Diet of Transylvania in 1570 provided a truly remarkable freedom of worship to Catholics, Lutherans, Calvinists, and Unitarians.

Orange's 1568 expedition as repulsing the 'spoilation and utter ruination' of the Netherlands by Alva's 'unspeakable bloodthirsty tyranny', and in 1572 William of Orange gave as one of the chief reasons for taking up arms that 'the name of the Inquisition shall be erased forever'. The identity of the republic was in significant part defined in the century following the Dutch Revolt by repudiation of religious persecution. As the important Amsterdam burgomaster and merchant Cornelius Hooft asserted, 'When we took up arms it was to throw off the yoke of tyranny, not with the intention of dominating the conscience of others'. He concluded that 'everyone should be entirely free in his religion, provided this freedom is not incompatible with that which God has given us the grace to acquire'.[2] This was the understanding of the Dutch Revolt provided to foreign observers of the Netherlands in the late seventeenth century, such as the English Ambassador Sir William Temple, whose 1673 *Observations Upon the United Provinces* declared that 'one of the great Causes of the first revolt in the Low-Countreys' was 'The Oppression of men's consciences, or Persecution in their Liberties, their Estates, their Lives, upon pretence of Religion'.[3] While over the century following the Dutch Revolt there had been an essentially Calvinist Dutch Reformed 'public church' in the Netherlands supported by public funds, which controlled the only buildings resembling churches, and whose ostensible membership controlled access to political office, there was no compulsion placed upon individuals to come to that church, and so it is usual to suggest that this was a 'public' rather than an 'established' church. Although in this chapter we will note many legal restrictions on religious expression in the Netherlands, it is important that there was no Dutch equivalent to the English Act of Uniformity containing penalties for refusal to attend the state church. One gained advantages such as the capacity to hold civic office from membership of the 'public church', but one did not suffer punishment simply for absence from that church.[4]

Moreover, in the century following the Dutch Revolt, the Netherlands accommodated large communities of every one of the most significant denominations of Protestant 'heresy' and heterodoxy who were burned, banned, and banished from other European countries. In the late sixteenth

---

[2] Israel, *Dutch Republic*, 372–3; W. Nijenhuis, *Ecclesia Reformata* (Leiden 1972), II, 177–8; van Gelderen, *Political Thought*; Hooft in Le Cler, *Toleration*, 293. It is unclear how extensive such a toleration was to be for Hooft in terms of his final words, and as a magistrate Hooft did not intervene to prevent the exile of Socinian preachers. On 'heresy' having been equated with 'treason' in the Catholic Netherlands, see J. Tracy, *Holland Under Habsburg Rule 1506–66* (Berkeley 1990), 151.

[3] W. Temple, *Observations Upon the United Provinces of the Netherlands* (London 1673), 25, 28–9, 35–6, 195; Israel, *Dutch Republic*, 639.

[4] J. L. Price, *Dutch Society 1588–1713* (Harlow 2000), 129–30. Temple saw no reason not to call the ordering of the profession of 'only' the 'Evangelical Religion' following 1583 the creation of 'the established Religion of this State': *Observations*, 197.

century, when the Anabaptists could not find toleration in almost the entirety of Western Europe and were being execrated, executed, or exiled as 'heretical', 'blasphemous', and 'seditious', they were tolerated in large numbers in the Netherlands. Severe measures had been taken in the Netherlands between 1523 and 1566 against Lutherans and Anabaptists as the Netherlands witnessed 'a persecution unmatched for its sustained intensity anywhere in Europe', and particularly large numbers of executions of Anabaptists occurred in the later 1530s during a period when there were significant attempts by Anabaptists to use force in the Netherlands and an Anabaptist attempt to seize control of Amsterdam. But partly because of the repudiation of 'Spanish tyranny' and the 'Inquisition' and its executions of Anabaptists, from the 1570s there was a stronger attempt in the Netherlands than in almost all other European locations to differentiate between truly 'seditious' Anabaptists, who deserved punishment only for their sedition, and the vast majority of peaceful and pacifist Anabaptists, who deserved toleration.[5]

The Parliamentarian side in the English civil wars of the 1640s drew considerable support from the desire of Calvinist Protestants to eradicate 'Arminianism' from the Church of England, leading to the establishment of prison sentences for Arminianism in the Blasphemy Ordinance of 1648. Even as late as the 1680s, Huguenot synods in France in the mid- and late seventeenth century regularly condemned positions which they saw as tending towards 'Arminian' heresy, such as Amyraldism, and Arminianism itself was not tolerated.[6] A similar Calvinist desire to eradicate 'Arminianism' dominated magisterial policy in the Netherlands from 1618 to the mid-1620s. But after 1630–1, the magistrates in the Netherlands effectively tolerated the worship of a significant Arminian community numbering in the thousands, and that community gained influence among the magistrates and the urban elite in towns such as Amsterdam. Like all congregations in the Netherlands other than the Reformed, even after they became effectively tolerated from about 1630–1 the Arminians were forbidden to construct buildings which appeared to be churches from the outside, or to have bells to summon worshippers, but like other tolerated churches they thereafter were able to build places for worship by reconstructing the inside of buildings, and it was widely known what these buildings were. On the inside, they were large and imposing places for worship; on the outside, they appeared to be ordinary houses and not churches. In this, they were symbolic of much of the

---

[5] Pettegree, *Emden and The Dutch Revolt*, 2–3; Duke, *Reformation*; Israel, *Dutch Republic*, 374ff.

[6] Grotius and a few like-minded Arminian exiles sheltered in France but they were not allowed to worship at Charenton.

carefully circumscribed practice of Dutch toleration in the seventeenth century.

Not merely was effective toleration for Arminianism established in practice in the 1630s, but during the period when the Arminians were proscribed from 1619 to the late 1620s, and during the period when they organised themselves as a sect in the 1630s, a significant Collegiant movement was developed by former Arminians. The Collegiants disliked sectarian organisation, had no ministry, and instead allowed members of the congregation to speak as the 'spirit' moved them in 'free prophecy'. By the 1630s, they had organised 'colleges' of merchants and professionals in Amsterdam, Rotterdam, Haarlem, and Leiden. They communicated with several other communions, including the Mennonites, and were from mid-century crucial to sheltering Socinian exiles and significantly influenced by Socinian emphases on 'reason' and toleration. The Collegiant movement admitted extremely heterodox thinkers, such as Spinoza. From many of these sources, members drew materialist conclusions that were to end before the century with the denial of the existence of both evil spirits and of the Devil by Balthasar Bekker.[7]

Socinians and other anti-Trinitarians had been punished and executed in both Protestant and Catholic Europe in the sixteenth century, and were then able to find shelter in significant numbers only in Poland and Transylvania. When toleration of Socinians was restricted substantially in Poland in the mid-seventeenth century and then finally ended in 1658–60, during a decade when essentially Socinian anti-Trinitarians like John Biddle and Paul Best were incarcerated in England under Oliver Cromwell as a way to avoid enforcing the provisions of the law which called for their execution in England, and when anti-Trinitarians were still subject to execution in France, many Socinians – such as Jonas Schlichting, sentenced to death for an anti-Trinitarian work in Poland – fled to the Netherlands. Even if their toleration there was to be restricted, as we will emphasise later, and they were allowed to worship only among the Arminian and Collegiant communities rather than in their own place of worship, only a few Socinians were imprisoned in or banished from the Netherlands.[8]

It was in the Netherlands, moreover, that several hundred English covenanting separatists, the Brownists, found shelter in the early seventeenth century, and many 'puritans' sheltered under Laud in the 1630s. As the Restoration nonconformist John Quick put it, 'The old Puritan ministers,

---

[7] Israel, *Dutch Republic*, 395; Israel, *Radical*; A. Fix, *Prophecy and Reason* (Princeton 1991); *idem*, 'Angels, Devils and Evil Spirits in Seventeenth-Century Thought: Balthasar Bekker and the Collegiants', *Journal of the History of Ideas* (1989), 527–47, at 527–30, 535.

[8] Tazbir, *State Without Stakes*, 179.

who could not out of conscience conforme...did shelter themselves from the storms of Episcopall persecution, and from the tyranny of the High Commission court, in the...English churches of the Netherlands, as in a Sacred Sanctuary'.[9] The politically radical Brownist Church in Amsterdam was to shelter important new waves of English regicidal refugees around 1660, and then supporters of the 'Rye House Plot' and Monmouth rebellion in the 1680s. In the generations of severe persecution of Quakers in England in the 1650s under Cromwell, and in the 1660s to 1680s under Charles II, many Quakers found greater tolerance in the Netherlands than in England or elsewhere in Europe.

Amsterdam and Rotterdam moreover held significant Catholic communities, and even by the late seventeenth century perhaps 20 per cent of the population of the Netherlands was Catholic. While this was a much smaller figure than in the late sixteenth century, it was still a significant portion of the population. Catholic worship was legally forbidden – and remained so until the late eighteenth century – but Catholics were in practice generally allowed freedom of private worship and trade, while forbidden from holding civic office of any kind, officially prevented from building their own churches, and banned from holding any form of religious procession, giving or receiving Catholic education, sending children abroad for a Catholic education, or living together in 'klopjes' – groups of females engaged in religious work.[10] In the 1670s, William Temple was to note that Catholic worship itself was not officially tolerated, but because it was 'connived at' it was in practice 'free', and that therefore Catholics were 'a sound piece of the state, and fast jointed with the rest; And have neither given any disturbance to the Government, nor exprest any inclinations to a change, or to any foreign power'. By 1691, the sometime English consul and spy in Amsterdam, William Carr, estimated in his *Accurate Description* that there were no less than '85 Houses or Chapels' for Catholic worship in Amsterdam alone.[11] Toleration of Catholic worship came under particularly fierce pressure in the late 1680s, in the wake of the Revocation of the Edict of Nantes and of the persecution of Waldensians, but even in these years practical toleration of

---

[9] J. Quick, 'Icones Sacrae Anglicanae' quoted in K. Sprunger, *Dutch Puritanism: A History of the English and Scottish Churches of the Netherlands in the Sixteenth and Seventeenth Centuries* (Leiden 1982), 285.

[10] J.A. Bornewasser, 'The Roman Catholic Church Since the Reformation' in J. Hebly (ed.), *Lowland Highlights* (Kampen 1972), 40–8, at 43–4. On Bayle holding that allowing processions was not necessary, see below, p. 556; such processions were elsewhere, of course, a major part of Catholic religious life in this period.

[11] Temple, *Observations*, 201–2; W. Carr, *An Accurate Description of the United Netherlands* (London 1691); P. Hoftijzer, '"Such Onely As Are Very Honest, Loyall and Active": English Spies in the Low Countries 1660–88' in P. Hoftijzer and C. Barfoot (eds.), *Fabrics and Fabrications* (Amsterdam 1990), 73–96, on Carr as spy.

private Catholic worship was not eliminated. And once again it should be stressed that the Netherlands was highly unusual as a Protestant country in allowing this significant if incomplete degree of toleration of Catholic worship. When Jurieu issued his *Policy* in 1681 and attempted to make the argument that Huguenots should be tolerated in France because Catholics were tolerated in their worship in practice in Protestant countries, it was only to the Netherlands that he could point.[12] The large degree of toleration offered to Catholics as well as to Protestant 'heretics' in the Netherlands was to provide an important context for the avowed multi-confessionality of the 'republic of letters' in journals published in the Netherlands, and for tolerationist arguments which attempted to separate Catholic worship and belief as tolerable from 'intolerable' Catholic political arguments. In the opening issue of Bayle's *Nouvelles*, he stressed the openness of the presses in the Netherlands to Catholic as well as to Protestant works.[13]

In the seventeenth century, Jews could not find admittance to England except in very small numbers by prerogative action; their statutory re-admittance was shelved after a full-scale debate during the English Revolution in 1656 which drew millenarian and conversionist support for a limited toleration, but which also witnessed opposition in England by writers such as William Prynne, who declared that Jews were child murderers and cannibals and rehearsed ritual murder allegations against them that had been voiced before their thirteenth-century expulsion from England. Jews had been expelled from France in the late fourteenth century and from Provence when that was recombined with France in the late fifteenth century, and while limited numbers of Jews had been readmitted to France in the sixteenth century by royal action, and their numbers by the late seventeenth century had reached several thousand, this readmittance was largely as Marranos veiling their Judaic beliefs with external Christian practices, and by immigration to outlying areas of France. In 1615, Marie de Medicis issued an order that renewed the fourteenth-century expulsion of Jews as the 'sworn enemies' of Christianity; even if the order was then ignored, it suggested the fragility of royal toleration. In 1619, a recent Portuguese immigrant, Catherine Rodrigues, was burned at the stake in St Jean de Luz, and riots against Marranos and the expulsion of Marranos from the town followed.[14] In 1652, a spate of anti-Semitic pamphlets in Paris charged Jews with ritual murder in connection with an outburst of interfaith violence. And although no pogrom or riots resulted, and although the Oratorian Richard Simon issued a pamphlet which attacked the repetition of ritual murder accusations

---

[12] Jurieu, *Policy*, 104–8.
[13] Bayle, *Nouvelles de la république des lettres* (Amsterdam 1684–7), 1st issue; see below, Part 3.
[14] Israel, *European Jewry*, 42–3, 56, 95–6, 132–4.

against Jews as an unjustified repetition of medieval accusations, in 1670 in Metz, the site of the largest Jewish community in France, Raphael Levy was burned alive following the accusation that he had stolen and murdered a Christian child. Soon after he commenced his personal reign, Louis XIV began to restrict the toleration and further admission of Jews. In 1663, he refused permission to Amsterdam Jews to settle in Dunkirk. Convinced that the Jews were a 'wicked people' who deserved expulsion, in the early 1680s Louis banned all Jewish immigration to France, and in 1683, immediately after the death of Colbert, the mercantilist defender of toleration of Jews, he expelled Jews from Marseilles and ordered Jews out of the French islands – an order then repeated in the 1685 Code Noir. In 1684, he proposed to expel further Jews from south-west France. It did not become clear until 1686 that Jews would not in fact be expelled from France. That this did not then occur owed something to the distinction drawn between Jews as tolerable non-Christians whereas Huguenots as 'heretics' were intolerable, and more to the economic importance of Jews to the French society at a moment when Huguenots were fleeing in large numbers. Jewish toleration was thus fragile in France, especially in the early 1680s.[15]

Jews were tolerated in the Netherlands and admitted in much larger numbers than in England until England gained a tolerationist Dutch king in 1688–9, and their toleration was less fragile than in seventeenth-century France, especially in the early 1680s. These comparisons with France and England are important, but they were not as important to understanding Dutch Jews' own experience of Dutch freedom to profess their religion as was the direct contrast to the personal experiences of persecution of many Jews who came to the Netherlands from Iberia and from Eastern Europe. The majority of the Jewish community in the Netherlands in the late sixteenth and early seventeenth centuries were Sephardic Jews who left behind an Iberia where they had been forced to profess Christianity while remaining observant Jews in private. The Netherlands provided for them, in Yosef Kaplan's words, the capacity to throw 'off the cloak of Christian conformity with which they had for so long concealed their true identity' and for many it thus realised a 'long-standing dream of an openly professed and full-blooded Jewish life'.[16] And in the second half of the seventeenth century they had good reason to contrast their experience of Dutch freedom with the growing force of the Portuguese Inquisition as it punished as 'Judaisers' increasing numbers of ostensible Christians who were found to

---

[15] *Ibid.*, 132–4. Simon's protest against ritual murder accusations was his *Factum servant de réponse au livre intitulé Abrégé du procès fait aux Juifs de Metz.*

[16] Quotations from Y. Kaplan, *From Christianity to Judaism* (English translation Oxford 1989), 106–7.

be practising Jews.[17] By the late seventeenth century, the majority of Jews in the Netherlands were Ashkenazi Jews who had fled to the Netherlands from pogroms in Germany, Poland, and Lithuania. They too experienced in the Netherlands liberation from personally experienced religious persecution.[18] It was the experience of liberation for Sephardic Jews which prompted the 1616 rabbinic celebration that 'since "this city is near enough to flee to" [Genesis 19:20] conversos of our time, great in number and prominence, have gone there and have entered under the wings of the Divine Presence'. It was this freedom which was celebrated in verse in the late 1680s by Miguel de Barrios, who asked the God of Israel to assist William III's invasion of England by declaring that 'To have a steadfast Faith, is pious love/and forcing the People that follow it/is not to imitate God who gives free/will and God will punish him/who tries to force the consciences of others'.[19]

The extent of Jewish toleration in the Netherlands should nonetheless not be overstated, particularly in the early seventeenth century. In 1598, shortly after Portuguese Jews had settled in Amsterdam, there was significant resistance to Jewish plans for synagogues, and public worship in a synagogue was officially condemned. An attempt to construct a synagogue was rebuffed by the city council in Amsterdam in 1612. Not until 1639 was a public synagogue inaugurated in Amsterdam. In 1606 and 1608, Jews were forbidden to buy land for a cemetery within the limits of the city of Amsterdam. From 1607 until 1614, Jewish dead had to be buried 25 miles from the city at Groet, near Alkmaar. In 1616, Jews in Amsterdam were warned to prevent all attacks on Christianity, not to attempt to convert Christians to Judaism, and not to have sexual intercourse with them, as well as ordered again not to construct a public synagogue. In both the early and the late seventeenth century, Jews were excluded from all long-established craft guilds except apothecaries, physicians, and booksellers, and faced other legal restrictions, such as being prevented from employing Christian maidservants. In common with all religions except the Dutch Reformed, they could not hold civic office. And Jews were not permitted even to live in some towns until the mid-seventeenth century and in Utrecht until long into the eighteenth century.

---

[17] D. Swetschinski, 'Kinship and Commerce: The Foundations of Portuguese Jewish Life in Seventeenth Century Holland', *Studia Rosenthaliania* (1981), 52–74, at 64.

[18] Y. Kaplan, 'The Portuguese Community in 17th Century Amsterdam and the Ashkenazi World', *Dutch Jewish History* 2 (Jerusalem 1989), 23–45; *idem*, 'Amsterdam and Ashkenazic Migration in the Seventeenth Century', *Studia Rosenthaliania* (1989), 22–44.

[19] M. Bodian, *Hebrews of the Portuguese Nation* (Indiana 1997), 63; H. den Boer and J. Israel, 'William III and The Glorious Revolution in the Eyes of Amsterdam Sephardi Writers: The Reactions of Miguel de Barrios, Joseph Penso de la Vega, and Manuel de Leao' in Israel (ed.), *The Anglo-Dutch Moment*, 439–61, at 449.

Moreover, much public expression of religious life and commitment was curtailed. As for Catholics, Jewish processional life was curtailed; in the case of Jews, however, such restrictions were generated as much within the community anxious to preserve that freedom it possessed as from without the community. In 1639, the Mahammad decreed that 'bridegrooms or mourners must not travel in procession, to avoid the problems which can occur with crowds and to avoid being noticed by the inhabitants of the city'. As late as 1690, it forbade members of the community to appear in costumes or masks in the streets during Purim 'since some of our enemies use this masquerading to demonstrate their ill intent to us'. And in 1700, it abolished the carrying of the Torah scrolls outside the synagogue on the Simhat Torah holiday because it had caused 'grave troubles and commotion amongst the gentiles'.[20] As early as the earliest Ascomot (Jewish communal regulations) of the Amsterdam Jewish community, they forbade proselytising in order not to endanger the 'freedom we enjoy' under pain of excommunication, and made the printing of a work critical of Christianity subject to a fine.[21]

But if these were significant restrictions on processions and public expressions of Judaic commitments, in 1605 the town council of Alkmaar resolved to allow Jews to 'have their religious worship' and the burgomasters of Haarlem, after initially resisting allowance of a public synagogue, resolved to allow both a public synagogue to be built and a cemetery to be acquired once fifty families had settled (though this number was not reached). They also resolved to permit Hebrew books to be printed 'on condition they refrain from blasphemy or derision of the Christians'. They explicitly allowed the hiring of Christian servants – though simultaneously the death penalty was provided for marriage or adultery with a Christian, and 'corruption' to Judaism or seduction to 'carnal intercourse' of servants was prohibited. Rotterdam provided for Jewish citizenship in 1610, and for worship in a synagogue once thirty families had settled, and in homes until then. Although resistant to the building of a public synagogue, in the early seventeenth century Amsterdam allowed private Jewish worship in homes. When pressing for a public synagogue elsewhere, Jewish merchants noted that they already possessed liberty of private worship in Amsterdam. As early as 1616, the author of a rabbinic query which was sent to Salonica declared that

Today a tranquil and secure people dwells in Amsterdam, and the officials of the city have sought to expand the settlement...they have allowed every man to believe in

[20] R. Melnick, *From Polemics to Apologetics* (Assen 1981), 8; Bodian, *Hebrews*, 62; Israel, *European Jewry*, 52.

[21] Melnick, *From Polemics*, 15. A 1664 order forbade the sale, loan or gift of books or manuscripts to Gentiles, presumably for the same reasons: Y. Kaplan, 'The Social Functions of the Herem', *Dutch Jewish History* (1984), 111–55, at 123.

divine matters as he chooses, and each lives according to his faith, as long as he does not go about the markets and streets displaying his opposition to the faith of the residents of the city.[22]

Later in the century, the toleration of public Jewish worship grew, while Jewish economic power grew significantly during the seventeenth century, and the Jewish community grew to perhaps 15,000. By 1700, the largest single concentration of Jews outside of the Balkans was in Amsterdam – about 6,000 people, or 3 per cent of the population of 200,000. In 1655, Rabbi Menasseh ben Israel proclaimed that 'in the Low Countries' Jews were 'received with great Charity and Benevolency', and in 1657 the States General declared that those of the Jewish nation 'are truly subjects of the state and as a consequence they are guaranteed enjoyment of the same rights and advantages...secured and obtained for the inhabitants of this state'. By the late seventeenth century, important parts of overseas trade in the Netherlands were controlled by Jewish merchants, brokers, insurance agents, and shipping agents, and there were Jewish printers and booksellers, physicians, apothecaries, diamond-cutters, and tobacco-spinners. Richer Sephardi merchants owned town houses that were so impressive that tourists came to gaze at them, and engravers such as Romeyn de Hooghe depicted some of their mansions.[23] By 1701, the English bishop Richard Kidder was able to declare in his *A Demonstration of the Messias* that

I have heard of a Rich Jew at Amsterdam, who treated a Christian very splendidly. When the Christian mentioned to him the present captivity of the Nation, the Jew smiled at it; and said, What is this Captivity? and protested, that he should not be willing to return to the Land of Canaan, where he could not expect the Conveniencies which he enjoyed where he was.[24]

In 1639, Amsterdam inaugurated a public synagogue. In 1642, Stadtholder Frederick Henry was accompanied by Queen Henrietta Maria of England to a

---

[22] A. Huussen Jr, 'The Legal Position of Sephardi Jews in Holland c. 1600' in J. Michman (ed.), *Dutch Jewish History* (1993), 19–41; O. Vlessing, 'New Light on the Earliest History of the Amsterdam Portuguese Jews' in *ibid.*, 43–75; H. I. Bloom, *The Economic Activities of the Jews of Amsterdam in the Seventeenth and Eighteenth Centuries* (New York 1969), 7; Bodian, *Hebrews*, 63.

[23] J. Israel, 'The Economic Contribution of Dutch Sephardi Jewry to Holland's Golden Age' in *idem, Empires and Entrepots* (1990), *passim*, esp. 444; *idem*, 'The Changing Role of the Dutch Sephardim in International Trade 1595–1715' in J. Michman (ed.), *Dutch Jewish History* 1 (1984), 31–51; *idem*, 'Sephardic Immigration into the Dutch Republic 1595–1672', *Studia Rosenthaliania* (1989), 45–53; *idem, European Jewry*, 127–8, 135, 180–1; den Boer and Israel, 'William III and the Glorious Revolution', 439–61; Kaplan, 'Portuguese Community', 23–45; *idem*, 'Amsterdam and Ashkenazic Migration', 22–44; Nijenhuis, *Ecclesia Rëformata*, II, 134.

[24] Kidder, *Demonstration* (1701), III, 460 in N. Matar, 'The Idea of Restoration of the Jews in English Protestant Thought 1661–1701', *Harvard Theological Review* (1985), 147. Locke read the work.

sermon there by Rabbi Menasseh ben Israel. In 1675, the Portuguese Jewish community built a new synagogue in Amsterdam which was both one of the largest buildings in Amsterdam and one of the largest synagogues in Europe. The English visitor William Mountague called it 'very fine' and perhaps the most impressive synagogue in the whole world, while a similarly impressed French visitor in 1687, Maximillian Misson, wrote that 'the Portuguese Jews here are extraordinary Rich, and their Synagogue is a stately building whereas that of the High-Dutch is but mean and contemptible'. Foreign visitors were impressed; Dutch residents were coming to take it as an accepted important place of worship. Dutch artists used the same pictorial styles to represent the Calvinist churches and the Jewish synagogue, which Yosef Kaplan has suggested shows 'that for the residents of the city, this Jewish site had earned a solid and well-established place on the map of Amsterdam and was seen as one of the accepted and familiar houses of worship in the city'. William of Orange visited the new Portuguese synagogue, continuing the stadtholder's tradition of recognition of public Jewish worship.[25]

By the late seventeenth century, the magistrates were clearly identified as supporting such extensive toleration of Jewish worship. At the end of the century, Surenhuis' influential Latin translation of the Mishna (1698–1703) was dedicated to the consuls of Amsterdam, who, it declared, had been 'tireless' in protecting Jews – adding that such Jews were understood as 'fallen not principally because of greed, or some depravity, but because of religious opinion that is indeed bad, but certainly not impious, and because of a kind of ignorance'.[26] The notion of a 'pious ignorance' here clearly demarcated Jews from the 'obstinate malice' against Christianity with which they were often charged elsewhere in Europe in this period. In 1658, the Spanish ambassador's secretary had similarly documented the support of the magistrates for Jewish worship in declaring in a report to Madrid which referred to the community of some 3,000 Sephardic (Iberian) Jews living in Amsterdam and the few hundred at Rotterdam that 'this nation has very considerable power with the magistrates of the city councils, and especially that of Amsterdam, for without doubt it is they who have the greatest commerce and who, consequently, yield the greatest advantage'. Significant parts of the costs of the invasion of

---

[25] W. Nijenhuis, *Ecclesia Reformata* (Leiden 1972), II, 134; Price, *Dutch Society*, 203–4; 'Misson and Menasseh Ben Israel' in Y. Kaplan, 'Gente Politica: The Portuguese Jews of Amsterdam Vis-a-vis Dutch Society' in *Dutch Jews as Perceived by Themselves and Others*, ed. C. Brasz and Y. Kaplan (Leiden 2001), 21–40; *idem*, 'For Whom Did Emanuel de Witte Paint His Three Pictures of the Sephardic Synagogue in Amsterdam', *Studia Rosenthaliania* (1998). On Menasseh ben Israel, see also R. Popkin (ed.), *Menasseh Ben Israel and His World* (Leiden 1989).

[26] F. Manuel, *The Broken Staff* (Harvard 1992), 96ff.

England in the Revolution of 1688–9 were borne by Jewish financiers in the Netherlands.[27]

Dutch toleration was thus fairly extensive in practice, especially after mid-century, and especially remarkable by comparison with other Western European societies. The Netherlands allowed to a degree unmatched by those other societies the worship of orthodox Protestants of the 'public church' and 'heretical' and 'schismatic' Protestants, Catholics, and Jews. And not merely was the Netherlands religiously the most tolerant society in Western Europe, but the reputation of the Netherlands was that it provided an extensive religious toleration. To most outside observers, this was a source for complaint and not compliment. The Welsh preacher Arise Evans declared in 1656, 'beware of Amsterdam. . .that provokes God in his face, in which Atheists and Devils have their abode'.[28] William de Britaine's 1672 *Interest of England* declared Holland 'a retreat for all rebels and a sanctuary to the worst of men' and suggested that all 'heresies, schisms, and anti-monarchical principles' had been 'hatch'd' there to spread contagion and poisoning to the kingdoms of Europe.[29] Dryden's 1673 *Amboyna* declared that 'interest's the God they worship in their State', and that the monarchy could 'own Religion's name/But states are atheists in their very frame'.[30] Even the radical Edmund Ludlow recorded critically that the Dutch 'prefer their Trade, before the honor of God and Christ', and Andrew Marvell wrote in the *Character of Holland* some much quoted words: 'Hence Amsterdam, Turk-Christian-Pagan-Jew/Staple of Sects and mint of schism grew/That bank of conscience, where not one so strange/Opinion but finds credit, and exchange'.[31]

For those foreign writers who supported religious toleration, as early as the first few decades of the seventeenth century the Netherlands was both the pre-eminent model to be cited and a significant source of inspiration for their ideas. The small number of tolerationist Baptists who were important in supporting religious toleration in early seventeenth-century England had spent time in the Netherlands and were significantly influenced both by the ideas of Dutch Anabaptism and by the tolerationist practices of the Netherlands. Their case for toleration in England unsurprisingly cited the Netherlands as a model. Thus, Leonard Busher, author of the tolerationist 1614 *Religion's Peace: Or a Plea for Liberty of Conscience* resided in the

---

[27] Israel, 'Economic Contribution', 417.
[28] A. Evans, *Light for the Jews* (1656), 53, in D. Katz, *Philosemitism and the Readmission of the Jews to England 1603–1655* (Oxford 1982), 158.
[29] W. de Britaine, *Interest of England* (1672), 14, in Pincus, 'Butterboxes', 338.
[30] J. Dryden, *Amboyna*, prologue sig. av in Pincus, 'Butterboxes', 339.
[31] Ludlow in J. Scott, *Algernon Sidney and the English Republic 1623–77* (Cambridge 1988), 174; A. Marvell, 'The Character of Holland' (written 1655? published 1665, 1681).

Netherlands, and was associated with the Mennonites, while Thomas Helwys' tolerationist English 1612 *Short Declaration of the Mystery of Iniquity*, issued immediately after his return to England, was preceded a year earlier by his Amsterdam *Declaration of Faith of English People Remaining at Amsterdam*. In their works, and those of the similarly Mennonite-influenced John Smyth, it was argued that church and state were separate, with the state devoted to secular ends, that toleration was to be extended to all peaceful religions, and that none possessed authorisation from God to use force against others for religious purposes. Many of the themes later central to tolerationist arguments of the 1680s and 1690s were rehearsed in these works. As Smyth put it in his *Confession of Faith*, the magistrate was to handle 'only civil transgressions, injuries, and wrongs of man against man, in murder, adultery, theft'. For Helwys, if any civil power could use force all could, and so a Catholic as a Protestant king would have 'the like power to compell all in his dominions to serve God as he commands'. Remarkably, Helwys added that even if the king did possess the truth, it would not help others: 'if they walk in the truth. . .in obedience to the king's power, either for fear or love' they would not be saved. And for Helwys, 'Let them be heretikes, Turcks, Jewes, or whatsoever it apperteynes not to the earthly power to punish them in the least measure'. For Busher, it was 'unnatural and abominable, yea, monstrous, for one Christian to vex and destroy another for difference and questions of religion'. These writers emphasised that the church was a voluntary organisation of believers, and that the vast majority of the world was sinful and to be excluded from communion. They simultaneously firmly distinguished the purposes of church and state, resorted frequently to excommunication from their own churches in pursuit of 'perfection', and cursed as damned those outside their communion. Their churches rarely held more than a few dozen members before splitting again, rather as the Dutch Mennonites excommunicated frequently and split into a series of often rhetorically warring factions who refused to communicate with one another.[32]

Succeeding generations of English writers continued to laud the Netherlands when defending toleration. Robert Greville, Lord Brooke, argued in his 1642 *A Discourse Opening the Nature of that Episcopacie which is Exercised in England* that England should imitate the United Provinces, which 'let every church please her selfe in her owne way, so long

---

[32] Sprunger, *Dutch Puritanism*, 80–3; McBeth, *English Baptist Literature*, 44; J. Coffey, 'Puritanism and Liberty Revisited: The Case for Toleration in the English Revolution', *Historical Journal* (1998), 964–5; W. Jordan, *The Development of Religious Toleration in England from James I* (Harvard 1936), 262–314, esp. 265, 270, 277–83; A. van Deursen, *Plain Lives in a Golden Age* (Cambridge 1991), ch. 17 stresses the tendencies of Mennonites both to split and to condemn each other ferociously.

as she leaveth the State to her selfe'. In his 1646 *The Arraignement of Mr Persecution* the tolerationist Baptist and Leveller Richard Overton concurred that England should imitate the Netherlands and cited 'Holland, Poland, Transilvania' whose 'weales, States, and Cities are well and peaceably governed' with 'divers Religions...in their Provinces' but 'all have one harmony in matters of state'.[33] In the Restoration, the English ambassador Sir William Temple recorded in his 1673 *Observations* that 'It is hardly to be imagined how all the violence and sharpness, which accompanies the differences of Religion in other countryes, seems to be appeased or softened here, by the general freedom which all men enjoy, either by allowance or by connivance'. Waxing lyrical, Temple wrote:

The differences in Opinion make none in Affections, and little in Conversation, where it serves but for entertainment and variety. They argue without interest or anger; They differ without enmity or scorn, And they agree without confederacy. Men live together like Citizens of the world, associated by the common ties of Humanity, and by the bonds of Peace, Under the impartial protection of indifferent laws, with equal encouragement of all Art and Industry, and equal freedom of Speculation and Enquiry.

He was clear that 'the great care of this state' had 'ever been, to favour no particular or curious Inquisition into the faith or religious principles of any peaceable man, who came to live under the protection of their laws, and to suffer no violence or oppression upon any man's conscience, whose opinions broke not out into expressions or actions of ill consequence to the state'.[34] Temple's *Observations* listed in 'the first rank' of causes of Dutch economic prosperity 'the persecutions for matter of Religion' across other countries, which attracted settlers to Holland by 'the general Liberty and Ease, not only in point of Conscience, but all others that serve to the commodiousness and quiet of life; Every man following his own way, minding his own business, and little enquiring into other mens'. Temple used his commentary on the Netherlands as an opportunity to make a more generalised claim for religious liberty, declaring that

the way to our future happiness, has been perpetually disputed throughout the world, and must be left at last to the Impressions made upon every man's Belief and Conscience, either by natural means or supernatural Arguments and Means...for belief is no more in a man's power, than his stature or his Feature; And he that tells me, that I must change my Opinion for his, because his 'tis the truer and the better,

---

[33] Nijenhuis, *Ecclesia*, II, 154; Robert Lord Brooke, *A Discourse* (London 1642), 91; R. Overton, *The Arraignement of Mr Persecution* (1646), 31, discussed in H. Rowen, 'The Dutch Republic and the Idea of Freedom' in D. Wootton (ed.), *Republicanism, Liberty and Commercial Society*, 310–40, at 336–7.

[34] Temple, *Observations*, 199–200, 205–6; cf. B. Kaplan, *Calvinists and Libertines* (Oxford 1995), 1; A. Pettegree, 'The Politics of Toleration in the Free Netherlands 1572–1620', in Grell and Scribner, *Tolerance*, 182–98, at 182.

without other Arguments, that have to me the force of conviction, May as well tell me, I must change my gray eyes for others like his that are black, because they are lovelier.

Giving voice to further arguments which were central to the tolerationist case of the 1680s and 1690s, in 1673 Temple condemned those who ended religious disputes 'in three words at last, which it might as well have ended in at first, That he is in the Right, and I am in the wrong'.[35]

As in Temple's work, which went through many editions, Dutch commercial success was a major argument for toleration in England in the Restoration, and particularly prevalent in works that were in this period coming to stress the importance of accommodating divergent 'interests' in a community. Such was the identification of religious liberty and the Netherlands that when the political economist Sir Josiah Child commented in 1665 on colonial policy that the English 'vainly' endeavoured to achieve religious uniformity at home, he noted that for reasons of trade they allowed 'an Amsterdam of Liberty in our Plantations'.[36] Charles Wolseley's 1668 *Liberty of Conscience the Magistrate's Interest* argued shortly after the Dutch naval victory of 1667 that England should imitate the Netherlands in order to better her: 'Liberty of Conscience would be a more serious blow to Holland than all the Victories yet gained'. The anonymous 1688 *A Letter From Holland Touching Liberty of Conscience* traced the prosperity of Amsterdam to the influxes of refugees under Mary and Laud, and Roger Coke's 1670 *Discourse of Trade* similarly stressed the increased industries of the Netherlands founded by refugees from Laud.[37] The leading London Whig Slingsby Bethel's 1671 *Present Interest of England*, reprinted in 1681 and 1689, identified Dutch commercial success as due to toleration in a work pleading for the English rulers to look to expand English commercial success and toleration. Bethel was to be a refugee in the Netherlands in the 1680s. The Whig lawyer William Petyt's 1680 *Britannia Languens* argued that 'the Dutch. . .allow liberty of conscience to Protestant dissenters' and suggested English imitation.[38]

The greatness and prosperity of the Netherlands was often attributed to their toleration in the Restoration by William Penn, a frequent visitor to the Netherlands and to the house of Benjamin Furly. Furly sheltered Locke in the Netherlands, and Penn's visits included one during the period of Locke's

---

[35] Temple, *Observations*, 191–3, 217–19.

[36] J. Child, *A New Discourse on Trade* (Glasgow 1751; originally 1665), 150–1, quoted in A. Pagden, *Lords of All the World* (Yale 1995), 36.

[37] C. Wolseley, *Liberty of Conscience the Magistrates Interest* (London 1668); *A Letter from Holland Touching Liberty of Conscience* (London 1688); R. Coke, *A Discourse of Trade* (1670), II, 53, in R. Walker, 'The English Exiles in Holland During the Reigns of Charles II and James II', *TRHS* 4, 30 (1948), 111–25, at 111.

[38] S. Bethel, *The Present Interest of England* (1671) cited and discussed in de Krey, 'Dissenting cases', 61; W. Petyt, *Britannia Languens* (1680) in Goldie, 'Huguenot Experience', 183.

residence there in the late 1680s. Penn was another of those stressing the role of 'interests', and Penn's revealingly titled 1675 *England's Great Interest* pointed to the Netherlands and asserted that 'Nothing else [than liberty of conscience] hath hindered Holland from truckling under the Spanish Monarchy, and being ruin'd above three score years ago, and given her that Rise to Wealth and Glory'.[39] His 1685 *Considerations Moving to a Toleration* asserted that the 'riches of a Nation are the bodies of men; for the greatness of a Kingdom certainly consists not in a vast continent of Ground, but in the Multitude of its Inhabitants; and the Thriving of the People, lyes in the encrease of Trade, Manufacture and Commerce'; establishing toleration 'would bring people that are persecuted in our Neighbour Nations about their Religion, to England, as it does, or hath done to Holland'.[40] In his 1670 *The Great Case of Liberty of Conscience* – a work which Locke possessed and listed under the heading 'Tolerantia' in his library catalogue – Penn focused on the 'practice of the greatest, wisest and learnedest Common-wealths, Kingdoms and particular persons' about toleration, and asserted 'Holland, then which, what place is there so improved in Wealth, Trade and Power, chiefly owes it to her Indulgence in matters of faith and worship'.[41]

Dutch toleration could even be made to serve, with qualifications, as a model for 'orthodox' Huguenots pleading in 1681 for Louis XIV to maintain toleration for 'orthodox' Huguenots in France. In his 1681 *Policy*, when he was still justifying toleration of 'orthodox' Protestants in France, Jurieu recorded that it was because of its toleration that the Netherlands grew strong and prosperous. He declared that the United Provinces included

in their bosom all the Religions of Europe…according to the rules of Policy, this general toleration is what makes the strength and power of that Republick: it is that which invites thither so great a number of people; it is what keeps up trade there. All those sects have different Interests in regard of Religion; but all conspire to the good and preservation of a State in which they enjoy a repose that they would not find elsewhere.

For Jurieu,

There is no body but knows, that the force of states depends on the multitude of Inhabitants: It is this that makes the United Provinces so powerful. It is incredible that so little a state can resist so powerful Enemies, and carry its name to the end of the world; which only proceeds from the prodigious multitude of inhabitants which are there. It is this that makes Arts flourish there, Necessity being the mother of Industry. It is the cause of Commerce, because the Territory being too little to nourish so many

---

[39] W. Penn, *England's Great Interest* (London 1675), 13, also discussed in Scott, *Restoration*, 133; Whiting, *Studies*, 140. On the rise of 'interest', see also Scott, *Sidney and…Republic*, ch. 13.
[40] Penn, *Considerations*, 5.
[41] W. Penn, *The Great Case of Liberty of Conscience* (London 1670), 37, 39; Locke, *Library*, 2954.

men, they have been obliged to go seek to the very ends of the World, the necessaries that their own Country could not furnish them with.[42]

Most foreign commentators were, then, clear that the Netherlands prized trade and commerce, drew economic strength from toleration, and were therefore tolerant. Such a view was widely shared within the Netherlands, although it met with considerable hostility from many Reformed ministers, and was recorded with some ministerial anxiety even amongst the tolerant Remonstrants. The Reformed minister Bartens lamented that Amsterdam was becoming increasingly godless instead of the city which had for him driven out Catholicism in the name of the true religion:

The whore on the Y can be bought with anybody's money: She serves Pope and heathen, Moor and Turk, She bothers about neither God nor the dear fathrland, She is concerned with profit alone, profit alone! Profit alone!

And even the Remonstrant minister of Amsterdam Gerard Brandt recorded with some degree of ambivalence that the town fathers

countenance only Calvinism, but for Trade's sake they Tolerate all others, except the Papists; which is the reason why the treasure and stock of most nations is transported thither, where there is full liberty of conscience: you may be what Devil you will there, so you be but peaceable: for Amsterdam is an University of all Religions, which grow confusedly (like stocks in a Nursery) without either order or pruning. If you be unsettled in your religion, you may try all, and take at last what you like best; if you fancy none, you have a pattern to follow of them that would be Church to themselves: its the Fair of all the sects, where the Pedlars of religion have leave to vend their Toyes, their Ribbands, and Phanatique Rattles; their Republic is more to them than Heaven; and God may be more safely offended there than the States General.[43]

Even though his works were proscribed and he complained as early as 1665 in a letter to Henry Oldenburg about suppression of freedom 'to philosophise' because of the 'excessive authority and impudence of the preachers', according to Spinoza's *Tractatus Theologico-Politicus*,

in this most flourishing Republic, this most outstanding city [of Amsterdam] all men, of whatever nation or sect, live in the greatest harmony...There is without exception no sect so hated that its followers are not protected by the public authority of the magistrates and their forces, provided that they harm no one, give each person his due, and live honorably.[44]

---

[42] Jurieu, *Policy*, 164–5, 200–1.

[43] Bartens in Melnick, *From Polemics*, 5; Brandt (1626–85) quoted in J. J. Murray, *Amsterdam in the Age of Rembrandt* (Norman, Okla. 1967), 25.

[44] A. Wolf, (ed.), *The Correspondence of Spinoza* (New York 1927), 206, cited in S. Smith, 'Toleration and Scepticism of Religion in Spinoza's *Tractatus*' in A. Levine (ed.), *Early Modern Skepticism and the Origins of Toleration* (Lanham, Md. 1999), 127–45, at 140; Spinoza, *Tractatus* in *Spinoza Opera* (Heidelberg 1925), III, 246; see especially Israel, *Radical*, *passim* on Spinozism and responses to it in the Netherlands and Europe.

Spinoza declared that 'all they bother to find out, before trusting goods to anyone, is whether he is rich or poor and whether he is honest or a fraud'. The poet Jeremias de Dekker declared similarly that the Exchange in Amsterdam was 'A strolling place where Moor with Northman bargained/A church where Jew and Turk and Christian gathered/A school of every tongue, a market field of every ware/An exchange which swells all exchanges in the world'.[45] Since an English observer in 1701 declared that out of every twenty shares in the East India Company which changed hands in Amsterdam, seventeen were handled by Jews, and Jonathan Israel has shown that Jews 'dominated the day-to-day dealings of the Amsterdam stock market', de Dekker's was not merely a pleasing poetic image.[46] And de Dekker's image of the Netherlands in the seventeenth century presaged the description of England and its Royal Exchange to be made so famous by Voltaire a century later as a leitmotif of the 'Enlightened tolerance' that Voltaire was then to identify with England and its exchange: 'where the representatives of all nations meet for the benefit of mankind. There the Jew, the Mahometan, and the Christian transact together as tho' they all profess'd the same religion, and give the name of infidel to none but bankrupts'.[47]

The Netherlands was thus significantly more religiously tolerant in practice than most other European societies, and widely cited as the epitome of a tolerant society both by opponents and supporters of toleration. The Netherlands was simultaneously and relatedly the most important centre of publishing in Europe, and more open than other societies in welcoming political as well as religious refugees, partly as a society aware of the economic benefits of immigration, partly as understanding itself as a refuge from persecution elsewhere, and partly because of strong support for republican 'freedom'. In the 1680s, Holland had five cities that were centres of publishing – Amsterdam, Rotterdam, Leiden, The Hague, and Utrecht – as many as Germany, France, and England combined. Amsterdam had more than a hundred printers and booksellers whose presses published, albeit often with fictious addresses and publishers, many works banned in other European countries – be they Spinozist 'atheist', Jewish, Catholic, 'heretical' Protestant or Reformed.[48] As Archbishop Bancroft sorrowfully noted in

---

[45] Spinoza, *Tractatus*, III, 246; Murray, *Amsterdam*, 60.
[46] Israel, 'Economic Contribution', 445; *idem*, 'The Amsterdam Stock Exchange and the English Revolution of 1688', *Tijdschrift voor Gescheidenis* (1990), 412–40, at 417.
[47] Voltaire, *Letters Concerning the English Nation* (1926 orig. 1733), 34; for a recent citation of that text in terms of Enlightenment thought, see R. Porter, *The Creation of the Modern World: The Untold Story of the English Enlightenment* (2000), 21.
[48] Hazard, *European Mind*, 88; D. Davies, *The World of the Elzeviers 1580–1712* (The Hague 1954); G. Cerny, *Theology Politics and Letters at the Crossroads of European Civilization* (Dordrecht 1987); C. Gibbs, 'The Role of the Dutch Republic as the Intellectual Entrepot of

1606, 'schismatic persons' had 'planted themselves in divers towns of the Low Countries, where they have liberty, without Impeachment or Contradiction, to publish in print many dangerous Books and Pamphlets in English'. The Brownists maintained their own press, while other puritans solicited Dutch printers such as the Arminian-inclined Jan Fredericksz Stam to print the works of such puritan luminaries as Burton, Prynne, and Bastwick. Several tolerationist works of Helwys and Busher were published in Amsterdam and circulated both in the Netherlands and in England.[49] Religious works were exported from Amsterdam and Leiden to the British American colonies. It was from Amsterdam that Socinian works began to be exported in significant numbers to England in the 1640s and 1650s, and from the Netherlands that Spinoza's works reached England in the Restoration.[50] Herbert of Cherbury's *De Religione Gentilium*, was first printed at Amsterdam in 1663.[51] In the seventeenth century, Amsterdam took over from Venice as the centre of Jewish book production, and from Amsterdam Hebrew books and Jewish texts in Spanish, Portuguese, and Yiddish were exported to the rest of Europe and the Middle East.[52] Such was the export trade that in the 1640s Menasseh ben Israel printed 4,000 copies of the Mishna and Emmanuel Benavist printed 8,000 copies of the Hebrew prayer-book at a time when both figures exceeded the numbers of the entire Jewish community in the Netherlands. In 1685, the city of Breslau decided not to establish a printing-press because 'in Amsterdam there are three important Jewish presses from which books are brought to Danzig and Memel by sea. In this way the Jews of Poland and Lithuania are furnished with these books'. Serving an international market, Jewish printers also aimed at a religiously ecumenical clientele: the Jewish printer Joseph Athias, given an exclusive right to print English Bibles by the States of Holland in 1670, claimed to have printed a million such Bibles for export and reading by every 'plow boy or servant girl' in England and Scotland. In the 1660s, the Moravian Jan Comenius established a Czech press in Amsterdam. The Armenian community, which settled in the 1640s, was printing its hymn-books and the first Armenian Bible there by the 1660s.

Europe in the 17th and 18th Centuries', *Bidjragen en Mededelingen betreffende de Geschiedenis der Nederlanden* 86 (1971), 323–49; H. F. van Nierop, 'Censorship, Illicit Printing and the Revolt of the Netherlands' and S. Groenveld, 'The Mecca of Authors? States Assemblies and Censorship in the Dutch Republic' both in A. Duke and C. Tamse (eds.), *Too Mighty to Be Free?* (Zutphen 1987), 29–44 and 63–86; C. Harline, *Pamphlets, Printing and Political Culture in the Early Dutch Republic* (The Hague 1987). England had London and Oxford; France had Paris and Lyons, and Germany just Leipzig.

[49] Winwood, *Memorials*, III, 95 quoted in Sprunger, *Dutch Puritanism*, 70–1; *ibid.*, 72–6.
[50] H. J. McLachlan, *Socinianism in Seventeenth Century England* (Oxford 1951).
[51] D. Pailin, *Attitudes to Other Religions* (Manchester 1984), 3.
[52] Israel, 'Economic Contribution', 427.

And a particularly lucrative part of the book trade was the printing of French works banned in France for export to France.[53]

It was thus considered appropriate when in 1687 Amsterdam was celebrated as the 'Mecca of authors'. Le Clerc was to say that had he lived anywhere else he could not have profited from so many volumes 'because so many books are no where so easily publish'd and sold, as at Amsterdam'. The editors of the Parisian *Journal de Trévoux* were in contrast to complain that they could not obtain in Paris the foreign publications they needed for review. The ethos of the 'republic of letters' was tied closely to the religiously tolerant practices of Dutch magistrates when in the advertisement to the reader of the first issue of his *Bibliothèque universelle* Le Clerc wrote that

The powers under whom we live permit all Christians to serve God according to the dictates of their conscience: we shall in some measure imitate the equity of the magistrates in reporting without prejudice the views of all Christian societies and the reasons why their authors defend them in those books which they now publish.[54]

This process of publication of works which were 'heretical' was thereby central to the organisation of the journals of the 'republic of letters' in the Netherlands in their tolerationist, ecumenical process of reviewing works and thus to be central to the 'early Enlightenment' – while simultaneously the editors of the journals, other than arguably but very importantly Bayle, explicitly refused to discuss works which could 'shake the foundations of Christianity' and thus, once again like the magistrates of Amsterdam, attempted to suppress the expression of atheistic views.[55] The 'republic of letters' was to be declared by its exponents an imagined transnational republic without territorial base, but in fact its territorial base in the hub of international publication in the Netherlands was vital.[56]

Again, it is worth stressing that the Netherlands was significantly freer than Britain and France in practices of publishing. In Britain for most of the period from 1660 to 1696, licensing acts were in force and many works could not be printed. Printers spent years in jail for issuing proscribed works, including in the years of lapse of the licensing laws during Exclusion when several

---

[53] Davies, *World*, 128–30.

[54] Groenveld, 'Mecca', 63; J. Le Clerc, *An Account of the Life and Writings of Mr John Le Clerc* (London 1712), 13 in R. Colie, 'John Locke in the Republic of Letters' in J.S. Bromley and E. Kossman (eds.), *Britain and the Netherlands* (1960), 111–29, at 119; Le Clerc, *Bibliothèque universelle*, I, preface and Colie, 'Republic', 120; *Journal de Trévoux* (1712), XIII, avertissement; M. Yardeni, 'Journalisme et Histoire Contemporaine a l'époque de Bayle', *History and Theory* (1973), 226; P. Dibon, 'Les Provinces-Unies, carrefour intellectuel de l'Europe du XVIIe siècle' in École practique des Hautes Études, *Annuaire 1965–6*, 98 (Paris 1966), 363–73.

[55] Le Clerc, *Bibliothèque universelle*, I, preface; Israel, *Radical*.

[56] F. Waquet and H. Bots, *La République des Lettres*; below, ch. 16.

'Whig' printers were imprisoned for publishing 'seditious' works. A significant number of Whig works were to be printed in the Netherlands and imported into England, and Whig works were very freely available in the Netherlands in the early 1680s. When John Twynn, printer of the resistance-supporting *Mene Tekel* was executed in England in 1663, an edition was issued in the Netherlands that had been paid for by the radical English exile community. The passage of the Blasphemy Act of 1698 after the lapse of the licensing Act in England in 1696 restored the former's prohibition of anti-Trinitarian works; tellingly, a Huguenot 'Socinian' resident in England, Jacques Souverain's 1690s assault on Trinitarianism was to be published in the Netherlands, from where it was reimported into England.[57]

France was less free still. Louis XIV prevented Huguenots from being booksellers and printers, and after 1685 banned Huguenot works entirely. Jurieu's *Policy* had to be smuggled out of France to the Netherlands in 1680 to be published, from where it was imported into France. Bayle's *Lettre* (later the *Pensées*) was refused publication in Paris in 1681, and Bossuet obtained the pulping of works such as the Oratorian Richard Simon's 1678 *Histoire Critique*, which asserted the interpretative status of the Catholic Church but did so by making it the only basis for support of such doctrines as the Trinity. It was placed on the Index in 1683. Both Bayle's work and Simon's work were published in the Netherlands (the former by Leers although fictiously by 'Pierre Marteau' at Cologne, and the latter by Elzevier with the editorial assistance of the anti-Trinitarian author Christopher Sand and the anti-Trinitarian Noel Aubert de Versé, the latter a tolerationist author). Antoine Arnauld's Jansenism was condemned as 'heretical' in France and publication of his 'Jansenist' works was banned in France. Arnauld came to reside in the Netherlands as a country more tolerant of publishing his religiously dissident views than was his own Catholic France. Many of the tolerationist works and journals of the 'republic of letters' were banned in France, although they then became among the earliest 'forbidden bestsellers' of the French Enlightenment in clandestinely imported copies as a consequence. Bossuet himself complained not merely that Simon's *Histoire Critique* was being 'circulated in a country where there are no restrictions, and among the enemies of the faith' but that when copies wormed their way into France 'They go the round, and pass from one reader to another' and were 'more eagerly devoured. . .because they are forbidden'.[58]

---

[57] Greaves, *Secrets*; Gillett, *Burned Books*; L. Schwoerer, 'Liberty of the Press' in J. R. Jones, *Liberty Restored?*; Walker, 'English Exiles'; Hoftijzer, 'Such onely', 78, 80; Groenveld, 'Mecca'; Harline, *Pamphlets*; [J. Souverain], *Le Platonisme dévoilé* (Cologne 1700), and *Platonism Unveil'd* (1700); see my 'Locke, 'Socinianism and Unitarianism' in M. A. Stewart (ed.), *English Philosophy in the Age of Locke* (Oxford 2000).

[58] Hazard, *European Mind*, 88–90, 193. My phraseology is of course intended here to evoke the title of R. Darnton's *The Forbidden Bestsellers of Pre-Revolutionary France* (New York

The Netherlands provided shelter not merely for religious but also for political refugees. It was to the Netherlands that many French religious and political refugees fled – though most proclaimed themselves religious rather than political refugees when soliciting protection and citizenship.[59] It was to the Netherlands that republicans such as Algernon Sidney retired from England. It was to the Netherlands that several of the regicides fled, and while they officially did not offer shelter to regicides, the authorities at Rotterdam helped the regicide Dendy to escape from English authorities in 1661, facilitated the escape of Cornet Joyce in 1670, and protested against the capture and transporting of Okey, Barkstead, and Corbet. It was to the Netherlands that many other plotters of resistance fled in 1682–3 and after the Monmouth rebellion of 1685. In 1685, the leading Whig grand juryman of 1681, Thomas Papillon, and his fellow shrieval candidate of 1682, Dubois, fled to the Netherlands. William Carr wrote to Archbishop Sancroft of Amsterdam as early as 1680 that 'This place hath been the Center or nest where all the Poysoned Phanaticall People of England, and other places resort to...this Citty...[and] was where first the English Brownist, Puritane, Anabaptist and Presbyterian...began their Plotts'. For Royalists, there were 'too many of his Majesty's unnatural subjects, residing and resorting in these parts' and 'Malice waxeth hotter and hotter'. In 1681, the Brownist Church in Amsterdam had among its members the sons of the Cromwellian Major-Generals Harrison and Haynes and the sons of the regicides Phelps and Blasgrave together with Henry Cromwell's son Oliver. It was two members of this church who printed the latest Whig tracts in the early 1680s, while a third, Abraham Keck, was to be Shaftesbury's host when Shaftesbury fled to the Netherlands in 1682 after he had planned but failed to raise armed resistance to the king in England. A fourth member of the church, Peter D'Aranda, was brother of a friend of Locke in the 1680s and 1690s, Paul D'Aranda, who was a go-between for Locke and his Dutch friend Philip van Limborch.[60]

Charles II and James II campaigned for these many radicals to be handed over. After the Monmouth rebellion, James II argued that should they be 'but connived there, they would still be contriving new designs to disturb me, for that restless and rebellious party will never be quiet'. But while the States General and States of Holland were willing under pressure to order their

1995). On the general topic of the influence of such forbidden works in corroding orthodox beliefs and hierarchies in eighteenth-century Europe, see also, *inter alia*, M. Jacob, *The Enlightenment* (Boston 2000); R. Chartier, *The Cultural Origins of the French Revolution* (London 1991); I. Wade, *The Clandestine Organisation and Diffusion of Philosophical Ideas* (Princeton 1938); and Israel, *Radical*, 98ff.

[59] Israel, *Radical*, 180–1.
[60] Walker, 'English exiles', 113–15; Hoftijzer, 'Such Onely', 74n.; Sprunger, *Dutch Puritanism*, 397–400, 410.

expulsion, and some of those sought moved to other cities in Europe, the authorities at Amsterdam argued that their town had always provided shelter for refugees and depicted many as falsely accused; other States refused to follow the lead of the States General, and many towns simply refused to comply. They claimed that many individuals could not be found, or significantly delayed the execution of warrants in order to allow escape. The bookseller John Dunton recorded in 1688 seeing 'several of Monmouth's friends' openly in Amsterdam in 1688. When army officers tried to kidnap Sir Robert Peyton in Rotterdam, they were resisted in the streets, and it was the potential kidnappers, and not Peyton, that the States of Holland ordered deported. In the one incident in the 1680s when Dutch magistrates complied with English desires for the return of accused rebels, when the Schout at Leiden detained the outlawed Armstrong in 1684 in order to gain the reward offered by the English government, he was himself ostracised by his fellow magistrates. Thomas Molyneux, a correspondent of Locke and a student in the Netherlands, recorded that the Schout by his action had 'incurred a great deal of hatred from the rest of the magistrates, and in general all the people of Holland, who think themselves obliged to rescue all men that come among them for refuge'. The magistrates of the city even sent a message to the parson of the English congregation in Leiden 'that he might assure any of his countrymen for the future they should constantly find refuge here, though they had been guilty of many and great misdemeanours at home, and they should not be delivered up on any pretence whatever'.[61] By gaining magisterial involvement in the return of Armstrong, however, the English authorities in fact outdid the French, who 'never succeeded in obtaining the extradition of a single fugitive French subject'.[62]

It was to the Netherlands that Gilbert Burnet fled, where he became a major political propagandist for William and Mary, including the very period (May 1687) in which Burnet was indicted *in absentia* for treason in Scotland. Burnet refused to return to Scotland, under whose law he would have faced interrogation by torture. Both William and the States General refused to extradite Burnet, although James II requested this on four separate occasions. Burnet was allowed to become a naturalised Dutch citizen in order that it could be claimed that he could only be arraigned in a Dutch court (and Locke and Shaftesbury both quickly became burghers of

---

[61] Dalrymple, *Memoirs of Great Britain and Ireland* (1771–3), II (b), 166–7; Bl Add 34508, fos. 52, 117; BL Add 41812 fo. 70; Add 41813 fos. 86, 204, Add 41814, fo. 139; Add 41819 fo. 245; Add 41820 fos. 175–6 in Miller, *James II*, 158–9; T. Molyneux, 'Correspondence with his Brother' in *Dublin University Magazine* 18 (1841), 314–490, at 485–6 and J. Dunton, *The Life and Errors of John Dunton* (1705), 199–215, at 211, cited in C. D. van Strien, *British Travellers in Holland During the Stuart Period* (Leiden 1993), 12.

[62] P. Zumthor, *Daily Life in Rembrandt's Holland* (Stanford 1994), 263.

Amsterdam for similar reasons, describing themselves as refugees for religious reasons). William even provided Burnet with a bodyguard. Having been outlawed in Scotland, Burnet was subject to individual assassination without penalty, and two plots were organised for his assassination. Moreover, Louis XIV let it be known that anyone who successfully kidnapped him would be given asylum in France.[63] Due to their fear of being kidnapped, Sir Thomas and James Stewart lived like vagrants, travelling under cover of darkness by barges around the canals of Amsterdam, and Locke hid under an assumed name, and for three months in 1685 was able to leave his house only under cover of darkness.[64]

Burnet unsurprisingly remained grateful to the Netherlands ever after, and waxed lyrical about its religious and political freedom from first setting foot there in the early 1680s through to looking back decades later. Burnet's *Original Memoirs* recorded:

One thing I drank in at Amsterdam (which sticks still with me and is not like to leave me) which is never to form a prejudice in my mind against any man because he is of this or that persuasion; for I saw so many men of all persuasions that were as far as I could perceive, so truly religious, that I never think the worse of a man for his opinions.

In his *History of His Own Time* the same broad sentiment remained. He declared:

I saw much peace and quiet in Holland, notwithstanding the diversity of opinions among them; which was occasioned by the gentlemen of the government and the toleration that made all people easy and happy...From there, where everything was free, I went to France, where nothing was free.[65]

Jacques Basnage celebrated the openness of the Netherlands to foreign immigrants and aligned it with its religious toleration in his 1719–26 *Annals of the United Provinces*.[66] The ex-professor of French at Leiden Jean-Nicolas Parival estimated in his *The Delights of Holland* that in 1685 half the population of Holland were foreigners or the descendants of foreigners.[67] In the 1680s, the Netherlands provided shelter not merely to Locke and

[63] Jones, *Revolutions*, 215–16; J. J. Hughes, 'The Missing "Last Words" of Gilbert Burnet in July 1687', *HJ* (1977), 221–7; Walker, 'English Exiles'; Hoftijzer, 'Such Onely'.

[64] Le Clerc, *Life*, 13–14; Walker, 'English Exiles', 121.

[65] Burnet, *A Supplement to Burnet's History of My Own Time, Derived from His Original Memoirs, His Autobiography* ed. H. C. Foxcroft (London 1902), 93; *idem, History* (1818), I, 219 in van Strien, *Travellers*, 20–1.

[66] J. Basnage, *Annales des Provinces Unies depuis les négociations pour la paix de Münster* (La Haye 1719–26) 2 vols, 13, 53, in M. Yardeni, 'La Tolérance Rétrospective: la perception de l'histoire des Pays-Bas et de l'Angleterre dans le refuge huguenot', in *Emergence*, 251–68, at 255.

[67] J-N. Parival, *Les Délices de Hollande* (1738), 22, in Zumthor, *Daily*, 261.

Burnet, political refugees who were defenders of toleration, but also for other major defenders of toleration in the 1680s whose exile was due to religious persecution: Pierre Bayle, Jacques Basnage, Henri Basnage de Beauval, Isaac Papin, Charles Le Cène, and Noel Aubert de Versé were all fleeing religious persecution in Catholic France, and Jean Le Clerc was fleeing religious persecution in Calvinist Geneva. The crucial arguments of these toleration-ists, published in the Netherlands as they were sheltering from persecution or political repression, will form the major story of Part 3 of this book. Without the shelter provided by the Netherlands, few if any of these works would have been composed or published and a major source of later 'Enlightenment thought' in defence of toleration and resistance would have been lost. Nineteenth-century Britain has become justly famous as a refuge for political radicals who were banned elsewhere in Europe; the Netherlands in the seventeenth century deserves a similar reputation.

RELIGIOUS INTOLERANCE IN THE NETHERLANDS

The Netherlands was, then, the most religiously tolerant society in Western Europe in the later seventeenth century, and provided shelter to political refugees who defended rights of resistance to all tyrants at a moment when both France and England were turning to absolutism and vicious intolerance in the 1680s. But enough of fanfares and trumpets. We have already noted some circumscription of toleration – including that churches other than those of the Reformed could not look like churches, that public synagogues were at points banned in the late sixteenth and early seventeenth century with allowance only of private worship, and that processions and proselytising were often forbidden. It is crucial to record both that the Dutch were unusually tolerant and that there had been and still was considerable opposi-tion in the Netherlands to a full or 'universal' religious toleration. Over the century in the Netherlands between 1580 and 1680 there had been only a gradual, at points interrupted, and potentially reversible trend towards full religious toleration. Many of the practices of toleration that have so far been described occurred by failure to enforce intolerant laws on the books, rather than by principled legislative enactment of toleration. There had been little theoretical defence of religious toleration composed by Dutch authors in the century from 1579 to 1681, and the majority of tolerationist arguments that were to be composed in the 1680s as the Netherlands served as the home of the 'early Enlightenment' were composed by recent refugees rather than by Dutch thinkers. The trend towards religious toleration, commenced in the 1570s, had been reversed after the Synod of Dort in 1618, when toleration was removed for Arminians and restricted for many others, including Catholics, whose toleration the Arminians had formerly promoted. And if the period from 1618 to 1630 is the most famous period when the move towards full religious toleration was decisively reversed for many Christians in the seventeenth-century Dutch republic, such religious toleration came under significant pressure and was restricted significantly in practice by legislation at other moments, especially in cities where the Reformed Church had won control, and especially for Catholics and anti-Trinitarians, but also for Jews, Mennonites, Quakers, and Lutherans.

As we will see in Chapter 11 in examining their arguments in some detail, over the century from 1579 to 1680 the ministers of the Calvinist Reformed Church were often outspoken advocates of restriction of toleration in practice and by law, and as the century progressed they had grown stronger in numbers, if somewhat more accepting of a slightly greater degree of religious toleration. Throughout the century, theirs was the publicly funded church and they occupied all buildings which looked like churches. After 1618–19, political office at all levels – including town regents and members of the States General – was formally confined to members of the Reformed Church. In the Grote Vergadering (Grand Assembly) of the seven provinces in 1651, the three elements declared to hold the republic together were the union, army, and 'religion' – the Reformed Church.

By the late seventeenth century, the Reformed Church was growing significantly in numbers. While both historians' estimates and contemporary estimates vary widely, J. L. Price has recently suggested that 'by the second half of the century over a half – and possibly as much as two-thirds by the end – of the population were members of the official church'. In Holland, the province of the large towns of Amsterdam, Leiden, and Rotterdam, Price identifies the towns as 'over three quarters Reformed' by the end of the century. I. Schoffer has concurred that as early as 1650 55 per cent of the total population of the Netherlands were members of the Reformed Church.[68] Even if concentration of Dutch Reformed strength in towns occludes the more substantial areas of Catholic, Lutheran, or Mennonite support in the countryside, it is clear that the Reformed community was growing rapidly and significantly in the urban centres of Holland, and that the more tolerant Arminian and Mennonite communities were both in significant decline. In the decade of the 1680s there were over 41,000 baptisms in the Reformed Church at Amsterdam, and just 565 baptisms by the Arminian community – a ratio of over 70 to 1. The Arminian community was by these years in 'precipitate decline': in 1670, the Rotterdam Remonstrant community was about 7,000, and by 1700 it was down to 6,000, or only one-eighth of the city population. This decline of the

---

[68] Price, *Dutch Society*, 130, 142–3, 198–9, 206; I. Schoffer, 'The Jews in the Netherlands: The Position of a Minority Through Three Centuries', *Studia Rosenthaliana* (1981), 85–105, at 86; cf. P. Burke, *Venice and Amsterdam* (Cambridge 1994), 109.

largely tolerant Arminian community occurred simultaneously with a decline in the numbers of the largely tolerant Mennonite community, the largest Anabaptist community in the Netherlands. It was therefore possible in the Netherlands in the 1680s to see the Reformed Church and its support for intolerance on the rise. Pressure against toleration mounted in the late 1680s, most notably against Catholics, but also against other groups. To the growth of the Reformed community, moreover, must be added the influx of largely orthodox Huguenots. Their anti-tolerationist activities will be discussed later in this chapter and their anti-tolerationist arguments will be discussed in Chapter 14. Here, it is necessary merely to note that they reinforced the anti-tolerationist proclivities of the Dutch Reformed Church, with whom they had much in common, and with whom they had had major contact over the previous century of dogmatic solidarity in support of 'international Calvinism': the Dutch Reformed confession of faith was based on that of the Huguenots.[69]

Moreover, if one turned from the current growth in the numbers of the Dutch Reformed and orthodox Huguenots to a survey of the history of the century from the Dutch Revolt to the 1680s, it became clear that the provision of religious toleration in the Netherlands had always been fragile, had suffered reverses and interruptions, and had rarely received sustained theoretical advocacy or legislative enactment, with many more Dutch writers arguing against full religious toleration than had come to its support. When one combined these observations on the history of toleration with observation of the pressures against toleration being exerted in the 1680s by the Dutch Reformed Church and by leaders of orthodox Huguenot refugees, the fragility of tolerationist practice and its significant limitations in the Netherlands became even more apparent. It was this perspective which was shared by many of those among the Huguenot refugees who supported universal religious toleration. It is this perspective which reverberates through those many pages of Bayle's *Dictionary*, in which he surveys and discusses the practices and moments of considerable intolerance in the Netherlands both in the 1680s and 1690s and throughout the preceding century of Dutch history. Jean Le Clerc, a refugee from Genevan orthodoxy who became an Arminian professor, also compiled a history of his new country from its beginnings as a republic to the Peace of Utrecht and lamented Reformed hostility to Arminianism.[70] Anti-Trinitarian Huguenot refugees to the Netherlands – and these probably included the

---

[69] Israel, *Dutch Republic*, ch. 27, esp. 641, 654–5; Duke et al. (eds.), *Calvinism in Europe: A Collection of Documents* (Manchester 1992); M. Prestwich (ed.), *International Calvinism 1541–1715* (Oxford 1985); P. Zagorin, *Rebels and Rulers 1500–1660* (Cambridge 1982), II, 73–4.

[70] Jean Le Clerc, *Histoire des Provinces-Unies des Pays-Bas* (Amsterdam 1727–8); R. Murris, *La Hollande et les Hollandais* (Paris 1925), 221.

tolerationist authors Noel Aubert de Versé and Charles Le Cène – had particularly acute reason to worry: as we will see, Socinianism was significantly suppressed even in the Netherlands. In order simultaneously to gain a sense of the perspective on Dutch intolerance over the previous century of a recent tolerationist immigrant such as Bayle, and an understanding of that intolerance as it had been practised, Bayle's commentaries in the *Dictionary* will be interwoven into the account which now follows of Dutch intolerance in the century from the Dutch Revolt to the 1680s.[71]

It is important to register first that from the very enunciation of 'freedom of religion' and 'freedom of conscience' in the 1570s, support for religious toleration had at many points been interpreted as restricted to a freedom of 'belief' or 'conscience' but not of practice, and that even to argue otherwise in the early years of the republic could spell trouble. In 1579, the argument that 'freedom of conscience' must involve liberty of practice of the sometime Secretary of the States of Holland, Dirck Coornhert, the most important sixteenth-century Dutch apologist for a truly extensive religious toleration, led to his condemnation by the States of Holland as a 'disturber of the peace'. The States of Holland had forbidden him to publish any theological works without their approval.[72] In 1595, Amsterdam banned Lutheran worship and threatened to expel Lutherans. Middleburg forbade Lutheran worship in 1589. Leiden expelled its Lutheran preacher in 1596 and did not allow another until 1606. Lutheran worship was forbidden at times in Leiden and Enkhuizen and other locations, and the Lutheran church at Rotterdam was demolished in 1624. The States of Holland ordered by placard in 1624 'that the preaching and other exercises of the Lutherans should be tolerated nowhere in the countryside'. This measure was repeated in the 1640s, although Lutherans were able to build a church on the Spui in Amsterdam, and published a Lutheran Bible in 1648.[73]

While Anabaptists were generally tolerated in the Netherlands after the late sixteenth century, this was true as long as they associated themselves with pacifist repudiators of resistance such as Menno Simmons – the Mennonites.[74] And at many times, toleration even for obviously peaceful Anabaptists was restricted by magistrates. Anabaptist worship was officially forbidden in Friesland from 1598, a proscription reinforced in later placards. In Groningen in 1601, an ordinance declared children who had not been baptised in the Reformed Church illegitimate, and gave ministers the right to

---

[71] See below, pp. 173–5.
[72] Coornhert challenged the notion that he was a disturber of the peace as equivalent to prior accusations against heretics of lèse-majesté: G. Voogt, *Constraint on Trial* (Kirksville, Mo. 2000), 88–90.
[73] Israel, *Dutch Republic*, 375–6, 476; Nijenhuis, *Ecclesia*, II, 151.
[74] C. Krahn, *Dutch Anabaptism: Origin, Spread, Life and Thought* (Pennsylvania 1981), 152.

enter houses in which they suspected that a Mennonite conventicle was being held. The States of Holland after 1618–19 decreed that tolerated churches 'in future will not be permitted in any other places than where they are already practiced' and used this measure to prevent construction of new Anabaptist churches. Even as late as 1643, the Anabaptist Weke Walles was banished from Groningen; he was expelled from Friesland in 1644 at the instigation of the synod (for preaching that Judas was 'a good man' and 'saved'). As Bayle noted about the case in the *Dictionary*, the Synod of Friesland was 'perpetually soliciting the States of that Province, to revive the Edict' of 1598 against Anabaptists, and in 1651 'their High Mightinesses' had decreed in response to an increase in Anabaptist congregations 'that the sect should be restrained and should not spread'. Bayle pointed to Voetius' *Politica Ecclesiastica* as 'generally speaking' arguing against the toleration of Anabaptists, and significantly compared the restriction of places of worship of the Anabaptists (which was established by the declaration of the States of Holland after 1618–19 that tolerated churches 'in future will not be permitted in any other places than where they are already practiced') to the restrictions placed on Huguenots in France before 1685: 'After the same manner, the Protestants, in France, were forbid all Places of religious Worship, which they could not prove they were in possession of at the time of the Edicts'.[75]

While they were largely tolerated from about 1630–1, the Arminian community were officially declared by the Synod of Dort in 1619 both 'heretics' and 'disturbers of the peace'. Following this judgment, about 200 Remonstrant preachers were deprived of their livings by the provincial and civic authorities; 70 were permitted to live in their Netherlands as long as they did not in future preach or engage in theological dispute in public, and another 80 were banished.[76] The leading Arminian theologian Episcopius was among those banished as part of the 'oppressed party', as Bayle put it in his extensive account of this intolerance towards Arminians in the *Dictionary*.[77] Many Arminians went into exile in France. In the early 1620s, those who stayed and attempted to preach in public were arrested and in some cases imprisoned.[78] In his *Het Interest van Holland*, first published in 1662, Pieter de la Court lamented that 'since the year 1618, we have begun to depart from that laudable maxim' of 'freedom of Religion' 'more and more', first 'with the Remonstrants, persecuting them by Placaets, Fines, and Banishments, and driving them into other lands'.[79] It was not until after 1625–6, and especially

---

[75] Bayle, *Dictionary*, Anabaptists D, H; Israel, *Dutch Republic*, 376, 709.
[76] Israel, *Dutch Republic*, 462.   [77] Bayle, *Dictionary*, Episcopius.
[78] Israel, *Dutch Republic*, 463–5.
[79] P. de la Court, *The True Interest and Political Maxims of Holland* (London 1702), 81.

after 1630–1, when the placards against them ceased to be enforced, when Arminian ministers were allowed to escape from confinement in Loevestein Castle, and when Episcopius was allowed to establish a covert church in Amsterdam and then from 1634 a seminary to train preachers, that Arminians became effectively tolerated in the Netherlands and were able to regain significant support among the regents in many towns.[80]

Before that date, in rhetorical attacks by the orthodox (essentially Calvinist) Gomarists, Arminians were depicted as 'polluting' the community and as theologically associated with Catholicism. A revealingly titled 1618 engraving *The Arminian Dung-Cart* placed Arminius on a 'dung cart' together with the Anabaptist David Joris and the spiritualist Dirck Coornhert; two Jesuits were shown directing the cart.[81] Surveying the accounts of the Gomarist-Arminian disputes published in contemporary and later accounts by both sides, it was clear to Bayle that such rhetorical attacks had been combined in the 1610s and early 1620s with considerable violence and threats of violence against Arminians as well as their banishment and silencing. Describing the disputes between Arminians and Contra-Remonstrants in his *Dictionary* entry on Episcopius, for instance, Bayle utilised the account in the preface to Stephen Courcelles' *Opera Theologica* to describe the period leading up to the Synod of Dort as a period when people were inflamed against the leading Arminian Episcopius 'whom they loaded with curses both in the Church and in the Street' and stressed that he 'hardly escaped being beaten, if not stoned to death' – the latter being the punishment for blasphemers. As Bayle noted, utilising Episcopius' successor Courcelles' account, a blacksmith seeing him go by had then gone

out of his forge with an Iron bar in his Hand, and began to run after him, crying out 'an Arminian, A Disturber of the Church': Episcopius would have been knocked on the Head by that fellow, if he had not run away, and if other people had not come to his Assistance.

According to Courcelles, as Bayle repeated, in 1617 the house of Episcopius' brother had moreover been 'plundered by the mob of Amsterdam, under the false pretence that several Arminians heard a sermon there'. Looking back, Bayle blamed the people who had 'alarm[ed] and terrif[ied] the Populace' as well as the failure in this period to maintain 'moderation'.[82] Courcelles' account of this violent treatment of Episcopius also received an English edition as part of the 1673 English edition of Episcopius' attack on the pretensions to infallibility of Catholicism, *The Popish Labyrinth*, which stressed that the blacksmith had intended to 'murther' Episcopius and that because of the

---

[80] Nijenhuis, *Ecclesia*, II, 150; Israel, *Dutch Republic*, 495ff.
[81] In Voogt, *Constraint*, 235–6.   [82] Bayle, *Dictionary*, Episcopius A.

hatred of 'the vulgar sort' for Arminianism, 'many hundreds of vile persons' had invaded his brother's house in a 'hostile manner' and 'as a Company of robbers'. They had 'drank up or spilled the wine and beer in the cellar' and then ransacked the house carrying away not merely money, but also 'clothes, linnen, pictures, books, houshold stuff, plate' and destroying what they could not carry away, 'leaving nothing there whole and untouched'.[83]

A similar account in its stress on the many levels of violence, threat, and banishment by civil authority was provided by Bayle in his extensive entry on the Arminian theologian (and arguably anti-Trinitarian) Vorstius, who was deprived of his academic position and banished by the States of Holland. Bayle indicated that the intolerant included the synod and minister who maintained 'the old doctrine of Calvin' and pressed that the States-General would take care that in future the churches of the low countries 'would not be polluted and defiled with such pernicious principles, heresies and blasphemies' and should suppress his works. As Bayle described it, using Dutch accounts, Vorstius' life was in danger because many thought that a person of his character 'ought not to be suffered to live'; they had forced him to 'change his habitation, and to be continually provided with a ladder at his window, in case they should attempt to break open his door'. On one occasion, his house being 'surrounded by armed men', such precautions were insufficient. Bayle declared that this was a 'religious zeal' which took away

all remorse of crimes...Those who designed to beat, rob, or assassinate Vorstius, to throw him into a dungeon, or load him with invectives, thought they did a very good action, and an acceptable service to God.

Such phraseology was strongly reminiscent of the images which Bayle employed in describing Catholic motivations and justifications of violence against Huguenots in his tolerationist 1686 *Philosophical Commentary*; this suggests that Bayle understood the Netherlands as having experienced similar persecutionary forces directed against Arminianism in the early seventeenth century. It is unsurprising that Arminians were not to feel secure in their own toleration, even in the late seventeenth century.[84]

Quakers received more toleration in the Netherlands than in England. But at various points and in various locations Quakers were persecuted in the second half of the seventeenth century even in the Netherlands, and members of the Reformed Church called for their suppression. In 1657, ministers of the

---

[83] S. Episcopius, *The Popish Labyrinth...unto which is Added The Life and Death of the Author* (London 1673), tr. J. K., 'life', 10–11.

[84] Bayle, *Dictionary*, Vorstius, F, I, K. On crowd violence against Arminians, see Israel, *Dutch Republic*, 491–2. For an entry by Bayle on an extreme anti-Arminian and anti-Socinian theologian at the Synod of Dort who was 'full of zeal and passion', and whose works Bayle indicated as 'worthy of oblivion', see *Dictionary*, Lubertus, notes.

Reformed Church in Rotterdam argued that Quakers such as William Ames were 'a sort of Heretics, and that they ought to be punished and their Meetings restrained', in the words of the Reformed minister Gerard Croese, who also declared that Reformed ministers hated them as 'Men of a Malignant seditious temper, whose assemblies were nothing else, but Seminaries of discord and wickedness'. The dyke-reeve of Rotterdam ordered Ames and Maertin Maertinson arrested and incarcerated in the city insane asylum. According to Ames, who issued *An Account of the Persecution and Imprisonment of William Ames and Maertin Maertensz*, he had been visited in this 'prison' by preachers who had said 'that the magistrates ought to punish such people...although they could not show wherein he had overstepped any just law of God or man'. Ames further claimed that 'some say we should be imprisoned, others that we should be banished, others that we should be burnt' – the last by a preacher in Overijssel, who allegedly had said moreover 'that we should be burnt with our books'.[85] In May 1661, the Rotterdam session of the Extraordinary Presbytery of Schieland argued that a 'stop should be put to the conventicles and visits of the Quaeckers', a sentiment reiterated at the Synod of South Holland in the following year, whose article VII opposed Quakers and Socinians together, a pairing later repeated in further assaults upon the toleration of both. Furly and Penn were acutely aware of the persecution of Quakers in Dutch-garrisoned Emden in East Friesland in the 1670s because of their joint visit there together, and Penn wrote a work pleading for toleration of Quakers, his *Account of the Travails of Mr Penn in Holland and Germany*, which described Emden as the city 'where friends have been so bitterly and barbarously used, the like hath scarcely been known in any place'. Here they had been 'banished some 30 and some 40 times and above'. He described the 1670s as seeing a 'sore and bitter tempest of persecution' and the scattering of a 'fine Meeting' as Quakers 'were sent away as fast as they return'.[86] In 1662, a Frisian edict was issued which prohibited all publications by 'erring spirits of the devil' and named not merely Socinians but also 'Quakers, Immersionists'. Although their most dramatic and repeated prohibitions were issued against Socinian works, Holland, Utrecht and Friesland in the 1670s and 1680s issued similar edicts banning a much wider range of books as blasphemous and harmful to the public Reformed religion, including Quaker works.[87]

At points in the later seventeenth century there were outbursts of crowd violence against the Quakers in Rotterdam itself. In 1675, Quakers in

[85] G. Croese, *History* (1696) II, 172 (202f.); Ames, *Een Beschrijvinge* in *idem De Valshe Propheten* (1659), 20–6, in W. Hull, *Benjamin Furly and Quakerism in Holland* (Pennsylvania 1941), 206–7.
[86] W. Penn, *An Account of the Travails of Mr Penn in Holland and Germany 1677* (London 1694), 199–201; Hull, *Furly*, 226.
[87] Groenveld, 'Mecca', 73 and notes 48 and 49.

Rotterdam recorded that 'within and without their regular meeting place' they had been 'treated and handled with violence and annoyance by divers sorts of men, not only young but of greater age, which is so publickly known that the thrown-in windowpanes and broken doors and benches are clear witnesses thereof'. The complaint was signed by Furly. The response of the burgomasters of Rotterdam was to order that the Quakers should be prevented from meeting and that the violence towards them thus would be prevented. When the Quakers presented another appeal, they were told that 'they should never receive freedom to hold a meeting at any place within the jurisdiction of the city'. This threat was not carried out, and Quakers met usually in Furly's house on the Scheepmakershaven which served as their meeting-house for over thirty years until 1695, but it suggests the pressures experienced by Quakers in worshipping in Rotterdam, and the fragility of toleration perceived by Furly, Locke's host in exile. The house on the Scheepmakershaven was both the site of Quaker meetings and of 'the Lantern' philosophical and literary society of which Locke was a member. It is, indeed, as much a measure of the fragility as of the existence of toleration for Quakers that in Amsterdam in 1686 the Quaker's quarterly meeting epistle declared that 'Our meetings are continued peaceable as from the Magistrates; and so it is likewise with the meetings of Rotterdam', and that the May 1687 epistle recorded that 'In Rotterdam, Haarlem and Alkmaar the Meetings are quiet and unmolested'. Such comments suggest how fearful of magisterial restriction and crowd violence Quakers were in the later 1680s. By sheltering in Furly's house in 1687–9, then, Locke was sheltering in the house of an author of works against persecution of the Quakers in England, the Netherlands, and elsewhere in Europe; the translator of others' works arguing for toleration; and a supporter of toleration for Quakers and Mennonites whom he understood as not being fully tolerated in the Netherlands. To offer a plea for toleration of Quakers in the 1680s – as Locke, Aubert, and others whose arguments we will examine in Part 3 did in their tolerationist works – thus involved pleading for the toleration of a group which was seen by many in the Netherlands, including particularly Reformed ministers, as both intolerable and 'abominable', and which at moments still faced and feared crowd violence against their worship.[88]

While Catholics in the second half of the seventeenth century were largely tolerated in the Netherlands, they had been the subject of many placards in the sixteenth and early seventeenth centuries, contributing to a sense of the

[88] Hull, *Furly*, 226–8, 232, 242–4, 263. Furly was, of course, conscious that England, in which his father had been incarcerated in the 1650s and 1660s, and in which his brother was incarcerated in the 1660s and still being fined in the 1680s, was far more oppressive for Quakers for most of the period 1660–89 than was the Netherlands.

fragility of their tolerance in the late seventeenth century. In 1573, celebration of the mass was prohibited in Holland. In 1581, just after the Union of Utrecht, a placard (ordinance) specifically forbade

any popish exercises such as masses, preaching, baptism and otherwise, by which any unrest and uproar might arise, nor any secret understanding with the enemy might be held, nor crafty attacks brought into play, and even if the same exercises might happen without large numbers at meetings, yet would serve not only to cause scandal and annoyance in the church to the detriment of the commonwealth, so it is that we have once more strictly forbidden and henceforth do forbid all such gatherings and meetings.

Similar placards were issued in 1622, 1629, 1641 and 1649.[89] From 1584, anyone who organised Catholic worship was subject to exile. Catholic churches and other establishments were seized and schools closed down.[90] All Catholic churches, chapels, and monasteries were confiscated. Jesuits, foreign and religious priests were at different points officially banned, and in the early seventeenth century Catholics were prosecuted for living in concubinage when they did not marry before a Protestant minister, and fined for having their children baptised in 'heretical' churches. Catholicism had been more tolerated in those towns controlled by the Arminians and their associates than in Contra-Remonstrant areas; the assault upon Arminianism in the late 1610s was followed by assault on Catholic worship. In many areas in the 1620s, priests lamented their 'miserable' condition. In 1622, it was reported in Gelderland that 'priests are rare owing to the harshness of the inhabitants and the severe persecution'. Although such assaults on Catholics became more sporadic again as magistrates relaxed their measures of the 1620s, and as Arminians began to regain some measure of toleration in the 1630s, nonetheless the potential for punitive measures against Catholics remained. When large-scale administration of the sacrament occurred in Zijdewind in 1649, the chapel was razed to the ground, the clergy were banished, and the local magistrates replaced.[91] In the mid-seventeenth century, de la Court complained that persecution of the Remonstrants after 1618 had been joined by that of the

Romanists, by disturbing them more and more in their Assemblies with severe Placaets, and more rigorous execution, notwithstanding that by the Prosperity of our own Government, the great increase of the Protestants, the Peace, and the King of Spain's renunciation of any Pretence, Right, or Title, for himself, or his heirs after him, to these United Provinces; the moving reasons of our first Placaets against the

---

89 Nijenhuis, *Ecclesia*, II, 147–8.
90 Le Cler, *Toleration*, 249–55; Israel, *Dutch Republic*, 373.
91 Israel, *Dutch Republic*, 382–4; Nijenhuis, *Ecclesia*, II, 148.

Romanists, seemed to have been taken away. So that now in order to enjoy their Liberty, they must pay a heavy tax annually, to the profit of the Bailiffs and Schouts.[92]

And even though Catholic worship became increasingly tolerated in the second half of the seventeenth century, Catholic priests were still subject to harassment and banishment; Catholic worship was permitted only in private where it was permitted, and in some places it remained banned entirely. In 1672, Sir William Temple recorded that Catholicism was not officially tolerated, being 'alone excepted from the common protection of their laws' because the States believed that it made men 'worse subjects than the rest, by the acknowledgment of a Foreign and Superior Jurisdiction'. Temple stressed that such toleration as existed in practice existed because what the constitution of the state did not allow by law was permitted through the 'connivance' of officials who in certain towns and for payment allowed Catholicism to be practised 'as free and easie, though not so cheap and so avowed'. William Carr, consul and spy in Amsterdam in the 1680s, noted that not merely were Catholic churches looked on as 'conventicles' but that they were 'many times shut up, and again opened at the Schout's pleasure'. Brandt similarly declared that all religions were tolerated in the Netherlands 'but the papists'.[93]

In the later 1680s, as the Dutch saw Catholic persecution in France and Piedmont and feared it in England, and as thousands of Huguenots and Waldensians flooded into the Netherlands, there were outbreaks of anti-Catholic rioting in Leeuwarden in July 1687, and votes by many of the provinces to restrict Catholic worship. In 1687, there was majority support in the states for a placard expelling Jesuits and other 'regular clergy', leaving only the secular clergy. If this placard had been enforced, the number of Catholic clergy in the Netherlands would have been halved. Leiden expelled the Jesuits in 1685, together with some other regular priests. The North and South Holland synods sent a delegation to Orange in 1687 to urge the passage of the placard against 'all regular priests whether Franciscans, Jesuits, or of whatever order they may be'.[94] It was only because William of Orange intervened in support of toleration for Catholics that a major restriction of Catholicism did not take effect; such measures apparently had the support of the majority of the Dutch population in the late 1680s.[95]

---

[92] De la Court, *True Interest*, 81.
[93] Temple, *Observations*, 200–2; Carr, *Accurate Description*, 15; Le Cler, *Toleration*, 249–55.
[94] Israel, *Dutch Republic*, 646–7.
[95] Such intolerance died down in the 1690s, as England became ruled by William and Mary and the threat to the very existence of Protestantism considerably receded, but intolerance towards Catholics flared up in anti-Catholic violence at various moments in the eighteenth century. Not until the end of the Dutch republic in 1795 was the official ban on Catholic worship completely lifted: M. E. H. N. Mout, 'Limits and Debates: A Comparative View of Dutch Toleration in the Sixteenth and Seventeenth Centuries' in *Emergence*, 37–47, at 45.

Although the Netherlands allowed Socinians to settle when banished from other countries, and rarely imprisoned them, Socinians were not officially allowed to print and circulate their works, nor to set up their own congregations, but only to worship with the Arminians, Collegiants and Mennonites. As Bayle noted in the *Dictionary*, using as his sources Reformed works in which restrictive measures against anti-Trinitarianism were advocated and approved, in 1653 and 1655 respectively the States of Holland and the magistrates of Utrecht had issued edicts forbidding any to bring 'Socinian heresies' into the country, to impart them to others, or 'to hold an assembly with such an intent'. Offenders were to be banished as both 'blasphemers' and as 'disturbers of the public peace'. The magistrates simultaneously instituted what Bayle called 'severe penalties' for impressions of Socinian books. The States of Holland placard of 1653 made printers of Socinian works liable to a fine of 3,000 guilders and a ban from the occupation for the first offence; a second offence brought banishment. Booksellers faced a 1,000-guilder fine. Even the fine for printers, let alone the loss of occupation and banishment, was triple the usual fine of 1,000 guilders for 'licentius' (uncontrolled printing), and that usual fine had recently been increased steeply. In 1655, Utrecht adopted the same punishments.[96] In 1678, the city of Utrecht reissued a placard against all 'Socinian, Arian, blasphemous and entirely pernicious books'. In 1642, Francis van Meurs served seven months in prison in Amsterdam for denying the immortality of the soul and Christ's divinity.[97] In the same year, the Dutch edition of the leading Socinian Johann Crell's *Bescrrijvinge van Godt en zijne eygenschappen* was publicly 'executed' and burned by order of the aldermen.[98] In 1669, Adriaen Koerbagh died in prison, having been tortured; he had received a ten-year prison sentence after having denied the Trinity, and having assaulted the incarnation, miracles, resurrection, immortality of the soul, and heaven and hell. His punishment was partly due to his 'Spinozist' leanings but it was also due to his Socinian sympathies; 'Spinozism' and Socinianism shared in many departures from 'orthodox' Trinitarian Christianity.[99]

Bayle noted in correspondence in 1701 that anyone publicly attacking the doctrine of the Trinity in Amsterdam was likely to be sent to prison.[100] In the *Dictionary* he stressed that those who thought that Socinians had a 'full liberty of conscience in the United Provinces, are little acquainted with

[96] Bayle, *Dictionary*, Socinus L; Groenveld, 'Mecca', 79.   [97] Zumthor, *Daily*, 93.
[98] Groenveld, 'Mecca', 85.
[99] Israel, 'The Intellectual Debate about Toleration' in *The Emergence of Toleration in the Dutch Republic* (Leiden 1997), 28–9; *idem*, *Radical*, 62–3, 185–96.
[100] Bayle, *Lettres*, III, 828, 835 quoted in Israel, *Dutch Republic*, 676.

History'.[101] While it was in the Netherlands that most Socinian works were in fact published, these Socinian works were usually given fictitious imprints. Tolerationist works were similarly often given fictitious German imprints, including that of 'Pierre Marteau' of Cologne.[102] As Jonathan Israel has stressed:

> The Dutch republic was undoubtedly freer than other European societies of the time and tolerated more churches and religions than any other, allowing numerous faiths to publish their books and rival interpretations of Scripture. Nevertheless, the Republic adhered to a comprehensive censorship which created a real and formidable barrier to the expression of certain kinds of religious and philosophical ideas.

Formal proscription of Socinian anti-Trinitarianism was, in Israel's words in *Dutch Republic*, the 'pivot of intellectual and theological censorship' from the 1650s to the end of the century.[103]

Not merely were anti-Trinitarian publications and preaching themselves proscribed, but individuals accused of being associated with Socinianism were forbidden to preach. In 1687–8, the synods of Friesland and North Holland condemned the Mennonite Foecke Floris as a 'Socinian' and attempted to prevent him from preaching. Floris' book was burned, and he was imprisoned for three weeks in Leeuwarden and banished from Friesland, and then threatened by the bailiff of Kennemerland with imprisonment in or expulsion from North Holland. Due to the personal intervention of Locke's host Furly, who thought Floris' case 'a matter of common concern to all Christians', William intervened to put a stop to the persecution, as Locke noted in describing these events in letters to Limborch in November 1688 – shortly before the Limborch-arranged publication in April 1689 of Locke's *Epistola de Tolerantia* in the Netherlands, a work which explicitly supported toleration for Socinianism and Anabaptism.[104] Synods regularly professed the need to institute effective surveillance of both Remonstrants and Mennonites suspected of harbouring Socinian tendencies. While officially tolerated, Arminians such as Limborch had good reason themselves to be fearful of such pressures and of the growing pace of accusations of Socinianism in the 1680s.[105] In his 1689 assault on Locke's *Letter Concerning Toleration*, the Anglican minister Thomas Long's *Letter on Toleration Deciphered* declared

---

[101] Bayle, *Dictionary*, Socinus, K.

[102] Israel, *Dutch Republic*. On Marteau, see Jacob, *The Enlightenment*, introduction.

[103] Israel, *Dutch Republic*, 915. Israel's more recent *Radical Enlightenment* has focused far more on the restrictions on 'Spinozism' than those on 'Socinianism'.

[104] Locke, *Correspondence*, 1090, 1092; Hull, *Furly*, 95; Israel, *Dutch Republic*, 914–15. In the 1690s, the Synod of North Holland resumed its demands for suppression of Floris' preaching and this was ordered by the bailiff in 1692.

[105] University Library, Amsterdam coll.hss.v.84; M. Jacob, 'Contemporary Enlightenment Historiography', *Geschiedenis*, 7–14.

that 'no Christian magistrate' had 'ever yet adventured on' an absolute toleration such as that Locke proposed, and continued:

For as for Holland which is objected from the very Foundation of their Establishment, Popery was excluded; nor could the Socinians or Arminians procure a toleration, tho' the latter were men of Great Learning and Peacable spirits.[106]

In the *Dictionary*, Bayle argued in the 1690s that most were 'in error' about Dutch religious liberty in thinking it truly extensive, when in fact much had been done even earlier in the century to try to ensure orthodoxy by 'many jealous, suspicious Persons and Inquisitors', and when the pressures for religious orthodoxy were growing rather than receding.[107] Bayle himself lost his professorial post at the École Illustre in the 1690s under accusations by Jurieu of heresy and atheism; his note in the *Dictionary* indicated that things had become worse 'since certain factious and haughty men' from France 'would make themselves formidable by some Attempts towards an Inquisition'. Even before that date, in 1691 Bayle wrote in a letter to a friend 'God preserve us from Protestant Inquisition', which in five or six years 'might make us long for the Roman one, as for a good thing'.[108] In his 1690 *Picture of Socinianism*, Jurieu argued that it was not religious diversity which made the Netherlands peaceful and prosperous, but that it was peaceful because such toleration was very significantly incomplete in a country with a desirably dominant Reformed religion and significantly suppressed sects. He was thus in agreement with Bayle about the lack of full religious toleration, while diametrically opposed to his advocacy of 'universal religious toleration'. Jurieu argued that only with 'indifference' could full toleration preserve the peace, and that such 'indifference' was undesirable where salvation was at stake.[109]

And the restrictions on toleration so far noted are only those of religious expression and worship. Many of the legislative condemnations of Socinian or Arian thought were combined with condemnations of 'atheist' or 'libertine' thought. We noted a moment ago that Adriaen Koerbagh died in prison, having been tortured and having received a ten-year prison sentence after denial of the Trinity in his 1668 *Bloemhof van allerley lieflijkheyd sonder verdriet* and assault on the incarnation, miracles, resurrection, immortality of the soul, and heaven and hell in his quickly suppressed

---

[106] [T. Long] *Letter on Toleration Decipherd* (London 1689), 16.
[107] Bayle, *Dictionary*, Blondel, D, note K.   [108] Bayle, *OD*, IV, 667 (17 Dec. 1691).
[109] P. Jurieu, *Le Tableau du Socinianisme* (The Hague 1690), and Rousseau, *The Social Contract*, IV, ch. 8, discussed in Dodge, *Political Thought*, 220; Israel, *Dutch Republic*. D. Wootton has also importantly pointed out that Dutch tolerationism was less compendious and more challenged than is often emphasised, while also recognising the Netherlands as vital as the most tolerant country in Europe.

significantly Spinozist- and Socinian-influenced 1668 *Een Ligt Schijnende in Duystere Plaatsen*. His Socinian- and Spinozist-influenced younger brother escaped the same fate only because he had not printed his very similar views.[110] Adriaan van Beverland's 1678 'libertine' attack on the doctrine of original sin, *De Peccato Originale* – a work whose 1679 edition saw the addition of a quotation of Hobbes and Spinoza – declared that Adam and Eve were guilty only of discovering sexual intercourse. The Synod of North Holland called Beverland's work a 'foul and blasphemous' treatise, and the States of Holland and Leiden University banned and burned the book and banished the man. Symbolically, it was William's apologist for religious toleration, Fagel, who ordered the book suppressed and the man arrested. Beverland then fled to England in 1680, a refugee for liberty for 'libertinism' crossing the sea in the opposite direction to Locke and Burnet, pleaders for liberty and not libertinism against the 'libertine' high culture of Restoration England.[111]

A small number of thinkers spoken of as 'libertines' or 'atheists', usually for the unorthodoxy of their public denial of a 'providential' God rather than because they avowed openly that no God existed, resided in the Netherlands in the late seventeenth century. One of these, Spinoza, has become world-renowned. These 'libertines' or 'atheists' found ways to publish clandestinely in the Netherlands. But this was often at substantial cost to themselves in terms of legal punishments and attacks on their works. Jonathan Israel has recently brilliantly reconstructed many of the dimensions of these 'atheist' or 'Spinozist' circles and the influences of such 'atheistic' or 'Spinozist' thought in the Netherlands (and elsewhere) in his *Radical Enlightenment*, and has emphasised that 'atheism' or 'Spinozism' was officially proscribed in the Netherlands. Spinoza's own works, such as the *Tractatus*, did not circulate easily but were rather called 'pestilentissimus' and banned. As Israel has put it, 'there were stringent limits on what could be published, openly declared, or even uttered in conversation...this ambivalent semi-tolerance...was the real hallmark of the Dutch republic...a partial toleration seething with tension, theological and political'.[112]

Such toleration as the Netherlands provided was, then, essentially 'religious' toleration. It did not extend to those considered to have no religion, and the Netherlands was fierce both in its legislation and in its execution of laws against 'immorality' or 'libertinism', and particularly against sexual 'immorality', and it attempted to proscribe and punish the printed publication

---

[110] Israel, 'Intellectual Debate' 28–9; *idem, Radical*, 62–3, 185–96; Groenveld, 'Mecca'.
[111] Israel, *Dutch Republic*, 475, 683–4; *idem, Radical*, 87–8; above, pp. 128–33 and below, pp. 706–18.
[112] Israel, *Dutch Republic, passim*, esp. 676; *idem, Radical*, 276.

of 'atheist' arguments. In the first years of the republic, under pressure from the synods, William of Orange had issued a placard of 1581 prohibiting the printing of 'offensive, seditious and scandalous books' which could lead the 'ignorant and inexperienced' to 'misunderstanding, disruption and sedition'. While the phrase 'hostile to the Christian religion' in a draft of this proposal was deleted, the language of 'offensive' and 'scandalous' books that could lead to 'misunderstanding' which survived in the promulgated edict was surely still intended to be much wider in its scope than seditious works. As such, it set the pattern for many later proscriptions of 'scandalous' atheistic and libertine works.[113]

In his *Political Arithmetic*, composed in 1671–7 and published in 1690, William Petty supported 'indulgence...in matters of opinion: though licentious actings, as even in Holland, be restrained by law'.[114] Israel has stressed that Dutch society was 'not less, but more, prone than other European societies to repress bawdiness, eroticism, undisguised homosexuality and street prostitution'.[115] If it was thought impossible to eliminate brothels in the maritime economies of such cities as Amsterdam,[116] and prostitution was therefore significant in the late-seventeenth-century Netherlands, street prostitution was almost unknown and brothels were concealed and probably significantly fewer than in Restoration London or Paris. Gregory Leti, a Milanese immigrant of 1683 and father-in-law of Jean Le Clerc, who became city historiographer of Amsterdam in 1685, declared that 'For every one of these *bordelli* to be seen in Amsterdam there are for sure ten in so-called "holy" Rome and more than twenty in Venice'. He stressed that Dutch women kept their necks, shoulders, and bosoms covered, in stark contrast to contemporary French fashions. And in his six-volume 1685 *Il ceremoniale historico e politico, opera utilissima a tutti gli Ambasciatori*, Leti argued that Dutch religious toleration was not, as alleged with 'horror' abroad, accompanied by 'license'.[117] Dutch magistrates attempted to suppress verbal and pictorial expression of sexuality. Erotic or pornographic works such as the *École des filles* (1669) were suppressed. The painter Jan Torrentius was sentenced to twenty years' imprisonment in 1628 for 'blasphemy', having composed pornographic paintings, and the famous engraver Romeyn de Hooghe was forced to flee Amsterdam after prosecution for his erotic

---

[113] Groenveld, 'Mecca', 67, seems more accurate to me here than van Nierop, 'Censorship', 29, who wishes to restrict the proscribed to 'seditious' works.

[114] Seaton, *Toleration*, 151.   [115] Israel, *Dutch Republic*, 683.

[116] Carr, *Accurate Description*, 70–1 declared some prostitution allowed because of the East India fleet but stressed that the Reformed ministers inveighed against it and identified it with certain known buildings rather than with the streets.

[117] Leti in Israel, 'Gregori Leti and the Dutch Sephardi elite' in *Jewish History* (ed.) A. Rapoport-Albert, 267–84, at 268–9.

engravings was initiated in the late seventeenth century. While Wijnand Mijnhardt notes that many of the 'seventeenth-century pornographic classics' were translated into Dutch in the 1670s and 1680s and that a few domestic works such as the 1681 *Het Amsterdamsch hoerdom* (*Amsterdam whores*) were published in the last two decades of the seventeenth century, he stresses also that 'Dutch writers did not take a leading role in producing pornography' and that such 'Dutch interest in translated and homemade pornography' was 'short-lived', in contrast to both British and French interest.[118]

The Dutch Reformed Church was strongly opposed throughout the century to many forms of entertainment, with the Synod of South Holland in 1640 banning from communion any who had attended a ball or had worn fancy dress, and assaulting 'various frivolities and worldly vanities...such as dancing, balls, scandalous misuse of God's good gifts in excessive eating and banqueting, wild hair of men and women, masquerades, comedies and tragedies, shameful dress, offensive exposure of the body'. Even walks in the country on Sundays were condemned by the Reformed Church since 'the sabbath was not established for the pleasure of sinful flesh'. Drinking, tobacco, jewellery, and plays all received consistorial censure. It was with reason that Oldenbarnevelt once defined the Dutch Reformed Church to the English ambassador as 'doubly puritan'. Temple noted that Reformed ministers were 'often very bold in taxing and preaching publiquely against the Vices, and sometimes the innocent Entertainments of persons most considerable in the Government, as well as of the vulgar'. While the Reformed Church took the lead in such preaching, the various Protestant churches in the Netherlands were without exception strongly opposed to 'sexual libertinism'. Support for Dutch Anabaptism in the sixteenth century was understood to have been generated partly because its austerity was understood to be even greater than that of the Reformed, desiring a purity without 'spot or wrinkle'. Menno Simmons asked women to avoid 'all unnecessary adornment and display, making or desiring no other clothes than those which are necessary'. Arminians' emphasis on the importance of morality included substantial emphasis on policing sexual morality. While it is important not to fall into too broad a caricature, a considerable portion of the Dutch population led 'plain lives' by comparison with the ostentation, luxury, and courtly 'libertine' culture of other European societies, including the 'Baroque' republic

---

[118] Israel, *Dutch Republic*, 434; W. Mijnhardt, 'Politics and Pornography in the Seventeenth and Eighteenth Century Dutch Republic' in L. Hunt, *The Invention of Pornography* (New York 1996), 283–300, at 283–6.

of Venice as well as the famously 'libertine' monarchies of Restoration England and Louis XIV's France.[119]

RELIGIOUS INTOLERANCE IN THE HUGUENOT COMMUNITY IN EXILE IN ENGLAND AND IN THE NETHERLANDS IN THE 1680S AND 1690S

The influx of thousands of orthodox Calvinist Huguenots into the cities of Rotterdam and Amsterdam in the mid-1680s added a considerable number of Calvinist Huguenots deeply hostile to anti-Trinitarianism to an atmosphere in Holland in which religious toleration was incompletely realised and threatened. To those French and English exiles who defended universal religious toleration in the Netherlands in the 1680s, these orthodox Huguenot refugee ministers were even more threatening supporters of intolerance than were their orthodox Dutch counterparts. Most exiled Huguenots, and most exiled British refugees in the Netherlands, neither spoke nor read Dutch, and tended to live, work, and worship within their own refugee communities. In the 1680s and 1690s, orthodox Huguenot leaders organised campaigns and established institutions to preserve their own confession of faith and international authority over the entire Huguenot community in exile, thereby continuing a drive for orthodoxy in the 1670s and early 1680s in France.[120] The huge Huguenot diaspora of the 1680s was led by a legion of clerics choosing exile in order to maintain their faith, who disagreed with Catholics about the identity of 'heretics' and 'schismatics' but agreed with Catholics that 'heretics' and 'schismatics' were to be punished by magistrates obliged to punish 'evil-doers' or to prevent heretics spreading their 'poison' to others. From orthodox Protestant leaders in the Netherlands and in England came works written in the late 1680s and 1690s condemning toleration as a 'poisonous' doctrine.

Orthodox Huguenot ministers had long defended orthodoxy within their own church in France, condemning unorthodox beliefs among French Protestants in a series of provincial and national synods from 1559 to 1659. They had long followed an essentially Calvinist confession of faith and had deprived of posts, promotion, and theological degrees any ministers

---

[119] Zumthor, *Daily*, 84–5; van Deursen, *Plain Lives, passim*; Burke, *Venice and Amsterdam*; Israel, *Dutch Republic*, 434; Temple, *Observations*, 204; Nijenhuis, *Ecclesia*, II, 158; *The Complete Writings of Menno Simmons*, 381, cited in Israel, *Dutch Republic*, 92, and the works of Pettegree and Duke cited throughout.

[120] The same pursuit of orthodoxy marked the Genevan church in the 1670s, and it was responsible for forcing into exile Jean Le Clerc, who had published an anonymous work, the *Theological Epistles*, which depicted a series of theological disputes – including one between a Socinian and a Trinitarian – ending in calls for charity and tolerance. Le Clerc was branded a 'Socinian' and forced to leave Geneva in order to avoid prosecution.

who challenged this confession. The Synod of Paris in 1559 established a strong and hierarchical structure of church discipline to protect and maintain 'uniformity' which attacked 'Heresie, Contempt of God, Schism, Treason, and Rebellion against the Church, or other grievous offences' and anathematised 'contentious persons' and 'rebels against the consistories'. It established a confession of faith strongly stating the orthodox Trinitarianism of one God and 'three persons' said to be 'taught in Holy Scripture'. Provincial and national synods thereafter combined to police the Huguenot ministry to remove any suspected 'heretics', and censured and suppressed suspect Huguenot books. The tolerationist Castellio's work was censured by the Huguenots at the Fourth National Synod at Lyons in 1563, and the Seventh National Synod at La Rochelle in 1571 'unanimously voted their Detestation of all those abominable Errors and Heresies' which Beza had reported as 'dispersed abroad in Poland and Transylvania' and as reviving the 'ancient Heretics' arguments and even those of 'Mahomet himself' against the 'Unity, Divinity and humane Nature of our Lord Jesus Christ'.[121] In the Protestant petition of 1561 to the king for temples to be allowed, their deputies explicitly declared that by the allowance of such temples 'the gate will be shut on all libertines, Anabaptists and other pernicious sects who might enter the church of God'.[122] The 1561 Synod of the Churches of Guyenne and Haut-Languedoc identified suppression of heresy as the duty of the magistrate, and forced one Jean Bonneau to retract his argument that it was wrong for the magistrates to punish heresy.[123]

Across the seventeenth century, this sixteenth-century combination of Presbyterian church government with provincial and national synods maintaining the faith remained central to Huguenot life. Pierre du Moulin, Pierre Jurieu's grandfather and author of an anathematising *Anatomy of Arminianism*, presided at the National Synod of Alais in 1620, which endorsed the doctrine of the Synod of Dort, with every member swearing an oath that 'I declare also and I protest that I reject and condemn the Doctrine of the Arminians' which was 'a Mask and Vizard for Popery to creep in among us'. Delegates took an oath to defend these resolutions to their 'dying breath'.[124] The 1623 National Synod of Charenton confirmed that they would 'never deviate' from the articles of Dort.[125] Although many

---

[121] Quick, *Synodicon*, I, clxiv; II, 4, 6, 46, 91.

[122] 'The Protestant Petition for Temples 1561' in D. Potter (ed.), *The French Wars of Religion* (New York 1997), 30.

[123] P. Benedict, 'Catholic-Reformed Co-existence in France 1555–1685' in Grell and Scribner, *Tolerance*, 70–1.

[124] Quick, *Synodicon*, II, 38–40; H. Nellen, 'Grotius' Relations with the Huguenot Community of Charenton 1621–35', *Lias* XII (1985), 147–77, at 149.

[125] Quick, *Synodicon*, II, 126–52.

Remonstrants, Grotius included, fled to France in the 1620s from their proscription in Holland after the Synod of Dort, they were not allowed to practise their religion as toleration in France was limited to 'orthodox' Protestant and Catholic communions. In Paris, Grotius joined a small like-minded community, which included Stephen Courcelles, who had been excommunicated by the Huguenot Church for his heterodoxy and became an Arminian. He lived for a time with Tilenus, who had taught theology at the Protestant Academy at Sedan until deprived of his post in 1618–19 because of Arminian sympathies. Uytenbogaert, Episcopius, and Grotius were three signators of a declaration framed by Grotius in 1621 which condemned the Huguenot Church for their hostility to Arminianism. In 1629 and 1634, Grotius declared in letters to friends that Huguenot ministers in France would be as intolerant if they gained power as were the Dutch Reformed in the Netherlands. When the leading Huguenot minister Daillé did propose admitting to communion at Charenton in 1640 some of the Remonstrants, he limited the offer only to the 'ignorant' people among them and explicitly excluded their clerics and leaders as 'blasphemers'. When Grotius died in 1645, André Rivet celebrated Grotius' death as that of the 'most malicious enemy' of our religion.[126]

When Moyse Amyraut articulated the universality of the offer of grace in ways that seemed to many fellow Huguenots in the 1630s to be reminiscent of Socinianism and Arminianism – but which was significantly divergent from both in its complex acceptance of predestination – Huguenot ministers such as the brothers Guillaume and André Rivet, again relatives of Pierre Jurieu, condemned Amyraut for spreading a 'poison', while others declared that he supported a 'monstrous doctrine'.[127] The now 68-year-old du Moulin campaigned against Amyraut and the spread of his ideas at Saumur, writing with an image of 'heresy' as 'disease' whose ancestry we will trace later that there were preachers 'whose skins showed the rash of these new ideas' and that none 'so infected' should be delegates to the national synod. When the national synod met in 1637 at Alençon it attempted to find ground on which to tolerate Amyraut's ideas, but was clear in so doing that he must reject 'Arminianism' and other similar 'heresies'. Similar controversies remained central to the Huguenot community until 1649, with repeated attempts by hardline Calvinists led by du Moulin, André Rivet, and their associates, to obtain condemnation of Amyraut, while Amyraut's supporters suggested that Amyraut was tolerable within the church only because he in fact supported predestination and clearly opposed

---

[126] H. Nellen, '*Disputando Inclarescet Veritas*: Grotius as a Publicist in France 1621–45' in Nellen and Rabbie (eds.), *Grotius Theologian*, 121–44, at 123; *idem*, 'Grotius' relations', 153–5, 163–8.

[127] Van Stam, *Controversy*, 33, 42–3, 62, 113–14 and *passim*.

'Arminianism'. It was relatedly from Amyraut that broader religious toleration received support in these years: Amyraut argued in his 1652–60
Christian Morality that only persuasion and example and not force could
convince people.[128]

The Huguenots met the growth of Independency or Congregationalism in
the English Revolution with horror. In 1645, the twenty-eighth National
Synod of Charenton learned that there had landed from England some 'going
by the name of Independents and so called for they teach every particular
church should be governed by its own laws, without any dependency or
subordination unto any person whatsoever in the authority of colloquies or
synods in matters of discipline and order'. The Assembly enjoined all provinces to prevent this religion getting 'footing' among us 'so Peace and
Uniformity in Religion and Discipline may be preserv'd inviolably',

fearing lest the Contagion of this Poyson should diffuse itself insensibly, and bring in
with it a World of Disorders and Confusions upon us; and judging the said sect of
Independentism not only prejudicial to the Church of God (because as much as in it
lieth, it doth usher in Confusion, and openeth a door to all kinds of Singularities,
Irregularities and Extravagancies, and barreth the use of those means, which would
most effectually prevent them) but also is very dangerous unto the Civil State; for in
case it should prevail and gain ground among us; it would form as many Religions, as
there be Parishes and distinct particular Assemblies among us.[129]

In 1670, orthodox Huguenots condemned the thought of Isaac
d'Huisseau, a Saumur theologian who argued for a reunion of all Christian
churches based on the limited fundamentals of Christianity found in
the Bible. D'Huisseau was anathematised as 'Socinian'. In 1676–7,
orthodox Huguenot ministers secured the condemnation of 'Pajonism' for
positions extending Amyraldism in ways which its enemies aligned with
'Arminianism' and 'Socinianism' in support for the hypothetically universal
offer of salvation, defence of free will, and support for mediate rather than
immediate operations of grace. By carefully examining Claude Pajon's own
thought, it was declared that he had himself not expressed 'pajonism', and so
the position said to be the implication of the man's works was condemned,
rather than the man.[130] In each of these two cases, of d'Huisseau and Pajon,
the individuals concerned had themselves stopped short of Arminianism, let

---

[128] Van Stam, *Controversy*, 90, 132–3, and *passim*; F. Laplanche, *L'écriture, le sacré et l'histoire* (Amsterdam 1986), 387–9, 484–9; Benedict, 'Catholic-Reformed', 73.

[129] Quick, *Synodicon*, II, 467 (partially cited in Parker, 'Huguenots', 17).

[130] O. Fatio, 'Claude Pajon et les mutations de la théologie réformée à l'époque de la Révocation' in R. Zuber et al. (eds.), *La Révocation de L'Édit de Nantes et le protestantisme français en 1685* (Paris 1986), 209–25; Laplanche, *L'écriture*; idem, *Orthodoxie et Prédication* (Paris 1965), 308–16; Rex, *Essays*, 142–4; B. Armstrong, *Calvinism and the Amyraut Heresy* (Madison 1969). Those studying or teaching at Saumur in the 1670s included the teachers Pajon, Amyraut, and Louis Cappel, and a group of students who

alone Socinianism, but had questioned the strictest predestinarian tendencies of Calvinism, had emphasised the importance of a 'working faith', and had reduced the number of fundamentals within Christianity in order to promote toleration amongst Christians.

The thought of Amyrault, Pajon, and d'Huisseau was significantly influential at the Protestant Academy at Saumur, which tended to elevate the role of reason and to stress the limited number of fundamentals within Christianity; orthodox Huguenots stressed instead the teaching of the Academy at Sedan. In the late 1670s and early 1680s, pastor Jacques Souverain was synodically condemned by the Synod of Poitou for views variously described as 'Pajonist', 'Arminian', and 'Socinian'.[131] The Pajonist Charles Le Cène, Pajon's nephew, was unable to secure a post at Orléans because he was held to have expressed 'Pelagian' and 'Arian' views in a sermon delivered at Charenton; and Isaac Papin, another Pajonist, had his theological degree issued with conditions. Le Cène and Papin were to become important supporters of toleration in the Netherlands and England in the late 1680s. Souverain and probably Le Cène were closest to Socinianism christologically by the 1690s at the latest, and in their hands 'Pajonism' took a further significant step towards Arminianism and Socinianism, although at the point of condemnation of Le Cène Pajon himself engaged in a debate with the leaders of the church at Charenton, denying that his nephew was 'heretically' inclined. Pajon suggested that the ministers of the church were the ones departing from the faith by asserting the necessity of subscription to articles of faith not found in Scripture and by imposing positions which made God author of sin in order to avoid 'Pelagianism'. For Pajon, Pelagianism itself would be better than such orthodox Calvinist positions. Others among the refugees who were supportive of toleration and who had formerly been educated at Saumur included Jean Le Clerc and Pierre Allix, a friend of Le Clerc and Limborch, and a protégé of Burnet. Allix was to be named in a petition of the Huguenot ministers in London in the 1690s specifying those for whom they wished promotion in the Church of England to be blocked because they were supporters of the 'poisonous' doctrine of toleration.

were to correspond with each other in the 1680s and 1690s, including Allix, du Temps, Papin, Le Clerc, and Jaques Cappel: Des Graves, 'les thèses soutenues a l'académie de Saumur', *BSHPF* (1979).

[131] The grounds of Souverain's deposition were the subject of contemporary disagreement: e.g. Trouillart stressed that Souverain was deposed for Socinianism (LP MS 1029, 65); C. Rey (*An Account of the Cruel Persecutions Raised by the French Clergy Since Their Taking Sanctuary Here* (London 1718), 31ff.) for Arminianism; see *Bulletin* (1903), 243; B. Sarazin, 'Les temples et les Pasteurs de Mouchamps', *BSHPF* (1909), 547–59, at 558–9; E. & E. Haag, *La France protestante*, 10 vols., (Paris 1846–1859), IX, 294; F. de Schickler, *Les Églises du Refuge en Angleterre* (Paris 1892), II, 333, 336; E. Haase, *Einführung in die Literatur des Refuge* (Berlin 1959).

It is important to stress, then, that in France in the 1670s there was official toleration of two religions – of Catholicism and of orthodox Huguenot thought. In France, anti-Trinitarianism was excluded from toleration by Catholics and Protestants alike. In France in 1676, Locke made precisely this point, writing in an entry about the procedures and importance of Protestant synods:

If any one holds tenets contrary to their articles of faith, the King punishes him, soe that you must be here either of the Romish or their church; for not long since it happened to one here, who was inclineing to and vented some Arrian doctrines, the Governor complained to the King. He sent order he should be tried, and soe was sent to Tholose where upon triall, he denying it utterly, he was permitted to scape out of prison; but had he owned it, he had been burnt as an Heretick.[132]

Locke thus knew that the attacks of orthodox Huguenots on anti-Trinitarians in the Netherlands in the late 1680s and 1690s were long-standing ones. It was only in the name of the continuation of toleration for orthodox Huguenots that Jurieu pleaded for 'toleration' under the terms of the Edict of Nantes in the early 1680s in his *Policy* and *Last Efforts*.

In exile in the Netherlands and in England in the 1680s and 1690s, the majority of orthodox Huguenot ministers continued their practices of intolerance towards unorthodox Protestants, and often repeated them against precisely those individuals whom they had already condemned in France, as they acted again, for instance, against Souverain, Le Cène, and Papin. There was to such ministers nothing incongruous in being intolerant when they had themselves been exiled because of intolerance: they understood their exile as undertaken in order to maintain the faith for which they were being persecuted, seeing this faith as the 'true faith' and their Catholic persecutors as part of the 'false' church illegitimately persecuting because they lacked the truth. In the Netherlands, 178 refugee pastors assembled at the synod signed a 'Declaration of Rotterdam' establishing that only Huguenot pastors signing an oath of adherence to the Walloon Confession of Faith in general, and to the tenets of the Synod of Dort in particular, were able to be ministers. The articles agreed by the Walloon Synod in 1686 described the synod itself as an association whose 'sovereign aim it is to safeguard the unity of belief [and] to secure the exclusion of all dangerous doctrine'. It declared 'no pastor eligible for admission to our body unless...his views are in accordance with our confession of faith' and 'disciplinary code'. A permanent censorship committee of four professors of theology and four pastors was established in 1686, and future meetings attempted to make this censorship effective by various institutional means. They called for 'orthodoxy', 'uniformity', and

---

[132] Lough, *Locke's Travels*, 40.

an end to 'dangerous innovation' in the Huguenot community.[133] In 1690, the Synod of Walloon Churches at Amsterdam condemned the proposition that 'the magistrate has no right, by virtue of his authority, to supress Idolatry and to hinder the progress of Heresy'. It 'solemnly' and unanimously declared that such an opinion was 'false, scandalous, pernicious, and equally destructive of Morality and Religion'. It forbade all persons in its communion to utter it in the pulpit as ministers, or even in private conversations as secular members of the Huguenot communion. Any ministers who were found supporting the view that the magistrate could not take action against idolatry and heresy were to be suspended from the ministry, and any private individuals who were found supporting it were to be refused the sacrament. Jurieu, decried by Pierre Bayle as 'the Promoter of These Synodical Decisions', further trumpeted these acts of the synod in his 1690 *Picture of Socinianism*, a work in which he assaulted as 'enemies' to Christianity Episcopius and Limborch, tolerant Arminians who supported the toleration of Socinianism.

Bayle attempted to convict these orthodox ministers and Jurieu in particular of inconsistency by arguing in the *Dictionary* that if the Huguenot ministers had been asked

while the Edicts of Persecution were pouring on their party, what they thought of the Conduct of a Prince, who inflicted Penalties on Those of his Subjects, who desired only the liberty of serving their consciences, they would have answered, that it is unjust; and yet, as soon as they are come into another country, they have pronounced their Anathema against Those, who condemn the use of penal laws, in order to suppress errors.

They had, Bayle suggested, 'changed their Opinion, while the Ruin of their churches, by the authority of the Sovereign, was quite fresh in their memory, and the Wound still bleeding'. He accused Jurieu of being the primary 'Turncoat'. Yet this analysis was deliberately lacking in nuance on Bayle's part. He knew very well that orthodox Huguenot ministers had not been in favour of a universal religious toleration before 1685, but had rather supported toleration only of orthodox Huguenots. He had himself published in 1687 Isaac Papin's tolerationist *Faith Reduced* with a preface of his own composition about the restrictions that had been placed on religious liberty within the Huguenot community in the late 1670s and early 1680s by requiring subscription to 'articles of faith' not found in Scripture. In the *Dictionary*, Bayle briefly recognised that Jurieu had spoken on both sides of the issue – for and against toleration – in his 1683 *History of Calvinism*,

---

[133] Article VI of the 1686 articles quoted and discussed in F. Puaux, *Les précurseurs de la Tolérance en France au XVIIe siècle* (Paris 1881) and in Hazard, *European Mind*, 92–3; Cerny, *Theology*, 63.

and attempted to treat this as a contradiction and to ridicule Jurieu as thinking himself allowed such contradiction by claiming personal inspiration. But in earlier writings such as the *Policy*, Jurieu had written only for the continued toleration of orthodox Huguenots, and had written against the toleration of unorthodox Huguenots in the 1670s and 1680s.[134]

Not merely did the Huguenot synods prohibit any minister or member of their church from declaring that magistrates could not act against idolatry and heresy, but they also condemned – as Socinian or demi-Socinian – works which asserted such a tolerationist argument, even if such an argument came from an author who was not himself a supporter of doctrinal positions which they identified as heretical. Many of the few dozen tolerationist works that were issued in the 1680s and early 1690s were condemned by these Protestant synods as 'pernicious', including, for instance, Noel Aubert de Versé's tolerationist 1684 *Pacific Protestant*, condemned as 'full of all sorts of abominable heresies and capable of seducing and infecting many people with its venom'. Indeed, Aubert had no less than three separate works condemned as pernicious by three different Walloon synods, who declared that it desired 'suppression of this heretic' as well as of his heresy.[135]

Jurieu organised an international campaign to prevent the employment of Aubert, and to condemn any who attempted to assist him; even when Aubert took an assumed name and tried to find work in Danzig, Jurieu tracked him down, prevented him from gaining a post, and organised the censure of a minister who had attempted to assist him. Jurieu organised a similar campaign against Papin in the late 1680s, who also ended up in Danzig seeking work and was also therefore unable to obtain it. In the 1690s, Jurieu regularly attacked the 'heresies' of other refugees, such as Bayle and Basnage, and Jurieu was responsible for Bayle losing his position at the École Illustre in 1693. Jurieu's efforts did not stop at the North Sea. He corresponded extensively with ministers in England in the late 1680s and early 1690s about the dangers of 'Socinianism' in the Huguenot community in England. In England, partly due to this encouragement from Jurieu, the French churches then attempted to institute a similar defence of orthodoxy. In August 1690, thirty-four Huguenot ministers in England wrote to their colleagues in the Netherlands about the need for concerted Huguenot efforts to maintain the 'capital points' of their faith against 'Arian' and 'Pelagian' views. They then attempted to obtain condemnation by the Huguenot ministers in London of the 'false, pernicious and scandalous' propositions related

---

[134] Jurieu, *Tableau*, 565; Bayle, *Dictionary*, Augustin H.
[135] P. Morman, *Noel Aubert de Versé: A Study in the Concept of Toleration* (New York 1987), 34, 40, 58. In 1685, there were twenty-six Walloon churches; by 1688, there were sixty-two: K. H. D. Haley, *The Dutch in the Seventeenth Century* (New York 1972), 170.

to 'Socinianism', 'the matter of tolerating', and 'internal grace' already condemned by the Walloon synods. In March 1691, ninety-six Huguenot ministers subscribed to their maintenance of the 'constant doctrine of the French Protestants', including anti-Socinian belief in Trinity, incarnation, and Christ's satisfaction, and anti-Pajonist belief in the necessity of regeneration by the internal operation of the Holy Ghost. 'The Opinions of Socinus' were explicitly 'detested' as 'Heresies which absolutely overturn the Foundations of the Christian Faith' with whose followers or teachers 'we can have no Religious Communion'. These Huguenot ministers exhorted their fellow ministers to attack Socinianism in private and in public. Such orthodox commitments and actions were then publicised in just such an attack, Claude Grosteste de La Mothe's Trinitarian 1693 *Two Discourses Concerning the Divinity of Our Saviour*.[136]

In October 1692, orthodox Huguenot ministers in England framed thirteen articles for subscription which stated strongly their commitment to the French confession of faith, to Trinitarianism, predestination, and to the anti-Pajonist 'internal and immediate operation of the Holy Ghost' as 'necessary' for 'our conversion'. The articles registered 'detestation' of Socinianism, and rejected several Socinian doctrines and the allegedly Socinian tenet that reason was to be 'judge' of the 'articles' of faith. They condemned moreover those who said they personally believed in the Trinity but could not find 'certain proofs' of it in Scripture and thought it legitimate to maintain communion with those who rejected it.[137] These ministers moreover petitioned William and Mary to prevent the spread of toleration and to prefer in their national churches only 'orthodox' and intolerant ministers. They singled out the reading of the Arminian Episcopius as pernicious as he was a 'demi-Socinien' committed to toleration of Socinians. For such orthodox ministers, there was no good reason to distinguish between those who were heretical and those who were not but believed that the 'heretical' should be tolerated: the latter was an unacceptable 'indifferentism'. They called toleration a 'poisonous doctrine'. In a document addressed to William and Mary, they called Socinianism subversive since it made of a king a 'mere man'. And they described toleration as a 'poisonous' doctrine leading to the murdering of souls. Educated by the Calvinist minister Trigland, William himself was a broadly tolerant Calvinist, but the one form of toleration which he notably

---

[136] Lambeth Palace (hereafter LP) MS 933, 67; Jurieu, *Tableau*, 559ff.; C. G. Lamothe, *Two Discourses Concerning the Divinity of Our Saviour* (London 1693), 64–8 (mispaginated as 57–60, 64); R. Gwynn, 'Disorder and Innovation: The Reshaping of the French Churches of London after the Glorious Revolution' in O. Grell, J. Israel and N. Tyacke (eds.), *From Persecution to Toleration* (Oxford 1991), 251–73, esp. 256–8; idem, *Huguenot Heritage*, esp. 105ff.; Cottret, *Huguenots*, esp. 207ff.

[137] LP MS 933 67.

did not himself promote in England – unlike that for Catholics and Jews – was toleration for anti-Trinitarians.[138]

These Huguenot ministers attempted to silence several ministers in the conformist French churches in London whom they viewed as 'heretical', including André de L'Ortie – the co-preacher with Jean Le Clerc in London in 1682–3, and author of a work which Locke read in his exile in the Netherlands.[139] When de L'Ortie protested that he had been falsely accused of Socinianism, they supplied a lengthy double-columned account setting his views against the orthodox Trinitarian views of another preacher, Testas of Threadneedle Street, with whom he had privately debated the Trinity.[140] Huguenot refugee ministers who were either probably anti-Trinitarian, such as Charles le Cène, or Trinitarian but 'Pajonist' and tolerant of those who were not Trinitarian, such as Isaac Papin, were unable to gain ministerial posts in England in the 1680s and 1690s. Charles Le Cène was forced to sell his library in order to feed his family; he apparently ended up being financially supported in the 1690s by Locke, by the Huguenot merchant Paul D'Aranda – who was accused by the orthodox ministers of being 'Socinian' himself and was the employer of the Socinian Huguenot Souverain, and by William Popple, also an alleged Unitarian, the tolerationist translator of Locke's *Letter Concerning Toleration*, and the employer of Papin.[141]

In the early 1690s, several other Huguenot ministers were forced from their pulpits, including the Socinian Jacques Souverain, a popular preacher at the new conformist church at the Quarry, Soho, and his colleague Daniel du Temps, whose burial expenses were allegedly refused in 1693 by orthodox Huguenot ministers because he was allegedly a 'dog of a Socinian'. In another remarkably unedifying series of events radiating around a deathbed, when Theodore Maimbourg died in 1692 as a reputed Socinian, orthodox Huguenot ministers commenced an investigation of four ministers who had attended him: Souverain, L'Ortie, du Temps, and du Temps' son-in-law. Pursuit of the investigations against du Temps continued after his death and

---

[138] See my 'Huguenot Thought after the Revocation of the Edict of Nantes' in R. Vigne and C. Littleton, *From Strangers to Citizens*.

[139] Locke read L'Ortie's *Défense du sermon de Mr Hesperien* in France in 1677: MS Locke f2 350–2, taking notes from it on Augustine and Erasmus; he had also taken notes from a work of Amyrault's *La vie de La Noue* in 1676: MS Locke f1 517; f2 10–13; and he purchased Pajon's *Examen des préjugés légitimes* and Claude's *Défense de la Réformation* by June 1677, and read the latter in December 1677: MS Locke f3 185–6, 380–1; MS Locke d1, 9, 37, 49, 77, 85; Lough, 'Locke's Reading', 235–6, 242, 248.

[140] LP MS 929, 54; LP MS 932, 1.

[141] On Papin and Le Cène see below, chs. 16–22. Papin could have become tutor for Locke's friend Edward Clarke but did not want the post. Papin stressed, after his conversion to Catholicism, in his *The Toleration of the Protestants* (London 1733), 55 that he had 'always followed the orthodox explications of holy scripture' and that Jurieu would have attacked him for anti-Trinitarianism if there had been 'the least proof'.

ended with anathematising him as a Socinian.[142] When in the mid-1690s there were disputes leading to a significant schism over Socinianism in the large Huguenot community at Canterbury, further proceedings against Socinian Huguenot ministers, again including Souverain, were called for by orthodox Huguenot ministers.[143]

It would be possible to tell the story in England so far, then, as a story of the maintenance by the majority of orthodox Huguenots of a distinct Huguenot identity in England and in the Netherlands, with Huguenots attempting to maintain in exile the orthodox faith for which they had gone into exile and attempting to police the beliefs of their fellow ministers as a separate religious community in England and internationally. This is indeed a considerable part of the story. Lamothe's *Discourses* affirmed that the articles to which French ministers had subscribed were those of the Confession of Faith of the Reformed Churches in France, and that he was giving written proofs of 'the constancy of our faith'. Focusing on Huguenot identity, constancy, and solidarity, he held that such a declaration would carry weight because of the great number of refugees and since it was on account of religion that they had been banished from their own country. Huguenot ministers of conformist and nonconformist congregations and various lay Huguenot leaders attempted at various moments to co-ordinate the refugee community as one community in England, as through a General Assembly from 1697.[144] Yet Lamothe was himself a conformist Anglican minister who held that it was the duty of French ministers to give public support to the 'best persons' in the Church of England who had defended the Trinity, and who had his *Discourses* published in an English translation. He argued that Huguenot ministers were testifying to their orthodoxy because they had been questioned on this matter by the Bishop of London, Compton. And he indicated that the articles to which they had subscribed were agreeable to the articles of the Church of England. The thirteen articles proposed in 1692 were similarly declared agreeable to those of the Church of England. Conformist French churches used the Church of England

---

[142] LP MS 933, 67; Rey, *Account*, 31ff.; Gwynn, 'Reshaping'. On Souverain, see also M. Mulsow, E. Labrousse, and S. Matton in S. Matton (ed.), *J. Souverain, Lettre à Mr xxx touchant l'apostasie* (Paris 2000); M. Mulsow, *Moderne aus dem Untergrund* (Hamburg 2002). Bayle drew attention to the reports of Maimbourg's Socinianism in the *Dictionary* (Maimbourg L, note E), directing readers to Simon's correspondence to show that he had 'openly died an Unitarian, and that he had been so a long time incognito'. R. Simon's *Lettres Choisies de M. Simon* (Rotterdam 1702), lettre VII, 77–9, discussed Maimbourg's manuscript 'Socinianism' with Justel as early as 20 March 1682.

[143] LP MS 1029, 65; Rey, *Account*, 31ff.; F. W. Cross, *History of the Walloon and Huguenot Church at Canterbury* (London 1898), *HSL*, xv, 157–8; *HSP* (1915–17), 263–92, at 291; Cottret, *Huguenots*, 181–4, 210.

[144] Lamothe, *Discourses*, 64–8; on the Assembly: Gwynn, 'Reshaping'; cf. also Whelan, 'Persecution'.

liturgy, translated into French, and the General Assembly, as only advisory, was permitted by the Bishop of London and Archbishop of Canterbury.[145]

We saw in Chapter 3 that the Toleration Act of 1689 provided indulgence from the penalties of the law for worship outside of the Church of England only to Trinitarian Protestants. English Socinians who publicly and repeatedly denied the Trinity faced fines and jail terms. Socinianism was still depicted in this period by many of its English opponents, as by its Huguenot opponents, as a heretical poison murdering souls. Over the next thirty years, it was repeatedly made clear that published anti-Trinitarianism was unacceptable in England.[146] It was to the Bishop of London, Compton, that orthodox Huguenots appealed against Souverain and du Temps in 1689, and Compton who pressed Souverain to stop preaching. It was Compton who requested proofs of Huguenot orthodoxy in 1691. Brocas, a leading Huguenot campaigner for orthodoxy, was Compton's chaplain.[147] It was Archbishop Tenison to whom the documents on L'Ortie were sent, and orthodox Huguenots were to appeal to him again over the Socinian schism at Canterbury.[148] Opponents of religious toleration among Huguenot refugees had considerable reasons to view their anti-Socinian intolerance as not merely maintaining their distinct faith and identity, but also as showing themselves, at English episcopal request, acceptable refugees because they were not 'heretical' refugees, and as integrating them into the English church and polity in identifying with a significant body within the Church of England in their orthodox commitments.[149]

We noted earlier that Bayle was deeply engaged with the practices of Huguenot intolerance in the 1680s and 1690s which in 1693 came to be directed against him personally as he was stripped of his post at the École Illustre. We have noted at different moments that Bayle feared a 'Protestant

[145] Lamothe, *Discourses*, 64–8; Gwynn, 'Reshaping', 254–5, 270–1.

[146] On heresy and 'poison', see, on example, Long, *Letter on Toleration*, 9, 17; on the blasphemy act, Levy, *Blasphemy*; on Whiston, J. Force, *William Whiston, Honest Newtonian* (Cambridge 1985); and on Whiston and Samuel Clarke, Levy, *Blasphemy*, 288–92; P. Miller, '"Free-thinking" and "Freedom of Thought" in Eighteenth-Century Britain', *Historical Journal* (1993), 599–618.

[147] For an attack on the role of Brocas (amusingly as 'Hocus') in fomenting persecution see [anon], *Reflections on Two Discourses Concerning the Divinity of Our Saviour* (London 1693), 22.

[148] LP MS 1029, 65 on the Socinian schism at Canterbury. Tenison attempted to silence debate on the Trinity in 1695.

[149] On the extent of contests over toleration and Anglican support for intolerance after 1689 and on the Bangorian Controversy see J. C. D. Clark, *English Society 1688–1832* (Cambridge 1985); idem, *The Language of Liberty* (Cambridge 1993); Harris, *Politics*; G. de Krey, *A Fractured Society* (Oxford 1985); G. Holmes, *The Divided Society* (London 1967); idem, *Britain after the Glorious Revolution* (London 1969); idem, *Politics, Religion and Society in England 1679–1742* (London 1986); idem, *The Trial of Doctor Sacheverell* (London 1973); J. Walsh, C. Heydon, S. Taylor (eds.), *The Church of England c. 1689–1832* (Cambridge 1986); Goldie, 'Political Thought', 102–36.

inquisition' in the 1690s because of these acts, and that at many points in the *Dictionary* he noted the recent increase in support for intolerance in the Netherlands due to the influx of Huguenot ministers desiring to impose their own orthodoxy on others. Here, it is important to indicate that not merely was Bayle exercised by the many dimensions of Huguenot intolerance in the Netherlands traced in this chapter, but that he was aware of Huguenot intolerance in England, recording that it was the brother of his opponent, the ex-Jesuit Louis Maimbourg of the *History of Calvinism*, who had campaigned for intolerance in France and who had become suspected in England of Socinianism, the ultimate Protestant heresy. He moreover discussed in another work the accusations of Socinianism against Souverain.[150]

We have seen in this chapter, then, that Bayle was deeply conscious of the lengthy history of moments of Dutch practices of intolerance through the course of the seventeenth century, and of the fragility and limitations of its practices of toleration in the 1680s and 1690s, that he saw this toleration as being under considerable threat from the added forces of intolerance in the Huguenot community, and that he was deeply aware of Huguenot intolerance within the Huguenot community in the 1680s and 1690s. We noted that he had reason to be suspicious of the tolerationism even of Arminians. It was against all of these Protestant practices of intolerance, as well as against Catholic intolerance that Bayle was to write many of his works in defence of toleration. Locke was similarly exercised by Huguenot intolerance both in the Netherlands and in England, and acutely aware through friendships with Limborch, Le Clerc, and Furly of the limitations that existed within Dutch tolerationism and of the need for support of such tolerationism from Arminians, Quakers, and Socinians alike. Locke had many affiliations with unorthodox and tolerationist Huguenots. He registered Aubert's *Treatise* in his personal copy with the paraph mark he often used for works of the highest intellectual significance, and probably used Aubert as a go-between with Jean Le Clerc. He tried to find employment for Papin with his friend Edward Clarke. He apparently helped to support Charles Le Cène financially. One of Souverain's unprinted anti-Trinitarian works is carefully recorded among Locke's volumes of manuscripts. Locke closely followed the measures undertaken by the orthodox ministers in the Huguenot community in the 1680s and 1690s. Locke's manuscripts include an account, in French, of the declaration of their anti-Socinian orthodox faith by French ministers in 1691, intended for others' subscription, personally endorsed by Locke at the end 'this was prepard but stopd'.

Throughout the late 1680s and early 1690s, during the composition, publication, and reception of Limborch's *History of the Inquisition*, which

---

[150] See my 'Huguenot thought after the Revocation of the Edict of Nantes' and 'Locke, Socinianism'.

Locke encouraged and instigated, Locke and Limborch saw its tolerationist arguments and its identification of persecution with inquisitorial practices as aimed not just at Catholic practices but equally at contemporary Huguenot practices. Limborch wrote to Burnet about the Huguenot practices of intolerance in the Netherlands during composition of the *History*. Burnet replied that 'the French refugees among us, seem as mad as they do with you' in a letter in which he celebrated publication of Limborch's *History of the Inquisition* and denounced Protestants as even worse than papists as persecutors because at least papists were 'more consistent in their fury' because they were committed to papal infallibility, whereas Protestants professed fallibility and then attempted nonetheless to decide what others should believe. Limborch wrote to Locke when composing the work was his 'daily occupation' in September 1690 that 'those whom it least behoved, people who had themselves barely escaped out of the hands of persecutors, have decided to show us an exemplar of the holy office'. In late 1692, Locke replied to another Limborch story that he had a tale about the 'French in this country which...surpasses it', referring to the report he had just received from William Popple. Popple had reported the 'most horrible breach of charity amongst the French refugiez here that ever was heard of', the attempts of orthodox ministers to enquire into the past behaviour of the charitable ministers, including Souverain, who had visited Maimbourg when he was dying to find out 'any by-past conversation of these men that may be an argument of their Heterodoxy'. Popple declared to Locke that 'some of the zealous Orthodox ministers' had animated the 'whole Orthodox Herd' and assembled on the cry of Socinianism 'a perfect Court of Inquisition, to the number of fourscore ministers, and are about making formularies and tests to choak all that have not so wide a swallow as themselves'. In 1694, Locke added in a letter to Limborch that 'the French theologians' zeal for orthodoxy seems to be blazing more fiercely in our colder climate...In an assembly convoked for that purpose they accused Cappel, a man, if any among the French, as it seems to me temperate and discreet, as suspect of heresy'. Cappel had refused to answer both when summoned and when visited privately; Locke reported to Limborch that this whole 'storm' was aroused because he had attended the funeral of Maimbourg, a man who was 'not orthodox to a hair's breadth'.[151]

---

[151] MS Locke c27 fo. 89a; Locke, *Correspondence*, letters 1567, 1572, 1590, 1608, 1630, 1692, 1698; Burnet to Limborch in Foxcroft, *Life of Burnet*, 314–15. Jacques Cappel, close friend at Saumur of Jean Le Clerc, had been accused of Arminianism and Socinianism at Saumur in 1682. In 1689, he published a commentary on the Old Testament, including a treatise on the state of souls after death which did not support the resurrection of the body.

There was, then, as multiple and international a practical context of intolerance for Locke as for Bayle. It was in contexts that included discussions about the activities by the French ministers against their colleagues suspected of 'Socinian' heresy, awareness through Furly of the dangers posed to Quakers in the Netherlands, and awareness through Limborch and Le Clerc of the dangers posed to Arminians in the Netherlands, that Locke not merely wrote and published his first three *Letters Concerning Toleration* between 1685 and 1692 and his 1695 tolerationist minimalist interpretation of Christianity, the *Reasonableness of Christianity*, but also instigated and encouraged the tolerationist writings of others, such as Limborch's 1692 *Historia Inquisitionis*. He wrote, furthermore, in immediate contexts of practices of Catholic intolerance in France and Piedmont; of Protestant intolerance towards 'orthodox' Protestant dissenters in England; and of intolerance towards anti-Trinitarians in all of these countries – intolerance towards anti-Trinitarians which was supported by very many of those who were themselves currently suffering persecution. Locke's arguments (like those of other defenders of religious toleration in the Netherlands in the 1680s who were also aware of very many of these international contexts of intolerance) were designed to support religious toleration simultaneously in all of these practical contexts of religious intolerance.

We have now established in the first part of this book all of the important practical contexts of religious intolerance within which the advocates of religious toleration were writing in the late 1680s and early 1690s. The arguments for religious toleration in the 1680s and 1690s were, however, simultaneously designed as intellectual replies to the many justifications of intolerance which were being offered in all of these contexts in the 1680s and 1690s, and as intellectual replies to the justifications of intolerance which had been offered throughout the past centuries of Christian history reaching back to the patristic period of Augustine. Indeed, the arguments for intolerance in the 1680s and 1690s were seen by both supporters and opponents as being in very many respects continuous with the arguments for intolerance developed over the preceding millennium of Christianity. The arguments for toleration offered in the 1680s and 1690s were also developments of arguments offered against these justifications of intolerance in early modern Europe. Before turning to the arguments of the 1680s and 1690s in defence of religious toleration in Part 3 of this book, it is therefore important now to turn in Part 2 to analysing at length the major intellectual justifications of intolerance, first as they were established and repeated from patristic to mid-seventeenth-century texts, and then as they were reiterated by Catholics, Huguenots, and Anglicans in the period 1660–1700. We will also consider very brief analyses of tolerationist arguments composed in early modern Europe before the 1680s.

PART 2

*Justifications of intolerance and the
emergence of arguments for toleration*

5

Patristic and medieval sources of early modern intolerance: anathematising heretics and schismatics as seditious, pestilential poisoners, 'libertines' and 'sodomites'

Early modern Europe inherited substantial anathematisation of heresy and schism from a host of late patristic and medieval works which were widely read, reissued, cited, and treated with reverence in the sixteenth and seventeenth centuries. For many clerics, these late patristic and medieval works provided central elements of their education and texts, after which they patterned their own devotional works and explications of doctrine. These works were authoritative not merely for the majority of Catholic theologians, who proclaimed the maintenance in their church of an unbroken tradition,[1] but also for 'magisterial Reformation' Protestants anxious to claim that it was they who represented the 'true church' in maintenance of its 'true faith' and who trumpeted their own reverence for patristic works, for the early creeds, and for the first four (or six) 'general councils'. Both Catholics confronting Protestantism as 'heretical' and 'schismatic', and 'magisterial Reformation' Protestants confronting 'radical Reformation' sects such as Anabaptists and anti-Trinitarians as 'heretical' and 'schismatic', understood and attacked these 'new heresies' as the revival of 'old heresies' already condemned by the Fathers and by the 'general councils' of the church. Both Catholics and 'magisterial Reformation' Protestants repeatedly issued historiographies of heresy and schism depicting these 'new heresies' and new 'schisms' as reiterations of the Arian heresy and Donatist schism of

---

[1] It was possible to challenge the notion of an unbroken tradition and yet to support the authority of the church to determine controversies, as Richard Simon did in the 1670s, but his works were not merely unusual but banned in France. Portions of this chapter were presented at the Durham conference 'Orthodoxies and Heresy' (July 1999) and the National Humanities Center (November 2000); I am grateful to the audiences for their comments.

the fourth century, and the lineage of Arians, Gnostics, Donatists, Waldensians, Albigensians, (Manicheans) and Hussites given by Catholics for Protestantism was in large part paralleled by the lineage of Arian, Gnostic, Pelagian, Donatist, and Manichean unorthodoxy used by many 'magisterial Reformation' Protestants to attack Anabaptists, anti-Trinitarians (Socinians) or Quakers on the one hand and the Catholic Church on the other.[2]

It was this perspective that 'new heresies' were but 'old heresies' revived which made many late sixteenth-century Catholics believe that Protestantism would be another short-lived heretical movement and made them view the Council of Trent as a repeat of the ancient councils which had 'always in the end prevailed', as the prefect of the seminary at Douai, Richard Bristow, put it in his 1574 *A Briefe Treatise of Diverse Plaine and Sure Wayes to Find Out the Truthe in this Doubtful and Dangerous Time of Heresie*.[3] It was this perspective, equally, which made an Anglican such as Richard Gardyner preach in 1637 in Christ Church Cathedral, Oxford, against Socinianism as 'the old Decay'd Heresies newly revived in these latter Days'. It was this perspective which made the Anglican Thomas Fuller and the Calvinist Presbyterian Daniel Featley attack (Ana) Baptists as 'Donatists new dippd'. And it was this perspective which made many Calvinists in early seventeenth-century England and the Netherlands condemn Arminianism as 'Pelagianism revived' and simultaneously as the theology of Catholicism or 'popery'. Such examples could quite literally be multiplied thousands of times in surveying early modern Europe.[4] And Catholicism and 'magisterial Reformation' Protestantism further agreed that the Devil was the central source of heresy and had 'seduced' believers throughout history with essentially similar ideas. As Bayle noted in the *Dictionary* – in combating this idea – it had been the 'constant opinion amongst Christians from the beginning, that the Devil is the author of all false religions; that he moves the Heretics to

---

[2] On old heresies revived see, for instance, John Heller, *Contra Anabaptistas* (1535) in S. Haude, *In the Shadow of 'Savage Wolves': Anabaptist Münster and the German Reformation During the 1530s* (Boston 2000), 59; J. Gaultier, *Table chronologique de l'état du christianisme...Ensemble le rapport des vieilles hérésies aux modernes de la prétendue réformation* (1609); P. Nicole, *Préjugés légitimes contre les calvinistes* (1671); B. Dompnier, *Le venin de l'hérésie* (Paris 1985), 49–50; B. Scribner, 'Practical Utopias: Pre-modern Communism and the Reformation', *Comparative Studies in Society and History* 36 (1994), 743–74 at 747–52.

[3] R. Bristow, *A Briefe Treatise of Diverse Plaine and Sure Wayes to Find Out the Truthe in this Doubtful and Dangerous Time of Heresie* (Antwerp 1574), 62, and the discussion in K. Campbell, *The Intellectual Struggle of the English Papists in the Seventeenth Century* (Lewiston 1986), 7.

[4] R. Gardyner, *A Sermon Preached in the Cathedral Church of Christ in Oxford on Christmas Day* (1637), 24, in McLachlan, *Socinianism*, 41; I. Horst, *Radical Brethren* (Nieuwkoop 1972), 27.

dogmatise, and inspires men with errors, superstitions, schisms, lewdness, avarice, intemperance'.[5]

For these many reasons, the anathematisation of heresy and schism in late patristic and late medieval works provided many of the terms within which they were discussed by anti-heretical and anti-schismatic writers from the Reformation and Counter-Reformation through to the end of the seventeenth century in England, France, and the Netherlands. In this chapter, I will briefly analyse these late patristic and late medieval depictions of heresy and schism, which declared it treasonous and seditious, murdering, poisoning, pestilential, libertine and sodomitical, before turning in Chapters 6–9 to analysis of the reiteration and massive expansion of these accusations against heresy and schism in early modern Europe, and to their combination with many other accusations against heretics and schismatics as these groups and individuals came to be associated ever more strongly with 'witches', 'atheists', and 'monsters'. This analysis of early modern anathematisations of heresy and schism from the Reformation to 1660 is important in order to understand the considerable force and character of anti-tolerationist argument in its own right, and to understand the arguments for intolerance of the later seventeenth century – discussed in Chapters 13–15 – since those arguments were reiterations of earlier arguments.

By describing the major contours of late patristic to early modern antitolerationist argument, we will simultaneously provide the context for understanding the character of tolerationist argument in the 'early Enlightenment', the subject of Part 3. Such tolerationist argument was not merely directed against the practices of intolerance of the 1660s to 1690s documented in Part 1, but was also composed in immediate response to the arguments offered in justification of intolerance in the 1680s and 1690s, and to these arguments for intolerance as arguments that had been developed throughout the history of Christianity since the late patristic period and reiterated massively since the Reformation.[6] This tolerationist set of

---

[5] Bayle, *Dictionary*, Paulicians H.

[6] An important caveat is perhaps necessary here. In this chapter I will not be attempting to describe the mentality of a 'persecuting society', nor the levels of intolerance in medieval society, and none of the complexities of the thought of a 'medieval church' which was not monolithic nor of 'The Inquisition', whose very capitalisation is the result of a process of reductionist historiography that was performed in the 'early Enlightenment'. I will, instead, be focusing on those elements of thinking about 'heretics' and 'schismatics' which were significantly repeated and extended in early modern Europe as parts of its anti-heretical and antischismatic literature, and then significantly repudiated in the course of the 'early Enlightenment' in its description of the mentality of the 'Middle Ages' as 'barbaric', 'ignorant', 'superstitious', and 'intolerant'. For an important recent criticism of the reductionism involved in describing this period sweepingly as that of a 'persecuting society', see Laursen (ed.), *Beyond the Persecuting Society*.

arguments of the 'early Enlightenment' was often issued by its authors as a defence of what they described as the more 'tolerant primitive Christianity' which they identified as having existed in the first three centuries of Christianity, and against the intolerance which they depicted as emerging in the late patristic period, as developed thereafter in late medieval Europe, and maintained and expanded by the majority of Protestants and Catholics in Reformation and Counter-Reformation Europe. These tolerationist arguments of the 'early Enlightenment' were simultaneously the expansion or further development of a small number of significant preceding tolerationist arguments, most of which had been issued by members of the sects of Anabaptists, anti-Trinitarians, Arminians, and Quakers most fiercely anathematised as heretical and schismatic, and thus as treasonous and seditious, murdering, poisoning, pestilential, libertine, and sodomitical. When Bayle composed his *Supplement* to his *Philosophical Commentary*, he suggested that only Arminians and Socinians had been defenders of 'universal toleration' in the recent centuries of Christianity, while using a pseudonym that evoked also Anabaptist and Quaker support for toleration. Chapters 10 to 12 will discuss some of the few but significant voices raised against intolerance before the 1680s, especially by Anabaptists, anti-Trinitarians, Arminians, and Quakers, whose arguments for toleration were often redeployed and developed further in the 1680s and 1690s. Important as these predecessors were, Bayle emphasised in 1688 that 'the doctrine of toleration is received only in a few dark corners of Christianity, while that of Nontoleration goes about everywhere'; the majority of Part 2 will be devoted to documenting the doctrines of intolerance that went 'about everywhere' in early modern Europe.[7]

PATRISTIC ANTI-HERETICAL AND ANTI-SCHISMATIC THOUGHT AND THE CONTRIBUTION OF AUGUSTINE

Heresy and schism were anathematised in many patristic commentaries which were very frequently reprinted and cited in early modern Europe, including texts specifically against heresy by Tertullian, the founder of Latin Christianity; by Origen, the most important Christian theologian of the second century; by Epiphanius; Irenaeus; Jerome; Ambrose; St John Chrysostom; St Gregory Nazianzen; Optatus of Milevis; and, most significantly of all, in epistles and treatises against heresy and schism by Augustine, the influence of whose works in succeeding centuries was such that he became known as the 'patriarch of persecutors'. Many of these patristic

---

[7] Bayle, *Philosophical Commentary* (1708), 745–7.

works were extended commentaries upon Paul's arguments that heresy and dissension – schism – were 'works of the flesh', that heresies were to be expected to manifest the faith, and that heretics were to be admonished and rejected. Augustine added to these commentaries on Paul a particularly crucial extended interpretation of Luke's Gospel parable of the wedding feast, which interpreted Jesus' injunction to go into the hedges and highways and to compel guests to come in as a legitimation of compulsion of heretics and schismatics back into the church.[8]

Many patristic fathers and then medieval writers who expanded their arguments in late medieval texts discussed the terms 'heresy', 'orthodoxy', and 'schism' themselves at length. They emphasised the source of heresy in a 'choice' made by individuals who did not have the right to choose what to believe but were instead required to believe what Christ had transmitted via the apostles and church. Thus, for Tertullian, the 'Greek word *haeresis*' indicated 'the sense of choice which a man exercises either to establish them or to adopt them. Therefore he [Paul] has called the heretic condemned by himself because he has chosen for himself something for which he is condemned. For us it is not lawful to introduce any doctrine of our own choosing'. In this account by Tertullian, heresy was a contradiction to the Scripture as 'epitomised' in the faith agreed among apostolic churches.[9] According to Cyprian's *Epistles* and *Sententiae*, the church was defined by its apostolic structure, with bishops as heirs to apostles possessing a right to obedience from the faithful; outside of this church there was no valid ministry, sacraments, Holy Spirit, or salvation. It was 'schism' to depart from such a church. Cyprian's writings were a particularly potent source for Roman Catholic opposition to much of Protestantism and for defences of High episcopalian Anglicanism; Archbishop Laud was depicted as *Cyprianus Anglicus.*[10]

Isidore of Seville, the sixth- and seventh-century bishop who composed an influential twenty-book encyclopaedic *Etymologies* which was still being published in new editions in early modern Europe a millennium later, added definitions of heresy, schism, and orthodoxy which resounded through the succeeding centuries. For Isidore, 'the name Orthodox means right-believing'. Indicating that such 'right-belief' was the basis of good actions, a notion that remained central for many anti-heretical writers into

---

[8] This section is indebted above all else to the brilliant article of Goldie, 'Theory of Religious Intolerance', 331–68. Cf also Coffey, *Persecution*; Zagorin, *Idea.*

[9] Tertullian, *Adversus Praxean*, 1; *De Praescriptionibus, passim*; E. Peters, *Heresy and Authority in Medieval Europe* (Philadelphia 1980), 30–1; S. L. Greenslade, 'Heresy and Schism in the Later Roman Empire' in D. Baker (ed.), *Schism, Heresy and Religious Protest* (Cambridge 1972), 1–4.

[10] Greenslade, 'Heresy', 5–7; G. Walker, *The Churchmanship of St Cyprian* (London 1968); Marshall, *Locke*, 36.

the late seventeenth century, Isidore continued, 'and, *as he believes*, in right-living'. *Haeresis* meant choice 'because each one chooses that which seems to him to be the best', including those who

contemplating their perverse dogma, recede from the Church of their own will. And so heresy is named from the Greek from the meaning of choice, since each decides by his own will whatever he wants to teach or believe. But it is not permitted to us to believe anything on the basis of our own will...we have the authority of the apostles, who...faithfully transmitted to the nations the teaching they received from Christ.

For Isidore, they are heretics 'who depart from the Church'. Since schism 'comes from the word for cutting...they delight in separating from the congregation', heresy and schism were linked conceptually as departures from the church. For Isidore, many heretics were schismatics, and vice versa.[11] These accounts thus tended to define 'heresy' by departure from the faith as recognised and taught by the 'apostolic church', and 'schism' as dividing that church, either with, or more often without, maintaining the 'true faith'. At many points, heresy was depicted as the worse of these two sins, but at many points they were yoked together and identified as two of the worst sins possible. Paul had linked heresy and schism, suggesting that the individual choice involved in heresy would result illegitimately in new societies alongside the Christian church; Augustine importantly emphasised that schism often led to heresy and to sedition, pointing to the failures of the Donatists (schismatics) to condemn the Circumcillions (seditious heretics) within their midst, and also declared that inveterate schism was itself 'heresy'.[12]

For Augustine, heresy involved not merely supporting, but persisting in false doctrine: 'opinionatedness' or 'obstinacy' was thus important to distinguish 'heresy' from 'error'. In the twelfth century, Gratian codified Augustine's account of heresy,[13] and, further emphasising obstinacy, Robert Grosseteste, Chancellor of Oxford University and Bishop of Lincoln, defined heresy in the thirteenth century in 'what became the standard definition' in late medieval Europe and persisted into the early modern period as 'an opinion chosen by human faculties contrary to holy scripture, publicly avowed and *obstinately* defended. *Haeresis* in Greek, *electio* (choice) in Latin'. The tendency of many clerics, however, was to declare that any defence of 'heretical' positions in the face of statement to heretics of the truth necessarily involved 'obstinacy'. In the 1640s and 1650s in England, and in the 1680s in France, the claim that those accused of being

[11] Peters, *Heresy*, 47–50.

[12] Augustine, *Contra Cresconium*, II, 4 in Greenslade 'Heresy', 8; J. Mueller, 'Milton on Heresy' in S. Dobranski and J. Rumrich (eds.), *Milton and heresy*, (Cambridge, 1998), 24–5.

[13] B. Gregory, *Salvation at Stake* (Harvard 1999), 76.

'heretics' and 'schismatics', such as Quakers in England or Huguenots in France, were 'obstinate' in maintenance of their 'error' was to remain central to the defence of intolerance, and denial of 'obstinacy' on the part of alleged 'heretics' was therefore to become central to Bayle's *Philosophical Commentary*, among other works.[14]

For these Fathers, and for their many medieval successors who drew extensively from their writings, it was in the 'apostolic church', based on apostolic teachings and derived from apostolic authority, that the 'rule of faith' was preserved against 'heretics'. In this account, the apostles had received true doctrine from Christ and had then passed this down to bishops who ruled the churches they founded; these bishops had then handed it on to their successors, and so on through the generations. The consensus of bishops and the apostolic succession were thus crucial to defining the true faith; as Vincent of Lérins put it in the fifth century, doctrines were true if they were held 'always, everywhere, by everyone'; his thought was extensively cited in the 1680s by Catholics in France, the subject of de Frontignères' 1684 *Warning of Vincent de Lérins, Defending the Antiquity and Universality of the Catholic Faith Against the Profane Novelties of all Heretics*, and criticised by Pierre Bayle, among others, in *Nouvelles*.[15] Tertullian explicitly argued that one was not even to discuss Scripture with 'heretics', who would merely abuse it. Paul's direction had, for Tertullian, been to 'admonish' heretics and not to 'discuss' it with them. For Tertullian, by standing against the apostolic tradition, 'heretics' properly could not even lay claim to the Scripture: they were quite literally not Christians.[16] Tertullian was to be particularly important to Bishop Bossuet, the most important Catholic apologist for the Revocation of the Edict of Nantes, whose sermons and *Pastoral Instructions* defining the church and its authority were significantly structured as commentaries on passages from Tertullian. From Tertullian, moreover, Bossuet was to draw the structuring notion of his crucial defence of intolerance towards Protestants, the *History of the Variations of the Protestant Churches*, that heresy 'naturally' bred further heresy. In this vein, Bossuet alleged that the first Protestant heresy of Lutheranism had naturally spawned the further Protestant heresies of the sixteenth century,

---

[14] Lambert, *Medieval Heresy*, 3–4; Peters, *Heresy*, 4, 167.

[15] *Avertissement de Vincent de Lérins, touchant l'antiquité et l'universalité de la Foi Catholique, contre les nouveautés profanes de tous les Hérétiques*; [Bayle], *Nouvelles*, 19/A.VIII; H. Bost, *Pierre Bayle et la question religieuse dans la Nouvelle de la République des Lettres* (Montpellier 1991), 248.

[16] Irenaeus, *Adversus Haereses*, ed. W. Harvey (Cambridge 1857), I, ix; II, viii; IV, xl; Origen, *Commentariorum Series*, 100 in Greenslade, 'Heresy', 1; Tertullian, *On Prescription Against Heretics*, in *Ante-Nicene Fathers*, ed. A. Roberts and J. Donaldson (Grand Rapids, Michigan 1986) *passim*, esp. ch. 5, 15–16; M. Colish, *The Medieval Foundations of the Western Intellectual Tradition 400–1400* (Yale 1997), 11.

such as Anabaptism and Socinianism, and then those of the seventeenth century, such as Quakerism. Tertullian's notion that discussion of Scripture was not needed against heretics was also to be important after the Revocation of the Edict of Nantes as Catholic writers declared that Protestants had wrongly given individuals the text of Scripture to interpret, instead of the church providing the interpretation for them and thereby maintaining the 'true' apostolic faith.[17]

Tertullian was thus a crucial patristic figure in his considerable impact on early modern definitions of 'heresy' and anti-heretical arguments. But writing before the Christianisation of the Roman Empire, Tertullian stressed the excommunication and rejection of heretics and schismatics rather than their coercion, and he claimed the right of Christianity itself to be tolerated in a pagan empire by arguing that 'the religion of an individual neither harms nor profits anybody else'. Tertullian was therefore to be cited *against* Catholic arguments for intolerance by Bayle in *Nouvelles* in 1686, with Bayle quoting Tertullian as suggesting that religion had to be embraced 'voluntarily and not by force' and regretting that later Fathers had adopted a maxim 'entirely opposed' to Tertullian's after the Christianisation of the Roman Empire.[18] A century after Tertullian, Lactantius was still stressing that 'there can be no true sacrifice under constraint...extorted by violence, imprisonment or torture'. Indeed, for Lactantius such coercion was not merely useless; it was harmful because it was 'sacrilege'. Those who accepted sacrifices offered 'with tears, moanings and bleeding limbs, deserve the curse of man'. Lactantius' (alleged) thought was similarly to be central to tolerationist argument in the 1680s as republished by Burnet, translated by Jacques Basnage, and reviewed by Henri Basnage de Beauval's *Histoire des Ouvrages des Savans*.[19]

The crucial theologian who justified the turn of Christianity to the use of state compulsion against heretics and schismatics was Augustine. Of all the major patristic writers on heresy and schism, none was to be as important as Augustine to medieval and early modern European thought in France, in the Netherlands, and in England. Augustine has been described by Marcia Colish as 'the single greatest authority, after the Bible, in western Christian thought' in medieval Europe, while one historian of the Counter-Reformation, A. D. Wright, with a pardonable exaggeration, has even labelled early modern Europe 'Augustinian Europe'.[20] Many of

---

[17] R.-J. Hesbert, *Bossuet: Écho de Tertullien* (Paris 1980), *passim*, esp. 147–55.

[18] Bayle, *Nouvelles*; idem, *OD*, I, 576; H. Bost, *Pierre Bayle et la Religion* (Paris 1994), 46.

[19] Tertullian, *Ad Scapulam*, ch. 2; Lactantius, *De Institutionibus divinis*, V, 21, in Le Cler, *Toleration*, I, 34–5; see below, p. 486.

[20] Colish, *Medieval*, 25; A. D. Wright, *The Counter-reformation* (New York 1982), chs. 1, 2, and *passim*; also A. G. Dickens, *The German Nation and Martin Luther* (1974), 83–98; Le Cler, *Toleration*.

Augustine's epistles used in the justification of compulsion of heretics and schismatics a passage of Luke's Gospel, *compelle intrare*, where Christ commanded his servants to 'go out into the highways and hedges, and compel them to come in, that my house may be filled'. For Augustine, the highways and hedges were 'heresies and schisms'. Augustine's *Treatise Concerning the Correction of the Donatists* defended the compulsion of schismatics into the church, and many of his other late writings and many of his other epistles reinforced the defence of magisterial punishment against schismatics contained in that letter. Augustine's thought served to justify coercion of schismatics who were not heretics, but also to yoke both together as he argued that schism tended to lead to heresy. All of Augustine's writings, including his many epistles, received widespread circulation in medieval Europe, and even wider circulation in sixteenth- to mid-seventeenth-century Europe. We will see in later chapters, as Joseph Le Cler, Mark Goldie, Elisabeth Labrousse, and others have importantly emphasised, that Bossuet and other defenders of the Revocation frequently cited Augustine's *compelle intrare* in defence of the Revocation, including in Bossuet's sermon at the moment of issue of the Edict of Fontaineblu, that many Presbyterian writers in mid-seventeenth century England and many Anglican writers in the Restoration cited the same passage in defence of intolerance against sects and then against nonconformists, and that so did many Huguenots led by Jurieu in the late 1680s and 1690s in arguing against unorthodox Protestants.[21]

In the course of his writings, Augustine made several distinctions that were central in anti-heretical and anti-schismatic writing in later centuries and still fundamental in late seventeenth-century Europe. The first was that one must distinguish an unjust persecution from a just persecution, and that Christ had only said that those who suffered for righteousness' sake were 'blessed'. According to Augustine:

There is an unjust persecution, which the ungodly operate against the Church of Christ; and a just persecution which the Churches of Christ make use of towards the ungodly...The Church persecutes out of love, the ungodly out of cruelty.[22]

For Augustine, the use of magisterial force to place pressure on heretics and schismatics was, moreover, not the denial but the essence of 'charity'. Magistrates thus using force were said to have turned their neighbour from the path that led to damnation for himself and to have prevented him from

---

[21] Labrousse, *Bayle*; *idem*, *Une foi*; Le Cler, *Toleration*; Goldie, 'Theory of Religious Intolerance'; H. Maisonneuve, *Études sur les origines de l'inquisition* (Paris 1960), 37–40; Peters, *Inquisition*, 11–67; E. Nelson, 'The Theory of Persecution' in *Persecution and Liberty* (New York 1921), 3–20; Zagorin, *Idea*, 24–33.

[22] Augustine, Epistle 185, 11, quoted in Le Cler, *Toleration*, I, 57.

infecting others, thus helping both the individual himself and others around him. In one of his Epistles, Augustine thus wrote that 'it is better to love with severity than to deceive with indulgence'. Indulgence was a 'mistaken kindness'. For Augustine, possessed himself by the zeal of the convert, there had been many like he himself had been who had not wanted to learn truth, 'but fear made us look twice and we recognised it'. For Augustine, the converted would end by 'thank[ing] God for having penetrated our negligence with the sting of fear'. Indeed, he declared that those who had been persuaded of the truth would come to thank 'joyously' those who had punished them. It was a description to be cited frequently in early modern Europe by those justifying using force in attempting conversions.[23]

Augustine further argued that faith adopted because of the use of force could nonetheless be said to have been adopted 'voluntarily'. Augustine argued that in judging the use of force

> You should not consider this constraint in itself, but the quality of the object to which one is constrained, whether it is good or bad. It is not that a man can become good in spite of himself, but the fear of suffering which he hates either makes him throw aside the obstinacy which held him back, or helps him to recognise the truth which he did not recognise. Consequently, this fear leads him to reject the falsehood he championed or seek the truth he did not know; thus he will come to attach himself voluntarily to what he first rejected.

Those who were 'first compelled by fear or pain...might afterwards be influenced by teaching'. Here, as Mark Goldie has emphasised, was an argument which tied force to education; many early modern anti-heretical writers were to justify coercion when harnessed to an 'educational' regime, and to oppose coercion if separated from such processes.[24]

For Augustine, the very definition and declaration of heresy served a crucial purpose. As he put it in the *Confessions*, quoting Paul, 'the refutation of heresies causes what your Church thinks to stand out: "For there must be heresies, so that those who are approved may become manifest among the weak"'.[25] The passage in which he wrote this was the conclusion of a discussion of his own former failure to understand and accept the doctrine of the Trinity. Discussing this passage in his account of Augustine's thought, *Augustinian Imperative*, William Connolly has focused on the ways in which the definition and expulsion of heretics for Augustine served to add both

---

[23] Quoted in Goldie, 'Theory of Religious Intolerance', 337, 347; Le Cler, *Toleration*, I, 57.

[24] Quoted in Le Cler, *Toleration*, 1, 56; Goldie, 'Theory of Religious Intolerance', 347; see also E. Peters, 'Destruction of the Flesh – Salvation of the Spirit: The Paradoxes of Torture in Medieval Christian Society' in A. Ferreiro (ed.), *The Devil, Heresy and Witchcraft in the Middle Ages* (Brill 1998), 131–48.

[25] Augustine, *Confessions*, Book 7, ch. 19, p. 178, ed. J. Ryan (New York 1960), cited and discussed in Connolly, *The Augustinian Imperative* (Sage 1993), 78.

solidity and determinacy to the faith on the one hand, and to add fervour in its defence on the other. Connolly has suggested that the act of definition of heresy often seizes precisely on contemporary points of debate within the faith, acting to close discussion by authoritatively expelling one of the parties. Thus, as Connolly emphasises, Pelagianism – centred on the belief in the potential universality of salvation – and Manicheanism – centred on the belief of separate principles of good and evil acting on the world – were defined as 'heresies' by Augustine and 'expelled' from the boundaries of the 'true faith' precisely as they were ideas then circulating within the faith, and because they involved the 'weak points' within Augustine's own account of that faith.[26]

Augustine moreover stressed the opposition to the 'true faith' of sinful propensities in two particularly important ways. Firstly, Augustine associated denials of the 'true faith' and worship in heresy and schism with sexual sins. Augustine's treatise against Parmenian, *Contra epistulam Parmeniani*, emphasised that St Paul had numbered among the 'fruits of the flesh', 'adultery, dissensions [i.e. schism], heresies, debauchery'. It was a key associative list, literally bracketing schisms and heresies with adultery and debauchery, and it was to be endlessly repeated in early modern Europe. Heresy had been spoken of as 'spiritual adultery' before Augustine; after Augustine, this was to receive more emphasis. Augustine's attack on the Manicheans, moreover, included declaration that their elect had attempted at their religious meeting to 'embrace' a woman and 'force her into sin'. Here, Augustine was in part taking over, but redirecting against the Manicheans as 'heretics' an image that Justin Martyr had recorded as part of the accusations made by pagans against early Christians, that Christian meetings were scenes of orgies. This was both a crucial move and a crucial misrepresentation: the Manichean Elect, a radical sectarian movement with which Augustine formerly had been associated, stressed asceticism and the spirit rather than matter, the renunciation of the body by fasting, and the avoidance of sexual activity which in begetting children helped to trap souls in matter and fostered the spread of the 'Kingdom of Darkness'. As we will see, in the late medieval period and repeatedly in the early modern period, Augustine's accusations against the Manicheans were to be turned against heretical sects' meetings as scenes of orgies which were said to be begun with the extinguishing of the lights, and many of the sects in the medieval period against whom this accusation was directed were, moreover, held to be revived 'Manicheans'.[27]

[26] Connolly, *Augustinian.*
[27] Augustine, *De Moribus Ecclesiae Catholicae et de moribus Manichaeorum*, II, ch. 7 in N. Cohn, *Europe's Inner Demons* (London 1975), 17; P. Brown, *The Body and Society*

Simultaneously, Augustine himself stressed the centrality within human sinfulness of sexual desires, and the forcefulness of such sinful propensities within humans unless aided by God's grace. Augustine here opposed diametrically the emphasis on free will of Pelagius, who asserted that unless humans were free to sin or do good works, they could not be held responsible for their sins and so could not deserve the punishment of eternal torment. To Augustine, one of the central failings of Pelagians was that they identified sexual urges as easily controlled by humans. Pelagians' heretical sense of the capacities of free will and of the potential universality of salvation were linked conceptually for Augustine to their greater acceptance of human sexuality and their diminution of the significance of Adam's Fall.[28] Augustine depicted the authority of the church being backed by the magistrate as necessary to counteract the propensity to sin which he identified as dominant in humans without grace and discipline due to original sin, a doctrine to which he gave a very heavy emphasis that was then to be maintained and expanded in early modern Europe not merely by Protestants such as Luther and Calvin, but also by Catholics such as the Jansenists in seventeenth-century France.[29] For Augustine, humans after Adam were born with a natural, inherited propensity to sin, and without grace they tended to adopt beliefs because these beliefs appealed to their corrupt passions. In this situation, there was a necessity for authority to counterbalance the effects of the sins that were disposing individuals towards false beliefs: that is, to errors and heresies. For Augustine, with the predestined elect small in number and sinful propensities predominant in humans without the grace given to the elect, the role for the magistrate in punishing to prevent chaos would always need to be considerable. The mind-set in which most around you were damned and only a small elect saved was one which could easily suggest that as sinful individuals most people did not deserve toleration; certainly, the English editor of the leading Arminian Episcopius' works in the 1670s thought that there was such a conceptual relationship.[30]

These conceptual relationships, between sinful propensities from 'original sin' leading to rejection of required beliefs, and intolerance as magisterial compensation aimed at counterbalancing sinful desires for false belief, were associative rather than logical entailments, and many of those who supported intolerance in early modern Europe did so on other grounds. It was thus common for many of those opposed to a strongly Augustinian (later

(New York 1988), 391–2; Lambert, *Medieval Heresy*, 13–14; R. Poole, *Illustrations of the History of Medieval Thought and Learning* (New York 1960), 85; R. I. Moore, *The Origins of European Dissent* (Oxford 1977; 1985), 27–8, 67.

[28] Brown, *Body and Society*, pt iii, esp. 410–11.

[29] Wright, *Counter-reformation*, *passim*; A. Sedgwick, *Jansenism in Seventeenth Century France* (Charlottesville 1977).

[30] Episcopius, *Popish Labyrinth*.

Calvinist) account of the sinful propensities caused by original sin to give many other reasons for justifying intolerance, as for instance high church Arminian Anglicans and many Catholics who stressed the authority of the church, bishops or Pope, tradition, and the importance of liturgical reverence. Moreover, the Baptist Roger Williams explicitly identified intolerance in his 1644 *Bloody Tenent* with the 'Arminian Popish Doctrine of Freewill' because to him free will was required for intolerance, since intolerance was absurd unless it 'lay in their owne power and ability to beleeve upon the Magistrates command'. For Williams, toleration was required precisely because man did *not* have such a 'free will'.[31] Despite Williams' account, however, there was a general association among Protestants in early modern Europe between support for a strong account of original sin and justification of intolerance, and the opposite correlation: tolerationist argument was to spread most in early modern Europe among those groups who questioned Augustinian accounts of human depravity from the Fall to varying but always significant degrees: Anabaptists, Arminians, Socinians, and Quakers.[32]

Viewed from this series of perspectives, it becomes logical that the clerical justifications of the Inquisition in the thirteenth century used Augustine's justification of compulsion specifically against what were termed revivals of 'Manicheanism' among the Albigensians or Cathars in the Albigensian Crusade, a crusade to defend the 'true faith' by the use of magisterial force that was encouraged and justified by clerics and the Pope; also, that much of the writing of the anti-tolerationists in early modern Europe was directed against the revivals of 'Pelagianism' which they perceived in both Arminianism and Socinianism; and that such anti-heretical writers repeatedly attacked those they perceived as 'heretics' in mid-seventeenth-century England as being 'Manicheans'.[33] Viewed in this series of perspectives, moroever, it becomes logical that tolerationists of the 1680s and 1690s devoted themselves extensively to attacking on many levels Augustine's defence of intolerance, composing personal invective against Augustine himself, and challenging the sexual associations of heresy and schism and the doctrine of original sin, while reviving precisely the questions within the faith which Augustine had attempted to close off, with Socinians and Arminians reviving discussions of free will, with Bayle reviving questions

---

[31] R. Williams, *Bloody Tenent* (1646) in *Complete Works* (New York 1963), 139.

[32] My thanks go to William Reddy for pushing me on this issue in a paper presented at the National Centre for the Humanities in 2000.

[33] On understanding medieval heresies, including the Cologne sectaries attacked by Eckbert of Schönau in the twelfth century, as 'Manichean' because of the influence of reading Augustine, and on the inclusion of Augustine's own anti-heretical writings in manuscript collections of monks concerned about 'heresy', see Lambert, *Medieval Heresy*, 30, 58; see below, p. 217.

of Manicheanism in the *Historical and Critical Dictionary*, and with various
tolerationists questioning the doctrine of the Trinity.

Important patristic authorities, such as Tertullian and especially
Augustine, thus set out a series of definitions of heresy and schism as opposed
to the 'true faith' maintained in the 'apostolic church', specifically defended
and defined as 'orthodox' the doctrines of original sin and Trinitarianism,
and extensively anathematised Manicheanism and Pelagianism. Such definitions of the faith received further clarification and assertion as 'orthodoxy' in
a series of creeds in the fourth century which were known as those of the
'general councils' of the church, enacted in the period immediately before
and after Augustine wrote his major works. The most important of these
were the Nicene and Athanasian creeds which defined with increasing
precision the doctrine of the Trinity as that of three co-equal co-eternal
persons in one substance. These creeds simultaneously anathematised anti-
Trinitarian heresies of the early patristic period and fourth century. The most
notable of those 'heresies' was Arianism, which followed Arius in holding
that Christ was a creature, subordinate to and not co-eternal with God the
Father. The next three general councils also condemned many other 'primitive' interpretations of the relationships, status, and nature of Christ and God
the Father which departed from Trinitarian orthodoxy. Indeed, as Thomas
Hobbes was to declare in his *Behemoth*, each of the first four 'general
councils' from Nicaea (325) to Chalcedon (451) had centred its dogmatic
concerns on one or other aspect of defence and definition of Trinitarianism,
and had condemned one after another departure from this.[34] As such,
'heresy' as an issue in the church became increasingly centred on 'blasphemy', on speaking inappropriately of the deity of Christ. The Trinitarian
definitions offered in these creeds were thereafter used by later church
Fathers and then by clerics through the centuries in defining 'heresy' as
those beliefs which stood against the first three creeds and these first four
general councils, either as these creeds and councils were said merely to have
declared what was already clearly stated in Scripture against those who had
latterly grown to oppose this – as Athanasius argued – or as having the
authority to decide matters of the faith *qua magisterium* or through the
promised guide of the Spirit.[35] Declaration of their own continued fidelity
to the faith established in these creeds and councils was to be central to both
'magisterial Reformation' Protestantism, and to 'Counter-Reformation'
Catholicism. Questioning of these creeds and councils as representing a
'corruption' introduced into Christianity and imposed both on the 'purity'
and 'simplicity' of the Gospels and on the toleration of divergent beliefs of

[34] T. Hobbes, *Behemoth*, (ed.) S. Holmes (Chicago 1990), 10.
[35] Greenslade, 'Heresy', 12; H. J. Margull, *The Councils of the Church* (Philadelphia 1966).

'primitive Christianity' were, however, to be central to the 'radical reformation' and then to the 'early Enlightenment'.[36]

As importantly, these creeds were issued in the epoch of the Christianisation of the Roman Empire, as for the first time Emperors turned from being pagan persecutors of Christianity to being 'protectors' of the Christian church. For the first time in Christian history, it thereby became possible for magisterial force to be used to punish those who departed from the creeds of the church, and Constantine used force against the Arians as well as against the Donatists. Magisterial force was thereafter usually employed by Trinitarians against anti-Trinitarians, as by Theodosius defending Trinitarianism after the Council of Constantinople, although Constantine's son Constantius importantly used magisterial force on behalf of the Arians against Trinitarians, leading Trinitarians such as Athanasius to turn to declaring at that point that magisterial persecution was never justified. He thereby provided one of the earliest examples of a repeated pattern of Christian thinkers over following centuries who justified toleration when persecuted and intolerance when they were the ones doing the persecuting. It was a pattern which was to convince tolerationists of the 'early Enlightenment' that they should be deeply suspicious of protestations of tolerance from any sect or theologian.

Magisterial force was used following Constantine not merely to defend the creeds, but also to ensure membership of a uniform church by punishment of 'schismatics' and by the addition in the early fifth century of civil penalties for those who were not baptised as infants. Once again, patristic thinkers from the fourth century onwards, 'magisterial Reformation' theologians, and Counter-Reformation Catholic theologians, joined hands in celebrating these roles of magistrates as protectors of the church who made laws to back its doctrine and to help to make people join and stay in the church. Such arguments often celebrated Christian emperors by interpreting the Mosaic theocracy as a godly precedent of an established religion backed by magisterial force. There was thus a strong tendency in these arguments to combine the messages of Old and New Testaments rather than to see the New Testament as abrogating the Old Testament. The magisterial proscription of blasphemy and idolatry in the Old Testament became expanded to include heresy – most easily in connection with anti-Trinitarianism, as this was to the orthodox simultaneously 'heresy' and 'blasphemy' in speaking against the deity (of Christ).

Once again, however, as we will see later, 'radical Reformation' Protestants were to challenge the arguments of both Catholics and

---

[36] H. Chadwick, *The Early Church* (London 1967); G. H. Williams, *The Radical Reformation* (Philadelphia 1962).

'magisterial Reformation' Protestants by questioning the role of the magistrate in the church in questioning punitive laws against 'heresy' and 'schism' and to back baptism. They emphasised the abrogation of the Old Testament in the message of the New, and understood the fourth century as the period of the key departure from 'primitive Christianity'. The 'corruption' of primitive Christianity was thus seen as cumulative by such 'radical Reformation' thinkers, being a compound corruption of Constantinian magistracy on the one hand, and of credal chains placed on individual believers on the other. Whereas they were understood by the vast majority of anti-heretical and anti-schismatic writers as reviving old heresies and schisms of the primitive church, they understood themselves as reviving the purity of the primitive church that had since turned to corruption, confessions, and coercion.

THE JUSTIFICATION OF EXECUTION, AND THE RHETORICS OF PLAGUE, PESTILENCE, POISON, MURDER, TREASON, SODOMY, AND LIBERTINISM FROM PATRISTIC TO MEDIEVAL WRITINGS

In Augustine's own thought, and in much of the subsequent literature about heresy throughout the entire period of its influence to the late seventeenth century, the use of force against heretics and schismatics was largely justified by it being required to reclaim them for the 'true faith' and church. This argument characteristically stopped short of justifying execution: obviously, the dead cannot be converted. Having initially been an opponent of magisterial compulsion, even when he turned to becoming its advocate, Augustine himself was reluctant to license more than 'moderate' measures of force. He explicitly condemned use of the rack and torture, and opposed execution. A notion of using 'moderate' punishments in compulsion, focused on reclaiming heretics to the truth, was therefore deeply 'Augustinian'; this notion was to be central to much 'Augustinian' intolerance in the 1680s, most notably in France in the 1680s, when many clerics stressed that they had not killed Huguenots but had in good Augustinian fashion only defended the use of 'moderate' force, such as fines and other temporal punishments, in order to reclaim these 'heretics' and 'schismatics' for the church. The repeated focus of Protestant propaganda on Catholics' use of 'the rack and torture' against Huguenots discussed in Chapters 1 and 2 was in part generated in order to show that Catholics had actually departed from their self-proclaimed Augustinian premises.

Yet, while much patristic anti-heretical literature continued to stress the desirability of conversion, late patristic and late medieval anti-heretical literature increasingly focused not only on the conversion of the heretics and schismatics themselves, but also on the fate of those others whom they might persuade to become heretics and schismatics, and to stress that the duties of justice (preventing harm) and charity (saving these potential converts' souls) required punishment, silencing, and even execution of heretics and schismatics. Here, the strongest emphasis was placed on the prime magisterial duty as that of service to the glory of God by protection of His church, and the central harm to subjects which magistrates were held to need to prevent was that to the soul, rather than threat to civil peace. Anti-heretical and anti-schismatic literature simultaneously stressed, however, that many heretics and schismatics were necessarily seditious or treasonous, challenging not just the church, but also the peace of the state, partly because challenging the authority of God was to challenge the authority of kings or emperors as God's representatives, and partly because when Christianity became the sole official religion of the empire (under Gratian and Thedosius) heretics became guilty of lèse-majesté.[37]

Anti-heretical literature had thus developed two positions which were to remain in some tension with each other throughout the early modern period, one which emphasised force to promote conversion and tended to deny that heretics should be killed, and the other which emphasised force to prevent the spread of heresy and the dangers posed by heretics to the ruling powers, which often legitimated the killing of heretics. Furthermore, even in the literature which justified the execution of heretics, when schismatics were held to have departed from the church in worship, but not in doctrine, they tended to be viewed as deserving compulsion back into the church, rather than death; however, since schism was often depicted as leading to heresy, the dividing line between them was often blurred as schism was assimilated to heresy. As early as 383, Priscillian became the first Christian to be executed for heresy by a Christian power, and anti-heretical laws were incorporated into Roman law from the *Theodosian Code* of 438 to the *Corpus Juris Civilis* of Justinian in the sixth century, and included in Gratian's *Digest*. Roman law condemnations of heresy clearly marked heresy as a 'crime' as well as 'sin', and they related it to sedition and treason, thus emphasising punishment for reasons other than conversion: the keeping of the peace and maintenance of rule against sedition and treason. For Origen, all heretics were 'traitors'. This association of heresy and schism with 'treason' and 'sedition' was thereafter to remain central into the early modern period, in which Origen's works circulated widely.[38]

Yet even though anti-heretical literature came to associate heretics and schismatics as seditious, and laws came to allow execution – focusing particularly on anti-Trinitarianism and rebaptism, central issues in the sixteenth

---

[37] Le Cler, *Toleration*, I, 46.   [38] Le Cler, *Toleration*, I, 46–61.

century for anti-Trinitarians and Anabaptists[39] – few heretics were executed before the late medieval period. It was not until the late twelfth and early thirteenth century that anti-heretical and anti-schismatic literature came to stress as strongly as 'moderate' punishment for the purposes of obtaining conversion (such as fines and the confiscation of property, supported in Augustinian fashion by theologians such as Peter Cantor) the full-blown justification of imprisonment and execution for unrepentant heretics in order both to punish them and to prevent them from spreading their heresies and schisms to others.[40] It was in the period of the third and fourth Lateran Councils, of the Albigensian Crusade in France and of the crusades against Muslims, and in the period of establishment of the episcopal and then papal inquisition, that heresy as a kind of treason against God, *crimen laese-majestatis divinae*, became central in anti-heretical literature. This placed heresy at the summit of human crimes ranked according to their threat to the authority of God and of the magistrate as representative of God; some historians have further argued that punishment of heretics itself then served to legitimate and to display the divine powers of monarchs.[41]

The late twelfth and early thirteenth century, with the establishment in various parts of Europe of episcopal and then papal inquisitions, with increasing argument for force in conversion in support of the crusades in the Middle East, and with the Lateran Council's statement that rulers who did not act against heresy could be excommunicated by the Pope, saw an increased statement that civil rulers were bound to use their force against heretics as the church and Pope determined.[42] It saw this increase in combination with, and in justification of, a series of major acts of intolerance against those considered 'heretics' and 'schismatics', most notably in what came to be called the Albigensian Crusade, in which the French king used massive force in the largely successful attempt to crush Albigensians and Waldensians. The identification of heresy and schism on the one hand, and 'treason' and 'sedition' on the other, was often repeated thereafter in defence of the use of force against the Waldensians, who refused oaths, and who were represented as challenging the prevailing structure of property distribution in favour of a more egalitarian distribution of property in an ascetic rejection of superfluity. Oaths were seen as central to obedience, and Bernard Gui summed up in the fourteenth century and handed on to later centuries the centrality of the issue of Waldensian refusal to take oaths in his specification

---

[39] The anti-Trinitarian Eunomians and Eutychians and the rebaptist Donatists were made subject to execution in 398, 452 and 413: Le Cler, *Toleration*, 46.

[40] Le Cler, *Toleration*, 82–9.

[41] Gregory, *Salvation at Stake*, n.51 to pp. 81–4; Clark, *Thinking With Demons* (Oxford 1997), c. 36ff., esp. 554; R. Muchembled, *Le Temps des supplices* (Paris 1992), 127–54.

[42] Peters, *Heresy*, 190.

of Waldensian belief in the Inquisitor's handbook: 'You are precisely regarded as a Waldensian heretic who believes any oath illicit and guilty'.[43]

Heresy was described as causing 'murder' for the soul and thus as worse even than murder of the body, as it was eternal murder and condemnation of the soul to torture through eternity, rather than the mere bodily cessation of temporal existence. This notion that heresy involved 'murder of the soul' had a long and ante-Nicene history, and was used by Augustine; late medieval anti-heretical literature often used it to argue that magistrates charged with the duty to punish murderers were thus charged with the duty to punish heretics. In the thirteenth century, Aquinas made clear that even murder was less bad than heresy in arguing that for their sin heretics deserved not just excommunication, but death itself:

> For it is a much graver matter to corrupt the faith which quickens the soul than to forge money, which supports temporal life. Wherefore if forgers of money and other evil doers are forthwith condemned to death by the secular authority, much more reason is there for heretics, as soon as they are convicted of heresy, to be not only excommunicated but even put to death.

Such heretics being executed by the civil power, their crime having been declared by the church, was for Aquinas 'not contrary to Our Lord's command'.[44] Aquinas deployed a fierce condemnation of heresy, in part to back an explicitly Augustinian understanding of original sin and a scholastic understanding of the Trinity of three consubstantial persons in one Godhead. For Aquinas, while it was important to think of the conversion of the heretic, after attempting such a conversion and failing – testimony once again to the crucial significance of 'obstinacy' – it was more important to think of the 'salvation of others' by punishing and silencing the heretic.[45]

In the anti-heretical and anti-schismatic literature issued by clerics in defence of the Inquisition and crusades, heresy was often imaged as a 'poison' for the soul, and heretics' punishments were repeatedly identified as more just than the punishments of those who poisoned and murdered the body. Once again, there were crucial patristic precedents, and again Augustine was the most important of these. Citing Galatians 5:19, Augustine had questioned why the schismatic and then heretical Donatists thought that it was 'right that the severity of the law is applied to poisoners,

---

[43] Bernard Gui, *Manuel de l'Inquisiteur*, ed. G. Mollat (Paris 1926–7), I, 74 in G. Audisio, 'How to Detect a Clandestine Minority: The Example of the Waldenses', *Sixteenth Century Journal* (1990), xxi, 2, 205–16 at 207; *idem*, *Le Vaudois* (Paris 1998). Waldensians were at some moments treated as heretics, at others as schismatics: B. Bolton, 'Papal Attitudes to Deviants 1159–1216' in D. Baker (ed.), *Schism, Heresy and Religious Protest* (Cambridge 1972), 84–5.

[44] Aquinas: 'Whether Heretics Should Be Tolerated' in Peters, *Heresy*, 182–3; Le Cler, *Toleration*, I, 97.

[45] R. Bainton (ed.), *Concerning Heretics* (New York 1935), 30.

and wrong when applied to heresies and unholy dissensions', when the apostle had 'put these last crimes on the same level with other fruits of iniquity. Would human power by chance be forbidden to deal with those crimes?'[46] Emperor Frederick II's *Liber Augustalis* of 1231 described heretics as deserving punishment using the image of poisoning. He attacked them as 'slaves to the vice of a word that means division' who strove to 'introduce division into the unity of the indivisible faith'. Diabolising them, he then declared that they were

sons of depravity from the father of wickedness and the author of evil who are resolved to deceive simple souls...serpents who seem to creep in secretly and, under the sweetness of honey, spew out poison...they mix up a potion of death as a certain very deadly poison.

For Frederick, who argued that a ruler had to draw the sword of 'righteous vengeance against them', heresy was a crime of treason, only 'more horrible because it is recognised that someone has attempted injury to divine majesty'. Heretics who were 'unwilling to relinquish the insidious darkness of the devil' should 'be condemned to death' and 'burned alive in the sight of the people'. Over the succeeding two centuries, similar punishments were enshrined in the laws of many Western European countries, partly due to the pronouncement of the Third Lateran Council that rulers who did not 'extirpate' heresy in their territories failed in their duties and could be excommunicated by the Pope. Punishment of heresy by public execution was enshrined in English law by the statute *de haeretico comburendo* – on the burning of heretics – of 1401, which provided that heretics were to be burned in a 'high place' before the people so 'that such punishment may strike fear into the minds of others, whereby no such wicked doctrine and heretical and erroneous opinions, nor their authors and favourers be sustained'.[47] The publicity and punishment thus afforded as a ritualised deterrent to heretics once again ranged them alongside the other capital crimes of murder, treason, arson, and counterfeiting.[48]

In anti-heretical literature heresy was, moreover, repeatedly described as a *pestis*, a disease. Here, again, it is crucial to stress that there were many important Pauline and patristic precedents. Tertullian had spoken of heretical 'words that spread like a cancer'; Jerome had spoken of the need to cut away the 'putrid flesh' of heresy in order to save the body; and Augustine had depicted heresy as a 'disease' in *The City of God* and had used the image in

---

[46] Augustine, *Contra epistulam Parmeniani*, I, X, 16 quoted in Le Cler, *Toleration*, I, 55. For details of the Albigensian Crusade, see J. Strayer, *The Albigensian Crusades*, (Michigan 1992); A. P. Evans in *A History of the Crusades* (Pennsylvania 1962) II, ed. K. Setton; Lambert, *Medieval Heresy*; R. I. Moore, *The Formation of a Persecuting Society* (Oxford 1987).
[47] Peters, *Heresy*, 207–8, 214–15. [48] Gregory, *Salvation at Stake*, 77.

his epistles of a physician who amputates a diseased member for the sake of the rest of the body. Spiritual infirmity was, moreover, often imaged in patristic writings through Leviticus' sanitary prescriptions. Much classical, patristic, medieval, and early modern thinking was structured around contrariety, and salvation in its literal meanings is the giving of health and life while disease obviously is the taking away of both. Rhabanus Maurus' ninth-century *On Medicine* was one among many medical texts which had classified diseases by the sins which they were understood to manifest bodily, writing that 'Leprosy is the false doctrine of heretics...lepers are heretics blaspheming against Jesus Christ'. Isidore of Seville had spoken of heresy as disease, 'an infection which when it catches one man quickly spreads to many'. The anti-heretical literature of late twelfth- and early thirteenth-century Europe, as R. I. Moore has particularly emphasised, repeatedly discussed heresy as a 'disease', as 'contagious' and 'infectious' as well as 'poisonous'. It is important to stress that, as Moore has put it, this interlinked series of images functioned not simply as 'a convenient metaphor, but a comprehensive and systematic model'. They produced a 'description of heresy and how it worked'. Heresy was frequently spoken of both as a 'cancer' – a word then used for external tumours or scabs – and as 'leprosy'. Guibert of Nogent representatively attacked Clement of Bucy as both a 'Manichean' and a carrier of 'the plague', and, applying the term for the sores of leprosy, described the Cathars as covered in the 'putrid tabes of heresy'. Eckbert of Schönau, canon of Bonn, wrote in 1163 that Cathar thought was endangering the church as a

most evil poison, which flows against it from all sides; for their message crawls like a cancer, and spreads far and wide like the progress of leprosy, corrupting the precious members of Christ.

The 'heretic' Henry of Lausanne was described as 'a leper, scarred by heresy' who was charged to say 'unceasingly' that he was 'a leper, a heretic, and unclean'. Henry was moreover said to 'infect other regions with his viper's breath'; the notion here was that of the poisoned breath of individuals polluting the air and thereby lodging in the viscera of their next victim as directly analogous to the spreading of other diseases. This was an image of the communication of heresy with an important early modern European future; we will meet the image later being used by Thomas Edwards and Ephraim Pagitt in works which were written in the 1640s against their fellow Protestants, whom they declared heretics.[49] As conspiracy means quite

[49] R. I. Moore, 'Heresy as Disease' in W. Lourdaux and D. Verhelst (eds.), *The Concept of Heresy in the Middle Ages* (Leuven 1983), 1–11; Moore, *Formation*, 62–3; Moore, *Dissent*, 246ff.; Gregory, *Salvation at Stake*, 87, on Jerome; Lambert, *Medieval Heresy*, 13, notes other images of heresy as poison and infection. Cf also Zagorin, *Idea*, 44.

literally 'breathing-together', there was even an important semantic association here between conspiracy and these notions of the spread of heresy and
schism.[50] Leprosy and 'cancer' were understood to require amputation of an
infected member. It was held – in an image handed on to almost ceaseless
reiteration in sixteenth- and early seventeenth-century Europe – that if left
unchecked, heresy like 'cancer' would spread to the healthy rest of the body.
Late medieval punishments of heretics themselves often reflected the notion
of transmission of heresy like disease. Not merely were heretics expelled or
burned, but after their deaths heretics' shelters were burned so that the
'disease' of heresy could not spread, exactly as the shelters of lepers and
their belongings were burned in case these harboured the disease.[51]

Association between leprosy and heresy further associated heresy with
'illegitimate' sexuality in the minds of many anti-heretical writers: leprosy
was understood to afflict those who were 'lecherous' and to be spread by
sexual transmission. Significantly, the language used for the spread of heresy
in many anti-heretical texts of the twelfth and thirteenth centuries (and into
the late seventeenth century) was that of 'propagation' and 'dissemina-
tion'.[52] Understood as though a disease associated with a sinful sexual
basis, heresy was often linked in the thirteenth-century literature with 'sodomy' and 'lustfulness'. Again, there were important patristic precedents;
again, the accusation in the late twelfth century and early thirteenth century
was associated with the campaigns against Albigensians and Waldensians.
We have seen that Augustine had associated Manichean meetings with orgies
as the most important of a series of ways in which he linked heresy and sexual
sinfulness. Epiphanius attacked the Adamites as motivated by 'insatiable
lust' in *Adversus Haereses*, although he denied that they engaged in sexual
orgies.[53] The Synod of Saragossa in 380 forbade the interpretation of
Scriptures in the nude by the congregations associated with the Manichean
Priscillian, the first heretic executed by Christianity in 383.[54] Tertullian's
Prescription Against Heresy, reissued frequently in early modern Europe,
included in his influential *Works* in the Paris edition of 1675, and cited by
Bossuet, had sexualised heresy as sin in declaring that it was a kind of
'adultery'.[55]

---

[50] The definition of 'conspiracy' was stressed by Justin Champion at the conference
'Conspiracies in Early Modern Europe'; the gloss on this is my own.
[51] Moore, *Dissent*, 250.
[52] The last three paragraphs utilise Moore, *Dissent*, 246–9; Bainton (ed.), *Concerning*, 25;
M. Barber, *The Two Cities* (London 1992), 188; Clark, *Thinking With Demons*, 354–5.
[53] Epiphanius, *Adversus Haereses*, 52; R. Lerner, *The Heresy of the Free Spirit* (Berkeley 1972),
22–3; cf. J. G. Turner, *One Flesh* (Oxford 1987), 82n.
[54] D. Cressy, *Travesties and Transgressions* (Oxford 2000), 257.
[55] Tertullian, *On Prescription*, xliv.

Thus depicted frequently as associated with sexual sinfulness, heresy in anti-heretical writings in the thirteenth century was at the least strongly associated with, and at times identified with, 'sodomy' – a term which, as Michel Foucault stressed in the *History of Sexuality*, joined together non-monogamous non-procreative sexual acts and all monogamous non-procreative sexual acts as 'sinful'. 'Sodomy' thus designated all non-procreative sexual acts between a man and a woman, even if married, as well as all sexual acts between two women, between two men, between an adult and child, and between a human and a beast. 'Sodomy' thus included but was not limited to male homosexual acts; male homosexual acts and bestiality were also referred to separately as 'buggery'. 'Sodomy' in both its narrower and wider descriptions was very often associated with 'lechery' and 'lustfulness' – that is, with what came to be termed in many texts of early modern Europe 'libertinism', a commitment to pursuit of sexual desires unrestrained by either 'law' or by monogamous, purposively procreative heterosexuality. Monogamous procreative heterosexuality was, in direct contrast, linked to the virtue of 'temperance', and all other sexual acts were linked to immoderate desires, or to immoderate licence having been given to desires. As John Boswell has remarked in *Christianity, Social Tolerance, and Homosexuality*, as the anti-heretical literature gathered new strength in the twelfth and thirteenth century, 'It became a commonplace of official terminology to mention "traitors, heretics, and sodomites" as if they constituted a single association of some sort'.[56] The Third Lateran Council of 1179 imposed sanctions on heretics and those committing 'sodomy'. The First Crusade involved both an increasing rhetoric against sodomy, and an increasing attack on Muslims as practising sodomy, while the Christian heretics or schismatics – the Cathars or Albigensians, and Waldensians – were simultaneously being frequently accused of 'sodomy'. The papal bull of Gregory IX of 1233 instructed the Archbishop of Mainz and Conrad of Marburg to develop a crusade against heretics in Germany, declaring that the meetings of the heretics ended with the lights being

extinguished, and they proceed to the most abominable fornication with no regard for shame or relationship. When it happens that more men than women are present, men satisfy their shameful lust together.[57]

The Aragonese Inquisitor Nicolas Eymeric's *Directorium Inquisitorum* of about 1368 – a work which was still being issued in new editions in Rome in 1578 – declared that the Waldensians held as an article of faith that

---

[56] J. Boswell, *Christianity, Social Tolerance, and Homosexuality* (Chicago 1980), 284, 92n.; M. Foucault, *History of Sexuality* (New York 1990); J. Goldberg, *Sodometries* (Stanford 1992), introduction.

[57] J. Trachtenberg, *The Devil and the Jews* (New York 1943), 205–6.

In the dark it is lawful to mate with any woman, without distinction, whenever and as often as they are moved by carnal desires. This they both say and do.

It was an accusation which was to be repeated in the early modern period by Catholics against Protestants, who were seen as being the lineal descendants of the Waldensians. The 1578 reissue of Eymeric furthered that accusation, as did histories of heresy by Catholic writers over a century later in the 1680s and 1690s. More generally, 'Buggery' as a term comes from French words 'bougre' and 'bougrerie', referring respectively to heretics and heresy, and the word for Cathar in various languages is the word for homosexual. The semantic condensation alone here indicates that association between 'heresy' and 'sodomy' was very strong in late medieval Europe. The evolution in late medieval Europe of the image of the witches' sabbaths as places of nocturnal orgies involving 'libertinism' and 'sodomy' owed much to the image of heresy in the anti-heretical literature, and was also strongly associated with the Waldensians. The terms 'valuderie, vauderie' became the name for the witches' sabbath and 'vaudoise' identified witchcraft in general; all of these words were derived from the heretical or schismatical Waldensians (the Vaudois).[58] In Chapter 2, we traced the centrality of the Waldensians to seventeenth-century accounts of Protestant ancestry and the importance of contemporary Waldensians as persecuted by Catholics in the 1680s; we will see later that a significant part of the Catholic legitimation of acts against Waldensians and Huguenots in the 1680s came from a continued attack on Waldensians as licentious and from an association of Huguenots with Waldensians.

Most of the late twelfth-century charges of 'sodomy' were, as Boswell puts it, 'formulaic' accusations rather than attempts on the parts of the anti-heretical writers to give an accurate reflection of the beliefs about the sexuality or sexual acts of those they accused.[59] Some of those accused of heresy, however, did advocate and practice a set of sexual standards divergent from the exclusively monogamous and exclusively purposively procreative sexuality considered 'orthodox' by the church. There is, for instance, considerable evidence that Cathars challenged Catholic justification of sexuality as serving procreation. But they did not do so in favour of 'libertinism', but rather in ascetic rejection of sexuality, in condemnation of procreation as the ensnaring of another soul 'in matter'. Indeed, their ascetic rejection of

---

[58] Nicolas Eymeric, *Directorium Inquisitorum* (Rome 1578), 206, in Cohn, *Europe's Inner Demons*, 37–8; Boswell, *Christianity*; C. Spencer, *The Heretic's Feast* (London 1993), 170–1, citing S. Runciman, *The Medieval Manichee* (Cambridge 1955); Trachtenberg, *Devil*, 206; R. Kieckhefer, *European Witch Trials: Their Foundations in Learned and Popular Culture 1300–1500* (1976); J. Russell, *Witchcraft in the Middle Ages* (Ithaca 1972); Briggs, *Communities*, 16, 19.
[59] Boswell, *Christianity*, 278–86.

sexuality as 'bodily' was so austere that Cathars forbade eating animals who reproduced sexually, and therefore did not eat meat or eggs. It was thus a substantial misrepresentation of their asceticism and rejection of marital pro-creative sexuality as merely a cover for voluptuousness that supported such accusations against them; such misrepresentations were to remain central in early modern Europe as applied to other 'heretical' sects. The ideas of Cathars were in many ways similar to those of the Manicheans, whom Augustine had attacked as covering their libertinism with asceticism and indulging in orgies, and it was as 'medieval Manichees', with citation of Augustine, that they were classified by the church which used force against them.[60]

Among the central tenets of the faith which anti-heretical texts had set out to defend was the orthodox doctrine of the Trinity of three co-equal, consub-stantial, co-eternal persons in the Godhead, a doctrine which had received its precise definition in tandem with accusations against heresy in the patristic period. Merely by being 'heresy', anti-Trinitarianism was often associated in late medieval literature with sexual 'libertinism' and with 'sodomy'. In addi-tion to their ascetic rejection of the body, Cathars did in fact deny the 'orthodox' doctrines of Trinity, incarnation, and resurrection. Holding that the material world was evil, they held that Christ could not have taken human form, died on the cross, and been resurrected. This rejection of the Trinity by Cathars was thus related directly to their holding that one should not create further material bodies to entrap souls and thus to their opposition to the standard of procreative sexuality considered orthodox by the church.[61] Here, then, the linkage between the heresy of anti-Trinitarianism, and attitudes about sexuality which challenged the 'orthodox' procreative sexual morality and which were attacked by the orthodox as supporting 'sodomy', was not merely a general association of heresy and 'sodomy', but a specific conceptual link in the thought of the 'heretics' themselves.

The process of association of heresy and anti-Trinitarianism with 'libertin-ism' in anti-heretial thought occurred again in fourteenth-century accusations against the 'brethren of the free spirit'. Some of these 'brethren of the free spirit' may have moved in an antinomian direction and become 'libertine'; at least most of these brethren, however, were once again instead austere repu-diators of the pleasures of the body, and once again for this reason they did not accept the orthodox doctrine of the Trinity. A fourteenth-century Franciscan chronicler attacking the heretical beliefs of the 'brethren of the free spirit' in remarkably crude language again indicates the conceptual linkage that was by

---

[60] Strayer, *Albigensian*, 28; Colish, *Medieval*, 251; Lambert, *Medieval Heresy*, 17; 24; Runciman, *Medieval Manichee*.

[61] Barber, *Two Cities*, 183–4.

now strongly present in the minds of their orthodox opponents between anti-Trinitarianism and 'libertinism'. In order to evidence the heretical beliefs of the 'brethren of the free spirit' he composed an account that alleged that when asked about the doctrine of the Trinity, a 'brother' had persuaded three women to take off their clothes and lie on their backs, had tied their contacting legs together (presumably to create three joined limbs in an obscene parody of the Trinity) and had then sexually violated them. The chronicler concluded that 'casting his lecherous eyes on their exposed shame' the 'heretic' had then said 'here is the holy trinity'.[62]

In the course of this chapter, then, we have seen that in much patristic and late medieval anti-heretical and anti-schismatic literature 'heresy' was viewed as an 'enormous crime', as a kind of blasphemy or 'treason' as lèse-majesté divine, and compared often to the crime of murder by poisoning but understood as worse as it involved murdering the soul and not merely the body. We have seen that it was imaged as a contagious, polluting, and insidiously spreading disease requiring amputation or segregation, and held to be sexually based and associated with 'lustfulness', 'sodomy', and 'libertinism'. Anti-Trinitarianism was particularly associated with such pilloried 'sexual nonconformity'. This pattern of accusations against heresy and schism – of treason and sedition; of murder of the soul, often by 'poisoning'; of disease requiring amputation or segregation; of 'libertinism' and 'sodomy' – was to be repeated many times in early modern Europe in arguments in justification of intolerance, including in the later seventeenth century.

The process of development of these associated accusations as justifying magisterial force against heretics and schismatics in patristic writings from after the first three centuries, and their use in the period of development of the episcopal and then papal Inquisition in the literature of inquisitors, crusaders, and defenders of papal authority, provided an agenda for the 'early Enlightenment' literature of toleration in the 1680s and 1690s. In these works, attack on doctrines of 'hereticide' and on the lesser punishments of heretics and schismatics still being strongly supported by anti-tolerationists involved declaring that these doctrines had been spawned in a period when patristic Christianity had become corrupted, credal and magisterial, and that they had then been developed further by late medieval papal and inquisitorial Christianity, when Christianity had been further corrupted, and thus were to be rejected as being a relic of ages which were to be typed as 'barbaric', 'ignorant', 'anti-Christian' and 'papist', in favour of what was declared the 'enlightened Christianity' of a return to the 'true primitive Christianity' before such persecution and credalism commenced. This was a major part of much of

---

[62] Lerner, *Heresy*, 10–11; Colish, *Medieval*, 250.

'early Enlightenment' thinkers' self-definition as promoting a 'liberating' and a 'reasonable' Christianity; we will meet very many such associations in later chapters, most obviously in discussing the *History of the Inquisition* by Philip van Limborch, a work instigated and encouraged by his close friend Locke, and in Bayle's *Philosophical Commentary*. In the works of this cadre of tolerationists, the attack on the anti-heretical and anti-schismatic writings and practices of late medieval inquisitorial Christianity thus joined hands with the 'early Enlightenment' attack on the late patristic Augustinianism standing behind the medieval Christian intolerance sketched a few moments ago. Such attack on late patristic and late medieval Christianity was simultaneously an assault on the dominant strands of Catholic and 'magisterial Reformation' Protestant thought in early modern Europe from the Reformation to the end of the seventeenth century. It is to delineating this thought, which reiterated earlier attacks on heresy and schism and joined them to increasingly central attacks on 'monstrosity' and 'witchcraft' in a period increasingly seen as that of the 'Last Days' before the millennium, that we now turn in Chapters 6 to 9.

6

Heresy and schism, sedition and treason, and 'contrarities' and 'inversions', in the 'Last Days'

Placing a series of theological and ecclesiological fissures at the heart of Christianity in the West, the Reformation thereby placed the issues and descriptions of 'heresy' and 'schism' at the centre of European intellectual life. In order to defend their own authority, Protestants and Catholics repeatedly defined and anathematised each other as 'heretical' and 'schismatic' deviations from the 'true church' and 'true faith'. As importantly, many 'magisterial Reformation' Protestants defined many 'radical Reformation' Protestant commitments and sects which emerged over the next two centuries as themselves 'heretical' and 'schismatic' deviations from the 'true faith' and 'true church', including Anabaptism, Socinian Anti-Trinitarianism, Arminianism, and Quakerism. 'Magisterial Reformation' Protestant leaders across Europe, including Zwingli, Melancthon, Bullinger, Calvin and Beza, thus turned the accusations of 'heresy' and 'schism' against Catholicism on the one side and against 'radical Reformation' Protestantism on the other. The 'radical Reformation' sects themselves added to the accusations of 'heresy' and 'schism' by anathematising each other; during the English Revolution, for instance, such accusations flowed backwards and forwards between Quakers, Baptists, Muggletonians, and Fifth Monarchists. And even Roman Catholics occasionally anathematised 'heresy' within their own church, as for instance in debates about grace between Jansenists and Jesuits in mid-seventeenth century France which led to the proscription of Jansenist publications as 'heretical'. The proscription here by Catholicism of the essentially Augustinian theology of Jansenism was the inverse of the most characteristic form of accusation within Protestantism, where it was Augustinian Calvinist theologians who tended to assault departures from Augustinianism as 'heretical'; this difference formed part of the reason that 'orthodox' Augustinian Calvinists claimed that most Protestant heresies involved support for 'Pelagianism' and 'popery'.[1]

---

[1] Sedgwick, *Jansenism in Seventeenth Century France*; A. Kors, *Atheism in Early Modern France* (Princeton 1990), ch. 8.

The Reformation simultaneously and relatedly contributed to a host of civil wars, rebellions, revolutions, and wars between polities in Western Europe over the two centuries following the 1520s, and gave considerable impetus to a massively increased articulation and development of political theories of obedience and of resistance. While obedience was most frequently stressed by religious writers concerned to gain the support of rulers or to show to rulers that nothing was to be feared from their religion, at moments when no other alternative existed for protecting their religion, many sixteenth-century theorists – Catholic and Protestant – composed theories of the duties and rights of resistance. Many writers who stressed obedience at one moment were forced by the alteration of their situation to justify resistance. Justification by Protestants of acts of resistance were deployed most notably in the sixteenth century in the wake of the 1572 St Bartholomew's Day Massacre of Protestant 'heretics' when many Huguenots turned to justifying resistance. As Quentin Skinner has brilliantly shown, some of the Protestant writers justifying resistance in the sixteenth century, such as George Buchanan, drew heavily upon scholastic and conciliarist (Catholic) thought and constructed their arguments for resistance on the grounds of natural rights and natural law rather than on the grounds of religious doctrine and duty, but other Protestants across Europe, including John Calvin, declared resistance to tyrants a religious duty to defend or establish the 'true faith'. Even though those Protestants constructing natural rights arguments on conciliarist bases intended thereby to compose non-denominational arguments, to many Catholics the practical association of the theories of resistance with those who were as Protestants both 'heretics' and 'schismatics' was alone sufficient to confirm the long-standing identification of 'heresy' and 'schism' with 'sedition' and 'treason' traced in the last chapter, while the specific claim of the duty of resistance to 'tyranny' in the name of 'true Protestant' religion made the association between Protestant 'heresy' and sedition central to their assaults on Protestants.[2]

Moreover, in many Catholic eyes there was considerable further evidence of Protestants who supported the founding of a 'dominion in grace' and the 'anarchy' of unrestrained 'conscience' in the sixteenth and seventeenth centuries to show that 'heresy' and 'schism' were inseparable from 'sedition' and 'rebellion'. Protestants were alleged to have fomented and supported the Peasants War of 1525, and some Protestants did, including the early

---

[2] See, magisterially, Q. Skinner, *The Foundations of Modern Political Thought* (Cambridge 1978); *idem*, 'The Calvinist Theory of Resistance' in B. Malament (ed.), *After the Reformation* (Pennsylvania 1980); also very importantly D. Kelley, *Beginning of Ideology* (Cambridge 1981); J. Franklin, *Jean Bodin and the Rise of Absolutist Theory* (Cambridge 1973); J. H. Burns and M. Goldie (eds.), *The Cambridge History of Political Thought 1450–1750* (Cambridge 1991), II.

Anabaptists Balthasar Hubmaier and Hans Hut. Anabaptists seized the town of Münster in 1534–5 in their effort to establish a reign of the saints on earth, involving both communism and polygamy, and attempted to seize Amsterdam in 1534–5. Some Anabaptists offered justifications of rights and duties of resistance to unjust authority.[3] Further confirmation for Catholic conviction about Protestant rebelliousness then came from the successful Protestant rebellion of the Netherlands against Spanish Catholic rule.[4] And in the seventeenth century came the *coup de grâce*: the English Civil Wars and Revolution, when Protestants took up arms against their ruler in significant part on the basis of a perceived religious duty to reform the religion of the Church of England from its allegedly 'heretical' tendencies to 'popery' and 'Arminianism', leading to a teeming liberty of Protestant sectarianism and execution of their king, Charles I. Defences of regicide, most famously Milton's *Tenure of Kings and Magistrates* and *Second Defence*, received widespread European circulations, and equally widespread European execrations. The authors and defenders of that act of regicide were seen both by many Catholics and by many 'magisterial Reformation' Protestants in other countries, including the Huguenot community in France anxiously repudiating its own monarchomach heritage, as the archetype of treasonable and seditious heretics and schismatics. Such English 'heretics' were persistently seen by European Catholics as revivals of the worst excesses of continental Anabaptism and of the allegedly 'Presbyterian' theories of monarchomachs.[5]

But it was not merely Protestants who seemed to Catholics to show that 'heresy' and 'schism' involved treason and sedition. The rulers of many nations became Protestant and were excommunicated by the Pope as 'heretical' and were then held by some influential Catholic writers to deserve deposition and assassination. Some Jesuit writers justified the legitimacy of measures being taken against 'heretical' rulers by subjects who did not have to 'maintain faith with heretics'; in Protestant polemic, all Jesuits were alleged to support such measures. English and French Protestant thinkers faced the issues of Catholic resistance theory in the sixteenth century when Elizabeth I in England and Henri of Navarre in France were declared

---

[3] Haude, *Shadow*; J. Stayer, *The German Peasant's War and Anabaptist Community of Goods* (Montreal 1991); *idem, Anabaptists and the Sword* (Lawrence, Kansas 1972); M. G. Baylor, *The Radical Reformation* (Cambridge 1991), *passim*, esp. xxiv–xxv.

[4] M. van Gelderen, *The Dutch Revolt* (Cambridge 1993); *idem, Political Thought*; P. Geyl, *The Revolt of the Netherlands* (1988).

[5] See below, ch. 13; *John Milton: Political Writings*, ed. M. Dzelzainis (Cambridge 1991); J. C. Davis, *Fear, Myth and History* (Cambridge 1986); Scott, *England's Troubles*. Continental writers often did not distinguish between British Presbyterians as repudiators of the act of regicide and Independents and other sects as its proponents.

unworthy to rule by the Pope. The papal excommunication of Henri of Navarre occurred in the practical context of Catholic resistance, as Paris declared itself 'resolved to suffer fire and famine rather than yield to the rule of a heretic'.[6] There were several attempts by Catholics to assassinate Protestant rulers, including plans to poison Elizabeth I in the 1590s and the Gunpowder Plot against James I in 1605, while in France a Catholic League assassin, Jacques Clément, killed Henri III in 1589 and resistance was justi-fied to Henri IV as a Protestant until – and to some degree after – his conversion to Catholicism; he, too, was assassinated by a Catholic. The Jesuit Mariana's 1598 *On Kings and the Education of Kings* specifically justified the assassination of Henri III. And Jesuit theorists such as Mariana simultaneously supported accounts of political society which asserted that political societies originated from the consent of the people and that tyrants could be resisted.[7]

The assassinations and attempted assassinations of English and French rulers – and that of William of Orange in the Netherlands – were declared in a huge volume of English polemic from the late sixteenth to the late seventeenth centuries to have involved active Jesuit participation; the Jesuit superior Henry Garnet was convicted (on slim grounds) of complicity in the Gunpowder Plot. Before moving towards supporting only passive disobe-dience in the 1620s, some English Catholics supported theories of resistance and regicide. The Oath of Allegiance issued in England in the wake of the Gunpowder Plot in 1605 specifically required English Catholics to declare that they abjured as a 'heresy' the doctrine that princes excommunicated by the Pope could be deposed or assassinated. It thus made explicit that such a Catholic view was simultaneously 'heresy' and the acme of treason. Since many Catholic clerics, particularly Jesuits, attacked rather than accepted the legitimacy of this Oath of Allegiance, the association of Catholic 'heresy' with 'treason' became even more pronounced in English Protestant thought, even though most English Catholics took the oath and declared that they did indeed deny the papal powers to depose or to legitimate assassination, there-after repeatedly attempted to make clear that they were loyal subjects, and later won recognition of their loyalty from Stuart kings. A persistent tension was thus set up in English thought between the potential loyalty of Catholics and the allegedly required and legitimated disobedience of Catholics. James I was to declare himself sorry 'to punish' the bodies of Catholics who were

---

[6] On Elizabeth, see Le Cler, *Toleration*, II, 358ff.; on Henri, see M. Wolfe, *The Conversion of Henri IV* (Harvard 1993), 35–8, and *passim*; on Paris, see P. Robiquet, 'Popular Insurrection as the Instrument of Aristocracy and Clergy' in J. Salmon (ed.), *The French Wars of Religion* (Boston 1967), 61; on Jesuit theorists, see Skinner, *Foundations*.

[7] Bayle, *Dictionary*, Mariana, G.

'quiet and well-minded men, peaceable subjects' for the 'errors of their minds' but feared the 'factious stirrers of sedition and perturbers of the commonwealth'.[8] This tension was to remain central into the late seventeenth century (and beyond). As alleged 'traitors' whose mere existence within the realm was adjudged sufficient crime, 189 Catholics, including 127 priests, were executed under Elizabeth I, and a further 40 priests died in prison; in 1588, the year of the failed Spanish Armada, 30 priests were executed in less than 4 months, and 24 more Catholics were sentenced to death by James I.[9]

In England in the late sixteenth century and throughout the seventeenth century, Catholic acts of excommunication, resistance, and assassination, and Catholic arguments supporting papal excommunication and the view that 'faith did not have to be kept with heretics', provided central topics for Protestant theorising. Much of James I's political writing was concerned with the threat of Catholic assassination and refutation of the argument that 'faith did not need to be kept with heretics', proving that plots for your own death do indeed concentrate the mind wonderfully. But the same topic also obsessed French Protestants throughout the century. Almost a century after Mariana's work, Bayle was to declare in the *Historical and Critical Dictionary* that 'nothing is more seditious than this book by Mariana', and Jurieu's 1681 *Policy* and 1682 *Last Efforts* both documented Catholic excommunications and assassinations in order to make the case that in France it was Catholics, not Protestants, who were the truly subversive subjects. There were in these actual instances of Catholic assassinations and arguments in defence of assassinations sources for declaration that Catholic 'heretics' and 'schismatics' were associated with 'sedition' and 'treason' in Protestant countries.[10]

In defences and definitions of the Church of England from soon after the Reformation there became a substantial tradition of attacking on the one hand Catholics as seditious 'heretics' and 'schismatics', and on the other hand many varieties of Protestantism – Presbyterian and 'puritan' as well as 'radical Reformation' – as equally seditious and treasonable. Such arguments pointed out forcefully that 'puritans' or 'Presbyterians' such as Buchanan

---

[8] B. Coward, *The Stuart Age* (London 1980), 110.
[9] Campbell, *Intellectual Struggle*; P. Holmes, *Resistance and Compromise* (Cambridge 1982); P. Hughes, *Rome and the Counter-Reformation in England* (Birmingham 1944); A. Marotti, 'Alienating Catholics in Early Modern England: Recusant Women, Jesuits and Ideological Fantasies' in idem (ed.), *Catholicism and Anti-Catholicism in Early Modern English Texts* (New York 1999), 10–5; Le Cler, *Toleration*, II, 363.
[10] James I, *The Political Works of James I* (London 1616; ed. C. McIlwain, Harvard 1918) and especially *A Premonition to All Most Mightie Monarches, Kings, Free Princes, and States of Christendome* (1609; 1616); Jurieu, *Policy, passim*; Bayle, *Dictionary*, Mariana G; Holmes, *Resistance and Compromise*; Morrill, *The Nature of the English Revolution*, 3.

and Calvin, and French monarchomachs such as François Hotman, had agreed with Catholic theorists such as Mariana in defending armed resistance. James I was almost as concerned with the potential for sedition from 'Puritans' as that from Catholics, and since his own tutor had been Buchanan, he had a particularly acute awarness of the point Marchamont Nedham was later to make in 1647, that 'A Scot and a Jesuit, joined in hand/ First taught the world to say/That subjects ought to have command/And princes to obey'.[11]

In terms of the generation of resistance theories and their place in rebellions and assassinations, then, there was much reason in early modern Europe to identify the alternative forms of Christianity typed by their opponents as 'heresy' and 'schism' with 'sedition' and 'treason'. There were two further crucial repeated elements to this association of 'heresy' and 'schism' with sedition and treason. Firstly, it was very often stated that peace could only be maintained in a polity with one religion, and it was held that the very existence of diversity of opinions necessarily caused turbulence. Here, it did not so much matter what the diverse opinions were, as that they were diverse opinions, and that because they were religious opinions and involved the conviction that those holding other views were damned and evil, they were particularly generative of animosity. This understanding of the danger of religious diversity seemed to many also to have received considerable documentation in the sixteenth and seventeenth centuries, as revolts, civil wars, and the English Revolution were understood by many contemporary commentators as caused primarily by religious divisions.[12] It is perhaps easiest to document the considerable force of the view that peace and security required only one religion in a state in the late sixteenth century by pointing to its strength in the thought of two *politiques*. Even Justus Lipsius, whose 1589 *Politicorum libri sex* was immediately controversial for arguing that a ruler should allow religious toleration 'for a time' when he was too weak to suppress 'vices', declared that 'one religion is the author of unitie; and from a confused religion there always groweth dissension' as part of his argument that a ruler had to 'enforce religious uniformity on his people, as far as possible'. It was for Lipsius an act of magisterial 'prudence' to 'burn' and to 'saw asunder' public heresy, and far better 'that one member be cast away, than that the whole body runs to ruin'. For Coornhert, who responded at the time to Lipsius with defences of religious toleration, and for Bayle, who still felt the need to respond to Lipsius' arguments a century later both in the

---

[11] Skinner, *Foundations*; Harris, *Politics*; Nedham in D. Wootton, 'Leveller Democracy and the Puritan Revolution' in Burns and Goldie (eds.), *The Cambridge History of Political Thought 1450–1750*, 434.

[12] Skinner, *Foundations*; R. Tuck, *Philosophy and Government 1572–1651* (Cambridge 1993).

Philosophical Commentary of 1686 and then at length in the *Dictionary* in
the wake of the revived 'reason of state' arguments for *in*tolerance surrounding the Revocation of the Edict of Nantes, Lipsius had thereby not condemned but instead had 'publickly approved the principles of persecution'.[13]
The force of conviction that uniformity was required for peace was similarly
illustrated in 1560 by Chancellor Michel de L'Hôpital, soon to be an important *politique* defender of toleration as a lesser evil than ruin of the state by
pursuit of uniformity, but in 1560 not yet convinced of this case. De
L'Hôpital asserted:

It is folly to expect peace, quiet and friendship among persons of various denominations. No sentiment is so deeply rooted in the heart of man as the religious sentiment,
and none separates one man more deeply from another...Hence the old proverb, One
faith, one law, one king. In such a diversity and opposition of sentiment it is difficult
for men to refrain from taking up arms; as the poet said, war follows closely on,
and accompanies, discord in speech.[14]

This case for the necessity of religious uniformity was often presented as
being axiomatic: diversity intrinsically threatened the state. But it was also in
early modern France an historical argument in which the religious uniformity
of the realm since the medieval punishment of the Albigensians and
Waldensians loomed large. Attacking the *politiques*, in 1563–4 Councillor
Jean Bégat of the Parlement of Burgundy declared that since the Albigensians
the subjects of France had not been divided by religion, and queried:

Who, then, are the people who wish to maintain that a Christian monarch can tolerate
two different sects in his kingdom without bringing about its ruin? Where in history
can they find a precedent, or from which place?

Since French kings had 'accepted the Christian faith', Bégat declared, there
had not been one 'who did not take care to maintain his subjects in the same
religion as his own'. Such an emphasis on uniformity since the time of the
conquest of the medieval Waldensians was to help to add further significance
to discussions in France of their punishment in 1685–92, and to that of
Huguenots as their alleged descendants.[15]

A second important association between heresy and schism and sedition
came in sixteenth- and seventeenth-century Europe from the importance

---

[13] J. Lipsius, *Politicorum libri sex* (1589), 62–5, and the discussions of it in Tuck, *Philosophy
and Government*, 58–9; in *idem*, 'Scepticism and Toleration in the Seventeenth Century' in
S. Mendus, *Justifying Toleration* (Cambridge 1988), 21–35, and van Gelderen, *Political
Thought*, 254–5; Bayle, *Dictionary*, Lipsius C; *idem*, *Philosophical Commentary*, 199.
Bayle asserted moreover in the *Philosophical Commentary* that Lipsius' arguments would
have supported pagan extermination of Christian preachers and the execution of Catholic
priests in Holland.

[14] *Oeuvres de Michel de L'Hôpital*, ed. Dufey (Paris 1824), I, 296–398 in Le Cler, *Toleration*,
II, 45.

[15] *Mémoires de Condé*, IV, 372 in Le Cler, *Toleration*, 78.

accorded to oaths. Oaths were considered by almost all political and religious theorists across early modern Europe to be vital for the security of the state. Oaths of allegiance backed by belief of divine punishment for disobedience were said to bind conscience far more powerfully than any terrestrial threats ever could. But many 'heretics' across the two centuries following the Reformation presented problems *precisely* in terms of their attitudes about oaths. Catholics were associated for Protestants with Jesuit theories of mental reservation and equivocation – that they could take oaths in forms of words or by mentally reserving a space for disobedience that would allow them to break them. They were associated with the doctrine that 'faith did not have to be kept with heretics', articulated extensively by Jesuit theorists, and attributed by Protestant polemicists to all Catholics and not just to Jesuit theorists. In this situation, it was thought that even the most carefully worded oath could not satisfactorily bind those who took it. Catholics were therefore seen by Protestant rulers as potentially politically subversive because their oaths could not be relied upon, and many attempts were made to find forms of oaths which would be binding. Equally, many 'radical Reformation' Protestant sects, including many Anabaptists, some Anti-Trinitarians, many Quakers, and some Baptists, refused to take oaths made to men and to government as they held that such oaths were forbidden by God (and in this conformed to the pre-existing image of 'heretics' and 'schismatics' from the Waldensians' refusal to take oaths). They were therefore held to be untrustworthy both by Catholics and by 'magisterial Reformation' Protestants. Every structure of authority could be seen as simultaneously undermined – or inverted – by such refusal. As Zwingli put it in responding to the Anabaptists' refusal to take oaths as seeking 'to destroy the magistracy':

Take away the oath and you have dissolved all order...Give up the oath in any state at once and in keeping with the Anabaptists' desire, the magistracy is removed and all things follow as they would have them. Good God, what confusion and up-turning of everything![16]

There were thus many reasons in the intellectual and political events of early modern Europe, and in positions taken by 'heretics' such as opposition to oaths and the adoption of resistance theories, for political observers to see ample confirmation of the long-standing association in anti-heretical and anti-schismatic literature of heresy and schism with sedition and treason, and for many such political writers to declare that heretics and schismatics could not be tolerated. This set of political concerns was paramount in much of the justification and motivation of persecution and punishment of those declared

---

[16] Zwingli cited in W. Klaasen, 'The Anabaptist Understanding of the Separation of the Church', *Church History* (1977), 421–36, at 423–4.

to be 'heretics' and 'schismatics' across early modern Europe. Political authorities enacting and enforcing penalties against religious 'dissidents' were unsurprisingly most concerned with the direct threats which they thought that heretics posed to their political authority.

Such arguments were urged repeatedly in the sixteenth century by Catholics and by 'magisterial Reformation' Protestants, who often added to them a series of even stronger stresses on religious reasons for punishing heresy and schism as they alleged that such heretics were 'poisoning' and 'infecting' others with their heretical views, and calling down God's punishments on the community. Heretics and schismatics were seen as needing punishments that 'purged' or 'cleansed' the body politic of such 'infection' and 'pollution': drowning and fire. Or they were seen as needing the punishment of blasphemers in the divinely instituted regime of Israel: stoning to death. Magistrates were held to be duty-bound to suppress heresy, idolatry, blasphemy, and sacrilege. Depicting the magistrate as a 'nursing father' to the church, in the *Institutes* Calvin argued that the civil magistrate was to provide that 'the true religion' be not 'violated and polluted by public blasphemies'.[17] As such, heresy had to be punished for religious reasons. For Calvin, heresy was moreover murder, poisoning, treason, sedition and lèse-majesté.[18] As such, heresy had to be punished for political reasons. Theodore Beza, the leader of Calvinism in succession to Calvin, made clear that both ends were important, but gave them a clear teleological theological priority:

The main end of human society is that God be honoured as He should be. Now the magistrate is set as guard and governor of this society...And though it be his duty, so far as in him lies, to take order that no discord arise among his subjects, yet, since the chief and ultimate end of human society is not that men should live together in peace, but that, living in peace, they should serve God, it is the function of the Magistrate to risk even this outward peace (if no otherwise it may be done) in order to secure and maintain in his land the true service of God in its purity...And it is impossible that he should so preserve and maintain religion unless he suppress by the power of the sword those who obstinately condemn it...those who would that the Magistrate should not concern himself with religion, either do not understand what is the true end of human society or else pretend that they do not.[19]

In their agreement with Calvin and Beza about both elements of this call to the use of magisterial force against heretics, many other 'magisterial Reformation' Protestant leaders, as Brad Gregory has recently stressed in *Salvation at Stake*, cited the precedent of the Mosaic Commonwealth,

---

[17] *Institutes*, tr. J. T. McNeill, *John Calvin on God and Political Duty* (New York 1956), 46f.
[18] Calvin, *Opera*, XXVII, 244–9; XLIV, 347–8; XXIX, 337–8, 532, 647, in Bainton (ed.), *Concerning*, 71–2.
[19] Beza, *De Haereticis* (Geneva 1554) in J. W. Allen, *A History of Political Thought in the Sixteenth Century* (London 1977), 96.

especially Deuteronomy 13:6 and Leviticus 24:14, which specified the punishment of 'false prophets'. In many of these arguments, the Mosaic theocracy served as divine positive law commanding punishment. Lutherans further cited these and other passages in 1557 as a part of 'natural law' which bound all authorities in their rule:

> For civil government should not only preserve the bodies of subjects as a shepherd preserves cattle or sheep, but should also uphold outward discipline and regulate government to God's honour, should remove and punish public idolatry and blasphemy.[20]

Sixteenth-century Catholic writers here agreed with 'magisterial Reformation' Protestants, and cited the same passages of the Old Testament and the same Mosaic precedent to the same effect of maintaining the religious duty of the magistrate to enforce 'true religion'. In the *Handbook of Commonplaces* (1525), which went through over one hundred editions by 1576, Eck identified Deuteronomy as having called for false prophets to be put to death for 'treason'. Antoine du Val argued:

> If it is right that thieves, murderers, and robbers are punished, is it not with greater reason that one ought to punish heretics, who steal the soul…Is it with good reason that a poisoner and corrupter of bodily health is punished? Then why would it not be more reasonable to punish one who deprives the soul of its wellbeing?

John Fisher similarly held that 'heresy' was 'the seed of the devil' and caused 'the murder of our souls' in a sermon of 1526 calling for heretics' execution. At the end of the century, according to Robert Bellarmine's *Disputationes de controversis christianae fidei*, heretics were to be killed as more harmful than bandits in killing the soul rather than the body, being both 'poisoners' and pestilential, because they 'fill the nation with unrest resulting from religious differences', and even as an act of 'charity' to them because

> To eliminate hardened heretics from this life is to do them a favour. The longer they live the more errors they concoct, the more people they will lead astray, and consequently the more eternal torment they will incur.

For many writers, Catholic and Protestant, French and English, a failure to punish heresy would moreover bring down God's judgment on the community, most notably in the form of plague. For the magistrate to fail to prosecute heresy and schism was thus to invite civil destruction of the community he was to protect.[21]

---

[20] Gregory, *Salvation at Stake*, 82–3.
[21] Gregory, *Salvation at Stake*, 84–5; Bellarmine in Tazbir, *State Without Stakes*, 147; J. Shakespeare, 'Plague and Punishment' in P. Lake and M. Dowling (eds.), *Protestantism and the National Church in Sixteenth Century England* (Croom Helm 1987), 106.

In his 1528 *A Dialogue Concerning Heresies*, Thomas More said that heretical works 'infect the reader and corrupt the soul unto everlasting death' and called for heretics' execution. For More, 'heresies breed disorders and fear of these have been the cause that princes and peoples have been constrained to punish heresies by terrible death'. Moreover, since heretics would themselves use force as soon as they were able, More argued,'he that would now suffer that sect to be preached or taught among Christian men and not punish and destroy the doers, were a plain enemy to Christ'. Given that heretics were subversives and desired to use their force against the 'truth' if able, for More princes were 'bound...that they shall not suffer their people to be reduced and corrupted by heretics, since the peril shall in short grow to as great, both with men's souls withdrawn from God and their goods lost and their bodies destroyed by common sedition, insurrection and open war, within the bowels of their own land'. He recommended a 'terrible death' for heretics. In his 1533 *Debellacyon of Salem and Bizance*, More similarly identified heresy as that 'by which a Christian becomes a traitor' and as 'considered by all spiritual and temporal laws as an equally great crime as treason committed towards a man on this earth'.[22]

More's friend Erasmus has become known for contributing significantly to the history of 'tolerationist' thought, particularly because of his arguments that it was a moral life and not dogma or ritual performance which was most crucial in Christianity, and that much was not 'known' but rather 'opinion'. Some passages of Erasmus' works in this vein were cited by Castellio in his important defence of toleration, *De Haereticis*. Grotius cited Erasmus in his 1622 *Apologetics* (*Verantwoordingh*) as favouring 'peace and accommodation' about diverse views about predestination. In the late seventeenth century, Erasmus became repeatedly represented as a proto-tolerationist by 'early Enlightenment' thinkers who identified an 'Erasmian tradition' and selected for emphasis Erasmus' most 'tolerationist' passages. Jean Le Clerc edited Erasmus' works and celebrated the pre-eminent contribution of the Netherlands to the 'Respublica Christiana' because of Erasmus and Grotius.[23] Hugh Trevor Roper has most notably followed this line of interpretation in identifying an 'Erasmian Enlightenment tradition', and J. G. A. Pocock has recently reinforced parts of this approach in his work on the multiple

---

[22] T. More, *A Dialogue Concerning Heresies* (1528) in *Works* (1557), 274–9; Allen, *Political Thought*, 75–6; G. Elton, 'Persecution and Toleration in the English Reformation' in W. Sheils (ed.), *Persecution and Toleration* (Oxford 1984), 163–87; T. More, *Debellacyon* in Rastell (ed.), *Works*, 995, in Le Cler, *Toleration*, 139.

[23] H. Grotius, *Verantwoordingh* (1622) and Jean Le Clerc (ed.), *Desiderii Erasmi Opera Omnia* (Leiden 1703), both discussed in J. Trapmann, 'Grotius and Erasmus' in H. Nellen and E. Rabbie (eds.), *Hugo Grotius, Theologian* (Leiden 1994), 77–98.

contexts of Edward Gibbon's thought.[24] Erasmus did indeed express many of these emphases. And he argued against the process of defining as a 'heretic' any who disagreed 'however little from St Thomas', instead of only 'if he deviated from the Gospel, the articles of faith or something of similar authority'. Erasmus stressed as crucial truths redemption, baptism, works, and the afterlife 'without which salvation is not possible', but he encouraged beyond these the definition of 'the smallest possible number of dogmas'. And he wrote explicitly that 'the more dogma there is, the more material for heresy'. Such credal minimalism and attempts to circumscribe the charges of 'heresy' itself were unquestionably important to later tolerationist arguments.[25]

Yet the 'Erasmian tradition' emphasising such passages distilled only Erasmus' more tolerationist pronouncements. Erasmus himself wrote at points in defence of the defining authority of the church, and while desiring reform of the church, identified himself as ready to 'suffer all things, even the most extreme, rather than become a member of any sect'. Like his very close friend More, he argued that there was heresy which was intolerable as

manifest blasphemy, and there is heresy…which makes for sedition. Shall we sheath the sword of the magistrate against this? To kill blasphemous and seditious heretics is necessary for the maintenance of the state.

Erasmus explicitly argued against the background of imperial edicts of execution of Anabaptists that Anabaptists were 'by no means to be tolerated. For the apostles command us to obey the magistrates, and these men object to obeying Christian Princes'. When the Lutheran Gerald Geldenhouwer published a citation of Erasmus' arguments in defence of toleration for heretics in 1529, Erasmus declared himself an opponent of those who opposed the execution of heretics and suggested that he wished only to ensure that magistrates did not immediately draw the sword upon any accusation of heresy and before an attempt had been made to convert the heretic. He was clear that the early apostles had not possessed the sword against heretics, but adamant that since then worldly powers had indeed been armed with real swords and not merely spiritual weapons with which to combat heresy. While desirous of stopping the 'plague' of Lutheranism by 'spiritual weapons', and convinced that executions of Lutherans generally encouraged rather than discouraged commitment to Lutheranism – once again expressing what was later an important tolerationist argument, that force created sympathy, admiration for and increased awareness of the ideas

---

[24] Trevor-Roper, *Catholics*; Pocock, *Barbarism and Religion*.
[25] Erasmus, *OE*, IV 101–6 in Le Cler, *Toleration*, I, 117; Erasmus, *OE*, V, 177–8 in Le Cler, *Toleration*, I, 126–7; G. Remer, 'Rhetoric and the Erasmian Defence of Religious Toleration', *History of Political Thought* (1989), 377–403, at 399n.127.

of those against whom it was used – Erasmus nonetheless declared that Lutherans were 'seditious'. And Erasmus wrote more generally and very significantly:

Let them burn, by all means, those who fight the teaching of the articles of the faith or of something of equal authority by the consensus of the Church.[26]

He argued that heresy was a monster which the magistrate should slay when able, and a disease to be amputated if possible. As Erasmus put it in *Vita Hieronymi*, 'in the matter of heresy, tolerance is a wrong, not a virtue'.[27] Erasmus declared France 'the most spotless and flourishing part of Christendom' because 'France alone remains not infected with heretics, with Bohemian schismatics, with Jews, with half-Jewish marranos, and untouched by the contagion of Turkish neighbours'. Erasmus contrasted France in these terms with Italy, Hungary, and Spain. One can only wonder what he would actually have said about the late seventeenth-century Netherlands, had he lived to see it.[28]

Royal officials in France supported heresy trials, Michael Wolfe notes, 'primarily because they beleieved religious dissent invariably led to sedition'. In the Edict of Fontainebleu of 1539, Francis I established lay trials for heresy in France and declared that 'such errors and false doctrines contain in themselves the crime of human lèse-majesté, sedition, and disturbance of our state'. For Francis I, subjects must denounce heretics 'just as everyone must run to extinguish a fire'. In 1545, the Waldensian strongholds of Cabrières, Merindol, and some twenty villages were destroyed with the deaths of perhaps 3,000 Waldensians; they were alleged to have been planning resistance.[29] But political arguments that heresy was seditious were usually combined with religious arguments for suppression of heresy as poison and plague. The 1551 Edict of Chateaubriand declared that Protestantism was becoming 'a plague so contagious that it infected and

---

[26] Erasmus, *Opera*, IX, 906C; X, 1575–6; *idem*, *Epistolarum Des. Erasmi libri XXXI* (1642), XXX, ep. 77 col. 1963D quoted in Bainton (ed.), *Concerning*, 40–2; Erasmus, *Opus Epistolarum*, V, 604–6, in Le Cler, *Toleration*, I, 118; Erasmus, *OE*, XI, 62, in *ibid.*, II, 13. For a recent account stressing Erasmus' tolerationism, see James Tracy, 'Erasmus, Coonhert and the Acceptance of Religious diversity in the Body Politic' in Berkvens-Stevelinck, *Emergence of Tolerance*, 49–62; but cf. M. Turchetti, 'Une question mal posée: Erasmus et la tolérance' in *Histoire de l'humanisme et de la Renaissance* LIII (1991), 379–95.

[27] *Vita Hieronymi* in *The Collected Works* (Toronto 1974), 61 44 in Bejczy, 'Tolerantia: a Medieval Concept', *Journal of the History of Ideas* (1997), 377, *passim*; Remer, 'Erasmian Defence', 377–403, at 380–1.

[28] Erasmus, *Collected Works*, IV (Toronto 1977), 279 and XXVII (Toronto 1986), 306, 314; *idem*, *Opera Omnia* (Amsterdam 1986), 58, all in R. Tuck, *The Rights of War and Peace* (Oxford 1999), 29–31, 41–2.

[29] W. Monter, *Judging the French Reformation* (Harvard 1999), 86; Le Cler, *Toleration*, II, 26; Wolfe, *Conversion of Henri IV*, 12.

contaminated many leading cities' with men, women, and children 'forcibly fed with this poison'. It banned Protestant books to 'purge and cleanse' the kingdom. Similarly, legislation in England deployed religious and political arguments for the suppression of 'heretical' books. The first royal proclamation listing prohibited books issued by Henry VIII in 1529 prohibited 'divers heresies and erroneous opinions' lately 'sown and spread among his subjects. . .to the intent as well to pervert and withdraw the people from the Catholic and true faith of Christ, as also to stir and incense them to sedition and disobedience against their princes, sovereigns and heads'.[30]

In the sixteenth and seventeenth centuries, such 'heretics' and 'schismatics' were understood to be involved not in a mere departure from the 'true faith' but in its direct diabolical antithesis, its inversion or 'contrary'. It is worth stressing here the importance of 'contrarieties' and 'inversions'. Intellectual and cultural historians, religious historians, and historians of science such as Stuart Clark, Michael Hunter, David Wootton, J. C. Davis, Patrick Collinson and Peter Lake have all recently crucially stressed that much thought in sixteenth- and early seventeenth-century Europe was structured in terms of 'contrarieties' and 'inversions'.[31] A host of social and cultural historians and literary scholars, led by Natalie Zemon Davis, M. Bakhtin, and E. P. Thompson, have simultaneously shown that 'inversion' was central to early modern ritual and intellectual life; Christopher Hill's *World Turned Upside Down* is but one of many works documenting the centrality of 'inversion' to political and religious thinking. As structured by the notion of reversal and antithesis – the world being either turned upside down or right side up – such 'inversion' is itself based on and strongly reinforcing of the notion of 'binary opposition'.[32] Drawing methodological sustenance from Quentin Skinner's analysis of 'meaning and understanding in the history of ideas',[33] Stuart Clark has particularly and brilliantly emphasised the 'predisposition' in the sixteenth and seventeenth centuries to 'see things in terms of binary opposition' and the 'extraordinary pervasiveness of the language of "contrariety", the most extreme of the relations of opposition'.

---

[30] Edict of Chateaubriand 1551 in Duke et al. (eds.), *Calvinism in Europe*, 60–1.
[31] Clark, *Thinking*; M. Hunter, 'Science and Heterodoxy: An Early Modern Problem Reconsidered' in D. Lindberg and R. Westman (eds.), *Reappraisals of the Scientific Revolution* (Cambridge 1990), 437–60; D. Wootton and M. Hunter (eds.), *Atheism from the Reformation to the Enlightenment*; Davis, *Fear*.
[32] Hill, *World Turned Upside Down*; Davis, *Society*; M. Bakhtin, *Rabelais and his World* (Cambridge, Mass 1968); E. P. Thompson, *Customs in Common* (London 1991). I wish to thank my many students over the past decade with whom I have discussed themes of inversions and contrarieties in many courses on 'popular culture in early modern Europe'.
[33] Q. Skinner, 'Meaning and Understanding in the History of Ideas', *History and Theory* 8 (1969), 3–53; S. Clark, 'Inversion, Misrule and the Meaning of Witchcraft', *Past and Present* (1980), 99.

Clark stresses the linguistic preference in the period for 'standardised forms of argument and expression based on antithesis, and a preoccupation with the extreme poles of the religious and moral universe'. All 'sciences' were held in the sixteenth and early seventeenth centuries to consist significantly of the 'comparing of contraries', with physicians thus relating 'health' to 'sickness', and the 'honest, just, and profitable' to be related by political philosophers and moralists to the 'dishonest, unjust, and domageable'. Surveying knowledge in 1604, William Cornwallis wrote that men cannot 'judge singlie, but by coupling contrarieties'; in 1651, the Spanish Jesuit Gracian wrote that 'the things of this world can be truly perceived only when looking at them backwards'. Discussing these (and other) important elements both of early modern thought about the constitution of the world itself, and of early modern forms and techniques of discourse about that world, Clark has stressed that 'Contrariety was...a universal principle of intelligibility as well as a statement about how the world was actually constituted'.[34]

As Clark shows very powerfully, many features of early modern religious thinking importantly partook of and massively reinforced the importance of these 'binary oppositions'. Doctrines of original sin and election in Calvinist thought centred on a polar opposition, contrasting human depravity and divine perfection, and absolute election and absolute reprobation. Beza's *Booke of Christian Questions and Answers* (tr. 1572) thus centrally discussed election and reprobation by utilising 'contrarities'. Much Calvinist thought stressed, with John Preston in *The New Covenant* in 1630, that 'there is no middle sort of men in the world, all are either sheep or goates...all are either elect or reprobates'. Demonology was based – as James VI and I put it in his 1597 work of that title, *Demonologie* – on the understanding that 'the Devill is the verie contrarie opposite to God' so that 'there can be no better way to know God, then by the contrarie'. The increased language of apocalyptic thought, including millenarianism, centred on the most uncompromising of contrarities – the battle against the Antichrist. It was central to much sixteenth- and seventeenth-century religious thinking, both Catholic and Protestant.[35]

---

[34] This entire paragraph, including all quotations, is drawn from Clark, *Thinking*; *idem*, 'Inversion'. For an important emphasis on binary opposition in the writings of male monastic medieval writers, see C. W. Bynum, *Holy Feast, Holy Fast* (Berkeley 1987).

[35] Clark, *Thinking*, ch. 22, 62–3, 137; P. Collinson, *The Birthpangs of Protestant England* (Basingstoke 1988), 146–8; *idem*, *The Puritan Character* (Los Angeles 1989), 25–9; Lake, 'Anti-popery'; W. Lamont, *Godly Rule* (London 1969); R. Bauckman, *Tudor Apocalypse* (Abingdon 1978); P. K. Christianson, *Reformers and Babylon* (Toronto 1978); K. Firth, *The Apocalyptic Tradition* (Oxford 1979); C. Hill, *Antichrist in Seventeenth Century England* (London 1990).

'Heresy' as the diabolical 'contrarie' to 'true faith' was a significant part of this series of polarities that was central to much early modern thinking, and both partook of these structures of binary opposition and helped to reinforce them. The 'heretical' was often held to be the 'anti-Christian', the polar opposite of the 'true faith', and as therefore needing to be punished severely as 'diabolic' and 'anti-Christian'. It was often said that failure to punish and remove such pollution and infection would itself call down God's punishments on the community, and that plagues or famines were themselves signs of God's desire to thus repent the failure to eradicate the diabolic sin from one's community. In France, François de la Noue, a *politique* who opposed this way of thinking as causing religious civil war, described the central contention of Protestants and Catholics that the other were wicked heretics as one of contrariety. He indicated that 'if a man say to one, "this man is a Protestant", by and by he will answere, "Then he is a wicked heretik", and saie to another, "This man is a Papist", and he also will say, "Then he is naught"'. This was so, de la Noue alleged, because men could say of a religious opponent only that 'his religion is contrarie to ours'.[36] In the sixteenth and early seventeenth centuries, such thinking thus divided the world into a series of 'binary oppositions' as many Protestants and Catholics claimed to be the 'godly' and demonised the other as 'anti-Christian', and within Protestantism many Calvinists similarly demonised Arminians, Socinians, Anabaptists, and Quakers.[37]

Yet it is crucial to stress that not all Protestants and Catholics supported such a series of binary oppositions. The features which Clark emphasises as most conducive to this vision of the world – Calvinist doctrines of election, commitment to the battle against the Antichrist, and demonology, suggest that two groups were most likely to conceive of the world in these strongly binary terms: Calvinist Protestants, and those Catholics strongly committed to demonology. In Clark's account, 'Radical Reformation' Protestants who attacked Calvinist doctrines of absolute election in favour of a more complex view of salvation as offered to many and accepted by those who utilised resistible grace provided by God were less likely to see the world in polarised terms and less likely to see 'heretics' as the demonic negations of 'true faith'. They were also less likely to believe in witches and demons. For those most committed to this 'binary opposition', however, those who themselves did not accept it by that very failure became assimilable to those who were seen as standing in binary opposition: to be 'indifferent' to the punishment of

---

[36] F. de la Noue, *The Politicke and Military Discourses of the Lord de la Noue*, tr. E. A. (1587), 47, in Clark, *Thinking*, 62; F. de la Noue, *Discours politiques et militaires* (Geneva 1614), 49–50, in Le Cler, *Toleration*, 133.

[37] Clark, *Thinking*, 540–5 discusses opposition to this attitude.

'heresy' was itself a sign of one's fellowship with the 'heretic' in a binary world-view, even if one did not oneself support the specific views anathematised as 'heretical'. We have noted in Chapter 4 that for many Calvinists – both Dutch Reformed and Huguenot – Arminians in the Netherlands and Amyraldists or Pajonists within the Huguenot community who supported the toleration of Socinians even if they were not doctrinally anti-Trinitarian became by this support effectively indistinguishable from Socinians themselves. We can now suggest that such a view was itself a conclusion of those seeing the world in these terms of 'binary opposition'. In England in the early seventeenth century, Laudians who did not hold that the Catholic Church or Pope was the Antichrist, or late sixteenth- and early seventeenth-century Cambridge thinkers who did not hold that strictly supralapsarian views were to be opposed strenuously, similarly gave sufficient reason for those English Calvinists who saw the world in these polarised terms to list them with the proscribed heresies as themselves tending to 'popery'.[38]

The tendency to demonise heretics and schismatics, supported most ardently by strict Calvinists and by significant numbers of Catholics with strong inclinations to demonology, thus joined hands with the strong association of heretics and schismatics with the 'seditious' and 'treasonable'. We noted in Chapter 5 that anti-heretical and anti-schismatic literature was structured around a conviction that new heresies and schisms were but 'old heresies and schisms revived'. In one extremely important way, however, the anti-heretical and anti-schismatic literature of the sixteenth to mid-seventeenth centuries stressed that such repetitions of 'old heresies and schisms revived' in new forms was occurring in a time of the most profound change, and argued that in this period the call for actions against heresies and schisms carried an unprecedented urgency. This was because the conviction that this was the period of the apocalyptic 'Last Days' before the coming of the millennium reached unprecedented levels in sixteenth-century to mid-seventeenth-century Europe. Historians such as Firth, Hill, Lamont, Christianson, and Clark have documented the centrality of such thinking in late sixteenth- to mid-seventeenth-century England, while scholars such as Delumeau, Crouzet, and Clark have shown its centrality in the same period in France. As Bob Scribner has stressed, the Reformation ideal of creating a reformed civic community identified threats to this new community as involving eschatological conflict, and considerably intensified the perception that these were the 'Last Days'.[39]

---

[38] See below, pp. 282–7 and Lake, 'Antipopery'; 'Whitaker' in P. Lake, 'The Significance of the Elizabethan Identification of the Pope As Antichrist', *Journal of Ecclesiastical History* (1980).

[39] Hill, *Antichrist*; Christianson, *Reformers and Babylon* (Toronto 1978); Clark, *Thinking*; D. Crouzet, *Les Guerriers de Dieu* (Seyssel 1990); Delumeau, *Sin and Fear*, ch. 21;

Scripture had spoken of the time of the 'Last Days' as a time of famine, pestilence, wars, false magic, portents, and false prophets. The notion of the prevalence in the 'Last Days' of 'false prophets' thus tied heretics to 'portents', and in sixteenth- and early seventeenth-century Europe this associated heretics frequently to 'monsters' as well as to other 'signs' from God, such as 'prodigious' comets or other 'celestial events' and to the false magic of witchcraft. As we will see in later chapters, all of these were perceived to be occurring at unprecedented levels in early modern Europe. The Strasburg preacher Kaspar Hedio declared representatively, in a work against the Anabaptists of Münster in 1535, that 'we are living in the endtime, in the days of misery, fear, distress, and blasphemy, when healthy, God-pleasing doctrine is assailed by so many horrifying errors, discord, and sects, and when the sun, the moon, and the stars give ample signs and warnings in the sky'. Three comets in two years were for Hedio clear signs from God; if more signs were needed, wars and pestilence provided them. Hedio applied this understanding directly to his opposition to the growth of Anabaptism and supported its fierce punishment as part of his interpretation of the time of portents which called upon the godly to institute punishments.[40]

This understanding of the character of the 'Last Days' tied 'false prophets' simultaneously to false magic, and in sixteenth- and seventeenth-century Europe it thus associated 'heretics' frequently to 'witches' in the period in European history – the sixteenth to mid-seventeenth century – in which witch trials and accusations reached their peak and numbered probably in the hundreds of thousands. Sixteenth-century Catholic France and Calvinist Scotland saw hundreds of executions, while England's witch trials peaked in exactly the same period as the peak of Calvinist strength and of accusations of 'heresy' in the English Revolution in the 1640s, when some of those accused of being 'heretics' in these years were also accused of being 'witches' – most notably Quaker women.[41] Witchcraft, like heresy, was treason against God and the magistrate; witchcraft, like heresy, involved harm to others by poisoning and spreading pestilence or disease; and witches, like heretics, were said to practice 'sodomy', 'libertinism', and 'seduction'. There

---

R. Scribner, 'Preconditions of Tolerance and Intolerance' in Grell and Scribner, *Tolerance*, 43. I became aware of A. Cunningham and O. Grell's excellent *The Four Horsemen of the Apocalypse* (Cambridge 2000), which examines early modern apocalyptic beliefs, after this book was written.

[40] K. Hedio, 'Radts Predigt', GFF 3425 aiiijr (1534) in Haude, *Shadow*, 23.

[41] B. Levack, *The Witch-Hunt in Early Modern Europe* (London 1995); J. Sharpe, *Instruments of Darkness* (London 1997); H. Trevor-Roper, *The European Witchcraze* (London 1978); L. Roper, *Oedipus and the Devil* (London 1994); Kieckhefer, *European Witch Trials*; W. Monter, *Frontiers of Heresy* (Cambridge 1990); K. Thomas, *Religion and the Decline of Magic* (London 1971); A. MacFarlane, *Witchcraft in Tudor and Stuart England* (New York 1970); M. Gijswijt-hofstra, 'Witchcraft Before Zeeland Magistrates and Church

was thus a strong isomorphism between heresy accusations and witchcraft accusations. Many historians have pointed to witchcraft beliefs as having been developed over previous centuries in significant part out of anti-heretical literature, and that the depictions of the sabbath in witch accusations 'largely derived from the accusations already made against groups of heretics', most notably against the Waldensians.[42] Witchcraft was understood to destroy familial authority and filial love in ways which directly replicated the charges earlier made against the Waldensians, the heretics whose meetings were held to be those of witches' sabbaths. Many of the French writers most committed to the duty of eradicating Protestantism as 'heresy' were precisely those Catholics most committed to demonology, most committed to identifying Protestantism and heresy generally with witchcraft, and most committed to providing a Waldensian ancestry for Huguenots. But important as these associations of actual accusations of both witchcraft and heresy simultaneously were, fear of heretics and the desire to see them punished did not require that they be accused of witchcraft itself: the similar but separate alleged occurrences of 'heresy' and 'witchcraft' at high levels were understood as mutually reinforcing confirmation that these were indeed the 'Last Days' in which authority would be challenged by both heresy and witchcraft, and would need to respond with force to both similarly.

It is worth emphasising that, rather as the evidence of civil wars and rebellions and the development of theories of resistance and consent provided evidence in religious opponents' eyes for the proclaimed associations between heresy, schism, and sedition, the period from the Reformation to the middle of the seventeenth century witnessed events that were easily interpretable in support of the view that one was living in a world conforming to the biblical description of the 'Last Days'. The period from the Reformation to the middle of the seventeenth century was a period of turmoils of civil wars and of wars between states, and of revolts, rebellions, and revolutions which carried high death tolls – the Thirty Years War in Germany involved the deaths of perhaps some 6 million people, or one third of the entire population. And it was a period of frequent and devastating famines and dearth, and a period of plagues and other diseases which literally decimated communities. It was a period when the image of the 'Last Days' of war and famine and pestilence seemed to receive ample confirmation. It was a period in which there were many reasons to apply the message commonly derived from the Bible, that God was punishing humans for their sins, and that

Councils, Sixteenth to Twentieth Centuries' in *idem* (ed.), *Witchcraft in the Netherlands from the Fourteenth to the Twentieth Century* (Rotterdam 1991), 103–18, at 106–9.
[42] Briggs, *Communities*, 16; Cohn, *Europe's Inner Demons*.

prominent among the sins of entire communities being punished was their failure to take adequate measures against the crying sins of 'heresy' and 'schism' now spreading rapidly in their midst in these 'Last Days'.

It is to the justification of intolerance towards the allegedly heretical and schismatic groups – including both 'magisterial Reformation' Protestants and Catholics to each other and the 'radical Reformation' sects to both – that we will now devote a series of chapters. We will examine in detail first in Chapter 7 the arguments against Anabaptism and anti-Trinitarianism, the two major Protestant 'heresies' of the sixteenth century, and their assimilation to 'atheism'. We will then turn in Chapter 8 to arguments between Protestants and Catholics, and particularly emphasise the Catholic anti-Huguenot arguments of the sixteenth and early seventeenth centuries, while also noting the Huguenot anti-heretical arguments of this same period. Both provide important backgrounds to the attitudes expressed by Catholics and by Huguenots in the 1680s and 1690s. We will turn in Chapter 9 to arguments in England, especially against Arminianism and Quaker thought, the two major Protestant 'heresies' of the seventeenth century. In Chapter 10 we will examine tolerationism as supported by some important advocates within these groups of alleged heretics and schismatics, and the responses to their arguments by anti-heretical writers. Chapter 11 will examine the important Dutch arguments for toleration in the sixteenth and seventeenth centuries, and the arguments for intolerance by many members of the Dutch Reformed Church in the same period. Chapter 12 will conclude this section with an equally brief but equally important discussion of intolerance and tolerance towards Jews and Muslims. Chapters 13 to 15 will then examine the arguments for religious intolerance in the later seventeenth century, and we will see that they reiterated many previous arguments for intolerance.

7

Catholic and 'magisterial Reformation' attacks on Anabaptism, anti-Trinitarianism, and atheism: sedition, 'libertinism', and 'sodomy'

We saw in Chapter 6 that there was a very strong reiteration by 'magisterial Reformation' Protestants as well as 'Counter-Reformation' Catholics of associations between heresy and schism and treason and sedition, and of the duties of magistrates to enforce true religion as well as to secure peace. In the 1520s and 1530s, both 'magisterial Reformation' Protestants and Catholics across Europe anathematised Anabaptism, the first major Protestant sect declared 'heretical' and 'schismatic' by both alike. Anabaptists refused to take oaths. Many opposed officeholding as based on the use of the sword. They opposed infant baptism, thereby challenging the identity of church and state and supporting the introduction of diverse sects into each polity. They questioned tithes and thus a public ministry. More broadly, they stressed 'inner inspiration' and 'conscience'. Most importantly, some radical Anabaptists attacked chapels and churches, participated in the Peasants' War in Germany in 1525, took part in the attempt to build a 'godly community' in Münster in 1534–5, and attempted to seize the city of Amsterstam in 1535. Anabaptists in Münster in 1534–5 not merely used force to elect their own king, formerly a tailor, but also used force to institute a community of goods and polygamy – the latter as a regime of polygyny involving execution of women who resisted such marriage. These radical Anabaptists – mainly the followers of Muntzer in 1524–5 and of John of Leiden in 1534–5 – were only a minority among Anabaptists and the majority repudiated Münster and declared themselves pacifists who had 'changed their swords into ploughshares', including the Mennonite followers of Menno Simmons and many Melchiorites of Strasburg, Swiss brethren in Zurich, and south German Anabaptists. But the radical minority in Münster provided the central image of Anabaptist disorder across Europe as horrifyingly combining everything that had been alleged of heretics and schismatics from late patristic and medieval times – communism, libertinism (polygamy), and sedition. Melancthon's judgment was typical: Anabaptists were relatedly thieves, murderers, and fornicators:

Like thieves, [they] had robbed [the citizens] of their belongings and set up a king; and, like murderers, they intended to subdue the land with the sword. In addition, they carried on all kinds of fornication. Thus their spirit revealed itself.

Melancthon and Bullinger agreed: Anabaptism was the work of the Devil. In 1546, Bullinger declared that 'by the grace of God we have always punished the vices of heresy and sodomy with fire, and have looked upon them and still look upon them, with horror'. The Hessian law of 1536–7 in response to Anabaptism declared simply and sweepingly that 'heresy always involves insurrection and destruction of all good customs and morals'.[1]

Many such condemnations of Anabaptism in the image of Münster were issued across Europe by 'magisterial Reformation' protestants and by Catholics alike, and in most European countries and polities from England to Zurich Anabaptists were executed, or at the least banished, in the aftermath of Münster. The Netherlands was a major participant in executions of Anabaptists in the later 1530s. Following an Anabaptist plot to take Amsterdam in 1534 and an attempt to seize the town in 1535, between February and July 1535, 62 'heretics' were executed at Amsterdam, and more than 200 were executed in Holland in 1534–6. In the 1535 'placard' of Charles V, it was declared that 'all those, male or female, who are found to be infected by the said condemned sect of Anabaptists...will...be put to death without delay...by fire'. The year 1535 saw the peak of Anabaptist executions, but large numbers of further radical Anabaptists who themselves defended and practised religious violence by seizing buildings and churches – Jorists and Battenburgers – were executed in 1539 and 1544, as 'for at least a decade heresy in Holland was equated with Anabaptism, and Anabaptism in turn with disorder, even rebellion'. In all, 617 Anabaptists were executed in the Low Countries in the sixteenth century.[2]

In the immediate aftermath of Münster, in 1535 in England Henry VIII issued a proclamation against Anabaptists' 'destestable heresies' and proclaimed the death penalty as the 'just' punishment. Perhaps fourteen Anabaptists were executed within months in England for their beliefs, which included condemnation of infant baptism, condemnation of the doctrine of the Trinity, and declaration that 'infidels' might be saved. Further

---

[1] Le Cler, *Toleration*, i, 196, 215; Melancthon, 'Verlegung' GFF no. 3439, aiiijv, quoted in Haude, *Shadow*, 21; Haude, *Shadow*, 22–5; Bullinger in J. E. Acton, *The History of Freedom and Other Essays* (London 1922), 175.

[2] G. Waite, *David Joris and Dutch Anabaptism* (Waterloo 1990), 73; *Placaert-boecken van Vlaanderen*, I (Ghent 1639), 118, in Le Cler, *Toleration*, ii, 192; Duke, *Reformation*, 88–9.

Anabaptists were later burned in England, and others were banished from the realm by Henry, Edward, and Elizabeth. 'Magisterial Reformation' Protestants in England were zealous in their condemnations of Anabaptism.[3]

Severely punished in the Netherlands and England, in the first half of the sixteenth century only a few communities, most notably independent German and Swiss cities, took care to discriminate between the Munsterites and other peaceful Anabaptists, and even their magistrates faced major external and internal pressures to punish Anabaptists. Bucer's *Dialogi* cited the example of Münster as evidence of the seditious consequences of Anabaptist thought and attacked Strasburg for tolerating Anabaptist sects, holding that God would send plagues to punish them if this continued. In a pattern to be repeated on many occasions by 'magisterial Reformation' thinkers over the next two centuries, Bucer anathematised not merely the Anabaptists themselves, but any who thought them tolerable, declaring that it was Satan, 'the creator of all destruction and enemy of all blessed order', who had made people think that political authorities needed only to look to external peace and not to the beliefs of citizens. Bucer had Augustine's epistles against the Donatists translated and appended to his work. In the midst of the next plague, in 1538, the magistrates heeded the warning, and issued mandates against the Anabaptists which declared them a threat to civic order and peace.[4] Other German cities were even quicker to punish Anabaptists. Having initially tolerated Lutherans and then ordered them burned in 1529 in response to an episode of the plague seen as punishment for tolerating heretics, the government of Cologne declared in 1533 that the 'secret poison' of heresy had infiltrated the city and heretics needed to be punished. Indicating the fears attached to news of Münster, the Cologne theologian John Heller's 1535 *Contra Anabaptistas* declared Anabaptists 'savage wolves' who would violate nuns and take property in justification of their punishment; libertinism and communism were here combined, as so often in accusations against heresy. A Catholic commentator recorded with pride in 1535 in Cologne: 'As soon as we in Cologne got hold of Anabaptists, Sacramentarians, or other sectarians and rebels, we burned, beheaded or drowned them...thanks be to God Cologne knows of no heresy in this city'.[5]

---

[3] Horst, *Radical, passim*, esp. 38, 61; P. Hughes and J. F. Larkin (eds.), *Tudor Royal Proclamations* (New Haven, 3 vols., 1964–9), I, 148–9, II, 227–8. Dr Carrie Euler has completed a doctoral dissertation examining, *inter alia*, 'magisterial Reformation' anti-Anabaptism. Although France faced little Anabaptist threat, hostility to Anabaptism was considerable, and when the zealous Calvinist Anne du Bourg argued in France in 1559 that Catholics should not be persecuting Protestants in France because they were not 'heretics', he made clear that he supported the punishment of 'Anabaptists' and anti-Trinitarians: Le Cler, *Toleration*, 31.

[4] Bucer in Haude, *Shadow*, 98, 100, 103.

[5] Haude, *Shadow*, 44–5. J. Heller, *Contra Anabaptistas*, fo. c5r in Haude, *Shadow*, 59; Haude, *Shadow*, 40, 43.

But it was not merely after Münster in 1534–5 that such measures were taken. Under an imperial edict of 1528, which accused Anabaptists of sedition and heresy and cited in justification of their punishment Roman law against the Donatists and Manicheans, Anabaptists had already been executed in the Holy Roman Empire for repetition of baptism. Nearly 700 Anabaptists were executed between 1527 and 1533, including 55 Anabaptists executed at Württemberg alone by 1531; by 1530, 4 years before any attempt had been made to build an Anabaptist kingdom at Münster, perhaps 1,000 Anabaptists had been executed across Germany. Indicating that such heretics were viewed as 'polluting' the community, such executions often involved rituals of purification by burning at the stake following the removal of the 'blasphemous tongue', as at Württemberg, or as in the drowning of many Anabaptists in Zurich.[6] Anabaptism was a crime punishable by death in Zurich as early as 1526, and Zwingli held that Anabaptists had 'severed themselves from the church' and with 'seditious intent' formed groups 'in order to bring about a schism'. Anabaptist actions and teachings thereby for Zwingli necessarily led to 'turmoil and rebellion against the government'.[7]

Such an assault on Anabaptists was based on the identification of Anabaptists with the understanding of heretics and schismatics handed on from late patristic and late medieval writings. As the leader of the Zurich Reformation, Zwingli's 1527 *In catabaptistarum strophas elenchus* was particularly influential in its association of Anabaptists with the Valentinian Gnostics who had been attacked by Irenaeus in the second century for debauching women they had seduced in the course of spreading their 'heretical' doctrines. Zwingli helped to spread the accusation further in consultations about heresy and co-ordinated efforts of Reformers against it. As he did so, he was simply taking over an accusation that Catholics had directed against 'Lutherans', and redirecting it against 'Anabaptists'. The imperial edict of 1528 attacked Anabaptists for holding both community of goods and community of women, and it had already become conventional by 1530 – several years before Münster – to accuse Anabaptists of practising the community of women and the community of goods. While there may have been some very minor licence on the basis of antinomianism, the structure of accusations against Anabaptists was primarily one taken over and applied to Anabaptists on the basis of these stereotypical accusations. That many Anabaptists did then support communism in Münster, at least in the form

---

[6] Bainton (ed.), *Concerning*, 52–3; Le Cler, *Toleration*, I, 200–2; C.-P. Clasen, *Anabaptism* (Ithaca 1972); W. Monter, 'Heresy Executions in Reformation Europe 1520–1565' in Grell and Scribner, *Tolerance*, 48–64, at 50–1.

[7] Zwingli in Le Cler, *Toleration*, I, 200.

of mutual apostolic aid via a community of goods, and the occasional rejection of a spouse as 'unworthy' by Anabaptist women together with the practice of polygamy, offered to anti-heretical writers confirmation for their accusation and understanding of the nature of heresy rather than providing the origin of the accusation of supporting community of goods, of women and 'libertinism'.[8]

Attacking Anabaptists as seditious and treasonous, as murderers and poisoners, later leaders of the 'magisterial Reformation' developed the accusation of 'libertinism' and 'sodomy' against them and linked it to the accusations of supporting communism in goods and anarchy in the state. Calvin held Anabaptists to have maintained that 'we are restored to the state of innocence whenever our judgment is suspended and we are carried away by our own libido'. For them, Calvin argued, the distortion of the command to 'increase and multiply' justified them to 'couple with one another whenever it suits them'. It is worthy of note that 'libertinism' and 'heresy' is here linked for Calvin in the claim to restore a state of innocence, a denial of the omnipresent effects since the Fall of original sin and lustfulness. This was to be a common refrain into the seventeenth century.[9]

The Anabaptists of Münster justified polygamy partly by the Old Testament example of David, and partly on the basis of its greater potential for fulfilling the biblical command to 'increase and multiply' and thus as the means to generate the eschatological number of 144,000 saints. To its many contemporary opponents, this regime was one designed to satisfy the 'lusts' of the male Anabaptist leaders; to many modern historians, it was both designed to satisfy such lusts and to establish a stringently patriarchal regime. There is very little question that patriarchal control of the female population of the city – of 5,000–6,000 women by 2,000 men – was among the aims of the Anabaptists, who monopolised positions of power in the city. Their edicts on polygamy required a marriage proposal from a man to be accepted under pain of death. Their justification was only of polygyny, and not of polyandry. The Anabaptist leader John of Leiden, who had sixteen wives, condemned one of his own wives to death for disobedience during his brief reign as King of Münster. In his 1534 *Restitution*, the leading Anabaptist theologian of Münster, Bernard Rothmann, included chapters on the 'Duty and Dominion of the Man in Marriage' and the 'Duty and Submission of the Woman in Marriage'. Rothmann, who took nine wives, declared that the new order was instituted in order to oppose women's power, as 'Women almost everywhere have taken control, and they lead men around like bears

---

[8] Scribner, 'Practical Utopias', 743–74, at 748–50.
[9] R. W. Collins, *Calvin and the Libertines of Geneva* (Toronto 1968); Kaplan, *Calvinists and Libertines*; Turner, *One Flesh*, 80–1; Horst, *Radical*, 30.

on a chain'. It is very likely, moreover, that male 'lusts' were indeed involved in the creation of this regime: John of Leiden explicitly argued that it was better 'that I have many wives than many prostitutes'.[10] The Anabaptists themselves declared, however, that they attacked 'lewdness', and they defended as part of their defence of polygamy the notion that 'increase and multiply' was the 'only legitimate purpose of matrimony' as an argument that such was *not* 'lustful'. They held that children were to be conceived in 'purity' free from the lusts of the flesh, and interpreted the nuptial consummation of Adam and Eve that they identified as having occurred before the Fall as 'pure' and to be imitated. Intercourse with anyone outside of the 'sacred community' of Anabaptists was forbidden in their effort to create a new 'holy nation'.[11]

Many Anabaptists were indeed 'heretics' in the sense that they supported doctrinal deviations from the faith considered 'orthodox' by both 'magisterial Reformation' Protestants and Catholics. Many Anabaptists questioned original sin, the condition of the soul after death, and orthodox accounts of the incarnation, at least in holding that Christ was not born of Mary. Many at least questioned, and some simply rejected, the doctrine of the Trinity. Some Anabaptists accepted the doctrine of the Trinity, wrote works against Socinian thought, refused communion with Socinians, and excommunicated anti-Trinitarian Anabaptists for anti-Trinitarianism. These included Menno Simmons, founder of the Mennonite Anabaptists, and many among the initial generation of Mennonites. But the Anabaptist leader David Joris, who condemned the execution of Servetus, himself declared:

There is but one God sole and indivisible, and it is contrary to the operation of God throughout creation to admit a God in three persons, or that three make but one, as it is taught in the Athanasian creed.

Joris adopted from the radical Anabaptist Melchior Hoffman the notion that Christ had 'heavenly flesh', not being born of Mary (a position in many ways a revival of the early Christian heresy of Docetism).[12] Here, as in the medieval period with the Cathars, there is thus a link between rejection of the doctrine of the Trinity and a challenge to 'orthodox sexual morality', although the vast majority of Anabaptists, such as Menno Simmons, repudiated not merely the Munsterites' use of force, but also their support for

---

[10] B. Rothmann, *Restitution* (Halle 1888), 83–91 in K. Sprunger, 'Anabaptist Women of the Radical Reformation', in R. Greaves (ed.), *Triumph Over Silence* (Connecticut 1985), 45–74 at 64–5; Williams, *Radical Reformation*, 508.

[11] Turner, *One Flesh*, 81; Williams, *Radical Reformation*, 371–8, 511–2. R. Po-Chia Hsia, 'Münster and the Anabaptists' in *idem* (ed.), *The German People and the Reformation*, 59.

[12] On Joris, see Waite, *David Joris*, 69; on Anabaptist anti-Trinitarianism, see E. M. Wilbur, *History of Unitarianism* (Harvard 1946), 40–8; Horsch, *Mennonites*, 324–5.

polygamy, and their anti-Trinitarianism.[13] Some followers of David Joris, who clearly rejected the doctrine of the Trinity, also seem to have been supporters of polygamy. One such, Geertgen Cornelius, 'admitted' under torture that communal nakedness in imitation of Adam and Eve had been practised: it is not clear whether torture caused the 'admission'. Joris himself was predisposed to patriarchal monogamy, but willing to accept polygamy; what was crucial to him was that sexual relations be entirely freed 'from the lusts of the flesh' which created 'children of the devil' in order to create children freed from 'original sin' to be pure apocalyptic servants of God.[14]

Support simultaneously for Anabaptism, anti-Trinitarianism, and challenge to the prevailing standards of sexual morality were thereafter central to the accusations against Bernard Ochino, a Franciscan turned Protestant who ended his life among the Anabaptists. Ochino argued in his *Dialogues* that one did not become a heretic by denying the Trinity, condemned intolerance towards Anabaptists, and in the very same work justified polygamy as a 'good thing and very profitable to mankind'. Ochino declared that only Europeans had condemned the practice of polygamy, and since he dated this condemnation after 600, his case for polygamy against clerical proscription was seen as related to his denial that belief of the Trinity was required because that was an imposition on Christianity after the primitive ages of the church. As with the Anabaptists in Münster, the central justification offered for polygamy by Ochino opposed sexual desires or saw them as needing to be moderated rather than celebrated. Polygamy for Ochino needed both a 'call from God' and the impulse not of the flesh but of the spirit 'that he may have children and bring them up in the fear of God'. As with the other Anabaptist defenders of polygamy, however, Ochino was quickly attacked for publishing 'horrible blasphemies' and 'filth', banished by the Zurich authorities, and represented as a 'libertine', 'sodomite', and 'monster' for questioning the doctrine of the Trinity and questioning the requirement of monogamy. Beza, as stout a defender of orthodoxy in conceptions of the family as in conceptions of the Godhead, wrote a major work against Ochino, *On Polygamy and Divorce*. He attacked Ochino in an associative assault as 'the secret favourer of Arianism, the patron of polygamy'. All were for Beza 'monstrous opinions'. When the aged Ochino visited Poland in 1564, he was accused by Polish Calvinists of having attempted to convert female market vendors to polygamy in Cracow – despite

---

[13] Williams, *Radical Reformation*, 511–13; W. Keeney, *The Development of Dutch Anabaptist Thought and Practice 1539–1564* (Nieuwkoop 1968), 91–2; C. Krahn, *Dutch Anabaptism* (The Hague 1968), 106, 108; Sprunger, 'Anabaptist', 50–1; Simmons in Le Cler, *Toleration*, I, 209–16.

[14] Waite, *David Joris*, 73, 105–6, 131.

knowing no Polish! The Polish Calvinist Simon Zacius similarly accused Polish anti-Trinitarians of celebrating their weddings naked in bathhouses because of their libertinism. Over a century later, the Catholic Moreri was still declaring that Ochino wrote 'to justify his libertinism'.[15]

Similar sets of images of heretics and schismatics to those drawn from patristic and especially late medieval writings were repeated frequently in England in the late sixteenth and early seventeenth century in attacks on the tiny 'heretical' sects which broke away from the Church of England and were declared to be associated with Anabaptism. The Family of Love was an important spiritualist movement in both the Netherlands and England, whose origins some scholars trace to David Joris. It was 'heretical'. Its leader Hendrick Niclaes posited the notion of perfectibility, questioned the notion of Christ's satisfaction as full payment for sin, and allegorised much in the Bible in ways that at the least left little room for an orthodox understanding of the Trinity. Some Familists were influenced by Dutch Anabaptism, and some denied the Trinity outright, although a few seem to have supported it. Others concealed their denials; the legitimacy of concealment (Nicodemism) was stressed by Familists. Familist works included questioning of the immortality of both soul and body, and of the reality of heaven and hell. Some, such as the Familist 'E. R.', were explicitly tolerationist, believing that it 'is not Christian like, that one man should envie, belie, and persecute an other, for any cause touching conscience'; others sought to justify state authority and liberty of conscience simultaneously in their 'Nicodemite' strategies.

To James I in the *Basilicon Doron*, the Family of Love was the epitome of 'vile' Anabaptism and 'puritanism'. From the late sixteenth century to the middle of the seventeenth, the Family of Love was depicted as not merely denying the Trinity but also as sanctioning both adultery and communism. As their anonymous 1606 defender put it in *A Supplication of the Family of Love*, these accusations were intended to make us 'seeme monstrous and detestable before the Magistrates'. One of the works against them was called *A Confutation of the Monstrous and Horrible Heresies Taught by H. N.* (1579); it suggested that their opinions belonged to the 'lowest pit of hell' and that their 'foule and...filthy' doctrines had made 'God, man: and man, God'. George Gifford's 1596 *Sermons Upon the Whole Booke of the Revelation* declared Familists and libertines 'filthy monsters'.[16] William

---

[15] R. Bainton, *The Travail of Religious Liberty* (Connecticut 1971), ch. 6; Williams, *Radical Reformation*, 511ff.; B. Ochino, *A Dialogue of Polygamy* (English tr. 1657); J. Cairncross, *After Polygamy was Made a Sin* (London 1974), 65–73; Tazbir, *State Without Stakes*, 72–3; Bayle, *Dictionary*, Ochino L.

[16] *A Supplication of the Family of Love* (Cambridge 1606), 47, in C. Marsh, *The Family of Love* (Cambridge 1994), 3; J. Knewstub, *A Confutation of the Monstrous and Horrible Heresies Taught by H. N.* (1579), 8r in Marsh, *Family*, 4; Davis, *Fear*, 122; A. Hamilton, *Family of*

Wilkinson's 1579 *Confutation of...the Family of Love*, which cited Augustine's attack on the Donatists against them, attacked them as 'libertines' who had been 'infected' by Niclaes' heresy, and drawing on continental repudiations of Anabaptism by Bullinger, Calvin, and Zwingli, associated them with 'libertine Anabaptists' who were declared 'the most pestilent sect of all others'.[17] Wilkinson depicted them as covered with 'ougly deformities' and as the most deadly Heresie of all since there was 'not almost any one particular erroneous and Schimsaticall phantasie, whereof the Familie of Love have not borrowed one braunche or other'. Thomas Rogers' 1578 *The Displaying of an Horrible Secte of Grosse and Wicked Heretiques* declared that they had 'infected sundrie simple men with this poysoned doctrine'.[18]

Niclaes' *First Exhortation* stressed 'pure procreating with undefiled love' and forbade the 'upright man and woman' to use their bed for 'lust'.[19] Nonetheless, in an accusation repeated over many years and publicised extensively during the 1640s, it was held that Familists believed it legitimate for 'one man to lye with another mans wife whilst he sleeps'. In 1607, *The Family of Love* depicted ignorant people holding ostensibly religious meetings at night for licentious reasons, and this was the central image handed on to the mid-century English Revolution, which saw a huge outpouring of literature against Familism.[20] Thomas Edwards was to repeat the charge in the 1640s.[21] Ephraim Pagitt tied them directly to the 'Priscillians' put to death after confessing 'what shamefull villanies he had committed with the women of his Sect'.[22] A royal proclamation of 1580 by Elizabeth I ordered burned the books of Hendrick Niclaes as 'lewd, heretical and seditious' – the linkage of terms is significant – and declared that the Family's leaders were to be 'committed to

---

Love (Cambridge 1981), 48–9, 133–4; George Gifford, *Sermons Upon the Whole Booke of the Revelation* (1596), 47, in J. D. Moss, 'The Family of Love and English Critics', *Sixteenth Century Journal* (1975), 44.

[17] William Wilkinson, *Confutation of...the Family of Love* (1579), 66ff., esp. 68, 70, 75.

[18] K. Poole, *Radical Religion from Shakespeare to Milton* (Cambridge 2000), 75, 83.

[19] Niclaes, *First Exhortation*, 205–6, in N. Smith, *Perfection Proclaimed* (Oxford 1989), 170.

[20] Knewstub, *Monstrous*, in Marsh, *Family*, 4v; Marsh, *Family*, 21–4, 33–4, 66, 106, 188, 241–2, 259; Elizabeth I, Proclamation 652 'Ordering the Prosecution of the Family of Love' in Hughes and Larkin (eds.), *Tudor Royal Proclamations*, II, 474–5; J. Halley, 'Heresy, Orthodoxy and the Politics of Religious Discourse: The Case of the English Family of Love', *Representations* (1986), 98–120, esp. 102–3; Hamilton, *Family of Love*, 114–16, 132–3; Davis, *Fear*, 122; Moss, 'The Family of Love and its English Critics', 35–52; W. G. Johnson, 'The Family of Love in Stuart England: A Chronology of Name-Crossed Lovers', *JMRS* 7 (1977), 95–112; Smith, *Perfection*, ch. 4; Turner, *One Flesh*, 85n. cf. also C. Marsh's essay on the Family of Love in Loewenstein and Marshall (eds.), *Heresy* (forthcoming).

[21] T. Edwards, *Gangraena*, (London 1646), ii, 141; for an example of a charge for this belief in 1588, see Essex ROD/ACA 16, fo. 64v in K. Thomas, 'The Puritans and Adultery: The Act of 1650 Reconsidered' in Pennington and Thomas (eds.), *Puritans and Revolutionaries* (Oxford 1978), 261.

[22] Pagitt, *Heresiography*, 99, in Poole, *Radical Religion*, 78.

prison, and to receive such bodily punishment and other mulct as factors of damnable heresies', although many were among the middling and well-to-do members of their communities and were only intermittently prosecuted.[23]

ANTI-TRINITARIANS

Support for the punishment of Anabaptists by 'magisterial Reformation' leaders thus often joined their 'heretical' beliefs, such as the questioning of the Trinity or original sin, to their practices and opinions declared to be seditious and libertine, such as communism, seizure of power, and lustful polygamy. At other points, however, 'magisterial Reformation' thinkers such as Melancthon argued that those who 'proclaim tenets that are frankly blasphemous, even if they are not rebels, should be done to death by the civil authority'.[24] Melancthon expanded on the theme in 1531, declaring that even those who did not 'teach seditious doctrines' were to be considered blasphemous and seditious for condemning public preaching, which must 'be prevented and repressed like any other sedition'.[25] For Luther, who approved that argument by Melancthon, heretics who taught 'matters contrary to the faith as it is clearly founded on the Scriptures and professed by all Christendom' including 'among other things that Christ is not God...as the...Anabaptists maintain' were not to be tolerated 'but punished as public blasphemers' who 'should be stoned'.[26]

As Anabaptism involved anti-Trinitarianism, then, execution was justified by 'magisterial Reformation' writers as a punishment of 'blasphemy'. Defences of the execution, and not merely of the 'moderate punishment' of 'heretics', were particularly frequently voiced in the sixteenth century by Protestants and Catholics in condemning anti-Trinitarianism. Some heretics were for Calvin to be educated, while others were to be punished, but anti-Trinitarian heretics who attempted to spread their views were to be executed. For Calvin, the 'rotten member' was to be amputated to save the body of the church; the 'poison' was to be prevented from spreading: 'the most extreme remedy may be applied so that the deadly poison may not fester'. For Calvin, it was not 'charity' to pardon heretics, allowing them 'to murder souls and to poison them with their false doctrine...that the whole Body of Jesus Christ be lacerated that the stench of one rotten member may remain undisturbed'.[27]

---

[23] Marsh, *Family, passim.*
[24] Melancthon, *Epist. Melancthon,* v, n.664 in Le Cler, *Toleration,* 161.
[25] Melancthon in Le Cler, *Toleration,* 162.
[26] Luther, *W,* xxxi, i, 208–9, in Le Cler, *Toleration,* 161.
[27] Calvin, *Déclaration pour maintenir la vraye foy que tiennent tous chrétiens de la trinité des personnes en un seul Dieu* (Geneva 1554), 35–6; Le Cler, *Toleration,* i, 334; Nijenhuis, *Ecclesia,* ch. 6. Cf also Zagorin, *Idea,* 79–82.

For Calvin, heretics were to be punished because 'They infect souls with the poison of depraved dogma'. It was using these terms that Calvin defended the execution of the anti-Trinitarian Michel Servetus, burned at the stake by Protestants in Geneva (and by Catholics elsewhere in Europe in effigy).

All of the major Protestant leaders across Europe joined hands with Calvin in defending the execution of Servetus when their opinions were solicited, including Bucer, Melancthon, Sleidanus, and Sturm, and they justified this in the language of removing a disease and a poison. The Schaffhausen clergy recommended repression 'lest his blasphemies like a cancer despoil the members of Christ'. The ministers of Basle identified such preventive punishment as apostolic and patristic, declaring that Paul had called 'pests' like Servetus a 'gnawing cancer' and that he had regarded heresy as worse than any other crime.[28] Bucer declared that Servetus' guts should have been pulled out of his body while he was still alive because his crime was so heinous.[29] The court's sentence declared that Servetus had first printed a work against the Holy Trinity, then continued in his errors despite remonstrances, and then printed in secret a book which contained these said heresies and blasphemies 'the more to spread the venom of his heresy'. This, it intoned, 'entails the murder and ruin of many souls'. He had 'with malicious and perverse obstinacy' maintained and spread opinions 'against the fundamentals of the Christian religion'. He had thereby tried to convert others 'a thing horrible, shocking, scandalous and infectious', trying to 'infect the world with your stinking heretical poison...For these and other reasons, desiring to purge the Church of God of such infection and cut off the rotten member', they declared that they had condemned him to be 'attached to a stake and burned with your book to ashes' which would 'finish' his life and 'give an example to others who would commit the like'.[30]

It was in defence of Servetus' execution that Beza published his 1554 *De Haereticis*, the most important and influential sixteenth-century Protestant defence of hereticide, republished many times in many languages over the next 200 years, and purchased by Locke in the Netherlands in the 1680s. It was in this work that Beza declared that 'the main end of human society is that God be honoured as He should be'. For Beza, heresy was a crime greater than any other crime, as it was a crime against God. Athanasius was invoked by Beza as giving the world 'his creed' (Trinitarianism) with such wonderful brevity, showing that from Scripture it could be proven that 'Christ is one with the Father and that three hypostases may be distinguished in one

---

[28] Calvin, *Opera*, VIII, col 810 in Williams, *Radical Reformation*, 613; R. Bainton, *Hunted Heretic: The Life and Death of Michel Servetus* (Boston 1953), 204; Nijenhuis, *Ecclesia*, cvi.
[29] S. Zweig, *The Right to Heresy* (1936), 98–9.
[30] The text of the judgment is in Bainton, *Hunted Heretic*, 208–9.

essence', and that it was 'Blasphemy' and the doctrine of 'devils' to declare the opposite. For Beza, as an 'obstinate' heretic and blasphemer Servetus deserved to die with the most excruciating death that could be invented. In his *Life and Death of Jean Calvin*, Beza reflected on Servetus as 'not a man, but rather, a horrible Monster, compounded of all the ancient and new heresies, and above all an execrable blasphemer against the Trinity' who had 'by the just judgment of God and man' 'ended by the punishment of fire'. Calvin had, for Beza, done 'the office of a faithful Pastor, putting the Magistrate in mind of his duty' that he might make sure that 'such a pestilence should not infect his flock'.[31]

Beza's and Calvin's attitudes about 'hereticide' were defended in sixteenth-century England by the major Protestant authors. Bishop Hugh Latimer held that false doctrine consumed 'like fire', burning everything laid within it. As authorities would put out a fire, so they should 'extinguish' heresy.[32] Bishop John Jewel argued forcefully in *An Answer to a Certain Book* (1567) that Protestants deserved the credit for burning Servetus. Jewel also defended in *An Answer* the burning of Joris, who condemned the execution of Servetus. Joris' name and the pseudonym under which he lived in Basle to avoid execution, Jean de Brugges, was to serve as part of the pseudonym chosen by Bayle for his tolerationist 1686 *Philosophical Commentary*, and Servetus' punishment was to be discussed in that work as a 'relic' of the 'barbarity' of 'popery' within Protestantism.[33] And anti-Trinitarianism was repeatedly punished by execution by fire in sixteenth-century England. Joan of Kent, Georg van Paris, Matthew Hamont, John Lewes, Peter Cole, and Francis Kett, were all burned in Protestant England for their 'heretical' and 'blasphemous' views of Christ and the incarnation between 1549 and 1589. That the execution of such anti-Trinitarian heretics was justified was maintained in full force into early seventeenth-century England, when the last two heretics executed for heresy in England, Bartholomew Legate and Edward Wightman, were both burned to death in 1612 as anti-Trinitarians. The 'heretic' William Sayer was considered worthy of death by the Bishop of Norwich, but the Archbishop of Canterbury, Abbott, was concerned that he should only be burned if he denied something expressly contained in the three creeds or first four general councils. If he did, however, deny 'the godhead of Christ and of the holie ghost' Abbott was clear that he too should 'frie...at the

---

[31] Beza, *De Haereticis*, 186 and *passim*; Allen, *Political Thought*, ch. 5; Bainton (ed.), *Concerning*, 108; Beza, *Life of John Calvin* in Duke, et al. (eds.), *Calvinism in Europe*, 16, 24.

[32] Gregory, *Salvation at Stake*, 84–6.

[33] On Joris, see Waite, *David Joris*, 69; on Anabaptist anti-Trinitarianism, see Wilbur, *Unitarianism*, 40–8.

stake'.[34] Even the allegedly moderate Bishop Hall, who wished to suggest that quietly held 'mere heresy' of an error in the fundamentals of the faith was permissible, declared that published 'mixed heresy' of 'blasphemy, infectious divulgation, seditious disturbance' was to be punished with execution. In the 1690s, John Locke was to collect papers on the executions of Legate and Wightman, intending that they should be part of a book against hereticide by his friend Philip van Limborch.[35]

ATHEISM AND ANTI-TRINITARIANISM

In anti-heretical literature, 'heresy' was often associated with 'atheism', and anti-Trinitarianism was particularly frequently associated with 'atheism'. As Michael Hunter has argued, it is likely that the investigation of the late sixteenth-century anti-Trinitarian and probably atheist playwright Christopher Marlowe was carried out as part of a wider 'heresy hunt' since the depositions in the case of Marlowe are preserved alongside examinations of sectaries and recusants.[36] Marlowe was accused in 1593 of 'heresy, treason, and sodomy'. He was said, among other things, to have stated that 'the first beginning of religion was only to keep men in awe', that he had 'as good a right to coin as the Queen of England', that Christ was the son of a carpenter and a bastard, that Christ had 'dishonestly' known the woman of Samaria and her sister, and that St John Evangelist was 'bedfellow to Christ' and 'that he used him as the sinners of Sodoma'. Marlowe was simultaneously alleged to have written a work denying the Trinity. As anti-Trinitariansim was understood to render Christ's nature merely creaturely and not divine, the conceptual linkage in the accusations against Marlowe is provided both by the general linkage alleged of heresy, sodomy, and treason, and also the more specific implication that 'sodomitical' human desires were associated with anti-Trinitarianism, as this allegedly rendered Christ human and not divine.[37]

---

[34] G. T. Buckley, *Atheism in the English Renaissance* (Chicago 1932), 54–60; Abbott in C. Burrage, *The Early English Dissenters in the Light of Recent Research 1550–1641* (Cambridge 1912), II, 171. In his *Disputation of Holy Scripture*, William Whitaker declared that there were 'none' who would tolerate 'him who should openly and publicly deny Christ' by reviving heresies denying the Trinity: Whitaker, *Disputation*, 20–1, in Lake, 'Significance', 166. Cf also Coffey, *Persecution*, 114–15.

[35] Jordan, *Toleration*, II, 153.

[36] M. Hunter, 'The Problem of "Atheism" in early modern England', *TRHS* (1985), 135–57, at 136.

[37] P. H. Kocher, *Christopher Marlowe* (Chapel Hill 1946), chs. 2–3; *idem*, 'Marlowe's Atheist Lecture' in C. Leech (ed.), *Marlowe: A Collection of Critical Essays* (New Jersey 1964), 159–66. On sodomy and heresy in Spanish territories, cf. Monter, *Frontiers of Heresy*,

In the late sixteenth century, the notion that the 'heresy' of anti-Trinitarianism was closely associated with 'atheism' was repeated in accusations of 'atheism' against the Earl of Oxford in 1581, as he was said to have declared both that 'The trinity [was] a fable' and that 'Scriptures [were] for pollicye'.[38] Anti-Trinitarianism was relatedly a form of 'atheism' for the leading 'puritan' divine William Perkins. According to Perkins, there were three degrees of atheism, from the highest, complete denial of the existence of God, through the middle level, worshipping the wrong thing – such as Gentiles worshipping moons or the sun – to the lowest degree, on which Perkins placed Turks, Jews, and Catholics as 'atheists'. In the case of 'Turks' and Jews, it was denial of the orthodox doctrine of the Trinity that for Perkins made them 'atheists'; Catholic denial of the satisfaction by Christ – his payment as himself God of a full equivalent for man's sins, such that works contributed nothing – helped make them 'atheists' in his eyes. While a Turk (i.e. a Muslim) recognised God as maker of heaven and earth and Christ as prophet, for Perkins 'yet his religion is atheism, for he conceiveth of God out of the trinitie, and so worshippeth nothing but an idol'. Jews similarly acknowledged one God, yet for Perkins they 'truly have no God' for they worshiped 'not that God in Christ, and so instead of the true God, frame an idol in their owne braine'. Catholics recognised the Trinity in unity, but by making works important, for Perkins they denied God's justice and mercy in Christ's satisfaction for sin, while they also placed the Pope in Christ's place, and their doctrine of the 'real presence' denied the nature of body and God. They were therefore 'atheists'. Here was a potent source for a Calvinist such as Perkins for the assimilation to Catholicism and to 'atheism' of Arminians and Socinians, as both were deniers of the satisfaction as a full payment by God (the Son) to God (the Father). For Perkins, the earth was too good to dwell upon for 'atheists' of the highest degree. Atheists who denied that there was a God committed in his eyes an offence greater than thieves and rebels, who deserved death, and so atheists deserved 'a most cruel death'.[39]

Atheism was often associated with denial of specific religious beliefs, such as the creation of the world from nothing; with preferring natural for supernatural explanations and questioning the extent of God's 'particular providence' in intervening in the world; with questioning the doctrine of the immortality of the soul; or with questioning the veracity of (all of) Scripture since it was (held to be) inconsistent. More generally, atheists were held to treat religion as merely a series of 'fables' which served 'civil

---

ch. 13. For a recent comparison of James' description of loving Buckingham as Christ loved John, see M. B. Young, *James VI and I and the History of Homosexuality* (Basingstoke 2000), 44–5.

[38] Hunter, 'Atheism', 149n.69.

[39] W. Perkins, *Works* (London 1608), 3 vols., II, 526–7; I, 130–3; cf. Hunter, 'Atheism'.

policy'. In the former set of senses, although not in the declaration that religion was merely a 'fable' publicly maintained for reasons of 'policy', there were close affinities between 'atheism' and questioning of specific 'orthodox' doctrines of Christianity among various 'heretical' groups in this period, and the affinities were most notable between atheists and Socinians. Thus, Socinians tended to support the eternity of the world or of matter rather than the creation *ex nihilo* which seemed to them unreasonable and unscriptural. They tended to stress the extensiveness of natural causes, to point to Scriptural contradictions, and to support mortalism, the denial of the natural immortality of the soul. All of these individual commitments were for Socinians held partly in order to rescue Christian beliefs from the objections that they argued would otherwise be open to them from atheists: they were intended not to support but to controvert atheism. Much of Socinian thought was directed to showing that atheism was itself 'unreasonable' and that Christianity was 'reasonable'. Nonetheless, in the eyes of orthodox Calvinists and Catholics, Socinianism had reason to look like a way station from doctrinal orthodoxy towards atheism, where contradictions in Scripture were not explained (as by Socinians) but instead used to suggest that Scripture should not be accepted at all, or where questioning of the natural immortality of the soul was not combined with stress on the sleep of the soul and the resurrection by God's power at the Day of Judgment (as by Socinians) but used by atheists to deny any personal resurrection.[40] Viewed from the perspective of an orthodox Calvinist, then, there was a logic to seeing Socinian heretics as closely resembling atheists. This set of associations thus added to the general conceptual pressure in the thought of many strict Calvinists and demonologically committed Catholics to associate 'heresy' and 'atheism' in a world which was perceived by them as structured around binary oppositions, especially the opposition of God and the Devil, in which 'heresy' was the opposite of 'true faith' and 'atheism' the opposite of any faith. A further assimilation was produced argumentatively by what was understood to be the process of conducting disputes. As Bayle was to declare to Pierre Coste, in connection with charges that Ralph Cudworth's principles led to atheism,

No one is unaware that in disputes, one objects to one's adversaries as many inopportune consequences as one can from their principles be it by alleging that they acknowledge these consequences...or by making an abstract of them whether they acknowledge them or not, or by declaring that they do not acknowledge them.[41]

---

[40] Hunter, 'Atheism', 140–1.
[41] Bayle, *Lettres*, ɪɪɪ, 1018–23 in Kors, *Atheism*, 295.

Anti-Trinitarianism was thus understood in England by many writers as being close to 'atheism'; it was, moreover, understood to be close to Judaism and Islam in denial of the doctrine of the Trinity and that Christ was God. This association further placed anti-Trinitarianism among many 'heresies' of 'foreign religions', many of which were also repeatedly attacked in this period as supporting 'sodomy' and 'libertinism'.[42] Thomas Becon's attack was capacious in its indictment, sexual in its content, and typical: 'the Jewes, the Mahometans, the Anabaptists...wyth all the rabble of heretickes and sectaries, have their churches also...unpure, filthy, stinking, vile, abhominable, ful of synne and wyckedness'. Early modern England was, moreover, among the inheritors of medieval associations of heresy, witchcraft, and 'sodomy' or 'buggery' and Henrician legislation was enacted simultaneously against witchcraft, prophecies, and buggery.[43] In the early seventeenth century, Sir Edward Coke listed in his legal treatise a similarly telling anti-Trinity: 'sorcerers, sodomites and heretics'. He argued that buggery was 'treason against the king of heaven; crimen laesae majestatis, a sin horrible, committed against the King; and this is either against the King celestial or Terrestial in three manners: by heresy, by buggery, by sodomy'.[44]

While anti-Trinitarianism was often seen as the heresy which was most particularly associated with atheism, as Michael Hunter and J. C. Davis have indicated, the more general accusation that 'heresy' and 'sectarianism' led to atheism was also widespread in sixteenth- and early seventeenth-century England. Roger Hutchinson's 1550 *Image of God or Layman's Book* identified Anabaptism as tending to atheism, attacking 'those who had said in their hearts that "there is no God"' or 'may easily be brought thereunto'. The important anti-Anabaptist writer Jean Véron similarly wrote his 1561 *Frutefull Treatise of Predestination and Providence* against the Anabaptists, whom he associated directly with epicurean atheism.[45] Thomas Heywood's *True Discourse of the Two Infamous Upstart Prophets* (1636) identified heresy as a route to atheism.[46] Knewstub's *Confutation* of the Familists called their belief 'atheism'. Cheynell's 1643 *Rise, Growth and Danger of Socinianisme* described 'Anabaptists and

---

[42] Cf. Monter, *Frontiers of Heresy*, 290–1.

[43] The statute of 1536, 25 Henry VIII c. 6, was also re-enacted in 1539, 1541, 1548, and 1563; Sharpe, *Instruments of Darkness*, 90; R. Warnicke, 'Sexual Heresy at the Court of Henry VIII', *Historical Journal* 30, 2 (1987), 247–68; Oldridge, *Devil*, 28.

[44] Coke, *Twelfth Part of the Institutes*, 36, discussed in A. Bray, *Homosexuality in Renaissance England* (London 1982), 20.

[45] Buckley, *Atheism*, 29–30, 64–8; M. Buckley, *At the Origins of Modern Atheism* (Yale 1987), 10; Hunter, 'Atheism', 138.

[46] Hunter, 'Atheism', 136n.5.

sectaries' as 'Famous Atheists' as well as accusing Arminians of supporting Atheism, and Socinians of being 'cursed Atheists'.[47]

To the notion that atheists were 'libertines', pursuing the pleasures of the world, and thereby close to allegedly 'libertine' heretics, was added at many points the notion that atheists had a mocking, scornful disposition or 'wit'. For Thomas Nashe in the late sixteenth century, it was 'superaboundance of witte' which made atheists. Hooker's *Ecclesiastical Polity* similarly saw 'scoffing' as increasing, and prevalent among atheists. Thomas Lodge's 1595 *Wits Miserie* identified the Devil 'Derision' as professing atheism and sitting 'in the chaire of pestilence'.[48] For Thomas Fuller in *The Profane State* (1642), scoffing by degrees 'abates the reverence of religion'. Such scorn was held to be diabolic. For Thomas Adams, 'The Chayre of the Scorner is the seate of Sathan'. For the deeply providentialist Thomas Beard, in the 1631 *Theatre of God's Judgements*, such scoffing was dangerous: he declared that a gentleman of Berkshire who had scoffed at religion was struck dead while out hunting as 'an example to all wicked Atheists, of God's justice'. To many anti-atheist writers, atheist commitment showed that one had only 'wit' devoted to fleeting pleasures of this life, but not the true intelligence which discerned clearly God's existence and the rules for attaining the everlasting pleasures of paradise.[49]

More broadly, Francis Bacon in 'Of Atheism' listed the primary cause of atheism as 'Divisions in Religion, if there be many; For any one maine Division, addeth zeale to both Sides; But many Divisions introduce Atheisme'. In 'Of Unity in Religion' he indicated that hearing of 'so many discordant and Contrary Opinions in Religion' as those of 'Heresies and Schismes' averted many from the church and made them 'scorners'. Bacon's essay 'Of Atheism' even made atheism itself a heresy – declaring that 'there is no heresy which strives with more zeal to spread...than Atheism'. At other points, the association of atheism, heresies, idolatry and witchcraft was stated by Bacon in the *Advancement of Learning* in ways that simultaneously differentiated and yet assimilated them:

The declinations from religion, besides the privative, which is atheism and the branches thereof, are three: Heresies, Idolatry, and Witchcraft; Heresies, when we serve the true God with a false worship; Idolatry, when we worship false gods, supposing them to be true; and witchcraft, when we adore false gods, knowing them to be wicked and false.[50]

---

[47] Buckley, *Atheism*, 50, 59.
[48] E. Gosse, *The Works of Thomas Lodge*, IV, 10–11, in Buckley, *Atheism*, 87.
[49] All in Hunter, 'Atheism'.
[50] F. Bacon, *Advancement of Learning*, in Clark, *Thinking*, 437; F. Bacon, *The Essayes*, ed. M. Kiernan (Cambridge, Mass. 1985): 53, 'Of Atheisme'; 11–12, 15, 'Of Unity in Religion'.

According to Richard Hooker's 1593 *Ecclesiastical Polity*, atheists' irreligious humour was 'much strengthened' by 'our contentions'. Pierre Charron's 1595 *Three Truths* anatomised the growth of atheism and held that 'interminable' theological disputes contributed greatly to its spread.[51]

Hooker's *Ecclesiastical Polity*, a work read carefully by Locke in 1681–2, divided atheists into two categories – those by whom God was not apprehended, who were 'but few in number, and for grossness of wit such, that they hardly and scarcely seem to hold the place of human being', and – more 'wretched' than these – those of 'riper capacity' whose 'evil disposition' made them try to persuade themselves that there was no God. The 'fountain and wellspring' of such atheism was a 'resolved purpose of mind to reap in this world what sensual profit or pleasure soever the world yieldeth'. The soul's immortality was for Hooker the central tenet which confuted such atheism, and established the 'principal spurs and motives unto all virtue': providence, resurrection, and eternal joys or endless pains. It was, for Hooker, impossible for men to think God's existence false 'without some scruple and fear of the contrary'. For Hooker, men fearing God are 'thereby a great deal more effectually than by positive laws restrained from doing evil'. Religion served as a 'bridle' on thoughts, not merely on outward actions. In the course of his discussion, Hooker used images of poison and licentiousness to describe atheism, as for most anti-heretical writers these images described heresy. He wrote of 'the spit-venom of their [atheists'] poisoned hearts' and declared that 'what their untamed lust suggesteth, the same their licentious mouths do every where set abroach'.[52]

'Atheists' were held to be intolerable. For Bacon, as for the vast majority of his contemporaries, religion was the 'chiefe band of humane Society'. Princes by the sword, and churches by their doctrines, were for Bacon both equally required to 'damn and send to hell' supporters of such views. Oaths were seen as central to political society, and supposed to work on conscience. As a 'puritan' petition put it in 1586: 'A conscience that feareth God is more violent than any rack to constrain him'. Or as Sir Edwin Sandys declared sonorously in *Europae Speculum*: 'The sacred, the sovereign instrument of justice among men, what is it, what can it be in this world but an oath, being the strongest bond of conscience'. Calvin's *Institutes* and the Anglican *Homily* both stressed very strongly that perjurers would be punished in the next world if not in this. Robert Backhouse described deceiving Royalists in civil war, but 'I never passed myself over to them by any oath or protestation, which alone admits of no equivocation, and without which they could have

---

[51] R. Hooker, *Of the Laws of Ecclesiastical Polity*, ed. A. S. McGrade and B. Vickers (London 1975), v, ch. 2, 223–6; Kors, *Atheism*, 27.

[52] Hooker, *Ecclesiastical Polity*, v, ch. 2, 223–6; Davis, *Fear*, 118–19.

no sufficient grounds of trust'.[53] *The Case of Concealment or mentall reservation* (1614) stated:

The safety of the King himself. . .every man's estate in particular, and the state of the realm in general, doth depend upon the truth and sincerity of men's oaths. . .The law and civil policy of England, being chiefly founded on the fear of God, doth use the religious ceremony of an oath, not only in legal proceedings but in other transactions and affairs of most importance in the commonwealth; esteeming oaths not only as the best touchstone of trust in matters of controversy, but as the safest knot of civil society, and the firmest band to tie all men to the performance of their several duties.

Daniel Featley, member of the Assembly of Divines, concurred in his 1646 *The Dippers Dipt* that oaths were necessary for

the execution of the magistrate's office and the preservation of human society. For without such oaths the commonwealth hath no surety upon public officers and minsters; nor kings upon their subjects; nor lords upon their tenants. . .nor [can] dangerous plots and conspiracies be discovered against the state.[54]

For Henry More, 'liberty of conscience' was the right of believers

provided they be not degenerated into Atheism and Prophaneness. For he that believes there is no God, nor reward, nor punishment after this life, what pretence can he have of claiming a right to Liberty of Conscience? Or how unproper is it to talk of his Right in matters of religion who professedly has no Religion at all, nor any Tie of Conscience upon him to make that wicked Profession.[55]

Atheists were thus clearly held to be utterly intolerable. And partly by the process of assimilation to atheists, anti-Trinitarian heretics were made to be almost equally intolerable in the eyes of many sixteenth- and early seventeenth-century thinkers. The association of anti-Trinitarian and Anabaptist 'heretics' with 'atheists' operated on many levels. It was suggested first that 'heretics' were almost 'atheists' and that 'heretics' tended by their specific doctrines towards 'atheism', including if they denied the knowledge of the true God of the Trinity in ways little distinguishable from denial of God altogether or supported materialistic theories said to deny a providential, omnipotent or omnipresent God. It was suggested next that 'heretics' caused contentions that fostered 'atheism' and that 'heretics' and 'atheists' were alike in tending to 'treason' and 'sedition'. It was suggested that 'heretics' supported their doctrines for 'libertine' or 'sodomitical' reasons that

---

[53] Sir Edwin Sandys, *Europae Speculum*, 45; R. Backhouse, *A True Relation of a Wicked Plot* (1644) in *Bibliotheca Gloucestrensis* (1823), II, 323 in C. Hill, *Society and Puritanism in Pre-Revolutionary England* (London 1964), ch. 11, 'From Oaths to Interest', 384–96.

[54] Anon, *The Case of Concealment* (1612), 51–2, in Hill, *Society*, ch. 11, 'From Oaths to Interest', 382; D. Featly,*The Dippers Dipt* (1646), 142, in Hill, *Society*, 383.

[55] H. More, *An Explanation of the Grand Mystery of Godliness* in *Theological Works* (1708), 361, in Colie, *Light*, 42.

were also the basis of 'atheism'. And it was suggested that 'heretics' misused their intelligence and often pridefully elevated it against the collective wisdom of the church and so were like 'atheists', who were said to substitute a celebration of their own superficial 'wit' for true intelligence and wisdom. 'Atheists', like 'heretics', were spoken of as spreading 'poisonous' doctrines and as 'pestilential', and as needing to be prevented from 'infecting' others. Both 'atheists' and 'heretics' were depicted as 'monsters' against 'nature'. Both were seen as having magistrates armed against them for the conjoint goods of civil peace to preserve the body and religious duty to preserve the soul.

In their sixteenth- and early seventeenth-century assault on the intolerable trinity of Anabaptists, anti-Trinitarians, and 'atheists', many 'magisterial Reformation' writers had thus handed on and expanded upon the assaults against 'heretics' and 'schismatics' as libertine and seditious, poisonous and murdering, that had long been iterated in late patristic and late medieval texts. Such assaults were frequently applied in sixteenth- and seventeenth-century disputes between Catholics and Protestants in France, in Huguenot assaults on unorthodox Huguenots, and in the English attacks on 'heretics' and 'schismatics' in the period leading up to and including the English Revolution. It is to these reiterations and reinforcements of the case against heresy and schism that we turn in the next chapters.

8

Anathematising heretics in sixteenth-and early seventeenth-century French religious polemic

The accusations that we met in the last chapter as repeatedly directed against anti-Trinitarians and Anabaptists as libertine, sodomitical underminers of the order of the family were made against Anabaptists and anti-Trinitarians by both Catholics and by 'magisterial Reformation' Protestants. In their form, however, they were very similar to the accusations that these Catholics and 'magisterial Reformation' Protestants repeatedly turned against each other in the sixteenth century. Not merely did each anathematise the other as seditious and treasonable, but they expanded at length upon the accusations of heresy, sodomy and libertinism in an escalating rhetoric of accusation and counter-accusation which fused with attacks on each other as diabolic antitheses of the 'true faith', witches, and 'monsters'.

Calvin and Beza were frequently denounced by Catholics as 'sodomites' as well as 'heretics'. Catholic pamphlets frequently depicted Luther as a lustful glutton driven by his sexual needs. Luther was attacked in Catholic images as a 'monster', 'libertine' preacher of 'sodomy', heretic, blasphemer, and poisoner.[1] Catholic attacks pointed to Protestant justifications of clerical marriage as revealing the 'lascivious' and 'voluptuous' motivations of Luther in condemning the 'angelic chastity' of Catholic clerics. Catholic theologians from the sixteenth century through to the works of Nicole and Arnauld in the late seventeenth century repeatedly attacked the Calvinists' doctrine of divine election and perseverance as intended to legitimate licence and to appeal to human corruption; it was for them an antinomian doctrine created precisely in order to facilitate libertinism.[2] Leaders of the 'magisterial Reformation' in their turn directed the same accusations against Catholic priests, depicted repeatedly as 'sodomites' and as devoted to 'concubines' and brothels. The Reformation placed images of the Pope as Babylonian

---

[1] M. Wiesner, 'Women and the Reformation' in R. Po-Chia Hsia, *German People*, 154; R. Scribner, *For the Sake of Simple Folk* (Oxford 1994), 329–31.
[2] Dompnier, *Le venin*, 79–81.

whore and Pope-prostitute at the centre of much of its propaganda.[3] In England, John Olde declared in 1557 that Catholicism's 'satanic nature' was shown by its adherents' love of 'whorish women and of fylthy and abominable sodomitical lustes'. William Lithgow asserted: 'Lo there is the chastity of the Romish priests who forsooth may not marry and yet miscarry themselves in all abominations, especially in sodomy, which is their continual pleasure and practice'.[4] In France, Protestant writers repeatedly attacked Catholic priests as lewd, depicted concubines and prostitutes kept by many priests, and at points attacked the Catholic clergy as being *mainly* 'sodomites'.[5]

The Reformation and Counter-Reformation both utilised extensive imaging of the opposite religion as counter to appropriate gender hierarchy, and simultaneously as supported particularly by women. As Natalie Zemon Davis and others have stressed, many Catholic works attacked Protestant women for challenging appropriate male authority by challenging the interpretative authority of the priest and church in their reading of Scripture and disputing with priests, and attacked women who published interpretations of the faith as lacking appropriate subjection to male authority. In *The Holy Household*, Lyndal Roper has stressed the extent to which Reformation theology was a 'theology of gender' intended to attack Catholic allowance of greater roles for women in arenas from marketing through convents in favour of an ideology of subservience within households directly supervised and directed by males.[6] Much polemic on both sides imaged the heretic not merely as female and insubordinate, but also as 'seductive' and 'diabolic'. The French anti-heretical writer Florimond de Raemond identified Satan as spreading heresy easily to the 'fragile sexe', and working in spreading his heresy to men exactly as he had done when tempting Adam, through female sexual seduction.[7]

As we noted in Chapter 6, the 'Last Days' were understood as a time of increased heresy and of increased false magic or witchcraft. It was also understood as a time of 'monsters' or the 'monstrous'. We have often noted claims from anti-heretical writers in early modern Europe that plagues and

---

[3] L. Roper, *The Holy Household* (Oxford 1989), 108–9; N. Z. Davis, 'Rites' in *idem, Society*, 159; Scribner, *For the Sake of Simple Folk*, 182–3.

[4] J. Olde, *Short Description*, 29v, in D. Oldridge, *The Devil in Early Modern England* (Sutton 2000), 25–6; Bray, *Homosexuality*, 18–19.

[5] Davis, *Society*, 158–9.

[6] Davis, 'City Women and Religious Change' in *Society*; Roper, *Holy Household*; N. Roelker, 'The Appeal of Calvinism to French Noblewomen in the Sixteenth Century', *Journal of Interdisciplinary History* (1971–2), 391–413; *idem*, 'The Role of Noblewomen in the French Reformation', *Archiv für Reformationgeschichte* (1972), 168–95.

[7] F. de Raemond, *Histoire de l'hérésie*, 847, in Dompnier, *Le venin*, 96; Butler, *Characters*, 62, in Marotti, 'Recusant Women', 1–34 at 4.

other forms of suffering were presaged by God sending 'signs' and 'portents' as warnings, and that plagues were understood as themselves sent by God as signs of his displeasure with heretics and with those who tolerated heretics. As such scholars as Niccoli, Hanafi, Labrousse, and Céard have shown, divination of signs and portents, including 'monsters', was a central topic of sixteenth- and early seventeenth-century European intellectual life.[8] The mid-sixteenth century has been called by Jean Céard 'the golden age' of monsters and prodigies. It has even recently been suggested, albeit somewhat hyperbolically, that 'interpretation of monsters' was no less than 'an alternative political science' and more popular than the treatises of Machiavelli.[9] Many thinkers from late fifteenth- to mid-seventeenth-century Europe strongly supported the notion that 'monsters' and 'monstrous births' – that is, physically deformed infants – were providential 'signs' revealing God's anger at sin and his intent either to castigate or to warn in order to encourage turning away from sins – including heresies and schisms. The very term 'monster' ('monstrum') was derived from *monere*, to warn or to threaten.[10] Such treatises as those of Machiavelli themselves often supported association between the appearance of monsters and portents and the destruction of a city by war or disease. Machiavelli wrote in his *Discourses* that it was 'clear from ancient and modern cases that no serious misfortune' falls on a city or province without signs and portents.[11] That this support was voiced in Machiavelli's *Discourses* on Livy was significant: Livy was one of the central classical sources for notions of prodigies and divination, influential both through his own works and through such Livian collections as Obsequens' *Prodigiorum Liber* and Lycosthenes' (Conrad Wollfahrt's) very popular 1552 *De Prodigiis*.[12] It is thus important that Jurieu, the strongest exponent of such signs in the 1680s was to cite Livy, while Jurieu's opponent in defence of toleration, Bayle, was to criticise Livy's credulous reporting of signs and prodigies in his *Pensées*, and that Locke noted the citation during the months of composition of his *Letter Concerning Toleration*. Augustine had recognised 'monsters' as 'portents' operating outside of the usual laws of nature, and although that latter fact made them in his view incapable of divination, others combined Augustine's view that 'monsters' were 'portents' with sources such as Livy, Pliny, and the Hebrew Bible, generating an account, as the seventh-century Bishop Isidore of Seville had long ago declared, that 'God wishes to signify the future through faults in things that

[8] J. Céard, *La nature et les prodigies* (Geneva 1977); Z. Hanafi, *The Monster in the Machine* (Duke 2000); O. Niccoli, *Prophecy and People in Renaissance Italy* (Princeton 1990); E. Labrousse, *L'entrée de Saturne au lion* (The Hague 1974); cf. also A. Paré, *On Monsters and Marvels*, tr. J. Pallister (Chicago 1982).
[9] Hanafi, *Monster*, 3.   [10] Hanafi, *Monster*, 3.   [11] Niccoli, *Prophecy*, xiii, ch. 2.
[12] Hanafi, *Monster*, 9.

are born'.[13] The Augustinian monk Edigio Canisio was one among many stating the widely shared view of his contemporaries when he opened the Fifth Lateran Council of 1512 with an oration on the 'monsters, portents and prodigies' as 'signs of celestial threats'.[14] John Ponet declared similarly in his 1556 *A Shorte Treatise of Politic Power* that 'there was never great miserie, destruction, plage or vistacion of God...but are before prophecied and declared by the prophets and ministers of goddes worde, or by some revelaciones, wondres, monsters in the earth, or tokens and signes in the elements'.[15]

'Monsters', then, were those declared 'monstrous' as they inverted the divine and natural order, and understood as interventions in the divine and natural order sent as signs and portents by God. Such portents included not merely 'monstrous births' but, as Ponet's reference to 'signes in the elements' makes clear, such events as the appearance of comets, or other occurrences in the skies then deemed by many writers to be 'prodigies' and 'signs'. Shakespeare perhaps put it best in the questioning of this view by a character in *King John*: 'No natural exhalation in the sky/No scope of nature, no distemper'd day/No common wind, no customed event/But they will pluck away his natural cause/And call them meteors, prodigies and signs/Abortives, presages, and tongues of heaven/Plainly denouncing vengeance'.[16]

In the 1570s, in a work translated into English in 1634, the royal surgeon Ambroise Paré described comets as 'celestial monsters' and as possessing 'beards' or 'hideous human faces'. Although Paré's work was important in giving natural rather than supernatural explanations to many of the 'portents', 'monsters', and 'marvels' which he discussed, Paré cited Pliny, Josephus, and Eusebius in describing the foretelling of the punishments of cities, such as that of Jerusalem 'after the Passion of Jesus Christ'.

For this book, the most important association drawn by these writers was the linkage of monstrosities, signs, and portents such as comets, with religious 'deviance'.[17] The French Catholic Ronsard wrote relatedly of seeing 'so many comets', 'so many new sects', and 'so many deformed monsters'.[18] His coreligionist compatriot Loys Le Roy's 1576 *On the Vicissitude and Variety of Things in the Universe* similarly linked the growth of 'factions and heresies' directly to the 'governing of celestial movements, and the concord of the

---

[13] L. Daston and K. Park, *Wonders and the Order of Nature* (New York 1998), 50.

[14] C. O'Reilly, 'Without Councils we Cannot be Saved', *Augustiniana* 27 (1977), 166–204 at 202–3, discussed in Niccoli, *Prophecy*, 46–7.

[15] Ponet, *Shorte Treatise*, 146, in K. Brammall, 'Monstrous Metamorphoses: Nature, Morality and the Rhetoric of Monstrosity in Tudor England', *Sixteenth Century Journal* (1996), 7.

[16] Shakespeare, *King John*, III, iv, 153–9, in A. Walsham, *Providence in Early Modern England* (Oxford 1999), 167.

[17] Walsham, *Providence*, 169.   [18] Delumeau, *Sin and Fear*, 139.

elements falling apart'.[19] The Protestant preacher Hedio wrote similarly of
the three comets in two years before the Münster Anabaptist kingdom as a
clear sign from God, and associated celestial signs with the rise of heresies
and discords in these 'Last Days'. Monsters as 'signs' were repeatedly associated in early modern Europe with religious sins, such as the corruption of
the clergy, alleged to be revealed in the quickly notorious alleged 'Monster of
Ravenna' of 1512, which in several anti-clerical accounts was said to be born
to 'a friar and a nun', but which in Roman Catholic accounts was said to be a
sign of the dangers of religious schism, which would turn the church itself
into a 'two-headed monster'.[20]

As Bob Scribner has shown in his extensive study of sixteenth-century
religious propaganda, and Daston and Park have shown in their discussions
of 'monsters' in early modern Europe, Luther and Melancthon deployed
accounts of monsters as central elements of their propaganda against
monks, utilising most notably a 'monstrous birth' said to resemble a monk
and another a 'popish ass' in a work translated into English in 1579, over
fifty years after its composition, entitled *Of Two Woonderful Popish
Monsters, to Wyt, of a Popish Asse,...and of a Monkish Calfe*. For
Luther, in a sermon on the Second Sunday of Advent, the Tiber had produced
an animal with 'the head of an ass, the torso of a woman, the foot of an
elephant for its right hand, fish scales on its legs, and a dragon's head at its
backside' in order to demonstrate anger at the papacy.[21] Many similar works
linking heresy, schism and monstrosity received English translations, such as
Boaistuau's very popular *Histoire prodigieuses*, translated by John Fenton as
Certaine Secrete Wonders of Nature (1569). Fenton and Boiastuau's account
of the 'Monster of Ravenna' interpreted a horn on its head as representing
'pride', its wings in place of arms as 'inconstancy', its claw on the end of one
leg as 'robbery' and 'covetousness', and the entirety as 'sodomy'. For Fenton,
the appearance of the monster indicated God's readiness to scourge men

---

[19] Hanafi, *Monster*, 9; Paré, *On Monsters*, ch. 38; Delumeau, *Sin and Fear*, 140–1. In their
initial account of monsters in 1981, Daston and Park employed what they have since rejected
as too teleological a model, suggesting the chronological replacement of supernatural monster beliefs with naturalistic scientific explanations, in favour of now suggesting that both
co-existed throughout the period up to 1750, although still dating a significant move from
supernatural to natural explanations in the late seventeenth century. Paré is a good example
of a sixteenth-century thinker who combined explanations, and important both as elevating
the natural and yet as supporting the supernatural; by the late sixteenth century, there was
increasing opposition to the notion of monsters as prodigies, including: Weinrich's 1595 *De
Ortu Monstrorum commentarius*; Riolan's 1605 *De monstro nato Lutetiae*; Liceti's 1616 *De
Monstrorum causis*, and Aldrovnadi's *Monstrorum historia*: Delumeau, *Sin and Fear*, ch. 4.
[20] Niccoli, *Prophecy*, 46–8; Haude, *Shadow*, 23.
[21] Daston and Park, *Wonders*; Scribner, *For the Sake of Simple Folk*, 125ff.; Delumeau, *Sin and
Fear*, 136–9; Niccoli, *Prophecy*, 126–7.

unless they returned from their 'abominable sins' to the cross of Jesus Christ.[22]

In late sixteenth- and early seventeenth-century England, monstrous births were repeatedly associated with the papacy and Catholicism, as in John Ponet's association in the *Short Treatise* between the increase of monsters and the Catholic tyranny of Mary and Philip, who executed 'all godly opponents'; Mary and Philip had provided a 'deformed head' to the 'body' of the state and caused similar births to occur in England. Ponet was one among many who attributed physical deformities to Catholics, such as the Catholic bishop Stephen Gardiner, who was said by Ponet to have a horse's nose, the devil's paws, and a griffin's feet. Bartholomew Traheron similarly wrote that the 'bloody beast Bonner' was visibly 'a most grislie, ugle, and horrible monster'. The notion that internal deformity and monstrosity (religion) would always be reflected in external deformity and monstrosity (physical appearance) was strong in much of this literature. These texts described the times of Catholic rule in England; J. L.'s 1590 *A True and Perfecte Description of a Straung Monstar Borne in the City of Rome* allied monstrous births to the papacy. In the early seventeenth century, monstrous births were increasingly alleged by Calvinist puritans in the contexts of 'popery', as having occurred in the context of disputes over the book of sports, and over the growing influence of Arminianism in England, testifying that these were 'ungodly' forces against which God was warning the community.[23] Physical 'monsters' here served to discredit as 'monstrous' those of opposing religious commitment, and thus to provide a physical centre to the more rhetorical claim that those of an opposing religion were 'monstrous', standing against the order of nature, and often concealed in appearance but revealed in behaviour as monsters.[24] Catholics in their turn repeatedly depicted Luther himself as a monster, and when Tomassino Lancellotti recorded in 1523 of these accounts a note about a monstrous monk who 'preached heresy' and who had been born of a cow in Saxony, he called him 'martin utero', his very naming of the monster itself being a play on the notion of monstrous births and heresies.[25] Sorbin's *Tractatus de monstris* asserted that 'before the time of heresies we did not see such monsters' in France; indeed, France 'did not know what monsters were, whereas now...each day' produces 'some new abberation'. Saxony 'ever

---

[22] Fenton, *Certaine Secrete Wonders* (London 1569), 140–140v; A. J. Schutte, 'Such Monstrous Births: A Neglected Aspect of the Antinomian Controversy', *Renaissance Quarterly* (1985), 92–3.

[23] Brammall, 'Monstrous', 11–13; Walsham, *Providence*, 219.   [24] Brammall, 'Monstrous'.

[25] Niccoli, *Prophecy*, 126–7.

since it was opposed to Christ by Luther's perfidious fraud, trembles beneath the proliferation of countless monsters'.[26]

Such associations of monstrous births with the religion declared heretical, the power of the imagination and uterus, and lust or libertinism were, then, extremely powerful and prevalent in Renaissance and sixteenth-century Europe.[27] In many cases, the deformity of the child was associated with alleged demonic influence in procreation. More broadly, in many cases the monster was associated with sexual 'libertinism', and often with 'sodomy'. In many cases, the alleged 'monstrosity' of deformed infants led to questioning whether such infants had souls, and to the refusal of baptism. Many were declared 'beasts'. In some cases, in early modern Christian as in many Western pre-Christian societies, babies born with physical deformities were killed, either by the use of force or by withholding of nourishment, and in some instances such actions were justified by the church. Indeed, in some instances in sixteenth-century France, even the mothers of such infants were condemned to death.[28]

LATE SIXTEENTH-CENTURY FRENCH CATHOLIC ANTI-HUGUENOT POLEMIC

Claude Haton was convinced that Protestants snuffed out candles and had sexual intercourse at nocturnal conventicles, involving a 'charité fraternelle et voluptueuse' caused by desire for 'carnal pleasure'. For Haton, the reading of the Bible in French even prompted 'incest'. We have met the exact accusation of the extinction of candles to begin sexual activities at conventicles before, in discussing Augustine, in accusations in the medieval period against Cathars and Albigensians, and before Augustine in Justin Martyr's account of pagan accusations against Christian conventicles.[29] And the same image of sexual licence at Calvinist conventicles was voiced by many other mid-sixteenth-century Catholics against Huguenots. The Franciscan

---

[26] Sorbin, *Histoires prodigieuses*, 628, quoted in Céard, *La nature*, 271; Delumeau, *Sin and Fear*, 139.

[27] Stephen Greenblatt names heretics as the first in a list of 'threatening Others' to whom one's opposition facilitated 'Renaissance self-fashioning': *Renaissance Self-fashioning* (Chicago 1980), 9.

[28] Hanafi, *Monster*, 2–3; Niccoli, *Prophecy*.

[29] M. Greengrass, 'France' in R. Porter and M. Teich (eds.), *The Reformation in National Context* (Cambridge 1994), 53–4; Haton, *Memoires*, 1:50–3 in Davis, 'Rites' in *idem, Society*; Haton and de Mouchy in B. Diefendorf, *Beneath the Cross; Catholics and Huguenots in Sixteenth Century Paris* (Oxford 1991), 54; cf. Haton's celebration of the 'conversion' of Huguenots following the St Bartholomew's Day Massacre in Benedict, *Rouen*, 148. More generally, see also M. Holt, 'Putting Religion Back into the Wars of Religion', *French Historical Studies* (1993), 524–51.

Thomas Beauxamis' 1562 *Resolution on Certain Portraits and Libels, Entitled with the Name of the Marmite* denounced the 'Satanic troop' of Huguenots whose assemblies were orgies and whose doctrines defended lubricity. He questioned: 'Who fails to see that this new faction gives free rein to all lasciviousness, given that it is an assembly of lustful apostates?'[30] Antoine de Mouchy made a similar accusation to that of Haton in his 1560 *Reply to the Heretics' Apology*. According to Mouchy, at the end of their worship Calvinists would retire to rooms where they

are so charitable towards each other…that the men are permitted (if they wish) to do shameful things with the women, and likewise the women with the men. For no one restrains, punishes, corrects…they live (as they put it) in total liberty and amity.[31]

Antonie du Val's *Mirror of the Calvinists* and the Sorbonne doctor Jean de la Vacquerie's 1560 *Catholic Remonstrance* joined in accusing Protestants of sodomy and incest, and even of perverting 'charity' to mean that no woman should ever refuse a man.[32] For du Val, heresy turned upside down all authority both in state and in family as it made wives, children, and servants of various opinions and 'factions and mutinies' followed, so that 'the husband is not in accord with his own wife, nor domestics and citizens with themselves, not the subjects with the ruler'. La Vacquerie accused Protestants not merely of ritual promiscuity in their conventicles, but of conspiring to raze the city of Paris, and argued that 'heresy is a crime, the most dangerous and stinking crime there is in a city or commonwealth' where 'religion is the primary and principal foundation of all order'.[33]

Such images of libertinism were repeatedly joined by images of heresy as poison and disease. Gentian Hervet's *Discourse on the Pillagers, Plunderers, and Burners of Churches* (1563) attacked Protestants' diabolic ministers and their 'pestilential little books full of poison'.[34] Hervet argued in an image we

---

[30] T. Beauxamis, *Résolution sur certains pourtraictz et libelles intituléz du nom de Marmitte* (Paris 1562), 3–4, 12, in P. Benedict, 'The Catholic Response to Protestantism' in J. Obelkevich, *Religion and the People 800–1700* (Chapel Hill 1979), 168–90, at 171; and in *idem, Rouen,* 56, 66.

[31] Antoine de Mouchy, *Réponse à quelque apologie que les hérétiques ces jours passés ont mis en avant* (Paris 1560), 41r, in Sypher, 'Image of Protestantism', *Sixteenth Century Journal* (1980), 59.

[32] Mouchy, *Response,* 34r, 38vff., 64r; du Val, *Mirouer,* 6, 10r, and La Vacquerie, *Catholique,* 15v, 40, both in Sypher, 'Image', 69. The Franciscan Jean Benedict argued in his 1610 *Compendium of Sins* that sodomy was linked to heresy and atheism as sodomites fell into even more miserable sins of 'apostacy, atheism, heresy' and died damned: J. Merrick (ed.), *Homosexuality in Early Modern France* (Oxford 2001), 2–4.

[33] Du Val, *Mirouer,* I, 28v–29r in Sypher, 'Image', 70; Holt, 'Religion', 44.

[34] Gentian Hervet, *Discours sur ce que les pilleurs, voleurs et brusleurs de L'Église disent qu'ils n'en veulent qu'aux Prestres* (1563) in Davis, *Society,* 317n.

have met before in Emperor Frederick II's *Liber Augustalis* of 1231, that a Carmelite suspected of Protestant heresy's arguments were

> but honey! It is but sugar! But let us look a bit under this sweetness to see if there may be some poison there, and if the wolf may not be hidden under wool so smooth.[35]

Antoine du Val likened Protestant heretics to skilled poisoners, adducing Scripture 'that they distort and falsify...to cover and disguise their poisons, in order that their venom be not readily apparent'.[36] For the poet Artus Desiré, heresy was a hydra-headed dragon, polluting the streams and rivers of the kingdom. France was becoming overrun simultaneously with blasphemy and sodomy. For Desiré, Genevan ministers had no scruples: they would

> kill their own father or anyone else...steal...bear false witness,...outrage,...cheat...poison...debauch in any way, or...mutiny and rebel against their lords.[37]

Desiré traced through time a 'tree of heretics' which he depicted literally as growing out of abnormal diabolic sexuality. The lower branches of this tree of heretics were occupied by Simon Magus and Donatus, and its middle branches included Arius, Priscillian, Pelagius and Wyclif, until it reached the uppermost branches, announcing the imminence of the Antichrist and occupied by Luther, Calvin, Bucer, Melancthon, and Oecolampadius, together with the Antichrist. It would be hard to create a more literal representation of the notions that heresies grew from the Devil, that new heresies were lineal descendants of old heresies, and that heresy and schism had spread their branches most widely in the time of the imminent Apocalypse.[38]

Jean Quentin declared to the Estates General on 1 January 1561 that Huguenots should be treated 'as enemies' and declared that it is the 'Prince's duty to use the sword he has received and to punish with death those who have let themselves be infected by the mortal poison of heresy'. Many Catholic preachers depicted the church as a body, and heresy as a cancer or gangrene. Pierre Dyvolé was one among many who compared sin to disease in a sermon on the mass, depicted the priests and sacraments as giving medicine, and heresy as a cancerous limb which had to be amputated in order for the rest of the body to be saved.[39] Simon Vigor, the most popular

---

[35] Hervet, *Sermon de Gentian Hervet, après avoir ouy prêcher un prédicateur suspect d'hérésie* in *idem, Recueil d'aucunes mensonges*, 19, quoted in Sypher, 'Image', 65.

[36] Du Val, *Mirouer*, 57v, in Sypher, 'Image', 66.

[37] Greengrass, 'France', 53–4; Desiré, *Passevent parisien*, 42–3; *idem, Les Grands Jours, passim* in Sypher, 'Image', 72–3; Crouzet, *Les Guerriers*, I, 191–200.

[38] A. Desiré, *L'arbe des hérétiques ou l'imminence antechristique annoncée par Artus Desiré* in Crouzet, *Les Guerriers* (Seyssel 1990), I, between 384 and 385.

[39] Quentin in LeCler, *Toleration*, II, 47; Barrington Moore, *Moral Purity and Persecution in History* (Princeton 2000), 40; Dyvolé, *Dix sermons de la saincte Messe*, 405; G. du Preau, *Des faux prophètes, séducteurs, amp; hypochrites...loups ravissans* (Paris 1563) in Diefendorf, *Beneath the Cross*, 150–1; Crouzet, *Les Guerriers*, I, 206–10.

preacher in Paris, depicted heresy as an infection needing amputation in the period leading up to the St Bartholomew's Day Massacre, and argued that if Huguenots were not killed – and he recommended a 'bitter death' – then they would 'kill you, either by poison, or some other means'. Other Catholics attacked an alleged Huguenot conspiracy said to be the result of a 'Theodor-Bezian infection'.[40] Catholic processions similarly emphasised that Huguenots were 'polluting' the community, and included 'purificatory symbols', such as the burning of candles and ringing of bells.[41]

As was emphasised by Natalie Zemon Davis in her now classic study of religious riots in sixteenth-century France, 'The Rites of Violence', and in various works by Barbara Diefendorf, Wylie Sypher, Donald Kelley, Mark Greengrass, and Denis Crouzet, among the results of these repeated imagings of Huguenots by Catholics in the 1560s and early 1570s as diseased, infectious, poisoning, arsonist libertines, sodomites, and witches was the legitimation, and to some extent also the inculcation, of extreme violence against their persons, enacted by children and women as well as by men in many riots throughout France and centrally in the St Bartholomew's Day Massacre of 1572. These riots and rituals were ones which physically as well as verbally treated those of the opposing religion as less than human, as 'polluting' the community, and as needing to be 'cleansed'. These riots and rituals of violence thus depicted as a duty to serve God – and to prevent God's further punishment of the community – the ritualised burning as well as massacring of Huguenots in 1572, in the St Bartholomew's Day Massacre. In that event, a subject of massive Catholic celebration in its initial moment (although later rejected as too violent), thousands of Huguenots were attacked on the streets and slaughtered in a repertory of ritualised actions against polluters.[42] René Benoist, curé of Saint-Eustache, invoked Old Testament occasions when God had 'animated the people to kill the false prophets without sparing a single one, thereby teaching us how grievously and without mercy the obstinate heretics should be punished and exterminated'.[43]

The association of Protestant heresy with witchcraft was frequent in Catholic demonological literature of the late sixteenth and early seventeenth centuries, which was strongly apocalyptic in its interpretation of these as the

[40] D. Kelley, 'Martyrs, Myths and the Massacre', in A. Soman (ed.), *The Massacre of St Bartholomew* (The Hague 1974), 181–202, at 199; Kelley, *Beginning of Ideology*; Davis, 'Rites' in *idem, Society*; Moore, *Moral Purity*, 51–2; Diefendorf, *Beneath the Cross*, 152–8.

[41] Benedict, 'Catholic Response', 171.

[42] There are some differences among these accounts which I here run together; for instance, Natalie Davis has stressed the collective rituals and Denis Crouzet the apocalyptic force of sixteenth-century thinking as prompting religious violence. Cf. Holt, 'Religion', 524–51; Benedict, 'Catholic-Reformed', 84–5.

[43] Davis, 'Rites' in *idem, Society*, 152–87; Diefendorf, *Beneath the Cross*, esp. 151–8; Holt, *The French Wars of Religion*; cf. also Moore, *Moral Purity*, 40.

'Last Days'. The demonologically obsessed Martin del Rio was merely one among very many such Catholic authors in the sixteenth and seventeenth centuries who traced the inseparability of heresy and witchcraft in a joint historiography from Simon Magus through the Waldensians to Lutheranism and Calvinism. For Del Rio, moreover, Lutheranism had 'infected' people in Trier, Germany with demonism and witchcraft; while England, Scotland, France, and Flanders had been 'poisoned' by the venoms of Calvinism. Demons inhabited heretics and witches.[44] Similarly, for the Catholic Nodé, Wyclif, Hus and Luther had all been heretics allied with witches, as Huguenots would prove to be over time. For Sebastien Michaelis, 'all Hereticks...naturally love Magicians and Sorcerers'. For the English Catholic Louvain theologian Stapleton, 'such is the affinity between them, being related in so many different ways...that there is not a Christian who does not fight against the outrages of heresy and magic with the same hatred, and dread them with equal detestation...Just as we imprison magicians by public authority, expel them from the community, and inflict terrible punishments on them, so we must take the same pains and use the same force against heretics. Just as the arts of magic, and their professors and books, cannot be suffered among Christians and are destroyed by sword and fire, so the same is decreed for heretics'.[45]

Summarising the writings of a series of Catholic authors of the late sixteenth and early seventeenth centuries, Stuart Clark has written that 'Their whole view of witchcraft was premissed on a historiography of heresy seen as the continuous expression of demonism'. Witchcraft accusations thus not merely shared many features with heresy accusations, but also drew heavily from and consciously repeated older accusations against heretics. To such Catholics, who had long held heresy and witchcraft to be associated, Protestantism was the latest in a long line of heresies associated with witchcraft. As Gillet pointed out in his 1605 *Enquiry Concerning Heresy*, witches rejected or subverted precisely the same parts of the faith attacked by Protestants – the Virgin, the saints, the sign of the cross.[46] For Stapleton,

just as the wonderful effects of the magic art...are produced...by the devil himself...so today the leading astray of the people by heretics does not happen because of the learning, eloquence, cunning or wickedness of the heretics themselves, but through that same Satan whose servants they are and who works through them.[47]

---

[44] M. Del Rio, *Disquisitionum magicarum* (Lyons 1608), 'Proloquium' in Clark, *Thinking*, 535.
[45] Stapleton, *Orationes academicae miscellaneae triginta quatuor* in idem, *Opera* (Paris 1620), II, 507; Michaelis in Clark, *Thinking*, 536–7.
[46] Gillet, *Subtile*, 217–18, in Clark, *Thinking*, 535–6.
[47] T. Stapleton, 'Cur magia pariter cum haeresi hodie creverit' in *Orationes* (see note 45), II, 502–7, quoted and discussed in Clark, *Thinking*, 535.

The Catholic Church in general was held by many early modern Protestants to be simultaneously 'heretical' and 'schismatic' from the 'true faith' and to be deeply involved in witchcraft, with its ritual structure based on false diabolic magic or witchcraft.[48]

POLITIQUE ARGUMENTS FOR TOLERATION, AND THE MAINTENANCE OF IMAGES OF HUGUENOTS AS 'MONSTERS' IN THE EARLY SEVENTEENTH CENTURY

After years of massacre and civil war in France, inspired in significant part by these hostile understandings of the other religious community, religious toleration by official recognition of pacific co-existence of Huguenots and Catholics in France was established with the Edict of Nantes in 1598. As early as the 1560s, there had been a move to extol 'the blessings of peace over the virtues of a just war'.[49] The mid- and late sixteenth century saw a major growth of such *politique* thought which stressed that magistrates were required to maintain the peace and that if pursuit of religious uniformity destroyed the peace, then magistrates could allow diversity of religions even though such religions were 'evil' and even though war against them would be 'just'. Castellio's *Advice to France Laid Waste* (1562) argued that one should not do to another that which you would not have them do to you', and that only restraint from killing enemies could allow the commonwealth to continue.[50] The *politique* chancellor de l'Hôpital had argued as early as 1562 that while it was folly to 'hope for peace, repose, and amity between peoples of different religions', and while the imposition of Catholic uniformity was 'good in itself', it was necessary to maintain the commonwealth when imposition would cause its ruin.[51] The author of the 1561 *Exhortation to Princes* took over the image of amputation of a rotten member used by anti-heretical writers, and declared that it was applicable only when this was possible:

Just as in the human body one has to amputate a rotten member at an early stage before the disease spreads...so the wise men of the world agree that as soon as new opinions begin to cling to a society, they should be cut off, by fire, sword, and death: that is to say, when their number is still small.[52]

---

[48] Clark, *Thinking*, 360.
[49] M. Greengrass, 'The Psychology of Religious Violence', *French History* (1991), 574.
[50] Skinner, *Foundations*, 250.   [51] Skinner, *Foundations*, 251.
[52] *Exhortation* in Le Cler, *Toleration*, II, 50. It was this argument which Jurieu was to use in his 1681 *Policy*: one could prevent a sect when small but could not do so when it was large because this was to endanger the state.

Bodin similarly argued in his *Six Books of the Commonwealth* that religious unity was the 'principal foundation of the power and strength of the state' and that 'disputations of religion' were the most likely causes of the 'ruin and destruction' of commonwealths, but that when the imposition of religious uniformity was not possible it was required that 'that religion or sect is to be suffered which without the hazard and destruction of the state cannot be taken away'.[53] Lipsius stressed that while magistrates had to obtain uniformity if they could, when this could not be obtained diversity could be allowed.[54] Representations of Huguenots through images of heresy and monstrosity, poison, pollution, and plague, died down considerably in France in the early seventeenth century. Images of Protestants as heretical 'monsters' were importantly countered by images such as those of Montaigne in his *Essays* that there was nothing more 'monstrous' than to cause civil wars and desolation for differences of religious opinions. Montaigne's *Essais* simultaneously identified many claims to knowledge as false and hubristic. And several other important French writers of the late sixteenth and early seventeenth centuries developed sceptical claims about humans' capacity for religious knowledge, and strengthened *politique* stresses on 'reason of state'.[55]

But for the Catholic Ligeurs, these *politiques* were as bad as were the heretics themselves, and heretics remained diseased poisoners and libertines deserving intolerance. Such images were therefore never completely removed from French thought in the late sixteenth and early seventeenth centuries, and the claims that politics should be governed by power or peace rather than directed to morality and godliness, and that much was unknown, were pilloried by many of these Ligeurs as the 'Machiavellian', 'atheist', or 'libertine' doctrines of a corrupt 'reason of state'. The more that such claims came to be associated in the seventeenth century with an increasingly articulate group of libertine *érudits* rather than obviously loyal orthodox Catholics, moreover, the more questionable such a stress on 'policy' and 'reason of state' was rendered in the eyes of many orthodox Catholics. Throughout the period from 1600–85, no decade was without religious riots, and these were particularly violent in the 1620s. Fears of massacre by those of the other religion spread on several occasions in the mid- and late seventeenth century, and Philip Benedict has suggested that while there was some local interconfessional intermarriage and other forms of local solidarity between Catholics and Protestants, religious endogamy and local hostility between Catholics

---

[53] Skinner, *Foundations*, 253.   [54] Tuck, *Philosophy and Government*, 58–9.
[55] Tuck, *Philosophy and Government*; M. Viroli, *From Politics to Reason of State* (Cambridge 1992); Skinner, *Foundations*; J. Pearl, *The Crime of Crimes* (Ontario 1999); N. Keohane, *Philosophy and the State in France* (Princeton 1980).

and Protestants grew rather than declined in the course of the seventeenth century in France.[56]

While after the Edict of Nantes Catholic Ligeurs were generally violent in word rather than in deed, Jonathan Pearl has recently documented the force of assault on Huguenots of fervent Ligeurs, showing that in opposition to the *politiques* a series of writers in the late sixteenth century and early seventeenth century continued to associate Protestant 'heresy' and 'witchcraft' in defences of religion against 'atheists, jews, philosophers and heretics'. Martin del Rio, who published a demonological treatise in 1599 – the year after the Edict of Nantes – that then went through twenty editions and was based on the thought of the Jesuit Jean Maldonat, continued to refer to heresy as a 'poison' and to say that 'witches are, for the most part, heretics'. For Jean Crespet in 1590, 'monsters' were born of the union of Catholics and 'heretics'. In a work published posthumously in 1605, Florimond de Raemond called Protestants 'ravishing wolves, monstrous dragons and deadly vipers', and further imaged Protestantism itself as a 'monstrous birth' in saying that Luther was 'godfather of this monstrous birth'. He declared that Protestants were of the army of Satan, 'an infernal monster' who committed 'crimes of divine and human treason'. He called for France to imitate the Spanish Inquisition. Heresy was for him a 'pestilential venom'. For the Jesuit Louis Richeome in 1603, 'Luther gave birth to monsters extreme in their impudence'. Richeome's 1608 *Huguenot Idolatry* depicted Protestantism as the heretical 'contrarie' to Catholicism. Calvin's doctrine was 'poison'. It was lèse-majesté divine, treason against God, the King of Kings, and 'against his Kingdom, the church'.[57] René Benoist's 'Opuscule, contenant plusiers discours de meditation et devotion' in Viel's 1610 *History* talked of Huguenots similarly as contraries to the truth, declaring that 'all good and holy things have their contraries'. For Benoist, in a list where the juxtapositions are extremely telling, Satan was now spreading 'carnal, licentious pleasures, heresies, black arts, lusts, blasphemies, false opinions'. Noel Taillepied, canon at Pontoise, wrote in his *History of the Views, Manners, Beliefs and Deaths of the Three Principle Heretics of Our Time* (1616) that heresy was a 'horrible and pernicious monster' and the source of sedition. For Taillepied, Satan had been loosed to 'seduce the nations'. In associations of heresy, atheism, and libertinism we have by now traced repeatedly, François Garasse, opponent of the libertine Charron, declared simply in 1622 that 'Libertine...signifies a Huguenot and a half' and depicted 'atheism' as 'an unhappy gangrene' starting where 'heresy' left off. Boucher's *Mystery of Infidelity* (1614) similarly declared that heretics were 'marked on the hand

---

[56] Benedict, 'Catholic-Reformed', 86–7, 90.
[57] Richeome in Dompnier, *Le venin*, 58, 76; Pearl, *Crime*.

with the mark of antichrist', that heresy was 'born in lust', and that heretics were 'traitors to religion'. Boucher said that the 'army of libertines' were the 'fruit of heresy'. Boucher's *Mystical Crown* (1624) declared the central magisterial duty to be the confounding of heresy, atheism, and Islam, and declared that heresy had spawned witchcraft, the highest degree of atheism. For Boucher, in every age witchcraft and heresy had paralleled each other in beliefs and in rituals; Lutheranism and Calvinism negated the true religion just as did witches' sabbaths, and witches flourished in Protestant nations.[58]

There was thus considerable pressure in the writings of such Ligeurs to resume intolerance towards Huguenots as diabolical opponents of the true faith. And even the *politique* arguments of many loyal Catholics were intrinsically double-edged. To many *politique* Catholic thinkers, Huguenots had gained toleration in 1598 as a recognition of their power, but they were never truly loyal and obedient subjects and were instead a heretical, intrinsically disloyal 'state within a state'. Further military campaigns in the 1620s against Huguenot strongholds were seen as necessary to prevent another manifestation of Protestant rebelliousness which otherwise would have threatened the state and king. And the *politique* argument that religious uniformity was desirable for peace, but that when the imposition of uniformity was impossible without ruining the state it was to be postponed, carried within it the strong assertion of the desirability of obtaining uniformity as soon as this was possible without ruining the state. The very success of the campaigns of the 1620s to reduce the threat of Protestant cities within the realm as a 'state within the state' thus simultaneously helped to allay the sense that Protestants posed a threat, and raised at exactly the same moment the question of whether the imposition of religious uniformity would still bring ruin to the state. As Protestant allegiance was declared to be in decline, this question only increased in pertinence as the century wore on.

The nature of the *politique* argument for toleration for Huguenots thus carried within itself the seeds of dissolution of toleration for Huguenots, and it was in a major way the fulfilment of the *politique* argument, rather than the abrogation of the argument, when Catholics justified the Revocation of the Edict of Nantes by saying that all Catholic kings of France had viewed the Edict as temporary and intended to extirpate the heresy of Protestantism as soon as they were able. Tolerationist argument would have required within *politique* argument a further declaration that intolerance in its very nature would cause endless sedition and turmoil and that toleration secured the peace, but this argument was absent from French *politique* thought. And as the Huguenots themselves almost entirely believed that magistrates had a

[58] Boucher, *Couronne* in Clark, *Thinking*, 387–8; Pearl, *Crime*, 63, 66, 83, 86, 87, 89, 91, 99; Clark, *Thinking*, 64, 328–9.

duty to suppress heresy, they offered little indeed in the way of argument that toleration or diversity was a good in itself. As Philip Benedict has put it, if Protestants were returning to Catholicism and the

crown's strength had increased to the point where it could no longer be argued that the revocation of tolerance for the Huguenots would produce an unacceptable level of internal warfare, what was the point of retaining a regime that had always been viewed as a necessary evil, especially when there was important symbolic capital to be obtained by doing away with it?[59]

Elisabeth Labrousse has similarly pointed to the way in which the Edict of Nantes reduced the temperature but did not remove the hostility between Catholics and Protestants, in noting that 'We should not fool ourselves; in the eyes of the most fervent, the Edict was only an armistice: to the hot war would succeed a cold war'.[60] The Catholic Ligeur anathematisations of Huguenots anatomised by Pearl and Clark provided part of the arsenal of this 'cold war' conducted in France from the Edict of Nantes to the Revocation of the Edict of Nantes. As the leading historian of Protestantism, E. G. Léonard, once remarked, the thing to be explained about the Revocation of the Edict of Nantes in 1685 is not that it happened, but that it did not happen sooner, given that such attacks on Huguenots did not disappear in the eighty years from 1598 to 1685, but instead received significant continued circulation.[61]

Such images of heretics and schismatics as infected, poisoning, monstrous and 'libertine' did not merely receive continued currency in seventeenth century France from Catholic quills; they also remained central to images deployed by the Huguenots themselves against Catholics, and especially against those within their own church who were seen by 'orthodox' Huguenots as having veered into 'heresy' or 'schism'. It was this set of images which underpinned the practices of intolerance in the Huguenot community against 'heresy' described in Chapter 4, which associated 'Heresie, Contempt of God, Schism, Treason, and Rebellion', and asserted that 'the gate will be shut on all libertines, Anabaptists and other pernicious sects who might enter the church of God'.[62] It was as 'poison' and as 'monstrous doctrine' that Arminianism and Amyraldism were rejected in the 1630s. When Du Moulin campaigned against Amyraut's influence at Saumur, it was against preachers

---

[59] M. Holt, *The French Wars of Religion* (Cambridge 1995), ch. 7; Benedict, 'Catholic-Reformed', 82–3.

[60] Labrousse, *Une foi*, 28.

[61] Labrousse, 'Understanding the Revocation of the Edict of Nantes From the Perspective of the French court' in R. M. Golden (ed.), *The Huguenot Connection: The Edict of Nantes, its Revocation, and Early French Migration to South Carolina* (Dordrecht 1988), 55; E. G. Léonard, *Histoire générale du protestantisme* (Paris 1961; London 1965–7).

[62] 'The Protestant Petition for Temples 1561' in Potter (ed.), *The French Wars of Religion*, 30.

'whose skins showed the rash of these new ideas' and with declaration that none 'so infected' should be delegates to the national synod. When the Huguenot Church rejected importation of Congregationalism from England in the 1640s, it was for fear that it would allow 'the contagion' of heretical 'poison' to spread. The same rhetoric was then applied in the 1670s against d'Huisseau and his followers.[63] Almost all Huguenots relied for the toleration of 'orthodox' Huguenots in France on *politique* arguments which were inherently subject to decay, and instead of generating theories of universal toleration, almost all Huguenots as orthodox Calvinists opposed such toleration for those within their own community whom they saw as becoming 'heretical'. When faced with a member of their congregation who developed Arminian inclinations, they excommunicated and execrated him; when faced with an anti-Trinitarian, they called for his burning, and throughout the century they maintained in speaking of such 'heretics' much of the rhetoric of 'poison', 'plague', and 'libertinism' with which heretics had been anathematised for centuries. Thus in France in the century after the Edict of Nantes, Catholic writers who supported the toleration of Huguenots did not generate theories which saw toleration as other than a forced *politique* compromise, a significant number of Catholic Ligeur writers saw such toleration as undesirable even as a compromise, and the vast majority of Huguenot writers themselves did not generate but rather opposed theories of universal religious toleration.

[63] Van Stam, *Controversy*, 33, 42–3, 62, 113–14, and *passim*.

Anti-heretical and anti-schismatic literature in England from the late sixteenth to the mid-seventeenth century

Much early and mid-seventeenth-century anti-heretical and anti-schismatic Anglican thought was structured in condemnation of 'puritanism' and of 'Anabaptism' or 'separatism' as heretical and schismatic, seditious and treasonous.[1] For Archbishop Laud, heresy and schism caused dissension both in church and state. For Laud, 'unity cannot long continue in the church, where uniformity is shut out at the church door'; banishment or other punishment was required for 'Anabaptists and Separatists'. As Kristen Poole has recently shown in *Radical Religion*, for many who wrote against puritanism 'puritans' were seditious, 'pestilential', and 'libertine'. In order to prevent challenges to family and state as well as church, and to prevent the spread of their 'infectious' doctrines, their punishment was required. David Owen's 1641 *The Puritane's Impuritie: of the Anatomie of a Puritane or Sepratist* asserted that 'amongst the whole brood of vices...there is none so great...none so leprous as this of Puritanisme'.[2] The 1642 *A Puritane Set Forth in His Own Lively Colours* asked 'What is a Puritan?' and answered: 'one of the pestilent party, the very plague of the Church and Commonwealth...one that breathes nothing but sedition'.[3] Many 'puritans' were identified with Anabaptism, as in Oliver Ormerod's 1605 *Picture of a Puritane*, in which an Englishman sought to know how 'Anabaptists did spend their time at their private conventicles' in Germany in order to understand the behaviour of English 'sectaries'. In Middleton's 1619 *Inner Temple Masque*, the nonconformist character declares himself 'born an Anabaptist'

---

[1] Modern historians have tended recently to use 'puritan' especially to designate conformists who desired further reformation, and stressed how few were 'separatists'. But polemics against 'puritanism' frequently made no such distinction, and repeatedly assaulted puritan schismatic tendencies and heretical tendencies, as Kristen Poole has recently noted (Poole, *Radical Religion*, 3). It is on the anti-heretical and anti-schismatic images of 'puritanism' which this chapter will focus; it intends to avoid the debate over the term. See especially P. Lake, *Anglicans and Puritans?* (London 1988).

[2] Jordan, *Toleration*, 132–42; Owen, *The Puritane's Impuritie* (1641), 1, in Poole, *Radical Religion*, 1.

[3] *A Puritane Set Forth in His Own Lively Colours* (1642), 2–3 in Poole, *Radical Religion*, 3.

before showing that he pretends asceticism only in order to conceal voracious libertine desires. Ben Jonson's *The Alchemist* invoked John of Leiden and Hendrick Niclaes in discussing religious nonconformity. Scores of other examples linking the accusation of 'puritanism' to Anabaptism and to over-turning sexual morality, church, and state, could be cited from early seventeenth-century Anglican assault on 'puritanism' and 'separatism'.[4]

But such hostility was met in the early seventeenth century by an increasing hostility to the forms of the Church of England and to the beliefs of many of its hierarchy as themselves 'popish' and 'Arminian' and therefore 'poisoning' and 'pestilential'. In charting English 'puritan' thought of the late sixteenth and early seventeenth century, Patrick Collinson has stressed that 'the lan-guage and social imagery of binary opposition were nothing if not scriptural and consequently almost mandatory for religious discussion'. He notes that 'puritans' insisted on the division of 'all into two, as if everyone had to be one thing or the other'. Collinson emphasises biblical sources, such as 'he who is not for me is against me', and that the appeal to these opposites in early modern Europe has to be understood in terms of the broader

prevalent mental and rhetorical habit of addressing every proposition or topic of investigation in terms of its contrary or antithesis, the method of binary opposition, or inversion.

For Collinson, it is this which explains the late sixteenth and early seventeenth-century binary emphases on Christ and the Antichrist and on the Devil and God; it also explains the level of antagonism to Catholicism as the 'polar opposite' of true religion.[5] Peter Lake has similarly written of anti-popery as 'in England, the most obvious and important example of that process of binary opposition, inversion, or argument from contraries'. Popery, he writes, was

an anti-religion, a perfectly symmetrical negative image of true Christianity. Anti-Christ was an agent of Satan, sent in to the Church to corrupt and take it over from within.

Anti-popery served simultaneously, according to Lake, as a way of think-ing designed to appeal to those whose vision of the polity was one emphasis-ing hostility, providing legitimation of such hostility as a fight of the 'godly' against the 'ungodly'. This helped to foster association in many early seventeenth-century Calvinist minds of 'Arminianism' with 'Catholicism', 'Pelagianism', and anti-Trinitarianism, all understood as the diabolical opposite to true Christianity. James I was a strict Calvinist who called

---

[4] Poole, *Radical Religion*, 49, 53, 54, 62, and *passim*.
[5] Collinson, *Puritan Character*, 26.; *idem, Birthpangs*, 147–8.

Arminius an 'enemie of God', advocated the suppression of Arminianism in the Netherlands, sent Calvinist representatives to the Synod of Dort, and suggested a quarantine to prevent the 'infection' from reaching England.[6] James I's Calvinist Archbishop of Canterbury Abbott similarly saw Arminianism as an 'infectious heresy' in condemning Samuel Harsnet and John Overall for expression of Arminian views, holding that the latter 'did infect as many as he could till by sharp rebuke and reproofs he was beaten from the public avowing these fancies'.[7] James I was deeply committed to Trinitarianism, declaring himself orthodox in believing

the three creeds. That of the Apostles, that of the Council of Nice, and that of Athanasius...in that sense, as the ancient Fathers and Councels that made them did understand them: to which three Creeds all the Ministers of England doe subscribe at their Ordination. And I acknowledge also for Orthodoxe all those other formes of Creedes, that either were devised by Counsels or particular Fathers, against such Heresies as most reigned in their times. I reverence and admit the first four generall Counsells as Catholique and orthodoxe: and the said foure generall counsels are acknowledged by our Acts of Parliament, and received as orthodox by our Church.

It was on this basis that in James I's eyes Arminius' successor at Leiden, Vorstius, deserved 'the stake' for questioning the orthodox doctrine of the Trinity in his *Tractatus Theologicus de Deo.*[8]

Significant similarities of doctrine helped to produce assimilation of Arminianism to Catholicism: both stressed works and accepted doubt about one's salvation in contrast to certainty conveyed by grace. And association of Arminianism to Catholicism in the late 1620s and 1630s was fostered by Laudians' stress on the ritual and episcopalian aspects of the church. Sir Walter Earle spoke in Parliament of 'Popery and Arminianism, joining hand in hand'. Francis Rous identified the dangers of the 'sect of Arminians' in 1629 by assaulting 'new paintings...laid on the old face of the whore of Babylon, to make her shew more lovely, and to draw so many suitors to her'. Henry Burton attacked 'Arminian heresyes which doe combine with popery'. William Prynne called Arminian errors 'in truth meer Popery'. Matthew Newcomen declared in *The Craft and Cruelty of the Churches Adversaries* (1643): 'First, bring in Arminian doctrines, then the popish will easily follow'. But the tendency to render all theological divisions into 'polar oppositions' helps to explain the tendency among orthodox Calvinist Protestants in seventeenth-century England to read almost all

---

[6] P. Lake, 'Calvinism and the English Church 1575–1625' in M. Todd (ed.), *Reformation to Revolution* (1995), 179–207; *idem*, 'Anti-popery', 73.

[7] PRO SP 105/95 fo. 9v in Lake, 'Calvinism'.

[8] C. McIlwain (ed.), *The Political Works of James I* (Cambridge, Mass. 1918), 122–3; N. Tyacke, 'Arminianism and English Culture' in A. Duke (ed.), *Britain and the Netherlands*, 7 (The Hague 1981), 94–117, at 96; Jordan, *Toleration*, II, 335–6.

sects taken to oppose the 'true orthodoxy' of strict Calvinism as being openly or covertly Catholic – even in such apparently unpromising cases as that of Quakerism as Catholicism-in-disguise.[9] And the general tendency to pillory new heresies as but 'old heresies revived' reared its head again as powerfully as ever, as when the Calvinist Archbishop Abbot's former chaplain Daniel Featley called his work against the Arminian Richard Montagu *Pelagius redivivus: or, Pelagius Raked out of the Ashes by Arminius and his Scholars*, and when the former delegate at the Synod of Dort, George Carleton, published *An Examination of those Things wherein the Author of the Late Appeal Holdeth the Doctrines of the Pelagians and Arminians to be the Doctrines of the Church of England*.[10]

'Arminianism' was execrated by Calvinists in early seventeenth-century England in the language central to assault on 'heresy' through the centuries.[11] In the reign of Charles I, as the new monarch became an apparent supporter of Arminianism instead of its opponent, the House of Commons' petition against Richard Montagu's *New Gagg for an Old Goose* declared that the opinions of 'Arminius and his sectaries have infested and had brought into great perill the states of the United Provinces' and called for measures to be taken so 'that their infectious and corrupt doctrine may spread itself no further'.[12] Thomas Bedford's 1624 *Luther's Predecessors* attacked Arminianism for having 'infected' some.[13] Sir John Jackson declared in the House of Commons that Archbishop Neile had 'poisoned' his see of Durham by appointing Arminians. Francis Rous' *Oyl of Scorpions* and *The Only Remedy* traced plagues and harvest failures as divine punishments for sins, including Arminianism.[14] Tying such portents to the threat of punishments by God, Burton's 1628 *Israel's Fast* attacked Arminians as traitors 'betraying us into our enemies hands, by making God our enemy'.[15] And for many 'puritans' Arminianism was 'libertine'. William Prynne's 1626 *The Perpetuity of a Regenerate Man's Estate* attacked the

---

[9] Lake, 'Anti-popery' see chapter 0. Earle, *Commons Debates*, 1629, 18–19 in N. Tyacke, *Anti-Calvinists* (Oxford 1987), 135; Rous in Jordan, *Toleration*, II, 125; H. Burton: PRO SP 16/335 fos. 148–9v in Tyacke, *Anti-Calvinists*, 228; Bedford, Prynne: J. Sommerville, *Politics and Ideology in England 1603–40* (1986), 221; M. Newcomen, *The Craft and Cruelty of the Churches Adversaries* (1643), quoted in J. Walter, *Understanding Popular Violence in the English Revolution* (Cambridge 1999), 222–3; Tyacke, 'Arminianism and English Culture', 94–117, at 100; P. Elmer, 'Saints or Sorcerers' in J. Barry et al. (eds.), *Witchcraft in Early Modern Europe* (Cambridge 1996), 145–76.

[10] Lake, 'Calvinism', 196–7.   [11] Tyacke, *Anti-Calvinists, passim*, e.g. 182, 198.

[12] Yates, *Ibis ad Caesarem*, III, 45–6 in Tyacke, *Anti-Calvinists*, 148; Tyacke, 'Arminianism and English Culture'.

[13] Tyacke, *Anti-Calvinists*, 150.

[14] *Commons Debates* 1628, IV, 320–1; Tyacke, *Anti-Calvinists*, 139.

[15] H. Burton, *A Plea*, sig. 3v; H. Burton, *Israel's Fast* (1628), sigs. B2v–B4 in Tyacke, *Anti-Calvinists*, 158.

Arminians as 'carnall, gracelesse, prophane and dissolute persons'. Arminians were declared 'libertines' morally and intellectually for their 'very lives and actions do prove their doctrines'. Their supporters were 'drunken', 'loose, licentious and voluptuous'. Prynne's 1628 *Healthes: Sicknesse* argued that playwrights were now teaching a 'libertine' religion of 'pelagian errors' as the 'empoysoners of all grace'. Thomas Randolph's 1630 play *Aristippus or the Jovial Philosopher* identified Cambridge theologians' support for Arminianism by claiming in a reference to Aristippus, founder of the Cyrenaic school of hedonism, that 'they are all so infected with Aristippus his Arminianism, they can preach no doctrine but sack and red noses'.[16] Here, as Nicholas Tyacke has shown, is a significant part of the background to the terms of the Grand Remonstrance of 1641 which described their opponents as 'Arminians and Libertines' doing the bidding of 'Papists'.[17] English rhetoric was here paralleling that of Contra-Remonstrants in the Netherlands who campaigned against toleration in 1637 by arguing that the town governments of Holland were full of 'libertines, Arminians, Atheists and concealed Jesuits'.[18] And 'Arminianism' and 'Laudianism' were frequently linked not merely to 'libertinism' but also to 'sodomy' and to 'popery'. The Bishop John Atherton's execution for 'sodomy' in 1640 was linked to his Laudian alleged sympathy with 'popery'.[19] As Lake has argued, the accusation of sodomy was central to the early seventeenth-century English literature of anti-popery in which tyranny, popery, and sodomy were linked and counterposed to a godly Protestant commonwealth, and in which alleged 'Arminians' were linked to 'popery'. In Lake's account, the images of Arminianism and Laudianism tending to 'sodomy' and 'libertinism' as to Catholicism were significant in helping to form opposition to the court from a 'puritan' direction, and they help to explain why the English civil wars occurred as what John Morrill has described as 'wars of religion', fought primarily for religious reasons.[20]

In his 1594 *Adversus Thomas Stapletoni Defensionem*, William Whitaker, a Cambridge theologian whose patrons included Archbishop Whitgift and the Earls of Essex and Leicester, declared that

[16] W. Prynne, *The Perpetuitie of a Regenerate Man's Estate* (London 1626), 22–5, 405–8; *God no impostor nor deluder* (London 1629); *The Church of England's Old Antithesis to New Arminianisme* (London 1629); *Healthes: Sicknesse* (London 1628), sigs. B7, D4; *Poetical and Dramatic works by Thomas Randolph* (ed. W. Hazlitt 1875), 10, in Tyacke, 'Arminianism and English Culture', 103–4, 112–13.
[17] *The Constitutional Documents of the Puritan Revolution*, 207; Tyacke, 'Arminianism and English Culture', 116–17.
[18] Israel, *Dutch Republic*, 536, 637; *idem*, 'Intellectual Debate'.
[19] Lake, 'Anti-popery'; Bray, *Homosexuality*, 72.
[20] Morrill, *The Nature of the English Revolution*, 37, also 61–4, 68, 71–2, 81–3.

Bellarmine compares heresy to a plague and rightly. For the plague does not hang about the outward limbs but attacks the heart, immediately poisons it with venom and suddenly destroys him who but a little before was in health; then it spreads a fatal contagion to others also, and...sometimes fills the state itself with whole corpses and funerals. In like manner heresy especially assails the hearts and expels faith from the mind then creeps further and disperses itself over many. If, then, you tender your salvation, approach not near so deadly a pestilence without an antidote or counterpoison'.

Even if supplied with an intellectual antidote, for Whitaker not everyone would find a 'fitting reply' to the arguments of papists or be able to judge their arguments. Therefore 'security' from conversion to Catholicism was to be ensured in part by preventing circulation of Catholic works, and in part by censuring those who doubted that the Pope was the Antichrist. For Whitaker, the Antichrist knew that none would now 'tolerate' any who spoke directly against Christ, as had the heretics of old (the anti-Trinitarians), but since the Antichrist 'must needs be opposite to Christ the same purpose must needs be gained in a more secret manner' by seeming to establish Christ but in fact destroying him through the 'Antichristianism of the papists, who leave indeed the nature of Christ intact, but make away with the offices of Christ and consequently Christ himself'. Thus for the Calvinist Whitaker, the Antichrist had worked in anti-Trinitarians in polar opposition to Christ in the first ages; now papists stood in the same place, seeming to assert Christ as God but, by removing the offices of satisfaction for sin and supporting justification by works, being anti-Trinitarian Antichrist still.[21]

Arminianism and Laudianism were thus anathema as approaching Catholicism in the eyes of a significant number of orthodox Calvinists of the early seventeenth century, while Catholicism itself was the archetype of the sinful: sodomitical, libertine, and diabolical. As Cynthia Herrup has recently shown, the trial of the Earl of Castlehaven in the 1630s, the most famous accusation, trial and execution for sodomy in seventeenth-century England, associated Castlehaven's 'sodomy' directly to his alleged Catholicism.[22] In 1612, Thomas Adams declared as 'essential' to the papacy 'perjury, sodomy, sorcery, homicide, patricide'.[23] In the late sixteenth century, David Lindsay called Catholicism 'a cistern full of sodomy'. William Lithgow asserted 'Lo there is the chastity of the Romish priests who forsooth may not marry and yet miscarry themselves in all abominations, especially in sodomy, which is their continual pleasure and practice'.[24] As Lake has

---

[21] Whitaker, *Adversus Thomas Stapletoni Defensionem* (Cambridge 1594); *idem, Disputation,* 20–1, in Lake, 'Significance', 166–7 and *passim.*
[22] Herrup, *House,* XIV, 14, 133.
[23] T. Becon, *Worckes* (1564), I, 314r in Oldridge, *Devil,* 28; Adams quoted in Oldridge, *Devil,* 28.
[24] Bray, *Homosexuality,* 18–20.

stressed, Protestants such as William Perkins celebrated marriage and held that celibacy was unnatural; they identified celibacy's celebration by Catholics as being like the rest of the idolatrous religion of Catholicism, an attack on Scripture and nature, which therefore led to covert promiscuity and buggery. Ephraim Pagitt declared in his *Heresiography* that Jesuits defended and maintained 'their idolatries and sodomitical uncleanness'.[25]

THE ASSAULT ON 'HERESY' IN THE ENGLISH REVOLUTION 1640–60

Much of the support for the initial fight against the king in the first English Civil War 1642–6 came from Calvinist Presbyterian desire to reform the Church of England in order to remove from it those elements that were seen as tending to 'popery', including the alleged spread of 'Arminianism' and Laudian 'popish' ritual, and to establish strict Calvinist theology and disciplinarian Presbyterian ecclesiology. Committed to the notion that God would punish failure to check the spread of false religion, puritans such as Preston repeatedly cited Gratian's declaration that 'whoever does not prohibit an evil which he could prohibit, commands it'. The Old Testament story of Phinehas killing as idolatrous a pregnant Moabitish woman and so lifting a plague was similarly frequently cited, as in Stephen Marshall's preaching to Parliament in 1642 in celebration that England now had a 'sprinkling of Phinehazzes'.[26] Such Presbyterian Calvinists were thus motivated by their perceived duty to prevent the spread of 'heresy' and 'idolatry' in England, and for many the heresies which then evolved in the years of the Civil Wars and Revolution were horrifying, even if they were to be expected as the explosion of heresies forecast for the period immediately before inauguration of the millennium.[27]

The Presbyterian Calvinist Thomas Edwards' 1646 *Gangraena* is probably the most famous of all assaults on 'heresy' during the English Revolution; it was certainly the single most influential. His book, Edwards declared, was required against heresies as it would be against thieves and witches, in an image in which the poison of heresy for the soul was compared to that of witches to the body:

If I knew a way to be laid by theeves, were it not my part to reveal it, so that travellers might not fall into their hands, ought I to conceal witches, who would conspire the

---

[25] Lake, 'Anti-popery'.

[26] C. Russell, 'Arguments for Religious Unity in England 1530–1650', *Journal of Ecclesiastical History* (1967), 201–26, at 222–3.

[27] I am simply leaving aside here many other causes of the English Civil Wars in concentrating only on those elements that tended most towards polarisation in the religious world-view of some strict Calvinists and their willingness to take up arms against the king. On the themes of consensus, see especially the many important works of Russell, Morrill, and Burgess.

death of the people? Now there is not theft so wicked, nor poyson so pernicious, as abominable Doctrine which tends. . .to overthrow all Christian Religion.[28]

As heresy was 'poison' to Edwards, so it was to Ephraim Pagitt in his 1645 *Heresiography*. To the question whether it 'be lawfull for the Magistrates to use the sword against Hereticks?', Pagitt answered:

Such whose Heresies are blasphemous in doctrine, or dangerous to the State, deserve death. The reason whereof is, because they corrupt the Faith. If such as poyson waters and fountains, at which men and beasts drink, deserve capital punishment, how much more they that as much as in them lyeth, go about to poyson men's souls.[29]

Similar images came from the leading Independent John Owen, who said of the works of the anti-Trinitarian John Biddle that they showed that

the evill is at the doore; there is not a Citty, a Towne, scarce a village in England, where some of this poyson is not poured forth.

As late as the 1650s, Owen declared that Calvin had been right to burn Servetus. For Owen in the 1650s, Socinianism was responsible for the 'flood' of 'scepticism, libertinism, and atheism' now 'broken upon the world' in which nothing was certain, 'nothing unshaken'. Like many other Calvinist Independents, Owen desired 'liberty of conscience' only for those who believed in the Trinity; his influence on the Cromwellian regime was part of the reason that its proclaimed 'liberty of conscience' was always trammelled by commitment to Trinitarianism and the satisfaction.[30]

As heresy was 'poisoning' for Edwards, Pagitt, and Owen, so it was 'pestilential'. Indeed, as is obvious from its title alone, the set of associations and image of heresy as 'disease' we have met many times in medieval anti-heretical literature gave the overriding image to Edwards' *Gangraena*. Edwards declared that every taking of a town or city by the Parliamentary army was 'a further spreading over this kingdom the gangrene of heresy and error'.[31] Edwards warned against going to sectaries' conventicles: 'Those private meetings are the nurseries of all errours and heresies, very pest houses'.[32] This was being written by Edwards in 1646. In 1644–5, there was a major outbreak of the plague in Bristol, causing the deaths of nearly a

---

[28] Edwards, *Gangraena*, 179. On the importance of heresy as poison and plague to intolerance in the English Revolution see crucially, albeit briefly, B. Worden, 'Toleration and the Cromwellian Protectorate' in W. Sheils (ed.), *Persecution and Toleration* (Oxford 1984) and also, brilliantly, Hughes in Loewenstein and Marshall, *Heresy*, forthcoming.

[29] Pagitt, *Heresiography* (London 1645), Epistle Dedicatory.

[30] Owen discussed in Worden, 'Toleration', 205. Cf. also J. Coffey's essay in Loewenstein and Marshall, *Heresy* (forthcoming).

[31] Edwards, *Gangraena*, I, III, 80.   [32] Edwards, *Gangraena*, 173.

quarter of the city's population by September 1645, while Oxford, Stratford-upon-Avon, Chester, Somerset, and Devon, saw major outbreaks of the plague and opening of pest-houses. That heresy was like a plague spreading over the land was a deeply fearful image in 1646, and that punishment of heresy was required to prevent the further development of the plague as God's punishment was a declaration with very deep immediate resonance.[33]

The Presbyterian Ephraim Pagitt's campaign in his 1645 *Heresiography* to 'cleanse' the city of London of 'heresy' suggested methods inherited from late medieval conceptions of heresy as a 'plague', and methods like those being applied against the plague itself. For Pagitt, in his dedication to the Lord Mayor, 'heresy being like the plague or pestilence which usually seizeth first upon the metropolis' required immediate action in London against the growing evil of 'this infectious and contagious malady'. Pagitt pointed out that they had engaged in a covenant to 'endeavour the extirpation of Popery, Prelacy, Superstition, Heresies, Schism, Prophaneness' and everything contrary to 'sound Doctrine' lest 'we partake in other men's sin, and thereby in danger to receive of their plagues'. He declared that allowing heretics had brought God's punishments by 'fire from heaven'. He praised the magistrates' great care in shutting up the sick, perfuming the streets, making fires and praying to God about the plague 'of all diseases most infectious', but then added that 'the plague of Heresie is greater, and you are now in more danger than when you buried five thousand a week'. Having described magistrates incarcerating the sick in pest-houses and setting wardens to keep the 'whole from the sick', he argued that they should similarly prevent heretics and sectaries gathering together in conventicles 'to infect one another'.[34]

Such notions of the infection, plague, and poison of heresy were widespread and extremely powerful among Calvinist Presbyterians in these years. The Solemn League and Covenant listed 'heresy' and 'schism' among the 'plagues' in committing those who took it to establish the nearest conjunction and 'uniformity' in religion and 'confession of faith' possible, and to endeavour the 'extirpation' of

Popery, prelacy...Superstition, Heresie, Schism, Prophaneness, and whatsoever shall be found to be contrary to sound Doctrine, and the power of Godlinesse; lest we partake in men's sins, and thereby be in danger to receive of their plagues.

---

[33] Porter, *Great Plague*, 28–30.
[34] Pagitt, *Heresiography*, Epistle Dedicatory; Edwards, *Gangraena*, 43–4. Edwards quoted Augustine at great length against the Donatist schism, and drew many direct comparisons between the sectaries of his day and Augustine's description of the Donatists.

In many works, the Baptists' act of baptism was imaged as spreading 'contagious diseases' rife among 'promiscuous anabaptists'.[35] When the Quaker Edward Billing was attacked by a mob, it was argued that there was no need to

> trouble...a magistrate with him. Dash out his brains...they are like dogs in time of plague. They are to be killed as they go up and down the streets, that they do not infect.[36]

Socinianism was similarly anathematised. According to the Presbyterian Matthew Poole in the 1653 *The Blasphemer Slain*, 'all Heresies lead to Hell' and 'none are more dangerous nor infectious than such as assault the Sacred Trinity'. For Poole, Socinianism was 'that hydra of Blasphemies' spreading the 'corruption of the people'. Francis Cheynell's 1643 *Rise, Growth and Danger of Socinianisme*, printed by order of the Committee of the House of Commons, attacked the introduction of 'damnable heresies' such as Socinianism, a 'pestilent heresy...which corrupts the very vitalls of Church and State'. The English Arminians and popish Socinians were declared 'such monsters' as are not to be found in all Africa'. The opening sentence of the book declared:

> The Socinians have raked many sinkes, and dunghills, for those ragges and that filth, wherewith they have patched up and defiled that leprous body which they account a compleat body of pure Religion.

For Cheynell, Socinianism had 'infected' Poland and Transylvania and then Italy with a 'monstrous body of errours and blasphemies'. Citing at various points the writings against heresies and schisms of Eusebius, Epiphanius, Tertullian, Augustine, and Optatus, Cheynell lauded the execution of Servetus as needed to 'kill the Viper'. He argued that Socinians' attempt to convert Jews and Turks to Christianity by not pressing the Trinity was to 'deny a prime article of our Christian faith', while Socinian denial of Christ's satisfaction 'overthrew the foundation of our faith'. Socinus had written several 'pestilent books, in which he hath most cunningly vented his poyson'; he had thereby been able 'to infect a people that were too willing to be infected'. Chapter 4 of Cheynell's book was entitled: 'Whether England

---

[35] A. Houghton, *An Antidote against Hen Haggars Poysonous Pamphlet* (London 1658), 241; T. Bakewell, *The Dippers Plunged* (London 1650), 7; J. Goodwin, *Catabaptism* (1655), 56, in J. F. McGregor, 'The Baptists: Fount of all Heresy' in B. Reay and J. F. McGregor (eds.), *Radical Religion in the English Revolution* (Oxford 1984), 42.

[36] Friends' House MS Portfolio i. 20, quoted (from the work of B. Reay) in K. Thomas, *Man and the Natural World* (Oxford 1983), 47.

Hath Been, or Is Still in Danger to be Farther Infected with Socinianisme'; the head of each verso page in the chapter simply bore the words: 'England infected'.

It was with the 'poisonous, pestilential heresy' of Socinianism that Cheynell associated the 'Latitudinarian' Anglican William Chillingworth, author of the eirenic *The Religion of Protestants*, which stressed the minimal fundamentals of Christianity and redefined heresy and schism. Indeed, for Cheynell, Socinians, Arminians, and Chillingworth were the children of 'Anabaptism' in its denial of the full satisfaction by Christ who had been 'poysoned' by an 'Arminian Libertinism' promising salvation to heretics and had opened the door to 'Atheistical Libertinisme'.[37] Completing the set of assimilations of Anabaptism, anti-Trinitarianism and atheism traced in Chapter 7, for Cheynell Anabaptism was itself 'atheism', as was indicated by the title of his fifth chapter: 'Shewes that the Famous Atheists (Anabaptists and Sectaries)...have been Raised or Encouraged by the Doctrines and Practices of the Arminians'. This chapter complained that Socinian-influenced 'men are turned Atheists' since God had taken 'unkindly' their denial of Christ's deity and 'had given them over to that cursed Atheism'. Cheynell recognised that Chillingworth did not take the positions that he was attacking, but condemned Chillingworth for not condemning those positions, alleging that one partook of the sins one failed to prevent. When Chillingworth died, Cheynell wrote another work, *Chillingworth Novissima*, in which he declared the desirability of burying Chillingworth's book as well as his body, to prevent it from 'infecting' others. Locke was repeatedly to recommend Chillingworth's *Religion of Protestants* as teaching children how to reason well; he took a series of notes on Chillingworth's tolerationist definitions of heresy and schism in 1682 and 1696, and was always strongly aware of the ways in which arguments about toleration in the 1680s and 1690s were replaying arguments from earlier periods. He labelled Cheynell's book the 'worst book ever written'.[38]

In 1648, at Presbyterian instigation but without significant Independent opposition, Parliament passed the first of two blasphemy statutes providing execution for many beliefs, and imprisonment for other beliefs, such as 'Arminian' belief in free will. Again assimilating anti-Trinitarianism and atheism, the death penalty was provided for any who argued that there was no God – atheists – *and* for a set of anti-Trinitarian beliefs such as that the

---

[37] F. Cheynell, *The Rise, Growth and Danger of Socinianisme* (London 1643), Epistle Dedicatory, 1–7, 13, 19–20, 39, 54–5, 67, 72; Trevor-Roper, *Catholics*, 187.

[38] J. Locke, *Some Thoughts Concerning Education* (Oxford 1989), ed. J. F. Yolton and J. Yolton, 240, 320; Marshall, *Locke*, 11, 94, 372; MS Locke d 10, 71, 157, 170.

'three are not one Eternal God, or that. . .Christ is not equal with the Father', or that the bodies of men were not resurrected. This law was passed partly in response to the anti-Trinitarianism of Paul Best and John Biddle. Few publicly supported Biddle or Best, whose works were burned, and whose persons were imprisoned for many years, in both cases probably contributing to their early deaths. Parliament condemned the Racovian Catechism, licensed by Milton, as 'blasphemous and scandalous', and it was burned in 1652.[39]

Although they had themselves taken up arms against their king and his ministers in the name of religion, revolutionary Presbyterian anti-heretical and anti-schismatic writers such as Edwards and Pagitt viewed themselves as having taken up arms primarily in order to crush the heresies of Arminianism and 'popery' spreading in England, and with no sense of irony they restated the link between 'heresy' and 'schism' on the one hand and 'rebellion' and 'sedition' on the other. Ephraim Pagitt's *Heresiography* declared that heretics were 'dangerous to the state'. Pagitt opposed preachers vending 'strange doctrine, tending to faction, sedition, and blasphemy'. Edwards' *Gangraena* attacked the 'sectaries' design and practise not to be only corrupting religion. . .but to be against magistracy and civil government. . .bringing an anarchy and confusion into church and state'. Presbyterians' arguments were in this sense close to the arguments of the Anglican Royalists against whom they had taken up arms to fight. In 1648, a Royalist declared that 'heresy is always the forerunner of rebellion'. *Eikon Basilike*, the most widely circulated work of the Revolution and published in more copies than the combined corpus of Hobbes, Harrington, Milton, and the Levellers, declared that rulers should never neglect 'a speedy reforming and effectuall Suppressing [of] Errours and Schimes' caused by 'seditious spirits'. It declared in a phrase whose condensed resonances are revealing that 'rebels' were 'Hereticall in point of Loyalty'. Alexander Ross's *Pansebia, or a View of all Religions* – issued in many editions into the Restoration – declared similarly:

Diversity of Religions beget envy, malice, seditions, factions, rebellions, contempt of Superiours, treacheries, innovations, disobedience, and many more mischiefs, which pull down the heavy Judgements of God upon that State or Kingdom, where contrary religions are allowed.[40]

---

[39] *Journals of the House of Commons* VII, 113–14, discussed in D. Loewenstein, 'Treason against God and State' in S. Dobranski and J. Rumrich (eds.), *Milton and Heresy*, 180; Hill, *World*, 166–7.

[40] Edwards, *Gangraena*, in Wootton, 'Leveller Democracy', 418; A. Ross *[Pansebia,] Or A View of all Religions* (4th edn 1664), 506, quoted in Katz, *Philosemitism*, 161.

NAYLER AND THE QUAKERS

The most substantial new 'schismatic' sect or 'heresy' born in the English Revolution was that of the Quakers. Like previous 'heresies' and 'schisms' through the centuries, it was quickly associated with allegedly similar heresies through the ages, and assaulted as deserving punishment in terms derived from anti-heretical and anti-schismatic literature: execution, banishment, or incarceration as segregation. Associations of heresy and schism with plague and poison, with evil-doing, with treason and witchcraft, and, more briefly, with 'libertinism', were all voiced in the extensive Parliamentary debates of 1656 over the Quaker James Nayler, whose understanding of the indwelling Christ in him, and whose entry riding into Bristol on Easter Sunday in imitation of Christ, convinced many that he was claiming to be God himself. Major-General Boteler was clear that magistrates had a duty to honour Christ; and to be 'a terror unto evil works'; they were not to 'punish murder and witchcraft, and let greater offences go, as heresies and blasphemy' which came 'under the same enumeration'.[41] For Bedford, heresies in the gospel were 'enumerated under the works of the flesh, and so to be punished by the magistrate'.[42] Many spoke of Nayler as infectious. Sir William Strickland urged that 'Such a leper ought to be separated from the conversation of all people'. Major-General Disprowe declared that 'it is such a leprosy that ought to be shut out from all others', and argued that a magistrate was 'to take heed that such persons do not infect others'. For Major-General Kelsey, who argued for Nayler's execution, Quakers were pernicious, 'spreading, infectious, and contagious'. For Sir Gilbert Pickering, 'Quakerism is as infectious as the plague' and men and women were to be kept away from Nayler. Even Lord Strickland, who argued against Nayler's execution as a blasphemer, wanted him shut up 'as one that has the plague upon him'. Nayler's final of a series of punishments was indeed to be shut up in perpetuity in prison, where he was to be kept from 'the society of all people', following punishments including severe whippings of up to 310 lashes, having his tongue bored through, and having his forehead branded with a B for blasphemer.[43]

Others, such as Mr Robinson, declared that they wanted to prevent Nayler from spreading his 'poisonous principles', while Major-General Goffe argued that Nayler had corrupted and 'poison[ed]'.[44] Many speakers were clear not merely that Nayler deserved death but that if they did not punish him, it would be a national sin deserving a 'national punishment' and 'bring blood upon this nation'.[45] For Nathaniel Bacon, Nayler's

---

[41] T. Burton, *The Diary of Thomas Burton* (London 1828), I, 26.   [42] *Diary*, 122.
[43] *Diary*, 35–6, 56, 71–2, 124, 155, 158.   [44] *Diary*, 77, 110.   [45] *Diary*, 34, 55, 71.

anti-Trinitarianism deserved the 'highest punishment' as destroying 'the very foundation of our faith and religion'.[46] When some argued for a lesser punishment than death, others replied that they would need to 'wash my hands of the guilt of giving less than death'.[47] For many of the speakers, Nayler deserved an excruciating death. Lord Whitlock recommended punishment as in the 'like case' of Lord Rochester's cook, who had been boiled to death: such was the punishment under English law until 1547 for poisoners, as worse than other murderers. Mr Bacon agreed. Many focused on Nayler's 'blasphemy' or 'horrid blasphemy' (saying that he was God), heresy (anti-Trinitarianism) and idolatry (promoting the worship of a creature), drawing Mosaic precedents for the execution of such individuals by stoning, and precedents from treason for hanging, drawing, and quartering.[48]

Participants in these debates frequently mentioned that Quakers undermined magistracy and ministry, and that Nayler needed to be punished to prevent the spread of Quakerism and challenge to the civil peace. Colonel Briscoe argued that Quakers were 'destructive to human society...Do not they all hold against the essence of Government'. It is important to stress that Quakers were seen as challenging simultaneously the entire structures of hierarchy as they refused hat honour, addressed others as 'thou' and 'thee', and rejected gender hierarchy in favour of the spirit or inner light that legitimated women preaching and prophesying to men. The Anglican Thomas Fuller's 1655 *Church History* spelled out the danger that Anglicans perceived in verbal refusal of recognition of social superiority:

We maintain that Thou from superiors to inferiors is proper, as a sign of command...but from inferiors to superiors, if proceeding from...affectation [hath] a tang of contempt...Such who now quarrel at the honour will hereafter question the wealth of others.

Against Nayler, one accusation was thus unsurprisingly that 'there is much talk by some of your friends of dividing up men's estates, and having all things common'. Quakers were seen as attacking ecclesiastical authority as it was reconstructed under Cromwell by their opposition to tithes, priests, and preachers in favour of that 'inner light' and prophesying. They were seen as attacking the entire structure of political authority by their opposition to oaths and their more general questioning of both magistracy and the law.[49]

It is worth stressing that Quakers trumpeted their disapproval of others' beliefs and practices, verbally attacking their forms of worship as antichristian, interrupting services and sermons, cursing those who defended

---

[46] *Diary*, 133.   [47] *Diary*, 108.   [48] *Diary*, 58, 68; Coffey, *Persecution*, 154.
[49] J. Nayler, *A True Discoverie of Faith* (1655), 13–14 in Moore, *The Light Within Their Consciences* (Pennsylvania 2000), 64; Hill, *World*, 247.

'idle worship and vain praise', and admonishing magistrates to act against them. William Simpson recorded going naked 'as a sign' through Colchester, Cambridge, London and other towns to show to Cromwell and his Parliament and priests 'how God would strip them of their power, and that they should be naked as he was, and should be stripped of their benefices'.[50] Quakers in Ireland challenged other ministers to public debate, questioning scriptural warrant for infant baptism and 'for singing druids experience in rhyme and metre, calling it an ordinance of God'. More than 300 instances of Quakers disturbing ministers in the 1650s ended up in the courts, and in 1654 Oliver Cromwell issued a 'Proclamation Prohibiting the Disturbing of Ministers' in order to try to prevent such disturbances of the peace.[51] There is no question, then, that the Quakers' challenge to the established hierarchies of the day in state, church, and family and their disruption of others' worship were important in causing hostility and the conviction that they should be punished. But it is as important to register that every one of these social and political issues was seen by those hostile to them as a direct consequence of Quakers' 'heretical' and 'schismatic' beliefs. Ephraim Pagitt's *Heresiography* called the Quakers a 'desperate, furious, bloody kennel, who in the generall liberty...of Hereticall, Atheisticall professions, have infected many innocent harmless' souls. They were an 'upstart branch of the Anabaptists', who worked to 'poyson the Scriptures'. It was on this basis that Pagitt's text recommended their execution. It was for 'blasphemy' that many others called for the most serious punishment. We need to avoid a proleptic secularisation in our treatment of Quakers and of responses to them: above all else, Nayler was to be punished because of his religious views and the danger of 'infection' that they posed.[52]

Only one contribution to the entire debate over many days on Nayler's punishment was made by Colonel Anthony Ashley Cooper, at this date a member of Cromwell's Council of State, and later first Earl of Shaftesbury and patron and friend of Locke. He argued against Nayler's execution and questioned whether Nayler's belief was indeed 'horrid blasphemy'. He further argued that instead of reducing Quaker converts by killing Nayler, this would 'lay a foundation for them', as martyrdom would encourage others to adopt his beliefs, thus stating what was to be a central tolerationist

[50] Cressy, *Travesties*, ch. 15.
[51] P. Kilroy, *Protestant Dissent and Controversy in Ireland 1660–1714* (Cork 1994), 84–5; B. Reay, 'Quakerism and Society' in J. F. McGregor and B. Reay, *Radical Religion in the English Revolution* (Oxford 1984), 157; R. Baxter, *One Sheet Against the Quakers* (1657), 4, in Moore, *Light*, 119. The Baptist convert to Quakerism Denis Hollister attacked the Baptists as seed of the bondwomen in *The Skirts of the Whore Discovered* and in *The Harlot's Veil Removed*: Moore, *Light*, 90–1.
[52] Pagitt, *Heresiography* (sixth edition, 1662), 257, Epistle Dedicatory. Cf. Moore, *Light*, 55.

argument in the 1680s and 1690s. However, Cooper did not at this point argue for toleration of Nayler and the Quakers, but rather for measures other than execution in order to 'suppress' the growth of Quakers, as they were indeed dangerous and becoming numerous, and he recommended Nayler's imprisonment so that he could not 'spread his leprosy'. In the 1650s, Locke, of low church Anglican or Presbyterian church background, was shocked and horrified by Nayler's views, recording that England had become a 'Bedlam' and that Quakers were mad, having overheated their brains by keeping on their hats. As we saw in Chapter 3, in the first three versions of his 1667 'Essay on Toleration', probably written at Shaftesbury's behest, Locke was to argue that if Quakers became numerous and thus dangerous, they were to be suppressed on the grounds of the civil peace. It seems likely that Shaftesbury probably found it as difficult as Locke to reach the argument of the fourth and final draft of that 1667 'Essay', which urged toleration even for Quakers.[53]

Nayler was far from the only Quaker attacked and punished in the English Revolution against a background of accusations that they infected and poisoned others. The Irish Minister Claudius Gilbert decried them as having 'infected divers of our citizens' in works such as *A Sovereign Antidote Against Sinful Errors, the Epidemical Plague of These Latter Days* (1658).[54] The courts in Devon and Cornwall in the 1650s ordered watches set up on highways and bridges 'for the preventing of this great contagion, that infects almost every corner of this Nation'.[55] Thomas Jenner's *Quakerism Anatomised and Confuted* (1670) attacked the 'spreading gangrene of Quakerism in the Kingdom', most notably attacking as 'heretical' their opposition to the doctrine of the Trinity of one God and three persons.[56]

And in the years of the English Revolution, as Peter Elmer has shown, Quaker heresy and infectiousness was very often linked with witchcraft, as heresy and witchcraft had frequently been linked throughout the centuries since medieval Waldensians were declared witches and heretics. As late as his autobiography in the 1690s, the Presbyterian Richard Baxter declared that 'when the Quakers first rose here, their Societies began like Witches, with Quaking and Vomiting, and infecting others, with breathing on them'.

---

[53] *Diary*; Marshall, *Locke*; Worden, 'Toleration' associates Cooper with several significant *politiques* who were said to represent the moderate view in these debates; they included also the Anglican Latitudinarian Matthew Hale. The Strasburg magistrates imprisoned the Anabaptist Melchior Hoffman for many years 'so that he may not do any more harm to others': in L. J. Abray, 'The Limits of Magisterial Tolerance in Strasburg' in Grell and Scribner, *Tolerance*, 106.

[54] Kilroy, *Protestant Dissent*, 140.   [55] Reay, 'Quakerism', 157.

[56] Thomas Jenner, *Quakerism Anatomised and Confuted* (1670).

Accusations that Quakers were witches and used the power of witches to 'seduce' others to their 'heresies' were legion in the 1650s. The Quaker leader George Fox was often alleged to have converted his followers by bewitching them, using magic objects or the power of 'fascination'. Many Quakers were subjected to the trials used to test if individuals were witches, such as 'pricking' the skin. A significant number of Quakers were prosecuted and imprisoned for witchcraft in the 1650s. Particularly prominent among those accused of witchcraft were Quaker women. Quaker works were condemned as diabolically inspired, and Quaker meetings were sometimes depicted as witches' sabbaths; at many points, Quakers were diabolised in the Protectorate Press.[57]

HERESY, MONSTROSITY AND GENDER IN THE ANTI-HERETICAL LITERATURE OF THE ENGLISH REVOLUTION

The set of associations traced in Chapters 5 to 7 between heresy and monstrous births, disordered imaginations, and lust, based in part on an understanding of the role of the maternal imagination articulated on the bases of Aristotle, Hippocrates, and Empedocles, received widespread circulation in Britain and its colonies.[58] In England, discussion of such 'monsters' occurred within widespread commitment to the understanding of 'portents' and 'prodigies' through 'divination' and 'prophecy', as documented by Daston and Park, Capp, Firth, Friedman, and others. Supporting this commitment was a further commitment to the extensiveness and frequency of God's immediate interventions in the operations of the world.[59] It was tellingly in the turbulent decade of the 1640s that the associations of monstrous births and heresy reached their peak in England and its colonies, in associations of heresy and disordered female imaginations. In a case analysed by Tom Laquer and Phyllis Mack, among others, in Massachusetts, Governor John Winthrop's tellingly titled *A Short Story of the Rise, Reign and Ruine of the Antinomians, Familists, and Libertines* recorded of the antinomian midwife

---

[57] Elmer, 'Saints', 145–79; *Certain Passages*, 9–16 February 1655 in Worden, 'Toleration'.

[58] M. H. Huet, *Monstrous Imagination* (Harvard 1993); P. Boucé, 'Imagination, Pregnant Women and Monsters in Eighteenth Century England and France' in G. S. Rousseau and R. Porter (eds.), *Sexual Underworlds of the Enlightenment* (Manchester 1987).

[59] Daston and Park, *Wonders*; B. Capp, *The Fifth-Monarchy Men* (London 1972); Firth, *Apocalyptic Tradition*; Jerome Friedman, *Miracles and the Pulp Press During the English Revolution* (London 1993). Even as late as the 1740s, by which time the belief was under significant attack, the *Gentleman's Magazine* contained no less than 92 articles on monstrous births due to the imagination of pregant women, and strongly associated these with women's insatiable sexual desire. Boucé has indicated the strength and currency of such beliefs until the late eighteenth century. Cf now also M. Fissel, *Vernacular Bodies*, (Oxford 2004).

Anne Hutchinson, expelled from Massachusetts for preaching heretical doctrine, that

Mistress Hutchinson being big with child, and growing towards the time of her labour...she brought forth not one...but 30 monstrous births or thereabouts at once; some of them bigger, some lesser, some of one shape, some of another...none of them...of human shape...looke as she had vented mishapen opinions, so she must bring forth deformed monsters; and as about 30 opinions in number, so many monsters.

Here, then, two notions were being joined by Winthrop – that the mother's disordered, heretical imagination had effected the foetus, and that God had signalled heresies to the world by the example of a monstrous birth, a prodigy of warning and punishment given to discourage heresy in the community. While these accounts usually stressed the primary or exclusive role in the deforming of the imagination of the mother, fathers' imaginations were also at times invoked, and in this case her husband was then also questioned 'in the church for divers monstrous errors'. Hutchinson's friend Mary Dyer, who later returned to London and converted to Quakerism, suffered a stillbirth; John Winthrop had the body excavated in order to prove from its 'deformity' that Dyer was a heretic, and reported this in accounts reprinted many times in the 1640s in London as well as Massachusetts. The Reverend John Elliott offered his further testimony to its truth in a letter to the Presbyterian Richard Baxter in 1660, blaming 'a great fomenting of those horrid opinions being the mother' of a 'creature' who was 'a woman, a fish, a bird, & beast all woven together'. Of both Hutchinson and Dyer, Winthrop recorded that they had 'in the time of the height of the Opinions' produced 'out of their wombs, as before they had out of their braines, such monstrous births'.[60]

Such ideas of heresy and monstrous births were widely circulated in England in the 1640s. *Strange News from Scotland* (1647) described a monster born to Baptist parents, and had that monster explicity declare that 'I am deformed for the sin of my parents', a sin identified as the desire provoked by 'heretical factious fellows' to 'see the utter ruin and subversion of all church and state government'. A local Anglican preacher John Locke recorded in *A Strange and Lamentable Accident That Happened Lately at Mears Ashby in Northamptonshire* (1642) that when in the beginning of Elizabeth's reign 'Moore and Geoffrey, two of the devil's agents, published their prodigious and heretical tenets, to the allurement of many faithful and constant believers. The year after were many monstrous births'. Mary Wilmore was said to have rejected the Anglican Church in the 1640s, saying

---

[60] T. Laquer, *Making Sex* (Harvard 1990), 122; Mack, *Visionary Women*, 40–3; D. Hall (ed.), *The Antinomian Controversy 1636–38* (Wesleyan 1968), 214.

she would rather 'my child should be born without a head than to have a head to be signed with the sign of the cross', and 'it pleased God about a month later, she was accordingly delivered of a monster...a child without a head'.[61]

Monstrosity in 'opinions' and monstrosity in 'breeding' were part of the accusations against Hutchinson; these accusations also involved further accusations very often combined with such alleged 'monstrosity – the infection and the seduction of others – in ways that drew these together with monstrosity in 'breeding'. Conventional deeply misogynist attitudes about female sexuality informed images of heresy; images of heresy then further reinforced those attitudes. Hutchinson was not merely depicted as a 'monster' in her opinions; she was also depicted as causing the 'infection of many' by her speech, as Thomas Shepherd put it, and she was said by Cotton Mather to be possessed of a capacity to 'seduce' others which he associated with the verbal skills of the 'first mother'. For Mather, Hutchinson was thereby the 'breeder and nourisher' of errors in the community. Shepherd similarly described her as using her fluent tongue 'to sowe her seed in us'. As Lisa Jardine, Barbara Kamensky and others have argued, the tongue was 'the specifically female sexual instrument', 'throughout' the literature of the period; as Jardine puts it, we 'find a willingness to slide provocatively from one sense to another – scolding = active use of the female tongue = female sexuality = female penis'. Jardine has emphasised that a woman's tongue as her organ of speech was repeatedly imaged as involved in an inversion of the appropriate generative act, and, like most inversions, partook of the associations it inverted. But even for men the tongue was viewed as a problematic member, as unruly, poisonous, and libertine, and compared often to the penis as directed by lusts rather than by reason. Many Christian writers spoke of the tongue as the 'wilde member', the 'unruly member', and 'the viper', and depicted it as spreading poison, including Bishop John Abernethy in *The Poysonous Tongue* (1622) and Richard Allestree in the 1674 *The Government of the Tongue*. Many compared it directly to the phallus, as did John Bulwer's 1649 *Pathomyatomia*, and the 1664 *Microcosmographia*; the comparison was usually one which emphasised that both were moved by lusts. So strong was the identification of 'tongue' and 'yard' or penis, that when the clitoris was rediscovered in the late sixteenth century, and depicted as a miniature penis, it was called the 'little tongue'.[62]

---

[61] All quoted and discussed in Jerome Friedman, *Miracles*, 50–6, 257.
[62] C. Mazzio, 'The Sins of the Tongue' in D. Hillman and C. Mazzio (eds.), *The Body in Parts* (New York 1997), 52–79; K. Park, 'The Rediscovery of the Clitoris' in *idem, Body*; B. Kamensky, *Governing the Tongue* (Oxford 1997), 75–8; L. Jardine, *Still Harping on Daughters* (1983), 121.

Uncontrolled speech was thus problematic for men, and associated with lust, and doubly problematic for women, and associated both with lust and with an inappropriate claim to speak. 'Heretical' speech was a *locus classicus* of uncontrolled speech. Hutchinson's speech was associated by her anti-heretical opponents in an image we have by now repeatedly met in anti-heretical literature with alleged support for the 'promiscuous and filthie cominge togeather of men and Woemen without Distinction or Relation of Marriage'.[63] Winthrop spoke of Hutchinson's 'infection', and 'seduction', and of women catching their husbands in heresy 'as by an Eve', and of how

as it is said of the Harlots dealing with the young man, Prov 7.21 with much faire speech they caused them to yeeld, with the flattering of their lips they forced them.

For Winthrop, in a structure of explanation about the relationship between right believing and right acting that we earlier saw in the anti-heretical thought of Isidore of Seville, their opinions had made them be 'very loose and degenerate in their practises (for these Opinions will certainly produce a filthy life by degrees)'.[64]

The attack on heresy as monstrous, infecting and seductive was thus associated with an attack on female speech as 'seductive' and 'infecting'. Women's speech was regularly associated with the spreading of poison, a notion we have seen repeatedly in anti-heretical literature. A ballad of 1638 was revealingly titled *The Anatomy of a Woman's Tongue, Divided in Five Parts: a Medicine, a Poison, a Serpent, Fire, and Thunder*. Before the Civil Wars and Revolution, conduct books, marriage manuals, and proverbs combined to stress that silence was the 'best ornament of women'. These texts particularly emphasised that women were to avoid 'discourse of state matters' and 'high points of divinity'.[65] The English Revolution of 1640–60, however, involved many women prophets, petitioners, pamphleteers, rioters, and attack by these on the authority of the king, the episcopal Church of England, and mainstream Presbyterianism and conservative Independency. Phyllis Mack has pointed to the significant proportion of female Quaker prophets, numbering over 300 in the years of the Revolution. Keith Thomas has stressed that women joined the Quakers in large numbers because the Quakers offered greater spiritual equality. Quakers allowed women to be preachers, and Dorothy Ludlow has pointed to women preachers and prophets among Baptists, Quakers, and Fifth Monarchists. Women petitioned Parliament in 1649 and claimed their 'interest in Christ, equal unto men'; and

---

[63] Kamensky, *Governing*, 75–8.   [64] Hall (ed.), *Antinomian*, 205–6, 216.
[65] Jardine, *Harping*, 121; L. Gowing, *Domestic Dangers* (Oxford 1996); D. Freist, 'The King's Crown is the Whore of Babylon: Politics, Gender and Communication in Mid-Seventeenth Century England', *Gender and History* (1995), 457–81.

7,000 Quaker women petitioned as 'hand-maids of the Lord' speaking against 'the Antichristian law and oppression of tithes' in 1659. Such women may have used a rhetoric declaring that they were weaker vessels, stressing the indwelling Holy Spirit rather than their status as female speakers, but they also proclaimed their equal capacity to speak as women with an equal interest in Christ, and their actions in speaking were radical even when their rhetoric was not.[66]

To Presbyterians and to almost all Independents or Congregationalists, groups such as Quakers, Baptists, and Fifth Monarchists in which women were prophets and preachers were 'heretical' and 'schismatic', and the prevalence of women in them served further to associate 'heresy' with false 'female' claims to 'inner inspiration' and with the inappropriate speaking of those who were said, as women, to need to be silent. Quaker women's preaching was declared by J. Miller in *Antichrist in Man* in 1655 as a 'monstrous' practice and 'against nature'. A 1641 print *A Discovery of Six Women Preachers* represented four women dancing around a topless sister; the same image was used in the same year to illustrate a pamphlet about prostitutes, the *Sisters of the Scabards Holiday*. The text itself claimed to have discovered women who taught that those husbands who would not obey their wives could be abandoned. Quaker women who accompanied James Nayler on his entry into Bristol in 1656 were examined as being either 'witches or whores'.[67] A full decade earlier, the London aldermen and common council had sent a delegation to the House of Commons in 1646 to complain of 'private meetings of Women Preachers', 'petticoat preachers', and 'apron apostles', and Parliament had arrested and interrogated some women preachers.[68] Thomas Edwards' anti-heretical 1646 *Gangraena* was thus one work among many typing heresy as a female disorder in attacking the preacher Katherine Chidley's 'unnatural' vociferousness for speaking with 'a great deal of violence' against ministers and for being 'so talkative and clamorous'. For Edwards in *Gangraena*, Chidley was spreading heretical 'poison'. Edwards moreover spoke of 'some women in our times, who keep constant lectures' wrongly 'taking upon them to preach'. Edwards attacked an Anabaptist 'shee-sectary' who allegedly proclaimed herself as good as

[66] K. Thomas, 'Women and the Civil War Sects', *Past and Present* (1958), 42–62; Mack, *Visionary Women*; D. Ludlow, 'Shaking Patriarchy's Foundations: Sectarian Women in England 1641–1700' in R. Greaves (ed.), *Triumph Over Silence* (Connecticut 1984); P. Crawford, 'The Challenges to Patriarchy: How Did the Revolution Affect Women?' in J. Morrill (ed.), *Revolution and Restoration* (1992), 112–28.

[67] J. Miller, *Antichrist in Man* (1655), 27, quoted in Reay, *Quakers*, 58, 69; T. Williams, 'Polemical Prints of the English Revolution' in L. Gent and N. Llewellen (eds.), *Renaissance Bodies* (1990), 101; Watts, *Dissenters*, 81; Crawford, 'Challenges to Patriarchy', 122.

[68] *Journals of the House of Commons* (1803), 4, 407, in Ludlow, 'Shaking Patriarchy's Foundations', 93 and 97.

Christ, and Mrs Attaway, the Baptist 'mistress of all the shee-preachers in Coleman Street', whom he alleged to have commended Milton's 1644 *Doctrine and Discipline of Divorce* and to have declared it useful for 'she had an unsanctified husband' and then to have promptly eloped with 'another woman's husband'. As Rachel Trubowitz has put it,

> Sectarian dissent is for Edwards a form of loud and unruly female discourse, and the figure of the woman preacher a symbol of the monstrous world turned upside down that the sectaries hoped to create.[69]

It is unsurprising, then, that for Edwards, declaring the need for magistrates to act against heresy, it was disruption of the family that served as image and justification for punishment of heresy: private Christians were to protest to magistrates 'how their Wives and children are stolen from them, and taken away against their wills; how they have no command of their servants, no quiet in their families'. For Edwards,

> If any persons should go about to steal from us our children, sons and daughters to carry them over beyond seas, and that in all parishes Children were taken away... what a cry there would be...Now behold there are worse spirits abroad then those, that go up and down from City to Country...to steal away our Wives, Children, Servants, and to carry them to worse places then New Plantations, namely to Hell.[70]

HERETICAL AND SCHISMATIC SECTS AS 'LIBERTINE' AND 'SODOMITICAL'

The discourse of heretical and schismatic 'monstrosity' in the English Revolution was thus one which drew upon long-standing anathematisation of heretics and schismatics as 'monsters', and did so against the background of a related series of attacks on the lower order's claim of authority as 'monstrous', on the undesirability of 'unruly' heretical male speech, and of a generalised attack on female speech and alleged challenge to male authority as 'monstrous'. Such alleged 'monstrosity' involved alleged 'libertinism'. Edwards' *Gangraena* (1646) attacked all separatists from the 'publick assemblies' as 'monsters' in an image which simultaneously made the separate churches themselves 'disordered mothers': he fulminated against those who joined 'separated Churches where these monsters daily breed'. Toleration was called a midwife for 'monstrous bastard and misshapen religious growths'. For Edwards, the New Model Army was made up of persons who were

---

[69] Edwards, *Gangraena*, I, 79–80, 170, cited in R. Trubowitz, 'Female Preachers and Male Wives: Gender and Authority in Civil War England' in J. Holstun (ed.), *Pamphlet Wars* (London 1992), 112–33, at 115–16; Ludlow, 'Shaking Patriarchy's Foundations', 96–7; K. Chidley, *A New Years Gift* (1645); Smith, *Perfection*, 12–13; Thomas, 'Women', 42–62.

[70] Edwards, *Gangraena*, 90, 174–5. Cf now also A. Hughes, *Gangraena*; Fissel, *Vernacular*.

strange monsters, having their heads of enthusiasme, their bodies of antinomianisme, their thighes of Familisme, their legges and feet of Anabaptisme, their hands of Arminianisme, and Libertinisme as the great vein going thorow the whole.

Thus, Edwards' image of heresy and schism united monstrosity simultaneously to wrong ideas, to a disfigured body, and to a 'nourishing vein' for all heretical ideas of 'libertinism'.[71] For Edwards, as for so many of his predecessors, no heresy was worse than anti-Trinitarianism. Edwards' very juxtapositions of Socinianism to libertinism in *Gangraena* were themselves telling: his list of associated heresies read 'Antinomian, Manifestarian, Libertine, Socinian...'[72] Ephraim Pagitt's *Heresiography* similarly focused on allegations about the 'lewd' actions and 'debauchery' of many groups, from Anabaptists through Familists to Quakers and Ranters. It stressed that Adamites called their meeting-place 'Paradise' and went naked there, an image central to scores of attacks on Adamites in the 1640s that were then transferred to Quakers and Ranters in the 1650s. Pagitt declared that Augustine had mentioned the Adamites, 'an old heresy' now 'renewed by the Anabaptists'.[73]

The sects of the English Revolution were imaged not merely as pestilential, infecting, monstrous poisoners, but also as 'libertines' and 'sodomites'. Woodcuts and pamphlets frequently imaged Quakers as libertines and even as committing bestiality, and often depicted other sects engaged in sexual orgies, with the women dominating, including many which depicted the 'Adamites', who were said not to hear the word or have the sacraments administered unless they were 'naked'. The Family of Love was repeatedly said to hold all in common 'as wife, children, goods, etc.'. For Baxter, Familists were, like Ranters, based on 'a Cursed Doctrine of Libertinism, which brought them to all abominable filthiness of life'. Familists were often pilloried as Ranters, about whom we will say more in a moment. In 1641, Familists were attacked for adoring 'Saints Ovid, Priapus, Cupid'. Edward Harris' *A True Relation of the Company of Brownists, Separatists, and Nonconformists in Monmouthshire* declared that these separatists had drawn 'divers honest men's wives in the night times to frequent their assemblies' and had caused 'many chaste virgins to become harlots and the mothers of bastards'.[74]

[71] Edwards, *Gangraena* (1646), Epistle Dedicatory, 2, 4, and 14; McBeth, *English Baptist Literature*, 70.

[72] Edwards, *Gangraena*, 13.

[73] Edwards, *Gangraena*, II, 15; Pagitt, *Heresiography*, *passim*; Williams, 'Prints of the English Revolution', 101; Cressy, *Travesties*, 260ff., 271.

[74] Freist, 'The King's Crown'; Watts, *Dissenters*, 81–2; R. Baxter, *Reliquiae Baxterianae* (London 1696), 76–7; J. Tickell, *The Bottomless Pit Smoaking in Familisme* (Oxford 1651); Huehns, *Antinomianism*, 62n.2 cited in Davis, *Fear*, 122; Edward Harris, *A True Relation of the Company of Brownists, Separatists, and Nonconformists in Monmouthshire* (1641), sig. A2 in Watts, *Dissenters*, 81.

Edwards was thus one among many identifying sects as sexually licentious, and linking their heretical or schismatic opposition to orthodox practices and beliefs to their licence. According to Edwards, a man had deprived a girl of her virginity on the ground that 'marriage was but an idle ceremony'. An Independent who had made advances to his maid had defended his actions on antinomian grounds. Baptists who baptised young maids at about one or two in the morning had been 'tempting them out of their fathers' houses' and their commitment to adult baptism and to immersion as Christ's order was made sexually motivated by desire to see the women naked. Edwards published a correspondence section which included an anonymous letter describing a bashful woman about to undergo baptism by immersion 'having pulled off all her cloaths to the naked skin, ready to go into the water...covered her secret parts with both her Hands' but was told by the 'dipper' that it was an 'unseemly sight to see her hold her hands downward, it being an ordinance of Jesus Christ, her hands with her heart should be lifted upwards towards heaven'.[75]

Once again, heresy was thus tied repeatedly to libertine sexuality in antiheretical writing. Many of these sects were attacked for anti-Trinitarianism. Many beliefs were expressed by the authors attacked as 'libertines' which spoke of the 'man Christ' and which denied the orthodox doctrine of the Trinity and incarnation together with other traditional doctrines of Christianity, such as the eternity of punishment, also associated with anti-Trinitarian thought. John Bunyan was later to allege that he had heard a man 'tempting a maid to commit uncleanness with him' by saying that 'if she should prove with child' she should say to the judge that she was 'with child by the Holy Ghost'. *A List of Some of the Great Blasphemers and Blasphemies* (1654) suggested that many women had made this claim. In the anonymous 1652 *The Ranters Monster*, a Ranter lady was alleged to have made this claim and to have argued that since Genesis taught that 'Woman was to be a helper for man,...it was not sin to lie with any man, whether Batchelor, Widdower, or married, but a thing lawful, and adjured thereunto by Nature'. She was alleged to have then given birth to a 'monstrous' offspring. A more direct association of the heretical attack on the virgin birth with sexual libertinism and with monstrosity would be very difficult to find. The text, as usual, was accompanied by a woodcut.[76]

In almost all of these allegations, it is the associations of heresy that we have traced over the earlier sections of this chapter which are central to the accusations of 'libertinism' against these sects. The sects did indeed challenge

---

[75] Edwards, *Gangraena*, in Watts, *Dissenters*, 113–14; Edwards, *Gangraena*, II, letters, p. 5 cited in Stevenson, 'Social Integration', 363–4.

[76] Turner, *One Flesh*, 85, 165; Hill, *World*, ch. 9; E. Hobby, *Virtue of Necessity* (Ann Arbour 1989), 28; C. Hill, *A Turbulent, Seditious, and Factious People* (Oxford 1988), 52; Davis, *Fear*, 90.

conventional notions of the family in various ways. Quakers argued that women influenced by the spirit could preach and prophesy, and accorded a greater degree of spiritual equality between men and women in a society in which most condemned such equality, although, as Phyllis Mack has shown, this should not be overstated; many women Quaker prophets claimed to speak with a male or 'neuter' voice. Quakers rejected Anglican marriage ceremonies as vestiges of popery and argued that those present were 'witnesses' to a marriage made by God, not by church ceremonial. Some in the Revolution, such as the privately anti-Trinitarian and publicly tolerant Independent John Milton, questioned the disallowance of divorce, and Milton countenanced a prelapsarian sexuality that was decidedly unorthodox and linked to some 'heretical' questioning of Genesis, as James Turner has shown.[77] But most of the accusations of libertinism against sects and heresies in the Revolution were caricatures of their questioning of orthodox sexual morality in order to render these sects 'libertine' supporters of sexual licentiousness. A few members of these sects may personally have been 'libertines' in behaviour – as in any religious group – but these sects excommunicated such individuals. And many in these sects spent much time denying that they were 'libertine' – most notably by writing extensively against the Ranters in the 1650s. Thus, the Quakers Richard Farnsworth in *The Ranters Principles and Deceits Discovered* (1655), John Audland in *The Innocent Delivered out of the Snare* (1655), Edward Burrough in *A Trumpet of the Lord Sounded out of Sion* (1656), Margaret Fell in *A Testimonie of the Touch-Stone for all Professions* (1656), and George Fox in *The Great Mystery of the Great Whore Unfolded* (1659) all stressed Quaker commitment to moral performance and all specifically attacked the Ranters as heretics and as 'libertines'. Indeed, many Quaker works specified in their titles themselves that they were attacking libertinism, as John Chandler's *A Seasonable Word and Call, to all those called Ranters or Libertines Throughout the Three Nations* (1659), and Robert Barclay's *The Anarchy of the Ranters and other Libertines* (1676).[78] Such attacks were surely intended to serve both to legitimate Quakers in the eyes of their contemporaries as being themselves not 'heretics' and 'libertines', and to help the emergent Quaker movement to define itself.[79] Quakers were similarly to condemn Muggletonians as 'heretics' in many works, while Muggleton himself denounced many leading Quakers as heretics.[80]

---

[77] Turner, *One Flesh*.   [78] Davis, *Fear*, 90.

[79] Davis, *Fear*, 88ff.; F. McGregor, 'Ranterism and the Development of Early Quakerism', *Journal of Religious History* (1977), 349–63; *idem*, 'The Baptists'.

[80] C. Hill, B. Reay, and W. Lamont, *The World of the Muggletonians* (London 1983); 'Testimony of a General Meeting of Friends for Münster' fo. 3 and A. Delemaine, *A Volume of Spiritual Epistles...of...Reeve and Muggleton* (1820), in Kilroy, *Protestant*

Attack on the Ranters and Quakers as heretics was also used by Baptists in order to defend Baptists as legitimate. The title of the Baptist Thomas Hicks' 1673 *Three Dialogues between a Christian and a Quaker* tells its story. For the anti-Trinitarian John Milton, the Ranter Clarkson was devoted to the flesh, but Milton also urged that 'anabaptism, famelism, antinomianism' were all sexually motivated: 'their opinions having full swinge, do end in satisfaction of the flesh'. And Lodowick Muggleton himself, condemned by many as a particularly extreme heretic and libertine, saw Ranters as to be attacked for their libertine 'Judgment' and 'Practice' which led to 'the Destruction both of soul and body'.[81] There was, then, in many works by those considered 'libertine' as they were 'heretics', the indignant repudiation of the charge, combined with levelling the very same charge against other sects who were typed by them as both truly 'heretical' and 'libertine'. Thus, if there was here the resolute denial by sects such as Quakers or even Muggletonians that their allegedly 'heretical' views were 'libertine', there was still a strong association by them of 'heresies' they alleged to be held by others with 'libertinism' or 'sodomy'. The association between 'heresy' and 'libertinism' was in this sense reinforced even by many among the most 'tolerant' of the sects in the years of the Revolution.

THE RANTERS

This brings us to the only 'religious grouping' who may actually have celebrated their own sexual 'libertinism' in revolutionary England: the Ranters. Historians' opinion is very strongly divided over whether the Ranters existed far more as 'fear' and 'myth', as J. C. Davis has argued,[82] or as real if temporary and fissiparous social and religious groupings, as historians such as Christopher Hill have argued, in a debate which has generated as much heat as light.[83] Nigel Smith has taken a slightly different tack, recognising Davis' objections to treating Ranters as a movement, but stressing that there were at the least some self-proclaimed Ranter individuals, and pointing out that 'if the Ranters were a fiction, they were one of their own as well as others making'. Smith then traces their 'representations or identities, pejorative or otherwise'. He shows that there were many affinities between

---

Dissent, 88; W. Penn, *The New Witnesses Proved Old Heretics* (London 1672). Fox declared that what Reeve had heard in his alleged commission was 'but a whispering of Satan': Fox, *Something in Answer to Lodowick Muggleton's Book*, 21, in T. Underwood, *Primitivism, Radicalism and the Lamb's War* (Oxford 1997), 15.

[81] Davis, *Fear*, 92; Hill, *World*; Underwood, *Lamb's War*, 18, 66; Turner, *One Flesh*, 90–1.

[82] Davis, *Fear*.

[83] Hill, *World*; A. L. Morton, *The World of the Ranters* (1970). For a much stronger argument about the reality of the Ranters than the evidence warrants, see N. Cohn, *The Pursuit of the Millenium* (Oxford 1970).

elements of their (self-) representation and those of many others stressing prophecy and 'begoddedness' – an intimate union with God – in the years of the Revolution.[84]

To their opponents, Ranters' heresies were understood to be directly associated with unrestrained – indeed with legitimated – sexual licence. The *Ranter's Religion* (1650), the first official attack on the Ranters, had, as J. C. Davis has shown, a title-page adorned by a woodcut of naked men and women.[85] The *Routing of the Ranters* (1650) identified them as delighting 'in gluttony and drunkenness, chambering and wantonness' and depicted their meetings as orgiastic. The Ranters were said by their adversaries, and allegedly by some who claimed to have been formerly Ranters themselves, to believe that he who 'commits adultery, incest, or buggers the oftenest' is 'most beloved' of God. It was said of them in *The Ranters Parliament* that they held that 'each Brother ought to take his Fellow-Female upon his knee, saying let us lie down and multiply, holding this lascivious action to be the chief motive of their salvation'.[86] It was suggested that Ranters believed that it was not sinful for 'hundreds of men and women (savage like) to lie with each other...in Houses, Fields or Streets, which is their constant course'.[87] Ranter women were depicted as sexually voracious and in sexual control; many texts depicted them as copulating openly with many men.[88] Many tied their libertinism directly to their preaching. Anthony Wood declared that the Ranter Abiezer Coppe preached 'stark naked many blasphemies' by day and then laid 'with a wench' who had heard him by night.[89] For Richard Baxter, they misinterpreted the word of God and so 'as allowed by God...many of them committed Whoredoms commonly'. According to Baxter, indeed, a 'Matron of great Note for Godliness and sobriety, being perverted by them, turned so shameless a Whore, that she was carted in the Streets of London'.[90]

To many, Ranters were 'infecting', 'monsters', and 'poisoners'. John Tickell, minister in Abingdon, attacked them in the 1651 *Bottomless Pit Smoaking in Familisme*, in language which by now we have seen has many patristic and medieval antedecedents, as those who 'will smile upon you, and cut your throat: use melting words, Honneysweet, smooth as oyle, but full of poyson'.[91] Humphrey Ellis' 1650 *Pseudochristus* attacked the spread of the

---

[84] Smith, *Perfection*, 8n. and *passim*.

[85] *The Ranters Religion* (1650), title-page in Davis, *Fear*, 78, 156.

[86] *The Ranters Parliament* in Davis, *Fear*, 175.

[87] Turner, *One Flesh*, 88; Levy, *Blasphemy*, 149.

[88] Davis, *Fear*, 106, who discusses these images in part in relation to charivari images of women on top and the work of N. Z. Davis.

[89] In Levy, *Blasphemy*, 139; Cohn, *Pursuit*, 316–17.

[90] Baxter, *Reliquiae Baxterianae*, I, 76; Levy, *Blasphemy*, 153.

[91] J. Tickell, *Bottomless Pit Smoaking in Familisme* (Oxford 1651), 37–40; Cohn, *Pursuit*, 296–7.

'poysonous infection' of the beliefs of William Franklin and Mary Gadbury, who were alleged to have expressed some Ranter antinomianism or perfectionist 'libertinism'.[92] In another text, a 'shee Ranter' was alleged to have said that she would think herself 'a superlative servant of Gods, if any man would accompany with her carnally in the open Market place'. This was immediately followed by the declaration 'O wretched people! O monstrous Times' and by the request that 'vigilant senators' would suppress 'these Monsters of mankind', the frame of 'these Schismaticks' being 'out of joint' as they were 'Devils clad in flesh'.[93] Other texts also aligned Ranters with schism, talking of them specifically as latter-day 'Donatist' sects, or with (Manichean) heretical belief in two gods, one good and one evil. It is difficult not to believe that one is hearing primarily the voice of the anti-heretical and anti-schismatic literature descending from Augustine and others, rather than hearing Ranters' actual beliefs being recorded.[94] Moreover, in a representation which surely owed much to Calvin's image of libertinism as based on the perversion of the order 'increase and multiply', much of this sexual libertinism was alleged to be justified specifically not by complete disbelief in the Bible but by wrong interpretation, by citations of the biblical text 'increase and multiply'; the accusation had such currency that the phrase 'well-wisher to the mathematics' became a slang term for a 'whoremaster'. The *Ranters Declaration* included the caption 'Increase multiply' on its title-page.

For John Bunyan, Ranters and atheists were similar in lacking a sense of sin; Ranters professed belief in God and atheists did not.[95] For many writers, Ranters were not merely heretics, but their heresy shaded directly into 'atheism'. Pagitt discussed the Ranters as 'atheists'. The *Faithful Scout* agreed. *Mercurius Politicus* declared in 1653 that the 'hideous atheism abounding in the Land' had created swarms of 'blasphemies, damnable Heresies, and licentious practices'.[96] The 'Ranter' Abiezer Coppe was imprisoned for blasphemy, and accused of believing that heaven involved being able to perform 'murder, Adultery, incest, fornication, uncleanness, Sodomie, etc'.[97] It was this set of associations which produced the 1650 Act against Atheism and Blasphemy, explicitly directed against those who 'monstrously' thought that 'the acts of Murder, Adultery, Incest, Fornication, Uncleanness, Sodomy, Drunkenness, filthy and lascivious Speaking' were not sinful.[98] Significantly, this Act was passed in the same period and directed at some

[92] H. Ellis, *Pseudochristus* (1650), in Cohn, *Pursuit*, 300.   [93] In Davis, *Fear*, 160.
[94] Davis, *Fear*, 79.   [95] Hill, *World*, 205; Davis, *Fear*, 121.
[96] Whiting, *Studies*, 272; *The Faithful Scout* 51, 2–9, January 1651, 393–6; *Mercurius Politicus*, 174, 6–13 October 1653, 2788, 2791, in Davis, *Fear*, 118–19.
[97] Levy, *Blasphemy*, 149.   [98] Cohn, *Pursuit*, 295–6.

of the same targets as the May 1650 Adultery Act for 'suppressing the detestable sins of incest, adultery and fornication'. By that Act in defence of 'monogamy', incest and adultery became felonies carrying the death sentence; fornication became subject to a three-month prison sentence, and brothel-keepers were to be whipped, pilloried, branded, and jailed for three years. As Keith Thomas notes, the Adultery Act was unique in English history as an attempt 'to put the full machinery of the state behind the enforcement of sexual morality'. The two acts were strongly related practically and conceptually. Indeed, they had been proposed initially as one law and had been split into two as they worked their way through Parliament in 1647. Thomas has noted that on fast days, Parliament had been warning that the allowance of sexual sins would cause God to punish the nation, and that the legislation made progress precisely on fast days. He has pointed, moreover, to the fear of sexual licence among the antinomian sects, and stressed that the bill was ordered presented *immediately* after the House condemned Coppe's *Fiery Flying Roll*.[99]

Viewed in the perspective of the anti-heretical and anti-schismatic literature traced during the course of this section and chapter, it is difficult not to believe that the Act against Atheism and Blasphemy and the accusations against Ranters reveal far more about the fears and the set of associations of acts and beliefs in the minds of legislators and heresiographers than they do about Ranter beliefs and practices, as J. C. Davis has argued – very strongly indeed – in *Fear* – but which some of the historians he criticised had also recognised, if not as strongly as he does.[100] James Turner has similarly traced many of these accusations to Calvin's attack on the libertines, to 'medieval inquisitions of popular heresy, and...patristic attacks on Gnostics and Adamites'. And many of the allegations are accusations central to the anti-heretical traditions derived from the Fathers. For instance, the accusation that the Ranters indulged in 'gluttony and drunkeness, chambering and wantonness' is not merely a straight rendition of Paul in Romans 13:13–14 rather than a description of their actual behaviour, but it is, moreover, an accusation that is based on the exact passage of Romans that sealed the conversion of Augustine himself.[101]

[99] Thomas, 'Puritans and Adultery', 257–82, at 256, 276–8; Davis notes the simultaneity of the Acts in *Fear*. Cf also now Fissell, *Vernacular*, 162–70.

[100] For strongly stated replies to Davis' strongly stated arguments, see E. P. Thompson, 'On the Rant' in G. Eley and W. Hunt (eds.), *Reviving the English Revolution* (London 1988), 153–60; C. Hill, 'Abolishing the Ranters' in *A Nation of Change and Novelty* (1993), 172–218; see also Davis' own 'Fear, Myth and Furore', *Past and Present* (1990), 98–103, and the contributions to *Past and Present* (1993) 'Debate: Reappraising the Ranters', 155–210.

[101] Turner, *One Flesh*, 85; Colish, *Medieval*, 29; Augustine, *Confessions* (Penguin 1961), 175–8. For the importance of this passage within Catholic missions to convert Protestants

Yet, once again, as in the case of Cathars, or the Anabaptists, it is important to note that some among those named as Ranters did indeed challenge the standard of orthodoxy of monogamous procreative sexuality, either through a heavily sexualised language of spirituality, or perhaps in a few cases by practices. Abeizer Coppe's several pamphlets, including the *Fiery Flying Roll* which prompted Parliamentary condemnation, celebrated 'base impudent kisses' and 'wanton kisses' with 'gypsies' and depicted these as a transformative action 'out of flesh into Spirit'. For Coppe, these 'external kisses' were 'the fiery chariots to mount me swiftly into the bosom of him whom my soul loves'. Coppe drew on the Song of Songs, speaking of being 'kist with the kisses of his mouth, whose loves are better than wine'. Concubines 'without number' were depicted as vehicles of transcendence. Coppe's language at many points took over the language of accusation against libertines and heretics as sexual monsters. He thus depicted a monstrous pregnancy of lust in writing in *A Second Fiery Flying Roule* that 'I have gone along the streets impregnant with that child [lust] which a particular beauty had begot', and declared that he had

sate downe, and eat and drank around on the ground with Gypseys, and clip't, hug'd and kiss'd them, putting my hand in their bosomes, loving the she-gypsies dearly.

He even consciously adopted the language of the 'plague' of heretics in order to mock public morality, depicting himself as David in 2 Samuel 6: 13–26 'plaguing' and 'tormenting' Mical, and reversed the image, declaring that he was 'utterly plagued' until he had been reborn in his – to others heretical – union with God.[102]

Here, as Nigel Smith has suggested, at the least the Ranters themselves helped to create some parts of the language of accusation against them and of their image as legitimators of libertine sexuality. It was after publication of Coppe's work that the main attack on Ranter beliefs in pamphlets as well as Parliament was launched, and his language itself provided seeming confirmation to many of his attackers of the fears they then expressed. Coppe seems to have stayed – even in his image of 'loving the she-gypsys' – at the level of imaginative, fornicatory metaphor, and centred his sexual imagery on 'base kisses' rather than other sexual acts, as Nigel Smith has emphasised; his fellow Ranter Lawrence Clarkson seems to have emphasised the need to act, and he may well have acted in a 'libertine' manner. Clarkson's *A Single Eye* declared that

in the seventeenth century, see K. Luria, 'Rituals of Conversion: Catholics and Protestants in Seventeenth Century Poitou' in Diefendorf (ed.), *Culture and Identity in Early Modern Europe*, 65–81, at 73.

[102] A. Coppe in N. Smith (ed.), *A Collection of Ranter Writings* (London 1983), 82, 106–8; Smith, *Perfection*, 58–9, 61.

there is no such act as drunkenness, adultery and theft in God. Sin hath its conception only in the imagination. . .What act soever is done by thee in light and love, is light and lovely, though it be that act called adultery.[103]

Coppe himself declared that the service of God was 'pure Libertinisme'. Others took the word 'libertine' and also did not apolgise but rather rejoiced in it: Tobias Crisp wrote that 'to be called a libertine is the most glorious title under heaven'.[104] In these writings, then, there was at the very least an intellectual, imaginary, rhetorical challenge to 'orthodox' (that is, procreatively legitimated monogamous) sexuality, and there may have been much more. The climate of rejection of religious formalism in its many guises, the antinomian potential within Calvinist theologies of predestination and their rendition in perfectionist language, and the widespread attack on parts of 'orthodox sexual morality' as papistically imposed, would all have been easy to combine in a revolutionary moment of questioning received values with the long-standing laxer attitudes about sexual morality of the population at large.[105]

To orthodox Presbyterian Calvinists, whose motivations for taking up arms against their King had included the desire to reform the Church of England, to *reduce* its lax allowance of a festival culture declared immoral, and to reduce the theological variations found within the national church by eliminating Arminianism and enforcing strict Calvinism, the Ranters provided the ultimate proof that the claim of 'conscience' could be made for any and every 'immoral' practice. And in the eyes of such orthodox Calvinists, they were joined at the hip to other radical sects, who also challenged familial authority in support of 'libertinism' and simultaneously and relatedly challenged the authority of the state, the national church, and the central doctrines of Christianity. If Anabaptism and anti-Trinitarianism provided for the sixteenth century the central examples of heretical and schismatic nightmares for the 'orthodox' in these 'Last Days', in the mid-seventeenth century in England in a period which many also thought was that of the 'Last Days' when heresies and schisms were multiplying before the second coming of Christ, the Quakers and especially the Ranters provided the heretical and schismatic nightmare of all nightmares.

---

[103] Hill, *World*, 215; Smith, *Perfection*. For other examples of fornicatory images and language which probably did not get performed in acts, see Turner, *One Flesh*, 81n.; for Clarkson as actor, see Turner, *One Flesh*, 90–1.

[104] Smith (ed.), *Collection*, 86; Hill, *World*, 186, 317; Turner, *One Flesh*, 91–2.

[105] Thomas, 'Puritans and Adultery', stresses both the extensiveness of laxer sexual morality in the population at large and of questioning received views about marriage and prohibited sexual relations; Smith, *Perfection*, gives a brilliant account of the many forms of antiformalism in these years; Hill, *World*, and Thompson, 'On the Rant', stress the closeness of antinomianism to strict predestinarian Calvinist theology and its potential for challenge to orthodox sexual morality; Turner, *One Flesh*, 86–7, suggests that there were probably 'scattered outbursts' of 'erotic frenzy' in these years.

——— 10 ———

Early tolerationist arguments and their condemnation

It was Anabaptists and anti-Trinitarians, attacked by 'magisterial Reformation' Protestants and Catholics as seditious communists and poisoning pestilential libertines and sodomites, who developed many (although not all) significant arguments for religious toleration generated in the sixteenth century. It was then Arminians, Quakers and seventeenth-century descendants of Anabaptists and anti-Trinitarians, attacked by exactly the same series of accusations, who generated many (although not all) significant arguments for religious toleration in the seventeenth century. Writing in the 1688 *Supplement* to his *Philosophical Commentary*, Bayle noted this lineage of tolerationist argument by declaring that Socinians and Arminians had been the only sects defending universal religious toleration in recent centuries and by giving himself a pseudonym which recalled both the Anabaptist David Joris and the Quaker George Fox. He wrote that the 'great subject of wonder' is that the 'doctrine of persecution' had 'prevailed to such a degree that there should not be one considerable sect which does not maintain it vigourously either in whole or in part'. He argued that there were some persons 'in every christian communion' who inwardly condemned, or even publicly opposed, the use of all violent methods for making men change their religion, but that he knew of none 'except the Socinian and Arminian sects' who 'professedly teach that all other means for converting Heretics or Infidels, but those of Instruction, are unwarrantable'. Socinians were said to be 'blended imperceptibly with other christians' and not to 'make a sect apart, except in a very few places of the world, and as for the Arminians, they are known in some towns in Holland'.

We have already met associations of support for toleration with these sects when we saw that Quakers and Baptists supported James II's toleration and noted their arguments; Baptists drew in part on Anabaptist arguments and influences. In this chapter, we will examine the contours of the arguments for toleration of these groups, and indicate the hostile response to them from the vast majority of their contemporaries who held that 'toleration' was a 'diabolical' commitment. When Bayle noted that Arminians and Socinians had generated arguments for universal religious toleration, he simultaneously noted that they were condemned by the vast majority of contemporary Christians as the doctrine of non-toleration went 'about everywhere' while that of toleration was reserved for the few 'dark corners' of Christianity inhabited by the few members of these sects.[1]

The leading Anabaptist Menno Simmons stressed in his *Foundation Book* both the religious duty of toleration and that use of force was antichristian. For Simmons, toleration was required as imitating Christ: 'Antichrist rules through hypocrisy and lies, with force and sword, but Christ rules by patience with his Word and Spirit. He has no other sword or saber'. Christ alone was the 'ruler of the conscience'. Magistrates were not to 'usurp the judgment and kingdom of Christ'. For Simmons, magistrates were called to punish 'manifest criminals, such as thieves, murderers, Sodomites, adulterers, seducers, sorcerers, the violent, highwaymen, robbers' and to 'do justice between a man and his neighbour' but not to impose religion on their subjects. Simmons' *Christian Baptism* similarly ended with condemnation of those Anabaptist sects which had wrongly used force and with the suggestion that magistrates were armed against all 'thievery, murder, perjury, sedition, rebellion or any other criminal act' but were not to impose on conscience.[2]

Many sixteenth- and seventeenth-century Anabaptists and anti-Trinitarians stressed the limited number of doctrinal requirements within Christianity and emphasised that they considered moral behaviour rather than dogma the vital element of Christianity. As Socinus put it, there were many things 'not essential for our salvation' in doctrine; a church was not apostolic 'because it teaches no doctrinal errors, but because it teaches no error in things that are necessary for salvation'.[3] The *Racovian Catechism*, issued in many editions in the seventeenth century which were read by tolerationist authors, declared that its own catechism was obligatory to no one but rather an expression of ideas, and celebrated the 'primitive' church as to be imitated as 'enlightening':

Let everyone be free to express his judgment in religious matters, provided we, too, be allowed to express our opinion on divine things without injury or insult. Such indeed is that freedom to prophesy which the holy Scriptures recommend to us so warmly, and of which the primitive Church of the Apostles gives us such an enlightening example.[4]

---

[1] Bayle, *Supplement* in *Philosophical Commentary* (1708), 745–7.
[2] Menno Simmons, *The Complete Writings* (Scottsdale, Penn. 1956), 190–3, 204, 284.
[3] *Bibliotheca Fratrum Polonorum*, I, 347 in Le Cler, *Toleration*, I, 413.
[4] *Catechesis Ecclesiarum Polonicarum* (1684), introduction, in Le Cler, *Toleration*, I, 416.

Many added that those who used force undermined their own credibility. As the leading seventeenth-century Socinians Jonas Schlichting and Johann Crell put it, those who used force, 'by resorting to violent means' showed that they lacked confidence in their arguments. Schlichting questioned whether heretics could be identified, defined a 'heretic' as simply someone with a different belief, and urged that if something bad was meant by the term then it was those who used force who fitted that definition. Centring the issue of toleration on the crucial notion of 'harmlessness' towards others, Schlichting asserted:

What is freedom of conscience under God alone if not the right to think what you choose, to freely preach what you think and to do whatever causes no harm to others?[5]

Both anti-Trinitarians and Anabaptists emphasised strongly against Augustinian notions of charitable coercion that 'charity' was a duty which required one to tolerate others as long as their beliefs did not transgress the 'fundamental' requirements of belief in Christianity, and that Christian love forbade the death or punishment by torture of 'heretics'. In these ways, their arguments tended to support an ecumenical inclusive Christianity in which all those crossing a very low threshold of beliefs were Christians.

Stressing the new life of believers in Christ through the presence of the Holy Spirit, Anabaptists such as Joris de-emphasised even the revelation of the word of God found in the Bible, and especially all later theological professions of faith formulated by men. For Joris,

The Christian faith is not a word pronounced by the mouth, but a true eternal force, a divine operation, which no one can know but he who receives it. It does not consist in a few specially formulated articles, nor in words outwardly pronounced.

No one could even speak of the 'true faith', Joris claimed, 'unless he has found it in himself'.[6] Menno Simmons similarly railed in his *Foundation Book* against restrictive definitions of Christianity by 'the sublety and philosophy of the learned ones...the many councils...customs and usages of long-standing' and 'imperial edicts' which were 'nothing but shifting sands'.[7] Many Anabaptists saw the establishment of Trinitarian orthodoxy at the Council of Nicaea of 325 as a moment in the corruption of the 'true church' involving the imposition of fine-spun philosophic doctrine. The proposition that Jesus was the son of God was for Anabaptists clear; that he was God eternally and consubstantially was not clear to all Anabaptists, but to many was instead an imposition on the word of God after the ages of 'primitive

---

[5] Tazbir, *State Without Stakes*, 158–9.   [6] R. Bainton, *David Joris* (Leipzig 1937), 80.
[7] Simmons, *Complete Writings*, 210–11.

purity'. Even more widely accepted among the Anabaptists – by those who upheld the doctrine of the Trinity and by those who questioned it – was that the imposition of infant baptism backed by civil penalties in 407 was a corruption which removed the true identity of the church as voluntary. The imperial Christianity derived from Constantine was often spoken of by Anabaptists as the 'fall' of the church, when civil power came to coerce people to a worship which should have been adopted freely. Both Anabaptists and anti-Trinitarians identified the Old Testament as surpassed by the New Testament, and by the processes of inner inspiration of the Holy Spirit. As the Swiss brethren put it in 1532, 'In the early church only those were received as members who were converted through repentance to newness of life'. Many rejected most of the precedents drawn from the Mosaic commonwealth and Old Testament that were central to their 'magisterial Reformation' contemporaries and Catholics.[8]

Anabaptist opposition to infant baptism, combined by most Anabaptists with a stress instead on the adult baptism of believers, involved stress on the voluntary nature of the church against a state church. Although the Anabaptists at Münster thought of themselves as building a kingdom and expected to conquer the world, most Anabaptists stressed instead the clear separation of church and state. As the Swiss brethren argued in 1532,

The true church is separated from the world and is conformed to the nature of Christ. If the church is yet at one with the world we cannot recognise it as the true church. We cannot admit that a true church is united with the worldly government.

Menno Simmons similarly taught that 'the whole evangelical scriptures teach that Christ's church was and must be a people separated from the world in doctrine, life and worship'. He described the failure to distinguish between 'the church and the world' of Catholicism, repeated in 'magisterial Reformation' Protestantism, as 'a condition which is so clearly contrary to Scripture'. For Simmons, one had to take communion in a church 'outwardly without spot or blemish, that is, without open transgression and wickedness'; most state churches were instead full of sinful transgressors.[9] Bullinger summarised the arguments of the Anabaptist Swiss brethren as including that faith was 'the gift of God' and so should not be compelled; that 'the secular kingdom should be separated from the church, and no secular ruler should exercise authority in the church'; that Christ had commanded preaching and not compulsion; and that Paul had restricted the punishment of the church against 'heretics' to their exclusion from the church.[10]

---

[8] Williams, *Radical Reformation*, 617–20; Horsch, *Mennonites*, 339.
[9] Horsch, *Mennonites*, 339–42.   [10] Horsch, *Mennonites*, 325–6, 339.

Anabaptists and anti-Trinitarians generally argued that political society was based on certain minimum requirements, which they themselves did not transgress, and that many diverse religious beliefs and sects could peacefully and prosperously co-exist within a state. As many anti-Trinitarians were sheltered in Poland from persecution elsewhere in Europe they pointed to Poland as a peaceful society in the sixteenth century in contrast to the rest of Europe, torn apart by religious warfare. For Przypkowski, author in the mid-seventeenth century of the 'most exhaustive Polish work on the mutual relations of Church and State', since they had 'different objectives and different ways of achieving them' the authorities of church and state 'should not interfere with one another'. The state accepted 'people of all faiths and conditions: idolaters, heathens, heretics, and those denying the name of Christ' as long as they were obedient and loyal. The rise of the church

did not set aside the secular authority, but brought about the establishment of mutual limits that the one did not encroach on the sphere of the other. Both when the State with compulsory authority encroaches on the government of the Church, and when the Church takes the sword which God himself has entrusted to it out of the hands of the civil authority, there is a violation of justice.

For Przypkowski, political authority was not to bring men 'to virtue, which it is impossible to compel, but to refrain from offenses and to observe the political order'.[11] Many Anabaptists and many sixteenth-century anti-Trinitarians were pacifists opposing military service or officeholding, holding that others would engage in these tasks and that the survival of the state therefore did not depend on their participation. When some refused oaths, they argued that their refusal was biblically based, and due to the seriousness with which they treated the duty to keep their word; they were therefore trustworthy. Thus stressing the weight of their own religious convictions as animating their refusal of oaths and undergirding their word, they opposed the toleration by civil society of 'atheists' as untrustworthy. Convinced by the force of their own religious commitments to be Anabaptists and anti-Trinitarians and to suffer martyrdom and exile for their beliefs, they had little sympathy for 'atheists' who denied such beliefs.[12]

At the same time as they emphasised that the state should not punish for religious reasons, many Anabaptists and many anti-Trinitarians tended to emphasise their own beliefs as the 'true beliefs', to practise spiritual, marital, and economic endogamy, and to practise a considerable level of excommunication. The very stress on the need to hold communion only in a church

---

[11] J. Przypkowski, *Animadversions* (1650) in S. Kot, *Socinianism in Poland* (Boston 1957), 184–5; Tazbir, *State Without Stakes*, esp. 157–60.
[12] Tazbir, *State Without Stakes*, esp. 157–60; Wilbur, *Unitarianism*; McLachlan, *Socinianism*.

'without spot or wrinkle' which was a major part of the rejection of a state church promoted large-scale excommunications for 'wickedness' and for variations in beliefs. At points, Anabaptists and anti-Trinitarians attacked both the Catholic Church and those Protestants supporting such beliefs as Trinitarianism as being committed to the vestiges of 'superstitious popery' and as 'antichristian' or 'Antichrist', repudiating any notion that such anti-christians should be tolerated within an ecumenical church constructed on the basis of minimal beliefs. Anabaptists such as Joris tended to stress the exclusivity of the 'true church' born of the spirit. Menno Simmons declared the first duty of excommunication to be about 'false doctrines', and called anti-Trinitarianism an 'abomination'. Moreover, while Simmons generally assaulted persecution, and even denied the use of 'bloodshed' in the passage which is about to be quoted, he held in his *Foundation Book* that magistrates were indeed to 'restrain by reasonable means, that is, without tyranny and bloodshed, manifest deceivers who so miserably lead poor helpless souls by hundreds of thousands into destruction'. He explicitly then listed as such deceivers 'priests, monks, preachers', and declared the magisterial duty to prevent them from introducing 'such ridiculous abuses and idolatry under semblance of truth as has been done until now'.

While many Anabaptists and anti-Trinitarians denied that the Mosaic theocracy was to be imitated, for Simmons, Moses was indeed to be imitated as he acted against 'the false prophets and priests of Baal' with their 'idol-atry'. It was clear that for the ex-Catholic Simmons such 'idolatry' was a central feature not merely of pagan religion but of contemporary Catholicism, which he declared worse than pagan idolatry. He attacked the inclusion in public assemblies, as 'it may be witnessed everywhere', 'of all manner of idolatry where the most high, blessed, and precious name of God is so sadly blasphemed, the blood of Christ despised, the Holy Ghost grieved, the truth violated, the lie commended, the poor souls deceived, and the blind, ignorant people not only directed to the water, bread, wine and the mass, but also to the dumb idols of wood and stone'. While at points Simmons suggested that one should 'depart' from Catholics and from the mass, as that was 'an abomination of abominations' and a 'bewitching seduction of Antichrist', at this point in his most influential work, the *Foundation Book*, he suggested that magistrates had *wrongly* 'sheathed' the 'sword of righteousness' about these actions.[13]

And for Simmons it was not merely Catholics who were promoters of 'deception, hypocrisy, blasphemy, abomination, and idolatry', but also Lutherans and Zwinglians whose 'office and service' issued 'from the

---

[13] Simmons, *Complete Writings*, 151–6, 190–210, 212.

bottomless pit'. The doctrine of all of these religious groups – the major ones in Europe at the moment he was writing – was held to be 'deceiving', and their divine service 'an open abomination and idolatry'. Partly because of the importance of the repudiation of the image of polygamous and licentious Anabaptist Münster, Simmons accented heavily the sexual purity and probity of his Anabaptists. In contrast, he assaulted all others as licentious. For Simmons, 'in Spain and Italy and in the cloisters' all 'manner of sexual perversion is practiced' far 'exceeding Sodom and Gomorrah', while all other religions than his brand of Anabaptism were declared by Simmons to be committed to sexual licence. All such were, for Simmons, promised in the Scriptures 'nothing but punishment, wrath, damnation, and the blackness of darkness, the flaming lake and eternal gnashing of teeth, weeping, wailing, fire, woe, and death'. Utilising the language of anti-heretical and anti-schismatic writers, Simmons appealed to the 'common people' to understand that the preachers of all of these religions other than his brand of Anabaptism were 'thieves and murderers, who with the sword of their false doctrine slay your poor souls and steal from you the Word and kingdom of the Lord'. He identified the Anabaptist leaders David Joris, Battenburg and John of Leyden as 'blasphemers' who deserved the punishment of the magistrates, and as also 'the theives and murderers' of your souls. Thus, having divided the world into five groups – Catholics, Lutherans, Zwinglians, the 'corrupt sects' of Anabaptism, and the 'true Anabaptist church', it was only the last group for Simmons which was the 'true church' and in which salvation was possible. For Simmons, there was only one true church of Christ and it only taught the 'pure unmixed' word of God and Christ dwelt within its members.[14]

While many tolerationist arguments were composed by anti-Trinitarians, they also placed significant restrictions on toleration and expressed deep hostility to Catholics, Trinitarians, and even some other anti-Trinitarians. Francis David, anti-Trinitarian assistant in Transylvania to Blandrata, disputed against the adoration of Christ: in his view, Christ was a man and should not be adored even after the resurrection, which most Socinians held conveyed divinity to him and thus permitted adoration. David thus began a schism among the anti-Trinitarians. The leader of Socinianism in Poland, Blandrata, had David thrown into prison as a heretic, and he died in captivity.[15] Polish anti-Trinitarians launched major destructions of Catholic shrines and crosses, and attacked Catholic processions in order to steal and

---

[14] Simmons, *Complete Writings*, 190–210, 212.

[15] Le Cler, *Toleration*, I, 405 on David. Cf. Bayle, *Dictionary*, Blandrata H. The level of hostility about the issue of worship of Christ was central to anti-heretical polemic in the late seventeenth century: Edward Stillingfleet declared that Socinians logically ought not to worship one they believed a creature, for that was idolatry, and Francis Fulwood called those who refused worship 'desperate enemies of our Lord and Saviour': Champion, *Pillars*, 118.

trample on the eucharist.[16] It was alleged that Servetus himself was such a strong opponent of Trinitarianism that he called Trinitarians 'atheists', called the Trinity a diabolic 'monster' with three heads, and called believers in infant baptism followers of the Devil. If this was accurate, in the levels of his anathematisation of Trinitarianism, there could seem to be the potential for an intolerance equal to that of the Trinitarians, were he to have been in power. Servetus himself declared in a letter to Calvin his own support for death to 'obstinate heretics' (while not thinking himself one), writing that

> St Peter punished by death Ananias and Saphira, of whom he had not hope of conversion, to show more clearly his detestation of their crime, and to make them an example for all others, or because the Holy Spirit, whom they had scorned, made plain by that measure that they were incorrigible and obdurate in their wrong. This crime simply deserves death before God and man.[17]

In their attitudes and behaviour towards those they considered 'heretics' and 'idolaters', then, there were reasons even within the practices and attitudes of the most tolerationist groups of the sixteenth century – anti-Trinitarians as well as Anabaptists – to fear that were they ever to have significant power they too easily might become significantly intolerant.

Many of the Anabaptist and anti-Trinitarian works written in defence of toleration in the sixteenth century and early seventeenth century were republished in the mid- and late seventeenth century and read by later authors of defences of toleration, including Locke, who purchased many anti-Trinitarian works in the 1680s and 1690s as individual works and as part of the eight-volume *Bibliotheca Fratrum Polonorum*. Other important defenders of toleration in the 1680s and 1690s who possessed many of these works included Bayle, who discussed many of them in his *Dictionary*, Limborch, whose personal library included many Socinian works and some Anabaptist works, and Charles le Cène, whose manuscript collection includes several Socinian works which he had translated with an eye to publication, and one of whose works was published together with an early seventeenth-century Socinian defence of toleration. Two other of the most crucial sixteenth-century arguments for toleration still in influential circulation in the late seventeenth century, written in opposition to Servetus' execution, came from associates of the Anabaptists and of Socinus. Both were cited by Bayle in the *Philosophical Commentary*, both were read by Locke in the 1680s, and both were possessed in personal libraries by other important defenders of toleration in the 1680s, such as the Arminian Limborch and the Quaker Furly. They are Sebastian Castellio's (Chateillon's) 1554 *De haereticis*

---

[16] Tazbir, *State Without Stakes*, 75; Horsch, *Mennonites*, 339.
[17] Bainton, *Hunted Heretic*, 208; Calvini, *Opera*, XIV, 708 in Le Cler, *Toleration*, I, 329.

an sint persequendi et omnino quomodo sit cum eis agendum doctorum
virorum tum veterum tum recentiorum sententiae – 'Concerning heretics,
whether they should be persecuted, and what is to be done about them,
illustrated by the opinions of learned authors both old and new', and Jacob
Acontius' *Satanae Stratagema* – 'Satan's Stratagems'. Castellio, professor of
Greek at Basle, was also author of a series of supplementary works expanding his case and defending himself against Calvin's and Beza's replies. He was
an associate of David Joris, whose comments on his French translation of the
Bible he had solicited, and to whom he provided shelter while Joris was
hiding under an assumed name. His *Four Dialogues* were to be punished by
Faustus Socinus in 1578. In these *Four Dialogues*, he attacked Calvinist
predestinarian thought, arguing that it did not square 'with the nature of
God. Nothing could be more contrary to God than the creation of sons...for
the purpose of punishing them'.[18] In Basle, Castellio very probably knew
Acontius, an Italian convert to Protestantism who became a naturalised
English subject and a defender of Dutch Anabaptists against Archbishop
Grindal in the 1560s.[19] Castellio's works were to be translated by Coornhert
in the Netherlands in 1581–2, and then issued again by the Remonstrant
Nicolaas Borremans, pupil of Courcelles and close friend of the Remonstrant
minister and tolerationist historian Gerard Brandt.[20] Important in the sixteenth century itself, these arguments became even more influential in the
seventeenth century, as very many of Castellio's and Acontius' arguments
were to be rehearsed in defence of toleration; they thus require analysis in
some detail.

Castellio placed his own arguments in two successive dedications to
Concerning Heretics, with the following text a tissue of citations from a
series of other authors.[21] For Castellio, 'you should allow everyone who
believes in Christ to do so in his own way'. For Castellio, it was wrong to
force anyone to beliefs he did not hold; force made only hypocrites: 'It is
preposterous to assert that those who are forced to profess a belief really
believe what they profess.'[22] For Castellio, 'the Trinity, predestination, free
will...the state of souls after this life and other like things' do 'not need to be
known for salvation by faith'. Even when known, they would not make man

---

[18] Bainton (ed.), *Concerning*, 10; S. Ozment, *Mysticism and Dissent* (Yale 1973), 172;
H. Guggisberg, *Sebastian Castellio* (Basle 1956); *idem*, 'The Defence of Religious
Toleration and Religious Liberty in Early Modern Europe: Arguments, Pressures, and Some
Consequences', *History of European Ideas* (1983), 35–50; Castellio, *De Praedestinatione*,
59, in Ozment, *Mysticism*, 184.
[19] J. Acontius, *Satanae Stratagema*, ed. R. E. Field as *Darkness Discovered* (New York 1978), v–vi.
[20] Wilbur, *Unitarianism*, 207; van Eijnatten, 'Lodestars of Latitude: Gerard Brandt's Peaceable
Christian c. 1664, irenicism and Religious Dissent', *Lias* (1999), 66.
[21] Zweig, *Right to Heresy*, 159; Skinner, *Foundations*, II, 245–8.
[22] Zweig, *Right to Heresy*, 210. On Castellio see now especially Zagorin, *Idea*, 98–142.

better. Men's 'perverse curiosity' engendered worse evils, as men were 'puffed up with knowledge or a false opinion of knowledge and look[ed] down upon others'. Although opinions were 'almost as numerous as men, nevertheless there is hardly any sect which does not condemn all others and desire to reign alone'. From this came 'banishments, chains, imprisonments, stakes, and gallows' as penalties for those 'who differ from the mighty about matters hitherto unknown, for so many centuries disputed, and not yet cleared up'. Castellio compared this to a prince who had commanded being greeted on his return by people 'clad in white garments' but who forgot this command in order to dispute about his 'person', and were killing each other 'because some said he would return on a horse, and others in a chariot'. The killing by magistrates of their subjects over such issues was, Castellio argued, repugnant to Christ, whose authority was nonetheless being claimed for such acts. Castellio declared that he did not see how one can 'retain the name of Christian if we do not imitate his clemency and mercy'.

Castellio declared that he hated 'heretics', and that the seditious should be punished for withdrawing people 'from their obedience'. But he held that 'heretics' had been ill defined, and argued that most of those called 'heretics' were not such. For Castellio, 'When I reflect on what a heretic really is, I can find no other criterion than that we are all heretics in the eyes of those who do not share our views'.[23] For Castellio, all Christians held that Jesus was the Son of God, Saviour and Judge of the world, but disagreed about other matters. The 'better a man knows the truth, the less is he inclined to condemn'. For Castellio, 'Let not the Jews or Turks condemn the Christians, nor let the Christians condemn the Jews or Turks, but rather teach and win them by true religion and justice'. Capacious in all of these ways, Castellio's tolerationist argument nonetheless had two important limits. For Castellio, if any denied the Lord God, this atheist 'is deservedly to be abhorred in the eyes of all'. Magistrates were to punish atheists. And while in general Castellio advocated toleration for alleged heresy, he argued that punishment with fines and banishment, although not death, was deserved by those whose 'heresies' and 'blasphemies' were such that they 'deny the creation of the world, the immortality of souls and the resurrection'.[24]

In the body of Castellio's text, which was composed of a tissue of citations of other thinkers, Castellio abstracted passages in which these other authors had condemned punishment of heretics or where they had argued that such punishments should not include the death penalty. These passages were often from authors who had justified such punishment elsewhere in their writings,

---

[23] Castellio, in Bainton (ed.), *Concerning*, 121–33; Zweig, *Right to Heresy*, 154, 156.
[24] Castellio, in Bainton (ed.), *Concerning*, 121–33; 'Dedication to Duke Christoph', 137–40; 'Dedication to William of Hesse'.

including Luther and Calvin. The net effect for readers surely included a sense that those who at one moment protested for liberty at other moments argued against it, a sentiment that was to be memorably expressed in Popple's preface to Locke's *Letter Concerning Toleration*, in its accusation that those who pleaded for liberty of conscience when out of power opposed it when they gained power. For instance, the Württemberg Protestant Johann Brenz was a signator of the 1557 memorandum at Worms which approved the death penalty for Anabaptists and the execution of Servetus, and which declared that the opinion of the Anabaptists about civil government 'in itself constitutes sedition'. But in 1528, Brenz had opposed the punishment of Anabaptists, and Castellio reproduced his entire text against this punishment in *Concerning Heretics*. For Castellio, citing the tolerationist arguments of Brenz, unbelief and heresy were subject to the spiritual sword of excommunication, and not to the civil sword which punished theft, murder, and adultery. The civil sword was simply 'to maintain the civil peace'. As long as heretics do 'violence to no man and keep the civil peace' they were not to be punished. Against the citations of the Mosaic theocracy, it was declared that 'Christianity is fundamentally different from Judaism'. Anabaptists were held by the orthodox to teach that goods should be held in common and so to be intolerable. In an argument to be rehearsed again by Aubert de Versé in the 1680s, it was pointed out in reply that even if so they did not 'teach that others should be forced to practice community of goods, and they themselves constrain no one'. They therefore should not be constrained. For Castellio, if every thing

> out of which sedition might conceivably at some time arise were to be suppressed with the sword, we should have to prohibit rigorously all banquets and business, assemblies and fairs and church gatherings, for experience shows that insurrection has been hatched at many a banquet, and many a fair has issued in a riot, and in many a church a conspiracy has been conceived.[25]

In his 1562 *Advice to France Laid waste*, Castellio argued that sedition and the spread of heretical doctrine were the dangers from suffering heretics to live. But sedition arose 'from the attempt to force and kill heretics rather than from leaving them alone, because tyranny engenders sedition'. While he admitted that false doctrine might be disseminated, he argued that the remedy must not be worse than the disease, and that 'the constancy of the heretics in martyrdom' would make many join them. Moreover, 'constantly' from 'the time of Christ to our own' Christians had been mistaken for heretics. Since Christianity had now broken into many sects and 'Each sect regards itself as Christian and the rest as heretical' a law for the persecution

[25] Castellio, in Bainton (ed.), *Concerning*, 50–8, 154–69.

of heretics would 'let loose a Midianite war of extermination'. For Castellio, those who used force, and not the heretics, were the murderers: 'Either the victim resists, and you murder his body, or he yields and speaks against his conscience, and you murder his soul'. For Castellio, such violence was 'monstrous'.[26]

In Castellio's *Contra libellum Calvini in quo ostendere conatur haereticos jure gladii coercendos esse* (the 'Reply to Calvin's Book in which he Endeavours to Show that Heretics Should Be Coerced by the Right of the Sword'), he argued that 'now that the man has been burned with his books, everybody is burning with a desire to read them'. Recognising that Jews and Turks were excluded from punishment, he argued that Calvinists, Jews and Turks would be the only ones that Calvin would not wish to kill in the world. He repeated that the Trinity, predestination, and election were matters about which many of the saints had known nothing, and that all things necessary for salvation were 'certain'. Calvin compared heresy to theft, rapine, adultery, and murder; for Castellio, these were punished to 'protect the bodies and possessions of the good', not 'to establish the kingdom of Christ'. To Calvin's argument that 'They infect souls with the poison of depraved dogma' and that the swords should therefore not 'be withheld from their bodies', Castellio replied: 'The envious, avaricious, and proud infect souls and beget their like by words and example...but the sword has no power against their bodies'. To Calvin's question 'Shall the whole body of Christ be mangled that one putrid member remain intact', Castellio replied that the metaphor was simply inapt: 'to kill a man is not to amputate a member'. To Calvin's argument that the penalties applied only to those who fell away from the truth, Castellio replied:

All sects hold their religion as established by the Word of God and call it certain. Therefore all sects are armed by Calvin's rule for mutual persecution. Calvin says he is certain, and they say the same. He says they are mistaken, and they say the same of him. Calvin wishes to be judge, and so do they. Who will be judge.[27]

In an unpublished manuscript, Castellio argued strongly against the doctrine of the Trinity of Athanasius; Athanasius' Trinitarian beliefs were described first as non-scriptural, obscure and enigmatic, and thus unsuitable for a creed which needed to be understood, and finally as simply ridiculous: as if

you should say, 'Abraham is an old man, Isaac is an old man, and Jacob is an old man; yet they are not three old men, but one old man'. If I were to beleive this, Athanasius, I should have to say farewell to reason, the noblest gift of God, by which

---

[26] Castellio, *Conseil à la France désolée* (1562) in Bainton (ed.), *Concerning*, 258–64; Le Cler, *Toleration*, II, 76–7.

[27] Castellio, *Contra libellum Calvini in quo ostendere conatur haereticos jure gladii coercendos esse*, in Bainton (ed.), *Concerning*, 265–87.

man most markedly differs from the beasts, and I would have to return to the nature and sense of the brute and should lack the capacity for belief.[28]

Acontius' *Satan's Stratagems*, also composed in Basle in the 1560s, promoted a similar effort to distinguish fundamental and non-fundamental matters. For Acontius, because of Satan, men thought that they were required to loath 'that Doctrine, which in some one or two points is accounted heretical'. It was very difficult to decide what is 'damnable error' because Satan endeavoured to persuade men 'that it is a weighty point'. Some 'prime...pillars of the Church' from zeal had damaged the church – a corruption 'then which there cannot be a more deadly plague'. Most contentions were over 'the punctilio's of religion and matters for the most part of small moment'. Those trying to 'poyson simple people' were not the heretics, but those who assaulted them. Schism hindered the spread of the gospel. Moreover, the bridling of opinion caused sects to grow in strength and then disquiet the commonwealth as 'in the so late sedition at Münster'.[29] For Acontius, everyone with a sword called themselves orthodox and others heretics; magistrates could not judge who were the heretics.[30] For Acontius, 'it is a property of mankind to err'. He suggested that in discriminating between what was necessary to know and what was not, that things were written 'that you can believe that Jesus is the Messiah, the Son of God and obtain life by him'. Yet part, at least, of anti-Trinitarianism Acontius declared to fail in these terms. Acontius identified Sabellius as having confounded the Son and Father – and so it was plain that he did not believe that Jesus was the Son of God, which for Acontius it was necessary for him to believe.[31] Acontius' *Satan's Stratagems* was translated into English as *Darkness Discovered* by John Goodwin and dedicated by John Dury to Samuel Hartlib. Dury complimented Acontius' 'moderation' in religion. Dury may have been responsible also for the translation into English of the Socinian John Crell's *Vindication of Liberty of Religion*. Acontius' arguments were placed into *Racovian Catechism* nine years later almost verbatim. Acontius' thought influenced Chillingworth, and was discussed at the circle at Great Tew which included Falkland, Hales, Chillingworth, and Hobbes. As such, it was discussed alongside the Socinian Crell's works. In these ways, it provided major impetus towards notions of toleration via latitude in ideas in the 1640s and 1650s. It was then transmitted on to the 1680s and 1690s both by its influence upon such works – as in Locke's repeated celebrations of Chillingworth – and by its own republications and circulations; Locke bought a copy in the 1680s in the Netherlands.[32]

---

[28] Castellio, *De arte dubitandi*, in Bainton (ed.), *Concerning*, 287–305.
[29] Acontius, *Satan's*, 16–23, 26–7, 45; Bainton, *Travail*, 104; Voogt, *Constraint*, 63.
[30] Acontius, *Satan's*, 96–100.   [31] Acontius, *Satan's*, 16–23, 27, 78–9, 83.
[32] Trevor-Roper, 'Great Tew' in *Catholics*.

ANABAPTIST AND ANTI-TRINITARIAN TOLERATIONISM CONDEMNED

To their 'magisterial Reformation' opponents, these tolerationist arguments were themselves 'heretical' arguments; they were to be expected from those who were heretics, and they further associated support for religious toleration with the communism, sedition, treason, murder, libertinism, sodomy, poison, and plague central to 'heresy'. The limitation of 'fundamental' truths by Anabaptists and anti-Trinitarians was held by magisterial Protestants to be 'heresy' and antichristian. The declaration that 'charity' was required to others by tolerating them was described as justifying leaving them in 'fundamental' and damning errors and thus to mistake 'true charity'. The questioning of original sin and suggestion of perfectibility was itself 'heretical' and damning. Viewing such 'heretics' as motivated by their lusts in desire for community of goods and community of women, for libertinism and sodomy, and as therefore proclaiming the rights of 'conscience', such heretics' tolerationism was seen as motivated by desire to support free rein for lusts. Political authority was held to have a duty to secure peace which could be maintained neither with a diversity of sects nor with anarchic and seditious claims of 'conscience', and a still greater duty to secure religious truth and salvation of souls. On every one of its central features, tolerationist argument was thus itself heretical and libertine, poisonous and murderous.

To every one of the leading 'magisterial Reformation' thinkers of the sixteenth century, no less than to contemporary Catholics, toleration was quite simply a 'diabolic doctrine'. This was the famous and influential description of 'toleration' given by Beza, the leader of continental Calvinism in succession to Calvin and the organiser of international campaigns to ensure Protestant orthodoxy. For Calvin himself,

whoever shall maintain that wrong is done to heretics and blasphemers in punishing them, makes himself an accomplice in their crime and guilty as they are. There is no question here of man's authority: it is God who speaks and clear it is what law he will have kept in the Church even to the end of the world. Wherefore does he demand of us a so extreme severity, if not to show us that due honour is not paid him, so long as we set not his service above every human consideration, so that we spare not kin nor blood nor life of any and forget all humanity when the matter is to combat for his glory.[33]

For Calvin, those who did not understand the duty of the magistrate to punish heresy were either simple and ignorant people who needed to be educated, libertines who wanted to secure liberty for their evil wills, or atheists.[34]

---

[33] Calvin, *Defensio orthodoxae fidei* (1554), 46–7; Allen, *Political Thought*, 86–7.
[34] Calvin, *Defensio*; Allen, *Political Thought*, 84.

When Castellio criticised Calvin's legitimation of the execution of Servetus and declared that he could find no more meaning to the term heretic than 'that we regard those as heretics with whom we disagree', Calvin issued a work that responded to Castellio as 'Satan'. Beza described Castellio as the 'chosen instrument of Satan' on the first page of his revised *New Testament*.[35] Beza coined the phrase 'Libertas Conscientiae Diabolicum Dogma' – literally, 'liberty of conscience is a diabolical doctrine'. Indeed, Beza declared, 'The contention that heretics should not be punished is as monstrous as the contention that parricides and matricides should not be put to death; for heretics are a thousandfold worse criminals than these'.[36] Using the Augustinian notion of true charity, Beza declared that we must not tolerate 'a few ravening wolves, unless we are prepared to deliver over to their fangs the whole flock of good Christians...shame on this reputed clemency, which is in reality the utmost cruelty'.[37] In his *Responsio ad defensiones et reprehensiones Sebastiani Castellionis*, Beza called Castellio an Anabaptist 'protector of all adulterers and criminals'. Under the influence of such strict Calvinist orthodoxy, at Basle a trial was ordered of Castellio under suspicion of heresy. He was accused of translating the work of the anti-Trinitarian Ochino, and of having helped to shelter the arch-heretic David Joris, who was discovered to have lived in Basle under the assumed name Jean de Bruges. Joris' body was exhumed, tried, and hanged on public gallows, then burned with heretical books in the market-place of Basle. Castellio died before the trial ended.[38]

TOLERATIONISM SUPPORTED IN EARLY AND MID-SEVENTEENTH CENTURY ENGLAND

Arguments for religious toleration were briefly deployed in the early seventeenth century and then extensively in mid-seventeenth-century England among the radical 'heretical' sects – most notably Quakers and Baptists – and by some Independents and others significantly influenced by Arminianism or Unitarianism (Socinianism), including such thinkers as the Baptist Roger Williams, the Baptist Leveller Richard Overton, the anti-Trinitarian and Arminian John Milton, and the Arminian-influenced Chillingworth and Hales. The arguments of a number of Dutch-Anabaptist-influenced English Baptist authors, including Leonard Busher, John Smyth, and Thomas Helwys in the early seventeenth century, were described earlier in this book; they declared that the church was a voluntary organisation, that the state was to protect individuals from harm from others

---

[35] Acontius, *Satan's*, viii–xi.   [36] Zweig, *Right to Heresy*, 168.
[37] Zweig, *Right to Heresy*, 169.   [38] Zweig, *Right to Heresy*, 215–19.

but not to use its force to promote salvation; and that Jews, Muslims, pagans and all varieties of Christians deserved toleration unless they were seditious. We have seen earlier in this chapter the arguments of Acontius, Castellio, various Socinians, the Racovian Catechism, and Anabaptists such as Joris, that it was necessary to distinguish firmly between fundamental articles and those not necessary to be imposed, that magistrates were only to prevent harm and not to impose religion, and that the attempt to impose in religion caused sedition and war. These and others of their arguments were to be expanded during the English Revolution, most notably in the Baptist Roger Williams' *Bloody Tenent* (1646), which attacked Calvin's and Beza's defences of persecution. According to Williams, it was the will of God since Christ that permission of 'the most paganish, Jewish, Turkish or Antichristian consciences and worships' was 'granted to all men'.[39] He was willing to accept that in a 'spiritual and mysticall account' Jews, Turks or antichristians were indeed 'ravenous and greedy wolves' but argued that they might nonetheless be 'peaceable and quiet subjects, loving and helpful neighbours, faire and just dealers, true and loyal to the civil government'.[40] He replied to the text 'compel them to come in':

compel them to Masse (say the papists): compell them to Church and Common prayer, say the Protestants: compel them to the Meeting, say the New English. In all these compulsions they disagree amongst themselves: but in this, viz, Compell them to pay in this they all agree.

For Williams in 1644, three factions were now striving to 'sit downe under the shadow of that Arme of Flesh': first, the prelacy; second, the Presbyterians who made the magistrate 'the Reformer of the Church, the Suppressor of Schismaticks and Hereticks, the Protectour and defendour of the Church', and third, the 'growing faction' of Independents who wanted to persuade England to imitate 'her daughter New England's practice' of intolerant congregationalism. Rendering the account of magisterial force global, Williams wrote that if magistrates must judge and punish they had to do so 'as they are persuaded in their own beleif and conscience', and if there was a duty to punish as persuaded in their own conscience, 'they must judge according to their Consciences, whether Pagan, Turkish or Antichristian'.[41]

For Williams, 'all civil states...are...essentially civil, and therefore not Judges, Governors or Defendours of the Spirituall or Christian State and Worship'. For Williams, one's worship did not hurt another. Magistrates' tasks were to defend the 'bodies and goods of others' and not their souls. For

---

[39] Williams, *Bloody Tenent*, III, 3–4. Generally on arguments for toleration in England in the 1640s, see Coffey, 'Puritanism and Liberty'; idem, *Persecution*; Zagorin, *Idea*.
[40] Williams, *Tenent*, 142. [41] Ibid., 201, 206, 299–300, 349–51.

Williams, it was true that souls were more precious than bodies, and that the loss of one soul was a greater mischief than cutting the throats of kings. But for Williams, whatever infection was 'breathed out from the lying lips of a plague-sicke Pharisee' not one of the elect of God whose names were taken could be infected since 'none die everlastingly but such as are thereunto ordained'. For Williams, all the souls in the world were either naturally dead in sin, or alive in Christ. If they were dead in sin, no man could kill them. Augustine's account of soul-killing as 'murder' by another individual therefore made no sense in Williams' predestinarian theology. Even though 'heresy' might be a 'poison', for Williams it would, moreover, not hurt the body 'when it is not touched or taken, yea and the antidotes are received against it'. Spiritual officers and not civil magistrates were appointed to provide 'spiritual antidotes and preservatives'. For Williams, spiritual weapons were proper against 'idolatry, false worship, heresie, schism' and force was 'vain, improper, and unsuitable'.[42]

For Williams, enforced uniformity was 'the greatest occasion of civill warre': 'Such persons onely breake the Cities or Kingdoms peace, who cry out for prison and swords against such who cross their judgement or practice in Religion'. Violence was wrongly used in an attempt to prevent by swords and guns what should be cleared by light alone. Yet for Williams, neither

disobedience to parents or magistrates, not murther nor quarelling, uncleannesse nor lasciviousnesse, stealing nor extortion, neither ought of that kinde ought to be let alone...but seasonably to be supprest, as may best conduce to the publicke safetie'.

No offender against the civil state 'by robbery, murder, adultery, oppression, sedition, mutiny is for ever to be connived at'. There was here the potential for a remarkably strict moral regime of magisterial punishing of quarrelling, and of 'uncleanness' and 'lasciviousness'. Williams recorded that 'an Heretic' was 'commonly defined to be such an one as is obstinate in fundamentalls'. But for Williams, 'fundmentals' were not clear beyond a very few required items of belief – and these were only the necessity of: repentance, faith, baptism, laying on of hands, the resurrection, and eternal judgment. Heretics were those who contended about 'unprofitable Questions and Genealogies' and 'is not such a monster intended in this place, as most Interpreters run upon, to wit, one obstinate in fundamentals'. For Williams, the punishment for a heretic was excommunication and not corporal punishment, fines, or banishment.[43]

Making a firm and crucial distinction between the business of one's soul as not affecting others and those actions which did affect the commonwealth, in April 1649 the sometime Baptist Leveller Overton differentiated those things

---

[42] *Ibid.*, 5, 125–6, 127, 148, 198, 208.   [43] *Ibid.*, 80–1, 85–8, 90–1, 96, 108–10.

in which 'as I am in myself in respect to my own personal sins and transgressions, so I am to myself and to God, and so I must give an account' from those things in which

I am in relation to the Commonwealth, that all men have cognizance of, because it concerns their own particular lives, livelihoods and beings, as well as my own; and my failings and evils in that respect I yield up to the cognizance of all men, to be righteously used against me. So that the business is, not how great a sinner I am, but how faithful and real to the Commonwealth; that's the matter concerneth my neighbour.[44]

The Levellers declared in *The Agreement of the Free People of England*:

That matters of religion, and the Wayes of Gods worship, are not at all intrusted by us to any humane power, because therein wee cannot remit or exceed a tittle of what our consciences dictate to be the mind of God, without wilfulle sinne: nevertheless the publike way of instructing the Nation (so it be not compulsive) is referred to their discretion.

It is worth noting here that they have accepted that there will be a public church, receiving magisterial support and income; what they have challenged is backing worship in such a church by compulsion. In the *Agreement of the Free People of England*, they stressed that 'nothing' had 'caused more distractions and heart burnings in all ages, then persecution and molestation for matters of consience in and about Religion' and declared that they did not 'empower our Representatives' to compel

by penalties or otherwise any person to any thing in or about matters of faith, Religion, or God's worship or to restrain any person from the profession of his faith, or exercise of religion according to his conscience.[45]

The Baptists and Levellers thus pursued toleration during the English Revolution most vigorously by specifying the differences of church and state and the central role of the state as preventing harm, and they articulated in the process a strong argument for toleration as a 'natural right', but also equally importantly questioned the very definition of 'heresy' that made it subject to magisterial punishment. The definition of heresy became a major topic of concern in these years, as it received strict definition in the Westminister Confession of Faith and in the writings of heresiographers such as Edwards and Pagitt, both of which anathematised Arminianism and anti-Trinitarianism. It was in this context that John Milton, privately an anti-Trinitarian on Christology and an Arminian on grace, repeatedly attempted to defend an extensive religious toleration for Protestant 'heretics' by redefining 'heresy', sometimes by rendering it a neutral term, and thus

---

[44] Haller and Davies, *Tracts*, 231, in Wootton, 'Leveller Democracy', 441.
[45] Houston, 'Monopolizing Faith' in A. Levine (ed.), *Early Modern Scepticism and the Origins of Toleration* (Lanham, Md. 1999), 148–9.

deserving of toleration, and at other times reserving its pejorative use for those persecuting others. Milton's *A Treatise of Civil Power* (1659) declared that 'heresie. . .is no word of evil note' in Greek. To Protestants whose

common rule and touchstone is the scripture nothing can with more conscience, more equity, nothing more protestantly can be permitted than a free and lawful debate at all times by writing, conference or disputation of what opinion soever, disputable by Scripture.

Milton noted that Paul had anathematised heresy and schism by associating them with 'uncleanness' and 'enmity', but for Milton this was to gloss the required choice 'which may be without discord' – 'heresy' – by the unacceptable division, 'schism'. For Milton, moreover,

He then who to his best apprehension follows the Scripture, though against any point of doctrine by the whole church received, is not the heretic; but he who follows the church against his conscience and perswasion grounded on the Scripture. . .No man in religion is properly the heretic at this day, but he who maintains traditions or opinions not probable by scripture; who, for aught I know, is the papist only; he is the only heretic, who counts all heretics but himself.

In *Areopagitica*, Milton accented the necessity of search and enquiry to such a degree that even holding to the truth could render one a heretic, writing that 'a man may be a heretick in the truth; and if he beleeve things only because his pastor says so, or the Assembly so determins, without knowing their reason, though his belief be true, yet the very truth he holds, becomes his heresy'. For Milton:

Where there is much desire to learn, there of necessity will be much arguing, much writing, many opinions; for opinion in good men is but knowledge in the making. Under these fantastic terrors of sect and schism, we wrong the earnest and zealous thirst after knowledge and understanding which God hath stirr'd up.

For Milton, 'the perfection' of the house of God 'consists in this, that out of many moderat varieties and brotherly dissimilitudes that are not vastly disproportionall arises the goodly and the graceful symmetry that commends the whole pile and structure'.[46]

By 1673, facing Anglican assault on nonconformist worship as schismatic, Milton turned to redefining 'schism' as well as 'heresy'. In *Of True Religion, Haeresie, Schism, Toleration, And What Best Means May Be Us'd Against the Growth of Popery* he argued that in its pejorative sense 'heresie therefore is a religion taken up and believed from the traditions of men and additions to the word of God'. The consequence for Milton was that 'Popery is the only or the greatest heresie: and he who is so forward to brand all others for

---

[46] Milton in Mueller, 'Milton on Heresy', 22–3, 26–7, 28–30.

Hereticks, the obstinate Papist, the only Heretick'. Heresy is 'in the will and choice profestly against Scripture'. Schism was now defined by Milton as involving separation in congregations. For Milton, errors in some points of doctrine, as among Lutherans, Calvinists, Anabaptists, Socinians, and Arminians, did not need to cause such separation, and Milton suggested the possibility of 'keeping their other Opinions to themselves, not being destructive to Faith'. Catholics – obstinate papists – were 'heretics'; and Milton argued that their political principles rendered their toleration deeply problematic. Catholics were also, for Milton, 'idolators', and as such their worship was intolerable in England. While he suggested that Catholics were not to be corporally punished except for their political principles, Milton argued that 'idolatry' involved 'grievous and unsufferable scandal giv'n to all conscientious Beholders' and privately 'offense to God' and so it must be removed:

First we must remove their idolatry, and all the Furniture thereof. . .If they say that by removing their Idols we violate their consciences, we have no warrant to regard Conscience which is not grounded on Scripture.

As Janel Mueller has put it, in the Restoration Milton

remained as committed as ever to foreclosing the possibility of tolerating Catholicism in England. He never could regard Catholicism in any other light than as a conjoint abrogation of political safety and true religion founded in Scripture and in un-constrained, individual choice.[47]

Tolerationist in a very important way in redefining heresy and schism, Milton was thus simultaneously markedly intolerant in his opposition to Catholicism on religious as well as political grounds. Viewed from the perspective of the 1680s and 1690s in the tolerationist circles of the Netherlands, this was an important limitation in Milton's argument, and in the *Dictionary* Bayle was to compose a lengthy footnote to his entry on Milton, in which he assaulted those who by alleging that the mass was 'idolatrous' denied toleration to Catholics on religious grounds.

TOLERATIONIST ARGUMENT CONDEMNED IN MID-SEVENTEENTH-CENTURY ENGLAND

As in the sixteenth century, many of these seventeenth-century (Ana)Baptists, Quakers, Arminians, and anti-Trinitarians were committed to positions which to orthodox Protestants were 'heresies'. Although they were often imprecise about their exact doctrinal position on the person of

---

[47] Milton, *Of True Religion* (1673), 6–7, 10–3; Mueller, 'Milton on Heresy', 33, 35–6.

Christ, it is clear that many Quakers did not support the doctrine of the Trinity in its definition of three persons in one Godhead, resisting this doctrine as non-scriptural and as generated in the patristic period. Unitarians such as Biddle and Best similarly opposed the doctrine of the Trinity, but were clearer that Christ was not eternal. Arminians supported free will and reduced original sin. Some Baptists asserted perfectibility. All of these groups were attacked by orthodox Protestants as sodomites, libertines, poisoners, pestilential, traitors, communists and murderers. Their defence of toleration served not to increase support for toleration but to confirm further in the eyes of the majority – whether Anglican, Presbyterian, or conservative Independent – that toleration was no less than a 'diabolical' doctrine. For most Presbyterians and most Independents, there were firm limits to what they thought tolerable, and even at their most tolerant what was emphasised was a 'liberty of conscience' limited to what it was said could be claimed by 'conscience' and not 'toleration'. As the Independent Thomas Goodwin put it in 1645,

if any man think I am pleading for liberty of all opinions, of what nature and how gross so ever, I humbly desire them to remember that I only plead for saints, and I answer plainly, The Saints they need it not.

It was because they stood outside of these limits that Quakers, Baptists and Socinians spent many years in prison in the 1650s. For the tolerant Baptist Roger Williams, Independents had 'cast down the crown of the Lord Jesus at the feet of the Civil Magistrate', aiming to 'perswade the Mother Old England to imitate her Daughter New England's practice' of intolerance.[48] For Thomas Case in 1647, in an image we have by now repeatedly met as used against previous 'heretics' such as Anabaptists, and as central to much anti-tolerationist literature, 'liberty of conscience' might in time 'improve itself into liberty of estates and liberty of houses and liberty of wives'.[49] For John Taylor in 1651, invoking a biblical image Thomas Long was to invoke against Locke forty years later, heretics were growing like 'locusts out of the bottomless pit'.[50] The anonymous author of *Antitoleration* declared quite simply in 1646 that tolerationism was itself a 'monster'.[51] For the anonymous author of *Sine Qua Non* in 1647, toleration would 'open a floodgate unto all Licentious liberty'.[52] For the Presbyterian Christopher Fowler,

---

[48] T. Goodwin, *The Great Interest of States and Kingdomes* (London 1646), 53; *An Apologetical Narration* (1643), 23–29; Williams, *Bloody Tenent*, 349–56, in A. Zakai, 'Religious Toleration and its Enemies', *Albion* (1989), 1–39, at 3, 12, 17, 33; see especially Coffey, 'Puritanism and Liberty'.
[49] Levy, *Blasphemy*, 143; Davis, *Fear*, 102.   [50] Levy, *Blasphemy*, 151.
[51] *Antitoleration* (1646) in Katz, *Philosemitism*.
[52] *Sine Qua Non* (1647), 3 in Davis, *Fear*, 102.

toleration was 'the whore of Babylon's back door'. For Daniel Cawdrey, it was the 'last and most desperate design of Antichrist'.[53]

These comments could be multiplied hundreds of times. Fortunately, this is unnecessary; the recent scholarship of J.C. Davis, A. Zakai, B. Worden and others has shown very clearly indeed that the majority of English Protestants in the English Revolution – conservative Independents as well as Presbyterians and Anglicans – were *opponents* of toleration to heretics and schismatics, and associated heresy and schism with sedition and treason. The Independent leaders declared in the 1643 *Apologetical Narration*:

> If in all matters of doctrine, we were not as orthodox in our judgements as our brethren themselves, we would never have exposed ourselves to this tryall and hazard and discovery in the Assembly.

They sought to 'unite the Protestant partie in this Kingdom, that agree in Fundamentall truths against Popery and other heresies'. Their sermons and complaints to the Westminster Assembly rang out against Anabaptists, Brownists, antinomians and Separatists. They stressed the duty of the civil magistrate to uphold 'pure religion'. William Walwyn noted that their argument for their own toleration 'was grounded...upon a remonstrance of the nearness between them and the Presbyterians, being one in Doctrine with them'. Independent ministers were responsible for publishing John Cotton's *Keys of the Kingdom of Heaven*, which asserted that 'the establishment of pure religion and the reformation of corruptions in religion, do much concern the public peace'. Richard Overton declared that these Independents and Presbyterians would 'not suffer Brownists, Anabaptists' and were 'against Toleration'. The Independent Joseph Caryl preached against 'loose libertine Protestants' who opposed those Independents and Presbyterians who 'agree in every doctrine of faith'. It was necessary to distinguish between 'liberty and libertinism' and 'whatsoever (I say) is an errour or heresie' was to be opposed and magisterially suppressed.[54]

Thomas Edwards should probably claim the final word of these intolerant Presbyterians and others. In 1646, Edwards wrote in *Gangraena* that Parliament must not 'let hereticks and sectaries do what they list, preach, write, spread their errours, destroy many souls'. For Edwards, 'Tis a golden saying of Luther, and worthy to be thought of in these times; Cursed be that

---

[53] C. Fowler, *Daemonium Meridianum. Satan at Noon* (1655), 167, and D. Cawdrey, *Sathan Discovered* (1657), 22, quoted in Worden, 'Toleration', 200.

[54] *An Apologetical Narration* (1643), 26; W. Walwyn, *The Compassionate Samaritane* (1644), 1–3; J. Cotton, *The Keys of the Kingdom of Heaven* (1644), 153; R. Overton, *The Arraignment of Mr Persecution* (1645), 19; J. Caryl, *The Arraignment of Unbelief* (1645), 2, 47; *idem, England Plus Ultra* (1645), 24–5, in Zakai, 'Religious Toleration and its Enemies', 6, 12, 13, 18, 20, 24, 28.

Charity which is kept with the losse of the doctrine of faith, to which all things ought to give place, Charity, an Apostle, an Angel from Heaven, yea, and I will adde, Parliaments'.[55] For Edwards, 'the issue of these Sects and Schismes will be, that all will end in a looseness and licentiousnesse of living'. If a toleration were granted, he concluded that 'men should never have peace in their families more, or even after have command of wives, children, servants'. This passage bore a marginal hand in Edwards' text, indicating that he expected it to be used by other preachers in their sermons persuading their hearers of the evil of toleration. And Edwards summed up: toleration was 'a most transcendent, catholique, and fundamentall evill'; as 'original sin' was the 'most fundamentall sin, all sin; having the seed and spawn of all in it: So a Toleration hath all errors in it, and all evils'.[56]

---

[55] Edwards, *Gangraena* (1646), II, 11.

[56] Edwards, *Gangraena* (1646), I, 156, in Russell, 'Arguments for Religious Unity', 206; *Gangraena*, II, 14, and I, 121–2, in Davis, *Fear*, 102–3.

11

Arguments for and against religious toleration in the Netherlands, c. 1579–c. 1680

We saw in Chapter 4 that religious toleration in the Netherlands was considerably greater in practice than in legislative provision, existing more because of deliberate failures to enforce anti-tolerationist laws than by principled enactment of full religious toleration. As has often been noted by Dutch historians, Dutch authors composed few principled defences of religious toleration across the ninety years from 1579 to 1670. Dutch toleration was celebrated more by observers than by the Dutch themselves.[1] But there were a series of important Dutch defenders of religious toleration during the century from 1579 to the 1680s. Indeed, Martin van Gelderen has shown that in connection with the 1579 Union of Utrecht there were important voices in the Netherlands which called for a widespread toleration of worship and beliefs as long as this did not transgress the requirements of civil peace and security, arguing that 'From this perspective the Dutch revolt as a defence of liberty was principally a fight for individual freedom of conscience and worship'.[2]

The 1578 *Admonition and Advice for the Netherlands* argued that none 'should force consciences' and that both Catholics and 'evangelicals' were guilty of persecuting. In an argument later central to advocacy of toleration, it stressed that forcing conscience was wrong as contrary to the rule of nature 'that one should not do unto others what you do not want them to do to yourself'. In a second equally crucial contention in later tolerationist argument, it traced 'sedition and domestic dispute' in the Netherlands to the practice of tyrannising and persecuting 'those who are held for heretics'. The 1579 *Good Admonition to the Good Citizens of Brussels* argued that every person should be able to 'accept and keep such religion as his conscience guides' and declared freedom of worship essential to such 'liberty of conscience'. And the 1579 *A Friendly Admonition to All Lovers of Liberty*

---

[1] Cf. E. Kossman, 'Freedom in Dutch Thought and Practice' in Israel (ed.), *The Anglo-Dutch Moment*, 281–98, at 292–98, esp. 292.

[2] Van Gelderen, *Political Thought*, 228.

and Peace argued that one should not 'cut each other's throat' for taking 'different ways' to the same destination, although, showing the difficulty of generating support for full religious toleration, it then explicitly denied toleration to Anabaptists and to the Family of Love. Written in the years of French argument on the basis of 'reason of state' that diversity in religion was problematic but might need to be accepted when the alternative was civil war and destruction, the Huguenot adviser to William of Orange, François Duplessis-Mornay, argued in his 1579 *Discourse on the Permission of Liberty of Religion, Called 'Religions Vrede' in the Low Countries* that while religious union was best for peace, where it could not be obtained without great cost one was to allow religious diversity as a lesser evil. The 1579 *Discourse Containing the True Understanding of the Pacification of Ghent* defended Dutch liberty 'of goods, of body, and of conscience' and asserted that 'the principal point of liberty is to have liberty of conscience, to which all are entitled by natural right'. The *Discourse* asserted straightforwardly that unless religious doctrine inclined directly to the subversion of the political order, religion did 'not affect politics'. Magistrates were charged simply to ensure that the polity was not disrupted because of religion. While the *Discourse* indicated that it was desirable to 'avoid diversity of religions', it argued that if this diversity could not be avoided peacefully, magistrates were to secure peace. Aggeas van Albada's 1581 *Acts of the Peace Negotiations which Took Place at Cologne* repeated the argument already advanced in the 1579 *Admonition and Advice* that the law of nature to not do unto others required toleration, as one clearly would wish to be tolerated by others. Albada stressed that faith could not be forced, that political authorities had been established to secure the 'body and goods' and not salvation, and that only toleration could secure peace.[3]

The most extensive series of defences of toleration in the period of the Union of Utrecht were by the spiritualist Dirck Volckertsz Coornhert, sometime secretary to the States of Holland, and author of the 1582 *Synod of the Freedom of Conscience*, 1589 *Trial of the Killing of Heretics and the Constraints of Conscience*, and a number of lesser-known works, including the 1582 *Means to Abate the Sects and Factional Strife in this Civil War Until Such Will Be Provided by Common Concord*, the 1581 *Request by the Catholics of Haarlem*, the 1583 *Examination of the Heidelberg Catechism*, and the 1590 *The Root of the Dutch Wars*. Coornhert's works were to be

---

[3] *Admonition and Advice for the Netherlands* (1578), fos. A8, C, F4–F5 in van Gelderen, *Political Thought*, 220; du Plessis Mornay, *Discours* (1579) in *ibid.*, 221–2; *Friendly Admonition*, fos. A2, A7 in *ibid.*, 222–3; *Good Admonition* (1579), 13–15 in *ibid.*, 223–4; *Discours* (1579), 31–2, 35, 64, 95 in *ibid.*, 224–5; A. van Albada, *Acts of the Peace Negotiations* (1581), 6, 129, 194, 299 in *ibid.*, 227–8; quotation at 228; Israel, *Dutch Republic*, 210–11.

particularly influential on later Arminian defences of toleration, and to be republished in his collected works at Amsterdam in 1630. The hostile 1618 engraving *The Arminian Dung-Cart* affiliated Coornhert and Arminianism in declaring that 'for Arminius' teachings he blazed the trail. . .we may justly call Arminians Coornhertists'.[4]

In one of Coornhert's two most important works contending for toleration, the 1582 *Synod of the Freedom of Conscience*, he argued that true members of Christ could err and still hold to the faith, and that all 'faction, dispute, condemnation, banishment, and persecution' should be renounced. The *Synod* paralleled Protestant claims to authority over 'conscience' with Catholic claims, and argued that since none was impartial it was simply not possible to judge between them which was the 'true church'. For Coornhert, who explicitly assaulted 'Genevan Popery', Beza had made the magistrate 'the servant of other people's cruelties, rather than the protector of God's truth'.[5] In his 1589 *Trial of the Killing of Heretics and the Constraints of Conscience*, he identified Calvin as having taken to Geneva from Catholic sources the fires used by Catholics to burn heretics. And in the 1590 *Root of the Dutch Wars* he wrote of persecution that 'The Reformed' were 'drawn to this by false doctrine, interpretation and glosses of people who follow in the well-trodden footsteps of the Catholic murderers'.[6]

Thus indicting the Catholic Church as the source of arguments for intolerance, Coornhert nonetheless himself remained a nominal, albeit not a communicating Catholic.[7] When Catholic worship was forbidden in April 1581 in Haarlem, he wrote a plea for the toleration of Catholics, the *Request by the Catholics of Haarlem*, arguing that 'two religions can indeed coexist peacefully in one town'.[8] In a debate which he himself publicised, he challenged the Reformed minister Cornelisz to show that the Catholic Church was not the 'true church' and suggested that the Reformed had only the form of the 'true church' without its substance.[9] And it was not merely the mainstream of 'magisterial Reformation' Protestantism that he challenged. He was hostile to what he saw as 'foundationalism' in the Anabaptist Menno Simmons' *Foundation Book*, with its implication that it

[4] *Den Arminiaenschen Dreck-waghen* in Voogt, *Constraint*, 235.
[5] Coornhert, *Synod, passim*; Voogt, *Constraint*, 95; Le Cler, *Toleration*, II, 278 (the synod is available in French as T. Coornhert (ed.), *À L'Aurore des Libertés Modernes: Synode sur la Liberté de Conscience*, ed. J. Le Cler and M.-F. Valkhoff (Paris 1979); van Gelderen, *Political Thought*, 247–50. Cf also Zagorin, *Idea*, 154–64.
[6] *Wercken*, II, cii, C in Voogt, *Constraint*, 100.   [7] Voogt, *Constraint*, 131.
[8] Coornhert, *Requeste der Catholijcken tot Haarlem* in *Wercken*, I, '537'(545)–546 discussed in Voogt, *Constraint*, 93.
[9] Voogt, *Constraint*, 183.

had identified something 'foundational' beyond the Scripture. He was hostile to the founder of the Family of Love Hendrik Niclaes' *Spiegel*, with its claims to complete Jesus' revelation. And he was hostile to the Anabaptist David Joris' claims of religious leadership. All seemed to him to be supporting their own authority instead of that of unmediated Scripture. In one dialogue, he attacked the exclusivism of the Anabaptists, cited the example of Münster against them, and suggested that if they were in power the Anabaptists might persecute. Coornhert argued that even the pacifist and significantly tolerationist Anabaptist Simmons spewed forth 'venom' in 'slandering and damning' those outside of the community, and on this basis had 'no doubt that if you should find the external sword in your hands, you would not save the bodies of these, similarly to the way that you do not save their names with your two-edged and defaming tongues'.[10]

Coornhert's 1589 *Trial of the Killing of Heretics and the Constraints of Conscience* utilised what was already by then becoming a staple of tolerationist argument, later to be central in the 1680s, in contending that the punishment of heretics was ruled out by the 'natural law, mentioned in God's word, what you wish people to do unto you, do that also unto them'. He stressed a further important element of much later tolerationist argument in indicting Calvin for failure to meet this standard, tying it specifically to his first justifying toleration when powerless and persecution when powerful. For Coornhert, as soon as Calvin had reached a position of secure power enabling him to do to others what he had first complained about when it happened to him, he had wrongly turned to persecute others.[11] In his 1579 *About the Constraint*, Coornhert similarly pilloried Calvin as having opposed force when 'he was still under, not beyond the power of the authorities', but then having supported it when he gained authority. And in his *Vre-Reden*, Coornhert wrote: 'Let everyone follow the law of nature: if you do not like being forced in your conscience, then do not force others either in word or in deed'.[12]

Coornhert argued that the government was ordained to protect and to administer justice but not to 'punish the errant in matters of faith'. Since faith was the gift of God alone, it was unjust to punish a man who had not received this gift. Princes ruled only over 'bodies and goods' and not over souls. By taking over the definition of 'heresy' of Peter Martyr, that 'heresy' involved the 'stubborn protection of doctrines which conflict with the divine scripture'

---

[10] Voogt, *Constraint*, 134–5; Coornhert, *Schijnedeught*, cccxlvA in Voogt, *Constraint*, 148–9; cf. van Deursen, *Plain Lives*, ch. 17.

[11] *Trial of the Killing of Heretics* (1589) in *Wercken* 2, fo. cxliA in Voogt, *Constraint*, 101; van Gelderen, *Political Thought*, 252–3.

[12] *Vre-Reden* in *Wercken*, ɪɪ, ccccxviiA in Voogt, *Constraint*, 120; E. Kossman and A. F. Mellinck (eds.), *Texts Concerning the Revolt of the Netherlands* (Cambridge 1974), 193.

engaged in to satisfy private 'lusts and benefit', Coornhert declared that for punishing heretics judges would need to know not only the truth about doctrine but also the content of people's hearts. And he stressed that such an 'impartial judge' was impossible to find. Coornhert here set out a structure of argument that was to be utilised again by Pierre Bayle in the *Philosophical Commentary* in the 1680s.[13] And in another argument endlessly repeated in later tolerationist polemic, Coornhert's 1590 *The Root of the Dutch Wars* identified concord, riches, and power with 'diversity'. The use of force was for Coornhert, in an image which was employed in the 1680s by Limborch, 'like oil on the flame': it increased rather than prevented sects. In an argument endlessly rehearsed in the 1680s, he declared that force could only produce 'impious or hypocritical people'.[14] Reversing the usual images applied to heresy, Coornhert's 1583 *Examination of the Heidelberg Catechism* attacked the attempt to constrain conscience as 'more harmful' than 'a disastrous fire'.[15]

Coornhert's 1579 *About the Constraint upon Conscience Practised in Holland* argued that the 'clear evangelical law' about heretics was that they were to be admonished and then avoided. Those who wished to punish heretics looked for a precedent in Moses or 'invent[ed] one' by stretching Scripture; they, and not alleged heretics, thereby 'reject[ed] Scripture'. He challenged the Haarlem burgomaster Niclaes van der Laan to 'quote one single clear sentence from the whole Bible in which it is said that God has ordered the political authority to kill heretics, to protect his church by their sword of steel, or to nourish, guide and preserve the souls of the subjects'. Since this could not be done, such political authorities were 'being disobedient' and openly dishonouring God. In an emphasis on the words of Scripture itself against the impositions of synods which was to become a central stress of tolerationist arguments of the late seventeenth century, for Coornhert it was crucial to 'accept the books of God's word', but Calvinists' 'glosses' either 'contain nothing else than what also stands written in the Holy Scripture, in which case they are not needed, or they contain something else, in which case they are not to be believed'.[16]

In some of his works, Coornhert's emphases on the words of Scripture alone, his attack on those who added glosses to Scripture, and his assault on the intolerance which he found in communions ranging from Catholic to

---

[13] Coornhert, *Synod, passim* in *ibid.*, 245–9; *idem, The Root of the Dutch Wars* (1590), in *Works*, II, fo. 180 in *ibid.*, 255; *idem, Trial, passim* in van Gelderen, *Political Thought*, 251–4.

[14] Coornhert, *Wercken* (Amsterdam 1630), I, 470ff. in Kossman and Mellinck, *Texts*, 191–6; van Gelderen, *Political Thought*, 255–6.

[15] Coornhert, *Wercken*, III, cccclxvir in Voogt, *Constraint*, 97.

[16] Kaplan, *Calvinists*, 98; Kossman and Mellinck, *Texts*, 192–3.

radical Anabaptist, turned clearly in the direction of proposing substantial magisterial restriction of public religious expression and even of the private possession of religious works, at least for an interim period until Christian peace and unity could be gained and settled. In the name of toleration, what Coornhert thus proposed amounted to a sweeping set of restrictions on the contemporary religious commitments of almost every single person in the Netherlands in his day. Coornhert's 1582 *Means to Abate the Sects and Factional Strife in this Civil War until Such Will Be Provided by Common Concord* thus argued that all religious worship should be restricted to the reading of Scripture, introducing no interpretations of Scripture at all since this was the source of conflict, and that the government should ensure such limitation.[17] He even argued that citizens should be forced to turn in all books which contained anything beyond 'pure Scripture' or be fined by the magistrate. Since the Scripture was 'pure', and anything beyond this was not, for Coornhert this would be like compelling people to use only a pure fountain to obtain water. It should not be understood as a restriction on one's religious freedom, which was clearly based on one's duty to follow Scripture. Against Coornhert's proposal of restricting public worship to reading the Scripture, however, the Reformed ministers Arent Cornelisz and Reinier Donteclock pointed out in their 1582 *Examination of the Unheard of Means...to Abate the Sects* that this was itself intolerance because it argued for governmental interference to prohibit interpretations of Scripture, and by the act of prohibiting many people's religious commitment in the name of toleration it essentially committed the government thereby to the 'plant[ing of] his own particular religion'.[18]

Part of the impetus for this vision of a restrictively simplified worship was that Coornhert was deeply spiritualist, and thought that outward worship was unimportant.[19] For Coornhert, Christianity had dispensed with ceremonial emphases in order to require focus on spiritual laws of love of God and of one's neighbour. When composing his entry on Coornhert in the *Dictionary*, it was this feature which Bayle most emphasised in the beginning of his entry; he was marking thereby the distance between Coornhert and almost all contemporary Christians.[20] Coornhert was deeply influenced by the mystical fourteenth-century *German Theology*, a work from which he and others drew the message of incarnation after the ascension – that is, of

---

[17] Coornhert, *Means to Abate* (1582) in van Gelderen, *Political Thought*, 243–4.

[18] Coornhert, *Means* in *Wercken*, cccxcviC[cccxcviiiC] in Voogt, *Constraint*, 107; van Gelderen, *Political Thought*, 243–4.

[19] He also countenanced salvation for pagans on the basis of following the law of nature, and argued that Jesus was comprised in the golden rule and so one could have Christ in his heart without knowing the historical Christ: Voogt, *Constraint*, 120–1.

[20] Voogt, *Constraint*, 14–15; Bayle, *Dictionary*, Koornhert.

the 'indwelling spirit' operating in believers. In one of his dialogues, a character criticised another who was attempting to define the Trinity by indicating that he could not even define the soul, and also attacked the doctrine of original sin as an 'invented doctrine'. Coornhert had thus moved far from orthodox Trinitarianism and into denial of the doctrine of original sin – a position associated especially with Socinianism. Discussing freedom and sin, he identified Calvinist doctrine as teaching in essence that God was the author of evil. Coornhert was thus clearly what almost all contemporary Catholics, almost all 'magisterial Reformation' Protestants, and many radical Reformation Protestants considered a 'heretic' and blasphemer.[21]

As such a spiritualist, Coornhert was one of several late sixteenth-century Dutch thinkers – the small number of others included Coolhaes and Duifhuis – who advocated widespread religious toleration, attacked the credal impositions of Calvinists, and drew sustenance from the mystical *German Theology*. Like Coornhert, Coolhaes denied the name Christians to Calvinists,

who cling so tightly to Calvin and his writings that they are not willing to deviate even a smidgen from them...Our office is to preach Christ, not Calvin. We are Christians, and for that reason we must give ourselves no other names and no one may follow anyone else but God.[22]

For Coolhaes, 'we can and readily should tolerate by our side all those who still live in the darkness of papism and similar sects as long as they do not commit acts of rebellion or other crimes which public authority is in duty bound to punish. Errors must be countered by the word of God'.[23] But while there are some affinities between the thought of a few other spiritualists and the thought of Coornhert, it is important to emphasise that in his time Coornhert was a relatively isolated figure. In theory, he was a tolerant Catholic, but in practice not a communicating member of any church, and deeply hostile to the persecutionary proclivities he discerned in all worships from Mennonite to Catholic. His works were banned by the States of Holland for 'disturbing the peace'. Coornhert was in many ways more important for his influence on a later generation than influential in his own. Partly due to his influence after his works were republished in Amsterdam in 1630, the later generation of Arminians repeated his emphases on the actual words of Scripture, fierce oppositon to Calvinist credalism,

---

[21] Voogt, *Constraint*, 49–50, 56, 66–80. For Calvin, Coornhert was a 'drunkard', who, 'under the guise of wanting to make Christians entirely spiritual, allows them to pollute their bodies by engaging in all sorts of idolatries': Calvin, *Réponse à un certain Hollandais*, in Voogt, *Constraint*, 15–16.

[22] Kaplan, *Calvinists*, 98–9.   [23] Le Cler, *Toleration*, 266–7.

stress on the ethics of reciprocity – do not be intolerant to others if you do not wish them to be intolerant to you – and emphasis on the limitations of governmental authority to securing the goods of body. While he did not share his 'spiritualist' emphases, Limborch attempted to present the spiritualist thought of Coornhert fairly and emphasised tolerance. And Bayle stressed Coornhert's significance with an entry in the *Dictionary*.

In the first generation of Arminians, before the tolerationist generations of Episcopius around 1630 and of Limborch around 1680, however, even Arminianism took up only a limited tolerationist position. Like Coornhert, the first generation of Arminians, including Arminius himself, tended to stress the limited number of fundamentals of Christianity, the words of Scripture, and the desirability of an inclusive and ecumenical church. They stressed the proneness of humanity to error through ignorance rather than malice, and the possibility of salvation for those in error. In all of these senses, they importantly countenanced a tolerable and indeed ineradicable variety of understandings. But they also strongly stressed the role of the civil magistrate as having the right to settle religious controversies, and cited the Old Testament as establishing this clearly.

Arminius had studied with Thomas Erastus – for whom the doctrine of magisterial supremacy over the church, Erastianism, is named – and his 1606 address on 'The Reconciliation of Religious Dissensions among Christians' called not merely for the attempt to conduct controversy in a moderate and reconciling manner, stressing all of the points about error just mentioned, but also for the magistrate to call and preside over a council to try to establish consensus about matters 'supported by clear testimonies from the Scriptures', by setting aside 'churches and their confessions' and 'schools and their masters' in attempting to establish the faith. The potential for magisterial imposition of religion here was indicated clearly by Reformed opponents of such a suggestion. Believing that the church was the repository of truth, and that it should recommend the 'true' and 'pure' religion to be supported by the magistrate, the Reformed Church assaulted this proposal of Arminius as being an unacceptable 'Erastianism' in which the magistrate might choose to impose the false and not the 'true religion'. Supportive of intolerance established by the magistrate on the orders of the church rather than by the orders of the magistrate over the church, they argued for determination of the controversy by the terms of the confession of faith and catechism of the Reformed Church. Arminius' leading modern biographer, Carl Bangs, notes among Arminius' probable motivations for his alternative model of the council a desire 'to set up a magisterially controlled assembly where his own views would prevail'. It is moreover unclear how extensive a membership was supposed to exist in such a council – whether Anabaptists or Socinians were to be admitted, for instance – and the declaration of the matters that were 'clearly testified to' in Scripture in Arminius' eyes may well have included the Trinity. Episcopius himself identified Arminian desires as having been either for a fair and impartial synod to settle disputed matters *or* for mutual toleration to accommodate differences, suggesting that toleration of differences was only one possible outcome of a magisterially controlled council.[24]

The leading Arminian Uyttenbogaert's 1610 *Treatise of the Function and Authority of a Superior Christian Magistrate* declared the States of Holland to have authority from God to 'watch carefully over the teaching given to subjects', to prevent 'idle disputes in the pulpit', and to 'not suffer your subjects to be disturbed, divided and torn apart by men that thrive on discord'. Signed by forty-four ministers, including Uyttenbogaert, the 1610 Arminian *Remonstrantie*, from which the name of 'Remonstrants' for Arminians was derived, called for a revision to the confession of faith and catechism. It is again possible to describe this demand for revision in two separate ways. One way is to interpret it as involving the desire to make the terms of the confession and catechism of the public church more flexible and inclusive, accommodating Arminian positions alongside strongly predestinarian positions but not precluding others from holding such strongly predestinarian views. In his 1613 *Ordinum Pietas*, Hugo Grotius, associated with Arminianism and with the so-called leader of the Arminian party, Oldenbarnevelt, supported the notion that Arminians wished 'freedom to entertain' their opinion, and cited Erasmus in favour of the notion that 'we define only the absolute minimum and leave to each individual his own free judgment on many questions, because many things are very obscure'. This would clearly be to revise the confession in a tolerant direction. Another way, however, is to suggest that the civil magistrate could have revised the confession in such a way as to reflect Arminian positions on disputed issues, and not merely to give them permission to continue their own beliefs alongside others' equally valid positions. And Grotius' *Ordinum Pietas* also raised that possibility, being clear that the magistrate was to summon synods, to determine their membership, and to determine what was taught, supporting the 'supreme judgment on public religion' of the 'supreme magistrate' and his 'right to decide on the faith of the Church in as much as it is public'.[25]

---

[24] Greengrass, *European Reformation*, 221; C. Bangs, *Arminius* (Nashville 1971), 275–80; D. Nobbs, *Theocracy and Toleration* (Cambridge 1938); Nijenhuis, *Ecclesia*, 139; S. Episcopius, *Opera Theologica* (Amsterdam-Gouda 1650–5), II, ii, 2, in Jordan, *Toleration*, 339; Grotius in H.-J. van Dam, '*De Imperio Summarum Potestatum Circa Sacra*' in H. Nellen and E. Rabbie (eds.), *Hugo Grotius, Theologian* (Leiden 1994), 22, and cf. Trapmann, 'Grotius and Erasmus' in *ibid.*, 84; cf. also J. Taurinus, On Mutual Tolerance (Utrecht 1616) discussed in Le Cler, *Toleration*, 307–8.

[25] H. Grotius, *Ordinum...Pietas*, ed. E. Rabbie (Leiden 1995), pp. 135, 169, 189 (paragraphs 40, 90, 118); cf. Tuck, *Philosophy and Government*, esp. 187 and J. den Tex, *Oldenbarnevelt* (Cambridge 1973), 2 vols., on Grotius' affiliations with Arminianism.

While the former way of reading Arminians as desiring greater flexibility and ecumenicism reflects most of the early generations of Arminian rhetoric closely, the latter possibility of support for public imposition of Arminian teaching has some evidence to support it. The years between 1609 and 1618 saw Arminian-inspired or -supported purges of Contra-Remonstrant ministers by magistrates, starting in 1609–10 in Alkmaar and Utrecht, but also including Rotterdam, den Briel, Hoorn, The Hague and Hillersburg, and there were deprivations of Contra-Remonstrant ministers after the decree of the States of Holland of 1614 forbidding pastors to treat controversial matters in the pulpit. In some cases, the measures taken included expulsion of pastors from the cities and the breaking up of Contra-Remonstrant worship; in one case, they involved the banishment of two citizens of Utrecht who wished to employ a Contra-Remonstrant preacher. Here, then, in the years immediately before the much more famous 1618 deprivation of Remonstrant ministers by the magistrates following the Synod of Dort, was magisterial suppression by Arminians of Contra-Remonstrant teaching. And Arminius himself was one of two ministers involved in protests to the magistrates against the Brownist separatist community. Contra-Remonstrants confronted the turn by Arminians to defence of full religious toleration when they were proscribed after 1618 as being opportunistic hypocrisy. In the sense that Arminians had employed magisterial power in an attempt to deprive their opponents of ministerial positions and had advocated magisterial judgment of theological controversy, they were not inaccurately represented by Cornelius Dunganus and Henricus Arnoldi as among those who defended toleration when out of power and yet denied toleration when in power. Reflecting on the denial of toleration to Arminians in the 1620s, the Contra-Remonstrant Buchelius had reason to argue that Arminians' period of domination had been harsh towards others.[26]

In the early years of Arminianism, such intolerance towards other Christians was combined with the desire of some Arminian and Arminian-associated thinkers to place increased restrictions upon Jewish worship and upon the Jewish community. In 1610, the burgomasters of Rotterdam had granted Jews a charter or contract for public worship and citizenship, but when the Remonstrants took power in Rotterdam, they rescinded this charter. When Arminian worship was forbidden following the Synod of

---

[26] Sprunger, *Dutch Puritanism*, 47–8; Pettegree, 'Politics', 196–7; Nijenhuis, *Ecclesia*, ii, 142–3; J. Israel, 'Toleration in Seventeenth-Century Dutch and English Thought', in *Britain and the Netherlands* (1994), 13–30, at 17; *idem*, *Dutch Republic*, 422–5, 435, 457; *idem*, 'Intellectual Debate', 11ff.; J. Pollman, *Religious Choice in the Dutch Republic* (Manchester 1999), 148; Tex, *Oldenbarnevelt*; Bangs, *Arminius, passim*.

Dort in 1618–19, the Arminian van Pauw complained that Jews had been allowed to 'intermarry' – a charge which he did not provide any evidence to document – and that Jewish synagogues continued to be allowed as tending to 'great obloquy, especially to the Remonstrants to whom the exercise of their religion was interdicted while that of the Jews was permitted'. It was the later Remonstrant historian Gerard Brandt who turned this complaint into the more tolerant claim that Arminians had noted the tolerance towards sects banished from England and 'even to the Jews who deny Christ whom the petitioners regard as their only Saviour' in order to campaign for their own toleration as well as others'; the original Arminian protest made Jewish worship intrinsically problematic.[27]

Moreover, when Grotius was pensionary of Rotterdam from 1613 and was therefore consulted by the States of Holland and Westvriesland about Jewish worship, he composed a *Remonstrantie*; this ended with a declaration which contended that 'the Jews are to be admitted to Holland' and that 'they are to be granted freedom of religion', but continued with the further declaration that admission and toleration was to occur 'provided that certain rules are laid down, in order not to endanger Christian religion and public order', which then was said to involve no less than forty-nine regulations. Grotius began the manuscript by criticising towns which granted 'extensive privileges' to Jews 'only with a view to private gain and trade, but not to the glory of God and the public weal'. He argued that it was 'high time, that those who are not motivated by private interest, but have the public weal in mind, are roused to direct that which has already happened in such channels that no offense is given'. Grotius proposed the allowance of up to three public synagogues. But he advocated that Christian preachers should have the right to preach Christianity in the synagogues and that Jews were to be compelled to listen to the sermons, a provision reminiscent of Pope Gregory XIII's recent 1584 institution of conversionist sermons in Rome. Grotius provided that Jews could have a printing-press. But he stipulated that Jews were not to be allowed to print any works containing 'blasphemy', suggested interdicting possession and printing of the Talmud, and referred in complimentary terms to the burning of the Talmud at Rome under Pope Clement VIII in 1601. Grotius proposed permission for Jewish schools but he forbade Jewish children from attending Christian schools on the grounds that Jewish children had already 'lighly infected' their classmates by attending Christian schools, and argued that 'experience' had shown 'the necessity of this prohibition'. He recommended banning the employment of Christian servants by Jews and banning Jews from intermarriage with 'the daughters of

---

[27] Huussen, 'Legal Position', 27; A. Kuhn, 'Hugo Grotius and the Emancipation of the Jews in Holland', *Publications of the American Jewish Society*, 31 (1928), 173–80.

the land'. He advocated Jews needing special permission to buy land, and opposed the purchase of land for a Jewish cemetry within city walls. And Grotius proposed strict limits on the ultimate size of the Jewish community in any town – 200 families for most cities and 300 for Amsterdam – together with a complete ban of Jews from the countryside. He suggested that this would prevent conspiracies 'which may be conceived in solitary places or also in towns, if they were allowed to become too numerous'. His proposals would have virtually ended Jewish immigration at the date of their composition, before the large-scale increases of the mid-seventeenth century as Ashkenazi Jews fled persecution in Eastern Europe. It was only within these severe limits that Grotius then became remarkably generous: this limited population was to be allowed freedom to trade in the same way 'as the other burghers and citizens without being encumbered with any special tribute'.[28]

Grotius devoted more of his manuscript to consideration of arguments against 'admission' than to arguments against 'toleration'. In this first category of arguments on admission to which he responded were arguments that no state could tolerate two religions, that Jews hated Christians, that Jews had murdered Christians in the remote and recent past, and that Jews had murdered children in order to ridicule Christianity. In the second category, on toleration, were arguments that no state was to tolerate idolatry and that Jews should not be allowed legal freedom when this was denied to Catholics. In each case, it is significant that Grotius himself argued *against* these arguments and in favour of both admission and toleration. He urged that conversion of Jews required their association with Christians, that hospitality was a mark of the Reformed Church, and that nations excluding foreigners were 'decried everywhere as barbarians'. He spoke of a 'natural community' of humankind. He argued that 'we have to practice natural love to every person without excluding anybody'. Expulsion was held to be 'against nature because it cuts off the communion established by nature'. He attacked the ill-treatment of Jews by many rulers throughout history, and praised Christian emperors who had tolerated Jews. Jews were, moreover, for Grotius to be 'beloved for the sake of the forefathers, who were specially chosen by God'. He argued that 'religion should not be forced upon anyone' and that imposition which created hypocrisy was sinful. And he declared Judaism far less dangerous than the Catholic religion, whose 'head and supreme ruler' was a 'notorious enemy of this state', and the meetings of

---

[28] J. Michman, 'Historiography of the Jews in the Netherlands', *Dutch Jewish History* 1 (Jerusalem 1984), 7–24, at 17–22; J. Meijer,'Hugo Grotius' Remonstrantie', *Jewish Social Studies* 17 (1955), 91–104; E. Rabbie, 'Hugo Grotius and Judaism' in H. Nellen and E. Rabbie (eds.), *Hugo Grotius, Theologian* (Leiden 1994), 99–120, at 107–10; Kuhn, 'Hugo Grotius', 175–6.

whose members were 'incomparably more dangerous' because they could conspire with foreign enemies, whereas Jews had neither a head 'nor a Prince of their religion'. Catholicism for Grotius involved both 'idolatry' and 'iconolatry', but Jewish worship for Grotius involved 'the worship of the true God, however mixed with unbelief'.[29]

In all of these arguments, Grotius was markedly tolerant. But this was not all that he said. Grotius also argued that it was inadvisable 'to admit any persons into the country who differ so greatly from us in their religious convictions', voicing the fear that this would weaken people's commitment to the faith necessary for salvation in a country 'in which many people are inclined to new departures and too inquisitive examination of things beyond human understanding'. He attributed much Jewish hatred of Christians to ill-treatment, but not all. He declared the need for 'judicial investigation' of ritual murder allegations, recorded that 'the concurrence of testimony of so many witnesses' and the 'large number of examples' rendered credible the accusations of ritual murder, and argued that 'the general implacable hatred of the Jews towards the Christians' gave reasons to find these accusations credible.

As Edward Rabbie has shown, Grotius was to be consulted many years later by a Polish nobleman who had been his student during Grotius' exile in Paris in the 1620s, Jerzy Slupecki, who was sceptical about 'ritual murder' accusations against Jews in the city of Lublin in 1636, and who wished to know from Grotius what the Talmud said, what allegations had been voiced in Western Europe, and whether clear evidence had been found. Grotius replied that Jews did hate Christians, as was written in the Talmud, that they had murdered dissidents, and that they believed that the blood of children was a cure for leprosy, which perhaps had inclined them to using this remedy. Grotius praised Slupecki's 'impartiality', and suggested that the accusations against them were primarily inspired by hatred of the Jews, but to praise 'impartiality' was not to praise scepticism. Grotius concluded that 'one should not believe everything of this, but neither nothing of it'. He held that while no similar blood-libels were recorded in Holland, this might merely be because Jews were lying low and had only been in Holland a short time, and added that Jews would not have been expelled 'without reason' from Holland and France.[30]

While Contra-Remonstrant ministers themselves at points had campaigned against freedom of Jewish worship, and while they were probably responsible for the order prohibiting construction of a public synagogue in

---

[29] Meijer, 'Hugo Grotius' Remonstrantie', 91–104; Rabbie, 'Grotius and Judaism'; Melnick, *From Polemics*, 14–15.
[30] Meijer, 'Hugo Grotius' Remonstrantie'; Rabbie, 'Grotius and Judaism'.

Amsterdam in 1612, the Contra-Remonstrant magistrates who were in sole control of Amsterdam after 1618–19 did not institute any of the restrictions advocated by Grotius and instead continued to permit Jewish worship and Jewish immigration to Amsterdam, even while forbidding Arminianism as 'heretical' Christian worship. They were here in part following a long-standing division made by theologians between the illegitimacy of forcing those to Christianity who had never adopted it and the legitimacy of punishing those who had departed from the faith. Noting the disparity between Contra-Remonstrant and Remonstrant attitudes and practices about toleration and Judaism in the early seventeenth-century Netherlands, Jozeph Michman has argued that 'Fortunately for the Jews the Remonstrants were defeated and eliminated from power'. This overstates Reformed toleration-ism, for there were Contra-Remonstrants who argued against toleration of Jews as well as those who provided it, and the leading Reformed Utrecht professor Gijsbertus Voetius in 1637 accepted the blood-libel and held that ritual infanticide accorded well with denial of the doctrine of justification by faith.[31] But it does importantly indicate one of the major limits of Arminian and Grotian tolerationism in the early seventeenth century.[32]

Grotius' tolerationism was more considerable within Christianity, and centred on reducing the essentials of Christianity. As Richard Tuck has indicated, Grotius' twenty-folio 1611 manuscript *Meletius* (not published until after Grotius' death and only recently discovered) argued that disagree-ments among Christians over points of philosophy on which they could not decide was a 'disease' which had a remedy: 'limiting the number of necessary articles of faith to those few which are most self-evident, and to inquire into the other doctrinal points which lead to the perfection of pious wisdom without prejudice, preserving charity and under the guidance of the Holy Scriptures'.[33] Although Grotius initially wished to find ways to defend the Trinity and satisfaction against Socinian opposition – and indeed to show that Arminians did not favour the 'noxious weeds' of Socinianism being planted in Dutch soil – over the course of his life, Grotius increasingly came to place the Trinity outside of self-evident articles and increasingly suggested that anti-Trinitarianism was tolerable. Grotius stressed the limited number of fundamentals within Christianity particularly importantly in his *De Veritate Religionis Christianae*, a work which sought to persuade

---

[31] G. Voetius, *Selectae disputationes* (Utrecht 1648–69), II, 77–102, cited in P. van Rooden, 'Conceptions of Judaism in the Seventeenth Century Dutch Republic', in D. Wood (ed.), *Christianity and Judaism* (Oxford 1992), 299–308, at 302; Michman, 'Historiography', 21.

[32] See Chapter 4 below, pp. 144–9; Rabbie, 'Grotius and Judaism', 110; Michman, 'Historiography', 21.

[33] Grotius, *Meletius* in Tuck, *Philosophy and Government* 184–6.

non-Christians of the truth of the Christian revelation, and which simply left out of its discussion such disputed issues as the Trinity.

Members of the Reformed Church assaulted Grotius as 'Socinian' both for this failure to state the single most important item of Christianity when attempting to persuade people of its truth, and for his own explications of Scripture in several of his works, some of which he issued in declared opposition to Socinian readings, but some of whose readings accepted rather than challenged Socinian positions or opposed them in ways thought by many readers to have weakened rather than strengthened Trinitarianism. Grotius refused to respond to the reply to his early work on the satisfaction issued by the leading Socinian John Crell, and instead engaged in a polite correspondence with Crell, and in an eight-year friendly correspondence with the leading Socinian Martin Ruar. Grotius may have moved closer to Socinian understandings of the Trinity himself as his life wore on. And Jan Paul Heering has shown that two of the books of Grotius' *De Veritate* are close to Socinus' *De Auctoritate Sacrae Scripturae*, describing these similarities as 'so striking that we cannot but assume that Grotius had Socinus' work at hand' during composition.[34] Other scholars have pointed to the similarity of the structure of Grotius' arguments in the first books of *De Veritate* with the arguments of the Socinian *Racovian Catechism*, and their firm departure from the traditional form of arguments for the veracity of Scripture and superiority of Christianity to Judaism in a direction paralleled only by such Socinian works.[35]

Grotius was, moreover, adamant in his opposition to Calvin. For Grotius, invoking for Calvin the text of John 8:44, which spoke of the Devil as a murderer from the beginning,

Immense evils must inevitably beset any kingdom where the rulers allow themselves to be led, not by God, but by the spirit of Calvin who is much closer to the spirit of Elias than to that of the Gospel...Far from us be that spirit who has been a murderer from the beginning.[36]

It was the emphases on the toleration of anti-Trinitarianism, the limited number of fundamentals, the hostility to Calvinism, and the criticism of the 'disease' of imposition as countered by enquiry with charity which were to be taken over most extensively by Le Clerc in the late seventeenth

---

[34] Grotius, *Meletius* in Tuck, *Philosophy and Government* 184–90, 195; Israel, *Dutch Republic*, 428–32, 440; J. P. Heering, 'Hugo Grotius' *De Veritate Religionis Christianae*' in H. Nellen and E. Rabbie (eds.), *Hugo Grotius, Theologian* (Leiden 1994), 41–52; Wilbur, *Unitarianism*, 548–50.

[35] See below, pp. 605–7.

[36] Grotius, *Opera Omnia Theologica*, III, 675 in Le Cler, *Toleration*, 321.

and early eighteenth century as he edited Grotius' *De Veritate* and added to it a section of his own composition which challenged sectarianism.[37]

Yet Grotius supported a public church, and while he had very importantly desired considerable latitude within that church – a form of toleration – he was reluctant to offer intellectual support for toleration outside the boundaries of such a church. For Grotius, other worships than that of the public church were to be 'connived at' rather than officially allowed.[38] Grotius' *Oratie*, which suggested that the division of the public religion was 'ruinous' in republics, similarly declared that Lutheran and Mennonite churches might be 'connived at' but not that they deserved toleration.[39] Grotius argued in his *De Imperio Summarum Potestatum circa Sacra* that 'As only the sovereign has the right to introduce the true religion, it is also his duty to suppress the false ones, either by lenient methods or by force'.[40] While he explicitly argued in his 1622 *Apologetics* that oppression for beliefs caused sedition, and that allowance of 'diversity of views in religious matters' would bring peace, Grotius' clear and strong preference was for containing such diversity within the bounds of one church to the greatest extent possible. Such a desire was still to be significant, although more muted, among Arminians later in the century, who read and discussed Grotius' works at length, and when Jean Le Clerc was, symbolically, to open the first issue of his *Bibliothèque universelle et historique* with a review of Grotius.[41]

Thus, while importantly supportive of the reduction of controversy within Christianity, the first generation of Arminians can hardly be classified as either practioners or supporters of a very full toleration, although there was some move towards a more tolerant and inclusive public church between Arminius in the late sixteenth century and first decade of the seventeenth century and Grotius by the 1620s and 1630s. As Jonathan Israel has noted, 'neither Arminius, nor Uyttenbogaert, nor any Arminian leader, during the period down to 1618, tried to construct a general theory of toleration or argued for a general toleration on principle'.[42] Instead, in the controversy against Contra-Remonstrants within Christianity, they had argued for magisterial force alongside their ecumenical stress on reducing controversy, and in places instead of it, and had supplemented this by desire to place increased restrictions on Jewish toleration. Bayle was an avid reader of

---

[37] See below, Part 3, pp. 665–6; Le Clerc, *Truth*.

[38] Grotius, *Remonstrantie*, in Israel, *Dutch Republic*, 502.

[39] H. Grotius, *Oratie*, 52 in Israel, *Dutch Republic*, 439.

[40] H. Grotius, *De Imperio* (Paris 1647), 185, in Le Cler, *Toleration*, II, 313.

[41] Israel, 'Toleration', 22.

[42] Israel, 'Toleration' at 17, 20. The works of Arminius make no plea for toleration: J. Arminius, *The Works of James Arminius*, ed. C. Bangs, tr. J. Nichols (Baker Books, Grand Rapids, Mich. 1986), I–III, *passim*.

earlier Dutch sources by both Remonstrants and Contra-Remonstrants, and a specific suspicion of Arminians' proclivity to be intolerant towards Contra-Remonstrants was probably influential on the attack on the tolerationism of Le Clerc by Bayle, particularly strongly expressed in his final works of the 1700s, which declared that Le Clerc and his fellow-Arminians were tolerant towards Arminians but intolerant towards Calvinists and all those who subscribed to the theology of Dordrecht.[43]

It was not until the works of Episcopius, leader of the Arminians in the later 1620s and 1630s and founder of the Remonstrant seminary in Amsterdam in 1634, that Arminians added to their continued desire for an inclusive public church stronger support for toleration outside of the church and support for diversity as a good in itself. It was at this date, relatedly, that the Arminians commenced construction of covert churches in Amsterdam (on the Keizersgracht in September 1630) and the Hague (on the Laan in 1631), having accepted that they would not in the immediate future be the leaders of the public church, and accepting at least temporarily a kind of 'sectarian' status. As Bayle noted in the *Dictionary*, Episcopius had 'introduced in his Party the Toleration of Religions'. For Bayle, 'no Divine' was thereby 'so opposite to St Augustine's Doctrine' and that of the 'whole [Catholic] church'. Henricus Arnoldi's 1629 anti-tolerationist *Vande Conscientie-dwangh* agreed: Episcopius' defence of toleration was unprecedented among Arminians, and also almost unprecedented within Christianity since, for Arnoldi, such a doctrine could not be found in the Bible, and resembled only the doctrine of Coornhert. Sixty years later Jurieu added his agreement to his Calvinist predecessor Arnoldi by calling Episcopius in his 1690 *Picture of Socinianism* the 'most dangerous enemy to the Christian religion and its mysteries' in the entire century. Jurieu then designated Limborch and Aubert among Episcopius' followers.[44]

Episcopius increased the preceding Arminian and Grotian stress on the limited number of fundamentals within Christianity and added a very heavy emphasis on toleration for 'heresy' and on 'liberty of conscience'. For Episcopius, heresies were not to be punished since they could not be judged.[45] For Episcopius, heresies were moreover not to be punished because force could not produce conviction. For Episcopius, humans were fallible and to persecute them for failure to accede to 'obscure' dogma was to condemn 'human nature' itself. It was unreasonable to 'insist upon maintaining an agreement on all points and niceties of doctrine...and we

---

[43] Israel, 'Toleration', 17 and n.15; Bayle, *OD*, IV, 3–106 esp. 31.
[44] Bayle, *Dictionary*, Episcopius G; [Jurieu], *Tableau du Socinianisme* (1690), 9–10, 154, 188, 336, in Israel, *Radical*, 358.
[45] Nobbs, *Theocracy*, 94–5, 102–4. Cf also Zagorin, *Idea*, 176–8.

hold the view that the liberty of diversity of judgments and understandings will not bear such fetters and shackles'. Confessions had generally in history been instruments of persecution, as men had 'appealed to them as unexceptionable rules; and he that swerved but a finger's breadth from them, although moved thereto by a Scriptural reference itself, was, without any further proof, accused and condemned for heresy'.[46] For Episcopius, in another important invocation of the argument from 'equity' or 'reciprocity', Calvinists who sought to impose their views on others deserved to be 'treated by others in the same way, and equally, did not deserve to have their complaints or petitions listened to, according to the rule: Do not unto others what you would not have done to yourself'.[47] For Episcopius, there was a central Christian duty of charity:

As the teaching of others is a work of charity, and God wants us to do all charity, every one should enjoy that freedom of conscience without which this kind of charity cannot be put into practice, otherwise one would have to protest with the Apostles and say: Judge for yourselves whether it is better to obey god than to obey man.[48]

Very significantly, Episcopius developed the argument that divergent views each contained fragments of the truth, and that diversity could thus be a good in itself. He held that 'free enquiry' was useful to discern the truth. Here the search for truth, rather than the holding of truth, was coming to receive the central emphasis it was to possess also in the later generation of Arminians at the end of the century. Whereas Arminius had maintained the doctrine of the Trinity, holding that there were three persons in one substance, and had not departed significantly from the Calvinist understanding of original sin in still holding that there was a privation that followed the Fall which inclined men to sin, Episcopius himself emphasised that neither original sin nor the Trinity were Scriptural terms, and did not use the language of persons in one substance that defined the Trinity for Calvinist contemporaries. Episcopius was not a Socinian: he held that Christ was eternally God. But he advocated the toleration of Socinians and moved Arminianism away from explicit commitment to the doctrine of the Trinity of three persons in one substance that had been held for centuries, and towards a phraseology which did not reject such a doctrine but rather rendered it an unnecessary explication.[49]

---

[46] Episcopius, *Opera Theologica* (Amsterdam 1650–5), II, ii, 1–3 and II, ii, 69 in Jordan, *Toleration*, 338–9, 342–3.
[47] Episcopius, *Opera Theologica* (Amsterdam 1665), II, ii, 185–6 in Le Cler, *Toleration*, 316.
[48] Episcopius, *Opera Theologica* (Amsterdam 1665), II, 2, 409–11 in Le Cler, *Toleration*, II, 305.
[49] Van Limborch, *Voor-reden* in Israel, *Dutch Rupublic*, 503–4.

For Episcopius, freedom to preach and to teach was essential to freedom of conscience, and it was vital to the security of the state. In his 1627 *Free Religion*, Episcopius depicted a Contra-Remonstrant who held that only the public church should be allowed to preach and teach openly, and that diversity would undermine the state, in debate with a Remonstrant who argued that such imposition would cause sedition. For Episcopius, sedition would be eliminated by freedom of religion, tying all citizens to the state which provided it and facilitating perception of religious truth on all sides. 'Free minds' were those which would willingly and devotedly serve the 'common interest'. For Episcopius, Catholics deserved toleration as long as they 'declare that they will conduct themselves as true and upright subjects according to the laws of the country', and took an oath of loyalty to the magistrate 'with express renunciation of all those maxims which would dispense them from such an oath'.[50] Episcopius personally extended hospitality to many people of different religions to visit him and converse at his house; among those who accepted this hospitality were both the French theologian and historiographer royal Samuel Sorbière and Rabbi Menasseh ben Israel.[51]

Together with these new and important arguments for freedom of conscience and worship, Episcopius stressed that if a public church was in 'error', public denunciation of that church was *not* approved. Public worship should be criticised privately. He declared 'I so love Christian peace and unity, that I would rather conceal my views on any unimportant truth, than to seek to obtain a species of vain glory from an exhibition of them'. Agreeing with the former generation of Arminians, Episcopius held that the Magistrate could set up the place and time of worship, and appoint the personnel and mode of administration in the 'public church'. The ruler was to constitute, command, and enforce the forms of 'public worship', the persons to conduct the worship, and the way it should be conducted. The ruler was to summon synods and classes. The magistrate's sword was held moreover to be invaluable against 'drunkenness, hate and works of the flesh'. While at moments Episcopius assaulted the Mosaic theocracy as an ideal for the Christian commonwealth, holding that Old Testament penalties were no longer valid for Christians, at other moments Episcopius argued that the Jewish church and state had in fact been a model not for intolerance but for a tolerant public religion allowing variation in opinions, and so:

The Jewish church sets us an example. It had many synagogues, many communities and rather serious differences existed between its members; yet there was only one

[50] Episcopius, *Vrye Godes-dienst* (1627) in Israel, *Dutch Republic*, 503–4; Israel, 'Toleration', 21; Episcopius, *Vrye Godes-dienst*, 44, in Israel, *Dutch Republic*, 504.
[51] C. Roth, *A Life of Menasseh Ben Israel* (Philadelphia 1934), 156–8.

temple, one rite, one worship. What prevents Christians from following that example?...If they hold the same fundamental truth, the same religion, the same hope and the same salvation, why should those who remain united in one communion, not occasionally divide into various groups according as they hold a different interpretation of non-essential truths.[52]

The argument that the Jewish commonwealth had actually been one which accommodated a variety of opinions was to be used again by Bayle, Burnet, and Limborch in the 1680s.

The model derived from the collected works of Episcopius published in Amsterdam in the 1650s and 1660s and thereafter was thus still one of a society in which there was a 'public church', supported by the magistrate, with a strong stress on subjects containing their criticism of the public church, even if that church was in error, together with a strong desire for inclusion within that church of a variety of differing opinions, even if there was added to this explicit support for the toleration of worship outside of its boundaries and a positive role for religious diversity. Such religious diversity was explicitly not meant to include diversity of moral (or sexual) practices: for Episcopius, the magistrate was armed to punish vice.[53] These emphases were to achieve a new and important lease of life in the latter half of the seventeenth century as Philip van Limborch, the inheritor of Episcopius' papers as well as his status as leading Arminian theologian, republished Episcopius' works. Limborch's 1686 *Theologia Christiana* explicitly suggested the desirability of as extensive a public church as possible, and asserted that Arminians had appropriately attempted to contain dispute privately as much as possible. Limborch sent Episcopius' works to his close friend Locke, who read some of them carefully, as well as developing similar arguments in his own writings, which Locke also read carefully.

When Bayle identified the groups who were the supporters of religious toleration in contemporary Christianity, he gave particular prominence to Arminians of the generation of Episcopius and then of Limborch and Le Clerc. Episcopius' works were particularly crucial, but other Arminian works and Arminian-associated works in the mid-seventeenth century were also influential on later arguments. In the course of petitioning for their toleration after 1618–19, Arminian leaders made the case that toleration conduced to economic welfare. In the petition of Remonstrant ministers at Leiden, for instance, they argued that liberty of worship was required for conscience, that they should not receive less toleration than 'other Christian sects in these provinces, yea even to the Jews themselves' and that

---

[52] Episcopius, *Opera Theologica*, II, ii, 189 in Le Cler, *Toleration*, 316; Jordan, *Toleration*, 340.
[53] Nobbs, *Theocracy*, 93–4; Jordan, *Toleration*, 340.

Besides, tis most certain, and none can be ignorant of it, that liberty of conscience, or the toleration of several Christian sects, has caused not only these provinces, and in particular the town of Leyden, to increase and flourish in riches and number of inhabitants, but also that it produces the same effect in several other countries; and that those which are governed by different methods, lose their people, their trade, and their wealth.[54]

The note struck here was to reverberate in later Arminian-associated defences of toleration. A defence of a public church with toleration for all outside of that church which similarly gave major consideration to the economic benefits of toleration was importantly expressed in the early 1660s by Pieter de la Court's 1662 *Het Interest van Holland*, a work so widely read it was said to have been discussed on canal boats and wagons, and which was then expanded and adapted slightly in his 1669 *Indication of the Salutary Political Foundations and Maxims of the Republic of Holland and West Friesland*, later translated into English as *The True Interest and Political Maxims of the Republic of Holland* (1702). De la Court, a radically anti-monarchical republican member of the Leiden mercantile elite, was a client of the largely tolerationist republican Grand Pensionary Johann de Witt, who read the earlier version of de la Court's work in manuscript and both deleted some sections and composed parts of several chapters. To a significant degree, then, de la Court's work expressed the primary magisterial ethos of the Dutch republic in the 1660s under de Witt. For his extensive support of religious toleration, de Witt was branded a member of the 'Arminian party', and it is clear that leading Arminians were prominent among his supporters.[55] De la Court held in the *Indication* that it was known by 'experience in all countries to be necessary, as tending to the common peace, that one Religion should prevail and be supported above all others, and accordingly is by all means authorised, favoured, and protected by the State' and he defended the exclusion of dissenters from this religion 'from all Government, Magistracys, Offices and Benefices'. But he was equally adamant that 'the exercise of other Religions at the same time be in some measure publickly tolerated, at least not persecuted'.[56] Honest dissenting inhabitants 'who fare well in this country' would not 'fall into. . .seditious thoughts, so destructive to themselves and the Country, so long as they are not embittered by persecution, but on the contrary will be obliged by such Liberty, easy and moderate Government, to shew their Gratitude to so good a Magistracy'. For de la Court, toleration was clearly in socio-economic terms a republican as counter-revolutionary policy, for thereby, 'the rascally

---

[54] Quoted in Jordan, *Toleration*, 341n.
[55] Scott, *Sidney and. . .Republic*, 210–14; H. Rowen, *John De Witt* (Princeton 1978), 391–5; Israel, *Dutch Republic*, 759–61.
[56] De la Court, *True Interest*, 58–66.

people, or those of Mean Estates, and ambitious and seditious Inhabitants, would be deprived of all Adherents, whom otherwise under the Cloke of Religion they might the more easily gain to carry on their ill Designs'.[57]

De la Court was clear that such toleration was to extend to Catholics since it was certain that 'by persecuting the Romanists we should drive most of the Strangers out of our Country' or make them want to 'bring this country into the hands of our Enemy'. It was for de la Court clearly 'pernicious' to the state to be intolerant, but he declared that it was opposed in addition to the principles of 'Reformed Subjects' who 'always used to boast that they fought for their liberty, and constantly maintained that several publick religions may be peaceably tolerated and practised in one country' and who used to boast of the strength of their religion if tested by 'its own Evidence and veracity'. He criticised the increased prohibitions of Catholic worship after 1618, questioning 'why should we prohibit that which is not hurtful to the State' and recommending permission of 'none but small Assemblies in Cities, in the Houses of known Citizens, with such Priests as are best approved of by the Rulers'. The State could face no danger from such 'well known Assemblies, where every one might have free access, and no matter of secrecy could be consulted of'. And he argued that even if Catholics were to attempt to possess the government if given liberty then they would be opposed by four-fifths of the inhabitants of the Netherlands and easily crushed.[58]

Stressing that the increase of the population was the central interest of the commonwealth because from that came both prosperity and security, for de la Court the best means to preserve inhabitants and to draw foreigners was 'the Freedom of all sorts of Religions differing from the Reformed'. It was by such means that foreigners chose to leave their own lands and 'to come and sit down in our barren and heavy-taxed country'. Previous persecutions had cost 'trafficking cities' such as Lübeck 'most of their Wealth', as the preachers had taught that it was 'better to have a city of an orthodox or sound faith, ill stocked with people, than a very populous, and Godly city, but tainted with heresy'.[59] For de la Court, the 'evangelical lesson, and the law of Nature' were one and the same in prohibiting intolerance: 'to do nothing to others but what they would have done to themselves'. Christian ministers following their 'Master's doctrine' should have sought to 'enlighten the Minds of Men with the Truth' and persuade them into 'the path that leads to salvation', the instruction into 'Christian virtues'. Such virtues consisting 'only in the inward thoughts of our Minds' were incapable of being 'put into us by any outward Violence or Compulsion'. Since religion was built on hopes of an afterlife to compensate for the miseries of this one, it was

[57] *Ibid.*, 378–9.   [58] *Ibid.*, 58–66, 80–2, 381.   [59] *Ibid.*, 58–66.

'impossible' to make men 'by compulsion to hope for such advantage, in that which he cannot apprehend to be well-grounded'. All force in religion was vain on this ground alone. Moreover, since all those persecuted 'reproach and hate their persecutors', it was evident that persecutors lost 'all their weight to perswade'. Animosity to persecutors did not even allow the persecuted to consider the reasons of their 'enemies'.[60]

Clergymen were described as teaching 'all that can have a tendency to their own credit, Profit, and ease' because of their 'human frailty'. They had done so even at the cost of 'ruin of the whole Country', prosecuting men 'Odio Theologico'. By the 'evil ambitious maxims of the clergy', dissenters were 'persecuted'. He noted that not merely under Catholicism, but 'even where the Reformed Clergy bear sway' in other countries, 'dissenting Assemblies are prohibited'. And surveying the history of the Netherlands itself, he noted that when William of Orange had given 'more liberty to those of different perswasions in the Service of God than was pleasing' to the Reformed preachers 'the principal and most refined' of them 'did in their Pulpits openly exclaim against him for an Atheist, and ungodly person'. He then described the Reformed as having not become reconciled to the stadtholder Maurice until he had colluded with them in favour of intolerance in 1618–19. And he described as contemporary his fear that the preachers would not 'keep within their due bounds' but would adopt 'an impudent boldness of expounding in the pulpit all Political Acts or Laws, under the pretext of God's word' unless the Reformed preachers 'pretending to a Revelation and special Assistance of God's spirit, or a special call to the Ministry' were not subject 'to Ambition and Covetousness as other Clergymen are'. It was necessary, according to de la Court, 'that rulers so govern the state that seditious and proud preachers shall not be able to subvert the Republic, and ruin the prosperity of the Land'.[61] De la Court was banned from the Lord's Supper and censured by the consistory of Leiden for the expression of these and similar views about the Reformed Church in his 1662 *Political Discourses* and *Interest of Holland*. When he reworked them in his *Indication*, the work was banned by the States of Holland, in response to a request from the Synod of South Holland, which execrated his 'detestable maxims directed against church and state'. His radically anti-monarchical republican hostility to the House of Orange was to fall into still further disfavour after the assassination of his mentor de Witt in 1672. But in his combination of arguments for toleration on economic, epistemological, theological, and juristic grounds, de la Court's works expressed a combination of arguments for religious toleration which was to be important again in the next generation writing in the 1680s.[62]

---

[60] *Ibid.*, 58–66, 82.   [61] *Ibid.*, 58–66, 380–1, 386–8.
[62] Israel, *Dutch Republic*, 751, 786–91; Rowen, *De Witt*, 396–7.

RELIGIOUS INTOLERANCE JUSTIFIED AND ADVOCATED
IN THE NETHERLANDS C. 1579–1680

We have by now seen, then, that the late sixteenth-century Revolt had involved enunication of the principle of 'freedom of religion' in the Union of Utrecht, and that some important works were composed around that Union which defended religious toleration. We have seen that in the works of Coornhert and then of some Arminians and their associates in the 1630s and thereafter a large number of arguments for toleration had been developed. Particularly in the works of Coornhert, Episcopius, and de la Court, and much more complicatedly in the case of Grotius, there had been major Dutch contributors to theories of toleration stressing variously spiritualist arguments for liberty of conscience, ecumenical opposition to dogmatic imposition, and the economic benefits of toleration, but all including emphases on human fallibility and error and all including opposition to the imposition of explications of dogmas, creeds and confessions. In each, there was support for a public but non-compulsory church and desire to reduce controversy by not contradicting others unnecessarily. Toleration as practised in the Netherlands had largely evolved as the allowance alongside one public church of various private practices of worship, occurring in buildings which did not appear to be churches from the outside, and with processions disallowed or discouraged for Catholics and for Jews. Sources of public enmity and disputation were thereby strongly discouraged or removed, and religion was increasingly rendered for the tolerated in the Netherlands what tolerationist writing often declared it to be, an essentially private matter between worshippers and their God.

But in the late sixteenth- and seventeenth-century Netherlands there were many arguments arraigned against toleration, especially by members of the Dutch Reformed Church, largely as expressions of the orthodox Calvinist commitments which those ministers shared with their brethren in England and France in the movement of 'international Calvinism'.[63] It is true that Dutch Reformed thinkers, also known as Contra-Remonstrants, were never entirely united in their commitment to the complete magisterial suppression of 'heresy'. The leading Reformed preacher and historian Jacobus Trigland, for instance, argued that laws against heresy should exist but very rarely be enforced. Many scholars have emphasised that Dutch Calvinists never presented a united commitment to the extirpation, banishing, or even punishment of 'heretics'. At many points, Reformed ministers stressed confutation of heretical or erroneous arguments by theological

---

[63] M. Prestwich (ed.), *International Calvinism 1541–1715* (Oxford 1985).

disputations or by printing works against them instead of advocating magisterial suppression of those views. Franciscus Junius wrote an *Eirenicum de pace ecclesiae Catholicae* which condemned as an 'infectious sickness of our own day' those who had become 'utterly reckless in investigating, weighing, judging, condemning and rejecting the ways of our brethren' and cursing those who 'have the knowledge of Christ only because they do not think in all things like ourselves'.[64] But many of the ministers in the Reformed Church did campaign for suppression and punishment of 'heretics' and their works in the course of the late sixteenth to late seventeenth century. And they were perceived as particularly intolerant throughout the century by Arminian and Arminian-associated writers. Grotius declared to the Huguenot Reformed minister in the Netherlands André Rivet that 'all true Calvinists are professed enemies to such liberty [of conscience], as is shown by what happened to Servetus at Calvin's hands'.[65] As early as 1601, Remonstrants saw attempts to enforce uniformity of Calvinist doctrine as 'the fanning of the old Spanish fire with a Genevan bellows'.[66] It was in arguing against the significant degree of intolerance that was actually supported by Trigland that Adriaan van Paets the elder first cut his polemical teeth in the mid-seventeenth century. In the late seventeenth century, many Dutch Calvinists remained opponents of toleration, and exponents of toleration in the Netherlands had reason to understand themselves as combating more than a century of Dutch Calvinist defences of intolerance.[67]

Junius might have condemned the condemning of others in his *Eirenicum*, but in 1565 he wrote *A Brief Discourse To King Philip* which pleaded for 'liberty of worship' only for Calvinists and Catholics in 'two ways of public worship'. He attacked the 'vile libertines who form separate sects' and who taught that one should serve God in 'spirit and liberty' instead of under 'discipline' and 'under this pretext they indulge in every possible villainy and abomination, in murder and plundering, in incest and adultery, thinking such things do not matter'. He condemned the Anabaptists 'in Münster and their likes' and argued that 'new and abominable sects full of sedition and mutiny, and horrible blasphemies against the majesty of God' which sprang

---

[64] Tuck, *Philosophy and Government*, 181, citing den Tex, *Oldenbarnevelt*, 434; Nijenhuis, *Ecclesia*, 135, 163ff.; F. Junius, *Ecclesia* in Nijenhuis, *Ecclesia*, II, 174–5; Kaplan, *Calvinists*; Duke, *Reformation*; Israel, *Dutch Republic*; van Gelderen, *Political Thought*; P. De Jong, 'Can Political Factors Account for the Fact that Calvinism Rather Than Anabaptism Came to Dominate the Dutch Reformation?', *Church History* (1964) 392–417.

[65] H. Grotius, *Opera Theologica*, III, 679, in Tuck, *Philosophy and Government*, 201; Le Cler, *Toleration*, II, 320–1.

[66] *Tsamenspreeckinghee can drie persoonen, over het regiereus Placcaet van Groninghen* (1601) ('The Conversation of Three Persons on the Rigorous Edict of Groningen') in Harline, *Pamphlets*, 9.

[67] Israel, 'Intellectual Debate'.

up every day would be prevented precisely by the strict discipline and correction 'of all vices and licentiousness' by the 'Reformed'.[68] This model of two tolerated orthodox religions against a toleration of 'radical Reformation' heresies was similar to that established in France, partly because of the substantial interaction between the Calvinist communities in the Netherlands and France which involved influxes of French Calvinists to the Netherlands under persecution in France and use of the Huguenot confession as the basis of the Dutch Reformed confession of faith, or Belgic confession. The churches spoke often of their 'holy concord' and 'union'.[69]

The 1579 Synod of Dort reacted to a report that Anabaptist 'false doctrine spreads like a cancer' reaching from the village of Zwartewaal to 'infect the whole of Voorne' by calling for the magistrates 'only to accept or allow those who take a valid oath to obey the authorities'.[70] The Reformed consistory of Leiden argued for the 'prohibition, constraint and punishment' of Mennonites, Roman Catholics, and all other religions in the very year of the Union of Utrecht, 1579; the national synod then asserted in 1581 the magistrate's godly office to 'sanction the church order made by the church'.[71] The Reformed Church asked magistrates to forbid Anabaptist conventicles and Catholic worship in 1579, and again in 1593 and 1595.[72] In reply to Anabaptist arguments which confined the government to temporal matters, the Reformed Emden minister Menso Alting argued in his 1579 *Protocol* that while conscience had to be free, it was free as liberty of thought only, and that religious expressions and worship fell under the duty of the magistrate to maintain 'both Tables of God's commandments'.[73] The foreword of the *Protocol* asserted that 'the Anabaptists plant and cherish nothing but shameful and terrible errors which overthrow the foundation of eternal salvation and destroy the well-being of the churches'.

As a result of the debate, the Frisian states prohibited Mennonite worship.[74] Alting condemned the support given by Caspar Coolhaes to the magisterial appointment of ministers as the 'daily vomiting forth of poison' which wounded 'my very soul' and declared that 'If the magistrate were not such an enemy to all religion he would never permit the man such freedom'. For his 'Erastian' tolerationism, Coolhaes was excommunicated by the Synod of Haarlem and prevented from lecturing at the University of

---

[68] F. Junius, *Brief discours envoyé au roy Philippe nostre sire et souverain Seigneur* (1566) in Kossman and Mellinck (eds.), *Texts*, 57–81; Kaplan, *Calvinists*, 83; Pettegree, 'Politics', 184; Nijenhuis, *Ecclesia*, II, 174–5.
[69] Greengrass, *European Reformation*; Pettegree, *Emden*.
[70] The 1574 Synod of Dort 88 in Duke et al. (eds.), *Calvinism in Europe*, 173–4.
[71] Van Gelderen, *Political Thought*, 230, 233.   [72] De Jong, 'Political', 402–3.
[73] Alting, *Protocol* (1579), 318 in van Gelderen, *Political Thought*, 240.
[74] Krahn, *Dutch Anabaptism*, 248.

Leiden.[75] The Reformed ministers Arent Cornelisz and Reinier Donteclock attacked Coonhert's 1582 *Means to Abate the Sects* in their 1582 *Examination of the Unheard of Means...to Abate the Sects*. For these authors, Coornhert's work was problematic because it was intolerant in the wrong way, in arguing for magistrates to enforce only the Scripture in worship. They reasserted the need for the government both to support 'true religion' and to prohibit 'false teachers'. Against Coornhert's 1582 *Synod*, they argued in a 1583 *Remonstrance* that freedom of expression involved 'pernicious licence' and the 'public desecration' of God's name. Those who undermined the 'true religion' and 'seduced' hearers were to be silenced by the magistrate. Calvin had called Coornhert a 'savage beast', and Lambert Danneau, who taught at Leiden in the early 1580s, imitated him in describing Coornhert as a rabid dog, a supporter of Satan, and the prince of 'libertines'.[76]

In 1584, Calvinist magistrates at Ghent resolved to expel from the community anyone outside of the Reformed Church. The 36th article of the Belgic confession, adopted by the Dutch Reformed Church, defined the office of magistrate as 'not only to have regard unto and watch for the welfare of the civil state, but also that they protect the sacred ministry, and thus may remove and prevent all idolatry and false worship...that the kingdom of Christ may be promoted'. The 1586 Synod of North Holland argued that since 'the course of the gospel is greatly hindered by the conventicles of the Anabaptists' they should 'be prevented' by the magistrates. The Calvinist statesman Marnix de St Aldegonde's 1595 *Thorough Refutation of the Teaching of Fanatics* called for Anabaptists to be exiled and their works suppressed.[77] He identified peaceful Anabaptists with the fanatics of Münster, and declared that if they were allowed to propagate their opinions, 'the foundations of the faith would be completely destroyed, piety demolished, and God's authority over the conscience completely smothered'. And he expanded his argument in a 1598 *Réponse apologétique*, which asserted that since those who were 'overtly heretical' had 'abandoned the field of the lord' they could be punished.[78] In 1596, 1598, 1600, 1604, 1612, 1618, and 1620, the Synod of Overyssel asked for magisterial suppression of both Anabaptist and Catholic worship. The minister Gellius Snecanus called Anabaptist teaching 'a revelation of the devil' at Leeuwarden

---

[75] Alting to Cornelisz 24 March 1580, quoted in A. Pettegree, 'The Calvinist Church in Holland 1572–90', in *idem* (ed.), *Calvinism in Europe 1540–1620* (Cambridge 1994), 160–80, at 167; Le Cler, *Toleration*, II, 267.

[76] A. Cornelisz and R. Donteclock, *Examination* (1582), fo. B, c2 in van Gelderen, *Political Thought*, 245; Danneau and Calvin in Kossman, 'Freedom', 293.

[77] Pettegree, 'Politics', 192; van Deursen, *Plain Lives*, 261; De Jong, 'Political', 397.

[78] Le Cler, *Toleration*, 288, 291.

in 1597, and the Provincial Synod of Groningen in 1595 called them the 'scum of Anabaptists'.[79] In 1587, the Synod of Friesland, a province with a high concentration of Anabaptists, demanded the expulsion of 'heretics' from the Netherlands, arguing that it was better to be a 'desert' than corrupt and prosperous. On no less than ten occasions between 1584 and 1610 the Synod of Friesland demanded suppression of Anabaptists under an edict that the magistrates issued in 1584. That the authorities issued edicts but did not enforce them did not stop the synod from issuing many further declarations, including the 1605 declaration that 'with a view to their ungodly opinions and doctrines' Anabaptists 'deserved to be punished with the denial of rights' and that this was 'the office of magistrates'. In 1614, they desired the magistrates to order that Mennonite and Catholic churches be 'broken down'.[80] The Synod of South Holland protested against the 'Englishmen named Brownists' in 1596 as 'an unlawfull assemblie established in schisme'. Franciscus Junius admonished them to return to communion in the Church of England. In 1599, the Synod of North Holland protested against Brownists and refused to recognise that the Brownists were a church, denying it the word 'church' ('*kerk*') in favour of 'gathering' ('*vergadering*').[81]

The Reformed ministers A. Geldorp and I. Bogerman translated Beza's call for the punishment of heretics, *De haereticis*, into Dutch in 1601, and in their preface questioned economic arguments for toleration: 'Must Satan now, instead of God, promote our commerce?'[82] In Groningen, the Reformed Synod demanded in 1597 that Anabaptists' 'meetings and exercise of their religion' be prevented according to edict and that nothing was allowed 'contrary to the Reformed Religion'. In 1601, an ordinance declared children who had not been baptised in the Reformed Church illegitimate, and gave ministers the right to enter houses in which they suspected that a Mennonite conventicle was being held. The Synod of Groningen requested prevention of 'the conventicles of Anabaptists, Papists' no less than twenty times between 1599 and 1620. And it further demanded the suppression of Mennonite works, proclaiming 'unusually frightful errors to the detriment of the true church of Christ'.[83] In 1607, a Reformed minister in Holland argued that the magistrates were not Christian unless they expelled everyone who was not a member of the Reformed Church.[84] For the Calvinist Jan Schurmann, while none could be forced to believe, all could be forced to listen to the pure gospel and to frequent the sacraments, and conversion could occur by that process. Oaths with Catholics as 'idolaters' should be broken and their worship

---

[79] De Jong, 'Political', 392–417; Nijenhuis, *Ecclesia*, II, 131.   [80] De Jong, 'Political', 406–7.
[81] Sprunger, *Dutch Puritanism*, 51–3; Nijenhuis, *Ecclesia*, II, 154.
[82] Krahn, *Dutch Anabaptism*, 249.   [83] De Jong, 'Political', 408–10.
[84] Kaplan, *Calvinists*, 61; de Jong, 'Political', 396.

suppressed. For Charles Galus of Arnhem, Catholics were not merely to be forbidden public worship but also forced to attend Reformed sermons.[85]

The Calvinist preacher Abraham Coster's Rotterdam 1608 *History of the Jews* attacked the desire of 'these unclean people' to establish a public synagogue 'in which they can perform their evil and foolish ceremonies and spew forth their gross blasphemies against Christ and his holy gospels, as well as their curses against the Christians and the Christian authorities'. The Calvinist consistory in Amsterdam campaigned from 1610 to 1612 against worship by Jews, accusing them of slandering Christianity and seducing Christian maidservants; the 1612 magisterial prohibition of the Neve Salom community from building a synagogue was in part the outcome of their campaign. The Reformed Church council in Amsterdam protested against the Jews' 'great freedom' and 'great nastiness' in 1619, 1620, 1623, and 1639 – 1639 being the year of inauguration of the public synagogue. We noted earlier that the Utrecht Contra-Remonstrant professor Gijsbertus Voetius supported the blood-libel in disputation against the Jews in 1637; as a religion, he placed Judaism on a scale below Roman Catholicism and near 'atheism'. His pupil and colleague Johan Hoornbeek's 1655 *Eight Books to Convince and Convert the Jews* deplored Jewish toleration in the Netherlands. The Contra-Remonstrant Professor of Theology at Breda, Antonius Hulsius, identified Judaism in the 1650s as the source of Christian heresies, writing that 'Nothing strange to the Christian truth has been introduced in the Church, which does not smell of this corrupted Judaism'. Even as late as 1677, the Leiden preachers were to complain that Jews were 'blaspheming' Christianity and to demand their punishment by the States General of Holland – despite the cause of this alleged 'blasphemy' being the conversations and disputations between Reformed ministers and Jews which they had themselves called for in hopes of converting the Jews to Christianity. Clearly, they had not intended there to be effectively stated opposition to their position in the debates. The Portuguese congregation was forced to forbid its membership, on pain of excommunication, to engage in such disputations, 'since such things are prejudicial to the preservation of our safety, stirring up as they do the ill will of the Gentiles among whom we live'.[86]

Reformed opposition to toleration within the state in the late sixteenth century was matched by a drive towards intolerance within the church. The Synod of Emden during the period of exile had required subscription to the orthodox Calvinist Belgic confession, and the North Holland Synod of 1573

---

[85] Kaplan, *Calvinists*, 61; Le Cler, *Toleration*, II, 242.

[86] Bodian, *Hebrews*, 59, 62; Huussen, 'Legal Position', 21; Kaplan, *From Christianity*, 272–3; van Rooden, 'Conceptions of Judaism', 302–4.

demanded that ministers 'read with understanding and afterwards to sign the same with ripe understanding'. In the 1570s and 1580s, the Reformed Church constructed an effective organisation of *classes* such that, as van Deursen puts it, 'the Calvinising process within the church of Holland was complete towards the end of the sixteenth century'. The Synod of North Holland stated in 1582 – in defence of excommunication – that 'Christian love' did not 'consist in having to tolerate every person in his disbelief without speaking against it or punishing it'. Freedom did not consist in 'someone's being allowed to feel and to believe whatever pleases him, as if each person could be saved in that belief'.[87] In 1574, a synod in Holland urged ministers not merely to exhort people to read the Bible but to warn them against reading 'unhealthy heretical works' and asked ministers to 'keep an eye open' during 'house visits' for any 'damaging books'. And they brought pressure to bear on booksellers such as Albrecht Hendriksz of Delft, who printed a Mennonite work in 1578.[88]

Such views received repetition and expansion in the seventeenth century as the Reformed turned against the accommodation of Arminianism within the church or state. As Temple noted in his *Observations*, the Contra-Remonstrants had 'ever valued themselves upon the asserting. . .of the true and purer Reformed religion', in contrast to the Arminians, who had prided themselves on asserting 'the truer and freer Liberties of the State'. In 1613, Lubbertus denounced the States of Holland for failing to protect the Reformed Church from the 'plague' of heresy of Conradus Vorstius, Arminius' successor at Leiden.[89] In defence of the 'true and purer' religion, Gomarus, leader of the Contra-Remonstrants, argued that the magistrate was to imitate the kings of Israel in serving the Lord by preventing heresy and punishing idolatry.[90] For Althusius in 1614, Grotius' *De Imperio* was a 'diabolical' work; it suggested that magistrates should prevent synods from imposing belief on the populace and 'persecuting those who err from the right way'.[91]

The professors of Leiden issued a *Confessionis Remonstrantium Censura* in defence of the condemnation of Arminianism at the Synod of Dort, arguing that Remonstrants were guilty of 'execrable Heresies' and 'corrupted from the beginning to the end' with 'sore[s]' and thereby that they had 'justly excited the Magistrates to use great Severity against that Party', as Bayle summarised and cited their case in the *Dictionary* in condemning this

---

[87] Kaplan, *Calvinists*, 35; van Deursen, *Plain Lives*, ch. 15.
[88] Reitsma, *Acta Synoden*, II, 167 in Harline, *Pamphlets*, 61; *ibid.*, 91.
[89] Israel, *Dutch Republic*, 428; Temple, *Observations*, 85–6.
[90] Temple, *Observations*, 85–6; Gomarus in Nobbs, *Theocracy*, 18.
[91] Van Dam, '*De Imperio*' in H. Nellen and E. Rabbie (eds.), *Grotius, Theologian* (Leiden 1994), 22.

intolerant work.[92] When the Arminian Theodorus Bomius published Castellio's *Advice to France Laid Waste* in the course of the debates over Arminianism and Gomarism, he was condemned by the Contra-Remonstrants for 'having taken Castalio's stinking bones out of the Grave again', as Bayle again pointed out in the *Dictionary*.[93] As they asserted that good works were necessary to justification, Arminians were advocates of 'popish error', as well as 'Socinians, Arians, and libertines'. Reformed polemic assaults even rendered them 'atheists'. One Amsterdammer summarised the teaching that he therefore understood to be that of the Remonstrants: 'that there is no God, no resurrection'.[94]

The Contra-Remonstrant minister of Amsterdam, Plancius, even accused Episcopius of plotting in France with Jesuits 'the Ruin of the Reformed Church, and of the United Provinces', a claim which Bayle repeated in the *Dictionary* as evidence that 'zeal makes people often persuade themselves, that an heretic is capable of the most Infamous Plots, and from this Persuasion, they easily pass on to another, which is, that they fancy that he actually contrives all the machinations of which they suppose him to be capable'.[95] Since Bayle had himself come under attack by this date from the Calvinist Jurieu, who had alleged that Bayle had conspired with France against the Netherlands, it is likely that Bayle was thinking of his own experience under Jurieu's persecution in recounting this accusation, viewing Calvinist persecutionary zeal as similar through time. And it was not merely France to which the Remonstrants were alleged by Contra-Remonstrants to have allied themselves in the early seventeenth century, but also Spain. As van Deursen has noted in surveying the Contra-Remonstrant literature of the early seventeenth century, Remonstrants were often accused of being 'really Catholics' and friends of Spain. Tolerating Remonstrants was thus likened by Contra-Remonstrants in the Netherlands to tolerating a fifth column intent on opening the gates to the Spanish army. Such was the generalised assault on Remonstrants as heretics and treasonable; once banned from preaching after the Synod of Dort, Remonstrant preaching itself became specifically treasonable. Hendrik Slatius, a banned Remonstrant preacher, who preached nonetheless, was sentenced to death in 1623 for lèse-majesté.[96]

After their banishment or required silence, Remonstrants abroad managed to have their works published in the Netherlands only by smuggling them back into the country. The 23-year-old student Jan Claesz, who smuggled Remonstrant works, was therefore prosecuted for transporting illegal

[92] Bayle, *Dictionary*, Episcopius F. [93] Bayle, *Dictionary*, Castalio H.
[94] Van Deursen, *Plain Lives*, 273, 275. [95] Bayle, *Dictionary*, Episcopius I.
[96] Temple, *Observations*, 84–5; van Deursen, *Plain Lives*, 273.

pamphlets in 1621 in the Court of Holland. The Remonstrant historian
Gerard Brandt's *History of the Reformation* recorded that the
Remonstrants published 'many tracts' in order to win people to their side
and that 'the States and magistrates tried to prevent this with edicts and other
measures, but if one bookseller or printer was caught, another was found,
who then published the work, either out of devotion to the cause or thirst for
profits'. But he noted that 'the costs of publication, because of the danger,
were extremely high'. Approximately 1,000 to 1,200 copies of smuggled and
officially 'seditious' Remonstrant pamphlets were published by Joris
Veselaer in 1620; in 1621, the Council of Amsterdam confiscated his
books, and fined him 200 guilders plus costs of his imprisonment and trial.
As late as 1628, printers wanted to be well paid for considering Arminian
publications 'in the event of difficulties'. Uyttenbogaert wrote to Episcopius
as late as 1630 that to put the place of publication and printer on a book was
'dangerous, neither the ruler of the place, nor the printer will like it'. The
censorship and suppression of Arminian works was supported by Reformed
synod after Reformed synod in the 1610s and 1620s. The Synod of
Appingedam in 1614 demanded that the 'burgomasters and council of
Groningen' should 'forbid the printing of anything that goes against God's
word and law'. The Synod of Zwolle campaigned against publication of the
'blasphemous' Remonstrant *Panorama* in 1619 and the Synod of Delft listed
'seditious and scandalous' tracts – terms applied to Arminian works – for the
States to proscribe. Even as late as 1640, the Reformed Synod of Gouda urged
'authorisation of religious censors' and 'an end to the intolerable license of
the press, the publication of many scandalous, popish, Remonstrant, and
Socinian books'. And as late as 1670, the Arminian Rotterdam printer Johan
Naeranus died before the court could bring to completion its intention to
prosecute him.[97]

Henricus Arnoldi of Delft composed the petition of the South Holland
Synod in 1628, which demanded suppression of Remonstrant conventicles as
politically and theologically subversive – as causing riots and sedition, and
spreading 'Pelagian' and 'Socinian' ideas. In his 1629 *Vande Conscientie-
dwangh*, Arnoldi argued moreover that 'free exercise of their pretended
religions' had never been allowed to 'Lutherans or Mennonites, and still
less to the godless Jews, in these lands'; such freedom of worship as existed
occurred only by 'secular authorities turning a blind eye'. He saw 'Freedom
of worship' as no part of the 'freedom of conscience' of the Union of
Utrecht.[98] For Arnoldi, the Arminians should be vigorously suppressed,
Lutherans and Mennonites tolerated only as long as they were silent and

---

[97] Harline, *Pamphlets*, 86, 97, 125–6, 136–8, 139, 183–6; Groenveld, 'Mecca', 85n.67.
[98] Arnoldi, *Vande Conscientie-dwangh*, 20, 93 in Israel, *Dutch Republic*, 500.

not 'conspiratorial', and Jews who 'insult the name of Christ' were not to be tolerated.[99] When the Arminian Abraham Halinck was imprisoned in Utrecht in 1627, Bernhard Bushof and Arnoldus Buchelius declared in justification of the punishment that such Arminians were 'pests in a republic and poison in the community, whatever appearance of godliness they were feigning'. Following the Contra-Remonstrant propagandist Festus Hommius, Buchelius held that Arminian questioning of strict Calvinist predestination revealed their sympathies with 'Libertinism, Socinianism and atheism'. Attempt to accommodate Arminianism would be the letting in of 'libertinism' and the opening of the 'window to atheism' under the 'specious name of moderation'. For Buchelius, the Utrecht sympathiser with Arminianism, Jan Nieupoort, belonged 'to the Epicurean herd rather than among the Christians'. A Contra-Remonstrant wrote hostilely in 1637 that the town governments of Holland were full of 'libertines, Arminians, Atheists and concealed Jesuits'; another in 1650 attacked 'Espaniolized, libertine Arminians' and hoped for a restriction of the practices of toleration.[100]

As Bayle noted in the *Dictionary*, the Synod of Holland had petitioned the States in 1628, arguing that Socinianism should not be tolerated and that if it were its toleration would make the United provinces 'stink all over Christendom'.[101] Regents often enforced the edicts against Socinian works, themselves declaring that Holland should not be 'the seminary of all blasphemies against God'. The council at Rotterdam in 1645 suppressed one hundred copies of a Socinian work translated into Dutch. The Faculty of Divinity at Leiden in 1653, in response to a request from the states for advice about a synodical petition to prohibit conventicles and books of Socinians, declared that nothing 'could be more horrid and abominable than the Socinian sect; that it differed but little from Paganism', and that the States should have 'a steady and holy resolution of removing all those blasphemies, and suppressing such wicked books'.[102] In mid-century, the Utrecht Calvinist Voetius campaigned to restrict toleration and for the eradication of any anti-Trinitarians and deists, including by investigation and eradication of any concealed anti-Trinitarians in Mennonite or Arminian confessions.[103] When the example of 'tolerationist' Poland was cited to him, Voetius noted increasing measures against Socinianism there and responded that even Poland now appropriately suppressed Socinianism.[104]

---

[99] Israel, *Dutch Republic*, 500–1.   [100] Pollman, *Religious Choice*, 146–50.
[101] Bayle, *Dictionary*, Socinus K.
[102] Bayle, *Dictionary*, Socinus L; Harline, *Pamphlets*, 126, 140.
[103] Voetius, *Politica Ecclesiastica*, II, 538–44, 551 in Israel, *Dutch Republic*, 638.
[104] Bayle, *Dictionary*, Socinus K.

There was here a move among the leading Calvinists from the mid-seventeenth century towards focusing on anti-Trinitarianism rather than Arminianism as 'intolerable', but they were still capable of attacking Arminians as really anti-Trinitarians themselves, or as being as bad as anti-Trinitarians by being aiders and abettors of anti-Trinitarianism. Not merely did Arminians advocate toleration for Socinians, but from the middle of the seventeenth century they admitted Socinians to worship with them, and held amicable correspondence with them. Arminian leaders such as Stephen Courcelles were involved in the publication of Socinian works in the Netherlands. As the century wore on, Arminians' commitment to the orthodox doctrine of the Trinity became increasingly unclear, and they were increasingly branded as Socinians or demi-Socinians. While by comparison with the 1620s Arminians were in the second half of the century increasingly accepted as tolerable even by the leading Dutch Calvinists, Arminian toleration was never sufficiently secure for them to feel it unquestionable even in the late seventeenth century.[105]

There was, relatedly, considerable opposition from the Reformed Church to the tolerant magisterial career of the republican Johann de Witt, personally an orthodox Calvinist but as a magistrate a supporter of the career of some Protestants the Reformed considered 'unorthodox', unwilling to enforce proscription of many 'heretical' works, and permissive towards Catholic worship when the Reformed protested against Catholics' 'exorbitant boldness'. De Witt was branded an 'Arminian'.[106] De Witt was the patron of Pieter de la Court, whose support for toleration caused him to be barred from communion and censured by the consistory of Leiden, and whose 1669 *Aanwysinge* was banned by the States of Holland at the request of the Synod of South Holland. De Witt attempted to prevent its suppression, thereby identifying him with de la Court's tolerationism and in opposition to many Reformed preachers. Raising Reformed hostility to de Witt still further, even though he attempted to suppress Socinian works, de Witt became identified permissively in the late 1660s and early 1670s with the Socinian and 'atheist' expressions of the Spinozists and Socinians such as Koerbagh, anathematised by the Reformed and punished by the magistrates.[107] When de Witt was physically assaulted in June 1672, a Calvinist pamphleteer issued a defence of the deed as necessary in order to protect the Calvinist churches. Calvinist preachers looked on as de Witt was assassinated by mob violence two months later in August 1672, and then defended the assassination by comparing it to the 'just killings' recorded in Scripture. Viewed with deep religious hostility by the Reformed because he

---

[105] Israel, *Dutch Republic*, 536, 637; *idem*, 'Intellectual Debate', 3–36.
[106] Rowen, *De Witt*, ch. 21.   [107] Israel, *Dutch Republic*, 786–91.

was tolerant and associated with 'Arminianism', parts of de Witt's body were sold as mementos, and other parts were roasted and eaten in the streets.[108] As de Witt's magisterial biographer Herbert Rowen has remarked, de Witt was not 'the ungodly man his enemies thought him to be, but his failure to do as they believed true religion required condemned him in their eyes...For he was tolerant in an age which was only beginning to think of such an attitude as a virtue and not a vicious crime'.[109] It is surely significant that Locke's closest friend in the Netherlands, Limborch, owned a portrait of de Witt, suggesting Limborch's appreciation for a man who was literally torn apart by a hostile crowd in 1672 in part because of his support for toleration and for his association with Arminianism.[110]

Reformed hostility to Arminianism and Socinianism persisted into the late seventeenth century. When the Reformed minister Maresius attacked the work of Lodowick Meyer in 1671 for a work that was called 'nearly Socinian' but not actually Socinian, he assaulted jointly 'indifferentism' and 'Socinianism or libertinism'. For many Reformed ministers in the Netherlands, 'indifferentism' slipped easily into Socinianism and was itself pernicious. 'Indifferentism' was the central charge made by many of the Reformed against the Arminians for their support of toleration for Socinians.[111] In the 1670s, the Remonstrant minister Gerard Brandt, a colleague of Limborch's in Amsterdam since 1667, began to issue his influential tolerationist *History of the Reformation*. Looking back over the history of disputes between the Remonstrants and Contra-Remonstrants in the early seventeenth century, the 1674 second volume of Brandt's *History* convicted the Contra-Remonstrants of having intolerantly imposed their own creed and confession, and argued in eirenic language for the public church to become theologically Latitudinarian – to be once again accommodating of diverse views. In 1657, Brandt had written a pamphlet in order to persuade Remonstrants not to join Contra-Remonstrant services out of a misguided ecumenicism, on the grounds that Contra-Remonstrant ministers had always sought to suppress Remonstrants and that only the magistrate could reduce their power and create a united church. The Contra-Remonstrants issued several responses to Brandt, including defence by Henricus Ruyl of appropriate condemnations of 'soul-destroying errors'. For Ruyl, Brandt's history was 'an Arminian history', written 'by an Arminian, from Arminian sources, for the benefit of the Arminians'. Ruyl attacked the proposal for reform of the public church as 'seditious'. The

---

[108] Rowen, *De Witt*, ch. 21, esp. 436.   [109] Rowen, *De Witt*, 436.

[110] P. van Limborch, *Catalogus Librorum* (Amsterdam 1712), 118. For emphasising the importance of de Witt to me very many years ago, I am deeply grateful to Orest Ranum.

[111] Israel, *Radical*, 209–12.

Provincial Synod of Holland in 1676 condemned Brandt's work as 'injurious' to the state and magistrates as well as the church. Although Fagel, William's tolerant adviser, was reportedly pleased with Brandt's work, and although it was dedicated to the Amsterdam magistrate and Arminian sympathiser Cornelius Cloeck, under pressure from the synod the States of Holland withdrew the privilege for publication it had formerly granted to the *History*. Brandt left the final two volumes to be published only after his death. Brandt was advised by friends and sympathisers that he should avoid the dedication of other works to Arminian sympathisers and that the magistrates would be displeased with his *History* itself – suggesting clearly the limited advance in the toleration of Arminianism since 1630, when Episcopius was similarly advised that the magistrates would be displeased if he put the place of publication on his work. As Peter Burke has noted in stressing the reasons for Brandt not to publish all the volumes in his own lifetime, 'it was only in the changed intellectual climate of the eighteenth century', and not in the precariously and partially tolerant atmosphere of the 1670s, 'that Brandt['s *History*] could become a classic'.[112]

Such attacks of the 1670s by Reformed ministers against 'indifferentism' and against proposals for latitude in theology within the public church as 'seditious', the assassination of de Witt, the identification of the Reformed Church with the growing strength of the Calvinist-educated William of Orange, and the rapidly increasing commitment of the population to the Reformed Church, together gave reason for Limborch to feel deeply troubled in the 1680s about the already significant restrictions on toleration for Socinians in the Netherlands and the threat that further restrictions might again pose to Arminians themselves. Limborch knew that the Arminian community was not merely very small but actually shrinking, was acutely aware of the violence formerly used against Arminians in the Netherlands, and of the fragility of their toleration in the 1680s. It was a message that was probably present in Limborch's mind when he looked at his portrait of de Witt, assassinated only a decade earlier by a crowd hostile to the toleration provided by a magistrate branded a member of the 'Arminian party'. When Limborch helped in the 1680s to shelter an English refugee hiding under an assumed name, John Locke, and associated with a Scottish refugee with good reason to fear kidnap and execution, Gilbert Burnet, it was thus not the act of someone serenely secure of his own tolerated status in a tolerant country, but the act of someone realistically fearful about the dangers posed to toleration in the 1680s even in the Netherlands.

[112] Van Eijnatten, 'Lodestars of Latitude', P. Burke, 'The Politics of Reformation History: Burnet and Brandt' in A. C. Duke and C. A. Tamse (eds.), *Clio's Mirror: Historiography in Britain and the Netherlands* (Zutphen 1985), 73–85, at 76–7.

12

Toleration and intolerance, Jews and Muslims

Sixteenth- and seventeenth-century Europe inherited from patristic and medieval sources two divergent ways of discussing the toleration of Jews and Muslims. In patristic and medieval works, those who justified the punishment of 'heretics' and 'schismatics' had usually argued that Jews and Muslims were to be tolerated in order that they could be persuaded to adopt Christianity. Such arguments usually represented Jews and Muslims as 'evil' or 'ignorant', but proclaimed that Christianity had to be adopted voluntarily, and that a greater evil was use of force to convert. Partly as a result of these arguments, in many European societies at the same time as 'heretics' and 'schismatics' were being punished and executed, Jews and Muslims were tolerated. In early modern Europe, these arguments were maintained in substantial force by anti-heretical and anti-schismatic writers justifying intolerance to heretics and schismatics and toleration to Jews and Muslims, including Catholic authors justifying the use of force against Protestants as 'heretics' and 'schismatics' and toleration of Jews in France in the late 1680s.

But while the majority of patristic and medieval texts supported toleration of Jews and Muslims, some patristic and medieval arguments instead justified use of force against Jews and Muslims, either for promotion of conversion, or more usually by accusing Jews and Muslims of many crimes that were said to deserve magisterial punishment, from coining and usury through to sodomy, poisoning, and ritual murder. Many of these accusations drew on the languages of 'poisoning', 'pestilence', and 'sodomy' being deployed against 'heretics' and 'schismatics'. The accusation of 'ritual murder' levied against Jews held that due to their hatred for Christianity they kidnapped and murdered Christian children in a ritualised mockery of the sacrifice of Christ. This series of accusations at moments fostered: trials and executions of Jews; pogroms; the expulsion of Jews from late medieval England and France; programmes of forced conversions in crusades against Muslims in the thirteenth century; similar programmes in Spain and Portugal in the fifteenth century, and the expulsion of Jews from the Netherlands under Spanish rule in the sixteenth century. Early modern Europe thus inherited not merely arguments for the toleration of Jews and Muslims, but also a series of anti-Semitic accusations and associated images of the banishment of Jews and Muslims from England, France, and the Netherlands. As we will see in this chapter, in the seventeenth century these accusations were repeated forcefully in arguments used to defeat a proposed large-scale readmission of Jews to England in the 1650s, and more sporadically in France, which readmitted Jews by royal order in the sixteenth century.

Following Augustine, many late patristic and medieval anti-heretical and anti-schismatic writers had argued that while 'heretics' and 'schismatics' should be compelled back into the church, one must not enter Christianity by a forced conversion, and that therefore Jews and Muslims were to be tolerated. The Fourth Council of Toledo in 633 opposed the use of force to convert non-believers at a time when heretics were subjected to punishments including execution. Both of the main collections of canon law, the 1140 *Decretum Gratiani* and the 1234 *Decretals* of Gregory IX, identified Jewish rites as not to be interfered with; Gratian contended that the judgment of those outside of the church was to be left to God. In the *Summa Theologica*, Aquinas declared that the 'non-believer must not be compelled to believe, because believing is a matter of free will'. While for Aquinas those who fell away from the church could be compelled back into the church, those who had never known 'the truth' had to be persuaded to accept it. Aquinas argued that Jews and non-believers were only to be punished when they committed a civil crime among Christians. While Aquinas identified the Jewish and Muslim religions as 'evil', he suggested that intolerance towards them might lead to greater evils, such as warfare and failure to convert them to Christianity. Referring to Aquinas' arguments, the thirteenth- and fourteenth-century commentators Hostiensis and Johannes Andreae repeated earlier canonist arguments in defence of toleration of Jews. In this extensive canonist literature, Muslims and 'pagans' were generally treated under the same headings and with the same arguments for toleration as Jews.[1]

Such arguments that Jews and Muslims were to be tolerated retained considerable support in the sixteenth and seventeenth centuries in France, England, and the Netherlands, including by authors simultaneously justifying punishing alleged 'heretics' and 'schismatics'. For instance, in his defence of Servetus' execution, the 1554 *Defense of the Orthodox Faith of the Sacred Trinity Against the Prodigious Errours of Michel Servetus*, Calvin argued that those subject to a just punishment were not Jews but heretics and schismatics as 'the apostates, who impiously alienate themselves from the

---

[1] Bejczy, 'Tolerantia'; P. Garnsey, 'Religious Toleration in Classical Antiquity' in W. Sheils (ed.), *Persecution and Toleration* (Oxford 1984), 1–28, at 19.

way of truth and attempt to drag others away to a similar defection'.[2] Calvin wrote similarly in his major defence of magisterial punishment of heretics and schismatics in his *Commentary on Deuteronomy* of his 'perplexity' and 'anguish' as coming not from the resistance of 'Turks' or 'Pagans' to Christianity, but from multiplication of those who 'tear up piece by piece, ripping asunder the union of our faith with the end of perverting the truth of God'.[3]

In a survey of these various discussions of the issue of treatment of the Jews and Muslims in the medieval canonist literature, István Bejczy has declared that the very 'concept of *tolerantia* was chiefly developed as an answer to the question of how ecclesiastical authorities should deal with the practices of the Jewish religion'. Bejczy here captures something important. Aquinas' notion of tolerating a lesser evil (Judaism, Islam) in order to avoid a greater evil (war, forced conversion) was important in promoting toleration of Jews and Muslims in medieval Europe, even as 'heretics' and 'schismatics' increasingly were being punished as 'Christianity became increasingly intolerant of religious dissent in practice as well as theory'. As Bejczy puts it, 'Tolerantia was a way of walking honestly towards outsiders; towards insiders, strictness prevailed'.[4] The contention that one should tolerate a 'lesser evil' to avoid a 'greater evil' was to be a source of early modern tolerationist practice and argument, as in the course of the sixteenth century Jews were readmitted to several countries and cities from which they had earlier been expelled, including France. It was an argument that some in the sixteenth century – including Erasmus, Molanus, and Becanus – were to attempt to extend to apply to 'heretics' and 'schismatics', and in the second half of the sixteenth century many *politiques* similarly held that 'toleration' of heretics and schismatics was a permissible evil in order to avoid the greater evil of incessant warfare.[5] In the contexts of the sixteenth-century wars of religion, this was a powerful and important practical argument for toleration in late sixteenth-century France. Bodin defended toleration of all religions, not just orthodox Protestants and Catholics, partly in these *politique* terms. *Politique* arguments cited the toleration of Jews by popes, and the argument that force should not be used in conversion, as in Charles Gravelle's *Politiques royales*, which declared that

the example of the popes should be followed, for they have tolerated the Jews, even though this is, formally, contrary to the Christian religion...It would be better to

[2] Calvin, *Opera Omnia*, 8, 475, in Melnick, *From Polemics*, 11.
[3] Calvin, *Commentary on Deuteronomy*, 13, in *Corpus Reformatorum*, in *Opera*, vol. 55, quoted in M. de Certeau, *The Writing of History* (New York 1988), 152.
[4] Bejczy, 'Tolerantia', 371, 375.
[5] Israel, *European Jewry*; Le Cler, *Toleration*; Bejczy, 'Tolerantia'.

leave the Jews to the judgment of God and to work to bring them to salvation by good doctrine and pious argument, since no one should be constrained in matters of belief.[6]

Royal orders for the toleration of Jews were issued in the mid-sixteenth century, reinforced by Richelieu in the 1630s, and again under Colbert. Such toleration continued to draw its main strength from arguments of 'reason of state' and from the works of the *politiques*. In 1671, Colbert had ordered that because of their economic contribution, Jews in Martinique

should enjoy the same privileges as all of the other inhabitants of those islands and that they should be allowed complete liberty of conscience, although necessary precautions should be taken that the exercise of their religion should not cause any scandal to Catholics.

In rebutting arguments circulating 'against the Jews' in 1673, Colbert had written of Marseilles that 'business generally increases' where Jews were resident and that 'commerce is the only issue' and not 'religion'. Against the desire of Louis XIV for expulsion of the Jews in 1683, Colbert contended that 'commerce is almost entirely in the hands' of Jews and that a 'general exodus from the kingdom would be dangerous'.[7] The Jewish contribution to the economy became accentuated in the wake of the flight of many Huguenots in the early 1680s. And the rhetoric of Catholic justification of punishment of Huguenot heretics specifically distinguished them from Jews who should be tolerated. In January 1686, at the same time as force was being used against Huguenots and readied against Waldensians, all expulsion orders against Jews were lifted. Colbert de Croissy, brother of the now deceased Colbert and minister for foreign affairs, issued decrees in 1686 and 1687 inviting 'foreigners' of any 'quality, condition, or religion' to trade in France. It was in 1686 that Jews in Bordeaux finally stopped presenting their children for baptism. In 1691, Bayonne started describing those formerly called 'marchands Portugais' as 'Juifs Portugais'.[8]

In France in the wake of the Revocation of the Edict of Nantes, when it became clear that entirely opposed policies would be pursued against heretics and schismatics on the one hand and Jews on the other, the distinction long drawn between Jews as tolerable and heretics and schismatics as intolerable reached new heights, creating a powerful reason indeed for tolerationists to

---

[6] C. Gravelle, *Politiques royales* (Lyons 1596), 225, and Colbert in A. Hertzberg, *The French Enlightenment and the Jews* (New York 1968), 22–4, 29–32; Israel, *European Jewry*, 42–3, 56, 95–6, 132–4.

[7] Gravelle, *Politiques royales*, 225, and Colbert in Hertzberg, *Enlightenment*, 22–4, 31–2; Israel, *European Jewry*, 42–3, 56, 95–6, 132–4.

[8] Hertzberg, *Enlightenment*, 20–28; P. Meyer, 'The Attitude of the Enlightenment Towards the Jew', *Studies on Voltaire* (1963), 1161–1205, at 1169–70. I am grateful to Jeremy Popkin for indicating to me at a conference presentation in 2000 the importance of underlining this point.

argue that the treatment accorded to Jews should be applied to heretics and schismatics. As we will see in Chapter 18, 'early Enlightenment' arguments for 'toleration' contended that 'heretics' and 'schismatics' should be treated as well as Jews and Muslims, even if they were considered 'evil'. Because of that distinction being made on the one hand by the leading Huguenot defender of intolerance to heretics and schismatics, Jurieu, and on the other hand by those Catholic authors defending intolerance to heretics and schismatics, many tolerationist authors in 1684–9 pressed the alleged incongruity of persecuting Christian 'heretics' and 'schismatics' and yet of tolerating Jews and Muslims. Advocacy of toleration for Jews and Muslims was thus an important theme, both in the arguments for toleration of heretics and schismatics *and* in the anti-heretical and anti-schismatic literature from the patristic period through to the late seventeenth century.[9]

But if the claim that Jews and Muslims should be tolerated represented one important tradition of Christian thought about Jews and Muslims, Christian authorities had also issued arguments and laws against tolerating Jews and Muslims in patristic, late medieval, and early modern Europe, and as residents in many Christian countries Jews had suffered trials and executions, pogroms, banishments, and forced conversions. It was alleged that Jews and Muslims were poisoners, pestilential, sodomites, and libertines, coiners and clippers, usurers, and fraudulent in transactions. In declaring that Jews should not be punished for their religious beliefs, Aquinas had declared that they could be punished for their 'civil crimes': these allegations were of 'civil' rather than 'religious' crimes. In addition, Jews were accused of being 'ritual murderers' who had kidnapped Christian children and had sacrificed them in mockery of Christianity and as therefore deserving punishment. It is impossible here to address the many complicated factors which resulted in specific incidents of violence against Jews and Muslims in medieval Europe, topics which have generated huge and crucial historiographies which defy simple summary. But it is important for understanding the terms of debate and discussion of toleration of Jews and Muslims in sixteenth- and especially seventeenth-century Europe which are the focus of this book to note that a number of these accusations against Jews and Muslims contributed at various moments to considerable violence, that these accusations were among those used to justify the magisterial expulsion of Jews from various countries in late medieval and early modern Europe, including England, France, and the Netherlands, and that many of these accusations and images of expulsion were handed on to early modern Europe.

---

[9] Aquinas, *Summa*, IIa IIae qu. 10 art. 8 c, art. 9 in Le Cler, *Toleration*, I, 72, 78, 120, 301; Bejczy, 'Tolerantia', 371.

In a frequently cited passage in the New Testament, John had recorded Christ's declaration that the Jews were of the Devil 'and the lusts of your father ye will do'. Constantine had prohibited synagogues and referred to these by the slang name in use for a 'brothel'. The Third Lateran Council of 1179 had enacted legislation against Jews and Muslims in the late twelfth century at exactly the same time as that against heretics, schismatics, and 'sodomites', and the Fourth Lateran Council of 1215 had made Jews as well as lepers wear identifying dress. Debates had occurred in medieval Europe over whether cohabitation of a Christian and a Jew constituted 'sodomy' equal to 'bestiality'. Writers such as Damhouder declared that it was, and Nicholas Boer cited the example of Jean Alard, who had several children with a Jew and was convicted of 'sodomy' in a case in which it was declared that 'coition with a Jewess is precisely the same as if a man should copulate with a dog'. A deacon was burned at Oxford in 1222 when convicted of bestiality because he had converted to Judaism in order to marry a Jew.[10] When lepers were accused of poisoning wells and burned in 1321 in Languedoc, it was claimed that they had been bribed to do so by Jews who were themselves in the pay of the Muslim King of Granada.[11] Jews were accused at various moments of poisoning wells in order to spread the plague, and when plagues struck in large quantity in the Black Death in the 1340s, some of these 'chastisements' for sin were blamed on Jews' alleged sinfulness. Banishment of Jews from the community, and killing of Jews, were at points legitimated on these bases. The period of the Black Death saw the massacre of Jews across Germany, and in Aragon, and Flanders, among other locations, in the 1340s.[12] The late twelfth century also saw a rash of accusations against Jews of ritual murders, and these were repeated many times in late fifteenth century and then in early Reformation Germany, as R. Po-chia Hsia has shown in *The Myth of Ritual Murder*; their repetition formed part of the context for Grotius' discussions of ritual murder accusations examined in Chapter 11.[13]

---

[10] E. Peters, *The Magician, the Witch and the Law* (Philadelphia 1978); Trachtenberg, *Devil*, esp. 187; Moore, *Dissent*, 249.

[11] M. Barber, 'Lepers, Jews, and Muslims: The Plot to Overthrow Christendom in 1321', *History* (1981), 1–17.

[12] Trachtenberg, *Devil*, ch. 7; P. Ziegler, *The Black Death* (New York 1969), 36–7, 97–109. Perhaps 350 massacres occurred, eradicating 60 large and 150 smaller communities of Jews; rulers often tried to prevent these.

[13] C. Holmes, 'The Ritual Murder Accusation in Britain' in Dundes (ed.), *The Blood Libel Legend* (Wisconsin 1991), 102; R. Po-chia Hsia, *The Myth of Ritual Murder* (Yale 1988); N. Matar, *Islam in Britain 1558–1685* (Cambridge 1998); *idem, Turks, Moors and Englishmen in the Age of Discovery* (New York 1999). The debt of this chapter and of Chapter 19 to the work of Nabil Matar will be evident in many notes; I also wish to express my gratitude to him for a series of personal conversations about these issues.

Periods of violence against Jews, although relatively rare in medieval Europe, were extreme. For much of the period before 1492, Jews were not banished from most European societies, but England, which expelled Jews for more than 300 years from the thirteenth century, is an important exception. In France and England, it was on the alleged grounds of such accusations of coining and ritual murder that Jews were expelled from England in 1290, that attempts were made to banish Jews from France in 1306 and 1394, and that Jews were expelled from Provence in 1498. Accusations of ritual murder, poisoning, spreading pestilence, coining, and fraud were repeated across other European countries as Jews were expelled from Bohemia in 1541 and 1557, from Saxony in 1536, and as they were banned from the papal states in 1569 as Pope Pius V declared Jews 'satanic'.

Whereas Calvin maintained that Jews should be tolerated and the Netherlands readmitted Jews during the years of a Calvinist 'public church', Luther ended his life supporting the expulsion of Jews. Luther identified Jews as being 'as full of idolatry and sorcery as nine cows have hair on their backs, that is, without number and without end'. He identified Jews as desiring to kill Christians if they could, arguing in *On the Jews and Their Lies* that while Jews denied poisoning and murdering children, 'all of this agrees with the judgment of Christ, that they are poisonous, bitter, venegeful, deceitful snakes, assassins, and the Devil's children, who stab and do harm secretly, because they dare not do it in the open'. Even though he recognised at one point that it 'may or may not be' the case that these accusations of ritual murder were true, he immediately stated that 'I know well, that they do not lack the full, whole, and ready will, wherever they could come to do it, in secret or openly'. Luther thought that he might have been made ill by Jews 'blowing hard at me' as he passed by, a notion drawing on the pollution of the air by Jews similar to that spoken of the 'contagion' of 'heresy'. He identified the 'blindness, hardness, [and] wickedness' of Jews with that of 'Turks' and of the hierarchy of the Roman Catholic Church, and attacked 'witches, Turks, Catholics, and Jews' as practising 'magic, idolatry and swindle'. By the end of his life, Luther supported the expulsion of Jews, confiscation of prayer-books and the Talmud, burning of synagogues, and complete proscription of Jewish worship.[14]

A number of other Reformation leaders, including Martin Bucer, similarly opposed the toleration of Jews, and the leading Catholic opponent of Luther, Johann Eck, agreed in writing a *Refutation of a Jewish Booklet* in which

---

[14] Hsia, *Ritual Murder*, 132–5; D. Katz, 'The Phenomenon of Philo-semitism' in D. Wood (ed.), *Christianity and the Jews* (Oxford 1992), 333; Israel, *European Jewry*; Trachtenberg, *Devil*, ix and 99; also *ibid.*, 51–2, 76, ch. 7; Katz, *Philosemitism*, 4; S. Ettinger, 'The Beginnings of Change in the Attitude of European Society Towards the Jews', *Scripta Hierosolymitana*, vii (1961), 193–219, at 194n.

he repeated many of the ritual murder and well-poisoning accusations against Jews to illustrate their 'murderous nature'. Rather as Luther had identified Judaic and Catholic idolatry, Eck condemned Protestants for being imitators of Jewish desecration of the host, and attacked the leading Protestant Osiander, one of the first non-Jewish writers to question the 'blood-libel'.[15] In this process of post-Reformation accusation and counter-accusation, the comparisons of Jewish worship and beliefs with those of the opposing Christian denomination seen as 'heretical' and 'schismatic' reduced willingness to tolerate Jews. And this process of assimilation of 'heretics' to 'Jews' was iterated metaphorically. Franciscus of Piacenza, a Catholic convert from Judaism, declared in 1602 that many Jews suffered 'bloody sores open on their bodies' together with other diseases, imaging Jews as infected in ways parallel to the late medieval imaging of 'heretics' as 'leprous' or 'cancerous'. Johann Fischart's 1575 Strasbourg *Wunderzeitung* depicted the birth to a Jewish woman of two pigs – simultaneously an association of Jews with swine which was common in this period, and with a 'monstrous birth', an image being deployed in huge quantity against 'heretics' in precisely this period.[16] In 1580, an epidemic in Aix-en-Provence was diagnosed by Thomas Flud, an English physician then resident in Aix, as caused by 'poison which the Jews rubbed on the knockers of doors'. Adding his own variation to the themes of ritualised mockery of Christ's sacrifice on the cross, Flud identified the poison as being the venomous saliva collected by Jews from the mouth of a captured Englishman whom they had tied to a cross, and whom they had had serpents sting.[17]

In England, where there were no known resident Jews in the sixteenth century, although there was a small underground community, John Foxe attacked Jews' 'uncircumcised hearts', which overflowed with 'spyderlike poyson'.[18] The execution in 1594 of Roderigo Lopez, Elizabeth I's Jewish physician, for involvement in planning to poison the queen has recently been suggested by the leading historian of Jews in England, David Katz, to have some merit: Lopez probably did plan to poison Elizabeth. This allegation drew upon and added further fuel to English associations of Jews and 'poisoning', as it specifically tied Lopez's intended poisoning to his Jewish religion as 'diabolical' and declared him a 'perjured murdering traitor, and Jewish doctor, worse than Judas himself'. Many English literary works of the

---

[15] Hsia, *Ritual Murder*, 126–31.   [16] Hsia, *Ritual Murder*; n. 14 above.
[17] Trachtenberg, *Devil*, 107–8.
[18] J. Foxe, *A Sermon Preached at the Christening of a Certaine Jew at London* (1578), Eiiir–Eiv in F. Felsenstein, *Anti-Semitic Stereotypes: A Paradigm of Otherness in English Popular Culture 1660–1830*, 37. It is estimated that there were perhaps 27 Jewish families in England before 1655; some 500 Jews by 1677, and perhaps 6,000 in the early eighteenth century: Felsenstein, *Anti-Semitic*, 45.

1590s and early 1600s included anti-Semitic representations focusing on accusations of poisoning and child murder. Christopher Marlowe's *Jew of Malta* (c. 1591), written before Lopez' case but revived in its wake, included as the immediate response to the suggestion that the Jewish eponymous villain Barabas has done something bad: 'what, has he crucified a child?', and Barabas himself boasted that 'sometimes I go about and poison wells'. Thomas Nashe's 1594 *Unfortunate Traveller* included a Jewish physician poisoner, and George Carleton's 1624 *A Thankful Remembrance of God's Mercie* declared that the 'practice of poysoning' was 'taught for Doctrine by the Romish Rabbies'.[19]

Most commentaries on contemporary Jews were written by travellers, and their accounts were similar to these literary images of Jews. Henry Blount's *Voyage into the Levant* (1636 2nd ed.), declared typically that Jews' 'more swarthy' complexion came in part from their 'wallowing in the dirt'. Tying his comments to an accusation which had been central to the expulsion of Jews from England in 1290, he attacked their 'extreme corrupt love to private interesse' and consequent 'continual cheating and malice' which rendered them incapable of 'civill society' as they lacked 'that justice, and respect to common benefit, without which no civill society can stand'.[20] John Warner, Bishop of Rochester, delivered in 1648 a sermon entitled the *Devilish Conspiracy, Hellish Treason, Heathenish Condemnation and Damnable Murder* committed by Jews against Christ which declared them a 'generation of vipers' and 'children of the devil'.[21] In the same decade, Alexander Ross identified Jews as not merely a 'blind, hard-hearted, stiff-necked people' but as 'merciless Extortioners, and cunning in the art of poysoning'.[22] In 1608, in Calvin's case Sir Edward Coke declared that 'infidels including Jews are subjects of the devil and perpetual enemies, with whom and Christians there is perpetual hostility and no peace'.[23] On this basis in the early seventeenth century, Jews were held to lack legal standing in England as witnesses or as plaintiffs. Justices of the Peace advised that 'an infidell, Pagan, or Jew' could not 'get anything in this realm' or maintain any action.

---

[19] D. Katz, *The Jews in England* (Oxford 1994), ch. 2, discusses these images in relation to the probable reality of Lopez's willingness to poison the queen. See Trachtenberg for the level of accusations over many centuries that Jewish physicians had poisoned or attempted to poison kings. See also S.L. Lee, 'Elizabethan England and the Jews', *Transactions of the New Shakespeare Society* (1888), 143–66; F. Felsenstein, 'Jews and Devils: Anti-semitic Stereotypes of Late Medieval and Renaissance England', *Journal of Literature and Theology* (1990), 15–28; idem, *Anti-Semitic*, 38, on Carleton; *Merchant of Venice*, III, i, 22.

[20] H. Blount, *A Voyage into the Levant* (1636), 114, 123, in Katz, *Philosemitism*, 168–9.

[21] Felsenstein, *Anti-Semitic*, 36.   [22] A. Ross, *Pansebeia*, 26, in Pailin, *Attitudes*, 77.

[23] M. Kohler, 'The Doctrine that "Christianity is a Part of the Common Law"' in *Publications of the American Jewish Society*, 31 (1928), 105–34, at 109–10.

As David Katz has shown for England, major sources of what he calls 'philo-semitism' were growing in England in the same period of the late sixteenth and early to mid-seventeenth centuries as these negative attitudes.[24] It was stressed by many writers that the Jews had been chosen by God. There was an increasing interest in Judaic literature and scholarship from Christian scholars. It was stressed that Jews upheld the authority of the Old Testament and that they provided important testimony against 'atheists'. Some more 'radical' or 'deistic' thinkers began to stress what was common among the different religions of the world, and in 'natural religion', and included Judaism within this survey. It is important to recognise, however, that all of these arguments were capable of positive or negative interpretations. Thus, stress on natural religion could accent either Jewish superstitious distance from a 'natural religion' or the commonalities of divergent 'religions'. Study of Hebraic literature could view what Christians and Jews shared positively or emphasise the distance between them as it elevated Hebraic over Judaic literature and was celebratory of the Old Testament as part of the Bible rather than of Jews as a people, the law and the Pharisees. It has been suggested by Nabil Matar that it is therefore better to speak of these as 'philo-hebraic' attitudes rather than 'philo-semitic' attitudes. The English in the early seventeenth century often held 'philo-hebraic' attitudes but rarely 'philo-semitic' attitudes.[25] Thus John Lightfoot, an author of works on the Jews later frequently consulted by Locke, identified the 'doctrine of the Gospel' as having 'no more bitter enemies than' the Jews, and continued his sentence: 'and yet the text of the gospel hath no more plain interpreters'. Lightfoot followed: 'To say all in a word, to the Jews their countrymen they recommend nothing but toys, and destruction and poyson; but christians, by their skill and industry, may render them most usefully serviceable to their studies, and most eminently tending to the inter-pretation of the new testament'. There was thus unquestionably an elevation of the study of Hebrew and Hebraic works in the early seventeenth century, and the elevation of the status of this literature by Christian authors in some cases can be shown through their personal dealings with Jewish rabbis, such as Menasseh ben Israel, to have involved an increase in respect for Jews as individuals, but it is more questionable if this involved a general elevation in Christian eyes of the status of Jews as heirs of Moses rather than as ancestors of Paul.[26]

It is a last element of 'philo-semitism' identified by Katz, the potential of Jews still to be heirs of Paul instead of Moses, which was to be most important in providing impetus in mid-seventeenth century England for the

---

[24] D. Katz speaks of 'philo-semitism' as 'a positive attitude towards the Jews'. Katz, *Jews*, 117–30; *idem, Philosemitism*, esp. 32–3.
[25] Matar, 'Restoration', 118.   [26] Manuel, *Broken Staff*, 131; Matar, 'Restoration'.

construction of tolerationist argument about Jews. Millenarian literature stressed the conversion of the Jews, and held that for such conversion they would need to be taught by Christians and to be scattered into 'all the nations'. English exclusion of Jews was seen by many as frustrating this end. Here, the apocalyptic expectations of the 'Last Days', linked earlier to anti-heretical intolerance, served to promote arguments for the readmission of Jews to England and to place the toleration of Jews on the agenda. And by raising the general issue of religious toleration and giving a significantly increased voice to Baptists, Quakers, and others who argued for a more extensive toleration, the civil wars and Revolution also served to raise to prominence the specific issue of the toleration of Jews. In a council of war resolution of December 1648, there had been support for toleration of 'of all Religions whatsoever, not excepting Turkes [Muslims], nor Papists, nor Jewes'. Proposals for large-scale readmission and toleration of Jews, including 'free use of their Synagogues', owed most to the convergence during the English Revolution of the height of millenarian expectation, pogroms in Eastern Europe in 1648, and the campaign by the Jewish community in the Netherlands for creation of another refuge. The moment was seen as particularly propitious by many who were committed to the notion that the 'end of days' would be inaugurated by the conversion of the Jews. The Baptist Henry Jessey, for instance, expected the 'conversion of the Jews probably before 1658'; the Independent John Tillinghast in 1656 'or thereabouts', and the mathematician William Oughtred thought that the conversion would occur in 1656. Such expectations placed contemporary Jews in a more positive light for many of these millenarians – though as pre-converts, rather than as holding to a religion valid in itself. Some in England saw economic contributions as reinforcing conversion as reasons for readmission: Major-General Whalley argued to Secretary Thurloe in 1655 that 'They will bring in much wealth into this Commonwealth: and where wee both pray for theyre conversion and beleeve it shal be, I knowe not why wee should deny the means'. Readmission and toleration of public synagogues was petitioned for by Rabbi Menasseh ben Israel from the Netherlands, where Jews had gained public synagogues and admission in large numbers by the late 1630s.[27]

Readmission and a limited toleration was supported by Oliver Cromwell, and debated at the Whitehall Conference of 1655. The more 'tolerant' members of a subcommittee which met at Cromwell's instigation in 1655 to consider Jewish readmission and declared that as 'to poynt of conscience we judge lawfull for the Magistrate to admit', simultaneously proclaimed

---

[27] Katz, *Philosemitism*, ch. 3, 99, 126; H. Jessey, *A Narrative of the Late Proceeds at White-hall* (1656), 1–2, in Katz, *Philosemitism*, 1; Whalley in Matar, 'Restoration', 118.

that to provide the full toleration of worship and life asked for by Menasseh ben Israel in imitation of the Netherlands contained terms which it would be 'very sinfull for this or any Christian state to receave them upon'. Public Jewish worship was declared 'evill in it selfe', and it was held that it might persuade Christians to become Jews. Jews were held untrustworthy in terms of oaths even by the most tolerationist of the members of the Whitehall Conference. Jews could only be readmitted, this group recommended, if they were allowed only private and not public worship, and prohibited from printing anything which 'in the least opposeth the christian religion in our language', from holding public office, and from employment of Christian servants. The Baptist Henry Jessey, a correspondent of Menasseh ben Israel, gave an account of the proceedings at the Whitehall Conference which suggested that 'most' there feared that the Jews would 'seduce' and 'cheat' the English, that the 'Major part' thought that Jews might be tolerated with suitable precautions, and that only a minority thought that there was a 'duty' to readmit Jews. Those who favoured toleration with precautions, including Jessey himself, had held that conversion could be promoted by readmission, and that safeguards against blaspheming, proselytising, and cheating would be sufficient. The smaller third group, including the Independents Philip Nye and the tolerant Independent Thomas Goodwin, held that England was punished by God for not admitting Jews, and focused their arguments on the duty of facilitating conversion.[28]

But opposition to readmission and regulated toleration of Jews was substantial, and revived many earlier accusations against Jews. If many Calvinists in continental Europe were supportive of toleration, many in England were fiercely opposed. The Calvinist Presbyterian Matthew Newcomen argued at the Whitehall Conference that, if readmitted, Jews might begin offering children to Moloch. Tying the issue directly to the question of toleration to Quakers and Ranters, which he also opposed, Newcomen held that while some might doubt that Jews were so unreasonable as to sacrifice children, Quakers' and Ranters' practices and beliefs were abhorrent to all reasonable individuals. Since one could see that Quakers and Ranters existed and were really abominable and intolerable, one had reason to believe the accusations against Jews, and to conclude that they too were abominable and intolerable.

In his 1656 *Anglo-Judaeus*, William Hughes of Gray's Inn declared that Jews made it their 'annual practice to crucifie children' and 'conspire against City and people [and] still clip and spoyl the coin'. Given their 'hatred against Christ', they would if readmitted imbrue 'their hands in the blood of young

---

[28] This and the next paragraphs are based on Katz, *Jews*, 117–30; *idem, Philosemitism, passim.*

and tender infants (crucifying them in scorn and derision of our profession)'. William Prynne similarly explicitly opposed readmission of the Jews in his *A Short Demurrer to the Jews*, dated 1656 but issued to delegates before the final meeting at Whitehall, as 'great clippers of money' who 'crucified children'. Prynne restated ritual murder accusations from 1144 and 1255, and declared that Jews 'almost every year crucify one child, to the injury and contumely of Jesus'. He wished his work to serve as a 'perpetual Barr to the Anti-christian Jews' re-admission into England', and not just for the present but for 'all future Generations'.[29] The Royalist James Howell similarly argued that, if readmitted, Jews would repeat the causes of their expulsion by Edward I 'for their notorious crimes; as, poysoning of wells, counterfeiting of coins, falsifying of seals, and crucifying of Christian children, with other villainies'. Even the Christian eirenicist John Dury attacked in his *A Case of Conscience* plans for Jewish readmission to England on the basis of Menasseh ben Israel's model for extensive toleration, arguing that Jews have 'ways beyond all other men, to undermine a state'. If not restrained, Dury declared that Jews would 'be oppressive', as they were now becoming 'in Germany'. Facing such opposition, the Whitehall Conference ended without supporting the readmission and toleration of Jews.[30]

Following the failure of the Whitehall Conference to support the readmission of the Jews and therefore to promote statutory action to provide toleration, an extremely limited readmission and toleration was extended to some Jews by Oliver Cromwell, using personal prerogative powers to allow private but not public worship. Charles II, then James II, and then William and Mary, renewed this provision of toleration by monarchical prerogative over 'foreign' and 'alien' communities. Under such royal rather than statutory provision of toleration, by 1677 the Jewish community in England had perhaps reached nearly 500 people, and the Jewish community in London was becoming sufficiently established that it began offering annual gifts to the Lord Mayor. In 1685, Samuel Hayne's *An Abstract of All Statutes Made Concerning Aliens Trading in England* declared that 'The jews are a sort of Persons admired at by most Trading People all the world over, as here in England for their Great Wealth'.[31] In 1684, when a defendant in a case tried to use Coke's judgment from 1608 that a Jew as an 'enemy' could not sue, the Court of King's Bench declared that as long as the king permitted Jews to live and to trade in England, they could indeed sue. The Jewish plaintiff then won

---

[29] W. Prynne, *A Short Demurrer to the Jews* (1656); W. Hughes, *Anglo-Judaeus*, 46–8 in Katz, *Philosemitism*, 220–3; Felsenstein, *Anti-Semitic*, 32.

[30] J. Howell, *The Wonderful and Most Deplorable History of the Latter Times of the Jews* (1653), sigs. A4, Bv–B2 in Katz, *Philosemitism*, 191; Katz, *Jews*, 129.

[31] S. Hayne, *An Abstract* (1685), 7, in Matar, 'Restoration', 144.

his case. Suggesting an important further legal move towards recognition of the 'trustworthiness' of Jews, their testimony was also accepted as witnesses in cases in the 1660s and 1680s, in direct contradiction to Coke's judgment.[32] At the same time, there continued to be significant scholarly interest in Judaism, and while much of it was philo-Hebraic, some might be called philo-Judaic, appreciative not merely of the scholarship of the Old Testament but more broadly of Judaic scholarship. Rabbi Isaac Abendana was commissioned in 1663 by Cambridge University to translate the Mishnah into Latin, and continued this activity when he then moved to Oxford University. Abendana was a correspondent of Robert Boyle, Locke's close friend, and of Henry Oldenberg, the Secretary of the Royal Society, who was also a correspondent of Rabbi Menasseh ben Israel. Boyle collected Hebrew books. Locke was clearly aware of such activities, reporting on Boyle's acquisition of Christian Knorr's 1677 *Kabbalah Denudata* in 1679 in letters to his friend Nicholas Toinard as part of the process of scholarly exchange of information in the 'republic of letters', in which Hebraic scholarship was considered vital to a proper understanding of the Bible, but in which there seems to have been an increasing appreciation for Jewish scholarship and for Jewish scholars. Locke's friend in the Netherlands, Limborch, also possessed a copy of this work.[33]

But opposition to the admission and toleration of Jews did not end at the Whitehall Conference. Thomas Violet's *A Petition Against the Jews* began the Restoration as many were to continue it by protesting against the toleration of a synagogue as early as 1661 and declaring it 'to the great dishonour of Christianity'. A series of petitions were presented to Richard Cromwell in the late 1650s, and then to Charles II in the early 1660s, which urged that Jews be expelled. In 1660, London financiers proposed that 'the former laws made against the Jews' should 'be put into execution' and furthermore that new ones should be enacted 'for the expulsion of all professed Jews out of your Majesty's dominion'. In 1664, Charles II had to employ his royal prerogative to crush a scheme for the expulsion of the Jews which was supported by the Earl of Berkshire and others. In 1673, Jews were accused of a 'riot' for meeting in a synagogue, since such meetings were illegal; Charles II had to intervene to order cessation of the prosecution. Given Jews' precarious status and wealth as traders, in 1680 the Earl of Anglesey saw an opportunity for such toleration to be turned to greater economic

---

[32] Katz, 'The Jews'; N. Matar, 'John Locke and the Jews', *Journal of Ecclesiastical History* (1990), 51, 56; Kohler, 'Christianity is a Part of the Common Law'.

[33] Matar, 'John Locke and the Jews', 49; *idem*, 'Restoration', 131; A. Coudert, 'John Locke and Francis Mercury van Helmont' in J. Force and D. Katz (eds.), *Everything Connects* (Leiden 1999); H. Graf Reventlow, *The Authority of the Bible and the Modern World* (London 1984); Limborch, *Catalogus Librorum*.

advantage to the king and carefully restricted: he proposed that Jews be made to pay increased taxes and required to live in a ghetto. His proposals were not established, but they suggest the continued fragility of Jewish toleration. In 1681, the high church Anglican George Hickes assaulted the toleration of Jews and nonconformists simultaneously in *Peculium Dei, a Discourse about the Jews*, in which he tied support for the toleration of Jews to rebellious claims to personal inspiration, Fifth Monarchist views, and the 'heresies' of the English Revolution. In 1685, at James II's succession, there was another attempt to prosecute 48 Jews for recusancy. Again a royal order to desist was required; James II produced such, and declared – in a far more explicit and generous recognition of rights to worship of different religions than had been conventional from his brother – that he did so because he wished Jews to 'quietly enjoy the free exercise of their religion whilst they behave themselves dutifully and obediently to his government'.[34]

It was thus in the midst of a fragile but important royal toleration for some few hundred Jews under Charles II that Gilbert Burnet issued in 1680 *The Conversion and Persecutions of Eve Cohan, now called Elizabeth Verboon*, an account of a Jewish woman baptised in October 1680 by his friend William Lloyd. Burnet suggested that 'Eve Verboon' had begun to be persuaded of the truth of Christianity in the Netherlands, but that her mother had therefore imprisoned her for nearly six months, keeping her from doors and windows lest Christians come to her aid, and threatening 'to poison her if she changed her Religion'. Her reading of Christ's resurrection was said to have 'confirmed' her belief, however, and so she was said to have escaped to England. Burnet recounted that Jews had then threatened her in England, planned her kidnap, accused her of bastardy for a child she had miscarried under their threats, and accused her and her husband of theft.[35]

For Burnet, these Jews' 'enraged cruelty' against her was linked to their 'ancestors in unbelief' who had 'with so bloody a malice crucified our Blessed Saviour' and now wanted 'revenge' on one 'resolved to believe in Him'. In a 'Conspiracy of the Jews', they had, according to Burnet, gained her and her husband's imprisonment for debt, and when her husband had attempted to attack her accuser for false imprisonment, had managed to get the sum in action registered incorrectly as 20 pounds instead of 200 pounds, 'so prevalent were the Arts. . .of the Jews'. Describing her baptism, Burnet identified a Jew as having attended to mock it. Burnet declared 'this recital' of these Jews'

---

[34] T. Violet, *A Petition Against the Jews* (London 1661), 2; Katz, 'The Jews', 222–3; Matar, 'John Locke and the Jews', 46–8; G. Hickes, *Peculium Dei* (1681), discussed in Matar, 'Restoration', 136.

[35] G. Burnet, *The Conversion and Persecutions of Eve Cohan, now called Elizabeth Verboon* (London 1680), *passim*.

actions was 'necessary, to let the Nation see what a sort of People these Jews are, whom we harbour so kindly among us; who, as they yet lie under the guilt of that innocent blood' continued in 'obstinate infidelity' and still 'thirst after the Blood of such of their Nation as believe in Him whom their Fathers crucified; and whom they in derision called often to this Convert "that hanged Man"'. Burnet's final paragraph said that he did not 'design to inflame any to Rage or Fury against the Jews, nor do I desire to have any force put upon their Consciences' but that 'so base a Conspiracy' needed to be 'severely punished' so that 'those Enemies of Christ, if they are suffered to live among us, yet may not again dare to adventure on such Practices, against those who forsake their blind superstition'. The 'signal punishment' of these 'Instruments of Wickedness' was called for in order to terrify others 'that they may no more, with Judas, for a little Mony, betray a Member of Christ, to be Crucified by them'.[36]

Burnet thus proclaimed the desirability of 'true conversions' from Judaism to Christianity, attacked the use of force to obtain conversions, and argued that he did not intend to have Jews' toleration removed, but represented Jews as enemies of Christ whose actions against current Christians were understood as based on malice, revenge, idolatry, and mercenary considerations in imitation of the Jews' crucifixion of Christ. He represented them as potential 'poisoners' of their own children, blasphemers of Christ as 'the hanged man', and mockers of baptism, and he alleged that a number of Jews were 'conspirators' against Protestant Christianity and should be punished severely.

We have no way of testing Burnet's claims. It is *possible* that *some* of what Burnet charged was true. We know from the excommunications of a number of Jews in the Netherlands that those who challenged its central tenets were cursed with the full force of an anathema, and Yosef Kaplan has shown that the pain of excommunication was threatened for theological disputes with Gentiles and for selling or loaning books to Gentiles. But there is a very substantial difference between pronouncing a curse with expulsion from one's communion and community on the one hand, and the accusations that Burnet has presented, which are a tissue of stereotypical accusations and inferences, and seem very much more likely to have been based on anti-Semitism than to have been true. The likeliest effects of the text on readers, despite Burnet's denial that this was his intent, were surely to raise questions about the toleration of Jews. It has been suggested by Nabil Matar that as the major impetus for readmission of Jews to England was expectation of their imminent conversion, the absence of such conversions generated hostility to the community that was admitted. It is quite possible that Burnet's assault

---

[36] *Ibid., passim.*

reflected such hostility in an entirely spurious series of allegations about why such conversions were in fact rare.[37]

The Jewish community in England expanded significantly in the wake of the Revolution of 1688–9, in which the armies of William III received significant finance and support from the Jewish community of Amsterdam. William maintained substantial relationships with the Jewish community in England and in the Netherlands in the 1690s. He visited the Portuguese synagogue in Amsterdam in 1690 on his return as Governor-King; the members of the synagogue had prayed for the success of his mission. He knighted one important Jewish supporter in England in the 1690s. But, as under Cromwell, Charles II, and James II, toleration was provided for Jews after 1689 only by royal prerogative and not by statute. The Act to establish religious toleration in 1689 did not include statutory provision of toleration for Jews. Indeed, William used the fact that toleration was dependent on royal support to extract large sums of money from the Jewish community in what David Katz has called a system of 'extortion'.[38] Nonetheless, support for the toleration of Jews did grow in England in the final decade of the century, due in part to commercial concerns. In 1692, the Chairman of the East India Company Sir Josiah Child's *A New Discourse of Trade* explicitly celebrated the contribution of Jewish financial capital to his company and argued that Jews would be long-standing residents of England.[39] Child combined anti-Semitic stereotypes with mercantilist argument for toleration of Jews as serving the 'public good': 'subtiller the Jews are, and the more Trades they pry into while they live here, the more they are like to increase trade, and the more they do that, the better it is for the Kingdom in general, though the worse for the English merchant'.[40] By 1697, the Court of Common Pleas expanded the precedent of the Court of King's Bench of 1684 providing that Jews could sue, and counsel in the case argued in part from the principle of 'humanity' taught by 'commerce' that 'A Jew may sue at this day, but heretofore he could not, for then they were looked upon as enemies. But now commerce has taught the world more humanity'.[41] When a proposal was made to include within the Blasphemy Act in 1698 a specific penalty for Jews, the House of Commons voted it down. And in 1701, the

---

[37] Kaplan, 'The Social Functions of the Herem', *Dutch Jewish History* (1984), 111–55; Matar, 'Restoration'.

[38] Katz, 'The Jews', 242; J. Israel and H. den Boer, 'William III and the Glorious Revolution in the Eyes of Amsterdam Sephardi Writers: The Reactions of Miguel de Barrios, Joseph Penso de la Vega, and Manuel de Leao' in Israel (ed.), *The Anglo-Dutch Moment* (Cambridge 1991), 439–61; idem, *European Jewry*, 130–4.

[39] Matar, 'Restoration', 145.

[40] Child, *A New Discourse of Trade*, 123–4, cited in Israel, *European Jewry*, 132.

[41] M. Kohler, 'Phases in the History of Religious Liberty in America with Particular Reference to the Jews II', *Publications of the American Jewish Historical Society*, 13 (1905), 7–36.

first public synagogue in England since the fourteenth century was dedicated, the Bevis Marks synagogue.[42]

As immigrants to and worshippers in the Netherlands and France, and as mid-century campaigners for their readmittance to England who were there-after readmitted in small numbers, Jews presented a major practical issue about religious toleration in each of the three countries at the centre of this book. In contrast, few Muslims set foot in any of these countries in the sixteenth and seventeenth centuries, except as ambassadors, sailors, and traders. Relations with Muslims were those of international trade, interna-tional warfare, or piracy, rather than questions of refuge and toleration. Most discussions of Islam and of Muslims in seventeenth-century England were strongly negative, and significant portions of philo-Hebraic sentiment were anti-Islamic, but there were important sources of what might be called philo-Islamic sentiment in some ways paralleling philo-Hebraic sentiment. Many authors sympathetic to toleration and anti-Trinitarianism stressed the similarities of Islam and Unitarian Christianity, and many authors sympa-thetic to toleration but not to anti-Trinitarianism stressed the toleration provided in Islamic countries, while many Trinitarian opponents of toler-ation and of anti-Trinitarianism also stressed the similarities of Islam to Unitarianism and pilloried the toleration provided in Islamic countries.

As has been shown by Nabil Matar, the leading scholar of representations of Islam in early modern England, Muslims were frequently represented in early modern England 'as a people who defied God, nature, and English law, and therefore deserved punishment'. For Joseph Mede, whose eschatological writ-ing was important to Locke and Newton, Saracens were 'locusts' by inter-pretation of the biblical text and of their appearance, since their plaited long hair looked like the 'tentacles of locusts'. For the revolutionary Independent Thomas Goodwin, the 'Saracen locusts, under their ring-leader Mohammed' had created a 'tyranny of Mohammedans in the east'. For Henry More in his 1680 *Apocalypsis Apocalypseos*, Saracens were 'Scorpion Locusts, it being the nature of the Scorpion perpetually to sting and transfuse her poison, as of these Saracens to proselyte the world to their Religion'. 'Turks' were for More 'monsters' who were 'made up of a horse and a Man...and have tails'. More spoke in 1680 of 'the Satanical Kingdom of Mahomet' and hoped that this kingdom would soon be conquered by Jews who would then convert to Christianity.[43] More thus expressed the major attitude which caused pre-conversionist philo-Judaic sentiment to undergird anti-Islamic sentiment. In most Christian eschatological schemes of the seventeenth century, the Jews were to be converted and 'the Turks' destroyed. Many philo-Hebraic

---

[42] Katz, 'The Jews'; Matar, 'John Locke and the Jews', 51, 56.
[43] Matar, *Islam*, 158–9, 162, 176.

arguments for the conversion of the Jews inaugurating the millennium countenanced the 'Restoration' of the Jews to their Holy Land by conquest of the 'Saracens', and countenanced the removal of Jews from European lands in order to undertake that task – showing, as Matar has noted, that philo-Hebraism might be opposed to long-term (or even short-term) toleration and admission of Jews in England. As supporters of such expected 'Restoration', in 1665 Henry Oldenberg wrote to Boyle to celebrate the expected conquest of Mecca by Sabbati Sevi, as he had earlier written to Menasseh ben Israel forecasting the return of the Jews to Palestine. The messianic expectations raised by Sabbati Sevi, forecast to conquer Palestine and then to inaugurate the conversion of the Jews, were considerable in England in 1665–6, with many works celebrating that Jews had 'slain great numbers' of the 'Turks', and that 'They give liberty of conscience to all, except the Turks, endeavouring the utter Ruine and Extirpation of them'.[44]

To many Protestant Englishmen, Muslims were not merely Satanic monsters to be conquered by Jews and Christians; they were also 'sodomites'. Leo Africanus had assured readers – in John Pory's 1600 translation – that the Christian Portuguese who had just conquered Azamur had done so because 'God...brought this calamity upon them, but onely for the horrible vice of sodomie, whereof the greatest part of the citizens were so notoriously addicted'. Richard Knolles' *Generall Historie of the Turkes* described them as 'very inclined to venery, and...for the most part all Sodomites'. William Lithgow declared in the late sixteenth century of Muslims that 'Those who have done buggery (as the most part of them do)...shall fall...to the profoundest pit in hell'. William Davis in 1614 wrote that Turks were 'altogether sodomites, and doe all things contrarie to a Christian' – the notion of contrariety here appearing in the contrast of Islam to Christianity as earlier in the book in the contrast of heresy to true Christianity. Many writers identified Islamic theology as responsible for Muslim 'sodomy' and 'libertinism'. For Meredith Hanmer, Muslims believed that 'the pleasures of the body hurt not nether hinder at all the foelicity of the life to come' and therefore were 'sodomites'. Thomas Calvert identified the Qur'anic paradise as promising Muslims the pleasures of the flesh and explicitly included 'lusts of Boyes'. As Matar puts it, 'By predicating the barbarous on the sodomite, English writers created the stereotype of the Turk and the Moor'.[45]

Yet alongside these highly negative images of Islam and of Muslims were a series of sources of more positive images. There was an upsurge of interest in Arabic scholarship. Chairs of Arabic was established at both Oxford and Cambridge in 1630s. The Oxford don Edward Pococke, author of a 1648

---

[44] R. R. *A New Letter from Aberdeen in Scotland* (1655) in Matar, 'Restoration'.

[45] Matar, *Turks*, 112 *et seq.*

Specimen Historia Arabum and celebrated for unlocking 'the treasures of the East', composed poems in Arabic to mark national events, including the Restoration of Charles II. The Latitudinarian Isaac Barrow, Cambridge Professor of Mathematics, determined that it was necessary to learn Arabic for the advancement of science, and others noted that crucial books of 'physicke, astrologie, rhetoricke' were written in Arabic. Locke's mentor Boyle declared that he found the study of Arabic scientific texts useful in his contest against 'groundless traditional conceptions'.[46] Even more importantly, rather as the seventeenth century saw the growth of scholarly philo-Hebraic arguments that the Jews were to be valued as 'forefathers' who had agreed in support of the Old Testament, or stressed the common elements of the three major religions, many writers accented major elements of agreement between Christians and Muslims. This was largely in order to add Muslim testimony to the grounds of credibility of Christianity, or from conviction in the middle of the seventeenth century that even the conversion of Muslims would be possible as conversionist eschatology was applied to Muslims in the writings of the German mystic Jacob Boehme, and of the Moravian theologian Jan Comenius (based in the Netherlands but a visitor to England in 1641–2 and a strong influence on tolerationist members of the Hartlib circle).[47] Thomas Traherne argued against Hobbesian 'atheism' in 1674 that 'Turks acknowledge the historical part' of the Bible. The 1685, *The Atheist Unmasked* similarly argued that 'Mahometans and Jews' joined Christians in worshipping the same 'creator', providing support for the existence of (the Christian) God. Whichcote celebrated that 'The Mahometans...acknowledge all that is related concerning Christ' and indicated that their disagreement was about a further textual interpretation of Scripture, that what Christ said of 'sending the spirit' and a comforter was meant of Mahomet. Isaac Barrow noted that the Qur'an admitted Christianity as once 'a true doctrine, proceeding from and attested to by God'. Richard Baxter noted that the 'Religion of the Mahumetans' confirmed Jesus as 'the Word of God and a great Prophet'. Arthur Bury, whose work was burned as a Socinian and thus 'heretical' work, took this theme farther than anyone in his 1690 *Naked Gospel*, arguing that from the 'prosperity of the Alcoran, we have an argument for the Divinity of the Gospel'.[48]

Such stress on the common ground between Muslims and Christians rendered Muslims associates in Christian arguments against 'atheists'. Such

---

[46] Matar, *Islam*; Champion, *Pillars*, ch. 4.

[47] Matar, *Islam*, ch. 4, esp. 137ff.; H. Trevor-Roper, *Religion, The Reformation, and Social Change* (London 1967), 288; M. Greengrass, M. Leslie, and T. Raylor (eds.), *Samuel Hartlib and Universal Reformation* (Cambridge 1994).

[48] Matar, *Islam*, 109; Champion, *Pillars*, 108.

arguments could be voiced by the most committed Christian intent also on indicating the superiority of Christianity over Islam and merely using Islamic agreement with Christians on some points to make points against those who accepted neither religion. On a second step, however, there was a profound division between on the one hand those Unitarians (and Deists) who further accented Muslim closeness to Christianity by stressing that both were anti-Trinitarian or non-Trinitarian religions and who defended toleration for Unitarians and Muslims, and on the other hand many Trinitarians who accented the distance between Islam and orthodox Christianity and condemned Unitarian 'heresy' and its toleration partly by associating it with Islam.[49]

Justin Champion and Nabil Matar have shown that it was very common for Trinitarian anti-heretical writers to associate anti-Trinitarianism with 'Mahometanism'. Thomas Calvert declared that 'If any Christians turne Mahometans, they begin with Arianisme, and Socinianisme, and then Turcisme is not so strange a thing'. Cheynell called the *Racovian Catechism* the 'Racovian Alcoran'. Robert South in 1698 called an anti-Trinitarian a 'Mahometan Christian'. Locke was denounced by Edwards for having a 'Mahometan faith'. As Edwards put it, Locke had 'consulted the Mahometan Bible' and had 'the faith of a Turk'. For Charles Leslie, Mahomet was 'an express unitarian', Unitarians were 'scouts amongst us for Mahomet', and 'the Alkoran' was 'vile heresy'.[50] All were writing against toleration for anti-Trinitarianism. And such intolerant Anglicans organised in the midst of the Unitarian controversy in 1688 the republication of the mid-seventeenth-century translation of the Koran by Alexander Ross, which identified Mahomet as a sensualist and impostor, and argued that Mahomet accepted the gospel but misread it as he 'endeavoureth to overthrow Christ's divinity with Arius and Nestorius'.[51]

As if to confirm every association thus made by Trinitarian anti-heretical writers, Stephen Nye's *Letter of Resolution Concerning the Doctrine of the Trinity* suggested that Muslims were more numerous in the world than Christians because Muslims proclaimed in the Koran the 'one Truth...the Unity of God', whereas Christians tried to persuade others to a false and absurd faith. Nye's earlier *Brief History of the Unitarians* similarly argued that the 'true Nazarene faith' had been maintained in 'Turkish and other Mahometan and Pagan Dominions' whereas Trinitarian Christianity was

[49] Space does not permit a discussion of deist or libertine arguments about Islam by such authors as Stubbe, Blount, and Toland. On these, see especially: Champion, *Pillars*; J. Jacob, *Henry Stubbe: Radical Protestantism and the Early Enlightenment* (Cambridge 1983).

[50] Matar, *Islam*, 48; Champion, *Pillars*, 102, 110–13.

[51] Matar, *Islam*, 80; Champion, *Pillars*, 104–5; Pailin, *Attitudes*, 135.

full of 'Novelties, corruptions, and depravations of genuine Christianity'. William Freke's 1690 *Vindication of the Unitarians* included many recognitions that the Koran contained, as it put it, 'above a hundred indictments' of the Trinity. Nye and Freke both supported anti-Trinitarianism and the toleration of anti-Trinitarians. Arthur Bury stressed that Islam was Unitarian and had therefore spread in the world, and he attacked Trinitarianism as a platonic clerical imposition upon Christianity, campaigning for toleration of anti-Trinitarians by arguing for the simplicity of 'primitive' Christianity, which had not known of the many articles of faith later required by 'orthodox' Christians. Every one of these works which either pilloried Unitarianism and toleration by associating Unitarianism with Islam, or supported Unitarianism and toleration by associating Unitarianism and Islam, was being read by Locke in the early 1690s.[52]

As Justin Champion has stressed, the notion of the similarity of Islam and Unitarianism was also invoked in an attempt in the 1680s by two self-styled Unitarian 'philosophers' to present a Moroccan ambassador visiting England with a manuscript addressing the ambassador as a representative of their 'fellow worshippers of that sole supreme Deity of the Almighty Father and Creator'. This held that the doctrine of the Trinity was 'such a contradictory absurdity that certainly our wise Maker and Lawgiver would never impose it, to be believed', and that unlike 'backsliding Christians' who believed in 'three co-equal and self subsisting persons' all 'Primitive Christians' had been worshippers of 'an only one God (without a Trinity of persons)' and without 'personalities or pluralities'. Within this stress on the very important agreement of Unitarian Christianity and Islam, it maintained that there were 'weak places' in the Muslim religion and that the ambassador should therefore convert to Unitarian Christianity. One of those involved with the preparation of this manuscript was surely Noel Aubert de Versé. In Tenison's papers, it is recorded that the 'Agent of the Socinians' was a 'Monsieur de Verze'. On 12 September 1682 it was reported to the Tory Secretary of State Sir Leoline Jenkins that

M. Aubert, The French minister who writ the Socinian papers directed to the Morocco Ambassador, which are in your hands, desires after some serious conferences with myself and others to enter into the communion and ordination of the church of England.

This information was provided to Jenkins by Edmund Everard, a Whig associate of Shaftesbury but by 1682, and perhaps earlier, a spy for the Tories. In 1686, Tyrrell was to describe Aubert in a letter to Locke as 'your author' in response to Locke having sent to Tyrrell Aubert's *Pacific Protestant*, an

---

[52] Matar, *Islam* 108; Champion, *Pillars*, 108–9, 111; Marshall, *Locke*.

important plea for toleration. Locke consulted Tyrrell for an account of the visit of the Moroccan ambassador, who was entertained at the Tyrrell household at Shotover Lodge, but it seems very unlikely that Locke was involved in the arguments being prepared for the ambassador. Aubert, as we will see in Part 3 of this book, was to be a member of the intersecting tolerationist circles around Locke, Bayle, Furly, Limborch and Le Clerc, and was perhaps employed by Locke to take books to Le Clerc and by Boyle to take phosphorous to Bayle. In the 1690s and early 1700s, Charles Leslie thundered against Socinianism in a series of works which attacked Locke and which also republished the Socinian arguments prepared for the Moroccan ambassador.[53]

Islam was thus central to tolerationist debates in England in the late seventeenth century because of the similarities alleged between Islam and anti-Trinitarianism. It was also central because the practice of Muslim toleration for Christianity was repeatedly rehearsed by many authors. Not all authors agreed. John Tillotson declared that 'As for the Religion of Mahomet, it is famously known to have been planted by force at first, and to have been maintained in the world, by the same violent means', and Isaac Barrow declared that Islam was a religion so 'gross' that it was 'agreeable to the 'fierce and savage over-runners of the world' and had 'diffused it self by rage and terror of arms; convincing mens minds only by the sword, and using no other arguments but blows. Upon the same grounds of ignorance and force, it still subsists; neither offering for, nor taking against it self any reason; refusing all examination, and upon extreme penalties forbidding any dispute about its truth'.[54] But in the seventeenth century it was generally understood against these declarations by Tillotson and Barrow that force was not used by contemporary Muslims, and that Muslims tolerated Christians within their dominions. This understanding was correct: in Smyrna in the second half of the seventeenth century there were mosques, synagogues, Roman Catholic, Greek Orthodox, and Armenian churches, and Protestant chapels – a level of toleration of public worship unmatched even in the Netherlands.[55] Knolles' *Generall Historie* recognised that Muslims 'converse with Christians, and Eat and Traffick with them freely; yea sometimes they marry their daughters, and suffer them to live after their own

---

[53] McLachlan, *Socinianism*, 318–19; Champion, *Pillars*, 104–5, 111, 115; *CSPD* (1682), 12 September 1682; Locke, *Correspondence*, II, 715; Matar, 'John Locke and the Turbanned Nations', 72; N. Matar, 'The Toleration of Muslims in Renaissance England' in J. Laursen (ed.), *Religious Toleration: The Variety of Rites* (New York 1999), 134. I am grateful to Dr Champion for having drawn the *CSPD* entry to my attention, and for discussion of this issue. Martin Mulsow intends to publish this manuscript and also discusses it in a forthcoming piece on Socinianism which he kindly sent to me.

[54] J. Tillotson, *Works*, I, 148, in Pailin, *Attitudes*, 103; Barrow in *ibid.*, 203–4.

[55] Matar, *Islam*, 25, 29–48.

Religion'. Edward Kellet noted that converts to Islam from Christianity yielded to 'allurements' and not to 'violence'. Blount noted that 'the Turke puts none to death for Religion'. George Sandys declared that 'they compell no man'.[56]

The tolerationist writers of the mid-century particularly often pointed to Muslim toleration as to be imitated. Henry Burton wrote in 1644 that toleration was not, as alleged, the 'Bugbear of all confusion, and disturber of the Civill state' and pointed to Turkey as a peaceful tolerant country. For Roger Williams, Turkey provided the evidence that it was possible for Jews, Turks and 'antichristians' to be 'peaceable and quiet Subjects, loving and helpful neighbours, faire and just dealers, true and loyall to the civill government'.[57] In 1661, Henry Oldenberg argued that German and Hungarian Christians preferred to live 'under ye Turk, because of liberty of conscience'. In 1690, Arthur Bury argued in the *Naked Gospel* that if one wished to use argument for the veracity of Christianity from its successful spread without force, then one would have to accord an advantage to Mahomet 'so the victories of the Alcoran over the Gospel must be evidence, that as the religion of Moses was better than that of the Canaanites, and the religion of Christ better than that of Moses; so must the religion of Mahomet be better than that of Christ'.[58] The 1683 *Strange and Prodigious Religions, Customs, and Manners of Sundry Nations* noted that 'I have heard many say, that it is better for a man that would injoy liberty of conscience, to live in the countreys professing Mahometanism than Papistry: for in the one he shall never be free from the bloody Inquisition; in the other he is never molested, if he meddle not with their Law, their Wives, or their Slaves'.[59] Here, at the height of Charles II's Tory repression of dissenters and at a date when measures against Huguenots were being widely reported, attention was drawn in English argument to the comparative tolerationism of Muslims. It was an association of which Tories tried to make much. The Tory *Heraclitus Ridens* in March 1681 identified nonconformist support for toleration as that of 'Protestant Mahometans' who,

according to the Law of the Alcoran, (which for propagating Religions was in the late times translated into English) are so zealous for Toleration of all Jews, Pagans, Turks, and Infidels; if they have but a Conscience, it is no matter of what colour or size it is, it must have Liberty.[60]

Perhaps the most influential works in the late seventeenth century that were to make the same case that Islamic toleration was extensive, however, were

[56] Matar, *Islam*, 31, 40, 106.   [57] Matar, 'Muslims', 129.
[58] Matar, *Islam*, 22, 106; Champion, *Pillars*, 108.   [59] Matar, *Islam*, 106.
[60] *Heraclitus Ridens*, 29 March 1681, cited in Matar, 'Muslims', 137.

Paul Rycaut's *The Present State of the Greek and Armenian Churches* (1678) and *The Present State of the Ottoman Empire* (1668), the latter of which had received two separate translations into French in the 1670s, one by Briot and one by Bespier. Rycaut was read by Locke and by Bayle, the latter of whom cited Rycaut on Muslim issues in his *Dictionary* more extensively than any other source. For Rycaut, conversion to Islam was not due to force but 'free choice'. Rycaut gave thanks 'to God, there is a free and publicke exercise [of Christianity] thereof allowed in most parts, and something of respect given to the clergy, even by the Mahometans themselves'. And he alleged that the legitimation of violence by Mahomet had not been continued by the vast majority of his followers.[61] As we will see later, Bayle used Rycaut's arguments in his case for toleration in the *Dictionary*, and Locke celebrated 'Mahometan' toleration in the *Letter Concerning Toleration*.

[61] Matar, *Islam*, 22, 106; J. Charnley, *Pierre Bayle, Reader of Travel Literature* (Berne 1998), 49–54, 85–6.

13

Catholic justifications of intolerance in the 1680s and 1690s

The Revocation of the Edict of Nantes was celebrated by a huge outpouring of propaganda in France.[1] In the funeral oration for Chancellor Le Tellier in January 1686, Bishop Bossuet declared that his audience had seen a scene unrivalled even by the Church Fathers, who

had not witnessed, as you have witnessed, the sudden dissolution of an inveterate heresy, the return to the fold of so many lost sheep that our churches are too small to hold them and finally the defection of false pastors who are ready to abandon those whom they have misled without even waiting for the order to do so.

The Revocation was 'this miracle of our times', and the 'sacred pens' of those who composed the annals of the church were to be taken up 'to place Louis with the Constantines and the Theodosiuses', and to 'publish abroad this miracle of our times'.

For Bossuet, previous Christian emperors had also suppressed heresy which 'with its venom, and discord retreated into hell, whence it had come'; Louis XIV was thus no less than a 'new Constantine...Theodore...Marcian... [or a] new Charlemagne' who should be saluted

as six hundred and thirty churchmen saluted his predecessors at the Council of Chalcedonia: You have affirmed the faith, you have banished the heretics: this is the worthiest work of your reign, its true character. Thanks to you, heresy is no more: God alone could have brought about this marvel.[2]

---

[1] The next two paragraphs and much of this first section are based particularly on G. Adams, *The Huguenots and French Opinion 1685–1787* (Ontario, Canada 1991), ch. 1, and P. Burke, *The Fabrication of Louis XIV* (Cambridge 1992).

[2] Bossuet, *Oraison funèbre de Michel le Tellier, Oraisons funèbres de Bossuet* (Paris 1959), 167–8 in Adams, *Huguenots*, 23; and in J. Truchet, *La Politique de Bossuet* (Paris 1966), 183–4, as quoted in P. Riley (ed.), Bossuet, *Politics Drawn from the Very Words of Holy Scripture* (Cambridge 1990), liii. The Assembly of the Clergy had long been arguing that Louis should imitate Valentinian, Theodosius, and Charles, and enact 'complete extirpation of heresy', as it put it in 1675. It specified that 'Freedom of conscience is looked upon by all Catholics as an abyss yawning at their feet...an open door to libertinism': P. Gaxotte, *The Age of Louis XIV* (New York 1970), 208.

Bossuet's panegyrical lead was followed by many other clerics in the late 1680s and early 1690s. The Jesuit Philippe Quartier celebrated Louis for 'having extinguished heresy'. Even the Oratorian Richard Simon, whose *Histoire Critique* had been ordered burned by Bossuet, wrote in defence of the Revocation. The Revocation was defended also by Fénelon, for whom the 'sacred bond of unity' was 'the only bond by which man's wayward spirit is restrained from plunging to perdition'.[3] Massillon celebrated that:

The profane temples are destroyed, the pulpits of seduction are cast down, the prophets of falsehood are torn from their flocks. At the first blow dealt to it by Louis, heresy falls, disappears, and is reduced either to hide itself in the obscurity whence it issued, or to cross the seas, and to bear with it into foreign lands its false gods, its bitterness, and its rage.[4]

Such was the outpouring of clerical celebration of the Revocation, indeed, that Bayle began *The State of Wholly Catholic France* (1686) with the request: 'Permit me, sir, to interrupt for a quarter of an hour your cries of joy and the universal felicitations over the total ruin of heresy'.[5]

Much of the literature celebrating the triumph over heresy and schism was heavily providentialist in proclaiming this the work of God. Bossuet was deeply committed to the extensive particular providential interventions of God in the world as author of major works such as *Particular Providence* (1681), and he attacked Malebranche as a 'heretic' for his account of God operating by general laws instead of particular providential interventions. For Bossuet, God particularly intervened via the actions of rulers. In Bossuet's *Universal History*, he had spoken of God holding the reins of every kingdom and attacked those who spoke of 'coincidence or fortune...What is coincidence to our uncertain foresight is concerted design to a higher foresight'. In the 1679 manuscript of his *Politics Drawn from the Holy Scriptures*, he identified France as enjoying 'the particular protection of God'. It is unsurprising therefore that Bossuet's *Funeral Orations* on Queen Marie-Theresa and Anne de Gonzague, the first in 1683 in the period leading up to the Revocation, and the second in its first month of operation in November 1685, stressed that God was particularly involved in the 'miraculous reign' of Louis XIV, contrasted to the preceding Civil War of the Fronde as intended by God as a 'sign' to 'show that he brings death, and that he brings resurrection; that he plunges all the way to hell, and then

---

[3] Adams, *Huguenots*, 24–5; Fénelon, *Sermon*, 6 January 1685, in Hazard, *European Mind*, 90; O. Douen, *L'intolérance de Fénelon* (Paris 1875); Quick, *Synodicon*, cxxiv; E. J. Kearns, *Ideas in Seventeenth Century France* (New York 1979), 121.

[4] Massillon in Smiles, *Huguenots*, 152–3.

[5] P. Bayle, *Ce que c'est que la France toute Catholique* (1686; ed. E. Labrousse, Paris 1973); N. Keohane, *Philosophy and the State in France* (Princeton 1980), 314.

withdraws'. It was within such deep providentialism, seeing intolerance towards the Huguenots as heretics as miraculously ordained and providentially 'signified', that Bossuet described the 'miracle' of the Revocation and the recalling of the Huguenots from heresy and schism to the church. For Bossuet in his January 1686 *Oration on the Chancellor Le Tellier*, the Revocation was not merely the act of Louis himself for 'God alone could have brought about this marvel'.[6]

Many other bishops agreed. The Bishop of Luçon saw the destruction of Protestant chapels as the result of the 'particular protection of God'. The Bishop of Viviers declared his happiness:

We have had the consolation of seeing the temples razed, the false pastors driven out, and heresy reduced to its last extremity. O daughter of Babylon who art to be destroyed.[7]

Whatever complex of motivations drove Louis to the Revocation – and his political desire to crush the major source of resistance to the French monarchy over the past century and a half was doubtless important – that he was doing God's will, inspired by God, and would be successful with God's assistance, were attitudes that Louis XIV himself expressed. In September 1685, he wrote that he could not doubt 'that it is the divine will which wishes to use me to bring back into its ways all those subject to my orders'. In the month of the Revocation, Louis wrote that if the bishops supported him 'I am persuaded God will – for his glory – consummate the work he had inspired in me'.[8]

But it was not merely clerics and the king who celebrated. Mademoiselle de Scudéry celebrated the Huguenots' conversion as a 'miracle' in November 1685, and declared that 'the compulsion by which he is bringing them back into the church will be salutary for them in the long run'. Implicitly betraying a doubt that immediate conversions due to force would be real, but without this reducing her support for the Revocation one iota, she then immediately continued 'At the very least, it will save their children, who will be brought up in the true faith'. Complimenting dragoons as 'excellent missionaries' and declaring that 'The preachers who are now being despatched will complete the task' of these 'booted missionaries', Madame de Sévigné similarly encouraged her son-in-law, the Lieutenant Governor of Provence, 'to disperse and punish bands of wretched Huguenots' who 'crawl from their hovels to pray to God'. She commended the authorities' anxiety to 'exterminate them'. For Madame de Sévigné, 'everything' about the Revocation was so 'admirable' that 'No monarch past or future can possibly outdo it'. Poems

---

[6] Riley, introduction to Bossuet, *Politics*; J. B. Bossuet, *Discourse on Universal History*, ed. O. Ranum (Chicago 1976).

[7] McManners, *Church*, II, 581.

[8] McManners, *Church*, 578; cf. Labrousse, 'Understanding the Revocation', 56.

in the *Mercure Galant* similarly celebrated Louis' unique and 'most glorious' triumph in destroying the 'insolent' and 'rebellious Heresy'.[9]

The prolonged burst of celebration of the Revocation and propaganda in its defence in the late 1680s saw the commissioning of much art, from popular propaganda such as medals and engravings utilised in prints and included in almanacs through to paintings and statues. Many medals were struck to commemorate the Revocation. One showed a triumphant Louis being crowned with the victor's laurels by a female figure representing the church; his sword pinned to the ground a head complete with writhing snakes – the Hydra-head of heresy. The image was surrounded by the inscription 'two million calvinists brought back to the church'.[10] And many other medals similarly imaged conquest of the 'Hydra-head' of heresy or associated Protestants with the Beast of the Apocalypse, among them a 1687 medal commissioned by Comte D'Avaux, Ambassador to the Netherlands, which depicted the Huguenot leader Jurieu as the Beast of the Apocalypse and indicated that 'Minister Iurius' written in Hebraic letters and taken as numbers added up to 666.[11]

Almanacs for 1686, as Barbara de Negroni and Robin Gwynn have shown, included many prints on the theme of 'the Destruction of Heresy'. In one representative image (see Figure 13.1), Louis XIV was shown surrounded by religious figures, with sword and church linked, illuminated by rays from the sun and the Holy Spirit, and placed in the upper (heavenly) regions above a (hellish) figure of Heresy, whose mask is removed to display a monstrous face and writhing serpents: Heresy, as so often in preceding centuries, was here imaged as monstrous and venomous in celebrating intolerance towards it.[12]

Statues celebrating the Revocation and Louis as triumphing over heresy were commissioned across France and for a series of prominent locales in Paris. The statue of 'Louis Victorious' by Desjardins for the Place des Victoires, which included a bas-relief of the Revocation, showed Louis crushing Cerberus underfoot. The municipality of Paris commissioned a statue by Antoine Coysevox for the Hôtel de Ville which showed Louis, sword in hand, in the process of slaying two monstrous incarnations of heresy, one with bat's wings and the other with hideous features. Many paintings were commissioned on the same themes in the later 1680s. The Académie Royale de Peinture chose the 'triumph of the church' and

---

[9] Adams, *Huguenots*, 20–1; Burke, *Louis*, 102.   [10] Burke, *Louis*, 132, fig. 58.

[11] M. Jones 'The Medal as an Instrument of Propaganda in Late Seventeenth and Early Eighteenth Century Europe', *Numismatic Chronicle* 142 (1982), 117–26, at 121–2; plates 15, 31.

[12] Almanac (1686) Huguenot Library, London; cf. B. de Negroni, *Intolérances* (Paris 1996), plate 5 after p. 120.

Figure 13.1 *Heresy Unmasked by Truth*. From an Almanac of 1686.
By permission of the Huguenot Library, London.

'heresy trodden underfoot' as themes for pictures, and Charles Le Brun's 1687 'L'Église victorieuse de L'Hérésie', commissioned by the Oratorians, depicted the church bearing a shield emblazoned with the image of the Sun King and accompanied by Truth and Faith, triumphing over Heresy, a monster whose forehead crawled with serpents in yet a further use of the classical Hydra-image.[13] Once again here, the Revocation saw the revival of many images of the Protestant heresy that had been staples of Catholic propaganda in prints in the sixteenth century, with images of Protestantism as 'heresy' that was disease, monstrosity, and diabolic.[14] As Bayle noted in the preliminary discourse to his *Philosophical Commentary*, Catholics in 1685–6 spoke of nothing but 'crushing the infernal Hydra of heresy'.[15]

LOUIS' ACTIONS AGAINST HUGUENOTS AND WALDENSIANS AS CRUSADES FOR THE 'TRUE FAITH', THE INQUISITION, AND EARLIER ATTACKS ON THE WALDENSIANS

Many Catholic apologists in France moreover celebrated the role of Louis XIV in his actions against the Huguenots and then against the Waldensians as an explicit imitation of previous Catholic rulers leading crusades for the 'true faith'. Maimbourg emphasised in the 1682 *History of Calvinism* that Luther and Calvin had taken over the medieval heresies of Waldo, the alleged founder of Waldensianism. He depicted the Waldensians as always a thorn in the side of French kings, and François I as having wielded force against Waldensians who were then living in Provence in an 'extermination' of heresy which saw 3,000 killed, villages sacked, and a town razed; this drew Maimbourg's qualified defence.[16] Châtelet had argued in his *Treatise*, first published in 1666 but reprinted both in 1680 and 1689, that

The royal ancestors of His Majesty exercised constant diligence inviolably to preserve the Catholic religion. They were always the unfailing protectors of the Church and of the Holy Apostolic See. They expelled the Arians; they bore arms and risked their lives against the Albigensians, whom they defeated and destroyed; they chastised the Waldensians of Lyons; in sum, they preserved any attack on Christianity in all places to which their authority extended.

He then immediately continued that 'In the last century a new monster rose up against the Church', with a birth 'abetted by impiety and revolt'. The 'glory' of cutting off 'the last head of this Hydra was reserved for His

---

[13] Burke, *Louis*, fig. 36; Adams, *Huguenots*, ch. 1.
[14] As Labrousse points out, before the Edict of Nantes Huguenots had increasingly been represented as 'schismatic' rather than 'heretical'; the Revocation saw the charge of 'heresy' revived and ranged alongside that of schism: Labrousse, *Une foi*, 99–101.
[15] Bayle, *Philosophical Commentary* (1708), 19.
[16] Maimbourg, *Histoire*, 70–1; Dompnier, *Le venin*, 77.

Majesty' Louis XIV in a 'long-awaited execution'.[17] The Waldensians had adopted Protestantism at the Reformation, and had taken on a shortened version of the Huguenot confession of faith as their own. In one Catholic propaganda image of 1688, two Waldensians were shown finding Calvin and Beza in Hell with the Devil, berating him for leading them astray with his 'damnable errors'.[18]

Partaking of the general understanding of Christian history as a series of repetitions of heresies, histories of the Inquisition became a major form of Catholic propaganda in defence of the Revocation in the later 1680s and early 1690s, depicting the Calvinists as later versions of the Waldensians and Albigensians against whom earlier French kings had fought in defence of the faith and in conjunction with the Inquisition. In 1686, the Jesuit La Valette authored a *Parallel of the Albigensian and Calvinist Heresy*, which argued that in the actions against them of Louis XIV and St Louis – each said to be significantly the eighth king born after the birth of the heresy – there was 'something divine'. In 1691, the Dominican Benoist published a *History of the Albigensians and Waldensians*, which sought to maximise the credit of the founder of his order by maximising Dominic's role in forcibly converting Albigensians and Waldensians in the thirteenth century.[19]

Perhaps the most important work, however, in this extensive Catholic campaign binding together the defence of the Inquisition in medieval France against the Albigensians and Waldensians with Louis XIV's actions against Huguenots and Waldensians was Bossuet's 1688 massive and enormously influential *History of the Variations of the Protestant Churches*, which provoked no less than fifteen responses from leading Protestants. It devoted over one hundred pages to the views of the Albigensians and Waldensians and their Wyclifite and Hussite descendants. For Bossuet, while the Waldensians initially were schismatics, whereas the Albigensians were 'Manichean' heretics, the Waldensians had become 'heretical' as they had adopted the ideas of the Reformation in the sixteenth century and were now both 'heretics' and 'schismatics'. As such 'ambitious apostates' who 'wallowed in the devil's doctrines' both Huguenots and Waldensians deserved to be banished from the realm.[20]

---

[17] Paul Hay du Châtelet, *Traité de la politique de France* (1666; 1680; 1689), ch. 5; tr. A. Soman in O. Ranum (ed.), *The Century of Louis XIV* (1972), 350–8, at 351–2. Pierre Nicole's *Préjugéz legitimés contre les calvinistes* (1671), 199, similarly declared that Calvinists were simply heretical followers of the ideas of Waldensians and Albigensians: Dompnier, *Le venin*, 50.

[18] Stephens, *Waldensian*, 205.

[19] La Valette, *Parallel de l'hérésie des Albigeois et de celle du calvinisme* (1686); J. Benoist, *Histoire des Albigeois & des Vaudois* (Paris 1691); Perry, *Theology*, 18.

[20] J. B. Bossuet, *Histoire des variations des églises protestants* (1688).

DEFENDING INTOLERANCE BY THE TRADITIONS OF INTOLERANCE: AUGUSTINIANISM AND VARIATIONS IN THE FAITH

Bossuet's *Variations* placed this association of the Waldensians and Huguenots as heretics within a general argument that the Catholic Church had maintained the truth throughout time, and that variation was a sure sign of heresy. Bossuet's preface cited Tertullian on the ways in which heresies bred further heresies, and on such variation as a sign of heresy; his work was structured around that insight. As a young scholar and priest, Bossuet had studied Tertullian at length, including his *Prescriptions against Heresy*, together with Augustine against the Donatists, Irenaeus against heretics, Epiphanius against heresies, and the 'great bishop' Optatus against the Donatist schism. The 'excellent', 'learned', and 'grave' Tertullian became one of Bossuet's two most revered sources in sermons and reading, orations and writings. He was outnumbered in frequency of quotation only by the 'incomparable' Augustine, for Bossuet the 'master of all preachers of the Gospel and doctor of doctors'. Augustine and Tertullian were Bossuet's central citations in identifying Protestantism as heresy in his *Conference with Claude*, a work called by Arnauld 'perfectly beautiful' and described by Fénelon in 1705 as Bossuet's most celebrated. In his sixth *Reflection on a Writing of Claude*, Bossuet spoke of Tertullian's anti-heretical *Prescriptions* as a 'divine work'. Augustine was equally revered, and after an exhaustive study of Bossuet's *Oeuvres* which brilliantly illuminated the extensiveness of Bossuet's patristic learning, Theodore Delmont called Augustine Bossuet's 'principal inspiration'.[21]

The Revocation saw the full revival of attack on Huguenots as heretics as well as schismatics. In the eighty years of operation of the Edict, it had increasingly become common to treat the Huguenots as 'schismatics' rather than as 'heretics', assaulting them for their unjust separation from the church, or to identify their heresy as following from their schism. Augustine's authority remained central. On Sunday 21 October 1685 – four days after the Edict of Fontaineblen, the Jesuit du Rosel recorded that Bossuet preached at Fontaineblen with 'a very fine and very fair dissertation' on the just performed abjuration of Protestantism of the Duke of Richmond, illegitimate son of Charles II, 'applying to it the gospel for the day. It was the parable of the King who invites to a solemn banquet people of every sort and who, when these decline to come, desires that both the good and bad should be obliged to come in – compelle intrare'.[22]

---

[21] *Ibid.*, preface; Kearns, *Ideas*, 120; A. Rébelliau, *Bossuet Historien du protestantisme* (Paris 1891); T. Delmont, *Bossuet et les Saints Pères* (Paris 1896), 13–17 (esp. 16), 26, 28–9, 39, 47, 81–2, 86–8, 96–7, 120–1, 125–7, 133–43, 158–80 (esp. 168), 294–8, 321–42 (esp. 323–4), 328–31, 358–9, 409.

[22] Du Rosel in Dunlop, *Louis XIV*, 276.

The 1685 *Conformity of the Conduct of the Church in France for Recovering Protestants with the Conduct of the Church in Africa for Regaining the Donatists* – soon to be the target of Bayle's attack in his *Philosophical Commentary* – was, as its title suggested, a deeply Augustinian case for compulsion against schismatics, and it included the text of Augustine's letters to Boniface and Vincent. It declared in good Augustinian fashion that the punishment of the Huguenots was a work of love and charity, and denied that they could legitimately be called martyrs because they did not suffer for the truth.[23] Louis Thomassin's 1686–8 two-volume *Treatise of the Unity of the Church and the Methods Christian Princes Can Use to Regain Those Who Have Separated* – similarly reviewed by Bayle in the *Nouvelles de la République* in November 1686 and responded to by him in the *Philosophical Commentary* – also made much of Augustine's defence of compulsion of the Donatists, following lengthy analysis of Augustine's letters by four chapters on Augustine's *De Unitate Ecclesiae* as establishing the precedent for compulsion of the Huguenots. For Thomassin, the 'peines douces' used by the Catholic Church against the Donatists had been, in good Augustinian fashion, 'acts of love', and were like preventing someone from throwing themselves off of a precipice (leading Bayle to retort in the *Nouvelles de la République* that in ordinary human language, as opposed to that of the church, the taking of goods, liberty, country and children were acts of violent severity and not of love).[24] Reviewing the justifications of intolerance given in France, Claude's *Account* accurately declared that Catholics had 'continually in their mouths that passage of the Gospel, *compelle intrare*, compel them to come in and the persecution which the orthodox of Afric offer'd the Donatists'.[25]

Together with Augustine's central authority, many Catholics defending the Revocation drew extensively from the entire history of the justifications of force against heretics and schismatics in the Christian tradition since patristic times. Thomassin reviewed, as Bayle was to put it, a 'great number of citations and reflexions' which 'testified' that the 'Fathers, Popes and Councils' had had frequent recourse to the secular arm against sects, none of which was stronger than the provision of the Justinian Code forbidding heretics from assembling and baptising under penalty of death.[26] Many Catholic works declared that maintenance of the true faith was the 'finest

---

[23] *Conformité de la conduite* (Paris 1685), 211; Labrousse, *Une foi*, 102–3; de Negroni, *Intolérances*, 87–8.

[24] Bayle, *Philosophical Commentary*, III 15; *Nouvelles*, Nov. 1686; *OD*, I, 688–90; de Negroni, *Intolérances*, 91; Labrousse, *Pierre Bayle*, II, 560.

[25] [J. Claude], *Account*, 45.

[26] Thomassin's defence of intolerance has been called by Elisabeth Labrousse a 'veritable encyclopedia' of arguments for intolerance: Labrousse, *Une foi*, 96; *idem, Pierre Bayle*, II, 560.

flower' of the French Crown. They defended punishment up to execution for heretics, as schismatics and as blasphemers. Ferrand wrote in his 1685 *Reply to the Apology for the Reformation*, opposing Jurieu's *History of Calvinism*, that since 'it is permitted to punish heretics with the extreme penalty, I do not condemn those who deliver them to it'. Catholics thereafter repeatedly defended the executions of those preachers who did not go into exile, but stayed and preached against the king's orders. But it was the Augustinian emphasis on faith and conversion and not execution which predominated in most Catholic accounts. The intolerance culminating in the Revocation of the Edict of Nantes was based on the notion of 'conversion' using compulsion, and not on the basis of execution for heresy and schism. Those who were executed after the Revocation were executed not as heretics and schismatics but as rebels, for resisting authority by force, even if their resistance was enacted in defence of their religion. Even as Ferrand allowed the legitimacy of execution, he stressed that the point of force was to help to achieve conversion.[27] As Arnauld put it in his 1681 *Apology for the Catholics*, written against Jurieu's *Policy*, 'coercion may be justified if it makes people willing to listen and examine'. Pastoral education was required in combination with the use of force, or such force was illegitimate.[28]

A series of Catholic accounts defending the use of force even looked back in time and argued that the massacres of Protestants in sixteenth-century France had been unjust, or attempted to skirt the issue. In his qualified defence of the use of force against Waldensians in his *History of Calvinism*, Maimbourg emphasised that the soldiers of François I had used force in sacking villages and towns in the sixteenth-century assaults on Waldensians and Huguenots in Provence only against those who refused a pardon for abjuring their heresy, and he declared the soldiers guilty of excesses in killing.[29] Maimbourg criticised the St Bartholomew's Day Massacre, declaring it a day to be buried in the shadows of an 'eternal oblivion', and devoting almost the entirety of his last book to the massacre. He argued that once heresy was established, it could *not* be reduced only by force. While heresy, in Maimbourg's eyes, had to be punished, force alone would not work. Indeed, for Maimbourg, the massacre had 'hardened hearts' but where the Bishop of Lisieux had refused to obey the king's orders, Protestants had converted.[30] Châtelet's *Treatise* had similarly argued against banishing Protestants both because it would deprive the state of many good

[27] Ferrand, *Réponse*, 249, in Perry, *Theology*, 16.
[28] A. Arnauld, *Apologie pour les catholiques* (Liege 1681), quoted in Goldie, 'Theory of Religious Intolerance', 350.
[29] Perry, *Theology*, 145–6.
[30] Maimbourg, *Histoire*, VI, esp. 476–7, 484–8; Perry, *Theology* 163–4.

families and because it 'would deny these wretches any hope of conversion and salvation', calling for the king to use justice mingling 'gentleness with severity' and 'indulgent' punishments. He hoped that learning 'the true mysteries of those doctrines which now offend them' would 'cause them to confess, as did St Augustine, that they have not correctly understood the teachings of the Church'. De Vallemont's 1687 *Panegyric on Louis* even went so far as to distinguish Protestant violence against Servetus, which involved execution, from Catholic force currently being used to reclaim heretics for the church which banished or converted 'heretics'. It was important to many Catholic arguments that intolerance in the 1680s was 'judicial' and 'restrained', and not that of massacre and large-scale execution, in contrast to St Bartholomew's Day. In the *Journal des Savans* in February 1685, the review of the methods that had been used against the Albigenses declared them legitimate, and noted that the Lateran Council had justified death, but stressed that the 'gentleness' of Louis XIV was better. In constructing his pre-Revocation arguments that the toleration of Protestants under the Edict of Nantes should be continued, Jurieu had depicted a Catholic character who denied that Catholics thought that the St Bartholomew's Day massacre was legitimate; even after the Revocation of the Edict of Nantes, this was to remain the major theme of Catholic defences of the use of religious violence.[31]

Bossuet expended much effort in the years after the Revocation enquiring into conversions and suggesting techniques to persuade those now coming to mass of the truth of the Catholic religion. He accepted that many initially attended worship unconvinced, but hoped that 'the effect of time and the grace of God' would gradually open them to persuasion.[32] In 1699, Archbishop Colbert of Rouen directed a *Pastoral Letter* to the Curés of his diocese on the methods to be used with the 'newly reunited'. For Colbert, Protestantism was a 'pernicious poison' and Protestants had been guilty of both heresy and schism, 'which the fathers have always regarded as the worst of all crimes and the most contrary to the spirit of Jesus Christ'. Their principles had encouraged 'vanity' and a spirit of

revolt and presumption, each one believing it a right to read the scripture not as a submissive child awaiting the resolution of doubt from pastors, but as a judge who must pronounce on all controversies and interpret the scriptures by his own lights.

The newly reunited were therefore to be taught that the very interpreting of Scripture by individuals made Scripture impossible to understand.

---

[31] Hay du Châtelet, *Traité* in Ranum, *Louis*, 355; M. P. L. L. de Vallemont's 1687 *Panégyrique de Louis le Grand* (Lyons 1687) in de Negroni, *Intolérances*, 88, and *ibid*, 79; Bayle, *Philosophical Commentary* (1708), 197–8, on *Journal*.

[32] Rébelliau, *Bossuet*, 304–7; McManners, *Church*, 580; E. E. Reynolds, *Bossuet* (New York 1963).

Identifying the church as acting 'according to the great principles of St Augustine', he opposed a 'false charity' which did not confute error. He argued that Protestants' errors could be demonstrated to them both by their inability to agree on fundamentals of Christianity, and their justifications of rebellion and bloody warfare. His ideal was of persuasion to true conversion, against false abjuration extracted by force.[33] Even Nicholas-Joseph Foucault, the Intendant responsible for aggressive dragonnades in Béarn and Poitou, recorded in his *Memoirs* – albeit in the midst of accounts of promoting 'conversion' by imposing dragoons, fines, imprisonments, sending Protestant women to the monasteries, sentencing men to the galleys, and ordering the execution of one minister – that he had attempted to foster true conversions by having bad priests replaced, had encouraged the sending of 'good controversialists' to dissuade those who retained their objections to Catholic faith, and had suggested the organising of worship to be reminiscent of Huguenots' customary forms and so to promote true conversion by 'accustoming' worshippers to the Catholic faith.[34]

It was because the Catholic case was organised first around the declaration that no force had been used, and then around a justification of force to aid in conversion but not in defence of execution for religion, that Bayle recognised in the preface to his 1686 *Philosophical Commentary* that the Catholic Church had changed its methods and justifications since medieval times. Yet he argued that this had not in fact involved any reduction in its 'barbarity' because as times had changed and become more 'polite' and 'humane', the penalties that were deployed were in many ways more barbaric than they had been in medieval times of general 'ignorance' and 'barbarity'. And he emphasised in both the preface and in the *Philosophical Commentary* itself that while execution was not ostensibly being used for religion, but only to punish those who resisted, torture, rape, and theft were employed by dragoons.[35] Jurieu's 1682 *Last Efforts* similarly argued that the very 'taking from us of all means of living' meant that Protestants 'must dye or change our Religion', recognising that it was 'true, the death now propos'd is not hanging or burning as formerly', but arguing that it was unclear that it was better to die 'by a long train of Miseries' than 'in a moment on a Gibbet'.[36]

---

[33] *Lettre Pastorale de Monseigneur L'Archévèque de Rouen, Aux Curés de son Diocèse, au sujet des nouveaux Réunis* (Rouen 1699), 6, 9–10, 12–15, 34–5, 44–5, quoted and discussed in M. Greenshields 'How to Convert Protestants' in M. Greenshields and T. Robinson (eds.), *Orthodoxy and Heresy in Religious Movements* (Lewiston 1992), 60–92; cf. Briggs, *Communities*, 219; Orcibal, *Louis XIV*, 128–32, and Armogathe, *Croire*, 105–26, on episcopal questioning of conversion en masse.

[34] Foucault, *Mémoires*, esp. 92.   [35] Bayle, *Philosophical Commentary*, preface.

[36] Jurieu, *Last Efforts*, 42–3.

In justifying the punishment of 'heretics' by civil authorities on the recommendation of the church, Bossuet cited Calvin and Beza and pointed out that all Protestant theologians except the Anabaptists and Socinians had written in favour of the punishment of 'heretics'. Bossuet replied to an attack on Catholic persecution by Jean Rou, an associate of Bayle, by pointing out that the 'express opinion of your own theologians' had been that they had been 'morally bound' to execute Servetus for 'having denied the divinity of the Son of God'. Bossuet thus pinned contemporary orthodox Huguenots on the horns of a dilemma. If they declared that the punishment of heresy was indeed a moral obligation placed upon princes, their claim against the Catholic Louis' intolerance became simply that of denying that their beliefs were heresy, and their defence of synodal authority in order to maintain the faith itself rendered problematic their simultaneous attack on the infallibility claimed by the Catholic Church. This was also pointed out against them by Maimbourg, Nicole, and Arnauld.[37] If they declared, however, that Protestantism rejected such punishment of heretics, they showed that Protestantism had veered from its dominant sixteenth-century 'magisterial Reformation' heritage, and that Protestantism was simply incapable of maintaining effectively the faith in the matter which almost all Protestant as almost all Catholic theologians understood to be the most fundamental point of Christian faith, the doctrine of the Trinity. The obvious consequence, for Bossuet, was that Protestants could not claim to be the 'true church'. While Bossuet diverged widely from the biblical critic Richard Simon on issues such as the application of critical biblical scholarship and the correct text of the Bible, having ordered Simon's *Histoire Critique* burned and pulped, on this issue Bossuet joined hands with Simon in the argument that Protestantism attenuated quickly into Socinianism and stood self-condemned on those grounds, and in supporting the authority of the Catholic Church as necessary in order to uphold the faith.[38]

It was partly due to this challenge that most Huguenot ministers, led by Jurieu, undertook the measures against anti-Trinitarianism in the 1680s and 1690s described in Chapter 4, defending their confession of faith and responding that Protestants had always and still validly punished and sought magisterial prosecution of anti-Trinitarianism. Viewed in this light, the international campaign against Socinianism and tolerationism of the 1680s and 1690s was in significant measure a campaign to counter Catholic accusations that Protestantism always tended to support more and more fundamental 'heresies'.[39]

---

[37] Dodge, *Political Thought*, 193.   [38] Bossuet in Adams, *Huguenots*, 22.

[39] Jurieu's 1681 *Policy* included attack on Catholics as spawning 'Socinian heresies' that were repudiated, according to Jurieu, by 'every Christian'.

The Catholic case that Protestantism had no recourse against Socinian heresy was further bolstered after 1689 by the conversion to Catholicism of two among the very small number of Protestant tolerationists who were being attacked by Jurieu for their Socinianism, Isaac Papin and Noel Aubert de Versé, both of whom then issued works which argued that only Catholicism could defend the true faith against such Socinian heresy. In his *The Toleration of the Protestants*, Papin argued that because of its support for liberty of individual conscience, Protestantism necessarily had to be tolerationist, and that it therefore necessarily tolerated Socinianism, then added to these two arguments that he used in the 1680s in defence of toleration the argument that Protestantism was false precisely because it therefore could not maintain the 'true faith'. Bossuet made much of the conversion of Papin from Protestant tolerationism to Catholicism in 1690, publicising it in his own works and personally receiving Papin into the church. After he returned to Catholicism in 1690, Aubert similarly defended Catholic authority as vital to combat Socinianism in a work issued as an attack upon precisely the arguments he had formerly used in defence of toleration; again, these attacks were given wide publicity by Catholic apologists.[40]

Accusations that Protestantism led to Socinianism and that Protestant principles had no recourse against Socinianism were among the central accusations that Catholics made against Protestants in the 1680s and 1690s in justifying the Revocation of the Edict of Nantes and Catholic authority. They similarly deployed assault on one other Protestant denomination in order to pillory all of Protestantism: the Quakers. Bossuet's 1689 *Third Exhortation to Protestants*, written against Jurieu, called Quakers 'the most extreme fanatics', and argued in an extensive analysis of Quaker thought about inner inspiration that Jurieu's own stress on inner inspiration bringing knowledge was 'exactly what the Quakers' taught. Antoine Arnauld's *Spiritual Testament*, written c. 1679 but published in 1692, described the Quakers as the worst heresy, symbolising what England had lost in giving up Catholic unity in giving rise to 'all the most bizzarre heresies in the world, and some of the most senseless', including those whose 'name suggests their mania...the Trembleurs' (i.e. Quakers). For Brueys' *History of Fanaticism*, Quakers were extreme fanatics awaiting the second coming. In seeking to defend toleration for all Protestant sects, including Quakers, Aubert's 1684 *Pacific Protestant* treated those thought intolerable in turn in an escalating ladder of the intolerable. Arminians came before Socinians, and both came before Quakers, as the group thought least tolerable of all in

---

[40] I. Papin, *La Tolérance des Protestants* tr. as *Toleration* (1733), *passim*.

French Catholic eyes.[41] In the early 1690s, an anonymous author published an attack on Quaker doctrines of inner illumination, rejection of baptism and the eucharist, rejection of the real divinity of Christ in favour of one merely symbolic, and reduction of the status of the Scriptures. Giving them a heretical Christian heritage, it declared them the offshoot of Anabaptism. It assaulted Quaker opposition to social hierarchy, symbolised in refusal of hat honour and personal forms of address, and accused them of wishing to invert political hierarchy, identifying Benjamin Furly as desiring to make himself the King of Rotterdam. It attacked the tolerationist arguments of Aubert's *Pacific Protestant*. This *Short History of the Birth and Progress of Quakerism and its Doctrines* is often identified as having been written by Philippe Naudé, but Locke and Furly, both of whom possessed the work and criticised it in correspondence about it, were convinced that it had been written by Aubert after his reconversion to Catholicism, rather as he had written first for and then against Socinian principles. Whoever was its author, it was cited in Catholic works assaulting Protestantism as tending to the worst of all heresies by focusing on the Quaker challenge to every hierarchy.[42]

Tolerationists and anti-Trinitarians thus faced in the 1680s and 1690s the need to respond to the intolerant acts of the Huguenot community and Dutch Reformed Church in the Netherlands, and to the joint Anglican and orthodox English nonconformist support of restrictions of full toleration to Trinitarian Protestants. They faced agreement on the part of 'magisterial Reformation' Protestants and Catholics over the past century that anti-Trinitarianism was intolerable, and wrote in the midst of a major debate between Catholics and 'orthodox' Protestants (such as Jurieu) in which anti-Trinitarianism was still being held intolerable in the 1680s and 1690s. And they not merely faced the accusation of anti-Trinitarianism against Socinians, but also faced that argument against Quakers as part of the general case that Quakers were extreme fanatics and subversives. Such a context was surely extremely pressing to Locke, who was living in the household of the Quaker Furly and busily reading Socinian works.

---

[41] Aubert de Versé, *Le Protestant pacifique* (Amsterdam 1684), *passim*.

[42] E. Phillips, *The Good Quaker in French Legend* (Philadelphia 1932), 3–7, 9, 12, 22–3, 28ff. French sources had long been fed a heavy diet of images of the Quaker James Nayler by the Cromwellian Paris news gazette *Les Nouvelles Ordinaires* in November and December 1656, and the 1669–72 *L'État présent de l'Angleterre* declared that Quakers were 'vermin or insects which spring up in the foulest refuse'. In the 1669 *L'Europe vivante*, Chappuzeau declared them deniers of Trinity, heaven and hell, and the resurrection; they were relatedly described as communists and anarchists. Chappuzeau here largely followed the hostile account of Quakers in the French version of Alexander Ross's work, *Les Religions du monde*, which received two French editions published in Amsterdam in the 1660s, and one in the year following the Revocation, 1686.

HERETICS: LIBERTINES AND SODOMITES, THE PESTILENTIAL
AND THE POISONING

Much of the Catholic case thus argued that Protestants were heretics treading in the footsteps of the heretical Waldensians and Albigensians; it depicted the Catholic Church as inheritors of the Inquisition in defence of the 'true faith' and as the only authority capable of maintaining a consistent faith over time against heretics and schismatics, and depicted Louis XIV in the role of former kings acting against heresy. Tying together medieval heretics such as Waldensians and Albigensians, 'magisterial Reformation' heretics such as Huguenots, and 'radical reformation' heretics such as Socinians, Catholic accounts in the 1680s and 1690s drew freely upon the inquisitorial accounts of Waldensians and Albigensians as sodomites and libertines, poisoners and the pestilential, and tied them in their turn to attacks on both the 'magisterial' and 'radical reformation'.

We have seen in Chapter 5 that the very words for the Vaudois – vauderie, valuderie – imaged Waldensians' meetings as witches' sabbaths, that is, as nocturnal orgies, and used against the Waldensians the language of poison and pestilence as well as of sodomy and libertinism. Benoit's history of the Waldensians, issued in direct defence of the authority of the Catholic Church and in indirect defence of the Revocation of the Edict of Nantes, accused the medieval Waldensians of 'sodomy', an accusation against them that Pierre Bayle thought worth noting to his correspondent in the 'republic of letters', Minutoli, in February 1691.[43] And many Catholic works simultaneously pressed accusations that Protestant leaders were 'sodomites' and 'libertines'. Varillas recorded every story that he could find about Calvin as debauched and criminal. Maimbourg's *History of Calvinism* depicted Beza as the debaucher of children and as a lover of both men and women in an account which declared that his 'atheism', 'impiety', and 'debauchery' had not precluded his becoming the international leader of Protestantism following Calvin. A lengthy account of Clement Marot, Protestant translator of the Psalms into French, was given, in which Maimbourg said that Marot had seduced the wife of his host in Geneva, and that while he should have been condemned to death under Genevan law, he had escaped with a whipping.[44] The convert from Protestantism David Gautherau gave prominent play to allegations of Protestants' immoral lives among his personal reasons for converting to Catholicism. Other Catholic apologists accused Protestant ministers of crimes up to and including murder.[45]

[43] Bayle, *OD*, IV, 652, letter cxiv.
[44] Maimbourg, *Histoire*, II, 96–9; III, 217–19 in Perry, *Theology*, 126–7.
[45] Perry, *Theology*, 213–14.

Protestant heresy and schism was repeatedly imaged in the 1680s and 1690s as not merely 'libertine' and 'sodomitical' but as a kind of 'poison' and 'pestilence'. We have noted the appearance of these images in iconographic forms at the beginning of this chapter; they were also central to texts. As Bernard Dompnier has shown in his brief account of the images of heresy as 'poison' in early modern France in the chapter which gives the title to his important book *Le venin de l'hérésie*, and as Elisabeth Labrousse has noted about French anti-heretical and anti-schismatic thought of the 1680s, Protestant 'heretics' were compared frequently with incendiaries, poisoners, and evildoers threatening the entire body politic, and as 'infecting' and 'polluting'. Labrousse stresses, appropriately, the levels of fear of plague and disease in a world before antibiotics and modern medicine.[46] Barbara de Negroni has similarly written of the prevalent images of heresy as 'contagious evil' and the centrality of justification of the Revocation as keeping the Catholic population from contamination.[47] Literalising the image of the 'heretic' as poisoner, Maimbourg wrote of the 'poisoning' of Président D'Oppède by a Protestant surgeon as 'one of the fruits of this heresy'.[48] Soulier's 1686 *History of Calvinism* described the French as then becoming 'infected with the poison' of heresy.[49] In the *History of the Religious Revolutions in Europe*, Varillas, who spent much of the 1680s locked in a fierce debate with Gilbert Burnet over the latter's *History of the Reformation* and whose works received thereby substantial notoriety and many Protestant replies, described Calvin's doctrines as a 'pestilence' corrupting 'innocent maids' and 'straightforward men'.[50] And Thomassin's influential *Treatise on the Unity of the Church* was, as Labrousse stresses, a veritable compendium of accusations of 'disease', 'poison', 'sodomy', and 'libertinism'. The 1702 Rotterdam edition of Richard Simon's *Selected Letters* included a letter on the allegations of Socinianism against Theodore Maimbourg which declared simply 'L'air d'Angleterre contagieux en fait de Religion'. The attack on Maimbourg as 'Socinian' in the text included assertion of his 'debauchery'.[51]

As early as his 1681 *Policy of the Clergy*, Jurieu described a Huguenot commenting on the increased restrictions being placed on Huguenots as treating them 'as if we were the Plagues of the Republick' and declared that it was 'as if we were infected, we are forbidden to approach Children that come into the world, we are banished from the Bars and Faculties, we are

[46] Dompnier, *Le venin*; Labrousse, *Une foi*, ch. 5, esp. 96–7.
[47] Labrousse, *Une foi*, ch. 5, esp. 96–7; de Negroni, *Intolérances*, 80.
[48] Maimbourg, *Histoire*, II, 79–93, in Perry, *Theology*, 146.
[49] Soulier, *Histoire*, I, 5–6, in Perry, *Theology*, 79.
[50] A. Varillas, *Histoire des révolutions arrivées dans l'Europe en matière de Religion*, 4 vols. (Paris 1686–9), II, bl x, 459ff. in Perry, *Theology*, 123.
[51] Simon, *Lettres Choisies*, lettre vii, 76–81.

removed from the King's Person'.[52] In his 1682 *Last Efforts*, Jurieu similarly saw it as necessary to refute the sixteenth-century allegations of 'libertinism' against Protestants now being revived in Maimbourg's work by declaring them simply the renewal of 'all the old accusations of the pagans against primitive christians' who had 'charged them with strange crimes' such as that 'they roasted little children and having made great cheer put out the lights and turned the place into a brothel'. Thus viewing the refutation of these accusations as important to defending the toleration of Protestants in France, this did not stop Jurieu himself deploying in these very works the image of the Catholic proponent of persecution of Protestants, Valentinois, as a 'lascivious she-wolf thirsting after the blood of the faithful', and it was not to stop Jurieu turning the same kind of accusations of 'libertinism' and of 'poison' and 'pestilence' against the tolerationists and unorthodox Huguenots and 'Socinians' in the Netherlands and England in the late 1680s and 1690s, as we will see in the next chapter.[53]

The power of images of pestilence and libertinism as undergirding intolerance towards Protestants thus received testimony from Jurieu in the process of attacking them in order to defend the toleration of orthodox Huguenots in 1681–2. As Barbara de Negroni has shown, many images of Protestantism in engravings and in almanacs issued to defend the Revocation depicted it as an illness bringing about death. *The Consistory of Desolate Error* thus placed the demonic figure of 'erreur' itself in the 'Chaire de Pestilence'. The vices listed in a book placed on the lap of the figure 'erreur' explicitly named both 'libertinism' and 'obstinacy'.[54]

THE CATHOLIC CASE AGAINST PROTESTANT HERESY IN THE 1680S AND 1690S AS 'SEDITION' AND 'TREASON'

As early as 1666, Châtelet had stated the case for uniformity of the faith as necessary to preserve the peace in his *Treatise on the Policy of France*. Significantly, the *Treatise* was reprinted in 1680 at the beginning of intensification of the campaign to convert Huguenots, and again in 1689. For Châtelet, 'There can be no doubt that, by the principles of Christianity and by the maxims of politics, it is necessary to reduce the King's subjects to a single faith'. He argued:

A king can have no object more worthy of his care and attention than to maintain in his realm the religion which he received from his ancestors. For diversity of belief, cult, and ceremony divides his subjects and causes them reciprocally to hate and despise one another, which in turn gives rise to conflicts, war, and general

---

[52] Jurieu, *Policy*, 100–1.   [53] Jurieu, *Last Efforts*, 164–5.
[54] De Negroni, *Intolérances*, 97, and plate 4, plate 6, and pp. 98–101.

catastrophe. On the other hand, unity of beliefs binds men together. Fellow subjects who pray to God in the same church and worship at the same altar will rarely be seen to fight except in the same armies and under the same flags. Since this maxim is universally true in the politics of Christian nations, and since our religion is the only one which offers salvation, princes are obliged to maintain it with all their might and to employ for its glory the sovereign power which they derive from its beneficence.

For Châtelet, one religion was necessary not merely because Protestants were of a different religion and contrariety always caused dissension, but because Protestants were of an intrinsically rebellious religion. He identified Protestantism as a 'monster' born and matured in 'impiety and revolt' with 'much blood shed' in the sixteenth century as kings tried 'to reduce the heretics to their duty'. He attacked contemporary Protestants as retaining 'the memory of their audacity and of their past rebellions'. In their hearts, he asserted, 'they nurse the same old hatred of order and discipline, and they are inclined still towards revolt, confusion, and anarchy'. In sum, there was reason for the king 'to consider that he has more than 100,000 potential enemies in the bosom of his realm as long as France harbours Huguenots...only waiting for a chance to rebel'. He should 'reduce them to a condition in which they cease to be a threat'.[55]

Many Catholic works, including Maimbourg's 1682 *History of Calvinism,* followed in identifying Calvinist heresy and schism with sedition. Maimbourg's *History of Calvinism* attributed the civil wars of the sixteenth century to religion and to the Huguenots. For Maimbourg, the Calvinists were France's greatest enemy, and 'heresy and sedition were one and the same thing'.[56] The lesson for princes, according to Maimbourg, was straightforward: 'they have no more dangerous enemies than the enemies of the Church...and...they can never reign peacefully if they do not apply themselves forcefully to snuff out their cabale and heresy'. For Maimbourg, Calvinism maintained itself 'by the most violent of methods...against all divine and human laws, which forbid subjects to take up arms against their Sovereign under whatever pretext'.[57] The Catholic convert Gautherau's 1684 *Wholly Catholic France,* issued under royal privilege in July 1684, identified sixteenth-century Huguenot pastors as having taught that rebellion was just, creating the 'independent Spirit of Huguenotism'. In the 1680s, the Parisian *Journal des Savans* reviewed all of these works, repeatedly focusing on the theme that the 'spirit of Calvinism' was necessarily rebellious.[58] Denys de Sainte-Marthe discussed the history of Protestant rebellion in Anabaptist Germany and Huguenot France in his *Reply* to Claude's

---

[55] Hay du Châtelet, *Traité,* ch. 5 in Ranum, *Louis,* 352–3.   [56] Perry, *Theology,* 143, 151.
[57] Maimbourg, *Histoire,* II, 122–3, in Perry, *Theology,* 152; Maimbourg, *Histoire,* IV, 268, in Perry, *Theology,* 159.
[58] Gauthereau, *La France,* I, 118–19, 129; Perry, *Theology,* 150.

Account of the Oppressions in 1688, and concluded that 'we had to forestall their evil designs' because 'it is practically impossible for them not to believe themselves obliged to exterminate us'.[59]

Bossuet's 1688 *Variations* described the 'conspiracy' of Amboise as caused solely by religion.[60] For Bossuet, deliberately employing language against the Protestants that Huguenots were now applying in their accusations about Catholic violence due to the Revocation of the Edict of Nantes, the sixteenth-century 'council of Protestants' had ordered 'bloody executions' and had tried to force Catholics to embrace the Reformation 'by taxes, by quartering soldiers on them, by demolishing their houses and uncovering their roofs'. For Bossuet, 'Those who left to avoid those violences were stripped of their goods'. Bossuet ended this historical sketch with sarcasm dripping from his quill: 'These are the men who boast of their meekness: one should but leave them alone, because they apply Holy Scripture to everything, and sing so melodiously their Psalms in rhyme'.[61] Bossuet's 1691 *Defence* of the *History of the Variations* further attacked Luther for supporting a false idea of spiritual equality that had led directly to Anabaptist communism and to rebellion, declaring against this that 'there are Seigneurs and Sovereigns...whose bodies subjects can in no wise attack without committing a crime'. For Bossuet, the 'rebellions of the Protestants are passed into dogma and authorised by the synods...it is under the Reformers and by their authority it fell into this excess, and these enormous abuses have the same authors as the Reform'.[62]

This case was largely made by attacking sixteenth-century Huguenots as rebellious. But it also included reference to Huguenot support for the revolt of the Prince of Condé in 1614–16, and to the resistance of Huguenots to Louis XIII in the 1620s.[63] And these examples were often part of a broader case against Protestants, including Luther and Calvin and their followers, which indicted the rebelliousness of the Dutch republic in the sixteenth century, and then again under de Witt, and of the English Revolution of the 1640s and especially in the regicide of 1649, as the natural consequences of Protestant thought. Not merely were such principles as those of the monarchomachs said to lead to civil war, then, but regicide itself was made a natural consequence of doctrines often spoken of by Bossuet as 'Presbyterian' or 'Calvinist'. And by the later 1680s and early 1690s, such

---

[59] McManners, *Church*, II, 580.   [60] Perry, *Theology*, 148.

[61] Bossuet, *Variations*, X, sec. LII in Perry, *Theology*, 161.

[62] J. B. Bossuet, *Défense de L'Histoire des variations* (Paris 1689), sec. LII, LIII–LIV in Perry, *Theology*, 116–17.

[63] Holt, *French Wars*; R. Briggs, *Early Modern France* (Oxford 1977); A. Lublinskaya, *French Absolutism* (Cambridge 1968); G. Hanlon, *Confession and Community in Seventeenth Century France* (Philadelphia 1993).

a case was being supplemented by even more recent examples of resistance theory in England and the Netherlands, focusing on the justifications of rebellion in the thought of Jurieu. Rather as the actions against the Waldensians and Huguenots in the 1680s confirmed in the minds of English Protestants that Catholic rulers could not be trusted to maintain toleration for their Protestant subjects, fulfilling what they had long been saying about such rulers, the actions and arguments of many Huguenots who argued in defence of the resistance of Protestant subjects, first in defending themselves when worshipping in the south of France in 1683–5 and then in taking up arms against their Catholic ruler in England and Ireland, James II, confirmed in the minds of many French Catholics that Protestant subjects could not be trusted to maintain obedience to their Catholic rulers, fulfilling what they had long been saying about Protestant subjects. From the examples of intolerant Catholic kings in France, English Protestants justified their resistance in England; from the examples of rebellious Protestant subjects in Germany, the Netherlands, England, and France, French Catholics justified their intolerance.

In 1687 Simon's *Letter on the New Converts* attacked Jurieu's *Pastoral Letters* for their justification of rebellion, arguing that

All your speeches and pamphlets tend towards the restoration of the Gospel in France by force of arms...You give men who are no better than rebels the quality of martyrs for Christ.[64]

Bossuet was adamant in the *Defence*: Christ had left to his disciples 'no power and no force whatever against the public power, when they were oppressed with as much injustice and violence as was Jesus Christ himself'.[65] And in his *Fifth Exhortation* against Jurieu, Bossuet declared that Protestant defences of rebellion in the 1680s – including that of William of Orange against the rightful ruler James II – had added a further layer of evidence to the general truth of Protestant rebelliousness. He excoriated Jurieu for arguing in defence of the Revolution of 1688–9 that 'the people are naturally sovereign' and contended that if one considered men as they naturally were before government 'one finds only anarchy...where each one can claim everything, and at the same time contest everything'. In such a state of 'anarchy' there was for Bossuet neither 'people' nor 'sovereignty'. Such theories for Bossuet had led directly to the 'judicial murder' of Charles I, caused by 'Cromwell and the fanatics' and defended by Milton, on the principles of 'the absolute sovereignty of peoples over their kings, and all

---

[64] Simon, *Lettre des quelques nouveaux convertis* (Paris 1687), 15, in Adams, *Huguenots*, 24.
[65] *Défense de l'histoire des variations* in *Oeuvres* (Paris 1841), IV, 418, quoted in Bossuet, *Politics*, ed. Riley, introduction, xxxviii.

the other principles which M. Jurieu, following Buchanan, still maintains'. Jurieu had amalgamated natural rights arguments for resistance with a providentialism equal to Bossuet's own, and with a reading of Scripture as supporting popular sovereignty and resistance, citing David as a king who had ascended the throne by the authority of the people who were 'masters of their crowns, and that they take them from, and give them to, whom they will'. For Bossuet, Jurieu thereby misread providence, and 'prodigiously abused' Scripture. Rebellious people did not have rights; David had not needed the 'authority of a rebel people' to be ruler; and God had not intervened to protect Protestant heresy.[66]

In one of the most famous passages composed by any early modern thinker, Bossuet declared that 'Majesty is the image of the greatness of God in a prince'. The power of God

> can be felt in a moment from one end of the world to the other: the royal power acts simultaneously throughout the kingdom. It holds the whole kingdom in position just as God holds the whole world. If God were to withdraw his hand, the entire world would return to nothing: if authority ceases in the Kingdom, all lapses into confusion...'What is done solely at the Emperor's bidding?' asks St Augustine. 'He has only to move his lips, the least of all movements, and the whole empire stirs. It is he who does all things by his command, in the image of God'.[67]

Kings were always to be obeyed for Bossuet, even if they acted against the 'true religion' and in defence of 'heresy' or 'schism'. Yet a good king understood the need to consult the church, as Charlemagne had over the Nestorian schism. His decision, which Bossuet held up for imitation, was 'nothing else than an absolute submission to the decisions of the church'. The 'priesthood and the empire are two powers which are independent, but united'.[68] In Bossuet's thought in this climacteric, the classical divine right theory of monarchy reached its apogee in France in service of a king imitating Charlemagne by following the advice of the church and defending the 'true faith' against 'heresy'. Absolutism, backed by strong providentialism, joined hands with uniformity of faith, backed by strong providentialism. Thus was the famous formula given flesh in France after 1685: 'Une foi, une loi, un roi'.

---

[66] Bossuet, *Cinquième avertissement* and *Sixième avertissement aux protestans sur les lettres du ministre Jurieu contre l'Histoire des Variations*, 403–4, 410; Bossuet, *Politics*, ed. Riley, introduction, lvii, lix–lxiv.

[67] Bossuet, *Politics*, ed. Riley, 160 (and introduction).

[68] Riley, introduction to Bossuet, *Politics*, lv. On Bossuet's absolutism, see Skinner, *Foundations*, II, 113.

14

Huguenot justifications of intolerance and debates over resistance in the 1680s and 1690s

In the later 1680s, Pierre Jurieu clearly became the leading Huguenot theologian of the Huguenot diaspora after the 1687 death of Jean Claude. In this role, he published a series of works against the toleration of 'heresy' and organised the international campaigns to maintain the Huguenot confession of faith in the Huguenot diaspora and to prevent the employment of 'Pajonist' or 'Socinian' Huguenots which were described in Chapter 4.[1] In the early 1690s, Jurieu's repeated assaults on toleration included an attack on Locke's *Letter Concerning Toleration*,[2] and he brought about the synodical censure of Bayle's *Dictionary*, and the loss of Bayle's academic position at the Ecole Illustre in 1693, accused Bayle of 'atheism' and 'libertinism', attacked Bayle's *Pensées, Philosophical Commentary*, and *General Criticism* as the most perniciously 'pyrrhonist' works ever written, and declared Bayle's writings more 'poisonous' than those of 'atheists' such as Hobbes or Spinoza.[3] For his writings and actions, Jurieu was a major target both of Catholic writers, who depicted as incoherent Jurieu's defence of toleration for 'orthodox' Huguenots in France and intolerance towards Socinianism, and of tolerationist authors, including Bayle, Le Cène, and Aubert, who condemned him for practising Protestant intolerance while opposing Catholic intolerance. Locke's tolerationist arguments of the 1680s and 1690s were partially designed to oppose Jurieu, whose *History of Calvinism* Locke read just before composing the *Letter Concerning Toleration*, and whose international campaign of intolerance towards 'unorthodox' Huguenots was very much on Locke's mind in the 1690s, as we saw in Chapter 4. Jurieu was simultaneously in these years the author of important defences of rights of resistance in connection with the Revolutions

---

[1] On these campaigns, see Chapter 4 above.
[2] Albeit following the attribution of that work to Jacques Bernard in the *Histoire des Ouvrages des Savans*: Dodge, *Political Thought*, 214.
[3] Jurieu, *Courte revue des Maximes de morale* (1691), cited in Dodge, *Political Thought*, 199; Jurieu, *Le Philosophe de Rotterdam* (Amsterdam 1706; ed. B. de Negroni, Fayard 1997), 135; P. Rétat, *Le Dictionnaire de Bayle et la lutte philosophique au xviii siècle* (Paris 1971), 16.

of 1688–91 in England and Ireland, as a theorist of 'natural rights' to resist unjust force, and of God's providential protections of the 'true religion' of Protestantism. As Jurieu's defences of resistance in the 1680s were seized on by Catholic writers as giving contemporary proof that Huguenot theorists remained true to their monarchomach heritage and merited intolerance as seditious, they were rejected by Huguenots such as Bayle, who defended absolutism in the hope of the return to France of the Huguenot community. Other Huguenot replies to Catholic accusations that they were intolerable as seditious required complex arguments to differentiate legitimate resistance to tyranny from seditiousness, and the Revolutions in England and Ireland caused extensive discussion in continental Europe. While this chapter will concentrate on explicating Jurieu's arguments against toleration in order to describe the heart of Huguenot intolerance in these years, it will also very briefly discuss Jurieu's thought on resistance and the Huguenot debate over resistance as this related to the issue of toleration.

INTOLERANCE JUSTIFIED BY JURIEU

Jurieu was the last commanding figure of sixteenth- and seventeenth-century 'international Calvinism' whose theological strictures were soon to be replaced even in Geneva itself, and like many earlier Calvinists Jurieu saw himself as living in the 'Last Days' when 'heresies' and the persecution of 'the true faith' were rising before the imminent millennial victory of 'the truth'. Jurieu was a grandson of Pierre du Moulin, the staunch champion of Calvinist orthodoxy against 'Arminianism' and 'Amyraldism' in the 1630s and 1640s, and related to André Rivet, a leading opponent of Arminianism, Socinianism, and Amyraldism as 'intolerable heresies'; Rivet and du Moulin had together written more than 160 works against Catholicism on the one hand and 'unorthodox' Protestantism on the other. Much of Jurieu's intellectual career involved taking on the mantle of his forebears as defender of orthodox Calvinist thought against Catholicism on the one hand and against Arminianism and Socinianism on the other.[4] Jurieu had joined combat within the Huguenot Church in defence of Calvinist orthodoxy as early as 1670, when Isaac D'Huisseau published a *Reunion of Christianity* proposing that Christians should reunite in one confession based on the 'points fondamentaux' in the Bible and by rejection of the various 'preoccupations' of particular communions. D'Huisseau called for the greatest 'latitudinism' imaginable in ceremony, government, and doctrine. Jurieu's first publication, *The Examination of the Reunion of Christianity*, attacked

---

[4] Howells, *Jurieu*, 11.

D'Huisseau on the ground that he had thus recommended opening communion to Arminians, Anabaptists, enthusiasts, and Socinians, who were, for Jurieu, 'monsters' and 'enemies of God'. For Jurieu, one should deal with such people not with 'tolerance' and 'moderation' but with 'horror'. While Jurieu argued that it was permissible to vary in one's exact understanding of the manner of operation of grace on the will, he held that it was not permissible to be 'Pelagian' and that Arminians, Anabaptists and Socinians were all 'Pelagian'. For Jurieu, while one might tolerate some variations if they could not be reduced without destroying the peace of the church, one must never tolerate those which destroyed Jesus' satisfaction for sin. In 1670–1, Jurieu spoke with the voice of Huguenot orthodoxy and D'Huisseau spoke only for a tiny tolerant minority. D'Huisseau was deposed from the ministry for 'Socinian' principles and condemned by his consistory, by the Academy at Saumur, and by the provincial synod at Anjou in 1670. In 1676–7, Jurieu similarly preached against and assisted in organising the condemnation of the Salmurian theology of Claude Pajon, whose restatement of the potential universality of grace was to him 'Pelagian', 'Arminian', and 'Socinian'.[5]

Hostility to such Protestant 'heresy' was maintained by Jurieu even in the course of advocating civil toleration of Huguenots in his 1681 *Policy* and 1682 *Last Efforts*. In arguing in the voice of a Catholic *politique* that it was not in the 'Interests of the King and State' to persecute Huguenots since a multitude of inhabitants were central to the power and riches of a state, Jurieu pointed to the Netherlands as including 'all the Religions of Europe', in which 'general toleration', 'according to the Rules of Policy' made the 'strength and power of that Republick'.[6] But even the *politique* character was made to express reservation: 'I do not examine at present if that so general toleration for all sorts of Sects is according to the principles of Religion; I am not very much of that Opinion'. Jurieu had his character attack the Arians as 'sworn enemies of Jesus Christ, and by consequence of the Christian religion', declare in arguing that the Huguenots deserved continued toleration in France, that the Huguenots received 'the six first general Councils, and detest all the Heresies that the Church has condemned', and state what was surely Jurieu's own view in saying that

The conduct of Gratian, a most Christian Emperor, who gave liberty of conscience and exercise to all the Sects, except the Eunomians, Manicheans, and Phonitians, merits to be considered, for it is the Model wise Princes ought to regulate themselves by. That is to say, that when they are obliged to tolerate Divers Sects, their toleration

<hr />

[5] P. Jurieu, *Examen de la Réunion du Christianisme* (Orleans 1671), 10–11, 103–4, 154; Howells, *Jurieu*, 12–15, 19–20.

[6] Jurieu, *Policy*, 159–62, 200–2; *idem*, *Last Efforts*, 28–9, 84.

ought not to reach to those who ruin the very foundations of Christianity, as the Eunomians, or Arrians, the Manicheans, and the Photinians did, who were what the Socinians are at present.

Jurieu's argument in the *Policy* thus suggested that orthodox Huguenots were tolerable in France, but that Socinians were not tolerable.[7]

Jurieu's later works in the 1680s repeated this significant anti-tolerationist strain of argument in the *Policy* in denying that toleration should extend to Socinians or their equivalents, and continued Jurieu's earlier intellectual as well as practical battles in France for Calvinism against 'Pajonism', 'Arminianism', and 'Socinianism'. For Jurieu in his works from the mid-1680s to the late 1690s, while it might be acceptable to tolerate others over matters which were relatively unimportant, this was impossible where sins of disbelief were 'mortal'.

Jurieu's theological intolerance was given epistemological and theological foundations. For Jurieu in his 1686 *True System*, the certainty of the elect that they possessed 'righteousness' came in part from God giving grace to the elect, informing their consciences. There was effectively no such thing as an 'erring conscience' in matters of religion. The soul itself sensed 'when a religion provides for it what it needs to be saved'.[8] Jurieu's *Rights of the Two Sovereigns* (1687), written both to attack Bayle's advocacy of universal religious toleration in the *Philosophical Commentary* and the religious 'indifference' of Socinians and Remonstrants in the Netherlands, declared that 'God himself is the absolute truth, that his understanding is the source of all truths and *therefore it is impossible to be orthodox with respect to God without being so with regard to the reality of things*'.[9] For Jurieu, error has no rights, and so there could be no duty to follow an erring conscience.[10]

---

[7] Jurieu, *Policy*, 4, 82–3, 164, 170, 197–8, 200–1.

[8] P. Jurieu, *Le Vray Système de L'église* (Dordrecht 1686), 426–8, discussed in T. Lennon, 'Taste and Sentiment: Hume, Bayle, Jurieu, and Nicole' in O. Abel and P. F. Moreau (eds.), *Pierre Bayle: la foi dans le doute* (Geneva 1995), 49–64, at 54; H. Bracken, 'Toleration Theories' in *Mind and Language: Essays on Descartes and Chomsky* (Dordrecht 1984), 90. Philippe Naudé, Professor of Mathematics at Berlin, argued in very similar terms to Jurieu, defending absolute predestination in *The Sovereign Perfections of God* (1708) against Le Clerc and Jacquelot, and arguing in a *Réfutation du commentaire Philosophique* (1718) that conscience was 'science avec Dieu', and that Bayle's notion of 'erroneous conscience' was simply false. He supported 'rigueurs' as necessary against 'heretics', and associated Bayle, Le Clerc, and Jacquelot as heretics: see Rétat, *Le Dictionnaire de Bayle*, 32–4; cf. also Calvin, *Opera*, II, 399–410; *Institutes*, III, ii, 2–14; 'Faith is lodged not in ignorance but in knowledge...By the Apostle John it is called knowledge (scientia) since he testifies that the faithful know themselves to be sons of God...faith is not apprehension, but is certitude' quoted in Bainton, 'Sebastian Castellio, Champion of Religious Liberty 1515–63' in *Castellioniana* (Leiden 1951), 33.

[9] P. Jurieu, *Des droits de deux souverains* (Rotterdam 1687; reprint Fayard 1997, ed. B. de Negroni), title-page, *au lecteur*, 27; also in Dodge, *Political Thought*, 204; my italics.

[10] Jurieu, *Le Vray Système*, 188–94, discussed in Lennon, *Reading Bayle*, 94.

For Jurieu, significant errors in the faith were usually the results of 'obstinacy', 'negligence', 'self-love', or 'sensuality'. Because all were due to 'principles of corruption', they did not merit toleration. Jurieu argued that most matters in theology were matters of 'right' rather than of 'fact'. He thereby denied the distinction made by Jansenists between the Pope's condemnation of a doctrine as heretical about which he was infallible, and 'the fact' that it had or had not been supported by those whose works were condemned by that same Pope, about which he was not infallible. This was a distinction which Bayle extensively deployed in his tolerationist works, including the *Dictionary*, as a way of suggesting that often those condemned simply understood a series of words differently from those who condemned them and were therefore not the 'heretics' they were understood to be. Jurieu saw such tolerationism as a meaningless cavilling about words. He argued that truths 'of right' wore on their face 'their distinguishing characteristics, and those who do not see them are not worthy of being excused. For it is cupidity, corruption of the heart, prejudice, pride – the human passions that cast them in shadow'.[11] Jurieu thus opposed a theology of certainty through regeneration providing knowledge not merely to Bayle's attempt to construct toleration on the equivocality of words and the rights of an 'erring conscience', but also against arguments propounded by many Latitudinarians in England and by Arminians in the Netherlands for proportioning assent to available evidence and accepting Christianity as a 'reasonable faith' which left much in that faith obscure and uncertain. For Jurieu, as Richard Popkin has put it, the logic of acceptance of belief on such 'reasonable' principles was itself unacceptably 'Pelagian' because it suggested that assessment of the evidence by reason was accessible to all humans and led to a saving faith. Intruding the claims of 'reason' to establish the faith as 'credible', it held the danger that Manicheanism might seem to reason to explain the world better than did Christianity – a possibility of which Jurieu had reason to be acutely aware by the 1690s because of Bayle's discussion of Manicheanism in the *Dictionary*.[12] Jurieu made clear in his 1695 *Defence of the Universal Doctrine of the Church* that the adherence of the will in faith was grounded in *sentiment* or *goût*, that is, in a kind of 'feeling' or 'taste'. Faith was not a proposition to be adhered to in proportion to the evidence in the object (as Latitudinarians argued); this was for Jurieu to make 'reason' the principle

---

[11] Jurieu, *Le Vray Système*, 187, in Lennon, *Reading Bayle*, 93.
[12] Jurieu, *Le Vray Système*, 286, 371, 455, 463; P. Jurieu, *La Religion du latitudinaire* (Rotterdam 1696), 317; discussed in R. Popkin, 'Hume and Jurieu: Possible Calvinist Origins of Hume's Theory of Belief' in *idem*, *The High Road to Pyrrhonism* (eds.) R. A. Watson and J. Force (San Diego 1980), 165; Bayle, *Dictionary* Nicole C.

of faith. Faith was not 'probable'; God gave an 'irresistible impulse' to the will to make it believe with certainty.[13]

Like many Calvinists before him, Jurieu distinguished firmly between intolerance as due to those who had held the 'true faith' and then lost it – 'heretics' and 'schismatics' – and those who had never known it, such as Jews or Muslims. In his 1681 *Policy* and 1682 *Last Efforts*, Jurieu criticised the measures taken against Jews by Manuel in forcibly baptising children in Portugal in the 1490s. For Jurieu in his *Picture of Socinianism* (1690), it was necessary to convert Jews by pacific means: one must not use force against them, at least as long as they did not publicly 'blaspheme' Jesus and did not try to 'seduce' anyone. Here, Jurieu was summarising the position which the majority of anti-heretical and anti-schismatic writers took about Jews and Muslims. But Jurieu's attitude towards the Jews was also importantly influenced by his reading of prophecy. Jurieu's 1686 *Accomplishment of the Scripture Prophecies*, which forecast in prophetic terms the miraculous restoration of 'true' Christianity, was dedicated 'to the Nation of the Jews'. For Jurieu, understanding the conversion of the Jews as the penultimate event before the 'Second Coming' of Christ, Jews would be converted by Christ himself in 1710–15 in a 'glorious and surprising apparition'. To use force against the Jews failed to recognise the approaching millennium. Ridiculing this millenarianism, the unorthodox Catholic Oratarion Richard Simon wrote a mock letter to Jurieu purporting to be a letter of appreciation from the rabbis of Amsterdam to Jurieu, the *Letter to Jurieu from the Rabbis of the Two Amsterdam Synagogues*. But the rabbis themselves understood Jurieu as a genuine supporter of their toleration: the Amsterdam Jewish community gave Jurieu a pension. It was said that for Calvin, only Calvinists, Jews and 'Turks' were truly tolerable; a similar thing could be said for the deeply Calvinist Jurieu in the late 1680s.[14]

For Jurieu, Jews were to be tolerated and would soon be converted to Christianity. But heretics and schismatics had known the truth and lost it. In *The True System*, Jurieu argued that 'heretics' who sought to teach their 'heresy' went beyond the realm of conscience, which was always necessarily free, and into the realm of external expression, which was not:

God alone is master of and judge of the heart. But it is false that actions, consequent upon false thoughts of the heart, are the province of conscience and God alone. Nothing is of the realm of conscience alone but what is contained within it and

---

[13] P. Jurieu, *Défense de la doctrine universelle de l'église* (Amsterdam 1695), 124, 145–6, 295–6; *idem*, *Le Vray Système*, 393–4; Bracken, 'Toleration Theories', 83–96, at 89; Popkin, 'Hume and Jurieu', 168; Lennon, 'Taste', 51, 54.

[14] Jurieu, *Accomplishment*, p*2r–v; II, 48, discussed in R. Popkin, 'Pierre Bayle and the Conversion of the Jews' in Magdelaine et al., *De l'humanisme*, 637; Jurieu, *Tableau*, 429–30; Popkin, 'Hume and Jurieu', 162.

does not leave it. But everything that leaves the conscience and has an effect outside it is the province of those to whom God has given the authority to rule actions and words. A magistrate does not rightfully punish a fanatic who believes that all goods should be held in common, but he rightfully punishes this fanatic if he wants to act on his principles and take the goods of others.[15]

Civil Magistrates were empowered to do good and to prevent evil. The public expression of heresy was an evil, just as theft was an evil. It could therefore be forbidden. It was true that it was the will of God that the lives of heretics be spared 'because His gospel is not the Gospel of blood'.[16] But, Jurieu argued in his 1683 *History of Calvinism*, and expanded in his *True System*, the preaching of heretics could and should be forbidden. If they then transgressed this command, they were to be punished as criminals. For Jurieu, deploying on behalf of his argument the image of heresy as 'poison' so central to the last century of international Calvinism, there was

plenty of difference between putting an heretic to death and preventing the poison of his heresy from spreading within the country. A Christian prince can not do the former according to the Gospel, but he is obliged to do the latter. He ought to impose silence upon a heretic and prohibit him under severe penalties from dogmatizing; and if the heretic violates this prohibition he may very legitimately be punished, but no longer as a heretic but as a violator of the Sovereign's mandates and laws.[17]

For Jurieu, people should be prevented from reading untrue books, and pastors who held that variant opinions from the truth were acceptable should not express their tolerance and contaminate others thereby.[18]

Similarly expressing another of the central elements of 'magisterial Reformation' Protestantism, for Jurieu in *The Rights of the Two Sovereigns*, magistrates had duties to conserve the purity of religion by their authority.[19] According to Jurieu, without Constantine's use of civil authority, three-quarters of Europe would still have been pagan, and without recent sovereigns' support of Protestantism, Europe would still have been papist. 'Faithful Christian Princes are everywhere leaders in the spiritual as well as temporal domain and...the protectors of the Church'. They were providentially ordained to suppress 'idolatry', 'superstition', and 'heresy'. The church had approved, Jurieu declared, the kings of Israel in suppressing idolatry; they had approved Christian emperors ruining paganism in forbidding the worship of false Gods, suppressing the books of false teachers, and

[15] Jurieu, *Le Vray Système*, 189–90, in Lennon, *Reading Bayle*, 97.
[16] Jurieu, *Le Vray Système*, 180–1, 198–9, in Morman, *Aubert*, 228.
[17] Jurieu, *Histoire du Calvinisme et celle du papisme mises en parallèle* (Rotterdam 1683), III, pt 4, 197; Jurieu, *Le Vray Système*, 181–99, discussed in Morman, *Aubert*, 228–9.
[18] Jurieu, *Le Vray Système*, 198–200, 405; *Tableau*, 412–577, discussed in Popkin, 'Hume and Jurieu', 172.
[19] Jurieu, *Des Droits*, 145.

providing for the preaching of the gospel; they had approved Christian emperors in attacking Arianism and replacing its teachers with teachers of the 'true faith'; finally, they had approved Reformed princes abolishing Catholicism.[20]

For Jurieu, tolerationists' response that if the 'orthodox' ruler had this power then so would the 'heretical' ruler, was simply wrong. He asked: because a king had the power to punish malefactors, would a tyrant have the right to punish the innocent? Because a king had the right to levy reasonable taxes to support the state, did a tyrant have the right to levy exorbitant taxes? Because a people had the right to refuse obedience to a tyrant, did they have the right to refuse obedience to their legitimate ruler? The case was for Jurieu no different in religion: because a king has the right to advance and defend the truth, did he have the right to establish heresy and idolatry? 'In a word', Jurieu declared, 'because the King had a right to serve God by his authority, did he have the right to employ the same authority to serve the devil?' It was clear in the maxim of St Paul, Jurieu asserted, that one 'could do nothing against the truth'. In saying that the orthodox ruler had the authority to suppress false religions, one might give 'occasion' to heretical rulers to persecute the true, but one did not give them the 'right'. Thus, Louis XIV may have believed that he had the right to punish Protestants, but he was wrong: however firm his belief in his religion, Protestantism was the true religion. For Jurieu in *The True System*, 'we can do all things on behalf of the truth, and we can do nothing contrary to the truth'. The apostles had a right to preach and a duty to do so as possessors of the truth. Heretics, quite simply, did not. An 'erring conscience' was the lieutenant of the Devil and not of God. God, the consummation of righteousness, could never move a 'conscience' to do wrong. Those with 'grace' *knew* the truth and could not sin; those without grace were led by the devil. A magistrate such as Louis XIV had the *power* to act against the true religion, but he did not have the *right* to act against true religion. His persecution was therefore illegal and tyrannical.[21]

Employing the *politique* arguments which had been developed in sixteenth-century France, Jurieu was at points willing to countenance a limited toleration of those sects which supported the 'foundations' of the Christian religion and which were long established in a society. Huguenots had by then clearly been long established in France and should have continued to be tolerated. But although he was willing to recognise that use

[20] Jurieu, *Des Droits*, 147–9; Labrousse, 'Diaspora', 246–7.
[21] Jurieu, *Des Droits*, 150–4; *idem, Le Vray Système*, 178–200, 491; *idem, Religion du latitudinaire*, 387; *idem, Lettres pastorales, seconde année* (Rotterdam 1686–9), 21–2; Popkin, 'Hume and Jurieu', 171; Morman, *Aubert*, 233–4.

of 'death, iron and fire' was contrary to the spirit of the gospel, Jurieu held that they could be used when God allowed schisms to develop rapidly, such that only violence could deal with them. Jurieu argued in general that magistrates had duties to preserve the purity of religion, and to act against 'heretics' and 'schismatics' as against 'idolaters'.[22] These arguments were perfectly balanced to justify the toleration of orthodox Huguenots in France and to justify intolerance towards unorthodox Huguenots. Although Jurieu declared it a 'natural right' possessed by 'every individual' to resist such 'cruel oppression' as that inflicted on Protestants by Henri IV in the sixteenth century, he firmly denied that right to Socinians. In his *Examination of a Libel*, Jurieu argued that while an innocent person who resisted an unjust judgment did not thereby sin, a justly condemned criminal who resisted was doubly guilty: Socinians were therefore for Jurieu required to submit to penal laws 'because of the authority of the sovereign magistrate who is the master of the affairs of religion and especially because these laws are just and because they are true heretics'. For Jurieu, those 'heretics' who resisted princes working to 'establish true religion are wrong and obstinate, because, being wrong in the heart of the matter and their resistance tending to the retention of a false religion, they are wrong in all the consequences'.[23]

Jurieu was alleged by Bayle and by two other tolerationist writers, Saurin and Henri Basnage de Beauval, to have preached in the Netherlands in January and February 1694 two sermons on the theme of Christ's requirement that one righteously *hate* the enemies of the faith, and to have intended to have them published. Bayle published a pre-emptive response to publication of this work that declared in its very title that this was a 'new heresy in morality'. If Jurieu had indeed preached such sermons, Bayle thereby forestalled Jurieu from publishing them. Bayle's *New Heresy in Morality* (1694), Saurin's *Examination of the Theology of Mr Jurieu*, and Henri Basnage de Beauval's *Considerations on Two Sermons of Mr Jurieu* all attacked Jurieu in ways that identified Jurieu's thought in largely similar terms, as did Bayle in repeating much of the *New Heresy* in his extended footnote in the *Historical and Critical Dictionary* entry on Zuerius. According to Bayle, Jurieu had preached that 'the sentiments of hatred, indignation, and wrath, are allowable, good, and commendable, against the enemies of God, that is, as he himself explained it, against the Socinians, and the other heretics of Holland, against the superstitious, idolaters, etc.'. According to Bayle, Jurieu had moreover preached that we

---

[22] Jurieu, *Le Vray Système*, 177, in Lennon, *Reading Bayle*, 91; Jurieu, *Des Droits*, 278–86; P. Jurieu, *Lettre de quelques Protestans pacifiques* (1685), 28.

[23] Jurieu, *Examen d'un libelle*, 146–51, 171–80, discussed in Dodge, *Political Thought*, 115–16.

ought not merely 'to hate the heresies and bad qualities of such people, but that we ought to hate and detest their persons'. For Jurieu, in Bayle's account, the Sermon on the Mount, with its requirement that one love one's enemies, was 'ill understood', and actually intended only about 'private' enemies; his audience was exhorted to 'hate the King of France, and to wish him ill; not, he added, because he has taken your goods and estates from you; but because he persecutes your religion'. If the Sermon on the Mount required qualification, Jurieu allegedly identified the 139th psalm of King David as requiring a more literal reading: 'Do I not hate them that hate me? I hate them with perfect hatred'. It is unlikely that Jurieu's thought had been rendered entirely accurately by his opponents such as Bayle; few opponents' thoughts were in the seventeenth century, and Bayle himself recorded that it was usual in debate to charge opponents with all the bad consequences which one could draw from an argument, whether fairly or not. Jurieu denied that he had said exactly what he was alleged to have said. It nonetheless seems likely that the broad pattern of argument here was indeed Jurieu's, since it was an argument against toleration that was in keeping with Jurieu's other works, and since Jurieu, unusually, kept silent rather than reply to Bayle, which he surely would have done if severely misrepresented.[24]

In *The Rights of the Two Sovereigns*, Jurieu argued that toleration was itself 'a Socinian doctrine, the most dangerous of all those of that sect, since it was on the way to ruin Christianity and place all religions on the same plane'. Jurieu's *The Picture of Socinianism* (1690) attacked as overthrowing Christian faith the definitions of 'charity' given by tolerationists – that it required forbearance towards others whom one held in error over obscure matters. For Jurieu, true charity, in good Augustinian fashion, was instead that which brought people to the 'true faith'. Jurieu was willing to recognise that it might seem useful to Protestants in their moment of persecution to oppose magisterial duties of defence of religious purity in religion. But he declared that when Protestantism would again be the religion of the magistrate in France, and even in Spain and Italy, it would clearly be to the advantage of the 'true religion' that magistrates were understood to be empowered in religion. In *The Rights of the Two Sovereigns*, Jurieu declared that as it was 'the authority of the Western Kings that has built the empire of popery, so it will be their authority which will destroy it'.[25]

Jurieu was convinced that God was about to restore 'true religion' in France, identifying in his 1686 *Accomplishment of the Scripture*

---

[24] Bayle, *Dictionary*, v, Zuerius, note P; *idem, OD*, II, 814–16; Saurin, *Examen de la Théologie de mr Jurieu*, 807–29 in Rex, *Essays*, 234–5.

[25] Jurieu, *Des Droits*, 14, in Wilbur, *Unitarianism*, 532; Rex, *Essays*, 191 and 191n., 193; Labrousse,' Diaspora', 247, 273–4n.

Prophecies the year 1689 as when 'The Reformation will rise up again in France. . .by royal authority. France will renounce Papistry and the kingdom shall be converted'. For Jurieu, this was the prelude to the end of the reign of the Antichrist between 1710 and 1715.[26] Jurieu's *Pastoral Letters* from 1686, to 1689, issued every two weeks at the same time that he was writing works such as *The True System* and *The Rights of the Two Sovereigns*, were dominated by an overpowering sense of God's providential and miraculous interventions in the world. In the *Pastoral Letters* in October 1686, Jurieu reported that persecuted Huguenots had heard voices singing the Psalms where Protestant temples had been destroyed; for Jurieu, God was signifying his approval of Protestant forms of worship. Jurieu next identified God as miraculously raising up Huguenot prophets, such as an illiterate shepherdess Isabeau Vincent, miraculously providing for communities who had lost their preachers. In August 1687, he identified thunderbolts from heaven as setting fire to Catholic altars, a church at La Rochelle burning, and the wind storm which blew the consecrated host into the mud as further 'signs' from God of His disapproval of Catholic worship and punishments directed against those involved in the persecution of His church. In October 1688, Jurieu reported armies seen fighting in the air. The Spirit of God inspiring prophets in Vivarais was for Jurieu in 1689 the 'most extraordinary event' since 'the time of the Apostles'. God's special providence, Jurieu argued, was made manifest in many signs to humanity, such as earthquakes, eclipses, and rainbows. While he recognised that to speak in 'this century' of such events as 'prodiges, de merveilles, de presages' might seem foolish, to deny these interventions was to 'ruin' the faith in a spirit of 'pyrrhonism' that was the 'most dangerous to religion'. Such a conviction of God's interventions to protect the 'true religion' and to signify his will undergirded Jurieu's anti-tolerationist view that Protestants should not justify full toleration and would have cause to regret such championing when a Protestant magistracy was established in France and the population was converted.[27]

To oppose the thought of Jurieu and the late international Calvinist intolerance which he represented, advocates of toleration such as Locke, Bayle, and Le Clerc would thus need a battery of arguments that were about natural philosophic explanations of events in the world as well as epistemological, philosophical, theological, and political arguments. And part of this battery was needed also against Jurieu's Calvinist contemporary at Geneva, François Turretin, who was author in the 1680s of a similar identification of

---

[26] Jurieu, *Accomplishment*, 18–36, 141, 151–2, 182; Delumeau, *Sin and Fear*, 529–30.
[27] Jurieu, *Lettres pastorales*, 15 October 1686, 1 December 1686, 1 August 1687, 1 October 1688, 15 October 1688, 15 March 1689; Bayle, *Dictionary*, Augustin H; Rex, *Essays*, 218–19.

the 'elect' as regenerate in their understandings and therefore as capable of *knowing* the truth, evacuating the concept of a 'tolerable' error in 'fundamental' matters. The *Institutio theologiae elencticae* (1679–85) of Turretin, who identified Geneva as a theocracy devoted to the true worship of God and was involved in the enforcement of the largely Calvinist Helvetic Confession of 1679, argued that the 'word regenerates the minds of the elect, creating it de novo...healing its depraved inclinations and prejudices'. For Turretin, grace infused a supernatural *habitus* of *theologia*, a divine wisdom; with this, 'the believer perceives things contrary to and remote from reason'. This creative word of God for Turrentin

lays the foundation for a full assurance of faith...which suffices for expelling doubt...this sense of knowledge suffices for discerning the true from the false and for rejecting erroneous and fatal doctrines, in as much as they are unable to subsist with the true essentials and fundamentals of religion, which fills each of the faithful.[28]

When Locke described his reading of two theological 'systems' to which he was opposed late in the process of composition and publication of his tolerationist *Reasonableness of Christianity* in 1695, he specified Turretin alongside Calvin as the two authors whose works he decisively rejected. In the 1680s, he had already noted the strongly negative review given to Turretin's work in one of the journals of the new 'republic of letters'.[29] In about the period in which Locke was writing his *Letter Concerning Toleration* – the winter of 1685 – he was reading and taking notes in his journal from Jurieu's 1683 *History of Calvinism*. Both the multiple tolerationist arguments of the *Letter Concerning Toleration* and Locke's tolerationist arguments in his 1695 *Reasonableness of Christianity* – the latter of which centred on the argument that only belief in Jesus as the Messiah is necessary to make a man a Christian, and that beyond that individuals are to read the gospel for what they divergently understand to be its further requirements for belief – are to be understood as in significant part directed against the Calvinist scholastic orthodoxy of Jurieu and of Turretin, and, standing behind both, the 'orthodox' intolerance of Calvin.

JURIEU AND THE 'ERRING CONSCIENCE': RELIGIOUS OPPONENTS AS 'DEISTS', THIEVES, 'LIBERTINES', AND 'SODOMITES'

According to Jurieu, whose *The Rights of the Two Sovereigns* condemned the final four sections of Bayle's *Philosophical Commentary* as these

---

[28] Turretin in Phillips, 'The Dissolution of François Turretin's Vision of Theologia: Geneva at the End of the Seventeenth Century' in J. Roney and M. Klauber (eds.), *The Identity of Geneva* (Connecticut 1998), 77–92, at 80.

[29] MS Locke, c. 33; Marshall, *Locke*.

advocated toleration for an 'erring conscience', composition of those chapters had been the sole purpose of Bayle's work. He attacked Bayle as arguing for the salvific as well as political legitimacy of the belief of everyone in the world, the 'Turk with the Alcoran; the Jew with the Law of Moses; the Pagan with his Idols; and all the erring sects of Christianity with their superstitions and heresies'. Depicting the work as establishing the most dangerous of all Socinian 'dogmas', toleration for Socinians, Jews, Mahometans, and pagans, including their allowance to preach, to dogmatise, and to make disciples, Jurieu attacked this as 'ruining Christianity' and establishing 'indifference' of all religions. For Jurieu, voicing the classic set of accusations of the last century of Calvinist assaults on toleration, arguments from an 'erroneous conscience' could legitimate murder, parricide, theft, adultery, and debauchery. Jurieu recognised that Bayle had explicitly argued in the *Philosophical Commentary* that 'atheists' were to be punished, but contended that by Bayle's other arguments they could not be punished validly. If they were in conscience convinced that there was no God, with conscience reduced in Bayle's terms to an 'interior sentiment' of having the truth, then for Jurieu it was wrong to argue, as Bayle had, that they had no claim of conscience to toleration of their opinion. To Jurieu, such an 'erring conscience' suggested that Turks, Jews and pagans were saved equally with Christians, and it was thus also a 'pure deism'.[30]

For Jurieu, the problem with tolerationist arguments such as those of Bayle was thus the problem incessantly raised against allegedly 'heretical' and 'schismatic' sects over the preceding century, that once one made potentially erroneous 'conscience' the standard, then one had no foundation to establish that certain things were wrong, such as theft, libertinism, and sodomy. Were the Lacedaemonians wrong to make theft licit? For Jurieu, by supporting an erroneous conscience Bayle had left no grounds on which to condemn the Lacedaemonians, and thus left no security for property. Jurieu linked this to the examples of Anabaptists convinced by their erroneous 'conscience' that communism was required. He pointed out that they had supported polygamy. And he charged that on exactly the same ground of unregulated conscience, if a man was persuaded in his conscience that 'sodomy' was legitimate, then he did no wrong.[31] Jurieu's *True System* attacked the argument from the rights of conscience as legitimating the right to steal, to commit sodomy, and polygamy. To Jurieu, to give all rights to an 'erring

---

[30] Jurieu, *Des Droits*, 13–14, 37, 39–41, 43, 53. In his final attack on Bayle, *Philosophe*, Jurieu repeated his accusation that the *Philosophical Commentary*'s arguments on conscience meant that atheists should not be punished as long as they were sincere, and linked it to the *Critique générale*, the *Pensées*, and the *Dictionary: Philosophe*, 182–3, 189–90; Jurieu, *Des Droits*, 37, 43, 53.

[31] Jurieu, *Des Droits*, 58.

conscience' was '*la maxime du monde la plus libertine*'. The entirety of Bayle's emphasis on the 'erring conscience' was thus for Jurieu a 'Theologie libertine'. In the 1690s, Jurieu assaulted Bayle as an 'atheist' and a 'libertine', as supporting a 'pure deism' of salvation for all religions and none, and as advancing a 'toleration' so capacious that it could be claimed by the 'atheist' and the 'sodomite'. Such an assault was held by Jurieu to show similarly unacceptable any toleration for such 'heresies' as Socinianism, as they were based on the same false claim to a conscience that was no longer anchored in God's immediate, irresistible grace.[32]

Bayle was not the only advocate of toleration whom Jurieu assaulted as supporting 'libertinism'. In explaining the Trinity in the 1680s, Jurieu had explained the union of God and humanity in Jesus, and matter and motion, by using as an 'emblem' the marriage of Adam and Eve, in which man was matter and woman movement. The anti-Trinitarian Aubert seized the opportunity to mock Jurieu's account of the doctrine of the Trinity by mocking Jurieu himself as sterile and impotent. According to Aubert, a wife ought to resemble matter as properly 'passive', submitting to the husband, and entirely dependent on him. But in his account of the Trinity, Jurieu had created a new 'species of woman', who instead unnaturally gave movement and motion to the husband. Jurieu had made man 'sterile' without his Eve, who gave 'motion' to his 'inert matter'; Aubert declared Jurieu thus 'impotent' without Mrs Jurieu. In his *Pamphlet Demanding Justice* – which Bayle declared 'so filled with filth that a prostitute could hardly read it without blushing' – Jurieu replied by attacking Aubert for incest, seduction, and murder, and called on the civil magistrates to punish him for impiety, blasphemy, and irreligious behaviour. Jurieu utilised accusations made in France against Aubert by Catholics. Aubert's sister had converted to Protestantism, and in a classic accusation derived in significant part from centuries of typing 'heretical' religions as 'libertine', Aubert's Catholic family had accused him of seducing her to Protestantism: hence incest. Following Jurieu's attack, the Walloon Synod of April 1687 asked the magistrate to 'repress with all his authority such scandalous licentiousness', as Aubert's anti-Trinitarian books and life were held, as ever relatedly, to have revealed.[33]

And Jurieu did not merely defend Calvinist orthodoxy and intolerance against Bayle and Aubert by assault on tolerationism as 'libertine' and 'sodomitical'; he simultaneously assaulted Catholicism as 'libertine' and 'sodomitical'. Jurieu's two-volume 1685 *Well-grounded Prejudices against*

---

[32] Jurieu, *Le Vray Système*, 184–204; Lennon, *Reading Bayle*, 92.

[33] N. Aubert de Versé, *Le Nouveau Visionaire* (Frankfurt 1686), 11–15; Morman, *Aubert*, 57–8, 189–91.

Papal Catholicism, for instance, argued that Pope Sixtus IV was 'more debauched and vicious than one can imagine' and that when he had been petitioned by the family of the Cardinal of Santa Lucca, he had allowed the practice of sodomy during the hottest three months of the year. According to Jurieu, Sixtus was himself debauched, and 'delighted with women's lewd embraces…[and] filthy lust'. The source for Jurieu here was du Plessis Mornay's *Mystery of Iniquity*. Sixtus was thus still serving, in Protestant polemic in the late seventeenth century, the role of the debauched permitter of sodomy among Catholics which he had held at the height of sixteenth-century Calvinist assaults on Catholicism, and heresy, sodomy and libertinism were once again, as ever in Calvinist accounts, held to be linked in Catholicism.[34] Jurieu's *Last Efforts* similarly attacked the 'Bishops that keep concubines' and the 'Monks, that are become Courtiers and Effeminate'.[35]

Jurieu's descriptions of 'heresy' as 'pestilence' and 'poison', and of toleration as a Socinian and 'poisonous' doctrine, were repeated in the 1680s and 1690s by many other orthodox Calvinist Huguenot ministers. The Synod of Amsterdam in 1690 thus condemned a policy which 'under the misleading names of charity and tolerance tends to insinuate into unsophisticated minds the poison of Socinianism'. The language used around the early 1690s by orthodox Huguenot ministers in England in a petition to William and Mary against toleration and against Socinianism declared that Socinianism was 'pestilential' and attacked those 'infected' by the 'evil' spirit of toleration for Socinians. The 'spirit' of 'tolerance' for Socinianism was itself called evil, and Arminians were denounced as 'demi-sociniens' for that very tolerance.[36] In his influential *History of the Edict of Nantes*, pastor Elie Benoist paused in his indictment of increasing Catholic intolerance towards Huguenots in the 1670s and 1680s to celebrate the condemnations of 'Pajonism' by the Huguenot synods in the 1670s and 1680s, and attacked ministers whose thoughts were 'infected with the doctrine of the Arminians, Pelagians and Socinians', whom he described as 'debauched' voluptuaries lacking 'honour' and 'modesty'.[37]

---

[34] P. Jurieu, *Préjugés légitimes contre le Papisme* (Amsterdam 1685), I, 246. Bayle's *Dictionary*, v, 157–61, declared that 'This petition to obtain the permission to practice sodomy never existed, and I could be sooner persuaded of the truth than of the likelihood of such a proposition'. Bayle declared that the accusation was ridiculous, that Jurieu had plagiarised it from du Plessis Mornay, that Jurieu had not checked his sources and that they were untrustworthy, and that such accusations were generally untrustworthy when made against those of another religion: Merrick, *Homosexuality*, XVI.

[35] Jurieu, *Last Efforts*, 10.

[36] Wilbur, *Unitarianism*, 532; Lambeth MS 933 77; my 'Huguenot Thought'.

[37] Benoist, *Histoire de L'Édit*, III, II, 515–16. His account declared du Temps suspected of Socinianism as early as the early 1680s, and declared that he had recently died an 'open Socinian'.

As we saw in the last chapter, in the 1680s Catholics often justified intolerance by associating Protestants with sedition. Huguenots had by the 1680s spent nearly a century professing obedience to the French monarchy. Pierre du Moulin's 1630 *Shield of the Faith* had argued typically that 'the powers that be are ordained of God; whosoever therefore resisteth the power resisteth the ordinance of God'. Huguenots of all theological complexions had joined hands in condemnation of the English Revolution.[38] As late as the early 1680s, Huguenots protesting against increasing restrictions upon their worship argued that they remained loyal subjects. Jurieu's *Policy* asserted Huguenot loyalty and declared that 'Thanks be to God, nothing can stagger our fidelity'. Jurieu's *Last Efforts* described the wars of sixteenth-century France as political wars in which Catholics and Protestants had been found on both sides, and not as religious wars caused by rebellious Calvinists. Forecasting that Protestants would preach 'in Caves, and Woods, and Cellars, and Darkness' and that some would resist, Jurieu attacked this resistance with argument that 'God never blesses the designs of defending a Religion by Arms, of Rebelling against our Prince, and making war under pretences of Piety.' He called resistance the 'very blackest of crimes'. The *Last Efforts* argued that Protestants sought 'only a gate' to go out of the country if toleration was not maintained. Even as late as his 1685 *Reflections on the Cruel Persecution Suffered by Protestants in France*, Jurieu still argued that subjects of a tyrannical prince would need to wait for the day 'when God will hold them to account for their rule'.[39]

Yet while Jurieu's 1683 *History of Calvinism* (which Locke read in exile in 1685 shortly before writing his *Letter Concerning Toleration*) repeated the argument that the sixteenth-century French civil wars had not been wars of religion, and stressed passive obedience in most cases, it also argued that resistance was possible for reasons other than religion, and that Christianity did not 'despoil men of the use of the law of nations and the right inseparable from human nature'.[40] Jurieu explicitly argued that 'defense against oppression as cruel as that suffered by the Protestants' in

---

[38] Du Moulin, *Bouclier* (1636), 556 quoted in Parker, 'Huguenots', 17; F. Puaux, 'L'évolution des théories politiques du protestantisme français pendant le règne de Louis XIV', *Bulletin de la Société de l'histoire du Protestantisme français*, LXII (1913), 388; E. Labrousse, 'The Wars of Religion in Seventeenth Century Huguenot Thought' in A. Soman (ed.), *The Massacre of St Bartholomew* (The Hague 1974), 243–51; Skinner, *Foundations*.

[39] Jurieu, *Last Efforts*, 24–8; *idem*, *Reflections*, 44–6, discussed in Dodge, *Political Thought*, 22.

[40] Jurieu, *Histoire*, II, 507–12; Dodge, *Political Thought*, 25; Howells, *Jurieu*, 40.

the St Bartholomew's Day massacre was 'a natural right inseparable from all men in whatever condition they find they are'. Obedience was declared due to true kings, but not to tyrants, and resistance to defend life against unjust force was declared legitimate. As Jurieu put it in discussing subjects of Turkish rulers, 'the right of self-preservation is inseparable from men and nothing can deprive them of it'. While for Jurieu the sixteenth-century theorists of resistance Buchanan and Paraeus had gone too far in defending rights of resistance as though applicable to all societies, he held that Buchanan's argument that kings could be resisted only when they violated consciences, persons, and properties of subjects was less radical than Catholic justifications of resistance to 'heretical' rulers, and held that there were some societies of limited government where Buchanan's principles were true. Jurieu attacked as a theology good 'for nothing' but to create 'tyrants' the argument that subjects were to submit to death when commanded things against justice and truth. The first Christians had let themselves be massacred, but one was not therefore to accuse those who loved life and defended themselves against unjust force of abjuring their Christianity by their acts.[41] In his 1684 *The Spirit of M. Arnauld*, completed at the end of 1683, Jurieu argued that nothing was so natural as self-defence, to 'resolve to repel force with force', and that Huguenots massacred for worshipping God in 1683 in France who armed themselves to 'repel force with force' did not 'act according to the laws of Christianity, which do not enjoin that, but they act according to the laws of nature'. He added 'I doubt that Christianity has come to abolish nature' and questioned whether a man who guarded his life 'against a violent aggressor' risked 'his salvation'. When one was commanded to stop worshipping, then it was better 'to obey God than man'. There was a duty to preach the truth even when this was forbidden by the magistrate. To meet to worship God was a 'natural right', and it did not constitute 'a rebellion', or the apostles would have been 'rebels'.[42] In an ostensible context of discussion of Hungarians, Jurieu wrote that 'kings are made for the people, not the people for the kings'.[43] Jurieu was to expand upon these arguments in his argument in 1689 in the *Pastoral Letters* that 'It is...very necessary to distinguish between Establishing Religion, and Defending of it', that 'christian morals do not permit the Establishment of Religion by Arms' but that natural rights of resistance to unjust force allowed

---

[41] Jurieu, *Histoire*, I, 513–15, 539, discussed in Howells, *Jurieu*, 40. Jurieu often strongly emphasised, however, not individual rights of resistance but the role of estates and assemblies: Dodge, *Political Thought*, 26–8, 70.

[42] Jurieu, *Histoire*, II, 367, 561–2; IV, 205; Jurieu, *L'Esprit de M. Arnauld* (1684), II, 365–9; Dodge, *Political Thought*, 26–8, 32–3; Howells, *Jurieu*, 41.

[43] Jurieu, *L'Esprit*, II, 293, quoted in E. Labrousse, 'Les frères enemis: Bayle et Jurieu' in *idem*, *Conscience et conviction* (Paris 1996), 164.

self-defence. For Jurieu, 'all the world is agreed that defence is lawful, and allowed by the laws of nature, to which the positive laws of god never make any contradiction'. These *Pastoral Letters* stressed the origins of government in consent, and that the magistrate could not impose false religion because the people did not possess rights of 'making war on God, trampling the laws underfoot, committing injustice, destroying true religion, and persecuting those who follow it'.[44]

Jurieu's avowal of rights of resistance was thus extensive by 1688–9. It was influential among the Huguenot refugee community. But in the early and mid-1680s, support for non-resistance and monarchical absolutism were still the dominant strands in Huguenot thought. Claude declared in a sermon at Charenton in 1676 that Huguenots needed the protection of the king, and that 'Every one would turn against us' if we lost 'his guardianship'. Claude's *Plaintes* disavowed the assemblies for worship in Dauphiné in 1683 and declared continued Huguenot support for absolutism. The 1683 *Letter on the Present Condition of the Protestant Churches in France* supported the assemblies but disavowed their use of arms.[45] Elie Merlat's *Treatise on the Absolute Power of Sovereigns*, written in 1682 and published in 1685, stressed the uncompromising devotion of Huguenots to absolute monarchy in France, and condemned anything beyond passive resistance, even if rulers violated conscience. Bayle had probably organised its publication in 1685, and Merlat's *Treatise* was positively reviewed in August 1685 by Bayle in the *Nouvelles de la République*. Bayle's review attacked what he identified as the 'few Protestants' like Milton and Buchanan who had defended resistance, described Merlat's view as preponderant among Protestants whatever Catholics alleged to the contrary, and called it the best opinion. If attacked by a ruler who violated their rights of conscience, true Christians were to suffer martyrdom rather than resist by arms. Bayle took essentially the same position in reviewing Fabricius' *De limitibus obsequii* in the July 1685 issue.[46]

With their toleration in France having been created by royal edict and maintained by monarchs until Louis XIV, such defences of royal power and non-resistance by Huguenots in the early and mid-1680s were usually combined with defences of toleration for Huguenots in France. Bayle's friend

---

[44] Jurieu, *Pastoral Letters*, Letter xvi, third year, 368, discussed in Dodge, *Political Thought*, 69; Jurieu, *Monsieur Jurieu's Judgment* (1689), 5–6.

[45] Labrousse, 'Diaspora', 222–83, at 223; *idem*, (ed.), *Avertissement aux protestants*, 33–4, 36–44, 54, 63, 69, 71–3.

[46] Labrousse 'Diaspora'; Quick, *Synodicon*; B. Walters, 'Pierre Bayle's Article on George Buchanan', *Seventeenth Century French Studies*, (1998), 163–73; Dodge, *Political Thought*, 7–10; Bayle, *Nouvelles*, August 1685, vii and OD, i, 352–4; *idem*, *Nouvelles*, July 1685, iii and OD, i, 86–9; Jurieu, *Policy*, 102; Bost, *Pierre Bayle et la Religion*, 49, 65.

Henri Basnage de Beauval, to be editor of the *Histoire des Ouvrages des Savans* with Bayle's assistance from 1687, argued in his 1684 *Toleration of Religions* in support for toleration and for royal authority. Bayle was also in 1686 involved in publishing a French translation of his patron Adriaan van Paets' letter to him, the 1685 *De nuperiis Angliae motibus Epistolae, in qua diversum a publica Religione circa Divina sentientium disseritur Tolerantia*, as the (1686) *Lettre de Mr H. V. P a Mr B*** sur la tolérance*. This work simultaneously defended James II's authority and religious toleration. For van Paets, those who had taken up arms against their prince under the 'specious pretext' of religion were wrong; James II succeeded to the throne by right of succession, had maintained his own religion because of his conviction that it was necessary, had voluntarily promised to maintain toleration for English Protestants, and could be trusted. Condemning the notion that a prince was not to allow subjects to be of a contrary religion, and that subjects were not obliged to obey a heterodox prince, van Paets united defence of toleration with condemnation of resistance due to religion. Paets, Bayle's patron, was associated with the tolerant Arminians.[47] The Huguenot refugee minister Daillon's *Examination of the Oppression of Protestants* (1687) argued for toleration under James II and that monarchs could never be resisted; subjects were rather to suffer cruel punishment, and even death, rather than resist. Daillon identified nothing in the Protestant religion that encouraged 'sedition or disorder'; and declared that the 'maxims' which guided the church included 'submission to a monarch whether good or evil', and such submission 'even where obedience owed to God' meant that no resistance to the king by a subject was allowed and that such subjects 'must endure cruel punishment and even death rather than resist'. These were held by Daillon in 1687 to be the 'maxims of holy Scripture' and of 'all doctors of our communion' who had written on the subject.[48]

There was much reason for Bayle to feel in the mid-1680s that the turn of Jurieu to justification of resistance was illegitimate and extreme. In a situation in which much Catholic justification of the use of force against Protestants in the mid-1680s came from their association with sedition in the sixteenth century, and in which their support for resistance on the part of Waldensians and English Protestants in 1688–9 provided confirmation that Protestants were seditious, it would have been perfectly logical for Bayle as a supporter of religious toleration to be convinced that the only way that Huguenots could return to France and secure toleration would be to continue to repudiate resistance – whether that resistance occurred in France, in

---

[47] F. R. Knetsch, 'Pierre Jurieu: Theologian and Politician of the Dispersion', *Acta Historiae Neerlandica* (Leiden 1971), 213–42, at 232; Labrousse, 'Diaspora', 270n.37.

[48] Daillon, *Examen de l'oppression des réformes* (1687); Walters, 'Bayle's article'.

England, or among the Waldensians, the last of whom could have chosen flight rather than resistance. Moreover, it would have been perfectly logical for Bayle, deeply opposed to the providentialist and prophetic justifications for such resistance emanating from Jurieu, Lloyd, or Burnet, to oppose any such justifications of apocalyptic resistance and to see them as likely to promote intolerance in their turn.[49]

The anonymous *An Important Warning to the Refugees, on their Approaching Return to France* (1690) is famously perhaps by Bayle, who did not claim to have written it, perhaps by a Huguenot who later converted to Catholicism, Daniel Larroque, who did claim to have written it, perhaps by them jointly, or perhaps even by another author. Contests about authorship among modern scholars continue largely because the *Important Warning* was one of the central texts of the European Protestant reaction to the Revolution of 1688–9 in England. On the balance of evidence, it seems likely that Bayle was its primary author.[50] For the author of the *Warning*, Jurieu preached sedition in the tradition of Buchanan and of the 'Presbyterians' who were held responsible for the execution of Charles I, and of the 'Presbyterian' principles which now dominated the Church of England's defence of the Revolution of 1688–9. Resistance was declared the 'most monstrous' doctrine in the world. A lengthy section on the Waldensians argued that while they had been treated unjustly, they had erred in using force. It was declared part of sovereign power to be able to banish whomever it pleased, and the only response allowed was to show the injustice of their treatment to the sovereign and to work 'by means of apology and supplication, but not to use overt force'. That the Waldensians had been banished for their religion aggravated their crime in resisting, as Jesus had clearly forbidden this in his prescription that when you were persecuted in one place you were to flee to another. A double infidelity was thus involved in armed resistance – firstly to the prince, and secondly to God.[51]

In September 1693, Bayle wrote a letter to his friend Minutoli on the 1691 French translation of Locke's *Treatises*. For Bayle, Locke had set out to prove the sovereignty of the people and that they could depose those they called sovereigns. He sorrowfully noted that this had become the 'gospel of the day' among Protestants, but noted that he still preferred the argument of de Daillon's 1687 *Examination of the Oppression of Protestants*. By 1693, Bayle clearly knew that the 'gospel of the day' had triumphed over such

---

[49] Labrousse, *Bayle*; Walters, 'Bayle's article'.

[50] E. R. Briggs, 'Bayle ou Larroque? De qui est l'Avis important aux réfugiés de 1690 et de 1692', in M. Magdelaine et al. (eds.), *De l'humanisme aux Lumières* (Oxford 1996), 509–24.

[51] Bayle, *Avis important aux réfugiés* (1690), in P. Bayle, *Oeuvres diverses*, II, 578–633, *passim*.

principles, even though these had been so strongly expressed as recently as 1687. The vast majority of Protestants in England and in the Netherlands, including the vast majority of the Huguenot exiles in the Netherlands, welcomed the resistance of the Waldensians and justified the Revolution of 1688–91 in England and Ireland. By 1693, Elie Benoist could declare in his *History of the Edict of Nantes* – dedicated in its French original issued at the Hague to the States of Holland and West-Friezland, and in its English translation issued by the leading Whig theorist John Trenchard by command of William and Mary – that

All Europe has considered of it, and all Kingdoms having approv'd the Revolution in Great Britain, have by consequence pronounced sentence in favour of the People against the Pretences of Sovereigns. Liberty has gained the point, and Arbitrary Power is generally condemn'd. The Rights of Subjects are clear'd up, and the Usurpations of Puissances are disapprov'd.

The text was issued in England to help to teach the 'Dutiful Respect, Obedience, and Acknowledgments' owed by English subjects 'by informing them what a Horrid Persecution Popery was preparing for them too'. Benoist's text was intended to show that Huguenots had been loyal for a century, and that they were not, as Catholics alleged, marked by a 'factious, libertine, and restless spirit'. But Benoist was clear that

though it is always to be desired that people will never take up arms, and though it is even helpful to overdo submission and patience, nevertheless there may be occasions when oppression is so evident, the good of the State so openly attacked, the holiest rights of Justice and Liberty violated with so little restraint, that the defence of the oppressed cannot be regarded as illegitimate, and one cannot fairly blame them for taking up arms for their safety.[52]

While a small number of Huguenots maintained non-resistance, including Bayle's friend Jacques Basnage, the predominant response of Huguenots to the *Warning* itself was to attack it and support resistance. The ninth to twelfth of the Tronchin du Breuil's 1690 *Letters on Current Affairs* replied to the *Warning*. It was in direct response to the *Warning* that Abbadie published in The Hague his 1693 *Defence of the British Nation* justifying Protestant resistance in Piedmont and in Britain. In 1707, Armand Dubordieu argued in *The Pride of Nebuchadnezzar* that while there are those 'among us who subscribe to the thesis of the power of Kings' they had 'undermined our churches'. He noted 'Thanks to God, I did not study my

---

[52] Bayle, *OD*, IV, 696; Walters, 'Bayle's article', 173; E. Benoist, *The History of the Famous Edict of Nantes* (1694), I, xliv–xlv; Epistle Dedicatory, sig. A2; *ibid.*, II, preface, discussed in Johnston, 'Elie Benoist', 479.

theology concerning the power of Kings in the works of Amyraut and Merlat, nor in the *Warning to the Refugees*'.[53]

As the apologists for religious toleration under James II could convince few in England that a Catholic monarch's toleration was indeed 'irrevocable' because their argument was undermined both by the actions of Louis XIV and Victor Amadeus II and by the intellectual justifications of revocations of supposedly irrevocable edicts offered by Catholic theorists, so the *Warning* provided an intellectual argument that Protestants were good subjects who would never support resistance that was undermined both by the actions of Protestants resisting monarchs in England and Piedmont (until Victor Amadeus changed sides) and by the intellectual justifications of these acts of resistance offered by Protestant theorists.

---

[53] J. Basnage, *Instructions pastorales* (Rotterdam 1720); A. Dubordieu, *L'Orgueil de Nebucadnetzar* (1707), preface, quoted in M. Yardeni, 'French Calvinist Political Thought 1534–1715' in M. Prestwich (ed.), *International Calvinism 1541–1715* (Oxford 1985), 315–37, at 335.

15

Justifying intolerance in England, c. 1660–c. 1700

Writing in the immediate aftermath of twenty years of civil wars and revolution which had seen their worship proscribed and their king executed, many Restoration Anglicans unsurprisingly saw these events as incontrovertible confirmation of the long-standing message of anti-heretical and anti-schismatic writings that 'heresy' and 'schism' were inseparably related to 'sedition'. They were often called 'twin sisters' in the Restoration. Roger L'Estrange's *Toleration Discussed* (1663) declared straightforwardly that 'uniformity is the cement of both Christian and civil societies'. As the Uniformitarian case was stated by 'the Cathedral' in the incarcerated Baptist Thomas Grantham's 1662 poetic dialogue *The Prisoner Against the Prelate*,

> It seems my union thou approvest not,
> This savours of sedition or some plot,
> The land shall never quiet be, untel,
> Rulers, by their Edicts, all sorts compel,
> To uniformity, in things Religious. . .

Richard Perrinchief's *A Discourse of Toleration* declared simply that the state 'cannot be safe while the Church is in a Tempest' in a section entitled 'The Consequences of Dissentions as to the Civil State'. Samuel Parker's 1670 *Discourse of Ecclesiastical Polity* similarly and famously argued that religious pluralism was 'destructive of the common peace and amity of mankind'. For Parker, 'wherever there is difference of Religion, there is opposition too; because men would never divide from one another, but upon grounds of real dislike'. When people separated into 'distinct sects and parties, they always confine all their kind influences to their own Faction, and look with a Malignant aspect upon all the rest of Mankind. . .and shatter in pieces that natural peace and common love, that preserves the welfare and

440

tranquillity of humane nature'. Agreement in religion was 'the first, if not the only foundation of peace'.[1]

When the king, more tolerant than his Parliament for the first eighteen years of his reign, proposed to dispense with penal laws in 1663, high church Anglican and Cavalier Members of Parliament condemned establishing 'schism' by law since in their view 'the most probable means to produce a settled peace and obedience through the Kingdom' was to maintain uniformity

> because the variety of professions in religion, when openly divulged, doth directly distinguish men into parties, and withal, gives them opportunity to count their numbers; which, considering the animosities that, out of a religious pride, will be kept on foot by the several factions, doth tend, directly and inevitably, to open disturbance.[2]

The Presbyterian John Corbet wrote in his 1660 *The Interest of England in Matters of Religion* that England was not suited to liberty:

> Multiformity of Religion publickly professed doth not well comport with the spirit of this Nation, which is free, eager, jealous, apt to animosities and jealousies, besides that, it hath ever a strong propension to Uniformity. Also, it is too well known, that the dividing of Church Communion is the dividing of hearts, and that we shall not live like brethren, till we agree to walk in one way.

For Corbet, toleration was not the daughter of 'Amity' but of 'Enmity' and commonly lasted 'no longer than mere necessity compels'. As one side feared to 'lose its authority' and the other feared it would lose 'its liberty', neither could feel safe under toleration, and each would contend for dominance.[3]

Because the monarch was head of the church, the structure of English government was viewed by many writers as posing an additional problem for toleration. When in 1662 a nonconformist preacher, Field, said in a sermon that 'the government of the Church of England is popish, superstitious', his prosecutor argued that he had in effect said that the king was a heretic 'to the disturbance of the Government'. Lord Chief Justice Robert Foster declared in response that 'The government of England is all one... The ecclesiastick is the prime part of the Government' and Field was convicted, jailed, and fined. The Latitudinarian Lord Justice Matthew Hale, who often tried to mitigate the effects of the laws against particular dissenters, nonetheless argued

---

[1] Roger L'Estrange, *Toleration Discussed* (1663), 86, in Spurr, *Restoration*, 48; McBeth, *English Baptist Literature*, 241; R. Perrinchief, *A Discourse of Toleration* (London 1668), 10ff.; Parker, *Discourse*, preface, VI, VIII, LIV, 168–9; Spurr, *Restoration*, 105; Schochet, 'Samuel Parker, Religious Diversity and the ideology of persecution' in R. Lund (ed.), *The Margins of Orthodoxy* (Cambridge 1995), 119–48.

[2] *CJ*, VIII, 442–3 in Beddard, 'Restoration', 168.

[3] J. Corbet, *The Interest*, 73–4, in Schochet, 'Toleration and Comprehension', 165–87, at 168.

similarly that the 'reasonableness and indeed necessity of this coercion in matters of religion is apparent, for the concerns of religion and the civil state are so twisted one with another that confusion and disorder and anarchy in the former must of necessity introduce confusion and dissolution of the latter'.[4] Once the Church of England was re-established in 1662, the act of separate worship was a breaking of the law. Anglican polemicists disregarding any distinction between disobeying a law and suffering its punishment, and resisting actively, turned this act into 'rebellion'; Samuel Parker declared such worship both 'notorious schism' *and* in itself rebellion,

for when a Religion is established by the Laws, whoever openly refuses Obedience, plainly rebels against the Government, Rebellion being properly nothing else but an open denial of obedience to the Civil Power.[5]

Restoration Anglican argument further identified nonconformists as 'enthusiasts' in claiming divine inspiration, and associated 'enthusiasm' directly with 'sedition' and with all of the threatening consequences long ascribed to heretics and schismatics in anti-heretical and anti-schismatic literature. For Hale, in a classic expression of the fear which had haunted Protestants from the moment of Anabaptist rebellion in the 1530s onwards, but which had an even longer history in the church,

he that pretends an inspiration or a divine impulse to disturb a minister in his sermon tomorrow may pretend another inspiration to take away his goods or his life.

Hale argued that such 'enthusiasts' could break down all 'religion, liberty, property, and authority...printing upon it and coining it with the pretense of religion of the impulse of God himself'. In the 1680s, the High-Anglican White Kennett similarly declared in his commonplace book:

Toleration and liberty of conscience in the church are as plausibly cried up as liberty and property in the state, and indeed from the same cause and with the same effect, a stiff, unwieldy, restless, humour hurrying to disorder, anarchy, and confusion.[6]

These generalised accusations that dissenters were 'seditious' received their most crucial sustenance, of course, from the association of dissenters with the civil wars and Revolution. As it was famously put by Robert South at the consecration of Bishop Dolben, 'they were the same hands and principles that took the crown from the King's Head and the mitre from the bishops'. When there was a proposal for comprehension and toleration in

---

[4] Levy, *Blasphemy*, 212; Lambeth 3496, 10 ('Of policy...in matters of religion') in Cromartie, *Hale*, 177.
[5] Parker *Discourse*, 105; Schochet, 'Parker' 134.
[6] Lambeth 3497, 26; Lambeth 3507, 77v, in Cromartie, *Hale*, 177; BL MS Landsdowne 960 fo. 69v in Spurr, *Restoration*, 105.

1667–8, Sir Peter Leicester informed a Cheshire grand jury that the nonconformist clergy were

the main occasion and drawers on of the late rebellion...so that if these men receive a toleration again, every man may easily guess what will follow.

The Westmoreland justice Sir Daniel Fleming was similarly convinced that nonconformists were 'fanatics' who supported the 'good old cause', and that they planned to 'undo us' civilly or by 'some martial method'. Parker's 1672 preface to Bishop Bramhall's *Vindication* identified the 'natural tendency of fanatick and enthusiastick principles, to wild and seditious practices' and argued that nonconformists were 'fermented with a republican leven'. In 1676, Parker declared simply that 'The Heads and Preachers of the severall Factions are such as had a great share in the late Rebellion'.[7] A series of minor 'rebellions' in the early years of the Restoration served only to confirm the association of dissent and seditiousness in the minds of many Anglicans, however much the vast majority of nonconformists repudiated these rebellions both in these years and then throughout the Restoration, and however much they were willing to suffer martyrdom for their religious convictions rather than resist the government that was persecuting them. As Robert Beddard has put it, 'After Venner's desperate Fifth Monarchy insurrection, in January 1661, few disputed the Cavaliers' axiom that religious dissent and political subversion were indistinguishable'.[8] Surveying the Restoration in his tolerationist 1687 *Good Advice* under James II, William Penn complained that it had been made 'a riot' to 'pray to god in humble and peaceable manner in a conventicle'. He argued that over the last thirty years in England some had been 'hanged, many banished, some imprisoned, some died', and 'abundant numbers' had been 'impoverished', and 'all for religion, though by barbarous use of words called for treason, sedition, routs and riots'.[9]

The Conventicle Acts of the early 1660s were officially aimed at providing

further and more speedy remedies against the growing and dangerous practices of seditious sectaries...who under pretence of tender consciences do at their meetings contrive insurrections, as late experience hath shewed.

The Five Mile Act was issued to take away the 'opportunity to distil the poisonous principles of schism and rebellion into the hearts of His Majesty's

[7] R. South, *A Sermon Preached...Upon the Consecration of...Dr John Dolben, Lord Bishop of Rochester* (1666), 25–6, in Beddard, 'Restoration', 167; Leicester, *Charges to the Grand Jury*, 46, in J. Spurr, 'Religion in Restoration England' in L.K.J. Glassey (ed.), *The Reigns of Charles II and James VII & II* (New York 1997), 90–124, at 121; Fletcher, 'Conventicle', 238, 242–3; preface to Bramhall, sigs. A4v; ch. 6 in Schochet, 'Between Lambeth', 200; Keeble, *Literary Culture*, 69.

[8] Greaves, *Enemies*; Beddard, 'Restoration', 163–4.   [9] Penn, *Good Advice*, 11–12.

subjects, to the great danger of the Church and Kingdom'. Orlando Bridgeman, Chief Justice of Common Pleas, defended the law against conventicles, meetings and assemblies at a trial of Quakers in 1665 under the Conventicle Act that led to their transportation, saying that 'we have had late experience of the danger of such meetings under colour of religion. And it is an easy matter at such meetings to conspire and consult mischief'. Justice John Kelying of King's Bench similarly defended the Conventicle Act in 1664 'for they meet to consult to know their numbers and to hold correspondency, that they may in a short time be up in arms'. He was clear in his own mind that this was not repression of conscience for religion, for

worshipping God according to their consciences...they may do in their families, but forsooth they cannot do that, but they must have thirty, forty or one hundred others to contrive their designs.[10]

Such accusations drew most heavily on the recent history of the English Revolution, but in an important sense that was only the final confirmation of what had long been said about 'schismatics' and 'heretics'. Restoration justifications of persecution drew ceaselessly on the accusations made by 'magisterial Reformation' authors against 'radical Reformation' sects. *An Answer to a Seditious Libel* was one among many works which derided the Quakers' attempt to discriminate their worship from intrinsically seditious 'conventicles', and asserted:

That they have been dangerous Germany hath well experienced by the rebellion of David George, the first of your sect. Such another was John of Leyden.

Such an accusation was then immediately tied to the claim that there was 'danger enough in your small meetings, but much more in your greater meetings of hundreds'; where 'five or six hundred more shall meet' they could find opportunity to 'make an insurrection [that] may set a whole city on flames'.[11]

The 'Exclusion Crisis' and then the revelations of the 'Rye House Plot' saw the restatement of the association of dissent, republicanism and sedition at ever higher levels, especially after 1681. Edmund Bohun, magistrate and funder of informers, was convinced that dissenters' real aim 'was the destruction of the monarchy and bringing in a republic'. Bohun recommended in *The Third and Last Part of the Address* 'an Universal Execution of the Laws against the Dissenters, Especially those against Conventicles' which were 'the seed-places where Factions are nursed up till they may be strong enough

---

[10] Braithwaite, *Second Period*, 7; *GBS*, I, 466 (MS Great Book of Sufferings, 44 vols., Friends Library London); Horle, *Quakers*, 106, 107; *GBS*, II, 57.

[11] These accusations are quoted and replied to in the Quaker George Whitehead's *The Popish Informer* (London 1670), 5–6, 13–14.

to grapple with and overturn the Government of Church and State'. The 1680 *A Satire Against Hypocrites* argued that 'They meet in private, and cry Persecution/When Faction is their end, and state confusion'. The 1681 *The Ghost of the Late Parliament to the New One to Meet at Oxford* attacked the 'Anti-monarchick Hereticks of State'.[12] This note reverberated through Roger L'Estrange's works, where it provided the key answer to the accusations of a 'Popish Plot'. L'Estrange's 1679 *Answer...to the Appeal from the Country to the City* retorted to the *Appeal from the Country*'s invocation of the image of the town ravaged by papists with a counter-image of the town ravaged by dissenters: 'Imagine you see the whole nation in a flame, and brought to the same extremities of fire and sword by the same schismatical malice which embroiled it before'. L'Estrange's 1680 *Further Discovery of the Plot* argued simply that 'you cannot be a friend to the State without being one to the church too'. The first part of L'Estrange's 1681 *Dissenters' Sayings*, issued immediately after the dissolution of the Oxford Parliament, attacked the revival of the sayings of 'the late King's Judges, the sufferers of the Kirk militant, and the whole band of covenanted martyrs'. The second part of the 1681 *Dissenter's Sayings* attacked the 'fanatic rabble' who had torn 'the Government to pieces' in the English Revolution and were attempting to do the same again.[13]

The first issue of L'Estrange's *The Observator* in April 1681 attacked the 'seditious doctrines' and the 'bloudy design that is carry'd on, under the name, and semblance, of Religion' declaring its aim to 'lift up the Cloke of the True Protestant' and to show 'the Jesuit that lies skulking under it'. A dissenter was part of 'a Confederacy; as being a combination against the Law'. Invoking the anti-heretical and anti-schismatic images of the past 150 years alongside those of the English Revolution as the lineage of the Restoration dissenters, L'Estrange argued that whoever made current nonconformists part of the 'Reformed Religion'

---

[12] E. Bohun, *The Third and Last Part of the Address*, VI–VII, in Harris, *Politics*, 100; *A Satire Against Hypocrites* (1680), 23 in Harris, *London Crowds*, 134; *The Ghost of the Late Parliament to the New One to Meet at Oxford* in [N. Thompson], *A Collection of 86 Loyal Poems* (London 1685), 28. This was a message reiterated ceaselessly by many Anglicans, lay and clerical. Berkenhead's *Cabala, or an Impartial Account of the Nonconformists Private designs* (1663) depicted Presbyterians as seditious, plotting to overthrow the state: P. W. Thomas, *Sir John Berkenhead* (Oxford 1969), 221.

[13] M. D. George, *English Political Caricature* (1959), I, 54; L'Estrange, *A Further Discovery of the Plot (1680)*, 18, in Knights, *Politics*, 191; Kitchin, *L'Estrange*, 269, 283. It is relatively rare to find Anglicans ordering sins in such a manner that separation from the church is made worse than personal immorality, though many tolerationist writings complain about this as the real Anglican priorities, but in *L'Estrange's Accompt Cleared* (London 1682), 7, L'Estrange writes that 'I take a Conventicle (even upon that day – Sunday) to be much worse than a tipling-house, as I take a Schism that breaks Christianity to be worse than a personal debauch'.

sets up a Reformation of a hundred and fifty colours and as many Heresies. The Anabaptists, Brownists, Antinomians, Familists. . .do all of them set up for Dissenting Protestants; but God forbid we should ever enter these People upon the roll of the Reformation.

He compared the Whig nonconformist publishers Smith and Harris with 'Protestant Muncer' as 'Profess'd Anabaptists' and described as the 'very Doctrine of the Sect to root out Magistracy, Cancel Humane Laws; Kill, and take Possession; and wash their feet with the Bloud of the ungodly'. Harking back to Presbyterian attacks on the Anabaptists, he encouraged readers to read Featley's *The Dipper's Dipt* and Pagett's *Heresiography* to show how 'Jack of Leydens successor murthered his Wife, to make way to his daughter' and then 'cut off his Wives Head in the Market place'. Penal law against dissenters was called that which 'upon experience, has been found so Necessary, that the bare Relaxing of it, cost the Life of a Prince, the Blooud of two or three hundred thousand of his subjects, and a twenty years Rebellion'.[14]

In November 1681 *The Observator* questioned 'because Popish treasons, and massacres are Diabolical; Are phanaticall treasons and massacres ever the more warrantable?'[15] For such Anglicans, only they stood squarely against the treasonable principles of Catholics on the one side and of nonconformists on the other, and Whigs' failure to understand that they supported quintessentially 'Jesuit' principles of sedition was absurd. In March 1682, L'Estrange made his 'Whig' character declare that there was

a great difference betwixt the Pope's Excommunicating of an Hereticall Prince; and the Generall Assemblys Excommunicating of an Antichristian, Episcopall Prince; betwixt a Popish Gunpowder-Treason, in the Cellers, under the Parliament-House; and a Gunpowder Commission to Kill and Slay within the walls of the Same House, above ground; though to carnal eyes they may both appear to Center in the same point.[16]

This declaration occurred in the midst of an issue of *The Observator* which described a Whig showing a Tory his library, composed partly of works asserting 'The Rights and Power of the People' and partly of 'political divinity'. This Whig library included works by excoriated 'radical Reformation' Quakers, Baptists, Socinians, and Muggletonians such as 'Cartwright, Brown, Barrow, Robinson, Hetherington, Trask, Nayler, Best, Biddle, Muggleton'. These were identified as a broader tradition of heretical and schismatic sedition by listing them together with the works of

---

[14] *Observator*, 13 April 1681.
[15] *Observator*, 12 November 1681, fo. 30r in J. Redwood, *Reason, Ridicule and Religion* (1976), 21.
[16] *Observator*, 11 March 1682 (no. 110).

the 'Muncerians, Apostoliques, Separatists, Catharists, Enthusiasts, Adamites, Huttites, Augustinians, Libertines, Georgites, Familists, Ranters-Seekers, Sweetsingers, Antinomians, Arians, Socinians, Millenaryes, Quakers'.

The Cheshire Tories presented an address in 1681 to the House of Commons asking for execution of the 'wholesome laws' against dissenters who had perpetrated 'the barbarous murder of the best of Kings'. The loyal party in Bristol sent an address to their Tory MPs in 1681 calling 'for the due Execution of the Statutes in being...against all Recusants and Dissenters whatever, their Prosecution being in our Opinion the only means (under God) to preserve the King's Person, our Religion, Liberty and Property, from the secret machinations and hellish conspiracies of the wicked and ambitious, whether Papists or Fanaticks'. The leading Whig polemicist Henry Care was burned in effigy in 1681, wearing a paper inscribed 'scisme, faction and restless rebellion'.[17] After the revelations in 1683 of the 'Rye House Plot' to kill the king, L'Estrange's rhetoric in *The Observator* reached new heights of invective:

If I were a Prince I would no more leave any schools, academies, synagogues, nurseries, seminaries, conventicles, cabals, consults of dissenters in my dominions than I would leave so many bitch-wolves.

In 1685, after the Monmouth rebellion had begun James II's reign on a note of sedition, L'Estrange declared in an issue against 'schism' that dissenting preachers – 'seditious Oracles' – were still keeping alive the 'embers' of revolt, so that a man could not yet 'sleep in his bed without Dreaming of Conflagrations, or the Dread of rising with his throat cut'.[18]

For Nathaniel Thompson in these years, in the *Loyal Protestant Intelligence*:

All conventicles are Treasonable presumptively...while men labour to withdraw the Love and Loyalty of the Subject from the Established Government of Church or State, thereby to weaken and discredit both, there must lie hidden a Treasonable Purpose.

In 1683, Judge Levin straightforwardly charged the grand jury at Stafford assizes that 'where disagreement was admitted in the church, there could be no agreement in the state'.[19]

The involvement in plots for insurrection and assassination in 1682–3 of such Baptists as Thomas Walcott, Richard Rumbold, and Joseph Keeling, and of Presbyterians such as John Hampden, helped to maintain the

---

[17] Harris, *Politics*, 105, 107.
[18] *Observator*, 388, in Kitchin, *L'Estrange*, 353n.; *Observator*, 28 September 1685, III, 88; *Observator* 21 August 1686, III, 202; Scott, *Restoration*, 47.
[19] *Loyal Protestant Intelligence*, no. 123 in Harris, *London Crowds*, 134; Cragg, *Puritanism*, 264n.3 to p. 32.

branding of the 'Rye House Plot' as a 'Presbyterian fanatic plot' and the 'damned plot...by Dissenters', even though the majority of those identified as actually involved were Anglicans rather than dissenters, even though the vast majority of dissenters issued repudiations of acts of resistance in general and of these plots in particular, and even though the dissenters who seem to have been involved were almost without exception not Presbyterians but rather a small number of Baptists and Congregationalists.[20] The category of dissenting and especially of 'Presbyterian' treason existed, court literature was directed at 1641 as come again, and the evidence of the 'Rye House Plot' was read in its light to condemn all dissenters as seditious. The 1683 Judgment and Decree of the University of Oxford asserted that it defended the king from 'the attempts of open and bloudy enemies, and the machinations of Traiterous Heretics and Schismatics' and then proceeded to anathematise many different strands of nonconformist arguments (and those of some Latitudinarian Anglicans such as Daniel Whitby).[21]

Given the force of justification of the prosecution of Protestant dissent as seditious in the years from 1681 to 1685, there was reason for Penn to declare in his 1685 *Considerations Moving to a Toleration* that the

General, nay only Arguments urged against a Toleration, is that Clamorous pretence of its Danger to the Government, through an indulging of Rebellious and Antimonarchical principles, which under the Mask and Cover of Tenderness of Conscience, have been, or may be diffused thro' the Kingdom, and several Republick Machinations and Poysonous Designs, have or may be hatcht and nourisht under the happy Consequences of Liberty of Conscience.

Penn asserted that the accusation that dissenters were all seditious was a 'weak pretext' that should 'quickly fall to the ground' when examined; only an 'imbecile' administration would persecute the 'innocent worship' of God and fail to distinguish the 'guilty' from the 'innocent'.[22] But despite the evidence of the pacificism under severe persecution of the vast majority of dissenters, associations of heresy and schism with treason and rebellion continued into the early years of the reign of James II. It was in the atmosphere of association of 'sedition' and 'schism' in 1685 that Richard Baxter was convicted of seditious libel and sentenced to prison for having allegedly criticised bishops; Judge Jeffries called him the 'main incendiary' in a nonconformist design to 'ruin the king and the nation'.[23]

---

[20] Lacey, *Dissent*, 158–9.
[21] Gillett, *Burned Books*, 508; cf. Scott, *Sidney and...Republic*; Wootton, *Divine Right*, 120–8.
[22] Penn, *Considerations*, Epistle Dedicatory.
[23] Levy, *Blasphemy*, 213; W. Orme, *The Life and Times of Richard Baxter* (1830), 2 vols., I, 443–68.

After 1687, James himself argued that dissenting worship was not intrinsically seditious, and such argument received major support in the tolerationist works issued in his support by Baptists and Quakers and a few others, and then in those issued in support of 1689. But even after 1689, the associations of heresy and schism with treason and sedition played a central role in the politics of the nation in England well into the reign of Anne (and beyond) in the hands of many high church Anglicans and non-jurors. For the high church Anglican Thomas Long, writing against Locke in 1689, 'If private assemblies be permitted unlimitedly, it will then be impossible to restrain Heresie and Impiety, yet they may meet to Plot against the Magistrate.' Times of heresie and schism, according to Long, made 'private meetings more dangerous than quiet times'. For Long, the 'variety of confessions in religion, when openly divulged',

doth directly distinguish men into Parties, and withal gives them opportunity to count their numbers; which considering the Animosities that out of a Religious Pride will be kept on foot by the several Factions, doth tend directly and inevitably to open disturbance.

No 'Security' was possible for Long with religious toleration, which simply could not 'be consistent with the Peace of Your Kingdom'. Long's work was composed of a tissue of citations of mid-seventeenth-century Presbyterians proclaiming toleration a 'poisonous' doctrine, and asserting magisterial duties to combat heresy and schism both in themselves for religious reasons and because they would cause sedition and treason.[24] When William proposed opening office to dissenters in 1689, many Tories resolved, according to Morrice, to 'clamour upon the Dissenters as obstinate, unreasonable, and factious, and so endeavour to raise a new persecution against them'. They then opposed successfully the alteration of the Corporation Act, proposed in order to make office open to Protestant dissenters. For much of the period after 1689, high church Anglicans continued to argue against toleration, by identifying in general schism and heresy with sedition, and in particular dissent with the English Revolution and 'Rye House Plot'. Tolerationist argument remained important in England after 1689 not merely in contending for an extension of toleration to those denied toleration, including Socinians, but also remained an important defence of toleration for those who had won toleration in 1689 and yet faced the hostility of the majority of the political nation at many moments in the eighteenth century.[25]

---

[24] [T. Long], *Toleration Decipherd, passim.*
[25] Morrice, *Entr'ing Book*, II, 504–5, 16 March 1689, in Schochet, 'Toleration and Comprehension', 183; Sacheverell, *The Political Union*, 17, 50–1, 53, 59, in Kenyon,

For many Restoration Anglicans, simply by being 'schismatics' nonconformists were 'seditious'. They were also in their eyes committing a religious sin, and therefore deserved punishment. As Gregory Hascard put it in his 1683 *A Discourse about Edification*, nonconformists were not 'sensible of the heinous nature' of the 'black sin of Schism and Separation'. The Latitudinarian preacher Robert Grove held that schism was 'the Separating ourselves from a True church, without any just occasion given' and lamented that 'the want of due apprehension of the sinfulness of this' was the 'main cause' of our divisions. Some Anglicans stressed that the Church of England was a national church which had power to reform itself from Rome, as Rome was 'schismatic' from the 'true faith' in its idolatry, and as magistrates had the right to organise churches along national lines; others stressed that 'schism' was the setting up of churches and altars against those commanded by bishops, utilising the increasingly popular Cyprianic definition of 'schism' as separation from the bishop. Anglicans repeatedly condemned 'causeless separation' and emphasised that there must be 'one church in one place', as William Sherlock put it.[26]

Images of heresy and schism as plague and poison did not die with the Restoration, not least because many earlier texts deploying such images were republished, including Pagitt's *Heresiography*, which was cited with approval by such Tory Anglican luminaries as Roger L'Estrange. The judge at the trial of the Baptist Benjamin Keach in October 1664 for *The Child's Instructor; Or, a New and Easie Primer* as a 'seditious, heretical, schismatical person' did not allow Keach to speak because that might allow him 'to seduce and infect the King's subjects'.[27] At his trial in 1670 for riot, Penn was declared by the Recorder Sir John Howell a 'pestilent fellow', who needed his mouth stopped.[28] Archbishop Sheldon declared nonconformity a 'disease' and that 'Tis only a resolute execution of this law that must cure this disease, all other remedies serve and will increase it'.[29] L'Estrange argued in the *Observator* in 1685 that schism was worse than the plague: 'For the

---

Revolution Principles, 92–3; Holmes, *Politics*, 184, 203, 208, 228; Clark, *English Society*; K. Haakonssen (ed.), *Enlightenment and Religion* (Cambridge 1996); M. Fitzpatrick, 'Toleration and the Enlightenment Movement' in Grell and Porter, *Toleration in Enlightenment Europe*; P. Miller (ed.), J. Priestley, *Political Writings* (Cambridge 1993); *idem, The Common Good* (Cambridge 1994).

[26] G. Hascard, *A Discourse About Edification* in *A Collection of Cases* (1694), 442; R. Grove in *A Collection of Cases and Other Discourses* (1694), 3; W. Sherlock, *Resolution in Cases*, xxiv, all cited in Spurr, 'Schism and the Restoration Church', *Journal of Ecclesiastical History* (1990), 408–24; in *ibid.*, 415–16.

[27] Gillett, *Burned Books*, 443–4.   [28] Braithwaite, *Second Period*, 70.

[29] Spurr, *Restoration*, 47.

one taints but the bodies of men; the other destroys their very souls'.[30]
L'Estrange's *Observator* of 1 August 1683 summed up the Oxford decree
ordering that heretical, schismatic and seditious books be burned, comparing
the books to bottles in the shop of an apothecary, saying that 'Tis the same
thing in Books, and Principles; Only a Poysonous Position does more hurt
than a Poysonous Drug. The one kills it's Hundreds, and the other it's
thousands'.[31] Parker's *Discourse of Ecclesiastical Polity* described nonconformist preachers as full of the 'poyson of asps' and 'stings of vipers', of
the need to 'lance their Tumour', and of their 'vicious and diseased
Consciences'.[32] Matthew Hale warned his children in his *Contemplations
Moral and Divine* that Quakers suffered a 'contagion as infectious, and much
more dangerous than the Plague in the Body'.[33]

And once again these images were maintained after 1689 by opponents of
religious toleration. For Long in 1690, heresy was a 'poison' to the soul
whose delivery to others must be prevented by the magistrate. For Long,
Locke's arguments were those of 'one of those Locusts that arose out of the
smoke of the bottomless pit...whose smoke darkened the Air and the Sun'.
Locke, for Long, had 'the face of a man' but was in reality a 'scorpion'.[34] In
1696, Thomas Aikenhead became the final person executed in Britain for
heresy or blasphemy; Lord Anstruther called him 'a monster in nature' for
'reviling the persons of the Trinity', a minister who visited him declared that
he had caught the 'plague of blasphemous deism', and Aikenhead's sentence
of death was upheld by the Scottish Privy Council so 'that there might be a
stop put to the spreading of that contagion of blasphemy'.[35] Writing against
Quakers' refusal to pay tithes, Francis Bugg, author of many works against
Quakers, presented a broadsheet to Parliament in 1699, *Some Reasons
Humbly Proposed to the Lords Spiritual and Temporal Assembled in
Parliament*, asking MPs to halt 'the Gangreen of Quakerism'. In 1695,
various Ministers of the Kirk in Scotland were saying in their pulpits that
Quakers 'are as dangerous to converse with as those that have the plague'.
And in 1709, Sacheverell attacked the calamity of toleration as 'an epidemical

---

[30] *Observator* 28 September 1685, III, 88.
[31] *Observator*, 1 August 1683, in Gillett, *Burned Books*, II, 511; for later political images of
poisoning and political radicalism, see D. Herzog, *Poisoning the Minds of the Lower Orders*
(Princeton 1998).
[32] Parker, *Discourse*, preface, X, XIX, XLIX–L, 11.
[33] Hale, *Contemplations Moral and Divine* (1699) III, 252, in R. Clark, 'Gangreen of
Quakerism', *Journal of Religious History* (1981), 404–29, at 423n.101; British Library
Stowe MS 163, 154, in Cromartie, *Hale*, 182–6.
[34] Long, *Toleration Deciphered*, 4–5.
[35] Levy, *Blasphemy*, 231–3; M. Hunter, 'Aikenhead the Atheist: The Context and
Consequences of Articulate Irreligion in the Late Seventeenth Century' in Hunter and
Wootton (eds.), *Atheism*, 221–54.

evil', a 'national calamity, an everlasting plague, that has slain its thousands and its ten thousands'.[36]

Many in the Restoration continued to associate heresy with the 'plague' also as the plague would be visited on England as a punishment for its permission of 'heresy' or 'schism', and for its preceding rebellion against the king. Thus, in 1665 the Form of Common Prayer for Fast Days drew attention to the passage in the Book of Numbers which described a visitation of the plague as God's punishment for a rebellion among the Israelites against Moses and Aaron. Parallels were drawn with those in England who strove 'both with their Princes and their Priests', and the question asked 'what wonder that there is wrath gone out from the Lord, and the Plague is begun?'[37] Matthew Griffith's *The King's Life-Guard* (1665) declared that God

had a controversy with this nation, for our ingratitude, schism, sedition, and rebellion; which he punished by sheathing that sword into our own bowels, that was so causelessly, and unlawfully, drawn against his anointed.[38]

1666 was described by Evelyn as a 'year of nothing but prodigies in this nation: plague, war, fire, rains, tempest, comets'. Evelyn saw these as deserved punishments and hurried to church.[39] The Great Fire laid waste to 89 of London's parish churches and 13,000 houses. To many Anglicans, it was a 'horrid theatre of divine judgment' combining 'severe judgments and almost miraculous mercy'. Many said that it was a judgment on London 'for the murder of the King and rebellion of the city', while Anglican clergy particularly laid 'blame on schism and licentiousness'. Simon Patrick declared that the 'more incurable this disease is...the more are they directed to acknowledge a supreme power that chastises men and corrects their disobedience'. For Richard Perrinchief, the succession of miseries were 'hasty messengers'.[40] Adam Littleton's sermons, collected in 1680, argued that God did 'not pour out all his indignation at once; but gives the people a time of probationership for judgement to see whether they will repent'. Many Anglicans thus drew the message that God was sending signs that toleration and nonconformity, atheism and profaneness, were sinful and were to be punished more effectively in future, in order to prevent further signs of his displeasure. It was in this atmosphere that the Anglican Cavalier-dominated House of Commons established its committee to consider the bill 'touching such books as tend to atheism, blasphemy, and profaneness, or

---

[36] Clark, 'Gangreen', 423n.101; Sacheverell, *Derby Sermon*, 15–16, in Holmes, *Trial*, 55.

[37] Porter, *The Great Plague*, 55.

[38] M. Griffith, *The King's Life-Guard* (1665), sig. A4 in Spurr, *Restoration*, 239.

[39] Evelyn, *Diary*, III, 477, in Spurr, *Restoration*, 56, 243.

[40] Patrick, *Works*, IX, 584–5 in Spurr, *Restoration*, 53; R. Perrinchief, *Sermon 7 November 1666*, 48, in Spurr, *Restoration*, 54.

against the essence and attributes of God the Father, Son or Holy Ghost, given to them in Scripture', or against the providence of God in governance of the world, or against the 'divine authority' of any of the books of Scripture received by the Church of England, or finally, in denial of immortality of the soul, 'resurrection of the body' and 'eternal rewards' in heaven or 'eternal punishments' in hell. In 1674, the bishops similarly told the king of the spread of atheism, profaneness, and the 'pernicious and destructive novelties of the various sects raised in the worst of times' that 'God has threatened [destruction] for such sins, unrepented and unpunished'. In 1678, the House of Lords similarly passed a bill 'for the better suppressing of those crying sins of atheism and blasphemy, and the turning away of God's wrath and his judgments from this land and nation'.[41] As L'Estrange put it in 1685, schism filled up 'the Measure of a Publique Iniquity' and made 'a Land ripe for vengeance' from God.[42]

DISSENTERS AS LIBERTINES AND SODOMITES

The justification over many centuries of intolerance towards many considered 'heretical' and 'schismatic' by identifying them with 'libertinism' and 'sodomy' continued in Restoration England. In his 1668 *A Discourse of Toleration*, Richard Perrinchief, prebendary to Sheldon, attacked heresy and schism by claiming that 'Heresies are reckoned among the works of the flesh'. He then turned to the historians who gave accounts of the 'Heresies and Schisms which arose' in the 'succeeding ages of the Church' as telling how

great Monsters they were which did bring them forth...The abominations of the Gnosticks are not to be named even by a sober Heathen, for the vilest acts of uncleanness which would dishonour even a Stewes, were taken up by them for Duties of Religion.

The bases of all sects, of all schisms and heresies, for Perrinchief, then as now, were 'lusts'.[43] Although he spent much time emphasising that the allowance of nonconformist conscience was even more threatening in itself to government than was 'lewdness and debauchery', in his *Discourse of Ecclesiastical Polity*, Parker asserted that the claim of conscience for separation from the Church of England would legitimate not merely the Presbyterians separating from the church and Independents from them but also Anabaptists from Independents, the Familists from Anabaptists, and Quakers from them, ending: 'The Gnosticks of old so abused this Pretense to justifie any

---

[41] A. Littleton, *Sermons* (1680), 3 vols., II, 237, in Spurr, *Restoration*, 244; *CSPD* 1673–5, 549, in Spurr, *Restoration*, 68; Tuck, 'Hobbes'; Spurr, *Restoration*, 74.
[42] [L'Estrange], *Observator*, 28 September 1685, III, 88.   [43] Perrinchief, *Discourse*, 4ff.

Seditious and Licentious Practices'.[44] Herbert Thorndike's 1670 *Discourse of the Forbearance, or the Penalties, which a Due Reformation Requires*, attacked the Quakers as no more Christians than the Gnostics and Manicheans, and called for them to be banished.[45] The anti-Quaker *Answer to a Seditious Libel* similarly associated the Quakers with David George and John of Leyden, leading the Quaker George Whitehead to repudiate the 'very blasphemous licentious doctrines' and support for polygamy of both.[46] According to the 1682 *No Protestant but the Dissenters' Plot* by Thomas Long, no Baptist 'stopped there: they are separatists, Arminians, Antinomians, Socinians, Libertines, Seekers, Familists'.[47] In his 1660 *Explanation of the Grand Mystery of Godliness*, Henry More wrote that all sects of the Revolution – including for him Adamites, Ranters, and Quakers – were sexually driven, with their attitude being that once perfected 'they cannot sin, do what they will'; sin being 'a Conceit [except] to those that know not their own Liberty'. The founder of the Family of Love was for More 'a Pimp' who encouraged orgies by 'lusty animadversions against Shamefacedness and Modesty in men and women'.[48] A small group of Familists survived into Restoration England, and Evelyn recorded in 1687 that James II had received an address from them in defence of his Declaration of Indulgence; they called themselves 'a sort of refined Quakers'. Elizabeth Rone published a broadside in 1680, *The Description of the Singers of Israel*, complaining that others in desiring to refuse them toleration

> charge us with Debauchery,
> and very many, and very gross evils,
> But those that come us for to try,
> shall find that you are lying Devils.[49]

Accusations of libertinism and sodomy were most frequently directed against Quakers, in part because Quakers refused Anglican marriage ceremonies, believing that marriage was the Lord's work, to which individuals were just 'witnesses'. In 1661, in ruling on an attempt to declare Quaker marriages unlawful, Judge Archer found for the Quakers; in order to do so, he said he believed of Quakers that 'they did not go together like brute beasts (as had been said) but as Christians'. Quakers had to defend themselves in court throughout the Restoration against accusations of sexual 'bestiality'

[44] Parker, *Discourse*, 177–8.
[45] H. Thorndike, *A Discourse of the Forbearance, or the Penalties, which a Due Reformation Requires* in Whiting, *Studies*, 188.
[46] *Answer to a Seditious Libel*; [Whitehead], *The Popish Informer*, 5–6.
[47] T. Long, *No Protestant but the Dissenters' Plot* (London 1682) in Whiting, *Studies*, 90.
[48] Turner, *One Flesh*, 84–5.
[49] *The Diary of John Evelyn*, ed. E. S. de Beer (1959), 867–8, in Marsh, *Family*, 246; E. Rone, *The Description of the Singers of Israel* in Marsh, *Family*, 246.

and libertinism, an accusation which they were forced to reject in works such as the 1671 *Quaker's Answer to the Quaker's Wedding*, which tried to turn the accusation back on the accuser as talking as one 'acquainted with a Brothel-Bed' and a 'Fond Libertine'.[50]

Sir John Berkenhead was a Laudian Royalist propagandist, editor of the official newsbook and censor of the press from 1660–3, a member of the committee who drew up the Act of Uniformity, and a Restoration member of parliament. He was an enemy of every dissenter, from Presbyterian to Quaker. In the Restoration, he was to speak in Parliament in defence of Laud, against Latitudinarianism, against Parliamentary ease to 'tender consciences', and in praise of Elizabeth and James I's uncompromising punishment of Protestant dissenters. Berkenhead was author of many popular broadsheets which attacked the dissenters by charging them with libertinism and sodomy (bestiality). His *The Four-Legg'd Quaker* (1659), reprinted in 1682 (and 1731), associated Quakers pictorially and in rhyme with the bestiality of sex with horses, the picture showing a Quaker chasing after a horse, and the monstrous result of sex between them, an animal that was half-horse and half-Quaker, wearing a Quaker's hat, being bridled by a demonic figure wearing a Quaker's hat (see Figure 15.1).

The accompanying text discussed several times the noted Quaker stronghold of Colchester, declaring in its first verse that 'In Horsley fields neer Colchester/A Quaker would turn trooper/He caught a Foal and mounted her/(O base!) beneath the Crupper'. It declared that Colchester was properly 'Coltchester', for sure as 'Horsley comes from Horse/From Colt was called Coltchester' – and linked its 'monstrous' offspring to Naples and Milan, foreign locations often associated with 'sodomy' in English accounts. Quakers' alleged bestiality – sex with horses in the fields – was directly linked in the text by Berkenhead to their refusal of social superiority: 'Though they salute not in the Street/Because they are our Masters/Tis now Revealed why Quakers meet/In Meadows, woods and pastures'. To grasp the antagonism here, it is worth remembering that many Quakers were meeting in woods and pastures to worship because the Conventicle Acts prohibited the worship by more than five together, and because many meeting-houses were attacked or forcibly closed, and that in recognition of the extent of such meetings the 1670 Conventicle Act had explicitly prohibited meetings in fields instead of merely households. Berkenhead linked the alleged bestiality to inappropriate preaching: 'This Centaur, unquoth other things/Will make a dreadfull breach/Yet though an Asse may speak or sing/O let not horses preach'. Its chorus, repeated

---

[50] Horle, *Quakers*, 15, 234–45, 248; *The Quaker's Answer to the Quaker's Wedding* (1671).

Figure 15.1 [Sir J. Berkenhead], *The Four-legg'd Quaker*
(n.p. 1659?). Bodleian Library Wood 416(70). By permission of the Bodleian
Library, Oxford.

throughout its many verses, and forming its final lines, were centred on an image of castration of Quakers to prevent sodomy: 'Help, Lords and Commons, once more help/O send us knives and daggers/For if the Quakers be not gelt/Your troops will have the staggers'.[51]

To a high Anglican such as Berkenhead a humorous refrain, this was founded in deep hostility to those against whom the violence of castration was imagined; castration was among the punishments for treason, and the regicide Hugh Peter was castrated and then had his genitals placed in his mouth. In the Restoration, Royalist propaganda often celebrated Charles' phallic power and prowess, and it was challenged in anti-Royalist literature in a set of images equally stressing phallic powers but condemning royal licence. The notion in Berkenhead's image that the king's opponents were inappropriately claiming phallic authority only to use it in an inappropriate manner, and that they therefore deserved 'gelding', was thus powerful symbolism in the heavily sexualised political language of the Restoration. The notion that Quaker men were inappropriately focused on animals rather than properly focused on the role they should be maintaining – control of their wives – was also part of the classic accusation against Quakers for allowing women to preach and prophesy.[52]

In passing, this piece several times referred to sexual intercourse between a Presbyterian elder's maid and a dog, and it bore the instruction: 'To the tune of the Dog and Elder's Maid'. It declared at its very beginning that the Quaker bestiality was ten times worse still than the foul intercourse between 'Swash' and 'Jane', because then a dog 'did play the man' but 'man now play'd the horse'. Berkenhead had used that theme before, firstly in the king's Oxford newsbook *Mercurius Aulicus* in 1643, when he attacked a 'holy Rebell' as a 'sodomite', and secondly in his August 1647 *Four Legg'd Elder*, in which a Presbyterian elder's maid, Jane, was said to have committed sodomy with a dog, Swash. The *Four Legg'd Elder* was then reprinted in a collection of verse at the Restoration, and again as a broadside in 1677. Its currency as an attack on Restoration nonconformists was referred to in the second part of *Absalom and Achitophel*.[53] Berkenhead's images retained substantial currency, and both were taken over by his successor as press censor, L'Estrange, and used in a manner that indicates that the audience was expected to get the message, in his *The Committee; or Popery in Masquerade* (1680). This broadside (see Figure 15.2), one of the most important produced during the 'Exclusion Crisis', depicted a 'Committee' made up of a Muggleton, a Ranter, a Quaker, an Anabaptist, an Independent, a Fifth

---

[51] J. Berkenhead, *The Four-Legg'd Quaker* in Reay, *Quakers*, 48.
[52] M. Stocker, *Judith: Sexual Warrior* (Yale 1998), 94 ff.; Thomas, 'Sects'.
[53] Berkenhead, *Four-Legg'd Quaker*, 48; Thomas, *Berkenhead*, 201–2.

Monarchist, Nayler, and an Adamite, presided over by John Presbyter, all of whom were declared to be 'a covenanting people', and all of whom were suggested to be doing the Pope's bidding as shown by an image of the Pope encouraging them by saying, in French, 'courage mes enfans'. All of them were depicted as intent on destroying law, monarchy and church in their pursuit of the alleged 'Popish Plot'.[54] The Adamite was depicted naked, as in scores of pamphlets of the English Revolution, in an image that was generally understood in prints of this period to signifiy that he was one of those who were 'so hot within/With lust, that they all clothing do disdain'.[55] But while this image of libertinism was important, it was not the central image of lust in the prints, for that was the attack on the Presbyterians and Quakers as both 'sodomitical' or bestial. In front of the table of the committee and almost at the centre of the print, L'Estrange placed both of Berkenhead's two images – on the left, a Dog named 'Swash' and an 'Elder's Maid', thus captioned in the clear expectation that readers would understand the reference; and on the right, a Quaker and a horse, bearing a caption based on a similar expectation, 'The Colchester Wedding'. It is to this quartet in the print that were given the words 'no bishops', 'no service book', 'No popish lords' and 'No evill counsellors'. In such high Anglican polemic, political opposition to monarchy, law, and religion was in essence religious opposition, and both involved 'sodomy' (bestiality). Here the resonances of accusations against heretics and schismatics over the centuries as libertines and sodomites, treasonous in state, and wayward in religion, received expression at the height of the 'Exclusion Crisis'.[56]

The Elder's Maid served similarly in a central image of Titus Oates in the midst of this crisis which, as the Restoration literary scholar Paul Hammond has shown, combined accusations of religious dissent, of 'amphibiousness' – of being Presbyterian, Quaker, Jesuit, Muslim, Calvinist, and Anabaptist – of 'sodomy', and of defence of resistance against monarchy. The accusation was that Protestant nonconformity in all its types was linked to being Muslim and Catholic, to resistance as opposition to established authority, and to resistance to 'orthodox' sexuality. The text depicted Oates as an 'Incarnate Imp of Hell' who was

> skilled in Turkish and Italic Fashion,
> In whom the Elders Mayd and Green combine,
> Both fleshly given, and yet both Divine,

---

[54] For excellent discussions of this image, see Harris, 'The Parties and the People', 141–2, and *idem, London Crowds*, 136, 139–40 (Harris does not make the point about bestiality).

[55] R. Heath, *Clarastella* (1650), 16, in Williams, 'Polemical Prints', 101; *ibid.*, 100–2 on sexual images of Adamites.

[56] Cf. Thomas, *Berkenhead*, 94, 145; George, *Political Caricature*, Plate 14.

Figure 15.2 R. L'Estrange, *The Committee; Popery in Masquerade* (1680), Bodleian Library. By permission of the Bodleian Library, Oxford.

> Hence Cap and Turbant both his Noddle grace,
> His mouths the centre of Protesting Face.

Stressing that his 'rascall side' was 'guarded with cold iron', it declared that his coat and cloak showed his deference to John Calvin and to John of Leiden as the justifiers of resistance for religion: 'To Calvin Jack and Jack of Leyden too,

> Whilst one hand holds a flayl, the t'other Sword,
> It paints a modern Holder forth oth' word.'

It then concluded that such was associated with sodomitical impulses:

> Buttond Schismatic Cassock girded notes,
> an Odd Amphibious Animal like O[ates]...View him All ore,
> he's Quaker Presbyter Musulman Jesuit and for Him not her.[57]

As Hammond has shown, not merely was such language commonly deployed against Oates, linking nonconformity to sodomy, but it was also used against the Whig nonconformist politics of the pamphleteer and poet Andrew Marvell, author of the crucial 1677 nascent Whig *Account of the Growth of Popery and Arbitrary Government*. As Hammond indicates, 'sodomy is a sign of religious and political nonconformity'.[58] Attacking dissenters and Whigs as libertines and sodomites was central to the Tory reaction of the early 1680s. The Baptist printer Francis Smith was attacked for 'libertinism'. Others reported Presbyterian ministers with 'no less than fifty Bastards', or discussed dissenting ministers who allegedly needed more than one prostitute at a time to satisfy them.[59]

Once again, such attacks on nonconformists as 'libertines' and 'sodomites' did not die with the provision of toleration for orthodox dissenters in 1689 but continued to be expressed after 1689 by those who wished to see that toleration restricted or removed. In 1706 and 1707, Francis Atterbury preached before the Lord Mayor of London that 'Libertinism hath erected its standard' under toleration. He declared that 'abominable impurities, not to be mentioned, have been openly and daringly practiced: we have declared our Sin, as Sodom, and have not hid it'.[60] When the leader of the Society of the Reformation of Manners, Thomas Bray, was involved in the prosecution of a Captain Rigby for attempted buggery in the 1690s, the accusations

---

[57] This paragraph is based on the extremely important article by P. Hammond, 'Titus Oates and 'Sodomy' in J. Black (ed.), *Culture and Society in Britain 1660–1800* (Manchester 1997), 85–101.

[58] P. Hammond, 'Marvell's Sexuality', *Seventeenth Century* (1996), 87–123, esp. 98.

[59] Harris, *London Crowds*, 147–8.

[60] F. Atterbury, *Sermons and Discourses on Several Occasions* (1735), II, 107, 131–2, in Kenyon, *Revolution*, 116.

against Rigby were recorded by Edward Harley as being simultaneously of 'sodomy' and of a 'horrid blasphemy'. Rigby was recorded as having attempted to persuade another by citing previous examples of the act and 'thereto spake blasphemous words'; the strong likelihood is that Rigby was suggesting Christ's alleged sodomitical activities.[61] And in the 1690s, John Edwards associated Locke's alleged 'Socinianism' with sexual impropriety and that sexual impropriety with foreign sexuality by attacking Locke in a phrase which was edited out of the printed text, but about which Locke came to hear and against which he protested, as a 'heretic', supporter of a 'Mahometan faith', and as living in the 'Seraglio at Oates' of Locke, Damaris Masham, and Sir Francis Masham. Here, the suggestion that Socinianism is an intolerable religious commitment is conveyed by its association with a foreign religion, Mahometanism, with a foreign sexual practice associated with that religion, the Seraglio, and with the sexual libertinism of Locke implied to have violated a marital union. Given both the importance of these associations in anti-tolerationist literature and the personal nature of the attack, it is not surprising that Locke responded with outrage, nor that Locke's tolerationist and other writings are replete with the attempt to distinguish religious 'liberty' from 'libertinism'.

NONCONFORMITY AND ATHEISM

For many Restoration Anglicans, religious nonconformity was held to be intolerable in part because it was held to breed atheism. Again, we have seen that this charge was made against heretics and schismatics in the late sixteenth and early seventeenth centuries in England, and across Europe in the early modern period. It was repeated extensively in the Restoration. Over 1,500 inhabitants of Durham petitioned in 1660 for the restoration of the 'ancient' government of the church, declaring that the loss of their orthodox clergy had 'caused us to be overrun with errors, heresies, schisms, and atheism'.[62] Denis Granville, high church Dean of Durham, wrote that 'licentiousness' was 'i. cause of sects. ii. cause of atheism'.[63] Matthew Hale declared that Congregationalism divided families and led observers to conclude that 'all religion is but a notion and cast off all'.[64] Richard Hollingsworth's *A Modest Plea* (1675) declared that 'The atheism that is at present so rife among us owes its growth to the changeableness of many men's principles who pretend to more than ordinary godliness'. William

---

[61] Bray, *Homosexuality*, 98, 137n.24; Herrup, *House*, 135.
[62] Hunter MSS 7/38, Dean and Chapter Library, Durham, in Beddard, 'Restoration', 162.
[63] Granville, II, 12, in Spurr, *Restoration*, 68.
[64] Lambeth 3507, 151v, in Cromartie, *Hale*, 178.

Jackson argued in *Of the Rule of Faith* (1675) that the 'licentious preaching' of 'reforming' Puritans had created such 'legions of heresies' that wise men had 'of late thought [it] a necessary work to prove that there is a God'.[65] Parker's 1670 *Discourse of Ecclesiastical Polity* repeatedly argued that if one allowed toleration for liberty of conscience, one could not close off the space that would be occupied by 'atheists'. He identified Hobbes and his followers as patrons of 'liberty of conscience'. Nonconformity led to atheism; claims for 'liberty of conscience' to license 'nonconformity' were worse still as they justified atheism itself. It was atheism which was for Parker the true nightmare. In the 1672 'preface' to Bishop John Bramhall's *Vindication of Himself*, Parker wrote: 'were it not for the Restraints of Conscience, that are tied on by the hands of the Priest, and the Laws of Religion, Man would be a monstrously wild and ungovernable Creature'.[66] The notion that atheism was intolerable as it dissolved oaths remained central. Tillotson's 1681 *The Lawfulness and Obligation of Oaths* contended that the necessity for oaths was

> so great that human society can very hardly, if at all, subsist long without them. Government would many times be very insecure.

Its obligation 'reaches to the most secret and hidden practices of men, and takes hold of them when no law can'.[67] Halifax's 1684 *The Character of a Trimmer* similarly declared that

> Religion hath such a superioritie above all things, and that indispensable influence upon all mankind, that it is as necessary to our living happily in this world, as it is to our being saved in the next. Without it man is...one of the worst Beasts nature hath produced, and fitt only for the Society of Wolves and Beares. Therefore in all ages it hath been the foundation of Government.

For Halifax, if a neighbouring nation 'worship and acknowledge no deitie at all, they may be invaded as publique enemies of mankind because they reject the only thinge that can bind men to live well with one another'.[68]

NONCONFORMITY AS 'POPERY IN DISGUISE'

In justification of intolerance throughout the Restoration, it was said that popery would come in via toleration, and that nonconformists were 'papists in disguise'. As an anti-separatist song *A New Year's Gift for the Rump*

---

[65] R. Hollingsworth, *A Modest Plea* (1675), 88; W. Jackson, *Of the Rule of Faith* (Cambridge 1675), 3–4, in Spurr, *Restoration*, 262.

[66] Parker, *Ecclesiastical Polity*, 212–13, in Schochet, 'Between Lambeth', 200.

[67] Tillotson, *Lawfulness and Obligation of Oaths* (1681), 6, in Hill, *Society*, 416.

[68] George Savile, Marquis of Halifax, *The Character of a Trimmer* (1684) in M. Brown (ed.), *The Works of George Savile, Marquis of Halifax* (Oxford 1989), 199–200.

(Oxford 1660) put it, 'Let 'em cry down the Pope, till their Throats are sore, / Their Design was to bring him in at the Back-Door'. *Heraclitus Ridens* made the same point twenty years later: 'Popery could never come into England, unless the Phanatiques let it in at the back door of Toleration'. Dissenters were declared by many Anglicans to be 'the great promoters of that interest, and it will be wholly owing to them, if ever it be introduced into these kingdoms'. Papists were said to 'take all shapes upon them, and all disguises' such as 'Agitators, Ranters, Levellers, and Quakers', making sects their 'Trojan horse'.[69] Thompson's *Loyal Protestant Intelligence* conjured up the image of a sickened Pope on hearing of the 'persecution of his dear Friends the Fanaticks in England' when the penal laws were enforced in 1682, and declared that the Pope was actually 'more troubled for them, then all the Persecutions of the Papists; for that all his hopes consists in their dissentions, and endeavours to root out the Church of England'.[70]

It had been common to attack Quakers as papists in disguise in the English Revolution. For William Prynne, author of *Quakers Unmasked, and Clearly Detected to Be but the Spawn of Romish Frogs* (1655) and *A New Discovery of Some Romish Emissaries* (1656), Quakers were 'but the spawn of Romish frogs, Jesuites, and Franciscan Fryers'. The 'Romish emissaries and vermin' had set out to 'reduce and divide the people' by broaching new opinions or 'old Heresies or Blasphemies'.[71] To Baxter in his *Quakers Catechism* and many other works, 'it is Papists that are their Leaders', creeping in among the sects to unsettle them and drive the nation to Catholicism. Works such as the 1655 attack on George Fox, *The Quaking Mountebank or the Jesuite Turn'd Quaker*, William Brownsword's *Quaker-Jesuit*, and Baxter's *Quakers Catechisme* attacked Quakers as papists in disguise. Baxter declared in 1664 that 'Many Franciscan friars and other Papists have been proved to be disguised speakers in their assemblies and to be among them: and its very like are the very soul of all these horrible delusions'.[72] In one pack of cards, the knave of hearts depicted a Catholic priest speaking at a Quaker meeting. L'Estrange's 1680 *The Committee, or Popery in Masquerade*, depicted the Quaker Isaac Pennington among those nonconformists doing the Pope's bidding in disguise.[73] Dryden's 1681 *His Majesty's Declaration Defended*,

---

[69] Harris, *London Crowds*, 53; *Heraclitus Ridens*, no.7 in Harris, *London Crowds*, 140; Spurr, *Restoration*, 49; Spurr, 'Religion in Restoration England' in L. K. J. Glassey (ed.), *The Reigns of Charles II and James VII & II* (New York 1997), 119.

[70] Thompson, *Loyal Protestant Intelligence*, 104, in Harris, *London Crowds*, 140.

[71] Prynne, *Quakers Unmasked, and Clearly Detected to Be but the Spawn of Romish Frogs* (1655), title-page and 9, in S. A. Kent, 'The Papist Charges Against the Interregnum Quakers', *Journal of Religious History* (1982–3), 180–90, at 181.

[72] *Reliquianae Baxterianae*, 77, in Whiting, *Studies*, 170.

[73] Harris, *London Crowds*, 119, 139.

issued in defence of the king's dissolution of the Parliaments at London and Oxford, suggested that 'Priests, Jesuits and Friars mingle amongst Anabaptists, Quakers and other Sectaries, and are their teachers'.[74] It was this polemic association of Quakers and Jesuits which provided the brutal repertoire of John Hellier, town clerk of Bristol, who arrested the Quaker Robert Gerrish in the Bristol meeting-house in 1682, forced him amongst the women, and ordered him to preach, addressing him as 'friar' and 'Pope' and the women as 'whores', and trying to force the women to kiss Gerrish.[75] As noted in Chapter 2, this theme helped to fuel the suspicion of Quaker support for James II's toleration to such a degree that William Penn was thought even more suspicious as a potential papist in disguise than was James II as an open Catholic. In 1678, Algernon Sidney wrote to his friend and sometime host Benjamin Furly that the Committee of the Commons was working that Quakers 'be distinguished from Papists'. Although Secretary Williamson declared that they were not Christians but 'abominable' deniers of the fundamentals of Christianity, and Sir Charles Wheeler agreed that Quakers were not Protestants, the Committee recommended toleration for Quakers.[76]

The Tory periodical *Heraclitus Ridens* declared in 1681 that it was a 'maxim, that the discords of England are the great Interest of France and Rome'.[77] There are many sources for this set of accusations. First, it was very frequently declared that nonconformists and Jesuits agreed in resistance theory, a point which Quentin Skinner has shown to be largely accurate as to lineage, and an association which Mark Goldie and Tim Harris have documented extensively in the Restoration.[78] As the Tory John Nalson put it in 1681 in *The Character of a Rebellion and What England May Expect from One*, Whigs and Jesuits agreed in 'their doctrines of murdering and deposing lawful princes'. This was a theme especially sounded in the period after 1679. The *Jesuits Letter of Thanks to the Covenanters of Scotland* (1679), George Hickes' *The Spirit of Popery Speaking out of the Mouths of Phanatical Protestants* (1680) and Nalson's other works *Foxes and Firebrands* (1680) and *A Letter from A Jesuit at Paris* (1678) made similar claims. So did *Simeon and Levi, Brethren and Iniquity. A Comparison Between a Papist and a Scotch Presbyter* (1679) and *Jockey's Downfall* (1679). *Interrogatories, or a Dialogue Between Whig and Tory* (1681) asked 'What is Term'd Popery? To Depose a King. What's true Presbytery?

---

[74] Dryden, *His Majesty's Declaration Defended* (1681), 17.
[75] In Horle, *Quakers*, 129.   [76] Hull, *Furly*, 57; Whiting, *Studies*, 174–5.
[77] Harris, 'The Parties and the People', 141.
[78] Skinner, *Foundations*; idem, 'Origins'; Goldie, 'John Locke'; Harris, *London Crowds*, esp. 144.

To act the Thing'. *Heraclitus Ridens* advertised a print of Pope Gregory XIII shaking hands with John Knox, inscribed 'Agreed in the main, that Heretical Kings may be Excommunicated, Deposed, and Murthered'.[79] One of the grand juries presenting dissenters in 1681 included the claim in their presentment that dissenters were disguised Jesuits.[80] In 1697, William Lancaster of St Martins in the Fields marked the anniversary of Charles I's death by declaring to the House of Commons that resistance theorists were 'vending among the people...jesuitical notions and speculations'.[81] It was as part of this refrain that Thomas Long in 1689 attacked a recently published work as the product of a 'jesuitical conspiracy', as intended to bring destruction to 'the state or church'. Its opening page declared the author of this seditious work issued from the bosom of Jesuitical conspiracy as 'one of those Locusts that arose out of the smoke of the bottomless pit whose smoke darkened the Air and the Sun'. He was one of those who had 'the face of a man' who were in reality 'scorpions'. Long identified 'what tends to this Sedition' as 'Privy Conspiracy and Rebellion, Heresie and Schism'. It should be remembered that the Litany ran 'From all sedition, privy conspiracy and rebellion...Good Lord deliver us'.[82] The work attacked by Long was Locke's *Letter Concerning Toleration*.

AUGUSTINIANISM

Augustinianism, as Mark Goldie has shown, provided 'the life-blood' of intolerance in England. Anglican preachers such as George Hickes endlessly applied Augustine's authority to the defence of Anglican intolerance during the height of intolerance in the early 1680s. Citing Augustine, Hickes defended the imprisonment of Protestant dissenters from the Church of England in a 1681 sermon *The True Notion of Persecution* as not being 'persecution' because persecution consisted 'not in the greatness of any man's suffering, which inconsiderate people chiefly look at, but in the righteousness of the cause'. For Hickes, it did not 'matter how much they are persuaded in their consciences, and to what degree they suffer'; blessed only were they 'who are persecuted for righteousness' sake'. It was this relatively subtle argument for intolerance based on 'moderate' penalties and backed by

---

[79] J. Nalson, *The Character of a Rebellion and What England May Expect from One* (1681), 4, in Harris, 'The Parties and the People', 141; Miller, *Popery*, 86; Harris, *London Crowds*, 134, 144.

[80] Miller, *Popery*, 190.

[81] W. Lancaster, *Sermon Before the House of Commons* (1697), 26–29, in Kenyon, *Revolution*, 72; Skinner, *Foundations*.

[82] Long, *Toleration Deciphered*, 4, 8–9, 16. This passage in the Litany was drawn to my attention by Miller, 'James II and Toleration', 11.

'sober' and 'friendly conferences' and 'reasoned arguments' which was widespread in the English Restoration, as among Catholics justifying the Revocation of the Edict of Nantes. Joseph Glanvill's 1681 *The Zealous and Impartial Protestant* declared that when dissenters were chastised for their prejudices, they would be made thereby more likely to consider the reasons of the Church of England impartially. The future Archbishop of Canterbury Thomas Tenison's 1685 *An Argument for Union* agreed that 'no man's mind may be forced, for it is beyond the reach of human power' but held that men could be moved by 'good governors' using force 'to move them, after a trial of fair means, to greater consideration'. Many other Anglican works of the Restoration made this kind of case, and in so doing they often noted as explicitly as had Tenison that force could *not* work on the understanding directly, but they held that it *could* bring individuals to consider the reasons given by churchmen who were to confer and reason with those who had been subjected to these penalties. They then added that even if force initiated the consideration which led to the conversion, it was thereafter both 'sincere' and 'free'; as Richard Perrinchief, editor of Charles I's works, argued in his 1664 *Samaritanism*, echoing Augustine's self-description of coming to faith, many 'who at first took upon them the profession [of true religion] under compulsion, afterwards embraced it sincerely and freely'. As Goldie has brilliantly stressed, what these Anglicans criticised in the persecution of Huguenots in France was that penalties had been employed on behalf of the 'false religion' against the 'true'. As French punishments were used against the 'true religion', those who suffered endured 'persecution'; but as Anglican punishments were used against 'unjust' and potentially seditious separation, they were instead legitimate 'punishments', and not 'persecution'. It is unsurprising that much tolerationist argument in the 1680s and 1690s focused on alleging that the intolerant had no good reason for certainty that theirs was the true religion and were 'abusing words' in distinguishing 'punishment' and 'persecution'.[83]

---

[83] Hickes, *The True Notion* in Goldie, 'Theory of Religious Intolerance', 360; Le Cler, *Toleration*, 1, 56; J. Glanvill, *The Zealous and Impartial Protestant* (London 1681), 34, discussed in Seaton, *Toleration*, 125, and Goldie, 'Theory of Religious Intolerance', 348; Perrinchief, *Samaritanism* (1664), 39, quoted in Goldie, 'Theory of Religious Intolerance', 340.

PART 3

The 'early Enlightenment' defence of toleration and the 'republic of letters' in the 1680s and 1690s

16

Tolerationist associations in the 1680s and 1690s and virtuous service in the cause of toleration in the 'early Enlightenment republic of letters'

In the 1680s, a handful of writers who had gathered in the Netherlands published a series of defences of 'universal' religious toleration in order to challenge simultaneously the multiple practices of religious intolerance described in Part 1 of this book and the multiple justifications of religious intolerance described in Part 2 of this book. Among these works, two have become lastingly famous: John Locke's *Letter Concerning Toleration* (composed 1685, published 1689), and Pierre Bayle's *Philosophical Commentary* (in four parts: Parts 1 and 2 in 1686, Part 3 in 1687, and a *Supplement* in 1688). The *Philosophical Commentary* was one of Bayle's many defences of religious toleration in the 1680s and 1690s, which also included his 1682 *General Criticism of Maimbourg's History of Calvinism*, his continuation of that work in his 1684 *New Critical Letters*, and his 1686 *The True State of Wholly Catholic France*. Bayle's March 1682 *Letter on the Comet*, expanded in September 1683 into his famous *Pensées*, or *Miscellaneous Reflections on the Comet*, was also indirectly supportive of religious toleration by assaulting as 'pagan' and 'superstitions' some beliefs which underpinned contemporary arguments for religious intolerance. Some of its readers in the 1690s and thereafter perceived among the implications of its arguments that atheists were not intrinsically seditious and injurious the suggestion that 'atheists' should be tolerated. The contemporary reading of Bayle as supporting 'atheism' was one cause of his removal from his position at the Ecole Illustre in 1693. Four years after his dismissal, Bayle published his masterwork, *An Historical and Critical Dictionary*, a further 'weapon in the war on religious intolerance on the one hand, and an outline of the history of philosophy on the other'. The *Dictionary* would become 'the arsenal of the Enlightenment' as it supplied ammunition for the arguments of Voltaire, Diderot, Jefferson, and others. In its many attacks on unenlightened theologians and metaphysicians it was, as Richard Popkin has written with pardonable hyperbole, 'one of the most exciting works of an age', serving as a '*Summa Sceptica* that deftly undermined all the foundations of the seventeenth century intellectual world' and thereby 'launched the Enlightenment'. Anthony Grafton has noted that the *Dictionary* became 'the favorite reading matter of just about every literate European for much of the next century'. By 1750 there had been nine French, three English, and one German edition of the *Dictionary*.[1]

In the eighteenth century, Bayle's tolerationist *Historical and Critical Dictionary* thus ranked in influence at least alongside, and arguably ahead of, Locke's tolerationist masterwork, *An Essay Concerning Human Understanding*. The *Essay* was brought to completion by Locke in his years in the Netherlands and first published in 1690. In it, Locke mounted extensive epistemological arguments for toleration, stressing fallibility and the limitations of human knowledge, the variations of words across time, and the difficulties attached to the meanings of many terms currently employed in specification and explication of doctrinal orthodoxy, including definitions of the terms 'person' and 'substance' which were central to contemporary Trinitarianism. Following the 1689 publication of his *Letter Concerning Toleration* in Latin in the Netherlands and in English translation in London, Locke further defended religious toleration in his 1690 *Second Letter Concerning Toleration* and his 1692 *Third Letter For Toleration*. A fourth *Letter* was left incomplete at his death in 1704. Locke supported toleration indirectly in his educational recommendations in *Some Thoughts Concerning Education*, and through his proposals in 1696 to abandon pre-publication licensing of works. And he issued a series of works, including his 1695 *Reasonableness of Christianity*, its 1695 and 1697 *Vindications*, and his posthumously published *Paraphrase upon the Epistles of St Paul*, which defended toleration among Christians by assertion that only a minimalist creed – belief in Jesus as the Messiah – was necessary to become a Christian, in combination with stress on the legitimacy of various interpretations of Scripture.[2]

---

[1] Labrousse, *Bayle*, 41; P. Bayle, *Historical and Critical Dictionary: Selections*, ed. R. Popkin (Indianapolis 1991), introduction, esp. ix, xix; A. Grafton, *The Footnote* (Cambridge, Mass. 1997), 194–5; T. Lennon, *Reading Bayle* (Toronto 1999), 7. Earlier versions of parts of this chapter were presented first to audiences at The University of Denver, and I am grateful to my former colleagues there for their comments. Material from this and succeeding chapters in this section of the book was also presented to many seminars and conferences, including: The Cambridge University Seminar in Early Modern British History; the Institute of Historical Research Seminar on Seventeenth-Century Britain; the British Society for the History of Philosophy Conferences on 'The Furly Circle' and 'Libertinism and Liberty'; the UCLA/ Clark Library Conference 'Materialist Philosophy, Religious Heresy and Political Radicalism'; the Seventeenth-Century Studies Conference 'Orthodoxies and Heterodoxy' at Durham, England, and the National Humanities Centre, North Carolina, seminar on the Enlightenment. I am grateful to all audiences for their comments.

[2] See below and Marshall, *Locke* on these works.

From an eighteenth-century perspective, Locke and Bayle tower over their contemporaries as late seventeenth-century defenders of religious toleration. We will study their works, particularly the *Philosophical Commentary* and *Letter Concerning Toleration*, in considerable detail, devoting more words to their analysis than to any other tolerationist works of the period. But it is worth emphasis that in the mid-1680s both men were still relatively obscure. Locke had by then published nothing beyond some trivial poetry, and his political patron, Shaftesbury, had died. Bayle had only recently begun his anonymous and pseudonymous publication of tolerationist works, and his responsibility for these works was not yet widely known. And Locke's *Letter Concerning Toleration* and Bayle's *Philosophical Commentary* were in the 1680s two among more than a dozen important arguments for religious toleration composed or published in the Netherlands; their later pre-eminence was not yet established. In order both to understand their arguments in context, and to understand the tolerationist arguments of the 1680s as a whole, their works will be considered in the remainder of this book as parts of a flotilla of arguments for toleration.

Among this flotilla were a series of works by close associates of both Bayle and Locke. Bayle's friend Henri Basnage de Beauval issued a 1684 *Toleration of Religions*, and one of Bayle's patrons, the Arminian-educated magistrate Adriaan van Paets, composed a Latin *De nuperis Angliae* (1685) then translated by Bayle into French as *La lettre sur les derniers troubles d'Angleterre* (1686). Isaac Papin argued for religious toleration in a manuscript of about 1684, *Faith Reduced to Its True Principles*, which was first printed by Bayle in 1687 with a preface of his own composition and perhaps without Papin's approval. Arguments for universal religious toleration included also Noel Aubert de Versé's 1684 *Pacific Protestant* and his 1687 *Treatise on Liberty of Conscience*, the latter a work which Bayle recommended in the *Dictionary* and a work in which Locke recorded in his personal library copy the special 'paraph' mark designating a work of the highest intellectual significance. Two important works defending toleration were composed by the 'Pajonist' Huguenot who evolved into an Arminianised-Socinian or Socinianised-Arminian, Charles Le Cène, his 1685 *Conversations* (*Entretiens sur diverses matières*) and his 1687 *Conversations* (*Conversations sur diverses matières*). The second part of the latter work was an unacknowledged translation of the leading Socinian John Crell's *Vindication of Liberty of Religion*, and the second part of the former work was a series of theological reflections, intended in significant part to buttress religious toleration, that were composed by the Genevan refugee turned Arminian Professor Jean Le Clerc. Publication of both of these volumes was secured by Le Clerc, who was also author of several other works indirectly or directly supportive of religious toleration in the 1680s, most notably his 1681 *Theological Epistles* and a series of lives of the early Fathers which undermined much of contemporary doctrinal orthodoxy by identifying it as late patristic philosophic accretion to the simple gospel of Christ. Le Clerc and Locke's close friend, the Arminian Professor of Theology Philip van Limborch, issued a tolerationist *Theologia Christiana* in 1686, a further tolerationist debate with Isaac Orobio de Castro in 1687, *De veritate religionis christianae*, and a tolerationist *History of the Inquisition* in 1692. Finally, several important tolerationist works were composed in the late 1680s in the Netherlands by an associate of both Locke and Bayle, Gilbert Burnet, soon to be Bishop of Salisbury but at this moment an anxious refugee. The most notable of Burnet's works was an edition of a work attributed to Lactantius, *De Mortibus Persecutorum* (1687), *The Death of the Primitive Persecutors*, which Burnet issued with an extensive preface against persecution that was then itself issued separately in several different editions and translations. Burnet also published an *Apology for the Church of England* (1687), which attacked that church for its recent Restoration persecutions while defending it as having been more tolerant in its practice and ethos than most other churches, several shorter texts in defence of toleration but against James II's prerogative tolerationism, and multiple editions of his account of his 'travels' in Europe, *Some Letters*.[3]

Symbolising the similarity of Protestant and Catholic arguments for religious intolerance, and the significance of contemporary Protestant as well as Catholic advocacy of intolerance in the eyes of the advocates of universal religious toleration in these years, many of these tolerationist works were written specifically against Protestant rather than or as well as against Catholic targets, and most notably against Jurieu's works, as he was the leading Protestant campaigner for intolerance towards unorthodox Protestants. Bayle's *Philosophical Commentary* was in its first two parts directed against Catholic arguments, and it suggested that Protestants were opposed to persecution on principle, but its 1688 *Supplement* was directed instead against the intolerant Protestant work which Jurieu had quickly written in reply to the first two parts of the *Philosophical Commentary*, and Bayle noted much more accurately in the *Supplement* that few Protestants had ever supported full religious toleration and that few now did so. Aubert's 1684 *Pacific Protestant* and his 1687 *Treatise on Liberty of Conscience* were both written against Jurieu, with whom Aubert carried on a running battle in the 1680s, during years in which Jurieu obtained Aubert's repeated condemnation by the synods of the Walloon Church in the Netherlands. Burnet's preface to *The Death of the Primitive Persecutors* attacked all persecutions,

---

[3] See below, Chapters 16 to 22. Papin and Le Cène both spent part of the period following the Revocation in the Netherlands and part in England.

Catholic and Protestant, and Burnet's widely circulated *Some Letters* attacked both Catholic and Genevan persecution. Limborch's 1686 *Theologia Christiana* assaulted the support for the doctrine of hereticide not merely by Catholics but by Calvin and Beza and 'some' of their Protestant followers.[4]

Of the defences of religious toleration which I have listed, almost all were published anonymously or pseudonymously, with only Limborch's *Theologia* and Burnet's edition of the Church Father Lactantius' (alleged) *De Mortibus Persecutorum* published under their own names; other items of Burnet's tolerationist works were issued anonymously under the imprint of Pierre Marteau of Cologne, a fictitious imprint which Margaret Jacob has recently identified as central to the works of 'the Enlightenment'.[5] Only two of these authors in the Netherlands in the 1680s were Dutch (Paets and Limborch), while one was English (Locke), one was Scottish (Burnet), four were Huguenot refugees (Le Cène, Papin, Basnage de Beauval, and Bayle); one was a refugee from Genevan persecution (Le Clerc); and one was an unorthodox French Catholic who had turned into an unorthodox Protestant (Aubert). Publishing anonymously or pseudonymously, these advocates of religious toleration were either political refugees deeply worried about their possible extradition, kidnapping or assassination during the years of composing these works, or they were religious refugees who had personally experienced religious persecution – from fellow Protestants as well as Catholics – and feared that this now would be repeated in the Netherlands.

As we saw in Chapter 4, although Locke and Burnet registered themselves as religious refugees in taking out Dutch citizenship, they were in exile in the Netherlands primarily for political reasons, and both were realistically fearful of execution in their own countries should they be extradited or kidnapped. Burnet became aware of the 'designe for seising on me and carrying me away', and in case God allowed him to 'fall into the hands of my Enemies from whom I expect neither favour nor Justice and who will perhaps deny me the benefit of pen paper and ink' he composed some manuscript 'last words' to be published after his death.[6] Sir Thomas Armstrong, an associate of Locke and Shaftesbury, was kidnapped in exile in Leiden and brought back to England and summarily executed without being able to obtain a trial in 1685 since he was a declared outlaw. Having probably helped to plan armed resistance to the

---

[4] On the theme of 'popery' and 'priestcraft', see important articles by Mark Goldie, including 'The Civil Religion of James Harrington' in A. Pagden (ed.), *The Languages of Political Theory in Early Modern Europe* (Cambridge 1987), 197–222, and Champion, *Pillars.*

[5] Jacob, *The Enlightenment*, introduction.

[6] Burnet, *History*, I, 300, quoted in Hutton, *Charles II*, 408; Hughes, 'Last Words', 221–7; B. Lenman, 'Providence, Liberty and Prosperity' in D. Hoak and M. Feingold (eds.), *The World of William and Mary* (Stanford 1996).

Stuart monarchy, and having composed in the Second Treatise a clearly treasonable justification of such plans, Locke in exile anxiously hid under assumed names, changed his location, and for a period went out only at night.[7]

Most of the other tolerationist authors had personally suffered religious persecution before writing their tolerationist works, and many of them were to suffer further religious persecution either for these tolerationist arguments or for other works. Bayle, Basnage de Beauval, Papin, and Le Cène were Huguenots who fled from France as the measures taken by Catholics against Protestant worship increased in the early 1680s. Bayle was unable to publish his early works in France, and because he had fled to the Netherlands in 1685 Bayle's elder brother Jacob was imprisoned and died. Bayle then lost his academic position in the Netherlands after an attack from Jurieu for works which Jurieu said promoted religious 'indifference' and 'atheism'. Having fled from France in 1685, Isaac Papin was in the later 1680s unable to find ministerial employment in various European countries due to a concerted campaign of Jurieu to brand him a tolerationist, and ended up converting to Catholicism. Having fled from France to avoid Catholic proscription of Protestantism, but having already faced Protestant censure in France as a 'Pajonist' viewed as close to 'Arminianism' and 'Socinianism', in the 1690s Le Cène was forced by deprivation of ministerial employment by the Huguenot campaigns against him as a 'Socinian' to live on charity, was described as selling his books to support his family, and had a later work officially condemned as Socinian by a Protestant synod. Aubert, who had been prosecuted by Catholics, converted to Protestantism and fled from France, but in the Netherlands he then had three separate works condemned in the mid-to-late 1680s by Protestant Walloon synods as 'pernicious' and as full of 'abominable heresies', and Jurieu organised another international campaign to prevent his employment.[8] Jean Le Clerc had fled from Geneva in the early 1680s under threat of Protestant prosecution for writing an anonymous work defending toleration for Socinians, his *Theological*

---

[7] See above, Chapters 1, 2 and 4; Marshall, *Locke*.

[8] See Chapter 4 above, and Chapters 17–22 below; Cerny, *Theology, passim*; Labrousse, *Bayle, passim*; Morman, *Aubert, passim*; Fatio, 'Claude Pajon', 209–27; E. Kappler, 'La controverse Jurieu-de la Conseillère', *BSHPF* (1937), 146–73; R. Zuber, 'Papiers de Jeunesse d'Isaac Papin', *BSHPF* (1974), 107–43; *idem*, 'Spinozisme et tolérance chez la jeune Papin', *Dix-huitième siècle* (1974), 218–27; E. Haase, 'Isaac Papin à l'époque de la Révocation', *BSHPF* (1952), 94–122; F. Puaux, *Les précurseurs français de la Tolérance en France au XVIIe siècle* (Paris 1881), esp. 91–4, 99, 108–10, 113–17; L. Simonutti, 'Between Political Loyalty and Religious Liberty: Political Theory and Toleration in Huguenot Thought in the Epoch of Bayle', *History of Political Thought* (1996), 523–54; [I. Papin], *The Toleration of the Protestants* (London 1733); S. O'Cathasaigh, 'Bayle and Locke' on Toleration', in M. Magdelaine, M.-C. Pitassi, R. Whelan, and A. Mckenna (eds.), *De l'humanisme aux Lumières, Bayle et la Protestantism* (Paris 1996), 679–92; my 'Huguenot Thought'.

Epistles, and found it difficult to secure a post for himself outside of the highly tolerant Arminian community in the Netherlands once he too was branded a 'Socinian' tolerationist. And while he was not personally subject to persecution, Margaret Jacob has indicated that in the later 1680s even the Dutch Remonstrant Professor Limborch had reason to be fearful about the response to his compositions and to fear that the practice of persecution of Arminianism might be reinstituted in the Netherlands, and even as late as 1700 he declared to Locke that if the 'prudence and benignity of the magistracy...did not restrain the clergy's fiery zeal the same tempest as formerly overwhelmed our predecessors would overwhelm us today'.[9]

In the 1680s and 1690s, this small intersecting group of political and religious refugees who advocated full religious toleration engaged in many important forms of mutual support, including mutual advocacy of religious toleration. They sometimes discussed their writings in each others' works in order to give them greater publicity and support. However, in a decade in which tolerationist argument was seen by many of their contemporaries not only as itself the 'vending' of a 'poison' but also as supportive of others who were 'vending' the 'poisons' of heresy and schism, they often sought to preserve each others' anonymity as much as possible by discussing works in the third person or anonymously. These tolerationists provided financial support for each other. They attempted to gain employment for each other with their associates. They provided letters of introduction to each other and to other friends in the 'republic of letters'. They purchased books for each other, informed each other of book auctions and new publications, and either carried books for each other or employed other intermediaries to do so. All of these were major services at a time of difficult travel and when many of these works were officially proscribed even in the Netherlands. And they met together to converse in intellectual circles, and conversed about issues central to religious toleration or about the major scientific enquiries of the day. They offered intellectual consideration of each others' arguments before their publication and often suggested improvements or additional arguments. They arranged for the publication of each others' tolerationist works, and helped to supply editorial assistance or translating assistance for such publications.[10]

---

[9] M. Klauber, 'Between Protestant Orthodoxy and Rationalism: Fundamental Articles in the Early Career of Jean Le Clerc', *JHI*, 611–36; A. Barnes, *Jean Le Clerc et la République des Lettres* (Paris 1938), ch. 2; S. Golden, *Jean Le Clerc* (New York 1972); J. Guichard, *Histoire de Socinianisme*, II, 564–97, esp. 565; Wilbur, *Unitarianism*, 585; Jacob, 'Contemporary Enlightenment Historiography', 7–14; University Library Amsterdam coll.hss.v.84 (Remonstrants MS, Afschrift v84): 'Aanteekeningen betreffende zijn leven. Loopende tot 1701'; Locke, *Correspondence*, 2795. I am grateful to Margaret Jacob for her insights into Limborch's fear of persecution and for the reference to his manuscript autobiography.

[10] See the next sections of this chapter for documentation of many instances; Locke's *Correspondence* shows that Locke was involved in very many of these mutual services.

In one of the most crucial developments, in the 1680s three new journals of the 'republic of letters', the *Nouvelles de la République des Lettres*, the *Bibliothèque universelle et historique*, and the *Histoire des Ouvrages des Savans*, were all founded and edited by individuals who were themselves also authors of works advocating religious toleration – respectively Pierre Bayle, Jean Le Clerc, and Henri Basnage de Beauval. They then gave to each other's tolerationist works – in some cases even to themselves – extensive reviews in these journals, one of whose central commitments was to religious toleration. These three editors were assisted in publishing these journals by the contribution of book reviews or in the editing of particular issues of these journals by others who were also authors of works on toleration – including Locke, Le Cène, and Jacques Basnage. These journals were crucial to the 'early Enlightenment' and to the defence of religious toleration, and both the journals and the tolerationist culture of the 'republic of letters' will be examined at length in later sections of this chapter.[11]

It is impossible to trace in this book every filament of the many webs of influence and of the many forms of mutual assistance which connected these individuals to each other, not least because many connections and many such services were doubtless never recorded, or have disappeared from the records. But it is important to indicate in this chapter that there was a very substantial web of alliance and mutual assistance between these individuals in campaigning for religious toleration. To say this is not to say that there were not at moments some very considerable tensions between individuals, such as between Le Clerc and Bayle, nor is it to deny that there were some particularly decisive rips in various fibres in the web of mutual support between them, most notably when in 1689–90 two advocates of toleration in the 1680s, Papin and Aubert, converted to Catholicism and became apologists for religious intolerance. But the mutual associations and assistance of these tolerationists for each other were vital in years when few supported universal religious toleration, when the supporters of such toleration came under rhetorical attack from many opponents of toleration, and when Jurieu organised international campaigns to prevent the employment of several of these individuals. In many cases, significant friendships developed in the course of these mutual associations, such as between Locke and Limborch; in others, more restrained or distant forms of co-operation and admiration came to exist, as between Burnet and Locke, or Locke and Bayle.

Locke, however, kept his composition of the *Epistola* secret from many other tolerationist authors, except Limborch, until after its publication. See also R. Colie, 'Locke and the republic of letters' and H. Bots and M. Evers 'Book News in Locke's Correspondence' in P. Hoftijzer and C. Barfoot (eds.), *Fabrics and Fabrications* (Amsterdam 1990), 297–312.

[11] See also Israel, *Radical*, ch. 7; Pocock, *Barbarism and Religion*, I, 63n; n. 82 below. Cornand de la Crose was Le Clerc's assistant editor for vols. 1–9 and edited vol. 11 of the *Bibliothèque universelle*; vols. 21–5 were edited by Jacques Bernard: Bots (ed.) *De Bibliothèque*.

The next section of this chapter will be devoted to documenting in slightly more detail some of the many connections among these advocates of toleration that have just been stated summarily, in order to give a slightly more developed picture of the many interactions and forms of assistance among this group, and to note a few tensions within the group. I will then turn to analysing the culture of the 'republic of letters' which these individuals simultaneously helped to define in the late seventeenth century, and in which they participated, including its 'republican' ethos of 'virtuous' service to the international and interconfessional community of scholars pursuing and defining the 'early Enlightenment'. I will examine briefly the associations between scientific enquiry and religious toleration in the 'republic of letters', and end this chapter by indicating and examining some elements of the commitment to religious toleration of the journals of the 'republic of letters'. The picture of the 'republic of letters' and of the many associations of the defenders of universal religious toleration thus presented will provide the platform for the discussion in the remaining chapters in this book of the arguments that were made in favour of religious toleration in the series of tolerationist works issued by these associated individuals, arguments which were also very often reiterated in summary form in the journals of the 'republic of letters' which the authors of defences of toleration were themselves simultaneously issuing.

THE MULTIPLE ASSOCIATIONS AND MUTUAL SUPPORT OF THE ADVOCATES OF RELIGIOUS TOLERATION IN THE 1680s

Locke and Jean Le Clerc became very close friends in the mid-1680s. They met for intellectual conversation during the years that Locke was in the Netherlands, and corresponded extensively when they were in different cities – Amsterdam and Rotterdam – during this period, and then for the rest of Locke's life after Locke's return to England. Quickly firm friends, as early as 1686 Locke was writing to Le Clerc of his 'regret' when absent from Le Clerc at his loss of 'conversation and the advantages I promised my self from it'. Le Clerc noted in his *Life* of Locke that they had spent 'many an hours Conversation' on 'Philosophical Matters' and celebrated the 'Pleasure and Profit' of their many conversations.[12] Their correspondence often revolved around issues that were important to the cause of religious toleration, usually by discussions of the kind of biblical criticism and patristic scholarship which undermined contemporary

---

[12] *Correspondence*, 866, 1011, 1067, 1069, 1120, 1126, 1127, 1148, 1172, 1184, etc.; Barnes, *Le Clerc*, 156ff.; J. Le Clerc, *The Life and Character of Mr John Locke* (London 1706), 11; L. Simonutti, 'Religion, Philosophy and Science: John Locke and Limborch's Circle in Amsterdam' in J. Force and D. Katz (eds.), *Everything Connects* (Leiden 1999), 295–324.

theological orthodoxy. They sent their works to each other, a significant number of which utilised the ideas of the other. Several of Le Clerc's works were dedicated to Locke, including his *Ontology*.[13] Le Clerc provided five pages of manuscript criticisms of the French edition of Locke's *Essay*.[14] Le Clerc wrote a *Life* of Locke: elegies of major figures were a major form of propagandising the values of the 'republic of letters' and 'early Enlightenment'.[15]

Locke's manuscripts show that he read many of Le Clerc's works very carefully and took extensive notes from them, including from many of the reviews and articles which Le Clerc composed for the *Bibliothèque universelle*. Locke's notes and his personal marks and page numbers registered in copies of the *Bibliothèque universelle* in his private library suggest very careful reading not merely of Le Clerc's reviews of others' contemporary works, but also of Le Clerc's own articles on the lives of the Fathers. These lives indirectly but significantly supported toleration by turning a critical eye on the patristic accretions of dogma to the simple gospel of Jesus. Locke's journals record passages from the *Bibliothèque Universelle* where he specifically noted the variant readings by different Fathers of biblical passages crucial to the doctrine of the Trinity. And Locke's personal interleaved Bibles show that he often recorded against biblical passages the interpretations offered in the course of Le Clerc's learned patristic scholarship in the *Bibliothèque*. Once again, these notes often had tolerationist purchase as they recorded variant readings, difficulties in interpreting passages of the text, and patristic accretions to the text. Locke's own works supporting toleration, including the *Reasonableness of Christianity*, *Vindications*, and *Paraphrase*, were influenced by such arguments.[16] Demonstrating the still broader significance of the new journals for structuring the reading and purchases of at least one of their most engaged contributors and readers, there is evidence that Locke's own book purchases during his time in the Netherlands and after his return to England were often based on his reading and recording of reviews of these new works in the *Bibliothèque universelle* and in the other learned journals of the republic of letters. MS Locke c33 is a

---

[13] Le Clerc, *Ontology* in *Locke Library*, 763; R. Hutchinson, *Locke in France* (Oxford 1991), 23; Golden, *Le Clerc*; M. C. Pitassi, *Entre Croire et Savoir: Le Problème de la méthode critique chez Jean Le Clerc* (Leiden 1987).

[14] Colie, 'Republic', 73.

[15] Barnes, *Le Clerc*; Golden, *Le Clerc*; Hutchinson, *Locke*, 28–30; Le Clerc, *Life of Locke* see below, pp. 515–17. Bayle defined provision of *éloges* of the learned as a central task of the journals of the republic in the first issue of the *Nouvelles*; on the importance of *éloges* in this period, see C. Paul, *Science and Immortality: The Eloges of the Paris Academy of Sciences (1699–1791)* (Berkeley 1980); on specific elegies, see below, pp. 515ff.

[16] See – for instance – Locke's library copies of the 1690 *Bibliothèque universelle* and its page lists at the back to Le Clerc's life of Gregory, the many references from the *Bibliothèque universelle* in Locke's interleaved Bibles, and MS Locke c33, 18–29.

manuscript book composed largely of summary recordings of the reviews from the *Bibliothèque universelle*, *Nouvelles de la République des Lettres*, and *Acta Eruditorum*. Among the many works whose review in the journals Locke noted was the extensive review of Bayle's *Philosophical Commentary* in the *Bibliothèque universelle*.[17]

Further indicating Locke's commitment to Le Clerc's new journal in the 'republic of letters', and symbolising the function of the new journal in assisting readers to develop their own critical techniques for analysing works and rejecting traditional authorities, Locke contributed two significant pieces of his own composition to Jean Le Clerc's *Bibliothèque universelle*. The first of these, in 1686, was an account of his method of commonplacing books which was later translated into English, German, and Dutch and also issued in several editions for eighteenth-century audiences. Locke's method allowed efficient comparison of the arguments of various authors, the recording of the comments of other critics on the value and status of their works, and the construction in miniature of a history of philosophy and theology through the ages. The net effects that this method was likely to produce in those employing it, including Locke himself, included corrosion of the status of authors as 'authorities', the fostering of a critical attitude towards preceding systems of metaphysics and theology, and the fostering of critical techniques of reading by empowered readers. More notable still was the publication in the *Bibliothèque* of the 'Extrait' of Locke's *Essay*, the first printed publication of part of his masterwork, which Le Clerc translated into French for Locke, and which was also quickly issued on its own in the Netherlands in 1688 as an *Abrégé D'un Ouvrage intitulé Essai Philosophique touchant l'entendement*. Le Clerc later also published in the *Bibliothèque universelle* summaries of sections of the *Essay Concerning Human Understanding*, including the attacks on innatism in book 1 which had not been included in the *Extrait*.[18]

It is perhaps worth emphasising that, aside from two early poems on Cromwell, it was in Le Clerc's *Bibliothèque* in the 1680s that Locke's first publications of any kind appeared in print. Moreover, not merely did Locke

---

[17] This statement about Locke's book purchases is based on an extensive comparison of Locke's purchases listed in his library, in such manuscripts as MS Locke b2, and in his personal journals MS Locke f9 (e.g. p. 81, 86, 88) and f10, the works reviewed in the journals of the 'republic of letters', and Locke's actual recording of many reviews of these works in the learned journals in summary fashion in his manuscripts, e.g. MS Locke c33, esp. 29v (on Bayle's *Philosophical Commentary* as reviewed in the *Bibliothèque universelle*; 39r–42v; MS Locke f30; MS Locke f32.

[18] *Bibliothèque universelle*, II (July 1686), 315–40; 8 (January 1688) 49–142; J. Yolton, *John Locke: A Descriptive Bibliography* (Bristol 1998), 318–22 on later editions of the method and Hutchinson, *Locke*, 11–12 for evidence of its influence; Hutchinson, *Locke*, 22, on the *Abregé*.

supply Le Clerc with books for review in the *Bibliothèque*, but he even more notably reviewed several of these books himself. He probably wrote the review of his empiricist medical friend Thomas Sydenham's *Scheduli Monitoria de Novae Febris Ingessu* (1686) in the *Bibliothèque* in September 1687, a review which brought Sydenham to the attention of many doctors on the continent who came to view him as their 'clinical guide'.[19] He probably wrote the review of Isaac Newton's *Principia Mathematica*, which brought Newton to the attention of many continental readers. Rosalie Colie long ago proposed that he might have written the *Bibliothèque*'s review of Bayle's *Philosophical Commentary*, but this does not seem accurate.[20]

Le Clerc defended Locke's thought in the *Bibliothèque universelle* from John Norris' 1690 *Cursory Reflections*, and then later defended Locke from Stillingfleet's assaults on his epistemology. Le Clerc published in the *Bibliothèque* a set of 'Rules of Criticism, for the Understanding of Ancient Authors', parts of which were based on the third book of Locke's *Essay*. Le Clerc's translations were used in a 1720 French edition of Locke's works, including *Of the Conduct of the Understanding*.[21] For over twenty years, Le Clerc repeatedly reviewed Locke's epistemology, educational works, methods of commonplacing, theological works, and the *Treatises* in his journals, praising the *Treatises* and attacking absolutist theory on several occasions.[22] Le Clerc helped instigate the French translation by his Arminian friend Pierre Coste of Locke's credal minimalist and thereby tolerationist *Reasonableness of Christianity*, and in 1708 praised that work and its *Vindications* in the *Bibliothèque Choisie*.[23] A French-language summary of the Latin edition of the *Letter Concerning Toleration* was issued in the *Bibliothèque universelle* in 1689. In his own copy of Thomas Pope Blount's *Censura Celebriorum Authorum*, Locke allowed himself the private vanity of copying passages from Le Clerc's review of the *Epistola* in the *Bibliothèque universelle*.[24] Le Clerc then reviewed Proast's reply to Locke's *Letter* and Locke's *Second Letter* in the *Bibliothèque universelle* in 1690,

[19] *Bibliothèque*, VI (Sept 1687); Locke, *Correspondence*, 926; Golden, *Le Clerc* (1972), 63; K. Dewhurst, *John Locke, Physician and Philosopher* (London 1963).

[20] *Bibliothèque*, III, 335–60 (August 1686); *Bibliothèque* 8 (1688), 436–50; J. Axtell, 'Locke's Review of the Principia', *Notes and Records of the Royal Society*, 20 (1965), 152–61; Colie, 'Republic'; Yolton, *John Locke*, ch. 7, 313–15.

[21] *Bibliothèque universelle*, x, 309–78; XX, 65–72; Colie, 'Republic', 70–1.

[22] *Bibliothèque universelle*, VI, 20–6; XIX, 365–91; XVII, 399–427; *Bibliothèque choisie*, VI, 342–411; XII, 80–170; XIII, 38–178; XVII, 234–41.

[23] Le Clerc, *Bibliothèque choisie* (1708), VI, 46ff.; Hutchinson, *Locke*, 17.

[24] *Bibliothèque universelle*, 15 (1689), 402–12; Sir T. Pope Blount, *Censura Celebriorum Authorum* (1690), 701 (Locke library copy, Bodleian Library).

placing Locke's replies to Proast's arguments immediately after his excerpting of Proast's arguments, thereby giving the reader the tolerationist argument replying decisively and repeatedly to the arguments for intolerance. And Le Clerc ended by stressing how Proast's arguments were inadequate in any circumstance and country other than that where the true religion happened to be established, and thus were alleged valid in England and not in France, and valid under Charles I but not under Cromwell, while Locke's arguments were in contrast valid 'all over the world'. Le Clerc mocked Proast as thus supporting a justice limited by the sea, and one which changed with the government.[25]

Locke and Le Clerc both became very close to Philip van Limborch in the 1680s. Limborch was Le Clerc's primary Dutch patron, who secured for Le Clerc a position as his most important colleague teaching philosophy at the Remonstrant seminary. Le Clerc supplied manuscript criticisms of works by Limborch, such as his *De Veritate Religionis Christianae*. Le Clerc preached Limborch's funeral oration and published his *Life*.[26] And Le Clerc reviewed many of Limborch's works in his *Bibliothèque universelle* and *Bibliothèque choisie*. In reviewing Limborch's *Theologia Christiana* in the *Bibliothèque universelle*, he stressed the tolerationism of Limborch in identifying the central Remonstrant beliefs as being that the Christian religion consisted principally of obeying the precepts of the gospel, that there were many doctrines in the Scripture that were not absolutely necessary to salvation, and that there were only a few essential or 'fundamental' articles which were clearly revealed. In publishing his *Funeral Oration* for Limborch in the *Bibliothèque choisie*, Le Clerc emphasised that Limborch was personally 'civil' and 'agreeable', that the Remonstrants believed that it was not legitimate to persecute anyone for religion, and that they did not damn those who erred in non-fundamental matters. Reinforcing these tolerationist emphases, the funeral oration ended with the celebration of the need for love for 'charity' and 'peace' as well as 'truth' and with the conviction that human understanding was fallible.[27]

Locke first met Limborch due to the extremely cold winter of 1683 and their shared interests in new scientific enquiry in the 'republic of letters': they met in January 1684 at the dissection of a lioness which had died due to the cold. Quickly very close friends due to their shared commitment to religious toleration, Limborch and Locke were thus, symbolically, brought together

---

[25] *Bibliothèque universelle*, XIV (1690), 365–91, esp. 388–91.

[26] Le Clerc, *Éloge* (1713); Barnes, *Le Clerc*, 98ff. and *passim*; J. Le Clerc, *Epistolario*, ed. M. Sina (Firenze 1987–), 7, 8, 9, 10, 11, 12, 13, 14, 15, 16, 17, 18, 19, 20, 21, 22, 23; L. Simonutti, *Arminianesimo e tolleranza nel seicento olandese* (Firenze 1984); Barnouw, *Limborch*, *passim*.

[27] *Bibliothèque universelle* II (1686), 21–51, esp. 22–3; VII (1687), 289–330; *Bibliothèque choisie* XXIV, 350–68, esp. 358.

first because of their shared concern with rigorous and impartial experimental scientific enquiries. Limborch and Locke were thereafter fellow members of intellectual circles for conversation while Locke was in the Netherlands, and corresponded for many years after Locke's return to England in 1689. They quickly began to discuss issues directly and indirectly connected to toleration in such correspondence, as for instance in their September 1685 discussion of the just-published Spinozist-influenced arguments questioning the inspiration of the entirety of the Scriptures of the *Sentimens des quelques théologiens*, a work definitely composed by Le Clerc, and perhaps associated with Aubert, and a work itself extensively reviewed in the journals of the 'republic of letters' and part of a major debate with the Oratorian biblical critic Richard Simon, author of a quickly banned *Critical History of the Old Testament*. Locke was to lament his distance from Limborch after that return to England as causing the absence of a very close friend, and to suggest that he truly resided not in England but in Limborch's heart. Locke was to suggest that Limborch had made the Netherlands during Locke's time there Locke's own country. We will also return to such notions of intellectual friendship and the significant *patria* of intellectuals in the late seventeenth century in later sections of this chapter.[28]

Locke wrote his *Letter Concerning Toleration* to Limborch, while he was hiding at the house of Veen in winter 1685, and Limborch arranged for the first Latin publication of Locke's *Letter* in the Netherlands and helped to persuade Locke that it should be printed.[29] He then kept Locke updated about its reception, telling Locke in September 1689 that 'the Dutch [translation] is on sale in our shops and is being read by many people with great approval'.[30] Locke constructively criticised arguments of Limborch's 1686 *Theologia Christiana* before its publication and celebrated it when it was published. Limborch celebrated Locke's 'discerning scrutiny and fine judgment' in thanking him for his 'scholarly observations' on the draft of the *Theologia Christiana*.[31] Locke similarly made suggestions when he read in manuscript Limborch's replies in defence of Christianity against Isaac Orobio de Castro's defence of Judaism; Limborch thanked him for improvements 'through which the entire disputation has appeared in a more elegant shape'.[32] In the 1690s, Locke was to solicit John Tillotson's approval of the

---

[28] P. T. van Rooden and J. W. Wesselius, 'The Early Enlightenment and Judaism: The "Civil Dispute" Between Phillippus van Limborch and Isaac Orobio de Castro', *Studia Rosenthalia* (1987); Barnouw, *Limborch*; Marshall, *Locke*; Locke, *Correspondence*, 834–5, and the Locke–Limborch correspondence in many volumes from 1685 until his death; Klauber, 'Fundamental Articles', 623.

[29] Locke, *Correspondence*, 1131, 1283; Locke, *Letter*, ed. Klibansky and Gough, introduction; M. Montuori, *John Locke on Toleration and the Unity of God* (Amsterdam 1983), xxii–xxvii.

[30] Locke, *Correspondence*, 1158, 1178.   [31] Locke, *Correspondence*, II, 832.

[32] Locke, *Correspondence*, 958, in van Rooden and Wesselius, 'Early Enlightment', 143.

dedication of Limborch's *Historia Inquisitionis* to Tillotson, and in the late 1680s and early 1690s Locke had instigated the composition and publication of that work by supplying to Limborch the manuscripts on which it was based and thereafter a host of letters encouraging its publication. Locke also discussed these manuscripts of the Inquisition with Benjamin Furly and Jean Le Clerc, and Le Clerc discussed them with Limborch. Limborch's *History of the Inquisition* was among the works most extensively reviewed in the *Histoire des Ouvrages des Savans* and the *Bibliothèque universelle*.[33] Locke was to consult Limborch himself in letters and to reread Limborch's works during the process of composition of his *Reasonableness of Christianity*, which owed much to Limborch's thought.[34]

Le Clerc published Le Cène's works, the 1685 and 1687 *Conversations* (*Entretiens* and *Conversations*), in one case with his own work as a second part. He sent these to others to read or with requests for journal review, and he himself reviewed Le Cène's *Conversations* in his *Bibliothèque universelle*. He employed Le Cène briefly to help to review others' works for the *Bibliothèque*. Le Clerc discussed issues of toleration and Limborch's tolerationist *Theologia Christiana* with Le Cène when the latter was in London in 1685. Locke and Limborch considered Le Cène for transcription work on Limborch's important tolerationist *History of the Inquisition*. Le Cène translated Locke's *Letter Concerning Toleration* into French, although this edition was not published for some reason. In the 1690s, Locke apparently financially supported Le Cène, and thus helped at least indirectly to fund Le Cène's work on a *Projet* for a new translation of the New Testament. That work was condemned as Socinian by the Synod of Brille, and Jacques Gousset identified it by careful analysis of its passages as an amalgam of 'poisonous' Arminian readings of grace and Socinian readings of the Trinity. Le Cène's extensive manuscript collection in the Huguenot Library, London, suggests strongly that this was indeed an accurate portrait of Le Cène's major commitments by the 1690s, combining post-Pajonist Arminianism on issues of grace and predestination with a Socinian Christology.[35]

[33] see Chapter 20 below.
[34] See below, pp. 518, 617, 671; Marshall, *Locke*.
[35] Barnes, *Le Clerc*, 103–4; Locke, *Correspondence*, 1154; Le Clerc, *Epistolario*, 54, 91, 100, 109, 118 [C. Le Cène], *Conversations sur diverses matières*; C. Le Cène and J. Le Clerc, *Entretiens sur diverses matières* (1685); Locke, *Correspondence*, 1158; Le Clerc, *Bibliothèque universelle*, v (1687), 212–27; Locke, *Correspondence*, 2192, 2197, 2238; J. Gousset, *Considerations théologiques et critiques sur le projet d'un nouvelle version française de la Bible* (Amsterdam 1698), *passim*, esp. preface 3 on 'poison'; Huguenot Library, London, MS R5, esp. v. 1–3, and 6–10; cf. E. R. Briggs, 'Les manuscrits de Charles Le Cène dans la Bibliothèque de la Huguenot Society of London', *Tijdschrift voor de studie van de verlichting* (1977), 358–78; J. Vercruysse, 'Crellius, Le Cène, Naigeon ou les chemins de la tolérance socinienne', *Tijdschrift voor de studie van de verlichting*, 24.

Locke's apparent support for Le Cène was provided through the instigation of Paul D'Aranda, a tolerationist merchant (and himself allegedly a Socinian). D'Aranda was also a go-between between Locke and Limborch, carrying books between them, and the man whose suspicions of Locke's authorship of the *Letter Concerning Toleration* Limborch confirmed, much to Locke's irritation. In the mid-1690s, D'Aranda employed as tutor the Socinian Jacques Souverain, one of whose lengthy unprinted Socinian works is recorded in Locke's manuscript papers. Locke had formerly recommended Souverain's employment as tutor to his own friend Edward Clarke, declaring him to have been approved of by a mutual tolerationist friend, William Popple. In the late 1690s, D'Aranda also arranged for Popple, the translator into English of Locke's *Letter Concerning Toleration*, to help to support Le Cène. In the late 1690s, therefore, the English translator of Locke's *Letter Concerning Toleration*, Popple, was helping to support a French translator of Locke's *Letter*, Le Cène, as apparently was the author, Locke, himself.[36]

Burnet was in these years a friend of Locke, if perhaps not a close friend, and they remained correspondents thereafter. Locke was to send his works to Burnet and to cite Burnet's *Pastoral Care* approvingly several times in his 1692 *Third Letter for Toleration*. Burnet was in these years moreover the close associate of many Arminians. Le Clerc translated some of Burnet's sermons in defence of the Revolution of 1688–9 into French, having already translated several of his other works into French. He, and also his assistant editor Jean Cornand, gave many of Burnet's works favourable reviews in the *Bibliothèque universelle*. He may have borrowed Burnet's edition of Lactantius from Locke in August 1688. Le Clerc published Burnet's *Life*, and in it he remarked that during his time in the Netherlands he and Burnet had frequently visited each other in Amsterdam and the Hague. They also corresponded frequently in these years, including exchanging letters about mutual acquaintances who defended toleration, and complaints about Jurieu's attempts to foster persecution of Socinianism in the Netherlands.[37] Le Clerc remained a correspondent of Burnet after Burnet's return to

[36] *Correspondence*, 1105, 1110, 1113, 1306, 2192, 2197, 2204, 2238, MS Locke f29, 33–4; Montuori, *Locke*, introduction; Locke, *Letter*, ed. Klibansky and Gough, introduction; Lambeth Palace MS 1029, 65, refers to D'Aranda as a known Socinian; my 'Huguenot Thought'; on Souverain, see MS Locke e17 175ff. and my 'Locke, Socinianism'; Labrousse, Mulsow, and Matton in J. Souverain, *Lettre*, ed. S. Matton.

[37] Locke, *Letter*, ed. Klibansky and Gough, introduction; Locke, *Third Letter* in *Works*, VI, 151, 172–3; Marshall, *Locke*; G. Burnet, *Trois sermons* (1689) (tr. J. Le Clerc); *Bibliothèque universelle*, I (April 1686), 466–7; III (September 1686), 130–8; VII (November 1687), 271–8; (1687), 529–54; Reesinck, *L'Angleterre et la Littérature Anglaise* (Paris 1931), 208–11; MS Locke f29, 12–13; J. Le Clerc, *Life of...Burnet* (London 1715); Le Clerc, *Epistolario*, 115, 117, 119, 133, 139, 172, 234, 237, 238, 253, 297, 328, 355.

England, and later asked for his help in gaining a post in England, though he worried about Burnet's increasing conservatism from his moment of departure from the Netherlands, and Burnet worried about Le Clerc's alleged Socinianism and refused such assistance. Le Clerc recommended Le Cène to Burnet, although when Le Cène's increasing Socinianism was drawn to his attention Le Clerc reduced his patronage of Le Cène.

Limborch sent copies of his works to Burnet and corresponded with Burnet. Burnet's chaplain William Jones translated Limborch's *Theologia Christiana* into English in 1706. Limborch and Burnet, and Limborch and Locke, corresponded about the anti-credal argument for toleration of Christians within one enlarged communion of Limborch's further friend and correspondent, Samuel Strimesius, in his *De pace ecclesiastica*. Limborch had that work bound together with Locke's *Letter Concerning Toleration* in copies shipped to England, and also sent it to Burnet. It was once again a work which was prominently reviewed in the *Bibliothèque universelle* – much more prominently than its circulation or its author's status would otherwise have suggested, although Bossuet elevated Strimesius' status when he responded to Strimesius in the course of his important series of *Exhortations to Protestants* against Jurieu. Locke took a note from Strimesius' work in 1687 in the midst of his memoranda from books reviewed in the learned journals.[38]

Burnet recorded that when he first came to Holland in 1687 'I was well acquainted with the Remonstrants', particularly with their 'Professors' Le Clerc and Limborch, and that

they were the best men I saw in Holland and of the clearest heads and best tempers; they had an excellent sense of the practical parts of religion (particularly of love and peace), and expressed great readiness to reunite with the Calvinists whenever they should come to cease from imposing their doctrines upon them; and thought that in these things and many others there ought to be more mutual forbearance.[39]

In the early 1690s, Burnet continued to exchange letters with Limborch, including a series of letters in celebration of Limborch's *History of the*

---

[38] Barnes, *Le Clerc*, 159–66; Le Clerc, *Epistolario*, 172, 225, 228; P. van Limborch, *A Compleat System of Divinity*, ed. and tr. W. Jones (1706); Limborch: Amsterdam University Library, Remonstrants MS III, D 17, 135; D 16, 66, 68, 79, 84, 85v, 89, 90, 93, 156–7, 163; Locke, *Letter*, ed. Klibansky and Gough, introduction; Montuori, *Locke*, introduction; Strimesius, *Dissertatio theologica de pace ecclesiastica* (Frankfurt 1689); *Bibliothèque universelle*, VIII (1688), 244–55; Bossuet, *Sixième avertissement*, II, 633–40; MS Locke c33, 20v. I am grateful to the librarian of the Remonstrants' manuscripts at the University of Amsterdam for providing me with photocopies of manuscripts and facilitating my research in Amsterdam, and to the librarian of The Queen's College, Oxford, for providing me with a photocopy of Strimesius' *De pace ecclesiastica*.

[39] Burnet, *History*, III, 92; Colie, *Light*, 24.

Inquisition. Burnet noted that this was a work which had expanded since their discussions of it in person in the late 1680s:

While we yet discussed the subject you were designing a short treatise, or a long introduction, animadverting on the zealous spirit which breathes fire and slaughter and tracing its progress. But as in all things you far transcend the hopes even of your friends, you have now favoured us with an entire volume, which leaves nothing unsaid...God grant your success may be proportionate.[40]

Limborch was a correspondent also of the tolerationist Pierre Allix, as were Le Clerc, Le Cène, Locke, Papin, and Bayle. Like many among this group of advocates of toleration, Allix had formerly been a student at the Huguenot Academy at Saumur. Allix corresponded with Limborch about the history of the Inquisition, and they supplied each other with manuscript information; the history of the Inquisition was to be the subject of two of Allix's works in the early 1690s and of Limborch's *Historia Inquisitionis*. Allix had corresponded with Limborch and Le Clerc while he had been a preacher at Charenton in the 1680s. Burnet and Allix were to be two of the most important defenders of the Revolution of 1688–9 in England, Allix being the most published of all Whig defenders of the Revolution in the 1705 Whig *State Tracts*. Allix was to be appointed Dean of Salisbury by Burnet when Burnet became bishop.[41]

Burnet held a multi-year friendship and correspondence with Jacques Basnage, who dedicated his 1690 *History of the Protestant Churches* to Burnet with explicit celebration of Burnet's 'friendship' and the benefits of his kind 'censures' – a common recognition of the debts for constructive criticism of arguments in manuscript. Basnage translated into French as the 1687 Utrecht *Histoire de la mort des persécuteurs de l'Église primitive* both Lactantius' *De Mortibus Persecutorum* and Burnet's extensive tolerationist prefatory commentary upon it; in his *Sixth Exhortation*, Bossuet attacked this as a plea for 'universal' toleration which reduced heresy to non-existence.[42] Basnage's brother Henri Basnage de Beauval reviewed this translation in the *Histoire des Ouvrages des Savans*, giving its preface a lengthier summary than Lactantius' work itself. And this extensive review was one of no less than fourteen articles which the *Histoire* devoted to Burnet's works.[43] Basnage continued to correspond with Burnet after his return to England, and Jacques Basnage introduced to Burnet the tolerant J. A. Turretin – tolerant son of the intolerant father and

[40] Foxcroft, *Life of Burnet*, 314–15.

[41] Limborch, Remonstrants MS III, D 4, 5, 6, 7, 9, 17, 19, 20, 114–20, 122; Le Clerc, *Epistolario*; Locke, *Correspondence*, 2653; Labrousse, *Bayle*, I, 123, 156, 211; *DNB*, Allix.

[42] Cerny, *Theology*, 90, 93–8, 100–4, 163, 205–8, 212, 263, 276; Bossuet, *Sixième avertisse-ment*, 654–5; [J. Basnage], *Histoire de la mort des persécuteurs de l'Église primitive* (Utrecht 1687).

[43] *Histoire des Ouvrages des Savans* (September 1687), 112–16; (March 1688), 319–27; (October 1699), 435–64; Reesink, *L'Angleterre*, items 859–72; Cerny, *Theology*, 96–7.

systematic Calvinist theologian François Turretin. Burnet employed Basnage to secure a Latin translation of his *Exposition of the Thirty-Nine articles.*[44]

Basnage was Bayle's undergraduate contemporary at Sedan, and one of the most important of Bayle's patrons; Basnage encouraged Bayle to apply for the Chair of Philosophy at Sedan. He tried to defuse or deflect many of the measures taken against Bayle by the Walloon consistory in the 1690s, and became Bayle's executor, one of his heirs, and the recipient of Bayle's theological and ecclesiastical books. He composed Bayle's *Elogy.*[45] Like Basnage, Bayle seems to have been close to Burnet in the later 1680s and early 1690s. He reviewed several of Burnet's works in the *Nouvelles.* And in the late 1690s he wrote that he hoped that Burnet's *Exposition of the Thirty-Nine Articles of the Church of England* would give reasons for and against particular theological positions such that differing points of view on the issue would become acceptable – an ethos close to Bayle's own. In the 1688 *Supplement to the Philosophical Commentary*, Bayle quoted from 'the English' – that is, Burnet's – preface to Lactantius' *Death of the Primitive Persecutors* for its tolerationist argument that 'the persecutions of Christian against Christian can't chuse but be unjust, because they have no demonstrative Evidence whereby infallibly to decide who is right and who wrong'. The work also received review in the *Histoire des Ouvrages des Savans* in 1687.[46] And Bayle not merely later corresponded with Burnet – congratulating him on his elevation to the see of Salisbury, for instance, and also later corresponding with others who corresponded with Burnet in one of the epistolary circles so central to the 'republic of letters' – but, more importantly for this book, he was in frequent contact with Burnet, and reported on various of his compositions in Rotterdam in July 1686. Burnet was thus corresponding with Papin while Bayle was editing Papin's tolerationist *Faith Reduced* and adding to it his own preface in defence of toleration, and while Locke was recommending Papin to Edward Clarke.[47]

Upon Bayle's illness in 1687 (and again in 1699–1711), the editorship of the journal *Nouvelles de la République*, founded by Bayle in 1684, perhaps went next to Jacques Bernard. Bernard was reported in the *Histoire des Ouvrages* to be the actual author of Locke's anonymously published

---

[44] Cerny, *Theology*, 90, 93–8, 100–4, 163, 205–8, 212, 263, 276; Marshall, *Locke*; Phillips, 'Geneva', 77–92; M. Klauber, 'The Eclipse of Reformed Scholasticism in Eighteenth Century Geneva', in J. Roney and M. Klauber (eds.), *The Identity of Geneva* (Connecticut 1998), 129–42.

[45] Labrousse, *Bayle*, 18, 20; Cerny, *Theology*, 105–18.

[46] G. Burnet (ed.), *A Relation of the Death of the Primitive Persecutors* (Amsterdam 1687); Bayle, *Philosophical Commentary* (1708), 533; *idem, Nouvelles*, (May/June 1687); (September 1687), 112–16; Bayle, *OD*, IV, 618, 630, 640–1, 684, 885; Cerny, *Theology*, 96.

[47] Bayle, *OD*, IV, 630 (July 1686); Cerny, *Theology*, 96; Labrousse, *Bayle*, I, 213n.; Reesinck, *L'Angleterre*, 172.

Epistola, a work which Henri Basnage de Beauval then compared with Bayle's *Philosophical Commentary*, suggesting that among friends of Bayle, Bayle's and Locke's (respectively pseudonymous and misattributed anonymous) arguments were seen as operating in tandem in these years. Bernard was a cousin of Jean Le Clerc and associated with Le Clerc in publishing the *Bibliothèque universelle*. Bayle meanwhile began to assist in the production of the *Histoire des Ouvrages des Savans* with its editor Henri Basnage de Beauval, author of *Toleration of Religions*. Bayle had reviewed *Toleration* in his *Nouvelles de la République* in June 1684, and over the next twenty years Bayle, Basnage de Beauval, and Jacques Basnage reviewed the tolerationist thought of Bayle, Locke, Limborch, Le Clerc, Burnet, and others in the *Histoire*. Locke's works were often reviewed in the *Histoire*.[48]

Bayle translated the tolerationist *De nuperis Angliae motibus Epistola, in qua diversorum a publica Religione circa Divina sentientium disseritur tolerantia* of Adriaan van Paets from Latin into French. Paets was Bayle's patron, and a correspondent of Le Clerc. Paets had been a student of Stephen Courcelles, the co-leader (with Episcopius) of the previous generation of Arminianism before Limborch and Le Clerc; Limborch's *Theologia Christiana* was a summary of the thought of Episcopius and Courcelles. Like many other Arminians, Paets stressed the limited number of fundamental elements of Christianity and their clarity in Scripture. And Bayle gave the work he had himself translated a lengthy fourteen-page review in the October 1685 issue of the *Nouvelles de la République des Lettres* – thereby, among other things, signalling to prospective purchasers that it was available in his French translation. Locke owned a Latin copy.[49]

---

[48] Basnage de Beauval, *Histoire des Ouvrages des Savans* (Sept–Nov 1689), 20–6; L. P. Courtines, *Bayle's Relations with England and the English* (New York 1938); Hutchinson, *Locke*, 15; Cerny, *Theology*, *passim*; T. Lennon, 'Bayle, Locke and Toleration' in M. A. Stewart (ed.), *Studies in Seventeenth-Century European Philosophy* (Oxford 1997), 192; Le Clerc, *Epistolario*, 108; Locke, *Letter*, ed. Klibansky and Gough, introduction, xxviii–ix; H. Basnage de Beauval, *Tolérance des Religions* (Rotterdam 1684); *Nouvelles*, June 1684; *Histoire*, *passim*, inc. I, 112–16 (Burnet); I, 439–55 (Limborch); VII, 457–65 (Locke's *Treatises*); VI, 20–6 (Locke, *Letter*); J. de Vet, 'John Locke in de "Histoire des Ouvrages des Savans"' in H. Bots (ed.), *Henri Basnage de Beauval & l'Histoire des Ouvrages des Savans* (Amsterdam), II, 183–270. As editor of the *Nouvelles*, Bernard reviewed Locke's *Paraphrase*: *Nouvelles* (1705), 448–56; (1706), 101.

[49] Labrousse, *Bayle*, I, 165–6; 172n.; 193; 217; Israel, *Dutch Republic*, 395, 638–9, 674ff.; 789–90, 912; *idem*, *Radical*, 332; A. van Paets, *Lettre de Mr M. V. P. a Mr B *** sur les derniers troubles* (Rotterdam 1686), 21; Bayle, *Nouvelles* (October 1685), 1082–95; Locke, *Library*, 2166a; S. O'Cathasaigh, 'Bayle's Commentaire Philosophique, 1686', *Studies on Voltaire and the Eighteenth Century* (1989), 159–77, at 163–4; J. Solé, 'Les débuts de la collaboration entre Adriaan van Paets, protecteur de Pierre Bayle à Rotterdam, et le gouvernement de Louis XIV' in *De l'humanisme*, 477–94; F. R. Knetsch, 'Jurieu, Bayle et Paets', *BSHPF* (1971), 38–57.

Burnet and Papin corresponded in 1687–8 about Papin's tolerationist work, *Faith Reduced*, a work which was not merely published by Bayle, but which had been written in the Bordeaux household of William Popple, who was in 1689 to be the English translator of Locke's *Letter*, who was later employed by the Board of Trade on Locke's recommendation, and who apparently was a financial supporter of Charles Le Cène in the 1690s. Locke recommended Papin to his tolerationist friend Edward Clarke for employment on the basis of Popple's recommendation of Papin. Bayle's and Le Clerc's journals reviewed several of the works of Papin and responses to these.[50] From the early 1680s, Papin and Le Clerc corresponded extensively about religious toleration and about many religious and philosophical issues, and they supplied each other with works. Papin further corresponded with Jacques Lenfant about toleration and about Le Clerc, and it was Lenfant who recommended Le Clerc to Bayle, and who corresponded with Bayle about his *Commentaire Philosophique*, and about Burnet's letters approving of the work of Papin.[51]

Papin's former employer Popple was in 1686 the author of *Rational Catechism* (1687), a work from which Locke took notes in 1688, and then in 1689 the English translator of Locke's *Letter Concerning Toleration*. Popple was a friend and correspondent on issues of toleration of William Penn, who was in turn a friend of Locke's 1687–9 host Benjamin Furly, who had translated Penn's earlier tolerationist writings into Dutch. Penn visited Furly in Rotterdam during Locke's time in the Netherlands. Popple's movements after leaving France following the Revocation are obscure, but in Lawton's 'Memoir of William Penn' he recorded that in 1687 Popple was living at Windsor, dining with William Penn and Lawton, that Penn was then 'bringing [Popple] out of trouble', and that Penn was visiting the French ambassador to 'solicit Mr Popple's business'.[52]

It is possible that Penn was Aubert's host when Aubert was in England in 1688–9: Aubert is recorded as having lived in Holland House, Penn's residence, and a location where Furly visited Penn for dinner. Penn had also been a student at the Protestant Academy at Saumur in 1663–4; this institution was attended by many of the advocates of toleration, and it shaped their tolerationist thought by emphasising an eirenic theology. In the 1680s, Aubert probably transported books between Locke and Le Clerc, and phosphorous

[50] Bossuet, *Sixième avertissement*, ii, 673–8; O'Cathasaigh, 'Bayle and Locke'; Le Clerc, *Bibliothèque universelle*, IX, 200–20.

[51] Bayle, *OD*, IV, 680; Le Clerc, *Epistolario*, 35, 36, 38, 39, 42, 54, 71, 74, 97, 101, 102, 104, 105, 106; Klauber, 'Fundamental Articles', 618; Labrousse, *Bayle*; Bossuet, *Sixième avertissement*, 673–8; Zuber, 'Papiers', 107–43.

[52] Locke, *Letter*, ed. Klibansky and Gough, introduction; Montuori, *Locke*, introduction; [Lawton], 'Mr Lawton's Memoir', 215–31, at 218–20; O'Cathasaigh, 'Bayle and Locke'.

between Bayle and Locke's friend Boyle, and he recommended books to Locke. Locke recommended Aubert's *Pacific Protestant* to Locke's own tolerationist collaborator Tyrrell, and Bayle recorded in a letter to a friend in 1684 that there was much of merit in Aubert's *Pacific Protestant*.

Bayle's *Nouvelles* reviewed another work of Aubert, albeit with some significant reservations about Aubert's Socinian materialist response to Spinoza's metaphysics. Aubert knew Locke's host Furly, who seems to have lent him money for a period before refusing to continue such funding. And he cited Bayle's 'excellent' *Philosophical Commentary* as 'admirably defending my cause' in his 1687 *Treatise*. Bayle returned the compliment, citing Aubert's *Treatise* in the *Historical and Critical Dictionary* as one of the four works to be read on the subject of toleration. Two of the others were his own *Philosophical Commentary*, and Adriaan van Paets' *De nuperis Angliae*, a work which Bayle had himself translated into French for publication. Adriaan van Paets was Bayle's patron, and he attempted to be Aubert de Versé's patron, offering him a position as tutor in his household.[53]

The fourth book which Bayle recommended in the *Dictionary* on the topic of toleration was Locke's *Letter Concerning Toleration*. Over the nearly twenty years from the mid-1680s to Locke's death in 1704, Bayle and Locke helped each other occasionally with book recommendations and the supply of tolerationist works. Bayle gave a series of other recognitions to the value of Locke's epistemological and other works in the *Dictionary*, although he did not refrain from one jibe at Locke, by referring to him as 'Dr Locke' (of the theological and not medical ilk), much to Locke's annoyance. Even in the early eighteenth century, by which time, as we will see in a few moments, their mutual acquaintance Le Clerc had fallen out with Bayle, Locke was continuing to pursue correspondence with Bayle via Furly about matters that varied from the best editions of Livy (an issue deeply connected to the understanding of 'superstition' and thus related to Bayle's *Pensées*) through to Bayle's opinion of the *Essay Concerning Human Understanding*. Locke declared then that he valued Bayle's opinion in the 'first rank'. In the 1690s,

---

[53] Bayle, *Dictionary*, 'Sanctesius'; Locke, *Letter*, ed. Klibansky and Gough, introduction; Aubert de Versé, *Traité de la liberté de conscience* (Amsterdam 1687; ed. B. de Negroni 1998), 77–8; *idem*, *Manifeste de Maître Noel Aubert de Versé* (Amsterdam 1687), 12–13, 19; Le Cène, *Conversations*; Locke, *Correspondence*, 1480; MS Locke f29 31 (1687); Morman, *Aubert*, *passim*, esp. 91n.162, 163, 164; M. Turchetti, 'La liberté de conscience et l'autorité du magistrat au lendemain de la Révocation', in H. Guggisberg (ed.), *La liberté de conscience* (Geneva 1991), 290–367; [Lawton], 'Mr Lawton's Memoir'; Bayle, *Nouvelles* (October 1684), 862–4; my 'Huguenot Thought'; on Furly promoting toleration in England in 1689, see Hull, *Furly*, 96, 159n.

Locke recommended the *Historical and Critical Dictionary* as one of the important pieces of reading for a gentleman.[54]

In June 1686, Sir Walter Yonge and John Freke, visiting Locke in Amsterdam, Haarlem, and Rotterdam, and Furly in Rotterdam, were meeting Bayle, who lived near Furly. A year later, upon hearing that Bayle was ill, Yonge was corresponding with Locke in terms which suggest that he knew of familiarity between Locke and Bayle.[55] Strongly anti-Catholic and anti-absolutist, Yonge and Freke were to be two of the most important tolerationist Members of Parliament in England in the 1690s and two of the members of the 'College' to whom Locke then gave political advice now that his former patron Shaftesbury was dead. In 1688, Locke sent Freke one of three copies of the *Abrégé* of the *Essay* from the *Bibliothèque*. Freke was the negotiator with the Churchills for publication of the *Essay*; he was also a celebrant of Locke's 'obliging and agreeable conversation'. Yonge wrote to Locke that he valued Locke's conversation 'at the highest rate' and even that the great 'advantage of his conversation' gave the very 'idea of happiness'. Both Yonge and Freke were among those to whom Locke sent copies of the new journals of the republic, including the *Nouvelles* and Le Clerc's *Bibliothèque universelle* (and the *Acta Eruditorum* and *Journal des Savants*) during his time in the Netherlands; Yonge solicited Locke's judgment of the quality of their entries.

Locke had the broader task of supplying a library for Yonge, judging which 'curious books' would be fit for Yonge's 'use', as Yonge declared that he did not desire a library for 'furniture' but rather for its intellectual matter. Locke's services for Yonge were thus somewhat similar to those of the journals themselves for other readers. Yonge moreover charged Locke to furnish him with 'such choice pieces as I fancy can hardly be had any where but in Holland'. Suggesting heavy emphases on toleration and on Arminianism in response to Yonge's desires, Locke's purchases for Yonge included the works of his Arminian friend Limborch, Grotius' eirenic *De Veritate*, and a work of Arminius himself, together with Bayle's *Philosophical Commentary*. Locke also supplied Yonge with Fontenelle's *History of Oracles*, a redaction of Anthonie van Dale's attack on the impostures of priests upon the credulity of the people, *De Oraculis Ethnicorum*. That was the book with whose review Bayle opened the *Nouvelles*, and a work which Locke read and from which he took extensive notes in his journal in 1683. And Locke supplied Yonge with Pufendorf's *De Jure Naturae*.

[54] Bayle, *Dictionary*, 'Sanctesius'; Locke, *Correspondence*, 3198; Bayle, *OD*, II 729; *OD*, IV, 695, 785, 803, 816, 831, 834, 840–1, 850, 853; MS Locke f8, 13 October 1685; P. Whitmore, 'Bayle's Criticism of Locke' in P. Dibon (ed.), *Pierre Bayle, Le philosophe de Rotterdam* (Paris 1959), 81–95; Lennon, 'Bayle'; Locke, *Some Thoughts*, 326.
[55] Locke, *Correspondence*, III, 944 and notes; M. Cranston, *Locke* (London 1957), 257.

Back in England, when Locke's close friend Edward Clarke was interviewing the apologist for toleration Isaac Papin for the post of tutor at Locke's recommendation in 1687, it was Yonge who served as translator between Clarke and Papin, whose *Faith Reduced* was written in the household of Popple, translator of Locke's *Letter*, and published by Yonge's acquaintance, Bayle. It seems clear that Papin could have had the job but was not resigned to such quasi-menial non-scholarly employment. Yonge was one of the Members of Parliament who supported the campaigns to disable many fierce Anglicans – those who had given up their charters to the king – from being members of corporations in 1689. He may at that point have been associated with the campaign for toleration of Furly, who had returned to England in order to assist in the campaign. Another of the supporters of this cause was Edward Harley, later to be associated with Locke; it was with the name of an unidentified Harley in 1694 that Locke noted the title of one of Le Clerc's tolerationist works in one of his journals. Freke's cousin was the anti-Trinitarian William Freke, author of *A Brief and Clear Confutation of the Doctrine of the Trinity*, burned by the hangman in London in 1694. With Locke's advice, Freke and Yonge were both opponents of the renewal of the Licensing Act in 1696, an act which Locke opposed partly on the grounds of its prohibition of 'heretical' works.[56]

That Yonge and Freke visited both Bayle and Locke in Rotterdam and Yonge then wrote to Locke with concern about Bayle's health is thus surely suggestive of awareness of mutual commitment to religious toleration on the part of all of the individuals concerned. That impression is reinforced by Locke having supplied Yonge with the *Philosophical Commentary*. Moreover, in approximately the same period Locke received compliments to be presented to the author of the *Philosophical Commentary* from Damaris Cudworth (later Masham), a woman with whom Locke had discussed religious issues in the years immediately before he left England in 1683, with whom he was to continue to discuss religion for the rest of his life, and who was to be Locke's hostess for the last years of his life. Damaris Cudworth (Masham) was a tolerationist author, and daughter of the largely tolerationist as credal minimalist and ecumenicist Cambridge Platonist and

---

[56] Locke, *Correspondence*, 876, 939, 944 (*inter alia*); Bayle, OD, IV, 696; MS Locke f7, 109 (recording Locke receiving twenty shillings from Yonge in June 1683 for a subscription for a book of martyrs!), 166ff. on Locke's reading of *De Oraculis* in 1683; MS Locke f9, 339; MS Locke f29, 90; MS Locke d10, 159; F. Ellis, 'John Freke and the History of the Insipids' in *Philological Quarterly* (1965), 472–83; O'Cathasaigh, 'Bayle and Locke'; W. H. Barber, 'Piere Bayle, Benjamin Furly and Quakerism' in *de l'humanisme*; on Furly promoting toleration in England in 1689, see Hull, *Furly*, 96, 159n.; Bayle, *Nouvelles*, I (1684); my 'Locke, Socinianism'; Israel, *Radical*, 152, 335; Champion, *Pillars*, 158–9 on the *History of Oracles*.

Latitudinarian Ralph Cudworth. It is possible that Locke had also provided Damaris Cudworth with Bayle's *Philosophical Commentary* to read, and she thought that he knew the author to whom she wished her compliments to be conveyed.[57]

Locke and Bayle were associates in the Netherlands at least partly through the tolerationist Quaker merchant Furly. Locke, Bayle, Burnet, Le Clerc, Limborch, and Basnage were all occasionally or regularly participants in a conversational circle which gathered at the house of Furly, with whom Locke lived for a significant part of his time in the Netherlands. Bayle, Basnage, and Henri Basnage de Beauval were also regularly members of a second circle for intellectual conversation which met nearby, and which included Adriaan van Paets the Younger, son of Bayle's benefactor, and the publisher of Bayle's tolerationist works, Leers. A third conversational and intellectual circle in the Netherlands was based around the Arminian community in Amsterdam and seems to have included Limborch and Le Clerc, with Locke as an occasional visitor. The houses of Bayle and Furly were very near each other; Furly described Bayle as his 'neighbour'.[58]

Furly's house and his extensive library of 4,400 volumes – which included many 'heretical' works – were at the epicentre of the early Enlightenment. Locke surely consulted Furly's library while living in his house for two years from 1687 to 1689. Locke and Furly procured many books for each other and for mutual associates, and after his return to England Locke used Furly as a conduit for sending books to Le Clerc for review in the *Bibliothèque universelle*. Their shared bookish interests were even reflected in the present to Furly by Locke of a bookcase with 'bookshelves for all sizes of books, invented by John Locke' intended to be 'convenient for transportation without removing the books from them'. Furly himself was a Quaker and as such to many of his contemporaries a 'heretic', and was himself the author or translator of many works defending Quaker thought. His circle also included other Quakers such as Kohlans and the Kabbalist Quaker van Helmont, who became very friendly with Locke, and who visited Locke in England in the 1690s. James Tyrrell, Locke's tolerationist friend in England, worried jocularly that Locke might himself be becoming too Quakerish in these years, and that he would return to England 'theeing' his acquaintance. It is likely that in this period Locke did gain a greater appreciation of Quaker thought and life, including its large degree of support for toleration: his

---

[57] Locke, *Correspondence*, III, 967, 975 (cf., however, J. Yolton's more cautious comments on the Locke–Cudworth correspondence: J. Yolton, *John Locke: A Descriptive Bibliography* (Bristol 1998), 313–15.

[58] Cerny, *Theology*, 87–92; Labrousse, *Bayle*, I, 217n.; Hull, *Furly*, 51; Barber, 'Pierre Bayle' 624–5; Locke, *Correspondence*, 1480.

journals show that he read Quaker works in these years and was attempting to find ways to accommodate Quaker accounts of the indwelling spirit with the status of Scripture, a task made easier by the tendency of Quaker writings by this date – such as those of Robert Barclay, whom Locke read – to be engaged in the same attempts themselves. We have noted in Chapter 4 Locke's increased sympathy for Quaker sufferings in the late 1670s and early 1680s. But the influence between Locke and Furly seems to have proceeded also in the other direction, with Locke influencing Furly as well as being influenced by Quaker thought. By the 1690s, Furly increasingly came to feel that even the Quakers were too restrictive a church and relatedly to attack the words 'Church' and 'Heretick' as themselves 'pernicious' in letters to Locke; while often defenders of a large degree of toleration, Quakers had had a pronounced tendency to anathematise those of other religions in the 1650s, and while this was lessened by the 1690s it remained a feature of many Quakers' commitments. Furly was an important practical as well as principled advocate of toleration, a financial and political sup-porter of toleration in England and the Netherlands, and a regular defender of toleration in discussion with William III himself. In Furly's house in the late 1680s many conversations were held which Locke himself described as 'heretical', and he referred to Furly's conversational circle, known as 'the Lantern', as the 'heretics of the Lantern'. That the conversational circle around Furly included Bayle, Basnage, Burnet, Limborch, Le Clerc, Kohlans, van Helmont, Furly, and Locke (among others) indicates that it was precisely the open-minded ecumenical tolerationist agreement of Quakers, Arminians, Socinians, and their associates that was important to this group.[59]

I will return to the ethos of these overlapping conversational circles in the Netherlands, and to consideration of the relationships between their prac-tices of discussion and the advocacy of religious toleration later in this chapter, indicating some divergences between the practices of Locke and of Bayle. What is important to note here is that these circles themselves pro-vided a major further series of mutual associations and assistance in these years; they drew together into intellectual discussions and personal famil-iarity many of the authors of tolerationist works, and included every one of the editors of the new learned journals of the 'republic of letters' that were founded in the 1680s.

In describing the mutual assistance, significant friendships, or at least respect and admiration among many individuals defending religious tolera-tion in the 1680s and 1690s, I have deliberately left until almost last two

---

[59] Locke, *Correspondence*; Hull, *Furly*; Cranston, *Locke*; *Biblotheca Furliana*, 352 quoted in Coudert, 'Locke', 96–7; my 'Locke and the Furly Circle'.

issues which will now complicate this story. The first of these is the status of two advocates of toleration in the 1680s who converted to Catholicism in 1690, Noel Aubert de Versé and Isaac Papin. The second is the later strained relationship between Le Clerc and Bayle. In each case, if there was friendship and trust between the group of advocates of toleration in the mid-1680s, it was to be betrayed; and considerable mistrust may have marked some of these relationships from as early as the 1680s.

From as early as the early 1680s there may have been good reason for wariness on the part of other tolerationists towards Aubert. As early as 1684, Bayle worried that Aubert wrote only for pay, had no principles, and could as easily write for as against any position. In this, Bayle was to prove eerily prophetic. Aubert was to reconvert to Catholicism in the 1690s, and to receive patronage from Bossuet to write anti-tolerationist works. He was to be understood by Furly and Locke – probably wrongly – to be the author of an anoymous swingeing attack on Quakerism, the *Short History of Quakerism*, which included a personal attack on Furly and appalled both Locke and Furly. It is possible that throughout his entire time in the Netherlands, Aubert was a spy. There is no evidence to suggest that Isaac Papin was a spy, and there seems to have been no wariness about him in the early or mid-1680s, but Papin also converted to Catholicism in 1690 and then he too published anti-tolerationist argument. He provided Bossuet with the correspondence between himself and Burnet in the late 1680s in which Burnet had endorsed a toleration so capacious that in the 1690s it could be used to embarrass him now that he had become a bishop of the Church of England.[60]

In a climate in which many spies and double agents were being employed against the refugee and exile populations, and when plots for assassination or capture of some of these individuals were laid, a certain wariness may have inflected some or even many of the relationships sketched in this chapter. The obsessive desire for anonymity which has often been noted by modern scholars as a feature of Locke's intellectual career surely owed something to his own entirely accurate perception that he was spied upon in England, and the need to hide under assumed names in the Netherlands and fear of death can surely only have increased Locke's wariness in his dealings with anyone and everyone. He certainly displayed considerable anger when Limborch confirmed to Guenellon that Locke was indeed the author of the *Letter Concerning Toleration*, as D'Aranda already suspected. Wariness may have been considerably more intense with a figure such as Aubert than with others; we have met Aubert in

---

[60] Morman, *Aubert*; Locke, *Correspondence*, 1480; as E. S. de Beer notes, the author of the *History of Quakerism*, which Locke attributed in his library to Aubert de Versé, presumably on the basis of this letter from Furly, was probably Philippe Naudé; Bossuet, *Sixième avertissement*, 673–8; Papin, *Toleration*.

the course of this book as a tolerationist who became an anti-tolerationist, as formerly accused of adultery, incest, and rape by both Catholics and by Jurieu, and preparing for the Moroccan ambassador in England an argument that that Ambassador's religious commitments were close to Socinianism and that he should convert to Socinian Christianity as that was superior to Islam. But rather than emphasising wariness and mistrust, it would surely be more accurate to think that many of the advocates of toleration saw their relationships with other tolerationists as being even more important and more than usually trusting because their support for full religious toleration was so narrowly shared, and because they were helping to shelter and protect each other at a time of danger. Even in the case of Aubert, while Bayle was clearly always suspicious of Aubert, Locke and Furly's letters communicate a sense that they felt truly betrayed by Aubert, whom Furly had probably supported financially and whom Locke may have employed to carry books. The evidence does not suggest that they had formerly suspected Aubert, but rather that they saw their trust as violated.[61]

The most complex relationship to describe is that between Bayle and Le Clerc. By the early 1700s, Bayle and Le Clerc were to write an almost vitriolic series of works against each other. Bayle was in that period accused by Le Clerc of writing works whose purpose seemed to be to incline men to atheism rather than to edify them. Among several places in which he thus discussed Bayle, in his 1708 review of Matthew Tindal's significantly Lockeian *Rights of the Christian Church* Le Clerc introduced an entirely gratuitous attack on Bayle's suggestion that atheists might be virtuous, recorded the importance of religion to political security, and noted that only the most extended charity on his part prevented him from impugning Bayle's motives in reducing *hatred* for atheists as themselves 'atheistic'. In return, Le Clerc was accused by Bayle in his 1703–7 four-volume *Reply to the Questions of a Country Gentleman* and in his posthumously published 1707 *Conversations of Maxime and Themiste* of composing defences of 'reasonable' Christianity that were no more capable of explaining the difficulties within Christianity than were other accounts, and which supported toleration only for those *opposed* to the theology of the Synod of Dort, even though Le Clerc proclaimed that they defended universal religious toleration.[62]

The latter charge was serious: what Bayle had said was that Le Clerc wished in effect to exclude from the right to toleration the majority of

---

[61] Morman, *Aubert, passim*; Locke, *Correspondence*, 1283, 1285, 1480.

[62] Labrousse, *Bayle*, 44–5; Le Clerc, *Bibliothèque choisie*, XII, 198ff.; *idem, Bibliothèque ancienne et moderne* (Amsterdam 1714–24), I, 204–20; *Bibliothèque ancienne et moderne* (1727), 367ff., esp. 394–5, 431; Stankiewicz, *Politics*, 226.

orthodox Huguenots and the majority of the orthodox Calvinist Dutch Reformed Church. And the former attack was intellectually serious, for a considerable portion of Le Clerc's *oeuvre* consisted precisely of attempts to found a 'reasonable' Christianity against what Le Clerc saw as on the one hand the excesses of Calvinist supralapsarianism in positing an 'unreasonable' and 'unjust God', and on the other hand the excesses of 'libertinism' in deploying that 'unreasonable' and 'unjust' God to declare that no God existed and that libertinism was more 'reasonable'. Moreover, while they took many years to mature, the seeds of mutual suspicion between Bayle and Le Clerc had been scattered as early as the mid-1680s. Le Clerc was perturbed as early as 1685–6, by Bayle's review of his (anonymous) part of the *Conversations (Entretiens)* in Bayle's *Nouvelles*, a review which recorded both that Le Clerc's work was 'heterodox' and that it attacked Augustine 'cruelly'. And Bayle alleged in the same period in a letter to a friend that he was concerned both about the open heterodoxy of Le Clerc and his clear bias towards Arminianism – an attitude which anticipated his criticism of the 1700s that Le Clerc truly wished for toleration only for anti-Calvinists.[63]

Yet while it is important to give appropriate emphasis to these differences between Bayle and Le Clerc, before describing a great gulf as having separated Le Clerc and Bayle as early as the 1680s it should be noted immediately that Bayle wrote privately to Le Clerc to indicate that in his view Augustine deserved to be cruelly treated, and that his comment in the *Nouvelles* would only encourage more readers to read Le Clerc's work. In his 1687 *Bibliothèque universelle* review of Le Cène's *Conversations*, Le Clerc compared an argument of Bayle's *Philosophical Commentary* to that of Crell's *Vindication of Liberty of Religion*, the second half of Le Cène's *Conversations*. Since Le Clerc had organised the publication of this work, this aligns Le Clerc's perception of the *Philosophical Commentary* in 1687 with arguments for toleration for whose printing Le Clerc was responsible. He, or his assistant editor Cornand, had already given Bayle's work an extensive review. And in reviewing Jurieu's 1687 attack on Bayle's *Philosophical Commentary*, Le Clerc (or Cornand) noted that given his preceding account of Bayle's work, readers would be very surprised to see the 'frightful picture' of it which Jurieu had given.[64]

Important as the separation between Le Clerc and Bayle was by the 1700s, then, one thus needs to be careful about dating the development of this chasm. Bayle came under fire for his alleged support for 'atheism' *in the 1690s*. When

---

[63] Bayle, *Nouvelles* (1685) in *OD*, I, 277; Labrousse, *Bayle*, I, 262ff.; Le Clerc, *Epistolario*, 84, 86–7; Mori, *Bayle Philosphe* (Paris 2000), *passim*.

[64] Le Clerc, *Epistolario* (1 May 1685), 86; Le Clerc, *Bibliothèque ancienne et moderne*, I, 204–20; *Bibliothèque universelle* (1687), III, 335–60; V 212–27, 334–52, but cf. Mori, *Bayle*.

Locke took notes from Bayle in 1685, even though he was reading a version of one of the central works of Bayle later specified as 'atheistic', the *Letter on the Comet*, he took *none* on the topic of 'atheism'; whereas when he took notes again in 1698, these notes were *entirely* on the topic of atheism. What had happened between 1685 and 1698 involved one issue that was simply about the edition of Bayle's work that Locke had read – in 1685, he had read the initial and short form of the argument about atheists in the 1682 *Lettre*, as opposed to the longer version Bayle had by then already published in the 1683 *Pensées*. But the transition in Locke's focus from highlighting the issue of 'superstition' in Bayle's work in 1685 to stressing only the issue of 'atheism' in Bayle's work in 1698 surely also reflected Jurieu's explicit attack on Bayle's support for toleration of 'atheists', which occurred in the early 1690s rather than in the 1680s.

It was in Bayle's *Dictionary* article on Manicheanism that Le Clerc found the central position which would lead him into fiery dispute against Bayle. Again, this entry in the *Dictionary* dates from the 1690s and not the 1680s. Moreover, the same impression (that the issue of alleged support for 'atheism' in Bayle's *Pensées* bubbled to the surface in the 1690s, and that in the mid-1680s many read Bayle's *Pensées* as the attack on superstition which it was on the surface rather than as offering covert support of atheism) is provided by noting that it was being reviewed in the learned journals in ways which did not discuss 'atheism' but rather emphasised, precisely like Locke's notes from Bayle, the issue of superstitions, miracles, and prodigies. Locke thus took a note in the 1680s from the review of Bayle's *Lettre* in the *Acta Eruditorum* which summarised the argument of that work as being that comets did not presage evil, and in which Locke noted: 'See in him miracles and prodigies treated of at large'. *No* mention was here made of atheism. And further suggestion still that the issue of Bayle's potential atheism became pressing in the 1690s rather than on the basis of initial publication of the *Lettre* or *Pensées* comes from the fact that Bayle was sending his work in the early 1680s to thoroughly orthodox Protestant friends and ministers who did not then accuse it of being supportive of 'atheism' but instead celebrated it, including the arch-orthodox François Turretin, as well as Jean-Robert Chouet, the latter of whom read the text several times with the kind of 'incomparable satisfaction' which would not have been registered for a work understood to support 'atheism'.[65]

In 1684–5 alone, Bayle and Le Clerc exchanged no less than fourteen surviving letters, and these letters included several times the declaration that they were each others' friends 'with all their heart'. In these years, as Bayle founded a learned journal in the 'republic of letters', Le Clerc offered to

---

[65] See the *Acta Eruditorum* review of the *Lettre*, 318–21; MS Locke f9, 91; MS Locke d10, 3 (Locke's 1698 note); Rex, *Essays*, 72–3; Labrousse, *Bayle*. I am grateful to Anthony McKenna for several discussions of Bayle.

Bayle advice on how to review works and they supplied each other with works. Le Clerc encouraged Bayle to give a more straightforward rendition of what was included in the work reviewed – what he called a 'faithful extract' – and thus to tone down Bayle's own editorial interventions and criticism. These letters between Le Clerc and Bayle came complete with a supply to each other of a series of directly or indirectly tolerationist works, including their own (anonymous) works – such as the Le Cène/Le Clerc *Conversations* and Bayle's *New Letters*.[66]

In his correspondence in the 1680s, Le Clerc praised Bayle's discussion of the 'erroneous conscience' as having been one of two particularly 'pleasing' elements of the *New Letters*, a work which Bayle had personally sent to Le Clerc. As late as 1707, Le Clerc called Bayle's *Philosophical Commentary* a 'very good work' in his *Bibliothèque choisie*, and later still he described it as 'the best work that he ever wrote' in his *Bibliothèque ancienne et moderne*. In other words, even when Le Clerc had indeed come to worry that Bayle might be a covert 'atheist' and that others of his works might be intended to incline people towards atheism, Le Clerc was still willing to commend the *Philosophical Commentary*. He also remained willing to commend several of Bayle's other tolerationist works of this period of the mid-1680s – the *General Criticism of Maimbourg*, the *New Letters*, and the *State of Wholly Catholic France*.[67] Moreover, Le Clerc's close friend and fellow preacher during the months he spent in London in 1683, André de L'Ortie, also declared in the early 1690s that Bayle's *Philosophical Commentary* was a 'very good book', and L'Ortie continued to assert that Bayle's work was 'very good' as an attack on all principles of persecution, even when this support for Bayle's work was cited against him by his fellow Huguenot refugees in England in the 1690s, in the course of allegations that they made to the Archbishop of Canterbury that L'Ortie's beliefs deserved deprivation of his ministerial position in the Church of England.[68]

---

[66] Le Clerc, *Epistolario*, 45 (26 April 1684), 49 (3 June 1684), 50 (8 June 1684), 51 (18 June 1684), 55 (16 August 1684), 57 (6 Sept 1684), 81 (14 April 1685), 84 (23 April 1685), 86 (1 May 1685), 87 (11 May 1685), 93 (18 July 1685), 94 (19 July 1685), 95 (21 July 1685).

[67] Le Clerc, *Epistolario*, 87 (11 May 1685); *Bibliothèque universelle*, III (1686), esp. 357, V (1687), 336; *Bibliothèque choisie*, XII (1707), 201ff.; *Bibliothèque ancienne et moderne*, XXVIII (1727), 367; cf. Mori, *Bayle Philosophe*, 287–8, for a rather different emphasis concerning the Le Clerc–Bayle relationship and these passages. As Dunn, 'Freedom of Conscience', 115, appropriately stresses, Bayle's 'attack upon religious persecution [in the *Philosophical Commentary*] was developed in explicitly religious terms...his publicly proclaimed regard for liberty of conscience rested solidly and obtrusively on his expressed faith in the Christian revelation'.

[68] Lambeth Palace MS 929, 54; MS 932, 1, and my 'Huguenot Thought'; also for discussions of the tensions surrounding L'Ortie but not his citation of Bayle, see Gwynn, 'Reshaping', 251–73; *idem*, *Huguenot Heritage*, 105ff.; Cottret, *Huguenots* esp. 207ff.

It is worth noting that even when the divisions between Le Clerc and Bayle were to have grown into full flower in the early 1700s, Locke and Bayle kept in contact with each other via Furly and Coste (who was also Le Clerc's close friend) until Locke's death, and that Bayle was helping to supply Locke with copies of Locke's hard-to-obtain tolerationist works as late as 1704. As we have noted, Bayle moreover kept on recommending Locke's *Letter Concerning Toleration* in the *Dictionary* as one of four works to be read on the topic of religious toleration, with two of the other three works being his own *Commentary* and his own translation of van Paets' work. Individuals such as Pierre Coste and Pierre des Maizeaux, both central figures in the popularisation of the works of the 'early Enlightenment' in the early eighteenth century, remained close to Le Clerc, Locke, and Bayle. Coste and des Maizeaux were involved in the publications of the works of all three authors in the early eighteenth century.[69] A tandem of Bayle's *Philosophical Commentary* and Locke's *Letter Concerning Toleration* was to be frequent and important in the eighteenth-century case for religious toleration. Bayle's own pairing of the two works in his own recommendation of only four tolerationist works in the *Dictionary* has already been indicated. François de la Pillonière was author of defences of toleration in the Bangorian Controversy, the most important controversy over toleration in early eighteenth-century England, and tutor to Benjamin Hoadly, the most important voice of tolerationism in England. The works which he identified as having persuaded him to become a tolerationist included both Locke's *Letter Concerning Toleration* and Bayle's *Philosophical Commentary*. When Locke's *Letters Concerning Toleration* were published in 1765, in an edition under the auspices of the leading radical Whig Thomas Hollis, the only tolerationist work other than Locke's own that was recommended by name was Bayle's *Philosophical Commentary*.[70]

It is important to stress all of this because the scholarly tendency over recent years has been to emphasise the distances separating Bayle and Le Clerc, and Locke and Bayle. It is possible to tell the story of their personal

---

[69] J. Almagor, *Pierre des Maizeaux (1673–1745), Journalist and English Correspondent for Franco-Dutch Periodicals 1700–1720* (Amsterdam 1989); Hutchinson, *Locke*, 11, 25–8; J. H. Broome, 'Bayle's Biographer: Pierre des Maizeaux', *French Studies* (1955), 1–17; G. Bonno, 'Locke et son traducteur français Pierre Coste', *Revue de littérature comparée* (1959), 161–79; J. Schosler, 'Les Editions de la traduction française par Pierre Coste de l'Essay Concerning Human Understanding de Locke', *Actes du VIIIe Congrès des romanistes scandanives* (Odense 1983), 315–24; Goldgar, *Impolite Learning*; cf. also Reesinck, *L'Angleterre*; Barnes, *Le Clerc*.

[70] F. La Pillonière, *Answer to Mr Snape's Accusation* (1717), 43–4; *idem, Third Defense* (1718), 98–124; Rey, *Account*; my 'Huguenot Thought'; C. Robbins, 'The Strenuous Whig, Thomas Hollis', *William and Mary Quarterly* (1950), 405–53; Patterson, *Early Modern Liberalism*.

and intellectual relationships and to accent only acrimony and distance, when it is necessary to capture collaboration and wary friendship as well, in order that the very important joint advocacy of toleration and the significant tolerationist practices of Le Clerc's and Bayle's journals in the 1680s and 1690s do not become neglected. What is needed in order to understand the relationship between Bayle and Le Clerc *in the 1680s*, in other words, is a sense *both* that there were some significant sources of tension in their dealings with each other as early as 1684–6, with seeds and early growths of the suspicions and acrimony which were later to blossom, and that at the same time Le Clerc and Bayle knew that (in opposition to the vast majority of their contemporaries) they shared a considerable amount in their mutual commitment to religious toleration, and were trying to help each other to promote that cause in the circulation of tolerationist arguments and in their foundation of learned journals of the 'republic of letters'.[71]

THE 'REPUBLIC OF LETTERS'

The relationships so far described between the handful of advocates of universal religious toleration in the Netherlands in the 1680s were particularly important ones for the individuals concerned. But many of the forms of mutual assistance between the members of this group – from the purchasing of books for others to meeting in conversational circles and discussing ideas or constructively criticising each others' unpublished manuscripts – were extensions of practices of association and assistance which had been evolving as duties among scholars in the emerging 'republic of letters' over the

---

[71] On the differences and distances between Le Clerc, Bayle, and Locke, see especially Mori, *Bayle, Philosophe*; S. Jenkinson, 'Two Concepts of Tolerance: Or Why Locke Is not Bayle', *The Journal of Political Philosophy* (1996), 302–21; H. Bracken, 'Toleration Theories: Bayle vs Locke' in E. Greffier (ed.), *The Notion of Tolerance and Human Rights* (Carleton 1991), 1–11; *idem*, 'Toleration theories'; Klibansky and Gough (eds.), Locke, *Letter*, introduction, xxxiv; J. B. Schneewind, 'Philosophical Roots of Intolerance and the Concept of Toleration' in M. Razavi and D. Ambrel (eds.), *Philosophy, Religion and the Question of Intolerance*, (New York 1997), 3–15; T. Todorov, *The Morals of History* (Minneapolis), 151–3. For a work stressing acrimony and hierarchical competition in the early eighteenth-century 'republic of letters', and discussing acrimony between Le Clerc and Bayle, see Goldgar, *Impolite Learning*. In the view of this author, Goldgar overstates the competition and acrimony in the republic and understates the attempts to aid and assist others. Goldgar further identifies the 'republic of letters' as developing out of 'a kind of conservatism, or even fear', as a republic which 'glossed over religious quarrels', and as a republic in which savants specifically chose to concentrate on 'the formal construction of scholarly society' instead of on 'the content of ideas'. In my view, for the 1680s and 1690s this understates the importance of ideas supportive of religious toleration and corrosive of authority in the 'republic of letters' at a time of politically sanctioned religious intolerance; it also understates the significance of the support for rights of resistance of authors such as Locke and Le Clerc.

previous two centuries, most notably in the 'natural philosophic' or 'scientific' community and in the highly classicised and often philologically focused communities of humanistic and ecumenical scholars from Erasmus and his 'Louvain circle' in the early sixteenth century through to the circles associated with Tew, with Grotius, with Mersenne, or with Hartlib in the seventeenth century.

Many of the issues of textual criticism discussed in the circles of the late seventeenth century were importantly influenced by their predecessors in intellectual exchange in the sixteenth and early seventeenth century.[72] Based on multiple interactions between individuals interested in discussing ideas, and thus on intellectual circles which gathered for discussion in person, on networks of correspondence to continue conversations at a distance, and on the widespread circulation of manuscripts and printed materials, the seventeenth century saw increased capacities for correspondence across Western Europe due to the development of postal networks, the multiplication of intellectual circles due to improved means of transport and thus greater possibilities for travel, increased commercial exchanges bringing greater communications, and the multiplication of the material for discussion due to the increased printing and distribution of works and the increased pace of scientific experiment.[73]

The evolution of these practices and possibilities for scholarly interaction then reached a further level in the 1680s. As Paul Dibon has indicated, while the idea of a 'Res Publica Literaria' or 'republic of letters' dates back to antiquity, and while the term was utilised with increasing frequency in sixteenth- and early seventeenth-century Europe, the 'republic of letters' as a self-consciously designated, institutionalised, and central form of scholarly interaction and criticism 'attained prominence and a degree of concreteness only in the late seventeenth century'.[74] The Huguenot refuge in the

---

[72] H. Bots and F. Waquet, *La République des Lettres* (Paris 1997), 12–13, 31–2, 37, 46, 81–3; *idem, Commercium litterarium* (Amsterdam 1994); Barnes, *Le Clerc*; R. Whelan, *The Anatomy of Superstition* (Oxford 1989), ch. 4; L. Jardine, *Erasmus, Man of Letters* (Princeton 1993); B. Rochot, 'Le P. Mersenne et les relations intellectuels dans l'Europe du XVII siècle', *Cahiers d'histoire mondiale* (1966), 55–73; A. Grafton, *Joseph Scaliger* (Oxford 1983, 1993); *idem, Defenders of the Text* (Cambridge, Mass. 1991); *idem, Forgers and Critics* (Princeton 1973); Q. Skinner, *Reason and Rhetoric in the Philosophy of Hobbes* (Cambridge 1986); Tuck, *Philosophy and Government*, 286–93; *idem*, 'Hobbes'; Greengrass et al. (eds.), *Hartlib*; H. Trevor-Roper, 'The Religious Origins of the Enlightenment' in *idem, Religion.*

[73] M. Ultee, 'The Republic of Letters: Learned Correspondence 1680–1720', *Seventeenth Century*, II (1987), 95–112; E. Eisenstein, *The Printing Press as an Agent of Change* (Cambridge 1979); Bots and Waquet, *La République.*

[74] P. Dibon, 'Communication in the Respublica Literaria of the 17th Century', *Res Publica Litterarum* (1978); A. La Vopa, 'Conceiving a Public: Ideas and Society in Eighteenth-Century Europe', *Journal of Modern History* (1992), 79–116; Goodman, *The Republic of*

Netherlands in the 1680s was central to crystallising this new level of the 'republic of letters' as it brought together a large number of Huguenot intellectuals and many temporary visitors in a few cities in the Netherlands, the country possessing the most extensive printing-presses in Europe and the most extensive tradition of publishing a diversity of works by authors of a diversity of faiths. It brought together several individuals already committed to extensive religious toleration and to support for scholarly and scientific enquiries conducted with 'curiosity' and 'critical' thinking, even if this involved challenges to contemporary theological orthodoxy. And, most importantly, in the very years of the 1680s when individuals such as Le Clerc, Bayle, and Basnage de Beauval were advocating religious toleration in their own works, and when they were assisting each other by many mutual services and gathering for discussions in conversational circles, they simultaneously gave to the 'republic of letters' a new level of prominence and a new level of definition by founding three new journals of the 'republic of letters' and discussing its ethos in these and other works. The first of these, Bayle's *News of the Republic of Letters*, communicated by its very title the new prominence being given to that 'republic of letters', and simultaneously helped by its very existence to give that 'republic' new distinction. As Dibon has put it, whereas 'the lifeblood' of the 'republic of letters' in the early and mid-seventeenth century of Grotius, Mersenne, and Oldenburg had been networks of 'correspondence' which made 'its activities known to its citizens', which heralded 'the appearance of books', and which spread 'news about research in progress', the 'flourishing of journals in the last years of the century' came to stand alongside such correspondence in these tasks and in 'coordinating the life of the republic'. Such correspondence was, of course, not replaced but rather joined by these journals: it is important to note that the polymathic and voluminous correspondence of Locke with other savants, very familiar to students of Locke, was similar in style, content, and size to that of Le Clerc, Limborch, Bayle, and others. But the journals gave the republic a new focus, and increasing numbers of such letters were concerned with material in or for the journals themselves.[75]

It is important to underline the sense of intellectual excitement that was associated with these journals and with participation in the activities of the late seventeenth-century 'republic of letters' more generally. To bookish individuals such as Bayle and Locke, the very activities of study and of

Letters, ch. 1; L. Daston, 'The Ideal and Reality of the Republic of Letters in the Entightenment' in *Science in Context* (1991); Barnes, *Le Clerc*, 13–14; Gordon, *Citizens Without Sovereignty*; Chartier, *Cultural Origins*.

75 Dibon, 'Communication'; Daston, 'Ideal'; H. Bots, 'L'Esprit de la République des Lettres et la tolérance dans les trois premiers périodiques savants hollandais', *XVIIe siècle* (1977), 43–57; Locke, *Correspondence*; Le Clerc, *Epistolario*; Simonutti, *Arminianesimo*; Limborch, Remonstrants MS; Bayle, *OD*, IV.

criticism involved considerable pleasure. Bayle remarked in 1692 that he found 'as much pleasure and happiness' in study as 'others do at the gaming-table and in the tavern' and Locke described study and intellectual criticism among friends as significant kinds of pleasure. But many others in this period were caught up in the sense that criticism and constructively critical conversation was pleasurable and exciting; we found the same notion being expressed to Locke, for instance, by such a figure as Sir Walter Yonge, who wrote to Locke that he valued Locke's conversation 'at the highest rate' and that the great 'advantage of his conversation' gave the very 'idea of happiness'.[76]

In the wake of such intellectual developments as: the revival of scepticism in the sixteenth century; the philological studies of Erasmus, Scaliger, Casaubon, Grotius, and others, focused in significant part on identifying and rejecting the authority of spurious texts; the questioning of traditional moral values by such thinkers as Montaigne; the attempts to refound morality by Grotius, Hobbes, Pufendorf, and others; the epistemological and ontological challenges to received understandings of the world of Hobbes, Descartes, and Spinoza; and the redescriptions of knowledge due to the 'natural philosophic' or 'scientific' works of Copernicus, Galileo, Kepler, Harvey, and several generations of 'Baconian' empiricist 'scientific' experiments in England, these new journals of the 'republic of letters' were associated in the 1680s and 1690s with an exciting perception that received wisdom in all fields of knowledge was in the process of being challenged, undermined, and rewritten.

As Anthony Grafton has noted, scholars of the 'High Enlightenment' of the 1790s often looked back and emphasised their debt to preceding critics and

In particular they stressed the importance of the scholars of the late seventeenth century, those avatars of the critical spirit of the Enlightenment and authors of *Critical Histories* of almost everything.

Among the figures whom Grafton then names as particularly crucial was Le Clerc, not merely the editor of three separate journals of the 'republic of letters', but an author who provided '*the* systematic statement of the principles of higher criticism, and offered dozens of examples to clarify them, in his *Ars Critica*'.[77] Grafton stresses, appropriately, that such scholars of the 1680s themselves owed a considerable amount to the scholars of the 1580s, and even before, who had begun to develop many of the forms of textual criticism which were to inspire the generation of the 1680s. It is as

---

[76] Bayle to Cuper, 1 December 1692 in Labrousse, *Bayle*, 16; Marshall, *Locke*; Locke, *Correspondence*, 876, 939.

[77] Grafton, *Forgers and Critics*, 72–4. For a critical contemporary review of Le Clerc's criticism, see *Histoire* (August 1697), 522–31.

important, however, to stress that by the 1680s and 1690s the criticism being practised had also become distinctively new by its very cumulation across many fields, with a quantitative change itself becoming a qualitative change in the critical attitude involved; that in the hands of many Protestant authors it was increasingly being wielded to support religious toleration and not the *magisterium* of the Catholic Church; and that it was understood by many of its practitioners and participants in the 1680s and 1690s to be more biting, more refined, and more 'enlightened' than had been the scholarship of previous generations of scholars. Bayle was once again the leading exponent of the notion that while much had been learned from sixteenth-century critics, current criticism was more 'enlightened'; in Acontius D in the *Dictionary*, he thus wrote:

I am of the opinion, that the sixteenth century produced a greater number of learned men, than the seventeenth, and yet the former was not so enlightened as the latter. While the reign of Criticism and Philology continued, every part of Europe produced prodigies of Erudition...[but now] a certain Genius more refined, and accompanied with a more exquisite discernment, has spread itself over the Commonwealth of Learning: People are now-a-days less learned, and more subtle.[78]

The process of holding everything or almost everything open to question, of examining alternative views, and of rejecting traditional authority, is the common thread linking many reviews and defining the character of these journals in the last two decades of the seventeenth century. It is important that the strands of criticism of theological orthodoxy involved in fields as diverse as archaeology, epistemology, astronomy, politics, and patristic studies were physically as well as intellectually woven together in the journals, and that their effect was thereby cumulative. In the act of reading these journals, a reader consulted works which reviewed literature which most viewed as 'heretical' on one set of pages, which included works of scholarship on the Fathers of the church which was often critical of contemporary theological orthodoxy on another set of pages, which had a section of works explicitly on the topic of religious toleration on another set of pages, and which had a section of works on the new 'science' on another set. 'Natural philosophy' was reviewed alongside patristic scholarship, investigations of classical and Christian morality alongside the natural law theorising of Grotius and Pufendorf, and the epistemological investigations of Locke and Leibniz alongside the archaeological conjectures of Thomas Burnet, the gravitational theories of Newton, and the medical empiricism of

---

[78] Bayle, *Dictionary*, Acontius D; cf. the comment on Bayle of his friend Basnage, quoted from the 1706 *Histoire des Ouvrages des Savans* in Cerny, *Theology*: 'Some have much knowledge and little genius and the others little erudition and much wit. But both shine in Mr Bayle's writings'.

Thomas Sydenham. All were reviewed alongside 'heretical' religious works and defences of religious toleration.[79]

It is equally crucial to focus on the expansion of the audience aimed at in these journals. Bayle stressed that his journal was aimed at an audience of thousands of readers, and not just at 'the learned'. The very range of materials covered was explicitly intended to appeal not to the limited range of the specialist and expert but to the allegedly capacious interests of the literate citizens of the 'republic of letters'. Here, then, was the taking of materials whose discussion had formerly been largely confined to specialists possessed of traditional university learning, most notably divines, and placing them instead into the hands of a critical lay public who were being asked thereby to use their reason to judge the views being presented to them. Jean Le Clerc explicitly stressed that his journal was intended to provide 'faithful extracts' of works precisely in order to allow the reader him or herself to make the judgment. It is this process which has led Dena Goodman to declare that the 'republic of letters' was the location in which individuals learned to use their reason publicly. And Le Clerc explicitly stressed in one of his works in 1700 that 'the republic of letters is at last become a country of reason and light, and not of authority and implicit faith as it has been too long'.[80] Thus was the central ethos of the 'early Enlightenment', and in many ways that of the 'High Enlightenment' itself, expressed in the journals of the 'republic of letters' and identified with the practices fostered by the journals of that republic.[81]

These journals are, then, fascinating works whose adequate analysis would itself fill volumes. It is clearly not possible to undertake that task here.[82] For the purposes of this book, what remains necessary in this chapter

---

[79] On Grotius and Pufendorf, see R. Tuck, *Natural Rights Theories* (Cambridge 1979) and *idem, Hobbes*, Tully, *A Discourse on Property: John Locke and his Adversaries* (Cambridge 1980), and J. B. Schneewind, *Invention of Autonomy* (Cambridge 1998); on Locke and Leibniz, see N. Jolley, *Leibniz and Locke* (Oxford 1984), and Riley, *Leibniz' Universal Jurisprudence* (Harvard 1996), Marshall, *Locke* and Porter, *Untold Story*; on Thomas Burnet, see Jacob, *Newtonians*; on Sydenham, K. Dewhurst, *Dr Thomas Sydenham*, (Berkeley 1966); on the general sense of questioning, Hazard, *European Mind.*

[80] Goodman, *Republic*, Le Clerc, *Epistolario*, 51; Marshall, *Locke*, 330; cf. *Five Letters Concerning the Inspiration of the Holy Scriptures*, p. 7: 'we live in an age of so much Light' that it is now unbecoming to sacred truths to build on 'unsound principles' and so the 'Doctrine of Implicit faith has lost its Vogue'.

[81] As Dena Goodman has put it, 'the republic of letters was the very center of the public sphere in which private persons learned to use their reason publicly': Goodman, *Republic*; cf. *idem Criticism in Action* (Ithaca 1989); Gordon, *Citizens Without Sovereignty*.

[82] For important studies of various aspects of these journals, see H. Bots (ed.), *Henri Basnage de Beauval en de Histoire des Ouvrages des Savans* (Amsterdam 1976); *idem* (et al.), *De Bibliothèque Universelle et Historique* (Amsterdam 1981); *idem, Circulation and Reception of Periodicals in the French Language During the 17th and 18th Centuries* (Amsterdam 1988); Bots and Waquet, *République*; G. N. M. Wijngaards, *De Bibliothèque Choisie (1703–13) van Jean Le Clerc* (Amsterdam 1986); A. Laeven, *The Acta Eruditorum Under the Editorship of Otto Mencke. The History of an International Learned Journal*

is: to indicate that this period saw the definition and celebration of the services of participants in the 'republic of letters' as a kind of virtuous service in a 'republic' that was devoted to toleration and enlightenment, critical reason and questioning; to examine the rather different inflections given to that notion of virtuous service in the practices and in the descriptions of the practices of Locke and Bayle, and to indicate that these journals themselves both advocated religious toleration and attempted to practise it to a significant degree in their structure.

THE REPUBLICANISM OF THE 'REPUBLIC OF LETTERS' AND THE PRACTICES OF CONVERSATION, CIVILITY, AND CRITICISM OF LOCKE AND BAYLE

The 'republic of letters' was republican. Crucially, the ethos defined for the processes of discovery, communication, and discussion of scholarship in these years centred precisely on the 'virtues' of a 'republic': on the duties of citizenship, of virtuous participation, of liberty, and of equality amongst its citizens. In his preface to the first edition of the *Nouvelles*, Bayle stressed that 'we are all equals'. In the entry 'Catius' in the *Dictionary* Bayle emphasised that 'liberty prevails in the Common-wealth of Learning' and that 'This Common-Wealth is a State extremely free'. Henri Basnage de Beauval, editor of the *Histoire* spoke very similarly of 'republican liberty of letters'.[83] Vigneul-Marville recorded as early as 1700 that there was never a republic 'greater, freer, or more glorious' than the 'republic of letters', which included all people without respect to condition, age, sex, and of diverse religions and manners, and 'of piety and libertinage'.[84] Reflecting on the history of the 'republic of letters' a century later, the *Histoire de la République des lettres* recorded that this was a republic precisely 'because it preserves a measure of independence, and because it is almost its essence to be free. It is the empire of talent and thought'.[85]

As was true of early modern republicanism more generally, with such 'liberty' was combined the 'duty' of service to the commonwealth as a 'republic'.[86] As Paul Dibon notes, 'it was the strict duty of each citizen of the republic to establish, maintain, and encourage communication, primarily by personal

Between 1682 and 1707 (1682–1707) (Amsterdam 1990); A. Desautel, *Les Mémoires de Trévoux* (Rome 1956); H. Bost, *Un 'intellectuel' avant la lettre: le journaliste Pierre Bayle* (Amsterdam 1994).

[83] Bots and Waquet, *République*, 26; Bayle, *Nouvelles*, I (1684), preface; Bayle, *Dictionary*, Catius; Barnes, *Le Clerc*, 14–15; Whelan, *Anatomy*, 87–8.

[84] Bots and Waquet, *République*, 18.   [85] Daston, 'Ideal', 367.

[86] J. G. A. Pocock, *The Machiavellian Moment* (Princeton 1975); *idem*, *Virtue, Commerce and History* (Cambridge 1985); Q. Skinner, *Liberty before Liberalism*; *idem*, *Machiavelli*; M. Peltonen, *Classical Humanism and Republicanism in English Political Thought* (Cambridge 1995).

correspondence or contact, with expanding networks of epistolary exchange remaining until the last years of the century the primary means of coordinating the life of the Respublica literaria'. The purchase of books, the communication of information about new publications, and the reporting of scientific advances, was a duty to other citizens of the intellectual and international republic. Locke was both a frequent participant in such activities and a frequent celebrant of such activities. He bought books for others and had others buy them for him; he alerted others to new publications, and reported new scientific discoveries and advances in personal reading for Shaftesbury and in letters to others, as well as celebrating them in his own writings, including the *Essay*. He frequently discussed the recent activities of the 'republic of letters', particularly referring to it by its English designation as the 'commonwealth of learning', and encouraged others to publish their contributions to that commonwealth as a duty to serve the public good, from the period of his association with Boyle and Sydenham in the 1660s and of his membership in the intellectual circle of Justel and Toinard in Paris in the 1670s through to the end of his life.[87]

As such communication in the republic of letters was based on intellectual merit and mutual service, within the network of associates who were corresponding and conversing it set aside – or at least held at arm's length – issues of social status in the other societies and nations to which the individuals belonged. Moreover, since letters were exchanged reciprocally, this itself strengthened 'the sense of equality which structured relations between among citizens of the republic'. Tony La Vopa has stressed that in both its ethos and in many of its practices – critical reflection, epistolary exchanges, conversational circles – the 'republic of letters' created a 'socially neutral zone' in which 'intellectual property, like landed property in classical republicanism, assured equality of citizenship'.[88] Like most conceptions of 'republicanism' of this period, as Waquet has stressed, this equality was understood to exist *within* the group of citizens of the 'republic of letters'; it was a kind of 'aristocratic republicanism' based on literacy in the wider sense of that term. It thus in practice excluded from participation in the 'republic' the vast majority of the population of early modern Europe. And while the ethos of the republic held it open to both ladies and gentlemen, in these years female participants in its discussions and publications were relatively rare. The capacity of Damaris Masham for the discussion of metaphysics was explicitly praised by Locke as greater than that of most men, but rare in ladies.[89]

---

[87] On Toinard, Justel, and Locke, see their correspondence in Locke, *Correspondence*, vols. I and II.

[88] La Vopa, 'Conceiving a Public'; Bots and Waquet, *République*.

[89] Bots and Waquet, *République*, 96–9; Marshall, *Locke*; S. Hutton, 'Damaris Cudworth, Lady Masham: Between Platonism and Enlightenment', *British Journal for the History of*

The interactions of individuals within the republic stressed not merely equality and the duties of citizens to serve the republic of the mind but also classical notions of the *amicitia* to be found among individuals – primarily gentlemen or aristocrats – of similar levels of virtue even if separated by physical distance. As Vossius had written to Ussher earlier in the century, '*scis enim, quam late pateat Respublica literaria, atque ut amicitiam eorum, qui ad hanc pertinent, nulla dissolvant regionum spatia*'.[90] As in classical understandings of 'republicanism', the ethos of 'loving friends' who were serving each other and their republic simultaneously was often contrasted explicitly with the potential corruption which surrounded monarchs and courts as that realm of hierarchy and flattery made impossible the necessary criticism possible between friends and equals in the republic. Jacob Graevius, significantly the most important translator and editor of Cicero's works in the late seventeenth-century Netherlands, wrote to Locke in 1689 that 'to be loved by you, my dear Locke, I account, believe me, of greater value than to be in the favour of potentates and kings'.[91] Locke himself celebrated the 'republic of letters' and his friendships in it with individuals such as Limborch by declaring that

some likeness of the golden age has returned. For forests used to be the only abode of virtue and benevolence, peace and good faith, for which there is hardly any place in the crowded cities of men.

In September 1686, Locke wrote to assure Limborch that 'I draw breath elsewhere but I live with my friends'. Such citizenship was often proclaimed, with reference to Cicero, as 'universal', as the 'citizenship' of the 'world', as it had been by the English heremeticist John Dee at the beginning of the century. And the freedom of publication and enquiry within the 'republic of letters' was increasingly conceptualised in contrast to the power of the Inquisition in the French and Spanish monarchical realms, tying the 'republicanism of letters' to 'Enlightenment criticism'. Bayle was one among many who contrasted the free publication and criticism of the 'republic of letters' directly with the processes of the Inquisition in 1685, noting that the

---

Philosophy (1993), 29–54; L. Simonutti, 'Damaris Cudworth Masham' in *Scritti in onore di Eugenio Garin* (Pisa 1987), 141–65; Goodman, *Republic*, ch. 1; C. Lougee, *Le Paradis des Femmes: Women, Salons and Social Stratification in Seventeenth Century France* (Princeton 1976); L. Schiebinger, *The Mind has no Sex? Women in the Origins of Modern Science* (Harvard 1989); M. Jacob (ed.) *Women and the Enlightenment* (Cambridge, Mass. 1989); G. Meyer, *The Scientific Lady in England 1650–1760* (Berkeley 1955). The *Bibliothèque Universelle* (1687), 370–8 (on Fénelon's *Education des Filles*); *Histoire des Ouvrages des Savans*, VII, 512–15 (on female philosophers); VIII, 27–34 (the equality of the two sexes). This is obviously a topic which requires and merits a lengthier analysis than can be provided here.
90 Dibon, 'Communication', 46–8; cf. Bots and Waquet, *République*, 120.
91 Locke, *Correspondence*, III, 1110; on Graevius discussing Cicero with Le Clerc, see, for instance, *Epistolario*, 182 (1691).

Inquisition was at that moment in the process of being established in France under its intolerant Catholicising monarchical absolutism. For Bayle, 'the best writers' were now discouraged in France, as it increasingly disapproved of any mind 'elevated above slavery and vulgar opinions'; but freedom still prevailed in 'the republic of letters'. In the years after the Revocation, during an outpouring of works on the Inquisition which were avidly reviewed in the new journals of the republic, this was a telling contrast indeed; it is unsurprising that Limborch's *Historia Inquisitionis*, extensively reviewed in the journals of the 'republic of letters', dwelled at length on the censorship of books, including Galileo's works, as scientific enquiry, toleration, free discussion and publication of ideas were linked and supported in the practices and the ethos of the 'republic of letters'.[92]

The influence of Cicero was central to the definition of the duties of republican citizens, whose services to each other and to the intellectual republic were themselves intellectual services, as to the definition of *amicitia*. Graevius' edition of Cicero's works was the most frequently reviewed set of classical texts in the journals of the 'republic of letters' in the 1680s and 1690s. Graevius' two volumes of Cicero's letters became the subject of particularly extensive review in the republic's journals and of discussion between Locke and Le Clerc. The first of the volumes of Graevius' edition of Cicero's works had originally been recommended to Locke in 1678 by Locke's friend in another important Parisian circle within the 'republic of letters', Nicholas Toinard; Toinard then quoted from them in his letters to Locke across many years.[93] Locke's favourite author of the last twenty years of his life was Cicero. Some of Locke's letters to correspondents equally familar with Cicero quoted from Cicero's letters or conceptualised the intellectual friendship involved in these relationships in the 'republic of letters' with reference to Cicero's conceptualisations of friendship, the most famous of which was *De Amicitia*. Like Cicero, and like the 'republic of letters' in general, Locke strongly emphasised the *amicitia* possible among virtuous equals, and he stressed that the processes of intellectual service to others in the 'republic of letters' created gentlemanly obligations which in good Ciceronian fashion were to be welcomed as the currency of virtue, gratitude, and duty. Thus, in a letter to Toinard in 1680, Locke declared that he feels some 'self-satisfaction because in Cicero's judgement it is the mark of a gentlemanly and grateful disposition to wish to owe the utmost to whom you owe much'. In his

[92] Bots and Waquet, *République*, 66; Locke, *Correspondence*, 834; P. Bayle, *Recueil de quelques pièces curieuses concernant le philosophie de Mr Descartes* (Amsterdam 1684); des Maizeaux, 'Life of Bayle' in *Historical and Critical Dictionary* (1734–), vol. I, xix; Limborch, *Historia Inquisitionis*.

[93] *Bibliothèque universelle* VII (1687), 85–94, 265–7; VIII, 492–3; xx, 73–85; journal 2 July 1678 in Lough, *Locke's Travels*.

educational writing, *Some Thoughts*, which itself started out as a series of letters from the Netherlands, Locke recommended to his gentle friend Edward Clarke, a visitor to him in the Netherlands, that 'if you would have your son speake well, let him be conversant in Tully to give him the true idea of eloquence'. Although Locke had thought that Cicero's letters showed how to 'say and do well' as early as the 1660s, Locke's focus on Cicero dates especially from 1682–3; 1683 was Locke's first year in the Netherlands. It was in his period in the Netherlands that Locke added a Ciceronian motif to the *Essay*'s title-page. In the 1690s, a passage from Cicero was again used by Locke for the motif of his *Of the Conduct of the Understanding*. Thus both of Locke's epistemological works, one of which was of course the work which he considered his masterpiece, bore quotations from Cicero on the title-page.[94]

Cicero's central location in the 'republic of letters' was similarly recognised by the image next to the title-page in Jean Le Clerc's *Bibliothèque universelle* (see Figure 16.1). It is the image of a scholar writing on paper on a desk, with illumination provided by a winged female figure bearing a torch who is, for a work which was both 'universal' and 'historical', intended surely as Mercury, the Muse of History. Above the scholar is a canopy, symbolic in this period of (aristocratic) honour and decorum and thus indicating the illustriousness of the scholar. Simultaneously, the canopy blocks the light from the window just visible behind it, focusing attention on the scholar's illumination by the torch-bearing Muse, and by the books whose spines the torch lights for us as viewers: enlightenment comes from the inspiration of books and the critical mind of the scholar. In front of the desk, three small winged figures clasp an ink fountain, a quill, and the tablet on which are inscribed the words 'Bibliothèque par Jean Le Clerc'. The image is thus of a book to form a library – a universal and historical library – as the summary of a library in which a scholar is reading and writing in order to send this 'universal and historical library' out into the world. The scholar is presented as condensing for readers who are about to read the volume the knowledge contained in the many books the scholar has read. The desk itself contains no books, probably implying the creative importance and imposing extent of the knowledge possessed by the scholar who is composing the journal.

Crucially, placed on one side of the figure is a column with baroque volutes containing a bust of Cicero, who is the only named figure in the library, and who is placed in a position where he presides over the figure of Le Clerc composing the *Bibliothèque* itself. On another column is a soldier with a weapon, a capital, and at the soldier's feet an owl – probably the owl of

---

[94] Locke, *Correspondence*, II, 556, 877; Locke, *Library* 721a and 721c; Marshall, *Locke*, 164.

Figure 16.1 J. Le Clerc, *Bibliothèque universelle et historique*
(Amsterdam 1718), title-page. (Library of Congress)

Minerva. It is notable that no religious image exists in this entire library. A journal of a 'republic' of scholarship and a 'universal and historical library', the title-page thus looks back most obviously to classical learning and to images that are not Christian but rather Roman and Greek, and its tropes of honour are given to a scholar working in a library in the service of a 'republic', with the republican Cicero being the sole human figure explicitly named as associated with this enterprise and joined with Mercury, Muse of History. Cicero occupied many roles in early modern Europe, including: a discriminating transmitter of Greek learning to the Romans; a mitigated sceptic; a scholar who produced work in a private library but always with an eye to its contribution to the public; an advocate of republican life and virtue – by participation in political life directly if possible, but through service to the community of letters and in communication of the desirability of a republic if that was not currently possible. All of these overlapping and related roles of Cicero are surely summoned simultaneously by this explicit invocation of Cicero as imitated by Le Clerc. Moreover, Cicero was understood to have been an author working solitarily, but to have been bound to his readers as 'friends' by bonds of considerable solidarity and significance.[95]

We have noted already that conversation was central to the 'republic of letters'; it is time now to stress that Cicero was central to conducting conversation. As Peter Burke has emphasised in *The Art of Conversation*, manuals on conversation in early modern Europe were little more than 'a series of footnotes to Cicero'. Cicero had set out a model of an urbane conversationalist who kept others' interest by keeping carefully to the topic under consideration, who limited the length of his discourses, who participated in conversations which included everyone and allowed people to take turns. The ideal conversationalist was to show respect to those with whom he was conversing, and to rebuke only rarely, only when absolutely necessary, with restraint, and only as constructive criticism. This model of Ciceronian conversation was central to conversation, and conversation was central to intellectual exchange in the 'republic of letters'. Even journals such as the *Bibliothèque universelle* themselves reviewed works which discussed models of conversation, such as the 1688 *Art of Pleasing in Conversation*; linking the ethos of conversation to the cause of Christian 'reunion' instead of 'animosity', the final page of the review turned to discuss conversions by force and dragoons as opposed to persuasion in conversation.[96]

[95] Le Clerc (et al.), *Bibliothèque universelle* in 26 vols. (1718), vol. 1, title-page. The journal was initially anonymous. I am especially grateful to Orest Ranum for extended discussions of this image and for his many suggestive comments.

[96] *L'Art de plaire dans la conversation* (Paris 1688); Cornand, *Bibliothèque universelle*, XI, 500–10; P. Burke, *The Art of Conversation* (Cambridge 1993).

As Dena Goodman and Françoise Waquet have both stressed, the correspondence of the 'republic of letters' took as its central models the correspondence of Cicero and of Erasmus, and took as its fundamental principles reciprocity, status based on merit, and fidelity to truth; to these principles needs to be added the very modelling of the urbane conversationalist himself.[97] In many ways, Erasmus' influence here as a model of conversation and scholarly co-operation reinforced Cicero's authority, and it was itself developed in response to Cicero. In the most important work to study Erasmus from the perspective of a scholar engaged in critical enquiries and co-operating and communicating with others, *Erasmus, Man of Letters,* Lisa Jardine has pointed out that Erasmus' self-portrait in his works was that of an intellectual centred on a 'Louvain circle', in correspondence involving the 'exchange of letters between intellectual friends'. And she has noted the revealing comment on Erasmus' letters by Barlandus: if you concealed the name of Erasmus, his letters 'could be taken to have been written by Cicero'. Erasmus' works were being revived and redescribed by many Arminians in the seventeenth-century Dutch republic, who made of him a proto-Arminian tolerationist and stressed his anti-dogmatic arguments and his sceptical arguments. Le Clerc not merely edited three of the major journals of the 'republic of letters', but he also issued an edition of Erasmus' works. Cicero's works were crucial in the sixteenth and seventeenth centuries, but in that most conversational, classicised, and Roman of centuries, the eighteenth, Cicero's works became, if possible, ever more influential.[98]

Ciceronian notions of discussion were surely among the influences on practices within the 'republic' in Locke's own composition of rules for a society or 'club' for conversation in the 1690s which were an amalgam of this essentially Ciceronian model of conversation, of Locke's own stresses on impartial pursuit of truth and 'charity' among differing opinions, and of the stress of many in the late seventeenth-century 'republic of letters' on communicating and propagating the truth. This 'dry club' was thus in Locke's words 'for the amicable improvement of mixed conversation'. The set of rules which Locke drew up required that everyone should sit in a circle in the order of their arrival and speak in order of their seating, removing any notion of social precedence among the speakers. Each individual was for Locke, as Cicero recommended, to focus their comments in discussion on what they

---

[97] Goodman, *Republic,* 17; Bots and Waquet, *République,* 66.
[98] Barlandus and Erasmus in Jardine, *Erasmus,* 19; cf., on the importance of Cicero in the sixteenth to eighteenth centuries, Q. Skinner, 'Sir Thomas More's Utopia and the Language of Renaissance Humanism' in A. Pagden (ed.), *The Languages of Political Theory in Early Modern Europe* (Cambridge 1987), 123–57; Peltonen, *Republicanism*; Champion, *Pillars*; Miller, *Common Good*; and Marshall, *Locke.*

had to say to the topic at hand with 'everyone endeavouring that their answers may not be onely loose Discourses on the Subject; but that they tend directly to...the Resolution of the Question proposed'. When any member thought 'that any appearance of growing warmth is fit to be stopd' they could immediately end any debate. Everyone was exhorted to keep in mind that the meeting was intended as a 'serious and impartial enquiry after Truth...with the maintenance of Charity under different Opinions'. Each individual proposed for membership was to testify that they 'love' and 'seek truth for truths sake; and will do his endeavour impartially to find, and receive it, himself, and to communicate and propagate it to others'.[99]

This ethos was central to Locke's descriptions of his own intellectual identity and to those of Locke provided by others with whom Locke interacted in the 'republic of letters'. Limborch lauded Locke as an 'indefatigable searcher after the truth', and Locke described himself as 'everywhere in search of truth alone'.[100] The Ciceronian model of the urbane conversationalist who was devoted to enquiry into truths and to the discussion, communication, and propagation of ideas also surely stood behind the notion of Locke given by Damaris Masham and Pierre Coste to Jean Le Clerc and used in his *Life of Locke*. Masham stressed that Locke was devoted to conversation, careful to enunciate criticism to friends on 'something which twas for their benefit to make known', and possessing 'not only the Civility of a well educated Person, but even all the Politeness that can be desired'. Coste stressed that Locke corrected others in a 'modest' way.[101] Jean Le Clerc also stressed in his *Life of Locke* that Locke had employed 'civility' and 'politeness' in his conversations with others, including 'Ladies'. Le Clerc moreover described Locke as having created rules for conversations and conferences in his time in the Netherlands which were very similar to those which have survived for the 'dry club'. Le Clerc thus noted that Locke had

desired that Mr Limborch and I with some other friends, would set up conferences, and that to this end we should meet together once a week, sometimes at one house, and then at another, by turns, and that there should be some question proposed, of which every one should give his opinion at the next meeting; and I have by me still the rules, which he would have had us observe, written in Latin with his own hand.[102]

These comments should all be understood as descriptions of Locke and of what was important to him in his practices of conversation, amply confirmed by his own manuscript rules and by his exhortations in the *Essay Concerning Human Understanding* to discussions conducted with civility. Locke practised as well as preached religious toleration. But when published in works

---

[99] MS Locke c25, 56; Marshall, *Locke*, 391.   [100] Locke, *Correspondence*, II, 793, 834.
[101] Le Clerc, *Life of Locke*; idem, *Bibliothèque choisie*, VI, 342–411.
[102] Le Clerc, *Life of Locke*, 28, 14.

such as Le Clerc's and Coste's *Lives* of Locke, these descriptions of his behaviour and attitudes should also be understood to have been shaped and presented as prescriptive accounts for readers. By discussing the conversational practices of Locke in his *Life of Locke*, Le Clerc understood himself to be offering suggestions to be imitated as well as descriptions of Locke's individual behaviour. Such lives were themselves understood both as products of the 'republic of letters' and they were ways to communicate and celebrate its values; Le Clerc's *Life of Locke* appeared in his *Bibliothèque choisie*, and Locke's *Some Familiar Letters* was examined in a later volume of that journal, with a review which emphasised both the philosophical issues which Locke had debated in his correspondence, and the tone of 'friendship' and 'civility' with which he corresponded with such friends as Limborch.[103]

The *Journal des Savants* had set out from its first issue to provide at their death the life of any person 'celebrated for his doctrine and his works' and to give both a catalogue of works and a description of their life. The intent here was to declare that such a life in service of scholarship was significant and laudable as much as it was to identify critically what was valuable about the specific works composed by an individual. And such lives quickly set out behaviour norms for scholars in the 'republic of letters' communicating with each other. This notion spread in the late seventeenth century with the multiplication of lives of scholars. When Coste published his 'Character of Mr Locke' in the *Nouvelles de la république des lettres* his account was at least as much about what one should value in behaviour in that republic as it was an account of the person Locke himself, with Locke declared to be dominated 'by thinking of others' and to have been a model of 'Affability, Good-humour, Humanity, Pleasantness', who was desirous not to 'make a shew of his own Science' but instead to inform himself about what others 'understood better than himself'. He was said to have been on these bases 'one of the politest men' who was 'as agreeable for his obliging and civil behaviour, as admirable for the profoundness and delicacy of his Genius'. Moreover, Coste asserted that Locke's attitude was more important than his 'Genius' in his being 'always...glad to prefer Truth to any of my opinions'.[104]

The ethos here, of 'civility' combined with desire to gain from another's knowledge and a willingness to change one's mind in response to this knowledge was central to the attitudes of the 'republic of letters' and to the 'early Enlightenment', and it was simultaneously central to the ethos of religious toleration in the works issued by defenders of religious toleration in the

---

[103] Le Clerc, *Bibliothèque choisie*, VI, 342–411; XVII, 234–41, esp. 239.
[104] *Nouvelles* (Feb 1705), 154–77; also printed as *The Character of Mr Locke in des Maizeaux's Collection of Several Pieces of Mr John Locke* (1720); partially discussed in Goldgar, *Impolite*, 122ff.

1680s and 1690s who were simultaneously the editors of the journals of the 'republic of letters'. Similarly, Locke's letters were themselves to be issued to the early eighteenth-century public as a modelling of 'such civill and polite conversation as friendship produces among men of parts, learning, and candour', as it was explicitly stated in the 1708 *Some Familiar Letters*. And the influence of this modelling of the laudable behaviour of the scholar through the image of Locke refracted in eighteenth-century texts of and about Locke was then to be handed on to the 'High Enlightenment'. It was, for instance, a model deployed in Diderot's *Encyclopaedia* entry on Locke, which described Locke as 'a foe of disputes, willingly consulting with others, counselling them in their turn, obliging to thinkers and personalities, finding everywhere an occasion to be informed or enlightened, curious about everything'. Diderot, it should be remembered, identified the *éloge* as 'an encouragement to virtue'.[105]

It is important to stress that as significant parts of 'early Enlightenment' toleration were formed by the combination of support for 'enquiry' in the desire to be 'informed or enlightened', of discussion conducted with 'civility', and of the avoidance of (religious) disputes, Locke's *Life* as modelled and presented in these works and then as represented in works such as Diderot's *Encyclopaedia* was probably more influential in spreading the notions and practices of religious toleration in the eighteenth century than the specific arguments in the *Letter Concerning Toleration* on the limited purposes of political society.

Recent scholarship from Roger Chartier, Margaret Jacob, Dan Gordon, Dena Goodman, and others has valuably refocused our attention from 'the Enlightenment' defined as a set of propositions or specific commitments to 'the Enlightenment' as a set of practices and processes of criticism and conversation, enquiry and curiosity. But there is a danger that the valuable emphasis here on process, on critical spirit, could occlude the central ideas and commitments that did equally define 'the Enlightenment'. What is needed first is to point to the importance of the symbiotic combination of these cultural processes and practices on the one hand and the specific commitments to 'tolerance' and 'civility' and 'humanity' stressed in older historiography on the other. And, secondly, it is important to stress that the 'early Enlightenment' combination of these commitments *and* practices in the late seventeenth-century 'republic of letters' was crucial in their evolution as the later commitments *and* practices of the 'High Enlightenment'.[106]

---

[105] Diderot, *Encyclopédie*, IX, 625–7; Israel, *Radical*, 13; Goldgar, *Impolite*, 149.
[106] Jacob, *Living the Enlightenment*; *idem*, *The Radical Enlightenment* (1981); Goodman, *Republic*; Chartier, *Cultural Origins*; Gordon, *Citizens*.

The model of Lockean conversation presented by Le Clerc and others and strongly celebrated in the eighteenth century thus stressed 'civility' and 'politeness', the prevention of dispute by stopping discussion which demonstrated 'warmth' on the part of the participants, and the maintenance of charity. It stressed *amicitia*, or the bonding of individuals in intellectual friendship. It stressed that it was possible to criticise such friends for their intellectual (or moral) failings but that doing so should be structured within very careful civility. It stressed that if one criticised opponents, one should be even more careful in the display of civility. It was an ethos which was celebratory of solidarity among friends and of the pacification of disputes by the silencing of disputes or the conducting of disputes in the most civil and polished manner. When disputation grew strong, the literal requirement in Locke's rules for conversation was the ending of the conversation with an imposition of silence. There is an important series of ways in which Locke's own works of religious interpretation of the 1690s and 1700s – the *Reasonableness of Christianity* and its *Vindications* and the *Paraphrase on the Epistles of St Paul* are themselves strongly marked by this ethos. Le Clerc was to remark in reviewing them in one of his journals that Locke had avoided many of the difficult issues in theological disputes. This was, I am now suggesting, a deliberate *silence* on Locke's part, as a policy associated with toleration and civility as it allowed variant views to be inscribed at those points where Locke was silent. We will see later that in his tolerationist *Theologia Christiana*, Limborch interpreted the duty of equity at one point as the duty of mutual silence, of not unnecessarily attacking others' views; we have already met in Chapter 11 the stress of Episcopius upon preferring silence to unnecessary dispute against publicly accepted religion.[107]

We have already noted that conversational circles provided one of the central forms of intellectual support among the advocates of religious toleration in the Netherlands, and that three circles, two of which were gathered a few streets from each other in Rotterdam and seem to have intersected in membership, were the most important: one gathered in the house and library of the merchant Furly, a second around Bayle and Jacques Basnage nearby – Bayle and Furly called each other neighbours – and a third, of largely Arminian scholars associated with Limborch and Le Clerc, was based in Amsterdam.[108] Furly's circle included Quakers and Arminians, and hosted among others Locke, Le Clerc, Limborch, and at least occasionally Burnet, Basnage, Bayle, and the publisher of many of their tolerationist works, Wetstein. It seems from the correspondence of Locke and others to have

---

[107] Le Clerc, *Bibliothèque ancienne et moderne; Bibliothèque choisie*, II, 284–305; XIII, 37–137.
[108] Cerny, *Theology*, 87–91; Labrousse, *Bayle*, I, 217n.52; Hull, *Furly*, 77, 87–9, 244; Cranston, *Locke*, 280–3, 291–7.

been a convivial affair, and was often referred to humorously. It is worth pausing here for a moment to note that it was in these years that Locke composed his description in the *Epistola* of the church as a voluntary gathering for worship explicitly paralleled by him to a circle meeting for intellectual conversation. The imaging of one – the church – by the other – the circle of friends discussing intellectual issues – is itself suggestive of his own highly intellectualised notion of the church as eirenic and inclusive in communion, discursive, rational, and voluntary in nature, and not a little 'heretical' in the expansiveness of its intellectual commitment. Locke referred humorously in these pieces to Furly's circle as the 'heretics of the Lantern', in precisely the years in which we will see later that he was attacking the conventional definitions of the term 'heresy'. Locke's 'dry club' in the 1690s included among its members William Popple, and the Unitarian responsible for the first usage of the term 'Unitarian', Henry Hedworth. Tolerationism was simultaneously often modelled on the notion of conversations curing 'prejudices', and in many cases it seems to have been in part promoted by the effects of such conversations promoting criticisms of contemporary orthodoxies. Locke's *Essay* described and advocated 'friends' discussing matters with one as good to cure one of one's 'prejudices'.[109]

Locke's was one very important model indeed of conversation, discussion, friendship, and civility in the 'early Enlightenment'. It shared some important features with the model increasingly constructed by Pierre Bayle, who was on occasion a member of Furly's discussion circle of 'the Lantern'. Des Maizeaux, an editor of the works of Locke and Bayle, declared in his life of Bayle in the 1734 English edition of the *Dictionary* that Bayle's 'manner of exposing the faults of an adversary without bitterness' was to be contrasted with that of Jurieu, for 'Mr Bayle writes like a gentleman, and Mr Jurieu like a bigotted old woman'. The notion of 'civil correction' here – the exposing of faults without bitterness and of the writing of a gentleman – was thus central to the method of Bayle as well as to that of Locke, and celebrated about both Locke and Bayle in the early eighteenth century. As Des Maizeaux stressed in his *Life of Bayle*, Bayle had 'embellished' his extracts with 'many ingenious and delicate reflexions' which were intended to serve 'not just the learned' but the 'polite world'.[110]

But Bayle's model of scholarship and his description of intellectual discussion in the 'republic of letters' contained not merely important similarities to that of Locke, but also some rather different emphases. In the *Dictionary* and in his published works of controversy, Bayle both attempted to offer a

---

[109] Marshall, *Locke*. As John Dunn once remarked, the only notion of a just society Locke had really experienced was that of circles of intellectual conversation.

[110] Des Maizeaux, 'Life' in Bayle, *Dictionary*, i, xvii, xx.

general definition of behaviour in the 'republic of letters' and to inflect it with his own accenting of confutation in combination with civility. Where Locke might be said to have stressed toleration through civility, charity among differing views, and silence, Bayle tended to stress the reasoned demolition of others' arguments leading to their inability to claim the right to impose their beliefs on others. The universal demolition here therefore included for Bayle the demolition of the very views of a 'reasonable' Christianity which were being espoused by both Le Clerc and by Locke. According to Bayle in the *Dictionary*, in the 'republic of letters' the 'Empire of Truth and Reason is only acknowledged' and 'innocent war is waged against any one'. For Bayle, devotion to truth required placing aside even kinship and friendship if they might impede the pursuit of truth: 'This places friends on their guard against friends'; and even family members against family members – fathers against children, and fathers-in-law against sons-in-law. Bayle invoked the 'right of the sword' in his image of the 'republic of letters' as a place in which individual rights from before the construction of the republic were maintained. For Bayle, in the 'republic of letters',

Everybody there is both Sovereign and under everybody's jurisdiction. The laws of the Society have done no Prejudice there to the Independency of the State of Nature: in that respect, every particular man has the Right of the Sword, and may exercise it without asking leave of those who govern.

For Bayle, the 'sovereign power' of the 'republic of letters' had left everyone within the polity itself in their 'pre-political liberty' to write against 'mistaken authors', showing 'public faults' in someone's book. Criticism conducted in a 'civil' manner, even if it resulted in the demolition of the reputation for learning of others, was justified in the 'interests' of 'reason' and 'truth' – the 'public good' of the 'commonwealth of learning'. In his description in his *Projet* of the aims of correcting mistakes in his *Dictionary*, Bayle similarly contrasted scholars unwilling to be corrected who were wrongly dominated by their self-love with those correctly serving the 'public interest'.[111]

I have suggested that the image of the 'republic of letters' in Locke's works resonated with his own practices in conversational circles, and in part reflected his own behaviour in those conversational circles, in a kind of intellectual and cultural symbiosis of commitment and practice. Bayle's image of the republic similarly resonated both in his own primary conversational circle discussing ideas and in his works. Bayle's primary conversational circle in the Netherlands was not the convivially humorous circle of the 'heretical' Lantern of Benjamin Furly, but instead one that emphasised

---

[111] Bayle, *Dictionary*, Catius D; *idem*, *Projet*, VI, 2980; Whelan, *Anatomy*, 88, 114.

the demolition of others' arguments in a circle which held Bayle's fellow advocates of toleration and close friends, the brothers Henri Basnage de Beauval and Jacques Basnage, the publisher of Bayle's *Dictionary* and other tolerationist writings, Leers, and Adriaan Paets, son of Bayle's republican tolerationist benefactor.[112] Bayle's group for conversation seems to have cleaved to his notion of the wielding of a post-Grotian sword in discussions which focused directly on religion and politics and on arguments and reply instead of civility and silencing. Charles le Vier recorded that they

dealt freely with the most sensitive matters, such as Religion and politics. Messrs patz [Adriaan van Paets] and de Beauval were ordinarily the attackers, and Mr Basnage often had to undergo violent Battles. He did not blush in admitting that he had very much benefitted from these conversations & that they contributed to cure him of several prejudices.[113]

At the end of his life, Bayle was to remark in a joke that resonates more and more as one examines his intellectual life that he was 'a good Protestant' because he protested 'against everything anyone says or does'.[114]

Rather as Locke's works of religious interpretation and defences of toleration resonated with the ethos involved in his conversational practices and his notions of the methods to conduct intellectual discussion, Bayle's works, and most notably the *Dictionary*, resonate vibrantly with these practices. In the second volume of his 1703–7 *Reply to the Questions of a Country Gentleman*, Bayle described reason as 'better suited to pulling things down than to building them up, and better at discovering what things are not, than what they are'. Many of his works focused precisely on the alleged mistakes and errors made by others, and on the demolition by reason of any and all of their particular commitments and claims that these were reasonable. The *Dictionary* was itself intended initially as a compendium of mistakes that had been made by others; it was expanded by Bayle to become much more than that, but retained that purpose throughout. Many of its entries addressed issues in order to suggest that reason was defeated in defending any and every proposition dear to any theologian's heart, from Le Clerc's 'reasonable Christianity' through Jurieu's Trinitarian Calvinism to Bossuet's Molinist Catholicism, and on to any and all of the other major religious commitments of the day.[115]

The central purpose of this method for Bayle was to support religious toleration by suggesting that no cleric could give good reasons to back any

---

[112] Cerny, *Theology*, 87–9.
[113] C. Le Vier, 'Eloge historique de M. Basnage', IV in Cerny, *Theology*, 89.
[114] Labrousse, *Bayle*, 46.
[115] Bayle, *Réponse*, II, cxxxvii; Labrousse, *Bayle*, 61; Bayle, *Dictionary*, *passim*.

theological or ecclesiological position. As des Maizeaux described Bayle's method in his *Life* in the 1734 *Historical and Critical Dictionary*:

Being persuaded that disputes about religion, which have been the occasion of infinite disorders in the world, proceed only from the too great confidence which the Divines of all parties have in their own understanding; he undertakes to humble them, and to render them more modest and moderate, by showing that even so ridiculous a sect as that of the Manicheans can raise such objections to them concerning the origin of evil and the permission of sin, which it is impossible to answer. He even goes further, and maintains in general that human reason is more capable of refuting and destroying, than of proving and building up.

There were, stressed des Maizeaux, no 'points in divinity' against which reason does not raise 'very strong difficulties'. We will consider later the possibility that one purpose of this method for Bayle was the support of 'atheism' itself, with the alternate possibility of fideism; here, it is important to stress that its central contemporary point in the 1690s and early 1700s was the support of religious toleration, and that des Maizeaux still saw that as its central purpose four decades later.[116]

SCIENTIFIC IMPARTIALITY AND COMMUNITY, LATITUDINARIANISM, AND THE SUPPORT FOR TOLERATION IN THE REPUBLIC

At the centre of the nascent international 'republic of letters' in the early and mid-seventeenth century was 'natural philosophy' or 'science'. International intellectual circles of correspondence were maintained by figures such as Mersenne in France and Oldenburg in England, who gathered and communicated discoveries from across Europe, and Mersenne hosted a particularly important and lively international circle for intellectual discussion in person. The seventeenth century witnessed a gathering pace of scientific investigations and discoveries, and an increase in the development of an international scientific community and of national scientific academies. These activities, institutions, and discoveries combined by mid-century into a sense that the bases of knowledge were themselves being refounded, as the seventeenth century witnessed the works of Galileo and Kepler, Harvey and Sydenham, Boyle and Newton, Descartes and Hobbes, Locke, Spinoza, and Leibniz, among many others. Whether one held with many French thinkers that Cartesianism was the wave of the future, or with many British thinkers that empiricist experiment was the essential technique, the sense that

---

[116] For des Maizeaux, Bayle's purpose was that of a sceptical fideist and not an atheist: 'there are doctrines which are certainly true, to which it opposeth unanswerable objections' but one should not 'regard these' but instead oblige limited human understanding to 'captivate itself under the obedience of faith'. Reason then acts on very reasonable principles: Bayle, *Dictionary*, lxxvi.

scientific investigations were changing and extending humans' understanding of the natural world was pervasive and exciting, and stimulated a heightened lay interest in the 'natural philosophy' that was reflected in the extensive gentle and noble membership of the new scientific academies, such as the Royal Academy, and in the foundation of a series of learned journals which reviewed scientific investigations for lay contemporaries across Europe – the English *Philosophical Transactions* and the French *Journal des Savants* of the 1660s, and then the Leipzig *Acta Eruditorum* of the 1670s.[117]

Commitment to and interest in such scientific investigations were capable of many different patterns of association with the distribution of political and religious power – as the names and divergent religious and political commitments of Descartes, Hobbes, Locke, and Leibniz are alone sufficient to illustrate. But if this variety of commitments and assocations means that any general statement of the relationship between science and toleration is immediately doomed, it is nonetheless crucial to register that several major strands of scientific investigation did tend to reinforce major elements of the cause of religious toleration. Most notably, the processes of questioning were at points in this period related, both generally and specifically; some scientific explanations began to undercut important parts of the case for religious intolerance; science had a particularly strong association with Latitudinarian toleration for speculative opinions and attitudes about the conducting of discussions without dogmatism, and considerable portions of scientific investigations and the collaborative nature of the scientific community were understood as aconfessional and impartial in ways which influenced the journals and the broader 'republic of letters'. Each of these relations will now briefly be addressed.

Firstly, and most broadly, processes of questioning the received views about the natural world were often similar to processes of questioning accepted propositions of doctrinal orthodoxy, especially where both specifically challenged the philosophical underpinnings of that orthodoxy in medieval

---

[117] See, *inter alia*, R. Hahn, *The Anatomy of a Scientific Institution: The Paris Academy of Sciences* (Berkeley 1971); A. Stroup, *A Company of Scientists: Botany, Patronage and Community at the Seventeenth Century Parisian Royal Academy of Sciences* (Berkeley 1990); M. Hunter, *Establishing the New Science: The Experience of the Early Royal Society* (Suffolk 1989); *idem, Science and Society in Restoration England* (Cambridge 1981); Greengrass et al. (eds.), *Hartlib*; C. Webster, *The Great Instauration* (London 1975); Jacob, *Newtonians*; B. Shapiro, *Probability and Certainty in Seventeenth Century England* (Princeton 1983); *idem, A Culture of Fact* (Ithaca 2000); R. Iliffe, 'In the Warehouse: Privacy, Property and Priority in the Early Royal Society', *History of Science* (1992), 29–68; D. Kronick, *A History of Scientific and Technical Periodicals: The Origins and Development of the Scientific and Technical Press 1665–1790* (New Jersey 1976); R. Birn, 'Le Journal des Savants sous l'Ancien Régime', *Journal des Savants* (1965), 15–35.

scholasticism or patristic platonism. The doctrine of 'substance' was, for instance, simultaneously central to 'natural philosophy' and to the accepted understanding of doctrines such as the Trinity of three 'persons' in one divine nature or 'substance'. From Spinoza through Descartes to Locke or Leibniz, no topic was more important to epistemological investigations than the nature and apprehension of 'substance', and it is not suprising that Leibniz saw as one of the most pressing issues in Locke's account of 'substance' its potential support for anti-Trinitarianism. The sense that received opinions in religion were to be questioned and challenged was, thus, not merely generally parallel to the sense that received opinions in 'natural philosophy' were to be challenged, but the very topics which were subject to questioning within and without the orbit of doctrinal orthodoxy were often similar in specific content.[118]

Furthermore, the processes of scientific investigation itself simultaneously tended to provide 'naturalistic' rather than 'supernatural' explanations for phenomena, including arguments, for instance, that comets and eclipses were natural phenomena subject to natural laws, rather than providential signs from God. Alleged 'monsters' were increasingly treated as abnormalities caused by natural processes, rather than supernatural signs. Since we saw earlier that the understanding of such phenomena as providential signs was bound up with interconfessional disputes, with the alleged spread of 'heresy' and 'schism' in the 'Last Days', and with justification of action against 'heresy' and 'schism', the move to render such phenomena 'natural' rather than 'supernatural' crucially undercut justifications of intolerance by undercutting argument that God was signalling his providential support for a particular 'true religion' and wishing to have 'heresies' and 'schisms' punished. Naturalistic explanations were simultaneously increasingly provided for wars, famines, and diseases, undercutting interpretation of these as signs of the imminence of the apocalyptic 'Last Days'. The assault on the understanding of these phenomena as 'supernatural', providential, and apocalyptic further often involved a mockery of claims to expertise of the clergy who had interpreted God's word in support of such signs; in maintaining his support for such miraculous interventions in the 1680s, Jurieu explicitly recognised that he was opening himself up to ridicule because of the increasing public acceptance of the arguments of seventeenth-century natural philosophers.[119] Naturalistic explanations often simultaneously involved the notion that the times of belief in preceding 'supernatural' explanations were times of 'superstition' and 'ignorance' maintained by priests, and the contrasting notion that this was a time of 'enlightenment' and 'progress' in the

---

[118] Jolley, *Leibniz and Locke*; Marshall, *Locke*.   [119] Cf. also Bayle, *Pensées*, introduction.

understanding of the operation of the world, also corroding the notions of cycles of repetitive or intensified heresies in the 'Last Days'.

Next, what was called 'Latitudinarianism', not merely in England but also in Jurieu's condemnatory 1696 *Religion of a Latitudinarian* in the Netherlands, had particularly strong associations with science and with religious toleration as advanced through an expansive freedom of speculative opinions. Joseph Glanvill suggested that natural philosophic enquiry provided a remedy for religious dispute because the very processes of enquiry 'disposed men's Spirits to more calmness and modesty, charity and prudence in differences of religion, and even silences disputes there'. Sir Peter Pett, lay Latitudinarian and an early defender of religious toleration in the circles around Locke and Boyle, saw a similar major influence from discourses of science on support for the cause of toleration. In a work which defended the cause of religious toleration, the *Happy Future State*, he wrote that 'the old way of arguing about speculative points in religion with passion and loudness...is grown out of use, and a gentlemanly candour in discourse of the same with that moderate temper that men use in debating natural experiments has succeeded in its room'.[120]

Focusing on such individuals as Glanvill, in a series of works the historian of science Barbara Shapiro has particularly importantly expanded upon this kind of association, linking together support for scientific enquiry and religious Latitudinarianism in late seventeenth-century England as 'the norms of scientific and Latitudinarian discourse clearly were interdependent'. As Shapiro has put it, Latitudinarians strongly opposed the speech and behaviour 'of the dogmatist, sure of his opinions and willing to force them on others'.[121] This vision encouraged a view that much was to be learned from the cumulative enterprises of many scholars working on individual experiments and sharing the results in a conversation about science conducted with great freedom for enquiry and investigation, for challenging accepted understandings, for stressing the limitations and fallibility of human understanding, and for the promotion of the basis of such fallibility of great freedom about 'speculative' matters. As has been stressed by Henry van Leeuwen, Shapiro, and myself (in preceding work), these attitudes were expressed in general fashion by Locke in the *Essay Concerning Human Understanding*.[122] Thus, while concentration on scientific investigation in the seventeenth century could involve withdrawal from the world of religious and political disputes and a kind of political quietism that was

---

[120] J. Glanvill in Shapiro, *Culture*, 164; Pett, *Happy Future State* quoted in Goldie, 'Pett'.
[121] Shapiro, *Culture*, 163–4.
[122] Van Leeuwen, *The Problem of Certainty in English Thought* (The Hague 1963); Shapiro, *Probability and Certainty*; Marshall, *Locke*.

willing to accept an intolerant religious regime in the state, as with Descartes, or a politics capable of supporting practices of toleration but assertive of the power of the sovereign to determine religious worship for subjects, as with Hobbes, it was often instead involved with the Latitudinarian desire to redescribe religious dispute to be more like the model of scientific discussion, with support of a wide freedom of enquiry and discussion conducted with 'civility' and with a desire to clearly identify 'facts'. It was not coincidental that Le Clerc's journals extensively discussed those thinkers with whom it identified a broad 'Latitudinarian' or 'Arminian' freedom for a variety of opinions in religion – including Erasmus and Grotius – and those scientific investigators, including Boyle, whose science was particularly identified as Latitudinarian.

The scientific community was religiously diverse, and there was a strong sense in which scientific investigation was understood as aconfessional, even while it was 'religious' in its overriding purpose as it was intended to confirm the divine order of God's natural world. One was understood to be a 'Christian natural philosopher' but not a Catholic or Protestant, Calvinist or Lutheran. As Shapiro has stressed, 'religious affiliation was not important in assessing the fidelity of the scientific witness', and the English Royal Society had Catholic members and 'communicated regularly with continental Roman Catholic virtuosi'. It even sought the information that could be provided by Catholic missionaries who were 'curious and philosophically given'. Many 'natural philosophers' saw concentration on their 'scientific' investigations as a way to build a cosmopolitan and ecumenical discourse across confessional lines at a time of bitter religious disputes between Catholics and Protestants and amongst the various varieties of Protestantism. Intellectual circles discussing 'science' across national boundaries often avowedly included many of different religious commitments, and consciously contrasted the intellectual co-operation at the centre of their circles with the bitter religious disputes preoccupying many of their contemporaries. The group which gathered to discuss science at Wadham College, Oxford, and the Royal Society were among many such scientific organisations which eschewed religious topics and disputes and stressed religious inclusiveness in membership.[123]

The *Philosophical Transactions* in England and the *Journal des Savants* in France, which summarised for an interested lay audience new discoveries and questioning in 'natural philosophy', were explicitly referred to as the models for the founding in the 1680s in the Netherlands of Pierre Bayle's *Nouvelles*, Jean Le Clerc's *Bibliothèque universelle*, and Henri Basnage de

[123] Shapiro, *Culture*, 123–4, 163.

Beauval's *Histoire des Ouvrages des Savans*. These later journals included summaries of scientific experiment and enquiry and extended to all of the topics of intellectual endeavour the notion of an international community of scholars communicating their discoveries and the questioning of received orthodoxies to an interested and extensive lay public. The structure of appeal of these journals to the laity to judge of matters that had formerly been primarily the province of clerical explanation made this lay public active participants in a process of education and enquiry challenging to theological orthodoxy and to the status of the clergy as experts. There was a substantial attempt to take the model of the *Philosophical Transactions* and the *Journal des Scavans* in their multiconfessional and aconfessional stance as the basis for the journals of the 'republic of letters' of the 1680s. Bayle and Le Clerc explicitly paid homage to the *Journal* and to the *Philosophical Transactions* as models for their journals, even as they sought to expand their intellectual enterprise considerably. Shapiro has recently emphasised in *A Culture of Fact* the centrality of 'impartiality' and verification by assessment of the 'credibility' of 'witnesses' within claims made in the seventeenth-century scientific community. Impartiality was central to the stated ethos of the new journals of the 1680s. Bayle, Le Clerc, and Basnage de Beauval all proclaimed that their journals would be aconfessional, that they would discuss ideas on their merits, and that they would state and summarise in the best light the arguments of Catholic and Protestant works alike. Le Clerc declared in the first issue of the *Bibliothèque universelle* that his journal would report 'without prejudice the views of all Christian societies and the reasons why their authors defend them'. Bayle celebrated the location of his journal in the 'republic of letters' in the physical space of the Netherlands as propitious because the Netherlands was unusual in the level of publication and circulation of the works of both Catholics and Protestants. He explicitly stressed that he would attempt to imitate the practices of the Netherlands as a country of free discussion of ideas and freedom of the press in his practices in the *Nouvelles*. And in the first issue in 1684, in the course of promising to review Catholic and Protestant books impartially and to provide *éloges* of great men in the republic, Bayle declared:

Here it is a question not of religion, but of learning. We must therefore lay aside all those terms which divide men into factions, and consider that point that unites them, which is the quality of being an illustrious man in the Republic of Letters.[124]

---

[124] Daston, 'Ideal', 374; Goldgar, *Impolite*, 184; Bayle, *Nouvelles* (1684), preface; Le Clerc, *Bibliothèque universelle*, I, preface; Israel, *Radical*, 146. The *Journal de Trévoux* was clear in opposition, in saying it would be neutral 'except when it concerns Religion, good morals, or the State: in which it is not permitted to be neutral': Goldgar, *Impolite*, 185.

The editors of the journals did not merely protest their impartiality; they made significant attempts to review Catholic as well as Protestant works and to be fair to these works in their summaries and reviews, particularly in those cases where Catholic works were on issues unrelated to intolerance. The journals often included sections identifying the works reviewed as Protestant or as Catholic to underline their rigorously religiously 'impartial' and thus 'scholarly' review. Here, then, were practices reflecting the interconfessional scholarly and especially 'scientific' communities of the seventeenth century, and heading towards the ethos perhaps expressed best in the *Bibliothèque italique* of 1727, that

justice, equity and politeness, whose rules people of letters must follow, more exactly than anyone, are so opposed to partiality, that an Author delivered over to this base passion is surely sullied in the spirit of *honnêtes* people of all Communions.[125]

Le Clerc defined his practice as editor 'of relating scrupulously the different points of view'. In giving his comments on the earliest edition of the *Nouvelles* to Bayle, Le Clerc recorded that Bayle was thought to have been too partial, and that it was best to give as straightforward and accurate an account of the ideas of a text as was possible in order to let readers judge for themselves, and not to make the reviewers' commentary the focus of the review. Such were *'fidèles extraits'*. It was this model which Le Clerc attempted to follow in most of his reviews. Bayle responded to such criticism by toning down his reviews and thus approaching more closely to a kind of scholarly impartiality. As early as the second issue of the 1685 *Nouvelles*, Bayle reported that he had been 'reliably warned that people do not like his taking sides in the matters of which he speaks, and that people would prefer that he confine himself in the limits of a disinterested Historian, who is sparing with his Reflections'. He thereafter attempted to some degree to follow the advice. As he did so, his reviews and summaries became closer to those of an impartial or neutral editor.[126] Le Clerc was seen as erring on the other side: Lenfant wrote to Le Clerc in 1687 that people found his extracts 'too dry' and recommended a middle ground between 'judging as Mr Bayle does, and not judging as you do. It seems to me too that one can judge without taking sides. And people even believe that it will be impossible for you to keep this promise of not judging'. Le Clerc was to respond by

---

[125] Goldgar, *Impolite*, 99.
[126] See p. 494 and n. 124 above; *Nouvelles* cited in Goldgar, *Impolite*, 98.

including at times more overt commentary, but he usually stayed close to his initial notion of *'fidèles extraits'*.[127]

An attempt to distinguish Catholic ideas on many issues from Catholic ideas on toleration was crucial to support in journals of the 'republic of letters' for the notion that many Roman Catholics in their beliefs other than those related to intolerance and political obedience were tolerable and important contributors to the republic. Such an attitude distinguished many individual Catholics from the recent intolerant actions of the Catholic Church. The tolerationist authors of the journals of the republic understood that intolerance was substantial in the Protestant churches of their day and similarly fostered a distinction between those who were intolerant in many different denominations and those who were tolerant in many different denominations. There was a firm distinction made by many of the tolerationist writers between 'popery', a term used to identify a religious affliction of many in different denominations who wished to impose their beliefs on others by using force, and Roman Catholicism. Limborch and Locke in the 1690s were frequently to note that 'popery' existed in all communions, as did good men.[128]

But there was in the 1680s a considerable tension between the attempt to be aconfessional or multiconfessional, and a series of Protestant or tolerationist commitments. The summarising of many accounts of contemporary religious persecution of Protestants by Catholics in the wake of the Revocation of the Edict of Nantes was a particularly prominent part of the journals, two of which were, after all, edited by Huguenot refugees who had fled into exile. Summarising such works as Bayle's own *Wholly Catholic France*, Jacques Basnage's *Considerations on the Condition of Those Who Have Fallen* (1686), reviewed by Bayle in the April 1686 *Nouvelles*, and his *Reply* to Bossuet's *Pastoral Letter* (1686), reviewed by Bayle in the October 1686 *Nouvelles*, or Daillon's *Examination of the Oppression of Protestants in France* (1687), reviewed in the *Bibliothèque universelle* in 1687 on the pages that led in to the review of part of Bayle's *Philosophical Commentary*, these journals themselves repeatedly stressed that brutal violence enforced the Revocation of the Edict of Nantes, in outlining the reports in these works of force used by dragoons to coerce profession of Catholicism and of 'victims' dragged 'to the altar' against their will. And the journals summarised, *inter alia*, Claude's and Basnage's arguments for toleration, including: that faith is a gift of God; that violence causes hypocrisy or 'atheism'; and that the Roman Catholic Church was 'very criminal' in supporting this persecution because it 'put

---

[127] Goldgar, *Impolite*, 112–13; Le Clerc, *Bibliothèque universelle* (1686–91).
[128] On Protestant intolerance, *Histoire* (November 1687), 372–92; *Nouvelles* (1686), 363–84; *Bibliothèque*, v (1687), 334–52; Marshall, *Locke*; Locke, *Correspondence*, 2498, 2516.

a King in place of God who alone has empire over conscience'. These works often asserted these positions in combination with the notion that the Roman Catholic Church was idolatrous and that salvation was not possible within it.[129] The journalists even at points mentioned their own works in the course of their reviews; Bayle, for instance, drew readers' attention to his own just published *State of Wholly Catholic France* in reviewing Claude's *Plaintes* in 1686.[130] Moreover, these authors often reviewed in their journals the specific works which they also attacked in their own tolerationist writings, and in so doing used some of the same arguments against them; Bayle for instance not merely made Brueys' *Reply* to Claude's *Plaintes* a major target in his *Philosophical Commentary*, but he also gave the work an unfavourable multi-page review in the *Nouvelles*, condemning the choice offered by Catholicism of converting under the pressure of dragoons or being imprisoned perpetually.[131]

The review in these journals of many works on the late patristic period onwards made clear that intolerance had a substantial history in the Catholic Church, and the works on the Inquisition which were issued in the late 1680s and early 1690s received significant notices in the journals, further strongly identifiying Catholicism, the Inquisition, and intolerance, and the opposition of the journals to the Inquisition. Many of the works reviewed discussed particularly the actions of the Catholic Church against the Albigensians and Waldensians and now against Protestants. In 1687, the *Histoire des Ouvrages des Savans* reviewed works on: martyrology and the punishment of heretics; Nicodemite strategies of professing what one was forced to profess; Ussher's arguments on schism; the debate between Burnet and Varillas on heresy and schism and history; works on the unity of the church; and Penn's *Good Advice to the Church of England*.[132] Claiming to be international and interconfessionally impartial, all three of the journals of the 1680s were quickly banned in France and condemned in Rome. The *Mémoires de Trévoux* was to be founded in Jesuit hands in the early eighteenth century in order to provide an alternative journal to defend the

---

[129] *Bibliothèque universelle*, V (1687), 471–5; Bayle, *Nouvelles* (November 1685), 1219–27; (February 1686), 230–1; (April 1686) article 8; (May 1686), 516–32; *Histoire* (February 1689), 560–70; Hazard, *European Mind*, 84; Cerny, *Theology*, 71–9.

[130] Bayle, *Nouvelles* (May 1686), 516–32, at 520.

[131] Bayle, *Nouvelles* (August 1686), 863–83, esp. 864–5; Bost, *Un 'intellectuel'*, 48–9.

[132] Bernard, *Bibliothèque universelle*, XX (1691), 197–227; XXIII, 361–409; Bayle, *Nouvelles*, (June 1686), 719–22; *Histoire des Ouvrages* (1687), article 2; V, 87ff., 100ff., 106ff., 112ff., 161–72, 180ff., 186ff., 258–67, 372ff., 479; (May 1693), 496–511; (Jan 1694), 229–49; *Acta Eruditorum* (April 1693), 169–76; (July 1693), 323–33.

Catholic faith against the Protestantism and 'heterodoxy' of these allegedly 'impartial' journals.[133]

If 'natural philosophy' had partly been concentrated upon by many scholars in the seventeenth century precisely because its discussion allowed them to set aside religious disputes, the expansion of scholarly enquiries covered by the journals of the 1680s to include survey of interconfessional polemic, patristic scholarship, and religious toleration, placed severe strain on the notion of an impartial review or the ability to avoid religious disputation. The act of selecting works to review often privileged a particular religious viewpoint, as Catholic works were reviewed less frequently than Protestant works in these journals, and as works defending intolerance were reviewed less frequently than works defending toleration. Le Clerc reviewed 'Arminian' works with such frequency that Bayle commented sourly that the first editions of the *Bibliothèque* revealed the folly of Le Clerc's own views. And Le Clerc included discussions of the debates between Arminians and Contra-Remonstrants in the early seventeenth century which condemned Contra-Remonstrant intolerance and declared Grotius and Uittenbogaert tolerationist. The opening review of Le Clerc's *Bibliothèque*, symbolically and revealingly, was of Grotius' works, thus celebrating an author who could be read in an anti-tolerationist vein, but whom Le Clerc chose to read in tolerationist fashion. Le Clerc contributed a host of reviews to the pages of his *Bibliothèque* which undercut contemporary Calvinist orthodoxy by suggesting that the early church had been anti-Calvinist and anti-Augustinian in its understanding of free will. He contributed many further reviews and a series of *Lives* of the Fathers which suggested cumulatively that many of the Fathers had intruded explications and explanations of doctrines and of the Scriptural text which were based on false and often meaningless theology. As he did so, he undermined the foundations not merely of the Dutch Reformed and Huguenot confessions of faith, but also much that was taken for orthodox in the Anglican articles and in contemporary explications of Trinitarianism. Many of Le Clerc's pieces were then published separately as individual works in their own right.[134]

Bayle tended to review more orthodox Calvinist works, and more works whose implications could very easily be taken as 'libertine'. Bayle's opening review of *Nouvelles* was of van Dale's *De Oraculis ethnicorum*, a work whose explicit attack was on the history of pagan cheats and impostures, but which could easily be seen – and should unquestionably be seen – as an attack on

---

[133] Hazard, *European Mind*, 87.
[134] For instance, Le Clerc, *Bibliothèque universelle*, x (September 1688), 379–463; xiv (1689), 139–398; J. Le Clerc, *The Lives of the Primitive Fathers* (London 1701).

Catholic imposition, and arguably on Christian imposition. Locke read *De Oraculis ethnicorum* in 1683, taking extensive notes from it in one of his journals, and we noted earlier that he supplied Fontenelle's redactive *History* to his anti-Catholic tolerationist friend Sir Walter Yonge. Among three rapidly produced English translations of Fontenelle was one which suggested that contemporaries were indeed reading it in a 'libertine' manner – a translation by the 'libertine' playwright Aphra Behn. Hazard's comment on the journals of such 'journalists' in these years remains largely accurate in terms of their location on the theological spectrum of the day: they were 'organs of nonconformity...[and]... mouthpieces of heterodoxy'.[135]

Even when Le Clerc or Bayle attempted to be impartial in the content of a review, and in the review of works defending and defining Catholic and Calvinist orthodoxy, the very act of *discussing* the arguments of every kind of Christian from Catholic to Socinian was explicitly tolerationist in ethos. Most contemporary Catholics and 'magisterial Reformation' Protestants did not believe that one should even read or discuss Socinian thought; the *Nouvelles* and *Bibliothèque universelle* both reviewed Socinian works. As such, the very act of reviewing Socinian thought was tolerationist, even if one explicitly criticised Socinian thought in the review itself, as Bayle did in his comments on Socinianism in the *Nouvelles* and Le Clerc at points did in the *Bibliothèque universelle*; and even such criticisms could serve the cause of toleration, as when Bernard criticised Socinians for their intolerance towards Francis David, the Socinian who had refused to adore Christ.[136] Moreover, when Bayle published in the *Nouvelles* a new attempt by Jurieu (anonymously) to explicate the doctrine of the Trinity and then published in the next issue a response to this argument which mocked the explication, the net effect was to open the Trinity itself to further critical debate and questioning from a Socinian direction as the author, perhaps Aubert, gleefully used the opportunity to ridicule Jurieu and Trinitarianism.[137]

When it was founded as the Catholic journal to maintain the faith in the early eighteenth century, the Catholic Parisian *Journal de Trévoux* noted explicitly that it was not legitimate to be 'neutral' in matters of 'religion', and it linked such 'indifference' directly to support for toleration. Bayle devoted an article of the *Nouvelles* to defence of the very act of

---

[135] Israel, *Radical*, ch. 20; Goldgar, *Impolite*, 113; Hazard, *European Mind*, 85–6.

[136] For instance, *Bibliothèque universelle*, ɪɪ, 34ff., 306ff.; ɪɪɪ, 543ff; v, 44; xxɪv (January 1693), 1–40; *Nouvelles*, ɪ (June 1684), 395–402; ɪɪɪ (September 1684), 721–31; v (May 1685) 566–7; *Histoire* (April 1692), 367–90.

[137] Bayle, *Nouvelles*, ɪv (July 1685), 727–45; v (August 1685), 923–9; Morman, *Aubert*, 189–92.

publishing and discussing Socinian works, and as he did so he sounded a clarion call for discussion of ideas that was to echo down through the Enlightenment. In article 9 of the July 1685 *Nouvelles*, entitled 'Reflexions sur la tolérance des livres hérétiques', an article which explicitly defended the publication and discussion of Socinian works, Bayle associated attempts to suppress Socinian works with the practices of the Inquisition.[138]

The process of reviewing in these journals a variety of religious arguments intended to be read by an enlightened laity and to be considered by them in a process of critical engagement of their reason to judge involved the journals in a degree of openmindedness and eclecticism that may be associated with the cause of toleration. Peter Gay has written that religious toleration had two intellectual corollaries in the Enlightenment: relativism and eclecticism. While this judgment is too summary, Gay does point to an important feature of these journals in noting that the sense that 'no system has the whole truth, and most systems have some truth' promoted by these journals often involved as a corollary attitude that 'discriminating selection among systems is the only valid procedure' and placed readers in a position of judging for themselves.[139] Here, Bayle's contributions to his journal in his years as editor from 1684 to 1687 involved a significant parallel to a stress in his overtly tolerationist works, such as the *Philosophical Commentary*, on being able to learn from many individuals of divergent backgrounds – religiously, philosophically, and politically. Here, Bayle may be said to have been expressing in his journal the virtue of open-mindedness and openness to others, a willingness to listen and learn, and curiosity. These are all attitudes which Michael Walzer has identified in *On Toleration* as one of five kinds of attitudes of tolerance.[140] Intended to bring reviews of new publications to the thousands of 'thinking' readers who were not professionally 'savants' (as Bayle put it to Le Clerc), who as a result of reading the works of the 'republic of letters' were members of an 'enlightened age', and who were explicitly to be rendered by this help an enlightened laity capable of challenging their clerics, as Le Clerc put it in the *Bibliothèque choisie*, these journals were tolerationist.

Finally, the journals frequently reviewed the newest works on toleration itself. By 1703, Le Clerc wrote in the *Bibliothèque choisie* that there was 'nothing of which people speak more today than tolerance and the principles of civil society'. Le Clerc's *Bibliothèque universelle*, Bayle's

---

[138] Bayle, *Nouvelles* (July 1685), 786–92, esp. 789; Hazard, *European Mind*, 101.
[139] P. Gay, *The Enlightenment, I: The Rise of Modern Paganism* (New York 1967), 163.
[140] M. Walzer, *On Toleration* (Yale 1997); cf. J. C. Laursen, 'Orientation', in Laursen (ed.), *Religious Toleration* (New York 1999), 2–5.

Nouvelles, and Basnage de Beauval's *Histoire des Ouvrages des Savans* all
very frequently devoted reviews to toleration as an issue, reviewing books
under section titles as 'La réunion et La tolérance' in a 1690 issue of the
Bibliothèque, to take just one example.[141] Moreover, by reviewing the
major works of political and moral philosophers on the issue of toleration, the journals themselves caused authors such as Pufendorf to write
new works on the issue of toleration and thereby not merely publicised
existing works on toleration but expanded the very terms of debate. In
1688, Le Clerc criticised in the *Bibliothèque* Pufendorf's *Introductio ad
Historiam praecipuorum regnorum...in Europa* for having defended the
necessity of a uniform religious establishment to peace in the state; Le
Clerc countered that religious pluralism was permissible in the state.
Stung by this journal criticism, Pufendorf issued a short pamphlet in
reply, the *Eclaircissemens de quelques endroits du Tome VIII. Samuelis
Pufendorfi Epistolae duae super Censura in Ephemeridibus eruditorum
Parisiensibus et Biblioteca Universali*, leading Le Clerc to then reply in the
journal, on the basis of the example of Holland, where true politics was
said to accord very well with 'Reason and Religion', that people must not
maltreat each other for opinions and that under toleration they did not
maltreat others.[142]

Perhaps most importantly of all, the journals often reviewed the
tolerationist works of their fellow journalists, fellow members of intellectual
circles for conversation, and correspondents about toleration. Thus,
for example, Le Clerc's journals reviewed the works of Locke, Limborch,
Burnet, Le Cène, Papin, Strimesius, Allix, Bayle, and the Basnage brothers
in addition to the works of Le Clerc himself. Bayle's and then Basnage's
journal similarly reviewed almost all of those just named. The reviews were
themselves written by others among these very individuals, by their close
associates, or by the authors themselves. And indicating the function of
publicising works that readers should then wish to obtain, the *Histoire des
Ouvrages des Savans*, published by Leers, told readers that he carried all of
the books reviewed in the journal. These reviews usually summarised the
major arguments of the works. Every one of the arguments which we will
now examine in Chapters 17 to 22 were discussed and summarised in the

---

[141] Dodge, *Political*, 172; Le Clerc, *Bibliothèque universelle*, XVIII (1690), 284–96. This
reviewed the *Projet de Réunion entre les protestans de la Grand Bretagne* (1689); the
Apologie pour les vrais tolérans (1690).
[142] Le Clerc, *Bibliothèque universelle* (1689), 472–86; (1688), 249–56; M. Bots, 'Le Plaidoyer
des journalistes de Hollande pour la tolérance' in *De l'humanisme*, 547–59; D. Doring,
'Samuel von Pufendorf and Toleration' in Laursen (ed.), *Beyond the Persecuting Society*
(Pennsylvania 1998); S. Zurbuchen, 'From Denominationalism to Enlightenment' in
Laursen (ed.), *Religious Toleration*, 191–209.

journals. Rather than engage in a repetitive rendition of such summaries and reviews here, since these arguments are to be the focus of our attention for the vast majority of the remainder of this book, we can now turn our full attention to the case for religious toleration made in the 'early Enlightenment'.[143]

[143] See most notably *Bibliothèque universelle*, V (1687), 212–27 (reviewing Le Cène's *Conversations*); III (1686), 335–60 and (1687), 475–81 (reviewing Bayle's *Commentaire*); (1689), 402–12 (reviewing Locke's *Epistola*); (1690), 365–91 (reviewing Locke's *Second Letter*); *Histoire*, I, (September 1687), 112–16 (reviewing Burnet's *De Mortibus*); II, 378–86; 529–40 (on Bayle's *Supplement*); (September 1689), 20–6 (reviewing Locke's *Epistola*); X, 24–39 (on Locke's *Third Letter*); (January 1696), 228–45 (on Basnage's *Traité*); (November 1696), 108–28 (on Saurin); *Nouvelles*, I (June 1684), 420–23 (on *Tolérance*); (October 1685), 1082–95 (reviewing van Paets' *De nuperis Angliae motibus Epistola, in qua diversorum a publica Religione circa Divina sentientium disseritur tolerantia*); cf. Goldgar, *Impolite*, 70.

17

Political and economic arguments for religious toleration in the 1680s and 1690s

Many of the advocates of religious toleration whose associations in the 1680s and 1690s we traced in the last chapter argued that magistrates were to use force to preserve society and to punish those who injured others, and that as forms of worship and religious belief neither threatened the peace and welfare of society, nor harmed others' rights or interests, they were to be tolerated.[1] Gilbert Burnet argued in his extensive preface to his 1687 edition of Lactantius' *Relation of the Death of the Primitive Persecutors* that others in society simply had no 'interest' in the belief and worship of their neighbours, as

those Actions which concern humane Society, belong indeed to the Authority of the Magistrate; but...our thoughts, with relation to God, and such Actions as arise out of those thoughts, and in which others have no interest, are God's immediate Province.

For Burnet, a magistrate imposing religion 'breaks in upon God's propriety, and upon that essential right of humane nature, of worshipping God according to our conviction, which is in us Antecedent to all humane Government, and can never become subject to it'. Johann Crell's *Vindication of Liberty of Religion*, republished by Charles Le Cène in his 1687 *Conversations*, argued that whoever obeyed the rules of civil society and did not disturb the peace should not be punished. Thieves were to be punished since they invaded other men's rights and disturbed 'the peace and tranquillity of other men', but those of other religions who lived peaceably with other men and did not commit anything against 'the laws of civil society' deserved to be tolerated.[2] Aubert's 1684 *Pacific Protestant* argued that magistrates should 'tolerate in

---

[1] For notions of liberty through 'harmlessness' as central to 'classical liberalism', see, J. Rawls, *A Theory of Justice* (Harvard 1971); Alan Ryan, 'Liberalism' in R. Gordon (ed.), *A Companion to Contemporary Political Philosophy* (Blackwell 1993).

[2] Burnet (ed.), *Death*, preface, 17–18; Crell, *Vindication of Liberty*, 11, 13; C. Le Cène, *Conversations*, 225–6, 230. To maintain near-contemporary English idiomatic translation, I generally quote throughout from the 1646 English translation, of Crell's *Vindication of Liberty*; Le Cène's translation into French was very close to this 1646 translation on the quoted points.

the commonwealth and in the state all kinds of people of whatever religion they may be, whatever heresy they may uphold, provided it does not ruin the society or the foundations of the state'.[3] The Arminian-educated magistrate and Bayle's patron Adriaan van Paets' *De nuperis Angliae*, published in Latin in 1685 and in French by Bayle in 1686, expressed his horror for the 'barbarities and cruelties' founded on claims that magistrates were to promote by force the 'eternal felicity' of their subjects and treat those of different religions as criminals, and stressed that magistrates should use force only for things which preserved this life.[4]

For Bayle in the 1686 *Philosophical Commentary*, the 'Right with which Princes are invested' was that 'of punishing with the sword those who exercise violence against their Neighbour, and who destroy the publick Security which every one ought to enjoy under the Protection of the Laws'. The magistrate was empowered to punish 'all such as injure their Neighbour...in his Person or Estate or Honor'. Bayle was adamant: 'every private person who does wrong to his Neighbour, who smites him, who robs him of his Goods, who forces him to Actions which he has an abhorrence for, is ipso facto guilty of the Violation of the Fundamental Laws of the Commonwealth'. A magistrate who ordered goods taken from his subjects for religious reasons was, for Bayle in the *Philosophical Commentary* and its 1687 *Third Part*, guilty of 'robbery' and of an 'abuse of that power with which God has entrusted him'. Princes for Bayle should never 'disturb any one in the possession of that Estate which he's come honestly by, and which he's entitled to by the municipal Laws, at least unless the urgent Occasions of the State require'. It was 'in the Hypothesis of Toleration' that Bayle found magisterial force applied properly 'because then we might say, that righteous Laws are such as tend to the Advantage of the State and of Religion, by means suited and proportion'd to the Natures of each' with religion 'promoted only by Instruction and Persuasion; and the publick Good of the state only by the Punishment of those, who won't suffer their Fellow-Citizens to live in quiet'.[5]

Locke's *Letter Concerning Toleration*, which Bayle recommended in the *Dictionary* to be read on toleration alongside his own *Philosophical Commentary*, declared that 'The commonwealth' was constituted only for

[3] Aubert de Versé, *Le Protestant pacifique*, 1–2; Morman, *Aubert*, 218. In quotations from Aubert's works throughout, as here, I have generally utilised Morman's translations of Aubert.
[4] van Paets, *Lettre*, 9–14.
[5] Bayle, *Philosophical Commentary* (1708), 248–9 (*Philosophical Commentary*, ed. Tannenbaum, 138; *De la tolérance: Commentaire philosophique*, ed. Gros (Paris 1992) (hereafter cited as *Commentaire philosophique*), 261–2), 375, 387–8, 392, 445–9, 451, 460; Bayle, *OD*, II, 446, 449, 450, 464, 466. Quotations of the *Philosophical Commentary* are throughout generally taken from the 1708 English translation, with occasional brief discussion of significant variations in meaning.

the 'procuring, preserving and advancing' of 'civil interests'. Such civil interests were the 'life, liberty, health, and indolency of body; and the possession of outward things'. The 'sole reason' for a man to enter into civil society was, for Locke, 'temporal good and outward prosperity'. In the *Letter*, Locke stressed that people were not forced to be rich or healthy. He took it as understood that in 'private domestic affairs, in the management of estates' everyone had to be left to follow their own course unless this was harmful to others or society; for Locke, religious worship was similarly essentially a private affair of the individual, a commerce between that individual and God. The responsibility for correct employment of an individual's spiritual estate was no more subject to public oversight than the correct employment of his financial or physiological estate.[6]

For Bayle, most theological doctrines were simply opinions which did not challenge the welfare of societies, and such opinions were in 'no way prejudicial, as sometimes Actions are, to the Prosperity, Power and Quiet of a State'.[7] Aubert argued that 'speculative' opinions deserved toleration, firmly distinguishing someone who preached 'heresy' in things which were 'purely speculative' from one who taught maxims destructive to the society.[8] Limborch's 1686 *Theologia Christiana* agreed: holding an 'error' in opinion did not disturb the public peace nor rob another of his possessions, and so was not subject to magisterial force. Limborch was here reiterating the argument which was made earlier by Episcopius, whose works he edited for publication.[9] Locke had argued since his 1667 'Essay on Toleration' that 'Speculative' opinions in their nature did not 'disturb the state or inconvenience my neighbour', and that a different manner of worship could not 'make me either the worse subject to my prince or worse neighbour to my fellow-subject', concluding that these had an 'absolute and universal right to toleration'. Locke maintained the same positions in his *Letter Concerning Toleration*, written initially for Limborch. For Locke, there was no 'harm' offered to another from one's use of a ceremony in worship, and where there

---

[6] Locke, *Letter* in *Works* (1794), v, 10, 22, 43, and *passim*; Bayle, *Dictionary*, Sanctesius; cf. Marshall, *Locke*. Locke's *Letter* is generally quoted throughout from the Popple translation included in Locke's *Works* (which Locke defended in the succeeding *Letters*, and which generally conveys his meaning well), with occasional discussions of and references to Locke's Latin original as published by Klibansky and Gough.

[7] Bayle, *Philosophical Commentary* (1708), 393–4; *idem*, OD, II, 451.

[8] Aubert de Versé, *Protestant*, *passim*, esp. 12; *idem*, *Traité*; Bayle, *Dictionary*, Sanctesius; Morman, *Aubert*, ch. 4.

[9] Limborch, *Theologia Christiana* (1700), 834, tr. as *Compleat System* (1706), 991. To maintain contemporary English idioms, I generally quote throughout from Jones' good (if at times reorganised or compressed) translation as *Compleat System* (on a significant variation, see below n.69).

was no injury to any individual or threat to peace and the good of the society, an act was not to be forbidden by the magistrate. According to Locke:

The magistrate ought not to forbid the preaching or professing of any speculative opinions in any church, because they have no manner of relation to the civil rights of the subjects. If a Roman Catholic believe that to be really the body of Christ, which another man calls bread, he does no injury thereby to his neighbour...The power of the magistrate, and the estates of the people, may be equally secure, whether any man believe these things or no.

For Locke, that an individual was headed towards perdition did not 'harm' another, and 'Neither the use, nor the omission of any ceremonies in those religious assemblies, does either advantage or prejudice the life, liberty, or estate, of any man'.[10]

For many of these tolerationist authors, magistrates were not to enforce morality except as necessary to prevent harm and threats to the peace and security of the society. Holding that many magistrates and many anti-tolerationist writers themselves recognised that magisterial duties to enforce morality were circumscribed, tolerationist authors emphasised the incongruity of the magisterial suppression of relatively unimportant religious opinions while magistrates left alone that much more important 'moral' part of religion. And they emphasised that allowance of 'heresy' did not imply its approval any more than allowance of immorality implied its approval. Van Paets assaulted as inappropriate those who neglected morality and made piety consist solely in 'conservation of dogmas'. He stressed the corrupt motivations of those who sought to please God by attacking others as 'heretics' instead of mortifying their passions.[11] Le Cène's *Conversations* republished Crell's argument in the *Vindication* that under persecution 'indemnity' and 'immunity' were granted to all who were 'drunken and covetous', and that 'harlots' were not prosecuted, without magistrates thereby approving of these. The argument often cited from Gratian in the seventeenth century, that those things you did not condemn when in your power you therefore approved of, met the reply that those whom magistrates 'did not suppress by force' were not therefore 'approved of'. Indemnity and immunity was, for instance, granted to all who were 'drunken' and 'covetous' without thereby approving of such behaviour and individuals. Liberty of religion for 'heretics' similarly did not require approval, but only 'not hindering' from 'attending religion...exercising, professing, defending and endeavouring to propagate it without any violence'.[12] Against the hereticidal doctrine that heretics deserved to be put to death by the magistrate because of their influence on others, Limborch's *Theologia Christiana* questioned: if so,

---

[10] Locke, *Political Essays*, 136–9; Locke, *Letter* in *Works*, 30, 40; Marshall, *Locke*, ch. 2, 8.
[11] Van Paets, *Lettre*, 7.
[12] Crell, *Vindication*, 12–13, 14–15, 17–18; Le Cène, *Conversations*, 231–2, 233–4, 236.

'why are not the covetous, the whoremongers, put to death, who by their examples do a great deal of mischief'?[13] Aubert argued in the *Treatise* that sins such as fornication, drunkenness, and debauchery were not punished by the magistrate even though they were clearly wicked. And in his *Pacific Protestant*, he was clear that magistrates had the power needed for the 'conservation' of the commonwealth but not over all 'morals'.[14] Bayle argued similarly in the *Philosophical Commentary* that for conversion of a 'young Rake' God could 'make use of a blow' or reduce him 'to beggary' in order to make him think 'upon things above', but that 'Mutilation, Calumnys, Imprisonment' should not be employed against these young rakes 'who transgressing no municipal Law of the State, are not justly punishable by the Magistrate'. Bayle noted that anti-tolerationists did not say that the magistrate should persecute 'a Gamester…a Whoremonger…a Drunkard'. He lambasted the current persecution of Protestants as a 'ridiculous' contest only for 'opinions' by pointing out that no dragoon in France was involved in a 'crusade for the Reformation of Manners' and that no 'convertist of manners' had called for the use of magisterial force against 'Luxury, Evilspeaking, Gaming, Fornication, Leud Discourse etc.' Bayle argued at one point that in fact there was more reason for punishment of the debauched and prodigal, since this could be practised 'for the good of society'; even then, however, for Bayle, rulers would not have the 'same right' over opinions since these did not have the same effect on society.[15]

As early as his 1667 'Essay on Toleration', Locke had argued that magistrates were not to force individuals to be healthy or wealthy, and that they should enforce morality only in those areas where it caused injustice and injury and threatened security. The *Letter Concerning Toleration* stressed that no one argued that magistrates should punish covetousness and idleness, even though they were sins, since they were 'not prejudicial to other men's rights, nor do they break the public peace of societies'. For Locke, 'it does not belong unto the magistrate to make use of his sword in punishing everything, indifferently, that he takes to be a sin against God'. Locke suggested that 'nobody corrects a spendthrift for consuming his substance in taverns'. Locke's *Second* and *Third Letters* of 1690 and 1692 reiterated the point, but under assault from Jonas Proast for promoting 'epicurism', and in the context of the increasing campaign for 'moral reformation' and of edicts against 'vicious, debauched, and profane persons' supported by his

---

[13] Limborch, *Compleat System*, 992; *idem, Theologia Christiana* (1700), 834.

[14] Aubert de Versé, *Traité*, 29–33; *idem, Protestant*, 12–13; Morman, *Aubert*, 226–7.

[15] Bayle, *Philosophical Commentary* (1708), 171–2 (*Philosophical Commentary*, ed. Tannenbaum, 99; *Commentaire philosophique*, 196–7); 393–4, 395–6; *idem, OD*, II, 450, 451.

Latitudinarian associates in the early 1690s, Locke increasingly came to stress in these *Letters* the magisterial promotion of a 'good life', and that magistrates should hinder the practices to which 'men's lusts' carried them. He argued in the *Second* and *Third Letters* that magistrates could act against 'luxury and debauchery', and he advocated 'severities against drunkenness, lasciviousness, and all sorts of debauchery'. As an adviser on the Poor Law in the 1690s, Locke recommended suppression of alehouses and attributed multiplication of the poor to the 'relaxation of discipline' and 'corruption of manners'. Having thus moved increasingly in his tolerationist writings towards magisterial action against such 'immorality' as 'drunkeneness' and 'debauchery', the notion that there were in fact greater reasons to act magisterially against immorality than against speculative opinions and religious worship voiced also by Bayle came to preponderate in Locke's own arguments. Again like Bayle, Locke was clear – even when he came to stress in the 1690s that there might be good reasons for magistrates to thus enforce such morality – that there were no such good reasons for a magistrate to act to enforce religious worship and speculative opinions.[16]

Anti-tolerationists very often pointed to the Mosaic theocracy as their central precedent for Christian magistracy. Bayle held in reply that the Mosaic theocracy was *sui generis*. While Moses and Elias had indeed acted against 'false prophets' and had punished them with death, this was not a precedent for Christian rulers. According to Bayle, Moses had had a special revelation of wonders and miracles, and Elias had probably had a special revelation that those he punished acted out of malice and so had deserved punishment, but it was impossible for other rulers lacking such individual inspiration to know others' motivations. Moreover, in Israel, religious laws were the 'fundamental laws of their commonwealth', and persuading anyone to worship another divinity than that of the state involved an 'overt act of high treason', an 'attempt of rebellion against the sovereign magistrate'.

For Bayle, all magistrates had the power of 'cutting off from the commonwealth' whatever necessarily 'destroys the security' of its members and 'tends to dissolve the society', and Moses had had that power since an act of alternative worship was necessarily rebellion, but in any other commonwealth this would not have been rebellion. For Bayle, Jews were further distinguished from Christians because their commonwealth had had neither commerce with others, nor a duty of religious propagation, whereas Christians had an obligation to 'instruct all nations'. It was, declared Bayle, 'morally impossible' that a Jew should 'attempt...Change' from the God of Abraham to a pagan divinity from 'any motive of Conscience' or

---

[16] Locke, *Letter* in *Works*, 22, 36; Marshall, *Locke* 377.

from any other principle than 'a spirit of Rebellion, Libertinism, or mere Malice', in which 'case he justly deserv'd to die'. For Bayle, 'in this case we declare that no Heretick has right to a Toleration'. If preachers could be 'fairly convicted of preaching Errors and heresy' when *knowing them to be such*, then they would have acted 'from mere Malice and worldly Interest' and so would have deserved 'the gibbet'. Bayle stressed, however, that 'under the present dispensation' it was impossible for rulers to 'tell whether a Heretick be sincerely or maliciously in error'.

For Bayle, the emperors whom Christians since Augustine had valorised for acting against the Arians and Donatists, Theodosius and Honorius, had lacked special revelation, and even if truth had been on their side against heretics and schismatics, 'the probability was much stronger on the other hand, that these methods would rather rivet 'em in their Errors, and produce false Conversions'. Magistrates should therefore now 'commit the care of punishing Hereticks to God alone' so long 'as they obey the laws'.[17] Rather as Episcopius had emphasised in the 1620s the allowed variations in beliefs in Israel in order to defuse Mosaic precedents for persecution, Bayle further turned away justification of actions against heretics on the basis of the Mosaic theocracy by arguing that Jews had in fact 'tolerated' all 'the different Sects' interpreting the 'law of Moses', including the 'most detestable heresies' within that religion, which 'by consequence destroy'd all Religion': the 'sect of Sadducees' who denied the immortality of the soul and the resurrection of the body. Mosaic practices thus could not stand as precedents for the punishment of heretics, even if accepted as precedents. Bayle concluded that if the convertists actually modelled themselves on the Jews, they would have to tolerate every different opinion on passages of Scripture but not tolerate Jews, 'pagans', or Muslims who stood beyond such variations – an ironic reversal of the justifications of force offered by contemporary Catholics.[18]

Many of the other defenders of toleration constructed similar arguments against Mosaic precedents for Christian intolerance. Limborch's 1686 *Theologia Christiana* attacked the arguments drawn from the Old Testament for punishment of 'heretics' and 'schismatics'. He stressed that Jewish laws were in general 'abrogated' in the Christian dispensation. He added to this that specific laws against apostates and idols were not applicable to punishments of those who worship the 'same god' but differed in the interpretation of Scripture, and that even 'False prophets' were clearly different from 'heretics'. For Limborch, as for Bayle, Moses had received a special

---

[17] Bayle, *Philosophical Commentary* (1708), 214–18 (*Philosophical Commentary*, ed. Tannenbaum, 121–3; *Commentaire philosophique*, 225–35), 405–6; *idem, OD*, II, 453–4.

[18] Bayle, *Philosophical Commentary* (1708), 218 (*Philosophical Commentary*, ed. Tannenbaum, 122–3; *Commentaire philosophique*, 236–7). Cf. Coffey, *Persecution*, 63.

commission. Finally, even if one still wished to hold that the Mosaic laws were 'binding', it was clear to Limborch that this would need to be after the same manner. The consequence was that the father would be required to inform against the son, and those punished should be stoned to death, as Deuteronomy held of 'apostates and blasphemers'.[19] Burnet's prefatory discourse on toleration before his edition of Lactantius' *Death of the Primitive Persecutors* argued that since Judaism was temporal, its punishments were for temporal crimes like coining, rather than for religious crimes like heresy. As he put it, Jews had held their rights by virtue of the Covenant, and it was just for them to put others to death if they violated these laws 'as it is lawful for us to put a man to death, that coins or clips Money'. But, Burnet continued, over religious opinions 'the case was different, even among the Jews: and therefore, tho the Doctrines of the Sadducees struck at the Foundations of all Religion, the Pharisees, when they had the upper hand, never carried the matter so far as to proceed to extremities against them'. Having thus undermined punishment of Christian heretics, even if Christian commonwealths were seen as imitating Judaic theocracy, Burnet firmly declared that whatever had been true under the 'Mosaical' dispensation was simply not true for Christians: Christians held their temporal rights by virtue of being members of a state or kingdom, as men, and not as Christians.[20] Crell's argument, republished by Le Cène, agreed that despite the opposition of the Sadducees to the 'resurrection of the dead' the Jews had not persecuted the Sadducees: 'although the greatest part both of the People and the Rulers believed them to erre exceedingly, nevertheless they were not expelled the city, neither exempted from being Magistrates, and bearing any other civil office'.[21]

Locke was clear in the *Letter* that Jews had had the right to punish idolators in the commonwealth of Israel. That commonwealth had been 'an absolute theocracy', in which there was no 'difference between that commonwealth and the church'. Its citizens who 'apostatize[d]' from the 'worship of the God of Israel' were therefore 'proceeded against as traitors and rebels, guilty of no less than high treason'. But no other commonwealth was 'constituted upon that foundation'. Indeed, 'there is absolutely no such thing, under the gospel, as a christian commonwealth'. Christ had 'instituted no commonwealth' and had not 'put. . .the sword into any magistrate's hand' with a commission to force men to his religion. Moreover, 'foreigners' and 'strangers' were not 'compelled by force to observe the rites of the Mosaical law'. The law of Moses was simply 'not obligatory to us Christians'.[22]

---

[19] Limborch, *Compleat System*, 987–8; *idem*, *Theologia Christiana*, 831.
[20] Burnet (ed.), *Death*, 18–20.
[21] Le Cène, *Conversations*, 241–2; Crell, *Vindication*, 22–3; cf. Aubert de Versé, *Protestant*, 20.
[22] Locke, *Letter* in *Works*, 37–8.

We saw in Chapter 13 that the Catholic case for the intolerance culminating in the Revocation of the Edict of Nantes was based largely on the pillars of sixteenth-century justification of intolerance, the need for a uniformity of religion to civic peace, and the support of Protestants for sedition, conspiracy, and resistance evidenced by sixteenth-century Huguenot resistance theories and rebellions. We saw in Chapter 15 that many Restoration Anglicans repeatedly voiced the same arguments, associating the Revolution of 1642–60 with contemporary 'heretics' and 'schismatics' and tying them to a lineage of sixteenth-century rebels from Anabaptists to Huguenot monarchomachs. And we saw in Chapter 14 that while denying that Huguenots were seditious, once in the Netherlands Jurieu argued that the Netherlands was peaceful because it was not in fact completely tolerationist and suggested that it was impossible to maintain diversity and peace unless people had become 'indifferent' about religion. The continued force of the view that diversity threatened security affected even some who condemned persecution in the 1680s. The natural law theorist Samuel Pufendorf, whose works were extensively discussed in the 1680s and 1690s, argued for freedom of belief as a 'natural right', condemned persecution, and argued that in many cases it was necessary for rulers to tolerate divergent confessions. But Pufendorf's *Introductio ad Historiam praecipuorum regnorum. . .in Europa* and others of his works and letters in the 1680s and 1690s stressed the desirability of a uniform religious establishment to peace in the state and held that confessional variations tended to produce tumult and sedition. Pufendorf advised the Swedish king that admitting Huguenot refugees could threaten his state, and argued that England and the Netherlands would enjoy greater security if their citizens were religiously united.[23]

Facing the long-standing staple of anti-tolerationist argument that diversity brought tumult, it is unsurprising, then, that Crell's argument, republished by Charles Le Cène in the 1687 *Conversations*, had registered the accusation in justifying intolerance that 'heretics' and 'schismatics' were seditious, and that diversity in its nature brought faction,

> because if liberty of Religion be permitted them, the Commonwealth will be divided into factions, and a way laid open for all discord, tumults, and. . .seditions: For the minds of the people are knit and united together by consent in Religion; but by difference and dissent therein they are divided and distracted; neither can it otherwise happen, but that they who are zealously affected to Religion, should rise up in arms

---

[23] Tuck, *Rights*, 163; Doring, 'Samuel von Pufendorf', esp. 188; this paragraph summarises and inflects parts of Doring's argument.

against them, at some time or other, whom they are fully perswaded do spread abroad ungodly and pestilent doctrine.

In the *Philosophical Commentary*, Bayle identified as an unsustainable commonplace the major argument of the anti-tolerationists that multiplicity of religion was 'dangerous' to government.[24] Several of the authors of works supporting religious toleration in the 1680s spent considerable effort refuting the anti-tolerationist stress on uniformity against sedition and diversity. To those who would object that liberty of religion would cause factions and thus tumults and seditions, Crell's argument, republished by Le Cène, replied that the attempt to impose uniformity by force was instead the most 'apt and commodious way' to stir up tumults. Magistrates who tolerated heretics gained their goodwill.[25] Aubert de Versé declared in the *Treatise* against the argument that civil wars always followed from states being religiously divided that civil wars followed not from diversity itself but from rulers favouring one party over others, who were treated badly. For van Paets, it was true that often the factious covered their 'criminal enterprises' under the cloak of religion; however, more often the 'entirely innocent' members of sects were 'maltreated' under the specious pretext of fear that they would mutiny. Magistrates who knew assemblies to be 'schools of virtue' and not of 'sedition' acted 'very unjustly' in punishing them, and if such failed to imitate completely the patience of primitive Christians, it was unjust to impute to them a design of revolt and punish them severely, especially when under toleration they showed that their fidelity was as great as that of other subjects.[26]

Bayle argued in the *Philosophical Commentary* that if multiplicity was indeed prejudicial to the state, it was only because individuals were 'not bearing with one another'. If instead 'each Party' did 'industriously cultivate that Toleration which I contend for, there might be the same Harmony in a State compos'd of ten different Sects, as there is in a Town where the several kinds of Tradesmen contribute to each others' mutual Support'. For Bayle, in an image of private religious commitment remarkable in its theme of bucolic religious retreat, the prince should protect and maintain an 'even balance of favours' of justice and 'thus Princes might always maintain their Authority intire, every private Person sit under his own Vine and his own Fig-Tree, worshipping God in his own way, and leave others to worship and serve him as they thought fit'. The arguments alleged of 'factious spirits', who, 'in order

---

[24] Crell, *Vindication*, 35–40; Le Cène, *Conversations*, 252–8; Bayle, *Philosophical Commentary* (1708), 243 (*Philosophical Commentary*, ed. Tannenbaum, 136; *Commentaire philosophique*, 258).

[25] Le Cène, *Conversations*, 252–8; Crell, *Vindication*, 35–40.

[26] Aubert de Versé, *Traité*, 14; van Paets, *Lettre*, 10–11.

to subvert the Constitution of the State, have pretended the necessity of a Reformation in Religion; and having drawn the People into their designs, have taken the field with Sword in hand' proved only, according to Bayle, that the 'best things are liable to Abuse'. Princes were obliged to examine any new teacher and 'where his Doctrines Tend, whether to the aggrandizing himself and his Party by civil Broils' and 'if he find this, he's to give him no quarter; he may exterminate him and his, tho the Man were never so much persuaded his Doctrine was divine'. Seditious preachers were, for Bayle, 'damnable, and the religion they preach, if they have any, is of a persecuting nature'.[27] To the argument that religious toleration necessarily 'creates confusions', which Bayle identified as 'pagan' in origin, Bayle replied that a commitment to the need for uniformity would have obliged pagan rulers to persecute Christianity, and that pagan arguments for uniformity had been 'much more reasonable then' than they were now because in the polytheistic and eclectic ancient world which at most required outward observance and not belief, it could 'justly be presumed' that one who had 'affected Noveltys' despite a religion 'so large and comprehensive' had no other design than 'forming political Cabals under a Pretence of worshipping the Gods'. With belief in the efficacy of one's worship required by Christianity, however, such a presumption of sedition in desire to alter forms of worship was simply no longer valid.[28]

It was against both the prevalent associations of conspiracy and sedition and against the broader case that diversity caused dissension and civil war that Locke had first argued in England in the final draft of his 1667 'Essay on Toleration' that religious oppression caused conspiracy and sedition, and that toleration in contrast caused peace and the uniting of the people to the magistrate. Locke had thus enunciated in outline in the 1660s the central elements of the case about toleration and sedition which he and many other tolerationists of the 1680s were to make in the Netherlands. In the *Letter*, Locke responded to the argument that diverse religious meetings were 'nurseries of factions and seditions' which endangered 'the public peace, and threaten[ed] the commonwealth'. He contended first that many such meetings were peaceful, and that there were 'such numerous meetings in markets, and courts of judicature' and 'a concourse of people in cities', without causing sedition and 'conspiracy'. It was a fallacy to make a simple 'agreement in matters of religion...in effect a conspiracy against the commonwealth'. If it was alleged that conventicles were seditious as they were

---

[27] Bayle, *Philosophical Commentary* (1708), 242–6 (*Philosophical Commentary*, ed. Tannenbaum, 135–7; *Commentaire philosophique*, 256–60).

[28] Bayle, *Philosophical Commentary* (1708), 30–2 (*Philosophical Commentary*, ed. Tannenbaum, 21–2; *Commentaire philosophique*, 71–3).

private meetings giving opportunities for 'clandestine machinations', then those to be blamed were 'those that forbid their being public', and not those who met privately. Locke's central reply, however, was to say that such meetings were at times seditious, but that if so this was caused by the oppression itself. Locke argued that the magistrate was afraid of other religions but not of their own 'because he is kind and favourable to the one, but severe and cruel to the other', and attacked the magistrate for using those of another religion 'as slaves; and how blamelessly soever they demean themselves, recompenses them' by 'prisons, confiscations, and death'. For Locke, 'if men enter into seditious conspiracies, it is not religion inspires them to it in their meetings, but their sufferings and oppressions' which make them 'willing to ease themselves'. Locke agreed that seditions were 'very frequently raised upon pretence of religion', but declared it just as true that 'for religion, subjects are frequently ill-treated, and live miserably'. Just and moderate governments were 'every where quiet, every where safe' but 'oppression raises ferments, and makes men struggle to cast off an uneasy and tyrannical yoke'. There was 'one thing only which gathers people into seditious commotions, and that is oppression'. Like many of these authors, Locke argued that toleration bound subjects to their prince. Taking away penalties against dissenters from the religion of the magistrate would make all things 'immediately...safe and peaceable', and those 'that are averse to the religion of the magistrate, will think themselves so much the more bound to maintain the peace of the commonwealth, as their condition is better in that place than elsewhere; and all the several separate congregations, like so many guardians of the public peace, will watch one another, that nothing may be innovated or changed in the form of the government: because they can hope for nothing better than what they already enjoy; that is, an equal condition with their fellow-subjects, under a just and moderate government'.[29]

The argument that toleration brought peace while oppression brought turbulence was regularly made by attacking clerical instigation of violence. Bayle's *Philosophical Commentary* associated clerics with the truly turbulent and spoke of the 'tumultuous Outcrys of a Rabble of Monks and Clergymen'. For Bayle, the 'disturbers of the peace' were those 'who won't suffer their Fellow-Citizens to live in the full and peaceable Enjoyment of all their Rights, Privileges, and Property'.[30] Aubert agreed in identifying clerics in the *Treatise* as having caused seditions, civil wars, and violence over religion, and he argued that magistrates who desired peace and stability should

---

[29] Marshall, *Locke*, ch. 2; Locke, *Letter* in *Works*, 47–50. Cf. Coffey, *Persecution*, 69–70.
[30] Bayle, *Philosophical Commentary* (1708), 243 (*Philosophical Commentary*, ed. Tannenbaum, 136; *Commentaire philosophique*, 257), 376–7; *idem*, OD, II, 447.

'mortify' and 'humiliate' such priests, and support instead as ministers only those who would promise and swear to preach and write in support of liberty of conscience, peace, and Christian toleration. Locke in the *Letter* attacked the 'avarice' and 'desire of dominion' of clerics who had animated ambitious magistrates and superstitious peoples against others, causing wars on 'account of religion'. For Locke, such preachers were the 'incendiaries, and disturbers of the public peace' who had sounded the 'trumpet of war' and who had favoured the dominion of princes as they endeavoured with 'all their might to promote that tyranny in the commonwealth, which otherwise they should not be able to establish in the church'.[31]

Diversity was allied in a number of tolerationist arguments with the fostering of prosperity and security. Bayle's *Philosophical Commentary* argued that one could have peace in a state with ten sects, just as with several kinds of tradesmen in town, but stressed also that in such a situation 'honest Emulation between them which shou'd exceed in Piety, in good works, and in spiritual Knowledge' would occur. Such competition 'must be the source of infinite publick Blessings'.[32] We have seen in previous chapters that theorists in the seventeenth century regularly linked Dutch toleration with Dutch prosperity, and with Dutch ability to withstand the attacks of other societies. Spain, England, and France had all fought wars with the Dutch in the past century, and all had lost to the Dutch. The Netherlands was in 1684–5 (before James II's toleration) the only substantial contemporary Western European Christian example of extensive toleration, and many of those writing in favour of toleration were themselves living in the Netherlands.

Aubert made much of the contrast of the Netherlands with Spain, which had formerly been so 'flourishing' and well-populated but which was now much reduced because of violence exercised over consciences and because of the power of the Inquisition. He stressed the flourishing under liberty of conscience of arts, sciences, manufacturing and commerce in the Netherlands, the riches and power of Amsterdam, and the devotion of the refugees there to its magistrates and laws. He emphasised that Amsterdam had the population and riches of a kingdom. In his *Parrhasiana*, Le Clerc similarly contrasted poor and Catholic Spain dominated by rapacious clerics with prosperous and tolerant Holland. At the time of translating Crell's *Vindication of Liberty of Religion* and issuing it with his 1687 *Conversations*, Le Cène was a religious refugee who had fled from France initially to the

---

[31] Aubert de Versé, *Traité*, 'adresse', 11–16; Locke, *Letter* in *Works*, 53–4. Cf. also Le Clerc, *Parrhasiana* (Amsterdam 1701), II, ch. 3.

[32] Bayle, *Philosophical Commentary* (1708), 243 (*Philosophical Commentary*, ed. Tannenbaum, 135–6; *Commentaire philosophique*, 257).

Netherlands (and then to England, before returning to the Netherlands), re-publishing the argument of a refugee to Poland. It is unsurprising that two locations adduced as evidence that toleration conduced to peace and security and intolerance to bloodshed and war were the Netherlands and France.[33]

We have seen in Chapter 12 that earlier theorists had often adduced Islamic society as a further example of peaceful toleration. When the advocates of toleration in the 1680s turned from the Netherlands to other contemporary societies for examples of toleration, they also focused especially on Islamic toleration as proof of the possibilities of peaceful toleration. Crell's argument, republished by Le Cène, argued that peace was feasible with diversity 'as we see it now a dayes to be under the Turk himself, who permits Christians...to exercise their own Religion'.[34] In his prefatory discourse to his edition of Lactantius, Burnet argued that while originally Mahomet had used force to convert others 'with all the Fierceness of rage', 'Mahometans' were 'so much softened' now and 'so gentle, that those of a Religion, which believes theirs to be only an Imposture, live secure under them, and know the Price that the Liberty of their conscience must rise to; and that being payed, they enjoy in all other respects the Protection of the Government, together with the Publick exercise of their Religion'. The notion that Islam was a 'softened' and 'gentle' religion involved exactly the terms which Burnet was emphasising in this work needed to become true of Christianity, as he held that Catholicism had departed from 'meekness' so that 'notwithstanding all the polishings of Learning and Civility that are in it, it is now the cruellest and most implacable society that has ever yet appeared in the world'. The contrast was for Burnet a 'shameful' reverse of the 'first beginnings of the two Religions'.[35]

Jurieu had pointed out in his 1683 *History of Calvinism* that 'Mahometans' were considerably more tolerant than Catholics. Jurieu described the conquest of Jerusalem by the Caliph Omar in 638 and stressed that the invaders had not tortured or raped, had left property intact, and had not persecuted for religion, but had left Christian churches standing and allowed freedom of worship. For Jurieu, Muslims had since then rarely had recourse to the use of force against Christians and had not exercised 'one thousandth' of the cruelties exercised by the Catholic Church. For Jurieu, more blood had been shed on St Bartholomew's Day in 1572 than in all Muslim persecution of Christians.

---

[33] Aubert de Versé, *Traité*, 8–10, 55; Morman, *Aubert*, 217; Le Clerc, *Parrhasiana*, 194–5; Golden, *Le Clerc*, 125–6; Le Clerc, *Bibliothèque universelle* (1688), 125; (1689), 472–86; Crell, *Vindication* (1646), 35–42; Le Cène, *Conversations*, 252–8. In his 1674 manuscript 'Trade', Locke identified 'freedom of religion' as essential to the promotion of trade; in his 1693 'For a General Naturalisation', he contrasted 'the poorest country in Europe', Spain, with Holland, 'abounding in riches': in P. Kelly (ed.), *Locke on Money* (Oxford 1991), 485–7.

[34] Crell, *Vindication*, 38; Le Cène, *Conversations*, 255.   [35] Burnet (ed.), *Death*, 23–4.

The 'Saracens' thus conducted themselves 'more evangelically' than Catholics, whose cruelty had for Jurieu 'surpassed the cruelty of the Cannibals'.[36] Whereas Jurieu indicted only Catholic persecution, Locke, who read Jurieu's work in about the period of composition of his *Letter Concerning Toleration*, and Bayle, who cited Jurieu's work on this topic extensively in the *Dictionary*, cited Islamic toleration in a more general indictment of all Christian persecution. Bayle stressed in his *Dictionary* that while 'Mahometanism' legitimated force, it did not use it, whereas Christianity legitimated only peaceful toleration, but did not maintain it.[37] Locke utilised the example of Islamic toleration to significant rhetorical effect in his *Letter Concerning Toleration* by depicting a potential situation of intolerance at Constantinople between Calvinists and Arminians – similar to that which had existed in the Netherlands earlier in the century, and which was still feared among the Arminian community. He argued that intolerance by one towards the other would appear utterly ridiculous to Muslims: would not 'the Turks', Locke asked, 'silently stand by and laugh to see with what inhuman cruelty christians thus rage against christians?'[38]

Bolstering their case for the peace which would reign in tolerant societies, many of the tolerationists further pointed to the times of the Roman emperors and to the peaceful tolerance of 'pagan' societies such as Athens. Le Cène, van Paets and Bayle made the same comparison in order to prove the possibility of societies encompassing diversity of opinion. In his 1687 *Conversations*, Le Cène pointed to the diversity of beliefs and sects in ancient Greece as greater than that today in Amsterdam without this having caused civil war amidst disputes between Pythagoreans, Peripatetics, Stoics, Pyrrhonians, Academics, Epicureans, Cynics, and others over such questions as good and evil, the nature of God, and the immortality of the soul. And he stressed that religious divisions had not then caused civil wars. Van Paets similarly discussed the different schools of philosophy in classical times who had disputed over the nature of 'the sovereign good' with peace, pointing out that Stoics had held one view of the highest good, Academics another, Peripatetics a third, and Epicureans a fourth, and had tolerated each other. For van Paets, furthermore, Christianity commanded 'patient' tolerance towards those who erred, and required their correction by 'reason' and not by force.[39]

Bayle not merely published van Paets' argument in Latin in 1685 and translated it into French in 1686, but he lauded it in the *Dictionary* as

---

[36] P. Jurieu, *Histoire*, 115–17; A. Gunny, 'Protestant Reactions to Islam in late Seventeenth-Century French Thought', *French Studies* (1986), 129–40.

[37] Bayle, *Dictionary*, Mahomet and notes; MS Locke f8, 289ff.

[38] Locke, *Letter* in *Works*, 18; Matar, 'Turbanned Nations', *Journal of Islamic History* (1991), 67–77.

[39] Le Cène, *Conversations* (1687), 110–12; van Paets, *Lettre*, 10–11.

unsurpassed as a compressed argument for religious toleration, declaring in *Sanctesius F* that 'without undertaking to read a long-winded work, one needs only read a small piece written at London, in 1685, by an illustrious magistrate of a town in Holland'. And he referred readers of the *Dictionary* to the 'encomium' upon Paets, that 'great man', which he had himself published in the *Nouvelles de la République*, underlining once again the role of the journals of the republic in celebrating toleration indirectly as well as directly. Bayle's review had summarised many of Paets' arguments. It is unsurprising, then, that Bayle's *Philosophical Commentary* of 1686 argued similarly to Paets that there had been no religious wars among pagan society with all its 'diversity'. As Bayle asserted,

To shew the Absurdity of those who pretend that Toleration causes Dissensions in the State, we need only appeal to Experience. Paganism was divided into an infinite number of Sects, which paid the Gods several different kinds of worship; and even those Gods which were supreme in one Country, were not so in another: yet I don't remember I have ever read of a religious war among the Pagans.

It was 'Non-toleration' which was 'the sole cause of all the Disorders which are falsly imputed to Toleration'. The debates in pagan society had been over the nature of the highest good, but they had been carried out peacefully:

The different sects of Philosophy ne'er disturb'd the Peace of Athens, each maintain'd its own Hypothesis, and argu'd against those of all the other Sects; yet their Differences concern'd matters of no small moment, nay, sometimes a Providence, or the Chief Good. But because the Magistrates permitted 'em all alike to teach their own Doctrines, and never endeavour'd by any violent Methods to incorporate one Sect into another, the State felt no inconvenience from this Diversity of Opinions; tho, tis probable, had they attempted this Union, they had thrown the whole into Convulsions.

The conclusion was therefore straightforward: 'Toleration therefore is the very Bond of Peace, and Non-Toleration is the Source of Confusion and Squabble'.[40]

To these arguments that intolerance had caused religious wars and sedition and that many societies had demonstrated that peace could be maintained with diversity, these tolerationists added the argument that if intolerance was justified by Protestants then there was no ground on which to attack contemporary Catholic persecution. We have seen that the decade of the 1680s was predominantly a decade of justifications of intolerance, both Protestant and Catholic, issued in many countries, and a decade of a massive forced exile for religion in which many of those exiled were opponents of full religious toleration rather than its supporters. It was a frequent complaint of those who

---

[40] Bayle, *Philosophical Commentary* (1708), 32–3 (*Philosophical Commentary*, ed. Tannenbaum, 22; *Commentaire philosophique*, 73–4).

defended toleration in these years that those who had been persecuted had not learned through their experience to be tolerant. Targeting particularly Protestant arguments for intolerance, tolerationists argued that the defence of intolerance rendered them incapable of protesting in a principled manner against Catholic intolerance.

As Bayle put it in his *Supplement* to the *Philosophical Commentary* against Jurieu's recent defences of intolerance: 'we are still of the mind of the first reformers, as to the punishing of Hereticks, which must needs enervate and pall the greatest part of our Remonstrances against the late Proceedings in France'. Bayle criticised those who 'judged very right' about the Church of Rome, that she had 'acted unjustly in persecuting them, but not that themselves did ill in compelling others'. For Bayle, this was indeed 'retaining all the Falsehood of the Doctrine'.[41] And, as we saw earlier, Bayle offered a similar indictment of the Huguenot refugee ministers in Augustine H in the *Dictionary*, arguing that they had proven one of the most remarkable examples of 'turncoats' offered by history (thereby ignoring the consistency of their opposition to the toleration of those they considered Protestant 'heretics'). They had, he asserted, 'changed' their opinion about toleration 'while the Ruin of their churches, by the Authority of the Sovereign, was quite fresh in their memory, and the wound was still bleeding. If they had been asked, while the Edicts of Persecution were pouring on their party, what they thought of the conduct of a Prince, who inflicted Penalties on those of his subjects, who desired only the liberty of serving God according to their Consciences, they would have answered, that it is unjust; and yet, as soon as they are come into another country, they have pronounced their Anathema against those, who condemn the use of Penal Laws, in order to suppress Errors'.[42]

This attack on Protestant intolerance was often combined in the 1680s with a broader attack on those who condemned persecution while out of power and justified persecution while in power. In previous chapters, we have seen such a complaint being frequently registered in earlier tolerationist arguments, and seen the ways in which many among even the most tolerant of preceding sects and individuals had fostered suspicion of their potential intolerance, as for instance in Socinian attacks on Catholic worship and their imprisonment of Francis David, or the levels of hostility expressed by Coornhert. Burnet argued that the 'plea of moderation' was a 'sanctuary of all unfortunate' people but that as soon as fortunes changed 'they insensibly got into that Principle which was so much decried by themselves, when their Affairs were in an ill condition'. He wanted to convince his readers instead

---

[41] Bayle, *Philosophical Commentary* (1708), 505; 753; *idem*, OD, II, 498, 555.
[42] Bayle, *Dictionary*, Augustine H.

that the doctrine of persecution was an 'infallible mark of an Antichristian church' so that 'if a Revolution in the State of Affairs' put them in power it would prevent them using 'others as hardly as they have been used by them'.

Burnet's *Some Letters* attacked Genevan requirements of subscription from their ministers. Given that Le Clerc had been exiled from Geneva after writing an unorthodox tolerationist work, it is unsurprising that this point was stressed in reviewing Burnet's *Letters* in the *Bibliothèque universelle*.[43] In his *Apology* – also published as *Apologie pour l'église d'Angleterre* – Burnet argued in characteristic Latitudinarian Anglican fashion that the Church of England was in fact the most tolerant church in practice, although the 'heats' of 'some angry and deluded men' and the intolerance fostered by the court might have obscured that important fact in the recent past. Burnet stressed what the Presbyterians had done in Scotland 'when the covenant was in Dominion' and 'what the Independents' had done 'in new england': they had 'carried the principle of rigour in religion' much further than the Church of England. Ignoring the tolerationist arguments of Baptists and Quakers, who had never held power over others, Burnet offered the behaviour of Presbyterians and Independents as further proof that the Church of England was 'the least persecuting' church in the world in her principles. He was sorry, he declared, that *all* parties have shown that 'as their turn came to be uppermost, they have forgot the same Principles of Moderation and Liberty which they all claimed when they were oppressed'. And he declared that he would much rather be persecuted for religion than persecute others.[44]

In his preface to his 1706 translation of Limborch's 1686 *Theologia Christiana* into English, Burnet's chaplain William Jones similarly attacked the earlier practices of Anglican persecution, writing that 'true it is there was a hot sort of spirit' prevailing when a late prince 'gave no quarter to those who would not conform to the Church of England'. Suggesting that 'this was partly owing to the unkind and severe usage which the Church of England men met with whilst dissenters were uppermost', Jones emphasised that 'we' had 'lived to see the error' of our ways, and that the 'best way of making dissenters proselytes' was by the 'force of arguments' and the 'energy of a holy life'. He condemned 'high churchmen' and identified the Latitudinarians as the 'best members' of the Church of England, for they were 'of a large and comprehensive charity, and breathe forth that universal love and peace'. He argued that 'To use foul and opprobrious language, to call hard names, to cast bitter reflections, and to keep at such a distance from

---

[43] Burnet (ed.), *Death*, 10; G. Burnet, *Some Letters* (Amsterdam 1686), *passim*; *Bibliothèque universelle*, v (1687), 538–44.

[44] Burnet, *Apology for the Church of England, passim*.

one another, as if we had daggers hid under our garments, is not the way for us to become friends: but an amicable deportment and Behaviour'.[45]

In his lengthy tolerationist manuscript of 1681–3, 'Critical Notes on Edward Stillingfleet', Locke had indicted Independents and Presbyterians for their intolerance in England and New England and declared that 'Churchmen of all sorts with power' were 'very apt to persecute and misuse those that will not pen in their fold'. Locke's *Letter Concerning Toleration* declared it worthy to be 'observed, and lamented' that when many had not had the 'power to carry on persecution, and to become masters, there they desire to live upon fair terms, and preach up toleration' but that as soon as they began to feel 'themselves the stronger; then presently peace and charity are to be laid aside'. Popple's preface to Locke's *Letter* expressed the need for impartial liberty, arguing against those who justified toleration only for themselves, and included many English dissenters in this accusation. Popple wrote that 'Our government has not only been partial in matters of religion, but those also who have suffered under that partiality, and have therefore endeavoured by their writings to vindicate their own rights and liberties, have for the most part done it upon narrow principles, suited only to the interests of their own sects'. Popple proclaimed the need for 'absolute liberty, just and true liberty, equal and impartial liberty' which had been 'not at all practised, either by our governours towards the people in general, or by any dissenting parties of the people towards one another'. Such suspicion of the potential for intolerance even amongst the most tolerant extended in Locke's circles in the 1680s and 1690s to Socinians and Quakers. Furly complained of Quaker rigidity in a series of letters to Locke in the 1690s. When accused of Socinianism in the 1690s, Locke rebutted this in part by condemning Socinians' 'zeal for their orthodoxy' and by declaring that even Socinians might persecute if they got power as 'the same genius seems to influence them all, even those who pretend most to freedom, the socinians themselves' who 'had they the power...would, I fear, be ready with their set of fundamentals; which they would be as forward to impose on others, as others have been to impose contrary fundamentals on them'.[46]

Having thus argued that only by tolerationist principles could the case against Catholic intolerance be made strongly by Protestants, and having indicted many Protestants for their failure to make that case, many of these advocates of religious toleration added that the arguments of the intolerant about the danger of diversity could have been voiced by pagan persecutors

[45] Limborch, *Compleat System*, preface.
[46] Marshall, *Locke*, 109–10; Locke, *Letter*, preface; *Letter*, in *Works*, 19–20; Locke, *Correspondence*, 1562, 1585, 1614, 1702, 1745; *idem*, *Vindication* in *Works*, VII, 167, 171–2; *Second Vindication* in *ibid.*, 295–6, 300, 359; my 'Locke, Socinianism'.

against Christianity. Crell's *Vindication*, republished by Le Cène, for instance argued that if one said that with diversity no peace was possible this would have armed 'heathens' against 'Christians' in the first age of the church. And for these advocates of religious toleration, argument for intolerance on the bases of the danger of diversity or the rights of magistrates to forbid preaching of heresy could be voiced against tolerating Christianity in their realms by contemporary Chinese, Japanese, or Muslim rulers, preventing evangelisation. Motivated in significant part by belief that toleration was the way to convert others to Christianity, many tolerationists combined support for toleration for Jews and Muslims with a general argument not merely for allowing Jews and Muslims to reside in European territories, but as parts of generalised support for international campaigns for conversion that were to include Japan and China as well as Islamic territories. This argument was in part rhetorical, but also a consequence of Jesuit missions in the seventeenth century and the deep concern with Japan and China of European intellectuals by the late seventeenth century. Aubert argued in the *Pacific Protestant* that Jurieu's intolerant principles would legitimate Japanese and Chinese rulers acting against Christians. And Bayle argued at length in the *Philosophical Commentary* that principles which legitimated constraint in religion would furnish reasons for the Chinese to exclude Christian missionaries. If aware of the true principles of Jesuit missionaries, Bayle held, the Chinese emperor would be right 'to order these men immediately out of his Dominions, as profest public pests'. The justification of compulsion was thus invalid because it meant that 'with Reason and Justice' China would remain unconverted.[47]

The final blow launched against magisterial arguments for intolerance on the grounds that such arguments would need to be universal was the claim that it was a necessary consequence of the legitimation of force that if one was obliged in religious matters simply to obey a prince, everyone would be, in Bayle's words, 'a Turk at Constantinople, an Arian under Constantius, a Pagan under Nero, a Protestant in Sweden, a Papist in Rome'.[48] Locke wrote: 'what power can be given to the magistrate for the suppression of an idolatrous church, which may not, in time and place, be made use of to the ruin of an orthodox one...the civil power is the same every where, and the religion of every prince is orthodox to himself. If therefore, such a power be granted unto the civil magistrate in spirituals, as that at Geneva, for example; he may extirpate, by violence and blood, the religion which is there reputed

---

[47] Crell, *Vindication*, 38; Le Cène, *Conversations*, 235–6; Aubert de Versé, *Protestant*, 18–19; Bayle, *Philosophical Commentary* (1708), 83–91 (*Philosophical Commentary*, ed. Tannenbaum, 51–7; *Commentaire philosophique*, 119–32); Elukin, 'Jacques Basnage', esp. 609.

[48] Bayle, *Philosophical Commentary* (1708), 480; cf. Seaton, *Toleration*, 99, 147, for some of the very many examples of this argument.

idolatrous; by the same rule, another magistrate, in some neighbouring country, may oppress the reformed religion; and in India, the christian'.[49] Such an argument was made not merely geographically but also chronologically, as by Aubert in *Pacific Protestant*, in arguing against Jurieu's 'bloody and barbarous' principles supporting magisterial force, which would have served to legitimate Anglicans and Puritans successively against each other, or the Roman emperors against Christianity itself.[50] And the argument most repeatedly made by Locke in the *Second* and *Third Letter* in attacking Proast's defence of Anglican imposition since Anglicanism was the 'true religion' was that defence of magisterial force would legitimate Louis XIV and the dragoons in France. As Locke put it on more than fifteen occasions in the *Second* and *Third Letters*, the case for magisterial force 'will as much promote popery in France, as protestantism in England', would justify 'the king of France' with 'his dragoons', and would 'excuse the late barbarous usage of the protestants in France, designed to extirpate the reformed religion there.'[51]

In some of these defences of toleration it was specified that it was not necessary to have public churches rather than private assemblies for worship, and various other restrictions were countenanced. Bayle argued in the *Philosophical Commentary* that there was no right to public religious procession or to public churches. He wrote that he did not think that 'having Public Churches' or 'walking in Processions thro the streets' was 'essential to Liberty in Religion'. For Bayle, such may 'contribute to the outward pomp' of worship but the ends of worship were served if they can 'assemble to perform divine Service, and to argue modestly in behalf of their own Persuasion, and against the opposite Doctrine, as occasion requires'.[52] In the *Treatise*, while Aubert argued very strongly that toleration conduced to peace, he nonetheless suggested that every ruler 'has the right to prevent all public professions or all public exercise of any Religion save his own or such as he might wish to accommodate; the reason is that Princes can legitimately presume that public assemblies are dangerous to the state and may give rise to revolt and sedition'. And he added that rulers could also legitimately forbid 'secret and private' assemblies if they became too numerous and gave offence to the ruler, could regulate the numbers attending such assemblies, and could punish those who violated these regulations. In the *Pacific Protestant*, Aubert had similarly argued that a ruler could restrict public

[49] Locke, *Letter* in *Works*, 35.   [50] Aubert de Versé, *Protestant*, 19–20.

[51] Locke, *Second Letter* in *Works*, VI, 64, 69, 72, 77, 87, 89; *idem*, *Third Letter* in *Works*, VI, 152, 181, 193, 194, 251, 286, 366, 400, 413.

[52] Bayle, *Philosophical Commentary* (1708), 237 (*Philosophical Commentary*, ed. Tannenbaum, 132; *Commentaire philosophique*, 251–2).

worship, while similarly identifying free public worship with 'affection' for and 'fidelity' to the ruler, and suggesting that a ruler could not legitimately forbid peaceful private worship.[53] In his *Theologia Christiana*, Limborch supported toleration and effectively recognised something of its character in the Netherlands in declaring that the magistrate was to establish public worship and to 'give those who dissent from him a free Toleration to serve God in their own way, which they think to be best, in their private Houses'.[54] Locke, who read part at least of the *Theologia Christiana* in manuscript in 1685, may even have been reacting to Limborch in arguing in the *Letter* that if others were allowed 'assemblies', 'observations of festivals', and 'public worship', these should with equal right be permitted to 'Remonstrants, AntiRemonstrants, Lutherans, Anabaptists, and Socinians'.[55]

In general, this group of tolerationists said that magistrates were not to establish religion by force, but positively encouraged magistrates to persuade others to what they considered the 'true religion' by reasonings, by exhortations, by personal example, and in many cases by providing 'public' support for that religion. Limborch's *Theologia Christiana* argued that the magistrate was to 'take care' that what 'he looks upon to be true' was 'taught in the public churches', to build public churches, and to give directions for worship. And he was to 'make use of all the mild methods imaginable' for 'inviting and perswading' dissenting subjects to communion with the 'public church'.[56] For Paets, the magistrate was to take care of ceremonies and public worship, and to provide for minsters from the 'public treasury'.[57] Bayle's *Philosophical Commentary* argued for magisterial attempts at persuasion using friendly conferences, books, and familiar instructions; it declared that the magistrate was to exert 'all imaginable care' to instruct and 'in endeavouring to convert those who are supposed to be in error, by Instructions, by charitable and calm Reasonings, by clearing up their Doubts, by Prayers to God in their behalf'. Princes as 'nursing fathers' to the church were for Bayle 'to see it be supply'd with sober and able pastors' and so to 'found and endow Colleges and Academies'; to 'spare no necessary charge for its Maintenance'; to 'punish ecclesiastics for vicious and scandalous lives'; and by their own 'good lives and wholesome laws excite all their people to the practice of virtue'. They were for Bayle to punish all who aimed to attack the established Church, and if new sects offer 'to insult the

---

[53] Aubert de Versé, *Traité*, 9–10, in Morman, *Aubert*, 221–2; Aubert de Versé, *Traité*, 29; *idem*, *Protestant*, 16–17.
[54] Limborch, *Compleat System*, 710–11; *idem*, *Theologia Christiana*, 582.
[55] Locke, *Letter*, ed. Klibansky and Gough, 102–3; Locke, *Letter* in *Works*, 52. Popple changed the list to name Presbyterians, Independents, Anabaptists, Arminians, Quakers, and others.
[56] Limborch, *Compleat System*, 710–11, 993; *idem*, *Theologia Christiana*, 581, 835.
[57] Paets, *Lettre*, 15.

Ministers of the establish'd religion' or to use violence against its communicants, they were 'to punish these sectaries' with requisite methods, and even 'with death' if warranted, because they had revealed their persecuting spirit, and aimed at the overthrow of the political laws.[58] For Aubert, magistrates could use all 'gentle' means against 'heretics' in order to persuade them to what they believed to be the 'true' faith, but not use force. The review of Bayle's *Third Part* of the *Philosophical Commentary* in the *Bibliothèque universelle* stressed that magistrates should support religion by persuasion, books, and sermons, but not by force. Locke's *Letter* said that magistrates had commission to admonish and exhort, to use all the methods of persuasion, but not to impose by laws backed by force. He wrote that magistrates could indeed 'make use of arguments, and thereby draw the heterodox into the way of truth, and procure their salvation' by 'teaching, instructing, and redressing the erroneous by reason' but not 'with penalties'.[59]

While much of this support for magisterial involvement in persuasion of others to the religion that the magistrate considered true can be understood as a natural polemical positioning by advocates of toleration faced by the justification of 'force plus consideration and conferences' then being voiced by many anti-tolerationists, it should also be understood to have been the commitment of all (or perhaps all but one) of these thinkers. With the possible exception of Bayle, all of these tolerationists themselves clearly believed both in the existence of a 'true religion' and in the magistrate's duty to foster the progress of the religion he thought true while not using force against those who disagreed with him. And these authors were publishing primarily in the Netherlands, where there was a 'public' religion but not an 'established' religion in the sense of one penalising those who did not attend its churches. Although they had been forced to become a kind of 'sect', in Arminian circles support for a 'public' church was still very strong, with continued desire for that 'public church' to increase its boundaries to readmit Arminians. This brought the Arminians close to those most eirenic strains of Latitudinarian Anglicanism which repudiated penal measures against dissent and wished to see the boundaries of the Church of England expanded to admit many dissenters through comprehension, the position supported by the Anglicans Locke and Burnet at various moments in the 1680s and 1690s.[60]

---

[58] Bayle, *Philosophical Commentary* (1708), 205, 246–7 (*Philosophical Commentary*, ed. Tannenbaum, 117, 137; *Commentaire philosophique*, 225, 260–1).

[59] Aubert de Versé, *Traité*, 103; Le Clerc/Cornand, *Bibliothèque universelle*, v (1687), 480–1; Locke, *Letter* in *Works*, 11.

[60] See Marshall, *Locke*, chs. 3 and 8 on Locke's significant desire for toleration through comprehension as well as toleration outside of the Church of England.

Two of the tolerationist authors directly raised the problem of a magistrate who believed in his conscience that he had the duty to use force against others. Defence of toleration which suggested that there was a duty to follow the determinations of one's conscience raised the awkward problem that many magistrates might well believe themselves duty bound to persecute. And after 1685, as Louis XIV was extolling the Revocation as a duty to God and as Catholic clerics were extolling him as duty-bound to punish heresy, this was not simply a theoretical issue within an argument about 'conscience' but rather an immediately pressing practical matter. In his 1687 *Treatise*, Aubert recognised that a magistrate might think that he had a duty to act against heresy as the consequence of the duty of following conscience, but argued that he would be guilty of vincible error if he used violence because of its clear biblical prohibition. And he argued that Louis XIV specifically should have followed his oath to maintain toleration for Protestants. Bayle's 1686 *Philosophical Commentary* had canvassed a similar combination of arguments, recognising that a magistrate might in conscience believe himself duty-bound to persecute others, but arguing that the evidence of natural light clearly testified to all, including magistrates, that intolerance was wrong. Bayle wrote that 'I don't deny but they who are actually persuaded that 'tis their Duty to extirpate Sects, are oblig'd to follow the Motions of their false Conscience'. But it did 'not follow' for Bayle that such magistrates 'act without sin'. He indicated that he hoped that everyone who examined his argument against taking in its 'literal sense' the passage of the Bible 'compel them to come in' might perceive those 'errors of conscience' which they were under as to persecution.[61]

This weakness in Bayle's arguments for toleration on the basis of rights of conscience which might generate a conscientiously persecuting magistrate was pointed out against Bayle immediately. Jurieu's 1687 *Rights of the Two Sovereigns* exploited the weakness by contending that it was simply useless to write a book against persecution based on the right of the 'erring conscience', as Bayle had done, when persecutors were convinced in their erring conscience that persecution was a duty. This provided Jurieu with reason to attempt to maintain his distinction between the right to punish of a magistrate who possessed the 'true religion', and the absence of such a 'right' from a magistrate who did not, however much he might be sure that he possessed the true religion and be sure that he therefore had a duty to impose that religion. Only on such grounds, Jurieu claimed, could one condemn the behaviour of Louis XIV and simultaneously support the establishment of

---

[61] Aubert de Versé, *Traité*, 'avertissement' and *passim*; Bayle, *Philosophical Commentary*, 306–7 (*Philosophical Commentary*, ed. Tannenbaum, 166–7; *Commentaire philosophique*, 311–12); cf. Mori, *Bayle*; Rex, *Essays*; Labrousse, *Bayle*.

true Protestant Christianity.[62] Such a criticism of Bayle's argument should not be seen as simply that of a critic of toleration such as Jurieu; the tolerationist Jacques Basnage's 1696 *Treatise on Conscience...with reflexions on the Philosophical Commentary* was to make the same point against Bayle. Tzvetan Todorov is thus making a point made first by Bayle's contemporaries when he points to this issue as a serious weakness in Bayle's argument, a weakness which makes Todorov prefer the argument of Locke.[63]

MAGISTERIAL AUTHORITY AND TOLERATIONISTS' ARGUMENTS ON RESISTANCE

Several tolerationist works stressed that magistrates could not possess authority over conscience since people could not give away a right they did not possess. Aubert's *Treatise* argued explicitly that civil society was established by consent, that people could not consent to give away a power that they did not possess, and that therefore magistrates could never be empowered to force others' consciences. For Aubert, the 'light of natural reason dictates to us that Monarchs have no other right...than that which resides naturally and originally in the people and of which the People have divested themselves in order to invest the Monarchs with it'. There was a clear right to religious worship in line with one's conscience: none had right over another's conscience and so this could not be transferred, while no one in their right mind would have given up right over their own conscience. The exercise of authority over conscience was 'tyranny'. For Aubert, Jurieu was worse than Hobbes and Spinoza in placing the public expression of religious views within the magistrate's control.[64] Locke held in the *Letter* that God did not give power to establish religion, and that man could not do so since he did not possess such a power. It was not committed to the magistrate by God 'because it appears not that God has ever given any such authority to one man over another, as to compel any one to his religion'. Moreover, no such 'power can be vested in the magistrate by the consent of the people; because no man can so far abandon the care of his own salvation, as blindly to leave it to the choice of any other, whether prince or subject, to prescribe to him what faith or worship he shall embrace'. Bayle's *Philosophical Commentary* left the origins of political authority open in arguing that all the power of princes came either from God or from man, but added that whichever was the source of political authority, a magistrate could not possess rights over conscience. God could not make

[62] Jurieu, *Des Droits*, 69; Mori, 'Bayle, the Rights of Conscience, the Remedy of Toleration', 50.

[63] Basnage in Dodge, *Political Thought*, 205; Cerny, *Theology*, 299–306; Todorov, *Morals of History*, 151–3; Mori, *Bayle*.

[64] Aubert de Versé, *Traité, passim*; cf. Morman, *Aubert*, ch. 4.

people subject against their conscience, and unless they were 'mad' men could not entrust the magistrate with a power to enjoin them to hate God.[65]

Some of the tolerationist authors whose works we have been considering discussed resistance in their tolerationist works of the 1680s and 1690s, or in other works in the 1690s and 1700s. We have examined Bayle's views, which stressed non-resistance, briefly in Chapter 14. In the *Supplement* to the *Philosophical Commentary*, Bayle argued that there was no crime that could be committed by a subject that was worse than 'that of rebelling against his lawful Prince', and at many points in the *Philosophical Commentary* itself he stressed the duties of obedience to rulers and that rulers could act against sedition. He opposed magistrates imposing their religion on their subjects by force, but countenanced no rights of resistance against such magistrates. He argued that any who acted against peace and property were to be 'cut off' by the magistrate who was 'armed' against all 'actual sedition, rapine, murder, perjury, and calumny'. Bayle combined his stress on the duty to follow conscience with arguing, as we saw earlier, that if a new preacher aggrandised himself or his sect and caused 'civil broils', magistrates were to use force against him. And, as John Laursen has shown, entries in the *Dictionary* expanded on the theme. For Bayle, torture and execution for treason was legitimate against Savonarola's 'factious spirit' and Jan Comenius' 'dangerous Fanaticism'. Both of these figures had prophetically supported invasion of other princes' territories. As Laursen has convincingly argued, behind both figures for Bayle stood the figure of Jurieu, prophetic justifier of revolution in England in the foreign invasion of William III.[66] We also saw in Chapter 14 that a number of Bayle's associates opposed rights of resistance, and that in his defence of James II as a Catholic by personal conviction who would allow all others to follow their own religious convictions and thus be tolerant, Paets argued against the religious pretext of taking up arms against a ruler of another religion.[67] Aubert wrote briefly in the *Pacific Protestant* that even though Christ had forbidden revenge this did not mean that Christianity should be thought to have deprived individuals of their 'natural right' to defend their lives against outrages, but he then condemned many acts of resistance to 'evil'.[68]

---

[65] Locke, *Letter* in *Works*, 10–11; Marshall, *Locke*; Bayle, *Philosophical Commentary* (1708), 114–16 (*Philosophical Commentary*, ed. Tannenbaum, 66; *Commentaire philosophique* 147).

[66] Bayle, *Philosophical Commentary* (1708), 517 and *passim*; *idem*, *OD*, II, 500; J. C. Laursen, 'Baylean Liberalism: Tolerance Requires Nontolerance' in Laursen (ed.), *Beyond the Persecuting Society* (Pennsylvania 1998), 197–215; Labrousse, *Bayle*, II, 553–4; J. Kilcullen, *Sincerity and Truth* (Oxford 1988), 91.

[67] Paets, *Lettre*, 4–6; Chapter 14 above.

[68] Aubert de Versé, *Protestant*, II, 96–8; E. R. Briggs, 'A Wandering Huguenot Scholar', *Huguenot Society Proceedings* (1970), 455–63.

While Limborch was clear in the *Theologia Christiana* that subjects were not to be forced to worship in the magistrate's religion, he stressed the general duties of obedience of subjects and argued that they were modestly to deny obedience to magistrates who attempted to use such force. He was adamant that they were not to seize public churches, which belonged to the magistrate. He argued that if a magistrate forbade separate assemblies and punished those who disobeyed his orders, subjects were to petition modestly for the liberty of exercising their religion, and if the magistrate proved inexorable they were to pray for a softening of the magistrate's heart and for constancy as they continued their private worship. And Limborch argued that if magistrates became tyrannical and imposed idolatry, subjects were to refuse to obey such commands, but that they were not to rebel under the pretext of piety. Turning to civil issues, Limborch argued that subjects were to pay even onerous taxes without rebelling or inciting others to rebel, and were to pray even for bad rulers. Stressing the honour due to rulers, he condemned conspiring and rebelling against rulers, citing in condemnation the actions of Absalom against David.[69]

In the *Letter Concerning Toleration*, initially written for Limborch in 1685 and first printed at Limborch's instigation in 1689, Locke argued that 'If any thing pass in a religious meeting seditiously, and contrary to the public peace, it is to be punished in the same manner, and no otherwise, than as if it happened in a fair'. In a sentence which Popple did not include in the English *Letter*, Locke declared that 'if a sermon in church contains anything seditious, it should be punished in the same way as if it had been preached in the market-place'. These meetings were 'not to be sanctuaries of factious and flagitious fellows'. Those who were 'seditious' for Locke ought 'to be punished and suppressed'. At the same time, as we saw earlier, Locke recognised that seditions were frequently raised upon pretence of religion, but argued that the stirs made were raised by the common disposition of mankind to 'shake off the yoke that galls their necks', and stressed that 'Just and moderate governments are everywhere quiet, everywhere safe'. And Locke argued in the *Letter* that where a magistrate believed that he had the right and judged it for the public good to make laws which took property from subjects who did not follow the same religion, and subjects believed the contrary, God was the only judge between them and would repay everyone at the last judgment according to their deserts in 'endeavouring to promote piety, and the public weal and peace of mankind'. Locke then wrote that 'in

---

[69] Limborch, *Theologia Christiana*, 582–5; *idem, Compleat System*, 711–15. Jones' translation introduced the theme of a 'natural right' of resistance based on princes using an arbitrary power contrary to the 'Original Constitution of the Country' and the laws 'by which he ought to govern'.

the mean while' subjects were to care for their own soul first and for the public peace second, adding immediately 'though yet there are few who will think it is peace' where 'they see all laid waste' (or, in Locke's own evocation of Tacitus, 'where they see a desert made'). Declaring that it was not his business to enquire into the rights of the magistrate in different nations, Locke held that there were contests between men by law and by force, and that where controversies arose without a judge to determine them it was true that the magistrate would have his will as 'the stronger' but that the question was not 'of the doubtfulness of the event, but the rule of right'.[70] And Locke wrote in the *Letter* of a situation under refusal of toleration where the 'leaders' of the church wrongly preached 'that heretics and schismatics are to be outed of their possessions, and destroyed' and where men were 'stript of the goods, which they have got by their honest industry' and were delivered up to others' 'violence and rapine' that nothing could be expected than that they should 'in the end think it lawful for them to resist force with force, and to defend their natural rights, which are not forfeitable upon account of religion, with arms as well as they can'.[71]

A complex set of positions on resistance emerged in the course of Burnet's writings in the Netherlands. Burnet's early publications in the Netherlands, gathered together and published as his 1687 *Six Papers*, argued against resistance for religion as he declared that he had preached in the Hague 'against the lawfulness of subjects rising in arms against their sovereign, upon the account of religion'. And he declared in the *Six Papers* the duty of subjects to 'bear all the ill Administrations that might be in the Government'. Burnet had been an opponent of armed resistance in the early 1680s in England. Even in his 1688 *Enquiry into the Measures of Submission*, Burnet argued that if one was persecuted religiously one was generally to fly or to submit if 'by the order of Divine providence, and of any constitution of government, under which we are born, we are brought under sufferings'. But, as we saw in Chapter 2, Burnet's *Enquiry* then crucially turned to a justification of resistance in arguing that when religion became a property, resistance could be used to defend that property; that if the laws of religion had made religion a property it became a 'right' of the subject; and that men were to judge of that 'invasion' of their rights as of all other such invasions. This was combined

---

[70] Locke, *Letter* in *Works*, 44, 51–2. Locke's own Latin text argued that man's first care should be of his soul and that he should 'do his utmost to maintain peace; though there are few who will think it is peace where they see a desert made': 'Prima animae cura habenda et paci quam maxime studendum; quanquam pauci sint qui ubi solitudinem factam vident pacem credant': Locke, *Letter*, ed. Klibansky and Gough, 130–1.

[71] Locke, *Letter* in *Works*, 53–4. Popple's translation spoke of 'natural rights'; Locke's own Latin of the 'rights which God and nature have granted them': 'jura sibi a Deo et natura concessa': *Letter*, ed. Klibansky and Gough, 146–7. Cf Marshall, *Locke*, 366; Zagorin, *Idea*, 265.

with argument in the *Enquiry* that when the legislative was 'invaded' the government had dissolved. Burnet's 1687 *History of the Valleys of Piedmont* supported the Waldensians' armed resistance as 'a natural and warrantable defence' against unjust oppression. And Burnet's defences of the Revolution in 1689 included a declaration of the legitimacy of resistance against attacks on liberty and property and against the invasion of freedom of conscience, 'the first and most sacred of all a Man's Rights'.[72]

Pierre Allix, Burnet's tolerationist protégé, Limborch's and Le Cène's friend, and Locke's correspondent, attacked divine right theories of absolutism and non-resistance as 'truly a Heresie in Matters of State' in his 1689 *Reflections upon the Opinions of Some Modern Divines Concerning the Nature of Government in General and that of England in Particular*. For Allix, such theorists had

endeavoured to delude the World, by alledging the Holy Scripture and Fathers, in favour of their opinions. But herein they have behaved themselves as the Heretics do, in citing the Scripture and Tradition in defence of their novelties.

Allix sought to show the 'original of the power' of kings, its 'extent', and the 'remedy' for 'abuse of it'. For Allix, there was no institution of rights of sovereignty in the 'law of nature'. Magistracy was founded to prevent invasion of what one's neighbour possessed by inheritance or industry. The choice of form of government was left to the people, from whom the magistrate derived his power. Allix argued that rulers could legitimately be absolute, and could revoke laws and dispense with them. They could not, however, lawfully overthrow the ends of government, divine laws, and the fundamental laws of the state. If government was bounded, duties of obedience ended where the magistrate issued commands beyond its bounds. Where consent was required to make laws and the magistrate tried either to make laws alone or to dispense with laws, subjects could resist. For Allix, the liberty of defending oneself was allowed to every individual by nature. While every failing of a king did not justify resistance, and individuals had an obligation to sacrifice their own private interest to the public, a tyrant could be resisted.[73]

Jean Le Clerc gave Locke's *Two Treatises* an extensive review in the *Bibliothèque universelle* in 1690, complimenting its 'moderation' and attacking those who supported the extremes either of elevating the rights of

---

[72] See Chapter 2 above, pp. 85–6; Burnet, *Six Papers*, esp. 7, 49–58, 59 (although cf. 25, where Burnet spoke of the suspension of the laws as subverting the government, as contrary to 'the Trust that is given to the Prince', and as putting men on 'uneasie and dangerous Inquiries' and as driving matters to 'a doubtful and desperate issue'); *idem, Enquiry*, esp. 7–9, 12–16; *idem, History*, 25.

[73] P. Allix, *Reflections upon the Opinions of Some Modern Divines Concerning the Nature of Government in General and that of England in Particular* (London 1689), *passim*.

sovereigns to such an extent that their subjects became 'slaves', or of supporting the rights of the people in such a way that the disorderly thought that there was no evil in 'shaking off the yoke' of political powers for very slight injuries thought to have been suffered and often changing the form of government. Le Clerc summarised many of Locke's replies to Filmer, and then many of his arguments in the Second Treatise, giving an extensive account not merely of Locke's arguments on the causes of the dissolution of government and defence of the rights of the people to judge when the prince or legislative power had exceeded their authority, but also of Locke's arguments that it was very difficult to get the people to amend the form of government to which they were accustomed (stressing illustratively the English preference for king and Parliament), that the people bore with even great mistakes by rulers, and that the power of the people to change the legislative power where necessary was an excellent way to prevent rebellion, as those who introduced arbitrary power were the 'true rebels'.[74]

This was one point at which Le Clerc reviewed English works discussing rights of resistance; his most influential such consideration in England was his review in the *Bibliothèque choisie* of the 1706 *Rights of the Christian Church* by Locke's Unitarian and later Deist friend Matthew Tindal. Tindal's book amalgamated a largely Lockeian case for natural rights, toleration, consent to civil society, and resistance, with a partially Harringtonian and strongly Erastian denial that the church was jurisdictionally separate from the state. Le Clerc identified Tindal's work as assaulting 'High churchmen' but suggested that it should be acceptable to all others in the 'enlighten'd' Church of England, 'the most illustrious of all the Protestant Churches'. Declaring the English people 'enlightened', Le Clerc asserted that he had 'scarce ever read a Book' that was 'so strong and so supported, in favour of those principles, which Protestants on t'other side the water commonly hold'. His 'abridgment' of Tindal's arguments stressed consent, natural rights, and resistance, all phrased in Lockeian fashion. It was held to be 'plain, that creatures of the same Kind, and created to the same advantages, are originally equal'. Every individual possessed a right of which he could not 'divest himself' and 'being thus obliged to preserve own life and person and endeavour to subsist as happily as Nature permits, he can neither give his Father, nor any other whatsoever, an absolute power over his Life'. Government was declared to have as its 'chief end' protection of acts 'not prejudicial' to others. Political power

---

[74] Le Clerc, *Bibliothèque universelle*, XIX (1690), 559–91. Cf also S. J. Savonius, 'Locke in French', *Historical Journal* (2004), 45–79 at 74.

must at first be placed by consent, either express or tacit, in the majority of the Members, who, when the greater multitude does not hinder, retain it themselves, or else commit it to some one, who acting as their representative, ought to be obeyed as long as he governs agreeably to the end for which he was established; yet who, when he acts contrary to that End, in the judgment of those who deputed him for that purpose, does in some sort make that Power naturally, as it were, revert to the People.

Those who 'come after' were 'presumed' to agree to laws and to preserving the authority of governors 'till they declare the contrary'. Government then owed its 'power of enforcing' observation of laws to the 'consent of the present Generation, which they sufficiently express in desiring to be protected by the Government in their Persons, Liberties and Estates, and also in agreeing to what is necessary to attain this End'. In most situations, this was the 'only way' most people had taken to show that they 'approve the Government'; and it was declared to be 'this which makes every one subject to the Government under which he lives'. Le Clerc summarised and declared as excellent advice Tindal's argument that the magistrate could punish those who 'preach up Persecution', and should restrict ecclesiastical preferments to those who had expressly renounced persecution. The English version of Le Clerc's review, *Mr Le Clerc's Extract and Judgment of the Rights of the Christian Church Asserted etc., translated from his Bibliothèque choisie vol. x*, identified Le Clerc as having been known as esteeming the Church of England so that he could not be thought to favour anything against 'the true Interest or Constitution of it', and complained that the adherents to arbitrary power had misrepresented 'the Patrons of Liberty' as being 'Levellers, Commonwealthsmen and enemys to the Prince's Prerogative'. Tindal and Le Clerc were thus identified as supporting both the royal prerogative and liberty, and the Church of England and toleration.[75]

This is a fair account of Le Clerc's positions. Le Clerc reviewed the republican regicide Edmund Ludlow's *Memoirs* and Clarendon's *History of the Rebellion*, arguing that Ludlow's work showed that Ludlow's party of 'independents' and 'violent republicans' of the English Revolution was 'odious'. They had not wanted peace to be made with the king, and the army had excluded from Parliament those Members of Parliament who were opposed to a court of justice to try the king. For Le Clerc, these 'Two Facts…in good Morality and Politicks, render culpable every thing the Presbyterians and Independents did against King Charles the First'. In his *Parrhasiana*, Le Clerc identified the 'happiness' of the people as the 'chief end' of government. Stressing that the Greeks and Romans had attacked tyranny, and that 'churchmen' had wrongly flattered temporal powers, he identified as the

---

[75] Le Clerc, *Mr Le Clerc's Extract and Judgment of the Rights of the Christian Church Asserted* (1708).

kind of government which deserved the praise of historians one in which subjects were 'only obliged to obey the laws, which are approved by a long usage, or enacted according to the usual manner', where subjects were capable of 'enjoying quietly one's Estate, and the Fruit of one's labour' without 'the apprehension of being deprived of it by any violent means', and of contributing to public charges only as much as they could bear 'without being overburdened'. He identified England as a country in which there was a limited obedience to a limited monarchy. And in his 1701 second volume of *Parrhasiana*, Le Clerc recommended Locke's *Second Treatise* in an essay on the means to render a commonwealth happy which praised the recent Revolution there as involving William III restoring liberty and the laws in England, while simultaneously stressing how very rare and extraordinary was such a revolution without disorder and effusion of blood.[76] In his support for the monarchy and its prerogative, in his support for the Church of England, Latitudinarianism, and toleration, and in his repudiation of those whose social and political challenges to monarch and church had occupied the more radical part of the political spectrum, Le Clerc was a 'moderate' defender of resistance. Le Clerc's general rendition of 'Lockeian principles' is close to the kind of ethos that Locke himself seems to have had, as a defender of rights of resistance *in extremis*.[77]

---

[76] Le Clerc, *Parrhasiana* (1700), 157–61; *idem, Parrhasiana* (1701), 138, 268–9; Golden, *Le Clerc*, 132; *Mr Le Clerc's Account of the Earl of Clarendon's History* (1710), 6; my 'Some Intellectual Consequences'. Cf also Savonius, 'Locke', 73–4.

[77] Another of Locke's friends, James Tyrrell, who defended resistance only in limited circumstances, added a dialogue to his *Bibliotheca Politica* to indicate that the principles of 1688–9, which he supported, did not justify the 'murder' of the royal martyr in 1649: Tyrrell, *Bibliotheca Politica* (London 1694); Kenyon, *Revolution*; my 'Some Intellectual Consequences'.

18

Toleration, 'heretics', and 'schismatics'

The tolerationists' contentions that magistrates were bound to prevent temporal harm and secure peace and that religious 'speculative' opinions and most forms of religious worship were 'harmless' to others diametrically opposed the antitolerationist argument of the past millennium that heretics and schismatics 'murdered' and 'poisoned' others by 'infecting' them with 'errors' which 'killed' their 'souls'. Bayle explicitly replied in the *Philosophical Commentary* to the characteristic argument of the intolerant that princes were 'armed against evil-doers' and therefore especially against 'heretics', who

affront the Divine Majesty, trample under foot his Sacred Truths, and poison the Soul, whose Life is our all, and ought to be infinitely dearer to us than that of the Body. They are worse than Poisoners, than Highwaymen or Banditti, who kill the body only, and ought consequently to be more severely punish'd.[1]

Bayle declared such arguments invalid because heretics 'offer Violence to no one' and undertook their actions towards their neighbour from love and desire to do 'great service to God'. Motivated to persuade others 'because they fancy they do great service to God' heretics might 'tell their Neighbour' that they thought him in error, and exhort and reason with him, but left him 'at full liberty'. For Bayle, injury and malice were the two 'grand Circumstances which authorise' magistrates to punish 'highwaymen and murderers' but not heretics. Bayle disagreed with the notion that the 'Poison shed into the Soul' by heretics was 'more fatal' than a murderer's act against the body; he stated that not merely was there 'full liberty of chusing or refusing' to believe the heretics and the motivation that 'he shall save his Neighbour's Soul', but a 'proper and saving Antidote' was available because preachers could argue against alleged 'heretics' and so 'prevent their seducing' others.[2]

---

[1] Bayle, *Philosophical Commentary* (1708), 247 (*Philosophical Commentary*, ed. Tannenbaum, 137–8; *Commentaire philosophique*, 260–1).

[2] Bayle, *Philosophical Commentary* (1708), 249–51 (*Philosophical Commentary*, ed. Tannenbaum, 137–9; *Commentaire philosophique*, 261–4).

Opposing justifications of 'hereticide' in his 1686 *Theologia Christiana*, Limborch similarly stressed that its supporters claimed that

thieves and robbers are justly put to death by the Magistrate; with much greater reason ought Heretics, who are compared to ravening wolves and to thieves and robbers. Again false coiners of money and poisoners are put to death; much more, they say, ought the falsifiers and corrupters of the word of God, who by the Poison of their false doctrines destroy the souls of men, to be cut off.

He answered that one should 'pity the sad estate of Christianity, when the Doctors thereof make use of such unnatural and inhuman arguments' and when they 'excite the poor populace to such a cruelty as is inconsistent with the meekness and moderation of a Christian'. For even if it were granted that 'Error in Religion were a crime' – which 'need not be granted' –

these crimes are so different, that no inference can be drawn from the one, which can affect the other. For error, if it be a crime, is committed directly against God, not against the Magistrate: since it disturbs not the publick peace, robs no man of his possessions, but proceeds from Principles of a Mistaken Concience, which is subject to the Cognizance of God alone, and not to that of the Magistrate, unless the Heretick be as great a Disturber of the Publick Tranquility, as Thieves, Robbers, etc. are.[3]

For Limborch moreover, even if the inference of force were correct, one would then need to know 'infallibly' who the heretics were, as 'thieves' were not put to death until the crime charged against them was 'fully made out'. Like Bayle, Limborch stressed heretics' good intention and that even if others were harmed, this was the result of their choice. He argued that whereas thieves knew they had done wrong, heretics believed that they had done well, that those who hurt others when intending to help them were 'not to be put to death', and that at worst heretics 'injure' none 'but the willing'.[4]

In his 1706 *History of the Jews*, Jacques Basnage identified among justifications of intolerance the contentions 'that the Church alone ought to reign; that Truth has its privileges which Falshood can never obtain' and the allegation that

the Erroneous poison and kill the Soul; and therefore deserve the punishment of murderers and Poisoners; which is the more justly inflicted, as the Death they cause is Eternal; and the Soul is more Excellent than the body.

Basnage pointed out that this argument was 'a Metaphor' and argued that a metaphorical similarity did not form a valid argument 'for punishing Poisoners and the Erroneous alike'. Introducing the theme of the consent of the supposed victims of heretics, these alleged crimes were, for Basnage, quite different because

---

[3] Limborch, *Compleat System*, 991; *idem*, *Theologia Christiana*, 833.
[4] Limborch, *Compleat System*, 992; *idem*, *Theologia Christiana*, 834.

A Murderer or Poisoner kill the Body against the Will, and without the Knowledge of the Person murdered…But the Erroneous have the Lamp of Reason to distinguish truth from error, and they voluntarily espouse it.

For Basnage, one should not base the 'persecution against the erroneous' on the 'equivocation of words'. Punishments

ought to be of the same nature with the crimes. Hereticks that poison the soul, ought to be chastised with a Spiritual Punishment, such as the denial of the Sacraments, and the Spiritual advantages reaped in the church, and the Murderer that kills the body ought to suffer a bodily punishment.

For Basnage, a similar abuse of words stood behind the notion that 'punishment' was not 'persecution'. One should not 'delude' oneself by taking 'Punishments for Persuasions' when persuasions did not rob one of liberty. If the church believed that it truly had the 'power to punish', for Basnage it should then 'speak sincerely' for 'cruelty and violence'. That it would not thus speak sincerely provided clear self-indictment.[5]

Johann Crell's *Vindication*, republished by Charles Le Cène in his 1687 *Conversations*, similarly attacked the 'injustice' involved in esteeming heretics 'as bad as thieves and robbers, or even worse than them, and to be ranked among those with whom no fellowship or society may be entertained, no promise made and kept'. In an argument which Crell had composed many years before Bayle's similar argument, it was contended that they

know not themselves to be heretiques, and would not be such if they knew it; but most strongly believe that they hold opinions concerning matters of Religion, which are true, pious, and altogether agreeable to the word of God, neither do, nor purpose to do wrong to any man.

Thieves knew that they invaded other men's rights, and sinned against the law of nature 'engraven in their hearts', and 'that which is of most force in this point, they disturb, violate, and destroy the peace and tranquillity of other men'. They were punished by magistrates as 'breakers of that common peace, which God ordained him to preserve'. Heretics lived 'peacefully with other men', did not know that they sinned, and did not 'commit anything against the laws of civil society'. They were not merely ignorant of harming other men's souls, but fully persuaded that they did not. Those accused and punished as 'heretics' often led blameless lives and were punished for 'mere error of judgement'. They who 'unwittingly destroy men's soules, as Heretiques are thought to do, are not to be dealt' with like those who 'kill their bodies'. One could thus reach a 'short conclusion': 'whoever observes the rules of civill society, neither disturb the peace and tranquillity of other

---

[5] Basnage, *History*, 639–41.

men, they cannot by any just authority be ejected out of a civill society, neither should they in any wise be denied peace and security'.[6]

Le Cène's own sections of the *Conversations* raised at a number of points in the voice of the character Agathon the notion that heresy was a contagious disease which needed the application of magisterial force to prevent infecting others; the character Philadelph replied that 'spiritual cures' were appropriate for what had been called a cancer and a gangrene, and emphasised the good intentions of those allegedly spreading this infection. For Aubert in the *Treatise*, a 'heretic' thought he was serving God, and was unwilling to give up his faith precisely because of his love for and fear of God. He was trying to do good to others by attempting to spread his ideas, and not trying to harm them. God would judge if such an individual was saved. In arguing against the toleration of heretics in his 1683 *History of Calvinism*, Jurieu had concluded that a heretic could be forbidden from preaching and then punished for disobeying the magistrate's orders, and thus not as an 'heretic' but as a violator of the orders of the sovereign. For Aubert, this argument was more to be expected from 'a Spanish Inquisitor than a minister of the gospel'. Bayle similarly noted in the *Philosophical Commentary* that if error was understood as a 'disease' of the soul, it should have a spiritual remedy such 'as argument and instruction'. The spiritual remedy of arguments and persuasions for any 'corruption' communicated by heretics to others was similarly endorsed by Jones' edition of Limborch's *Theologia Christiana*, which declared that to prevent 'corruption' by 'heretics' that 'they are to be opposed by all the Arguments that can be taken from Reason and Scripture'.[7] Bayle maintained the language of heresy as 'pestilential', but only to follow earlier writers such as Coornhert and Milton by redefining heresy as consisting of intolerance. It was intolerance that was actually the 'pestilential heresy': 'let the worst come to the worst, those Sects so run down on the score of their speculative Heresys are...at least as good as those who boast themselves Orthodox...considering their Doctrine of compelling is a Heresy in Morality, a practical and most pestilential Heresy' which more than balanced any 'speculative' falsehood.[8]

Locke had explicitly considered the notion of 'infection' as an argument for intolerance in a manuscript of 1676, 'Toleration B'; Locke replied to the notion that heretics 'will infect others':

---

[6] [J. Crell], *Vindication*, 6–7, 10–13; Le Cène, *Conversations*, 229–32.

[7] Le Cène, *Conversations*, 30–1, 105–9, 114; Aubert de Versé, *Protestant*, 7; *idem*, *Traité*, *passim*, esp. 55–7; Morman, *Aubert*, 228–9; Bayle, *Philosophical Commentary* (1708), 387; Limborch, *Compleat System*, xxii.

[8] Bayle, *Philosophical Commentary* (1708), 753; *idem*, OD, ii, 555.

If those others are infected but by their own consent, and that to cure another disease that they think they have, why should they be hindered any more than a man is that might make an issue to cure palsy, or might willingly have haemorrhoids to prevent an apoplexy?

Rhetorically posing the anti-tolerationist reply to this argument, and then meeting that reply with a further response of his own, Locke first noted that the anti-tolerationist would answer such a question by saying that the contagion required removal of the contaminated, since otherwise 'all people will run into this error', and responded first by invoking the provision of antidotes to their arguments, and then by shifting to the argument that if such antidotes failed there was no danger to the ruler of the polity posed by the multiplication of error because:

This supposes either that it is true and so prevails, or that the teachers of truth are very negligent and let it, and that they are to blame; or that people are more inclined to error than truth; if so, then, error being manifold, they will be as distant one from another as from you, and so no fear of their uniting, unless you force them by making yourself an enemy to all by ill-treatment.

Locke similarly recognised and responded in 1676 to a further argument that others should not be tolerated as they were 'distempered' because 'we fear their rage and violence'. He declared that if such fear existed as a 'symptom' 'because you treat them ill' then you should 'change' your method of dealing with them and thereby remove the 'distemper'. Even if a 'distemper' had a 'tendency to rage', one was to 'watch it' and to apply 'fit remedies'; if those observed were instead 'perfect innocents, only a little crazed' then a magistrate was to 'let [them] alone'.[9]

In the *Letter Concerning Toleration*, Locke himself used the metaphor of heresy as contagious disease but blunted its effects in noting that people who were out of power preached up toleration, and could 'bear most patiently, and unmovedly, the contagion of idolatry, superstition, and heresy, in their neighbourhood', but wished to use force against it as soon as they had power. He further met the imagery of 'heresy' as 'disease' by arguing that magistrates did not enforce health, and that even if they were to try to do so, they would not provide 'by law, that they must consult none but roman physicians, and shall every one be bound to live according to their prescriptions[?]'. Magistrates would not enforce that 'no potion, no broth be taken, but what is prepared either in the Vatican, suppose, or in a Geneva shop'. In a situation in which one had a 'weak body, sunk under a languishing disease, for which, I suppose, there is only one remedy, but that unknown' it did not belong 'unto the magistrate to prescribe me a remedy'. People were not treated for other

[9] 'Toleration B 1676' in Locke, *Political Essays*, ed. Goldie, 246–9.

diseases without their consent; even if religious errors were a disease they should not be treated in ways they had not approved for themselves. And he adopted the notion of 'poison' only in order to turn it against the notion of medicinal remedies for the soul from the magistrate: 'you will in vain cram a medicine down a sick man's throat, which his particular constitution will be sure to turn into poison'.[10]

In the early 1690s, Locke returned to the issue of disease and its images in tolerationist debate by questioning the applicability of the treatment to the disease, attacking Proast's notion of punishing dissenters to make them consider, when some dissenters had surely considered, and some of the Church of England had not, as being

just as reasonable, as if, a lethargy growing epidemical in England, you should propose to have a law made to blister and scarify and shave the heads of all who wear gowns: though it be certain that neither all who wear gowns are lethargic, nor all who are lethargic, wear gowns.[11]

And Locke suggested that the issue of toleration was like the issue of a patient with 'kidney stones'. It was true that a 'man may have the stone' and that it 'may be useful' to him to cut him, yet this did not 'justify the most skilful surgeon in the world' by force making him 'endure pain and the hazard of cutting' without commission. It was, for Locke, as for Bayle, Limborch, Aubert, and Le Cène, important that any doctor have 'consent'; the magistrate could not be a doctor for the soul because no 'consent' was possible where one's eternal fate was at issue.[12] It is important here to note that Locke was using primarily images of non-contagious diseases such as kidney stones and of one's own suffering of those diseases, thereby not so much meeting the language of harmful disease spreading contagiously as countering it with images of disease as essentially private, and of treatments such as surgical excision from a patient's body, rather than of excision from the polity to prevent others from being effected. When Locke did speak of 'epidemical' diseases, he focused on consent, or on the inability to deliver medicines in any logical curative manner. And he alleged that the partial application of force made it a remedy for disease 'like the helleboraster, that grew in the woman's garden for the cure of worms in her neighbour's children: for truly it wrought too roughly, to give it to any of her own'.[13]

We have seen repeatedly that heretics and schismatics were associated in anti-heretical literature not merely with disease but with theft, violence,

---

[10] Locke, *Letter* in *Works*, 20, 23–5, 28.
[11] Locke, *Second Letter* in *Works*, VI, 92–4; Seaton, *Toleration*, 260.
[12] Locke, *Second Letter* in *Works*, VI, 113; R. Vernon, *The Career of Toleration* (Montreal 1997), 83.
[13] Locke, *Letters*, in *Works*, VI, 94, 99, 164–9, 273, 277–8, 285–6, 324.

sexual libertinism, and challenges to familial authority. Bayle replied to this in the *Philosophical Commentary* in part by arguing that if aiming at the end of conversion justified the use of any means, then it could justify the overturning of all morality, allowing the use of violence, theft, and even rape in order to promote conversion to the 'true religion'. Alleging that these had been the methods employed by dragoons to coerce Protestant 'conversion', he thus suggested that if any were the 'true heretics' who were truly libertine and dismissive of rights to property, it was such Catholics. And he reinforced the accusations metaphorically. The Catholic polemicist Ferrand had defended the Revocation by arguing that the Catholic Church was 'a mother recalling her disobedient children' by force; Bayle replied that the Protestant pretension was that 'far from being that Spouse of Jesus Christ who is the Mother of all true Christians', the Roman Church was instead 'really an infamous Harlot, who has seiz'd the House, by the Assistance of a band of Ruffians, Cut-throats, Hell-hounds; who has turn'd the Father and Mother out o' doors, has murdered as many of the Children as she cou'd...forc'd others to own her for lawful Mistress, or reduc'd 'em to live in exile'. The Catholic Church was thus in Protestant eyes 'an abominable Harlot, who has seiz'd upon the House by downright force, and turned out the true Mistress and true Heirs, to make room for her Lovers, and the Accomplices of her Whoredom'.

Bayle did not himself subscribe to either the Protestant or Catholic pretension about the other denomination, as he asserted even before he embarked on the comparison that one needed to build on solid reasoning on principles common to both sides and *not* on pretensions. But he nonetheless argued that the punishments of Protestants by Catholics were the 'more unnatural and monstrous' the more that one granted her own assumption that Protestants were errant 'children', and that if one granted equally the Protestant pretension about Catholics, then Protestants were more justifiably revenging 'a mother' shamefully chased out of her own house by a 'Prostitute'. A significant rhetorical sleight of hand was thus involved in presenting these images while proclaiming each to be the pretensions about the other. Bayle had not registered Catholic images of Protestants as sexual libertines, thieves, and murderers and countered them by Protestant images of Catholics as libertines, thieves, and murderers, but had instead concentrated on Protestants being morally upright if 'rebellious children' and then given full voice to the set of Protestant associations and images that left a reader with 'monstrosity' and 'sexual transgressions' associated only with Catholics.[14]

---

[14] Bayle, *Philosophical Commentary* (1708), 12–15 (*Philosophical Commentary*, ed. Tannenbaum, 14–15; *Commentaire philosophique*, 58–60).

REDEFINING HERESY AND SCHISM

Thus far, the description of the tolerationist case has concentrated on their responses to anti-heretical and anti-schismatic writing which took for granted that alleged 'heretics' and 'schismatics' were indeed 'heretics' and 'schismatics', and then suggested that even if that was true they were 'harmless' or harmed others only with the consent of those others and while intending to do them good. Accepting that alleged heretics and schismatics were indeed heretics and schismatics, it denied that they were 'poisoners' and 'pestilential' and to be treated like murderers and highwaymen. But many of the advocates of religious toleration did not accept that 'heretics' and 'schismatics' were correctly identified. They also questioned the capacity of humans to identify heresy accurately, or redefined 'heresy' and 'schism' so that the 'heretics' and 'schismatics' were held to be the *imposers* of belief and worship and not those departing from the imposed orthodoxy and practices.

For Bayle, the very definition of 'heresy' was in contest. It was, as he put it in the 1688 *Supplement* to the *Philosophical Commentary*, 'impossible to define heresy'. And in the *Third Part* in 1687, Bayle pointed to the central distinction made by Augustine to distinguish 'good' and 'bad' persecutions as one that

amounts only to this; that the Orthodox Persecutors persecute for orthodoxy, and the Heterodox for Heterodoxy: a ridiculous Tautology, of no manner of Service for coming at the Knowledg of that which is under Enquiry.[15]

As he had argued at length in the first two parts of the *Philosophical Commentary* in 1686, if one gave power to the 'orthodox' to impose their religion, this would be claimed by all 'as each Party believes itself the Orthodox'. It was 'plain' therefore that if persecution was indeed commanded in the gospel, 'each sect wou'd think itself obliged' to persecute. If taken literally, the text of Luke 'compel them to come in' would be used by 'every sect' including *against* the 'truth' creating 'a continual War between People of the same Country, either in the Streets or in the open Field' and between 'Nations of different Opinions'.[16] As Bayle stressed in the *Third Part* of the *Philosophical Commentary* in reply to Augustine, if the right of violence against all other religions came from the claim to possession of the truth, then each sect will challenge with 'the same Reason and Excuses' and there would be no other remedy 'than the discussing all the Controversys between 'em from the very Source and Beginning; a Discussion which wou'd take up the

---

[15] Bayle, *Philosophical Commentary* (1708), 424, 600–1; *idem*, OD, II, 458, 519.
[16] Bayle, *Philosophical Commentary* (1708), 144 (*Philosophical Commentary*, ed. Tannenbaum, 84–5; *Commentaire philosophique*, 172–3).

Life of Methusalem upon any one Article'. For Bayle, under 'an Impossibility of mutually convincing each other', both sides should consent to the common laws of society and morality for peace.[17] For Bayle in the 1688 *Supplement*, God would not have left his church destitute of other remonstrances than praying for Persecutors to

> examine into a boundless Ocean of Controversys, so entangled with Cavil and Illusion, thro the Knavery and false Zeal of Controvertists, that there's no Patience but must be quite tir'd out with hearing and weighing the Answers, Replys, and Rejoinders of both Partys upon the minutest Point in contest.[18]

Coornhert had suggested in the sixteenth century that it was very difficult to find a 'judge' who would be capable of determining controversies. Bayle, who constructed an entry on Coornhert for the *Dictionary*, expanded this argument massively in the *Supplement* to the *Philosophical Commentary*. He argued that many judges had limited understandings and capacities to judge. It was, for Bayle, less difficult to discover if a person who was accused of murder, adultery, or poisoning was guilty than whether a doctrine was 'heretical'. He here turned to what was to be one of his favourite themes in many works, the famous dispute within Catholicism in the 1660s about Jansenism. Five propositions had been condemned at Rome; Jansen had replied that these propositions in his work could be received in an 'Heretical Sense', but that he did not support them in this sense. Jansen held that the Pope was infallible in determining matters of right, and thus in condemning a proposition as 'heresy', but not in matters of 'fact', such as determining whether another individual actually held the 'heretical' belief or had expressed it in a particular text. For Bayle, this illustrated the difficulty of determining even the simplest dispute over heresy, where both sides accepted the same ecclesiastical authority, lived at the same moment in the history of Christianity, and so had a fair chance of understanding each others' propositions. If that dispute could not be settled easily, the dispute between Catholicism and Calvinism had no hope of being settled without 'endless Broil and Contention'. And for Bayle, debate between Catholics and Calvinists had occurred when in time and 'stile' those debating the issue were the same; study of the Fathers and of Scripture itself multiplied massively the issues of time and style. In order to settle the kinds of disputes that had arisen during the history of Christianity, magistrates would need to understand the disputes, and this meant that they would need: a professional skill in metaphysics to settle the disputes over free will and omnipotence; to have a mastery of the Greek and Hebrew languages; to be students of 'critical

---

[17] Bayle, *Philosophical Commentary* (1708), 438; *idem, OD,* II, 461.
[18] Bayle, *Philosophical Commentary* (1708), 540–2; *idem, OD,* II, 506.

divinity'; to understand the 'customs of the Jews in our Saviour's Days'; and to be aware of the issues surrounding the 'copyists' of the Bible – alleged in the critical biblical scholarship issued in the late seventeenth century to have altered or mistranscribed whole passages of the text of Scripture. Even when possessed of such skills, they would then need impartially to weigh the 'Reasons' of each party, their 'reciprocal Objections', their solutions for these objections, their replies to these solutions, and their rejoinders to these replies. It was clear, in sum, that in order to make a determination about the matters in contoversy in religion, magistrates would need to 'surpass the Strength, the Patience, and Parts of most Judges in the World'.

The consequence was for Bayle clear: either that there was 'no Tribunal upon Earth for judging of Heresy', or one accepted that the judge was very fallible indeed in determining what was 'heresy'. In the latter situation, it was very likely that the judge would err, and would declare the 'orthodox' to be the 'heretic', and the 'heretic' to be 'orthodox'. It could not possibly be the case that such a magistrate ought to be empowered to use force. Bayle's significant output of competing opinions discussed in the *Dictionary* in the 1690s was surely intended not merely to show the difficulties of each position, but also to 'surpass the Strength, the Patience, and Parts' of most Readers and thus to promote toleration.[19]

In the *Supplement* to the *Philosophical Commentary*, issued in part to combat Jurieu's reply to the first two parts of the *Commentary*, Bayle explicitly phrased the question 'whether it be easy to give the Definition of Heresy'. Bayle noted that some said that 'heresy' involved beliefs maintained with 'obstinacy' against 'the church', but replied that this simply raised the question of the definition of 'obstinacy'. Some instead said that heresy was determined by 'the Church', but this simply raised the question which was the 'true Church'. Some said that a heretic was one who denied a fundamental truth of the Christian religion – but this raised the question of the 'mark' of a 'fundamental' truth. Thus, not merely was 'heresy' itself in dispute, but every one of the major attempts to ground a way to define heresy were themselves the 'source of endless discussion'.[20] As Bayle put it, 'the Term which St Paul makes use of, is extremely equivocal, and one might write a Book on the different Fates of this Word, and the different Significations it has born'. For Bayle, if 'heresy' was to be truly defined in its 'ill Sense' in Pauline terms, it consisted of the 'Attempt' to 'advance particular doctrines, and form a Party in the Church', motivated by pride, contention, and jealousy. It involved unnecessarily opposing a doctrine known to be good or at least very tolerable in order to make onself 'Head

[19] Bayle, *Philosophical Commentary* (1708), 591–7; *idem, OD,* ɪɪ, 518–19.
[20] Bayle, *Philosophical Commentary* (1708), 600–4; *idem, OD,* ɪɪ, 519–20.

of a Party'. It was 'restless', involving a 'turbulent humour' and 'Discord in the Church'. It was not to be applied to those who peacefully varied from others in their opinions and worship.[21]

It had been particularly common in late patristic, medieval, and early modern attacks on variants of anti-Trinitarianism to accuse anti-Trinitarians of 'corruption', including sexual 'libertinism'. Noting that 'heretics' were accused of being corrupt, Bayle argued forcefully that most sects had preached a severe morality and that most of the doctrines about which Christians had divided and to which the term 'heresy' was applied were 'speculative' and not 'carnal'. Various sects of Christians were 'all agreed about the Doctrines which teach Men to live soberly and righteously' but 'divided about Points which tend not to make the Yoke of Christian Morality either heavier or lighter'. For instance, for Bayle, just as Catholics did Protestants an injustice in saying that it was their corruption which prevented them from seeing the truth of Catholicism, so Socinians were done an injustice by Protestants in saying that a 'Corruption' prevented them from 'their finding the Doctrine of a Trinity in Scripture'. No greater burden of morality would be placed on them if they believed 'a Trinity of Persons in the Unity of the Divine Nature' than in their belief in 'a God one in Nature and Person'.[22]

Isaac Papin's *Faith Reduced*, which Bayle published from manuscript, argued at considerable length against the denomination of individuals as heretics because they did not follow articles in confessions of faith that had added to the express terms of Scripture. For Papin, it was those who claimed an empire over consciences and sought to impose their understanding of Scripture on others who were really the 'heretics'.[23] The first two of the dialogues in Le Cène's 1687 *Conversations* voiced a series of arguments about the toleration necessary among Christians and from magistrates, with the character Philadelph declaring it better to change one's thoughts in following the light of reason than to preserve those one had because of the prejudices of birth, education or chance, and arguing that one could not identify others as heretics unless they erred in matters that were 'clear and distinct' in the Holy Scripture and attempted to impose their views on others by force. Philadelph held that it was very difficult to know of what the alleged 'crime' of heresy consisted. And he contended that indirect or direct attack on the Trinity of persons in the divine nature did not constitute a

[21] Bayle, *Philosophical Commentary* (1708), 668–9; *idem*, OD, II, 535–6.

[22] Bayle, *Philosophical Commentary* (1708), 344–5 (*Philosophical Commentary*, ed. Tannenbaum, 184; *Commentaire philosophique*, 344).

[23] I. Papin, *La Foi réduite à ses véritables principes* (Rotterdam 1687), 3–4, 7, 16–18, 27–8, 30–2, 47–8, 50, 56–8.

'blasphemy' deserving of magisterial force, pointing to a variety of different beliefs as consistent with the words of Scripture and with salvation.[24]

Reviewing the *Conversations* in the 1687 *Bibliothèque universelle*, Le Clerc stressed its attack on those who would persuade the magistrate to use force against heretics, that persuasion and not force was legitimate, and condemned the calling by some of all Christians who were not of their sentiments 'heretics' and 'blasphemers'. Le Clerc's own earlier *Theological Epistles* had depicted a debate between a Socinian and a Trinitarian which had seen both claiming Scriptural support for their views, and which ended with an exhortation for each to allow the other to hold their beliefs in peace and charity, without accusing the other of 'heresy'. It was this work which caused Le Clerc to flee Geneva branded as a 'Socinian'.[25]

In his *Theologia Christiana*, Limborch declared that 'The Errors which the Scripture does not condemn as damnable, ought not to be call'd Heresies'. 'Hereticks' truly defined were 'Persons erring in points necessary to salvation' and not those 'that are simply erroneous, or who holding the same Fundamentals with our selves, do yet dissent from us in the Explication of some Doctrines not destructive of salvation'. A person with 'due reverence' for Scripture, who looked on Scripture as the 'only rule of faith' and desired to admit nothing as 'fundamental' but what may be 'clearly maintained and demonstrated to be such by Scripture', would not 'easily fall into such damnable errors as are destructive of faith'. Limborch pointed out that according to 'present usage', a heretic was identified as a 'man who maintains an opinion contrary to that commonly entertained, or even approved of by a synod; or rather who maintains a grievous errour contrary to the truth publickly received'. It was on this false basis, he noted, that the 'opinion of the Romanists' was that 'heretics' should have 'all sorts of punishments inflicted, even death'. He noted that by some Catholics 'the most exquisite kinds of death' were recommended, and that this opinion had been put in practice 'exceeding by far even Heathen Cruelty'. But he stressed that Calvin and Beza had maintained this opinion just as strongly as had Catholics. For Limborch, assaults on heretics had been invented in order to 'hide the Turpitude of that Opinion'. For Limborch, one that errs deserved to be pitied, not punished. Error was the fault of the understanding and not of the will. Stressing that men were not infallible, Limborch held that some whom 'we' think are 'heretics' might well be 'professors of the truth' whilst 'without knowing it' we may be 'patrons of very gross errors'. At most, moreover, heretics 'are only erroneous,

[24] Le Cène, *Conversations*, 1–121, esp. 4–5, 24–5, 38–9, 52–3, 69, 72–3, 78–81.
[25] Le Clerc, *Bibliothèque universelle*, v (1687), 212–27; Le Clerc, *Liberii de sancto amore epistolae theologicae* (1681); Klauber, 'Fundamental Articles'; Barnes, *Le Clerc*; Golden, *Le Clerc*; on Locke's notation of Le Clerc's work in the 1690s, see my 'Locke, Socinianism'.

but not wicked men'. Calvin had urged that the magistrate bears the sword not in vain. For Limborch,

The magistrate bears the sword...to restrain the wicked and ungodly; before he can punish, it must appear that such or such a person is of that number. Since then in the dissensions about the more obscure and secret mysteries of Religion it is not as yet determined by an infallible judgment on whose side the truth lies, it cannot likewise appear where the crime is. Add to this, that error is an offence that does not merit punishment.[26]

Not merely Bayle, but many of these authors questioned the central definition of heresy given in the church over the centuries, that it must involve 'obstinacy' in order to be punished, by attacking the capacity of others to know that another was being 'obstinate'. For Paets in *De nuperis Angliae*, translated into French by Bayle as the *Lettre...sur les derniers troubles d'Angleterre*, what was named 'obstinacy' by some was 'constancy' to others. It was in his view possible to distinguish between them only if one adopted the notion that 'obstinacy' was 'persevering in known evil'. But by this definition, one could 'never accuse a man who errs of being obstinate'. Paets argued that he did not mean to say that one who erred was not blameworthy; it was quite possible that such an individual had not chosen well, and had not employed himself as he should have. But since this was dependent on very many circumstances that were little known to men, they had to be left to be judged by God.[27] For Le Cène in the 1687 *Conversations*, only God could know the internal convictions of others necessary to identify 'obstinacy'.[28]

Bayle's *Philosophical Commentary* launched a similar but longer assault on the central tradition in the church of defining 'heresy' as an error in the faith maintained 'obstinately'. He noted that his opponents charged that violence was 'not designed to force conscience' but only applied against 'those who neglect to examine truth' with what 'they call obstinacy'. Bayle then stripped away this argument by presenting layer upon layer of objections which culminated in the notion that one 'must be God himself to know' obstinacy. For Bayle, if by saying that they could punish 'obstinacy' they meant one who persists in errors after they appeared to them to be 'gross errors' – when such an individual was 'convinced in his conscience' of this – then indeed such an individual should not be tolerated because their motivation had to be 'caprice and malice'. But humans could not read others' hearts, and thus could never know (short of a personal revelation from God) if this was true of another. For Bayle, there was simply no criterion to distinguish 'constancy' from 'stubbornness', but by a 'begging' of the

---

[26] Limborch, *Compleat System*, 982–6, 990, 1010–2; *idem, Theologia Christiana*, 827, 829, 833, 835, 846–7.
[27] Paets, *Lettre* (Rotterdam 1686), 16–21, esp. 19–21.　　[28] Le Cène, *Conversations*, 74–5.

question, or by bestowal of fine names on one's self and reproach on others. Any attempt to appeal to the 'evident' qualities of 'evidence' in order to convict another of 'obstinacy' was doomed to failure because for Bayle evidence was itself 'a relative quality'. One could not say 'that what appears evident to us is so to others'. People varied in their situation, point of view, and the proportion between things and their 'organs' or 'habits', 'education', or other influences on them. One could therefore not pronounce them 'obstinate' because they did not perceive things as you did on the basis of the same 'evidence'. And any appeal to 'obstinacy' as evidenced by the failure to be able to answer objections was doomed for Bayle, because his opponents were unable to 'say that a Peasant, a Shopkeeper, or Roman Catholick Gentlewoman engaged in an Argument of Religion' with the Anglicans' leading theologians, such as Stillingfleet, or with the Huguenot leaders such as du Moulin, would 'be able to answer all the Objections' raised by such learned disputants. In all disputes, Bayle claimed 'he who has a ready Wit, a voluble Tongue, a subtle Head, improv'd by Logick, and a great Memory, shall always get the better' even of learned but less facile arguers, without therefore being correct that theirs' was the 'true religion'. To conclude that one who was 'foiled' in an argument defended the 'bad Religion' was simply 'absurd'. It was, for Bayle, obvious from this that it was not a 'Mark of Falsehood in any Religion, that all who profess it, are not able to answer every Difficulty which a learned Controversist of the opposite side may suggest'. It was perfectly possible for an individual to suspect that some 'subtle Questions' were 'mere Cavils' and appropriately to stick to his side.

Indeed, in the 1688 *Supplement*, Bayle argued that given that the results of examination could well be to throw individuals into 'Doubts and distracting Thoughts' the very 'refusal' to examine was in some circumstances a 'good'.[29] Bayle was acutely aware that few were capable of being learned, and that it was necessary to support the toleration of those who could not in fact win disputes if one was to defend toleration instead of intolerant expertise. His position in the 'republic of letters' was combined with a sense that most were not capable of leisure and learning. He tended therefore to stress the differential requirements of individuals. For Bayle, 'every one ought to set apart some Portion of his time for Instruction, and even be ready to renounce what he had believ'd most true, if it be made appear to him false'. But alongside such readiness to give up opinions had to be an equal readiness to assert some: one could not be 'a Sceptick or Pyrrhonist in

---

[29] Bayle, *Philosophical Commentary* (1708), 151–66 (*Philosophical Commentary*, ed. Tannenbaum, 87–95; *Commentaire philosophique*, 177–92), 653–5; *idem, OD*, ɪɪ, 532–3.

Religion all his Life long' but instead had to adopt 'some Principles, and act acording to them'.[30]

In his prefatory discourse to Lactantius, Burnet assaulted the explanation that heresy involved 'obstinacy' as its 'peculiar character' to separate it from 'error'. For Burnet, 'obstinacy' had to mean 'continuing in Errour after one is convinced of it'; it was being misapplied to many who were not thereby 'heretics'. For Burnet, merely adhering in an opinion or a mistake in judgment should not be called a 'work of the flesh'. If it proceeded from 'Interest, Pride, or Discontent' then it was indeed a work of the flesh; but it might well be a mistake of judgment from the limitations of the human understanding alone. Burnet, whose work was cited by Bayle in the *Supplement*, may perhaps have been intending to point to the *Philosophical Commentary* in declaring that 'I will not enter' into 'so troublesome an enquiry as it would be, to examine how far an Erroneous Conscience acquits one before God', and indicating that even without entering into such a controversy it was clear that it 'must be left to' God because it was very difficult indeed to know when others were sincere.[31]

For Bayle, not merely was 'heresy' subject to widely varying definitions, but so was blasphemy, and for the 'blasphemer' to be punishable that individual had to think that what he expressed was indeed 'blasphemy'. A Socinian who denied the Trinity was *not* a blasphemer in making such a denial because *he* did not believe in a Trinity as he was 'persuaded in his erroneous conscience that there cannot be three persons each of which is God, but there must be three gods'. Such an individual therefore did not speak against the divinity he acknowledged. Bayle compared the Jew pillaging the temple of Jerusalem and the Greek pillaging the temple of Delphos. One of these temples was consecrated to God, the other to Apollo. If one were to judge impiety on the basis of truth, only the first was impiety. But for Bayle, these were equally 'impious' acts, because to a Greek Apollo was the 'true God' and his 'conscience' therefore required the honouring of what were in fact 'false Gods'. For Bayle, if one claimed to define 'blasphemy' for another, 'there is nothing fixed' but 'a mere begging the question in dispute and a perpetual circle' or the use of a dictionary to one's own advantage.[32]

Among many places in which Locke discussed heresy, and offered redefinitions, the most important was his *Letter Concerning Toleration*, which argued that men of different religions could not be 'heretics or

---

[30] Bayle, *Philosophical Commentary* (1708), 292–3 (*Philosophical Commentary*, ed. Tannenbaum, 160; *Commentaire philosophique*, 299).

[31] Burnet (ed.), *Death*, 36–7.

[32] Bayle, *Philosophical Commentary*, 266–9, 299–301 (*Philosophical Commentary*, ed. Tannenbaum, 148, 163–4; *Commentaire philosophique*, 277–9, 305–6).

schismatics to one another', and that Turks and Christians were of different religions since they had a different rule of faith and worship, the holy Scriptures and the Koran. He then added, however, that while Catholics and Lutherans both professed faith in Christ and were both called Christians, they were actually of different religions because 'these acknowledge nothing but the holy Scriptures to be the rule and foundation of their religion; those take in also traditions and decrees of popes, and of all these together make the rule of their religion'. He next added that it follows 'First, that heresy is a separation made in ecclesiastical communion between men of the same religion, for some opinions no way contained in the rule itself. And secondly, That amongst those who acknowledge nothing but the Holy Scriptures to be their rule of faith, heresy is a separation made in their christian communion, for opinions not contained in the express words of Scripture'.

For Locke, the declaration that Protestants and Catholics could not be heretics to each other rendered both unjustified in punishment of the other as 'heretical'. In discussing those who separated for opinions not in 'the express words of Scripture', Locke argued that such a separation of worship occurred first when a majority or stronger part of a church separated from others by excluding them from communion because those others would not profess belief of opinions not in 'the express words of Scripture', but that in that case those excluding others were the heretics, because 'he only is an heretic who divides the Church into parts, introduces names and marks of distinction, and voluntarily makes a separation because of such opinions'. Separation alternatively occurred when an individual separated himself from communion with a church because such a church did not profess opinions which the holy scriptures do not 'expressly teach'. Again, this was the 'heretic', erring 'in fundamentals, and...obstinately against knowledge. For when they have determined the holy Scriptures to be the only foundation of faith, they nevertheless lay down certain propositions as fundamental, which are not in the scripture' and separated because others would not acknowledge them, or make them necessary and fundamental. For Locke, applying implicitly a rule of equity or reciprocity, 'however clearly we may think this or the other doctrine to be deduced from scripture, we ought not therefore to impose it upon others, as a necessary article of faith...unless we would be content also that other doctrines should be imposed upon us in the same manner'. Turning this to a *reductio ad absurdum*, Locke declared that one might then be compelled to receive and profess 'all the different and contradictory opinions of Lutherans, Calvinists, Remonstrants', and Anabaptists.[33]

---

[33] Locke, *Letter* in *Works*, 55–8.

For Locke, the distinction between the purposes of civil society and those of the church, his claim that any principles would need to be universal and thus valid for 'infidel' rulers and Christian alike, and the inefficacy of force to persuade, were sufficient to show that even if it were manifest which church was in fact 'orthodox', it would still not gain the right to punish others. But Locke noted that it would be claimed that the 'orthodox church' has the 'right of authority over the erroneous or heretical'. And he asserted that this was

in great and specious words, to say just nothing at all. For every church is orthodox to itself; to others, erroneous or heretical. Whatsoever any church believes, it believes to be true; and the contrary thereunto it pronounces to be error. So that the controversy between these churches. . .is on both sides equal; nor is there any judge. . .upon earth, by whose sentence it can be determined.

Locke condemned the 'injustice' and 'pride' of those who 'rashly and arrogantly' took upon themselves to 'misuse the servants of another master'.[34]

Locke not merely thereby launched the central attack on definitions of heresy that was necessary to defeat the anti-heretical case for intolerance in the 1680s and 1690s, but he simultaneously assaulted the accusation of 'schism' that had served to underpin much Restoration Anglican intolerance and which was also being deployed by Catholics against Huguenots in the 1680s. He began the *Letter Concerning Toleration* with an attack on the pretension of some of the 'antiquity of places and names, or of the pomp of their outward worship' and the pretension of others of the 'reformation of their discipline', and indicated that these were not, as claimed, a 'characteristical mark' of the true church. He ended the *Letter* with an assault on the term 'schism' as well as on the term 'heresy'. For Locke, heresy as a word in 'common use' was applied only to 'the doctrinal part of religion'. Schism was 'a crime near akin' to heresy. Both words, Locke declared, signified ill-grounded separations in ecclesiastical communion about unnecessary things. It was only 'use', the 'supreme law in matter of language' which had determined that 'heresy' related to 'errors in faith' and 'schism' to 'those in worship or discipline'. But if one pursued such usage, 'schism' was then 'a separation made in the communion of the church, upon account of something in divine worship, or ecclesiastical discipline, that is not any necessary part of it'. Nothing was necessary in Christian communion if it had not been communicated by 'Christ our legislator, or the apostles, by inspiration of the Holy Spirit' in 'express words'. If someone did not make a separation on the basis of anything 'not manifestly contained in the sacred text', to whatever extent they might be 'nicknamed by any sect of Christians, and declared by some, or all of them, to

---

[34] Locke, *Letter* in *Works*, 18–19.

be utterly void of true christianity' they were not 'schismatic'. Having begun by assaulting Catholic and Protestant claims to be the 'true church' on the basis of government and discipline, by its attack on the definition of 'schism' Locke had thus ended the *Letter* by levelling alike the Anglican pretension that Protestant dissenters were 'schismatic', the Catholic accusation that Huguenots were 'schismatic', and the Dutch Reformed accusation that Arminians were 'schismatic'. In its context, it was a powerful argument for toleration, briefly stated. Locke himself noted that he could have explained this 'more largely, and more advantageously' but declared that he had said sufficient to make his case. The remarkable brevity of Locke's case for toleration was one of the features which Le Clerc celebrated in his review of the *Letter* in the *Bibliothèque universelle*.[35]

In his *Theologia Christiana*, part at least of which Locke read in manuscript in 1685, Limborch similarly replied to anti-tolerationist arguments which cited Romans 16:17 on 'schism'. For Limborch, the crucial reply was that the causers of divisions were not those who dissent by 'a simple error of the Mind' but those who 'cause divisions and offences', which meant those who 'convert things not necessary, preach'd by the apostles, into things necessary, or desire to tie up others to the sense he gives of the Apostles words; and upon the account of a disagreement in matters of less moment causes a Schism in the Church'. The correct inference from the biblical text condemning schism was therefore that we should avoid those who cause schisms upon account of errors which were not fundamental and who cast dissenters out of the church.[36] It was, moreover, for Limborch 'more tolerable to be infected with an error' that was 'not damnable' than it was 'to make an unnecessary truth the pretence of a schism'. If men erred, provided that they were 'sound' in the 'fundamentals of the faith' and 'want not piety', they might be saved, 'but if we want Charity, tho we had all faith it will profit us nothing'.[37]

Addressing two issues which had caused many disputes within the Church of England as well as within continental Christianity, ceremonies and church government, Limborch rendered both indifferent, stressing the duties of toleration and peace. For Limborch, it was clear that 'ceremonies', which had caused more disputes in religion than other important issues were 'no part of true holiness'. All controversies about them were then 'to be reckoned among things less necessary'. Noting that excessive ceremonial might prejudice 'inward' worship, as in the Catholic Church, Limborch held that these ceremonial emphases could 'in themselves' be 'tolerated as infirmities in those persons', and stressed that ceremonies could not 'be prescribed as

---

[35] Locke, *Letter*, in *Works*, 5, 57–8; Le Clerc, *Bibliothèque universelle*, xv, 402–12.
[36] Limborch, *Compleat System*, 1008; *idem, Theologia Christiana*, 845.
[37] Limborch, *Compleat System*, 1010; *idem, Theologia Christiana*, 847.

necessary' to others without violating 'Christian Liberty'. Discussing an issue which had caused more significant debates and disputes in many Protestant communions in the sixteenth century and early seventeenth century than had issues of doctrine, he argued that church government by 'bishops' or 'presbyters' had no right to be reckoned among things necessary to salvation because 'they are neither clearly determined in Scripture, neither do they strike at, much less are they destructive of the Practice of Piety'. His opinion was simply 'that it is the Duty of every Man to comply with that Form of Church-Government which prevails in the Place wherein he lives, when tis instituted only for the sake of observing outward order: Provided care be taken, that under pretence of keeping good order, the Liberty of Conscience be not oppress'd, and that no rule of faith be prescribed to the church besides what is contain'd in the word of God'.[38]

HERETICS, SCHISMATICS, MONSTERS, AND COMETS

We have seen in Part 2 that 'heretics' and 'schismatics' were regularly associated with 'monsters' in early modern anti-tolerationist literature. This association, like that of heretics and schismatics with poisoners and the pestilential, was partly metaphoric, though even as metaphor it was a condensed expression of hostility towards heretics and schismatics which represented them as diametrically opposed to the 'normal', and the associa- tion of heretics and monsters was for many anti-heretical and anti-schismatic writers 'factual' and not merely metaphorical: as in the case of Ann Hutchinson, 'heretics' and 'schismatics' were held to give birth to 'monsters' as their imaginations were disordered and as God sent providential signs of his desire for the punishments of 'heresies' and 'schisms'. Heresies and schisms were understood to be spreading alongside and related to the pro- liferation of 'monsters' in these 'Last Days' in early modern millenarian apocalypticism. These accusations were often combined with other notions of 'signs' sent by God of his intended punishment of the world for 'heresy' and 'schism' should these remain unpunished, understood to vary from comets and eclipses to other sights in the skies, such as battling armies. Alleged documentations of these signs of God's support for Protestantism were deployed extensively by Jurieu in the 1680s in his propaganda in defence of Calvinist orthodoxy.

At both the metaphoric and literal levels, defenders of religious toleration in the 1680s and 1690s challenged these images and associations of alleged 'heretics' and 'schismatics' with 'monsters'. They replied that heretics and

---

[38] Limborch, *Compleat System*, 1004–5; *idem, Theologia Christiana*, 842.

schismatics were not 'monsters' but rather that persecutors were 'monsters' opposed to 'humanity'. As they constructed this structure of argument that 'monstrosity' violated the duties of 'humanity', they centrally defined 'humanity' as involving a behavioural norm of toleration and charity, and made intolerance 'inhumane' and so 'monstrous'. As Peter Gay has stressed, the ethos of 'humanity' was to be central to the Enlightenment. And several of these advocates of religious toleration challenged simultaneously the structure of supernatural explanation of monsters, eclipses, visions, and comets as 'signs' sent from God such that 'heresies' and 'schisms' needed magisterial force to be applied against them in order to avert God's further wrath and punishment. Most notably and most quotably, the prevalence of testimony to these occurrences and explanations of these events in terms of prodigies and signs in the accounts of many historians, including Livy, was replied to by the observation of Bayle in the *Pensées* that 'the credit of historians runs low, because, generally speaking, they are but wretched philosophers'.[39]

Bayle noted in the *Philosophical Commentary* that the French clergy had encouraged Louis XIV to persecute Huguenots by extolling the 'current and avowed doctrine of the Church of Rome, that Hereticks, of whom they form a more hideous Idea than of any Monster, may and ought to be punished'. For Bayle, it was the 'convertist' who was actually the 'monster' against whom many of the accusations usually directed at 'heretics' should be directed. In the wake of the violence against property and persons committed by the dragoons in France and justified by the Catholic clergy, the very term 'convertist' Bayle declared to have now come to mean a 'Mountebank…Counterfeit…Pilferer, Maroder, a Soul void of Pity, void of Humanity, void of natural Equity', and 'a Man who proposes by tormenting others to expiate for his own Lewdness past and to come, and for all the irregularities of a profligate Life'. Indeed, a convertist was no less than

a Monster, Half-Priest and Half-Dragoon, who like the Centaur of the Fable, which in one Person united the Man and the Horse, confounds in one Actor the different Parts of a Missionary who argues and a Foot-Soldier who belabours a poor human Body, and rifles a Cottage.[40]

It was in the context of reply to accusations of heretics as 'monsters' that Locke's metaphorical argument in the *Letter Concerning Toleration* performed important work in its identification of the 'monstrosity' of the very doctrine of intolerance:

---

[39] P. Bayle, *Miscellaneous Reflections* (1708), 10. I generally quote from this 1708 translation of the *Pensées*.

[40] Bayle, *Philosophical Commentary* (1708), 3–4 (*Philosophical Commentary*, ed. Tannenbaum, 10; *Commentaire philosophique*, 48–9).

The toleration of those that differ from others in matters of religion is so agreeable to the Gospel of Jesus Christ, and to the genuine reason of mankind that it seems monstrous for men to be so blind, as not to perceive the necessity and advantage of it, in so clear a light.[41]

And by the late seventeenth century, there was a gradually growing opposition in elite intellectual culture to the associations of heresy and 'monstrosity'. In 'medical theory', the development of animaculate theory tended to render the mother's role that of nurturing the foetus and thus reduced the influence ascribed to her imagination. As Daston and Park have crucially stressed, in scientific investigation there was a move to record the evidence of an alleged 'monstrosity' and to discuss it in a secular vein, segregating the 'natural' and 'supernatural'. Robert Boyle, whose literary executor was Locke, recorded 'natural wonders' in lists of 'strange reports', which he treated separately from 'supernatural phenomena'. He sent a report on a 'monstrous Calf' – part-colt, part-calf – to the *Transactions of the Royal Historical Society*, offering details of, but no explanation for, this 'monster'; this reticence involved commitment to the empirical collecting of information and accounts of 'monsters' from which explanations of attested occurrences were then to be generated, a decisive step away from the explanations provided by notions of God's providential interventions central to preceding periods of interconfessional intolerance. Elsewhere, Boyle stressed the 'ordained regularities' of God, and that nature as a 'nursing mother' produced some deformities not because God intervened but precisely because God did not intervene. Edward Tyson, Fellow of the Royal Society, similarly published an account of a 'man-pig' in the 1699 *Transactions*, which stressed causes such as the physical pressure on the womb of the mother.

Surveying the study of 'monsters' in early modern Europe, Daston and Park have noted that understandings of 'monsters' and 'signs' shifted considerably from a pre-Reformation emphasis on 'monsters' as marking the 'traditional sins' of sodomy, avarice, pride, and worldliness, to monsters as marking during the next two centuries blasphemy, religious error, heresy, conspiracy, and sedition – a set of accusations which we have in Part 2 seen to be interrelated accusations against 'heresy'. They further indicate that the entire structure of belief in monsters and supernaturally caused eclipses and comets began to decline in England around the 1670s, as there was a move towards anatomical lessons, towards embryology, and towards natural explanations for phenomena in the skies.[42] Barbara Shapiro has recently noted similarly

---

[41] Locke, *Letter*, ed. Klibansky and Gough, 65 ('*Tolerantia eorum qui de rebus religionis diversa sentiunt, Evangelio et rationi adeo consona est, ut monstro simile videatur homines in tam clara luce caecutire*').

[42] Daston and Park, *Wonders*, 183–9, 209.

that 'over time, many if not all "marvellous" or "monstrous" matters of fact came to be viewed as having natural explanations'. She notes that the Oxford mathematician Seth Ward had treated comets by the 1680s as 'regular repeated natural appearances'. It was Locke's *bête noire* of the 1690s, the fiercely traditional Calvinist anti-heretical writer John Edwards, who then opposed Ward's account with the traditional Calvinist insistence that comets were, as Shapiro puts it, 'singular events portending political change or signalling God's displeasure' in his 1684 *Cometomantia*. What is being emphasised here is how important the shift from supernatural to naturalistic explanations was to tolerationist argument: it is significant that Edwards was both a defender of supernatural explanations for comets and a fierce anti-heretical intolerant Calvinist.[43]

While at first sight many of the natural philosophic and epistemological commitments in Locke's *Essay Concerning Human Understanding* and elsewhere appear to stand at a distance from Locke's tolerationist thought, they can be linked to the decoupling of 'heresy' from being the associate of a 'monstrous' and monster-generating imagination. Thus, the scientific investigations of Leeuwenhoek on the processes of generation, which Locke cautiously endorsed, the account of ideas and of chains of ideas rather than of images imprinted on the understanding that was central to Locke's epistemology in the *Essay Concerning Human Understanding*, and Locke's move towards an account of madness as the false association of ideas rather than as a consequence of sinfulness or divine grace, all combined to provide conceptual opposition to earlier sixteenth- and seventeenth-century notions of 'monstrous imaginations' which resulted in 'monstrous' generations, and to undercut the bases of intolerance from the associations of 'monsters' and 'heresies' documented earlier in this book. In discussing the boundaries of species and classifications of humans as part of his discussions of real and nominal essence, Locke raised the question in the *Essay Concerning Human Understanding* of whether nature 'always attains the essence it designs' in the production of things, noting specifically that 'irregular' and 'monstrous' births in 'diverse sort of animals' had been observed as giving 'reason to doubt' either nature's regularity on the one hand or the accounts of the 'monsters' on the other. Locke's arguments tended to exclude the notion that God had sent 'monsters' as 'signs', suggesting that physical abnormalities were due to physical or natural variations and not to supernatural interventions. Locke moreover indicated that it was wrong for many to determine that individuals were 'monsters' as opposed to 'humans' by their 'shape' rather than by their 'descent'. He pointed to debates over human

---

[43] Shapiro, *Culture*, 102–3.

foetuses whose status had been given only by the difference of their outward configuration and pilloried those who would have 'excluded' from humanity some born deformed and who would have 'executed' people with physical abnormalities. Locke stressed that there was 'no reason' why 'a visage' slightly different could not consist with a rational soul. The net effect of Locke's argument was thus to suggest that many formerly classified as 'monsters' were humans with slightly different external appearances; they were clearly not to be interpreted as 'signs' from God of the need to punish 'sins' such as 'heresy'.[44]

Here, many of Locke's arguments ran in significant parallel not merely to many English 'Latitudinarian' scientists such as Boyle but also to those of Bayle, from whose assault on the belief in comets, monsters, and other signs as 'superstitious' belief in 'prodigies' and 'miracles' in the first version of the *Pensées*, the *Letter*, Locke took notes in 1685 in the period leading up to his composition of the *Letter Concerning Toleration*. Bayle was the most important figure in assaulting accounts of God's extensive providential interventions through prodigies and signs and miracles in the 1680s and 1690s. Bayle's *Pensées* assaulted pagan superstition and asserted that comets were natural objects obeying general natural laws and not 'signs'. Bayle's *Pensées* also explicitly assaulted belief in many other things being taken for 'signs', such as 'monsters' and 'eclipses'. It proffered for these supposedly supernatural events similarly 'naturalistic' explanations. There were many levels and layers to Bayle's argument in the *Pensées*, which on its surface is merely a Christian attack on pagan superstitions, but which may be read also as a Protestant attack on Catholic maintenance of pagan superstitions, or as an 'atheist' attack on Christian maintenance of pagan superstitions. Almost all scholars agree that in the guise of a Christian attack on pagan superstition there is at the least an attack on Catholic superstition; many scholars go further and suggest that the same logic of arguments as make it an attack on Catholicism because Catholicism is largely composed of pagan superstitions make it a covert attack on Christianity itself, for Christianity is largely composed of pagan superstitions. Here, it is important merely to record that its arguments undermined the allegations of many in early modern Europe that 'signs' had been sent by God to encourage magisterial intolerance towards heresies and schisms.[45]

The central argument of the *Pensées* was an assault on what it argued was still then the general opinion, that comets were among the signs sent by God

---

[44] Locke, *Essay*, 3.6.16–26; cf. M. H. Huet, *Monstrous Imagination* (Harvard 1993), and, more broadly on the powers of the imagination and Locke, U. S. Mehta, *The Anxiety of Freedom: Imagination and Individuality in Locke's Political Thought* (Ithaca 1992).

[45] Cf. esp. Mori, *Bayle*; P. Bayle, *Various Thoughts on the Occasion of a Comet*, ed. R. Bartlett (SUNY 2000); MS Locke f8, 293ff.

as warnings to humanity to repent. To this it linked assaults on many other occurrences taken as 'signs', such as eclipses and monsters, earthquakes, fires, and plagues. We saw in Part 2 that these were indeed taken to be 'signs' that God wished for action against 'heresy' and 'atheism' in England, including in 1665–6, and that many of these events had been adduced by both Catholic and Protestant clerics in post-Reformation Europe, who argued that they required that magistrates punish 'heresy' and 'schism' and indicated that humans were living in the 'Last Days'. Pointing to the 'two dreadful comets in 1665', Bayle questioned the widespread interpretation in early modern Europe that such signified the rise of 'heresies' and 'schisms'. He asked 'Have Heresies and Schisms taken their Rise from these years?' He then dismissed this notion, among others, over several following pages by itemising the many good things that had followed after these comets, and concluded by placing such an interpretation within the realm of astrologers to be mocked rather than that of theologians to be followed, declaring that one should 'laugh at the astrologers, who declared they presaged dreadful events in the world, Schisms and monstrous Heresys in the Church'. Bayle immediately moved on in the next paragraph to argue that following these comets there had not been bad 'heresies' and 'schisms' requiring punishment, but instead reconciliation of theologians who had 'been long together by the Ears'. He thus introduced in the *Pensées* the disputes of the 1660s between Jansenists and Jesuits, which he interpreted as having been prevented from becoming schismatic by a magisterial order silencing the disputes among clerics, rather than by punishing one party as 'heretics' and 'schismatics'. For Bayle, comets were not presages of evil or signs that God intended to punish men who had failed to take his warning and had failed to punish heresies and schisms, as had been believed in preceding theological writing discussed earlier in this book, because such beliefs had built on pagan superstitions and on man's credulity with 'Christians...as far gone in the Folly of finding presages in every thing, as Infidels themselves'.[46] And not merely was belief in comets as 'signs' presaging the growth of heresy and schism identified with 'superstition' or 'idolatry' by Bayle – so in the *Pensées* was belief in 'monsters' such as 'a dog with two Faces' or 'a Calf with six feet' being taken as prodigies. According to Bayle, Virgil and Lucan bore witness to belief in prodigies, such as the 'clashing of arms in the air' or 'monsters'. But for Bayle, these had been used not to promote 'the reformation of manners' or 'condemning false Opinions in the worship of God', but processions and superstitious acts such as 'destroying perhaps all the Monsters to be found in the land'. For Bayle,

---

[46] Bayle, *Miscellaneous Reflections*, 67–8, 78–81, 152.

'true Philosophy' showed that 'the Production of Monsters' were 'properly natural Effects, as those daily and ordinarily produced'.[47]

And similarly naturalistic explanations were also offered by Bayle at various points in the *Dictionary* as he attacked claims that God intervened extensively through miracles in order to favour a particular religion, drawing his readers' attention to false claims of recent miracles. In Constance B, for instance, he recorded Spanheim's questioning of the alleged miraculous protection of that city, claimed for Catholicism against Protestantism. Bayle observed that 'there is not a country...where Winds, Rains, the Rise of Rivers, etc. have not favoured or destroyed Military Enterprises' and argued that there was 'no probability' that God 'should supersede the general Laws of nature, but in cases where the preservation of his Children requires it'. Bayle argued that people were 'strangely inclined to think themselves favoured by miraculous benefits', and noted that if this had been a Protestant town, Spanheim might well have written exactly the opposite argument in support of the miracles. And he continued with an attack on Jurieu: 'There are some Ministers who see a Miracle in all Events, which concern their Party. Mr Jurieu, for example, finds one everywhere, and lately in what happened to those in the Cévennes'. Such a mind-set on Jurieu's part was for Bayle associated with Jurieu's prophetic fanaticism. In the entry Comenius in the *Dictionary*, which John Laursen has convincingly identified as intended to target Jurieu as well as Comenius, Bayle attacked Comenius as 'infatuated with Prophecies, and Revolutions, the Fall of Antichrist, the Millennium and suchlike whims of a dangerous Fanaticism: I say dangerous, not only in relation to orthodoxy, but also in relation to Princes and States'. Part of Bayle's purpose here was to attack Jurieu's prophetic support for William III's invasion of England; part was surely once again, as so often in Bayle's *Dictionary*, to undermine the Protestant intolerance advocated by Jurieu.[48]

---

[47] Bayle, *Miscellaneous Reflections*, 121–5. Cf. Bayle's effective mockery of belief in the need to have pious thoughts during lovemaking or one's child would be born deformed – a notion central to earlier seventeenth-century associations of disordered heretical imaginations and monsters – in the entry Arodon in the *Dictionary*; D. Wootton, 'Bayle, Libertine?' in M. A. Stewart, *Studies in Seventeenth Century European Philosophy* (Oxford 2000).

[48] Bayle, *Dictionary*, Constance B, Comenius; Laursen, 'Baylean Liberalism', 197–215, at 210.

19

Toleration and Jews, Muslims, and 'pagans'

TOLERATION

Religious toleration was explicitly extended in the series of tolerationist works of the 1680s and 1690s to Jews, 'pagans', and 'Mahometans' or 'Turks' (Muslims). Bayle wrote of toleration that 'Pagans, Jews and Turks have a right to it' and that 'the Turk and Jew ought to be tolerated in a Commmonwealth'. He emphasised that not merely Muslims and Jews but the 'very pagans' were 'entitled to a toleration'.[1] Aubert wrote in his *Treatise on Liberty of Conscience* that Magistrates did not have the right to forbid their subjects' religious profession whether 'jewish, pagan, mahometan, [or] christian'.[2] Locke similarly wrote in the *Letter* that 'neither pagan, nor mahometan, nor jew ought to be excluded from the civil rights of the commonwealth because of his religion'. He described as deserving toleration in the *Letter* the 'innocent pagans' of America who were 'strict observers of the rules of equity and the law of nature, and no ways offending against the laws of society', and asserted:

If a Jew does not believe the New Testament to be the word of God, he does not thereby alter any thing in men's civil rights. If a heathen doubt of both Testaments, he is not therefore to be punished as a pernicious citizen.

Locke 'readily grant[ed]' that the opinions of pagans and Jews were 'false and absurd', but he held that they caused no harm to the 'safety and security of the commonwealth, and of every particular man's goods and person'. They were therefore to be tolerated.[3]

This argument followed naturally from tolerationists' contention that magistrates could not forbid harmless worship, but it was also used by

---

[1] Bayle, *Philosophical Commentary* (1708) 260–6; (*Philosophical Commentary*, ed. Tannenbaum, 145–50; *Commentaire philosophique*, 271–82).

[2] Aubert de Versé, *Traité*, 30–1, 76, and *passim*; Morman, *Aubert*, ch. 4.

[3] Locke, *Letter* in *Works*, 40, 36, 52; Armitage, *Ideological Origins*, 96–8; Matar, 'Turbanned', 67–77, at 75.

these authors to make a case for toleration of 'heretical' or 'schismatic' Christians by pointing to the general acceptance of toleration for Jews and Muslims, and arguing how incongruous it was to punish Christians but not Jews or Muslims. For Locke, it was readily acknowledged that an 'injury may not be done unto a Jew' in a Christian country by compelling 'him, against his own opinion, to practice in his religion a thing that is in its nature indifferent'. For Locke, it was obvious that 'if these things may be granted to jews and pagans, surely the condition of any christians ought not to be worse than theirs, in a christian commonwealth'. Bayle argued that there was 'no solid reason for tolerating any one sect, which does not equally hold for another', and that 'twere needless insisting in particular for a Toleration of Socinians, since it appears that Pagans, Jews, and Turks have a right to it'. Crell's argument in the *Vindication*, republished by Le Cène in 1687, recorded that to tolerate was not to approve opinions and that men 'without any scruple of conscience, allow Jewes and in some place Mahometans...liberty of religion' without thereby approving of their 'errors'.[4]

There was thus an attempt to extend the logic of the general acceptance of toleration for Jews, Muslims, and even 'pagans' to the toleration of Christians who were alleged to be heretics. But in terms of Jews and of 'pagans' in colonies, toleration was also an immediate practical issue in the Netherlands, England, and France. We saw in Chapter 4 that Jews had a large presence in the Netherlands, and their toleration had been a central issue of discussion in the seventeenth century. We saw in Chapter 3 that Jews had a small but increasing and publicly contested presence in Restoration England and in the English colonies, and an important one in support of the Dutch-led venture known as the Revolutions of 1688–91. We saw in Chapters 4 and 10 that the toleration of up to 10,000 Jews in France was under threat and increasing restriction by Louis XIV in the early 1680s, and that Jewish toleration was not reinforced in France until 1686, when this occurred partly as the result of the long-standing distinction drawn between Jews as 'tolerable' and 'heretics' as 'intolerable'. To assert staightforwardly that Jews should be tolerated in the mid-to-late 1680s was thus to make a case with immediate practical bearing in England, France, and the Netherlands. Over the course of the sixteenth and especially the seventeenth centuries, the toleration of 'pagans' had also become a substantial practical issue in the 'colonial' territories of all of these powers. To none of the tolerationist authors of the 1680s and 1690s was it a more immediate issue

---

[4] Locke, *Letter* in *Works*, 31, 52; Bayle, *Philosophical Commentary* (1708), 265–6 (*Philosophical Commentary*, ed. Tannenbaum, 147; *Commentaire philosophique*, 276); Crell, *Vindication*, 14; Le Cène, *Conversations*, 233.

than to Locke. As the probable author of the appropriate sections on toleration of the *Fundamental Constitutions of the Carolinas*, Locke himself had
discussed this issue in the provisions of its articles, which held that toleration
was deserved by 'pagans', or 'heathens', and Jews in providing that

> since the natives of that place, who will be concerned in our plantations, are utterly
> strangers to Christianity, whose idolatry, ignorance, or mistake gives us no right to
> expel or use them ill...[and so that] heathens, Jews, and other dissenters from the
> purity of the Christian religion may not be scared and kept at a distance from
> it...therefore any seven or more persons agreeing in any religion shall constitute a
> church or profession, to which they shall give some name to distinguish it from
> others.[5]

For Locke in the *Letter*, 'No man whatsoever ought' to be 'deprived of his
terrestrial enjoyments, upon account of his religion', and he made explicit that

> Not even Americans, subjected unto a Christian prince, are to be punished either in
> body or goods, for not embracing our faith and worship. If they are persuaded that
> they please God in observing the rites of their own country, and that they shall obtain
> happiness by that means, they are to be left unto God and themselves.[6]

Muslims presented a less immediate practical issue for toleration in
England, France, the Netherlands, and their colonial territories, but the
strength of Islam, its successes in gaining conversions of Christians to
Islam, the failures of Christians to convert Muslims, and the possibility of
Muslim preachers and traders residing in North-Western Europe, rendered
toleration of Muslims a live issue in debates over toleration. Bayle was
willing to countenance the Mufti (of Constantinople) sending missionaries
to Christian countries, and explicitly paralleled this to the Pope sending
Christian missionaries into the Indies. In the *Philosophical Commentary*,
he argued that Muslim preachers should not be punished, but rather that one
should 'bring them to a conference' in order to 'undeceive them'. Bayle
argued that he wished that Muslims and Christians would exchange missions
and toleration with us for 'the Christian religion wou'd be a great Gainer'.
'Pagans' and 'Mahometans' could 'never make any Progress among us', he

---

[5] Locke, *Fundamental Constitutions of the Carolinas* (21 July 1669), PRO 30/24/47/3, ff. 58–9
in Locke, *Political Essays*, 178; Armitage, *Ideological Origins*, 96–8; Matar, 'John Locke and
the Jews'; L. Huhner, 'The Jews of North Carolina Prior to 1800', *Publications of the
American Jewish Society*, 29 (1925), 137–48; *idem*, 'The Jews of South Carolina from the
Earliest Settlement to the End of the American Revolution', *Publications of the American
Jewish Historical Society*, 12 (1904), 39–61.
[6] Locke, *Letter* in *Works*, 35; cf. Armitage, *Ideological Origins*, 97–8; *Third Letter*, in *Works*,
VI, 235 and 396, where Locke discusses 'pagans' in the king's 'Plantations' and the abomina-
tion due to pagan worship which ought to be discouraged by the preaching of the gospel but
not by force.

asserted, but 'ours might reap a plentiful harvest'. For Bayle, the toleration of Muslims was due from Christians by the eternal law that religion was a matter of conscience and because Muslims allowed Christians to exercise their religion in their territories. Further stressing that principles and practices of toleration needed to be universal to be valid, he declared at one point that Muslims could not 'even be banished' if they did not disturb the peace, or else pagans would have been justified in imprisoning the apostles. While Bayle recognised the possibility that 'reasons of state' might, and sometimes did, require that Muslims should be banished in newly conquered Muslim territories, he held that except in such a situation one could not 'expel' Muslims from towns nor hinder 'their having mosks, or assembling in their own houses'.[7]

Locke was in general equally clear that Muslims were to be tolerated, writing as we saw a moment ago that 'neither pagan, nor mahometan, ought to be excluded from the civil rights of the commonwealth because of his religion'. There is, nonetheless, one explicit restriction on toleration for Muslims in Locke's *Letter*. Locke specifically excluded from toleration those Muslims who are 'bound to yield a blind obedience to the mufti of Constantinople; who himself is entirely obedient to the Ottoman Emperor, and frames the famed oracles of that religion according to his pleasure'. For Locke, such a Muslim could not profess himself 'a mahometan only in religion, but in every thing else a faithful subject to a christian magistrate'. Locke said that 'this mahometan, living amongst Christians, would yet more apparently renounce their government, if he acknowledged the same person to be head of his church, who is the supreme magistrate in the state'.

Several points need to be made here. Firstly, Locke was clear and emphatic that all other 'Mahometans' than these subjects of the Mufti were to be tolerated, explicitly listing Muslims with Jews and pagans at several points as deserving toleration in the *Letter*. Locke's *Second* and *Third Letter* both defended the 'largeness' of the *Letter*'s toleration, which 'would *not* have Jews, Mahometans, and Pagans excluded from the civil rights of the commonwealth'. That this was Locke's position was, moreover, clear to Locke's opponents on the basis of the *Letter*, including Jonas Proast, who focused on it in his reply, *The Argument of the Letter Concerning Toleration Briefly Considered and Answered* (1690). Proast's first two sentences pointed out that while Locke began his *Letter* talking about the 'mutual Toleration of Christians', Locke ended it by saying that 'neither Pagan, nor Mahumetan, ought to be excluded from the Civil Rights of the Commonwealth because of his Religion'. And if the exclusion of blindly obedient subjects of the Mufti

---

[7] Bayle, *Philosophical Commentary* (1708), 261–3 (*Philosophical Commentary*, ed. Tannenbaum, 145–6; *Commentaire philosophique*, 272–3).

but toleration of all other Muslims is taken literally, the numbers of Muslims whom Locke intended to exclude from toleration in England or the Netherlands would be small indeed.[8] The general scholarly tendency has been to suggest that this passage should be taken simply as an oblique reference to the Pope, who claimed infallible authority. By showing that Locke read John Greaves' publication of Robert Withers' *A Description of the Grand Signior's Seraglio*, Matar has recently provided us with historical grounds for a rhetorical association of the Mufti and the Pope to have been made by Locke, since Greaves' work described the Mufti as 'a circumcised Pope' who 'yields an infallible obedience to all the Emperor inspires him with'. Matar then reads Locke as having had the Pope in mind in making his comments on the Mufti, in addition to having the Mufti in mind, and places more of his rhetorical emphasis on the issue of the Pope. At this particular point in the text the analogy is surely one that for Locke worked to make the case that those obeying the Mufti with a blind obedience were intolerable, thus identifying a category of Muslims who were intolerable, while also underlining the difficulty that Catholics posed for toleration for Locke – an issue which will be explored further in Chapter 22. In considering Muslim toleration, probably reliant on the image of the Mufti presented by Greaves, Locke was probably intent in this particular part of this passage on denying toleration to those Muslims – probably a small number – whom he held to be an actual political threat.[9]

LOCKE ON TOLERATION OF JEWS, MUSLIMS AND PAGANS BEFORE 1685 AND IN 1685–92

Locke's personal questioning of the distinction in most anti-heretical and anti-schismatic arguments between 'heretical' and 'schismatic' Christian worship as intolerable on the one hand and Muslim and Jewish worship as tolerable on the other hand had started *before* Locke's own tolerationist commitment. As early as his own anti-tolerationist writings of about 1660, the *Two Tracts Upon Government*, Locke had not upheld this distinction. In 1660, Edward Bagshawe, Locke's colleague at Christ Church, argued in his *Great Question Concerning Things Indifferent in Religious Worship* that

---

[8] Locke, *Letter* in *Works*, 47; *idem, Second Letter; idem, Third Letter*; J. Proast, *The Argument of the Letter Concerning Toleration Briefly Considered and Answered* (Oxford 1690), 1–2; Matar, 'Turbanned'.
[9] Matar, 'Turbanned', 75–6. A somewhat similar argument to this was presented by Jeremy Waldron to a seminar in political and moral thought at Johns Hopkins, of which I am the Director, and has since been published in his *God, Locke and Equality* (Cambridge 2002), 221.

tis agreed that a Christian magistrate cannot force his religion on a Jew or a Mahomedan, therefore much less can he abridge his fellow Christian in things of lesser moment.

In his anti-tolerationist reply to Bagshawe's work, the *Two Tracts*, Locke did not argue that the magistrate had no power over Jews and Muslims because force could not be used against those outside of Christianity, but that the magistrate possessed power over all 'indifferent, matters', and that he would not *exercise* such power in the case of non-Christians for this might be perceived as supporting this kind of worship. In defence of the right of the magistrate over parts of Muslim worship as 'indifferent', Locke displayed ignorance of Koranic codes, which require a set schedule of worship, require worship in the direction of Mecca, and (together with the Sunna) require ablution and prostration, in contending that it was not 'unlawful for a Christian magistrate to prescribe either time or place or habit to a Mahomedan for his worship if his Alcoran hath left them undetermined', although he did then add that 'in those that are determined he ought not to be forced as being made by the doctrine of his religion no longer indifferent'. Moreover, in his defence of magisterial intolerance towards Protestant dissenters at the date of these *Two Tracts*, Locke replied to Bagwell's charge that Protestant dissenters from the Church of England should not be treated worse than Jews and Muslims with a smug declaration that 'Whatever other country do, England is clear of this imputation' and by pointing out that 'those of different religions' paid heavier taxes that were 'far heavier than the occasional penalties of nonconforming offenders'.[10]

But when Locke shifted to argument for the toleration of nonconformists' worship, in his 1667 'Essay on Toleration', he did so by utilising something closer to Bagshawe's argument, although it was the royal practice of toleration of Jewish worship as a continuation of Cromwell's policy of prerogative toleration that seems to have been his impetus in what was probably a manuscript of advice for Shaftesbury and the king. Locke proposed that

tis strange to conceive upon what grounds of uniformity any different profession of Christians can be prohibited in a Christian country, where the Jewish religion (which is directly opposite to the principles of Christianity) is tolerated; and would it not be irrational, where the Jewish religion is permitted, that the Christian magistrate, upon pretence of his power in indifferent things, should enjoin or forbid anything, or any way interpose in their way or manner of worship?[11]

[10] J. Locke, *Two Tracts Upon Government*, ed. P. Abrams (Cambridge 1969), 130, 168; Matar, 'Turbanned', 68–9; *idem*, 'John Locke and the Jews'. I am grateful to Nabil Matar both for drawing the former article to my attention and for discussions of the issues of Locke and toleration at several conferences; this chapter is significantly indebted to his analyses at many points.
[11] Locke, 'Essay on Toleration' in *Political Essays*, 140; Matar, 'Turbanned', 71; *idem*, 'John Locke and the Jews', 48; cf. Coudert, 'Locke'.

This practical awareness on Locke's part of the royal toleration of Jews was thus one factor helping him to argue as early as 1667 that Protestant dissenters should be tolerated in England – although since this argument appeared only in the final, fourth draft of the 'Essay on Toleration', it should be understood to have been a useful collateral argument rather than motivationally important in his switch from support for intolerance to support for toleration. Two further European examples that Locke personally witnessed in the 1660s and 1670s are likely to have then reinforced this argument that Christian dissenters deserved toleration where Jews were tolerated, and to have added impetus to his argument for toleration of Jews. In 1665, in a visit to Cleves, where Locke witnessed a great degree of religious toleration practised, he recorded that 'Jews, Anabaptists and Quakers' co-existed peacefully. In so doing, he was recording the toleration and peaceful co-existence of the three groups whose toleration in England was most decried, and in the case of Quakers the sect about whose toleration he himself had had questions as late as his first drafts of the 'Essay on Toleration'. In 1675, Locke also recorded that in France Jews were tolerated as well as orthodox Protestants but not 'heretics', as he visited the Jewish quarter in Avignon 'where they have a synagogue'.[12]

Probably once again even more important in promoting Locke's explicit support for the toleration of Jews in England and elsewhere, however, was Locke's colonial involvement. In the late 1660s, he was involved with drafting constitutions for the Carolinas which provided that Jews and heathens and 'other dissenters from the purity of the Christian religion' should be tolerated both for the commercial success of the colony and so that they could be 'won over to embrace, and unfeignedly receive the Truth'. It is important to note that in helping to draft this constitution, Locke was not working with a *tabula rasa*. In a 'declaration and proposals' issued on 25 August 1665, settlers to the Carolinas had already been offered 'in as ample a manner as they might desire, freedom and liberty of conscience in all religious or spiritual things'. Jews had probably first settled in the Carolinas from Barbados in 1665, and Locke was probably aware of the toleration of Jews in Barbados. Thomas Violet's 1660 *A Petition against the Jews* assaulted the Jewish presence not merely in the metropole but throughout the king's dominions, and argued specifically against tolerating Jews in Barbados that they 'engross' trade and 'eat the children's bread' and 'do so swarm'.[13]

---

[12] Locke, *Correspondence*, 177; Lough, *Locke's Travels*, 12; Matar, 'John Locke and the Jews', 49, 53.

[13] Locke, *Political Essays*, 178; Armitage, *Ideological Origins*, 97–8; Matar, 'John Locke and the Jews'; Chapter 11 above; Katz, *Jews*; Huhner, 'The Jews of North Carolina', 137–48; *idem*, 'The Jews of South Carolina', 39–61.

The provisions for toleration and settlement of Jews in Barbados and the appeal to settlers for Carolina thus all importantly presaged article 97 of the *Constitutions*, which explicitly contended that 'those who remove from other parts to plant there will unavoidably be of different opinions concerning matters of religion, the liberty of which they will expect to have allowed them' and which concluded, as we saw earlier,

that jews, and other dissenters from the purity of the Christian religion may not be scared and kept at a distance from it... therefore any seven or more persons agreeing in any religion shall constitute a church or profession, to which they shall give some name to distinguish it from others.

The Constitution provided that there were punishments for disturbing or using reproachful or abusive language against any religion and for molesting or persecuting another for their opinions or their way of worship. And it was held that anyone over seventeen had to be of some religion: atheists were banned from the colony as untrustworthy. In very many ways, the Constitution's language on all of these issues is close to that which Locke utilised at many points in other works, and it seems likely that he had a significant role in the composition of its language about toleration, and thus of its advocacy of toleration of Jews and 'pagans' but not 'atheists'.[14]

Locke thus arrived in the Netherlands in the 1680s having already argued that Jews should be tolerated in his 1667 tolerationist 'Essay on Toleration' and in his participation shortly afterwards in drafting the *Fundamental Constitutions*. And he arrived in the Netherlands having observed and commented favourably in the 1660s and 1670s on the toleration of Jewish worship in Cleves and France. Witnessing the toleration of Jews in the Netherlands in the 1680s surely then reinforced this already significant commitment to the toleration of Jews. Amsterdam's synagogues may also have accented to Locke the limitation of the toleration provided to Jews in England by the actions of Cromwell and Charles II, which had involved permission only of private worship: from 1660 to 1674, the small Jewish community in England had used a house in Duke's Lane, London, and from 1674 a house in Creechurch Lane, London. Locke composed in the *Letter* a passage whose rhetorical questioning proclaimed a right to public worship for Jews and not merely private worship as in England:

If we allow the jews to have private houses amongst us, why should we not allow them to have synagogues? Is their doctrine more false, their worship more abominable, or

---

[14] Locke, *Political Essays*, 178; Armitage, *Ideological Origins*, esp. 97–8; Matar, 'John Locke and the Jews'; Huhner, 'The Jews of North Carolina', 137–48; *idem*, 'The Jews of South Carolina', 39–61.

is the civil peace more endangered, by their meeting in public than in their private houses?[15]

The Tory Anglican Jonas Proast replied to these arguments by Locke in his series of assaults between 1689 and 1691 on the *Letter Concerning Toleration*. He attacked Locke's extensive toleration as good for the 'Advancement of Trade and Commerce', which he declared 'some' seemed to place above 'all other considerations'. And he suggested in his *Third Letter* that Jews could 'seduce' Christians to Judaism, and argued that 'though we are bound to desire their conversion' it was to be sought 'without endangering the Subjects of Christ's Kingdom, to whom he has a special regard'. For Proast, Jews were to be excluded from the civil rights of the commonwealth. As Locke noted in his *Second Letter*, the 'first thing' which Proast had been 'startled at' was not excluding 'so much as a pagan, mahometan or jew' from the civil rights of the commonwealth. Locke was clear in response that Jews were to be tolerated like any other citizen who did not break the laws, and Locke suggested that he supported endenisation of Jews, the monarchical process of naturalisation, some 150 years before statutory naturalisation was to be provided in England.[16]

TOLERATION AND CONVERSION

At the same time that he was arguing for civic rights for Jews, Locke also argued in his defences of the *Letter Concerning Toleration* in the early 1690s – by which time he was back in England, and English issues were once again at the centre of his arguments – that his argument for the toleration of Jews was intended in part to facilitate their 'conversion'. As Locke turned increasingly to extensive biblical exegesis in the 1690s and early 1700s, he collaborated extensively with Isaac Newton, who was committed to interpretations of the 'Restoration' of the Jews to their own land of Palestine. And Locke read and took notes, including dates of conversion and the millennium, from other works committed to the notion of this restoration, including *Seder Olam: or the Order, Series, or Succession of all the Ages, Periods, and Times of the Whole World* by his former associate in the Furly circle, Franciscus Mercurius van Helmont, who became such a friend that he visited Locke in England. In his posthumously published *Paraphrase*, Locke spoke of Jews as going to be restored to the 'land of promise' before the millennium.

---

[15] Locke, *Letter*, 52; Matar, 'John Locke and the Jews', 52–4. This is Popple's English phrasing; cf. Locke, *Letter*, ed. Klibansky and Gough, 144–5 for Locke's own effectively identical Latin phrasing.

[16] Proast, *Argument*, 2; *idem, Third Letter*, 3; Locke, *Second Letter* in *Works*, 62; *Third Letter* in *Works*, 229–33; Matar, 'John Locke and the Jews'.

Locke was a convinced 'Restorationist'.[17] Analysing Locke's notes and brief statements in his works on the theme of Jewish restoration, Matar has suggested that the concern of many of the thinkers around Locke, including both Newton and Boyle, involved support for the restoration of the Jews to Palestine in part as a more generalised support for the prophetic status of the Bible against the assaults of 'deists' and 'atheists' on prophecy and miracles: by validating this prophecy, the Bible itself received further validation. And Matar has also importantly suggested that Locke was committed by the later 1690s and early 1700s (at the latest) to the view that the future home of the Jews was Palestine and thus that their presence in England was to be 'short-lived'. He suggests that this involved a change of mind on Locke's part after composition of the first *Letter Concerning Toleration*, a change in which Locke's support for the conversion of the Jews and return to Palestine increased. Matar suggests, therefore, that while Locke's commitment to the toleration of Jews in England was significant, in the 1690s and early 1700s it was deeply inflected by conversionist intentions.[18]

The notion that in the later 1690s and early 1700s Locke was conversionist and believed in the restoration of the Jews to Palestine is persuasive. But in terms of his tolerationist thought, and in terms of analysing his conversionist thought itself, it is important to note that Matar does not produce evidence that Locke himself viewed the conversion of the Jews and the millennium as imminent. He notes particularly Locke's notes from the 1694 English translation of van Helmont's *Seder Olam*, and Newton's influence on Locke. These notes, based on van Helmont, suggested, as Arthur Wainwright has noted, that the fullness of the Gentiles would occur in 1702, the conversion of the Jews in 1732, and the millennium in 1777. But Wainwright points out that it is not clear if Locke agreed with such a dating. This should be underlined. Locke's notes carry no clear suggestion of approval. Locke did not agree with a number of van Helmont's other positions – as van Helmont's biographer Alison Coudert has noted in arguing that Locke's thought on toleration of Jews does *not* seem to have changed due to an increasing emphasis on conversion. Moreover, if any prophetically inclined individual influenced Locke's own interpretations significantly, it seems more likely that Locke would have agreed with Isaac Newton's dating than with van Helmont's, as Newton apparently had a deeper influence on Locke's interpretation of prophecy in the 1690s and early 1700s than van Helmont, and

---

[17] Locke, *Second Letter* in *Works*, 62; Ms Locke 17 fos. 2, 58–60; Matar, 'John Locke and the Jews'; J. Locke, *A Paraphrase and Notes Upon the Epistles of St Paul*, ed. A. Wainwright (Oxford 1989), 2 vols, I, 55–6 and 56n.

[18] Locke, *Paraphrase*, ed. A. Wainwright (Oxford 1987), II, 577–8; Matar, 'John Locke and the Jews'. Cf now also A. Sutcliffe, *Judaism and Enlightenment* (Cambridge 2003), 218–20.

since Locke's notes in his private Bibles include some specifically from Newton on the interpretation of prophecy. But while Newton may have refused to identify the exact dates involved, as Matar notes, Newton's interpretation of prophecy, as Stephen Snobelen has recently shown, saw the conversion of the Jews as 'centuries away' – a temporal distance 'from his own time', which Snobelen contrasts to the dating of several of Newton's contemporaries and calls 'startling'. Newton apparently believed in a call to Jews to return to and rebuild Jerusalem occurring no earlier than 1895 or 1896, and he dated the end days (years) between 2000 and 2050 AD. Given such dates, Snobelen appropriately emphasises that Newton's thought gave 'no direct political context for his belief in the return of the Jews', and that on Newton's part there is 'no evidence of involvement in efforts to convert the Jews in his time'.[19]

If Locke was influenced by Newton on the question of dating the return of the Jews to Palestine, Newton's dating would have meant that such a commitment to conversion and return to Palestine exerted no meaningful influence on Locke's arguments for the toleration of Jews in England. And one very brief comment that Locke made in his published tolerationist writings perhaps suggests that he did not believe in an imminent restoration. In replying to Proast's citation of Kings as nursing fathers and mothers to the church, Locke argued that 'If we may judge of this prophecy by what is past or present, we shall have reason to think it concerns not our days'. He encouraged Proast to understand that this promise would not be enacted 'till the restoring of Israel', this being 'the time designed by that prophecy', indicating that he did not think that this prophecy was 'to be fulfilled in this age'.[20] Even if Newton did not influence Locke towards Newton's distant dating of the conversion and restoration to Palestine, there is insufficient reason to conclude that Locke accepted van Helmont's dating or any other which placed the conversion and restoration in the near term. Since Locke was explicitly committed to the toleration of Jews until whatever might be the date of their future restoration, and since it seems most likely that for him this was to occur in the distant future, Locke's position seems closer to the demands for Jewish citizenship in England and public worship in synagogues in England that had been expressed by Rabbi Menasseh ben Israel in the mid-seventeenth century than it was to those Christian conversionists who expected imminent Jewish conversion and who had argued in the mid-seventeenth century that Jews should not be readmitted to England because

[19] S. Snobelen, 'The Mystery of this Restitution of All Things: Isaac Newton on the Return of the Jews', in J. Force and R. Popkin (eds.), *Millenarianism and Messianism in Early Modern European Culture: The Millennial Turn* (Leiden 2001), 95–118, esp. 107–11. I am extremely grateful to Stephen Snobelen for providing me with a pre-publication copy of this important article.

[20] Locke, *Third Letter*, in *Works*, VI, 370–1.

they needed to be relocated imminently to Palestine, and who in the 1680s and 1690s were still expecting such a conversion within a few years.[21]

Locke unquestionably thought that Christianity was the superior religion to Judaism, which he declared both 'false' and 'absurd' in the *Letter*, and he unquestionably thought both that the Jews would be converted to Christianity before the millennium and that before that happened they would be restored to Palestine. But the evidence suggests that he simultaneously wished Jews to be tolerated in England (and elsewhere) in the immediate and probably the medium-term future. Locke's conversionist commitments and expectations of 'Restoration' thus did not blunt his argument for toleration of Jews in England, an argument which was to continue to be influential long after the date at which most of his contemporaries expected the restoration of Jews to Palestine. In the late eighteenth century, Joseph Priestley and Richard Price were influenced by Locke in their arguments for a wide toleration that included Jews, as was Thomas Jefferson in America. And in 1813, the pseudonymous authors 'Abraham, Isaac and Jacob' identified Locke in 'their' joint *The Lamentations of the Children of Israel Representing the Hardships they Suffer from the Penal Laws* as being a supporter of the toleration of Jews in their continuing campaign for statutory toleration of Jews in England.[22]

In supporting toleration of Jews at the same time as desiring their conversion and himself producing a series of arguments in his *Reasonableness of Christianity* to show that Christianity was the true religion and Christ the Messiah, Locke's arguments were also close to those of his friend Philip van Limborch. It was to Limborch that Locke had written his *Letter Concerning Toleration*, with its arguments for the toleration of Jews. And this work was written for Limborch in the midst of a debate about the merits of Judaism and Christianity between Limborch and Isaac Orobio de Castro, a former Marrano who had immigrated to the Netherlands in 1662 and had become there an important anti-Christian polemicist in Spanish and Portuguese. In 1687, Limborch published an account of this dispute, *De veritate religionis christianae amica collatio cum eruditio judaeo*, which presented both sides in the debate, although since it was structured as a rebuttal of Orobio's arguments and gave his own arguments considerably more pages, it cannot be called an entirely balanced account. It was a work to which Le Clerc gave a forty-one page review in the *Bibliothèque universelle*. Here again,

---

[21] Matar, 'John Locke and the Jews'; Coudert, 'Locke'; Snobelen, 'The Mystery'. I would suggest that the evidence is insufficient to merit Matar's overall conclusion of a shift in which 'From wishing to liberate them from Christian constraint and establish them legally in England, Locke turned to zealous conversionism and 'Restorationism'.

[22] Abraham, Isaac and Jacob, *The Lamentations of the Children of Israel* (1813) discussed in Matar, 'John Locke and the Jews', 45.

Le Clerc's journal of the 'republic of letters' was being used to advance both ecumenical Christian arguments and tolerationist arguments. Locke consulted in manuscript Limborch's arguments and those of Orobio, recording in February 1685 that he was studying repeatedly 'those writings of your own and of Don Balthasaar which you lent me some time ago', and making suggestions for improvements in 1685–6. Limborch thanked Locke for his improvements. He was drafting the third part of his response in September 1685 – that is, probably shortly before Locke composed his *Letter Concerning Toleration* for Limborch.[23]

In a political and religious situation in the Netherlands which provided toleration for Jewish worship, but where it was deeply problematic for Jews to argue against Christ in public disputations with Christians because this could be considered to violate the requirement that their toleration did not include attack on Christianity and 'blasphemy', Orobio was constrained to avoid direct argument against Christ's divinity and to argue against Christianity instead through questioning how the Old Testament gave proof that belief in the Messiah was essential for salvation, how Israel would perish through disbelief in the Messiah, and how the Old Testament prefigured the New Testament. Even with such carefully cautious argumentation, once Limborch published his arguments Orobio was saved from the censure of the Ma'amad for holding a forbidden public disputation against Christianity only by the fact that he died one week after the appearance of the work.

As P. T. van Rooden and J. Wesselius have shown, Limborch's argument in reply to Orobio radically departed from previous Christian disputes against Judaism in which it had been conventional to assert on textual grounds the triune nature of God, the need for reconciliation with God due to original sin, the necessity to such reconciliation of a 'God-man', and Jesus' fulfilment of that role. This traditional structure of argument had been deployed in many accounts, including that in the fifth book of Grotius' *De veritate religionis Christianae*. Limborch instead turned the question to the prophetic and law-giving status of Moses, and argued that Christianity completed Judaism, with a Messiah vaguely promised in the Old Testament and clearly revealed in the New, with a clear doctrine brought by Christ, and with the same but better grounds for acceptance of Christ as those for Moses. The 'clarity' of doctrine for Limborch was largely that Christ had reinforced the duties of natural law, and Limborch discussed the argument that the Jews had not known the promise of the afterlife. For

---

[23] Le Clerc, *Bibliothèque universelle* (1688), 289–330; van Rooden and Wesselius, 'Early Enlightenment'; Kaplan, *From Christianity*, 273–85; Israel, *European Jewry*, 221–4; *idem*, *Dutch Republic*; *idem*, *Radical*, 466ff.; Simonutti, 'Religion'.

Limborch, the miracles clearly established in the New Testament were sufficient to establish this revelation. For Limborch, the Jews of Old Testament times had not needed to know Christ in order to be saved, and he emphasised that Christians worshipped the same God as Jews.[24]

Although giving no attribution, in the course and structure of these arguments Limborch was deploying (as van Rooden and Wesselius and Luisa Simonutti have shown) Spinozist arguments against the reliability of the Old Testament and the Mosaic authorship of the Pentateuch. Limborch's friend Le Clerc not merely read but lauded Spinoza's biblical critcism, and sought to distinguish where it was valid – in its criticisms on the Pentateuch, *inter alia* – from where it erred – in its denial of miracles, *inter alia*. And Limborch's arguments, as van Rooden and Wesselius have shown, were also derivative of some of the most advanced biblical criticism of the pre-Adamite philosopher La Peyrère (who countenanced two separate Messiahs), and of the worries about the textual traditions of the Bible voiced by the Oratorian biblical critic Richard Simon and by the leading Huguenot biblical scholar Louis Cappel. Orobio himself tangentially noted these sources of Limborch's arguments in suggesting that they were borrowed from the 'Pre-Adamite pseudo-scholars, the atheists and political theologians'. Two further sources for Limborch's arguments in his *De Veritate* are here important. Where Grotius had argued in the then usual Christian fashion in book 5 of his *De Veritate*, in books 1 to 3 he had reversed the usual pattern of argument, from the usual contention that the New Testament could be said to fulfil the Old Testament and thus be proven true, to the suggestion that it was its miracles and success in the world which together testified to the status of the New Testament. It was this method of the first book of Grotius' *De Veritate* which Limborch followed in his argument, and which Limborch explicitly noted to Le Clerc had been suggested to him by reading Grotius.

But it is important that the sources of this argument did not stop with Grotius. For the arguments of Grotius' *De Veritate* were close indeed to those of the Socinian *Racovian Catechism* of 1609, which defended the validity of Christianity through its miracles and success in the world, and to Socinus' own works, such that it has been declared that Grotius must have had these works in hand in his process of composition. Orobio himself suggested that Limborch's argument was ultimately owed to a Socinian source. Owing a debt to such a Socinian source and method, albeit mediated to Limborch by Grotius, Limborch was thus influenced in his important new pattern of Christian apologetic by the methods of Spinoza and of the

---

[24] P. van Limborch, *De Veritate Religions Christianae* (Gouda 1987); van Rooden and Wesselius, 'Early Enlightenment'; Kaplan, *From Christianity*, 273–85; Matar, 'John Locke and the Jews'.

Socinians. While it is important to register that Arminians in the first generation of Arminianism were close to many parts of Calvinism, for all of their opposition to its specific tenets on predestination, by the time of the generation of Limborch and Le Clerc there was considerable reason to think that the Arminians were increasingly in the process of becoming the 'demi-sociniens' which their opponents had long accused Arminians of being.[25]

By adopting this derivatively 'Socinian' method of arguing for the truth of Christianity on the basis of its testimony and clarity, with arguments thought to be persuasive to 'reasonable' individuals, Limborch was thus turning away from the usual Christian emphases on the Trinity and satisfaction and their concomitant stresses on the unique salvific requirements and provisions of Christianity. And he was turning towards a method of argumentation thought to be convincing to 'reasonable' individuals when it was offered as part of a 'civil discussion', as the title of the work itself indicated, and as an appeal to reasoned arguments. Limborch described the use of force against Orobio de Castro at length in order to condemn the Inquisition in Spain. Limborch then explicitly declared that preceding Christians were responsible for having 'repelled' Jews from Christianity by their behaviour. Here, Limborch was expanding in part upon the arguments of his predecessor Episcopius, whose *Two Discourses on the Causes of Jewish Unbelief* (1650) had described Christian behaviour as having been so 'barbaric' in its use of force, cruelty, and massacres that Christians had made Jews reject Christ. While Episcopius did briefly note that Jewish education itself taught a hatred of Christianity, he had been adamant that molestation by Christians had fortified this, as had 'absurd' and 'ridiculous' doctrines of Catholics such as transubstantiation, and as had sectarian wars among Christians.[26] Limborch's fellow Arminian professor Jean Le Clerc's 1699 *Parrhasiana* argued that medieval libels against the Jews condemned those making them, and his *Treatise of the Causes of Incredulity* recommended Limborch's work itself as offering good arguments for the conversion of Jews.[27]

In recognition of Limborch's manner of argumentation, attempts at reasoned and civil persuasion, and repudiation of the use of force, Orobio's own argument in the text declared that Limborch was a 'civil' and 'honest' disputant. And while Limborch cannot be said to have provided by his publication an equal representation of his opponents' arguments as he

---

[25] Simonutti, *Arminianesimo*, 78–83; van Rooden and Wesselius, 'Early Enlightenment', *passim*; cf. Le Clerc and Spinoza's biblical criticism discussed in Klauber, 'Fundamental Articles'.

[26] Manuel, *Broken Staff*, 109–10.

[27] Le Clerc, *Parrhasiana*, I, 299; *idem, A Treatise of the Causes of Incredulity* (1697), 67–9; Yardeni, 'Bayle', 253.

allowed himself the benefit of the final word, a structure providing what he thought to be rebuttals of his opponents' arguments, and considerably more words, he did state Orobio's arguments both clearly and about as fairly as the structure of the disputation then permissible in the Netherlands allowed, and he provided an image thereby of a 'civil' debate for others. It is important to stress that this method of arguing was itself crucial, as these disputants attempted to turn acrimonious religious polemic which they associated with intolerance into channels of 'civility' and polite persuasive arguments. Many tolerationists associated with Locke understood that in their controversial works they were attempting to set out a model of disputation for others that would itself foster tolerance. In Le Clerc's *Life of Locke*, he was to stress that 'two things' had been notable in the way in which Locke had handled the 'controversy' with Stillingfleet over Locke's works in the 1690s. The first was the subject-matter, but the second was 'the manner wherein that was handled'. Le Clerc thus celebrated the 'strength of Mr Lock's reasonings' with which Le Clerc thought that Locke had clearly demonstrated the advantages of his position against Stillingfleet, but gave at least equal celebration to the way in which Locke was 'yet very far from abusing the Advantages he had, but always detected and refuted his [Stillingfleet's] errors with Civility and Respect'.[28]

That Limborch recorded Orobio's arguments fairly and civilly meant that he recorded Orobio's questioning of the historical reliability of traditions about the life of Christ and about the history of early Christianity. Thereby, Limborch was simultaneously and unintentionally to provide 'clandestine literature' with many arguments it was to use against Christianity in succeeding years. And Limborch's own turn to reliance on 'miracles' as testified to in a text to whose validity as a text those miracles were themselves said to support created the kind of circular argument deserving of Hume's later acid commentary. Limborch's 'Socinian' move away from traditional arguments in disputations against Jews that had formerly focused on establishing Christianity as forecast in the Old Testament and on Christ's divinity, and towards 'reasonable' arguments that focused on the internal evidence of the New Testament and its 'miracles', thus helped to provide the 'reasonable' ground for both Jewish and 'atheist' questioning of the status of that text.[29]

Thus, both John Locke and Philip van Limborch desired conversion of Jews and advocated toleration of Jews. A third important tolerationist author, Jacques Basnage, was equally desirous of the conversion of Jews and supportive of toleration of Jews. Basnage's 1706 *History of the Jews* was

---

[28] Le Clerc, *Life of Locke*; Limborch, *Collatio*, 50, in van Rooden and Wesselius 'Early Enlightenment', 146. Cf Sutcliffe, *Judaism*, 166–70.

[29] Van Rooden and Wesselius, 'Early Enlightenment'; Israel, *Radical*, 466.

simultaneously the first history of the Jews in post-biblical times as a continuation of Josephus, an important defence of toleration, an indictment of medieval ignorance and barbarity, a celebration of Protestantism, and a description of the many maledictions which had fallen upon Jews for their rejection of Christ.[30] His discussion of Chilperic, 'a bad king' who 'thought to do himself honour by forcing the conscience of the Jews and compelling them into baptism' was in part surely intended as an indirect indictment of Louis XIV's attack on the Huguenots, but it was also a direct attack on the use of force against Jews. Basnage wrote of the Reformation that

people then began to sense the barbarism and the gross ignorance of the monks and ceased to accuse the Jews of the murder of children, a libel which had brought so many troubles down on them and had caused torrents of their blood to be shed.[31]

For Basnage, Jews had been accused often of crucifying Christian children as the renewal of their 'Fathers crime' against Jesus and of the use of blood diabolically mingled with the host in conjuration. For Basnage,

this accusation is found repeated every where, since the Twelfth Century: Historians support it by a great number of Miracles which God has wrought to take exemplary Vengeance upon the Jews' impiety, without being able to amend them.[32]

This gave Basnage the opportunity to launch an attack simultaneously on Catholic monks for their artifices, on the medieval Catholic laity for their ridiculous beliefs and 'superstition', and on intolerance to Jews. For Basnage, 'these Miracles and Crimes are equally false'. For Basnage, Jews had repeatedly said that the accusations against them involved 'calumny' and had shown 'a thousand Discoveries' of the 'Artifice of Monks or other Christians, who threw into their Houses the dead Body of a Child or a Man, to have the pretence of charging them with the Murder'. Noting that Jews abhorred 'human sacrifices', he declared these accusations among 'pretenses' to incense kings and people against Jews, and that it was impossible to believe that they had so departed from 'prudence' and 'humanity'.[33]

In passages strongly reminiscent of Bayle's *Philosophical Commentary*, Basnage indicted the hypocrisy and dissimulation used in order to justify punishment that was held not to be persecution. It was for Basnage ridiculous when some endeavoured to 'soften' this notion and 'change the common meaning of words, and colour Violence with the pretext of charity for the Errroneous. They call it an Holy Severity'. Citing Thomassin's *History of Edicts*, Basnage ridiculed Thomassin's suggestion

[30] Yardeni, 'Bayle', 245–58; Elukin, 'Jacques Basnage', 602–30. Cf Sutcliffe, *Judaism*, 81–5.
[31] Basnage, *Histoire de la religion des juifs* (Rotterdam 1706–7), IV, 1, 425 and V, 2,064, in Yardeni, 'Bayle', 245–58, at 248; Elukin, 'Jacques Basnage', 602–30, at 608.
[32] Basnage, *History*, 642.   [33] *Ibid.*, 642–3.

that the edicts against Jews were 'not violent constraints, but inducements to remove the impediments to your instruction and conversion'. Such Christians said that the repudiation of liberty of conscience, removal of children, exile and confiscations were 'persuasions' rather than 'violences' or 'constraints'. It was claimed that 'Fathers, Husbands, and Masters, exercise gentle chastisements upon their children, wives and servants, to reduce them to their duty'. And the ultimate hypocrisy for Basnage was that the church which 'abhors' the spilling of blood held itself only to deliver up to the secular arm those who needed to be punished and was therefore 'an indulgent and charitable mother, who has no hand in the Murder of her Children'. Basnage wished that the church would act 'with more sincerity'. For Basnage, 'enemies' of the Christian religion had not been shown in their 'true light' but had always been represented as 'odious by metaphorical terms, and drawing cruel and barbarous consequences from them'. The greatest men in Christianity had been guilty of this 'zeal'; but it was necessary now not to imitate them but to learn 'more equity'. For Basnage, if drawn 'in its natural colours' the Inquisition could not ever have been justified. It was only by obscuring these true colours that the church had been able to defend the institution. The 'truth' was 'no other ways salutary, than in proportion as it is known, and voluntarily embraced. Corporal pains and Punishments ought to be inflicted for faults that disturb civil society'. Acts of punishment were acts 'of inhumanity and barbarity, which ought never to be seen among Christians'.[34]

Basnage was a close friend of Bayle. Bayle was adamant in many works, including the *Philosophical Commentary*, that Jews deserved toleration. In the *Dictionary* at many points Bayle condemned arguments for the use of force against Jews, for instance complimenting Pope Gregory the Great for denying that force could be used against Jews while attacking him for arguing that force could be used against heretics, supplying lengthy arguments for toleration of Jews and heretics and referring readers to his own *Philosophical Commentary*. Bayle similarly paralleled intolerance to Jews with intolerance to others in condemning both in entries such as Apion E. According to Bayle, as the Jews had refused orders to worship Caligula, Apion had drawn upon the hatred of the Egyptian nation to the Jewish nation 'time out of mind' and had rendered 'the Jews odious to Caligula' by 'Accusations of Impiety' and 'captious points'. Bayle continued immediately: 'Thus false zealots act, at this very day, to support themselves in a most unjust authority over Conscience, as well as all other Concerns. This can never be too often repeated'. Occasionally, however, Bayle noted that Jewish

---

[34] *Ibid.*, 639–42.

hostility to other religions could present problems for their toleration. In 'Drusilla A' in the *Dictionary*, Bayle noted that as the Jewish religion condemned all other religions, it had tested even the tolerantly eclectic and polytheistic Romans. He wrote:

> I know the Romans were very easy in tolerating Religions; but there is a vast difference between tolerating a religion which does not contemn yours, and tolerating a Sect that anathematises and damns you. And this is what the Jews did with respect to all other Religions.

But even at this point Bayle noted that the Romans had required the conversion of Drusilla herself only when she was to marry the Roman commander Felix because at that point it became a problem that she viewed 'the Religion of the Romans as abominable'; the implication was still supportive of toleration of Jews who were out of power, whatever their attitude about other religions.[35]

A number of Bayle's representations of Jews were strongly negative. Bayle assaulted Jewish credulity in miracles, as in the *Dictionary* article on Ezekiel, one of the 'four great Prophets, whose writings make up part of the Old Testament', where he spoke of the Jews as 'infatuated with their Superstitions, and absurd Whims' and having therefore told many stories about miracles at his tomb; Bayle stressed the prayers of those who wished to conceive. Adding a biting tone of ridicule, he noted that such prayers were for people themselves or for their barren cattle or horses. The point here for Bayle was unquestionably in part to ridicule Jews for their 'superstition'. But the more important point for Bayle was not the ridiculing of Jews as much as the depicting of these 'many Fables' as revealing the origins of many Christian beliefs. For Bayle, such beliefs were clearly the source of central Catholic practices. He declared that these stories showed that 'invocation of the Saints has long since been a practice of the Jews'. Bayle gave Protestant readers a few sentences to feel triumphant in having purged themselves of such false beliefs. But then Bayle very quickly pulled the rug out from under Jurieu:

> The Protestants have reason to lament the shameless Credulity of this People, and the confidence of their writers in publishing a hundred thousand foolish stories; but every one ought to learn by what passes in his own Party, that in this place the Declivity is very slippery. How many things are practiced by the Protestants nowadays, which would not have been approved a hundred years ago? I am satisfied the Author of the *Pastoral Letters* [Jurieu] has published more false Miracles than he ought to have done: but I am certain that he had many more sent him than what are in his Letters.[36]

---

[35] Bayle, *Dictionary*, Gregory the Great, Rem E; Drusilla A; Yardeni, 'Bayle'.

[36] Bayle, *Dictionary*, Ezekiel; Constance B; Yardeni, 'Bayle'.

It is within this structure of directly or indirectly assaulting contemporary Christian practices and beliefs as 'superstitious' or 'idolatrous' and identifying pagan and Judaic sources for such beliefs that Bayle excoriated Judaic beliefs and practices. Bayle wrote extensively on 'rabbinic judaism', 'idolatry', and 'superstition'. But almost all scholars agree that the primary point of this was not to indict Judaism alone but by implication to indict contemporary Catholicism, while some scholars further argue that it was intended simultaneously to indict contemporary Christianity as full of superstition. Bayle repeatedly mocked miracles, and none more than that of Jonah and the whale. Bayle's article on Jonah linked the story in the margin to the fable of Hercules, quoting Homer and Lycophron on Hercules having spent three days in the belly of a whale. By a process of isolating these statements against Judaism from their multiple resonances against contemporary Christianity, Bayle has been associated with Enlightenment anti-Semitism by some writers, including Arthur Hertzberg and Haydyn Mason. It is certainly true that, for Bayle, 'superstition' and 'idolatry' were to be condemned, and that, for Bayle, they were prevalent in Judaism, but what was under assault by Bayle was not Judaism alone, but rather all religious claims that Bayle deemed 'superstitious', 'credulous', 'enthusiastic', or 'fanatical' – which meant, for Bayle, most claims and many actions of all religions. While he wished to see many of these elements of religion purged from religions, and used arguments mocking many of these elements towards that end, it was not necessary for Bayle that a religion not be superstitious for it to be tolerated – it was only necessary that it not be politically dangerous. Jews, for Bayle, deserved both ridicule for superstition and religious toleration – as, for Bayle, did most, and perhaps all, contemporary Christians.[37] Bayle discussed the conversion of Jews at a number of other moments in the *Dictionary*. But as Richard Popkin has emphasised, what is most striking about Bayle's accounts of conversion in the *Dictionary* in their context is that they do not celebrate conversion to Christianity nor condemn conversion away from Christianity.[38]

SINCERITY, MORALITY, AND THE POSSIBILITY OF SALVATION

We have seen that in the 1680s many advocates of toleration explicitly defended toleration for Muslims alongside toleration for Jews and Pagans.

---

[37] Hertzberg, *Enlightenment*; H. Mason, *Bayle and Voltaire* (Oxford 1963), 28–9; for criticisms of Hertzberg, see R. Schechter, 'Rationalizing the Enlightenment: Postmodernism and Theories of Anti-Semitism' in D. Gordon (ed.), *Postmodernism and the Enlightenment* (New York 2000), 93–116.

[38] Popkin, 'Bayle and the Conversion'.

At points, this was combined with conversionist argument not merely about Jews and pagans but also about Muslims, as it was argued both that Muslims should be allowed to reside in Christian countries in order to be converted, and that a tolerant Christianity should be supported in order that Muslim rulers would not have reason to exclude Christian preachers from their domains. Such conversionist thought often expressed its confidence in the superiority of Christianity over other religions while arguing for those other religions to be tolerated. Tolerationist argument went further still at various points, however, in stressing the sincerity of Muslims and even their laudable morality.

In the *Dictionary*, Bayle suggested that Mahometans had falsely claimed that Mahomet had done miracles, and that one might attack Mahomet himself for his nine wives and criticise polygyny for its effects on women. But Bayle quoted the accounts of Richard Simon and Pierre Chardin as well as Paul Rycaut against the commonly held view that Muslims were morally lax and that their religion encouraged this laxity, quoting Simon both as identifying that Islamic morality 'consisted in doing good and avoiding evil' and comparing Islamic moral theology favourably with the casuistry of Christians. Bayle indicated that Islamic morality included not injuring others and the 'epitome of the law and the prophets, Do to your neighbour, what you would that he should do to you'. In general, in the *Dictionary*, Bayle gave a favourable picture of Muslim beliefs and especially of their practices of toleration, largely by using the arguments of Paul Rycaut's *State of the Ottoman Empire*. Indeed, at a point where Rycaut questioned Muslim sincerity in providing toleration, Bayle criticised Rycaut's evidence and argument and proclaimed Muslim tolerance more forcefully than Rycaut.

For Bayle, while Islam in its prophetic foundation legitimated force, it had not thereafter practised it, in direct contrast to Christianity, which had denied the use of force in its foundation but thereafter had practised it. Recognising that Christians were tolerated in Islamic territory, Bayle argued that if the Western church had dominated in 'Asia' in place of the 'Saracens' and 'Turks' then there would have remained no trace of the Greek Church, and no toleration for Mahometanism, in contrast to the toleration the 'Infidels' had given to Christianity. It was for Bayle ridiculous for Christians to reproach Mahometans with having used violence to propagate the Koran when Christians had propagated their religion by greater force. For Bayle, the 'Turks tolerate all religions, although the Alkoran enjoins them to persecute the infidels' whereas the Christians were persecutors, despite the fact that 'the Gospel forbids' all such persecution. Thus, in Bayle's *Dictionary*, while Mahomet was presented as a fraud, as lustful, and as legitimating the use of force in religion, in direct contrast to the role of Christ in preaching peace and love and tolerance, a significant part of the Muslim moral code was suggested to be similar to the Christian, and in the part of morality that counted most to Bayle, support for religious toleration, many Muslims were depicted as far ahead of most Christians in their practices.[39]

Various of the passages in Locke's works such as the *Essay Concerning Human Understanding* record deep hostility to alleged Muslim practices and to the Islamic religion. We saw in Chapter 10 that extensive seventeenth-century discourses attacked Muslims as 'libertines' and 'sodomites' and Islam as validating such acts; in the *Essay*, Locke sketched this idea, writing in one of his many illustrations of the absence of innate moral ideas (in a passage that followed immediately after discussions of cannibalism and atheism elsewhere in the world) that the 'saints, who are canonized amongst the Turks, lead lives, which one cannot with Modesty relate'. Modesty was then presumably preserved for female readers by his immediately recounting in Latin only 'A remarkable passage to this purpose' in a book about concubines that was 'not every day to be met with'. Locke then immediately added further confirmation by indicating that 'More of the same Kind, concerning these precious Saints amongst the Turks, may be seen in Pietro della Valle, in his letter of the 25th of January 1616'.[40]

But in a little-noticed but important passage of the *Third Letter for Toleration* to which Nabil Matar has called our attention, Locke wrote:

> You cannot but allow there are many Turks who sincerely seek truth, to whom yet you could never bring evidence sufficient to convince them of the truth of the christian religion, whilst they looked on it as a principle not to be questioned, that the Koran was of divine revelation. This possibly you will tell me is a prejudice, and so it is; but yet if this man shall tell you it is no more a prejudice in him, than it is a prejudice in any one amongst christians, who having not examined it, lays it down as an unquestionable principle of his religion, that the Scripture is the word of God; what will you answer to him?[41]

It perhaps needs emphasis that Locke has here canvassed the notion that many Muslims sincerely seek truth and may have as good (or as bad) a series of reasons for their commitment to the Koran as most Christians have for their commitment to the gospel during a period in which arguments for toleration amongst Christians were assaulted by pillorying the toleration of the 'Alcoran' and in an atmosphere where John Edwards was soon to assault Locke's minimalist and allegedly 'Socinian' Christology in the *Reasonableness of Christianity* as being itself a 'Mahometan faith'.

---

[39] Bayle, *Dictionary*, Mahomet, L, O, P, AA, Charnley, *Bayle*, 49–54, 78–86.

[40] Locke, *Essay*, I.3.9; idem, *Reasonableness* in *Works*, VI, 85; idem, *Paraphrase*, I, 3, 30–1; 1 Corinthians 2: 4–5.

[41] Locke, *Third Letter* in *Works*, 298; Matar, 'Turbanned', 74.

Locke further wrote in a letter to James Tyrrell in defence of the account of moral ideas in the *Essay Concerning Human Understanding* against others' criticisms that

The Alcoran of the Mahometans...being taken for a divine law it would have served men who made use of it and judged of their actions by it to have given them notions of morality or Moral Ideas.

In this letter to Tyrrell on the source of 'moral ideas', Locke indicated that he was not investigating of 'any supposed divine revelation', whether it was 'true or false', and he cited as equivalent in this sense the laws of Moses and Jesus Christ, the Alcoran and the 'Hanscrit [sic: Sanscrit] of the Bramins'. He noted that 'perhaps you or your friends would have thought it more worth their censure if I had put them in and then I had lain open to I know not what interpretations'. The double caution here is worth noting: Locke is not discussing even in a private letter to Tyrrell the 'truth' claims of these different religions, recognising that there were reasons to avoid publishing such a consideration explicitly in the *Essay* since he understood that it might be construed by others censoriously. But neither form of Locke's character-istic caution about what he put into print excludes the *possibility* that Locke was thinking that many who would subscribe to these 'false' bases of moral argument might be sincere in their subscription, and that this sincere sub-scription might in the eyes of God be acceptable in their situations. In combination with the passage in the *Third Letter* just cited, it appears that Locke himself *may* perhaps have been thinking of the potential salvation of Muslims (and others) who attempted to live to a moral code which they had accepted on sincere grounds, even if to him their religion was 'false'.[42]

In the late seventeenth and early eighteenth centuries there was a move to oppose Calvinist accounts of the restricted salvation of the predestined Christian elect and to recognise the possibility of salvation for those who had never heard of Christ but who sincerely tried to live morally in their religions. At the time of Robert Burton's *Anatomy of Melancholy* in the early seventeenth century, it was declared to be a 'Socinian' view to hold that if someone was 'honest' and lived 'soberly and civilly' whether 'jew, turk, or anabaptist' then such an individual could be saved. By the late seventeenth century, this view was coming to be shared not merely by many Socinians but also by some Arminians and Cambridge Platonists. Nonetheless, it remained to many orthodox Calvinists a 'Socinian' view which proved that these other denominations were indeed becoming (or had become) 'Socinian' or 'demi-Socinian'. The traditional Calvinist John Owen argued in his 1672 *Discourse Concerning Evangelical Love* that the possibility of salvation was confined

---

[42] Locke, *Correspondence*, IV, 1309; Matar, 'Turbanned', 75.

to those with knowledge of Christ; while it might appear unjust for God to have thus banished from salvation a majority of the world's population, this was the wisdom of God (and in fact the just deserts of all of sinful humanity, with only a small number mercifully saved). But for Henry More, in his 1668 *Divine Dialogues*, supralapsarian Calvinism was quite literally diabolic:

For the object of their Worship is a God-idol of their own framing, that acts merely according to Will and Power, sequestered from all respect to either Justice or Goodness...which is the genuine idea of a Devil...

More emphasised that what was crucial to salvation was 'sincerity' in the search for truth or the attempt to live to a moral standard. More had vilified Islam as the 'Satanic Kingdom', but he was committed to the possibility of a post-mortem redemption and argued that one should not damn

the very best and most conscientious Turks, Jews, and Pagans to the pit of Hell, and then to double lock the door upon them, or to stand there to watch with long poles to beat them down again, if any of them should offer to emerge and endeavour to crawl out...

George Rust's 1661 *A Letter of Resolution Concerning Origen* similarly held out the possibility of universal salvation, or *apocatastasis*.[43] The Baptist John Bunyan, who had come under the influence of Quakers questioning the restriction of salvation, wrote:

How can you tell but that the Turks had as good Scriptures to prove their Mahomet the Saviour, as we have to prove our Jesus is? And, could I think that so many ten thousands, in so many countries and kingdoms, should be without the knowledge of a right way to heaven; if there were indeed a heaven, and that we only, who live in a corner of the earth, should alone be blessed therewith? Every one doth own his own religion rightest, both Jews, and Moors, and Pagans! And how if all our faith, and Christ, and Scriptures, should be but a think-so too?[44]

In the Restoration, the Latitudinarian Isaac Barrow suggested that Christ was 'Saviour of all men'. The Grotian or Arminian Presbyterian Baxter distinguished between Christ's procurement of our pardon and salvation by his sacrifice and Christ as the object of man's faith, or as believed in by man. The first – Christ's procurement of salvation – was necessary for salvation but had been available since the creation of humanity, and was available to all men whether they believed in Christ or not. Locke's friend Tillotson declared that the 'good' among the heathens had been accepted by God and not excluded from the blessing of the Messiahs 'tho they were ignorant of him'.[45] Le Clerc argued in his *Treatise of the Causes of Incredulity* that 'there was no Injustice' in some nations having knowledge

[43] H. More and G. Rust in P. Harrison, *Religion and the Religions in the English Enlightenment* (Cambridge 1990), 48–57.
[44] Bunyan in Hill, *Turbulent*, 75.   [45] Pailin, *Attitudes*, 60; Porter, *Untold Story*, 100–2.

of Christ and others not, 'provided' God 'requires no more than he has given...if he judges all nations according to their portions of knowledge, as he infallibly will do'. Limborch argued in his *Theologia Christiana*, considering American Indians to whom Christ had never been preached, that 'No man is obliged to know those things, which God has not, or will not reveal to him, nor will any man be damned for the want of such a Knowledge'. He argued that God could save those who 'live agreeably to the Law of Nature' without 'faith in Christ'. Aubert's *Treatise* questioned how could 'incredulity', if unavoidable, be charged to individuals. For instance, American Indians were unaware of Christ, and had not had the opportunity to become aware. Such was 'invincible ignorance'. They had to have the possibility of being saved, or God would be unjust. God had therefore provided salvation for those who had tried to live well even if they had not ever heard of Christ.[46] And Locke clearly argued in the *Reasonableness of Christianity* that God would deal appropriately with those who had never heard of Christ, and clearly indicated the possibility of their salvation. According to Locke, God would not 'require any one should believe a promise of which he has never heard'. Many 'to whom the promise of the Messiah never came' would have had to try to find their duty by the light of nature and would be forgiven for failures to live up to it. In the period after Locke and Tillotson, Limborch, and Aubert, support for the possibility of salvation for those outside of Christianity who lived morally upright lives and who had not specifically rejected Christ was to become a widespread attitude among European Christians in the eighteenth century. In the process, in its move towards a salvific universalism of sincerity and moral obedience, the mainstream Christian 'early Enlightenment' took a considerable step beyond the Calvinists' acceptance of toleration for Jews, Muslims, and 'pagans' whom the Calvinists had nonetheless believed damned unless they could be persuaded to adopt Christianity or were given the gift of faith.[47]

---

[46] Le Clerc, *Treatise*, 181–2; Limborch, *Compleat System*, 362–6; Aubert de Versé, *Traité*, 77–8.
[47] Locke, *Reasonableness* in *Works*, VII, 125–33, esp. 132–3; Porter, *Untold Story*, 101.

20

The historical argument for toleration and 'early Enlightenment' advocacy of 'humanity' and 'civility'

In the 1680s to 1700s, the advocates of toleration frequently presented as a major part of their arguments for toleration a historical case which identified the period of justifications of the use of magisterial force in religion as a time of overwhelming 'barbarism', 'superstition', and 'ignorance'. They posed in contrast as a set of related values 'humanity', 'tolerance', 'civility', 'politeness', 'reason', and 'critical' scholarship.[1] This historical understanding was created as part of a new classification in the late seventeenth century of the previous periods of history which first deployed the terms 'the Middle Ages' and 'the Reformation'. Gerard Brandt's 1676 *History of the Reformation* and Burnet's 1679 *History of the Reformation* were the first two works to designate themselves as histories of 'the Reformation' with a capital R and were simultaneously Protestant tolerationist arguments, while Christoph Keller's (Cellarius') 1696 *Modern History (Historia Nova)*, which brought the term 'Middle Ages' into currency, began its account of 'modern history' with 'the Reformation'.[2] In these years, the identification of the 'Middle Ages' as a period of 'barbarism' and 'ignorance' was simultaneously fostered by the publication of many Protestant histories of 'The Inquisition', most notably *The History of The Inquisition* by Locke's friend Philip van Limborch. And even when the Inquisition was not the central focus of works, it was nonetheless a major theme. Brandt's *History of the Reformation* thus included in book 3 'A Dreadful Picture of the Inquisition' and identified the rejection of 'the Inquisition' in the Netherlands as central to its political and religious liberty. These accounts of the Inquisition were works that were designed to reply to the historical case being presented in the Catholic defences of the Revocation of the Edict of

---

[1] On Enlightenment values, see, *inter alia*, P. Gay, *The Enlightenment, an Interpretation: Volume II. The Science of Freedom* (London 1970); Pocock, *Barbarism and Religion*; Jacob, *Living the Enlightenment*; Porter, *Untold Story*; N. Hampson, *The Enlightenment* (London 1968); Israel, *Radical*; J.-A.-N. de Caritat, Marquis de Condorcet, *Sketch for a Historical Picture of the Progress of the Human Mind* (London 1955).

[2] Burke, 'Politics of Reformation History', 73–85, at 73.

Nantes which identified contemporary Protestantism with Albigensian and Waldensian heresies, and which celebrated the Catholic Church's actions throughout time against 'heresies'. The authors of these Protestant histories of 'the Inquisition' not merely assaulted the medieval period as a period of 'barbarism' and 'ignorance', exemplified by the institution of 'the Inquisition', but also designated their own period as one of 'enlightenment' against such 'barbarism' and 'ignorance', whose first step had been taken at 'the Reformation', but which now needed a further step to be taken in order to establish religious toleration, since most Reformation thinkers had themselves been intolerant.[3]

These histories were thus constructed around a notion of 'progress' from barbarism to enlightenment and were decisively Protestant. In England, they were, moreover, often 'Whig'. Symbolically, Burnet's *History of the Reformation* was officially celebrated by the Exclusionist and Protestant tolerationist House of Commons in the period of the first emergence of the 'Whig party'; that 'Whig party' was based on the notion of either excluding or bridling a potential future Catholic ruler, and Burnet himself described his primary message as warning of the dangers of a future Catholic ruler plunging England back into the 'barbarism' of executions for religion. Burnet suggested that England had escaped from such 'barbarism' in 'the Reformation' but could easily return to it by adopting an absolutism identified as 'French', 'tyrannical', Catholic, and 'barbaric', and in all of these ways not appropriate to 'English liberties'. This historiographical case in works on 'the Reformation' and on 'the Inquisition' thus presented the argument that Europe was now locked in a combat between an institution, the Catholic Church, which it typed as maintaining medieval 'barbarism' and 'superstition', its many Protestant imitators who were wrongly maintaining the last vestiges of this barbaric 'Popery' in defending religious intolerance, and a tolerationist Protestantism, which was declared to be an 'enlightened' and 'reasonable' Christianity. These writings presented themselves as reviving true 'primitive Christianity' and the 'polished' and 'civil' times of Roman toleration, and thereby presented as a major part of argument for the 'early Enlightenment' an argument about the virtues and vices of previous ages, and of the relationships between 'barbarism and religion'.[4]

Burnet's prefatory discourse to his 1687 edition of Lactantius' *De Mortibus Persecutorum, A Relation of the Death of the Primitive Persecutors* thus declared that when the Roman Empire had fallen, 'and those polishings of

[3] See below; also Peters, *Inquisition*, 153–4 and ch. 6.

[4] Champion, *Pillars*, 27–32; M.A. Goldie, 'Priestcraft and the Birth of Whiggism' in N. Phillipson and Q. Skinner (eds.), *Political Discourse in Early Modern Britain* (Cambridge 1993); cf. also Pocock, *Barbarism and Religion*, I, *passim*.

learning and civility with it', this decline and fall had 'brought on a Night of Ignorance, that can scarce be apprehended, by those who have not read the Writings of the following ages'. For Burnet, 'superstition' had then grown on the 'ruins of learning, and eat up all' with the 'Northern people being mufled up in Ignorance, and wrought on by Superstition' leavened 'with Cruelty' until at last 'heresy' had come to be 'reckoned the greatest of all Crimes'. For Burnet, Catholicism had thus departed from 'meekness' and 'notwithstanding all the polishings of Learning and Civility that are in it, it is now the cruellest and most implacable society that has ever appeared in the world'. The 'present scene of affairs' in France and Piedmont in 1685–87 for Burnet led one's mind 'naturally' to think of 'modern persecutors' in terms of the characters of 'ancient persecutors' who had 'delivered themselves up to all the Brutalities of sensual Pleasure'. It was crucial to revive against such persecution not merely the 'politeness' of the Roman period but also that of the tolerationist 'primitive Christianity' of the 'first ages' which had stood 'against all cruelty', and thereby to reject the 'barbarism' that he alleged had followed the Christianisation of the Roman Empire. Burnet celebrated Lactantius as the 'politest writer of his time' and as amply testifying that even at the beginning of Constantine's reign persecution had not yet been supported by magistrates.[5]

Van Paets' *De nuperis Angliae*, translated as the *Lettre* by Bayle in 1686, contrasted 'ancient' Christians' reliance on reasons, arguments, and prayers which had made Christianity flourish with the false zeal for persecution which reigned among modern Christians as they supported a 'barbarous' opinion.[6] And the contrast of Catholic 'barbarity' with 'politeness' was a significant argument of Bayle's *Philosophical Commentary*. We noted earlier that few Huguenots were executed in the 1680s in France, and that Catholic polemicists had increasingly repudiated the violence of the late sixteenth century and stressed instead Augustinian arguments for 'moderate' penalties to aid conversion. In the wake of the Revocation, Catholics suggested that Protestant polemic against the Revocation was engaging in malicious aggravation of the violence used against Huguenots in focusing on the gibbet, taxes, and quartering. Bayle did recognise that some change had indeed occurred in the methods of the persecutors. But he declared that while he had not made the 'most odious' acts of Catholics his standard in representing their violence after the Revocation, Catholics were still separating families, thrusting individuals into dungeons, and depriving them of the means of subsistence. He stressed in opposition to such methods that Christ

---

[5] Burnet (ed.), *Death*, tr. and preface to Lactantius, *De Mortibus Persecutorum*, 4, 8–9, 20, 25–7, 33–4, 37, and *passim*. Cf Coffey, *Persecution*, 48–9, 63.

[6] Van Paets, *Lettre*, 8–9.

condemned 'the very Thought and Look of Inhumanity and Injustice'. And he replied by invoking his time as an era of 'politeness' and 'civility' that had been shattered by persecuting Catholics as they remained mired in medieval bigotry; their lesser punishments were still marks of 'barbarity'. In the preliminary discourse to the *Commentary*, Bayle declared that 'civility and politeness' had reigned 'in the manners of this age', that all that was 'rough and shocking in the Manners of our Ancestors is quite worn off; to that rustick and forbidding air of former times, there has succeeded an universal Gentleness and exceeding Civility, all Christendom over'. For Bayle, this laudable development had, however, just been interrupted by the Revocation because 'popery' had remained brutal and 'savage'. It was, Bayle declared, a false religion which did 'not mend its ways' through the passage of time but was instead 'still animated as much as ever with a spirit of cruelty and fraud'. For Bayle, 'Popery alone feels no change' from the change in manners and 'she alone still keeps up her ancient and habitual ferocity'.

This provided Bayle with the platform for his assault on the justification of contemporary intolerance as involving only 'moderate' punishments, writing in 1686 that 'This Fierceness of Popery' was not to be computed, 'as some undertook to do about a year ago, by a parallel between the Growth of the Politeness of this Age, and the Diminution of Punishments which it has of late made use of for converting'. For Bayle, 'We affirm, there's as much Barbarity in Dragooning, Dungeoning, Cloistering, etc People of a contrary Religion, in such a civiliz'd, knowing, genteel Age as ours; as there was in executing 'em by the hands of the common Hangman, in Ages of Ignorance and Brutality, before People had purg'd off the Manners of their Ancestors'. According to Bayle, it was worse for those who lived in a time which had become 'polish'd by an Improvement of the Sciences and nobler Arts', and where individual persecutors had themselves lived alongside those of another religion, to 'prosecute, disquiet, torment and vex' their neighbours, than it had been for those who had 'not purg'd off the Barbarousness of their Race' to execute strangers. That the contemporary 'barbarism' of Catholicism was at least the equal of its ancestors became even clearer, according to Bayle, when one took into account the edict of 1686, which provided death for Protestant worship and 'which is executed without delay upon all who have the Courage' to make the least defiance. The *Philosophical Commentary* assaulted the 'cruel extremities' being used in France in a 'civilized age and country which passes for very polite', and it indicted 'popery' as one of the false religions which were 'always excepted out of the number of those things whose Nature may be humaniz'd'.[7] For Bayle, in the first two parts of

[7] Bayle, *Philosophical Commentary* (1708), 7–9, 29, 186, 189 (*Philosophical Commentary*, ed. Tannenbaum, 11–12, 21, 108; *Commentaire philosophique*, 52–4, 71, 211).

the *Philosophical Commentary*, 'popery' thus stood in contrast to Protestantism, which, even if it did still persecute, generally now allowed people either to leave 'with their Effects' or allowed 'serving God privately in their own way'.[8]

In Bayle's depiction, by its revived persecutions Catholicism had identified itself with a medieval past of 'barbarism' and cruelty, and had become thereby a religion out of harmony with its time of increasing 'civility' and 'humanity'. As Peter Gay has stressed in examining eighteenth-century thought, the philosophers' later efforts at defending and disseminating 'humanity' as a value was a central project of the Enlightenment and applied against many forms of cruelty or 'barbarism'. The virtue of 'humanity' was especially invoked in the 'early Enlightenment' as a part of the tolerationist case that rejected medieval 'barbarism' as 'inhumane'. And Bayle repeatedly contrasted to this inhumane barbarism an age of 'civility' and 'politeness'. As J. G. A. Pocock, Anna Bryson, and Lawrence Klein, among others, have particularly stressed for England, and as Norbert Elias and Roger Chartier have emphasised for France, the values of 'politeness' and 'civility' were central to the Enlightenment; here we meet them as values central to the 'early Enlightenment' case for religious toleration which contributed significantly to their elevation in the Enlightenment.[9]

Bayle recognised that the Catholic Church had indeed supported explicitly only 'moderate' penalties in its justification of the Revocation of the Edict of Nantes rather than the executions it had formerly advocated, but argued that the moderate use of penalties had in its internal logic no limits. If a mild persecution added to the numbers of the church, then a fierce persecution would add more. Bayle scorned as merely the 'Prettiest conceit' the argument of the Catholic apologist Ferrand that those who execute heretics 'do well but not quite so well' as those who did not carry it so far. Catholic arguments were still 'justly chargeable with the wheel, gibbet, torture' and with 'the most inhuman' massacres since they called for them 'by a just and very natural consequence' when lesser means were insufficient. And Bayle noted that while Catholic clerics had initially justified 'moderate' penalties, penalties of death and slavery had been instituted in 1686 for maintaining Protestant worship when forbidden, or for helping others to escape from France. Not merely by their internal logic, but by the rapid escalation of

---

[8] Bayle, *Philosophical Commentary* (1708), 234–5 (*Philosophical Commentary*, ed. Tannenbaum, 130–1; *Commentaire philosophique*, 248–9).

[9] Gay, *The Enlightenment*, II, 398; N. Elias, *The Civilizing Process* (New York 1978); N. Philipson, *Hume* (London 1989); L. Klein, *Shaftesbury and the Culture of Politeness* (Cambridge 1994); Pocock, *Virtue, Commerce and History*; A. Bryson, *From Courtesy to Civility* (Oxford 1988); Chartier, *Cultural Origins*.

punishments in the wake of the Revocation, the Catholic Church was justly chargeable with supporting immoderate penalties.[10]

The pattern of indictment by Bayle of Catholic punishment as immoderate even when it was proclaimed to be 'moderate', and as logically necessitating fiercer punishment if milder punishment was justified, ran parallel to the indictment of Proast and Anglican punishment deployed by Locke in his defences of the *Letter Concerning Toleration* in 1690 and 1692. Proast defended only 'moderate' penalties as being used to 'persuade' people by counterbalancing the force of the 'passions' which were alleged to have hitherto prevented their perceiving the truth; he repudiated 'fire' and 'the sword'. Locke replied to Proast's argument that the logic of this argument necessarily made greater punishments justified. If one could legitimately apply a small quantity of coercion, then one could legitimately apply a greater force, and there was simply no stopping point. Locke traced the development of religious persecution through the century and a half after the Reformation until it reached its culmination in the Restoration, and his point here was not merely the historical point that there had in fact been a tendency to increase punishment as lesser punishments had not worked, but also that such a process of increased punishments was inherent in the logic of punishment itself. And Locke stressed that Proast's claim that Anglicans supported only 'moderate' penalties was open to the serious practical objection that the penalties that the Anglicans had called 'moderate penalties' had in fact involved not merely fines but the loss of estates, and liberty, and then incarcerations which had led to the deaths of many dissenters in 'noisome prisons' in the Restoration. These were in fact not 'moderate' punishments.[11]

For Bayle's friend and associate Henri Basnage de Beauval's 1684 *Toleration of Religions*, the period from the eleventh and twelfth centuries to the Reformation had been a time of great 'ignorance' and 'superstition', when there had been little care to instruct the people and vices had gone unpunished as the clergy were motivated by interest and ambition, when clerics had strengthened the yoke they imposed on consciences and usurped secular authority.[12] In Chapter 19 we noted the many arguments for toleration of Jews mounted in Henri's brother Jacques Basnage's 1706 *History of the Jews*. Here, it is important to stress that this *History* was a classic Protestant Enlightenment work which contributed to typing the 'Middle Ages' as a period of 'barbarity', 'ignorance' and 'superstition', and identified

[10] Bayle, *Philosophical Commentary* (1708), 190, 195–7, 200–4 (*Philosophical Commentary*, ed. Tannenbaum, 109, 111–15; *Commentaire philosophique*, 212, 216–18, 221–5).

[11] Bayle, *Philosophical Commentary*; Locke, *Second Letter*; idem, *Third Letter*; cf. Vernon, *Toleration*.

[12] Basnage de Beauval, *Tolérance des Religions*, 68–73.

the medieval period as the period during which persecution of the Jews had developed and the Protestant Reformation as the crucial beginning of 'toleration' and 'persuasion'. Chapter 11 of book 7 of *The History of the Jews*, on the medieval period, was named 'The Reasons of the Christians Making Severe and Ignominious Laws against the Jews', and gave an account of the ages in which 'the Jews were exposed to cruel Persecutions', either from

> the Fury of the People, who accus'd them of several crimes, that they might have a pretence to punish them; or from the Authority of Princes, who fancy'd they ought to destroy that Nation, whose ancestors had crucified the Messiah; and to Violence, added a multitude of Edicts and Declarations.[13]

As we saw in Chapter 19, Basnage depicted the Reformation as the time when

> people then began to sense the barbarism and the gross ignorance of the monks and ceased to accuse the Jews of the murder of children, a libel which had brought so many troubles down on them and had caused torrents of their blood to be shed. People no longer recounted wonders concerning the stolen host which miraculously gave forth blood, in whose name it was always possible to arouse the fury and the violence of the crowd.[14]

In his *Second Vindication of the Reasonableness of Christianity*, Locke similarly assaulted 'these thousand years and upwards' of 'schism, separations, contentions, animosities, quarrels, blood and butchery' that had 'harassed and defamed' Christianity. For Locke, including in the *Reasonableness* and its *Vindications*, there were 'dark' periods of history to be contrasted with those of 'light' – the former being both the period when the 'jews and pagans' were sunk in idolatry, polytheism, and 'priestcraft', and the millennium of persecutions until his day. They were contrasted to the period after the 'gospel' when Christ had brought the afterlife 'to light' and had reinforced natural law, stressing morality as the essential element of religion. Much of the rhetoric of 'light' against 'darkness' in the 'early Enlightenment' that was generated and utilised by Locke's closest friends was that of the revival of the light of the gospel, evoked from *within* and not *against* Christianity. In the 1690s, William Molyneux celebrated Locke for having abridged the priestly 'empire of darkness, wherein. . .the subjects wander deplorably yet the rulers have their profit and advantage'. Or, as Le Clerc put it in his *Parrhasiana* in 1700, the 'republic of letters' had become a republic of 'light' and 'reason' and not of traditional authority and 'implicit faith'. It was 'implicit faith', and not faith itself, which they saw as 'darkness', and a 'reasonable faith' which they saw as 'light'.[15]

---

[13] Basnage, *History*, 638.
[14] J. Basnage, *Histoire des juifs*, IV, 1,425 and V, 2,064, in M. Yardeni, 'Bayle', 245–58, at 248; Elukin,'Jacques Basnage', 608.
[15] Locke, *Letters, passim*; *Reasonableness, passim*; Marshall, *Locke*, 330, 351.

Much of the indictment of medieval religious intolerance was conducted by the creation of an image of the Inquisitor and the Inquisition as exemplary of medieval intolerance; such images very frequently deployed contrasts of darkness and light, and of barbarity and toleration. Bayle used his *Dictionary* at many points to assault the 'barbarity' of the 'Inquisitor'. As he put it in his entry on Vergerius, 'We can never too often represent the villainy and injustice annexed to the profession of Inquisitor'.[16] He dwelt in great detail in the *Dictionary* on the Inquisitors who 'entered houses to search for suspicious books', who excommunicated 'those who did not detect persons suspected' of heresy, even if this violated 'consanguinity' or 'gratitude', and who spread 'terror everywhere'. In the entry on Bartholomew Carranza, the sixteenth-century Dominican Archbishop of Toledo under Philip II who had become suspected of Lutheran sympathies and was therefore incarcerated on 'suspicion' of heresy, Bayle noted the indignation of the people against his 'oppressed innocence' but stressed that it should have instead been directed at 'That unjust Tribunal, which had been so long persecuting an innocent man; and, at least, they should have made it appear, that they wished his wicked Judges might be stigmatised with some Mark of Infamy'. It was the part of 'wise men', Bayle suggested in this note, to behold the 'Iniquity' of the Inquisition and to adore the divine providence 'which suffers the Tribunal of the Inquisition, a real Abomination introduced into the Holy Places, not only to reign and triumph thus long in so many Christian countries, but also to enlarge its phylacteries, and spread its roots everywhere'. Here, Bayle's argument may have been intended to suggest that not merely Catholicism but also Protestantism was overrun by inquisitorial practices as its 'roots spread everywhere'. In his correspondence in the early 1690s, Bayle depicted the Protestant persecution led by Jurieu as a Protestant Inquisition.

A similar indictment of 'inquisitors' was registered in Bayle's entry in the *Dictionary* on Cornelius Agrippa of Nettesheim, a 'very learned man of the sixteenth century' who had been persecuted by monks who 'suspected, whatever they did not understand, of Errour or Heresy' and was forced to leave a city 'which the seditious Inquisitors had made an Enemy to Learning, and true Merit'. Bayle stressed in the text that this was 'the fate of all countries, where such Persons grow powerful, of whatsoever religion they are'. And he made clear that Agrippa had been troubled, and that his friend James Faber Stapulensis had been 'pulled to pieces' for the serious intellectual crime of refuting the 'common opinion' of 'three husbands' of St Anne and for considering her 'monogamy'. In the notes, Bayle indicated that Agrippa had intended to compose a work against the Dominicans as 'chief

---

[16] Bayle, *Dictionary*, Vergerius C; Peters, *Inquisition*, ch. 6, esp. 173.

Directors of the Inquisition' who were 'indulgent to the Errours of their brethren' and yet 'severe against the equivocal protestations of other Persons'. Underlining still more clearly the failure of 'equity' involved in such behaviour, Bayle stressed that the people foolishly celebrated the 'zeal of an Inquisitor, who discovers Heresy wherever he thinks fit' but would not allow recrimination against their own 'pernicious Doctrines'. The note ended by accusing Dominican Inquisitors of the vices of 'treason' and 'heresy' and of 'enormous crimes'.[17]

'The Inquisition' thus symbolised religious intolerance and hypocrisy for Bayle in the *Dictionary*, and the Inquisitors were themselves guilty of precisely the crimes alleged by them against others. Many tolerationist works were published by other Protestant authors in the late 1680s and early 1690s on the history of 'the Inquisition' which made the same arguments, and which replied also to Catholic arguments that the current punishment of Huguenots and Waldensians was justified as the medieval punishment of Waldensians and Albigensians had been justified. Pierre Allix, Huguenot tolerationist associate and correspondent of Limborch, Le Clerc, Burnet, and Locke wrote in England two histories of the use of force against the Waldensians and Albigensians intended as contemporary tolerationist arguments, as refutations of Catholic justifications of force against Huguenots and Waldensians, and as assaults on the use of force as a relic of medieval 'barbarism'. Allix's 1690 *Some Remarks on Ancient Churches of Piedmont* gave 'a compendious view of the horridness of the Inquisitor's Proceedings'. It declared that the Inquisitors had 'not omitted any cruelty' and had put 'vast numbers' of men and women 'to tortures', had used the 'fury of soldiers and cruelty of executioners to root them out', and had used cruelties on those even wars spare: old men, women and 'suckling children'. Allix's accounts of the violence used against the Waldensians travelled from medieval persecution to contemporary persecution, and ended with 'The Business of 1686'. For Allix, the Inquisition was the epitome not merely of violence but also of injustice. The Inquisitors had used a 'devilish cheat' to make it appear that their victims had proclaimed themselves as guilty 'by their own confession', had employed its punishments against any who spoke up for them, and had obliged princes to break treaties that they had made for their defence. The selection of actions used first against medieval Waldensians and recently against contemporary Huguenot and Waldensians is obvious. Noting that the violence against the Waldensians had been justified in part because they were called 'unclean and filthy people', Allix argued that in fact this was true not of the Waldensians but was true of their 'great accusers' who had 'made use of the Inquisition to

---

[17] Bayle, *Dictionary*, Carranza, esp. note D; Agrippa, esp. note S; Peters, *Inquisition*, 173.

ravish their Wives and daughters'.[18] Making use of a distinction that Bossuet had himself drawn between Waldensians as 'schismatics' and Albigensians as Manichean heretics, Allix argued that the accusation of 'heresy' against the Waldensians had been employed inappropriately in order to justify the persecution of 'those who set themselves against the Errors and Superstitions' of the Church of Rome, though indeed they had nothing in common with the Manichees'. The Waldensians were in fact 'the nursery of Protestantism' and the defenders of 'apostolical purity' against Roman 'corruptions in matters of faith, her idolatry, her false and superstitious worship, and her horrid Tyranny'. 'Never' for Allix, 'did the Church of Rome give in a more incontestable evidence of hir own Antichristianism, than by her insatiable Thirst after the Blood of those Christians'.[19]

Allix's *Some Remarks* was one of the two most influential Protestant works on the history of the Inquisition in these years. By far the more influential was Philipp van Limborch's *History of the Inquisition*, a work which one of the leading contemporary historians of 'the Inquisition', Edward Peters, declares that of 'the first great historian of the inquisitions'. Limborch utilised primarily Catholic sources and a very few Protestant sources in order to evidence the development of 'the Inquisition', and proclaimed that he did so with the desire to portray the institution accurately. He thereby, however, presented an account of the emergence of what he termed one institution, with the reductiveness involved in the capitalisation 'the Inquisition'. Where modern historians have shown that the inquisition was a highly variable set of institutions that were diverse in their prosecution of 'heresy', and that many of these institutions were lenient in such prosecution while others were fierce, the influence of Limborch's *History* exerted a considerable force in identification of 'the Inquisition' as the barbaric and intolerant monolith later execrated by 'High Enlightenment' writers. Limborch's work was the single most important history of the Inquisition, republished and translated frequently in the eighteenth century, and the source for many later accounts.[20]

It is worth pausing before analysing some of Limborch's arguments to stress that Limborch's *History* needs to be understood as not just the product of his own thought but also as one of the most important products of the network of advocates of religious toleration. The *History* was composed at Locke's instigation, in that Locke provided Limborch with the manuscript of the inquisition at Toulouse against Albigensians and Waldensians, which prompted its composition and which was published with Limborch's *History*. Locke moreover encouraged its composition in letters over many

---

[18] Allix, *Some Remarks*, 266–7. [19] *Ibid.*, 129–39, 167, 183ff., 195, 238ff., 291–5ff.
[20] Peters, *Inquisition*, ch. 6 and *passim*, quotation at 166.

years and obtained permission for its published dedication to his own tolerationist friend (and Limborch's correspondent), Archbishop Tillotson. As
Locke once noted, the manuscript of the inquisition at Toulouse had been
sent to Limborch 'on my suggestion and incitement'.[21] Locke's own identification of those who preserved the 'truth' in medieval times as the
Waldensians is suggested by his comment in the 1692 *Third Letter for
Toleration*, issued in the same year as the *History*: 'if truth must have either
the law of the country, or actual miracles to support it, what became of
it after the reign of Constantine the Great, under all those emperors that
were erroneous or heretical? It supported itself in Piedmont, and France, and
Turkey, many ages without force or miracles'.[22] The *History* was composed
with the support also of Furly, in whose hands the manuscript of
the Inquisition initially resided in the later 1680s, and who in the 1690s
purchased the manuscript for his personal library from its then owner, Sir
William Waller. Again tying the 'Whig' and Protestant causes together in
the 'early Enlightenment', Waller was a fiercely anti-Catholic Whig Justice of
the Peace who had been Locke's and Shaftesbury's associate during the
'Exclusion' campaign; Locke and Shaftesbury were leading Whigs, Furly
was a leading supporter of Whigs in 1688–9, and Tillotson was a known
Whig in 1681–3 and the leading Whig Archbishop of Canterbury from 1689.
The *History* was composed with the extensive encouragement of Le Clerc,
Limborch's fellow professor at Amsterdam and, like Locke, a member of
Furly's 'Lantern' discussion group. Le Clerc was also to identify his political
attitudes strongly with Whig thought in the 1690s and 1700s. Locke, Le
Clerc, and Furly discussed with each other their encouraging of Limborch's
publication as well as encouraging it directly in letters to and in conversations with the author. Limborch's work was also composed in the midst of
correspondence and exchange of manuscripts with Allix, Burnet's protégé as
chaplain at Salisbury and leading Whig defender of 1688–9. And it was
composed in the midst of discussions with Burnet, who celebrated its publication in 1692, and who led Whig defences of 1688–9. When it was

---

[21] Locke, *Correspondence*, 1023, 1068, 1134, 1147, 1215, 1242, 1262, 1509, 1516, 1518,
1523, 1527, 1553, 1562, 1567, 1572, 1826, 1852, 1878; A. Nickson, 'Locke and the
Inquisition of Toulouse', *British Museum Quarterly* 26 (1971–2), 83–92. I first presented
papers on Limborch's *History* to the Cambridge University Seminar in British history and the
Institute of Historical Research Seminar in British history in 1998–9 and am grateful to those
and other audiences for their comments. Luisa Simonutti has also examined Limborch's
History in two very important articles: 'Limborch's *Historia Inquisitionis* and the Pursuit
of Toleration' in A. Coudert, S. Hutton, R. Popkin, and G. Wiener (eds.), *Judeo-Christian
Intellectual Culture in the Seventeenth Century* (Dordrecht 1999), 237–55, and 'Between
History and Politics: Philip van Limborch's *History of the Inquisition* in J. Laursen (ed.),
Histories of Heresy in Early Modern Europe (New York 2002), 101–18.

[22] Locke, *Third Letter for Toleration* in *Works*, VI, 444.

published, Locke sent copies of the *History* on Limborch's behalf to Burnet, Tillotson, and to the Earl of Pembroke, a leading Whig politician.[23]

The intellectual engagement of Locke and Furly with the manuscript of the inquisition at Toulouse was considerable in the later 1680s, as they discussed issues of baptism and heresy, *inter alia*. Locke wrote at one point to Furly when Locke was away from Rotterdam and thus could not study the manuscripts with Furly that 'I long to know what this new gang is that you have found, which we took for Waldenses, and for that as well as some other lanterne reasons, I wish the printers could dismisse me'. There is perhaps a hint here that 'the Lantern' itself was discussing the manuscript; at another point, Locke wrote to Furly in what may be another such hint that he enviously pictured Furly with the manuscript on one side and 'the Lantern' on the other. There is more than a hint that Locke and Furly were puzzling over the intricacies of medieval belief described in the inquisitorial records and trying to classify the individuals accused of 'heresy' and to distinguish the Waldensians from other groups. Locke admonished Furly not to part with the manuscript until he returned, since he had to have his 'time with it', and worried about Waller taking the manuscript back. Locke seems to have himself visited publishers in the Netherlands in the late 1680s, in attempts to obtain a publisher for the manuscript, as did Furly and Le Clerc, suggesting that Locke was attempting to gain a publisher in the Netherlands for the records of the inquisition against the medieval Waldensians during the period when Waldensian refugees were arriving in the Netherlands, when Catholic apologists were asserting the continuity of actions of their church against medieval Waldensians and against contemporary Huguenots and Waldensians, and when James II was providing as a Catholic ruler a toleration in England and Ireland that was suspect as a revocable edict in part because of actions against the Waldensians.[24]

It is important to stress how central was Locke's focus on the institution of 'the Inquisition' as the image of intolerance writ large. He read Gabriel Dellon's account of the Inquisition in November 1687 and referred in correspondence sarcastically to the desirability of fully exposing 'that Evangelical method'. Dellon's work was among those on the Inquisition reviewed in the journals of the republic, including the *Ouvrages des Savans*.[25] In 1687, when Locke was separated from Furly and from the Lantern discussion group which was held at Furly's house, Locke

---

[23] Remonstrants MS III D 4–7, 9, 17, 19–20, 114–20, 122; Locke, *Correspondence* 1539, 1562, 1572.

[24] Locke, *Correspondence*, 991, 993, 995, 1004, 1008, 1009, 1010, 1033, 1034; cf. MS Locke ch. 27, fo. 48 dated [16] '77'.

[25] Locke, *Correspondence*, 979; *Histoire* (oct 87), 258–67; *Bibliothèque universelle*, VII, 290.

recommended that Furly should lend an ear to 'that instructive discours and leave for a while your processes, condemnations, prisons and executions to take a little fresh air in those unconfined spaces where separate souls wander at liberty'. Here was Locke, like Bayle in 1685, imaging the conversational practices and intellectual freedom of their circles in the Netherlands as the antithesis of the Inquisition.[26] Most importantly, according to Locke's celebratory epistles to Limborch which greeted its publication, Limborch's *Historia* was a work which had 'dragged forth that mystery of iniquity from darkness into light and exposed it openly to the world.'[27] He declared that

the Christian world will owe a great deal to your scholarship and to your lucubrations on this theme; by them with fidelity and industry you have dragged forth from the darkness and made known to the world these secret mysteries alike of iniquity and cruelty that have been so sedulously concealed.[28]

It was a book which Locke saw as necessary 'at this time, for the Christian world, for there we have the fountain-head of all persecution carried on under the cloak of religion; there is the foundation of that ecclesiastical tyranny which lesser sects preach and strive after, inspired by that example'. It was a 'mirror' in which to see the image of all such tendencies.[29] Most strikingly, when he read it, Locke declared that

You have dragged that work of darkness and the hidden practices of execrable cruelty out of their dens into so clear a light that, should any vestiges of humanity remain among those henchmen of the church, or rather of Antichrist, they would at least feel shame for so unrighteous and so fearful a tribunal, where all law, human and divine, and justice, are set at nought.

It was a work which should give courage against 'such inhuman tyranny, under whatever semblance of religion or concord it again seeks to creep in'. Indeed, for Locke,

if any unlearned commoner should read through your account he would feel at once that religion, charity and justice were wanting there where every rule of equity and every way of pronouncing judgment throughout the world are violated, and deeds so inhuman, so cruel, and so very far from the spirit of the Gospel are perpetrated. I therefore consider the work worthy of translation into the vernacular of every people.

It was a work which Locke thought would be good for 'teaching the vulgar, instructing the learned, and making everyone steadfast'.[30]

Locke, Limborch, Burnet, and Popple pointed in their mutual correspondence to the contemporary persecutions of Huguenots by their fellow Huguenots in the 1690s as evidence that many Protestants were guided by the same principles of intolerance as many Catholics. Limborch also

[26] Locke, *Correspondence*, 991.   [27] *Ibid.*, 1601.   [28] *Ibid.*, 1375.   [29] *Ibid.*, 1398.
[30] *Ibid.*, 1804.

identified the arguments of his *History* as designed against much Dutch Contra-Remonstrant behaviour, writing to Locke in 1693 that 'Many of the counterremonstrants are buying and reading it' and that so far he had not heard complaints from them, for

> they are glad the romanists' sores are uncovered. Meanwhile let them believe that what is said to others is said to themselves also. I detest persecution, not because it is Popish, but because it is contrary to the spirit of the Christian religion; so, whether Rome or Geneva sets it up, for me it is alike condemned.[31]

In 1690, Limborch indicted the intolerance of Jurieu as similar to that of the 'Holy Office' as he would describe it in the *History of the Inquisition*, and asserted that 'If kings are prepared to lower their sceptres and fasces to these people we shall soon have a new Holy Office, yielding nothing to the old in cunning or cruelty'.[32] And he wrote to Locke in 1692 that

> The remarks I shall make on religious persecution in this treatise, which is apparently directed solely against Romanists, will now perhaps be received with calmer spirits; though if I were to intermingle with them even the scantiest allusions to the Reformed they would be rejected at first sight by the zealots. People are usually less offended by seeing their own faults censured in others; and perhaps some of them will be taught better things.[33]

Locke replied that he agreed with Limborch that 'Theological zeal, as I see it, is always and everywhere the same and proceeds in the same way'. He complimented Limborch's indirect attack on all persecution in the guise of an attack only on Roman Catholic persecution:

> You do rightly in condemning persecution on account of religion in Romanists only. If you should pick out and stigmatise for its cruelty any particular sect among Christians you will be commended by the rest of them, though persecution is the same everywhere and plainly popish; for any church whatsoever lays claim in words to orthodoxy and in practice to infallibility.[34]

The same aim of Limborch's *History* of indirectly condemning all persecution and the fault of Protestants for inconsistently proclaiming fallibility in principle and infallibility in practice was clear also to Burnet, whose copy of the *History* was forwarded to him by Locke on Limborch's behalf. Burnet greeted the appearance of the work in 1693 in a letter to Limborch by noting that

> It is a scandal that so many among the Reformed, who are always, and justly, taxing the Church of Rome with cruelty, should act in the very same spirit whenever they have the power. They do not see, or they will not acknowledge, that the Papists, who claim Infallibility, are less guilty and more consistent in their fury than those who, if you take them at their word, admit themselves liable to error. Judged by their deeds, however, they claim the power of deciding and pronouncing what must be believed.

[31] *Ibid.*, 1581, 1640, 1708. [32] *Ibid.*, 1317. [33] *Ibid.*, 1447. [34] *Ibid.*, 1473.

Burnet declared that

While we yet discussed the subject you were designing a short treatise, or a long introduction, animadverting on the zealous spirit which breathes fire and slaughter and tracing its progress. But as in all things you far transcend the hopes even of your friends, you have now favoured us with an entire volume, which leaves nothing unsaid...God grant your success may be proportionate.[35]

Limborch's *History of the Inquisition* thus needs to be understood as a work which operated on several tolerationist levels simultaneously. It defended the Waldensians against accusations of 'heresy' and claimed them both as the forefathers of Protestantism and as having been tolerable in their beliefs, thus undermining Catholic arguments for the punishing of Huguenots on the same grounds as the punishing of Waldensians. The Catholic case had represented the Waldensians as not merely 'heretics' but also as 'libertines' and 'sodomites'; Bayle had thought that attack worthy of note in his correspondence. Limborch's *History* assaulted Catholic clerics as perpetuating the commitments and behaviour of their medieval forefathers, whom it attacked as themselves having been the very 'sodomites' and 'libertines' that they had instead accused the alleged heretics of being. It identified arguments for the punishment of 'heresy' with the Inquisition, drawing on the 'Black Legend' against the Spanish Inquisition. Simultaneously, Limborch indirectly accused Protestant defences of the use of force against 'heresy' of being also the relics of an age and of an institution which it described as 'barbaric'. It was thereby intended to have considerable contemporary purchase as an argument against contemporary intolerance in all of its forms, as Locke, Limborch and Popple corresponded throughout its composition about current situations of Protestant persecution as the Huguenots erected what Popple called a 'court of Inquisition' against unorthodox – allegedly Socinian – Huguenots or their tolerationist supporters in the 1690s.[36]

In his *History of the Inquisition*, Limborch identified the medieval period as one when the 'most absurd opinions came to be established by the Violence of the Popes'. In this period of medieval Christianity, so 'deep was the ignorance that had spread it self over the world, that men, without the least regard to knowledge and learning' had received with 'blind obedience' everything taught by ecclesiastics. Ignorance was widespread, and the severity of the laws such that people 'durst not even so much as whisper against the received Opinions of the Church'. It 'was the entire study and endeavour of the Popes, to crush in its Infancy, every doctrine that any way

---

[35] Foxcroft, *Life of Burnet*, 314–15.
[36] Locke, *Correspondence*, 1317, 1368, 1567; my 'Huguenot Thought'; Chapter 4, above.

opposed their exorbitant power'. Limborch identified the Inquisition as started by Dominic in 1208, 1212 or 1215, and he identified Dominic as a 'bloody and cruel man'.[37] To this image of 'superstition' and 'ignorance', Limborch added extensively the image of bloody cruelty in extended accounts of the development of the punishments of 'the Inquisition', which began early in the text in Limborch's account, and were then repeated at many later points as he travelled around Europe with each successive stage of extension of 'the Inquisition'. Limborch thus recounted extensively the 'burning and slaughter and imprisonment' of heretics, noting – to give one random instance – the imprisonment of Raymond de Termis, who had died in prison but not before they had 'burnt in one large fire his Wife, Sister, and Virgin Daughter, with some other noble Ladies'. The setting up of the office of the Inquisition was described as 'a tyranny' involving the exposing of 'fortunes and lives'. The Inquisition was declared a 'hateful tribunal' because of its 'excessive cruelty'.[38]

For Limborch, as for Bayle in the *Dictionary* and for Allix in *Some Remarks*, 'the Inquisition' was the epitome not merely of cruelty but also of injustice. Limborch indicted it for 'many notorious and manifest acts of injustice'. Several chapters discussed the manner of proceeding on accusations and on witnesses in order to show this 'injustice'. And Limborch dwelled on descriptions of torture which he identified as used precisely when one could not be convicted otherwise because of want of proof. Limborch emphasised not merely the actual processes of torture but also the threat of torture. And he described in grim detail how individuals were carried to a place, stripped, and 'hoisted' on the rack; or how individuals being questioned had had their hands tied behind their backs, and weights tied to their feet, and were then hoisted and kept there as their limbs were stretched or let down with a jerk so that they became disjointed.[39] Limborch gave an excruciatingly detailed account of the inquisitorial procedures used against the former Marrano, with whom he had debated in the 1680s, Isaac Orobio de Castro, when he had not yet escaped from Portugal and had been suspected of 'Judaising'. Orobio had been imprisoned for three years. In questioning him, he was tied up in his clothes till he nearly expired, his thumbs were tied with small cords causing extreme swelling and his blood to burst out; then he was tied to the wall by his fingers and toes, hanging by cords, until he felt like 'dissolving in flames'. Pain was added to his shins by a 'sharp ladder'; ropes were tied around his wrists and a weight was placed on them. The clear implications of the account were that such force was 'barbarous', that the threat of force had created only hypocritical dissimulation

[37] Limborch, *History*, I, 41, 58, 60. [38] *Ibid.*, 58, 66, 71, 82. [39] *Ibid.*, II, 212–22.

in public and the practice of Judaism in private in Iberia as elsewhere, and that such force was both useless to convert someone and counterproductive, as it had increased Orobio's hatred towards Christians and Christianity itself.

Bringing his *History* to a resounding conclusion, the final chapter of Limborch's introduction was entitled 'An Enumeration of the Several Instances of Injustice and Cruelty Practised in the Tribunal of the Inquisition'. According to Limborch, the 'principal iniquities and injustices of this tribunal' included: that they attempted to oblige all to inform against others, including wife against husband and son against father; that any witness but an avowed 'mortal enemy' was admitted to testify; that torture was often ordered with only one witness and when one was merely suspected; that no defence was allowed against unknown witnesses; that one became one's own accuser, and that judges were deceitful. For Limborch, concluding this account,

as no one ought to assume to himself the Power of Judging concerning it, but God the searcher of hearts, to him only let us leave it to pass the true Judgment concerning every man's belief. Let us in the mean while detest the Tyranny of the papists, and strive to reduce those who, in our Judgment, hold Errours, into the way of truth, by the good Offices of Charity and Benevolence, without arrogating to our selves a Judgment over the Consciences of others.

While Limborch recognised that it was indeed true, as Catholic authors repeatedly claimed, that for most of the history of 'the Inquisition' only secular magistrates could punish, according to Limborch this had simply involved them enacting the orders of the Inquisition and was thus a power 'only to put to death those who were condemned for heretics by the ecclesiastics'. The church could not escape its responsibility for punishment, nor occlude its usurpation of civil authority. With the sole exception of Venice, where, following Paolo Sarpi, Limborch held that secular control over the Inquisition was maintained, he held that the magistrate in the period of 'the Inquisition' 'became a mere slave to the Inquisitors' and their 'slave and tool'.[40] Like very many tolerationist accounts of these years which epitomised persecution by 'the Inquisition', Limborch saw the culmination of 'the Inquisition' as occurring in Spain. He declared it unclear, in a countenancing of different possibilities which registered only stressed zeal or secular motivations, if the Inquisition was established there because of the 'blind zeal' of Ferdinand and Isabel, for greater peace and security, or for effecting the Spanish design of acquiring the 'universal monarchy' of Europe by endeavouring to secure the goodwill of the Pope. But he was clear that whichever of these

---

[40] *Ibid.*, 81, 88, 97. On Sarpi, cf. D. Wootton, *Paolo Sarpi* (Cambridge 1983).

had motivated the bringing of the Inquisition to Spain, the 'pretence' they had employed was first the 'licentiousness' of the times, and second that 'commerce' with 'moors' and 'jews' had led to the 'infection' of some Christians.[41] He here designated as merely 'pretences' two of the major themes of anti-tolerationist literature which were countered repeatedly in tolerationist literature in these years: notions of 'licentiousness' and pretences of 'infection'.

Limborch extensively traced not merely the process of punishments for religious beliefs and worships, making the Inquisition the archetype of religious intolerance, but relatedly traced the process of prohibition of books by the Catholic Church, making the Inquisition the archetype of intellectual intolerance. Here, Limborch looked back far beyond the establishment of 'the Inquisition' for the origins of the prohibition of books. According to Limborch, the first to 'prohibit books of religion' had been Antiochus Epiphanes; this had then been followed by Diocletian, the most 'cruel persecutor of the christian faith' as he had condemned 'the sacred books' to the fire. Thus identifying the prohibition of books as a 'Heathen' practice hostile to Christianity, Limborch was clear that it had entered Christian practice at the moment so many tolerationists identified negatively, the moment when the empire became Christian and forcefully Trinitarian, when Constantine had commanded the books of Arius to be burned under penalty of death. And he noted that Theodosius had then done the same to the books of Nestorius, another crucial critic of orthodox Trinitarianism (and the subject as such of analyses by Bayle and Hobbes).

It is worth noting that Limborch's lineage for proscription of books was thus 'pagan', 'antichristian', and then Trinitarian. For Limborch, the papacy had then usurped the minds of Christians as well as pagans and Trinitarians, as after 800 the Pope had for Limborch 'usurped. . .many branches of the civil government', prominent among which was that the Pope took control of 'forbidding the reading of books'. As the Spanish Inquisition served as the culmination of Inquisitorial force, so the creation of 'the Index' in the 1550s served Limborch as the culminating image of the proscription of books. Limborch particularly stressed that the books it had prohibited had included even those of Catholic doctors, and he specified that it had proscribed many books defending 'the authority of princes' against the 'unlawful usurpations' of ecclesiastics. It is unsurprising that Limborch's *History of the Inquisition* was placed on the Index immediately after the first copies had reached Rome, and that Limborch described this in letters to Locke as a topic not for commiseration but for celebration. Limborch suggested that he could not expect a 'more lenient sentence' for an account

---

[41] Limborch, *History*, I, 119; II, 221–2, ch. 42.

which tears from darkness, and exposes publicly to the eyes of the whole world, its arts and cruelties, which it wishes to be hidden, and unknown to all men; and shows this tribunal as not to be venerated for its holiness but execrated for its unrighteousness, cruelty, frauds, and impostures.[42]

For Limborch, the 'whole office' of the Inquisition was the 'extirpation of heretical pravity'. It was to Limborch therefore desirable to define such 'heretical pravity'. Properly to be a 'heretic' in the terms of the Inquisition, it was for Limborch necessary firstly to have professed the Catholic faith – that is, to have been baptised. It was necessary secondly to have erred in understanding matters of faith, which to Catholics meant in points determined by general councils or the Pope as necessary to be held or as injoined by 'apostolic tradition'. And it was necessary thirdly to have displayed 'obstinacy' of will. For Limborch, the use of force against such alleged heretics was ridiculous. He noted the reluctance to debate with heretics by Scripture that was underwritten by Tertullian's recommendation that no victory was possible through that route, mocking its later renditions in recording that

Simancas gives a merry reason why they punish hereticks so severely, instead of convincing them by Scripture of their Error and false Doctrine. We must not contend with Hereticks by Scripture, because by that our victory will be uncertain and doubtful. 'tis no wonder they defend doctrines which have no foundation in Scripture by force.[43]

And Limborch applied the classic arguments of the tolerationists in holding that 'greater gentleness' is used towards

thieves, traytors and rebels, those enemies of mankind, than toward miserable hereticks; who, endeavouring to worship God with a pure conscience, and regulate their lives by the gospel rule, yet oppose some doctrines of the church of Rome.

It was worse 'in that church', he complained, 'to oppose certain opinions by the clear light of the word of God' than to live an impious and profane life. Limborch noted, in a passage that may well be reflective of his experience of Calvinist opposition to the Arminians' toleration of Socinianism, that it was among the most unjust provisions of the Inquisition that 'all persons' were obliged to 'discover heretics' and if they did not, they were declared 'favourers of heretics'.

In order to make the most powerful case that Waldensians had indeed been a kind of proto-Protestants, but that they had neither been 'heretics' nor justly punishable when the Catholic Church had used force against them in the thirteenth century, Limborch needed to distinguish Albigensians as

---

[42] Limborch, *History*, 223–31; Locke, *Correspondence*, 1823.   [43] Limborch, *History*, II, 2–3.

'Cathar heretics' from the Waldensians. He thus committed himself to the notion that while the 'Albigenses and Waldensians' had been united in their opposition to papal power, in their belief that every oath was unlawful and sinful, in their conviction that power to hear confession had not been given either to the Church of Rome or to the Pope, and in their opposition to indulgences and purgatory – the proto-Protestant similarities are evident throughout this list – the sentences of the inquisition of Toulouse nonetheless gave 'evident proofs of differences in opinions' between them. For instance, some had believed that God only could absolve sins; but others believed that 'laicks' could absolve. Only the Albigenses, committed to the view that the 'church of Rome' was 'a mother of fornications', 'the Temple of the Devil and the Synagogue of Satan', were said to believe in 'two gods and lords', one of whom was evil and one good, and of the creation of worldly things by the 'evil' one. Here, then, for Limborch as for Allix, was the clear ground to declare that the Waldensians had not been 'heretics', that the use of the Inquisition against them had been unjust even in its own terms, and that the imitation of its use in the present day against Huguenots who were also not 'heretics' was similarly unjust.

More remarkable still was Limborch's willingness to find some grounds for defence even of the Albigensians who were Manichean. Allix's *Some Remarks* had expressed the conventional view among Protestants and Catholics of the day that Manicheans were 'the most wild heresie the devil could ever suggest' and that they had found many followers in the region among the Albigensians. He had suggested that the Waldensians had been unjustly persecuted, but had made only a very tentative gesture in that direction for some of the Albigensians less 'tainted' with heresy.[44] For Limborch, while there were indeed among Albigensian beliefs some 'Manichean mistakes' which should be owned, it was more 'to be wondered at' that they 'throw off so many errors, than that they should retain some'. The move to call these 'mistakes' and 'errors' here was immediately to take the Albigensians out of the realm of the justly punishable 'heretic' even as they were 'Manichean', and thus a far cry from Allix's description of Manicheanism as the 'worst heresy' of the Devil. For Limborch, by contemporary standards the Albigensians were anti-Trinitarian heretics: 'As to the incarnation of Christ', they had held 'That the Lord did not take a real humane Body, nor real humane Flesh of our Nature; and that he did not really arise with it, nor do other things relating to our salvation; nor sit down at the Right hand of the Father with it, but only with the likeness of it'. They had held that God had never entered into the womb of Virgin Mary, and that

---

[44] Allix, *Some Remarks*, 129, ch. xv.

it was 'impossible for God to be incarnate'; God had never humbled himself so much as to take on a body.

According to Limborch, the Albigensians had moreover denied the resurrection of bodies, and held that souls shall come to judgment but not in bodies, imagining 'a sort of spiritual bodies' and that souls were 'spirits banished from heaven because of their sins'. In Limborch's account, the Waldensians in contrast did not subscribe to any of these positions. The 'Waldenses' were 'plain men of mean capacities' and they were closest among contemporary denominations to 'Mennonites'; most Mennonites, as we saw in Chapter 11, were Trinitarian Anabaptists.[45] But here again Limborch sought to make not merely the Waldensians but also the Albigensians undeserving of the use of inquisitorial force, and his argument served to make a simultaneous present-day case for toleration not merely of Mennonites, who were like Waldensians, but also for Socinians, who were somewhat like Albigensians. For Limborch, very often enemies gave 'very vile and odious Accounts of the Doctrines they held; as will appear by comparing the several Places in which they describe them. For the same opinion, which in one place appears extremely erroneous; in another, when tis more fully explained, and without Spite, is harmless enough; of which the single instance of the Resurrection of the Dead is full Proof. For sometimes the Albigenses are accused, that they deny the Resurrection of the Dead; which yet in another Place is more distinctly explained thus, that the Dead shall arise with spiritual Bodies'. In Limborch's day, Socinians denied the resurrection of the body but not the resurrection of the dead; the failure to recognise the distinction was among the reasons for their association with 'atheists'. Limborch has by clear implication made Socinians tolerable, and has simultaneously criticised those who attacked them as denying any resurrection because of their denial of the resurrection of the self-same body. By the end of his life, Locke seems to have held such a notion that the person was resurrected but not the body; he was attacked as a Socinian and an 'atheist' by his opponents.[46]

In discussing the Albigensians, Limborch faced the same series of associations which we have traced repeatedly in this book against those who denied the orthodox accounts of the Trinity or the resurrection: that they were not merely 'heretics' but also 'libertines' and 'sodomites', as they not merely denied 'the resurrection', but justified 'men and women to lie promiscuously with one another'. For Limborch, these 'untrue' accusations had been made against them because it was the 'way' of papists to attack all of 'impurity and lust' who left their church. But Limborch did not assert this in order to remove

[45] Limborch, *History*, 43–58, 114ff.   [46] *Ibid.*, 50–1.

the accusation of libertinism and sodomy from religious dispute, but rather to redirect it. Like Allix, he asserted its untruth as an allegation against Waldensians and Albigensians in order to repay it with interest against Catholics, helping thereby to hand on from the 'early Enlightenment' to 'the Enlightenment' the considerable Protestant Reformation hostility to monks and priests as sexually licentious and sodomites:

nothing is more notorious, than that their Monks and Priests, who are forbid the Remedy of a Chaste and honourable matrimony, abandon themselves without shame to the most impure embraces, and infamously wallow in carnal pleasures.

Limborch raided the corpus of the Catholic reformer Erasmus' writings in order to describe in detail that '11,000 priests' had openly kept 'whores' and to allege that many monasteries were 'private stews'. He even added for good measure that some monasteries had buried the girls they had abused. According to Limborch, one confessor of nuns had 'laid with 200 of them'. For Limborch that 'the Inquisition' itself provided punishment for priests who 'solicit women', and 'what is much worse' boys in the 'sacrament of confession' gave proof not that Catholics disapproved of these practices, but rather that these 'crimes' were 'frequent'. The understanding of the opposing religion as one of 'libertines' and 'sodomites' and reversing the appropriate use of the sacraments as reversing 'normal' sexuality is here as strong in Limborch's response as it had ever been in Catholic attacks on 'heresy'.[47]

And still Limborch was not finished. Limborch argued that when a papal bull had been brought into Spain that 'confessors provoking women to lewd actions' were to be punished, the consequence was that 'so large a number of women went to the Palace of the Inquisitors in the City of Seville only, to make their Discoveries of these most wicked confessors, that twenty secretaries, with as many Inquisitors, were not sufficient to take the Depositions of the Witnesses'. They therefore had had to assign a second thirty days for reports, then a third, and then a fourth. And Limborch stressed that in its punishments 'sodomy' was 'esteemed a much smaller crime than that of heresy'. This for Limborch held the message that the

truly pious man, who fears god, and is most careful of his eternal salvation, may be accounted an heretick by the portuguese inquisitors whereas a sodomite cannot but be the vilest of men

and yet could receive lesser punishment.[48]

Here, we meet a major strain of argument for religious toleration, in which the arguments of 'early Enlightenment' thinkers such as Limborch and Locke still accused many Catholic clergy of being 'libertines' and 'sodomites',

[47] *Ibid.*, 50–4.   [48] *Ibid.*, II, 78–9, 82.

which defended the toleration of alleged 'heretics' and 'schismatics' by distinguishing them firmly from the 'libertine' and the 'sodomite', and which emphasised that the 'libertine' and 'sodomite', was truly 'intolerable' and 'vile'. In its denial of toleration to 'libertines' and 'sodomites', this distinction is a crucial component of argument for *religious* toleration; we will return to this topic in Chapter 22.

'TOLERANT PRIMITIVE CHRISTIANITY' AND INTOLERANT LATE
PATRISTIC CHRISTIANITY

The 'Middle Ages' were thus depicted in works defending religious toleration as a period when 'barbarism' and 'superstition' and 'darkness' had reached its height, before the first light of dawn in the Reformation, and recently the development of 'enlightened' civil and religiously tolerant Christianity. But it was not merely the 'Middle Ages' that was condemned and the current period of Christian 'Enlightenment' that was lauded. At exactly the same time as they assaulted medieval Christianity, many of these authors made an extended case that the 'primitive Christianity' of the first three centuries had been tolerant and was now being revived and imitated in the 'early Enlightenment', and that much of patristic Christianity – especially the thought of Augustine – was to be condemned as standing behind the intolerance of both the 'Middle Ages' and of the 'magisterial Reformation'.

Limborch's *History of the Inquisition* identified toleration as the commitment of Christians up to the fourth century:

This was that most harmless perswasion of the Primitive Christians, before the World had yet entered into the Church, and by its Pomp and Pride had perverted the Minds, and corrupted the manners of its professors.

For Limborch, Constantine had initially pursued the appropriate policy for rulers. He had rebuked Bishop Alexander for his 'needlessly inquisitive' questioning of Arius' beliefs, and he had chided Arius for 'imprudent answers about an unnecessary question'. But he had then been persuaded to call the Council of Nicaea and had instituted Christian magisterial religious persecution. Limborch condemned both Arian and Athanasian persecution. The structure of Limborch's *History of the Inquisition* was thus a call for a return to tolerant primitive Christianity against patristic, medieval and Reformation intolerance: the toleration of 'the Enlightenment' was to be the 'toleration' of 'primitive Christianity' revived.

For Limborch in the *Theologia Christiana*, departure from the practice of the primitive church by condemning dissenters had involved descent into 'inhumanity', and it would have damned the Fathers of the primitive church themselves since the intolerant came to

> pronounce all, who err even in the least matters, to be guilty of eternal damnation. They confess, if we mind the rule of God's word, that all error is damnable; since whoever preaches any other Gospel than what is preach'd, tho it were an Angel from heaven, is anathema, or accursed, and every Error is in their account a new Gospel: And thus they are under a necessity of damning all who dissent from them; which is not only repugnant to the very Genius of Christianity, but likewise barbarous and inhuman. 'Tis damning men by whole-sale, and throwing the very fathers of the Primitive Church, those Glorious Lights of the Christian Religion, into Hell, since they (as well as other Men) were not without their Failings and Errors in some lesser Matters.

For Limborch, in the 'primitive church' 'heretics' were not put to death, but were instead the 'persecutors of others, and the first inventors of the most exquisite punishments'. In translating Limborch's *Theologia Christiana* into English, Burnet's client William Jones underlined his hostility to the anathematisation of others for alternative religious commitments, and noted that some think synods 'have done more harm than good to the Christian Religion being generally compos'd of men on one side only, who are warm in their Debates, and violent in their Decisions and Proceedings against others of the contrary Party'.[49]

The structure of Burnet's edition of Lactantius as well as his 'Preface of some length', which he added to 'swell up the bulk of this small Book' in order to consider 'the grounds on which those cruel and persecuting doctrines and practices are founded', conveyed exactly the same message that the Christians of the 'first ages' had opposed 'cruelty', that the fourth century had been the time of corruption of Christianity, which was then extended further in the Middle Ages and maintained in the Reformation, and that this corruption was now to be removed in a return to 'primitive Christianity'. For Burnet, even when the empire had first become Christian, 'heathens' had continued to be tolerated and employed. The 'first severity' of Christians had come in the 'banishing of Arius'. Because the Arians had been 'violent' against the 'orthodox', Burnet held that such banishment was legitimate, but that any further magisterial force than that of banishment was not legitimate, and that it was the violence and not the unorthodoxy of the Arians which legitimated the limited use of force against them. Burnet declared this the

> utmost extent of civil authority in those matters: for certainly a Government may put such persons out of its protection, that are enemies to its peace, and so banish them

---

[49] Limborch, *Compleat System*, preface, xx, 997, 986; *idem, Theologia Christiana*, 837; Peters, *Inquisition*, 167–8; Limborch, *History*, I, 6–7.

upon great occasions, giving them leave to sell their estates, and to carry with them all that belongs to them.[50]

For Bayle, who cited Burnet's edition of Lactantius in the *Supplement* to the *Philosophical Commentary*, there was a need to reason on universal principles, something which he alleged the first Christians had done in defence of toleration and not of intolerance. He noted that while Tertullian might now be being cited extensively by defenders of intolerance and the Revocation such as Bossuet, he had actually argued against and not for the use of magisterial force in religion; we noted in Chapter 5 that Tertullian had in fact argued for toleration of Christians by magistrates as not 'harming' others, thereby expressing in miniature the central political tolerationist argument of the 1680s and 1690s. For Bayle, the 'primitive church' had prevailed 'without the Assistance of the Secular Power, and in spite of all the Opposition of the World'.[51] For Bayle, the Christianisation of the Roman Empire had first introduced magisterial force and so corruption into the heart of Christianity. 'Temporal greatness' had become the aim 'of princes and counsellors'. It was a 'scandal to Christianity that the fathers' who had been so prodigious against persecuting pagans and Arians had then turned to the defence of persecution. The reign of Theodosius had been 'perfectly Priestridden'. While he noted that 'heretics' had sometimes acted 'cruelly' against the 'orthodox', he stressed that the 'orthodox' were particularly aggressive, for they had 'implored' Constantine to use the secular arm before the Arians had ever used 'any violence'. It was also true that in support of Arianism, Constantius and Valens had employed 'great violence' against the orthodox, but even that had not reached the heights employed by the 'orthodox'. He noted that 'ever since the court of France' had become 'infatuated with the Spirit of Persecution', many had been 'employed in compiling... all the Laws...of...Christian Emperors against Arians, Donatists, Manicheans, and other sectaryes'.[52]

Bayle was here expressing the arguments about tolerant 'primitive Christianity' that were common to many tolerationist authors of the 1680s and 1690s. He was thereby in the company not merely of many contemporary advocates of toleration, but also specifically of Socinian predecessors, and the linkage between the interpretations of Bayle and the Socinians was made explicit by Jean Le Clerc. As we noted in Chapters 7 and 10, Socinians had had dual reason to render the fourth-century period of Constantinian

[50] Burnet (ed.), *Death*, preface, 9, 28–33, and *passim*.
[51] Bayle, *Philosophical Commentary* (1708), 38 (*Philosophical Commentary*, ed. Tannenbaum, 24–5; *Commentaire philosophique*, 77–8).
[52] Bayle, *Philosophical Commentary* (1708), 220–5 (*Philosophical Commentary*, ed. Tannenbaum, 125–30; *Commentaire philosophique*, 239–43).

Christianisation of the Roman Empire problematic: the fourth century had been the period of imposition of Athanasian Trinitarian orthodoxy. Celebration of tolerant 'primitive Christianity' had for them been celebration simultaneously of the period before magisterial force was deployed by Christians and before imposition of Trinitarian orthodoxy. Reviewing Charles Le Cène's *Conversations* in the 1687 *Bibliothèque universelle*, Le Clerc noted that its second part was a translation of the Socinian Johann Crell's *Vindication of Liberty of Religion* and suggested that in the treatment of the conduct of 'primitive Christians' Bayle's *Philosophical Commentary* was an 'embellishing and amplifying' of Crell's work.[53]

Many of the tolerationist works of the 1680s explicitly attacked Augustine, and the 'Augustinian imperative' to attack heresy that was revered by Protestants such as Jurieu at least as much as by Catholics such as Bossuet, whose public justification of the Revocation of the Edict of Nantes at his sermon at the moment of that Revocation was explicitly based on Augustine. In his preface to Lactantius, Burnet identified Augustine as being a man with a 'heat of imagination' who misinterpreted the Bible. It was true that Burnet tried to restrain his criticism of Augustine, emphasising that the contest with the Donatists had grown so 'fierce and intolerable' that it 'broke in' on other churches when Donatists had 'committed outrages' on bishops. Yet Burnet indicated that Augustine had inappropriately justified 'severity in general', zealously, and because of his own deficiencies. And immediately after identifying Augustine's misinterpretation of Luke's *compellare* on the basis of his 'uncorrect Eloquence' and failure to 'examine critically' the 'true meaning' of Scripture, Burnet indicted Augustine as bringing about the 'night of ignorance', declaring that 'with that Father the Learning of the Western Church fell very low, so that his Works came to be more read in the succeeding Ages, than the writings of all the other Fathers: and in this, as in other things, men that knew not how to reason themselves, contented themselves with that lasie and cheap way of copying from him, and of depending on his Authority'. Giving Burnet's attack on Augustine further circulation and publicity, Henri Basnage de Beauval translated Burnet's work into French, and published a review of Burnet's work in the *Histoire des Ouvrages des Savans*.[54]

---

[53] Le Clerc, *Bibliothèque universelle*, v (1687), 212–27.

[54] Burnet (ed.), *Death*, preface, 28–33; Cerny, *Theology*, 96; Basnage de Beauval, *La mort des persécuteurs*. This analysis of Burnet's response to Augustine and of Henri Basnage de Beauval's and Bayle's reactions to it was explored in my 2000 paper at the National Humanities Centre, North Carolina, and I am grateful to the audience for their comments. Burnet's reaction has also been discussed by John Coffey in *Persecution*; both Coffey and I are indebted on the theme of opposing Augustine especially to Goldie, 'Theory of Religious Intolerance'.

Assaulting the reprint of Augustine's letters in the revealingly entitled *The Conformity of the Conduct of the Church of France for Reuniting Protestants with Africa in Reuniting Donatists,* Bayle devoted the entire third part of his *Philosophical Commentary* to an attack on Augustine. For Bayle, Augustine had had such 'zeal' that he believed he did God 'good service' as he 'wrested scripture'.[55] In order to prove that 'heretics' and 'schismatics' were justly persecuted, Bayle argued that Augustine had inappropriately 'painted' the 'errors of adversarys in the frightfullest colours' and had made it appear that he justified punishment only against the 'restless' while actually justifying the punishment of all 'even the most meek and inoffensive'. While no one had ever doubted that it was the duty of princes to 'enact wholesom Laws against Hereticks who disturb the publick peace, who are of a turbulent persecuting spirit, and so forth', Augustine had made it appear that all 'heretics' were turbulent and had ignored the duty to restrain the orthodox of a factious and turbulent spirit. Augustine's attempt to distinguish 'good' and 'bad' persecutions came to no more for Bayle than that the orthodox may persecute for orthodoxy and the heterodox may not persecute for heterodoxy – a simply ridiculous tautology.[56]

Understanding the huge power exercised by Augustine's influence, and responding to the republication of Augustine's epistles to justify the Revocation, Bayle then replied to each of Augustine's major arguments for magisterial force in turn. Augustine had argued that it was an act of 'charity' and 'goodness' to reclaim someone who was 'ready to throw himself down a precipice in...a raging fever'. But for Bayle, while it was true that to save the life of a madman one did not need his consent, 'as to the hereticks there is no doing him any good with regard to Salvation, except his Consent be had'. For Bayle, 'Where the Heart is not touch'd, penetrated and convinc'd, the rest is to no purpose; and God himself cannot save us by force, since the most efficacious, and the most necessitating Grace, is that which makes us consent the most intirely to the Will of God, and desire the most ardently that which God desires'.[57] Bayle traced to Augustine similarly the argument that the 'rod' was useful to correct the 'listlessness' of dissenters; in an explicit attack on Augustine, he argued that this filled men with fears of temporal punishments and hopes of temporal advantages, an 'ill state for discerning the true reasons of things from the false'.[58]

---

[55]   Burnet (ed.), *Death,* 31–2; Bayle, *Philosophical Commentary* (1708), 369–502, esp. 370–1; *OD,* II, 445–96, esp. 445.
[56]   Bayle, *Philosophical Commentary* (1708), *Third Part, passim,* esp. 372ff.; *OD,* II, esp. 446.
[57]   Bayle, *Philosophical Commentary* (1708), 382–4; *OD,* II, 448–9.
[58]   Bayle, *Philosophical Commentary* (1708), 389–90; *OD,* II, 450.

For Augustine, correction was the act of a friend, and the magistrate might chastise as a friend. For Bayle, a friend was indeed 'not afraid of telling his Friend disagreeable Truths, of reproving him roundly, of contradicting him...and of resisting his Appetites'. A pastor might even 'rattle and teaze' his own flock out of 'vices'. But in dealing with 'strangers' it was far better to approach them with 'Civility; Men being much more apt to be embitter'd and confirm'd in their Opinions by harsh Treatment, than determin'd to change and forsake em'. And there was no magisterial right to inflict punishment due to the friend's capacity to give 'wholesom Reproof'.[59] Finally, in an argument about the consequences of an unregulated claim of conscience and free will which we have met repeatedly in Part 2 of this book, Augustine argued that if 'profaneness' was permitted because of 'free will' then 'adultery' might be permitted on the same ground. Princes were to 'ordain penalties' of laws of 'honesty and sobriety' and all acknowledged their 'justice'. Every transgression against them was 'wilful, malicious and under conscience of its being displeasing to god'. For Bayle, a Christian was 'justly punished' who 'renounced God' because by his own principles he was guilty of 'blasphemy and sacrilege'. He who committed adultery was 'agreed' that it was a 'wicked action'. Judges were able to know that there was a 'knowledge' of acting wickedly. But this was simply not true of the alleged profanation of heresy.[60] To such extensive replies to Augustine in the *Philosophical Commentary*, Bayle also added reply in the *Dictionary* entry 'Augustin H', including assaulting Augustine as 'a Turncoat in his opinion' who had wrongly turned from toleration to justification of penal laws against heretics.[61]

In a letter to Locke, Limborch declared that one cannot 'but find fault... most of all with the teaching of Augustine' against the Donatists. It was against the intolerance of Augustinian and post-Augustinian Christianity that Limborch directed his recommendation in the *Theologia Christiana* of a 'return to the ancient simplicity which prevailed in the primitive church'. Le Clerc challenged Augustine's authority at many points, including declaring that his epistles in defence of the use of force contained 'little piety' and attacking him for misinterpreting Luke with the 'most cruel opinion imaginable'.[62] And Augustine's authority as the 'patriarch of persecutors' was also questioned indirectly by the subscription to Arminian accounts of grace against Augustinian accounts of predestination of such advocates of toleration as Le Clerc, Le Cène, and Limborch. When Bayle reviewed Le

---

[59] Bayle, *Philosophical Commentary* (1708), 390–2; *OD*, ɪɪ, 450.

[60] Bayle, *Philosophical Commentary* (1708), 461–7; *OD*, ɪɪ, 468.

[61] Bayle, *Dictionary*, Augustin H.

[62] Locke, *Correspondence*, 1393; Limborch, *Compleat System*, 1020; Le Clerc, *Account*, 41–2; J. Milner, *Animadversions on le Clerc's Reflections* (London 1702), 50; Goldie, 'Theory of Religious Intolerance'.

Clerc's 1685 *Conversations* in the *Nouvelles*, he noted that Augustine had been 'cruelly treated' (although, as noted in Chapter 16, when Le Clerc protested against this review by Bayle, Bayle responded that 'cruel' treatment could be 'unjust', or 'just', and that he had encouraged many to read the work by his comment).[63] The attack on Augustine was thus multi-faceted, including arguments for the necessity of human co-operation in achieving salvation which revived possibilites within the faith which Augustine had attempted to close off as 'heretical'. It assaulted Augustine not merely by repudiating his late commitment to intolerance but by representing him as zealous and a misinterpreter of the Bible and by subjecting to criticism many of his central theological commitments. The central problem in religion in 'enlightened' Christian eyes in the late seventeenth and early eighteenth century was in the process of changing from a focus on 'heresy' and 'schism' to a focus on 'superstition', 'ignorance', 'barbarism', and especially 'intolerance'. And the repudiation involved was not merely of 'The Inquisition' but also of Augustine, not merely of Bossuet but also of Jurieu, not merely of Counter-Reformation Catholicism but also of 'international Calvinism'.[64]

---

[63] Le Clerc, *Epistolario*, 86.
[64] Cf. Connolly, *Augustinian*, 78–9; M. Prestwich (ed.), *International Calvinism 1541–1715* (Oxford 1985).

21

Epistemological, philological, theological, and ethical arguments for religious toleration

FORCE AND THE NATURE OF THE UNDERSTANDING

Advocates of toleration repeatedly asserted that the understanding could not be forced since belief was not within the power of the will. As Burnet put it in his preface to Lactantius, 'a man...thinks as he thinks, and cannot think otherwise, because he would have himself do so'. A man was 'not the master of his own mind, much less is any other man the Master of it'.[1] Crell's argument in the *Vindication*, republished by Le Cène in his 1687 *Conversations*, declared that violence should not be used because it could not 'cause a man to think otherwise than he doth'.[2] Bayle argued in the *Philosophical Commentary* that violence was 'incapable' of 'convincing the Judgment' and was a 'mistaken way of establishing a Religion'.[3] Locke had argued in his tolerationist 1667 'Essay on Toleration' that 'no man can give another man power (and it would be to no purpose if God should) over that over which he has no power himself'. It was 'evident' that a man could not 'command his own understanding'. Locke's *Letter* restated this position: 'such is the nature of the understanding, that it cannot be compelled to the belief of any thing by outward force'. For Locke, 'no man can, if he would, conform his faith to the dictates of another'. Confiscation of Estate, 'Imprisonment, Torments, nothing of that nature can have any such efficacy as to make men change the inward Judgment that they have framed of things'. Penalties 'in this case are absolutely impertinent; because they are not proper to convince the mind'. It is 'only Light and evidence that can work a change in mens opinions; which Light can in no manner proceed from corporal sufferings, or any other outward penalties'.[4]

---

[1] Burnet (ed.), *Death*, preface 15–16.   [2] Crell, *Vindication*, 46; Le Cène, *Conversations*, 263.
[3] Bayle, *Philosophical Commentary* (1708), 60–1 (*Philosophical Commentary*, ed. Tannenbaum, 36; *Commentaire philosophique*, 99–101).
[4] Locke, *Political Essays*, ed. Goldie, 137; Locke, *Letter* in *Works*, 11–12. Locke had himself argued that the understanding could not be forced in his anti-tolerationist *Two Tracts*, but had there given the magistrate power to force outward compliance: *Two Tracts*, 129–30.

Anti-tolerationists, however, also held that the understanding could not be convinced directly by force, and argued instead that force could work indirectly, for instance by soliciting consideration of arguments which could persuade people. As Bayle noted in the *Philosophical Commentary*, Catholics alleged in defence of the Revocation of the Edict of Nantes that the offer of the 'Comforts of Life' and the 'Dread of Misery' could 'rouze' individuals from their 'slumber' and put them to 'an Examination of the two Religions' of Catholicism and Protestantism, thus indirectly helping to make them choose the 'true religion' of Catholicism. Locke similarly noted in the *Second Letter concerning Toleration* that this was the 'plea made use of to excuse the late barbarous usage of the protestants in France'.[5] In order to rebut this kind of argument, many of the advocates of toleration turned from the argument that force could not produce conviction as it could not work on the understanding to the argument that the use of force was harmful to examining impartially the evidence for the 'true religion'. Van Paets' 1685 *De nuperis Angliae*, translated by Bayle in 1686, attacked the argument that force could be used to make individuals examine the evidence properly, alleging that it did the opposite by making people place in the balance not merely the reasons on both sides but fear of the 'present evil' of torments. Bayle argued similarly in his own 1686 *Philosophical Commentary* that punishments and rewards served not to calm people's passions and judge by impartial reason but instead to make people judge 'under the disadvantages of all those Mists and thick Darkness, which a conflict of several violent Passions must needs produce in the Soul'. The use of force upset the 'Ballance of Evidence' by providing a 'counterballance' of 'temporal Advantage'.[6] In the *Second Letter*, Locke similarly mocked the notion that force could allow men to 'weigh matters of religion carefully, and impartially' by suggesting that 'Discountenance and punishment put into one scale, with impunity and hopes of preferment put into the other, is as sure a way to make a man weigh impartially, as it would be for a prince to bribe and threaten a judge to make him judge uprightly'. Given that Locke thought that judicial dependence on royal favour had fostered the dangers of absolutism described in Chapters 1 and 3, this was a powerful indictment indeed.[7]

Many tolerationists contended that when used against the wicked, force caused either profession without belief, the sin of 'hypocrisy', or atheism. Van Paets declared that force created hypocrites unfaithful both to God and to

---

[5] Bayle, *Philosophical Commentary* (1708), 63, 150–2 (*Philosophical Commentary*, ed. Tannenbaum, 37, 88–9; *Commentaire philosophique*, 102, 177–9); Locke, *Second Letter*, in *Works*, 87.

[6] Van Paets, *Lettre*, 17–18; Bayle, *Philosophical Commentary* (1708), 151–5 (*Philosophical Commentary*, ed. Tannenbaum, 88–91; *Commentaire philosophique*, 179–81).

[7] Locke, *Second Letter* in *Works*, 97.

their sovereign. Bayle's *Philosophical Commentary* identified 'hypocrisy' and religious indifference among the natural consequences of the use of force.[8] Aubert's *Treatise* condemned force as causing 'hypocrisy'. Crell's *Vindication*, republished in Le Cène's 1687 *Conversations*, declared that the use of force created 'hypocrites', and that hypocrisy was an abomination to God, harmful to the church by creating 'secret enemies', and harmful to hypocrites by bringing them 'eternall destruction'. Moreover, when 'Conscience' was suppressed in 'those men' with less honesty and virtue than there 'ought to be', the counterfeiting of belief in order to avoid punishment led to 'atheism' and 'profaneness'. In his own sections of the *Conversations*, Le Cène argued that the use of force to coerce profession of a religion which was not believed developed insensibly into a general indifference to religion and finally to impiety.[9] For Locke in the *Letter*, 'All the life and power of true religion consists in the inward and full persuasion of the mind...Whatever profession we make, to whatever outward worship we conform, if we are not fully satisfied in our own mind that the one is true, and the other well pleasing unto God, such profession and such practice...are...great obstacles to our salvation...we add unto the number of our other sins, those also of hypocrisy, and contempt of his Divine Majesty'.[10]

If promotion of hypocrisy and atheism were held to be the likely effects of force being used against those disposed to evil, Bayle argued that someone persuaded of the truth of his own religion would be confirmed in it by the martyrdom of fellow believers.[11] Crell's *Vindication*, republished in Le Cène's *Conversations*, declared that in men of 'greater honesty and integrity' the love of their religion was 'inflamed and increased by persecution'. And it urged that force increased 'heresies' as those who endeavoured to suppress another man's religion made their own religion suspect by seeming to 'distrust their cause' if debated by argumentation. Use of force diminished the credit 'of their Religion, which animates and stirs them up to so much cruelty against innocent and harmlesse men'. Le Cène himself argued in the *Conversations* that the use of force backfired as martyrdom made people more interested in the ideas of those punished.[12] And Limborch argued

---

[8] Van Paets, *Lettre*, 7–8; Bayle, *Philosophical Commentary* (1708), 63 (*Philosophical Commentary*, ed. Tannenbaum 36; *Commentaire philosophique*, 101).

[9] Aubert de Versé, *Traité*, 9, 28–9; Crell, *Vindication*, 46–7, 55–6; Le Cène, *Conversations*, 121, 263–5, 271–3.

[10] Locke, *Letter* in *Works*, 11. In the *Second Letter*, Locke argued that those who could most easily be compelled were those 'who have nothing of religion at all; and next to them, the vicious, the ignorant, the worldling, and the hypocrite': 115.

[11] Bayle, *Philosophical Commentary* (1708), 183–4 (*Philosophical Commentary*, ed. Tannenbaum, 104; *Commentaire philosophique*, 207–8).

[12] Crell, *Vindication*, 26–9, 56–8; Le Cène, *Conversations*, 103–4, 244–7, 272–4.

similarly in his 1686 *Theologia Christiana* that martyrdom made people more interested in the ideas of those who were martyred, encouraging the adoption of their views, because it offered a testimony to the martyrs' conviction and rendered their heresy 'plausible'.[13]

Since Locke stated axiomatically in the *Letter* that force could not enlighten the mind, Proast was quick to restate against the *Letter* the anti-tolerationist arguments that force worked 'indirectly'. Locke did, however, buttress his axiomatic argument that force could not work on the under-standing by arguing even in the brief *Letter* that *if* force could effect a change in belief, since there was but 'one way to heaven' but all magistrates would be empowered, those saved would owe heaven to their place of birth, while the vast majority would miss salvation as 'ignorance, ambition, or superstition' had established religions in their domains. Locke pressed this point on Proast repeatedly in his defences of the *Letter*, refusing to narrow the debate to only one country – England – in which both agreed that the 'true religion' was established.[14] And Locke further argued in the *Second* and *Third Letter* that if force could work indirectly then it was more likely to produce error than truth because those in error were 'apter to use force', and because there were perhaps a hundred magistrates in error for every one who held the truth. Noting that force was used only against those who were not members of the national religion, Locke stressed that many outside of the national religion would have examined their religious beliefs, whereas many within the national church would not. Since force was justified as required in order to make people examine their beliefs, it could not on its own terms legitimately be applied only against dissenters. Indeed, since 'interest' naturally led those who laid aside 'conscience, or the care of their souls' into the national church, for Locke one could 'rationally presume' that the national church had more communicants who had not 'considered' than 'any congregation of dissenters'.[15] Reviewing the arguments of Proast and Locke in the *Bibliothèque universelle*, Le Clerc recapitulated Locke's arguments that magistrates most inclined to use force were most likely to be in error, that many more magistrates erred than held the truth, and that justifying magisterial use of force to defend 'true religion' led to the Inquisition in Spain and Portugal, and to the dragonnades in France.[16]

---

[13] Limborch, *Compleat System*, 984; *idem, Theologia Christiana*, 829.
[14] Locke, *Letter* in *Works*, 12; *Second Letter* in *Works*, 64, 76, 94–5, 111; *Third Letter for Toleration* in *Works*, 151–3, 220–1, 251, 281, 333, 366–7.
[15] Locke, *Second Letter* in *Works*, 73–8, 93–5; *Third Letter* in *Works*, 225, 244–8, 256–8, 305–6, 337–53, 372–3, 378–9. By the time of the *Fourth Letter*, Locke spoke of 499 magistrates out of 500 as holding false religions: *Fourth Letter* in *Works*, 567.
[16] Le Clerc, *Bibliothèque universelle*, XIX (1690), 367, 377–9.

THE RIGHTS OF CONSENT AND CONSCIENCE, THE DUTIES OF EQUITY
AND CHARITY, AND THE 'GENTLENESS' OF CHRISTIANITY

The advocates of toleration combined with their stress on the inefficacy or negative effects of the use of force arguments that God himself required a voluntary or consensual worship which could not proceed from force, that toleration was required by 'liberty of conscience', and that the duties of equity and charity in imitation of Christ and the apostles required the toleration of others. Whereas anti-tolerationists argued that it was possible for forced worship to be 'voluntary' and for force to produce a post-facto celebration of a resulting conversion, tolerationists argued that unforced consent was vital to worship being truly free and voluntary. Aubert's *Pacific Protestant* argued that religion was a voluntary obedience and sacrifice of the heart which could not proceed from force. Aubert's *Treatise* argued that God detested a 'forced profession'. Bayle's *Philosophical Commentary* argued that the 'inward disposition' was the 'essence of religion' and that the gospel required men to follow it through reason rather than be forced as a 'slave'.[17] Crell's *Vindication*, republished by Le Cène, quoted Lactantius in arguing that 'nothing is so voluntary as Religion, which if the minde of him that sacrifeth dislike, then it...becomes none at all'.[18] Locke argued in the *Letter* that no one could consent to vest power over religion in the magistrate 'because no man can so far abandon the care of his own salvation, as blindly to leave it to the choice of any other'. Lacking power over their own minds, they could not give that power to another. Instead, they were to join 'free and voluntary' societies to worship God 'in such a manner as they judge acceptable to him'. He repeated the argument in his *Second Letter*, and stressed in the *Third Letter* that 'every man has a right to toleration' because force being used against a man 'to bring him to a religion, which another thinks the true' would have been an injury in the state of nature, and protection from such injury was one of the ends of setting up any commonwealth.[19]

The advocates of toleration repeatedly asserted that toleration was required by liberty of conscience and by the right of God over conscience. Aubert's *Treatise* identified the 'fundamental reason' for toleration of all sects as based on the 'indispensable and necessary obligation' of obeying 'conscience', even if in error. Bayle's *Philosophical Commentary* declared the 'rights of conscience' directly 'those of God himself', and conscience 'the

---

[17] Aubert de Versé, *Protestant*, 3; *idem, Traité*, 30; Bayle, *Philosophical Commentary* (1708), 59, 68–9 (*Philosophical Commentary*, ed. Tannenbaum, 35, 40–1; *Commentaire philosophique*, 99, 106–7).

[18] Crell, *Vindication*, 46; Le Cène, *Conversations*, 263.

[19] Locke, *Letter* in *Works*, 10, 13; *Second Letter* in *Works*, 127; *Third Letter* in *Works*, 212.

Voice and Law of God in him, known and acknowledged as such by him, who carrys this Conscience about him: So that to violate this Conscience is actually believing, that he violates the Law of God'. For Bayle, 'Every one should follow the Dictates of his Conscience'. The extensive defence of the rights of an erroneous conscience is perhaps the most famous element of Bayle's entire *Commentary*; for Bayle, 'we are obliged to follow the suggestions of an erroneous conscience'.[20] Papin's *Faith Reduced*, as Bayle emphasised in his preface, stressed that the authority of councils or synods must never prevail over individuals' 'consciences'. Papin declared that 'the spirit of Christianity is a spirit of liberty of conscience' and argued that the apostles and Fathers had never attributed power to councils to dominate over consciences.[21] For Limborch in the *Theologia Christiana*, intolerance was invalid because 'Hereby the Liberty of Conscience is oppressed, so that a Man dare not freely profess that, to which he thinks he is obliged for the Glory of God'. Every man was 'bound to serve God sincerely according to the full perswasion of his own Conscience' and no man could 'lay a violence upon another Man's conscience, without encroaching upon the Prerogative of Heaven'. For Locke in the *Letter*, men had to be 'left to their own consciences', and 'No way whatsoever that I shall walk in, against the dictates of my conscience, will ever bring me to the mansions of the blessed'.[22]

The advocates of religious toleration alleged that toleration was required not merely by 'liberty of conscience', but also by the duties of equity and charity. Limborch stressed 'this one most equitable Law of Nature written in all our Hearts, Whatsoever ye would that Men should do unto you, even so do unto them...For tis highly reasonable that we should be under the Obligation of the same law, which we would have prescribed to others'.

---

[20] Aubert de Versé, *Traité*, 67–8, and *passim*; Bayle, *Philosophical Commentary* (1708), 95, 115, 210, 349, and *passim* (*Philosophical Commentary*, ed. Tannenbaum, 56, 66, 119, 186; *Commentaire philosophique*, 129, 146, 230, 347). Cf Kilcullen, *Sincerity*; Zagorin, *Idea*.

[21] Papin, *Foi réduite*, preface, 105–6.

[22] Limborch, *Compleat System*, 984–5; *idem*, *Theologia Christiana*, 828–9; Locke, *Letter* in *Works*, 28. All such definitions of 'conscience' tied it to belief in God. Bayle held in the *Philosophical Commentary* that it was evident that conscience was 'a Light dictating that such a thing is good or bad' and that acting against conscience was a sin because it was against the will of God. Only in 1703, in his *Reply to the Questions of a Provincial*, did Bayle come to suggest that atheists *might* have a conscience, writing first in conventional terms that 'if conscience signifies a judgment of the mind that stimulates us to take certain actions because they were commanded by God under the promise of a reward, it is certain that an atheist with a conscience would be a monster', but then adding 'But if by conscience you mean only the judgment of the spirit that stimulates us to do certain things because they are in conformity with reason and lead us from certain things because they are contrary to reason, it is not at all impossible that an atheist should have a conscience': Bayle, *Réponse*, OD (1727–31), III, 986a, in Mori, 'Bayle', 57.

Since we would not wish to be persecuted, we should not persecute others. Invoking the 'light of nature' in his *Pacific Protestant*, Aubert stressed that as 'I do not have any right to force others to hold my opinions, no-one has the right to force me to adopt his'. In his *Treatise*, he invoked the rule of doing unto others as the great 'maxim' authorised by Christ and showing that magistrates should not force others. Burnet concurred in his preface to Lactantius that the rule of doing 'to others that which we would have others do to us' ought to let persecutors see 'how differently they act'.[23] For Bayle, all moral laws 'ought to be regulated by that Idea of natural Equity, which...enlightens every Man coming into the world'. Catholics using force against Protestants were 'void of natural Equity'. Le Clerc joined the chorus, *inter alia*, in his *Life of Locke*, where he complimented Locke's *Third Letter* and condemned those who 'when it is in their power, persecute others because they differ from them in their Notions; and...would think it very hard, if they were on the weaker side, to be persecuted...themselves'.[24]

Such equity could be invoked in support of liberty of public expression of one's religious views, but while Limborch went on to suggest that some liberty of public expression was required by equity in the following passage, his discussion began by emphasising that it might also call for mutual silence in order to avoid public disputations breaking peace, as he argued that 'if any man should embrace a doctrine for true which is different from the received doctrine of the church', an advocate for the church should

consider how much liberty he must allow to the other of maintaining and defending the doctrine he looks upon to be true...If therefore he should think it reasonable, for the preservation of the Peace of the Church, that the other should say nothing of that Doctrine, he ought also to injoin silence to himself. On the other hand, should it happen, that another should dissent from the common Doctrine of the Church, he will consider how much Liberty he would desire (were he of his opinion) of proposing and maintaining his Tenets, and will grant the same to his dissenting Brother, without any Violation of the Peace of the Church.[25]

Arminians such as Limborch had often refrained from public disputation in the Netherlands in the seventeenth century, and Limborch went on to stress strongly their reluctance to dispute publicly with Contra-Remonstrants. In their correspondence, Locke and Limborch often criticised others' works not so much for their particular doctrinal positions as for their unnecessary disputatiousness. The emphasis on mutual silence as much as on public

[23] Limborch, *Compleat System*, 1015; *idem, Theologia Christiana*, 850; Aubert de Versé, *Protestant*, 3–4; *idem, Traité*, 29–30; Burnet (ed.), *Death*, 20.
[24] Bayle, *Philosophical Commentary* (1708), 3, 49 (*Philosophical Commentary*, ed. Tannenbaum 10, 30; *Commentaire philosophique*, 49, 89–90); Le Clerc, *Life of Locke*, 17–18.
[25] Limborch, *Compleat System*, 1015; *idem, Theologia Christiana*, 850.

expression in Limborch's thought was significant; there are ways to read much of Limborch's and Locke's attitudes about the disputed issues of the Trinity in the late seventeenth century, for instance, as an example of attempting to practice tolerant, equitable silence.

In order to combat the intolerant Augustinian defence of forcibly saving souls as an act of 'charity', Limborch also spoke of 'equity' as required by the law of charity. For Limborch, intolerance was 'repugnant to the law of charity, the chief of the Christian laws', as this 'chief Christian law' prescribes us 'this most equitable rule, whatsoever ye would that Men should do unto you, even so do ye unto them. Now there is no man, if by chance he should unwittingly fall into error, that would be willing any violence should be offered to him upon that account'. In order to further combat the Augustinian notion of the charitable saving of others' souls, many advocates of toleration further defined the duty of charity as a duty of 'gentleness' in opposition to force and cruelty, stressing both the imitation of Christ and the apostles, and that Christianity was essentially a religion of gentleness. For Burnet, the 'character' of the Christian religion was charity, and the doctrine of persecution was 'a more infallible mark of an Antichristian church, than all the other Characters are of an Infallible church, to which those pretend, that have died themselves so red in the Blood of others'. The Doctrines of 'Meekness and Charity' were 'such main Ingredients' of the gospel that Christ had made them 'the Characters by which his Disciples may be every where known'. Christ was a 'pattern for Humility and Charity'. Le Cène argued that the doctrine of Christ was a doctrine 'of peace and charity'. Crell's argument, republished in Le Cène's *Conversations*, declared the Christian requirement to 'make good the law of charity to all men' and that Christ's example, to be imitated, was one of 'great lenity and gentleness towards erroneous persons'. It stressed that while cruelty drove people away, 'the praise...of meekeness, equity, gentleness, and moderation...would gaine their good wills and affections, which being once gained, it is an easie matter to perswade them of the truth which is founded upon solid arguments'.[26]

Le Clerc's portion of the 1685 *Conversations* emphasised the many scandalous violations of 'Christian charity' in disputes over predestination. In his own *Treatise*, Le Clerc depicted those who zealously defended doctrines and lacked charity as contemporary Pharisees 'a very ill sort of men' who caused incredulity in others as they confused 'Abuse of Religion with Religion it self'. For Le Clerc, those who argued for the use of force were 'strangers to

---

[26] Limborch, *Compleat System*, 983–4; *idem, Theologia Christiana*, 828; Burnet (ed.), *Death*, 9, 20, 23; Le Cène, *Conversations*, 17, 74–7, 244–8, 274–9; Crell, *Vindication*, 26–31, 58–63; cf. Coffey, *Persecution*, 59.

the true Proofs of Christianity, as well as to the Spirit of Charity and Moderation, which is the Life and Soul of the Gospel'. Behaving towards another 'charitably...if he be in any erroneous Opinion as to Religion, especially when it has little or no influence upon his Manners' was 'one of the principal branches...of that general love of our Neighbour'. Yet, Le Clerc observed, 'no part of Christian Theology has been so long neglected as this has been'; only in 'the last Age, and especially in the present' had 'any reflection...been made upon it'.[27]

Enumerating those damning errors which would in fact prevent individuals from inheriting the kingdom of God, Limborch effectively damned Calvin and Beza as well as many Catholic clerics when he declared in the *Theologia Christiana* that one such was 'the Error of the Romanists and of some Protestants concerning Hereticide, which is destructive of Charity, the chief precept of the New Covenant'. For Limborch, Jesus had recommended 'peace and charity as the characteristical mark by which his genuine disciples might be known'.[28]

Van Paets' *De nuperis Angliae* stressed that the example of Christ was of 'gentleness'. Papin's *Faith Reduced* declared that God had 'expressly commanded' that Christians were to have 'charity and friendship' for each other, and Jesus had said that it was by this that his disciples would be known. If one thought another wrong, then one was to converse and reason with them with a spirit of charity and gentleness, humility and support. Aubert's *Treatise* identified Christ as the 'divine herald of charity' and condemned those preachers who did not teach charity as ministers of Satan and not of Christ.[29] Bayle's *Philosophical Commentary* identified Jesus as an example of humility and meekness. For Bayle, one had to transcribe 'almost the whole New Testament' if one wished 'to collect all the proofs it affords us of that Gentleness, and Long-suffering, which constitute the distinguishing and essential Character of the Gospel'. The 'whole Tenor and Spirit of the Gospel' supported toleration, and argument for the use of force from the passage of Luke involved the use of one 'small sentence tending this way in the whole Gospel, and that a Piece of a Parable too, with the word compel at the tail on't, a Word which on a hundred other occasions signifies the pressings of Civility and Kindness to keep a Friend, for example, to dine with us'.[30]

---

[27] Le Clerc and Le Cène, *Entretiens*, 271–2; Le Clerc, *Treatise*, 132–8, 151, 190–1.
[28] Limborch, *Compleat System*, 1003, 1011; *idem, Theologia Christiana*, 841, 848.
[29] Van Paets, *Lettre*, 7; Papin, *Foi réduite*, 13, 15; Aubert de Versé, *Traité*, 16–17.
[30] Bayle, *Philosophical Commentary* (1708), 65, 69–71, 174 (*Philosophical Commentary*, ed. Tannenbaum, 39, 41–2, 100; *Commentaire philosophique*, 108, 198).

Locke began the *Letter* by arguing in its first sentence that 'toleration' was 'the chief characteristical mark of the true church'. He indicted those who boasted of their reformation or 'of the orthodoxy of their faith' as marks of men striving for empire over one another in asserting that 'if he be destitute of charity, meekness, and good-will in general towards all mankind...he is certainly...short of being a true christian himself'. Both the 'gospel and the apostles' had held that 'no man can be a Christian without charity, and without that faith which works, not by force, but by love'. Attacking the declaration by those who used force that they were acting out of charity, Locke argued that 'like the captain of our salvation' they should 'tread in the steps, and follow the perfect example of that prince of peace, who sent out his soldiers to the subduing of nations, and gathering them into his church, not armed with the sword, or other instruments of force, but prepared with the gospel of peace, and with the exemplary holiness of their conversation. This was his method'.[31] Locke's prose pulsed with scorn in these pages for those who proclaimed that they used force as a duty of charity as he appealed 'to the consciences of those that persecute, torment, destroy, and kill other men upon pretence of Religion, whether they do it out of Friendship and Kindness towards them, or no'. He declared that he would not be persuaded until he saw them correct 'their Friends' for their 'manifest' sins 'by the Infliction of Torments, and exercise of all manner of Cruelties'. It could not, for Locke, be 'out of a principle of Charity, as they pretend' that they deprived people 'of their estates, maim them with corporal punishments, starve and torment them in noisome prisons, and in the end even take away their Lives'. Those who were 'cruel and implacable towards those who differ from him in Opinion' but indulgent towards iniquities and immoralities demonstrated that they were motivated by desire for terrestrial power and not Christian charity.

Locke's *Second Letter Concerning Toleration* declared that the gospel was 'mild, and gentle, and meek'.[32] That these were important emphases of Locke's works was emphasised by Le Clerc's review of Locke's *Second Letter* in the *Bibliothèque universelle*, which stressed that in its account Christianity was a religion of 'gentleness and charity'. Le Clerc's *Life* of Locke similarly celebrated Locke's *Letters Concerning Toleration* and assaulted Christians defending intolerance as using religion 'to defend those practices which it expressly forbids'.[33]

Although political scientists nowadays tend to pass by Locke's argument in the *Letter* for toleration on the basis of charity and concentrate on his more 'political' arguments, there is no question that for Locke, as for his contemporaries arguing for toleration, the duty of charity was a crucial

---

[31] Locke, *Letter* in *Works*, 5–9.   [32] Locke, *Second Letter*, in *Works*, 76.
[33] Le Clerc, *Bibliothèque universelle*, XIX (1690), 377; *idem, Life of Locke*, 18.

argument for toleration as charity was the most important duty of Christianity, and also polemically central in order to reply to the central contemporary argument for intolerance from 'charity'. That Locke's opening lines and first three pages of his *Letter Concerning Toleration* were on the duty of charity clearly indicates its overriding importance to him; invocation of the duty of charity also animated much in his other works. In a number of these works, Locke specifically tied the 'gentleness' of 'charity' directly to opposition to imposition of the explication of articles of faith and obscure doctrines. Thus, in the *Third Letter for Toleration*, Locke invoked those 'generous principles of the Gospel, which so much recommend and inculcate universal charity, and a freedom from the inventions and impositions of men in the things of God'. Locke's *Vindication of the Reasonableness of Christianity* bemoaned that the Christian church had been 'so cruelly torn, about the articles of the christian faith, to the great reproach of Christian charity'. On the closing page of his *Second Vindication*, he identified charity as 'a virtue much more necessary than the attaining of the knowledge of obscure truths, that are not easy to be found; and probably, therefore, not necessary to be known'. In his *Paraphrase on the Epistles of St Paul*, Locke rendered 1 Corinthians 13:9 about charity towards errors in explication of Scripture by paraphrasing the biblical text 'for we know in part, and we prophesy in part' with 'for the knowledge we have now in this state and the explication we give of Scripture is short partial and defective'.[34]

The legitimacy of varying beliefs: the pressures of education and custom, fallibility, and sincere error

Several advocates of religious toleration stressed that beliefs were formed by pressures and circumstances beyond the control of individuals, and that variations of beliefs because of these circumstances were not blameworthy. They stressed that much of humanity was unable to reason extensively because denied the leisure and capacity to read and reflect which would allow them to judge critically for themselves, and that it was reasonable for such individuals to rely on others who possessed learning or authority, leading to a tolerable variation of beliefs. For Basnage de Beauval, error could be due to a 'prejudice of education', to 'defect of intelligence or the effect of some other human infirmity'. And he was 'persuaded that God will punish injustice more severely than error' due to such education and imperfections.[35] In his preface to his edition of Lactantius, Burnet stressed that

---

[34] Locke, *Third Letter* in *Works*, 544–5; Locke, *Vindication* in *Works*, vii, 169; *idem, Second Vindication* in *Works*, vii, 424; Locke, *Paraphrase*, i, 1 Corinthians 13.
[35] Basnage de Beauval, *Tolérance des Religions*, 49–50.

men were 'much governed by fancy' and that education was 'so powerful' with most of mankind that they were 'scarce able ever to overcome it'. For Burnet, these constraints might be escaped by a few men 'that think much, and that Reason well, that are freed from the biass that Interest, Honour, Kindred and Custom, do give them, and that have leisure to examine matters carefully', but such a capacity was given to very few men, and for Burnet fewer still utilised it.[36] For van Paets, those with 'leisure and ability to study' were obliged to 'search' and to understand issues that the 'ignorant and stupid' were not. It was for van Paets a consequence that the necessary articles of belief varied between individuals and consisted 'in a certain extent which only God knows'.[37] For Bayle, there was a necessity of bestowing time on the 'affairs of this life' and an 'almost unsurmountable subjection to the Prejudices of Education'. For Bayle, children naturally grew up accepting their parents' views. For almost all people it was 'owing to Education that they are of any one Religion rather than another'. For Bayle, this was the result of human's natural condition, and not blameworthy. A reasonable variety of beliefs necessarily followed.[38] And when Bayle did stress duties of enquiry, it was sincere effort that he praised. For Bayle, God required 'no more of us than to examine and search after [truth] diligently'. God 'in the present Condition of Man exacts no more from him than a sincere and diligent search after Truth'. It was enough if he 'sincerely and honestly consults the Lights which God has afforded him; and if, following its discoveries, he embraces that Persuasion which to him seems most reasonable and most conformable to the will of God. This renders him orthodox in the sight of God'.[39]

For Locke in the *Essay Concerning Human Understanding*, first drafted in the 1670s in England and massively expanded in the 1680s in the Netherlands, most men adopted views from 'the opinion of others'. Men frequently adopted them because of the credit of the proposer or from an opinion that the proposer was inspired by God. For Locke, it could not 'reasonably' be expected that they should renounce their opinions in order to submit to an authority which they did not recognise. If they suspected that those who wished them to renounce their opinions were motivated by 'Interest, or Design', which 'never fail[ed]...where men find themselves ill-treated', it was unreasonable even for those who had not regulated their assent properly to accept others' authority. For Locke, men would do well to 'commiserate our mutual ignorance, and endeavour to remove it in all gentle

---

[36] Burnet (ed.), *Death*, 12–13.   [37] Van Paets, *Lettre*, 34.

[38] Bayle, *Philosophical Commentary* (1708), 331–6, 346 (*Philosophical Commentary*, ed. Tannenbaum, 179–85; *Commentaire philosophique* 332ff.).

[39] Bayle, *Philosophical Commentary* (1708), 331, 337, 340 (*Philosophical Commentary*, ed. Tannenbaum, 178, 180–1; *Commentaire philosophique*, 332, 339–40); Kilcullen, *Sincerity*, 84–5.

and fair ways of information, and not instantly treat others ill, as obstinate and perverse' because they would not accept opinions. It is worth pausing here to emphasise that when in the *Essay* Locke specifically opposed treating others as 'obstinate and perverse' for failure to accept opinions, he clearly must have had in mind the arguments for intolerance towards heretics traced in this book, and that will have been clear to his contemporary readers. Locke spent several pages of the *Third Letter for Toleration* challenging Jonas Proast, who had defended 'moderate penalties' as useful against those who were not 'desperately perverse and obstinate' to define who was thus 'desperately perverse and obstinate', and emphasised that 'The King of France...when he came to dragooning' had found few 'so desperately perverse and obstinate, as not to be wrought on'.[40]

For Locke in the *Essay*, those who had not thoroughly examined to 'the bottom' all of their 'own Tenets' were 'unfit to prescribe to others'. These were both 'few in number' and found so 'little reason to be magisterial in their opinions' that 'nothing insolent and imperious is to be expected from them'. Locke stressed that in theological questions it was difficult to gather 'all the Particulars before us, that any way concern the Question' and men lacked the 'leisure, patience and means' to collect proofs. It was unavoidable that men would have 'several opinions'; this ought to lead men to 'maintain Peace, and the common offices of Humanity, and Friendship, in the diversity of Opinions'. Accenting sincerity in the search for truth over its attainment, for Locke 'he that...seeks sincerely to discover Truth...may have this satisfaction in doing his Duty as a rational Creature, that though he should miss Truth, he will not miss the reward of it'. One who did not search 'however he sometimes lights on Truth, is in the right but by chance; and I know not whether the luckiness of the accident will excuse the irregularity of the proceeding'.[41]

In his other writings, Locke further stressed the difficulties of those without leisure and literacy, and stressed sincerity in the search for truth. In the *Second Letter Concerning Toleration*, he argued that the use of force by national religions would promote false religion because most national religions were false and the 'greatest part of mankind, being not able to discern between truth and falsehood, that depend on long and many proofs, and remote consequences; nor having ability enough to discover the false grounds, and resist the captious and fallacious arguments of learned men versed in controversies; are so much more exposed...to be led into falsehood and error' than into truth. Locke attacked the arguments of Proast that force

<hr>

[40] Locke, *Essay*, III, ix–x; IV, xv–xvii, xx; *idem*, *Third Letter* in *Works*, 270–4, 283; Marshall, *Locke*, 351–7.

[41] Locke, *Essay*, IV, xvi, 3–4; xvii, 24; Marshall, *Locke*, 351–7.

should be used against those who had not examined the grounds of their religious commitments by arguing that 'if you will punish men till this be done, the countryman must leave off ploughing and sowing, and betake himself to the study of Greek and Latin; and the artisan must sell his tools, to buy fathers and schoolmen, and leave his family to starve'. For Locke, 'it is beyond the power or judgment of man, in that variety of circumstances, in respect of parts, tempers, opportunities, helps, etc men are in, in this world, to determine what is every one's duty in this great business of search, inquiry, examination; or to know when any one has done it'.

In the *Third Letter for Toleration*, Locke argued that understanding the Athanasian Creed was beyond the capacities of most in the population, writing that any one acquainted with 'a country parish' could not think that 'all the ploughmen and milkmaids at church understood all the propositions in Athanasius' Creed', and immediately adding that he himself thought that none would understand them all. Implicitly attacking the damnatory clauses of the Athanasian Creed still officially accepted in the Church of England (albeit opposed by John Tillotson, Archbishop of Canterbury and Locke's friend), Locke declared that he could not think himself authorised to pronounce them damned on this basis.[42] In the *Reasonableness* and its *Vindications*, Locke stressed that God seemed to have 'consulted the poor of this world, and the bulk of mankind' in designing necessary articles of religion 'that the labouring and illiterate man may comprehend': belief in Jesus as Saviour, resurrected, and now Lord, Judge and King.[43] In a lengthy note in his commonplace book 'Error' (1698), Locke argued that a 'ploughman that cannot read, is not so ignorant but he has a conscience, and knows in those few cases which concern his own actions, what is right and what is wrong'. If he sincerely obeyed this light of nature he would be led 'into all the truths in the Gospel that are necessary for him to know'. Accepting Christ as Lord and Master and sincerely attempting to live well was 'knowledge and orthodoxy enough for him, which will bring him to salvation' and was an 'orthodoxy which nobody can miss, who in earnest resolves to lead a good life'. All men were 'ignorant of many things contained in the Holy Scriptures' and held 'errours concerning doctrines delivered in the Scriptures'; this indicated that such 'cannot be damnable'. Ignorance in 'speculations which they have neither parts, opportunity, nor leisure to know' would not damn.[44]

The advocates of toleration in the 1680s and 1690s faced not merely the Catholic Church proclaiming its infallibility, but also the claims of an

---

[42] Locke, *Second Letter* in *Works*, 78, 102–3; *Third Letter* in *Works*, 410.
[43] Locke, *Reasonableness* in *Works*, VII, 157; Locke, *Vindication* in *Works*, VII, 175–7.
[44] J. Locke, *The Life and Letters of John Locke*, ed. P. King (London 1884), 282ff.; Marshall, *Locke*, 443–5.

inspired conscience delivering certainty composed by Protestants such as Jurieu, and Huguenot claims to be following synodical doctrine. In reply, they stressed fallibility. In his portion of the joint Le Cène–Le Clerc 1685 *Conversations*, Le Cène stressed that the Synod of Dort was not infallible.[45] Papin's *Faith Reduced* and its preface by Bayle declared that charity was necessary over 'dogmas' about which one could not have 'infallible certainty'. And Papin stressed that one should hold to the 'terms of Scripture' rather than to the explications of theologians or synods who were not 'infallible'.[46] Le Cène's 1687 *Conversations* warned against judging others as heretics when one was not infallible and might oneself be in error. Errors were 'inseparable from human nature'. In his preface to Lactantius' *Death of the Persecutors*, Burnet denied that 'there is such an infallible distinction in one man's nature from another, that the one is more like to be in the right than the other: Since therefore, among all those that differ, some must be in the wrong, those that have the power in their hands, may possibly be of the wrong side'.[47] In his *Life of Burnet*, Le Clerc stressed that 'if we would but consider that no Man is infallible, and that consequently one Man has no right to impose his Opinions on another, but only to require, that he do him no wrong, as he would expect no wrong himself, it would be very easie to bear with each other in the same society, nay in the same church, provided they imposed no other rule of faith or manners, but the holy scripture'.[48] In his *Life of Locke*, Le Clerc assaulted 'the strange and unaccountable temper of some men, who though they are fully convinced that their clear and distinct knowledge is of a very small extent, and that they are easily mistaken in the Judgments they pass of things' would yet persecute.[49]

Locke argued in the *Letter* that 'Princes indeed are born superior unto other men in power, but in nature equal. Neither the right, nor the art of ruling, does necessarily carry along with it the certain knowledge of other things; and least of all of the true religion.'[50] In the *Essay*, Locke stressed that Scripture was infallible, but that men could not 'but be very fallible in their understanding of it'. He urged that it would 'become us to be charitable one to another in our Interpretation or Misunderstandings of those Ancient Writings'. And he firmly distinguished faith from knowledge, arguing that religious opinions were held with varying degrees of probability short of the certainty of knowledge. Even those who were personally inspired by God were unable to communicate that inspiration to others, so

---

[45] [Le Cène and Le Clerc], *Entretiens*, 9.
[46] Papin, *Foi réduite*, preface, 33, 37–8, 45–7, 50–4.
[47] [Le Cène], *Conversations* (1687), 2–3; Burnet (ed.), *Death*, 16.
[48] Le Clerc, *Life of...Burnet*, 12.   [49] Le Clerc, *Life of Locke*, 17.
[50] Locke, *Letter* in *Works*, 25.

those to whom they attempted to communicate their revelation lacked certainty. In the *Third Letter*, he stressed that since 'remote matters of fact' were 'not capable of demonstration' no magistrate could demonstrate the fundamental articles of Christianity and magistrates therefore could have only 'faith...and not knowledge; persuasion, and not certainty'. Magistrates could not know 'the truths necessary to salvation' and if magistrates had a duty to use force to bring men to true religion it would be only 'to that religion which he believes to be true'.[51] In the *Second Vindication of the Reasonableness of Christianity*, Locke defined orthodoxy as 'right opinion' and then stressed that such orthodoxy 'has always modesty accompanying it, and a fair acknowledgement of fallibility in ourselves'. There was 'nothing more ridiculous' than for any man or company of men 'to assume the title of orthodoxy to their own set of opinions, as if infallibility were annexed to their systems...' and from thence 'erect to themselves a power to censure and condemn others...The consideration of human frailty ought to check this vanity'.[52]

And Bayle particularly strongly opposed arguments for certainty from gracious inspiration providing the basis for intolerance. Bayle noted in the *Philosophical Commentary* that he was 'free to own that tis Grace which makes us perceive' the 'Sense of Scripture' but stressed that even if this was accepted, it 'does not...afford us any certain and convincing Argument of the Sense which we believe true'. Bayle declared that faith afforded no 'Criterion of Orthodoxy' other than 'the inward Sentiment and Conviction of Conscience', and that this was a criterion common to the most 'heretical' souls. And in the entry Nicole in the *Dictionary*, Bayle sought to undermine the route to certainty of belief provided by Jurieu's theology of grace delivering both the knowledge of the truth to those graciously regenerated and the 'taste' of truth identifying it to them as 'truth'. He assaulted Jurieu's *True System* for arguing 'that the Faithful do not embrace Orthodoxy, by evident proofs, but by proofs of sentiment, and that they discern truth by taste, and not by distinct ideas'. For Bayle, 'when...Divines...reduce the analysis of faith to taste', they should support toleration. Identifying Jurieu's hypotheses of taste as 'the most proper that could be thought of to confirm' the tolerationist arguments of the *Philosophical Commentary*, Bayle suggested that in a logical debate, one would say that

I believe...because I have the taste and perception of it; and I also do the same, would another say. I do not pretend to convince you, would one say, by evident reasons, I know that you are able to elude all my proofs: nor I neither, would another say....I am persuaded, would the first add, that the internal operation of the spirit of God, has led

[51] Locke, *Third Letter* in *Works*, 144–5; Marshall, *Locke*, 354.
[52] Locke, *Second Vindication* in *Works*, 376.

me to Orthodoxy; and so am I, would the second affirm. Let us then dispute no more, let us persecute one another no more, would be their mutual resolution...Your taste would serve you in the room of a demonstration; just the same thing as in the article of eatables, we trust more to our palates, and the good effects they have upon our health, than to the speculative arguments of a Cook or a Physician; though we are not able to give any reason why these meats either please or strengthen us. Let us therefore agree on all sides not to disturb one another, and let us content ourselves with praying to God one for another.[53]

THE LEGITIMACY OF VARYING BELIEFS: 'FUNDAMENTAL ARTICLES', EXPLICATIONS, PHILOLOGY, AND PHILOSOPHY

Many of the advocates of toleration urged that Scripture distinguished between articles necessary to salvation and those that were not necessary, and that most disputes among Christians had been unnecessary disputes about opinions not required for salvation. They argued that Christians should require no more for communion – that is, for ecclesiastical toleration – than what was necessary to salvation, and that they should not persuade magistrates to punish over issues not necessary to salvation. Many specified the only fundamental doctrinal points of Christianity as contained in the Apostles' Creed. Papin's *Faith Reduced* celebrated the 'brevity and simplicity of [the] apostles creed', and Bayle's preface to it identified only 'holy scripture and the apostles creed' as deserving to be rules of belief. Aubert's *Pacific Protestant* specified the Apostles Creed together with the moral requirements of Christianity in the Ten Commandments as the fundamentals of Christianity.[54] Le Cène's *Conversations* stressed the limited numer of 'fundamental truths' of Christianity and the attempt to understand Scripture itself, declaring that everything necessary was contained in the Apostles' Creed, which required belief in one God; in one redeemer, Jesus Christ, who died and was resurrected for us; in the Holy Spirit; in the final judgment, and in the resurrection with eternal punishment and reward. It declared that the partisans of the Synod of Dort had erred in anathematising any who denied their articles as 'heretics', and quoted Chillingworth in arguing that the Bible was the religion of Protestants, and not the creed of any particular sect.[55] For Strimesius in *De pace ecclesiastica*, the fundamental doctrines were: faith in Jesus Christ as the unique mediator between God and men, sanctification, and faith animated by charity. Nothing else was fundamental.[56] Some advocates of toleration

---

[53] Bayle, *Philosophical Commentary*, 341 (*Philosophical Commentary*, ed. Tannenbaum, 183; *Commentaire philosophique*, 340–1); *Dictionary*, Nicole C; Lennon, 'Taste'.

[54] Papin, *Foi réduite*, preface; 2; Aubert de Versé, *Protestant*, 21.

[55] Le Cène, *Conversations*, 8–11, 24–7, 38–48, 52–3, 56.

[56] Strimesius, *De pace, passim*.

further stressed that the very definition of fundamental articles would vary between individuals, as people had different abilities and circumstances and only God knew what was necessary to each to believe. Van Paets opposed articles being held to be absolutely necessary. For van Paets, sects divided over 'necessary articles' should avow that they were divided over non-necessary matters rather than abandon the principle of the Reformation in declaring that knowledge of necessary articles was not easy to acquire. Bayle stressed that invocation of the 'fundamentals of Christianity' settled nothing, for what was fundamental to one was not to another. And he noted that even if such fundamentals could be shown to be violated, toleration would still be owed, as it was to Jews.[57]

In the *Theologia Christiana*, Limborch set out to 'enquire what the Duty of the Church is with respect to those that are simply erroneous, or who holding the same Fundamentals with our selves, do yet dissent from us in the Explication of some Doctrines not destructive of salvation'. In order to achieve this, he sought to 'establish the difference between Articles necessary to salvation, and those which are not' by showing by what 'signs and tokens a necessary article ought to be distinguished from that which is not necessary', and that 'a mutual toleration ought to be admitted between Persons dissenting from each other in Articles not necessary'. For Limborch, 'some Divines, averse to Peace and Unity, and breathing forth nothing but strife and Contention' had called 'so clear and manifest a truth' as the very distinction between fundamental and non-fundamental doctrines 'into Question', and even 'expressly' denied it by 'declaring that all articles are fundamental, and that every error in Religion renders a Man guilty of eternal Damnation'. For Limborch, the distinction between fundamental and non-fundamental articles was scriptural and apostolic, and Scripture made a 'manifest distinction between the Foundation and that which is built upon it'. Salvation could be obtained even when one 'built upon' the foundation 'vain, inefficacious and erroneous Doctrines'. Scripture required only 'two things as necessary to salvation, viz, Faith in God and Jesus Christ, and Obedience or Holiness of Life grounded upon the Expectation of the Divine Promises'. But although 'there really is but one Foundation of Salvation, viz, the Lord Christ Jesus, yet upon the account of the various Effects it has upon the Work of our Salvation, it may be...branch'd out into many Particulars, which shall all agree in one and the same truth...Under these things evidently expressed in the Scripture, we comprehend those which are so necessarily annx'd to them, that they may be deduced from them by a necessary connexion, and which have been believed by all Christians, at all Times and in all Places. The

---

[57] Van Paets, *Lettre*, 33–4; Bayle, *Philosophical Commentary* (1708), 269–70 (*Philosophical Commentary*, ed. Tannenbaum, 149; *Commentaire philosophique*, 280).

summary of which is contain'd in that which is vulgarly call'd the Apostles Creed'. Furthermore, since 'those things are necessary, without which the Practice of Piety and the Hopes of Eternal Life cannot subsist', 'the Doctrine concerning the Resurrection of Jesus Christ' was vital. For Limborch, 'If all the Doctrines of Christianity were to be examined by these Rules' it would be found 'that those which are necessary are very few in comparison of those many that are either not necessary, or are very useless and hurtful'. It would be understood that 'The Controversies among Christians about Doctrines necessary to salvation are very rare, and that they generally agree in these points, especially if they have a due regard for the Scriptures'. Limborch declared that 'every truth necessary to be believed in order to [achieve] eternal salvation...is comprehended under one single truth, that Jesus is the Christ'.[58]

Le Clerc, Limborch's Arminian protégé and friend, voiced similar themes in many of his own works from the 1680s to the 1730s, in his extensive correspondence, and in editing his journals from the 1680s to the 1700s. In 1684, Le Clerc declared that 'God has not given us the truth of the Gospel to make us philosophers...That which relates to the necessary truths of religion which are sufficiently general and few in number, the New Testament leads us much more certainly than abstract reasoning. We are much more convinced of the truth of the Christian faith than we could be by Metaphysical reasoning which is full of obscurities and contradictions'. For Le Clerc, it was necessary 'that Scripture contains the instructions...so clearly that even the most simple can understand them; otherwise it would be necessary to seek light outside of Scripture. If Scripture contains the fundamentals in a manner so clear that they are proportionate to the most simple, one would not need to resort to Tradition; and if they could only be understood by scholars, the simple people would have to refer to the educated or to Tradition'. Specifying what it was necessary to believe, Le Clerc listed: the resurrection; that there was a God as referred to in the Scripture; that God was 'merciful; and that he loves virtue and hates vice, and that he does not lie, and that he is all powerful and eternal and able to make us happy if he wishes. It is not necessary to know any more than this to obey him'.[59] In editing Grotius' *On the Truth of Christianity*, Le Clerc followed Grotius in declaring that prudent men took knowledge from 'the fountain', not from 'the creed or confession of faith of any particular church' but 'only the Books of the New Testament'; in

---

[58] Limborch, *Compleat System*, 497, 994–9; *idem*, *Theologia Christiana*, 403, 835–8. Locke drew attention in May 1695 to Limborch's declaration that the single truth necessary for salvation was that Jesus is the Christ, in correspondence with Limborch: *Correspondence*, 1901; Locke, *Reasonableness*, lxv; V. Nuovo, *Locke and Christianity* (Bristol 1997).

[59] Le Clerc, *Parrhasiana*, 30–1; Le Clerc to Chouet, 18 December 1684, Universiteits Bibliotheek, Amsterdam MS N 24 fo. 89 & *Sentimens*, 405, 407, in Klauber, 'Fundamental Articles', 629–31; M. C. Pitassi, *Entre croire et savoir*.

explication of doctrine, he followed the example of the Apostles' Creed and 'avoided all Expresssions which have caused any Controversies amongst Christians'. The only requirement that could be imposed on Christians was 'that they embrace whatever they think is contained in the books of the New Testament'.[60]

Many of the advocates of toleration specifically condemned the imposition of 'explications', stressing the words of Scripture against imposed catechisms and creeds. Papin's *Faith Reduced* argued against adding explications, including the use of 'barbarous' terms to explicate the inexplicable relationship of Father, Son and Holy Ghost. Noting that anti-tolerationists argued that by their explications they added nothing and merely 'explained the sense' of Scripture, Papin argued that while claiming to follow Scripture alone, they added their own interpretations and traditions.[61] In his *De pace ecclesiastica*, Strimesius argued against the imposition of confessions of faith and articles of faith requiring belief in obscure doctrines. He stressed the duty of reunion among Christians and argued that it should be achieved by return to the word of Scripture. For Strimesius, explications were not fundamental articles. If they involved the imposition of a particular sense on Scripture against others who followed the words of Scripture, this was to prefer human judgment to God's, to suggest that God lacked power to reveal clearly what was necessary to salvation, and to contradict the Protestant doctrine of the perfection and clarity of Scripture. All of these features of Strimesius' argument were emphasised in its lengthy 1688 review in the *Bibliothèque universelle*. In 1689, Burnet declared that he had 'often marvelled at the effrontery with which the Reformed Churches, to whom Ecclesiastical Infallibility is abhorrent, can require from all their members these forms of subscriptions; by which one is bound to acquiesce in every proposition which has found place in the Confession of Faith; though it is not easy for an honest man...to swallow at a gulp, a complete system. And should there ever dawn a hope of reconciling the Churches, the plan adopted must be, not to endeavour after unity of opinion, which cannot be expected, but so to arrange it that such as differ in opinion may live peaceably side by side'.[62]

In many of his writings, Le Clerc particularly stressed historical and philological attempts to understand the express words of Scripture against the imposition of philosophic explications of obscure doctrines in the text. Le Clerc's portion of the 1685 *Conversations* centred on argument designed to 'destroy the prejudice' in favour of metaphysical reasoning in general, and anathematised the application of Platonic, Aristotelian, Cartesian, and

---

[60] Grotius, *De veritate*, ed. J. Le Clerc, 299–300.   [61] Papin, *Foi réduite*, 2ff., 10, 27, 33.

[62] Strimesius, *De pace ecclesiastica*, *passim*; Cornand, *Bibliothèque universelle*, VIII (1688), 296–307; Foxcroft, *Life of Burnet*, II, 275–6.

Malebranchian metaphysics to explain 'articles of faith'. Le Clerc declared the necessity of distinguishing fundamental articles from those which were not, and the great importance to both the 'republic of letters' and to Christianity itself of reviving long-exiled 'charity and peace'.[63] He condemned many theologians for destroying religion and putting in its place philosophy, and for creating 'a religion entirely metaphysical'. His first discourse argued that such philosophic theologians had replaced the word of God with 'purely human reasonings', and attacked 'scholastic subtleties' and 'contradictions'. Le Clerc argued that about many things God had given knowledge of what it was necessary to know, while leaving much unknown. He attacked the use of violence against those who would not receive 'explications', and the torturing of the prophets and apostles to make them speak as metaphysicians, and crucially itemised almost all major doctrines then being imposed by force as 'orthodoxy' in listing 'various speculations of metaphysical theologians about the Trinity, the necessity of satisfaction, original sin, grace, free will, the existence of bodies, and various other matters'. His following discourses documented 'various articles of religion obscured by the subtleties of metaphysicians' and various passages of Scripture badly interpreted by metaphysicians. Among those he attacked most forcefully for their 'metaphysical theology' were the 'predestinarians' of the Synod of Dort, whom he accused of developing a novel doctrine which had manifestly destroyed the compassion and sincerity of God. For Le Clerc, they were among the theologians rendering Christianity 'ridiculous'; in order to save Christianity from ridicule, they needed to be opposed. And he explicitly attacked theologians unwilling to be 'content with the words of Scripture' who had developed many words to define the doctrine of the Trinity which could not even be translated into French from Latin because they were meaningless.[64]

Le Clerc was at least primary author of the 1685 *Opinions of Some Divines*, issued anonymously in reply to Simon's *Critical History*, which attacked interpretation of the Scripture by catechisms and creeds as the substitution of human authority for divine, and complained that 'each group forms its own idea of religion or rather follows that of the society in which they were born...and haughtily condemns whatever appears contrary to their catechism. Thus the phrase "Analogy of faith" is virtually equivalent to the words "church", "orthodox", and "heretic". Each group "pretends to be the Church of orthodoxy, and holds such a title with much pride and vanity"'. The work included two letters – very probably both also by

---

[63] Le Cène and Le Clerc, *Entretiens*, sig. a4v–sig. a6r; 240–1.
[64] Le Cène and Le Clerc, *Entretiens*, sig. a4v–sig. a6r; 207–382, esp. 225–6, 231, 235–6, 270–1, 291–7.

Le Clerc – which argued that the Bible was not entirely inspired, and that the purpose of the Bible was to make good men and not good critics. These letters attacked theologians' 'subtleties' in explication of words which had created endless disputes and debates and thus lost the spirit of Christianity itself.[65] The *Opinions* urged that claiming that every word in the Bible was inspired and quibbling over irrelevant matters opened to ridicule from libertines the authority of Scripture and of clerics, and argued that an emphasis on moral duty and a desire to distinguish the fundamentals of Christianity from the niceties of theologians was the desirable response. Locke and Limborch were among those who discussed the work, with Locke noting the importance of finding a criterion thus to distinguish 'fundamentals' of Christianity.[66]

Le Clerc criticised several of the Fathers for their adoption of Platonic and scholastic explications of Christianity in a series of *Lives* of the Fathers which he published initially in his *Bibliothèque universelle* and later as separate works. Le Clerc's *Life of Eusebius* tied orthodox Trinitarianism to Platonic philosophy, and attacked the application of the term 'heretic' to any who denied explications of the gospel based on philosophy. His *Life* of Gregory Nazianzen declared of Gregory's praise of the church of Nazianzum a 'considerable commendation, viz, that they made piety to consist, not in speaking much of God, but in being silent and obeying him'. He continued: 'If ancient and modern Divines had endeavoured to deserve that Praise, Christianity would not have been torn by so many disputes, nor would it be so now'. Le Clerc's discussion immediately following this laudation was of Trinitarianism and anti-Trinitarianism, and it declared that the words 'substance' and 'hypostasis' should not be used since they were not scriptural. Le Clerc then declared persecution 'odious'. Le Clerc's account of Clemens Alexandrinus identified Clement as explaining Christ's divinity through Platonism and as having 'explicated' Christianity by doctrines found in the philosophers. He attacked Gregory's writings as 'full of figures' and thus a breeding ground for obscurity. For Le Clerc, many divines spoke obscurely because 'they do not apprehend things more clearly than they speak them'. Locke's copies of the *Bibliothèque* in his private library include many page references to Le Clerc's critical *Lives* of the Fathers, suggesting that he had studied them very carefully; it is exceedingly likely that this message received Locke's assent.[67] Many of Le Clerc's reviews of others'

---

[65] Le Clerc, *Sentimens*, 449, in Klauber, 'Fundamental Articles', 621–3; Pitassi, *Entre croire*.

[66] Morman, *Aubert*, 46–52; Marshall, *Locke*, 338–41.

[67] Le Clerc, *Bibliothèque universelle*, x (1688), 379–496; Golden, *Le Clerc*, 140–1; Le Clerc, *Lives*, 28–31, 183–4, 202; *Bibliothèque universelle* in Locke's *Library*, page references to e.g. 23, 34, 89, 125 (Bodleian Library).

works in the *Bibliothèque universelle* and *Bibliothèque choisie* stressed the unimportance of 'speculative articles' and challenged the imposition of explications, and in his review of Locke's *Reasonableness* he stressed that reliance on Scripture and opposition to imposed explications was the fundamental principle of the Reformation itself.[68]

Le Clerc's *Parrhasiana*, a miscellaneous work of criticism, attacked the ancient poets as filling their poetry full of the 'trash of the pagan divinities' and identified the danger in reading them of losing 'good taste and right judgement'. This prepared the ground for assertion that the 'same effects' came from 'reading of authors of a quite different character', 'the fathers of the church, but especially the latines'. Le Clerc criticised modern readers for 'being resolved beforehand to find them polite and solid, and humbly to sacrifice their reason to them' when in fact their writings were full of 'false thoughts and ill reasonings' and their imagination had been 'heated by the enthusiasms of a false rhetoric'. For Le Clerc, the Fathers and philosophers after Christ's day were not 'just reasoners' or methodical arguers; that 'which keeps up this language...is that every man cites the fathers in theological controversies and desires to have them of his own side; yet this could not be done with any advantage, if people were generally persuaded that they were bad orators and yet worse logicians'. It took their antiquity to make us 'bear with them'. Undermining their authority, Le Clerc recommended instead the need for clear reasoning in order to 'enlighten' the mind. And he argued that it was important to stress both that 'speculative errors don't corrupt the manners of those who are engaged in them' and that the mixture of good and bad 'in the conduct of life is almost equal between the orthodox and the heretics'.[69]

In the *Letter Concerning Toleration*, Locke argued that it was 'more agreeable to the church of Christ, to make the conditions of her communion consist in such things, and such things only, as the Holy Spirit has in the Holy Scriptures declared, in express words, to be necessary to salvation' than 'for men to impose their own inventions and interpretations upon others, as if they were of divine authority; and to establish by ecclesiastical laws, as absolutely necessary to the profession of Christianity, such things as the Holy Scriptures do either not mention, or at least not expressly command'. He argued that those who professed articles which seemed to them agreeable to Scripture did well, but that such 'consequences deduced from Scripture' ought not to be obtruded on others to whom these were not 'indubitable doctrines of the Scripture'. And he identified not merely Lutherans and Calvinists but also Remonstrants and Anabaptists among those sects

[68] Le Clerc, *Bibliothèque choisie*, II, 302.
[69] Le Clerc, *Parrhasiana* (1700), 5–7, 87–8, 96, 129.

whose opinions had been presented by 'the contrivers of symbols, systems, and confessions' as necessary deductions from the Scripture, indicting the arrogance of those who thought that they could 'explain things necessary to salvation more clearly than the Holy Ghost'.[70]

In the *Essay*, Locke argued that the signification of words depended on 'the thoughts, notions, and ideas of him that uses them' and were 'unavoidably of great uncertainty, to men of the same Language and Country'. This was magnified in 'different countries and remote ages, wherein the speakers and writers had very different notions, tempers, customs, ornaments, and figures of speech'. Many men, well satisfied of the 'meaning of a text if scripture' had 'by consulting commentators, quite lost the sense of it' and 'drawn obscurity upon the place'. The 'several sects of Philosophy and Religion' had exacerbated the problem by coining 'insignificant' words in order to affect 'something singular', to support 'strange Opinions', or to cover weaknesses in their hypotheses. The 'mischief' of perplexed meanings, especially due to the Schoolmen, had 'obscured and perplexed the material Truths of Law and Divinity'. The precepts of 'natural religion' were legible; those revealed in 'Books and Languages' were liable to 'the common and natural obscurities and difficulties incident to Words'. For Locke, it would 'become us to be more careful and diligent in observing the former, and less magisterial, positive, and imperious, in imposing our sense and interpretations of the latter'.[71]

Locke maintained many of these arguments in the 1690s. In his 1692 *Third Letter*, he argued that those are most 'authors and promoters of sects and divisions, who impose creeds, and ceremonies and articles of men's making...who narrow Christianity within bounds of their own making, which the gospel knows nothing of'. He contended that the 'bond of unity might be preserved, in the different persuasions of men concerning things not necessary to salvation, if they were not made necessary to church communion'. He railed against 'needless impositions and moot points in divinity' being 'established by the penal laws of kingdoms'. He condemned 'articles and distinctions set up by men without authority from Scripture'. For Locke, 'an agreement in truths necessary to salvation, and the maintaining of charity and brotherly kindness with the diversity of opinions in other things' was 'that which will very well consist with christian unity, and is all possibly to be had in this world, in such an incurable weakness and difference of men's understandings'.[72] For Locke in the *Third Letter*, even the Apostles' Creed, which contained 'all the credenda necessary to salvation', was not to be

---

[70] Locke, *Letter* in *Works*, 15, 56–7.
[71] Marshall, *Locke*, 353–5; Locke, *Essay*, III, *passim*, esp. cix, x.
[72] Locke, *Third Letter*, 237–40; Marshall, *Locke*, 375–6.

imposed by the magistrate because it contained in addition things not 'absolutely necessary to salvation'. For Locke, creeds which were not in the 'words of divine revelation' and which claimed to 'explain and determine the sense of some obscure and dubious places of Scripture' included 'explication not being of divine revelation, [which] though sound to one man, may be unsound to another, and cannot be imposed as truths necessary to salvation'. In *Some Thoughts*, Locke recommended educating children by using the Cambridge Platonist and Latitudinarian John Worthington's catechism because it had all its 'answers in the precise Words of Scripture, a thing of good example, and such a sound form of words, that no Christian can except against'.[73]

Locke's 1695 *Reasonableness* and its *Vindications* urged that the only necessary belief to become a Christian was that Jesus was the Messiah. Christians were then to search Scripture for themselves and to believe what they understood it to state as doctrine. In the *Second Vindication*, he accused sects who judged the meaning of Scripture by their 'systems' of turning Scripture into 'a nose of wax, to be turned and bent, just as may fit the contrary orthodoxies of different societies'. Locke complained that 'almost every distinct society of christians' – including Socinians – 'magisterially ascribes orthodoxy to a select set of fundamentals, distinct from those proposed in the preaching of our Saviour and the Apostles'. Locke stressed in the *Vindication* and *Second Vindication*, in reply to John Edwards' protests that the *Reasonableness* had ignored many fundamental articles of Christianity, such as the Trinity and satisfaction, that it was 'every christian's duty to read, search and study the holy scriptures: and make this their great business'. A 'sincere endeavour' to understand them was required. Where there was obscurity, 'either in the expressions themselves, or by reason of the seeming contrariety of other passages', a 'fair endeavour', as much as 'circumstances' permitted, secured from sinful error 'which way soever our inquiry resolves the doubt, or perhaps leaves it unresolved'. Everyone was obliged to believe as a 'fundamental article' what 'he understands to be truth, delivered by our Saviour, or the apostles commissioned by him, and assisted by his Spirit'. The result was that 'almost every particular man' would end with a 'distinct catalogue of fundamentals' and that 'no body can tell what is fundamental to another, what is necessary for another men to believe'. This 'catalogue of fundamentals, every one alone can make for himself: no body can fix it for him; no body can collect or prescribe it to another'.[74] Locke stressed that Anabaptists, Quakers, Arminians, Socinians, Lutherans and papists disagreed on 'fundamentals', and that even when they agreed

---

[73] Locke, *Third Letter* in *Works*, 153–4; Marshall, *Locke*, 372.
[74] Locke, *Vindication*, 165, 176; Locke, *Second Vindication* in *Works*, VII, 228–34, 244–5, 289, 295–6, 351, 390, 408.

about texts, 'all men do not understand those texts alike, and some may draw articles out of them quite different from your system; and so, though they agree in the same texts, may not agree in the same fundamentals'.[75] For Locke, even if Edwards could generate a list of articles, there was a question about who was 'to explain your articles', and an expectation that they would be differently explained by 'papists' and the 'Reformed', by 'Remonstrants' and 'anti-Remonstrants', and by Trinitarians and Unitarians. It was doubtful if 'any articles, which need men's explications' could be as clearly understood as the proposition that Jesus is the Messiah, which did not 'need any explication at all'.[76]

Locke stressed that the gospel had been preached to the simple and ignorant. Suited to their understandings, and to the limited capacities which they possessed for leisure and study, it did not require belief in philosophic explications of obscure doctrines. In the *Vindication*, he expanded upon his declaration in the 1692 *Third Letter* that the Apostles' Creed itself contained unnecessary articles, pointing out that that creed declared that Christ was 'born of the virgin Mary, suffered under Pontius Pilate, was crucified, dead, and buried' but that even Edwards did not press these as fundamental doctrines which Locke had ignored. But he stressed particularly that the Apostles' Creed had been taken in the first ages of the church to contain 'all things necessary to salvation', and that it was 'well for the compilers of that creed, that they lived not in Mr Edwards's days' for he would have charged them with Socinianism for their failure to declare the Trinitarian 'doctrines he collects out of John i and John xiv'.[77] Locke's *Paraphrases on the Epistles of St Paul*, his final and posthumously published work, sought to interpret Paul's epistles by examining his style, purposes, and the possible contemporary meanings of the texts, by eschewing all later philosophic accretions, and by emphasising that since they were directed to those who were already Christians, they had not been intended as an explication of necessary matters of belief for those entering Christianity.

Le Clerc's reviews of Locke's religious writings in his various journals of the 'republic of letters' emphasised these themes, in which, as we have just seen, Locke's arguments often paralleled Le Clerc's own arguments, together with those of many other apologists for toleration in the 1680s and 1690s (and those of several important predecessors in argument for toleration whose works Locke purchased and read or re-read in this period, including Acontius and Chillingworth). Reviewing the *Reasonableness of Christianity* in the *Bibliothèque choisie*, Le Clerc stressed Locke's argument that the only required belief for baptism was that Jesus Christ was the Messiah, which

---

[75] Locke, *Second Vindication*, 217–18.   [76] Locke, *Vindication*, 178.
[77] Locke, *Vindication* in *Works*, 166–7, 169.

necessarily further required an attempt to understand Scripture and to believe sincerely all that one understood to be the doctrine of Jesus Christ, and to perform his commandmants, but did not require study of 'controversies' and 'difficult speculations'. And he stressed that according to Locke Christians were not obliged to receive a certain number of articles from some theologian, but all that they found in the New Testament to be the will of God. What was fundamental for one was not fundamental for another.[78] Reviewing the *Paraphrase* in his *Bibliothèque choisie*, Le Clerc noted Locke's concentration on explicating Paul by examining his intended audience in the composition of his letters rather than in terms of the philosophy which had especially influenced theologians' explications of the Old and New Testament: Platonism and then scholasticism. And he stressed that it was 'vain' to explicate Scriptural expressions by 'our philosophy'.[79]

This series of arguments about fundamental articles, explications, philology and philosophy advanced by many apologists for toleration in the 1680s and 1690s clearly excluded the central doctrine of 'orthodoxy' for the past millennium, the doctrine of the Trinity, from the list of 'fundamental' or 'necessary' articles of Christianity, whatever the personal views of these authors were about the doctrine of the Trinity (which seem to have included views that varied from broadly Trinitarian through to Christologically Unitarian).[80]

---

[78] Le Clerc, *Bibliothèque choisie*, II, 285–8, 294–5; MS Locke c9, 20; MS Locke c33, 20; MS Locke d10, 131.

[79] Le Clerc, *Bibliothèque choisie*, XIII, 37–73, at 60–2.

[80] The advocates of toleration discussed in this section of the book – from Aubert and Le Cène to Burnet – were all attacked as 'Socinians'. Burnet seems to have remained a Trinitarian who opposed the imposition of Trinitarianism in the 1680s and then countenanced communion with Socinians, but became worried by the 1690s, as he became an Anglican bishop, about Socinian hostility to Trinitarians as 'idolaters' for worshipping a 'creature'. Aubert in the 1680s, and probably Le Cène by the 1690s, and perhaps earlier, seem to have been Christologically Unitarians. Le Cène's manuscript collection includes many works by Socinians which he seems to have translated with an eye to publication. Aubert and Papin were to convert to Catholicism in the 1690s and to give among their reasons for conversion that Protestantism was required to tolerate Socinians. Consistently believing that Protestantism must tolerate Socinianism, in the 1680s this was for them an argument for toleration, and in the 1690s an argument that they must convert because Protestantism lacked the principles to justify punishing the heresy of Socinianism. Limborch supported the eternal deity of Christ, but also suggested a subordination of Christ and the Holy Spirit to the Father. Le Clerc's position on the Trinity is hard to classify. Le Clerc stressed that he opposed the use of terms in explication of the Trinity and the subleties of the scholastics. He was on several occasions to issue works which he proclaimed opposed Socinus in upholding 'two natures' in Christ and that Christ was the 'most high God'. He registered to Locke his desire to separate his thought from contemporary Unitarianism. Stressing historical and philological approaches to Scripture, he interpreted the Logos in St John's Gospel as Divine Reason, apparently a quality rather than a substance, and left it unclear how he might subscribe to the positions of orthodox Trinitarianism without their concepts and language. Sympathetic readers of Le Clerc's works worried that he was unorthodox, while unsympathetic readers concluded that he was a Socinian or at least a Sabellian heretic and so 'three

Argument that the non-Trinitarian Apostles' Creed contained all fundamental articles implicitly rendered Trinitarianism unnecessary. And many other arguments surveyed over the preceding pages more explicitly rendered contemporary Trinitarianism either doctrinally unnecessary or a questionable belief. Le Clerc's *Theological Epistles* depicted two students unlearned in philosophy studying the Bible and then debating; one had become a Unitarian and the other a Trinitarian. Le Clerc concluded the debate by arguing for moderation and charity, with toleration of different opinions, as long as both sides maintained the opinions that God has all perfections and that Christ died to save men.[81] Le Clerc's portion of the 1685 *Conversations* assaulting metaphysical theology argued that if men had held to 'the simplicity of Scripture' there would have been fewer disputes among Christians; these had arisen from the formation of a metaphysical idea of the doctrine 'more exact and distinct' than Scripture's own terms furnished. They should have been content to say that there was a 'certain distinction' in the sole divine essence. He attacked the word 'Person' as not appropriate to aid understanding of an 'incomprehensible' matter. And he attacked the further explications of this doctrine by Trinitarians who had 'invented terms'. The words 'essence, substance, hypostasis, person and manner of being' were all 'so obscure' and had been differently understood by the Fathers. He condemned the metaphysicians for not being content with the terms of Scripture for expressing what it was necessary to believe about the doctrine, and for inventing new terms as if they were better able to express the point than Jesus and the apostles. Recognising that the terms were 'ambiguous', Le Clerc questioned the authority by which they could determine the sense of Scripture and impose the necessity of understanding them in their 'explication'. For Le Clerc, the imposition of absurd and contradictory explanations of the doctrine had aided in the rejection of Christianity by Jews and Muslims, had given Socinians ample ammunition, and had led many to 'libertinism'.[82] For Limborch, much contemporary orthodoxy consisted of words 'of which there is no mention made in Scripture, but such as merely depend on human traditions and decrees', such as 'many Superstitions in the Church of Rome' and many 'Phrases and

quarters Socinian'. Burnet thought that Le Clerc had not cleared himself of the accusation of Sabellianism even in replying to the accusations of Socinianism, and in the 1690s refused to help Le Clerc obtain an English position. Le Clerc's accounts of the thought of the Fathers provided ammunition for Unitarians wishing to document the perversion of primitive Christianity by philosophic impositions and for charging that the Trinity was such an imposition. Jacques Souverain, a Unitarian persecuted by Huguenot ministers, utilised and cited extensively many of Le Clerc's arguments from various of his works in composing two essentially Socinian (or Artemonite) attacks on Trinitarianism, one of which was copied into Locke's personal papers.

[81] Le Clerc, *Epistolae*; Klauber, 'Fundamental Articles'; Barnes, *Le Clerc*, 62.
[82] Le Cène and Le Clerc, *Entretiens*, 291–7; my 'Locke, Socinianism', 136.

manners of expression not used in Holy Writ', but instead invented and received by 'the consent of many persons, nay of whole Councils, for the better Explanation of some one doctrine' to which 'no man is tied up. . .since they are not Scriptural expressions. Such are the Words Trinity, Person, Homoousion, Merit, Satisfaction, with the like, which are not only of a doubtful meaning, but are also no where to be met with in Scripture in the same sense which is at present applied to them'.[83] Locke's *Second Reply* to Stillingfleet denied that the propositions that 'there are three persons in one nature, or there are two natures and one person' were in the Bible, and added that 'whoever shall say that they are propositions in the Scripture, when there are no such words, so put together, to be found in holy writ, seems to me to make a new scripture in words and propositions, that the Holy Ghost dictated not'.[84]

Aubert's *Treatise* condemned the way in which those who did not understand the Trinity and incarnation as did others had been called 'blasphemous' Unitarians when they had attacked the follies and 'contradictions' of scholastics, and its final two chapters argued for toleration among various explications and suggested that contemporary Trinitarianism was diametrically opposed to the beliefs of the first centuries and included incomprehensible phrases, such as hypostatic union. Aubert's *Pacific Protestant* argued that there was a duty to tolerate all Christians who accepted the fundamental points of Christianity, including Socinians who differed on their 'explications' of words such as 'satisfaction' but held the essential doctrines of Christianity. He noted that Arminians such as Episcopius and Courcelles had argued that there was a duty to tolerate Socinians in the church. And he attacked various terms of orthodox Trinitarianism as explications that were 'incomprehensible, contradictory, and inexplicable'.[85] Le Cène's 1687 *Conversations* argued that before the Council of Nicaea, the eternal generation of the Son had been regarded as a matter of 'little importance'.[86] Papin's *Faith Reduced* argued against the imposition of 'barbarous' terms 'forged in the Schools' and unknown in Scripture for explicating the 'inexplicable' relationship between Father, Son and Holy Ghost.[87] For Strimesius, not merely political but also ecclesiastical toleration was to be provided for moderate Socinians who only doubted particular doctrines, or the explications that the 'orthodox' gave to those dogmas. If Socinians did not themselves condemn others, they could be admitted to worship. While Bayle criticised Socinianism in the *Dictionary*, and in the *Philosophical Commentary* criticised the extensiveness of Socinians'

[83] Limborch, *Compleat System*, 999–1000; *idem, Theologia Christiana*, 839.
[84] Locke, *Second Reply*, in *Works*, III, 343.
[85] Aubert de Versé, *Traité*, 20, chs. 6–7; *idem, Protestant*, II, 20–77.
[86] Le Cène, *Conversations*, 80–3.   [87] Papin, *Foi réduite*, 3.

application of reason, he declared in the *Commentary* that Socinians deserved toleration, were not blasphemers because they did not deny a God in whom they believed, and were not motivated by corruption to deny the Trinity. In the *Supplement*, he pilloried as the source of continued religious controversies the application of reason and faith by his contemporaries who used the 'purest ideas of natural reason' and incontestable philosophy against the real presence by arguing that 'whatever implies a contradiction' was impossible, but then defended the doctrine of the Trinity against Socinianism with statements of the 'incomprehensibility of the divine nature', the 'darkness' of our 'weak reason' and the need to captivate reason to the 'yoke of faith'.[88]

These advocates of toleration also made clear that on other doctrines for which they were being anathematised and denied toleration in the 1680s and 1690s, Socinians and others held tolerable beliefs. Contemporary 'orthodoxy' upheld the resurrection of the same body and immortal soul, and anathematised those who denied this as having no certainty of the resurrection of the same individuals to reward and punishment. But Limborch, Le Clerc, and (from the date of his revisions to the *Essay*) Locke declared this an imposition on scriptural Christianity, which spoke only of the resurrection of the dead. As we saw in Chapter 20, in his *History of the Inquisition*, Limborch declared tolerable those medieval heretics who had disbelieved in the resurrection of the same body but believed in the resurrection of the dead. For Limborch, the 'Resurrection of the Dead' was 'the foundation of our whole salvation', but it was not 'necessary to determine, whether the same numerical bodies are to be raised again, or whether God will produce at the resurrection other spiritual and glorious bodies in their steads, and unite them to the souls of the faithful'.[89] In his edition of Grotius' *De veritate religionis christianae*, Le Clerc testified that it was not necessary that the matter that is raised 'should be numerically the same with that the dying man carried to the grave with him'; 'provided it be the same soul' it could be called the resurrection of the body 'when a like one is formed by God out of the earth and joined to the mind'. In his *Treatise of the Causes of Incredulity*, Le Clerc identified himself as knowing that the Dead shall rise but not 'distinctly the manner and Circumstances of the Resurrection'. In the first editions of the *Essay*, Locke spoke of the resurrection of the bodies of the dead. But Locke amended later editions of the *Essay* to declare that Scripture spoke only of the resurrection of the dead and not of the same numerical body. His defence of the *Essay* against Edward Stillingfleet's argument that the

---

[88] Bayle, *Philosophical Commentary* (1708), 265–7, 344–5, 612–13 (*Philosophical Commentary*, ed. Tannenbaum, 147–8, 184; *Commentaire philosophique*, 276–80, 344); Bayle, *OD*, II, 522.

[89] Limborch, *Compleat System*, 1002; *idem, Theologia Christiana*, 841.

Christian faith required belief in resurrection of the same body acknowledged that the resurrection of the dead was 'an article of the Christian faith' but spent more than thirty pages in denying that the resurrection of the same body was such an article. His posthumously published *Paraphrase* denied that the resurrection would be of the same body.[90]

Orthodox Calvinist Huguenots in the 1680s, led by Jurieu, identified 'fundamental articles' of Christianity as rejected not merely by Socinians but also by Arminians, Amyraldists, Pajonists, Quakers, and Anabaptists. As we saw in Chapter 4, requiring subscription to the articles of the Synod of Dort to qualify for ministry in the Huguenot Church, these Huguenots maintained in exile the long-standing exclusion from the ministry of Amyraldists, Pajonists, and Arminians formerly practised in seventeenth-century France, deprived several authors of works on toleration of ministerial positions, and specifically condemned their works in synods in the Netherlands. In this context, in the 1680s, many of the advocates of toleration specifically defended the views of these groups as deserving toleration. Aubert's *Pacific Protestant* stressed that Arminians deserved ecclesiastical as well as civil toleration, and condemned supralapsarian arguments for reprobation to sin.[91] The 1685 *Conversations* by Le Cène and Le Clerc defended the importance of mediate grace through education and example against the condemnation of that account as 'Pelagian heresy' by Jurieu and others, offered alternate readings to orthodox Calvinism on original sin, free will, and predestination, and attacked the requirement that ministers had to accept all of the articles of the Synod of Dort or be declared heretics. Le Clerc itemised unnecessary metaphysical explications as including those about 'the necessity of satisfaction, original sin, grace, free will'.[92]

Limborch argued that it was not necessary to believe 'Such things as are not clearly expressed in Scripture, but deduc'd from thence by obscure subtle and far-fetched consequences, for the discovering of which there is need of great parts, or which are only founded on metaphysical speculations of which nature are many of those points disputed in the schools, about the nature, essence, attributes, and decrees of God'.[93] Le Cène's still unpublished manuscript collection includes a volume of protests against the condemnation in France of Pajonist thought. Pajon's nephew Papin attacked in *Faith Reduced* the practices of provincial synods in imposing articles of faith, and

---

[90] Grotius, *Truth*, ed. Le Clerc (London 1827), 110n.; Le Clerc, *Treatise*, 222; Locke, *Second Reply in Works*, III, 303–34; Locke, *Paraphrase*, I, 52 and 1 Corinthians 15:50.

[91] Aubert de Versé, *Protestant*, 32–188, esp. 32, 57, 137–41 and II, 9–22.

[92] Le Cène and Le Clerc, *Entretiens, passim*, esp. sig. a4v–sig. a6r; 7, 225–6, 231, 235–6.

[93] Limborch, *Compleat System*, 1000; *idem, Theologia Christiana*, 839.

was issued with a preface by Bayle underlining his opposition to the actions of French ministers. For Le Cène, the partisans of the Synod of Dort had erred in anathematising any who denied their articles as 'heretics'.[94] Le Cène cited Burnet as condemning the methods of the clergy of France for 'pronouncing positively' on 'mysterious points', such as the order of decrees and manner of operation of grace, thereby assuming the power they condemned in the Catholic Church.[95] Burnet's *Some Letters* condemned Genevan persecution about issues of free will and its condemnation of the 'middle way' of Amyraut. Having become Bishop of Salisbury after the Revolution of 1688–9, Burnet maintained the toleration through inclusiveness of Anglicanism about disputed issues of free will in his *Exposition of the Thirty-nine Articles*. In his preface to Papin's *Faith Reduced*, Bayle stressed the laudable inclusivity of varying views of the Church of England (which Papin had joined in England in 1685–6 before his return to the Netherlands in 1687, and before his attempts to find employment in Hamburg and Danzig were thwarted by the intolerant reach of Jurieu). In his *Historical and Critical Dictionary*, Bayle surveyed many of the divergent opinions held by Jesuits, Jansenists, Calvinists, Arminians, and many others about God's omnipotence, omniscience, humans' free will, and the existence of evil, *inter alia*. He criticised many of their attempts to explicate these doctrines as inadequate, and criticised many of the practices of intolerance based on commitment to such explications as the sole and certain truth. And he reported at various points the views of such authors as Milton that toleration of a wide variety of different explications of Scripture, from Calvinist to Socinian, was legitimate.[96]

In decades in which, as we saw in Chapters 1 to 4 and 13 to 15, Quakers and Anabaptists remained among the most anathematised of sects by many of the intolerant, Catholic and Protestant alike, and when Quakers and some Anabaptists suffered or feared persecution and violence, several of the advocates of toleration specifically defended toleration for Quakers and Anabaptists. Aubert's *Pacific Protestant* defended as erroneous but tolerable Anabaptists' denial of baptism and officeholding and stressed that Quakers had suffered all indignities and even death with 'angelic patience' and that their behaviour conformed to the model of Jesus Christ. And he argued that opposition to Quakers because of their refusal of hat honour and familiarity in speech was due to the 'vanity and ambition' of foolish men who wished to

---

[94] Papin, *Foi réduite*, preface; Le Cène, *Conversations*, 8–11; Huguenot Library MS R5; my 'Huguenot Thought'.

[95] [Le Cène and Le Clerc], *Entretiens*, 8–9.

[96] Burnet, *Some Letters* (1724), 62–4; Burnet, *Exposition of the 39 Articles*, *passim*; Papin, *Foi réduite*, preface; Bayle, *Dictionary*, esp. Manicheans, Pauliciens, Milton; Kilcullen, *Sincerity and Truth*, 57.

tyrannise over others.[97] In the *Theologia Christiana*, Limborch discussed those who had religious objections to oaths, such as Anabaptists. He identified as 'errors' which did not force individuals 'to violate any one precept' of Christianity and which did not make them bad subjects the views that it was 'unlawful for a Christian to bear the office of a magistrate' or to 'take an oath'. For Limborch, oaths and magistracy were 'highly necessary for the preservation of the public tranquility' but since such as Anabaptists did not exclude others holding office, but merely declined it themselves, were moved by 'reverence' for divine prohibitions to abstain from taking oaths, and were 'subject to same penalty as a perjured person' if they failed in keeping their word, they could be trusted sufficiently for political society to operate.[98] Locke explicitly named Anabaptists among others to be tolerated in his *Epistola de Tolerantia*, and in his translation of the *Epistola* as the *Letter Concerning Toleration* Popple added Quakers to the list alongside Anabaptists.[99]

[97] Aubert de Versé, *Protestant*, 77–98, 101–20.
[98] Limborch *Compleat System*, 1003; *idem*, *Theologia Christiana*, 841–2.
[99] Locke, *Letter*, ed. Klibansky and Gough, 142 and n.64. Locke explicitly named 'Remonstrants, Anti-Remonstrants, Lutherans, Anabaptists or Socinians'; Popple's translation amended the list for a primarily English audience to 'Presbyterians, Independents, Anabaptists, Arminians, Quakers, and others'.

22

Toleration and the intolerant, Catholics, 'atheists', 'libertines', and 'sodomites'

In the 1680s and 1690s, the advocates of universal religious toleration at many points in their writings denied the right to toleration to the intolerant, to at least some Catholics, to 'atheists', and to 'libertines' or 'sodomites'.[1] This chapter primarily will document these significant forms of intolerance within arguments for religious toleration. We will also see, however, that some of the advocates of religious toleration attempted to qualify some of these denials of toleration. The intolerant were clearly denied rights to toleration by Bayle and Locke, but Bayle canvassed briefly at one point the possibility of toleration even for the intolerant. Rights to toleration were often denied to at least some Catholics in Protestant countries, but some of these authors attempted to distinguish the political denial of toleration to some Catholics from religious intolerance to all Catholics, and suggested that some Catholics were tolerable in at least private worship. The supporters of religious toleration who discussed the issue denied toleration to atheists. But some of Bayle's arguments could be read as implying that 'atheists' were tolerable, especially the arguments he developed over the twenty years following the suggestion in his *Pensées* that atheists were not necessarily intrinsically worse citizens than believers. And while Locke was generally adamant that 'atheists' were not to be tolerated, both in his *Letters* on toleration and in other works such as the *Essay Concerning Human Understanding*, there is a glimpse in a passage added to a later edition of the *Essay* of Locke perhaps questioning whether 'atheism' was necessarily inimical to political obedience. These advocates of religious toleration repeatedly denied that they supported toleration for 'sodomites' and

[1] Thanks are due to the many audiences who commented on elements of this chapter at many seminars and conferences, including particularly the British Society for the History of Philosophy Conference 'Libertinism and Liberty' (1999); the UCLA/Clark Library Conference 'Materialist Philosophy, Religious Heresy and Political Radicalism' (1999); the Seventeenth-Century Studies Conference 'Orthodoxies and Heterodoxy' at Durham, England (1999), and the National Humanities Centre, North Carolina, seminar on the Enlightenment (2000).

'libertines' (even if they supported positions others then considered 'libertine', such as the possible legitimacy of polygamy, of divorce, and of women's capacity to prophesy).[2] But Bayle, once again, may have intended to imply broader support for sexual 'libertinism' in his *Dictionary*.[3] Each of these qualifications to intolerance supported by the advocates of religious toleration will be discussed in this chapter, as this chapter charts the fast-flowing currents of intolerance in the works of the advocates of *religious* toleration in the 1680s and 1690s.

THE INTOLERANT

Some of the advocates of 'universal religious toleration' argued straightforwardly that the intolerant had no right to toleration, and included under this description the intolerant of any profession or denomination. Bayle's *Philosophical Commentary* set it down as a general principle that 'the party which, if uppermost, would tolerate no other, and would force Conscience, ought not to be tolerated'.[4] For Locke in the *Letter*, those who 'attributed' to themselves and to their own sect a 'particular privilege' to impose a religion, whether or not they yet had the capacity to enforce this, 'have no right to be tolerated by the magistrate', and there was a need for a preacher to own and to teach the duty of tolerating in order to be tolerated: the right to toleration did not extend to 'those that will not own and teach the Duty of tolerating All men in matters of meer Religion'. In his 1667 'Essay on Toleration', Locke had similarly declared that 'it is unreasonable that any should have a free liberty of their religion who do not acknowledge it as a principle of theirs that nobody ought to persecute or molest another because he dissents from him in religion'.[5] Locke's straightforward declaration that one had to own and teach toleration to have a right to be tolerated was noted by Locke's contemporaries. Reviewing and criticising Locke's arguments in his 1690 *Argument of the Letter Concerning Toleration Briefly Considered and Answered*, Jonas Proast noted that the third of Locke's three requirements 'to qualify them for the benefit of the Toleration he endeavours to promote' was 'That they own and teach the Duty of tolerating all men in

---

[2] See for Locke on polygamy and divorce, Locke, 'Essay on Toleration'; on divorce, Locke, *Treatises* and Locke's *Observations* on Nye's *Discourse on Natural and Revealed Religion*, MS Locke c27, 93–5; and on women prophesying, Locke, *Paraphrase*. On these topics, see Wootton, *Political Writings*, introduction; Weil, *Political Passions*, 28–31; Locke, *Paraphrase*, ed., Wainwright, I, 44.

[3] Wootton, 'Bayle, Libertine?'.

[4] Bayle, *Philosophical Commentary* (1708), 233 (*Philosophical Commentary*, ed. Tannenbaum, 130; *Commentaire philosophique*, 249).

[5] Locke, *Letter* in *Works*, 46; 'Essay on Toleration' in Locke, *Political Essays*, ed. Goldie, 152.

matters of meer Religion'.[6] These advocates of religious toleration held that the intolerant could have no claim of injustice for denial to them of a right that they would themselves deny to others. As Bayle put it, those who would not tolerate did not have the 'right' to be tolerated because 'a religion which forces conscience has no right to plead it'. But even though such intolerant individuals did not have a 'right' to toleration, Bayle suggested at one point that even the intolerant pagans in previous centuries should have been granted toleration when they were 'so low' that 'there was no danger of their ever recovering Power enough' to enact intolerance.[7] Bayle here effectively anticipated the argument of John Rawls' *Theory of Justice*, that a supporter of the principle of toleration should extend toleration even to those who do not accept it as far as is compatible with security. As Rawls put it, 'while an intolerant sect does not itself have title to complain of intolerance, its freedom should be restricted only when the tolerant sincerely and with reason believe that their own security and that of the institutions of liberty are in danger. The tolerant should curb the intolerant only in this case'.[8]

TOLERATION OF CATHOLICS

The advocates of religious toleration in various works clearly assaulted Protestant as well as Catholic intolerance. Many spoke of themselves as opposing the desire to impose on others, whether by Protestants or Catholics. But in designating the intolerant of their day who did not deserve to be tolerated, these advocates pointed especially to contemporary Catholic intolerance and placed it within the history of extensive Catholic intolerance through the centuries. In his 1682 *General Criticism of M. Maimbourg's History of Calvinism*, Bayle condemned the 'spirit of bloody violence' in Catholicism and pointed to centuries of crusades and inquisitions.[9] In the *Dictionary* entry on Milton, Bayle noted from Toland's *Life of Milton* Toland's summary of Milton's argument that 'Popery' ought 'to be wholly deprived of the benefit of a toleration, not as it is a religion, but as it is a tyrannical faction which oppresses all others' and declared that it had been 'time out of mind the sect which persecutes most, and incessantly torments both the body and soul of other Christians wheresoever it can do it'. According to Bayle, this meant that the 'most zealous advocates of toleration

---

[6] Proast, *Argument*, 1–2; N. Tarcov, 'John Locke and the Foundations of Toleration' in A. Levine, *Early Modern Skepticism and the Origins of Toleration* (Lanham, Md. 1999), 179–80.

[7] Bayle, *Philosophical Commentary* (1708), 264 (*Philosophical Commentary*, ed. Tannenbaum, 147; *Commentaire philosophique*, 275).

[8] Rawls, *A Theory of Justice*, 216, 220.

[9] Bayle, *Critique générale* in OD, 1717–31, II, 106–7, in Mori, 'Pierre Bayle', 45–60, at 46.

do chiefly design its exclusion'. Bayle attacked Catholics' claim that they were appointed to 'banish, imprison, torture, kill, and dragoon, all those who refuse to be converts to the gospel, and to dethrone the princes who oppose its progress'. And he pointed to the argument of his own *Philosophical Commentary* that Chinese rulers should therefore have excluded Catholics from their territories.[10] In the *Philosophical Commentary* itself, Bayle immediately followed his general declaration of the denial of the right to toleration to the intolerant with identification of Catholics as thus intolerant. He suggested that councils and popes had approved persecution 1,000 times, that Catholic princes had committed all manner of 'barbarous cruelties', and that Catholic clergy had extolled the 'current and avowed doctrine of the Church of Rome, that Hereticks, of whom they form a more hideous Idea than of any Monster, may and ought to be punished' with the result that 'Prudence and common sense' required that rulers should consider papists as 'a Party of Men who look on all Government in the hands of Protestants with an evil eye' desiring to 'extirpate what they call Heresy'. Writing pseudonymously in the guise of an Englishman in his *Philosophical Commentary* in 1686, Bayle argued that Catholics would 'not forbear three years, nor fail bringing those to the Stake who did not go to Mass had they once more the Power in their own hands'. The fact that English Catholics were now declaring 'That nothing is more unjust than vexing men on the score of conscience' was for Bayle 'ridiculous...perfidious and insincere in them, Qualitys inseparable from their Nature for so many Ages past'.[11]

For Bayle in the 1686 *Philosophical Commentary*, the rule of toleration was not 'the falseness of Opinions' but 'their influence with regard to the publick Peace and Security'. Bayle was clear: toleration was not deserved for 'those Opinions...tending directly, and in the nature of them, to the Disturbance of the State, and endangering the Sovereign's Authority'. Bayle declared that it was 'just' that Protestant states who had shaken off popery 'make the most severe laws against its Re-admission', and that Protestant states with Catholics within their territories made the 'severest' laws and put them 'in Execution' against them. Measures against them were a 'precaution against all attempts on their part'. According to Bayle, constraint against papists in Protestant countries had no other aim than 'to prevent their disturbing the State, which the Principles of their Religion directly lead to'. Moreover, for Bayle in the 1688 *Supplement*, those who refused oaths refused securities of 'obedience' and may justly be 'expelled on this score'.

---

[10] Bayle, *Dictionary*, Milton O.
[11] Bayle, *Philosophical Commentary* (1708), 6–7, 231–3, (*Philosophical Commentary*, ed. Tannenbaum, 11–12, 129–30, *Commentaire philosophique*, 52, 247–8).

For Bayle, 'a Roman Catholic with regard to a Protestant sovereign' was in this situation because his religion viewed oaths as null. This was 'ground enough' for a Protestant sovereign 'never having an intire Confidence in a Catholick Subject'.[12] Bayle thus explicitly allowed severe laws against Catholics and the banishment of Catholics. And in one passage he declared that 'as for a Stranger, who may be surprized in the clandestine Exercise of some religious function, if he be punished', this was 'not so much on the score of religion, as on that of his being a Fryar or Monk in masquerade, and a presumption that he's come to burn, poison, play the Spy, or carry on some hellish Conspiracy; of which there have been a hundred Examples'. Bayle may well have intended thereby to render legitimate the grounds on which Catholic priests had been executed in England in the sixteenth and seventeenth centuries; des Maizeaux, in translating the *Commentary* in 1708, thought so and added the words 'by death' to indicate the punishment of such clerics, and Bayle's own preliminary discourse to the *Philosophical Commentary* spoke of clandestine monks in the reign of Elizabeth, James I and Charles I who had acted against those sovereigns and attempted to overthrow the government.[13]

Writing in the guise of an Englishman before James' prerogative provision of toleration and opening of office to Catholics by suspension of the penal laws and Test Acts, in the *Philosophical Commentary* Bayle advocated 'just precautions' to prevent Catholics holding public employments and 'trusts'. Nothing was declared 'more reasonable or more necessary' than laws to prevent Catholics from making use of such positions 'for the better executing the black and horrible Maxims of Persecution'. These were 'just' laws given Catholics' 'compelling and deposing Principles inconsistent with the publick safety'.[14] But it was thus acts against officeholding rather than laws against worship which Bayle focused upon most specifically in the *Commentary* in discussing measures to provide Protestant rulers or countries with security, and the *Commentary* also suggested the desirability of tolerating the private worship of Catholics. Bayle noted that Protestant rulers had often treated 'papists' with 'tenderness' as long as they obeyed the laws, citing Holland and Cleves and the reign of Charles II in England as examples. He argued that Catholics could not defend intolerance to Protestants on the grounds of Protestant intolerance towards them since Protestants allowed Catholics

[12] Bayle, *Philosophical Commentary* (1708), 229–31, 771–3 (*Philosophical Commentary*, ed. Tannenbaum, 129–31; *Commentaire philosophique*, 245–7); Bayle, *OD*, II, 559–60. Cf. also *idem Critique générale* in *OD*, II, 105–6, in Lennon, 'Bayle', 193.

[13] Bayle, *Philosophical Commentary* (1708), 18–19, 62–3, 240 (*Philosophical Commentary*, ed. Tannenbaum, 16–17, 133; *Commentaire philosophique*) 254.

[14] Bayle, *Philosophical Commentary*, 7, 18–20 (*Philosophical Commentary*, ed. Tannenbaum, 11, 16–17; *Commentaire philosophique*, 52, 62–4).

voluntary exile or 'serving God privately in their own way'. And Bayle argued that laws against Catholics should not lead to Catholics being 'exposed to insults in their persons' nor to 'disturbing them in the Enjoyment of their Estates, or the private Exercise of their Religion, or for doing them any injustice in their Appeals to Law, or for hindering them' from bringing up their children 'in their own Faith'. Bayle further added in the *Supplement* when discussing the lack of security for Protestant rulers which legitimated the non-toleration and banishment of Catholics that he did not think that Catholics should in fact be banished 'where they behave themselves quietly'.[15]

Arguments for toleration of Catholic worship while supporting maintenance of Test Acts to prevent Catholics from holding office in Protestant countries were voiced by two works which Bayle cited in the preface to his *Supplement* to the *Philosophical Commentary*. In his edition of Lactantius' *Death of the Primitive Persecutors* in 1687, Burnet argued that it was 'exream tender in our present circumstances' to discuss 'how far Protestants ought to tolerate Papists'. It was, for Burnet, 'most unreasonable' for those 'to pretend to it, who we are sure must destroy us as soon as it is in their power to do it'. For Burnet, the 'breach of faith, and the rage of persecution...in France and Piedmont' provided clear arguments against 'lenity towards them'. Yet Burnet also declared simultaneously that most Catholics were 'not so formidable as to raise our fears and jealousies to so high a pitch', distinguishing the situation in England and the Netherlands from that in France and Piedmont. He recommended that a distinction be made in England and the Netherlands between intolerance towards Jesuits and other regular priests, who were clear supporters of intolerance, and toleration for 'secular priests', which might make further severity justified if they were 'restless' under such 'easy circumstances'. Burnet contended that he would 'rather' the Church of England was 'persecuted by the Church of Rome' than that it 'persecute Papists'.[16] In works attacking, *inter alia*, James II's suspension of the Test Acts, gathered together into *Six Papers* and published in England and the Netherlands in 1687, Burnet had argued that a ruler could not have security of obedience and that a subject could not have security of the maintenance of his property and religion on the bases of the

---

[15] Bayle, *Philosophical Commentary*, 229–30, 235, 772–3 (*Philosophical Commentary*, ed. Tannenbaum, 129–31; *Commentaire philosophique*, 245–7, 250); Bayle, *OD*, ΙΙ, 560.

[16] Burnet (ed.), *Death*, 46–51; Bayle, *Philosophical Commentary* (1708), 533; *idem*, *OD*, 504. Bossy argues in *The English Catholic Community*, ch. 9, that there were probably more secular priests in England in the Restoration than Jesuits and Benedictines, especially in the wake of the 'Popish Plot', when the number of Jesuit missionaries fell to about 90. In the Netherlands, the numbers of secular priests and regular priests were probably about equal in the later 1680s: Israel, *Dutch Republic*, 646–7.

position of many Catholic priests, that faith did not have to be kept with heretics. He argued that Test Acts in England were justified as the only security of Protestantism and liberty, and attacked James II's suspension of laws against Catholic office-holding by prerogative powers as subverting the government. He voiced his deep suspicion of the current toleration provided by James II in 1687 as intended to lay men asleep until they were to be 'destroyed', and argued that the provision of 'general toleration' in 1687 would give way to a religion 'which must persecute all equally'. But he simultaneously indicated that as long as the protection of the Test Acts was maintained he supported English 'charity' towards Catholics, that they should live at ease, and that Parliament should review penal laws against Catholics as well as dissenters.[17]

Fagel's *Letter*, which Burnet translated into English, and which Bayle also cited in the *Supplement* to the *Philosophical Commentary*, argued simultaneously for Test Acts and Catholic toleration. He declared that 'no Christian ought to be persecuted for his Conscience, or be ill used because he differs from the publick and established Religion'. But at the same time it was held to be vital that laws were to remain in vigour 'by which the R. Catholicks are shut out of both Houses of Parliament, and out of all Publick Employments, Ecclesiastical, Civil and Military'. This involved for Fagel no 'severity against the Roman Catholics upon account of their Consciences; they are only provisions qualifying men to be Members of Parliament, or to be capable of bearing office'. Fagel declared that Catholics could not be employed without threatening the security of the Protestant religion, and that it was shown by 'plain Reason' and 'the experience of all Ages, the present as well as the past' to be 'impossible' that Catholics and Protestants could live peaceably when 'mixed together in places of Trust and Publick Employment'. But toleration without capacity to hold office was a 'great...favour' to Catholics in a Protestant nation since it offered 'the free Exercise of their Religion' and since it was more tolerant to Catholics than were Catholics who aimed wherever it was possible for them safely to 'absolutely suppress the whole Exercise' of Protestantism 'and severely persecute all those that profess it'.[18]

LOCKE AND THE TOLERATION OF CATHOLICS

At many moments from the 1660s to the 1690s, Locke expressed considerable fear of Catholic threats to Protestant rule in England and Ireland. In his

[17] Burnet, *Six Papers, passim,* esp. 4–6, 22–5.
[18] Fagel, *Letter,* 1–4; Bayle, *OD,* II, 503; on the circulation of Fagel's letter, see Jones, *The Revolutions,* 226–8.

1667 'Essay On Toleration', Locke opposed toleration for Catholics, arguing that they took up their religion 'in gross' and that this included political principles inimical to obedience and security, including papal authority to 'dispense with all their oaths, promises, and the obligations they have to their prince, especially being (in their sense) a heretic'. For Locke in 1667, papists 'where they have power, they think themselves bound to deny it to others'. For Locke, 'it being impossible. . .to make papists, whilst papists, friends to your government, being enemies to it both in their principles and interest. . .I think they ought not to enjoy the benefit of toleration'.[19] As we saw in Chapters 1 and 2, Locke repeated such worries on many occasions from the 1670s to the 1690s. Thus, in the 1670s in France, Locke recorded the French Catholic belief that faith does not need to be kept with heretics and their desires for re-Catholicisation of England and resumption of lands lost at the Reformation. Throughout the 'Exclusion Crisis', Locke was deeply fearful of French and Irish Catholic armies supporting the re-Catholicisation of England, and in his 1681–3 'Critical Notes on Edward Stillingfleet' he spoke of Catholics as the 'common enemy' of Protestants and called for Protestants to be stirred up against Catholics as 'People that have declared themselves ready by blood, violence, and destruction to ruine our religion and Government', as 'enemies' or 'spies' within, with commanders whom they 'blindly' obeyed declaring war 'and an unalterable design to destroy us'.

In the early 1680s, the Shaftesbury circle, of which Locke was a significant member, was responsible for issuing propaganda which identified all papists as committed to violence against Protestants and committed to the belief that faith was not to be kept with heretics; such propaganda adduced Catholic treatment of Huguenots and Waldensians as evidence. Locke was associated with Shaftesbury's 1681 'Irish Plot' accusations of French and Irish Catholic plans for the reconquest of England. And the same fear of French and Irish Catholic troops conquering England was dominant again in Locke's argument in 1690 that the battle in Ireland between Irish Catholic forces together with French troops against William's international Protestant army was a battle between 'popery' and 'slavery' on one side and 'liberty' and 'property' on the other. In Locke's terms, Irish Catholic supporters of James II were 'rebels' against the rightful monarchs, William and Mary, whose title over Ireland as well as England was established in England; the results of a conquest of England by 'foreign' dragoons he then described as rape, torture, and execution, together with forcing of conscience.

Yet as early as his 'Essay on Toleration', Locke did not argue that Catholic worship was intolerable as 'idolatrous', and explicitly identified the

---

[19] H. Fox Bourne, *Life of Locke* (London 1867), I, 187–8; Locke, *Political Essays*, ed. Goldie, 152.

desirability as well as the difficulty of finding principles on which Catholic worship and speculative beliefs could be tolerated while political principles that threatened security could be neutralised. In 1672, as part of the Cabal administration, Shaftesbury had supported royal indulgence towards Catholic worship, and Locke was probably also then its supporter. Locke spoke very briefly in the 'Critical Notes' in 1681–3 not merely of Catholics as enemies but also of the possibility of a 'regulated toleration' which would exclude Catholic priests but tolerate obedient English Catholics. He declared then that if Catholics were punished 'for anything but being the subjects to a Prince that hath declared enmity and war to us I think they have hard usage', and added that if there were no more papists than those 'amongst us' then they should have been treated 'as other dissenters'.[20]

Locke thus displayed at many moments a desire to distinguish loyal and tolerable from seditious and intolerable Catholics in England, albeit often in the context of recording reasons why such a distinction was exceedingly difficult or currently impossible to make. One further manuscript among his papers also suggests that Locke was interested in finding a way to make such a distinction. In a hand that is perhaps that of Locke's amanuensis, Sylvanus Brownover, is a manuscript endorsed 'The Particular Test for Priests' and 'T. Walsh'; the title 'Test' is written by Locke. It is a response, presumably by Locke himself, to Peter Walsh's *Some Few Questions Concerning the Oath of Allegiance*, a work which Locke owned in its 1674 edition. Since Brownover worked for Locke from 1678 until the late 1690s, if the hand is Brownover's, then it was presumably composed at some point in these years. Walsh, a Franciscan priest who was to be excommunicated in 1670 and thereafter worshipped in the Church of England, was in the 1660s the major Catholic clerical defender of an attempt by Irish Catholics to prove that they were loyal to the Crown by subscription to a Remonstrance which identified Charles II as to be obeyed in temporal matters, and which denied any papal powers to the contrary. This Remonstrance had been signed in 1661 by 121 leading Irish Catholic nobility and gentry, but by only 70 priests and a Catholic bishop, while being rejected by nearly 2,000 Catholic priests in Ireland, and condemned both by the theological Faculty at Louvain and by the Pope. The English court required subscription to the Remonstrance, and then tolerated those Catholics who took it. Those who refused were harassed, imprisoned, deported, or forced into hiding. If he was reading Walsh and reviewing the history of the Remonstrance, most probably in the 1670s,

[20] Marshall, *Locke*, 81–3, 90–1, 110–12; MS Locke c34, 7–11, 26; Locke, 'On Allegiance and the Revolution' in Locke, *Political Essays*, ed. Goldie, 306–13; G. A. J. Rogers, 'Locke and Religious Toleration' in *La naissance de l'idée de tolérance 1660–89* (Rouen 1998), 121–35, at 131–2; Chapter 2 above.

Locke had ample reason to think it important to identify loyal Catholics who were willing to take an oath to the English Crown and thus capable of being tolerated, including not merely lay Catholics but priests such as the Franciscans, forty-four of whom supported the Remonstrance, and yet at the same time had even more ample reason to think that the majority of Irish Catholic clergy did indeed maintain positions which dispensed with oaths to Protestant rulers and upheld the papal supremacy – positions which Locke had long identified with sedition.[21]

Locke's apparent response, the 'Particular Test', was to propose an oath to be taken by 'English' Catholic priests other than Jesuits that they 'utterly renounce and abjure' a series of 'positions or doctrines'. Its first two provisions required abjuration of papal infallibility and the rights of councils of the church to issue decrees binding on all Christians. The remaining nine 'positions' dealt with the question of political obedience and enumerated for denial every item which might allow Catholics to break their allegiance. The 'Particular Test' proposed requiring repudiation of papal powers to depose, to legitimate assassinations of rulers, and to dispense with oaths of allegiance, together with denial of the powers of priests to back the breaking of oaths, and the legitimacy of mental equivocation and reservations in the taking of oaths. The list included renunciation of the proposition 'that it is lawful not to keep faith with heretical princes'. This manuscript then suggested that it be made treason to assert, maintain or defend in word, writing, or otherwise, the papal power to depose or to raise resistance.[22] If this manuscript was of Locke's composition, as seems likely, then it shows that Locke was concerned with finding a way to discriminate between loyal and disloyal Catholic priests, and not merely between the Catholic laity and all priests, and that he was thinking of admitting secular or Franciscan priests as long as they would abjure the political principles that he held made some Catholics intolerable, while thinking that Jesuits were utterly intolerable.

---

[21] Connolly, *Religion*, 19–21; Bagwell, *Ireland*, III, ch. 43; B. Fitzpatrick, *Seventeenth Century Ireland: The War of Religions* (Totowa N.J.), 222–3, 227–30, 233–45; Burnet, *History of His Own Time*, I, 194–5; J. Evelyn, *Diary*, 6 January 1686. There are also two very hostile analyses of Walsh by J. Brennan, which stress his 'Gallicanism' and elevation of divine right monarchy, and show a clear preference for the thought of Bellarmine: J. Brennan, 'A Gallican Interlude in Ireland', *Irish Theological Quarterly*, 24, 217–37 and 283–309. We await a new study of Walsh by A. J. Brown, a student of John Morrill.

[22] The text is in Locke, *Political Essays*, ed. Goldie, 222–4; cf. Rogers, 'Locke', 131–2. Much of the 'Particular Test' replicated the 1605 Oath of Allegiance. Locke went further than Walsh in arguing against papal and conciliar infallibility, and in his discussions of mental equivocations and the possibility of divines legitimating disobedience. It is not clear what territory Locke intended the Test to cover; in its reference to English priests it may have been meant for England.

Locke's *Letter Concerning Toleration* was written in winter 1685 in a country, the Netherlands, in which Catholics were tolerated in practice in private worship but legally denied toleration and actually as well as legally denied office. It was written during a winter in which local regents, such as those in Leiden, had already started to expel Jesuits. It was probably written within weeks of the Revocation of the Edict of Nantes, after huge influxes of Protestant refugees to the Netherlands, and during a period of publicity about violence against Huguenots which identified such violence as based in part on the principle that faith did not need to be kept with heretics. It was written before James II had yet moved to tolerate Protestant dissenters and open office to Catholics. In the *Letter*, Locke argued that there was no right to toleration for those who held that 'faith is not to be kept with heretics', for those who held that 'kings excommunicated forfeit their crowns and kingdoms', and for those who would not teach toleration, as these and similar doctrines showed that they were ready 'to seise the government, and possess themselves of the estates and fortunes of their fellow-subjects' when they were able to do so. For Locke, there was no right to toleration for a church constituted 'upon such a bottom, that all those who enter into it, do thereby, *ipso facto*, deliver themselves up to the protection and service of another prince'. The Pope was the obvious such 'foreign prince', and Locke's disparaging reference to the 'frivolous and fallacious distinction between the court and the church' underlined that his reference was to Roman Catholicism.[23]

These comments have usually been taken, both by Locke's near contemporaries, and by many but not all scholars since, as showing that Locke simply excluded all Catholics from toleration. A century later, Locke was to be criticised by Joseph Priestley for denying toleration to Catholics. Priestley held that Locke's work was admirable for its time but criticised Locke for 'hesitating' or being 'staggered' at the thought of tolerating opinions no longer considered dangerous, including Roman Catholicism. Many others who cited and published Locke's *Letters Concerning Toleration* in the eighteenth century, including the leading 'Whig' Thomas Hollis, saw Locke's principles in the *Letter* as supportive of their own campaigns to deny toleration to Catholics on political grounds. Even Catholics arguing for toleration on the grounds that Catholics did not hold the alleged beliefs, such as the late eighteenth-century Benedictine Joseph Wilks, understood Locke's arguments as having been intended to deny toleration to Catholics on political grounds.[24]

---

[23] Locke, *Letter* in *Works*, 45–7; cf. *idem*, *Letter*, ed. Klibansky and Gough, 130–3, and notes 55 and 56, including on the support of various Catholics for deposition by papal excommunication.

[24] M. Fitzpatrick, 'Joseph Priestley and the cause of Universal Toleration', *The Price–Priestley Newsletter* (1977), 5–8; Miller, *Common Good*, ch. 5; Patterson, *Early Modern Liberalism*, ch. 1, 7.

As we saw in Chapters 1 and 2, in the period between 1685, when it was written, and 1689, when it was printed, Catholics' belief that faith does not have to be kept with heretics was cited frequently by Protestants as one reason that Catholics had revoked the Edict of Nantes, and then as a reason that Victor Amadeus revoked toleration for the Waldensians. The identification in the *Letter* of those who held that faith does not need to be kept with heretics as intolerable would have been understood by any contemporary audience as directed at many contemporary Catholics. Even though many Protestant preachers would have come within the denial of toleration to those who would not themselves teach toleration, the primary identification of those who were intolerant in these years was Catholic priests; intolerance was frequently said to be an essential principle of Catholic priests, especially of Jesuits, and by some authors was said to be a required principle of Catholicism itself. Locke's denial of toleration on this ground would thus have been read in its immediate context as denying toleration especially to many Catholic priests, and potentially also to many lay Catholics.

Yet Locke did not specify in the *Letter* against how capacious a group of Catholics his comments were directed, and he argued in the *Letter* at a number of points that in terms of their worship and religious speculative beliefs, Catholics deserved their worship to be free. There was a growing perception in the years of composition and printing of the *Letter* that many Catholics denied the political principles condemned by Locke. English Catholics arguing in support of James II's toleration, such as John Gother in *A Papist Represented and Misrepresented* (1685), identified the 'misrepresented' Catholic as thought 'to keep no faith with any that are reputed heretics by his Church; and that whatsoever promises he has made (tho never so positive and firm with this sort of people) he may lawfully break'. Gother argued that instead Catholics were taught 'to keep faith with all sorts of people of whatsoever judgment or persuasion that be, whether in communion or no'. Gother's work was influential, reaching its third editon by 1687; William Sherlock convened a meeting to discuss its rebuttal. Among the many answers it received was Edward Stillingfleet's 1687 *The Doctrines and Practices of the Church of Rome Truly Represented*. Stillingfleet said that he was glad to find 'utterly disowned' this 'principle so destructive to all humane Society' and hoped that Catholics' rejection of 'whatever Opinions and Practices there may have been of that kind formerly' would mean that the debate would not now be revived.[25] Locke owned neither Gother's nor Stillingfleet's work, and most of this debate took place after his composition

---

[25] J. Gother, *A Papist Represented and Misrepresented* (London 1685), 41, 64; E. Stillingfleet, *The Doctrines and Practices of the Church of Rome Truly Represented* (London 1687), 124; Speck, *Reluctant*, 179–81.

of the *Letter Concerning Toleration* although before its printing; nonetheless, the identification of many Catholics as repudiating politically subversive principles had been presaged in the attempt of Walsh and other Catholics to demonstrate Catholic repudiation of these principles earlier in the Restoration, and Locke had probably responded to that work with an effort to distinguish tolerable from intolerable Catholics before 1685.

The combination of Locke's comments in the *Letter* suggest that during composition of the *Letter* in winter 1685, Locke was once again struggling over how to discriminate between the series of associated political principles which for him made Catholics intolerable, and the religious worship and other religious beliefs of Catholics which deserved toleration. It seems probable that in writing the *Letter* Locke thought that at least *some* Catholics in England and the Netherlands were politically as well as religiously tolerable, as they did not hold that faith did not have to be kept with heretics, nor that excommunicated kings were deposed, and were themselves tolerant, and yet at the same time thought that very many Catholics, especially but not merely Jesuits, were indeed *in*tolerable, and wished to register both of these positions in the *Letter*.[26]

That Locke was desirous during the period of composition of the *Letter* to find a way to distinguish between some Catholic worship and belief as tolerable and some Catholic political commitments as intolerable is suggested by his expressed desire to do so in earlier works, such as the 1681–3 'Critical Notes' – even if that work suggested that because of Catholic forces surrounding England this was not then possible – and by his attempt to do so in 'the Particular Test for Priests', if that work predates the *Letter* and was by Locke. It is suggested also because a number of Locke's associates in England supported toleration of Catholic worship in the later 1680s, including William Popple, who in 1689 was to be the English translator of Locke's *Letter Concerning Toleration*, and whom we met in Chapter 2 as author in 1688 of *A Letter to Mr Penn*, discussing a 'fair and secure liberty' for Catholics, and as author of *Three Letters*, declaring Catholics deserving of toleration of worship.[27]

---

[26] See Marshall, *Locke*; Rogers, 'Locke', 131–2; Israel, *Radical*, 266; Lennon, 'Bayle', 191. Jeremy Waldron made a somewhat similar argument to this – on the grounds of textual analysis of the *Letter* rather than contextual argument – in a paper presented in 2000 to a seminar in The Johns Hopkins Programme in Political and Moral Thought, of which I am the Director; it has now been published in his *God, Locke and Equality*, 218–23.

[27] Popple, *A Letter to Mr Penn*, 5; idem, *Three Letters, passim*. The *Three Letters* supported Parliamentary enactment of universal liberty of conscience and a 'Test against persecution' to exclude from all offices 'persecuting Papists, and Protestants'. On Popple as author, see Robbins, *Absolute*, 3–5, and notes.

Also significant are the ways in which some of Locke's associates (such as Bayle and Burnet) who were also arguing for toleration in the 1680s were struggling to find positions rendering Catholics tolerable in their worship in Protestant countries, while declaring that many Catholic priests were intolerable; they identified the problems for security and toleration posed by Catholics who held the positions Locke specified as intolerable – including support for intolerance and the view that faith does not need to be kept with heretics. Political issues had been important in Arminian thought on the toleration of Catholics; Limborch, to whom Locke wrote the *Letter*, edited the works of Episcopius, who had proposed in his 1627 *Free Religion* that Catholics were tolerable as long as they had 'declare[d] that they will conduct themselves as true and upright subjects according to the laws of the country', and took an oath of loyalty to the magistrate 'with express renunciation of all those maxims which would dispense them from such an oath'. And Limborch's 1686 *Theologia Christiana*, part at least of which Locke read and commented on in manuscript form in 1685, identified the Pope as the Antichrist on the basis, *inter alia*, of the lengthy papal commitment to persecution in an account which stressed the torments imposed by the Inquisition, papal bulls directed to ensure that rulers punished 'heretics', and papal excommunications not only of private individuals but of whole communities.[28]

Whatever the exact nuances of Locke's belief about the toleration of Catholics in the *Letter*, for the longer history of provision of toleration to Catholics it is also important that Locke's *Letter* identified 'idolatry' as subject to variant definition, argued that accusation of idolatry gave no basis for persecution, and contended that worship in the forms of the mass did not constitute grounds for the denial of toleration. As Locke asked,

what power can be given to the magistrate for the suppression of an idolatrous church, which may not, in time and place, be made use of to the ruin of an orthodox one? For it must be remembered that the civil power is the same every where, and the religion of every prince is orthodox to himself.[29]

For Bayle, similarly, those Protestants who forbade Catholic worship in their countries not for political reasons but for 'idolatry' in the mass plainly exceeded the bounds of justice. Reviewing Bayle's arguments in the *Bibliothèque universelle*, Le Clerc or Cornand stressed that if force could be used by Protestant magistrates to burn Catholics as idolators in England and Holland, this would arm Catholics to punish Protestants as sacrilegious

---

[28] Episcopius, *Vrye Godes-dienst*, 44, in Israel, *Dutch Republic*, 502; Limborch, *Theologia Christiana*, 781–2; *idem*, *Compleat System*, 925–6. Jones added a passage to Limborch's discussion, on the 'Dragoons and Gallies, Fines, Confiscations and Banishment' used to 'root out the remainders of the Northern Heresy, as they term it'.

[29] Locke, *Letter* in *Works*, 35.

in France.[30] Locke and Bayle denied thereby the legitimacy of a ground for intolerance which some other mid-seventeenth-century defenders of 'liberty of conscience' had cited in denying toleration to Catholics: the alleged 'idolatry' of the mass. The removal of 'idolatry' as a justification of intolerance, such that intolerance was solely justified on the political grounds of Catholics' threat to security was to help to make it possible a century later to defend toleration for Catholics by examining if Catholics were *politically* intolerable, and this was finally to help to lead to official Catholic toleration in England and Ireland. While he depicted Locke as denying toleration to Catholics, the Benedictine monk and campaigner for Catholic emancipation Joseph Wilks saw him as preparing the ground on which it was possible to argue for Catholic toleration, writing in 1791 that 'since Locke published his letters on toleration the dispute has been less whether the Catholic tenets be true or false, then whether they were reconcileable with good government'. While understanding Locke as wrongly denying toleration to Catholics, Priestley and Jefferson saw themselves in part as extending Locke's own principles of worship as tolerable if harmless in declaring that Catholics deserved toleration.[31]

THE DENIAL OF TOLERATION TO ATHEISTS

As we saw in Chapter 7, in early modern Europe atheists were generally held to be intolerable as they did not believe in divine sanctions to back oaths and did not have the pleasures and pains of a rewarding and punishing God to motivate them to perform duties otherwise to their disadvantage. Atheists were held to have no 'conscience' to claim 'liberty of conscience', and since they did not believe they had a duty to worship, they had no claim to toleration of worship. It was often declared that 'atheists' were atheists because they desired there to be no God in order to avoid punishment for their vices, and that many 'atheists' had attempted to doubt the existence of God but could not eradicate the belief that there was indeed a God: they were understood to be 'atheists' in their actions, or 'practical atheists', but not in their beliefs. The notion that there were truly no 'speculative atheists' partook of a long-standing belief in universal consent to the existence of a deity; Augustine had declared that there was no nation so barbarous as to deny the existence of God. Before the late seventeenth century, almost all authors of

---

[30] Bayle, *Philosophical Commentary* (1708), 770; *idem, OD,* II, 559; *Bibliothèque universelle,* v (1687), 481.

[31] Fitzpatrick, 'Priestley', 3–30, at 3; Miller, *Common Good,* 321ff.; Patterson, *Liberalism,* ch. 7. Priestley and Jefferson also gave arguments for toleration of Catholics on grounds that were not extensions of Locke's arguments.

works defending religious toleration in early modern Europe themselves supported these views of atheists and denied that atheists merited toleration. Many defenders of religious toleration in sixteenth- and seventeenth-century Europe who were accused of being close to atheism because they were 'heretics' – including Anabaptists and mortalist and materialist Socinians – were adamant that they were not atheists; they denied that atheists deserved toleration by differentiating tolerable religiously committed and moral 'heretics' from intolerable immoral 'atheists', including by distinguishing the religious objections to oath-taking of trustworthy Anabaptists from untrustworthy atheists' irreligious disbelief in God.[32]

The advocates of religious toleration in the 1680s who discussed atheists, including Aubert, Locke, and Bayle, explicitly denied toleration to 'atheists'. For Aubert, heretics were people of good intention, and peaceful even if in error in their desire to serve God; 'atheists' who denied the existence of God or Providence, for Aubert the same thing, were in contrast corrupt and threatening. For Aubert, the magistrate was to hunt down 'cabals' of atheists as inimical to society and all civil authority. Alleged to believe that all goods were common, that one could steal, and that all laws were merely political inventions of rulers, they were not to be allowed to preach against the beliefs necessary to civil society.[33] In the *Letter*, Locke argued – in Popple's flowing words in the English translation – that 'promises, covenants, and oaths, which are the bonds of humane society, can have no hold upon an atheist. The taking away of God, tho but even in thought, dissolves all' – or, in a less flowing and more literal translation: 'neither faith (*fides*) nor agreement nor oaths, the bonds (*vincula*) of human society can be stable and sacred for an atheist: so that, if God is once taken away, even simply in opinion, all these collapse with him'. Locke argued that a man who undermined and destroyed religion 'can have no pretence of religion whereupon to challenge the privilege of a toleration'.[34] In the *Third Letter*, Locke declared to Proast that whereas his 'zeal' against reputed heretics and schismatics was inappropriate, 'I do not...blame your zeal against atheism'. And he argued that it was inappropriate of Proast to charge support for atheism on supporters of

---

[32] Kors, *Atheism*; Buckley, *Atheism*; Hunter, 'Aikenhead', in Hunter and Wootton (eds.), *Atheism*; Hunter, 'Atheism'.

[33] Aubert de Versé, *Traité*, 13–15, 31–3; Morman, *Aubert*, 223; Mori, *Bayle*, 291. For Le Clerc, atheists did not deserve toleration, since belief in God was 'very necessary for the conservation of civil society'. In his review of Matthew Tindal's *Rights of the Christian Church*, Le Clerc attacked the notion 'That Religion is not necessary to Society, and that a Commonwealth of Atheists might as well subsist, as the very best among the ancient Pagans'. Le Clerc, *Bibliothèque ancienne et moderne*, XXVI, 243; *idem, Treatise*, 262–3; *idem, Mr Le Clerc's Extract*, 11; Golden, *Le Clerc*, 82.

[34] Locke, *Letter* in *Works*, 47; J. Dunn, *Rethinking Modern Political Theory* (Cambridge 1985), 43.

religious toleration, 'who deny atheism, which takes away all religion, to have any right to toleration at all'.[35] In the 1695 *Vindication of the Reasonableness of Christianity* Locke described atheism as a crime 'which, for its madness, as well as guilt, ought to shut a man out of all sober and civil society'. And as John Dunn has stressed, in a manuscript entry of the 1690s, 'Ethica B', Locke wrote:

If man were independent he could have noe law but his own will noe end but himself. He would be a god to himself, and the satisfaction of his own will the sole measure and end of all his actions.

It was this emphasis on God's punishments and rewards persuading individuals to act virtuously and obediently which dominated much of Locke's thinking, and was predominant in the *Essay* where Locke described 'pleasure tempting' men to vice as counterbalanced by the hand of God prepared to 'take vengeance'. He described the atheists recorded in classical times as having had their names 'branded' on history, and most 'atheists' in Europe as 'profligate wretches' who needed the magistrate's force applied to them as well as their 'neighbour's censure' in order to keep them from proclaiming themselves 'atheists' by words as 'openly' as their lives did. Locke thus recommended the suppression of atheist speech in Europe in the *Essay*, as in the *Letter*. Standing behind this notion of 'profligate wretches' was unquestionably the view that most atheists in contemporary Europe were such because they were 'libertines' who wished there not to be a God in order for their disorderly and immoral lives to go unpunished. As John Dunn has suggested, Locke's concern was with focusing hedonically motivated humans on the pleasures and pains of the afterlife or punishment at the resurrection: he was concerned with individuals not otherwise having enough motivational reason to maintain oaths, promises, and compacts that would be to their apparent terrestrial disadvantage. James Tully has phrased the point well: 'For Locke, as for almost all his contemporaries, only belief in a God who punishes the wicked and rewards the virtuous in an afterlife provides most individuals with the motive – self-interest – sufficient to cause them to act morally and legally'. Trust stood at the conceptual centre of Locke's thought: atheists were not trustworthy.[36] And the exclusion of atheists defended in the *Letter Concerning Toleration* was by 1685 a long-standing commitment on Locke's part. In the 1668 *Fundamental Constitutions of the Carolinas*, which Locke helped to draft, atheists were to be excluded from the colony. In the 1667 'Essay on Toleration', atheists

---

[35] Locke, *Third Letter*, vi, 414, 416.
[36] Locke, *Essay*, 1.3.13; 1.4.8; *idem, Vindication*, in *Works*, vii, 161–2; Dunn, *Rethinking; idem, The Political Thought of John Locke* (Cambridge 1969); Locke, *Letter*, ed. Tully, 8.

were declared 'the most dangerous sorts of wild beasts, and so incapable of all society'. Belief in God was 'the foundation of all morality, and that which influences the whole life and actions of men, without which a man is to be counted no other than one of the most dangerous sorts of wild beasts, and so incapable of all society'. In 1770s and 1780s, Joseph Priestley and Thomas Jefferson were among those who reflected on Locke's arguments and sought to extend them on the issue of religious toleration. For both, by his own principle of 'harm', Locke should have extended toleration to atheists. As Jefferson put it, 'it does me no injury for my neighbour to say there are twenty gods, or no god. It neither picks my pocket nor breaks my leg'. As Priestley put it, Locke's thought was 'certainly admirable' for its moment, but Locke was wrong to be 'staggered at the thought of tolerating Atheism'. Atheists were not intrinsically dangerous, and should be tolerated.[37]

That atheists had no claim to toleration since they did not believe in God was supported not merely by Aubert and Locke, but also apparently explicitly endorsed by Bayle in the *Philosophical Commentary* in 1686. Bayle specifically denied that his defence of the rights of conscience opened the door to atheists to 'vend any speculative doctrines' and so to 'declaim against God and Religion'. He then argued that he denied this conclusion because the magistrate by the law of order was obliged to promote public welfare and security and 'may and ought to punish those who sap or weaken the fundamental laws of the state', 'among whom are customarily placed all those who remove Providence and all fear' of the 'justice of God' ['*au nombre desquels on a coutume de mettre tous ceux qui otent la providence, et tout la crainte de la justice de Dieu*'].[38] Bayle continued that if this reason was insufficient, a further reason was that an atheist 'incapable of being prompted to vend his Tenets from any Motive of Conscience, can never plead that Saying of St Peter, it is better to obey God than Men; which we look upon with reason as the Barrier which no secular Judg can get over, and as the inviolable Asylum of Conscience. An atheist, void as he is of this main Protection, lies justly exposed to the utmost rigor of the Laws...and the moment he vends his notions, after warning once given him, may be justly punished as a Mover of sedition; who believing no Restraint above human Laws, presumes nevertheless to tread them under foot'. And he ended: 'I shall insist no farther upon this answer: I'm satisfied the least discerning Reader will presently perceive its force, and thus my Doctrine is entirely secured against all Attempts of

---

[37] Locke, *Political Essays*, 137; Fitzpatrick, 'Priestley'; Miller, *Common Good*, 316ff., 346.

[38] Bayle, *Philosophical Commentary* (1708), 307–9 (*Philosophical Commentary*, ed. Tannenbaum, 167–8; *Commentaire philosophique*), 312–13. (The English translation of Bayle's passage '*au nombre...*' is here adapted slightly from Tannenbaum; on des Maizeaux's 1708 translation, see below).

Impiety, because it allows that the Secular Power may in this case take what methods shall seem most fitting. But the case is different with regard to a Teacher of new Doctrines, who may plead the Glory of God...in behalf of his teaching...and allege...Conscience...Such a Man must be argued with from the Word of God or the Lights of Reason'.[39]

This is a complex commentary on atheism and magisterial force; as Giunluca Mori especially has emphasised recently, it is worth pausing over. By the phrase 'are customarily placed' – '*on a coutume de mettre*' – Bayle is not *himself* endorsing the view that atheists do undermine society; indeed, the phrase is simply unnecessary unless intended to suggest the author's distance from such a 'customary' view. The reference to these arguments as able to persuade the 'least discerning reader' perhaps signals the desire for different reasoning by a more discerning reader. The passage suggests that the atheist be punished as seditious for expressing views when commanded not to, and not for expressing or holding them *per se*. Bayle's argument about toleration and atheists in the *Philosophical Commentary* thus differs from the other cited tolerationists' arguments in indicating that atheists could be punished by the magistrate as they were understood to threaten society, not because they did *in fact* do so, and that atheists could be punished for the venting of their opinions after having been given a warning, not for holding atheist views. For Locke in the *Letter*, atheists 'dissolved all', even if they were atheists only 'in idea', while Aubert encouraged the magistrate to search for 'cabals' of atheists. Bayle seems to have wanted at the least to provide toleration for atheists who held atheistic views in private but did not proselytise on behalf of their beliefs. It was close to a commonplace that 'speculative atheists' did not want to spread their opinions, lacking evangelical motivation. D'Assoucy declared in 1675 that 'speculative atheists' desired to keep their views 'under lock and key', while the *Works of the Learned*, reviewing and paraphrasing Bayle's friend Jacques Basnage in 1704, noted that atheists 'ordinarily' sought 'seclusion' and were 'little concerned for applause'.[40]

Before writing the *Philosophical Commentary* in 1686, Bayle had already described some 'speculative atheists' as virtuous and pacific in his 1682 *Letter on the Comet* and its expansion as the 1683 *Pensées*, and had firmly separated action and principles in direct challenge to the conventional understanding of the necessary immorality of the atheist. For Bayle in the *Letter* and *Pensées*, many factors came into play to make 'speculative' atheists act morally, justly, and pacifically: the threat of magisterial punishment, the

---

[39] Bayle, *Philosophical Commentary* (1708), 307–9 (*Philosophical Commentary*, ed. Tannenbaum, 167–8; *Commentaire philosophique*, 312–13).
[40] Mori, *Bayle*, 291–2 ; Kors, *Atheism*, 57, 78.

desire to receive honour and praise, and the temporal advantages of much virtuous behaviour. In the *Pensées*, Bayle initially raised the conventional argument that 'If we consider Atheists by their Disposition of Heart, we find, that not restrained by the Fears of Divine Judgment, nor drawn by the Hopes of heavenly Favour, they must abandon themselves to whatever indulges their Passions'. But Bayle then provided a riposte to this argument by noting that there were in fact 'no annals' of atheist nations, and that therefore we could not know 'to what Excesses a People may run, which have no God', rendering accusations against atheists conjectural. For Bayle, a society of atheists might be moral and just. It was true that 'very severe laws' very 'well executed' would be necessary in such a society against theft, murder, and other crimes, but these laws were necessary everywhere, and not merely in atheist societies. Indeed, it was such 'Human Justice' which provided 'for the most part the Base of Human Vertue'. Bayle further argued that many people acted morally because of the forces of approval and disapproval in their societies. As long as magisterial force executing severe laws was further backed by attaching 'Honor and Infamy' to many things, a society of atheists might well be made to perform moral and civil actions:

As the ignorance of a First Being, the Creator and Preserver of the World, would not bereave the Members of this society of a Sense of Glory and Contempt. Reward and Punishment, or of all the passions which reign in the rest of Men, nor wholly extinguish the Light of Reason; one should find Persons among them of integrity in common dealing, some who relieved the Poor, opposed Violence, were faithful to their Friends, despised Injuries, renounced sensual Pleasures, did no wrong; prompted. . .either by a love of Praise. . .or a design of gaining friends and Welwishers.

For Bayle in the *Pensées*, this was a conjecture, but no more of a conjecture about a society of atheists than the usual conjecture that it was simply impossible to sustain such a society. Bayle concentrated even more heavily on the argument that records showed that atheists had done no worse than idolaters because idolaters had done the worst that could be done. For Bayle, theistic 'ancient Heathens' had been motivated by 'the beastliest unnatural Impurity, boundless Ambition, black Spite and Envy, insatiable Avarice, savage Cruelty, and deepest Perfidiousness'. And he noted that even Christians had committed thefts, murders, debaucheries, and all sorts of crimes, despite avowed belief in a gospel which forbade them all, and in a rewarding and punishing God who would retribute to them for their deserts.[41]

Bayle's central contention was that the 'true Springs' of peoples' actions were not, as the vast majority of his contemporaries who wrote about

[41] Bayle, *Miscellaneous Reflections*, 258–96, 329–79; *idem, Pensées*, paras. 129–46, 161–82; Bayle, *Various Thoughts On the Occasion of a Comet* (SUNY 2000), paras. 129–46, 161–82.

atheism held, the conviction of theists that there was 'a Providence ruling the world, from whom nothing is hid, which recompenses the Vertuous with endless Felicity, and the Wicked with everlasting Pains', nor the beliefs of an atheist who considered transitory 'Pleasures as his Chief End, and Rule of All his Actions'. Instead, man 'hardly ever acts by fixt Principles', and individual factors such as 'the bias of his Constitution, [and] the Force of inveterate Habits' directed actions. Many individual atheists were described by Bayle as having been virtuous, including both atheists in classical times, and the few famous early modern atheists, such as Vanini. Indeed, according to Bayle in the *Pensées*, instead of libertinism leading to atheism, most voluptuaries either concealed their atheism or were not atheists, since the disapproval of the world reduced their terrestrial pleasures. Libertinism was more likely to be attached to those professing Christianity than to those professing atheism. Bayle registered a similar argument in the 1690s in the *Dictionary*, in his reflections on Spinoza, to Bayle a 'systematical atheist' of a 'new method' but of similar beliefs to many classical atheists. According to Bayle, Spinoza was a 'good, moral man' and while this was 'strange' it was not more surprising 'than to see men live an ill life, though they be fully persuaded of the truth of the Gospel'. Spinoza's atheism was 'speculative', and he had withdrawn from the pleasures of the world. He did not dogmatise and did not speak disrespectfully of God. He was sociable, affable, temperant, and just.[42] As Mori has stressed, in his *Continuation* of the *Pensées* Bayle contrasted such an atheist favourably with many contemporary Christians in arguing that for the Spinozist,

Reason, respect for the public, human honour, the hideousness of injustice would frequently enough stop [him] from doing wrong to others. But a man who is persuaded that in exterminating heresies he advances the reign of God...would trample all laws of morality, and far from being halted by remorse, he will feel pushed by his conscience to use all sorts of means...to establish orthodoxy on the ruins of heterodoxy.[43]

We can now return to the passage in the *Philosophical Commentary* examined earlier. The argument that many individual 'speculative' atheists acted morally, and that atheists had many reasons for acting morally and civilly, was already present in Bayle's 1682 *Lettre* and 1683 *Pensées*. As Mori has argued, it seems likely that Bayle's carefully phrased passage in the 1686 *Philosophical Commentary* that atheists could be punished because they were commonly understood to overturn the fundamental laws of the state

---

[42] Bayle, *Miscellaneous Reflections*, 269–75, 294, 353–61; *idem, Pensées*, paras. 133–6, 146, 174–5; *idem, Various Thoughts*, paras. 133–6, 146, 174–5; Bayle, *Dictionary*, Spinoza; Bayle, *OD*, III, 955, 968a; Mori, 'Pierre Bayle', 56.

[43] Bayle, *OD*, 1727–31, III, 955 in Mori, 'Pierre Bayle', 58.

was an apparent or tactical and not a real endorsement by Bayle himself of this common view, and voiced in order to persuade others to the cause of religious toleration in a situation where the denial of toleration of 'heretics' was more immediately pressing than that for atheists because of the religious violence being practised against alleged heretics, in a situation where advocacy of toleration for atheists would have reduced support for religious toleration.

But if Bayle was intending to imply to careful readers that the usual argument against tolerating atheists was not actually supported by the author of the *Philosophical Commentary*, in terms of tracing the reception and influence of that work on the issue of toleration of atheists – including tracing the ways in which Bayle's contemporaries such as Locke and Le Clerc probably read that work – it is important that Bayle's reservation about the usual argument was implicit in the *Philosophical Commentary*. There was therein no explicit extension of the reservation about atheists' challenge to the fundamental laws of society implied in the phrase 'are customarily placed'. There was no argument in the *Philosophical Commentary* for tolerating atheists' proselytisation. If Bayle wished careful readers to ponder this issue, he surely wished most readers to think that the author of the *Commentary* had supported the suppression of atheists' speech. The review in the *Bibliothèque universelle* summarised its arguments with no sign that it thought them intended to undermine rather than to support intolerance towards atheists. Even when he had come to be Bayle's polemic enemy in the 1700s, Le Clerc selected the *Philosophical Commentary* for praise when he was attacking Bayle's arguments in the *Pensées* and other works about atheists' potential for peaceful virtue. Le Clerc's fellow preacher and friend André de L'Ortie complimented *The Philosophical Commentary* as a 'very good' work, even when this endorsement was made a charge against him by orthodox Huguenot ministers; there is no sign that he read that work as supporting atheism. Never shy about accusing their opponents of atheism, the orthodox Huguenot ministers charged de L'Ortie with Socinian sympathies for endorsing Bayle's work and not with atheism; they thus recognised its argument for toleration of Socinianism but not of atheism as part of its argument for the 'universal' religious toleration they condemned. When an English translation of the *Philosophical Commentary* was issued in 1708, it made atheists those '*we* commonly reckon' to undermine society: its translator, Pierre des Maizeaux, thus effectively presented Bayle as himself among those reckoning that atheism undermined political society.[44] Bayle

---

[44] Lambeth Palace Library, MS 932, 1; my 'Huguenot Thought'; Le Clerc/Cornand, *Bibliothèque universelle*, III (1686), 357–8; Le Clerc, *Bibliothèque ancienne et moderne*, 367, 384, 391–2, 431; *ibid.*, XXVI, 243, 253; Bayle, *Philosophical Commentary* (1708), 307–8.

phrased his comments in the *Philosophical Commentary* to make the reading of his argument as supporting the suppression of atheists' speech both plausible and the readiest reading for most readers. As such, Bayle's argument in the *Philosophical Commentary* merits being listed alongside those of other authors of works explicitly defending only *religious* toleration in the 1680s. It is perhaps worth noting, moreover, that even the *Lettre* and *Pensées* did not directly declare atheists tolerable, and that Bayle sent the *Pensées* to friends and correspondents such as the Genevan defender of orthodoxy François Turretini, and the more 'liberal' minister Jean-Robert Chouet, who praised it in terms they would not have applied if they had read it as supporting the toleration of atheism. They apparently read it instead as an attack on idolatry and superstition, its explicit themes.[45]

We noted that in the *Essay* Locke endorsed the notion that atheists were 'profligate wretches' who should be suppressed by magisterial force. But in his amendments to the fourth edition to this passage in the *Essay*, Locke himself noted that there had in fact been, and still were, nations of 'atheists'. The passage of the *Essay* within which these sentences were placed, which argued against innatism on the grounds that some individuals and societies have no idea of God, continued to condemn atheists; Locke did not amend his notion that the 'profligate wretches' of Europe should be suppressed by magisterial force. He did not change the declaration that individual atheists in classical societies had their names 'branded' on the records of history. And in contrast to some of the travel literature which Locke was reading and citing about 'Indian' and African societies, Locke did not suggest in introducing 'atheist' nations that such societies were benign and peaceful, but rather held that they existed without 'arts' and 'discipline' and were 'immoral' and 'uncivil', writing that

> Besides the atheists taken notice of amongst the Ancients, and left branded upon the Records of History, hath not Navigation discovered, in these latter Ages, whole Nations...amongst whom there was to be found no notion of a God, no Religion?...There are Instances of Nations where uncultivated Nature has been left to itself, without the help of Letters and Discipline, and the Improvements of Arts and Sciences.

There is little move here towards the notion of a *civil* society of atheists. But Locke then added a very short passage recognising two societies either of 'atheists' or in which the ruling class and the learned were 'atheists': the Kingdom of Siam (now Thailand), and the Empire of China. He continued:

> But there are others to be found, who have enjoyed these in a very great measure, who yet, for want of a due application of their thoughts this way, want the Idea, and Knowledge of God.

[45] Rex, *Essays*, 72–3.

Locke noted that his readers would probably be surprised, as he himself had been, to find that Siam was atheist. He indicated that on the basis of the account which showed that Siam was entirely atheist – Simon de la Loubère's 1691 *Kingdom of Siam* – China was also entirely atheist. And he continued that even if one did not accept such a description of China, that on the basis of many other Jesuit accounts at the least the 'ruling Party' and the society of the literati in China were 'atheist'. It is true that Locke was primarily recognising these societies in order to bolster his case against innatism. In 1700, one of the learned journals of the emergent 'republic of letters', the *Works of the Learned*, reviewed the *Essay's* denial of innatism, and noted that 'travelers have met peoples who have no notion of the Divinity'. As Alan Kors has shown, by the time that Locke wrote this passage in the revised editions of the *Essay*, this position had been stated in a host of travel writings and was becoming commonplace. But even if further documentation of anti-innatism was Locke's primary purpose, the discussion of China and Siam involved presentation of the image of at least one highly-ordered political society of atheists, the kingdom of Siam, which until 1688 was engaged in commercial exchanges with the court of France and witnessing attempts by French missionaries to convert the king and population to Christianity.

Siam was the subject of significant discussion in many European texts in the period from 1688 to 1705, which depicted it as a highly developed and highly ordered society. La Loubère's 1690 *Kingdom of Siam*, which Locke quoted, declared that the Siamese did not worship false Gods but instead knew 'of no Divinity, neither true nor false'. And La Loubère was clear that the people were moral, that there was a low murder rate, and that there was less theft than in Europe. And while Locke's added passage was neutral on the question of whether China was entirely atheist or had only its 'ruling party' and learned as 'positive atheists' but not the rest of its population, it is clear that for Locke at least the latter was true, and it is clear that Locke was open to the possibility of the former. Locke thus registered that not merely the kingdom of Siam but even the flourishing stable empire of China might be entirely atheist. The obvious question that is raised by this brief recognition of atheistic Siam and potentially atheistic China is of Locke's repeated denial of toleration to atheists on the grounds that they are politically untrust-worthy as not being bound by oaths and not being religiously motivated to refrain from injuring and harming others. The possibility is surely raised that Locke was recognising that theism was not universally necessary to a viable and stable political order.[46]

---

[46] Locke, *Essay*, 1.4.8; *Histoire des Ouvrages des Savans* (1700), 294–5; Kors, *Atheism*, 218; S. de la Loubère, *The Kingdom of Siam* (Oxford 1986).

In the same period that Locke was adding this recognition of Chinese and Siamese atheism to the *Essay*, Bayle was developing his arguments about atheism. Bayle's *Pensées* had argued in the 1680s that atheists were not necessarily vicious, an analysis he then supported by the example of individual atheists who were virtuous, by the contention that many other forces dictated that many atheists lived virtuous lives, and by general argument that principles and practices were often disjunctive. Bayle explicitly declared in 1683 that there were no nations of atheists, opposing his own 'conjectures' about what a society of atheists might be like to others' 'conjectures'. As Joy Charnley has stressed, at this point Bayle showed no awareness of works such as Lescarbot's *Histoire de la Nouvelle France*, Sagard's *Histoire du Canada* or Cieza de Leon's *Chronica del Peru*, works to which he was to refer first in the 1697 *Dictionary* and then in the *Continuation* of the *Pensées*. Charnley shows that Bayle came to argue that there were in fact atheist nations on the basis of his reading of travel literature in the 1690s; his works from 1704 to 1707, the *Continuation* of the *Pensées* and the *Reply to the Questions of a Provincial Gentleman* contained discussions of moral and pacific atheist societies, especially of the moral pactific and atheist Chinese, and in the *Continuation* there were no less than seventeen references to China and Siam. Bayle was thus discovering evidence for the existence of stable atheist societies in roughly the period in which Locke was discovering this evidence from travel literature, and adding this argument to his later works in roughly the same period that Locke was adding recognition of Siam and China to the revised editions of the *Essay*. Having taken notes in 1685 from Bayle's *Lettre*, Locke took a few notes on atheism from the *Pensées* themselves in 1698, and he continued even when Bayle was attacked by Le Clerc to declare to Furly that he valued Bayle's opinion 'in the first rank'. And Locke's brief recognition of the existence of the atheist societies of Siam and perhaps China in the *Essay* brought Locke some way towards the position taken by Bayle, although Locke added his recognition of Siam and China as no more than a passing comment within an analysis of the falsity of innatism and in a section which even with this small addition still called for the magisterial suppression of atheism.[47]

David Wootton has indicated that there are a number of features of Locke's thinking which suggest that Locke was at various moments over many years exploring the possibility of secular foundations for virtues that would be sufficient for the maintenance of a polity. In a manuscript 'Morality', Locke apparently tried to find a way to found human society purely on naturalistic terrestrial considerations in which compacts

---

[47] Charnley, *Bayle*, 129–37 citing Bayle, *Continuation*, 6, 20, 55; Bayle, *Réponse*, II, 298; MS Locke f8, 293–6; MS Locke d10, 3; cf. also MS Locke f9, 91.

determined property in order to avoid a state of 'war', 'rapine' and 'force'. In translating Pierre Nicole's *Essais de morale*, Locke translated a work which suggested that much of the functioning of society could be achieved by the functioning of self-interest – although extra-terrestrial rewards remained important to Nicole. Nicole's *Essais* set out significant parts of the case that Bayle was to take further in the *Pensées* in holding that many virtuous actions and actions contributing to society's welfare were undertaken because of men's corrupt self-love. In the *Essay* itself, Locke noted that considerable portions of virtue were established by the law of opinion in many societies, as they were productive of terrestrial advantages. Such arguments also point towards arguments increasingly made by Latitudinarians in the late seventeenth century which focused on the terrestrial rewards yielded by true virtue. In the *Essay* itself, Locke noted moreover that 'Hobbists' had reasons for virtue in the punishment of a sovereign, and that the philosophers of classical times had reasons for virtue in their view of the intrinsic dignity of virtue.

Such manuscripts and passages of the *Essay* do indeed suggest that Locke was thinking about the possibilities of a series of motivations other than divine reward and punishment providing incentives for virtue and for political obedience. Yet they also are generally short, fairly rudimentary, and often combined with passages emphasising that Locke still believed that there was a pressing need for divine reward and punishment. Locke's *Reasonableness*, for instance, raised the possibility of virtuous behaviour based on the dignity of virtue in the theories of some classical philosophers in a passage which suggests that Locke found this an inadequate basis for motivations to virtue. To redeploy Priestley's language about Locke and atheism cited earlier, when read alongside such other discussions, the passage Locke added to the *Essay* about Siam and China suggests that Locke may have moved from being 'staggered' at the notion of politically viable societies of atheists to being 'surprised', and to have moved towards, but not subscribed to, Bayle's emphatic questioning of the conventional association of virtue and political stability with theism.

Wootton has suggested that Locke may have been influenced by his reading of Bayle, and has cited in this regard Locke's 1680s reading of Bayle's *Lettre*. But Wootton has not noted the changes in Bayle's arguments on the issue of atheist nations, nor Locke's inserted discussion of Siam and China in the *Essay*. Locke's notes from the 1682 *Lettre* were entirely on the topic of prodigies and superstitions, and not on the topic of atheism. If Locke was influenced by reading Bayle into questioning whether atheists were potentially virtuous and thus able to support a political order, it is more likely to have been in Locke's reading of Bayle in the late 1690s, as Locke was also reading travel literature such as La Loubère's work, rather than in the mid-1680s, when none of Locke's notes on Bayle's *Lettre* were on the issue of atheism, when reviews of Bayle's *Lettre* focused not on atheism but rather on superstition and prodigies, and before Jurieu's nose had caught the taint of atheism in the *Pensées*. And even if he was influenced by Bayle's argument, Locke amended his argument in the *Essay* to register that there were surprising atheist societies while leaving intact the *Essay*'s demand for magisterial suppression of atheists. Bayle was in these years using many of the same materials to build a more extensive case that atheists were not more vicious and turbulent than Christians, and providing a plethora of arguments from which to conclude that 'speculative' atheists were in fact tolerable.[48]

LIBERTINES AND SODOMITES

Many of the advocates of religious toleration explicitly denied that they supported toleration for 'libertines' and 'sodomites'. In order to understand these rejections of toleration for 'libertinism' and 'sodomy', it is important first to recall the many layers of accusation that supporters of toleration were supporters of 'sexual libertinism' charted in this book, and then to discuss the actual support for 'libertinism' of various authors in the mid-to-late seventeenth century in works to which several of the advocates of religious toleration had themselves replied. As we have seen, heretics and schismatics had been associated with 'sexual libertines' in patristic literature, in medieval inquisitorial accusations against Catharism and Waldensianism, in polemic attacks of early modern 'magisterial Reformation' Protestants and Catholics against each other, and in the attacks of both against radical Reformation Protestants, culminating in late seventeenth-century assaults by Anglicans against dissenters in England, by Catholics against Huguenots in France, and by orthodox Huguenots and Calvinists against 'unorthodox' Protestants in the Netherlands. We have seen that religions other than Christianity – especially Islam – had also been associated frequently through the centuries with sodomy, adultery, and fornication. We have seen that advocacy of toleration for alleged heretics and schismatics, Jews, and Muslims, was often depicted as supporting the 'sexual libertinism' and 'sodomy' alleged against all of these groups. Such associations of 'libertinism' with 'heretics', 'schismatics', Jews, Muslims, and toleration itself created substantial polemical cause for advocates of toleration to deny that they supported libertinism and sodomy, particularly as this charge was explicitly directed against their works by such authors as Jurieu in the 1680s and 1690s.[49]

---

[48] Wootton (ed.), *Locke Political Writings* (London 1993); *idem*, 'Locke, Socinian or Natural Law Theorist?'

[49] On the denial of toleration to adulterers, sodomites, and the lascivious by predecessors arguing for toleration see the discussions of Simmons, Castellio, and Williams in Chapter 10.

This was not, however, the only cause of denial by these advocates of religious toleration that they supported 'libertinism'. There was considerable circulation of 'libertine' ideas in the later seventeenth century, and a strong association between such 'libertinism' and support for toleration, which created both the strong desire and further polemical need on the part of many advocates of religious toleration to deny that they supported 'libertinism' and 'sodomy' and its toleration in arguing for religious toleration. By the later seventeenth century, there were numbers of 'libertines' – often also called 'atheists' or 'deists' – who often drew upon the materialist or monist thought of Hobbes and Spinoza in undermining or ridiculing central doctrines of Christianity such as the personal resurrection, the creation *ex nihilo*, original sin, and the Trinity. Although the works of a number of such 'libertines' were issued with brief invocations of God and in ostensible opposition to 'libertine' opinions, they described these 'libertine' opinions at length and inadequately rebutted them, and in the eyes of most of their contemporaries such 'libertine' authors were 'atheists' or 'deists' who at the least denied or mocked the providence of God and the importance of Christianity, or challenged the existence of God and undermined religion altogether.[50]

Various of these 'libertines' advocated sexual 'libertinism' in combination with the intellectual 'libertinism' of challenging orthodox Christianity, such as Rochester in England and Beverland in the Netherlands. Others expressed only intellectual 'libertinism', such as Charles Blount, significant portions of whose works were derived from Hobbes and Spinoza. Rochester's poetry, which quickly became infamous in England in significant manuscript circulation and anonymous print editions, questioned the doctrine of the creation *ex nihilo*, the personal resurrection, and original sin, in connection with apparently advocating adultery, fornication, and sodomy. As Burnet put it, Rochester had 'tried to fortifie his Mind...by dispossessing it all he could of the belief or apprehensions of Religion'. For Rochester, 'believing mysteries...made way for all the Juglings of Priests', and miracles and prophecies were to be counted among the many 'strange stories' which were believed because the 'boldness and cunning of Contrivers' met 'the Simplicity and Credulity of the People'. Forms of Worship were 'the Inventions of Priests, to make the World believe they had a Secret of Incensing and Appeasing God'. Disbelieving 'that there was to be either reward or punishment', and

---

[50] D. Berman, A *History of Atheism in Britain* (London 1988); *idem*, 'Disclaimers as Offence Mechanisms in Charles Blount and John Toland' in M. Hunter and D. Wootton (eds.), *Atheism from the Reformation to the Enlightenment* (Oxford 1992), 255–72; Champion, *Pillars*; Israel, *Radical*; Redwood, *Reason*; R. Pintard, *Le Libertinage érudit* (Paris 1943).

believing God at most a 'vast power' unconcerned with humanity, Rochester saw gratification of natural appetites as legitimate unless it caused injury to another or to one's own health. The 'restraining a man from the use of women, except one in the way of marriage…he thought unreasonable impositions on the freedom of man'. In his poem 'Upon Nothing', widely circulated in manuscript, printed in two pirated editions in 1679, and placed in the posthumous 1680 edition of his poetry immediately after a Senecan translation recording that man after death was 'nothing', Rochester mocked both orthodox Christian accounts of the creation and of the resurrection of the body and (allegedly immortal because immaterial) soul. The tone of the poem's treatment of orthodox Christianity is indicated by its capacity to be sung to the tune of 'Which nobody can deny'. 'Upon nothing' assaulted the central Christian doctrine of the resurrection in suggesting that the truly wise were those who lived as though there were no afterlife, in pursuit of terrestrial pleasures, since they would receive nothing after this life – that is, no punishment – while the fools were those who had restrained themselves in this life in their pursuit of celestial reward, who similarly would receive nothing: 'Yet this of thee the wise may truly say/Thou from the virtuous nothing dost delay/And to be part of thee the wicked wisely pray'. Rochester pilloried the 'dull Philosophies' of priests and philosophers, who vainly defined, distinguished, and devised accounts of a non-existent afterlife. In other works, Rochester similarly advised his readers: 'Let's wisely manage this last span/The momentary life of man/And still in pleasure's circle move/ Giving our days to friends, and all our nights to love'. To such 'libertinism', Rochester's poetry added poetic support of sodomy. One of his songs celebrated 'a sweet soft page of mine/who does the trick worth forty wenches', and one of his poems described a penis which 'Stiffly resolved, 'twould carelessly invade/Woman or boy, nor ought its fury stayed/Whe'er it pierced, a cunt it found or made'. To opponents of such views, in Rochester's *oeuvre* there was clear evidence that intellectual 'libertinism' challenging the doctrines of Christianity was intellectually associated with sexual 'libertinism' and 'sodomy'.[51]

[51] See my 'Libertinism and Liberty', forthcoming in J. Champion et al. (eds.), *Libertinism*; G. Burnet, *Some Passages of the Life and Death of…Rochester* (London 1680), preface, 13, 15, 22, 36, 38–9, 52–4, 60, 65–6, 72–4, 100–1; John Wilmot, Earl of Rochester, *The Complete Works* (London 1994), introduction, xiv, 26, 28–9, 37, 201–2, 402–4; R. Parsons, *A Sermon Preached at the Funeral of the Rt Honorable John Earl of Rochester* (Oxford 1680), 9; D. C. Allen, *Doubt's Boundless Sea* (London 1964), ch. 6, 201, 218; C. Hill, 'John Wilmot, Earl of Rochester (1647–80)' in *idem, The Collected Essays of Christopher Hill*, v.1, 298–317; *idem, The English Bible and the Seventeenth Century Revolution* (London 1993), 424–5; W. Chernaik, *Sexual Freedom in Restoration Literature* (Cambridge 1995), chs. 2–3, esp. 28–9, 98–101; Berman, *History of Atheism*, esp. 52–6; Redwood, *Reason*, 42–3; Champion, *Pillars*, 1, 121, 158; J. G. Turner, 'The

The deep Christian commitments of most of the advocates of religious toleration focused upon in this book rendered them opponents of 'libertinism', both as intellectual attack upon Christianity and when explicitly combined with sexual libertinism. Several of the authors whom we have met as advocates of toleration composed works whose central purpose was to oppose the arguments of 'libertinism', including Burnet and Le Clerc. Burnet personally attempted to convert Rochester to Christianity and issued a very popular work condemning Rochester's 'libertinism' which documented this attempt. Burnet's *Some Passages* provided 'reasons' to reject Rochester's 'libertinism' as 'unreasonable'. To Burnet, Rochester's acceptance of restraint where injury was caused gave reason why the 'free use of women' was illegitimate: because if 'a man's wife is defiled, or his Daughter corrupted' this injured *him*. For Burnet, 'Men have a Property in their Wives and Daughters...to defile the one, or corrupt the other, is...unjust and injurious'. Libertinism thus caused harm, and since only the harmless deserved toleration, libertinism did not deserve toleration.[52] And Burnet deployed a further argument central to support of religious toleration in order to suggest that lack of restraint was 'unreasonable': application of 'the rule of equity' that one should not do to others what one would not have done to oneself.[53] Burnet argued that there was 'sufficient' evidence for belief in Christianity, arguing that the authority of Scripture was confirmed by miracles with sufficient attestation unless one were unreasonably to reject the kind of witnesses accepted every day in court. But rather than defending patristic and scholastic explications of doctrines that were challenged by 'libertines' as unreasonable, Burnet himself condemned 'too much Curiosity among the Fathers' and the 'subtilties' added by 'the School-men'.[54] For Burnet, it was reasonable to think that there would be another life because those who imitated God were not favoured fully 'in this state'. Rochester had questioned the need for the 'tricks' of Christianity, asserting the sufficiency of philosophy and a few moral rules. Burnet replied that philosophy was a

Libertine Sublime: Love and Death in Restoration England', *Studies in Eighteenth Century Culture*, 19 (1989), 99–115; Weil, 'Sometimes', 125–53; Kent, *Gender*, 29–30; D. Griffin, *Satires Against Man* (Berkeley 1973), 266–80, esp. 274–5; M. Thormahlen, *Rochester: The Poems in Context* (Cambridge 1993), 141–61; J. Lamb, *So Idle a Rogue* (London 1993), 214–17; T. Barley, 'Upon Nothing: Rochester and the Fear of Non-entity' in E. Burns (ed.), *Reading Rochester* (New York 1995), 98–113; H. Erskine-Hill, 'Rochester: Augustan or Explorer?' in G. Hibbard (ed.), *Renaissance and Modern Essays* (1966), 51–64; D. Quentin, 'The Missing Foot of "Upon Nothing"' and P. Hammond, 'Rochester's Homoeroticism' in N. Fisher (ed.), *That Second Bottle* (Manchester 2000).

[52] Burnet, *Some Passages*, 39–42, 109–15; Hill, 'Rochester', 307, 314–15; cf. Burnet, *Six Papers*, 4; J. Rudolph, 'Rape and Resistance: Women and Consent in Seventeenth Century English Legal and Political Thought', *Journal of British Studies* (2000), 157–84.

[53] Burnet, *Some Passages*, 39–42, 45–53, 109–15.

[54] Burnet, *Some Passages*, 63–4, 74–5, 77–80, 84–5, 92–3, 101–7; cf. Shapiro, *Probability and Certainty* and *Culture*.

matter of 'fine Speculation', that few had the capacity to 'apply themselves' to such notions, that philosophy had 'few Votaries', and that philosophy had 'no Authority in it to bind the World to believe its Dictates' while its 'evidences' were not suited to the simple. Christianity had instead offered authority, appropriately 'allarming Evidences', and 'sufficient assurance' of rewards because of the promises of Christ, confirmed by miracles, and the Resurrection of him who had promised resurrection to others.[55]

In 1696, Le Clerc, Burnet's correspondent and in the mid-1690s his prospective client, issued a 1696 *Treatise* which paralleled a number of these arguments as it aimed to show that 'Unbelievers act against all good Sense in refusing their Assent to the Gospel'. Le Clerc identified 'Persons of Quality' and gentlemen and nobles associated with corrupt courts as most likely to 'doubt of the Truth of Christianity' or to believe it false both because of their vicious 'dispositions' and their desire to be elevated above the 'vulgar'. He indicted 'prideful' Epicurean philosophers, who looked upon 'Religion in general as mere Superstition, or as a Trick of Politicians to impose upon the simple', and who seasoned their 'conversation and debauches' with 'Railleries against Religion'. He attacked the disposition of unbelievers to question what they called 'incredible mysteries' and improbable miracles, defended the reality of miracles in the first ages of the church as sufficiently witnessed, and urged that such miracles testified to authority of Scripture. In his account of the importance of Christianity, Le Clerc stressed that Christ had grounded upon a 'new Foundation' belief in a future life and its rewards and punishments. Le Clerc and Locke corresponded about the *Causes of Incredulity*, and Locke's close friend William Molyneux attempted to find Le Clerc a post in Ireland after reading his *Causes of Incredulity* and corresponding with Locke about it. Locke's English publisher Churchill issued the English edition of Le Clerc's *Treatise*, and advertised in it both Locke's *Reasonableness* and Samuel Bold's *Vindication* of the *Reasonableness*.[56]

It is unsurprising, then, that parallel arguments were set out in Locke's *Reasonableness*, a work which was perhaps in part written to oppose the 'libertinism' of Charles Blount by definition of a reasonable Christianity to be accepted on reasonable grounds, and which Locke said was written against deists and to persuade those who 'wholly disbelieved' or doubted the truth of Christianity. Blount was Rochester's correspondent and friend, and Blount's correspondence with Rochester on the immortality of the soul was published in Blount's works in the midst of Blount's own ridiculing of

[55] Burnet, *Some Passages*, 56–7, 85–7, 92–8, 116–17.
[56] Le Clerc, *Treatise*, VI, 3–4, 19–22, 31–5, 262–4, 307ff., and *passim*; Golden, *Le Clerc*, 34–5; Locke, *Correspondence*, 1916, 1999, 2014, 2170, 2202, 2221, 2228, 2310, 2376.

many elements of contemporary Christianity, including the doctrines of the Fall, original sin, the Trinity, the creation *ex nihilo*, the resurrection, and the notion of personal reward and punishment. Blount's works extensively described anti-resurrectional arguments while briefly suggesting that (only) Revelation founded the doctrine of immortality of the soul. He indicated that the 'fable' of immortality had been deployed by politicians as it was thought useful to inculcate obedience and virtue. The tone of Blount's mockery of conventional Christianity is perhaps best captured by part of the contents list of his 1693 *Oracles of Reason*, as published in his 1695 *Miscellaneous Works*: 'Nature good in the Morning, Curs'd in the Evening; the Elaborate Work of an Almighty Architect of a whole week, all ruin'd in a few Hours by so silly a Beast as a Serpent'. Others of Blount's works also effectively ridiculed orthodox Christianity, albeit in the guise of defending it from 'libertine' ridicule, including his effective parallel in his *Two First Books of Philostratus* of Christ with Apollonius, a proclaimed miracle-worker but really a magician performing 'tricks'.

Blount was often called a 'deist', as were others whose arguments were included in Blount's *Oracles of Reason* and *Miscellaneous Works*; it is likely that opposing such questionings of the necessity of Christianity was among Locke's purposes in composing the *Reasonableness*, which he described as having been intended to show to 'deists' that Christianity was necessary. Like Burnet and Le Clerc, Locke stressed that Revelation brought knowledge of the afterlife backed by authority and clearer incentives for the practice of virtue, that there was sufficient evidence for belief in Christianity, and that miracles had provided confirmation of the truth of Christianity. Like Burnet and Le Clerc, Locke stressed the words of the gospel rather than defending philosophical exegeses of Christianity which others ridiculed and saw as reasons to reject Christianity. And Locke, like Burnet, stressed that few had the leisure or capacity of enquiry, that philosophy had no authority to bind the world to its dictates, and that it was not suited to the 'simple'. For Locke, Christianity had answered these needs.[57]

---

[57] Marshall, *Locke*, ch. 9, esp. 406–8; Nuovo, *Locke and Christianity*, xxxiii–xxxvi; Locke, *Reasonableness*, introduction, esp. xxvii–xxxi (where the editor, Higgins-Biddle, points out that Locke was not billed for two volumes of Blount's works until August 1695, but does not show that Locke did not know of Blount's works earlier; cf. Locke's 1694 notation of Blount's *Oracles* in MS Locke f29, 152); Champion, *Pillars*, 1, 7–8, 10, 22, 100, 114, 121, 134–5, 139–40, 142–8, 162–4, 166, 211, 220, 235; C. Blount, *Oracles of Reason* (London 1693), 87; Milton, 'Rye House', Locke, *Correspondence*, IV, 1312; S. Snobelen, 'Socinianism, Heresy and John Locke's *Reasonableness of Christianity*', review article, *Enlightenment and Dissent* (2001); D. Berman, 'Deism, Immortality and the Art of Theological Lying' in *idem*, *History of Atheism*; *idem*, 'Disclaimers as Offence Mechanisms'; Allen, *Doubt's Boundless Sea*; L. Simonutti, 'Spinoza and the English Thinkers' in W. van Bunge

Locke was, moreover, aware of and opposed to Rochester's libertinism. Not merely was Rochester's libertine correspondence with Blount questioning the immortality of the soul and personal resurrection republished in Blount's works, some of which Locke came to possess, but Rochester's poem mocking the creation *ex nihilo*, the Fall, and personal resurrection with reward and punishment, 'Upon Nothing', is among Locke's manuscript poetry collection and was endorsed in 1679 by Locke himself with the words 'noething' and 'Verses'. Rochester's libertinism was epitomised as the 'free use of wine and women', and Rochester was the most notorious libertine of a Restoration court devoted to the 'free use of wine and women'; this ethos, and probably its association with Rochester, was surely in Locke's mind in arguing in his educational writing for teaching restraint to the sons of gentlemen because 'if the child must have grapes or sugar plums when he has a mind to them...why, when he is grown up, must he not be satisfied too, if his desires carry him to wine or women'. Rochester's poetry may itself have been in Locke's mind when discouraging the reading of poetry by gentlemen's sons because poetry advocated licence; Rochester's poetry was the most notorious Restoration poetry advocating licence. Rochester was (with his personal friend Hobbes) the prime representative of egoism later repudiated by the Third Earl of Shaftesbury; the Third Earl was educated personally by Locke.[58]

Opposition to contemporary libertines' arguments against Christianity, and the strong association of such arguments with the actual sexual libertinism of such thinkers as Rochester, thus influenced the composition of a series of important works in defence of 'reasonable' Christianity by the authors of defences of religious toleration discussed in this book, and very probably also influenced the desire of several of the advocates of religious toleration to declare in their works advocating religious toleration that their support for toleration was not intended to provide toleration for 'libertinism'. In addition, the late seventeenth-century 'libertines' whom they attacked themselves tended to support religious toleration, creating a polemical need for authors such as Locke to identify themselves as not sharing such 'libertine' motivations in their own advocacy of toleration. At many moments, the Restoration

and Klever (eds.), *Disguised and Overt Spinozism Around 1700* (Leiden 1996), 191–211; Israel, *Radical*, 126, 340, 362–4, 601–6; Redwood, *Reason*, 14, 26, 35, 42, 44, 46, 57, 59, 62, 75, 80, 81, 85, 99–100, 111, 113, 118–20, 122–3, 125, 128, 130, 132, 135, 139, 153, 163, 180, 220; Harrison, *Religion and the Religions*, 77–85; J. V. Price, Introduction to C. Blount, *The Oracles of Reason* (London 1995); J. King, *Mr Blount's Oracles of Reason, Examined and Answered* (Exeter 1698), esp. 2–3, 16–17, 26, 33–5, 42; Hunter, 'Aikenhead', 221–54, at 240, 248; M. Benitez, *La Face cachée des Lumières* (Paris and Oxford 1996).

[58] MS Locke c32, 12; H. Love, *The Culture and Commerce of Texts* (Amherst 1998), *passim*; Rochester, *Works*, 198, 298–9; Wootton, *Locke*, introduction; *Locke Library*, item 1728; Lambeth MS 930 55; Klein, *Shaftesbury*, 63–4; Locke, *Some Thoughts*, 103–5, 230–1; J. Tully, 'Governing Conduct' in his *An Approach to Political Philosophy: Locke in Contexts* (Cambridge 1993).

court of England was both 'libertine' and tolerationist, headed by a king – Charles II – whose support for religious toleration was associated in part with his own sexual libertinism. Even when that king became resolutely religiously intolerant in the later 1670s and 1680s, court 'libertines' such as Rochester, Buckingham, and Sedley, remained supportive of religious toleration, and some became associated with Whig Exclusionist support for toleration. Tolerationist Whigs' arguments for excluding James from the succession in favour of the king's illegitimate son, Monmouth, included works which questioned 'orthodox sexual morality' in order to make the case for the succession of an illegitimate son. Hobbes, who became an Exclusionist just before his death, was associated with support for religious toleration in the years of the cabal as well as during Exclusion, and published assaults on punishment of heresy. His leading followers in England, including Blount, were proponents of religious toleration.[59]

Only Bayle, among the defenders of religious toleration considered at length in this book, was probably more accurately described as an intellectual 'libertine' rather than as its committed opponent. It is impossible to document this in the space available here, but there are many passages in Bayle's works which, as Mori recently has suggested, register libertine arguments and discuss central doctrines of Christianity in a mocking tone. Bayle ridiculed accounts of miracles in ways that suggest questioning not merely of the beliefs in particular providence of a Jurieu, but of Christianity itself. Some entries discussed claims that Apuleius and Apollonius had done miracles to equal or surpass those of Christ in such a manner that readers would see miraculous testimony to Christ's divinity as questionable. Like many contemporary 'libertines', Bayle ostensibly disparaged such 'libertinism', but also like many contemporary 'libertines', his accounts of the objections to Christianity recorded these at great length and provided often weak or mutually contradictory replies to them. Bayle may also have intended to support intellectual 'libertinism' by extensive attacks on the pretensions of such authors as Le Clerc, Limborch, Burnet, and Locke, to have defined a 'reasonable Christianity' against the challenges of intolerant orthodoxy on the one hand and unreasonable libertinism on the other. And as Bayle seems probably personally to have been intellectually 'libertine', so there are grounds to believe that he may have been intellectually 'sexually libertine'.

---

[59] Rochester, *Works*, 227–9; Tuck, 'Hobbes', 153–71; *idem, Philosophy and Government*, 338–45; Lacey, *Dissent*, 43–4, 80, 116; R. Thomas, 'Comprehension and Indulgence' in G. Nuttall (ed.), *From Uniformity to Unity* (London 1962), 200–1; T. Harris, P. Seaward and M. A. Goldie (eds.), *The Politics of Religion in Restoration England* (Oxford 1990), 7, 9, 11, 14, 90, 139–40, 142, 145–6; Love, *Culture and Commerce*, 243, 252; G. Tarantino, *Martin Clifford* (Firenze 2000); Hobbes, *Behemoth*, xlvii–xlviii, 8–9; Simonutti, 'Spinoza'; Weil, 'Sometimes'; Weil, *Political Passions*, 24.

David Wootton has shown that many passages of the *Dictionary* are capable of being read as supporting sexual 'libertinism', that many entries in the *Dictionary* treated issues of sexual behaviour as practical rather than moral issues, and has suggested that letter seventeen of Bayle's *Nouvelles lettres critiques* (1685) even suggested that the sexual exclusivity of marriage was irrational because women were an inexhaustible source of sexual pleasure and private property should be established only over 'scarce resources' such as land and not over inexhaustible resources such as women.[60]

Yet if a personal support for 'libertine' criticisms of Christianity and even intellectual support of sexual 'libertinism' is the most persuasive reading of Bayle's own private commitments, and arguably also the most persuasive reading of works such as the *Dictionary* once attuned to every nuance of his arguments, it is important that Bayle veiled any such personal libertinism within ostensible piety, declared himself a fideist Christian, and at many points attacked libertinism. It was ostensibly as a fideist Christian, and not as an avowed 'libertine', that Bayle attacked Le Clerc and others. Bayle denounced the sexual behaviour of many Catholics as 'libertine' and 'sodomitical'. He attacked the thought of Rochester. He repeatedly denied that he was a libertine and denounced libertinism with rhetoric substantial enough to have convinced many recent scholars that he was a fideist Christian who had accepted many challenges to reasoned explications of the faith but who maintained that faith by faith. Bayle's *Philosophical Commentary* itself attacked the use of force as exposing Christianity to the mockery of 'libertines'.[61] Attacked more than any other advocate of toleration except Aubert as being a 'libertine' himself, Bayle had many polemical reasons to declare that he was an opponent of libertinism and not its advocate.

In the 1680s and 1690s, the advocates of religious toleration focused upon in this book thus faced a series of associations of toleration with 'libertinism' and, with the probable exception of Bayle, all were hostile to the increasing circulation of 'libertine' challenges to Christianity, which was significantly associated with support for sexual libertinism. Although, as we saw in Chapter 17, many of these advocates of religious toleration at moments suggested that drunkenness or debauchery were not punished by magistrates,

---

[60] Bayle, *Dictionary*, 'Eve A'; 'Apollonius'; 'Pomponazzi'; Mori, *Bayle, passim*; Wootton, 'Bayle, Libertine?'; A. McKenna, 'L'Eclaircissement sur les Pyrrhoniens, 1702' in *Le Dictionnaire de Pierre Bayle* (Amsterdam 1997), 297–320; *idem*, 'Rationalisme moral et fideisme' in H. Bost and P. de Robert (eds.), *Pierre Bayle, Citoyen du Monde* (Paris 1999), 257–74; Champion, *Pillars*, 143; for more fideistic readings, see especially Labrousse, *Bayle* and Popkin (ed.), *Historical and Critical Dictionary*, selections, introduction. I am grateful to Jonathan Israel, Anthony McKenna, and Justin Champion for conversations about Bayle and 'libertinism'.

[61] Bayle, *Philosophical Commentary* (1708), 146 and *passim*; Bayle, *Dictionnaire* (Rotterdam 1702), III, 3145, in *Rochester: The Critical Heritage*, 183.

and although Bayle in the *Philosophical Commentary* explicitly suggested that 'rakes' stood beyond the purview of magisterial force, these advocates of religious toleration simultaneously argued forcefully and explicitly in their defences of religious toleration that they did not defend toleration of 'libertinism' and 'sodomy'. Aubert denied the legitimacy of personal attacks on him by Jurieu, who accused him of rape and incest, and his writings attacked the toleration of adultery, sodomy, and fornication. For Aubert in the *Treatise*, 'libertine sodomites' were 'open atheists' and the 'pests of society'; the magistrate must punish such. Aubert firmly distinguished the 'conscience' of a Pelagian or Nestorian heretic from that of an impious man who thought it legitimate 'to commit incests, adulteries, and sodomies'. For Aubert, if there were contemporaries who revived the 'infamies' attributed to the Gnostics and Priscillians, then magistrates had not merely the right but the duty to repress them. He argued that such were not to be executed, but instead were to suffer such punishments as 'perpetual imprisonment' and being sent to the 'galleys'. Enumerating crimes against which the magistrate was authorised to use the sword in the *Pacific Protestant*, Aubert listed adultery.[62] Bayle similarly was attacked for supporting 'libertinism', and attacked 'libertinism' and 'sodomy' in the *Philosophical Commentary* and its *Supplement*. He argued that his defence of conscience would not allow the preaching of 'sodomy, adultery, and murder'. He argued that his emphasis on an erroneous conscience did not legitimate behaviour such as that of the ancient Gnostics and Adamites. And in the *Supplement* he devoted a section to the attempt to turn the accusation of supporting 'sodomy' back against persecutors, suggesting that since persecution justified actions which conduced to conversion but were otherwise illegitimate, such arguments could be used to justify even 'sodomy', such that even 'sodomy might be a pious action according to modern persecutors' and 'we may bid fair for sanctifying the...sin....which deserves burning the most of any crime that can be named...Sodomy'.[63]

Locke argued in the *Letter* that he supported 'liberty' and not 'libertinism and licentiousness'. He argued in the *Letter* itself that 'adultery' and 'fornication' were punishable as crimes and so not to be tolerated on civil grounds; therefore they could not be defended via religious toleration. In a response to the centuries of accusations that heretics' and schismatics'

---

[62] Aubert de Versé, *Traité*, 32, 42–4, 99; *idem*, *Protestant*, 4.

[63] Bayle, *Philosophical Commentary* (1708), esp. 737–9; *idem*, *OD*, II, 551–2. In his 1696 *Treatise of the Causes of Incredulity*, Le Clerc declared that a prince who 'would abrogate all those Laws prohibiting Adultery' would cause 'Disorders' in the commonwealth. And he contrasted Christian societies with good laws with commonwealths whose laws suffered 'some Crimes which are very prejudicial to Society', naming among the latter Greek and Roman societies 'horribly addicted to Fornication and Sodomy': *Treatise*, 88, 197–9.

meetings were 'licentious' and 'libertine' orgies, accusations which we have seen were being repeated in Restoration England and post-Revocation France, Locke argued explicitly in the *Letter* that

if some congregations should have a mind to sacrifice infants, or, as the primitive Christians were falsely accused, lustfully pollute themselves in promiscuous uncleanness, or practise any other such heinous enormities, is the magistrate obliged to tolerate them...No. These things are not lawful in the ordinary course of life, nor in any private house; and therefore, neither are they so in the worship of God, or in any religious meeting.

Locke expanded on this theme in his defences of that *Letter* in the 1690s, declaring that he condemned 'debauchery', and as he did so he stressed that the magistrate ought to punish such debauchery and coerce people to lead a 'good life'. These short but important passages should be understood, moreover, as parts of a repeated attack by Locke on 'sexual libertinism' in his published works in the 1680s and 1690s. His *Two Treatises* argued that 'adultery' and 'sodomy' were both against 'the law of nature', which made procreation the only legitimate purpose of sexual activity, and declared that the 'security of the marriage bed' was necessary to procreation. In the *Paraphrase on the Epistles of St Paul*, Locke identified sodomy as against nature and condemned it straightforwardly and fiercely. His *Paraphrase* reiterated Paul's condemnation in Romans 1:26–28 of 'shamefull and infamous lusts and passions', of women who changed their 'natural use into that which is against nature' and of men who 'leaveing the natural use of the women burned in their lusts one towards another, men with men practiseing that which is shamefull'. Locke's note expanded that they 'debase and dishonour themselves by unnatural lusts'.[64]

In his *Essay*, as we saw earlier in this chapter, Locke attacked the 'profligate wretches' who wished there to be no God so that they could satisfy their lusts, and called for their suppression by the magistrate. It is important to stress that in context these passages involved practical justification in the 1690s of suppression of sexual 'vice' because they were issued in the midst of a campaign led by the religiously tolerationist Burnet and others of Locke's friends among the Latitudinarians, and supported by friends such as Furly, who wrote to Locke in 1690 simultaneously in defence of religious toleration and in support of the laws against 'immorality and debauchery' being 'rigorously executed'. As we noted in Chapter 3, in the 1690s bawdy-houses were closed, prostitutes arrested, and a trial instigated by Thomas Bray

---

[64] Locke, *Letter* in *Works*, 33; *Third Letter*, 373, 416, 468–70, 485–6; Locke, *Essay*, I, iii.13; Locke, *Some Thoughts*, 103–5; Locke, *Treatises*, II, 59; Locke, *Paraphrase*, Romans 1:26–7; Marshall, *Locke*, 378–83; Wootton, *Locke*, introduction, 191; Weil, *Political Passions*, 24–5, 29.

(Locke and Burnet's associate) which led to a prison sentence for attempted sodomy against Captain Rigby. For many defenders of religious toleration, what had finally been achieved in England in the 1690s was the desirable reverse of the intolerance of much of the Restoration, with toleration for (orthodox) religious dissenters and sexual repression replacing religious intolerance and sexual licence.[65]

For Burnet, support of such punishment of sexual licence in the 1690s was, however, maintained in a period which saw his support for religious toleration itself become increasingly limited, as he defended the 1698 Blasphemy Act, which provided penalties including imprisonment not merely for those who denied Revelation but also for those who denied the Trinity. Burnet supported this Act by attacking both atheists and Socinians in England. He differentiated Socinians in England from Socinians elsewhere in correspondence with Limborch which declared that the Act was intended to impose a check on 'the licentiousness of the irreligious, so as to hinder them from openly venting their blasphemous fury against religion' and which asserted that Socinians now 'openly argue in favour of free love, even without the formality of divorce. Such doctrines, propagated among the crowd, and almost universally discussed, have produced such a dissolution of manners as gives us the most melancholy prospect'. Responding to Limborch's opposition to religious persecution, Burnet trumpeted the urgent need for 'repression' of 'blasphemous fury against religion'. Having received this letter from Burnet, Limborch reported to Locke that Burnet had declared that the Blasphemy Act was directed against 'men who impugn all revelation' and that 'they openly defend promiscuous intercourse'. Locke responded that the Act was directed not against those who impugned all Revelation, but rather against those who questioned 'a certain interpretation of divine revelation' [The Trinity], that he had not heard 'any talk of' what Burnet had said about Socinian support for 'promiscuous sexual intercourse', and that such was alleged by Burnet in order to 'rouse ill-will' because those who did not 'dare openly to profess persecution, try to introduce it under another name and to veil it with false accusations'.[66] In the later 1690s, then, Burnet became more religiously intolerant as he aligned Socinians in England with intellectual and sexual libertinism and defended 'repression' for such Socinians as well as libertines, whereas Locke continued to deny that Socinians should be punished, as he denied that they were libertines, and noted that sexual allegations were commonly deployed by the religiously intolerant in order to legitimate religious

---

[65] Marshall, *Locke*, 380–3; Locke, *Correspondence*, 2596, 2615; S. Burtt, *Virtue Transformed* (Cambridge 1992), ch. 2; D. Rubini, 'Sexuality and Augustan England', *Journal of Homosexuality* (1988), 349–81; Herrup, *House*, 134–5.

[66] Foxcroft, *Life of Burnet*, II, 347–8; Locke, *Correspondence*, 2596, 2615.

intolerance. But both Burnet and Locke supported intolerance towards actual 'libertines' and 'sodomites'.

In both England and the Netherlands, the early eighteenth century was a period of increased definition of 'the homosexual' and of increased prosecution of homosexual acts. In England in the eighteenth century, homosexuals were punished fiercely while in general sporadically; in the Netherlands, where there had been one capital sentence against 'sodomites' in Breda in 1629, one in Utrecht in 1676, and one in Amsterdam in 1686, a hundred men and boys were to be executed for homosexuality in the 1730s.[67] In the 1730s, it was once again opponents of religious toleration who led the campaign, as Justus van Effen and others identified 'sodomy' with the toleration of Huguenots said to have brought the related sins of 'heresy' and 'sodomy' to a Dutch republic whose tolerance had therefore drawn upon its people God's punishments, including an epidemic of pile-worm. But the supporters of religious toleration of the 1680s and 1690s discussed in this book had themselves been apologists for intolerance towards homosexual acts, and supporters of religious toleration in the 1730s did not challenge this sexual repression.[68]

It was not until the period from the middle of the eighteenth century to the early nineteenth century that a significant number of theorists, including Beccaria and Montesquieu, came to criticise earlier arguments for the punishment of sodomy, indicting medieval barbarism as involved in the punishment of 'sodomy' as it was in the punishment of 'heresy'.[69] In some of the lengthiest considerations, Jeremy Bentham composed manuscripts attacking the punishment of homosexuality. For Bentham, it was much worse to 'thirst after a man's blood who is innocent, if innocency consists in the doing of no harm to anyone' than it was to have this 'taste'. He argued that he could not see how a Protestant could 'with consistency condemn the Spanish for burning Moors or the Portuguese for burning Jews: for no paederast can be more odious to a person of unpolluted taste than a Moor is to a Spaniard or a Jew to an orthodox Portuguese'. Rather as Priestley and Jefferson extended the tolerationist arguments of the 1680s and 1690s a century later by arguing

---

[67] L. Crompton, *Byron and Greek Love* (Berkeley 1985), ch. 1; Herrup, *House*; Bray, *Homosexuality*; A. Huussen, 'Sodomy in the Dutch Republic During the Eighteenth Century', in P. Maccubin (ed.), *'Tis Nature's Fault* (Cambridge 1987), 169–78, esp. 171; T. van der Meer, 'The Persecution of Sodomites in Eighteenth Century Amsterdam: Changing Perceptions of Sodomy', *Journal of Homosexuality* (1989), 263–307; R. Trumbach, 'The Birth of the Queen: Sodomy and the Emergence of Gender Equality in Modern Culture 1660–1750' in M. Duberman, M. Vicinus and G. Chauncy (eds.), *Hidden from History* (London 1991); idem, 'Sodomitical Subcultures, Sodomitical Roles, and the Gender Revolution of the Eighteenth Century' in Maccubin (ed.), *'Tis Nature's Fault*.

[68] Gibbs, 'Some Intellectual and Political Influences', 255–87, at 271.

[69] Crompton, *Byron and Greek Love*, ch. 1, esp. 16–17, 31–3; Huussen, 'Sodomy', 174.

for the toleration of Catholics and atheists as 'harmless', so Bentham extended these arguments in order to legitimate the toleration of homosexual acts. But whereas by the late eighteenth century argument for the toleration of atheists and Roman Catholics was beginning to become acceptable in England and the Netherlands, it was to take much longer for such arguments for the toleration of homosexual acts to become acceptable; Bentham left his arguments for the toleration of homosexuality unpublished, as he worried that their publication would lead others to repudiate his utilitarianism.[70] Anxious to defend religious toleration at a time of massive religious intolerance, many of the apologists of the 'early Enlightenment' analysed in this book challenged the centuries-old association of heretics with libertines and sodomites, but did so in the name of religious toleration and sexual repression.

[70] Crompton, *Byron and Greek Love*, ch. 1, esp. 28–9, 39, 42; *idem*, 'Offences Against One's Self: Paederasty', *Journal of Homosexuality* (1978), 3, iv, 389–404; 4, i, 91–107.

BIBLIOGRAPHY

PRIMARY SOURCES

Manuscripts

MS Locke b2
MS Locke c1
MS Locke c25
MS Locke c27
MS Locke c32
MS Locke c33
MS Locke c34
MS Locke c42
MS Locke d1
MS Locke d9
MS Locke d10
MS Locke e17
MS Locke f1
MS Locke f2
MS Locke f3
MS Locke f5
MS Locke f8
MS Locke f9
MS Locke f10
MS Locke f28
MS Locke f29
MS Locke f30
MS Locke f32
PRO 30/24/4/63
BM Add MSS 38847
Huguenot Library, London, MS R5, v.1–10
Lambeth Palace MS 929, 54
Lambeth Palace MS 930, 55
Lambeth Palace MS 932, 1
Lambeth Palace MS 933, 67, 77
Lambeth Palace MS 1029, 65

University Library, Amsterdam coll.hss.v.84; Remonstrants MS III, D17, 4, 5, 6, 7, 9, 16, 17, 19, 20, 66, 68, 79, 84, 85v, 89, 90, 93, 114–20, 122, 135, 156–7, 163.

PRINTED WORKS

An Appeal from the Country to the City (London 1680)

Avertissement aux Protestants des provinces (1684; ed. E. Labrousse, Paris 1986)

A Brief Account of the Designs which the Papists have had Against the Earl of Shaftesbury, Occasioned by his Commitment, July 2 1681 (London 1681)

Catechesis Ecclesiarum Polonicarum (1684)

The Further Information of Stephen Dugdale (London 1680).

His Majesty's Declaration Defended (London 1681)

The Horrible Persecution of the French Protestants in the Province of Poitou (London 1681)

[To the King's Most Excellent Majesty] The Humble Address of the Atheists, or the Sect of the Epicureans (London 1689)

The Humble Address of the Distressed Protestants in France (London 1681)

The Information of Robert Jennison (London 1680)

The Information of Edward Turberville (London 1680)

Letter From a Gentleman in the City to One in the Country (London 1680)

Letter From a Person of Quality Concerning His Majesty's Late Declaration (London 1681)

A Narrative of Popish Plots (London 1678)

Popery and Tyranny or the Present State of France (London 1679)

Popish Treachery, or a Short Account of the Horrid Cruelties Exercised on the Protestants in France. Being a True Prospect of What is to be Expected From the Most Solemn Promises of Roman Catholic Princes (London 1689)

The Prince of Orange's Engagement for Maintaining and Securing the Protestant Religion, and Liberties of the People of England (London 1689)

The Proceedings Against the Right Honorable Earl of Shaftesbury 24 November 1681 (London 1681)

Reflections on Two Discourses Concerning the Divinity of Our Saviour (London 1693)

The Several Informations of John McNamara, Maurice Fitzgerald and James Nash Relating to the Horrid Popish Plot in Ireland (London 1680)

A Short Account of the Persecution of the Waldensians (Oxford 1688)

The Sighs of France in Slavery (London 1689)

To the King, Lords and Commons in Parliament Assembled, the Case of the People Called Quakers Stated (1680)

A True Narrative of the Horrid, Hellish Popish Plot, the Second Part (London 1680)

The True Speeches of Thomas Whitebread, William Harcourt, John Fenwick, John Gavan, and Anthony Turner before their Execution at Tyburn June 20th 1679 (London 1679)

Abbadie, J., *Défense de la nation Britannique* (The Hague 1694)

Acontius, J., *Satanae Stratagema*, ed. R.E. Field as *Darkness Discovered* (New York 1978)

Allix, P., *Reflections Upon the Opinions of Some Modern Divines Concerning the Nature of Government in General and that of England in Particular* (London 1689)

Allix, P., *Some Remarks Upon the Ecclesiastical History of the Ancient Churches of Piedmont* (London 1690)

Ancillon, C., *L'irrévocabilité de L'Édit de Nantes, prouvée par les principes de droit & de la politique* (Amsterdam 1688)

Arminius, J., *The Works of James Arminius*, ed. C. Bangs, tr. J. Nichols (Mich. 1986), vols. I–III

Bacon, F., *The Essayes*, ed. M. Kiernan (Cambridge, Mass. 1985)

Basnage de Beauval, H., *Histoire des Ouvrages des Savans* (1687–1709)

Basnage de Beauval, H., *Tolérance des Religions* (Rotterdam 1684)

[Basnage, J.], *Histoire de la mort des persécuteurs de l'Église primitive* (Utrecht 1687)

Basnage, J., *History of the Jews* (London 1708)

Baxter, R., *Reliquiae Baxterianae* (London 1696)

[Bayle, P.?], *Avis important aux réfugiés* (1690), in P. Bayle, *Oeuvres diverses*, II, 578–633

Bayle, P., *Ce que c'est que la France toute catholique* (1686; ed. E. Labrousse, Paris 1973)

Bayle, P., *Historical and Critical Dictionary*, ed. P. des Maizeaux (London 1734)

Bayle, P., *Historical and Critical Dictionary: Selections*, ed. R. Popkin (Indianapolis 1991)

Bayle, P., *Miscellaneous Reflections* (London 1708)

Bayle, P., *Nouvelles de la république des lettres* (Amsterdam 1684–7)

Bayle, P., *Oeuvres diverses* (1727–31); ed. E. Labrousse (Paris 1964–82), 5 vols.

Bayle, P., *Pensées diverses sur la comète*, ed. A. Prat (Paris 1939)

Bayle, P., *Philosophical Commentary* (London 1708)

Bayle, P., *Philosophical Commentary*, ed. A. Tannenbaum (New York 1987)

Bayle, P., *De la tolérance: Commentaire philosophique*, ed. J.M. Gros (Paris 1992)

Bayle, P., *Political Writings*, ed. S. Jenkinson (Cambridge 2000)

Bayle, P., *Recueil de quelques pièces curieuses concernant la philosophie de Mr Descartes* (Amsterdam 1684)

Bayle, P., *Various Thoughts on the Occasion of a Comet*, ed. R. Bartlett (SUNY 2000)

Benoist, E., *Histoire de L'Édit de Nantes* (Delft 1693–5), 5 vols. in 3

Benoist, E., *The History of the Famous Edict of Nantes* (London 1694)

Benoist, E., *Historie der Gereformeerde kerken van Vankryk* (Amsterdam 1696)

Benoist, J., *Histoire des Albigeois & des Vaudois* (Paris 1691)

Beza, T., *De Haereticis* (Geneva 1554)

Blount, T., *Censura Celebriorum Authorum* (London 1690), Locke Library, Bodleian Library

Blount, C., *Great is Diana of the Ephesians* (London 1680)

Blount, C., *Miracles No Violations of the Law of Nature* (London 1683)

Blount, C., *Miscellaneous Works* (London 1695)

Blount, C., *Oracles of Reason* (London 1693)

Blount, C., *The Two First Books of Philostratus* (London 1680)

Bossuet, J.B., *Avertissements aux Protestans* (Liège 1710)

Bossuet, J.B., *Cinquième avertissement* and *Sixième avertissement aux protestans sur les lettres du ministre Jurieu contre l'Histoire des Variations*, in Bossuet, *Oeuvres*, vol. IV (Paris 1841)

Bossuet, J.B., *Conference With Mr Claude* (London 1687)

Bossuet, J.B., *Défense de L'Histoire des variations* (Paris 1689)

Bossuet, J.B., *Discourse on Universal History*, ed. O. Ranum (Chicago 1976)

Bossuet, J.B., *Histoire des variations des églises protestants* (1688; 1841)

Bossuet, J.B., *History of the Variations of the Protestant Churches* (Dublin 1836)

Bossuet, J.B., *Politics Drawn from the Very Words of Holy Scripture*, ed. P. Riley (Cambridge 1990)

Boyer, P., *The History of the Vaudois* (London 1692)

Burnet, G., *An Apology for the Church of England with Relation to the Spirit of Persecution for which she is Accused* (1688)

Burnet, G., *The Conversion and Persecutions of Eve Cohan, now called Elizabeth Verboon* (London 1680)

Burnet, G., *An Enquiry into the Measures of Submission* (London 1688)

Burnet, G., *History of His Own Time* (London 1724–30)

Burnet, G., *History of the Persecution in the Valleys of Piedmont* (Amsterdam and London 1687)

Burnet, G., *History of the Reformation* (London 1679–80)

Burnet, G., *Mystery of Iniquity* (London 1673)

Burnet, G., *Reflections on Mr Varrillas' History of the Great Revolutions which have Happened in Europe in Matters of Religion* (Amsterdam 1686)

Burnet, G., *A Relation of the Barbarous and Bloody Massacre of About an Hundred Thousand Protestants* (London 1678)

Burnet, G. (ed.), *A Relation of the Death of the Primitive Persecutors* (Amsterdam 1687)

Burnet, G., *Sermon...December 1688* (London 1689)

Burnet, G., *Sermon...Jan 31 1689* (London 1689)

Burnet, G., *Sermon 5 November 1689* (London 1689)

Burnet, G., *Six Papers* (1687)

Burnet, G., *Some Letters* (Amsterdam 1686)

Burnet, G., *Some Passages of the Life and Death of...Rochester* (London 1680)

Burnet, G., *A Supplement to Burnet's History of My Own Time, Derived from His Original Memoirs, His Autobiography*, ed. H.C. Foxcroft (Oxford 1902)

Burton, T., *The Diary of Thomas Burton* (London 1828)

Care, H., *Animadversions* (London 1687)

Care, H., *Answer to the Letter to a Dissenter* (London 1687)

Care, H., *A Discourse for Taking Off the Tests and Penal Laws* (London 1687)

Care, H., *The Legality of the Court* (London 1688)

Care, H., *A Word in Season* (London 1679)

Carr, W., *An Accurate Description of the United Netherlands* (London 1691)

Castellio, S., *Conseil à la France désolée* (1562) in Bainton (ed.), *Concerning*

Castellio, S., *Contra libellum Calvini in quo ostendere conatur haereticos jure gladii coercendos esse*, in Bainton (ed.), *Concerning*, 265–87

Castellio, S., *De arte dubitandi*, in Bainton (ed.), *Concerning*, 287–305

Cheynell, F., *The Rise, Growth and Danger of Socinianisme* (London 1643)

Clarke, S., *A General Martyrology* (London 1677)

[Claude, J.], *An Account of the Persecutions and Oppressions of the Protestants in France* (London 1686)

Condorcet, J.-A.-N. de Caritat, Marquis de Condorcet, *Sketch for a Historical Picture of the Progress of the Human Mind* (London 1955)

Court, P. de la, *The True Interest and Political Maxims of Holland* (London 1702)

[Crell, J.], *A Learned and Exceeding Well-compiled Vindication of Liberty of Religion* (London 1646)

D'Assigny, S., *A Short Relation of the Brave Exploits of the Vaudois* (Dublin 1699)

Edwards, J., *Some Thoughts Concerning...Atheism* (London 1695)

Edwards, T., *Gangraena* (London 1646)

Episcopius, S., *Opera Theologica* (Amsterdam-Gouda 1650–5)

Episcopius, S., *The Popish Labyrinth...Unto Which is Added The Life and Death of the Author*, tr. J.K. (London 1673)

[Everard, E.], *The Great Pressures and Grievances of the Protestants in France* (London 1681)

Fagel, G., *A Letter Writ by...Fagel...to James Stewart* (Amsterdam 1688; letter dated 4 November 1687)

Fagel, G., *Their Highness the Prince and Princess of Orange's Opinion About a General Liberty of Conscience* (London 1689)

[Ferguson, R.], *No Protestant Plot* (London 1681)

[Ferguson, R.], *The Second Part of No Protestant Plot* (London 1682)

[Ferguson, R.], *Third Part of No Protestant Plot* (London 1682)

Fontaine, J., *Memoirs of a Huguenot Family* (Suffolk 1986; originally published 1722), also published as Jacques Fontaine, *Mémoires d'une Famille Huguenote*, ed. B. Cottret (Languedoc 1992)

Foucault, N.-J., *Mémoires* (Paris 1862) in W. Church, *The Impact of Absolutism in France* (New York 1969), 87–95

Fowler, E., *The Great Wickedness, and Mischievous Effects of Slandering* (London 1685)

Fox, G., *Concerning Persecution in All Ages to this Day* (London 1682)

[Furly, B.], *Bibliotheca Furliana* (Rotterdam 1714)

Goodwin, T., *The Great Interest of States and Kingdomes* (London 1646)

Gother, J., *A Papist Represented and Misrepresented* (London 1685)

Gousset, J., *Considérations théologiques et critiques sur le projet d'un nouvelle version française de la Bible* (Amsterdam 1698)

Grotius, H., *Ordinum...Pietas*, ed. E. Rabbie (Leiden 1995)

Guichard, J., *Histoire du Socinianisme* (1723)

Halifax, George Savile, Marquis of, *The Character of a Trimmer* in *The Works of George Savile, Marquis of Halifax*, ed. M. Brown (Oxford 1989)

Halifax, George Savile, Marquis of, *A Letter to a Dissenter* (1687) in M. Brown (ed.), *The Works of George Savile, Marquis of Halifax* (Oxford 1989)

Hay du Châtelet, P., *Traité de la Politique de France* (1666), ch. 5, tr. A. Soman in O. Ranum (ed.), *The Century of Louis XIV* (1972), 354

Hobbes, T., *Behemoth*, ed. S. Holmes (Chicago 1990)

Hooker, R., *Of the Laws of Ecclesiastical Polity*, ed. A.S. McGrade and B. Vickers (London 1975)

James I: *The Political Works of James I* (London 1616; ed. C. McIlwain, Harvard 1918)

Jurieu, P., *Accomplishment of the Scripture Prophecies* (London 1686)

Jurieu, P., *Courte revue des Maximes de morale* (1691)

Jurieu, P., *Défense de la doctrine universelle de l'église* (Amsterdam 1695)

Jurieu, P., *Les derniers efforts de l'innocence affligée* (Amsterdam 1682)

Jurieu, P., *Des Droits de deux souverains* (Rotterdam 1687; reprint Fayard 1997, ed. B. de Negroni)

Jurieu, P., *L'Esprit de M. Arnauld* (1684)

Jurieu, P., *Examen de la Réunion du Christianisme* (Orleans 1671)

Jurieu, P., *Histoire du calvinisme et celle du papisme mises en parallèle* (Rotterdam 1683)

Jurieu, P., *Last Efforts of Afflicted Innocence* (London 1682)

Jurieu, P., *Lettre de quelques protestants pacifiques* (1685)

Jurieu, P., *Lettres pastorales* (Rotterdam 1686–9)

Jurieu, P., *The Pastoral Letter* (London 1689)

Jurieu, P., *Le Philosophe de Rotterdam* (Amsterdam 1706; ed. B. de Negroni, Fayard 1997)

Jurieu, P., *Policy of the Clergy of France to Destroy the Protestants of that Kingdom* (London 1681)

Jurieu, P., *La Politique du Clergé de France* (Cologne 1681)

Jurieu, P., *Préjugés légitimes contre le Papisme* (Amsterdam 1685)

Jurieu, P., *La Religion du latitudinaire* (Rotterdam 1696)

Jurieu, P., *Le Tableau du Socinianisme* (The Hague 1690)

Jurieu, P., *Le Vray Système de l'église* (Dordrecht 1686)

King, J., *Mr Blount's Oracles of Reason, Examined and Answered* (London 1698)

King, W., *Europe's Deliverance from France and Slavery* (London 1691)

King, W., *The State of the Protestants of Ireland under James* (Exeter 1691)

La Loubère, Simon de, *The Kingdom of Siam* (1693; reprint Oxford 1986)

Lamothe, C.G., *Two Discourses Concerning the Divinity of Our Saviour* (London 1693)

La Pillonière, F., *Answer to Mr Snape's Accusation* (London 1717)

La Pillonière, F., *Third Defense* (London 1718)

La Valette, *Parallel de l'hérésie des Albigeois et de celle du calvinisme* (Paris 1686)

[Lawton], 'Mr Lawton's Memoir of William Penn' in *Memoirs of the Historical Society of Pennsylvania*, III, ii (Philadelphia 1836), 215–31

[Le Cène, C.], *Conversations sur diverses matières de religion* (Amsterdam 1687)

Le Cène, C. and Le Clerc, J., *Entretiens sur diverses matières de théologie* (1685)

Le Clerc, J., *An Account of the Life and Writings of Jean le Clerc to 1711* (London 1712)

Le Clerc, J., *Bibliothèque ancienne et moderne* (Amsterdam 1714–24)

Le Clerc, J., *Bibliothèque choisie* (Amsterdam 1703–18)

Le Clerc, J. (et al.), *Bibliothèque universelle et historique* (Amsterdam 1718), 26 vols.

Le Clerc, J., *Epistolario*, ed. M. Sina (Florence 1987–)

Le Clerc, J., *Histoire des Provinces-Unies des Pays-Bas* (Amsterdam 1727–8)

Le Clerc, J., *Liberii de sancto amore epistolae theologicae* (1681)

Le Clerc, J., *The Life and Character of Mr John Locke* (London 1706)

Le Clerc, J., *Life of...Burnet* (London 1715)

Le Clerc, J., *The Lives of the Primitive Fathers* (London 1701)

[Le Clerc, J.], *Mr Le Clerc's Extract and Judgment of the Rights of the Christian Church Asserted* (London 1708)

Le Clerc, J., *Parrhasiana* (Amsterdam 1699, 1701; London 1700)

[Le Clerc, J.], *Sentimens des quelques théologiens* (Amsterdam 1684)

Le Clerc, J., *A Treatise of the Causes of Incredulity* (London 1697)

L'Estrange, R., *Dissenters' Sayings* (London 1681)

L'Estrange, R., *L'Estrange's Accompt Cleared* (London 1682)

[L'Estrange, R.], *The Observator* (London 1681, 1682, 1685, 1686)

Limborch, P. van, *Catalogus Librorum* (Amsterdam 1712)

Limborch, P. van, *A Compleat System of Divinity*, ed. and tr. W. Jones (London 1706)

Limborch, P. van, *De Veritate Religionis Christianae* (Gouda 1687)

Limborch, P. van, *Historia Inquisitionis* (Amsterdam 1692)

Limborch, P. van, *History of the Inquisition*, tr. S. Chandler (London 1731), 2 vols.

Limborch, P. van, *Theologia Christiana* (Amsterdam 1686, 1700)

Lloyd, W., *A Sermon Preached at the Funeral of Sir Edmund Berry Godfrey* (London 1678)

Lloyd, W., *A Sermon Preached Before Their Majesties...5 November 1689*

Lloyd, W., *A Sermon Preached...May 29 1692* (London 1692)

Locke, J., *The Correspondence of John Locke*, ed. E.S. de Beer (Oxford 1978–)

Locke, J., *An Essay Concerning Human Understanding*, ed. P. Nidditch (Oxford 1978)

Locke, J., *A Letter Concerning Toleration*, ed. R. Klibansky and J. Gough (Oxford 1968)

Locke, J., *A Letter Concerning Toleration*, ed. J. Tully (Indianapolis 1983)

Locke, J., *The Library Catalogue of John Locke*, ed. P. Laslett and J. Harrison (Oxford 1965)

Locke, J., *The Life and Letters of John Locke*, ed. P. King (London 1884)

Locke, J., *Locke: Political Writings*, ed. D. Wootton (New York 1993)

Locke, J., *A Paraphrase and Notes Upon the Epistles of St Paul*, ed. A. Wainwright (Oxford 1989), 2 vols.

Locke, J., *Political Essays*, ed. M.A. Goldie (Cambridge 1997)

Locke, J., *The Reasonableness of Christianity*, ed. J. Higgins-Biddle (Oxford 1999)

Locke, J., *Some Thoughts Concerning Education*, ed. J. and J. Yolton (Oxford 1989)

Locke, J., *Two Tracts Upon Government*, ed. P. Abrams (Cambridge 1969)

Locke, J., *Two Treatises Upon Government*, ed. P. Laslett (Cambridge 1963)

Locke, J., *The Works of John Locke* (London 1794)

Locke, J., *The Works of John Locke* (London 1801)

[Long, T.], *Letter on Toleration Decipherd* (London 1689)

Long, T., *No Protestant but the Dissenters' Plot* (London 1682)

Maimbourg, L., *Histoire du calvinisme* (Paris 1682)

Marsollier, J., *Histoire de l'Inquisition et son origin* (1692)

Marvell, A., *Account of the Growth of Popery and Arbitrary Power* (London 1677)

Mede, J., *A Key to the Revelation* (London 1627)

Mencke, O., *Acta Eruditorum* (Leipzig 1682–)

Migault, J., *Journal de Jean Migault*, ed. Y. Krumenacker (Paris 1995)

Milner, J., *Animadversions on le Clerc's Reflections* (London 1702)

Milton, J., *Considerations Touching the Likeliest Means to Remove Hirelings Out of the Church* (London 1659)

Milton, J., 'On the Late Massacre in Piedmont' in *Poems* (London 1673)

Milton, J., *Political Writings*, ed. M. Dzelzainis (Cambridge 1991)

Morland, S., *The History of the Evangelical Churches of the Valleys of Piedmont* (London 1658)

Nicole, P., *Préjugés légitimes contre les calvinistes* (1671)

Ochino, B., *A Dialogue of Polygamy* (English translation, London 1657)

Paets, A. van, *De nuperis Angliae motibus Epistola, in qua de diversum a publica Religione circa Divina sentientium disseritur tolerantia* (Rotterdam 1686)

Paets, A. van, *Lettre de Mr H.V.P. a Mr B*** sur les derniers troubles* (Rotterdam 1686)

Pagitt, E., *Heresiography* (London 1645)

[Papin, I.], *La Foi réduite à ses véritables principes* (Rotterdam 1687)

[Papin, I.], *The Toleration of the Protestants* (London 1733)

Paré, A., *On Monsters and Marvels*, tr. J. Pallister (Chicago 1982)

Parker, S., *A Discourse of Ecclesiastical Polity* (London 1670)

Parsons, R., *A Sermon Preached at the Funeral of the Rt Honorable John Earl of Rochester* (Oxford 1680)

Penn, W., *An Account of the Travails of Mr Penn in Holland and Germany 1677* (London 1694)

Penn, W., *Considerations Moving to a Toleration* (London 1685)

[Penn, W.], *The Continued Cry of the Oppressed for Justice* (London 1675)

Penn, W., *A Defence of the Duke of Buckingham's Book of Religion* (London 1685)

Penn, W., *England's Great Interest* (London 1675)

Penn, W., *Good Advice to the Church of England, Roman Catholick, and Protestant Dissenter* (London 1687)

Penn, W., *The Great and Popular Objection Against the Repeal of the Penal Laws and Tests Briefly Stated and Considered* (London 1687, 1688)

Penn, W., *The Great Case of Liberty of Conscience* (London 1670)

Penn, W., *The New Witnesses Proved Old Heretics* (London 1672)

Perkins, W., *Works* (Cambridge 1608), 3 vols.

Perrinchief, R., *A Discourse of Toleration* (London 1668)

[Popple, W.], *A Letter to Mr Penn* (London 1688)

[Popple, W.], *A Rational Catechism* (London 1687)

[Popple, W.], *Three Letters Tending to Demonstrate How the Security of This Nation Against All Future Persecution for Religion, Lys in the Abolishment of the Present Penal Laws...and the Establishment of a New Law for Universal Liberty of Conscience* (London 1688)

Proast, J., *The Argument of the Letter Concerning Toleration Briefly Considered and Answered* (Oxford 1690)

Quick, J., *Synodicon in Gallia Reformata or the Acts, Decisions and Canons of Those Famous National Councils of the Reformed Church in France* (London 1692)

Rey, C., *An Account of the Cruel Persecutions Raised by the French Clergy Since Their Taking Sanctuary Here* (London 1718)

Robinson, H., *Liberty of Conscience* (London 1643)

Savile Correspondence, ed. W.D. Cooper (London 1858)

Simmons, M., *The Complete Writings* (Scottsdale, Penn. 1956)

Simon, R., *Lettres Choisies de M. Simon* (Rotterdam 1702)

[Somers, J.], *[The Security of Englishmen's Lives or] The Trust, Power, and Duty of the Grand Juries* (London 1681), *passim*

[Souverain, J.], *Le Platonisme dévoilé* (Cologne 1700)

[Souverain, J.], *Platonism Unveil'd* (1700)

Stillingfleet, E., *The Doctrines and Practices of the Church of Rome Truly Represented* (London 1687)

Stillingfleet, E., *The Unreasonableness of Separation* (London 1681)

Stouppe, J., *A Collection of the Several Papers Sent to his Highness the Lord Protector* (London 1655)

Strimesius, S., *Dissertatio theologica de pace ecclesiastica* (Frankfurt 1689)

Temple, Sir J., *The Irish Rebellion* (London 1646)

Temple, W., *Observations Upon the United Provinces of the Netherlands* (London 1673)

Tertullian, *On Prescription Against Heretics* in A. Roberts and J. Donaldson (eds.), *Ante-Nicene Fathers* (Grand Rapids, Mich. 1986)

[Thompson, N.], *A Collection of 86 Loyal Poems* (London 1685)

Tyrrell, J., *Bibliotheca Politica* (London 1694)

Ussher, J., *Gravissimae Quaestionis de Christianum Ecclesiarum in Occidentis*(1687)

Varillas, A., *Histoire des révolutions arrivées dans l'Europe en matière de Religion*, 4 vols. (Paris 1686–9)

Versé, N. Aubert de, *Le Nouveau Visionaire* (Frankfurt 1686)

Versé, N. Aubert de, *Manifeste de Maître Noel Aubert de Versé* (Amsterdam 1687)

Versé, N. Aubert de, *Le Protestant pacifique* (Amsterdam 1684)

Versé, N. Aubert de, *Traité de la liberté de conscience* (Amsterdam 1687; ed. B. de Negroni 1998)
Wake, W., *A Second Defense of the Exposition of the Doctrine of the Church of England* (London 1687)
[Walsh, P.], *Some Few Questions Concerning the Oath of Allegiance* (London 1674)
[Whitehead, G.], *A Brief Account of Some of the Late and Present Sufferings of the People called Quakers* (London 1680)
[Whitehead, G.], *The Popish Informer* (London 1670)
Wilkinson, W., *Confutation of...the Family of Love* (London 1579)
Williams, R., *Bloody Tenent* (1646) in *Complete Works* (New York 1963)
Wilmot, J., Earl of Rochester in Ellis (ed.), *The Complete Works* (London 1994)
[Wissowatius, A.], *Bibliotheca Fratrum Polonorum* (1692)

SECONDARY SOURCES

Abray, L.J., 'The Limits of Magisterial Tolerance in Strassburg' in Grell and Scribner, *Tolerance*, 94–107
Acton, J.E., *The History of Freedom and Other Essays* (London 1922)
Adams, G., *The Huguenots and French Opinion 1685–1787* (Ontario, Canada 1991)
Allen, D.C., *Doubt's Boundless Sea* (Baltimore 1964)
Allen, J.W., *A History of Political Thought in the Sixteenth Century* (London 1977)
Almagor, J., *Pierre des Maizeaux (1673–1745), Journalist and English Correspondent for Franco-Dutch Periodicals 1700–1720* (Amsterdam 1989)
Anderson, A.B., 'Sociology of Persecution', *Journal of Religious History* (1977), 247–62
Armitage, D., *The Ideological Origins of the British Empire* (Cambridge 2000)
Armogathe, J., *Croire en liberté* (Paris 1985)
Armstrong, B., *Calvinism and the Amyraut Heresy* (Madison 1969)
Asch, R. (ed.), *Three Nations* (Bochum 1992)
Ashcraft, R., *Revolutionary Politics and Locke's Two Treatises of Government* (Princeton 1990)
Ashley, M., *James II* (Minneapolis 1977)
Audisio, G., 'How to Detect a Clandestine Minority: The Example of the Waldenses', *Sixteenth Century Journal* 21 (1990), 2, 205–16
Audisio, G., *Le Vaudois* (Paris 1998)
Axtell, J., 'Locke's Review of the Principia', *Notes and Records of the Royal Society*, 20 (1965), 152–61
Bagwell, R., *Ireland under the Stuarts* (London 1909–16)
Bainton, R. (ed.), *Concerning Heretics* (New York 1935)
Bainton, R., *David Joris* (Leipzig, 1937)
Bainton, R., *Hunted Heretic: The Life and Death of Michel Servetus* (Boston 1953)
Bainton, R., 'Sebastian Castellio, Champion of Religious Liberty 1515–63' in *Castellioniana* (Leiden 1951)
Bainton, R., *The Travail of Religious Liberty* (Connecticut 1971)
Baird, H.M., *The Huguenots and the Revocation of the Edict of Nantes* (New York 1895)
Bangs, C., *Arminius* (Nashville 1971)
Barber, M., 'Lepers, Jews, and Muslims: The Plot to Overthrow Christendom in 1321', *History* (1981), 1–17

Barber, M., *The Two Cities* (London 1992)

Barber, W.H., 'Pierre Bayle, Benjamin Furly and Quakerism' in *De l'humanisme aux Lumières* (Paris and Oxford 1996)

Bardon, J., *A History of Ulster* (Belfast 1992)

Barnard, T.C., 'The Cult and Culture of Improvement in Ireland' in M. Greengrass (ed.), *Samuel Hartlib and Universal Reformation* (Cambridge 1994), 281–97

Barnes, A., *Jean Le Clerc et la République des Lettres* (Paris 1938)

Barnouw, P., *Philippus van Limborch* (The Hague 1963)

Bartlett, T., *The Fall and Rise of the Irish Nation: The Catholic Question 1690–1830* (Savage, Md. 1992)

Bate, F., *Declaration of Indulgence* (London 1908)

Baxter, S., *William III and the Defense of European Liberty* (New York 1966)

Baylor, M.G., *The Radical Reformation* (Cambridge 1991)

Beddard, R.A., 'The Commission for Ecclesiastical Promotions 1681–4: An Instrument of Tory Reaction', *Historical Journal* (1967), 11–40

Beddard, R.A., 'The Restoration Church' in J.R. Jones (ed.), *The Restored Monarchy 1660–88* (London 1979), 155–75

Bejczy, I., 'Tolerantia: a Medieval Concept', *Journal of the History of Ideas* (1997), 365–84

Benedict, P., 'Catholic-Reformed Co-existence in France 1555–1685' in Grell and Scribner, *Tolerance.*

Benedict, P., 'The Catholic Response to Protestantism' in J. Obelkevich, *Religion and the People 800–1700* (Chapel Hill 1979), 168–90

Benedict, P., *Rouen During the Wars of Religion* (Cambridge 1981)

Benitez, M., *La Face cachée des Lumières* (Paris and Oxford 1996)

Berkvens-Stevelinck, C. (ed.), *The Emergence of Tolerance in the Dutch Republic* (Leiden 1997)

Berman, D., 'Disclaimers as Offence Mechanisms in Charles Blount and John Toland' in M. Hunter and D. Wootton (eds.), *Atheism from the Reformation to the Enlightenment* (Oxford 1992), 255–72

Berman, D., *A History of Atheism in Britain* (London 1988)

Birn, R., 'Le Journal des Savants sous l'Ancien Régime', *Journal des Savants* (1965), 15–35

Blet, P., *Les Assemblées du Clergé et Louis XIV* (Paris 1972)

Bloom, H.I., *The Economic Activities of the Jews of Amsterdam in the Seventeenth and Eighteenth Centuries* (New York 1969)

Bodian, M., *Hebrews of the Portuguese Nation* (Indiana 1997)

Bolle, P., 'Deux évêques devant la Révocation: Le Camus et Cosnac' in R. Zuber and L. Theis (eds.), *La Révocation de L'Édit de Nantes et le protestantisme français en 1685* (SHPF: Paris 1986), 59–74

Bolton, B., 'Papal Attitudes to Deviants, 1159–1216' in D. Baker (ed.), *Schism, Heresy and Religious Protest* (Cambridge 1972)

Bonno, G., 'Locke et son traducteur français Pierre Coste', *Revue de littérature comparée* (1959), 161–79

Bornewasser, J.A., 'The Roman Catholic Church Since the Reformation' in J. Hebly (ed.), *Lowland Highlights* (Kampen 1972)

Bossy, J., *The English Catholic Community 1570–1850* (Oxford 1976)

Bost, H., *Pierre Bayle et la question religieuse dans la Nouvelles de la République des Lettres* (Montpellier 1991)

Bost, H., *Pierre Bayle et la Religion* (Paris 1994)

Bost, H., *Un 'intellectuel' avant la lettre: le journaliste Pierre Bayle* (Amsterdam 1994)

Boswell, J., *Christianity, Social Tolerance, and Homosexuality* (Chicago 1980)

Bots, H. (et al.), *De Bibliothèque Universelle et Historique* (Amsterdam 1981)
Bots, H., *Circulation and Reception of Periodicals in the French Language During the 17th and 18th Centuries* (Amsterdam 1988)
Bots, H. and Waquet, F., *Commercium litterarium* (Amsterdam 1994)
Bots, H., 'L'Écho de la Révocation dans les Provinces-Unies' in R. Zuber and L. Theiss (eds.), *La Révocation de L'Édit de Nantes et le protestantisme français en 1685* (Paris 1986), 281–98
Bots, H., 'L'Esprit de la République des Lettres et la tolérance dans les trois premiers périodiques savants hollandais', *XVIIe siècle* (1977), 43–57
Bots, H. (ed.), *Henri Basnage de Beauval en de Histoire des Ouvrages des Savans* (Amsterdam 1976)
Bots, H., 'Le Plaidoyer des journalistes de Hollande pour la tolérance' in *De l'humanisme*, 547–59
Bots, H. and Bastiaanse, R., 'Le Refuge huguenot et les Provinces-Unies, une esquisse sommaire', in M. Magdelaine and R. von Thadden (eds.), *Le Refuge huguenot* (Paris 1985), 63–82
Bots, H. and Waquet, F., *La République des Lettres* (Paris 1997)
Bots, H. et al. (eds.), *Vlucht naar de Vrijheid de Huguenoten in Nederland* (Amsterdam 1985)
Boucé, P., 'Imagination, Pregnant Women and Monsters in Eighteenth Century England and France' in G.S. Rousseau and R. Porter (eds.), *Sexual Underworlds of the Enlightenment* (Manchester 1987)
Bracken, H., 'Toleration Theories' in *Mind and Language: Essays on Descartes and Chomsky* (Dordrecht 1984), 83–96
Bradshaw, B. and Morrill, J. (eds.), *The British Problem* (Basingstoke 1996)
Braithwaite, A.W., 'Early Tithe Prosecutions', *JFHS* (1960), 148–56
Braithwaite, A.W., 'Imprisonment Upon a Praemunire', *JFHS* (1962), 38–40
Braithwaite, A.W., *The Second Period of Quakerism* (Cambridge 1961)
Brammall, K., 'Monstrous Metamorphoses: Nature, Morality and the Rhetoric of Monstrosity in Tudor England', *Sixteenth Century Journal* (1996)
Bray, A., *Homosexuality in Renaissance England* (London 1982)
Brennan, J., 'A Gallican Interlude in Ireland', *Irish Theological Quarterly*, 24, 217–37 and 283–309
Briggs, E.R., 'Bayle ou Larroque? De qui est l'Avis important aux réfugiés de 1690 et de 1692' in M. Magdelaine et al. (eds.), *De l'humanisme aux Lumières* (Oxford 1996), 509–24
Briggs, E.R., 'Les manuscrits de Charles Le Cène dans la Bibliothèque de la Huguenot Society of London', *Tijdschrift voor de studie van de verlichting* (1977), 358–78
Briggs, E.R., 'A Wandering Huguenot Scholar', *Huguenot Society Proceedings* (1970), 455–63
Briggs, R., *Communities of Belief* (Oxford 1994)
Briggs, R., *Early Modern France* (Oxford 1977)
Brooks, P.N. (ed.), *Reformation Principle and Practice: Essays in Honour of A.G. Dickens* (London 1986)
Broome, J.H., 'Bayle's Biographer: Pierre des Maizeaux', *French Studies* (1955), 1–17
Brown, P., *The Body and Society* (New York 1988)
Bryson, A., *From Courtesy to Civility* (Oxford 1988)
Buckley, G.T., *Atheism in the English Renaissance* (Chicago 1932)
Buckley, M., *At the Origins of Modern Atheism* (Yale 1987)

Burgess, G., *The New British History* (London 1999)

Burke, P., *The Art of Conversation* (Cambridge 1993)

Burke, P., *The Fabrication of Louis XIV* (Cambridge 1992)

Burke, P., 'The Politics of Reformation History: Burnet and Brandt' in A.C. Duke and C.A. Tamse (eds.), *Clio's Mirror: Historiography in Britain and the Netherlands* (Zutphen 1985), 73–85

Burke, P., *Venice and Amsterdam* (Cambridge 1994)

Burns, J.H., and Goldie, M. (eds.), *The Cambridge History of Political Thought 1450–1750* (Cambridge 1991)

Burns, R.E., 'The Irish Popery Laws', *Review of Politics* (1962)

Burrage, C., *The Early English Dissenters in the Light of Recent Research 1550–1641* (Cambridge 1912)

Burtt, S., *Virtue Transformed* (Cambridge 1992)

Bynum, C.W., *Holy Feast, Holy Fast* (Berkeley 1987)

Campbell, K., *The Intellectual Struggle of the English Papists in the Seventeenth Century* (Lewiston 1986)

Capp, B., 'Arson, Threats of Arson, and Incivility' in Harrison and Slack (eds.), *Civil Histories* (Oxford 2000)

Capp, B., *The Fifth-Monarchy Men* (London 1972)

Céard, J., *La nature et les prodigies* (Geneva 1977)

Cerny, G., *Theology Politics and Letters at the Crossroads of European Civilization* (Dordrecht 1987)

Chadwick, H., *The Early Church* (London 1967)

Champion, J., *The Pillars of Priestcraft Shaken* (Cambridge 1992)

Champion, J., 'Willing to Suffer' in McLaren and H. Coward (eds.), *Religious Conscience, State and Law* (Albany 1999), 13–28

Charnley, J., *Pierre Bayle, Reader of Travel Literature* (Berne 1998)

Chartier, R., *The Cultural Origins of the French Revolution* (Durham 1991)

Chernaik, W. and Dzelzanis, M. (eds), *Marvell and Liberty* (Basingstoke 1999)

Chernaik, W., *Sexual Freedom in Restoration Literature* (Cambridge 1995)

Christianson, P.K., *Reformers and Babylon* (Toronto 1978)

Church, W., *The Impact of Absolutism in France* (New York 1969)

Clark, J.C.D., *English Society 1688–1832* (Cambridge 1985)

Clark, J.C.D., *The Language of Liberty* (Cambridge 1993)

Clark, R., 'Gangreen of Quakerism', *Journal of Religious History* (1981), 404–29

Clark, S., 'Inversion, Misrule and the Meaning of Witchcraft', *Past and Present* (1980), 98–127

Clark, S., *Thinking With Demons* (Oxford 1997)

Clasen, C.-P., *Anabaptism* (Ithaca 1972)

Claydon, T. and McBride, I. (eds.), *Protestantism and National Identity* (Cambridge 1998)

Claydon, T., *William III and the Godly Revolution* (Cambridge 1996)

Clifton, R., 'The Fear of Popery' in C. Russell (ed.), *The Origins of the English Civil War* (Oxford 1973)

Coffey, J., *Persecution and Toleration in Protestant England 1558–1689* (Harlow 2000)

Coffey, J., 'Puritanism and Liberty Revisited: The Case for Toleration in the English Revolution', *Historical Journal* (1998)

Cogswell, T., *The Blessed Revolution* (Cambridge 1989)

Cohn, N., *Europe's Inner Demons* (London 1975)

Cohn, N., *The Pursuit of the Millenium* (Oxford 1970)

Colie, R., 'John Locke in the Republic of Letters' in J.S. Bromley and E. Kossman (eds.), *Britain and the Netherlands* (London 1960), 111–29

Colie, R., *Light and Enlightenment* (Cambridge 1957)

Colish, M., *The Medieval Foundations of the Western Intellectual Tradition 400–1400* (Yale 1997)

Colley, L., *Britons* (Yale 1992)

Collins, R.W., *Calvin and the Libertines of Geneva* (Toronto 1968)

Collinson, P., *The Birthpangs of Protestant England* (Basingstoke 1988)

Collinson, P., *The Puritan Character* (Los Angeles 1989)

Connolly, S.J., 'The Penal Laws' in W. Maguire, *Kings in Conflict* (Belfast 1990), 157–72

Connolly, S.J., *Religion, Law and Power: The Making of Protestant Ireland* (Oxford 1992)

Connolly, S.J. (ed.), *United Kingdoms?* (Dublin 1998)

Connolly, W., *Augustinian Imperative* (Sage 1993)

Cottret, B., 'Glorieuse révolution, révocation honteuse? Protestants Français et Protestants d'Angleterre' in M. Magdelaine and R. von Thadden (eds.), *Le Refuge huguenot* (Paris 1985), 83–96

Cottret, B., *The Huguenots in England* (Cambridge 1991)

Coudert, A., 'John Locke and Francis Mercury van Helmont' in J. Force and D. Katz (eds.), *Everything Connects* (Leiden 1999), 89–114

Courtines, L.P., *Bayle's Relations with England and the English* (New York 1938)

Coward, B., *The Stuart Age* (London 1980)

Cragg, G., *Puritanism in the Age of the Great Persecution* (Cambridge 1957)

Cranston, M., *Locke* (London 1957)

Crawford, P., 'The Challenges to Patriarchy: How Did the Revolution Affect Women?' in J. Morrill (ed.), *Revolution and Restoration* (London 1992), 112–28

Cressy, D., *Travesties and Transgressions* (Oxford 2000)

Cromartie, A., *Sir Matthew Hale 1609–76* (Cambridge 1995)

Crompton, L., *Byron and Greek Love* (Berkeley 1985)

Crompton, L., 'Offences Against One's Self: Paederasty', *Journal of Homosexuality* (1978), 3, iv, 389–404; 4, i, 91–107

Cross, F.W., 'History of the Walloon and Huguenot Church at Canterbury', *HSL* xv (London 1898), 157–8; *HSP* (1915–17), 263–92

Crouzet, D., *Les Guerriers de Dieu* (Seyssel 1990)

Curtayne, A., *The Trial of Oliver Plunkett* (London 1953)

Dam, H.-J.van, '*De Imperio Summarum Potestatum Circa Sacra*' in H. Nellen and E. Rabbie (eds.), *Grotius, Theologian* (Leiden 1994)

Darnton, R., *The Forbidden Bestsellers of Pre-Revolutionary France* (New York 1995)

Daston, L., 'The Ideal and Reality of the Republic of Letters in the Enlightenment' in *Science in Context* (1991)

Daston, L. and Park, K., *Wonders and the Order of Nature* (New York 1998)

Davies, D., *The World of the Elzeviers 1580–1712* (The Hague 1954)

Davis, J.C., 'Fear, Myth and Furore', *Past and Present* (1990), 98–103

Davis, J.C., *Fear, Myth and History* (Cambridge 1986)

Davis, N.Z., *Culture and Society in Early Modern France* (Stanford 1975)

De Beer, E.S. (ed.), *The Diary of John Evelyn* (1955)

De Certeau, M., *The Writing of History* (New York 1988)

Deijk, F., 'Elie Benoist: Historiographer and Politician after the Revocation of the Edict of Nantes', *Nederlands Archief voor Kerkgeschiedenis* 69 (1989), 54–92

De Jong, P., 'Can Political Factors Account for the Fact that Calvinism Rather Than Anabaptism Came to Dominate the Dutch Reformation?', *Church History* (1964), 392–417

De Krey, G., *A Fractured Society* (Oxford 1985)

De Krey, G., 'London Radicals and Revolutionary Politics' in T. Harris, P. Seaward and M. Goldie (eds.), *The Politics of Religion in Restoration England* (Blackwell 1990), 133–62

De Krey, G., 'Rethinking the Restoration: Dissenting Cases for Conscience 1667–72', *HJ* (1995), 53–83

Delmont, T., *Bossuet et les Saints Pères* (Paris 1896)

Delumeau, J., *Sin and Fear* (New York 1990)

Den Boer, H. and Israel, J., 'William III and the Glorious Revolution in the Eyes of Amsterdam Sephardi Writers: The Reactions of Miguel de Barrios, Joseph Penso de la Vega, and Manuel de Leao' in Israel (ed.), *The Anglo-Dutch Moment*, 439–61

De Negroni, B., *Intolérances* (Paris 1996)

Desautel, A., *Les Mémoires de Trévoux* (Rome 1956)

DesGraves, L., 'Les Thèses soutenues a l'académie de Saumur', *BSHPF* (1979)

Deursen, A. van, *Plain Lives in a Golden Age* (Cambridge 1991)

De Vet, J., 'John Locke in de "Histoire des Ouvrages des Savans" ' in H. Bots (ed.), *Henri Basnage de Beauval & l'Histoire des Ouvrages des Savans* (Amsterdam 1976–84), ii, 183–270

Dewhurst, K., *Dr Thomas Sydenham* (Berkeley 1966)

Dewhurst, K., *John Locke, Physician and Philosopher* (London 1963)

Deyon, S., 'La Destruction des temples' in R. Zuber and L. Theis (eds.), *La Révocation de L'Édit de Nantes et le protestantisme français en 1685, SHPF* (Paris 1986), 239–59

Dibon, P., 'Communication in the Respublica Literaria of the 17th Century', *Res Publica Litterarum* (1978)

Dibon, P., 'Les Provinces-Unies, carrefour intellectuel de l'Europe du XVIIe siècle' in École practique des Hautes Études, *Annuaire 1965–6*, 98 (Paris 1966), 363–73

Dickens, A.G., *The German Nation and Martin Luther* (London 1974)

Diefendorf, B., *Beneath the Cross; Catholics and Huguenots in Sixteenth Century Paris* (Oxford 1991)

Dodge, G., *The Political Thought of the Huguenots of the Dispersion* (New York 1947)

Dompnier, B., *Le venin de l'hérésie* (Paris 1985)

Doring, D., 'Samuel von Pufendorf and Toleration' in Laursen (ed.), *Beyond the Persecuting Society* (Pennsylvania 1998)

Douen, O., *L'intolérance de Fénelon* (Paris 1875)

Duke, A., et al. (eds.), *Calvinism in Europe: A Collection of Documents* (Manchester 1992)

Duke, A., *Reformation and Revolt in the Low Countries* (London 1990)

Dunlop, I., *Louis XIV* (London 1999)

Dunn, J., 'The Claim to Freedom of Conscience' in *idem, The History of Political Theory* (Cambridge 1996)

Dunn, J., *Locke* (Oxford 1984)

Dunn, J., *Political Obligation in its Historical Context* (Cambridge 1980)

Dunn, J., *The Political Thought of John Locke* (Cambridge 1969)

Dunn, J., *Rethinking Modern Political Theory* (Cambridge 1985)

Eijnatten, J. van, 'Lodestars of Latitude: Gerard Brandt's Peaceable Christian c. 1664, Irenicism and Religious Dissent', *Lias* (1999), 57–75

Eisenstein, E., *The Printing Press as an Agent of Change* (Cambridge 1979)

Elias, N., *The Civilizing Process* (New York 1978)

Ellis, F., 'John Freke and the History of the Insipids' in *Philological Quarterly* (1965), 472–83

Ellis, S. and Barber, S., *Conquest and Union* (London 1995)

Elmer, P., 'Saints or Sorcerers' in J. Barry et al. (eds.), *Witchcraft in Early Modern Europe* (Cambridge 1996), 145–76

Elton, G., 'Persecution and Toleration in the English Reformation' in W. Sheils (ed.), *Persecution and Toleration* (Oxford 1984), 163–87

Elukin, J., 'Jacques Basnage and the History of the Jews: Anti-Catholic Polemic and Historical Allegory in the Republic of Letters', *Journal of the History of Ideas* (1992), 603–30

Erskine-Hill, H., 'Rochester: Augustan or Explorer?' in G. Hibbard (ed.), *Renaissance and Modern Essays* (London 1966), 51–64

Ettinger, S., 'The Beginnings of Change in the Attitude of European Society Towards the Jews', *Scripta Hierosolymitana*, 7 (1961), 193–219

Farr, J. and Roberts, C., 'John Locke on the Glorious Revolution: A Rediscovered Document', *Historical Journal* (1985), 385–98

Fatio, O., 'Claude Pajon et les mutations de la théologie réformée à l'époque de la Révocation' in R. Zuber et al. (eds.), *La Révocation de L'Édit de Nantes et le protestantisme francais en 1685* (Paris 1986), 209–25

Felsenstein, F., *Anti-Semitic Stereotypes: A Paradigm of Otherness in English Popular Culture 1660–1830* (Baltimore 1995)

Felsenstein, F., 'Jews and Devils: Anti-Semitic Stereotypes of Late Medieval and Renaissance England', *Journal of Literature and Theology* (1990), 15–28

Ferguson, J., *Robert Ferguson the Plotter* (Edinburgh 1887)

Finkelstein, N., *The Other 1492* (New York 1989)

Firth, K., *The Apocalyptic Tradition* (Oxford 1979)

Fissell, M., *Vernacular Bodies* (Oxford 2004)

Fitzpatrick, B., *Seventeenth-Century Ireland: The War of Religions* (Totowa New Jersey)

Fitzpatrick, M., 'Joseph Priestley and the Cause of Universal Toleration', *The Price–Priestley Newsletter* (1977), 3–30

Fitzpatrick, M., 'Toleration and the Enlightenment Movement' in Grell and Porter, *Toleration in Enlightenment Europe*

Fix, A., 'Angels, Devils and Evil Spirits in Seventeenth-Century Thought: Balthasar Bekker and the Collegiants', *Journal of the History of Ideas* (1989), 527–47

Fix, A., *Prophecy and Reason* (Princeton 1991)

Fletcher, A., 'The Enforcement of the Conventicle Acts' in W. Sheils (ed.), *Persecution and Toleration* (Oxford 1984), 235–46

Force, J., *William Whiston, Honest Newtonian* (Cambridge 1985)

Ford, A., 'The Protestant Reformation in Ireland' in C. Brady and R. Gillespie (eds.), *Natives and Newcomers* (Dublin 1986)

Foster, R., *Modern Ireland* (London 1988)

Foucault, M., *History of Sexuality* (New York 1990)

Fox Bourne, H., *Life of Locke* (London 1876)

Foxcroft, H., *Life of Burnet* (Cambridge 1907)

Franklin, J., *Jean Bodin and the Rise of Absolutist Theory* (Cambridge 1973)

Freist, D., 'The King's Crown is the Whore of Babylon: Politics, Gender and Communication in Mid-Seventeenth-Century England', *Gender and History* (1995), 457–81

Friedman, J., *Miracles and the Pulp Press During the English Revolution*, (London 1993)

Froude, J., *The English in Ireland in the Eighteenth Century* (London 1901)

Garnsey, P., 'Religious Toleration in Classical Antiquity' in W. Sheils (ed.), *Persecution and Toleration* (Oxford 1984), 1–28

Garrisson, J., *L'Édit de Nantes et sa révocation* (Paris 1985)

Gaxotte, P., *The Age of Louis XIV* (New York 1970)

Gay, P., *The Enlightenment, an Interpretation: Volume II. The Science of Freedom* (London 1970)

Gelderen, M. van, *The Dutch Revolt* (Cambridge 1993)

Gelderen, M. van, *The Political Thought of the Dutch Revolt* (Cambridge 1992)

George, M.D., *English Political Caricature* (Oxford 1959)

Geyl, P., *The Revolt of the Netherlands* (London 1988)

Gibbs, C., ' The European Origins of the Glorious Revolution' in W.A. Maguire (ed.), *Kings in Conflict* (Belfast 1990), 9–28

Gibbs, C., 'The Role of the Dutch Republic as the Intellectual Entrepot of Europe in the 17th and 18th Centuries', *Bijdragen en Mededelingen betreffende de Geschiedenis der Nederlanden* 86 (1971), 323–49

Gibbs, C., 'Some Intellectual and Political Influences of the Huguenot Emigres in the United Provinces c. 1680–1730', *Bijdragen en Mededelingen betreffende de Geschiedenis der Nederlanden* 90 (1975), 255–87

Gijswijt-hofstra, M., 'Witchcraft Before Zeeland Magistrates and Church Councils, Sixteenth to Twentieth Centuries' in *idem* (ed.), *Witchcraft in the Netherlands from the Fourteenth to the Twentieth Century* (Rotterdam 1991), 103–18

Gillett, C.R., *Burned Books* (New York 1932)

Goldberg, J., *Sodometries* (Stanford 1992)

Golden, R.M. (ed.), *The Huguenot Connection: The Edict of Nantes, its Revocation, and Early French Migration to South Carolina* (Dordrecht 1988)

Golden, S., *Jean Le Clerc* (New York 1972)

Goldgar, A., *Impolite Learning* (Yale 1995)

Goldie, M.A., 'The Civil Religion of James Harrington' in A. Pagden (ed.), *The Languages of Political Theory in Early Modern Europe* (Cambridge 1987), 197–222

Goldie, M.A., 'The Hilton Gang', *History Today* (1998), x, 26–32

Goldie, M.A., 'The Huguenot Experience and the Problem of Toleration in England' in C.E. F. Caldicott et al. (eds.), *The Huguenots and Ireland* (Dublin 1987), 175–203

Goldie, M.A., 'James II and the Dissenters' Revenge', *Bulletin of the Institute for Historical Research* (1993), 53–88

Goldie, M.A., 'James II and the Whig Collaborators', *Historical Journal* (1992)

Goldie, M.A., 'John Locke's Circle and James II', *Historical Journal* (1992), 557–86

Goldie, M.A. and Spurr, J., 'Politics and the Restoration Parish: Edward Fowler and the Struggle for St Giles Cripplegate', *English Historical Review* (1994), 572–96

Goldie, M.A., 'Priestcraft and the Birth of Whiggism' in N. Phillipson and Q. Skinner (eds.), *Political Discourse in Early Modern Britain* (Cambridge 1993)

Goldie, M.A., 'Sir Peter Pett, Sceptical Toryism and the Science of Toleration in the 1680s' in W. Sheils (ed.), *Persecution and Toleration* (Oxford 1984), 247–74

Goldie, M.A., 'The Political Thought of the Anglican Revolution' in R.A. Beddard, *The Revolutions of 1688* (Oxford 1991), 102–36

Goldie, M.A., 'The Revolution of 1689 and the Structure of Political Argument', *Bulletin of the Institute for Research in the Humanities* (1980), 473–564

Goldie, M.A., 'The Theory of Religious Intolerance in Restoration England' in W. Sheils (ed.), *Persecution and Toleration* (Oxford 1984), 331–68

Goodman, D., *Criticism in Action* (Ithaca 1989)

Goodman, D., *The Republic of Letters* (Ithaca 1994)

Gordon, D., *Citizens Without Sovereignty* (Princeton 1994)

Gowing, L., *Domestic Dangers* (Oxford 1996)

Grafton, A., *Defenders of the Text* (Cambridge, Mass. 1991)

Grafton, A., *The Footnote* (Cambridge, Mass. 1997)

Grafton, A., *Forgers and Critics* (Princeton 1973)

Grafton, A., *Joseph Scaliger* (Oxford, 1983, 1993)

Greaves, R. and Zaller, R., *Biographical Dictionary of British Radicals in the Seventeenth Century* (Brighton 1982)

Greaves, R., *Deliver Us From Evil* (Oxford 1986)

Greaves, R., *John Bunyan and English Nonconformity* (Hambledon 1992)

Greaves, R., *Secrets of the Kingdom* (Stanford 1992)

Greaves, R., 'Shattered Expectations? George Fox, the Quakers, and the Restoration State 1660–85', *Albion* (1992), 237–59

Greenblatt, S., *Renaissance Self-fashioning* (Chicago 1980)

Greengrass, M., 'France' in R. Porter and M. Teich (eds.), *The Reformation in National Context* (Cambridge 1994)

Greengrass, M., *The Longman Companion to the European Reformation c. 1500–1618* (London 1998), 166–70

Greengrass, M., 'The Psychology of Religious Violence', *French History* (1991), 467–74

Greengrass, M., Leslie, M. and Raylor, T., (eds.), *Samuel Hartlib and Universal Reformation* (Cambridge 1994)

Greenshields, M., 'How to Convert Protestants' in M. Greenshields and T. Robinson (eds.), *Orthodoxy and Heresy in Religious Movements* (Lewiston 1992), 60–92

Greenslade, S.L., 'Heresy and Schism in the Later Roman Empire' in D. Baker (ed.), *Schism, Heresy and Religious Protest* (Cambridge 1972)

Gregory, B., *Salvation at Stake* (Harvard 1999)

Greig, M., 'The Reasonableness of Christianity: Gilbert Burnet and the Trinitarian Controversy', *Journal of Ecclesiastical History* (1993), 631–51

Grell, O. and Porter, R., *Toleration in Enlightenment Europe* (Cambridge 1999)

Grell, O. and Scribner, R., *Tolerance and Intolerance in the European Reformation* (Cambridge 1996)

Griffin, D., *Satires Against Man* (Berkeley 1973)

Groenveld, S., 'The Mecca of Authors? States Assemblies and Censorship in the Dutch Republic' in A. Duke and C. Tamse (eds.), *Too Mighty to Be Free?* (Zutphen 1987), 63–86

Guggigsberg, H., 'The Defence of Religious Toleration and Religious Liberty in Early Modern Europe: Arguments, Pressures, and Some Consequences', *History of European Ideas* (1983), 35–50

Guggigsberg, H., *Sebastian Castellio* (Basle 1956)

Gunny, A., 'Protestant Reactions to Islam in late Seventeenth-Century French Thought', *French Studies* (1986), 129–40

Gwynn, R., 'The Arrival of Huguenot Refugees in England 1680–1705', *Proceedings of the Huguenot Society* 21 (1969), 366–73

Gwynn, R., 'Disorder and Innovation: The Reshaping of the French Churches of London after the Glorious Revolution' in O. Grell, J. Israel and N. Tyacke (eds.), *From Persecution to Toleration* (Oxford 1991), 251–73

Gwynn, R., 'England's First Refugees', *History Today* (May 1985)

Gwynn, R., *Huguenot Heritage* (London 1985)

Haag, E. and E., *La France protestante*, 10 vols, (Paris 1846–1859), vol. IX

Haakonssen, K. (ed.), *Enlightenment and Religion* (Cambridge 1996)

Haase, E., *Einführung in die Literatur des Refuges* (Berlin 1959)

Haase, E., 'Isaac Papin a l'époque de la Révocation', *BSHPF* (1952), 94–122

Hahn, R., *The Anatomy of a Scientific Institution: The Paris Academy of Sciences* (Berkeley 1971)

Hale, J., *The Civilization of Europe in the Renaissance* (New York 1994)

Haley, K.H. D., *The Dutch in the Seventeenth Century* (New York 1972)

Haley, K.H. D., *Shaftesbury* (Oxford 1968)

Hall, D. (ed.), *The Antinomian Controversy 1636–38* (Wesleyan 1968)

Halley, J., 'Heresy, Orthodoxy and the Politics of Religious Discourse: The Case of the English Family of Love', *Representations* (1986), 98–120

Halliday, P., *Dismembering the Body Politic* (Cambridge 1998)

Hamilton, A., *Family of Love* (Cambridge 1981)

Hammond, P., 'Marvell's Sexuality', *Seventeenth Century* (1996), 87–123

Hammond, P., 'Rochester's Homoeroticism' in N. Fisher (ed.), *That Second Bottle* (Manchester 2000)

Hammond, P., 'Titus Oates and "Sodomy"' in J. Black (ed.), *Culture and Society in Britain 1660–1800* (Manchester 1997), 85–101

Hanafi, Z., *The Monster in the Machine* (Durham 2000)

Hanlon, G., *Confession and Community in Seventeenth Century France* (Philadelphia 1993)

Harline, C., *Pamphlets, Printing and Political Culture in the Early Dutch Republic* (The Hague 1987)

Harris, T., 'The Bawdy House Riots of 1668', *Historical Journal* 29, 3 (1986), 537–56

Harris, T., 'Lives, Liberties and Estates: Rhetorics of Liberty in the Reign of Charles II' in *idem* (ed.), *The Politics of Religion in Restoration England* (Oxford 1990), 217–42

Harris, T., *London Crowds* (Cambridge 1987)

Harris, T., 'London Crowds and the Revolution of 1688' in Cruickshanks (ed.), *By Force or by Default* (Edinburgh 1989)

Harris, T., 'The Parties and the People: The Press, the Crowd and Politics "Out-of-doors" in Restoration England' in L.K. Glassey (ed.), *The Reigns of Charles II and James VII and II*, 125–51

Harris, T., Seaward, P. and Goldie, M.A. (eds), *The Politics of Religion in Restoration England* (Oxford 1990)

Harris, T., *Politics Under the Later Stuarts* (London 1993)

Harrison, P., *Religion and the Religions in the English Enlightenment* (Cambridge 1990)

Hart, A. Tindal, *William Lloyd, 1627–1717: Bishop, Politician and Prophet* (London 1952)

Haude, S., *In the Shadow of 'Savage Wolves': Anabaptist Münster and the German Reformation During the 1530s* (Boston 2000)

Hazard, P., *The European Mind 1680–1715* (1935; tr. 1953–64)

Heering, J.P., 'Hugo Grotius' *De Veritate Religionis Christianae*' in *Hugo Grotius Theologian*, 41–52

Herrup, C., *A House in Gross Disorder* (Oxford 1999)

Hertzberg, A., *The French Enlightenment and the Jews* (New York 1968)

Herzog, D., *Poisoning the Minds of the Lower Orders* (Princeton 1998)

Hesbert, R.-J., *Bossuet: Écho de Tertullien* (Paris 1980)

Hibbard, C., *Charles I and the Popish Plot* (Chapel Hill 1983)

Hill, C., 'Abolishing the Ranters' in *idem, A Nation of Change and Novelty* (London 1993), 172–218

Hill, C., *Antichrist in Seventeenth-Century England* (London 1990)

Hill, C., *The English Bible and the Seventeenth-Century Revolution* (London 1993)

Hill, C., 'John Wilmot, Earl of Rochester (1647–80)' in *idem, The Collected Essays of Christopher Hill* (Amherst 1985), I, 298–317

Hill, C., *Society and Puritanism in Pre-Revolutionary England* (London 1964)

Hill, C., *A Turbulent, Seditious, and Factious People* (Oxford 1988)

Hill, C., Reay, B. and Lamont, W., *The World of the Muggletonians* (London 1983)

Hill, C., *The World Turned Upside Down* (New York 1972)

Hobby, E., *Virtue of Necessity* (Ann Arbour 1989)

Hoftijzer, P., ' "Such Onely As Are Very Honest, Loyall and Active": English Spies in the Low Countries 1660–88' in P. Hoftijzer and C. Barfoot (eds.), *Fabrics and Fabrications* (Amsterdam 1990), 73–96

Holmes, C., 'The Ritual Murder Accusation in Britain' in Dundes (ed.), *The Blood Libel Legend* (Wisconsin 1991)

Holmes, G., *Britain After the Glorious Revolution* (London 1969)

Holmes, G., *The Divided Society* (London 1967)

Holmes, G., *Politics, Religion and Society in England 1679–1742* (London 1986)

Holmes, G., *The Trial of Doctor Sacheverell* (London 1973)

Holmes, P., *Resistance and Compromise* (Cambridge 1982)

Holt, M., *The French Wars of Religion* (Cambridge 1995)

Holt, M., 'Putting Religion Back into the Wars of Religion', *French Historical Studies* (1993), 524–51

Horle, C., *The Quakers and the English Legal System 1660–89* (Pennsylvania 1988)

Horsch, J., *Mennonites in Europe*, (Scottsdale, Penn. 1950)

Horst, I., *Radical Brethren* (Nieuwkoop 1972)

Houston, A., 'Monopolizing Faith' in A. Levine (ed.), *Early Modern Scepticism and the Origins of Toleration* (Lanham, Md. 1999), 147–64

Howells, R., *Pierre Jurieu: Antinomian Radical* (Durham 1983)

Hsia, R. Po-chia, 'Münster and the Anabaptists' in *idem* (ed.), *The German People and the Reformation* (Cornell 1988)

Hsia, R. Po-chia, *The Myth of Ritual Murder* (Yale 1988)

Huet, M.H., *Monstrous Imagination* (Harvard 1993)

Hughes, A., *Gangraena and the Struggle for the English Revolution* (Oxford 2004)

Hughes, J.J., 'The Missing "Last Words" of Gilbert Burnet in July 1687', *HJ* (1977), 221–7

Hughes, P., *Rome and the Counter-Reformation in England* (Birmingham 1944)

Hughes, P. and J.F. Larkin (eds.), *Tudor Royal Proclamations*, 3 vols. (New Haven 1964–9)

Huhner, L., 'The Jews of North Carolina Prior to 1800', *Publications of the American Jewish Historical Society*, 29 (1925), 137–48

Huhner, L., 'The Jews of South Carolina from the Earliest Settlement to the End of the American Revolution', *Publications of the American Jewish Historical Society*, 12 (1904), 39–61

Hull, W., *Benjamin Furly and Quakerism in Holland* (Pennsylvania 1941)

Hunt, W., 'Spectral Origins of the English Revolution' in G. Eley and W. Hunt (eds.), *Reviving the English Revolution* (London 1988), 305–32

Hunter, M., 'Aikenhead the Atheist: The Context and Consequences of Articulate Irreligion in the Late Seventeenth Century', in Hunter and Wootton (eds.), *Atheism*, 221–54

Hunter, M., *Establishing the New Science: The Experience of the Early Royal Society* (Suffolk 1989)

Hunter, M., 'The Problem of "Atheism" in Early Modern England', *TRHS* (1985), 135–57

Hunter, M., 'Science and Heterodoxy: An Early Modern Problem Reconsidered' in D. Lindberg and R. Westman (eds.), *Reappraisals of the Scientific Revolution* (Cambridge 1990), 437–60

Hunter, M., *Science and Society in Restoration England* (Cambridge 1981)

Hutchinson, R., *Locke in France* (Oxford 1991)

Hutton, R., *Charles II* (Oxford 1989)

Hutton, S., 'Damaris Cudworth, Lady Masham: Between Platonism and Enlightenment', *British Journal for the History of Philosophy* (1993), 29–54

Huussen, A. Jr, 'The Legal Position of Sephardi Jews in Holland c. 1600' in J. Michman (ed.), *Dutch Jewish History* (1993), 19–41

Huussen, A., 'Sodomy in the Dutch Republic During the Eighteenth Century' in P. Maccubin (ed.), *'Tis Nature's Fault* (Cambridge 1987), 169–78

Hylton, R.P., 'The Less-favoured Refuge: Ireland's Nonconformist Huguenots at the Turn of the Eighteenth Century' in K. Herlihy (ed.), *The Religion of Irish Dissent 1650–1800* (Dublin 1996), 83–99

Iliffe, R., 'In the Warehouse: Privacy, Property and Priority in the Early Royal Society', *History of Science* (1992), 29–68

Israel, J., 'The Amsterdam Stock Exchange and the English Revolution of 1688', *Tijdschrift voor Gescheidenis* (1990), 412–40

Israel, J. (ed.), *The Anglo-Dutch Moment* (Cambridge 1991)

Israel, J., 'The Changing Role of the Dutch Sephardim in International Trade 1595–1715' in J. Michman (ed.), *Dutch Jewish History* I (Jerusalem 1984), 31–51

Israel, J., 'The Dutch Contribution to the Glorious Revolution' in *idem*, *The Anglo-Dutch Moment* (Cambridge 1991)

Israel, J., *Dutch Primacy in World Trade* (Oxford 1989)

Israel, J., *The Dutch Republic* (Oxford 1995)

Israel, J., 'The Economic Contribution of Dutch Sephardi Jewry to Holland's Golden Age' in *idem*, *Empires and Entrepots* (Oxford 1990)

Israel, J., *European Jewry in the Age of Mercantilism* (Oxford 1985)

Israel, J., 'Gregori Leti and the Dutch Sephardi Elite' in A. Rapoport-Albert (ed.), *Jewish History*, 267–84

Israel, J., 'The Intellectual Debate about Toleration' in *The Emergence of Toleration in the Dutch Republic* (Leiden 1997), 3–36

Israel, J., *Radical Enlightenment* (Oxford 2001)

Israel, J., 'Sephardic Immigration into the Dutch Republic 1595–1672', *Studia Rosenthaliania* (1989), 45–53

Israel, J., 'Toleration in Seventeenth-Century Dutch and English Thought', in *Britain and the Netherlands* (1994), 13–30

Jacob, J., *Henry Stubbe: Radical Protestantism and the Early Enlightenment* (Cambridge 1983)

Jacob, J., *Robert Boyle and the English Revolution* (New York 1977)

Jacob, M., 'Contemporary Enlightenment Historiography in the Netherlands' in *Geschiedenis documentatieblad van de Werkgroep "Sassen" Wisjbegeerte in Nederland*, Jaargang 5 (1994), 7–14

Jacob, M., *The Enlightenment* (Boston 2000)

Jacob, M., *Living the Enlightenment* (Oxford 1991)

Jacob, M., *The Newtonians and the English Revolution* (Hassocks 1976)

Jacob, M., *The Radical Enlightenment* (London 1981)

Jacob, M. (ed.), *Women and the Enlightenment* (Cambridge, Mass. 1989)

Jardine, L., *Erasmus, Man of Letters* (Princeton 1993)

Jardine, L., *Still Harping on Daughters* (Sussex 1983)

Jenkinson, S., 'Two Concepts of Tolerance: Or Why Locke Is not Bayle', *The Journal of Political Philosophy* (1996), 302–21

Johnson, W.G., 'The Family of Love in Stuart England: A Chronology of Name-Crossed Lovers', *JMRS*, 7 (1977), 95–112

Johnston, C., 'Elie Benoist, Historian of the Edict of Nantes', *Church History* (1988), 468–88

Jolley, N., *Leibniz and Locke* (Oxford 1984)

Jones, J.R., *First Whigs* (London 1961)

Jones, J.R., *The Revolutions of 1688 in England* (New York 1978)

Jones, M., 'The Medal as an Instrument of Propaganda in Late Seventeenth and Early eighteenth Century Europe', *Numismatic Chronicle*, 142 (1982), 117–26

Jordan, W., *The Development of Religious Toleration in England I* (3 vols.) (Harvard 1936)

Joutard, P., *Les Camisards* (Paris 1994)

Joutard, P., 'The Revocation of the Edict of Nantes: End or Renewal of French Calvinism?' in M. Prestwich (ed.), *International Calvinism 1541–1715* (Oxford 1985), 339–68

Kamensky, B., *Governing the Tongue* (Oxford 1997)

Kaplan, B., *Calvinists and Libertines* (Oxford 1995)

Kaplan, Y., 'Amsterdam and Ashkenazic Migration in the Seventeenth Century', *Studia Rosenthaliana* (1989), 22–44

Kaplan, Y., 'For Whom Did Emanuel de Witte Paint His Three Pictures of the Sephardic Synagogue in Amsterdam', *Studia Rosenthaliana* (1998)

Kaplan, Y., *From Christianity to Judaism* (English translation, Oxford 1989)

Kaplan, Y., 'Gente Politica: The Portuguese Jews of Amsterdam Vis-a-vis Dutch Society' in C. Brasz and Y. Kaplan (eds.), *Dutch Jews as Perceived by Themselves and Others* (Leiden 2001), 21–40

Kaplan, Y., 'The Portuguese Community in 17th Century Amsterdam and the Ashkenazi World', *Dutch Jewish History*, 2 (Jerusalem 1989), 23–45

Kaplan, Y., 'The Social Functions of the Herem', *Dutch Jewish History* (1984) 111–55, at 123

Kappler, E., 'La Controverse Jurieu-de la Conseillère', *BSHPF* (1937), 146–73

Katz, D., 'English Charity and Jewish Qualms' in A. Rapoport-Albert and S. Zipperstein (eds.), *Jewish History* (1988), 245–66

Katz, D., *The Jews in England* (Oxford 1994)

Katz, D., 'The Jews of England and 1688' in O. Grell, J. Israel and N. Tyacke (eds.), *From Persecution to Toleration* (Oxford 1991), 217–49

Katz, D., 'The Phenomenon of Philo-semitism' in D. Wood (ed.), *Christianity and the Jews* (Oxford 1992)

Katz, D., *Philosemitism and the Readmission of the Jews to England 1603–1655* (Oxford 1982)

Kearns, E.J., *Ideas in Seventeenth Century France* (New York 1979)

Kee, R., *Ireland* (London 1995)

Keeble, N., *The Literary Culture of Nonconformity* (Leicester 1987)

Keeney, W., *The Development of Dutch Anabaptist Thought and Practice 1539–1564* (Nieuwkoop 1968)

Kelley, D., *The Beginning of Ideology* (Cambridge 1981)

Kelley, D., 'Martyrs, Myths and the Massacre', in A. Soman (ed.), *The Massacre of St Bartholomew* (The Hague 1974), 181–202

Kelly, P., 'Locke and Molyneux: The Anatomy of a Friendship', *Hermathena* (1979), 38–54

Kelly, P. (ed), *Locke on Money* (Oxford 1991)

Kelly, P., 'Lord Galway and the Penal Laws' in C. Caldicott (et al) eds, *The Huguenots and Ireland* (Dublin 1987), 239–55

Kent, S., *Gender and Power in Britain 1640–1990* (London 1999)

Kent, S.A., 'The Papist Charges Against the Interregnum Quakers', *Journal of Religious History* (1982–3), 180–90, at 181

Kenyon, J., *The Popish Plot* (London 1972)

Kenyon, J., *Revolution Principles* (Cambridge 1977)

Kenyon, J., *The Stuart Constitution* (Cambridge 1986)

Keohane, N., *Philosophy and the State in France* (Princeton 1980)

Kieckhefer, R., *European Witch Trials: Their Foundations in Learned and Popular Culture 1300–1500* (London 1976)

Kilcullen, J., *Sincerity and Truth* (Oxford 1988)

Kilroy, P., *Protestant Dissent and Controversy in Ireland 1660–1714* (Cork 1994)

Kitchin, G., *Sir Roger L'Estrange* (London 1913)

Klaasen, W., 'The Anabaptist Understanding of the Separation of the Church', *Church History* (1977), 421–36

Klauber, M., 'Between Protestant Orthodoxy and Rationalism: Fundamental Articles in the Early Career of Jean Le Clerc', *JHI*, 611–36

Klauber, M., 'The Eclipse of Reformed Scholasticism in Eighteenth Century Geneva' in J. Roney and M. Klauber (eds.), *The Identity of Geneva* (Connecticut 1998) 129–42

Klein, L., *Shaftesbury and the Culture of Politeness* (Cambridge 1994)

Knetsch, F.R., 'Jurieu, Bayle et Paets', *BSHPF* (1971), 38–57

Knetsch, F.R., 'Pierre Jurieu: Theologian and Politician of the Dispersion', *Acta Historiae Neerlandica* (Leiden 1971), 213–42

Knights, M., *Politics and Public Opinion* (Cambridge 1995)

Kocher, P.H., *Christopher Marlowe* (Chapel Hill 1946)

Kocher, P.H., 'Marlowe's Atheist Lecture' in C. Leech (ed.), *Marlowe: A Collection of Critical Essays* (New Jersey 1964), 159–66

Kohler, M., 'The Doctrine that "Christianity is a Part of the Common Law"' in *Publications of the American Jewish Society*, 31 (1928), 105–34

Kohler, M., 'Phases in the History of Religious Liberty in America with Particular Reference to the Jews II', *Publications of the American Jewish Historical Society*, 13 (1905), 7–36

Kors, A., *Atheism in Early Modern France* (Princeton 1990)

Kossman, E., 'Freedom in Dutch Thought and Practice' in Israel (ed.), *The Anglo-Dutch Moment*, 281–98

Kossman, E. and Mellinck, A.F. (eds.), *Texts Concerning the Revolt of the Netherlands* (Cambridge 1974)

Kot, S., *Socinianism in Poland* (Boston 1957)

Krahn, C., *Dutch Anabaptism: Origin, Spread, Life and Thought* (Pennsylvania 1981)

Krahn, C., *Dutch Anabaptism* (The Hague 1968)

Kronick, D., *A History of Scientific and Technical Periodicals: The Origins and Development of the Scientific and Technical Press 1665–1790* (New Jersey 1976)

Kuhn, A., 'Hugo Grotius and the Emancipation of the Jews in Holland', *Publications of the American Jewish Society*, 31 (1928), 173–80

Labrousse, E., *Bayle* (Oxford 1983)

Labrousse, E., *L'Entrée de Saturne au lion* (The Hague 1974)

Labrousse, E., *Une Foi, une loi, un roi?: Essai sur la Révocation de L'édit de Nantes* (Paris 1985)

Labrousse, E., 'Les Frères enemis: Bayle et Jurieu' in, *idem, Conscience et conviction* (Paris 1996)

Labrousse, E., *Pierre Bayle* (The Hague 1963–4)

Labrousse, E., 'The Political Ideas of the Huguenot Diaspora (Bayle and Jurieu)' in R.M. Golden (ed.), *Church, State and Society under the Bourbon Kings of France* (Lawrence, Kans. 1982), 222–83

Labrousse, E., 'Les Réponses du Refuge à la *Pastorale* aux N.C. De Meaux' in T. Goyet and J.-P. Collinet (eds.), *Journées Bossuet* (Paris 1980), 343–60

Labrousse, E., 'Understanding the Revocation of the Edict of Nantes From the Perspective of the French Court' in R.M. Golden (ed.), *The Huguenot Connection: The Edict of Nantes, its Revocation, and Early French Migration to South Carolina* (Dordrecht 1988), 49–62

Labrousse, E., 'The Wars of Religion in Seventeenth Century Huguenot Thought' in A. Soman (ed.), *The Massacre of St Bartholomew* (The Hague 1974), 243–51

Lacey, D., *Dissent and Parliamentary Politics* (New Brunswick 1969)

Laeven, A., *The Acta Eruditorum Under the Editorship of Otto Mencke. The History of an International Learned Journal Between 1682 and 1707* (Amsterdam 1990)

Lake, P., *Anglicans and Puritans?* (London 1988)

Lake, P., 'Anti-popery: The Structure of a Prejudice' in R. Cust and A. Hughes (eds.), *Conflict in Early Stuart England: Studies in Religion and Politics 1603–42* (Harlow 1989)

Lake, P., 'Calvinism and the English Church 1575–1625' in M. Todd (ed.), *Reformation to Revolution* (1995), 179–207

Lake, P., 'The Significance of the Elizabethan Identification of the Pope As Antichrist', *Journal of Ecclesiastical History* (1980), 161–78

Lamb, J., *So Idle a Rogue* (London 1993)

Lambert, M., *Medieval Heresy* (Cambridge 1992)

Lamont, W., *Godly Rule* (London 1969)

Laplanche, F., *L'écriture, le sacré et l'histoire* (Amsterdam 1986)

Laplanche, F., *Orthodoxie et Prédication* (Paris 1965)

Laquer, T., *Making Sex* (Harvard 1990)

Laursen, J.C., 'Baylean Liberalism: Tolerance Requires Nontolerance' in *idem* (ed.), *Beyond the Persecuting Society* (Pennsylvania 1998), 197–215

Laursen, J.C., 'Orientation' in Laursen (ed.), *Religious Toleration: The Variety of Rites* (New York 1999), 1–11

La Vopa, A., 'Conceiving a Public: Ideas and Society in Eighteenth Century Europe', *Journal of Modern History* (1992), 79–116

Le Cler, J., *Toleration and the Reformation* (New York 1960)

Lee, S.L., 'Elizabethan England and the Jews', *Transactions of the New Shakespeare Society* (1888), 143–66

Leeuwen, H. van, *The Problem of Certainty in English Thought* (The Hague 1963)

Lenman, B., 'Providence, Liberty and Prosperity' in D. Hoak and M. Feingold (eds.), *The World of William and Mary* (Stanford 1996)

Lennon, T., 'Bayle, Locke and Toleration' in M.A. Stewart (ed.), *Studies in Seventeenth-Century European Philosophy* (Oxford 1997)

Lennon, T., *Reading Bayle* (Toronto 1999)

Lennon, T., 'Taste and Sentiment: Hume, Bayle, Jurieu, and Nicole' in O. Abel and P.F. Moreau (eds.), *Pierre Bayle: la foi dans le doute* (Geneva 1995), 49–64

Léonard, E.G., *Histoire générale du protestantisme* (Paris 1961; London 1965–7)

Lerner, R., *The Heresy of the Free Spirit* (Berkeley 1972)

Levack, B., *The Witch-Hunt in Early Modern Europe* (London 1995)

Levy, L., *Blasphemy* (Chapel Hill 1993)

Loewenstein, D., 'Treason Against God and State' in S. Dobranski and J. Rumrich (eds.), *Milton and Heresy*

Lougee, C., *Le Paradis des Femmes: Women, Salons and Social Stratification in Seventeenth Century France* (Princeton 1976)

Lough, J., 'Locke's Reading During His Stay in France', *The Library* (1953)

Lough, J., *Locke's Travels in France* (Cambridge 1953)

Love, H., *The Culture and Commerce of Texts* (Amherst 1998)

Ludlow, D., 'Shaking Patriarchy's Foundations: Sectarian Women in England, 1641–1700' in R. Greaves (ed.), *Triumph Over Silence* (Connecticut 1984)

Luria, K., 'Rituals of Conversion: Catholics and Protestants in Seventeenth Century Poitou' in Diefendorf (ed.), *Culture and Identity in Early Modern Europe*, 65–81

McBeth, L., *The Baptist Heritage* (Nashville 1989)

McBeth, L., *English Baptist Literature on Religious Liberty to 1689* (New York 1980)

McClure, K., 'Difference, Diversity and the Limits of Toleration', *Political Theory* (1990), 361–91

MacFarlane, A., *Witchcraft in Tudor and Stuart England* (New York 1970)

McGregor, J.F., 'The Baptists: Fount of all Heresy' in B. Reay and J. McGregor (eds.), *Radical Religion in the English Revolution* (Oxford 1984)

McGregor, J.F., 'Ranterism and the Development of Early Quakerism', *Journal of Religious History* (1977), 349–63

Mack, P., *Visionary Women* (Berkeley 1992)

McKenna, A., 'L'Eclaircissement sur les Pyrrhoniens, 1702' in *Le Dictionnaire de Pierre Bayle* (Amsterdam 1997), 297–320

McKenna, A., 'Rationalisme moral et fideisme' in H. Bost and P. de Robert (eds.), *Pierre Bayle, Citoyen du Monde* (Paris 1999)

McLachlan, H.J., *Socinianism in Seventeenth Century England* (Oxford 1951)

McManners, J., *Church and Society in Eighteenth-Century France* (Oxford 1998)

Magdelaine, M. and R. von Thadden (eds.), *Le Refuge Huguenot* (Paris 1985)

Maguire, W.A., 'The Land Settlement' in *idem* (ed.), *Kings in Conflict*, 139–56

Maisonneuve, H., *Études sur les origines de l'inquisition* (Paris 1960)

Manuel, F., *The Broken Staff* (Harvard 1992)

Margull, H.J., *The Councils of the Church* (Philadelphia 1966)

Marotti, A., 'Alienating Catholics in Early Modern England: Recusant Women, Jesuits and Ideological Fantasies' in *idem* (ed.), *Catholicism and Anti-Catholicism in Early Modern English Texts* (New York 1999), 1–34

Marsh, C., *The Family of Love* (Cambridge 1994)

Marshall, J., 'Huguenot Thought After the Revocation of the Edict of Nantes' in R. Vigne and C. Littleton, *From Strangers to Citizens* (London 2000)

Marshall, J., *John Locke: Resistance, Religion, and Responsibility* (Cambridge 1994)

Marshall, J., 'Libertinism and Liberty', forthcoming in J. Champion et al. (eds.), *Libertinism*

Marshall, J., 'Locke, Socinianism, and Unitarianism' in M.A. Stewart (ed.), *English Philosophy in the Age of Locke* (Oxford 2000), 111–82

Marshall, J., 'Some Intellectual Consequences of the English Revolution', *The European Legacy* (2000), 515–30

Mason, H., *Bayle and Voltaire* (Oxford 1963)

Matar, N., 'The Idea of Restoration of the Jews in English Protestant Thought 1661–1701', *Harvard Theological Review* (1985), 115–48

Matar, N., *Islam in Britain 1558–1685* (Cambridge 1998)

Matar, N., 'John Locke and the Jews', *Journal of Ecclesiastical History* (1990), 45–62

Matar, N., 'John Locke and the Turbanned Nations', *Journal of Islamic History* (1991), 67–77

Matar, N., 'The Toleration of Muslims in Renaissance England' in J. Laursen (ed.), *Religious Toleration: The Variety of Rites* (New York 1999)

Matar, N., *Turks, Moors and Englishmen in the Age of Discovery* (New York 1999)

Matton, S. (ed.), *Lettre à Mr *** touchant l'apostaise* (Paris 2000)

Mazzio, C., 'The Sins of the Tongue' in D. Hillman and C. Mazzio (eds.), *The Body in Parts* (New York 1997), 52–79

Meer, T. van der, 'The Persecution of Sodomites in Eighteenth Century Amsterdam: Changing Perceptions of Sodomy', *Journal of Homosexuality* (1989), 263–307

Mehta, U.S., *The Anxiety of Freedom: Imagination and Individuality in Locke's Political Thought* (Ithaca 1992)

Meijer, J., 'Hugo Grotius' Remonstrantie', *Jewish Social Studies* 17 (1955), 91–104

Melnick, R., *From Polemics to Apologetics* (Assen 1981)

Merrick, J. (ed.), *Homosexuality in Early Modern France* (Oxford 2001)

Meyer, G., *The Scientific Lady in England 1650–1760* (Berkeley 1955)

Meyer, P., 'The Attitude of the Enlightenment Towards the Jew', *Studies on Voltaire* (1963), 1161–1205

Michman, J., 'Historiography of the Jews in the Netherlands', *Dutch Jewish History* 1 (Jerusalem 1984), 7–24

Mijnhardt, W., 'Politics and Pornography in the Seventeenth and Eighteenth Century Dutch Republic' in L. Hunt, *The Invention of Pornography* (New York 1996), 283–300

Miller, J., *The Glorious Revolution* (London 1983)

Miller, J., 'The Immediate Impact of the Revocation in England' in C.E.J. Caldicott, H. Gough and J.-P. Pittion (eds.), *The Huguenots and Ireland* (Dublin 1987), 161–74

Miller, J., *James II* (Hove 1978)

Miller, J., 'James II and Toleration' in E. Cruickshanks (ed.), *By Force or Default?* (Edinburgh 1989)

Miller, J., *Popery and Politics* (Cambridge 1973)

Miller, P., *The Common Good* (Cambridge 1994)

Miller, P., '"Free-thinking" and "Freedom of Thought" in Eighteenth Century Britain', *Historical Journal* (1993), 599–618

Miller, P., ed. J. Priestley, *Political Writings* (Cambridge 1993)

Milton, A., *Catholic and Reformed* (Cambridge 1995)

Milton, J.R., 'Dating Locke's Second Treatise', *History of Political Thought* (1995), 356–90

Milton, J.R. and Milton, P., 'Selecting the Grand Jury: A Tract by John Locke', *HJ* (1997), 185–94

Milton, P., 'John Locke and the Rye House Plot', *HJ* (2000), 647–68

Monter, E.W., 'The Death of Co-existence: Jews and Moslems in Christian Spain 1480–1502' in R.B. Waddington and A. Williamson (eds.), *The Expulsion of the Jews: 1492 and After* (New York 1994)

Monter, W., *Frontiers of Heresy* (Cambridge 1990)

Monter, W., 'Heresy Executions in Reformation Europe 1520–1565' in Grell and Scribner, *Tolerance*, 48–64

Monter, W., *Judging the French Reformation* (Harvard 1999)

Montuori, M., *John Locke on Toleration and the Unity of God* (Amsterdam 1983)

Moore, B., *Moral Purity and Persecution in History* (Princeton 2000)

Moore, R., *The Light Within Their Consciences* (Pennsylvania 2000)

Moore, R.I., *The Formation of a Persecuting Society* (Oxford 1987)

Moore, R.I., 'Heresy as Disease' in W. Lourdaux and D. Verhelst (eds.), *The Concept of Heresy in the Middle Ages* (Leuven 1983), 1–11

Moore, R.I., *The Origins of European Dissent* (Oxford 1978)

Mori, G., *Bayle Philosophe* (Paris 2000)

Mori, G., 'Pierre Bayle, the Rights of Conscience, the Remedy of Toleration', *Ratio Juris*, x (1997), 45–60

Morman, P., *Noel Aubert de Versé: A Study in the Concept of Toleration* (New York 1987)

Morrill, J. (ed.), *The Impact of the English Civil War* (London 1991)

Morrill, J., *The Nature of the English Revolution* (London 1993)

Morrill, J., 'The Religious Context of the English Civil War', *TRHS* (1984), 155–78

Morrill, J. (ed.), *Revolution and Restoration* (London 1992)

Morton, A.L., *The World of the Ranters* (London 1970)

Moss, J.D., 'The Family of Love and English Critics', *Sixteenth Century Journal* (1975)

Mours, S., 'Les Pasteurs à la Révocation de L'Édit de Nantes', *BSHPF* (1968), 67–105

Mout, M.E.H.N., 'Limits and Debates: A Comparative View of Dutch Toleration in the Sixteenth and Seventeenth Centuries' in *Emergence of Tolerance*, 37–47

Muchembled, R., *Le Temps des supplices* (Paris 1992)

Mueller, J., 'Milton on Heresy' in S. Dobranski and J. Rumrich (eds.), *Milton and Heresy* (Cambridge 1998)

Mullett, C.F., 'Toleration and Persecution in England 1660–89', *Church History* (1949), 18–43

Mulsow, M., *Moderne aus dem Untergrund* (Hamburg 2002)

Murdoch, T., 'The Quiet Conquest: The Huguenots 1685–1985', *History Today* (1985)

Murray, J.J., *Amsterdam in the Age of Rembrandt* (Norman, Okla. 1967)

Murris, R., *La Hollande et les Hollandairs* (Paris 1925)

Nellen, H., '*Disputando Inclarescet Veritas*: Grotius As a Publicist in France 1621–45' in Nellen and Rabbie (eds.), *Grotius Theologian*, 121–44

Nellen, H., 'Grotius' Relations with the Huguenot Community of Charenton 1621–35', *Lias* XII (1985), 147–77

Nelson, E., 'The Theory of Persecution' in *Persecution and Liberty* (New York 1921), 3–20

Nenner, H., *By Colour of Law* (Chicago 1977)

Niccoli, O., *Prophecy and People in Renaissance Italy* (Princeton 1990)

Nickson, A., 'Locke and the Inquisition of Toulouse', *British Museum Quarterly* 26 (1971–2), 83–92

Nierop, H.F. van, 'Censorship, Illicit Printing and the Revolt of the Netherlands' in A. Duke and C. Tamse (eds.), *Too Mighty to Be Free?* (Zutphen 1987), 29–44

Nijenhuis, W., *Ecclesia Reformata* (Leiden 1972)

Nobbs, D., *Theocracy and Toleration* (Cambridge 1938)

Nuovo, V., *Locke and Christianity* (Bristol 1997)

Nusteling, H.P. H., 'The Netherlands and the Huguenot Emigres' in *La Révocation de L'Edit de Nantes et les provinces-unies 1685* (Amsterdam 1986), 17–34

O'Cathasaigh, S., 'Bayle and Locke on Toleration' in M. Magdelaine, M.-C. Pitassi, R. Whelan, and A. McKenna (eds.), *De L'humanisme aux Lumières, Bayle et la protestantisme* (Paris 1996), 679–92

O'Cathasaigh, S., 'Bayle's Commentaire Philosophique, 1686', *Studies on Voltaire and the Eighteenth Century* (1989), 159–77

Ogg, D., *England in the Reign of Charles II* (Oxford 1934)

O'Higgins, J., *Anthony Collins* (The Hague 1970)

Ohlmeyer, J. (ed.), *Ireland From Independence to Occupation* (Cambridge 1995)

Oldridge, D., *The Devil in Early Modern England* (Sutton 2000)

Orcibal, J., *Louis XIV et les Protestants* (Paris 1951)

Orme, W., *The Life and Times of Richard Baxter* (London 1830), 2 vols.

Outram, D., *The Enlightenment* (Cambridge 1995)

Ozment, S., *Mysticism and Dissent* (Yale 1973)

Pagden, A., *Lords of All the World* (Yale 1995)

Pailin, D., *Attitudes to Other Religions* (Manchester 1984)

Park, K., 'The Rediscovery of the Clitoris' in D. Hillman and C. Mazzio (eds.), *The Body in Parts* (New York 1997), 171–93

Parker, D., 'The Huguenots in Seventeenth-century France' in A.C. Hepburn (ed.), *Minorities in History* (New York 1979), 11–30

Parkin, J., *Science, Religion and Society* (Rochester 1999)

Patterson, A., *Early Modern Liberalism* (Cambridge 1997)

Patterson, A., *Marvell: The Writer in Public Life* (New York 2000)

Paul, C., *Science and Immortality: The Eloges of the Paris Academy of Sciences (1699–1791)*(Berkeley 1980)

Pearl, J., *The Crime of Crimes*, (Waterloo, Ontario 1999)

Peltonen, M., *Classical Humanism and Republicanism in English Political Thought* (Cambridge 1995)

Perry, I., *From Theology to History* (The Hague 1973)

Peters, E., 'Destruction of the Flesh – Salvation of the Spirit: The Paradoxes of Torture in Medieval Christian Society' in A. Ferreiro (ed.), *The Devil, Heresy and Witchcraft in the Middle Ages* (Leiden 1998), 131–48

Peters, E., *Heresy and Authority in Medieval Europe* (Philadelphia 1980)

Peters, E., *The Inquisition* (Berkeley 1989)

Peters, E., *The Magician, the Witch and the Law* (Philadelphia 1978)

Pettegree, A., 'The Calvinist Church in Holland 1572–90', in *idem* (ed.), *Calvinism in Europe 1540–1620* (Cambridge 1994), 160–80

Pettegree, A., *Emden and The Dutch Revolt* (Oxford 1992)

Pettegree, A., 'The Politics of Toleration in the Free Netherlands 1572–1620' in Grell and Scribner, *Tolerance*, 182–98

Phillips, E., *The Good Quaker in French Legend* (Philadelphia 1932)

Phillips, T., 'The Dissolution of François Turretin's Vision of Theologia: Geneva at the End of the Seventeenth Century' in J. Roney and M. Klauber (eds.), *The Identity of Geneva* (Connecticut 1998), 77–92

Phillipson, N., *Hume* (London 1989)

Pincus, S., 'From Butterboxes to Wooden Shoes: The Shift in English Popular Sentiment from Anti-Dutch to Anti-French in the 1670s', *HJ* (1995), 333–61

Pincus, S., *Protestantism and Patriotism* (Cambridge 1996)

Pintard, R., *Le Libertinage érudit* (Paris 1943)

Pitassi, M.C., *Entre croire et savoir: Le problème de la méthode critique chez Jean Le Clerc* (Leiden 1987)

Pocock, J.G. A., *The Ancient Constitution and the Feudal Law* (Cambridge 1957)

Pocock, J.G. A., *Barbarism and Religion* (Cambridge 1999–)

Pocock, J.G. A., 'British History: A Plea for a New Subject', *New Zealand Historical Journal* (1974), 3–21

Pocock, J.G. A., 'The Limits and Divisions of British History: In Search of the Unknown Subject', *American Historical Review* 87 (1982)

Pocock, J.G. A., *The Machiavellian Moment* (Princeton 1975)

Pocock, J.G. A., *The Political Works of James Harrington* (Cambridge 1977)

Pocock, J.G. A., *Politics, Language and Time* (New York 1971)

Pocock, J.G. A., *Virtue, Commerce and History* (Cambridge 1985)

Pollman, J., *Religious Choice in the Dutch Republic* (Manchester 1999)

Poole, K., *Radical Religion from Shakespeare to Milton* (Cambridge 2000)

Poole, R., *Illustrations of the History of Medieval Thought and Learning* (New York 1960)

Popkin, R., 'Hume and Jurieu: Possible Calvinist Origins of Hume's Theory of Belief' in *idem*, R.A. Watson and J. Force (eds.), *The High Road to Pyrrhonism* (San Diego 1980)

Popkin, R. (ed.), *Menasseh Ben Israel and His World* (Leiden 1989)

Popkin, R., 'Pierre Bayle and the Conversion of the Jews' in Magdelaine (et al.), *De l'humanisme*, 635–43.

Porter, R., *The Creation of the Modern World: The Untold Story of the English Enlightenment* (2000)

Porter, S., *The Great Plague* (Sutton 1999)

Potter, D. (ed.), *The French Wars of Religion* (New York 1997)

Price, J.L., *Dutch Society 1588–1713* (Harlow 2000)

Price, J.V., Introduction to C. Blount, *The Oracles of Reason* (London 1995)

Puaux, F., 'L'Evolution des théories politiques du protestantisme français pendant le règne de Louis XIV', *Bulletin de la Societé de l'histoire du Protestantisme français*, 62 (1913)

Puaux, F., *Les Précurseurs de la Tolérance en France au XVIIe siècle* (Paris 1881)

Quentin, D., 'The Missing Foot of "Upon Nothing"' in N. Fisher (ed.), *That Second Bottle* (Manchester 2000)

Rabbie, E., 'Hugo Grotius and Judaism' in H. Nellen and E. Rabbie (eds.), *Hugo Grotius, Theologian* (Leiden 1994), 99–120

Rawls, J., *A Theory of Justice* (Harvard 1971)

Reay, B., 'Quakerism and Society' in J.F. McGregor and B. Reay, *Radical Religion in the English Revolution* (Oxford 1984)

Reay, B., *Quakers in the English Revolution* (New York 1985)

Rébelliau, A., *Bossuet Historien du protestantisme* (Paris 1891)

Redwood, J., *Reason, Ridicule and Religion* (London 1976)

Reesinck, H., *L'Angleterre et la Littérature Anglaise* (Paris 1931)

Remer, G., 'Rhetoric and the Erasmian Defence of Religious Toleration', *History of Political Thought* (1989), 377–403

Rétat, P., *Le Dictionnaire de Bayle et la lutte philosophique au xviii siècle* (Paris 1971)

Reventlow, H. Graf, *The Authority of the Bible and the Modern World* (London 1984)

Rex, W., *Essays on Pierre Bayle and Religious Controversy* (The Hague 1965)

Reynolds, E.E., *Bossuet* (New York 1963)

Rietbergen, P., 'William III of Orange (1650–1702). Between European Politics and European Protestantism: The Case of the Huguenots' in *La Révocation de L'Édit de Nantes et les Provinces-Unies 1685* (Amsterdam 1986), 35–50

Riley, P., *Leibniz' Universal Jurisprudence* (Harvard 1996)

Robbins, C., *Absolute Liberty* (Hamden, Connecticut 1982)

Robbins, C., 'The Strenuous Whig, Thomas Hollis', *William and Mary Quarterly* (1950), 405–53

Robiquet, P., 'Popular Insurrection as the Instrument of Aristocracy and Clergy' in J. Salmon (ed.), *The French Wars of Religion* (Boston 1967)

Rochot, B., 'Le P. Mersenne et les relations intellectuels dans l'Europe du XVII siècle', *Cahiers d'histoire mondiale* (1966), 55–73

Roelker, N., 'The Appeal of Calvinism to French Noblewomen in the Sixteenth Century', *Journal of Interdisciplinary History* (1971–2), 391–413

Roelker, N., 'The Role of Noblewomen in the French Reformation', *Archiv fur Reformationgeschicte* (1972), 168–95

Rogers, G.A. J., 'Locke and Religious Toleration' in *La naissance de l'idée de tolérance 1660–89* (Rouen 1998), 121–35

Rooden, P. van, 'Conceptions of Judaism in the Seventeenth Century Dutch Republic', in D. Wood (ed.), *Christianity and Judaism* (Oxford 1992), 299–308

Rooden, P.T. van and Wesselius, J.W., 'The Early Enlightenment and Judaism: The "Civil Dispute" Between Philippus van Limborch and Isaac Orobio de Castro', *Studia Rosenthaliania* (1987)

Roper, L., *The Holy Household* (Oxford 1989)

Roper, L., *Oedipus and the Devil* (London 1994)

Rose, C., *England in the 1690s* (Oxford 1999)

Roth, C., *A Life of Menasseh Ben Israel* (Philadelphia 1934)

Rowen, H., 'The Dutch Republic and the Idea of Freedom' in D. Wootton (ed.), *Republicanism, Liberty and Commercial Society*, 310–40

Rowen, H., *John De Witt* (Princeton 1978)

Rubini, D., 'Sexuality and Augustan England', *Journal of Homosexuality* (1988), 349–81

Rudolph, J., 'Rape and Resistance: Women and Consent in Seventeenth Century English Legal and Political Thought', *Journal of British Studies* (2000), 157–84

Runciman, S., *The Medieval Manichee* (Cambridge 1955)

Russell, C., 'Arguments for Religious Unity in England 1530–1650', *Journal of Ecclesiastical History* (1967), 201–26

Russell, C., *The Fall of the British Monarchies* (Oxford 1991)

Russell, J., *Witchcraft in the Middle Ages* (Ithaca 1972)

Ryan, A., 'Liberalism' in R. Gordon (ed.), *A Companion to Contemporary Political Philosophy* (Oxford 1993)

Sabean, D., *Power in the Blood* (Cambridge 1984)

Sachse, W., *John, Lord Somers* (Manchester 1975)

Sachse, W., 'The Mob and the Revolution of 1688', *Journal of British Studies* (1964), 23–40

Sarazin, B., 'Les Temples et les Pasteurs de Mouchamps', *BSHPF* (1909), 547–59

Savonius, S., 'Locke in French', *Historical Journal* (2004), 47–79

Schama, S., *The Embarrassment of Riches* (New York 1987)

Schechter, R., 'Rationalizing the Enlightenment: Postmodernism and Theories of Anti-Semitism' in D. Gordon (ed.), *Postmodernism and the Enlightenment* (New York 2000), 93–116

Schickler, F. de, *Les Églises du Refuge en Angleterre* (Paris 1892)

Schiebinger, L., *The Mind Has No Sex? Women in the Origins of Modern Science* (Harvard 1989)

Schneewind, J.B., *The Invention of Autonomy* (Cambridge 1998)

Schneewind, J.B., 'Philosophical Roots of Intolerance and the Concept of Toleration' in M. Razavi and D. Ambrel (eds.), *Philosophy, Religion and the Question of Intolerance* (New York 1997), 3–15

Schochet, G., 'The Act of Toleration and the Failure of Comprehension: Persecution, Nonconformity, and Religious Indifference' in D. Hoak and M. Feingold (eds.), *The World of William and Mary* (Stanford 1996), 165–87

Schochet, G., 'Between Lambeth and Leviathan' in N. Phillipson (ed.), *Political Discourse in Early Modern Britain* (Cambridge 1993)

Schochet, G., 'Samuel Parker, Religious Diversity and the ideology of persecution' in R. Lund (ed.), *The Margins of Orthodoxy* (Cambridge 1995), 119–48

Schoffer, I., 'The Jews in the Netherlands: The Position of a Minority Through Three Centuries', *Studia Rosenthaliania* (1981), 85–105

Schosler, J., 'Les Editions de la traduction française par Pierre Coste de l'Essay Concerning Human Understanding de Locke', *Actes du VIIIe Congrès des romanistes scandanives* (Odense 1983), 315–24

Schutte, A.J., 'Such Monstrous Births: A Neglected Aspect of the Antinomian Controversy', *Renaissance Quarterly* (1985)

Schwoerer, L., *The Declaration of Rights 1689* (Baltimore 1981)

Schwoerer, L., 'Liberty of the Press' in J.R. Jones, *Liberty Secured?* (Stanford 1992)

Scott, J., *Algernon Sidney and the English Republic 1623–77* (Cambridge 1988)

Scott, J., *Algernon Sidney and the Restoration Crisis* (Cambridge 1991)

Scott, J., *England's Troubles* (Cambridge 2000)

Scribner, R., *For the Sake of Simple Folk* (Oxford 1994)

Scribner, R., 'Practical Utopias: Pre-modern Communism and the Reformation', *Comparative Studies in Society and History*, 36 (1994), 743–74

Scribner, R.,'Preconditions of Tolerance and Intolerance' in Grell and Scribner, *Tolerance*

Seaton, A., *The Theory of Toleration Under the Later Stuarts* (Cambridge 1911)

Sedgwick, A., *Jansenism in Seventeenth Century France* (Charlottesville 1977)

Sell, A., 'Through Suffering to Liberty: 1689 in the English and Vaudois Experience', in *idem, Commemorations* (Cardiff 1993)

Shakespeare, J., 'Plague and Punishment' in P. Lake and M. Dowling (eds.), *Protestantism and the National Church in Sixteenth Century England* (London 1987)

Shapiro, B., *A Culture of Fact* (Ithaca 2000)

Shapiro, B., *John Wilkins* (Berkeley 1969)

Shapiro, B., *Probability and Certainty in Seventeenth Century England* (Princeton 1983)

Sharpe, J., *Instruments of Darkness* (London 1997)

Simms, J., *William Molyneux* (Dublin 1982)

Simms, J.G., 'The Establishment of Protestant Ascendancy 1691–1714' in T. Moody and M. Vaughn (eds.), *A New History of Ireland* (Oxford 1986), vol. IV

Simonutti, L., *Arminianesimo e tolleranza nel seicento olandese* (Florence 1984)

Simonutti, L.,'Between History and Politics: Philipp van Limborch's History of the Inquisition' in J. Laursen (ed.), *Histories of Heresy in Early Modern Europe* (New York 2002), 101–18

Simonutti, L., 'Between Political Loyalty and Religious Liberty: Political Theory and Toleration in Huguenot Thought in the Epoch of Bayle', *History of Political Thought* (1996), 523–54

Simonutti, L., 'Damaris Cudworth Masham' in *Scritti in onore di Eugenio Garin* (Pisa 1987), 141–65

Simonutti, L., 'Limborch's *Historia Inquisitionis* and the Pursuit of Toleration' in A. Coudert, S. Hutton, R. Popkin, and G. Wiener (eds.), *Judeo-Christian Intellectual Culture in the Seventeenth Century* (Dordrecht 1999), 237–55

Simonutti, L., 'Religion, Philosophy and Science: John Locke and Limborch's Circle in Amsterdam' in J. Force and D. Katz (eds.), *Everything Connects* (Leiden 1999), 295–324

Simonutti, L., 'Spinoza and the English Thinkers' in W. van Bunge and W. Klever (eds.), *Disguised and Overt Spinozism Around 1700* (Leiden 1996), 191–211

Skinner, Q., 'The Calvinist Theory of Resistance' in B. Malament (ed.), *After the Reformation* (Pennsylvania 1980)

Skinner, Q., *The Foundations of Modern Political Thought* (Cambridge 1978)

Skinner, Q., 'Hobbes on Sovereignty: An Unknown discussion', *Political Studies* (1965), 213–18

Skinner, Q., 'Meaning and Understanding in the History of Ideas', *History and Theory* 8 (1969), 3–53

Skinner, Q., *Reason and Rhetoric in the Philosophy of Hobbes* (Cambridge 1986)

Skinner, Q., 'Sir Thomas More's Utopia and the Language of Renaissance Humanism' in A. Pagden (ed.), *The Languages of Political Theory in Early Modern Europe* (Cambridge 1987), 123–57

Smiles, S., *The Huguenots* (New York 1868; reprint Baltimore 1972)

Smith, N. (ed.), *A Collection of Ranter Writings* (London 1983)

Smith, N., *Perfection Proclaimed* (Oxford 1989)

Smith, S., 'Toleration and Scepticism of Religion in Spinoza's *Tractatus*' in A. Levine (ed.), *Early Modern Skepticism and the Origins of Toleration* (Lanham, Md. 1999), 127–45

Snobelen, S., 'The Mystery of this Restitution of All Things: Isaac Newton on the Return of the Jews', in J. Force and R. Popkin (eds.), *Millenarianism and Messianism in Early Modern European Culture: The Millennial Turn* (Leiden 2001), 95–118

Snobelen, S., 'Socinianism, Heresy and John Locke's *Reasonableness of Christianity*', review article, *Enlightenment and Dissent* (2001)

Solé, J., 'Les débuts de la collaboration entre Adriaan van Paets, protecteur de Pierre Bayle à Rotterdam, et le gouvernement de Louis XIV' in *De l'humanisme*, 477–94

Sommerville, J., *Politics and Ideology in England 1603–40* (1986)

Speck, W., *Reluctant Revolutionaries* (Oxford 1988)

Spencer, C., *The Heretic's Feast* (London 1993)

Sprunger, K., 'Anabaptist Women of the Radical Reformation', in R. Greaves (ed.), *Triumph Over Silence* (Connecticut 1985), 45–74

Sprunger, K., *Dutch Puritanism: A History of the English and Scottish Churches of the Netherlands in the Sixteenth and Seventeenth Centuries* (Leiden 1982)

Spurr, J., *England in the 1670s* (Oxford 2000)

Spurr, J., 'Religion in Restoration England' in L.K. J. Glassey (ed.), *The Reigns of Charles II and James VII & II* (New York 1997), 90–124

Spurr, J., *The Restoration Church* (Yale 1991)

Spurr, J., 'Schism and the Restoration Church', *Journal of Ecclesiastical History* (1990), 408–24

Stam, F.P. van, *The Controversy Over the Theology of Saumur* (Amsterdam 1988)

Stankiewicz, W.J., *Politics and Religion in Seventeenth Century France* (Berkeley 1960)

Stayer, J., *The German Peasant's War and Anabaptist Community of Goods* (Montreal 1991)

Stayer, J., *Anabaptists and the Sword* (Kansas 1972)

Stephens, P., *The Waldensian Story* (Lewes 1998)

Stevenson, W., 'The Social and Economic Status of Post-Restoration Dissenters 1660–1725' in M. Spufford (ed.), *The World of Rural Dissenters 1520–1725* (Cambridge 1995), 332–59

Stevenson, W., 'Social Integration' in M. Spufford (ed.), *The World of Rural Dissenters 1520–1725* (Cambridge 1995), 360–87

Stocker, M., *Judith: Sexual Warrior* (Yale 1998)

Stouten, J., 'Quelques textes littéraires sur la Révocation de L'Édit de Nantes' in *La Révocation de L'Édit de Nantes*, 77–84

Strauss, L., *Spinoza's Critique of Religion* (New York 1965)

Strayer, J., *The Albigensian Crusades* (Michigan 1992)

Strien, C.D. van, *British Travellers in Holland During the Stuart Period* (Leiden 1993)

Stroup, A., *A Company of Scientists: Botany, Patronage and Community at the Seventeenth Century Parisian Royal Academy of Sciences* (Berkeley 1990)

Swetschinski, D., 'Kinship and Commerce: The Foundations of Portuguese Jewish Life in Seventeenth Century Holland', *Studia Rosenthaliania* (1981), 52–74

Sypher, W., 'Image of Protestantism', *Sixteenth Century Journal* (1980), 59–84

Tarantino, G., *Martin Clifford* (Florence 2000)

Tarcov, N.,'John Locke and the Foundations of Toleration', in A. Levine, *Early Modern Skepticism and the Origins of Toleration* (Lanham, Md. 1999), 179–95

Tazbir, J., *A State Without Stakes. Polish Religious Toleration in the Sixteenth and Seventeenth Centuries* (New York 1973)

Tex, J. den, *Oldenbarnevelt* (Cambridge 1973), 2 vols.

Thomas, K., 'The Puritans and Adultery: The Act of 1650 Reconsidered' in Pennington and Thomas (eds.), *Puritans and Revolutionaries* (Oxford 1978), 257–82

Thomas, K., *Man and the Natural World* (Oxford 1983)

Thomas, K., *Religion and the Decline of Magic* (London 1971)

Thomas, K., 'Women and the Civil War Sects', *Past and Present* (1958), 42–62

Thomas, P.W., *Sir John Berkenhead* (Oxford 1969)

Thomas, R., 'Comprehension and Indulgence' in G. Nuttall (ed.), *From Uniformity to Unity* (London 1962)

Thompson, E.P., *Customs in Common* (London 1991)

Thompson, E.P., 'On the Rant' in G. Eley and W. Hunt (eds.), *Reviving the English Revolution* (1988), 153–60

Thormahlen, M., *Rochester: The Poems in Context* (Cambridge 1993)

Todorov, T., *The Morals of History* (Minneapolis 1995)

Trachtenberg, J., *The Devil and the Jews* (New York 1943)

Tracy, J., 'Erasmus, Coornhert and the Acceptance of Religious Diversity in the Body Politic' in Berkvens-Stevelinck (ed.), *Emergence of Tolerance*, 49–62

Tracy, J., *Holland Under Habsburg Rule 1506–66* (Berkeley 1990)

Trapmann, J., 'Grotius and Erasmus' in H. Nellen and E. Rabbie (eds.), *Hugo Grotius, Theologian* (Leiden 1994), 77–98

Trevor-Roper, H., *Catholics, Anglicans, and Puritans* (London 1989)

Trevor-Roper, H., *The European Witchcraze* (London 1978)

Trevor-Roper, H., *Religion, The Reformation, and Social Change* (London 1967)

Trubowitz, R., 'Female Preachers and Male Wives: Gender and Authority in Civil War England' in J. Holstun (ed.), *Pamphlet Wars*, (London 1992), 112–33

Truchet, J., *La Politique de Bossuet* (Paris 1966)

Trumbach, R., 'The Birth of the Queen: Sodomy and the Emergence of Gender Equality in Modern Culture 1660–1750' in M. Duberman, M. Vicinus, and G. Chauncy (eds.), *Hidden from History* (London 1991)

Trumbach, R., 'Sodomitical Subcultures, Sodomitical Roles, and the Gender Revolution of the Eighteenth Century' in P. Maccubin (ed.), *'Tis Nature's Fault* (Cambridge 1987)

Tuck, R.,'Hobbes and Locke on Toleration' in M.G. Dietz, *Thomas Hobbes and Political Theory* (Kansas 1990), 153–71

Tuck, R., *Natural Rights Theories* (Cambridge 1979)

Tuck, R., *Philosophy and Government 1572–1651* (Cambridge 1993)

Tuck, R, *The Rights of War and Peace* (Oxford 1999)

Tuck, R., 'Scepticism and Toleration in the Seventeenth Century' in S. Mendus, *Justifying Toleration* (Cambridge 1988), 21–35

Tully, J., *An Approach to Political Philosophy: Locke in Contexts* (Cambridge 1993)

Tully, J., *A Discourse on Property: John Locke and his Adversaries* (Cambridge 1980)

Tully, J. (ed.), *Locke, A Letter Concerning Toleration* (Indianapolis 1983), introduction

Tully, J., *Strange Multiplicity* (Cambridge 1995)

Tumbleson, R., *Catholicism in the English Protestant Imagination* (Cambridge 1998)

Turchetti, M., 'La Liberté de conscience et l'autorité du magistrat au lendemain de la Révocation' in H. Guggigsberg (ed.), *La Liberté de conscience* (Geneva 1991) 290–367

Turchetti, M., 'Une Question mal posée: Erasmus et la tolérance' in *Histoire de l'humanisme et de la Renaissance*, 53 (1991), 379–95

Turner, J.G., 'The Libertine Sublime: Love and Death in Restoration England', *Studies in Eighteenth Century Culture*, 19 (1989), 99–115

Turner, J. G., *One Flesh* (Oxford 1987)

Tyacke, N., *Anti-Calvinists* (Oxford 1987)

Tyacke, N., 'Arminianism and the Theology of the Restoration Church' in S. Groenveld and M. Wintle (eds.), *The Exchange of Ideas* (Zutphen 1991), 68–83

Tyacke, N., 'Arminianism and English Culture' in A. Duke (ed.), *Britain and the Netherlands*, 7 (The Hague 1981), 94–117

Ultee, M., 'The Republic of Letters: Learned Correspondence 1680–1720', *Seventeenth Century*, 2 (1987), 95–112

Underdown, D., *Revel, Riot and Rebellion* (Oxford 1985)

Underwood, T., *Primitivism, Radicalism and the Lamb's War* (Oxford 1997)

Vercruysse, J., 'Crellius, Le Cène, Naigeon ou les chemins de la tolérance socinienne', *Tijdschrift voor de studie van de verlichting*, 244–320

Vernon, R., *The Career of Toleration* (Montreal 1997)

Vigne, R., 'Avenge O Lord Thy Slaughtered Saints: Cromwell's Intervention on Behalf of the Vaudois', *Proceedings of the Huguenot Society* (1983)

Vigne, R., 'The Good Lord Galway. The Irish and English Careers of a Huguenot Leader: Biographical Notes', *Proceedings of the Huguenot Society*, 24, (1988), 532–50

Viroli, M., *From Politics to Reason of State* (Cambridge 1992)

Vlessing, O., 'New Light on the Earliest History of the Amsterdam Portuguese Jews' in J. Michman (ed.), *Dutch Jewish History* (1993), 43–75

Voogt, G., *Constraint on Trial* (Kirksville, Mo. 2000)

Wade, I., *The Clandestine Organisation and Diffusion of Philosophical Ideas* (Princeton 1938)

Waite, G., *David Joris and Dutch Anabaptism* (Waterloo 1990)

Waldron, J., *God, Locke and Equality* (Cambridge 2002)

Walker, G., *The Churchmanship of St Cyprian* (London 1968)

Walker, R., 'The English Exiles in Holland During the Reigns of Charles II and James II', *TRHS*, 4, 30 (1948), 111–25

Wall, E. van der, '"Antichrist Stormed": The Glorious Revolution and the Dutch Prophetic Tradition' in D. Hoak and M. Feingold (eds.), *The World of William and Mary*

Waller, M., *1700: Scenes From London Life* (London 2000)

Walsh, J., Heydon, C, and Taylor, S. (eds.), *The Church of England c. 1689–1832* (Cambridge 1986)

Walsham, A., *Providence in Early Modern England* (Oxford 1999)

Walter, J., *Understanding Popular Violence in the English Revolution* (Cambridge 1999)

Walters, B., 'Pierre Bayle's Article on George Buchanan', *Seventeenth Century French Studies* (1998), 163–73

Walzer, M., *On Toleration* (Yale 1997)

Warnicke, R., 'Sexual Heresy at the Court of Henry VIII', *Historical Journal*, 30, 2 (1987), 247–68

Watts, M., *The Dissenters* (Oxford 1978)

Webster, C., *The Great Instauration* (London 1975)

Weil, R., *Political Passions* (Manchester 2000)

Weil, R., 'Sometimes a Scepter is only a Scepter: Pornography and Politics in Restoration England' in L. Hunt, *The Invention of Pornography* (New York 1993), 125–53

Whelan, R., *The Anatomy of Superstition* (Oxford 1989)

Whelan, R., 'Persecution and Toleration: The Changing Identities of Ireland's Huguenot Refugees', *Proceedings of the Huguenot Society* (1998), 20–35

Whiting, C., *Studies in English Puritanism* (London 1931)

Whitmore, P., 'Bayle's Criticism of Locke' in P. Dibon (ed.), *Pierre Bayle, Le philosophe de Rotterdam* (Paris 1959), 81–95

Wiesner, M., 'Women and the Reformation' in R. Po-Chia Hsia, *The German People and the Reformation* (Cornell 1988)

Wijngaards, G.N.M., *De Bibliothèque Choisie (1703–13) van Jean Le Clerc* (Amsterdam 1986)

Wilbur, E.H., *History of Unitarianism* (Harvard 1946)

Williams, G.H., *The Radical Reformation* (Philadelphia 1962)

Williams, T., 'Polemical Prints of the English Revolution' in L. Gent and N. Llewellen (eds.), *Renaissance Bodies* (London 1990)

Wolfe, M., *The Conversion of Henri IV* (Harvard 1993)

Wood, N., *Locke and Agrarian Capitalism* (Berkeley 1984)

Wootton, D., 'Bayle, Libertine?' in M.A. Stewart, *Studies in Seventeenth Century European Philosophy* (Oxford 2000)

Wootton, D., *Divine Right and Democracy* (London 1986)

Wootton, D., 'Leveller Democracy and the Puritan Revolution' in J. Burns and M. Goldie (eds.), *The Cambridge History of Political Thought 1450–1750*

Wootton, D. (ed.), *Locke: Political Writings* (London 1993)

Wootton, D., 'Locke, Socinian or Natural Law Theorist?' in J. Crimmins (ed.), *Religion, Secularization and Political Thought* (London 1989), 39–67

Wootton, D., *Paolo Sarpi* (Cambridge 1983)

Wootton, D. and Hunter, M. (eds.), *Atheism from the Reformation to the Enlightenment*

Worden, B., 'Toleration and the Cromwellian Protectorate' in W. Sheils (ed.), *Persecution and Toleration* (Oxford 1984)

Wright, A.D., *The Counter-reformation* (New York 1982)

Yardeni, M., 'Bayle and Basnage on Post-Commonwealth Jewish History', *European Studies Review* (1977), 245–58

Yardeni, M., 'French Calvinist Political Thought 1534–1715' in M. Prestwich (ed.), *International Calvinism 1541–1715* (Oxford 1985), 315–37

Yardeni, M., 'Journalisme et Histoire Contemporaine a l'époque de Bayle', *History and Theory* (1973), 222–9

Yardeni, M., 'La Tolérance Rétrospective: la perception de l'histoire des Pays-Bas et de l'Angleterre dans le refuge huguenot', in *Emergence*, 251–68

Yolton, J., *John Locke: A Descriptive Bibliography* (Bristol 1998)

Young, M.B., *James VI and I and the History of Homosexuality* (Basingstoke 2000)

Zagorin, P., *How the Idea of Religious Toleration Came to the West* (Princeton 2003)

Zagorin, P., *Rebels and Rulers 1500–1660* (Cambridge 1982), II

Zakai, A., 'Religious Toleration and its Enemies', *Albion* (1989), 1–33

Ziegler, P., *The Black Death* (New York 1969)

Zook, M., *Radical Whigs and Conspiratorial Politics in Late Stuart England* (Pennsylvania 1999)

Zuber, R., 'Papiers de Jeunesse d'Isaac Papin', *BSHPF* (1974), 107–4

Zuber, R., 'Spinozisme et tolérance chez la jeune Papin', *Dix-huitième siècle* (1974), 218–27

Zumthor, P., *Daily Life in Rembrandt's Holland* (Stanford 1994)

Zurbuchen, S., 'From Denominationalism to Enlightenment' in Laursen (ed.), *Religious Toleration*, 191–209

Zweig, S., *The Right to Heresy* (1936)

INDEX

Titles in the series

Printed in Great Britain
by Amazon.co.uk, Ltd.,
Marston Gate.